Commentary on the PSALMS

COMMENTARY ON THE
PSALMS

2 volumes in 1

J. J. Stewart Perowne

Foreword by Walter C. Kaiser, Jr.

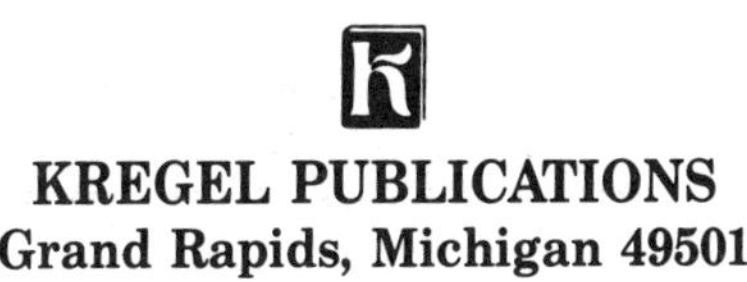

KREGEL PUBLICATIONS
Grand Rapids, Michigan 49501

Commentary on the Psalms, by J. J. Stewart Perowne (2 vols. in 1). Foreword by Walter C. Kaiser, Jr.

Cover Design: Don Ellens

Library of Congress Cataloging-in-Publication Data
[The book of Psalms]
Perowne, J. J. Stewart (John James Stewart), 1823-1879.
Commentary on the Psalms / by J. J. Stewart Perowne; foreword by Walter C. Kaiser, Jr.
p. cm.
Reprint. Originally published: The book of Psalms. 4th rev. ed. London: George Bell & Sons, 1878-1879.
Includes index.

1. Bible. O.T. Psalms—Commentaries. I. Perowne, J. J. Stewart (John James Stewart) II. Title.
BS1424.P37 1989 223'.2077 89-11054
CIP

ISBN 0-8254-3485-8 (pbk.)
ISBN 0-8254-3486-6 (hardcover)

1 2 3 4 5 Printing/Year 93 92 91 90 89

Printed in the United States of America

CONTENTS

VOLUME ONE

INTRODUCTION

THE PSALMS

VOLUME TWO

THE PSALMS, continued

FOREWORD

John James Stewart Perowne was born March 13, 1823 in Burdwan, 60 miles northwest of Calcutta, India. His studies took him to Corpus Christi College in Cambridge where he earned the B.A., 1845; M.A., 1848; B.D., 1856; the members' prize Latin essay; and the Hebrew scholar award.

In 1847 Perowne was ordained as a deacon and in 1848 he was ordained into the priesthood of the Church of England. Later he served as select preacher to the university in 1853, 1861, 1873, 1876, 1879 and 1882. Among the numerous posts he held in his very productive and busy career were: vice-principal of St. David's College, Lampeter, 1862-72; examining chaplain to the bishop of Norwich, 1865-78; prelector in theology in Trinity College, Cambridge, 1872-78; Hulsean professor of divinity, 1875-78; Margaret preacher, 1874-75; Whithall preacher, 1874-76; member of the Old Testament company of Bible revisers, 1878-84; royal commission on ecclesiastical courts, 1881-83; honorary chaplain to the queen, appointed in 1875; dean of Peterborough in 1878; and bishop of Worcester in 1890. Perowne retired in 1881 and died on November 6, 1884 near Gloucester, England.

One of the high points of his career came in 1864 when his two volumes, *The Book of Psalms: A New Translation With Introductions and Notes Explanatory and Critical*, appeared. These two volumes proved to be so popular and helpful that they would go through nine separate editions, the last appearing in 1898. In 1869 his Hulsean Lectures for 1868 were published under the title of *Immortality*. Perowne also served for many years as the editor for *The Cambridge Bible for Schools*. In that famous series, he personally contributed the volumes on Haggai and Zechariah (1888), Obadiah and Jonah (1889), and Malachi (1898).

However, it was his two volumes on the Psalms that had the greatest impact on his day and ours. His comments on each of the Psalms are always filled with a judicious balance between an appropriate overview of the message of the whole psalm and a careful selection of the necessary background of technical and critical details. Especially noteworthy is his long discussion of the theology of the Psalms in his elaborate introduction. While he takes up such theological topics as the spiritual appreciation of the ceremonial aspects of the Law, assertions of innocency and uprightness by the psalmist, imprecations or cursings in the Psalms, and the hope for a future life in the Psalms, his longest and best discussion is reserved for the important issue of the interpretation of the messianic hope in the Psalms. Here Perowne successfully maneuvers past the Scylla of modern rationalism's denial of any messianic presence in the Psalms and the Charybdis of the patristic and medieval writers who affirmed that every psalm had some direct prophetic reference to Christ and his Church.

Perowne chose, instead, to side with the reformers' view of the presence of the Messiah in the Psalms. He did not agree, however, with the Bishop Horsley principle that declared whenever a part of a Psalm is applied to our Lord, we are bound to explain the whole Psalm of Him. Instead, Perowne announced, ". . . we have our Lord's own authority for taking a portion, not only of a Psalm, but even of a particular passage in a Psalm, as prophetic of Himself and the circumstances of His life" (p. 47, 4th edition).

Even though Perowne's study on the Psalms could in no way anticipate the great advances that have come in the twentieth century following such giants as Hermann Gunkel and Sigmund Mowinckel, or the new studies on poetry that have appeared in the last third of the twentieth century; nevertheless, the mark it has made will still stand. Even apart from these later advances, Perowne is still able to do what some of the moderns with all their new insights are unable to do since they often do not approach the text with the same reverential humility or with the same regard for the author's truth-intention. It is a pleasure, therefore, to commend this work once again to all serious students of the Word and to those who wish to hear what the Spirit of God is saying to the church in our generation.

WALTER C. KAISER, JR.

Academic Dean
Trinity Evangelical Divinity School

PREFACES TO PREVIOUS EDITIONS

The Fourth Edition

Although the fourth edition of this work does not differ very materially from those that have preceded it, either in the translation or in the notes, yet in one respect it will, I hope, be found much more complete and accurate. In preparing it, I have had the advantage of consulting many original authorities in Talmudical and Rabbinical literature which before were not within my reach, and I have consequently been able to correct several errors of quotation from these sources, some of which have found their way into many commentaries, one writer having often merely copied and repeated the blunders of another. And, further, I have had throughout the valuable assistance of Dr. Schiller-Szinessy, the learned Reader in Talmudical and Rabbinical Literature in this University, who is a master of Jewish lore, and who has most kindly spared no labour in verifying and correcting my references. Their greater accuracy is, in a large measure, due to the conscientious care which he has bestowed upon them, and of which I am the more sensible, because I know that it has been bestowed notwithstanding the pressure of other numerous and heavy engagements. It is a pleasure for me to take this opportunity of expressing my obligations to him, and my sense of the ready kindness with which his learning is always placed at the disposal of others.

Cambridge,
March 7, 1878

The Third Edition

In preparing a third edition of this work for the press, I have availed myself of the following critical aids and authorities:

1. Baer's critical text of the Psalter. His preface on the metrical accentuation of the Poetical Books deserves notice.
2. Field's admirable edition of Origen's *Hexapla.* I have corrected by reference to it many quotations which were given in my former editions on the authority of Montfaucon.
3. Moll's Commentary in Lange's *Bibelwerk.*
4. The second edition of Delitzch's Psalter.
5. The third edition of Ewald's work on the Psalms.
6. The second edition of Hitzig's Commentary.
7. Dr. Kay's Psalms with Notes.
8. Professor Conant's Translation.
9. The second edition of Dr. Phillip's Commentary.

My special thanks are due to R.L. Bensly, Esq., Fellow of Gonville and Caius College, who has been so kind as to revise the sheets of the work as it passed through the press; to his knowledge and accuracy I am greatly indebted.

Trinity College, Cambridge
April 22, 1873

The Second Edition

The second edition of this work will not be found to differ very materially from the first. I have made a few additions, more particularly to the critical notes in some of the earlier Psalms; and I have corrected errors wherever I have discovered them, or where they have been pointed out to me by friends. All the references have been carefully revised. Many of the apparent mistakes in the references of the first edition were due to my having used the Hebrew Bible, without taking due care to mark where the Hebrew divisions of chapters or verses varied from the English. Where these differ, it will now be found, I hope, that both references are given, those to the Hebrew text being enclosed in square brackets. If, however, the double reference has still been omitted in some cases, it may be borne in mind that in all Psalms which have an inscription, the inscription is reckoned as a verse (occasionally as two verses) in the Hebrew text, whereas this is not the case in the English. Consequently, the first verse in the English may be the second or even the third in the Hebrew, and so on all through. In the critical notes the references are always to the Hebrew text.

In revising my translation I have approached in several instances more nearly to the Authorized Version, and I have more frequently than before left the literal rendering of a clause for the note, giving the freer and more idiomatic in the text. In doing this, I have listened to the suggestions of my critics, some of whom, not agreeing in other respects, have agreed in censuring my translation. And now as there is at last some reasonable hope that a revision of our Authorized Version will be undertaken by competent scholars, this question of translation possesses far more than a merely personal or temporary interest. Even a translator who has failed, if he has done his work honestly and conscientiously, may be a beacon, if he cannot be a guide, to those who come after him. I shall therefore be pardoned perhaps, if I discuss more fully than I should otherwise have done, some of the points that have been raised.

The objections that have been brought against me are of this kind. One of my reviewers observes that, after having said that I had not "needlessly departed" from our Authorized Version, I have "judged it needful often enough to give an entirely new air to my translation." Another writes: "The gain which is acquired by the greater accuracy of the version by no means compensates for the loss of harmony and rhythm and sweetness, both of sound and of association. An English reader could understand the Psalms *no better*, and he could not enjoy them *half so well*." I have been charged with going directly against "existing standards of public tastes and feeling," in following the Hebrew order of the words, where such order is not the most natural in English. This is "to undo the work of such men as Wordsworth and Tennyson." Again, "in the original, the paronomasia or alliteration [to preserve which the structure of the sentence in English has been made to accommodate itself to the structure in Hebrew] amounts only to a delicate hint, which may pass unnoticed except to an observant eye; in the translation it obtrudes itself as a prominent feature of the style." And both critics concur in thinking that I have myself fallen into the very errors in point of taste which I have condemned in other translations.

Now I may at once say that to some extent, if not to the whole extent alleged by the reviewers, I plead guilty to the indictment. I have carried minute and punctilious accuracy too far. I have sometimes adhered too closely, without any adequate and compensating result, to the order of the words in the Hebrew. It will be an evidence of the sincerity of my repentance on this head, that in the present edition I have in many instances corrected both the one fault and the other. But I cannot concede all that the critics demand of me.

1. In the first place, I did not say, in the preface to my first edition, that I had not "needlessly departed from our Authorized Version," but that I had "not needlessly departed from *the sound English* of our Authorized Version;" and my meaning was evident, because I immediately gave as

instances of departure the use of the verb "to seize" and of the noun "sympathy."[1]

2. In the next place, I feel quite sure that those who lay so much stress upon "harmony and rhythm and sweetness," are thinking more of the Prayer-Book Version of the Psalms, than of that of King James' translators. The former is far more musical, more balanced, and also more paraphrastic than the latter; and from constantly hearing it read in the church services, we have become so thoroughly habituated to it that almost any departure from its well-known cadences offends the ear. Indeed our familiarity with this version is such, that not only would most English churchmen having occasion to quote a verse of a Psalm quote it as it stands in the Prayer-Book, but they would often be very much surprised if they were told that the very sense of the Bible version was different. Of the multitude of persons who are familiar with the phrase, "The iron entered into his soul," how many are aware that the rendering in our Bible is, "He was laid in iron"? There can be no question as to which is the more rhythmical and the more expressive; but there can also be no question that the Authorized Version faithfully represents the Hebrew, which the other does not. It would be no difficult task to quote a number of passages from the Bible version of the Psalms which fail essentially in rhythm just because they are faithful to the original.

Take for instance the following (Ps. 58:7): "Let them melt away as waters *which* run continually: *when* he bendeth *his bow to shoot* his arrows, let them be as cut in pieces."

Now contrast with this the freer but inaccurate rendering of the Prayer-Book version: "Let them fall away like water that runneth apace; and when they shoot their arrows, let them be rooted out."

Again, the Bible version of 59:19 is: "God shall hear and afflict them, even He that abideth of old. Because they have no changes, therefore they fear not God."

Whereas the Prayer-Book version (again very inaccurate, but much smoother) is: "Yea, even God, that endureth for ever, shall hear me, and bring them down: for they will not turn nor fear God."

In the Bible, 68:19 stands: "Thou, O God, didst send a plentiful rain, whereby Thou didst confirm Thine inheritance, when it was weary."

In the Prayer-Book version it is: "Thou, O God, sentest a gracious rain upon Thine inheritance, and refreshedst it when it was weary."

---

1. So it ought to have stood: the verb "to sympathize" was put by mistake for the noun "sympathy." I have only used it once in Ps. 69, and there to express a Hebrew noun which occurs nowhere else.

Or compare the two versions in 49:7-9, or in 130:1-4, and the same phenomenon presents itself, as it does in many other instances; the Bible is the more accurate, the Prayer-Book the more rhythmical version. But if this is the case, then in estimating a new translation, the object of which is avowedly to give as exactly as possible the sense of the original, justice requires that it should be compared with the language of the Authorized Version, not with that of the Prayer-Book.

3. Thirdly, I have been censured for adhering too closely to the *form* of the Hebrew, both in its idiom and in the structure of the clauses. Perhaps I have gone too far in this direction. But before a question of this kind can be decided, it is important to lay down as clearly as possible to the mind what it is we aim at in a translation. "There are two maxims of translation," says Goethe: "the one requires that the author of a foreign nation be brought to us in such a manner that we may regard him as our own; the other, on the contrary, demands of us that we transport ourselves over to him, and adopt his situation, his mode of speaking, his peculiarities. The advantages of both are sufficiently known to all instructed persons, from masterly examples." Each of these methods "is good," says Mrs. Austin, the accomplished translator of Ranke's *History of the Popes*, "with relation to its end—the one when matter alone is to be transferred, the other when matter and form." And she adds very truly: "The praise that a translated work might be taken for an original, is acceptable to the translator only when the original is a work in which *form* is unimportant." She instances Pope's *Homer* as essentially a failure, because we want to know not only *what* Homer said, but *how* he said it. "A light narrative," she continues, "a scientific exposition, or a plain statement of facts, which pretends to nothing as a work of art, cannot be too thoroughly naturalized.

Whatever may be thought of the difficulties in the way of this kind of translation, they are slight compared with those attending the other kind, as anybody who carefully studies the masterpieces in this way must perceive. In the former kind the requisites are two: the meaning of the author, and a good vernacular style; in the latter, the translator has, as far as possible, to combine with these the idiomatic tone of the author—to place him before the reader with his national and individual peculiarities of thought and of speech. The more rich, new, and striking these peculiarities are, the more arduous will the task become; for there is manifestly a boundary-line, difficult if not impossible to define, beyond which the most courageously faithful translator dares not venture, under pain of becoming unreadable. This must be mainly determined by the plasticity of his language, and by the taste of his fellow-countrymen. A German translator can effect, and may venture, more than an English; an

English than a French —and this, not only because his language is more full and pliant, but because Germans have less nationality, and can endure unusual forms of speech for the sake of gaining accurate insight into the characteristics of the literature of other countries."[2]

It is on these grounds that Mrs. Austin defends her own "Germanisms" in her translation of Goethe into English. It is on similar grounds that I would defend "Hebraisms" in the rendering of the Psalms and the poetical portion of the Hebrew Scriptures into English. In the poetry of a people, more than in any other species of literature, *form* is of importance. Hence we find Mrs. Austin, whose skill as a translator has been universally admitted, not shunning inversions of language in her translations from Goethe, where "fidelity" and "literalness" are her object. Thus, for instance, the lines in the *Metamorphose der Pflanzen*:

> "Dich verwirret, Geliebte, die tausendfaltige Mischung,
> Dieses Blumengewühls über dem Garten umher;"

are rendered by her:

> "Thee perplexes, beloved, the thousandfold intermixture
> Of this flowery throng, around in the garden."

And again,

> "Blattlos aber und schnell erhebt sich der zärtere Stengel,
> Und ein Wundergebild zieht den Betrachtenden an,"

is translated:

> "Leafless, however, and rapid, up darts the slenderer flower-stalk,
> And a wonderful picture attracts the observer's eye."

I have in the same way deliberately preferred, where the English idiom did not absolutely forbid it, to retain the order of the words in the Hebrew, because I felt that in sacrificing the *form*, I should be inflicting a loss upon the reader. However, as I said, in revising my work I have somewhat modified my practice in this respect, and have contented myself on several occasions with putting the more literal rendering in a note.

4. Besides being guilty of too great "punctiliousness" and "inelegance," where idiom and harmony are concerned, I have sinned, according to one of my reviewers,[3] in the introduction of the word "Jehovah" instead of "the Lord," which has for centuries been its customary equivalent. The change, he says, would be perfectly legitimate, if I were professing to make everything give way to verbal exactness. But as I

---

2. *Characteristics of Goethe*, vol. i., pp.xxxv—xxxvii.
3. *Saturday Review*, July 2, 1864.

allow other considerations to come in, he thinks that the perpetual recurrence of the Hebrew form of the word is in the highest degree strange and unpleasant. "As the name had fallen out of use in the Jewish church, and never became current in the Christian, our old translators did well to prefer the idea to the name; and the attempt to bring back the name seems now to force into prominence its local and national character, where everything calls for a word which has nothing local or national about it." In reply to these objections, it might be almost sufficient to observe that in retaining the Hebrew name I have only followed the example of every modern translator of eminence. But, of course, it is still a question for consideration, whether there are sufficient grounds for the change.

I think there are very cogent grounds, which the reviewer in his dislike of novelty, or his dislike of Puritanism, has entirely overlooked:

1. In the first place, our translators in their use of the word "Lord" make no distinction between two names, "Jehovah" and "Adonai," perfectly distinct in Hebrew, and conveying different conceptions of God.

2. In the next place, it is well known that whole Psalms are characterized, just as sections of the Pentateuch are characterized, by peculiar names of God, and it is surely of some importance to retain as far as possible these characteristic features, especially when critical discussions have made them prominent, and questions of age and authorship have turned upon them.

3. What the reviewer regards as a disagreeable innovation, has been held by very good authorities to be a desirable emendation in our Authorized Version. "Why continue the translation of the Hebrew into English," says Coleridge, "*at second hand*, through the medium of the Septuagint? Have we not adopted the Hebrew word *Jehovah*? Is not the *Κύριος*, or Lord, of the Septuagint, a Greek substitute in countless instances for the Hebrew, *Jehovah*? Why not, then, restore the original word; and in the Old Testament religiously render *Jehovah*, by Jehovah; and every text in the New Testament, referring to the Old, by the Hebrew word in the text referred to?"[4]

No one could be a better judge on such a point than one who, like Coleridge, was both poet and critic; and it is observable that he would have carried the change even farther than to confine it to the Old Testament. And the late Professor Blunt, quoting this passage, remarks that "though we may not agree with him to the full extent of his conclusion that 'had this been done, Socinianism would have been scarcely possible

4. Coleridge's *Remains*, iv. p. 226.

in England,' yet we cannot doubt that the imperfect translation of the divine name has had its effect in fostering it."[5]

4. If owing to merely superstitious scruples the name fell out of use in the Jewish church, and if owing to a too slavish copying of the Greek and Latin versions our own version lost the word, these are reasons of no force whatever against a return to the original use. It is no doubt a question how the word should be written when transferred to another language. "Jehovah" certainly is not a proper equivalent for the Hebrew form; for it is well known that the Jews, having lost the true pronunciation of the name, transferred to it the vowels of the other name "Adonai," which in reading they have for centuries substituted for it. Some of the Germans write, "Jahveh," others "Jahaveh;" and Hupfeld, despairing of any certainty as to the vowels, retains merely the consonants and writes "Jhvh." Probably the most correct equivalent in English would be "Yahveh" or Yahaveh," but this would look pedantic, and would doubtless shock sensitive eyes and ears far more than the comparatively familiar form, Jehovah. Nor must it be forgotten that this Hebrew form is sometimes, though rarely, admitted by our translators, as is also the still less euphonious form, Jah.

5. Lastly, I cannot feel that it is any objection that the use of the Hebrew name "forces into prominence its local and national character." On the contrary, if we are to read the Old Testament with anything like discerning appreciation, if we are not to confound the New Testament with the Old, as the majority of ancient commentators and a large number of modern commentators do, thus effacing altogether, as far as in them lies, the progressive character of Revelation, we shall be anxious to retain all that is distinctive and characteristic in the earlier Scriptures, that we may give to each portion its proper value. We shall not wish to efface a single character by which God helps us the better to trace His footsteps, but shall thankfully remember that He who "in many portions and in many manners spake to the fathers by the prophets, hath in these last days spoken to us in a Son."

Having said so much on this subject of translation, I will venture to add a few words on the proposed revision of our Authorized Version.

It appears to me a matter of real congratulation to the church that such a revision has at length been seriously entertained by Convocation. I do not share the feelings of those who look upon any attempt to correct manifest errors with dislike and apprehension. Indeed the objectors have in this instance suffered their fears very grossly to exaggerate the evil against which they protest. Nothing surely can be more moderate, or

5. Blunt, *Duties of the Parish Priest*, Lect. II. p. 41.

more cautiously framed, than the language of the resolution adopted by the Southern Province in Convocation. They only advise that those passages in the Authorized Version should be amended "where plain and clear errors . . . shall on due investigation be found to exist." Yet it has been assumed, by nearly every writer and speaker who is opposed to revision, that revision is equivalent to reconstruction. It has been assumed that a commission would not leave of the existing structure one stone upon another—would scarcely even make use of the stones of the old building for the construction of the new. The whole strength of the objectors' case rests on this assumption. Yet, even setting aside the distinct avowal of the resolution to the contrary, scholars and men of taste and judgment are not likely to agree together to be guilty of any such ruthless demolition. The probability is that among those to whom the task of revision would be entrusted, there would be found many men whose veneration for our Authorized Version is quite as great, and quite as intelligent, as that of those who object to any alteration. Men of this kind would not be for rash and hasty corrections, or for trivial emendations. They would not suffer wanton injury to be done. They would religiously preserve the fine old diction, the mother idiom, the grace and the strength of the existing version. These are too precious a heritage, they would feel, to be lightly sacrificed. Keeping close to the terms of the resolution, they would only give a true rendering to passages which have *undoubtedly* been wrongly translated.

With the overthrow of this assumption, all the other arguments against revision lose their force. It has been said, for instance, that the specimens of new translations which have lately appeared are not such as to hold out any prospect of improvement in the new version. They may be more literal, but they are less idiomatic than the authorized translation. But it is one thing for an individual to put forth a translation which he believes gives the nearest and most literal rendering of a book; it is another thing to revise an existing translation. In the former case, the utmost liberty may be claimed in the latter, the work has its own obvious limitations. The difference is the difference between the architect who builds a new church as a rival to the old, or with the view of securing some particular advantages, acoustic properties for instance, which the old did not possess, and the architect who restores an ancient and glorious cathedral, removing only defects and scrupulously preserving all its characteristic features.

So, again, with regard to the objection that the new version would not gain universal acceptance, as that of 1611 has done; this surely depends upon the manner of its execution. No doubt even those comparatively few and moderate corrections which alone are designed would at first be regarded with some suspicion, especially because, as the Bishop of St.

David's pointed out, clergymen and dissenting ministers would thereby be robbed of some of their favorite texts. No doubt there would be some sharp criticism of the work. But if learned men of all parties, non-conformists as well as churchmen, are associated in the revision, and if the revision is wisely and carefully made within the assigned limits, there seems no very obvious reason why the new book should not find acceptance gradually, and eventually supersede the old. If it did not, it would fall by its own demerits, and no amount of "authority" would ensure its success.

The limitation of the revision to "plain and clear errors," does away also with the objection, of which so much has been made, that the faith of the ignorant would be unsettled if they were led to suppose that what they had been accustomed to receive as the Word of God, was not the Word of God. This is precisely the kind of argument, which would have stopped the Reformation. And the objectors seem to forget that the mischief they apprehend is already done, when ministers of religion give, as they often do, corrections of the existing version in their pulpits, and when designing men lay hold of manifest mistranslation as an instrument whereby to shake the faith of the multitude in the Bible.

One more objection only I shall notice. It has been argued that no essential doctrine would be affected by the change, and that therefore the change is not worth the risk which it entails. Those who rely most on this argument are the very last who ought to make it. For though it may be quite true that no doctrine of importance would be touched, yet holding, as they do, that "all Scripture is given by inspiration of God," they ought to hold that its exact sense is everywhere of importance. But I am not prepared to admit the allegation in all its breadth. There are passages in our Bible where great truths are at least grievously obscured by a wrong translation. Take, for instance, that very striking prophecy[6] in the latter part of the eighth and the beginning of the ninth chapter of the Prophet Isaiah. Perhaps there is no more remarkable prophecy in the Bible; yet it is worse than obscure as it stands in our Authorized Version. The sense given in the Authorized Version is even the exact opposite of the true sense. The prophecy ceases to be a prophecy at all. The prophet had been speaking of a thick darkness which should settle upon the land. Men in their perplexity, instead of seeking counsel of God and His Word (8:19, 20), were seeking to necromancers and to "wizards that *chirp*" (E.V. *peep*, i.e. pipe like birds, the Latin *pipiare*), and that mutter. The inevitable result was a yet more terrible hopelessness.

---

6. This is the passage to which the Bishop of Llandaff referred in his speech in Convocation.

> And they shall pass along hardly bestead and hungry; and it shall come to pass that when they shall be hungry, they shall fret themselves, and they shall curse their king and their God; and they shall look upward, and they shall look to the earth, and behold trouble and anguish, and distressful gloom. But the darkness is driven away. For there shall no more be gloom where there was vexation. As in the former time He lightly esteemed the land of Zebulun and the land of Naphtali, so in the latter time He hath made her glorious by the way of the sea, beyond Jordan, Galilee of the nations. The people that walked in darkness have seen a great light: they that dwell in the land of the shadow of death, upon them hath the light shined. Thou hast multiplied the nation, Thou hast increased their joy: they joy before Thee according to the joy in harvest, and as men rejoice when they divide the spoil. For Thou hast broken the yoke of his burden and the staff (laid upon) his shoulder, the rod of his oppressor, as in the day of Midian. For every greave of the greaved warrior in the battle-tumult, and the garment[7] rolled in blood, shall be for burning, for fuel of fire. For a child in born unto us, a Son is given unto us; and the government shall be upon His shoulder, and His name shall be called Wonderful, Counsellor, Mighty God, Father of Eternity,[8] Prince of Peace."

I have purposely abstained from any needless departure here from the Authorized Version. I have only corrected "plain and clear errors."

The alterations which I have made in the above passage are such as I believe, with one exception (that at the end of 8:22, "but the darkness is driven away"), would be accepted by all Hebrew scholars. And I would ask any one who recollects that this important passage is read every Christmas day in the ears of the people, and who has felt how impossible it is to extract any intelligible sense from it, whether the mere correction of acknowledged errors would not be an immense boon, whether it would not make at least one great prophecy concerning Christ shine with tenfold brightness? Are such corrections valueless? Would any injury or any loss follow from them? If not, is it not at least worthwhile to make the trial, to see whether we can improve without injuring our Authorized Version?

Since the first edition of this volume was published, several works have appeared in England bearing more or less directly on the interpretation of the Psalms. Bishop Wordsworth's *Commentary* is well known. It keeps to the beaten track of ancient exposition. *The Psalms by Four Friends* is a fresh and suggestive contribution to the literature of the subject. But it is impossible not to feel some regret that men who have done their work in other respects so well should have followed so arbitrary an authority as Ewald in his chronological arrangement. The

7. Properly, the soldier's cloak.

8. Or perhaps, "Father of the age to come," or "Author of a new dispensation."

Rev. Charles Taylor in his book, *The Gospel in the Law*, has treated with learning and ability many of the questions connected with the intrepretation of the Messianic Psalms and the Psalms of Imprecation. Still more recently, Dr. Binnie of Stirling has published a work on the Psalms, in which he discusses their history and poetical structure, their theology, and their use in the church. In his chapters on the theology of the Psalms, he maintains the most commonly received views respecting the Messiah, a future life, the imprecations, etc., but he handles these subjects with learning and moderation. I must not omit to add to these works, Professor Plumptre's volume of *Biblical Studies*, in which he has republished a very interesting paper on "the Psalms of the Sons of Korah."

I have had so little leisure for the revision of my own volume that I have not been able to make all the use of these different works which I could have desired. But I am indebted to them as well as to many correspondents, known and unknown, for valuable suggestions, which perhaps at some future time I may be able to turn to better account.

St. David's College, Lampeter
March 14, 1870

The First Edition

This work is designed to be a contribution to the study of the Old Testament. In preparing it for the press, I have kept before me the wants of two classes of readers; those who have, and those who have not, an acquaintance with the original text; and I am led to hope that thus the commentary will be more widely useful than if it had been merely popular on the one hand, or exclusively critical on the other.

It will be seen, that I have endeavored to accomplish three things.

1. In the first place, I have given a new translation of the Psalms, which it has been my object to make as faithful and as accurate as possible, at the same time that I have sought to avoid rather than to imitate that punctiliousness of rendering which, especially among our commentators on the New Testament, has been so much in fashion of late. In many instances, this too scrupulous accuracy is so far from helping to the better understanding of an author, that it has exactly the reverse effect. The idiom of the English language is sacrificed to the idiom of the Greek; and nothing whatever is gained by the sacrifice. What is supposed to be extreme accuracy is, in fact, nothing but extreme inelegance. The consequence is, that the hybrid English, which is designed to represent the Greek so exactly, stands bald and ragged, in the garb of a beggar as well as a foreigner, and fails to convey any intelligible idea at all, unless

it be to a reader who already is acquainted with the Greek. The Old Testament has not as yet been subjected, to the same extent, to this starving, denaturalizing process, though it has not altogether escaped. Indeed, it would be no difficult matter to cite passages from recent English translations, rendered evidently with the greatest care and apparent fidelity to the original, which are wanting in all the essentials of a good translation, having neither rhythm, nor force, nor elegance. I am not so presumptuous as to assert that where others have failed, I have succeeded. I can only say I have striven to the utmost to produce a faithful but not a servile translation.

Perhaps it is hardly necessary to add, that a new translation implies no disparagement to our Authorized Version. To the many excellences of that version, no one can be more alive than I am: the more it is studied, the more these will be appreciated; the more its noble simplicity, its unapproachable grandeur, its rhythmic force of expression will be felt. But it is obvious that, since the time when it was made, our knowledge of the grammar of the Hebrew language, of the structure of Hebrew poetry, and of many other subjects tending to the elucidation of the sacred text, has been largely increased. A modern interpreter is bound to avail himself of these new stores of knowledge, and may reasonably hope to produce, at least in some passages, a more accurate rendering of the Hebrew than that which our translators have adopted. But, as a rule, I have not needlessly departed from the sound English of our Authorized Version. Two or three words not used by our translators, such as the verb "to seize," and the noun "sympathy,"[1] I have ventured to employ where they seemed to me, in the particular passage, most exactly to convey the meaning of the original words. I have also adhered more closely than is usual in the English Version, to the order of the words in the Hebrew, because in many instances, as might be expected in a language so antithetical in its structure, the special force of certain words is thus maintained, or some delicate shade of meaning more clearly brought out, which would otherwise be lost. How far the attempt thus made has been successful, it is for others to judge.

2. In the next place, I have endeavored by means of Introductions to the several Psalms, and by Explanatory Notes, to convey to the English reader a true idea of the scope and meaning of each. Here I have availed myself of the best commentaries, ancient and modern. I have used them freely, but have laid it down as a rule to express my obligations, and to give the name of the writer from whom I have borrowed. If in some few

---

1. Both of these words are good old English words, and used by our best writers. The first is as old as R. of Gloucester, the second as early at least as Spenser. Shakespeare's is "condolement."

instances I may have neglected to observe this rule, it has not been done intentionally. From the Fathers I have gleaned but little, their style of exposition being such as to lead them to disregard the literal sense, and to seek for mystical and allegorical interpretations. For the first true exposition of Scripture, of the Old Testament more especially, we must come to the time of the Reformation. Here, Luther and Calvin hold the foremost place, each having his peculiar excellence. Luther, in his own grand fearless way, always goes straight to the heart of the matter. He is always on the look-out for some great principle, some food for the spiritual life, some truth which can be turned to practical account. He is preeminently what in modern phrase would be called *subjective*, as a commentator. Every word of Scripture seems to him instinct with life and meaning for himself and his own immediate circumstances. But on that very account he not unfrequently misses the proper and original force of a passage, because he is so intent on a personal application; not to mention that he cannot always shake himself free of the allegorical cobwebs of patristic interpretation. They still cling to the mane of the lion, who in his strength has trodden down the thicket.

Calvin, on the other hand, may justly be styled the great master of exegesis. He is always careful to ascertain as exactly as possible the *whole* meaning and scope of the writer on whom he comments. In this respect his critical sagacity is marvellous, and quite unrivalled. He keeps close, moreover, to the sure ground of historical interpretation, and, even in the Messianic Psalms, always sees a first reference to the actual circumstances of the writer. Indeed, the view which he constantly takes of such Psalms would undoubtedly expose him to the charge of Rationalism, were he now alive. In many parts of Psalm 45 he boldly denies any Messianic meaning at all. In expounding Psalm 72, he warns us against a sophistical application of words to Christ, which do not properly belong to Him. In writing on Psalm 40, he ventures to suggest, that the quotation from it in the Epistle to the Hebrews is not made in accordance with the genuine sense of the passage as it stands in the Psalm. I quote these things simply to show what has been said by a man who, though of course a damnable heretic in the eyes of the Church of Rome, is by a considerable section of our own church regarded as a high and weighty authority.

Even Luther is not guilty of those forced and unreal expositions which, it is to be feared, are now becoming common. In writing on Psalm 20 he says: "This Psalm almost all expounds of Christ. But such an exposition appears to me to be too farfetched to be called literal." Calvin's method of interpretation, in this and similar instances, will be abundantly evident to any one who will read the following commentary, where I have constantly and largely quoted from him. In some cases, as in Psalm 17, where he denies all reference to a future life, I have felt constrained to differ from him: in others, as in the Imprecatory Psalms, I have thought that he hardly carries out his own principles consistently. But of the general soundness of his principles of exegesis, where he is not under the influence of doctrinal prejudices—as, indeed, he rarely is in his commentary on the Psalms—I am thoroughly convinced. He is the prince of commentators. He stands foremost among those who, with that true courage which fears God rather than man, have dared to leave the narrow grooves and worn ruts of a conventional theology and to seek truth only for itself.

It is well to study the writings of this great man, if only that we may learn how possible it is to combine soundness in the faith with a method of interpretation varying even in important particulars from that commonly received. Nothing, I believe, is so likely to beget in us a spirit of enlightened liberality, of Christian forbearance, of large-hearted moderation, as the careful study of the history of doctrine and the history of interpretation. We shall then learn how widely good men have differed in all ages, how much of what we are apt to think essential truth is not essential, and, without holding loosely what we ourselves believe to be true, we shall not be hasty to condemn those who differ from us.

Among more modern commentators, I am indebted chiefly to the Germans. The valuable works of De Wette, Tholuck, Stier, Delitzsch, Ewald, Hupfeld, and Bunsen, I have always consulted with advantage.[2] Ewald is very often arbitrary, no doubt, and with many of his conclusions I am quite unable to agree: but his intuitive faculty is admirable, and much may be learned from him even where I with others may deem him most at fault. He holds deservedly a high position, but he would hold a higher, were he less severe and unjust in his condemnation of those who differ from him. Hupfeld's *Commentary* is the most exhaustive that has yet appeared, and, in point of grammatical analysis, by far the most masterly. Indeed, I know of none, on any part of the Old Testament, at all to be compared to it in these respects. Delitzsch represents a different school both of grammatical interpretation and of theology. He has a very extensive acquaintance with Talmudical and Rabbinical lore, and leans to the Jewish expositors. In depth and spiritual insight, as well as in the

---

2. No candid reader of this volume will, I hope, be left in doubt how far I agree, or disagree, with writers who differ so widely from one another as some of those just named. But to lay down exactly here the theological position of each of these writers would be a difficult and delicate task, and one to which I do not feel I am called.

full recognition of the Messianic element in the Psalms, he is far before either of the others. The laborious dulness of Hengstenberg renders it a tedious task to read his *Commentary*; and the English translation makes matters ten times worse.[3] The notes in Bunsen's *Bibelwerk* are, as a rule, excellent; in many instances where I have ventured to dissent from Hupfeld, I have had the pleasure of finding myself supported by Bunsen in my rendering of a passage. It is a matter of deep regret that the illustrious author did not live to witness the completion of a work in which his learning and his piety both shine so brightly, and which he had so greatly at heart.[4]

English expositors who have preceded me on the same path, have not, I hope, been overlooked. Bishop Horne's *Commentary*, the notes of Hammond and Horsley, the work of the Rev. G. Phillips (now President of Queen's College, Cambridge), and Mr. Thrupp's *Introduction*, and other works more or less directly bearing on the interpretation of the Psalms, have been consulted.[5] Dean Alford, in his *Commentary* on the Epistle to the Hebrews, has everywhere recognized and maintained, as it seems to me, the soundest principles of interpretation with reference to the Psalms, more especially the Messianic Psalms, and it is only to be regretted that this able expositor has not devoted some of that time and those energies to the elucidation of the Old Testament, which, in their devotion to the New, have already borne noble fruit. And here I cannot refrain from expressing my wish that our great English scholars had not been so exclusively occupied with the criticism and interpretation of the New Testament, to the comparative neglect of the Old.[6]

---

3. I give two specimens taken at random. "By the lowly is to be understood such a person, as at the time feels his lowliness; as also under the proud, he who is such in his own eyes, are to be thought of." - Vol.iii. p. 489. "The hero David, the *deforcer* of the lion, and the conqueror of Goliath." *Ibid.* xix.

4. In many things I differ materially from Bunsen, nor do I appear as the advocate of all his theological views; but of this I am sure, that in England he has been greatly misunderstood and misrepresented: and I cannot refrain from expressing my admiration of one who, amidst the anxious demands of public duties, could find time for the prosecution of studies as manifold and various as they were important, and who to the splendour of vast attainments, and the dignity of a high position, added the better glory of a Christian life.

5. The notes which accompany the Tract Society's *Paragraph Bible* deserve high commendation. They are brief, and to the point, and, without any affectation of learning, often give the correct sense of difficult passages. An unpretending, but useful little volume, has also been published by Mr. Ernest Hawkins, containing annotations on the Prayer-Book Version.

6. This is a reproach which is not likely to attach to us much longer. Dr. Pusey has already led the way in his elaborate commentary on the Minor Prophets, a work full of erudition. We are also promised a commentary on the whole Bible, under the editorship of the Rev. F. C. Cook, which is intended to convey to

The contrast between ourselves and the leading German commentators is in this respect, very remarkable. In Germany, those who have been most successful in their elucidation of the Greek text of the New Testament, have, in most cases, come to it well furnished and equipped with Hebrew lore, De Wette, Bleek, Tholuck, Umbreit, Stier, Delitzsch, and others to whom we owe some of the most valuable commentaries on the Gospels and Epistles, are men who have interpreted, with no less ability and success, various portions of the Old Testament; and it is impossible not to feel how materially their familiarity with the latter has assisted them in their exposition of the former. To Bleek and Delitzsch we are indebted for the two most thorough and exhaustive commentaries which have yet been written on the Epistle to the Hebrews. A glance at Dean Alford's volume will show, what it is no disparagement to him to remark, how largely he has borrowed from their accumulated treasures. Of that Epistle, perhaps more than any other portion of the New Testament, it may be safely said that it cannot be understood without a profound and accurate knowledge of the Pentateuch, the Psalms, and the Prophets. But the same remark holds good of the other books. As both Testaments were given by inspiration of the same Spirit, as both speak one truth, though in divers manners and under different aspects, it is obvious that the more complete our understanding of the one, the more complete also will be our understanding of the other.

3. Lastly, I have appended a series of notes, in which I have discussed the criticism of the text, the various readings, the grammatical difficulties, and other matters of interest rather to the scholar than to the general reader. These have been placed separately, for the most part, at the end of each Psalm, in order not to embarrass those who know nothing of Hebrew.

Here, as indeed in the notes generally, it will be seen that I have been fuller in the later Psalms than in the earlier. The reason for this is, that I had at one time hoped to finish the whole work in the compass of one volume, a design which I was afterwards compelled to abandon. But I trust that in no instance has any essential point been overlooked. For the

---

English readers the results of the most recent investigations into the criticism and interpretation of the sacred text. There is no lack of scholarship in England fully equal to such a task. Such accomplished scholars as the Deans of St. Paul's and Westminster, Mr. Grove, Mr. Plumptre, and many of the contributors to Smith's *Dictionary of the Bible*, have already cast a flood of light on the history, geography, antiquities, etc. of the Old Testament. The Bishop of Ely, in his *Lectures on the Pentateuch and the Elohistic Psalms*, and Mr. Pritchard, in his reply to Bishop Colenso, have given further and abundant proof that the criticism of the Old Testament is no unknown field to our English divines.

ordinary grammatical rules and constructions, the lexicon and grammar must be consulted; I have only handled those more exceptional cases which present some real difficulty, verbal, textual, or grammatical. The critical aids of which I have availed myself are the following:

1. The well-known collections of Kennicott and DeRossi, whence the various readings of the principal manuscript have been gathered. These various readings are, unhappily, of comparatively little value in ascertaining the true text of the Hebrew Bible, as none of the manuscripts are of any high antiquity. A useful digest will be found in Dr. Davidson's *Revision of the Hebrew Text of the Old Testament.*

2. The Versions. The text of the Septuagint which I have followed is that of Tischendorf's last edition. For the other Greek versions, Montfaucon's edition of Origen's *Hexapla* has been used.

The Chaldee, Arabic, and Syriac versions have been consulted in Walton's *Polyglot*, and the last also in Dathe's edition of the *Syriac Psalter*. For Jerome's versions I have used Migne's edition of 1851. I have also made use of the Anglo-Saxon version, and the ancient Latin version which accompanies it, which were edited by Thorpe.

Besides these, I have constantly had before me the versions of Luther, Diodati, Mendelssohn, Zunz, and others.

To these aids I must add Furst's *Concordance*, and the *Thesaurus* of Gesenius, both of them wonderful monuments of learning and industry. The grammars which I have used are those of Gesenius, the English edition by Davidson, based on the sixteenth German edition (Bagster, 1852); and Ewald's *Lehrbuch*, (1855). The commentaries already referred to, especially those of Hupfeld and Delitzsch, have assisted me materially here, as well as Reinke's on the Messianic Psalms. I have also found Maurer and DeWette of service, more so, indeed, critically than exegetically: Hitzig and Olshausen I only know at second-hand.

To three friends I am under great personal obligation: to the Rev. J.G. Mould, formerly Fellow and Tutor of Corpus Christi College, Cambridge, and the Rev. C. Pritchard, formerly Fellow of St. John's College [now Savilian Professor of Astonomy in the University of Oxford], for many valuable suggestions; and to Mr. W. Aldis Wright, the learned librarian of Trinity College, who has carefully revised a great part of the work. I am only sorry that the earlier sheets had been printed before he saw them, and contain therefore many more inaccuracies, I fear, than the later.

Thus I have explained what I have done, or, rather, what I have attempted to do. Many faults there must be; but, to quote the words of

Calvin, "Even if I have not succeeded to the full extent of my endeavors, still the attempt itself merits some indulgence; and all I ask is, that each, according to the advantage he shall himself derive therefrom, will be an impartial and candid judge of my labours."

Among the students of Hebrew in England it is a pleasure for me to think that I may count many of my former and present pupils, many who have heard from me in the lectureroom of King's College, London, or of St. David's College, Lampeter, the explanations and the criticisms which I have here placed in a more permanent form. I cannot help indulging the hope that they will welcome the book as coming from one who can never cease to feel the liveliest interest in all that concerns them. It would be no common gratification to me to know that it had served in some instances, perhaps, to continue a work which I had begun, or had even revived a study which the pressure of a busy life had compelled some of them to lay aside.

And now I commit to the Great Head of the Church this attempt to interpret some portion of His Holy Word, humbly beseeching Him to grant that it may bring forth fruit to His glory and the edification of His Church.

Truth has been my one object, I can truly say, mindful, I hope, that truth can only be attained through "the heavenly illumination of the Holy Ghost." Yet I would not forget what Luther has so beautifully said, that none can hope to understand for himself or teach to others the full meaning of every part of the Psalms. It is enough for us if we understand it in part. "Many things doth the Spirit reserve to Himself that He may ever keep us as His scholars, many things He doth but show to allure us, many more He teacheth to affect us; and as Augustine hath admirably said, No one hath ever so spoken as to be understood by every one in every particular, much more doth the Holy Ghost Himself alone possess the full understanding of all His own words. Wherefore I must honestly confess, that I know not whether I possess the full and proper (*ligitimam*) understanding of the Psalms or not, though I doubt not that that which I give is in itself true. For all that Saint Augustine, Jerome, Athanasius, Hilary, Cassiodorus, and others, have written on the Psalter is very true, though sometimes as far as possible from the literal meaning . . . One falls in one thing, another in another . . . others will see what I do not. What then follows, but that we should help one another, and make allowances for those who err, as knowing that we either have erred, or shall err, ourselves. . . . I know that he must be a man of most shameless hardihood who would venture to give it out that he understands a single book of Scripture in all its parts: nay, who would venture to assume that one Psalm has ever been perfectly understood by any one? Our life is a beginning and a setting out, not a finishing; he is best, who shall have approached nearest to the mind of the Spirit."[7]

St. David's College, Lampeter
March 1, 1864

7. Luther, *Pref. in Operationes in Psalmos.* (Tom. xiv., p. 9, Ed. Irmischer.)

INTRODUCTION

CHAPTER 1

David and the Lyric Poetry of the Hebrews

THE Poetry of the Hebrews is mainly of two kinds, lyrical and didactic. They have no epic, and no drama. Dramatic elements are to be found in many of their odes, and the Book of Job and the Song of Songs have sometimes been called Divine dramas ; but dramatic poetry, in the proper sense of that term, was altogether unknown to the Israelites. The remains of their lyric poetry which have been preserved—with one marked exception, the Lament of David over Saul and Jonathan—are almost entirely of a religious character, and were designed chiefly to be set to music, and to be sung in the public services of the sanctuary. The earliest specimen of purely lyrical poetry which we possess is the Song of Moses on the overthrow of Pharaoh in the Red Sea. It is the worthy expression of a nation's joy at being delivered, by the outstretched arm of Jehovah, from the hand of their oppressors. It is the grandest ode to liberty which was ever sung. And it is this, because its homage is rendered, not to some ideal spirit of liberty, deified by a people in the moment of that passionate and frantic joy which follows the successful assertion of their independence, but because it is a thanksgiving to Him who is the one only Giver of Victory and of Freedom. Both in form and spirit it possesses the same characteristics which stamp all the later Hebrew poetry. Although without any regular strophical division, it has the chorus, "Sing ye to Jehovah, for He hath triumphed gloriously," &c.; it was sung evidently in antiphonal measure, chorus answering to chorus and voice to voice; it was sung accompanied by dancing, and to the music of the maidens playing upon the timbrels. Such is its form. In its spirit, it is like all the national songs of the people, a hymn sung to the glory of Jehovah No word celebrates the prowess of the armies of Israel or of their leaders: "Thy right hand, O Jehovah, is become glorious in power; Thy right hand, O Jehovah, hath dashed in pieces the enemy." Thus it commemorates that wonderful victory, and thus it became the pattern after which all later odes of victory were written. The people from whom such poetry could spring, at so early a period of their history, could not have been the rude ignorant horde which some writers delight to represent them; they must have made large use of Egyptian culture, and, in these respects, in poetry and music, must have far surpassed their Egyptian masters.

Early lyric fragments

Some fragments of poetry belong to the narrative of the wanderings in the wilderness. One of these (Num. xxi. 14, 15), too obscure in its allusions to be quite intelligible now, is quoted from a book called "The Book of the Wars of Jehovah," which was probably a collection of ballads and songs, composed on different occasions by the watch-fires of the camp, and, for the most part, in commemoration of the victories of the Israelites over their enemies. Another is the little carol first sung at the digging of the well in the plains of Moab, and afterwards, we may presume, commonly used by those who came to draw water. Bright, fresh, and sparkling it is, as the waters of the well itself. The maidens of Israel, we may believe, chanted it one to another, line by line, as they toiled at the bucket, and thus beguiled their labour. "Spring up, O well!" was the burden or refrain of the song, which would pass from one mouth to another, at each fresh coil of the rope, till the full bucket reached the well's mouth.*

* See the article on the Book of NUMBERS, in Smith's *Dictionary of the Bible*, vol. ii. p. 583.

The Blessing of the High Priest (Num. vi. 24-26), and the chants which were the signal for the Ark to set forward when the people journeyed, and for it to rest when they were about to encamp, are also cast in the form of poetry. But these specimens, interesting as they are in themselves and from the circumstances which gave birth to them, are brief and fugitive. A far grander relic of that time has survived. The Ninetieth Psalm is "The Prayer of Moses the Man of God," written evidently towards the close of the forty years' wandering in the desert. It is touched with the profound melancholy of one who had seen his dearest hopes disappointed, who had endured trials of no common kind, who had buried his kindred in the desert, who had beheld the people that he led out of Egypt smitten down by the heavy wrath of God, who came to the borders of the Promised Land, looked upon it, but was not suffered to enter therein. It is the lofty expression of a faith purified by adversity, of a faith which, having seen every human hope destroyed, clings with the firmer grasp to Him of whom it can say, "From everlasting to everlasting Thou art God." This Psalm is like the pillar of fire and of a cloud which led the march of Israel—it is both dark and bright. It is darkness as it looks, in sorrowful retrospect, upon man; it is light as it is turned, in hope and confidence, to God.

Poetry in the time of the Judges.

During the stormy period which followed the first occupation of Canaan, poetry was probably but little cultivated. Yet it would be a mistake, as Dean Milman has pointed out,* to conclude that the whole period from Joshua to Samuel was a period of "alternate slavery and bloody struggles for independence," or that, during the greater part of it, the Israelites were subject to foreign oppression. Such seems by no means to have been the case. The wars of the time were wars, not of the whole people, but of the several tribes with their immediate neighbours. The conflicts were confined to a very limited area; and out of a period of about four hundred and sixty

* *History of the Jews*, vol. i. p. 219 (2d edition). See also Mr. Drew's *Scripture Studies*, p. 143.

years, more than three hundred were, it may be inferred from the silence of the narrative, years of peace and prosperity. The struggles for independence, however, which did take place, were such as roused the national spirit in an extraordinary degree : it was the age of heroes; and the victory, in one instance at least, was commemorated in a poem worthy of the occasion. Of the song of Deborah Dean Milman says : "The solemn religious commencement, the picturesque description of the state of the country, the mustering of the troops from all quarters, the sudden transition to the most contemptuous sarcasm against the tribes that stood aloof, the life, fire, and energy of the battle, the bitter pathos of the close—lyric poetry has nothing in any language which can surpass the boldness and animation of this striking production."

David.

But the great era of lyric poetry begins with David. Born with the genius of a poet, and skilled in music, he had already practised his art whilst he kept his father's sheep on the hills of Bethlehem. That he was no mean proficient on the harp is evident from his having been sent for to charm away the evil spirit from Saul, in those fits of gloomy despondency and temporary derangement to which that unhappy king was subject. It is probable that he had added careful study to his natural gifts, for we find him closely associated with Samuel and his schools of prophets—men who, like himself, were both poets and musicians. The art which he had thus acquired, and thus carefully studied, was his solace through life. His harp was the companion of his flight from Saul and of his flight from Absalom. It was heard in the caves of Engedi, on the broad uplands of Mahanaim, on the throne of Israel. We have songs of his which date from all periods of his life; from the days of his shepherd youth to his old age, and within a short time of his death. Both his life and his character are reflected in his poetry. That life, so full of singular vicissitudes, might of itself have formed the subject of an epic, and in any other nation but that of the Hebrews would certainly have been made the groundwork of a poem. It is a life teeming with romantic incidents, and those sudden turns of fortune which poets love to describe. The latter portion of his history, that which begins with his great crimes, and which traces step by step their fearful but inevitable chastisement, is itself a tragedy —a tragedy, in terror and pathos, equal to any which the great poets of the Grecian drama have left us, and, in point of human interest as well as Divine instruction, incomparably beyond them.

Life of David in his Psalms.

But the Poets of Israel did not make their national heroes, however great, the subjects of their verse, or, if they did, no works of this kind have come down to us. Designed to be the great teachers of a pure faith to men, chosen of God to speak His words, to utter the yearnings and the hopes of men's hearts towards Him, they were not suffered to forget this their higher vocation, or, when they did forget it, their words perished. Even the fame of Solomon could not secure for his thousand and five songs, which were probably merely of a secular kind, the meed of immortality. Hence it is that we have no Hebrew Poems on the life of David ; and hence also it is that the perils and adventures through which he passed are not described in David's songs as they would have been by more modern poets. We are often at a loss to know to what particular parts of his history, to what turns and circumstances of his fortunes, this or that Psalm is to be referred. Still it is impossible to read them and not to see that they are coloured by the reminiscences of his life. A Psalm of this kind, for instance, is the Twenty-third.* He who speaks there so beautifully of the care of God, under the figure of a shepherd, had known himself what it was to tend his sheep—" to make them lie down in green pastures," to lead them to the side of the brook which had not been dried up by the summer's sun. Another image in that Psalm we can hardly be wrong in conjecturing is borrowed from personal experience. It was scarcely a figure for David to speak of God as spreading a table for him " in the

* Even Ewald almost inclines to allow that this may have been a Psalm of David's, though his final verdict is in favour of a later, though not much later, poet.

presence of his enemies." It was "in the presence of his enemies" that Barzillai and others brought their plentiful provision of "wheat, and barley, and flour, and parched corn, and beans, and lentiles, and parched pulse, and honey, and butter, and cheese of kine, for David, and for the people that were with him, to eat, when they were hungry, and weary, and thirsty in the wilderness." (2 Sam. xvii. 28, 29.)

Or take, again, the Eighteenth Psalm, which we know from the express testimony of the history, as well as from its inscription, to be David's, and which is on all hands admitted to be his. How thickly sown it is with metaphors, which, in his mouth, have a peculiar force and beauty. Such are the names by which he addresses God. Thrice he speaks of God as a rock: "Jehovah is my rock, my fortress, my buckler, the horn of my salvation, my high tower." And again, "Who is a rock, save our God?" And yet again, "Jehovah liveth, and blessed be my rock."* How suitable are such epithets as coming from one who when hunted by Saul had so often taken refuge among the rocks and fastnesses, the almost inaccessible crags and cliffs, of Palestine. As he had escaped by swiftness of foot, so he tells how God had made his feet like the feet of the hinds or gazelles, which he had so often seen bounding from crag to crag before his eyes, and had set him "upon high places" beyond reach of the hunter's arrow. To the same class of metaphors belong also others in the same Psalm: "Thy right hand hath holden me up," "Thou hast made room for my steps under me, that my ankles have not slipt;" whilst the martial character of the whole is thoroughly in keeping with the entire tenor of David's life, who first, as captain of a band of outlaws, lived by his sword, and who afterwards, when he became king, was engaged in perpetual struggles either with foreign or with domestic enemies.

It would be easy to multiply observations of this kind. One other feature of his poetry, as bearing upon our present subject, must not be overlooked. It is full of allusions

* Ps. xviii. 1, 2. See also verses 30, 31, 46. Compare lxii. 2, 6, 7, where, in like manner, God is thrice called a rock.

to sufferings, to distresses, to persecutions; it abounds with complaints of the faithlessness of friends, of the malice of enemies, of snares laid for his life; it tells of constant perils and wonderful deliverances. Such expressions might naturally have come from David's lips again and again. But they are general, not special. Saul is not mentioned, nor Doeg, nor Ahithophel, nor Shimei. Very rarely is there an allusion of which we can say with certainty that it connects itself with one particular event rather than with another. We have enough to convince us that the words are David's words, but not enough to tell us under what pressure of calamity, or by what joy of deliverance, they were called forth. Shepherd, courtier, outlaw, king, poet, musician, warrior, saint—he was all these; he is all these in his Psalms, yet we can lay our finger but upon one or two that seem to exhibit him in one of these characters rather than in another. The inference is obvious: the Psalms were designed not to be the record of a particular life, but to be the consolation and the stay of all those who, with outward circumstances widely different, might find in them, whether in sorrow or in joy, the best expression of feelings which they longed to utter.

Inner life of David.

But if the Poems of David throw comparatively little light on the external circumstances under which they were written, they throw much upon his inner life. And here their value cannot be over-estimated. The notices of the history, indeed, leave us in no doubt as to the reality of his faith, the depth and sincerity of his piety. But the Psalms carry us further. By the help of these we see him, as we see but few men, his heart laid open in communion with God. We see the true man, in the deep humiliation of his repentance, in the invincible strength of his faith, in that cleaving to God in which he surpassed all others. How imperfect, if we had nothing but the narrative in the Books of Samuel to guide us, would be our knowledge of that saddest page in David's history, when "the man after God's own heart" became stained with the double crime of adultery and murder. We might have pictured to ourselves, indeed, the workings of a terrible remorse. We might have imagined how often, as he sat alone, his uneasy thoughts must have wandered to that grave beneath the walls of Rabbah, where the brave soldier whom he had murdered lay in his blood. We might have tried to fill up with words of confession and penitence and thanksgiving, those few syllables, "I have sinned," which are all the history records. But what a light is cast upon that long period of remorseful struggle not yet turned into godly sorrow, by those words in the Thirty-second Psalm: "While I kept silence, my bones waxed old through my roaring all the day, for Thy hand was heavy upon me day and night, and my moisture was turned into the drought of summer." What a keen, irrepressible sense of his crime in that cry in the Fifty-first: "Deliver me from bloodguiltiness, O God, thou God of my salvation." What a knowledge of sin not only in act, but in its bitter and hidden root—a sinful nature, in the acknowledgement, "Behold, in iniquity I was brought forth, and in sin did my mother conceive me." What a yearning for purity, for renewal, for conformity to the will of God, in that humble earnest pleading, "Create for me a clean heart, O God, and a steadfast spirit renew within me." What a clinging, as of a child to a father, in the prayer, "Cast me not away from Thy presence, and take not Thy Holy Spirit from me." What a sense of the joy of forgiveness and reconciliation, when, raised up again and restored, he says, "Blessed is he whose transgression is taken away, whose sin is covered. Blessed is the man to whom Jehovah reckoneth not iniquity, and in whose spirit there is no guile." It is confessions, prayers, vows, like those recorded in his Psalms, which reveal to us the true man, which help us better to understand him than many histories, many apologies.

Character of David.

But as David's life thus shines in his poetry, so also does his character. That character was no common one. It was strong with all the strength of man, tender with all the tenderness of woman. Naturally brave, his courage was heightened and confirmed by that faith in God which never, in the worst extremity, forsook him. Naturally warm-hearted, his affections struck their roots deep into the innermost centre of his being. In his love for his parents, for whom he provided in his own extreme peril—in his love for his wife Michal—for his friend Jonathan, whom he loved as his own soul—for his darling Absalom, whose death almost broke his heart—even for the infant whose loss he dreaded,—we see the same man, the same depth and truth, the same tenderness of personal affection. On the other hand, when stung by a sense of wrong or injustice, his sense of which was peculiarly keen, he could flash out into strong words and strong deeds. He could hate with the same fervour that he loved. Evil men and evil things, all that was at war with goodness and with God—for these he found no abhorrence too deep, scarcely any imprecations too strong. Yet he was, withal, placable and ready to forgive. He could exercise a prudent self-control, if he was occasionally impetuous. His true courtesy, his chivalrous generosity to his foes, his rare delicacy, his rare self-denial, are all traits which present themselves most forcibly as we read his history. He is the truest of heroes in the genuine elevation of his character, no less than in the extraordinary incidents of his life. Such a man cannot wear a mask in his writings. Depth, tenderness, fervour, mark all his poems.

The Third Psalm, written, there can be little doubt, as the title informs us, on his flight from Absalom, combines many traits:—his undaunted courage: "I laid me down and slept; I awaked; for Jehovah sustaineth me: I will not fear ten thousands of the people, who have set themselves against me round about" (ver. 5, 6); his strong conviction that he had right on his side, and that therefore his foes would be overthrown: "Thou has smitten all mine enemies on the cheekbone; Thou hast broken the teeth of the ungodly" (ver. 7); the generous prayer for his misguided subjects: "Thy blessing be upon Thy people" (ver. 8).

So again, in the Fifth Psalm, what burning words of indignation against the enemies of God and of His chosen: "Punish Thou them, O God; let them fall from their counsels; in the multitude of their transgressions cast them away; for they have rebelled against Thee" (ver. 10). (Comp. vii. 14-16.) In the Seventh, what a keen sense of injury, what a lofty, chivalrous spirit: "O Jehovah my God, if I have done this; if there be iniquity in my hands; if I have rewarded evil unto him that was at peace with me; (yea, rather, I have rescued him that without any cause was my enemy:) let the enemy persecute my soul, and take it; yea, let him tread down my life upon the earth, and make my glory abide in the dust" (ver. 3-5). In the Fifteenth, what a noble figure of stainless honour, of the integrity which can stand both before God and before man! In the Sixteenth (ver. 8-11), Seventeenth (ver. 8-15), and Eighteenth (ver. 1, 2), what deep personal affection towards God, an affection tender as it is strong, yet free from the sentimentalism which has so often degraded the later religious poetry of the Church!

One Psalm in particular exhibits with singular beauty and truth both sides of David's character. It is the Sixty-third. The same tenderness of natural affection, the same depth of feeling, which breathes in every word of his elegy upon Jonathan, is here found chastened and elevated, as he pours out his soul towards God. It is the human heart which stretches out the arms of its affections, yearning, longing for the presence and love of Him who is more precious to it than life itself. This is the one side of the Psalm. The other is almost startling in the abruptness of its contrast, yet strikingly true and natural. It breathes the sternness, almost the fierceness, of the ancient warrior, hard beset by his enemies. From that lofty strain of heavenly musing with which the Psalm opens, he turns to utter his vow of vengeance against the traitors who are leagued against him; he triumphs in the prospect of their destruction. They shall perish, so he hopes, in his sight, and their carcases shall be the prey of jackals in the wilderness.

I have lingered thus long upon David, upon his character and his writings, because, in even a brief outline of Hebrew poetry, he, of necessity, occupies a foremost place, and because the Book of Psalms is almost identified with his name. Nor must it be forgotten, that he not only thus personally contributed more than any other individual to the great national collection of religious songs and hymns, but that he may be said to have founded a school of sacred poetry among the Jews. Asaph, Heman, and Ethan (or Jeduthan) whom he appointed as his three chief musicians, were all, it would appear, poets; the first of them so famous as to have reached to a position almost equal to that of David himself. Some of the Psalms, it is true, which go by his name could not have been written by him, as they bear manifest traces of later times. Others are, with more probability, ascribed to him. And these, the Psalms of the sons of Korah, and a few which are anonymous, have many resemblances of thought and expression to those of David. He was the model after which they copied; his the fire which kindled theirs. So great a poet inevitably drew a host of others in his train.

Solomon.

Under Solomon, religious poetry does not seem to have flourished. His own tastes and pursuits were of another kind. The Proverbs can scarcely be called poetry, except that they are cast in a rhythmical form. They are at least only the poetry of a sententious wisdom; they never rise to the height of passion. The earlier portions of the Book contain connected pieces of moral teaching, which may be styled didactic poems. In two passages especially (iii. 13-20, viii. 22-31), where Wisdom is described, we have a still loftier strain. But there was no hand now to wake the echoes of the harp of David.* Lyric poetry had yielded to the wisdom of the *mâshâl*, the proverb, or parable; the age of reflection had succeeded to the age of passion, the calmness of manhood to the heat of youth. Solomon is said, indeed, as has already been remarked, to have written a thousand and five songs (1 Kings v. 12), but only two Psalms, according to their Hebrew titles, go by his name; and of these, one, the Seventy-second, may

* Unless, indeed, we assume with Delitzsch that Psalm lxxxviii. which is attributed to Heman, and Psalm lxxxix. to Ethan, were written in the time of Solomon. From 1 Kings iv. 31 it may perhaps be concluded that Asaph was already dead.

perhaps have been written by him: the other, the Hundred and Twenty-seventh, most probably is of much later date.

Besides these, two other of the Poetical Books of the Bible have been commonly ascribed to Solomon. One of them bears his name, "The Song of Songs which is Solomon's;" the other, whether written by him or not, represents with singular truth and fidelity the various phases of a life like that of Solomon. But Ecclesiastes is not a Poem. It is the record of a long struggle with the perplexities, the doubts, the misgivings, which must beset a man of large experience and large wisdom, who tries to read the riddle of the world, before his heart has been chastened by submission, and his spirit elevated by trust in God. The Song of Songs is a graceful and highly-finished idyll. No pastoral poetry in the world was ever written so exquisite in its music, so bright in its enjoyment of nature, or presenting so true a picture of faithful love.* This is a Poem not unworthy to be called "the Song of Songs," as surpassing all others, but it is very different from the poetry of the Psalms.

Poetry in the time of Jehoshaphat and Hezekiah.

From the days of Solomon till the Captivity, the cultivation of lyric poetry languished among the Hebrews, with two memorable exceptions. These were in the reigns of Jehoshaphat and Hezekiah. Both monarchs exerted themselves to restore the Temple worship, and to provide for the musical celebration of its services. To both, in circumstances of no common peril, were vouchsafed wonderful deliverances, which called forth hymns of praise and thanksgiving.† Both were engaged in meritorious efforts for the promotion and cultivation of learning. Jehoshaphat appointed throughout his dominions public instructors, an institution similar, apparently, to that of the Corlovingian *missi;* Hezekiah, who has been termed

* This is not the proper place to enter upon the question of the religious meaning of this Book: I am speaking of it simply as poetry. But I may say generally that I accept the interpretation of the poem given by Dr. Ginsburg in his valuable commentary. No objection can be made to that interpretation, on the score of the place that the Book occupies in the Canon, which would not apply equally to Deborah's Song, or to the Lament of David over Saul and Jonathan.

† 2 Chron. xx. 21, 29; xxix. 25, 30.

the Pisistratus of the Hebrew history,* established a society of learned men (Prov. xxv. 1), whose duty it was to provide for the collection and preservation of all the scattered remains of the earlier literature. To their pious labours we are doubtless indebted for many Psalms which would otherwise have perished. The arrangement of some portion, at least, of the present Psalter, it may reasonably be supposed, was completed under their superintendence. Smaller separate collections were combined into one; and this was enriched partly by the discovery of older hymns and songs, and partly by the addition of new.† A fresh impulse was given to the cultivation of Psalmody. The use of the ancient sacred music was revived, and the king commanded that the Psalms of David and of Asaph should be sung, as of old time, in the Temple. He himself encouraged the taste for this kind of poetry by his own example. One plaintive strain of his, written on his recovery from sickness, has been preserved in the Book of the Prophet Isaiah (chap. xxxviii.). In some Latin Psalters, several Odes, supposed to belong to the time of the Assyrian invasion, have his name prefixed to them.

How far any of the Psalms found in our existing collection can be placed in the time of Jehoshaphat is doubtful; on this point critics are divided: but there can be no doubt that several are rightly assigned to the reign of Hezekiah. Amongst these are a number of beautiful poems by the Korahite singers. The Forty-second (and Forty-third) and Eighty-fourth Psalms were written, it has been conjectured‡ by a Priest or Levite carried away into captivity by the Assyrians. The Forty-sixth, Forty-seventh, and Forty-eighth still more certainly refer to that period. These must all have been written shortly after the overthrow of Sennacherib and his army. The first has many striking coincidences of thought and expression with the prophecies of Isaiah, delivered not very long before under Ahaz. The last opens with a vivid picture of the approach

* See Delitzsch, *Commentar über den Psalter*, ii. 377.
† For the proof of this see below, Chapter IV.
‡ Bleek, *Einl. in das A. T.*, p. 168.

of the Assyrian army, and of its sudden and complete overthrow—a picture rivalling in its graphic force and concentrated energy the delineations of the same Prophet in sight of the same catastrophe—and concludes with a grand burst of religious and patriotic exultation, such as might naturally be called forth by an occasion so memorable. Religion and patriotism are here blended in one, and find, united, their truest and noblest expression.* To the same period of the Assyrian invasion may be referred the Sixty-fifth and Seventy-sixth Psalms,† and possibly, also, the Seventy-fifth.

But from this time till the return from the Captivity, comparatively few Psalms were written. It is probable, indeed, that as there was no period during the existence of the Jewish monarchy when the voice of Prophets was not heard, so also there was no long period during which the sweet singers of Israel were altogether silent. The Prophets themselves were Psalmists: Jonah (chap. ii.), Isaiah (chap. xii.), Habakkuk (chap. iii.), were all lyric poets. It would be but natural that, in some instances, their sacred songs should be incorporated in the public liturgies. After the Exile, when the Prophets took so active a part in the rebuilding of the Temple and the restoration of its services, this seems almost certainly to have been the case.‡ Before the Exile the same thing may have happened. Two Psalms, the Thirty-first and the Seventy-first, have been supposed by eminent critics to have been written by Jeremiah; a supposition which derives countenance from their general character, from the tone of sorrowful tenderness which pervades them, from the many turns of expression like those to be met with in the writings of the Prophet, and, in the case of the latter Psalm, also from its Inscription in the Septuagint, accord-

---

* See the Notes on these Psalms.

† The Seventy-sixth is expressly styled in the Inscription of the LXX. *ὠδὴ πρὸς τὸν ᾿Ασσυρίον.* With less probability they entitle Ps. lxxx. *ψαλμὸς ὑπὲρ τοῦ ᾿Ασσυρίου.*

‡ Several of the later Psalms are, by the LXX. Syriac and Vulgate, said to have been written by Haggai and Zechariah. See the Article ZECHARIAH in Smith's *Dictionary of the Bible.*

ing to which it was a favourite with the Rechabites and the earlier exiles.

The Babylonish Captivity.

Even in Babylon itself some Psalms were written. There the Hundred and Second Psalm was evidently composed, towards the close of the Seventy Years, and in prospect of the speedy restoration of the captives to the land of their fathers; there possibly, also, at an earlier period, the Seventy-fourth and the Seventy-ninth, which describe with so much force of pathos the sack of Jerusalem, the burning of the Temple, and the horrible slaughter of the inhabitants.

Still, during the five hundred years which elapsed from the death of David to the time of Ezra, a period as long as from the days of Chaucer to our own, no great successors to David appeared; no era but that of Hezekiah, as has already been observed, was famous for its sacred singers. Here and there a true Israelite, in his own distress, or oppressed by the sins and calamities of his nation, poured out his complaint before God; or for his own or his people's deliverance sang aloud his song of thanksgiving. And some few of these songs and complaints may have been collected and added to the earlier Psalms; some even, whose authors were unknown, may have been ascribed to David, the great master of lyric poetry. But what Eichhorn has remarked, remains true, that the Psalms belong, as a whole, not to many, but chiefly to two or three periods of Jewish history,—to the age of David, to that of Hezekiah, to the return from the Babylonish Captivity.

This, indeed, is only in accordance with what has been observed in other nations, that certain great crises of history are most favourable to poetry. From the throes and travail-pangs of a nation's agony are born the most illustrious of her sons in arts as well as in arms. The general commotion and upheaving, the stir and ferment of all minds, the many dazzling occasions which arise for the exercise of the loftiest powers,—all these things give a peculiar impulse, a higher aim, a nobler resolve, to those who, by the prerogative even of their natural gifts, are destined to be the leaders of the intellectual world. Hence, likewise, poets appear in clusters or constellations; for only in seasons of great peril, or signal and splendid triumph, are those deeper and stronger feelings called forth which are the soul of the truest and most perfect poetry.

Revival of Lyric Poetry after the Exile.

Such a crisis to the Jews was the Return from the Captivity. And, accordingly, to this period a very considerable number of Psalms, chiefly in the Fourth and Fifth Books, may without hesitation be referred. The Jews had carried with them to Babylon their sacred music, and the Psalms of David and his singers. The familiar words associated with so many happy memories, with the best and holiest hours of their lives, must often have soothed the weariness of exile, even if their hearts were too heavy to sing the song of Jehovah in a strange land. The fact that their heathen masters "required of them a song" to enliven their banquets, shows how great a skill in music they possessed, and how well it was appreciated. Nor did exile make them forget their cunning. When the first joyful caravan returned under Zerubbabel, we are particularly informed that it comprised *singing men and singing women.* The first expression of their joy was in Psalms. Many of the beautiful little songs in that exquisite collection entitled "Pilgrim Songs," or "Songs of the Goings-up," must have been first called forth by the recollection of their *going up* from Babylon to Jerusalem, if not first sung by the way. They are full of touching allusions to their recent captivity, full of pious affection for their land, their city, their temple. They were afterwards comprised in one volume, and were then intended for the use of the pilgrims who *went up* from all parts of the Holy Land to keep the yearly festivals in the Second Temple. For the worship now restored there, and restored with something of its former splendour, notwithstanding all that had been irreparably lost when the beautiful house wherein their fathers had worshipt was laid in ashes, many hymns and songs were especially composed. Amongst these was that long series of Psalms which open or close with the triumphant Hallelujah, a nation's great thanksgiving, the celebration of a deliverance so wonderful, that it eclipsed even that which before had been ever regarded as the most signal instance of God's favour towards them, the deliverance of their fathers from the bondage in Egypt. One portion of these Psalms (cxiii.—cxviii.), "the Hallêl,"* or, as it was sometimes called, "the Egyptian Hallêl," as if with the purpose of bringing together the two memorable epochs of the national history, was sung at the great festivals in the Second Temple, at the Passover, at Pentecost, at the Feast of Tabernacles, and also at the Feast of Dedication and at the New Moons. This was doubtless "the hymn" which our Lord and His Apostles are said to have sung† at His last solemn Passover before He suffered.

Nearly all these later Poems are in character and style unmistakeably different from the earlier. They have the air and colouring of another age, of a different state of society. They are, for the most part, no longer individual, but national, a circumstance which of itself, perhaps, in some instances abates their interest. They want the terseness, the energy, the fire, of the Psalms of David. They have neither the bold vehemence nor the abrupt transitions which mark his poetry. They flow in a smoother and a gentler current. We hardly find in the Anthems which were intended for the service of the Second Temple the vigour, the life, the splendour, the creative power, conspicuous in those which, when the Ark was carried to its resting-place on the holy mountain, rolled from the lips of "the great congregation," like "the voice of many waters," beneath the glorious canopy of a Syrian heaven. The last age of Hebrew Poetry, if poetical excellence alone be considered, was scarcely equal to the first. But it has its own peculiar interest: it was a second spring, and it was the last.

Maccabean Psalms.

One question remains to be considered before we conclude this rapid and necessarily very imperfect sketch

* Delitzsch, *Psalmen*, ii. 160 n. (1st Edit.) He points out that "the Great Hallêl" is the name, not of these Psalms, but of Ps. cxxxvi.

† Matt. xxvi. 30; Mark xiv. 26.

of Hebrew Lyric Poetry. Are any of the Psalms in our present Psalter later than the times of Ezra and Nehemiah? Three or four critics, with that strange perverseness so often to be found in minds naturally rather acute than profound, have insisted that more than one-half of the entire collection is as late as the days of the Maccabees. But this singular literary heresy apart, the verdict is almost unanimous the other way; the large majority have maintained that not a single Psalm in the collection can be brought down to a period so late. It has been argued and repeated again and again, that the history of the Canon precludes the possibility of Maccabean Psalms. That history shows us, it has been said, that the whole volume had long before received its recognised place as a Canonical book. The argument advanced on this side of the question rests on the following grounds:—First, in the Prologue to the Book of Ecclesiasticus, written some time before the outbreak of the Maccabean struggle, a threefold division of the Scriptures is recognised,—the Law, the Prophets, and "the other books of the fathers." This last expression has been generally supposed to denote that division of the Scriptures commonly called the Hagiographa, and in which the Psalms were comprised. Secondly, we are told in the Second Book of Maccabees (ii. 13), that Nehemiah made a collection of the sacred writings which included "the works of David." Hence it has been inferred that the Psalter was finally brought to its present shape, and recognised as complete, in the time of Nehemiah. But this is thoroughly to misunderstand the nature of the formation of the Canon, which was manifestly a very gradual work.* Even granting that by "the works of David" we are to understand a general collection of Psalms, it does not follow that the collection contained the exact number, neither more or less, now comprised in the Psalter. The Canon itself was not closed under Nehemiah. Additions were made by him to other Books. Why should not additions be made at a later

* See Prof. Westcott's able article on the CANON in Smith's *Dictionary of the Bible.*

period to the Psalter? Ewald himself, who strenuously maintains that no Psalms are so late as the Maccabean period, admits nevertheless that under Judas Maccabeus a large number of books were added to the Canon—the Proverbs, the Song of Songs, Ecclesiastes, Job, Daniel, Esther, the Chronicles.* But if so, on what possible grounds can it be alleged that the Psalter, merely because collected into a whole under Nehemiah, was finally closed against all later additions?

A far stronger argument on that side of the question would be found in the Septuagint Version, if it could be shown that the translation of the Psalms was finished at the same time with that of the Pentateuch under Ptolemy Lagi (B.C. 323—284). This, however, cannot be proved, though the expression in the Prologue to Ecclesiasticus may seem to imply it. But it is worthy of notice, that the writer of the First Book of the Maccabees is evidently acquainted with the Alexandrine Version, and that this Version, though it ascribes some Psalms to Haggai and Zechariah, mentions none of a later date.

The question, therefore, still remains an open one; and there is no reason, so far as the History of the Canon is concerned, why we should refuse to admit the existence of Maccabean Psalms. Psalms like the Forty-fourth, the Seventy-fourth, and the Seventy-ninth, seem more easily explained by referring them to that period of Jewish history than to any other; though the last two, as has already been remarked, may, not without some show of probability, be referred to the time of the Chaldean invasion.†

Such, in its merest outline, is the history of Sacred Psalmody among the Hebrews. It occupies between its extreme limits a period of a thousand years, from Moses to Nehemiah, or perhaps even to a later age. During a large portion of that period, the Psalms shine like "a light

---

* The passage in 2 Maccabees ii. 13 is as follows :—*ἐξηγοῦντο δὲ καὶ ἐν ταῖς ἀναγραφαῖς καὶ ἐν τοῖς ὑπομνηματισμοῖς τοῖς κατὰ τὸν Νεεμίαν τὰ αὐτά, καὶ ὡς καταβαλλόμενος βιβλιοθήκην ἐπισυνήγαγε τὰ περὶ τῶν βασιλέων καὶ προφητῶν καὶ τὰ τοῦ Δαυὶδ καὶ ἐπιστολὰς βασιλέων περι ἀναθεμάτων.*

† See more on this subject in the Introduction to those Psalms.

in a dark place." They tell us how, amidst corruption, idolatry, and apostasy, God was truly loved and faithfully worshipt. Not only as "given by inspiration of God" are they a witness to the fact that God was teaching His people. So far they are what the Prophetical Books are. Psalmists as well as Prophets were chosen by Him to be the interpreters of His will, to declare His truth. Both the one and the other are the organs and vehicles of the Divine communications. But there is this further significance in the Psalms. They are not only, not chiefly, it may be said, the voice of God to man. They are the voice of man to God. They are prayers, indeed, far beyond merely human utterances; they are prayers which the Spirit of God himself has given as the model of all prayer and intercession. But they bear witness at the same time to the reality of the soul's spiritual life in those who uttered them. Truly divine, they are also truly human. They go infinitely beyond us; they have a depth and height, and length and breadth of meaning, to which the best of us can never fully attain. We feel that they rise into regions of peaceful and holy communion with God to which we may aspire, but which we have not reached. But meanwhile they have a reality which satisfies us that they are the true expression of human hearts pouring themselves out towards God, though often themselves carried beyond themselves through the power of the Holy Ghost.

There are times, no doubt, when we read one and another of these Psalms with something like a feeling of disappointment. There are times when we cannot repress the wish to know more of the circumstances which called them forth, of the feelings, the views, the hopes, with which they were written. We ask ourselves what the peril is from which the Sacred Poet has barely escaped; who the enemies were whose machinations so terrified him; what the victories, the successes, the deliverances, which he celebrates with such loud songs of thanksgiving. We should read them, we think, with fresh interest, could we tell with certainty when and by whom they were written. But if we could do this, if the picture of those circumstances were clear and well-defined, we might lose more than we should gain. For the very excellence of the Psalms is their universality. They spring from the deep fountains of the human heart, and God, in His providence and by His Spirit, has so ordered it, that they should be for His Church an everlasting heritage. Hence they express the sorrows, the joys, the aspirations, the struggles, the victories, not of one man, but of all. And if we ask, How comes this to pass? the answer is not far to seek. One object is ever before the eyes and the heart of the Psalmists. All enemies, all distresses, all persecutions, all sins, are seen in the light of God. It is to Him that the cry goes up; it is to Him that the heart is laid bare; it is to Him that the thanksgiving is uttered. This it is which makes them so true, so precious, so universal. No surer proof of their inspiration can be given than this, that they are "not of an age but for all time," that the ripest Christian can use them in the fulness of his Christian manhood, though the words are the words of one who lived centuries before the coming of Christ in the flesh.

CHAPTER 2

The Use of the Psalter in the Church and by Individuals

DEEP as is the interest attaching to the Psalter as the great storehouse of Sacred Poetry, and vast as is its importance considered as a record of spiritual life under the Old Dispensation, scarcely less interest and importance attach to it with reference to the position it has ever occupied both in the public worship of the Church and in the private life of Christians. No single Book of Scripture, not even of the New Testament, has, perhaps, ever taken such hold on the *heart* of Christendom. None, if we may dare judge, unless it be the Gospels, has had so large an influence in moulding the affections, sustaining the hopes, purifying the faith of believers. With its words, rather than with their own, they have come before God. In these they have uttered their desires, their fears, their confessions, their aspirations, their sorrows, their joys, their thanksgivings. By these their devotion has been kindled and their hearts comforted. The Psalter has been, in the truest sense, the Prayer-book both of Jews and Christians.

The nature of the volume accounts for this; for it is in itself, to a very great extent, the converse of the soul with God. Hence it does not teach us so much what we are to do, or what we are to be, as how we are to pray; or, rather, it teaches us what we are to do and to be through prayer. "This," says Luther, "is the great excellence of the Psalter; that other books, indeed, make a great noise about the *works* of the saints, but say very little about their *words*. But herein is the pre-eminence of the Psalter, and hence the sweet fragrance which it sheds, that it not only tells of the works of the saints, but also of the words with which they spake to God and prayed, and still speak and pray."

Psalms as used in the public Liturgies.

Nor is the influence of this Book on the Church at large and on our public Liturgies less remarkable. "The primitive Church," says Bishop Taylor, "would admit no man to the superior orders of the clergy, unless, among other pre-required dispositions, they could say all David's Psalter by heart." * Tertullian, in the second century, tells us that the Christians were wont to sing Psalms at their agapæ, and that they were sung antiphonally. From the earliest times they formed an essential part of Divine Service. We learn from Augustine and other writers, that, after the reading of the Epistle, a whole Psalm was sung, or partly read, partly sung—taking them in the order in which they stood in the Psalter—and that then followed the reading of the Gospel.† Hilary, Chrysostom, Augustine, all mention the use of the Psalms in the public service, and describe them, sometimes as being sung by the whole congregation, at others as being recited by one individual, who was followed by the rest. The practice of antiphonal chanting was common in the East, and was introduced by Ambrose into the Western Church. Either the congregation sang the verses of the Psalm alternately, in two choirs, the one answering to the other, or, sometimes, the first half of the verse was sung by a single voice, and the other half by the whole congregation.

Use of particular Psalms.

We learn from the Talmud, as well as from the Inscriptions of the LXX., that certain Psalms were appointed in the Second Temple for the service of particular days. The same custom also obtained in the Christian Church. The Morning Service used to begin with Psalm lxiii., the Evening Service with Psalm cxli. In Passion Week, Psalm xxii. was sung. Since the time of Origen, Seven Psalms have received the name of Penitential Psalms, which were used in the special additional services appointed for the

* *Sermon on the Whole Duty of the Clergy.* Works (Eden's edit.), vol. viii. p. 507.

† August. *Serm.* 176, Opp. tom. v. pp. 1212-14. Paris, 1837.

season of Lent. These were Psalms vi. xxxii. xxxviii. li. cii. cxxx. cxliii.*

Use of the Psalter in the Church of Rome: In the Church of Rome, Psalms occupy a prominent place in the Service of the Mass. The oldest Mass-books consist of three parts: the Sacramentary, containing the prayers of the officiating priest; the Lectionary, containing the lessons from the Bible; and the Antiphonary, containing the Psalms and antiphons, or verses from the Psalms and Prophets which served as the Introit, and received the name from their being sung responsively. The term "gradual" in the Mass is a remnant of the ancient custom before referred to. The Psalm which was sung before the Gospel was called *Responsorium graduale*, because it was intoned by two voices from the steps (*gradus*, whence the name) of the *ambon*, and then taken up by the people. In the Seven Canonical Hours, as they are called, the Psalms form no inconsiderable part of the service; and the Romish priest prays them daily in his Breviary. Our own Church has provided for the daily recital of some portion of them in her services, and has so distributed them in her Liturgy, that the whole book is repeated every month. In a very large part of the Reformed Churches they take the place of hymns. Thrown into metrical versions, they are probably sung by most congregations of professing Christians amongst ourselves, little as any metrical version has succeeded in preserving the spirit and glow of the original. In many places, especially among Protestant communities abroad, it is usual to bind up the Psalter with the New Testament, from the feeling, doubtless, that, more than any other part of the Old, it tends directly to edification. Nor is this feeling modern, or peculiar to Protestants. Two facts will show how widely it has prevailed. The one is, that when the Council of Toulouse, in 1229, forbade the use of the Bible to the laity, a special exception was made in favour of the Psalter:

in the Church of England:

in other Protestant Churches.

* The *seven* Psalms were selected with reference to the sprinkling of the leper seven times in order to his cleansing, and the command to Naaman to wash himself seven times in the Jordan, or, as others say, as corresponding to the seven deadly sins. (See Delitzsch on Ps. cxliii.)

the other is, that the Psalter was the first portion of the Hebrew Bible which ever issued from the press.

To follow the history of such a Book, to listen to the testimonies which have been borne to it by God's saints in all ages, must be a matter of no little interest. I will, therefore, set down here some of the most striking of these testimonies.

I will first cite Athanasius, Bishop of Alexandria in the fourth century, who, in his Epistle to Marcellinus, prefixed to his Interpretation of the Psalms, professes to tell him the opinion of an old man whom he once met, concerning the Book of Psalms. He says: Athanasius.

"He who takes this Book in his hands, with admiration and reverence goes through all the prophecies concerning the Saviour which he finds there as in the other Scriptures; but the other Psalms he reads as if they were his own words, and he who hears them is pricked at the heart as if he said them himself." No one, he goes on to observe, can take the words of the Patriarchs, or Moses, or Elijah, to himself, and use them always as his own; but he who uses the Psalms "is as one who speaks his own words, and each one sings them as if they had been written for his own case, and not as if they had been spoken by some one else, or meant to apply to some one else." Again: "To me, indeed, it seems that the Psalms are to him who sings them as a mirror, wherein he may see himself and the motions of his soul, and with like feelings utter them. So also one who hears a psalm read, takes it as if it were spoken concerning himself, and either, convicted by his own conscience, will be pricked at heart and repent, or else, hearing of that hope which is to God-wards, and the succour which is vouchsafed to them that believe, leaps for joy, as though such grace were specially made over to him, and begins to utter his thanksgivings to God" (§ 12).

Again: "In the other Books (of Scripture) are discourses which dissuade us from those things which are evil, but in this has been sketched out for us how we should abstain from things evil. For instance, we are commanded to repent, and to repent is to cease from sin; but here has been sketched out for us how we must repent, and what we must say when we repent. And again, Paul hath said: 'Tribulation worketh patience for the soul, and patience, proof,' &c.; but in the Psalms we find written and engraven how we ought to bear afflictions, and what we should say in our afflictions and what after our afflictions, and how each one is proved, and what are the words of them that hope in the Lord. Again, there is a command in everything to give thanks; but the Psalms teach us also what to say when we give thanks. Then when we hear from others, 'They that will live godly shall be persecuted,' by the Psalms we are taught what we ought to utter when we are driven into exile, and what words we should lay before God, both in our persecutions and when we have been delivered out of them. We are enjoined to bless the Lord and to confess to Him. But in the Psalms we have a pattern given us, both as to how we should praise the Lord and with what words we can suitably confess to Him. And, in every instance, we shall find these divine songs suited to us, to our feelings, and our circumstances" (§ 10).

These words of Athanasius are doubly interesting when we remember what his own life had been; how often he had been driven into exile; what persecutions he had endured; from how many perils he had been delivered.

Ambrose. Let us hear next Ambrose, Bishop of Milan in the fourth century, in the preface to his Exposition of Twelve of the Psalms of David.* "Although all divine Scripture breathes the grace of God, yet sweet beyond all others is the Book of Psalms." . . . "History instructs, the Law teaches, Prophecy announces, Rebuke chastens, Mortality [? Morality] persuades: in the Book of Psalms we have the fruit of all these, and a kind of medicine for the salvation of man." . . . "What is more delightful than a Psalm? It is the benediction of the people, the praise of God, the thanksgiving of the multitude, . . . the voice of the Church, the harmonious confession of our faith," &c.†

* Opp. Venet. 1748, tom. ii. *In Psalmum I. Enarr.*

† Afterwards, in enumerating other excellences of the Psalms, he throws a curious light on the state of the churches in Milan during the

With deep feeling Augustine narrates what the Psalms were to him in the days of his first conversion to God. "What words did I utter to Thee, O my God, when I read the Psalms of David, those faithful songs, those pious breathings which suffer no swelling spirit of pride, when I was as yet uninstructed in all the truth and fulness of Thy love, a catechumen in that country-house, keeping holiday with the catechumen Alypius, whilst my mother remained with us, in the garb of a woman, (but) with the faith of a man, with the calmness of an old woman, with the affection of a mother, with the piety of a Christian. What words did I utter to thee in those Psalms; how was my love to Thee inflamed thereby; how did I burn to recite them, were it possible, through the whole world, against the proud swelling of men! And yet they are sung through the whole world, and there is none who is hidden from Thy heat.* How vehement and how sharp was my grief and indignation against the Manicheans;† and yet, again, how I pitied them because they knew not these sacraments, these medicines, and showed their insanity in rejecting the antidote which might have restored them to sanity! How I wish they could have been somewhere near me, and, without my knowing that they were there, could have seen my face and heard my words when I read the Fourth Psalm, in that retirement in which I was, and have known all that that Psalm was to me!" And then he goes through the whole Psalm, describing the feelings with which he read it, and the application which he made of it to his own case—an application very wide indeed of the proper meaning of the Psalm, but one which, nevertheless, poured light and peace and joy into his soul. Augustine.

We pass on to the time of the Reformation. Let us hear how two of its great master spirits speak. "Where," Luther.

---

celebration of Divine Service. "What difficulty there is," he says, "to procure silence in the church when the Lessons are read! If one speaks, all the rest make a noise. When a Psalm is read, it produces silence of itself. All speak, and no one makes a noise."

* In allusion to Ps. xix. 7.

† Because, as rejecting the Old Testament, they robbed themselves of the Psalms.

says Luther, in his Preface to the Psalter (published in 1531), "will you find words more aptly chosen to express joy, than in the Psalms of praise and the Psalms of thanksgiving? There thou mayest look into the heart of all the saints, as into fair delightful gardens, yea, even into heaven itself, and note with what wonderful variety there spring up therein, like so many exquisite, hearty, delightful flowers, sweet and gladsome thoughts of God and His benefits. On the other hand, where canst thou find deeper, sadder, more lamentable words of sorrow than are to be found in the Psalms of complaint? There again thou mayest look into the heart of all the saints, as into death, yea, as into hell. How dark and gloomy it is there with the manifold hiding of God's countenance! So likewise when the Psalms speak of fear or hope, they speak in such manner of words that no painter could so paint the fear or the hope, and no Cicero or master of oratory could express them to the life more happily."

Again, in the Preface to his *Operationes in Psalmos*,* he observes: "This Book is, in my judgement, of a different character from the other books. For in the rest we are taught both by word and by example what we ought to do; this not only teaches, but imparts both the method and the practice with which to fulfil the word, and to copy the example. For we have no power of our own to fulfil the law of God, or to copy Christ; but only to pray and to desire that we may do the one and copy the other, and then, when we have obtained our request, to praise and give thanks. But what else is the Psalter, but prayer to God and praise of God; that is, a book of hymns? Therefore the most blessed Spirit of God, the father of orphans, and the teacher of infants, seeing that we know not what or how we ought to pray, as the Apostle saith, and desiring to help our infirmities, after the manner of schoolmasters who compose for children letters or short prayers, that they

* D. Martini Lutheri Exegetica Opp. Latina, Ed. Irmischer, tom. xiv. p. 10. This Preface bears the date Wittenbergæ, sexto calen. Aprilis, Anno M.D.xix. I have to thank Dr. Binnie (*The Psalms, their Teaching and Use*, p. 381) for correcting an error in the reference in the first of my two quotations from Luther.

may send them to their parents, so prepares for us in this Book both the words and feelings with which we should address our Heavenly Father, and pray concerning those things which in the other Books He had taught us we ought to do and to copy, that so a man may not feel the want of anything which is of import to his eternal salvation. So great is the loving care and grace of our God towards us, Who is blessed for evermore."

The following passage from Calvin's Preface to his Commentary will show the high value which he set upon the Psalms. "If," he says, "the Church of God shall derive as much benefit from (the reading of) my Commentaries, as I have myself derived from the writing of them, I shall have no reason to repent of the labour I have taken upon me. . . . . How varied and how splendid the wealth which this treasury contains it is difficult to describe in words; whatever I shall say, I know full well must fall far short of its worth. . . . This Book, not unreasonably, am I wont to style an anatomy of all parts of the soul, for no one will discover in himself a single feeling whereof the image is not reflected in this mirror. Nay, all griefs, sorrows, fears, doubts, hopes, cares, and anxieties—in short, all those tumultuous agitations wherewith the minds of men are wont to be tossed—the Holy Ghost hath here represented to the life. The rest of Scripture contains the commands which God gave to His servants to be delivered unto us; but here the Prophets themselves, holding converse with God, inasmuch as they lay bare all their inmost feelings, invite or impel every one of us to self-examination, that of all the infirmities to which we are liable, and all the sins of which we are so full, none may remain hidden. It is a rare and singular advantage when, every hiding-place having been laid bare, the heart is cleansed from hypocrisy, that foulest of plagues, and is brought forth to the light. Lastly, if calling upon God be the greatest safeguard of our salvation, seeing that no better and surer rule thereof can be found anywhere than in this Book, the further any man shall have advanced in the understanding of it, the greater will be his attainment in the school of God. Earnest

Calvin.

prayer springs first from a feeling of our necessity, and then from faith in the promises. Here the readers will both best be awakened to a due sense of their own evils, and warned to seek the proper remedies for them.

"Moreover, whatever would serve to encourage us in our prayer to God is shown us in this Book. Nor yet are they only promises that meet us here; but we have often set before us one who, with the invitation of God calling one way, and the hindrances of the flesh another, girds himself bravely to prayer; so that if ever at any time we be harassed by doubts of one kind or another, we may learn to wrestle against them, till our soul takes wings and mounts up with glad freedom unto God. Nor that only, but that through hesitations, fears, alarms, we may still strive to pray, till we rejoice for the consolation. For this must be our resolve, though distrust shut the door to our prayers, that we must not give way when our hearts are shaken and restlessly disturbed, till faith comes forth victorious from its struggles. And in many passages we may see the servants of God, so tossed to and fro in their prayers that, almost crushed at times, they only win the palm after arduous efforts. On the one side the weakness of the flesh betrays itself; on the other the power of faith exerts itself. . . . This, only in passing, is it worth while to point out, that we have secured to us in this Book, what is of all things most desirable, not only a familiar access unto God, but the right and the liberty to make known to Him those infirmities which shame does not suffer us to confess to our fellow-men. Further, the sacrifice of praise, which God declares to be a sacrifice of sweetest savour and most precious to Him, we are here accurately instructed how to offer with acceptance. . . . Rich, moreover, as the Book is in all those precepts which tend to form a holy, godly, and righteous life, yet chiefly will it teach us how to bear the cross; which is the true test of our obedience, when, giving up all our own desires, we submit ourselves to God, and so suffer our lives to be ordered by His will, that even our bitterest distresses grow sweet because they come from His hand. Finally, not only in general terms are the praises of God's goodness uttered, teaching us so to rest in Him alone, that pious spirits may look for His sure succour in every time of need, but the free forgiveness of sins, which alone reconciles God to us, and secures to us true peace with Him, is so commended, that nothing is wanting to the knowledge of eternal salvation."

He adds, that his best understanding of the Psalms had come to him through the trials and conflicts which he had himself been called upon to pass through ; that thus he was not only able to apply better whatever knowledge he had acquired, but could enter better into the design of each writer of the Psalms.

Hooker, reasoning in his immortal work with the sectaries of his times, and defending the use of Psalms in the Liturgy, says : Hooker.

"They are not ignorant what difference there is between other parts of Scripture and the Psalms. The choice and flower of all things profitable in other books, the Psalms do both more briefly contain and more movingly also express, by reason of that poetical form wherewith they are written. . . . What is there necessary for man to know which the Psalms are not able to teach ? They are to beginners an easy and familiar introduction, a mighty augmentation of all virtue and knowledge in such as are entered before, a strong confirmation to the most perfect among others. Heroical magnanimity, exquisite justice, grave moderation, exact wisdom, repentance unfeigned, unwearied patience, the mysteries of God, the sufferings of Christ, the terrors of wrath, the comforts of grace, the works of Providence over this world, and the promised joys of that world which is to come, all good necessarily to be either known, or done, or had, this one celestial fountain yieldeth. Let there be any grief or disease incident unto the soul of man, any wound or sickness named for which there is not in this treasure-house a present comfortable remedy at all times ready to be found. Hereof it is that we covet to make the Psalms especially familiar unto all. This is the very cause why we iterate the Psalms oftener than any other part of Scripture besides ; the cause wherefore we inure the people together with their minister, and not the minister alone, to read them as other parts of Scripture he doth." *

Donne.

Donne says: "The Psalms are the manna of the Church. As manna tasted to every man like that he liked best, so do the Psalms minister instruction and satisfaction to every man, in every emergency and occasion. David was not only a clear Prophet of Christ himself, but of every particular Christian; he foretells what I, what any, shall do, and suffer, and say." †

Francke.

In later times we find similar testimonies repeated in great abundance. A. H. Francke, in his *Explanation of the Psalms with a View to Edification* (Halle, 1731, Part I. p. 904), thus expresses himself: "So long as a man has not the Spirit of Christ, so long as he does not deny himself, and take up his cross daily and follow Christ, no Psalm seems sweet to him. He has no pleasure therein; it seems to him all like dry straw, in which he finds neither strength nor juice. But when he is himself led through a like course of suffering and affliction, when he is ridiculed, scorned, and mocked by the world for righteousness' sake and because he follows Christ, and sees what it is to press through all the hindrances which meet him from within and from without, and to serve God the Lord in truth,—then it is that he observes that in the heart of David far more must have gone on than that he should have troubled himself merely about his outward circumstances. He is conscious, in his daily struggle, of the same enmity, which has been put by God between Christ and Belial, between those who belong to Christ, and those who belong to the devil, and that precisely the same contest in which so much is involved is described in the Psalms; and of which, in fact, even the First Psalm speaks, when it says, 'Blessed is the man who walketh not in the counsel of the ungodly,' &c. He therefore that denies himself and the world, with all its greatness, with all the riches and the favour of men, who will have nothing but God's word as his rule, and seeks

* Hooker, *Eccl. Pol.*, Book v. ch. xxxvii. § 2.

† Donne, *Sermon* lxvi. Works, vol. iii. p. 156 (Alford's edit.) See also the Introduction to Psalm lxiii.

to take a cheerful conscience with him to his death-bed, learns by experience what a real struggle it costs to effect this. But he who learns this, learns also how to understand the Psalms aright."

Herder.

From many passages which might be quoted from Herder's writings I select one: "Not merely as regards the contents, but also as regards the form, has this use of the Psalter been a benefit to the spirit and heart of men. As in no lyric poet of Greece or Rome do we find so much teaching, consolation, and instruction together, so has there scarcely ever been anywhere so rich a variation of tone in every kind of song as here. For two thousand years have these old Psalms been again and again translated and imitated in a variety of ways, and still so rich, so comprehensive is their manner, that they are capable of many a new application. They are flowers which vary according to each season and each soil, and ever abide in the freshness of youth. Precisely because this Book contains the simplest lyric tones for the expression of the most manifold feelings, is it a hymn-book for all times." *

Bishop Horne.

From Bishop Horne's Preface to his Commentary, I will quote a few lines, partly because of the striking coincidence of expression which they exhibit with two passages already quoted, the one from Donne, and the other from Calvin.

"Indited," he says, "under the influence of Him to whom all hearts are known, and events foreknown, they suit mankind in all situations, grateful as the manna which descended from above and conformed itself to every palate. . . . He who hath once tasted their excellences will desire to taste them again; and he who tastes them oftenest will relish them best.

"And now, could the author flatter himself that any one would take half the pleasure in reading the following exposition, which he hath taken in writing it, he would not fear the loss of his labour. The employment detached him from the bustle and hurry of life, the din of politics, and the noise of folly; vanity and vexation flew away for a

* *Abhandlungen und Briefen zur schönen Literatur.* Sämmtliche Werke. Th. xvi. p. 17.

season, care and disquietude came not near his dwelling. He arose, fresh as the morning, to his task; the silence of the night invited him to pursue it: and he can truly say that food and rest were not preferred before it. Every Psalm improved infinitely upon his acquaintance with it, and no one gave him uneasiness but the last, for then he grieved that his work was done. Happier hours than those which have been spent in these meditations on the songs of Sion, he never expects to see in this world. Very pleasantly did they pass, and moved smoothly and swiftly along: for when thus engaged, he counted no time. They are gone, but have left a relish and a fragrance upon the mind, and the remembrance of them is sweet."

Irving.

Irving in his Preface to Bishop Horne's work writes:

". . .The songs of Zion are comprehensive as the human soul and varied as human life; where no possible state of natural feeling shall not find itself tenderly expressed and divinely treated with appropriate remedies; where no condition of human life shall not find its rebuke or consolation: because they treat not life after the fashion of an age or people, but life in its rudiments, the life of the soul, with the joys and sorrows to which it is amenable, from concourse with the outward necessity of the fallen world. Which breadth of application they compass not by the sacrifice of lyrical propriety or poetical method: for if there be poems strictly lyrical, that is, whose spirit and sentiment move congenial with the movements of music, and which, by their very nature, call for the accompaniment of music, these odes of a people despised as illiterate are such. For pure pathos and tenderness of heart, for sublime imagination, for touching pictures of natural scenery, and genial sympathy with nature's various moods; for patriotism, whether in national weal or national woe; for beautiful imagery, whether derived from the relationship of human life, or the forms of the created universe; and for the illustration, by their help, of spiritual conditions: moreover, for those rapid transitions in which the lyrical muse delighteth, her lightsome graces at one time, her deep and full inspiration at another, her exuberance of joy and her lowest falls of grief, and for every other form of the natural soul, which is wont to be shadowed forth by this kind of composition, we challenge anything to be produced from the literature of all ages and countries, worthy to be compared with what we find even in the English Version of the Book of Psalms." *

This array of testimonies, so various and yet so accordant, shall be closed with three from our own time. The first, unhappily a mere fragment, is from one of the most original thinkers and most eloquent preachers whom our Church has in these later times produced. The second is from the dying bed of one who was the ornament and the pride of a sister Protestant Church on the Continent. The third is from a devout and attached member of the Church of Rome.

F. W. Robertson.

"The value of the public reading of the Psalms," says the late F. W. Robertson of Brighton, "is, that they express for us, indirectly, those deeper feelings which there would be a sense of indelicacy in expressing directly. . . . There are feelings of which we do not speak to each other; they are too sacred and too delicate. Such are most of our feelings to God. If we do speak of them, they lose their fragrance; become coarse; nay, there is even a sense of indelicacy and exposure. Now, the Psalms afford precisely the right relief for this feeling: wrapped up in the forms of poetry (metaphor, &c.), that which might seem exaggerated, is excused by those who do not feel it: while they who do, can read them, applying them without suspicion of uttering *their own* feelings. Hence their soothing power, and hence, while other portions of Scripture may become obsolete, they remain the most precious parts of the Old Testament. For the heart of man is the same in all ages." †

"It is this truth of human feeling which makes the Psalms, more than any other portion of the Old Testament, the link of union between distant ages. The historical books need a rich store of knowledge before

---

* Collected Works, vol. i. pp. 386, 387.

† *Sermon IX.* (Second Series), p. 119.

they can be a modern book of life; but the Psalms are the records of individual experience. Personal religion is the same in all ages. The deeps of our humanity remain unruffled by the storms of ages which change the surface. This Psalm (the Fifty-first), written three thousand years ago, might have been written yesterday: describes the vicissitudes of spiritual life in an Englishman, as truly as in a Jew. 'Not of an age, but for all time.'"*

A. Monod. Adolphe Monod, whilst suffering from the cruel malady of which he died, speaks thus to the friends who were gathered about his sick-bed: "We must read the Psalms in order to understand the sufferings of David. The Psalms discover to us the inner man of David, and in the inner man of David they discover to us in some sort the inner man of all the Prophets of God. Well, the Psalms are full of expressions of an unheard-of suffering. David speaks in them constantly of his evils, his sicknesses, his enemies without number: we can scarcely understand, in reading them, what he means by the enemies of which he speaks so constantly; but they discover to us at least an inner depth of affliction, of which, with the mere history of David in our hands, we should scarcely have formed an idea. It is one of the great advantages of the Psalms." He then refers to the Thirty-eighth Psalm as an illustration. Subsequently he says: "The capital object of the mission which David received of God for all generations in the Church was the composition of Psalms. Well, he composes his Psalms, or a great part of them, in the midst of the most cruel sufferings. Imagine then, bowed down by suffering, physical, moral, and spiritual, you were called upon to compose a Psalm, and that from the bosom of all these sufferings, and at the very moment when they were such as those which he describes in Psalm xxxviii., should issue hymns to the glory of God, and for the instruction of the Church. What a triumph David gains over himself, and what a humiliation it is for us, who in our weakness are mostly obliged to wait till our sufferings are passed, in order to reap the fruit of them ourselves, or to impart the benefit

---

* *Sermon VII.* (Second Series), p. 96.

to others. But David, in the midst of his sufferings, writes his Psalms. He writes his Thirty-eighth Psalm whilst he undergoes those persecutions, those inward torments, that bitterness of sin. I know it may be said that David wrote that Thirty-eighth Psalm coldly, transporting himself into sufferings which he did not feel at the time, as the poet transports himself into sufferings which he has never experienced; but no, such a supposition offends you as much as it does me: it is in the furnace, it is from the bosom of the furnace, that he writes these lines, which are intended to be the encouragement of the Church in all ages. O power of the love of Christ! O renunciation of self-will! O grace of the true servant of God! O virtue of the Apostle,* and virtue of the Prophet, virtue of Christ in them, and of the Holy Ghost! For never man (of himself) would be capable of such a power of will, of such a triumph over the flesh." †

Frederic Ozanam, writing shortly before his death to a Jew who had embraced Christianity, says: "The hand of God has touched me, I believe, as it touched Job, Ezechias, and Tobias, not unto death, but unto a prolonged trial. I have not, unfortunately, the patience of these just men: I am easily cast down by suffering, and I should be inconsolable for my weakness, if I did not find in the Psalms those cries of sorrow which David sends forth to God, and which God at last answers by sending him pardon and peace. Oh, my friend, when one has the happiness to have become a Christian, it is a great honour to be born an Israelite, to feel one's self the son of those Patriarchs and Prophets whose utterances are so beautiful that the Church has found nothing finer to place on the lips of her children. During many weeks of extreme languor the Psalms have never been out of my hands. I am never wearied of reading over and over those sublime lamentations, those flights of hope, those supplications full of love, which answer to all the wants and all the miseries

F. Ozanam.

* He had shortly before mentioned St. Paul as an instance like that of David.

† *Adieux à ses Amis*, &c. pp. 101-106. 7e édit. Paris, 1859.

of human nature. It is nearly three thousand years since a king composed these songs in his days of repentance and desolation, and we still find in them the expression of our deepest anguish and the consolation of our sorrows. The priest recites them daily; thousands of monasteries have been founded in order that these Psalms might be chanted at every hour, and that this voice of supplication might never be silent. The Gospel alone is superior to the hymns of David, and this only because it is their fulfilment—because all the yearnings, all the ardours, all the holy impatience of the prophet find their accomplishment in the Redeemer issued of his race. So great is the bond between the two Testaments, that the Redeemer Himself had no name dearer to Him than that of *Son of David.* The two blind men of Jericho called Him by it, and I often cry out to Him with them, 'Son of David, have mercy on us!'" * It is said of Ozanam in his sufferings that "it was sufficient to recite aloud some verses of the Psalms while he was suffering most to make him forget his own pain and the distress of those who were striving to alleviate it." †

How great, then, is the history of the Psalms! David sang them, and Isaiah, and Jeremiah, and all the Prophets. With Psalms Jehoshaphat and Hezekiah celebrated their victories. Psalms made glad the heart of the exiles who returned from Babylon. Psalms gave courage and strength to the Maccabees in their brave struggles to achieve their country's independence, and were the repeated expression of their thanksgivings. The Lord of Psalmists, and the Son of David, by the words of a Psalm, proved Himself to be higher than David; and sang Psalms with His Apostles on the night before He suffered, when He instituted the Holy Supper of His Love.‡ In His last awful hour on the Cross He expressed in the words of one Psalm, "His fear and His need of God," and in the words of another gave up His spirit to His Father. With Psalms, Paul and Silas praised God in the prison at midnight, when their feet were

---

* *Life of Frederic Ozanam*, O'Meara, pp. 438, 439.
† Ibid. p. 451. ‡ Matt. xxvi. 30.

made fast in the stocks, and sang so loud that the prisoners heard them. And after his own example, the Apostle exhorts the Christians at Ephesus and Colossæ to teach and admonish one another with Psalms and hymns and spiritual songs. Jerome tells us, that in his day the Psalms were to be heard in the fields and the vineyards of Palestine, and that they fell sweetly on the ear, mingling with the songs of birds, and the scent of flowers in the spring. The ploughman as he guided his plough chanted the Hallelujah, and the reaper, the vine-dresser, and the shepherd sang the songs of David. "These," he says, "are our love songs, these the instruments of our agriculture." Sidonius Apollinaris makes his boatmen, as they urge their heavily-laden barge up stream, sing Psalms, till the river-banks echo again with the Hallelujah, and beautifully applies the custom, in a figure, to the voyage of the Christian life.* With the verse of a Psalm, "Turn again, then, unto thy rest, O my soul," the pious Babylas, Bishop of Antioch, comforted himself, while awaiting his martyrdom in the Decian persecution, saying, "From this we learn that our soul comes to rest when it is removed by death from this restless world." Paulla, the friend of Jerome, was seen by those who were gathered around her in her last hour to move her lips, and when they stooped to listen, they heard the words, "How lovely are Thy tabernacles, O Lord of hosts." A Psalm was the best utterance for the overflowing joy of Augustine's heart at his conversion,† and a Psalm was his consolation when he lay upon his death-bed.‡ With the words of Psalms, Chrysostom comforted himself in his exile, writing thus: "When driven from the city, I cared nothing for it. But I said to myself, If the empress wishes to banish me, let her banish me; 'the earth is the Lord's, and the fulness thereof.'" And again: "David clothes me with armour, saying, 'I will speak of Thy testimonies before kings, and will not be ashamed.'" With the

* "Curvorum hinc chorus helciariorum
Responsantibus Alleluia ripis
Ad Christum levat amnicum celeusma.
Sic, sic psallite, nauta et viator!"

† See above, p. 27. ‡ See Introduction to Psalm xxxii.

words of a Psalm, holy Bernard expired. With the words of a Psalm, Huss and Jerome of Prague gave up their souls to God, without fear, in the midst of the fire. Chanting the twelfth verse of the Hundred and Eighteenth Psalm with voices that rose high above the din of battle, the Protestant army rushed to victory at Courtras. With the voice of a Psalm, Luther entered Worms, singing brave defiance to pope and cardinals, and all the gates of hell. With Psalms, that faithful servant of God, Adolphe Monod, strengthened himself to endure the agonies of a lingering and painful disease. And in the biography of a late eminent prelate of our own Church, no page possesses a deeper interest, a truer pathos, than that which records, that for many years before his death the Fifty-first Psalm had been his nightly prayer.* And what shall I say more? The history of the Psalms is the history of the Church, and the history of every heart in which has burned the love of God. It is a history not fully revealed in this world, but one which is written in heaven. It is a history which, could we know it, might teach us to hush many an angry thought, to recall many a bitter, hasty, uncharitable speech. The pages of that Book have often been blotted with the tears of those whom others deemed hard and cold, and whom they treated with suspicion or contempt. Those words have gone up to God, mingled with the sighs or scarcely uttered in the heart-broken anguish of those whom pharisees called sinners, of those whom Christians denounced as heretics or infidels, but who loved God and truth above all things else. Surely it is holy ground. We cannot pray the Psalms without realizing in a very special manner the communion of saints, the oneness of the Church militant and the Church triumphant. We cannot pray the Psalms without having our hearts opened, our affections enlarged, our thoughts drawn heavenward. He who can pray them best is nearest to God, knows most of the Spirit of Christ, is ripest for heaven.

---

* *Memoir of Bishop Blomfield*, vol. ii. p. 266.

CHAPTER 3

The Theology of the Psalms

THERE are some topics connected with the interpretation of the Psalms which have been the subject of so much discussion that it was scarcely possible to treat them satisfactorily in the notes. I propose, therefore, in this chapter to handle them more at large. How far we are to look in the Psalms for predictions of the Messiah, or the hope of a future life; in what sense the assertions of innocence which meet us on the one hand, and the imprecations of vengeance on the other, are to be understood: these, and questions like these, must present themselves to every thoughtful reader of the Psalms; and to give some answer to these questions will now be my endeavour.

The Messiah

I. The first question, and the most important, is this: What is the nature of the Messianic hope, as it meets us in the Psalms?

On this subject it may be said broadly, that three views have been entertained.

Modern Rationalistic views.

1. There have been expositors, more especially in recent times, who have gone so far as to affirm that none of the Psalms is in any proper sense Messianic, or that if the hope of the Messiah finds expression at all, it is traced in colouring so faint, in outlines so uncertain, that it ceases to be anything more than a vague anticipation at best. With such interpreters I shall not attempt to argue. To me the whole history of the Jewish nation becomes the most unintelligible of all enigmas, apart from the hope of Him who was to come. This hope is interwoven with all the tissues of the web of that history, and is the stay and the

strength of all. Nor can I understand how, with the historical fact before us of the promise given to David, we can hesitate to admit that in *his* Psalms, at least, some references to that promise would be found. A hope so great, a promise so distinctly given, must, by the very necessities of the case, have occupied the mind of David, and have reappeared in his Psalms. It would be far more perplexing to account for the absence than for the presence of the Messianic hope in his writings.

Patristic and Mediæval writers.

2. Others, again, and more especially the Patristic and Mediæval writers, have gone to the opposite extreme. To them every Psalm has some direct prophetical reference to our Lord, to the circumstances of His life, or His passion. So Tertullian takes the whole of the First Psalm as a prophecy of Joseph of Arimathea; Augustine gives to each a reference to Christ and His Church; and Albertus Magnus, asserting that it is a well-known fact that the whole Book is concerning Christ (*constat quod totus liber iste de Christo est*), interprets the First Psalm "of Christ, and His body the Church."

Views of interpreters since the Reformation.

3. But all sober interpreters since the time of the Reformation, following the guidance of Luther and Calvin, have avoided both extremes of error. On the one hand, they have recognised the existence of the Messianic element; on the other, they have abandoned those strained and fanciful interpretations by which violence is done to the plain language of many Psalms, when they are regarded as predictive of our Lord.

Common interpretation of Messianic Psalms.

Still much difference of opinion exists, more especially amongst English commentators, as to the principle of interpretation to be followed in those Psalms which are confessedly Messianic. One class of expositors, of whom Bishop Horsley may be taken as a chief representative, have laid it down as a certain principle, that whenever any part of a Psalm is by any of the writers of the New Testament applied to our Lord, there we are bound to explain the whole Psalm as prophetical of Him. Nay, every Psalm, it has been contended, which may reasonably be held, even without express New Testament sanction, to be Messianic, is Messianic in all its parts from first to last. For, it is urged, we are otherwise left without compass or star to guide us. Where, if this principle be abandoned, are we to draw the line, or what is to be the criterion of interpretation? Can we take one verse, and say, This applies to David; and another, and say, This applies to Christ? Does not our application of the Psalm thus become vague and arbitrary? Left without any standing rule or principle of interpretation, each can take or reject what he pleases.

But, in the first place, this canon of interpretation fails, because it, at least tacitly, assumes that in all these Psalms the writer is consciously uttering a prediction; that the Psalmist, although he is speaking, it may be, in some lower sense of himself, has ever consciously before the eye of his mind One greater than he, in whom he knew that his words would find their ultimate fulfilment. But there is no proof that such is the case, but rather the reverse. In many Psalms it seems very evident that the writer is speaking of *himself*, of *his own* sufferings, of *his own* deliverance, apparently without thinking of another; although being a prophet, and therefore a type of Christ, he is led to use unconsciously words which, in their highest and truest sense, are applicable only to Christ.

In the next place, the difficulties involved in the canon of interpretation to which I refer are far more serious than those which it is intended to surmount. It compels us constantly to take words and phrases in a sense which is obviously not their proper and natural sense. We find in many of these Psalms, passages of which are said to have been fulfilled in the circumstances of our Lord's life or passion, confessions of sinfulness, maledictions of the writer's enemies, expressions of hatred and revenge, none of which can, in their plain literal sense, be transferred to our Lord. It is therefore necessary, in order that the canon may hold in its application, to give to all such words and expressions a very modified and altered meaning; an expedient to which we surely ought not to resort, unless no other way of escape were open to us. The words of Scripture may have a far *deeper* meaning than that which lies on the surface, but surely not an altogether *different* meaning—a meaning which can only be extracted by ingenious contrivances, or by doing violence to the simplest rules of language. If, in order to maintain some rule of interpretation which we assume to be necessary, we are compelled to introduce words and thoughts into passages where those words are not found, it may be worth while to ask ourselves whether our rule itself is not bent and twisted, and fit only to be thrown away.

The Fortieth Psalm.

Let us test the rule, then, in one or two well-known instances. In the Fortieth Psalm there occurs a passage, the Septuagint Version of which is quoted in the Epistle to the Hebrews. The quotation runs thus: "Wherefore when He cometh into the world He saith: Sacrifice and offering Thou wouldest not, but a body hast Thou prepared me: In burnt-offerings and sacrifices for sin Thou hast had no pleasure. Then said I, Lo, I come; in the volume of the book it is written of me, to do Thy will, O God." The citation is made in illustration of the writer's argument against the perpetuity of the Jewish sacrifices. He shows that those sacrifices were but a part of a Law which was a shadow of good things to come, a Law which confessed its own incompleteness, which contained the elements of its own dissolution, which itself prophesied the destruction of its own body of death, and its resurrection to a life spiritual and eternal. He argues that the very *repetition* of those sacrifices is a proof of their incompleteness: and further, that the nature of the sacrifices was such, that they could have only a typical, not a moral efficacy. "It is impossible that the blood of bulls and of goats should take away sin," &c. With these he contrasts the offering of Christ, the great virtue of which lay in the fact, that it was the offering of an obedient will, and therefore essentially moral and spiritual in its character. And in order to express this truth in a forcible manner, and to put it in a light which for his readers would have an especial attraction, the writer of the Epistle claims the words of the Psalmist as having found their fulfilment in the mouth of Christ. The fact that the passage as cited by him from the Version of the LXX. differs in a material point from the Hebrew text, however interesting and instructive in itself, has no bearing on my present argument. What it is of importance to observe is, that those words quoted as having found their highest realization, their most perfect meaning, in the lips of our blessed Lord,* are followed by other words in the Psalm, which in their plain grammatical sense cannot possibly be considered as spoken by Him. For what follows this lofty expression of a ready obedience, of a will in harmony with the will of God? A sad confession of human sinfulness and misery. A cry for mercy, as from one who has sinned, and who has suffered for his sin. "Thou, O Jehovah, wilt not refrain Thy tender compassions from me. . . . For evils have come about me without number; My iniquities have taken hold upon me that I cannot see: They are more than the hairs of my head, And my heart hath failed me." Then follow further, a petition for help, and a prayer for confusion on his enemies. Now, how is this latter part of the Psalm made to apply to Christ? How, in particular, are the words in ver. 12, "my iniquities," interpreted? That I may not be guilty of any exaggeration, I will quote Bishop Horsley's note on the passage: "*Ærumnæ meæ* [my distresses], says Houbigant; piously thinking that the person who speaks throughout the Psalm had no sins with which to charge himself. But since God 'laid upon Him the iniquities of us,' therefore the Messiah, when He is personated in the Psalms, perpetually calls those iniquities His own, of which He bore the punishment."

But of the two explanations Houbigant's is the more tolerable. The word rendered "my iniquities" might, in accordance with the opinion of competent scholars, be rendered "my punishments," the word being the same as in Gen. iv. 14, where our Authorized Version has, "my punishment is heavier than I can bear." But even then, as punishment for personal guilt is meant, it is obvious that

* This, I think, it may fairly be concluded, considering the general nature of the argument of the Epistle, is the writer's view, although it is not expressly said that the Scripture was fulfilled.

only by a remote, and circuitous, and tortuous method, can the proposed application be made.

Examination of Horsley's interpretation.

But as to Horsley's own interpretation, it is far more indefensible than that which it is intended to supersede. The passage which he quotes in support of his interpretation fails really in its most essential particulars. For that does express the very idea which here is not expressed, and which is only assumed, but not proved, to be implied. There we do not find "our iniquities" spoken of as the iniquities of Christ, but they are distinctly said, on the one hand, to be "the iniquities of us all," and as distinctly said on the other, to have been "*laid* upon Him." Nor will similar passages which are sometimes appealed to in the New Testament bear the stress of the argument drawn from them. We are reminded, for instance, that our Lord is said "to bear our sins in His own body on the tree;" and that we even read that "God made Him who knew no sin to be sin for us;" and it is contended that such language justifies the interpretation which Horsley has given of the Psalm. But I ask, is there no difference between these alleged parallel passages? Is not the difference, on the contrary, so great, that the one cannot be fairly explained by the other? Surely it is one thing for us to be told that God *made* Christ sin; and it is quite another thing for our blessed Lord himself to speak of the iniquities of others as His own. As a fact He never does so. And the step in the argument is prodigious. The two ideas have scarcely an intelligible connection. The one expression seems even to exclude the other. A judge might condemn an innocent man to death in behalf of the guilty, but surely that innocent man would never speak of himself as guilty. Rather would he hold fast his integrity, as that which gave additional worth to his self-sacrifice.

The Forty-first Psalm.

Let us take one more instance, if possible still more strikingly conclusive against the mode of interpretation which I am impugning. It shall be taken from the next Psalm in the series, the Forty-first. If this Psalm be the composition of David, there can be little doubt that he had in his mind the cruel desertion of some friend, perhaps

Ahithophel, in the season of his extremity, 2 Sam. xv. 31; xvi. 20, &c. The words of the 9th verse, which so feelingly describe the bitterest drop in the cup of sorrow, the faithlessness of a known and trusted friend, are by our Lord himself applied to the treachery of Judas.* But it is very instructive to observe the manner in which the quotation is made, especially where, as in this instance, it is introduced with the formula, "That the Scripture may be fulfilled." Our Lord drops from the quotation words which could not apply to Himself: "Mine own familiar friend in whom I trusted;" for He never did trust Judas. He knew from the beginning who should betray Him. It is clear, then, that we have our Lord's own authority for taking a portion, not only of a Psalm, but even of a particular passage in a Psalm, as prophetic of Himself and the circumstances of His life. Indeed, in this Psalm the difficulties are absolutely appalling, if we try to expound it throughout of Christ. How, then, interpret the 4th verse: "Heal my soul; for I have sinned against Thee;" or the 10th, "But Thou, O Jehovah, be gracious unto me, And *raise me up, that I may requite them*"? Horsley's note on the former verse is one of the most remarkable instances of a forced interpretation which it was ever my lot to meet with. He says: "In this Psalm the Messiah is the speaker, who in His own Person was sinless. But the words may be rendered, 'Surely I bear blame before Thee,' *Personam peccatoris apud te gero.* So the word חטא is used, Gen. xliii. 9, of the A. V." Kennicott renders the sentence as a question, "Have I sinned against Thee?" But Horsley was quite right in adding, "But I much doubt the use of the particle כִּי as an interrogative." It would be as reasonable to make ὅτι or γὰρ an interrogative in Greek. To return, however, to Horsley's explanation, what meaning after all does it convey? What sense is there in saying, "Heal my soul, for I bear the blame before Thee. Heal my soul, for I am not a sinner, but only in the character of a sinner"? Such interpretations *introduce* the idea

* 'Αλλ' ἵνα ἡ γραφὴ πληρωθῇ, ὁ τρώγων μετ' ἐμοῦ τὸν ἄρτον ἐπῆρεν ἐπ' ἐμὲ τὴν πτέρναν αὐτοῦ. John xiii. 18.

which their authors think they find in a passage, and then the passage itself is said to contain the idea.

We need not carry this argument further. It is wonderful, indeed, that so arbitrary a canon of interpretation should have been invented, that it should have been maintained so perseveringly, and that its manifest defects should not have made its soundness suspected.

Analogy of Prophecy.

Besides these inherent difficulties, the canon has all analogy against it, as well as the authority of the New Testament writers. It has analogy against it; for no one thinks of expounding the prophetical books in this manner. Thus, no one contends that because part of a prophecy is Messianic, therefore every portion of it must be Messianic. No one, for instance, would argue that *the whole* of Isaiah's prophecy delivered to Ahaz, on the invasion of Rezin and Pekah, must be applied down to its minutest details to Christ, because St. Matthew leads us to see a fulfilment of one portion of his announcement in the birth of Jesus of Nazareth. Why should we apply to the Psalms a rule which we do not apply to the Prophets?

Quotations in the New Testament.

But in the next place, the invariable practice of the New Testament writers overthrows the canon referred to, and establishes for us a safe and consistent rule of interpretation. *Never does any writer of the New Testament, Evangelist or Apostle, never does our Lord himself, sanction the application of any passage of the Old Testament to Him in which the writer confesses and deplores his own sinfulness.* This fact of itself ought to be a guide to us in our interpretation. It is a beacon against the shoals and quicksands of human error. Frequently and freely as the New Testament writers cite passages from the Old Testament, and especially from the Psalms,* as fulfilled in Christ—some perhaps which, without their authority, we should hardly have dared so to interpret—they most cautiously abstain from that perversion of language which in modern theology has been pushed to such an extreme. To them it would

* It is a remarkable fact, that of all the citations in the New Testament, from the Old, which have a Messianic reference, nearly one-half is made from the Psalms.

have seemed nothing short of an awful profanation to have spoken of the sins laid upon Christ as His sins. They would never have thought it possible to speak of Him as a sinner, who to them was the Holy One of God. Words which expressed devotedness, self-sacrifice, high and holy aspirations, these they felt, and we all feel, however true in some sense of a righteous Israelite of old, uttering them in the communion of his heart with God, and carried beyond himself while he uttered them, were infinitely truer, yea, only true in the fullest sense, of Him who came not to do His own will, but the will of Him who sent Him. Hence these, even where no direct prediction was intended, were more fitting in His mouth than in theirs. So likewise the language of sorrow, the cry poured out from the depths of a troubled spirit, however truly expressive of the feelings of a pious Jew bowed down by calamities, persecutions, miseries untold, never came with so true a force of utterance from any lips as from the lips of Him, whose sorrows and whose sufferings were such as it hath not entered into the heart of man to conceive.

Typical character of Messianic prophecy in the Psalms.

What, then, is the conclusion at which we arrive from these observed facts? Surely it is this: that the Psalms to a large extent foreshadow Christ, because the writers of the Psalms are types of Christ. And it is of the very nature of a type to be imperfect. It fortells in some particulars, but not in all, that of which it is the type. Were it complete in itself, it would not point further; through its very incompleteness it becomes a prophecy. Now, the Psalms are typical. They are the words of holy men of old—of one especially, whose life was fashioned in many of its prominent features to be a type of Christ. But just as David's *whole* life was not typical of Christ, so neither were all his words. His suffering and his humiliation first, and his glory afterwards, were faint and passing and evanescent images of the life of Him who was both Son of David and Son of God. But the sorrowful shadow of pollution which passed upon David's life, *that* was not typical, and, therefore, the words in which it was confessed are not typical or predictive, or capable of application to our Lord.

Once let us firmly grasp this idea, that any Psalm in which a suffering saint of God under the Old Testament addresses God has but a typical reference to Christ, where it has any such reference at all, and we are freed at once from all embarrassment of interpretation. Then we can say without hesitation: Every word in that Psalm is the true expression of the feelings of him who wrote it; the suffering is a real suffering; the sorrow is a real sorrow; the aspiration, so high, so heavenly, is a real aspiration; the joy and the triumph of deliverance are real; the confession of sin comes from a heart to which sin is a real burden. But the sorrow, the suffering, the aspiration, the joy, the triumph—all but the sin—never found all their fulness of meaning save in the life and on the lips of the Perfect Man.

In accordance with the character of Jewish history.

Another great advantage of this system of interpretation is, that it not only saves us from a forced and unnatural interpretation of language in particular instances, but that it falls in so completely with the whole history of the Old Testament. That history is throughout typical. We have the key to its meaning in that quotation by the Evangelist Matthew: "Out of Egypt have I called my son." The history of Israel and the history of Christ are, in a certain sense, one. And as the history of Israel was fashioned to be typical of the history of Redemption, in its capital features, so the history of the great representative characters in Israel was designed to foreshadow, each in some distinct particular, the life of Christ. Christ our Lord is Prophet, Priest, and King. All these offices find their highest significance in Him; and, accordingly, those who bore these offices in the Mosaic economy were, in their several degrees, types of Christ.

The Prophet.

1. The Prophet was the teacher of the truth which he had received by solemn commission from the mouth of God. He came to the people, as one sent by God, bearing the message of God on his lips. He spake of truth, of righteousness, of mercy; he revealed God's will, he threatened God's judgements; he rebuked the prevalent formalism and the prevalent hypocrisy. He was the

majestic witness for God against the Priest whose lips no longer kept knowledge, against the King who forgot that he was the servant of the Highest, and against the people who clung to the letter of the Law with the more scrupulous tenacity, in proportion as they forgot and departed from its spirit. But the Prophet himself did not speak *all* the truth. He often spoke dimly; he revealed only those portions and fragments of truth which it was his especial mission to proclaim. Such was the Prophet in his teaching. But what was he in his life? He went in and out before the people, and he was one with them. He was better, for the most part, than those whom he rebuked, but there were blots and imperfections in his life. Sin, and error, and infirmity might be seen even in the teacher sent from God. The true Prophet had not yet come. God gave His people the type, but with His own hand He brake it in pieces before their eyes, that they might wait for the Great Prophet of His Church, for Him who should not only teach the Truth, but be the Truth; for Him who should not only speak the Word, but be the Word; the only-begotten Son, who, alike in life and speech, should declare the Father unto men.

2. So likewise was it with the Priest. The Jewish High Priest was the intercessor between man and God. As the Prophet was the messenger from God to man, so the Priest was the representative of man with God. He was taken from among men. Once in the year he entered into the most holy place, there to make atonement for sin. But that holy place itself was typical and shadowy; it was but the figure of heaven. The victim whose blood was there sprinkled to make atonement, showed that the earthly sanctuary needed itself to be cleansed. The blood was the blood of a dumb animal, which could never take away sin. The High Priest confessed his own imperfection in the very act of atonement, because he must offer sacrifice, first for his own sins, and then for the sins of the people. The Priest, therefore, though a representative of the people, was an imperfect representative, entering into an imperfect sanctuary, offering an imperfect sacrifice. The Priest.

God gave His people the type, but He brake in pieces the type before their eyes, and thus He led them to look for the true Priest, for Him who should make atonement with His own blood and for ever put away sin by the sacrifice of Himself; whose sympathy would be perfect, because He could bear all hearts in His; whose sacrifice would be perfect, because it was the sacrifice of Himself; whose intercession would be all-prevalent, because He ever liveth at the right hand of God.

The King.

3. There was another prominent character in the Jewish theocracy. The King was emphatically the Anointed of God, His vicegerent upon earth. He was to be the witness for a Divine Government, the pattern of the Divine righteousness, filled with the spirit of wisdom and understanding. "Give the King Thy judgements, O God, and Thy righteousness unto the King's son." Such was the prayer uttered, perhaps, by Solomon, and conveying in its expression the true conception of what a king should be, as ruling by the grace of God, and, in some sort, even representing God to man. God made a covenant with David, gave him promises great and glorious, seated his son upon his throne. But that son disappointed all the hopes which once gathered around him so brightly. The morning of his reign which was so fair, like a morning without clouds, was quickly overcast, and his sun set in the disastrous gloom of a gathering tempest. He who had been the mirror of justice and wisdom ended by cruelly oppressing his subjects. Too surely and too lamentably was it made evident, that he was not the righteous king whose rule was to be a blessing to the world. He was not the defender of the poor and the scourge of evil-doers; his dominion was not from sea to sea, nor from the river to the ends of the earth. After him the sceptre which he had held was broken in twain. And as one after another of his descendants sat upon David's throne, the earthly hope waxed fainter and fainter. If for a moment it revived with the pious Hezekiah, with the good Josiah, it was but to sink at last into a deeper darkness. Wrong and violence were in the city; and none sat

in the gate to do justice. The poor cried, but he had no helper; the oppressed, and there was none to deliver. The king was stained with crimes, and used the almost despotic power of an oriental prince unscrupulously and without remorse. The fair image of righteousness, associated with the very name of king, and of which the bright ideal had never been conceived as it was in Judaism, where was it to be found? The true Son of David was not yet come. Men's hearts and eyes failed them for longing and looking for His coming. God took the earthly type and brake it in pieces before their eyes, that they might thus wait for Him who should be King of Righteousness and King of Peace.

Two only of these figures appear in the Psalms.

Of these three principal figures in the Jewish typical system, two appear prominently in the Psalms, the Prophet and the King. This is what might be expected. The Priest was typical by his acts rather than by his words. And sacrifice and ritual might be enjoined and described in the Law, but they find no place in the Psalms. They are mentioned only to be depreciated. Hence in one Psalm only does Messiah appear as Priest, and there He is both King and Priest. There, moreover, He stands as a Priest after the order of Melchisedec, and not after the order of Aaron. But with regard to the other two offices — those of Prophet and King — the Messianic Psalms may be divided into two classes, according as they are represented by the one or the other of these two characters.

Prediction of the Messiah as King.

1. We have a series of Psalms — the Second, the Twentieth, the Twenty-first, the Forty-fifth, the Seventy-second, the Hundred and Tenth—in all of which a King is celebrated. In one Psalm a King is described who goes forth conquering and to conquer; in another, a King whose reign is a reign of righteousness and peace. In another, the occasion of the royal nuptials has been selected as the subject. In all, some Jewish monarch, either on his accession, or at some critical period of his reign, is the immediate object before the eyes of the inspired Poet. But in all the monarch grows larger and

fairer than the sons of men. He is seen ever in the light of the promise made to David, and in that light he is transfigured. Human he is, no doubt: many words spoken of him pertain only to a human king; but many also are higher; many cannot, except by force of exaggeration, be made to apply to one who wears the frailty together with the form of man. There is but one interpretation by which the apparently discordant elements in these Psalms can be held together. It is that according to which the Psalms are regarded, not as simply predictive, but as properly typical in their character.

As Prophet and Sufferer.

2. Many other Psalms there are, which, in the New Testament, are said to have their fulfilment in the sufferings of Christ. In these, again, the writer himself is a type of Christ, and he is so in his character as a prophet, or preacher of righteousness. In all these Psalms, a servant of God appears as a sufferer, and a sufferer for righteousness' sake; often, indeed, confessing that he suffers the just punishment of his sins *at the hands of God*, but always complaining that he is unjustly persecuted *of men.* In such Psalms, more particularly, as the Twenty-second and Sixty-ninth, we find, moreover, language used which implies that the sufferer occupies a prominent position, and that he is, in some sense, the representative of Israel in his sufferings. The issue of those sufferings is to be a subject of joy and thanksgiving, not to himself only, but to all who, like himself, fear God, and endure persecution for His Name's sake. Hence the Psalmist, both as prophet and as righteous sufferer, is a type of Christ; for every Jewish prophet or preacher was also conspicuous as a sufferer, a martyr for the truth.

These two not united in the Psalms.

But we never find these two characters—that of the suffering prophet and the victorious king—united in the same Psalm. This, of itself, is surely remarkable. This of itself teaches us how purely typical the Psalms are, so far as their Messianic import is concerned. Everywhere we find imperfection, everywhere only a partial representation of that which could not, as yet, be conceived of in its completeness.

Lastly, there is another remarkable circumstance, which lends ample confirmation, were confirmation needed, to the view I have advocated. It is this. Nowhere in the Psalms are the redemption of the world and Israel's final glory bound up with the coming of the Messiah. The Messiah is, for a time at least, associated with the present, and only with the present. The Anointed of God is David, or Solomon, till both the one and the other fail to fulfil the longings of men's hearts. But the Advent to which Israel looks forward is the Advent of JEHOVAH. It is He who is Israel's true King. It is His coming which shall be her redemption and her glory; but His coming is never identified with the coming of the Messiah.* The early hope and the heavenly run on in parallel lines, but they never meet. In the light of the New Testament only do we see how David's Son is also his Lord.

All these facts, then, point in one direction. The fact that the Messiah and the Divine deliverer are not as yet seen by the Psalmists to be the same; the fact that the King and the Sufferer are two, not one; the fact that the New Testament writers never quote confessions of sinfulness as in any way applicable to Christ, whilst they do quote other words expressive of devotion or suffering as so applicable: all these tend to the same conclusion, namely, that whilst all the great characters of Israelitish history are typical of Him, they are so only partially and imperfectly. Hence we can freely and safely adopt this principle of interpretation in all cases. We can see in every Psalm which may reasonably be regarded as Messianic, a primary reference to the writer and to his own circumstances; and, so far as confessions of sin meet us, an exclusive reference; whereas in all else, without maintaining a conscious prophecy, we can recognise the language of a type waiting its proper accomplishment in the Antitype.

Relation of the Psalmists to the Law.

II. We turn now to the relation in which the Psalmists

* See this beautifully stated by Delitzsch, in the note which I have quoted on Ps. lxxii.

stand to the Law of God. And here we may notice, first the strong affection expressed for the Law of God in itself and, next, the remarkable recognition of its higher and more spiritual requirements, as contrasted with its merely ceremonial enactments.

1. We have, first, the expression of a strong personal affection for the Law of God. "The Law of Jehovah," it is said in the Nineteenth Psalm, "is perfect, restoring the soul; the testimony of Jehovah is sure, making wise the simple. The statutes of Jehovah are right, rejoicing the heart; the commandment of Jehovah is pure, enlightening the eyes. . . . The judgements of Jehovah are truth, they are righteous altogether. More to be desired are they than gold, yea than much fine gold; sweeter also than honey, and the droppings of the honeycomb. Moreover Thy servant is enlightened by them, and in keeping of them there is great reward." In the First Psalm, where the character of the righteous man is pourtrayed in contrast with that of the wicked, it is summed up in these words: "In the Law of Jehovah is his delight, and in His Law doth he meditate day and night." The longest Psalm in the whole collection, the Hundred and Nineteenth, might be entitled "The Praise of the Law;" for it sets forth in ceaseless variety of application the value of the law, the statutes, the judgements of God. What then was this Law, which seemed so precious, so infinitely beyond all gold and silver, to the Psalmists of Israel, which was to them as a light to their feet, and as sweet food to their mouth, and which was their meditation all the day? Is it the same Law which to St. Paul seems so bitter, which he views as the strength of sin, as making him feel his wretchedness, as pronouncing his condemnation? Calvin has thrown out the question in his Commentary on the Nineteenth Psalm, and has partly answered it. "How," he asks, "shall these things agree, that the Law restores the soul, and yet is a dead letter; that it cheers the heart, and yet brings with it the spirit of a slave and inspires us with terror; that it enlightens the eyes, and yet, by putting a veil before them, darkens the light within?" "St. Paul," he replies, "and the

Psalmist, are regarding the Law from two different points of view. David does not speak of the Law as opposed to the Gospel, but of the Law as including the promise. To him the Law is not merely the code, the bare precepts, but the whole revelation of God, so far as it was then given, including Christ Himself, on whom the adoption of Israel rested. St. Paul, on the other hand, had to do with perverse interpreters of the Law, who were for separating it from the grace and spirit of Christ; whereas, apart from Christ, the Law, inexorable in its requirements, can only expose the whole world to God's wrath and curse." This, no doubt, is true so far as it goes. St. Paul was looking at the Law merely as a covenant of works: "The man that doeth these things, he shall live by them;" and he felt deeply his own inability to live by them. He saw, on the one hand, the holiness of God reflected in the Law, and, on the other hand, the impossibility of keeping the Law. The impossibility of keeping it filled him with terror and dismay, but, so far as it was the reflection of God's holiness, he could say, as truly as David, "I *delight* in the Law of God after the inner man." He too could say, "The Law is holy, and the commandment is holy, and just, and good." Viewed in itself, viewed as an expression of the mind of God, it was all that the Psalmist declared it to be. It was only when it was looked at as an instrument of justification that it became clothed with terror. When a man heard that in order to be saved he must obey the Law, and when conscience told him that he was a perpetual transgressor of the Law, then, indeed, he saw nothing but condemnation. But this relation to the Law, so distinctly felt, so clearly understood, is peculiar to the Gospel. The work of the Spirit of Christ has given us, it cannot be doubted, a deeper insight into the nature of sin, and therefore, also, into the condemning power of the Law. But, under the Old Testament, the opposition between the Law and sin does not appear with anything like the same sharpness of outline. The love and affection which are expressed towards the Law here, are expressed towards it regarded simply as the reflection of the pure, and perfect, and holy will of God. To the spiritually-minded Jew under the Old Testament, that Law was not merely an outward letter of restraint; his heart and conscience consented thereto.* And one capital object of the teaching of the Prophets was to represent it in its truly spiritual meaning, and so to set it forth as a proper object of affection to every heart which waited upon God.

Spiritual appreciation of the Ceremonial part of the Law.

2. But, again, we find in the Psalms a thoroughly spiritual appreciation of the ceremonial part of the Law. Samuel had already led the way here. "Hath the Lord as great delight in burnt-offerings and sacrifices as in obeying the voice of the Lord? Behold, to obey is better than sacrifice, and to hearken than the fat of rams." The same truth in one Psalm (the Fortieth) is represented as having been immediately communicated by Divine teaching to the writer of the Psalm. David may both have learnt it from Samuel, when he was living among "the sons of prophets," and have had the lesson confirmed by the direct inspiration of the Holy Ghost. "Burnt-offering and sacrifice," he declares, "Thou wouldest not. The sacrifices of God are a broken spirit." In the grand prophetic strain of the Fiftieth Psalm, the relation of sacrifice to obedience is no less explicitly taught; the comparative worthlessness of the one, the real value of the other. It is of importance to bear in mind, that this, and this only, is the view taken of the Mosaic sacrifices by the spiritually-enlightened Jew under that dispensation. He evidently did not regard those sacrifices, as so many Christian writers have regarded them, as having, in the case of those who offered them in penitence and faith, a spiritual efficacy. Their only efficacy to him was the efficacy which the Law itself assigned to

* Luther, in commenting on those words of the First Psalm, "His delight (or, as he renders it, *will*) is in the Law of Jehovah," beautifully observes: "Now this will is that pure satisfaction of the heart, and, so to speak, pleasure in the Law, which does not ask what the Law promises, or what it threatens, but only this, that the Law is holy, just, and good. It is, therefore, not only a love of the Law, but a loving delight in the Law, which neither by any prosperity nor by any adversity can the world and the prince of the world take away or overcome, but through the midst of want, infamy, the cross, death, hell, it forces its victorious way; for it shines forth chiefly in adversities."

them; they were the instruments of restoring him, when he had transgressed, to his place as a member of the theocracy, a citizen of the visible kingdom of God. But they did not confer, or convey, *the remission of sins.* They were external, and their efficacy was external. They were *typical,* no doubt, of Christ's sacrifice; and the forgiveness which they procured, and which resulted in the re-admission of an offender to the privileges of his Jewish citizenship, was typical of the forgiveness of sins under the Gospel dispensation. But it is no less certain that the legal sacrifices did not take the place in the Old Testament of the sacrifice of Christ in the New, that it was not *through his sacrifices* that the Old Testament believer looked for the forgiveness of his sins. Had it been so, we could not have found the constant opposition between sacrifice and obedience, the studied depreciation of sacrifices, which meets us everywhere in the Psalms and the Prophets, and which is, in fact, fully confirmed by the whole argument of the Epistle to the Hebrews. How far the Jewish believer saw into the typical meaning of his sacrifices, is a question which cannot now be answered. It is however somewhat remarkable that the Prophets, earnestly as they expostulate with the people on the subject of their sacrifices, never say one word on this aspect of them, never speak of this their hidden meaning. But the typical meaning and the real efficacy are two very different things. In truth, as has been ably argued,* if we assign to the type the virtue of the antitype, if we make the remission of sins procured by the one co-extensive with the remission of sins procured by the other, we destroy the type altogether. The sacrifice had no moral value. Hence the Psalmist says, *not* sacrifice *but* a broken heart. Could he have said this, if through the sacrifice he looked for forgiveness of sin?

Assertions of innocence in the Psalms.

III. We find in the Psalms, on many occasions, assertions of uprightness, of innocence, of freedom from transgression, which almost startle us. Such expressions,

* See the clear and satisfactory statement of the whole question in Dean MacDonnell's *Donnellan Lectures.* Appendix to the First Sermon.

indeed, have sometimes given offence, as if they savoured of a self-righteous spirit. But a little reflection will show how mistaken such a notion is. We have but to turn to the passages in which they occur to see at once that the words are not the words of a proud boaster, ignorant alike of his own heart and of the law of God. Take, for instance, such passages as these: "Thou hast proved my heart; Thou hast visited me by night; Thou hast tried me and findest no evil thought in me; neither doth my heart transgress" (Ps. xvii. 3). The words are bold words, no doubt. Such an assertion of innocence is one which we might tremble to make. But it is not self-righteous. It is not the utterance of the Pharisee, "God, I thank Thee I am not as other men are, or even as this publican." It is made solemnly in the presence of God, with a direct appeal to Him as knowing the heart: "From Thy presence let my judgement go forth; Thine eyes behold uprightness" (ver. 2). It is fully explained by other language immediately preceding: "Give ear to my prayer which (is uttered) *by no deceitful lips*." These last words show us the sense in which such a passage is to be taken. The Psalmist is not asserting his freedom from sin, but the uprightness and guilelessness of his heart towards God. He is no hypocrite, no dissembler; he is *not consciously* doing wrong.

Language equally strong, or stronger, we find again in the next Psalm: "Jehovah rewarded me according to my righteousness, according to the cleanness of my hands did He recompense me. For I have kept the ways of Jehovah, and have not wickedly departed from my God. . . . I have also been perfect with Him, and have kept myself from my iniquity." Such words are, no doubt, enough to make us pause and look within, and ask ourselves if we can utter them in sincerity, but they are manifestly not said in a boastful, arrogant spirit. The whole Psalm is full of a childlike trust and confidence in God, the very opposite of the spirit of self-righteousness. It may be, perhaps, that we meet with such expressions more frequently in the Psalms than we do in the New Testament, because the sense of sin under the old dispensation was not so deep as under the new. That it was not, and could not be, the New Testament itself teaches us. The Law was given to restrain outward acts, but it could not touch the conscience. There were foreshadowings of the sacrifice of Christ, but that sacrifice had not been offered. And therefore, as the power and efficiency of that atonement could not be understood, so neither could all the depth and malignity of sin be discovered. The Spirit of God, though He undoubtedly was the source of all righteousness then, as now, in the hearts of believers, yet did not, it is plain, exercise the same influence as He does in the present dispensation. We are distinctly taught that, till the Ascension of Christ, "the Holy Ghost was not given." That gift, it is intimated, was in some special sense the great glory and privilege of the Christian Church. "It is expedient for you that I go away; for if I go not away the Comforter will not come to you, but if I depart I will send Him unto you." Nor was the distinguishing feature of His mission the imparting only of extraordinary miraculous gifts. In His other operations, also, He works now as He did not then. Coming as the Spirit of the Father and the Son, it is His office in a sense before unknown, because connected immediately with the work of Christ and His going to the Father, to convince the world of sin, of righteousness, and of judgement. All, therefore, that was taught under the legal economy on these subjects, though true, because taught by the same Spirit, yet was nevertheless comparatively imperfect, because He had not yet come as sent by the risen Saviour.

Still, while we admit this, because the whole tenour and scope of God's Revelation compel us to admit it, we must not forget how true, how real, how widely different from anything to be met with elsewhere in the ancient world, is the sense of sin expressed in the Psalms. It may be, no doubt, and it often is, first awakened by suffering. The sharpness of the rod seems the measure of the transgression. It may be that more frequently acts of sin are regarded than the bitter root whence these spring—the sinful nature. So far as this is the case, we may allow that such representations are in accordance rather with the Old Testament than with the New. But even granting this, we have still the truest view of sin before us in the Psalms. We do find there (in the Fifty-first Psalm) the confession of a *sinful nature*, as well as of sinful acts. We find the confession that all sin, as sin, is committed against God, even when the act is done against our neighbour. We find the ever-living consciousness that God looks at the heart, and not merely at the outward act. "The righteous God trieth the hearts and reins." We find the blessedness of forgiveness stated in words which the Apostle Paul cites in his Epistle to the Romans, when asserting the doctrine of justification by faith. We find the need, and the longing for sanctification through the Spirit, plainly and feelingly declared.

Imprecations in the Psalms.

IV. One other point, bearing upon the moral position of the Psalmists, remains to be considered, and it is, perhaps, that which has occasioned more real perplexity than any other. We find in some of the Psalms terrible denunciations of the writer's enemies, withering anathemas, imprecations so awful that we almost tremble to read them. How are we to explain the occurrence of such prayers for vengeance? Are they justifiable? Are they, not the mere outbursts of passionate and unsanctified feeling, but the legitimate expression of a righteous indignation? Or are they Jewish only, and not Christian? And if so, then how are we to reconcile this with a belief in the Divine authority and inspiration of the Scriptures? Such language is certainly very different from anything that we meet with in the New Testament; and yet, if it is not legitimate, if we may not use it ourselves, then how can it be said to be given by inspiration of God?

This is a real difficulty, and it seemed so real a difficulty even to a mind like that of Arnold, that he took refuge in what must be called a non-natural interpretation, and argued that such language could be lawfully used now, only with reference to the enemies of our soul's peace. Yet it is obvious how impossible it is to carry out this principle of interpretation. How, for instance, in wrestling with spiritual enemies, could we adopt with any definite meaning such words as these: "Set Thou a wicked man over him, and let Satan stand at his right hand. When he shall be judged, let him be condemned; and let his prayers become sin. Let his days be few, and let another take his office. Let his children be fatherless and his wife a widow," &c. It is manifestly out of the question: the gulf is too wide between the original sense and the attempted application.

I have so fully explained, in a note on the Thirty-fifth Psalm, what I believe to be the right principle of interpretation in passages of this imprecatory character, that I need not go over the ground again. I will only make two remarks. First, let the English reader be on his guard against the well-meant assertions of Bishop Horne and other writers, that the verbs which are correctly rendered in our Authorized Version as optatives might, with equal propriety, be rendered as futures. This method of translation would escape from the difficulty by giving us predictions for imprecations. Thus, for instance, instead of reading: "*Let* his days be few: *let* his children be fatherless," &c., these expositors would have us read: "His days *shall be* few: his children *shall be* fatherless," &c. But this is an expedient which does violence to the most certain rules of language. The tense in Hebrew which by the older grammarians is commonly called the future, and, by the more recent, either the present or imperfect, but which I venture to think ought to be called the aorist, has two forms. One of these is used to denote sometimes present, sometimes past, sometimes future action. The other, an apocopated or shortened form, is used to denote the expression of a wish.* It is this last which occurs in all the

* In order to make this clear to a person ignorant of Hebrew, I will attempt an illustration from the Latin. *Amabit*, "he will love," is the third person future of *amo;* now suppose that instead of employing a distinct form, as the Latin language does, to express "let him love," it were to convey this optative meaning by contracting the future *amabit* into *ambt*, such a process would, as nearly as possible, represent what takes place in Hebrew.

passages where the English Version has employed, and rightly employed, the auxiliary verb "let" as an equivalent. This, then, is certain: we have in the Psalms imprecations, prayers for vengeance, and not merely the threatening of God's wrath against impenitent sinners. The verbs are optatives, not futures.

My next remark is designed to meet, if possible, a misrepresentation of my meaning in what I have said in the Note before referred to. I have there endeavoured to show that, whilst we need not suppose that the indignation which burns so hotly is other than a righteous indignation, yet that we are to regard it as permitted under the Old Testament rather than justifiable under the New. Surely there is nothing in such an explanation which in the smallest degree impugns the Divine authority of the earlier Scriptures. In how many respects have the harsher outlines of the legal economy been softened down by "the mind that was in Christ Jesus." How much of it is declared to be antiquated, even though it still stands for our instruction in the volume of the Bible. How clearly our Lord Himself teaches us, that His Spirit and the spirit of Elijah are not the same. Yet surely no prophet of the Old Testament occupies a higher place, as an inspired messenger of God, than the prophet Elijah. Our Lord does not condemn the prophet for his righteous zeal: He does forbid the manifestation of a like zeal on the part of His disciples. As in the Sermon on the Mount He substitutes the moral principle for the legal enactment, so here He substitutes the spirit of gentleness, meekness, endurance of wrongs, for the spirit of fiery though righteous indignation. The Old Testament is not contrary to the New, but it is inferior to it.

And there is a peculiarity in the circumstances under which our Lord's remarks were uttered when He forbade His disciples to call down fire from heaven upon the Samaritan village, which makes His remarks on that occasion strictly applicable to the question we are discussing. The disciples, it is plain, were not actuated by selfish or interested motives. It was not their own quarrel, but their Master's, in which they were engaged. The insult had been offered to Him, and therefore they would have avenged Him as Peter did, when he drew his sword and cut off the ear of Malchus. Their indignation was righteous, as Elijah's indignation was righteous. But because they were disciples of the Gospel of peace, not the stern soldiers of an exclusive and peremptory law, the zealous work of vengeance was forbidden them. Surely, then, we are justified in saying that the imprecations in the Psalms, though springing from a righteous zeal for the glory of God, and not from any mere thirst of personal revenge, still are not such as a Christian can lawfully, in their natural sense, use now. They may have their lesson for us, nevertheless. They may show us what zeal for God is; how it consumes one who is truly filled by it. They may be a warning against laxity of belief, indifference, softness of spirit, even whilst we know that our zeal is to be a zeal of love, not of hate; our fervour, a fervour of devotion to God, rather than of opposition even to those whom we may count to be His enemies. The imprecations which may not pass over our lips, where one of our own enemies, or even one of God's enemies, is concerned, may still remind us that there is a holy jealousy of love, may rouse us to greater moral earnestness, may rebuke us, and put us to shame because we are neither cold nor hot. Such words of Scripture may be profitable for reproof, if they are not profitable for doctrine.*

Hope of a Future Life.

V. Before we quit the general subject of the Theology of the Psalms, one other topic requires a few words of notice. I have touched upon it frequently in the Notes, but an allusion to it here will not be out of place. What do we gather from the Psalms with respect to a future life? Does the hope of that life, and of the resurrection of the dead, occupy any prominent place among those motives by which the saint of God strives to sustain his faith amidst the wrong-doing which he sees in the world, the persecu-

* See Coleridge's *Confessions of an Enquiring Spirit*, Letter III.; and Dean Stanley's *Jewish Church*, Lect. XI. p. 249, &c. I have said more on the subject in my *Sermons*. Sermon V.

tions to which he is exposed, the sorrows and the sufferings which lay so heavily upon him? Very rarely indeed is this motive appealed to: still more rarely is it made a ground of consolation in the midst of suffering. Some half-dozen passages in the Psalms are all that can be pointed out, where the bright hope of everlasting life casts its light upon the present. In this, as in all things else, God's revelation was gradual. At no time could they who trusted in God and loved Him dream that their trust and love were only for this world. But in the life of Abraham, nothing is said of his hope after death. In the life of Moses it is the same. With David the hope begins to assert itself; it is not, indeed, clear; it speaks in no certain accents; but still it wears the aspect, and utters the voice, of a hope. It is a hope of that which *may* be, rather than of that which *shall* be: but yet, even in its weakness, it tramples upon the world, and time, and death. With Isaiah this hope becomes clearer. Ezekiel, in the parable of a national resurrection, draws his image from the resurrection of the dead. Daniel asserts it in language which cannot be mistaken. From this time onward it becomes an undoubted article of Jewish belief. They who deny it are counted for a sect, and our Lord confutes them with an unanswerable argument drawn from the books of Moses. Finally, by His Resurrection, life and immortality were brought to light; and from the days of the Apostles to the present hour, Jesus and the Resurrection have been the prominent subjects of all Christianity, and a future life the most consoling hope in all times of affliction, and in the presence of death. But it was otherwise with the fathers of the Jewish Church. God was teaching them the capital truth on which all other truth was to rest, that He, and nothing else, was their sufficient portion. "I am thy shield, and thy exceeding great reward," this was His great word to Abraham. It was by this that Abraham lived. All else was promise; this was present possession. The promised land he could never call his own; the promised seed was given to him only to be demanded back by Him who gave it. The whole discipline of Abraham's life had this purpose in it; to lead him to find in the everlasting God, his strength, his portion, his all. He was called "the friend of God;" and he who had God for his friend could need, could have, nothing more; for all was implied in this. On this fact Abraham's life was built; on this the lives of all his true children. The Jews were not merely designed to be witnesses to the world of the unity of God. They were this, no doubt; but they were far more. They were witnesses to a better truth,—that the Eternal God loves men, and calls them His children and His friends, and that men can be, and know themselves to be, His friends and His children. It is of this truth that the Psalms are full. They give proof in every verse of the reality of a communion and fellowship between the living God and His creatures. The poetry of the Hebrews, it has been well said, is a "poetry of friendship between God and man."* And it seems to have been designed that the truth of this Divine communion should occupy so commanding a position, that no other truth should be suffered, as it were, to come into competition with it.† This was to stand alone in its grandeur, because it is upon this that man's life must be built. We must rest upon the broad foundation of faith before we can have the hope which maketh not ashamed. If hope is the anchor within the veil, faith is the victory which overcometh the world. We cannot wonder, therefore, that so little, comparatively, is said of a future life in the Psalms. It was not yet time. God was training His children to lean only upon Him. When the fulness of the time was come, the veil was rent away, Paradise opened, and the Church militant made one with the Church triumphant.‡

---

* "Eine Freundschaftspoesie der Menschen mit Gott sollte sie seyn; eine Kindespoesie schwacher Menschen vom väterlichen höchsten Wesen, die sich an seinen Bund erinnern, auf sein gegebenes Wort beziehen, und ihr Herz durch Thaten Gottes stärken."—HERDER, *Sämmtl. Werke*, i. 213.

† See Dean Stanley's *Jewish Church*, Lect. VII. p. 154, and Mr. Isaac Taylor's admirable work, *The Spirit of the Hebrew Poetry*, where this abstinence from the theme of a future life is strikingly brought out.

‡ I have discussed this whole question more fully in my *Hulsean Lectures* on "Immortality," Lect. III.

Nature of differences between the Old Testament and the New.

I have thus endeavoured to trace some of those differences between the Old Testament and the New, which meet us in the Psalms; and which meet us peculiarly there, because there, more than anywhere else, we can see what the life of the saints, their true life, was towards God. Such an attempt must be made carefully, lest we either exaggerate differences on the one side, or fail to see them on the other. That there are differences, our Lord Himself has taught us. In His Sermon on the Mount, and in the discourse with His disciples before referred to, He has distinctly recognised them. It is for us to strive to see them in His light, not according to our own prepossessions. We read the Old Testament now with our Christian illumination; we read it, therefore, in a Christian sense; we cannot help doing so. But we should also remember, that that sense is not the sense which it once possessed; but one which has superseded, or softened, or transfigured the other. We must not attribute to them of old time a knowledge and an insight which they did not possess, even whilst we thankfully use their words as the best expression of our own Christian faith, and hope, and love.

Let me venture here to add a comparison by which I have sometimes endeavoured to illustrate to my own mind the difference between the Old Covenant and the New. They who belonged to the former were like men living in a valley, above whose heads hung heavy masses of vapour, hiding from them the mountain-peaks which rose near, and the light resting on their summits. Now and then, through a sudden rift in the vapour, there stole a ray of light, and lingered for a moment on some favoured spot in the valley beneath. Now and then some one dwelling in that favoured spot, and endowed with a keener sight than the rest, followed that ray of light, till his eye rested upon the mountain summit. It was but for a moment that he was permitted to see such things, yet it was long enough to make him rejoice in hope; long enough to make him a preacher to others of what he had himself been privileged to see. We, on the other hand, stand on the mountain-top on which the Sun has risen, on which the full light now shineth. The vapours which once hid the valley are rolled away. To us the whole landscape is disclosed. We see, therefore, not the mountain only, but the valley. We see it far more truly than those who dwelt in it, for we see, not a part only, but the whole. We see it, not by means of a partial illumination only, mist and light struggling and confused, but all unveiled in its cloudless splendour. We see both mountain and valley, radiant with a Divine glory, bright with the everlasting sunshine of God.*

* A further discussion of some of the topics treated of in this Chapter will be found in the Appendix to Vol. II. of this Edition.

CHAPTER 4

The Position, Names, Divisions, and Probable Origin and Formation of the Psalter

Place of the Psalter in the Bible.

I. *Place of the Psalms in the Bible.*—The Psalter is a part of the third great division of the Hebrew Bible, which is styled the K'thubhîm, or Hagiographa. In this division it has commonly occupied the first place, and hence we find the whole of the Old Testament summed up under the three names of the Law, the Prophets, and the Psalms.* This order, however, has not been uniformly followed. It is observed in the German MSS. and in most printed editions, where the several Books stand as follow: Psalms, Proverbs, Job, and then the Five Megilloth, as they are called, viz. the Song of Songs, Ruth, Lamentations, Ecclesiastes, Esther. But the Massoreth and the Spanish MSS. arrange differently: Chronicles, Psalms, Job, Proverbs, the Megilloth, Daniel, Ezra, Nehemiah; the intention being, no doubt, thus to bring the Books of Chronicles into immediate juxtaposition with the Books of Kings, but with the obvious disadvantage of separating Chronicles from Ezra and Nehemiah. According to the Talmud the order is: Ruth, Psalms, Job, Proverbs; the Book of Ruth being prefixed as a kind of Prologue to the Psalms, because David was descended from Ruth. But the natural order is that which places the Psalms first, as representing, in a considerable portion of it, the age of David; and then Proverbs and Job, as representing the age of Solomon.

Names of the Psalms.

II. *Names of the Psalms.*—The Psalms are called, in our Hebrew Bibles, by the general name of תְּהִלִּים (*T'hillim*), "Praises, Songs of Praise," or סֵפֶר תְּהִלִּים, "Book of

* Luke xxiv. 44.

Praises;" frequently written in a shorter form, תִּלִּים (or with the Aramaic termination תִּלִּין), or even still further abbreviated, by rejection of the final *Mem*, into תִּלִּי (*Tilli*).* It is remarkable, however, that only one single Psalm, the 145th, is styled a *T'hillah*, or "Song of Praise," in its Inscription; and as most of the Psalms are not, strictly speaking, hymns, but rather of an elegiac or didactic character, it has been thought surprising that they should be styled collectively "Songs of Praise." De Wette, indeed, objects to the title, as not representing sufficiently the general character of the Book; but a more suitable one could, perhaps, hardly be found; for thanksgiving is the very life of the Psalms, even of those in which there breathes most the language of complaint. "To the Glory of God" might stand as the Inscription of each. The narrative Psalms praise, whilst they record, His mighty deeds; the didactic Psalms declare His goodness as worthy of grateful acknowledgment; the Psalms of sorrow are turned into songs of joy, in the recollection or anticipation of His saving help. "The verb הִלֵּל,"† says Delitzsch, "includes both the *Magnificat* and the *De Profundis*."

Another name, given, however, not to the whole Psalter, but only to a portion of it, is תְּפִלּוֹת (*T'philloth*), "Prayers." At the end of the Seventy-second Psalm there is appended a notice, which is designed, as some have supposed, to apply to the Second Book, but which more probably applies to the whole collection ranging from Ps. i. to Ps. lxxii., "The *prayers* of David, the son of Jesse, are ended." Here, as in the former instance, the name is not borrowed from the Inscriptions of the Psalms, for only one in that collection, namely the Seventeenth, is expressly styled "a Prayer." In the later Books a few other Psalms are entitled "Prayers;" such are Psalms lxxxvi., xc., cii., cxlii.

---

* Hippolytus attempts to express the title in Greek letters: Ἑβραῖοι περιέγραψαν τὴν βίβλον Σέφρα Θελείμ, and Jerome in Latin (in the Preface to his translation *juxta Hebraicam Veritatem*): "Et titulus ipse Hebraicus SEPHAR THALLIM, quod interpretatur volumen hymnorum Apostolicæ auctoritati congruens non plures libros, sed unum volumen ostendit." In later Jewish writings, the feminine form תְּהִלּוֹת occurs.

† "To praise;" retained in the English, Hallelujah.

But here, again, the title, as a general title, is justified by the contents of most of the Psalms. Psalms, it is true, like the First, the Second, the Thirty-third, the Thirty-seventh, contain no address to God, and many others, which contain petitions and supplications, are not throughout in the form of prayers. And yet, if prayer be the eye of the heart turned towards God, then each Psalm is a prayer, just as Hannah's Song of Praise is styled a prayer. "And Hannah *prayed* and said," &c. Thus the very names of the Psalms, "Praises and Prayers," not only tell us what they are, but remind us, in the language of the Apostle, "in everything, by prayer and supplication, *with thanksgiving*, to make known our requests unto God."*

In the Septuagint, the whole collection is styled ψαλμοί (Psalms), songs sung to a musical accompaniment; and, elsewhere in Hellenistic Greek, sometimes ψαλτήριον, a word properly denoting, in the first instance, a stringed instrument (*psantêrin* in the Book of Daniel; English, *psaltery*), and then the song or songs sung thereto (English, *psalter*). In the N. T. the Psalter is called βίβλος ψαλμῶν, "the Book of Psalms" (Luke xx. 42, Acts i. 20). From the LXX. the name was adopted by the Vulgate, and so came into general use in the Christian Church.

Division of the Psalter into Books.

III. *Existing Division of the Psalms.*—The Psalms are divided in our Hebrew Bibles into five Books, the close of each of the first four being marked by a doxology: the 150th Psalm itself, perhaps, as Delitzsch suggests, occupying the place of a doxology at the end of the last. These Books are distributed as follow: Book I. contains Psalms i.—xli.; Book II. Psalms xlii.—lxxii.; Book III. Psalms lxxiii.—lxxxix.; Book IV. Psalms xc.—cvi.; Book V. Psalms cvii.—cl. Hilary (*Prol. in Librum Psalmorum*) mentions this division, and observes on the *fiat, fiat* (Amen, Amen),

* The Massoreth styles the Psalter, הלילא, *Hallêla*. In Syriac it is called *ketobo demazmûre;* in the Koran, *zabûr;* this last meaning in Arabic nothing more than "writing," or "scripture," though Delitzsch conjectures it may be a corruption of *mizmor*, whence, in Jewish oriental manuscripts, is formed a broken plural, *mezâmîr*. In the O. T. there occurs no plural of *mizmor*. In later Hebrew, both *mizmorim* and *mizmoroth* are occasionally employed as names of the Psalms.

with which the several Books conclude, but thinks himself bound by the authority of the Apostle (Acts i. 20), who speaks of *the Book* of Psalms, to reject this division. On the other hand, he considers it absurd to call them "the Psalms of David," because the names of so many other authors are given in the Inscriptions. Cassiodorus, in like manner, declares for one Book instead of five, but strangely assigns the existing fivefold arrangement to Jerome, who, in the Preface to his Psalter, expressly discards it. Augustine (on Ps. cl.) is of the same opinion, confessing that he can discern no reason for the division. Hippolytus, on the other hand, whose words are afterwards quoted by Epiphanius, styles the Psalter "a second Pentateuch." His words are: *Τοῦτό σε μὴ παρέλθοι, ὦ φιλόλογε, ὅτι καὶ τὸ ψαλτήριον εἰς πέντε διεῖλον βιβλία οἱ Ἑβραῖοι, ὥστε εἶναι καὶ αὐτὸ ἄλλον πεντάτευχον.* In accordance with this is the Midrash on Psalm i. 1: "Moses gave to the Israelites the Five Books of the Law, and corresponding to these (כנגדם) David gave them the Book of Psalms, which consists of Five Books." "This division," says Delitzsch, perhaps somewhat fancifully, "makes the Psalter the counterpart of the Law, which it also resembles in this, that as in the Law Jehovistic and Elohistic sections alternate, so here a group of Elohistic Psalms (xlii.—lxxxiv.) is inserted between two groups of Jehovistic Psalms (i.—xli; lxxxv.—cl.). The Psalter is also a Pentateuch, the echo of the Mosaic Pentateuch from the heart of Israel; it is the fivefold Book of the congregation to Jehovah, as the Law is the fivefold Book of Jehovah to the congregation."

The doxologies which stand at the end of Psalms xli., lxxii., and lxxxix., stand there appropriately, as marking the close of certain groups, or distinct collections of Psalms. But there seems no such natural appropriateness in the position of the fourth doxology. There is no reason, as Ewald has observed, why Psalm cvi. should be separated from Psalm cvii. It was placed here, therefore, by the last collector or editor of the Psalms, in order to make up the fivefold division. Three divisions already existed from an earlier date. The rest of the Psalms, from Psalm xc. to cl., gradually collected, most of them after the Exile, would have formed one long Fourth Book, out of proportion to the rest, but for this division, which, making two Books out of one, brought the whole into conformity with the arrangement of the Law. It is not improbable, indeed, that this division into Five Books was made after the model of the Pentateuch; but when, or by whom, it was made, it is now impossible to say. All that we know is, that the division is as old as the Book of Chronicles, and therefore as old as the time of Nehemiah; for in 1 Chron. xvi. 35, 36, there is a free citation of verses 47, 48, of the 106th Psalm, the latter of which forms the doxology with which the Fourth Book concludes. But this doxology, there is every reason to suppose, was added later than any of the others. The first three Books represent, in the main, three original collections, as we shall see; the First belonging to the early period, the Second and Third to what may be called the middle period of the Jewish monarchy.

Principles on which the formation of the Psalter rests.

IV. *The gradual formation of the Psalter.*—1. One of the first things which strikes us in an examination of the Inscriptions, is that for the most part groups of Psalms by the same author are brought together. This fact is an indication that originally a number of smaller collections must have existed independently, which were afterwards united in one. The First Book consists, with two or three exceptions, of Psalms of David; the Second, of a series of Psalms by the sons of Korah, and another series by David; the Third, of two minor collections, one supposed to be by Asaph, and the other by the sons of Korah. In the Fifth we have one group of "Pilgrim Songs," and another group of "Hallelujah Psalms," each of them manifestly, in the first instance, distinct hymn-books or liturgies.

2. Again, a new Book frequently begins with a new collection, and this is followed by a series of Psalms, intended to be a supplement to the preceding Book. So, for instance, Book II. was a Korahite selection, enlarged by the addition of a number of Psalms of David, which had escaped the notice of the compiler of the First Book.

3. The same Psalm occurs in different Books, with some

variation, such as would be due partly to accident in its transmission from mouth to mouth, partly to design where it had been adapted to new circumstances, and to express particular feelings. The fact, however, that certain Psalms (the 14th and 53rd, the latter part of the 40th and the 70th, the 57th, 60th, and 108th) are thus repeated in different Books, proves incontestably that these Books were originally separate collections.

Use of the Divine Names.

4. The distinct use of the Divine Names lends a characteristic feature to some of the Books. Thus, in the First Book, Jehovah occurs 272 times, and Elohim but 15. The next two Books are chiefly Elohistic, at least as far as Ps. lxxxiv. From Ps. lxxxv. to the end of the Psalter, the name Jehovah again becomes prevalent, and to such an extent, that in Books IV. and V. it occurs 339 times, and Elohim, of the true God, but once (cxliv. 9). It is owing to this peculiarity in the use of the Divine Names, as it would seem, that the Korahite Ps. lxxxiv. is subjoined to the Elohistic Psalms of Asaph, which immediately precede. Of David's 71 Psalms, 18 are Elohistic; of the Korahite, 2; of Asaph's, all. Add to these one of Solomon's, and 4 anonymous ones, and we have in all (reckoning Pss. xlii. xliii. as one) 44, in which the name Elohim predominates. They form the middle portion of the Psalter, and have preceding them 41, and following them 65, Jehovistic Psalms.*

---

* Delitzsch, *Ueber den Psalter*, II. 388.

No probable explanation of this phenomenon has yet been given. Ewald supposes that the collector of the Second Book purposely changed the name throughout all these Psalms from Jehovah to Elohim, influenced perhaps by the same sort of superstitious feeling which prevents the modern Jews from uttering the sacred Name Jehovah. But there is no foundation for such an hypothesis, nor is it consistent with the fact that the later Psalms have, by preference, the name Jehovah. The attempts of Hengstenberg and others, and recently of some English critics, to show that the two names are always used with reference to their distinct meaning—Jehovah as the covenant God of Israel, Elohim as God the creator and governor of the world—must be regarded as equally unsatisfactory. One fact entirely overthrows it, viz., that *the same Psalm* appears both in a Jehovistic and an Elohistic recension. Bishop Colenso's theory is the most extravagant of all. As, according to him, Samuel introduced the name Jehovah, so this name is first found in the later Psalms of David, and in those

Extent of the several collections.

Let us now examine the several Books more closely, and endeavour to ascertain how far the original collection extended. The First Book consists entirely of Psalms attributed to David, with the exception of four, which in the Hebrew text are without any name; the First, the Second, the Tenth, and the Thirty-third. But the first was regarded usually (see Introduction to the Psalm) as a general prologue to the Book, and according to an ancient arrangement, the Second Psalm was united with the First. In the version of the LXX., the Tenth Psalm forms one with the Ninth; and the Thirty-third, however wrongly, is called a Psalm of David. In later Books we find in the same way shorter collections of songs supposed to be David's, and these for the most part grouped together.

But did the original collection end here, or did it extend beyond the First Book? At first sight we might be disposed to think that it extended as far as Psalm lxxii., which closes with a notice implying that up to that point none but Psalms of David, or Psalms at least of his time, had been collected. This collection, too, it might be argued, was formed by Solomon, who concluded it with a Psalm either written by himself, or, as some have conjectured, composed by David originally, and reduced to its present form by Solomon. It is far from improbable, as I have pointed out in the Introduction to Psalm i., that that Psalm was written by Solomon, and by him prefixed to the first collected edition of his father's poetry.* We might

---

portions of the Pentateuch which are later than Samuel, the Elohistic Psalms being earlier than the Jehovistic sections of the Pentateuch. But all the facts are against such a theory. The Psalms of the First Book (which he scarcely notices) are, by the consent of all critics, the earliest in the collection, and these are Jehovistic. Many of David's *later* Psalms (as the 51st, the 60th, the 63rd, &c.) are Elohistic; many of his earlier, Jehovistic. Other Psalms of the age of Hezekiah (or at the earliest of Jehoshaphat), as xlvi.—xlviii., and Psalms confessedly of the period of the Exile, are Elohistic. How impossible, then, it is to contend that Elohim is a mark of antiquity in a Psalm, Jehovah of a more recent date. This has been well argued by Professor Harold Browne (now Bishop of Ely), in his Reply to Bishop Colenso. His criticisms, both on the Psalms and on the Pentateuch, are, I rejoice to find, on many important points, confirmatory of my own.

* I can now add a circumstance in favour of that hypothesis, for the notice of which I am indebted to my friend Mr. George Grove. He

thus suppose the royal editor to have published the book with a preface and a conclusion of his own. But the internal evidence of the Second Book overthrows this hypothesis. The First Book contains few Psalms that can be certainly assumed to be later than the time of David. The Second Book contains some unquestionably Davidic songs, and one of Asaph, which may possibly be the genuine work of Asaph the seer. But it contains also a series of Psalms ascribed to the Korahite singers, many of which, it is perfectly clear, could have been written by no contemporary of David. The 46th Psalm (perhaps the 47th) and the 48th are almost certainly as late as the time of Hezekiah, and are songs of triumph celebrating the defeat of Sennacherib. By some critics, indeed, they are placed in the reign of Jehoshaphat, but no commentator of repute has placed them earlier. The date of the 44th has been much questioned, but it may perhaps be Maccabean, as Calvin was disposed to think. It contains an assertion of national innocence strangely at variance with all that we know of the earlier history of Israel, and with the uniform language of the Prophets. The 65th, 66th, and 67th Psalms may be referred most probably to the times of the Assyrian invasion, the 71st to the time of Jeremiah, and indeed it may have been written by the Prophet himself; the 69th seems to have been as late even as the Exile.

First collection of Psalms.

The internal evidence, then, leads irresistibly to the conclusion, that the original collection was of smaller compass, and consisted, we may reasonably suppose, of those Poems mainly, if not exclusively, which are now classed in the

---

remarked to me that the writer of the First Psalm must, he thought, have been a dweller in Northern Palestine, or one familiar with its scenery. To such a person the image of the tree planted by the channels of waters, whose leaf does not wither, would be far more natural than to an inhabitant of the southern district, where the streams only run in winter, and are soon dried up. Now Solomon, we know, had his summer-palace of Lebanon, and must consequently have often passed through a country which would have suggested the image employed in the Psalm. Indeed, would not such a phenomenon be *more* striking to one who saw it occasionally, than to one who had it constantly before his eyes?

First Book. These, I incline to think, were first collected by Solomon, who would naturally provide for the preservation and transmission of his father's poetry, the more so as the musical services of the Temple were by his direction conducted with the utmost magnificence, though he himself apparently contributed little or nothing to the anthems and liturgies of that service. It is not, however, necessary therefore to assume that *all* the Psalms of the First Book were written by David or his contemporaries; for at a later period some might have been added to the collection as first made by Solomon.

Collection under Hezekiah.

The next collection was probably not completed till the time of Hezekiah. To "the men of Hezekiah" we owe the preservation of many proverbs of Solomon not included in the first collection of his Proverbs (xxv. 1). To them we may in like manner be indebted for the discovery and preservation of many of those Psalms attributed to David, which we find grouped together in the Second Book. The peculiarity of this Book is, that it consists first of a group of Psalms attributed to the sons of Korah, then of a single Psalm said to be by Asaph, then of another group mostly bearing the name of David. In the Third Book we meet with a similar phenomenon. Here we have but one Psalm, the Eighty-sixth, which is said to be a Psalm of David, and we have first a group of Psalms called Psalms of Asaph (lxxiii.—lxxxiii.), and then a group of Korahite Psalms, forming a supplement to those in the Second Book, precisely as David's Psalms in the Second Book form a supplement to those in the First.

Now we are told, in 2 Chron. xxix. 30, that Hezekiah, when he kept that great Passover which filled all Jerusalem with joy, and which seemed the beginning of a better and happier time, appointed the Levites "to praise Jehovah in the words of David and of Asaph the seer." Such a fact harmonises exactly with what we have seen as to the formation of the Second and Third Books of the Psalms. Psalms of David are contained in the one, Psalms of Asaph in the other. And what more likely than that the compiler (or compilers) of these two Books should have appended the remark at the end of lxxii. 20, in order to intimate that he knew of no more Psalms which could with any show of reason be assigned to David? The fact that we have but one Psalm going by his name in the Third Book, lends colour to the supposition that the person who compiled that Book wrote the words which now stand as the conclusion of Psalm lxxii.

Collection under Ezra and Nehemiah.

No further additions were made to the Psalter till the times of Ezra and Nehemiah, when it was enriched by a large number of songs written during and after the Exile. To this period are due, in the main, the Fourth and Fifth Books. With these later Psalms were incorporated, however, some gleanings from earlier times; some precious relics of the ancient Psalmody of Israel not hitherto classed in any collection, and possibly preserved some of them only by oral repetition from father to son. The Fourth Book opens with a Psalm said to be "a Prayer of Moses, the Man of God." Then follows a series without names, and in this Book two only, the 101st and 103rd, are said to be by David. In the Fifth Book we have fifteen more attributed to him, some obviously by mistake, others, as the 110th, beyond all doubt rightly so attributed. From all this we conclude, first, that the formation of the present Psalter was a gradual work; and next, that though several individual Psalms have been dislocated, so as to disturb the chronological order, another order having been substituted for that of sequence in time, yet that in the main, the oldest Psalms stand first; the latest, last. The most ancient songs, those of David and of David's time, are chiefly contained in Pss. i.—xli. In xlii.—lxxxix. mainly those of the middle period of Hebrew poetry. In xc.—cl. by far the majority are of a later date, composed during or after the Babylonish captivity.

But as in the Prophecies of Isaiah, Jeremiah, Ezekiel, so here the chronological order seems to be recognised, only to be crossed and broken by another. The groups, as a whole, are chronologically disposed, but not so the several Psalms. Here a different principle of arrangement has been observed, and one to a great extent of a merely external kind. Psalms are placed together, sometimes because the instruction conveyed in both is the same; sometimes because the same word or expression occurs in both: thus, for instance, Ps. li. (David's) follows Ps. l. (Asaph's), because both disparage the sacrifices of slain beasts, as compared with the personal sacrifice of a broken heart and an obedient will: again, Psalm xxxv. follows Psalm xxxiv., because in both mention is made of "the Angel of Jehovah." Psalms liv. and lv. are associated, because in ver. 4 of the one we have "O God, hear my prayer;" and in ver. 2 of the other, "Give ear, O God, to my prayer."*

This principle being once recognised, we may understand how it comes to pass that later Psalms may be found in the earlier Books, and earlier Psalms in the later. Psalms by the same author would, almost as a matter of course, be characterised by certain peculiarities of expression. Some proof of this will be given in the next chapter. Hence, many such Psalms, originally placed together, would be left as they were first placed, and others, again, would be inserted here and there, where some link of affinity suggested that a place might be found for them. Thus it was that the chronological order held its ground partially; and thus we can account for the exception to, and deviation from, that order. Beyond this, it would be folly to attempt to go. To give a reason for the place of each Psalm, is as impossible as to give a reason for the order of the different Suras in the Koran; though there, in like manner, we see a general principle adhered to, the larger Suras coming first, and the smaller afterwards, without any regard to chronological sequence. In the *Divan* of Armul Kais, the Poems are differently arranged in different MSS., without any apparent reason or plan being discernible. In the Vedas, on the other hand, it has been

* Delitzsch, both in his *Commentary* and in his *Symbolæ ad Psalmos illustrandos*, has endeavoured to show that the order of all the Psalms rests upon a principle of this kind. Qimkhi (on Ps. ii.) says: The reason why one Psalm follows another in a particular order is not known to us, only we know that they are not arranged chronologically.

noticed that there are the same external points of connection as in the Psalms. Invocations addressed to the same divinities (as in the Psalms the same Divine Name), hymns referring to the same circumstances, and prayers for similar occasions are usually classed together.*

Psalms differently numbered in the Hebrew and Septuagint.

V. *Numbering of the Psalms.*—Two other points require some notice: (1) the separation of the several Psalms from one another; and (2) the integrity of each in the form in which we have them in our existing collection.

(1) As regards the first, every Psalm which is provided with an Inscription, is by that very circumstance separated from the Psalm immediately preceding: but it is otherwise with those which have no Inscription. Here, in the MSS. of the original collection, there would be little to distinguish between the end of one Psalm and the beginning of the next; nothing more, perhaps, than a small space between the two; or, at the most, the beginning of the Psalm would be marked by the beginning of another line. Hence copyists might easily make mistakes, and we find that the LXX. (who are followed by the Vulgate) make, in four instances, a distribution different from that of the Hebrew text. They combine Pss. ix. and x., and also cxiv. and cxv. into a single Psalm. On the other hand, they divide cxvi. into two, ver. 1—9, 10—19; and in like manner cxlvii. into two, ver. 1—11, 12—20.

The following table will exhibit the respective arrangements of the two texts:—

HEBREW.	LXX. VULGATE.
Ps. i.—viii.	Ps. i.—viii.
ix., x.	ix.
xi.—cxiii.	x.—cxii.
cxiv., cxv.	cxiii.
cxvi.	cxiv.—cxv.
cxvii.—cxlvi.	cxvi.—cxlv.
cxlvii.	cxlvi., cxlvii.
cxlviii.—cl.	cxlviii.—cl.

In these cases, the division in the Hebrew text seems preferable to the other. There are several other instances

* Stähelin, *Einleitung*, pp. 382, 383.

in which, although the two texts harmonize, yet the existing division appears doubtful.

Thus, it is almost certain that Pss. xlii., xliii., were originally but one poem. Less probably the same may have been the case with cxiii., cxiv.; and cxvii. (which is only two verses) may have originally belonged to cxviii.

On the other hand, some Psalms which now appear as one have been formed, it has been conjectured, out of two. As, for instance, Ps. xix. ver. 1—6, and ver. 7—14; xxiv. ver. 1—6, and ver. 7—10; xxvii. ver. 1—6, and ver. 7—14; xxxii. ver. 1—7, and ver. 8—11.

But in most of these cases there is little reason for disturbing the existing arrangement.

Changes introduced into the Psalms in the course of time.

(2) Many of the Psalms have not come down to us in their original form. (*a*) Later additions, omissions, and other alterations have been purposely made, in order to adapt them to special occasions. (*b*) Owing to a long-continued and widely-spread oral transmission, various lesser changes in the text would of necessity take place. We have an instance of the variations which would thus arise in comparing the two versions of the Eighteenth Psalm, the version which is found in 2 Sam. xxii. being the more popular of the two. Other examples of deviation, partly accidental, partly due to design, may be found on comparing Ps. lxx. with the latter portion of Ps. xl., from which it was both detached and altered; and Ps. liii. with Ps. xiv. In the last instance the changes seem to have been made purposely to adapt the Psalm to a particular emergency.

We have a striking instance of addition to an ancient poem in Ps. li., of which the two last verses were obviously added at the time of the return from the Exile, the Psalm itself having been written by David, as the title correctly informs us.

Psalm cviii. is compounded of portions of two other Psalms, lvii. 8—12, and lx. 7—14. Similarly the Psalm given in 1 Chron. xvi. 8—36, is a composition from Pss. xcvi., cv., and cvi. 1, 47. It is possible, in like manner, that the two parts of Ps. xix. were borrowed from two originally distinct poems, and designedly placed together by some later hand. Design is manifestly shown in the juxtaposition of the two, the glory of God in nature, and the glory of God in His Law; and, at the same time, the style of the two portions is widely different.

It is plain, then, that these ancient Hebrew songs and hymns must have suffered a variety of changes in the course of time, similar to those which may be traced in the older religious poetry of the Christian Church, where this has been adapted by any means to the object of some later compiler. Thus hymns once intended for private use became adapted to public. Words and expressions applicable to the original circumstances of the writer, but not applicable to the new purpose to which the hymn was to be put, were omitted or altered. It is only in a critical age that any anxiety is manifested to ascertain the original form in which a poem appeared. The practical use of hymns in the Christian Church, and of the Psalms in the Jewish, far outweighed all considerations of a critical kind; or rather these last never occurred. Hence it has become a more difficult task than it otherwise would have been to ascertain the historical circumstances under which certain Psalms were written. Some traces we find leading us to one period of Jewish history; others which lead to another. Often there is a want of cohesion between the parts of a Psalm; often an abruptness of transition which we can hardly account for, except on the hypothesis that we no longer read the Psalm in its original form.

CHAPTER 5

The Inscriptions of the Psalms

THE Inscriptions of the Psalms are chiefly of three kinds.

I. Those which mark their musical or liturgical character.

II. Those which assign them to particular authors.

III. Those which designate the particular circumstances under which a Psalm was composed.

Any of these may occur separately, or be combined to form one Title.

I. We distinguish here between what may be called the liturgical and the musical notices.

Liturgical notices.

i. To the former belong such formulæ as the often repeated לַמְנַצֵּחַ (*lam'natsäach*), "For the Precentor," or leader of the Temple choir. E. V. "To the Chief Musician." It occurs fifty-five times in the Inscriptions. The word is derived from נצח, "to be strong;" in the Piel, "to have the mastery;" and is used in 2 Chron. ii. 17, in the general sense of "leader." It may mean, therefore, either the leader of the band, or of the singers; or, perhaps, rather (comp. Hab. iii. 19; Pss. iv., vi.) the person to whom the song was given in order that it might be set to music for the Temple service, and who superintended the practice of the Levitical choirs.* In three Psalms (xxxix.,

* Ewald, *Poet. B.* i. 171; Delitzsch, *Psalm.* ii. 391. Stähelin, *Einl.* 374. In this case the לְ may be used in a sense more nearly approaching its use when prefixed to the names of the authors of the Psalms. It may mean not "*for*" the Precentor, but "*of*" the Precentor, as signifying that the musical accompaniment of the Psalm came from him.

lxii., lxxvii.) the name of Jeduthun (or Ethan) is added, who we know was one of David's three famous choir-masters. It is worthy of remark that, except in the case of two Psalms (lxvi., lxvii.), which are anonymous, this title is only prefixed to Psalms of David, Asaph, or the Korahites.

לְלַמֵּד (*l'lammêd*), "For teaching," Ps. lx. This may perhaps intimate that the Psalm was intended to be taught publicly by the Levites to the people, but it may also mean that it was to be taught to the Levites themselves. Delitzsch connects it with 2 Sam. i. 18, where David gives his elegy to be sung when the children of Judah are taught the use of the bow, לְלַמֵּד ב׳ י׳ קָשֶׁת, or the song itself may have been entitled "the bow."

לְהַזְכִּיר (*l'hazkîr*), "To bring to remembrance," Ps. xxxviii. and lxx. (see note on the Title of the former). In 1 Chron. xvi. 4, it is joined with לְהוֹדוֹת וּלְהַלֵּל, "to give thanks and to praise," as a part of the special duties of the Levites who were set by David before the Ark, and there it would seem to mean "to call to memory," so as to praise and celebrate the goodness of Jehovah. Delitzsch (on Ps. xxxviii. 1) connects it with the אַזְכָּרָה (*azkarah*), or "offering of incense," at the time of offering which these Psalms were to be sung. Ewald, on the other hand, admitting that such may have been its use, interprets it "to use as incense," and supposes it to mean a prayer offered in the Temple, which ascends to heaven, and *reminds* God of men, Ps. cxli. 2, Rev. viii. 4.

לְתוֹדָה (*l'thodah*), "For thanksgiving," Ps. c., Delitzsch explains in like manner, as a direction that the Psalm should be sung when the thank-offering was offered: Ewald, that it should be sung as a thanksgiving.

ii. Notices of a musical kind. Such are, (*a*) the different names by which a Psalm is described. Musical notices.

שִׁיר (*shîr*), "A song," xlvi., the most general name, and מִזְמוֹר (*mizmôr*), "A Psalm," properly as sung with instrumental accompaniment, from זָמַר, which means both "to sing" and "to play."* These two are frequently united (שִׁיר מִזְמוֹר), xlviii., lxvi., lxxxiii., lxxxviii., cviii., and in the reverse order, מ׳ שׁ׳, xxx., lxvii., lxviii., lxxxvii., xcii.), which may perhaps be explained, as Stähelin suggests, by the fact that there were different editions of the same Poem; for in lxv., lxxv., lxxvi., the words are separated from one another by intervening words, which shows that they are not merely a compound expression, but represent the same Psalm in two different musical aspects.

מִכְתָּם (*michtam*), LXX. *στηλογραφία*, Ps. xvi. (see note [a] there) and lvi.—lx.; perhaps a "Golden Poem," or it may be connected with the Arabic كَتَمَ, "to hide," and so "a mystery," "a song of deep import."

מַשְׂכִּיל (*maskil*), LXX. *συνέσεως, εἰς σύνεσιν*, "A finely, skilfully constructed Ode," xxxii. (see note there), xlii., xlv., lii.—lv., lxviii., lxxiv., lxxviii., lxxxviii., lxxxix., cxlii. So I think Ewald has rightly explained the word, and some such meaning is rendered necessary by its use, not in the Inscription, but in the body of the Psalm, in xlvii. 7 [8], where as following זַמְּרוּ, it must mean either "in a skilful strain," or, "a skilfully constructed song."

שִׁגָּיוֹן (*shiggaion*), Ps. vii. (see note there), perhaps "An irregular or dithyrambic Ode," from שׁגה, "to wander." The LXX. render it by *ψαλμός*, the Arab. "a lament," the Syr. "a hymn." But all these renderings are doubtful, as in Hab. iii. we find עַל שִׁגְיֹנוֹת, "*Upon shigionoth,*" the preposition denoting, in the Inscriptions of the Psalms, either the instrument *upon* which, or the melody *after* which, the Psalm was to be sung. Ewald, however (*Poet. B.* i. 176), explains "After the manner of dithyrambs," or "To dithyrambic measures," and contends that עַל is used as in the phrases "Upon 'Alamoth," "Upon the Sheminith

* Ewald (*Poet B.* i. 24) has rightly explained the root-idea as expressing that which is *pure*, *clear*, *well-ordered.* Hence (1) in its lower sense (in the active form of the verb) it is "to purge," "to prune," *putare*, *amputare*, said of taking away the superfluous wood of a vine, or of "snuffing" a candle; (2) it means also *computare*, "to number," and so to "arrange" in proper rhythm, and with proper music to sing and play, as *numerus* = *ρυθμός, ἀριθμός.* It is used of a song as accompanied by any instruments, not merely stringed instruments, as is evident from the Aram. זְמָר, Dan. iii. 5, 6, which means *music* in general.

(octave)," to denote, not the melody to which the Psalm was to be sung, but a particular kind of music.

Four other names occurring in the Inscriptions are not properly of a musical character. These are :—

(1) תְּהִלָּה (*t'hillah*), "A praise," only found in Ps. cxlv., though properly applicable to a large number of the Psalms. All which were composed on any occasions of joy, triumph, thanksgiving, and designed for public worship, might fittingly be described as "praises" or "hymns." Other names.

(2) תְּפִלָּה (*t'phillah*), "A prayer," Ps. xvii., lxxxvi , xc., cii., cxlii. (See also Hab. iii.) A whole collection of David's songs are styled "the Prayers of David," lxxii. 20.

(3) שִׁיר יְדִידוֹת (*shîr y'dîdoth*), "Song of loves," Ps. xlv., a song, that is, the subject of which is love.

(4) שִׁיר הַמַּעֲלוֹת (*shîr hamma'aloth*), "Song of the ascents." LXX. ᾠδὴ τῶν ἀναβαθμῶν. Ital. and Vulg. *canticum graduum*. E.V. "Song of Degrees." Ps. cxx.—cxxxiv. This has been variously explained. *a*. Gesenius, who is followed by Delitzsch and others, supposes that by this title the peculiar rhythmical structure of these Psalms is denoted, according to which, a word or expression in one verse is taken up and repeated in the next, this being done in a sort of ascending scale or ladder, whence the name. But there are two objections to this view: first, that all the Psalms bearing this title have not this rhythmical structure; and next, that this structure is not peculiar to these Psalms. It is found also in Ps. xxix., in Is. xvii. 12, xxvi. 5, &c., and in the song of Deborah, Judg. v. *β*. Some of the later Jewish expositors suppose that these fifteen Psalms were sung upon the fifteen *steps* leading from the court of the men to the court of the women; but the Talmud (*Middoth*, ii. 5; *Succa*, 51 *b*) only compares the fifteen Psalms to the fifteen steps, and gives a different explanation of the title elsewhere (*Succa*, 53 *a*). *γ*. Others, again, explain "songs of the goings-up," *i.e.* from Babylon, songs sung by the exiles on their return, comp. Ezra vii. 9, where the return is spoken of as הַמַּעֲלָה מִבָּבֶל. "the going-up from Babylon." And there can be no doubt that Songs of Degrees.

the contents of most of these Psalms favour such an explanation. δ. But the plural הַמַּעֲלוֹת makes it more probable that the yearly "goings-up" to keep the great festivals at Jerusalem are meant. Hence the title "song of the goings-up"="a pilgrim song." That the caravans "went up" with singing, is evident from Is. xxx. 29. The allusions to the Exile are readily explained by the fact that these Psalms, or some of them, were composed for the pilgrimages to the Second Temple.

Instruments. (*b*) Particular instruments by which the Psalm was to be accompanied, when sung.

אֶל־הַנְּחִילוֹת, "To the flutes," or with flute accompaniment, or wind instruments, Psalm v., seems equivalent to אֶל־הֲלִילוֹת.

בִּנְגִינוֹת, "With stringed instruments," Ps. iv., vi., liv., lv., lxvii., lxxvi.; and עַל־נְגִינַת, "*Upon* a stringed instrument," lxi.

But Ewald objects to the first, that flutes were not used in the Temple-service. To this Delitzsch (on Ps. v.) replies, by referring to Is. xxx. 29, and compares 1 Sam. x. 5, 1 Kings i. 40, which would at least show that the flute (*châlîl*) was used in religious services, and flutes are mentioned in the Mishna and Gemara, *Erachin* 10 *a*, among the instruments of music used in the Second Temple.

To the interpretation of *'al n'gînath* Ewald also objects, because he says the preposition ought to be בְּ, not עַל, though, as he admits that the latter preposition is employed in xcii. 4, this objection is not fatal to the common view (*Poet. B.* i. 175.)

Measures. (*c*) A particular tone or measure to which the Psalm was to be adapted.

Two of these, עַל־עֲלָמוֹת, Ps. xlvi., "After the manner of maidens," and עַל־הַשְּׁמִינִית, Ps. vi., xii., "Upon the octave (below)," occur also in the historical books, 1 Chron. xv. 20, 21, and it has been conjectured that the former refers to the high voice of the women singers, the soprano,—the latter to the deep voice of the men, the bass, upon the lower octave. Ewald objects, in one place, that we have no evidence that the Hebrews were acquainted with the octave in music; in another, he observes that the prep. עַל cannot be here employed to denote different kinds of *melodies*, because these two, "Upon 'Alamoth" and "Upon the Sheminith," were to be united in the same solemn procession. It is equally plain that the two words do not mean instruments, because they are in each case associated with instruments; the first with the lute (*nabla*), the second with the harp (*kinnor*). But there is no reason why different voices, sopranos and basses, or tenors and basses, should not have sung together. He finds the first formula again probably at the conclusion of Ps. xlviii., where the present Massoretic reading is עַל־מוּת, and again in the Inscription of Ps. ix., where he supposes עַל־מוּת לַבֵּן to be a longer form of the same notice. He would read עֲלָמוּת, one word, as it is found in some MSS., and suggests that it is a noun formed after the analogy of יַלְדוּת, and that thus the inscription may mean "youthful vigour hath the son."

עַל־הַגִּתִּית, Ps. viii., "Upon the Gittith," or, as the form of the word seems to imply, "after the Gittite manner," or "manner of Gath," some particular measure or style of music which had been borrowed from the Philistines, and named after one of their chief cities, as among the Greeks there were Phrygian and Lydian measures, &c.

עַל־יְדוּתוּן, "Upon, *i.e.* after the manner of, Jeduthun," one of the famous singers of David, who was perhaps, as Ewald suggests, the inventor of this particular measure.

עַל־מַחֲלַת, Ps. liii., and joined with לְעַנּוֹת, lxxxviii., "To sing after the manner of Machalath," may possibly be an inscription of the same kind, though other interpretations of it have been given. See note [a] on Ps. liii.

(*d*) A particular melody after which the Psalm was to be sung. Popular airs already in vogue were adapted to the service of the Temple. Such is the case, Delitzsch observes, with a great deal of the old Church music; and the hymns of the Synagogue (the Pijut) are set to old popular tunes. Inscriptions of this kind are to be found in Ps. xxii. "After the song beginning, Hind of the dawn;" Ps. lvi.

Particular melodies.

"After the song, The silent dove in far-off lands," or perhaps "The dove of the distant terebinths." Similarly we find "Destroy not," Ps. lvii.—lix., lxxv., these being probably the first words of some well-known song; and "After lilies," xlv., lxix., "After lilies, the testimony," lxxx., or "After the lily of the testimony," lx.; though some would explain this of a lily-shaped instrument. Perhaps the Inscription of Ps. ix. admits of a like interpretation. The preposition עַל may there denote that the Psalm was to be sung to an air beginning with the words, "Death of the son," or, as Delitzsch would render, "Death makes wise." See above under (*c*).

The older interpreters regarded all these expressions as so many mottoes or devices, designed to convey, with enigmatical brevity, the purport and meaning of the Psalm. Thus, for instance, in Ps. xxii., "the hind" was emblematical of suffering; "the dawn," of deliverance. In lvi. "the silent dove" was innocence suffering in patience, and so on. Paulus Melissus, in his translation of the Psalter (1572), was the first who suggested what may now be called the generally received explanation; and J. H. Alsted, in his *Triumphus Bibliorum Sacrorum* (1625), anticipated and even surpassed, says Delitzsch, all modern investigations on this subject. That this class of notices is properly musical, is evident, from the fact that they only occur in those Psalms which have "For the Precentor (or Chief Musician)" in their Inscriptions. They are clearly therefore not intended, as Hengstenberg still takes them, to denote the subject of the Psalm.

Psalms not all intended for the Temple service.

Though the Psalms, as a whole, were collected for liturgical use, still it may be doubted whether they were all originally intended for the public worship of the Sanctuary. Psalms like the 3rd, the 4th, the 7th, seem, as Stähelin remarks, to have been composed with no such purpose. These and other Psalms, especially in the First Book, appear rather, like the Olney Hymns, to have been the outpouring of personal feeling, the utterance of the sorrows and joys of the heart in its communion with God, with a view to private edification, and the relief of feelings which it was almost impossible to restrain (see Ps. xxxix.).* Indeed, the Psalms of the First Three Books, Pss. i.—lxxxix., are in this respect different from the remaining Psalms, which are of a less personal and more general character. It may perhaps be owing to this circumstance, as Stähelin has suggested, that לַמְנַצֵּחַ, "For the Precentor," which occurs fifty-five times in all, in the Inscriptions, is found fifty-two times in the First Three Books. In the case of the latter Psalms, it was understood, as a matter of course, that they were designed for the Temple service; but in the case of the earlier Psalms, this direction, "For the Precentor," was prefixed with the very object of making them liturgical. The three Psalms, cix., cxxxix., cxl., where this direction appears in the later Books, are such as, by their contents, required to be thus clearly marked as intended for public worship. Whereas, on the other hand, Psalms like the 8th, the 29th, the 33d, in the First Book, did not require any such specification, because from their general character they might at once be assumed to be liturgical.

The Selah.

The same conclusion may be drawn from the occurrence of another musical sign, which, though not found in the Inscriptions of the Psalms, may be noticed here; namely, the Selah. In the Fifth Book this occurs but four times, and of this number three times in one Psalm, the 140th, perhaps because, like the words "For the Precentor," it stamped the Psalm with a liturgical character.

It is almost hopeless to attempt to give a satisfactory explanation of this word Selah. By the Targum, the Talmud, and Aquila, it has been rendered "eternity," because in Ps. lxi. 5, and lxxxix. 38, it seemed to stand parallel with עוֹלָם, "for ever;" by Ab. Ezra, "Amen;" by Gesenius, "Pause, stillness, rest:" he derives it from סלה, or סלא, which he doubtfully connects with שׁלה, but such an interchange is hardly defensible, and, moreover, the meaning thus obtained does not apply where the Selah stands in the

* Reuss appears to me to be entirely mistaken in regarding all, or nearly all, the Psalms as national, not individual, even when the expression of feeling is in the first person singular.

middle of a verse, or interrupts the sense, as in lv. 19 [20], lxvii. 7 [8], 33 [34], Hab. iii. 3, 9, or at the end of a Psalm, as in iii., ix., xxiv., where the "rest," *i.e.* the cessation of the music or singing, would be understood of itself, and would not need to be pointed out. Others, again, would connect it with סלל, and explain it in the sense of "elevation," "lifting up," whether of the voice or of the music. As, however, it is most frequently introduced at the end of a strophe, it would seem more probably to imply the intervention at the particular place of a musical symphony. Hence the LXX. render it *διάψαλμα*. And in the hopeless perplexity and darkness which beset the whole subject of Hebrew music this may be accepted as the least improbable interpretation. The word derived from the root "to lift up," was intended as a direction to the musicians to strike up in a louder strain. During the singing, the accompaniment would be soft and gently modulated. At particular parts the voices would cease, and then the louder instruments, such as the trumpets, &c., would be heard with full effect. So that, as Ewald says, the word would be equivalent to "Up! Aloud!" or in German, *die Musik laut!* This musical sign is clearly very ancient, inasmuch as it is found in all the old Versions, and inasmuch also as even then its meaning was matter of debate and uncertainty.

For a full discussion of this subject, I would refer to Mr. Wright's Article in Smith's *Dict. of the Bible*, where the various hypotheses are discussed. In this and in his other Articles on the Titles of the Psalms, he has exhausted the question, but not without admitting how little that is really satisfactory can be said.

Each of these various notices was intended, though we have now lost the key to them, to give to the Psalm to which it was prefixed, as has been said, its proper musical or liturgical designation, and, except the Selah, they are all found in the Titles of the Psalms.* Further, as regards

* The only possible exception to this rule is in Ps. xlviii., where a musical notice *may* have been placed at the end (see note there), as it is also in Hab. iii. 19.

the order of the notices themselves, the direction "For the Precentor" stands, as a rule, first, and then the particular instrument, or melody, to which the Psalm was to be sung. The exceptions to this are in xlvi., where the name of the author is inserted between the musical references, and lxxxviii., where the words "A song. A Psalm of the sons of Korah," precede them. It is possible that in these instances the title was not correctly copied.

Why it is that in the heading of one Psalm we have only "For the Precentor," why in another the particular instrument is added, and in a third the particular tone or melody to which it was to be sung, cannot now be explained. There seems to be no reason, in the nature of the case, for these variations. All we can infer from the existing irregularity is, that these variations must have been as old as some of the separate collections, and that it was with them as with our modern hymn-books, some of which have prefixed to each psalm or hymn the tune to which it is to be sung, while others are published without such direction.

Authors of the Psalms.

II. We have next to consider those Inscriptions which give us the name of the Author.

This is always prefixed with the preposition לְ, "belonging to." So a Psalm is said "to belong to" David, or Solomon, or Asaph, according as it was written by one or the other. Out of the Psalter we find the same usage in Is. xxxviii. 1, and Hab. iii. 1; and a similar one exists in Arabic. In some instances we have only the name, with the preposition prefixed: in others we have the fuller form of expression, שִׁיר ל׳, *song of* . . . , or, מִזְמוֹר ל׳, *Psalm of* . . . , or the rarer words denoting the particular kind of poem, such as שִׁגָּיוֹן, מִכְתָּם, מַשְׂכִּיל, &c., on the meaning of which see above, p. 86. In one or two instances we find what may be called an historical description of the Poem, joined with the name of the author, as is the case with some of the Pilgrim-Songs, and also with the title of Psalm xxx., "Song of the Dedication of the House."

1. *David.*—His name is prefixed to all the Psalms in the First Book, with the few exceptions already noticed; and

to most of the Psalms in the second half of the Second Book, li.—lxx., except lxvi. and lxvii. After this his name appears once in the Third Book, Ps. lxxxvi.; twice in the Fourth, ci. and ciii.; fifteen times in the Fifth, cviii., cix., cx., cxxii., cxxiv., cxxxi., cxxxiii., cxxxviii.—cxlv. In all, therefore, he is said to have written seventy-three Psalms. In two Psalms of the First Collection, the high title of "servant of Jehovah" is added to his name.

2. *David's Singers.*—These appear in the Second and Third Books, as already noticed.

(*a*) *The Sons of Korah.*—Eleven Psalms, xlii.—xlix. (xlii. and xliii. being reckoned as one), lxxxiv., lxxxv., lxxxvii., and lxxxviii. (according to the first of its two inscriptions), are ascribed to them. According to Num. xxvi. 58, 1 Chron. vi. 22, ix. 19, xii. 6, they were one of the oldest Levitical families, long before the time of David, and related to the still more ancient family of Kohath, the son of Levi. In the time of David, Heman the son of Joel, a member of this family, became famed for his skill in music and song; and hence, apparently, the Korahites obtained the name of "singers" (2 Chron. xx. 19). Hence it is that in the Inscription of Ps. lxxxviii. we have, first, the general title assigning it to "the sons of Korah," and then the special, assigning it to Heman.

(*b*) *Asaph.*—He is said to have written twelve Psalms, l., lxxiii.—lxxxiii. He is one of the three famous singers of David, and holds amongst them, indeed, the foremost place, 1 Chron. xvi. 5, and xv. 17—21. In later times, he alone ranks with David, Neh. xii. 46, 1 Chron. vi. 29—32. In the books of Ezra, Nehemiah, and Chronicles, the "sons of Asaph" are mentioned in the same way as the "sons of Korah" in the Inscriptions.

(*c*) *Ethan, the Ezrahite.*—He is named only as the author of one Psalm, the Eighty-ninth. He is the third of David's great singers. See the passages quoted above.

Of these three leading men we know but little more; the notices of them in the historical books are but scanty. It would seem, however, that whilst (according to 1 Chron. vi.) each of the three was descended from one of the three great Levitical houses of Kohath, Gershom, and Merari, yet a comparison of 1 Kings v. 11 [E. V. iv. 31], and Pss. lxxxviii., lxxxix., with 1 Chron. ii. 6, might rather lead us to conclude that Heman and Ethan were originally, like David, of the tribe of Judah, and only because of their high reputation and their great skill in music, which led them to establish and train Levitical choirs, were afterwards, by way of honour, enrolled in the tribe of Levi, as we find in the post-Exile Books.*

3. Besides these seventy-three Psalms of David, and twenty-four of his singers', we have, according to the Hebrew Inscriptions, two of Solomon's, lxxii. and cxxvii.

4. One Psalm, the Ninetieth, is attributed to Moses, "the man of God."

5. The LXX., in the title of Ps. cxxxvii., add to the name of David that of Jeremiah (τῷ Δαυὶδ Ἱερεμίου), and in the titles of cxxxviii., cxlvi.—cxlviii., give the names of Haggai and Zechariah, whereas the three last have no inscription in the Hebrew text. In lxxi. they add to the name of David, "Of the sons of Jonadab, and of those who were first led captive."

About a third, therefore, of the Psalms are anonymous.

Such Inscriptions, how far trustworthy.

The question here arises, how far are these Inscriptions trustworthy? That in some cases the authors themselves may have prefixed their names to their poems may be granted. It may have been so, perhaps, in such instances as Is. xxxviii. 9, Hab. iii. 1; yet it would be too much to infer, from these passages, that such was the custom of the Hebrew poets. There still remains the remarkable fact, not to be accounted for on that hypothesis, that so large a number of Psalms, especially of those in the Fourth and Fifth Books, are anonymous.† Why is this? Why is it that David's name, and those of his singers, figure so prominently, whereas scarcely another author is mentioned?

* Ewald, *Poet. Büch.* i. 212, 213.

† In particular, it is strange that none of the Psalms are, in the Hebrew, ascribed to any of the Prophets, though some of them, as Isaiah and Habakkuk, are conspicuous as religious poets. The LXX. do assign some of the later Psalms to Jeremiah, Ezekiel, Haggai, and Zechariah.

It has sometimes been argued that we have evidence of David's own custom in this respect, in the title of Ps. xviii., as confirmed by 2 Sam. xxii. 1; but in the title of Ps. xviii. David is styled "the servant of Jehovah," and judging by the analogy of such cases as Deut. xxxiv. 5, Josh. i. 1, xxiv. 9, Judg. ii. 8, it seems most likely that this title was not bestowed upon him till after his death, and consequently that the Inscription was not written by him. Nor is the question settled by an appeal to the practice of the Arabian poets.* For there seems every reason to doubt whether it was a custom with them to inscribe their poems with their names; otherwise there could not be so much uncertainty respecting the authorship of very much of their poetry.† The same uncertainty has been observed in the case of the hymns of the Vedas, and those in the Zendavesta.‡

When we come to examine the Psalms more closely, and to compare their contents with their reputed authorship, we find ourselves compelled very often to reject the latter. Not only is it very difficult to believe that the author of Pss. iii., iv. could have been the author of Pss. ix., x.; not only is it evident, as in the inscription of Ps. cxxvii., where a misunderstanding of the words "except Jehovah build the house," which were supposed to allude to the building of the Temple, led the Psalm to be ascribed to Solomon, that the Inscriptions must sometimes have been due to the guess of a later collector; but what is still more astonishing, some of the Inscriptions involve us in glaring anachronisms. Psalms lxxiv., lxxix. for instance, which describe the destruction of Jerusalem, and the burning of the Temple, are said to be Psalms of Asaph, the contemporary of David.

Attempts to defend the Inscriptions.

An attempt has sometimes been made, in order to maintain at all hazards the correctness of the Inscriptions, to explain such anomalies. Hengstenberg, for instance, and

* Keil in Hävernick's *Einleit.* p. 131.

† Stähelin, *Einleit.* p. 387.

‡ De Wette, *Comm. Einl.* p. 77. Rückert, *Hamasa*, i. pp. 23,29; see also p. 45, where a poem of the famous Muhelhil Ibn Nobata, is ascribed to an unknown author.

Keil, would give a different meaning to the preposition לְ, in cases like the last mentioned. According to these critics, it denotes here, not that these Psalms were written by Asaph, but only that they were written by the family of Asaph, his name being prefixed because of his celebrity as head of the Levitical choir. But as Stähelin observes, this is really to make "the sons of Asaph" guilty of a literary imposture, in prefixing the name of their ancestor to their own productions, in order to clothe them with a fictitious splendour. Besides, as we have in the corresponding form of Inscription "the sons of Korah," there seems no reason why we should not have had here, "the sons of Asaph." Such facts prove convincingly that *all* the Inscriptions are not trustworthy, and consequently that they must be tested by a careful examination of the style and contents of the Psalms to which they are severally prefixed. The question may, however, be asked, How came Psalms which are so manifestly not the work of Asaph, to be ascribed to him? Can we *account for* the Inscription in such instances? Perhaps we can.

These Psalms are stamped by several peculiarities, which have been partly pointed out by Delitzsch, and still more fully by Stähelin.

Peculiarities of Psalms attributed to Asaph.

(1) In these Psalms God is for the most part spoken of as JUDGE; as exercising that judgement for His own glory, both in Israel and among the nations of the world. See Psalms l., lxxv., lxxvi., lxxxii. Psalm lxxiii., though it does not expressly mention God as Judge, is an acknowledgement of His righteous judgement upon earth; the more impressive, because it is the result of many doubts and questionings. Similarly, Pss. lxxviii. and lxxxi. are in substance records of the Divine judgement in the history of Israel.

(2) I may add, God is described frequently in these Poems as the SHEPHERD, and Israel as the flock, lxxiv. 1, lxxvii. 20 [21], lxxviii. 52, 71, 72, lxxix. 13, lxxx. 1 [2]. The figure is employed elsewhere in the Psalms of the *people* of Israel, only in xxviii. 9, xcv. 7, c. 3.

(3) In the next place, we find in these Psalms God

Himself introduced as speaking, and that not merely in a brief and passing manner, as in other Psalms, but in a sustained and solemn discourse, continued through several verses: l., lxxv., lxxxi., lxxxii.

(4) In several of these Poems we find references to the giving of the Law on Sinai, to the march through the wilderness, and to other portions of the ancient history of Israel, such as do not occur at least in the Psalms of the first Two Books. Comp. l., lxxiv., lxxviii., lxxx., lxxxi., lxxxiii.

(5) In all these Psalms, both the Divine Names, Jehovah and Elohim, occur, and the former usually towards the end, where the language of the Psalm changes to supplication. See lxxiii. (where, however, 'Adonai Jehovah), lxxiv. 18, lxxvi. 11 [12], lxxx. 19 [20], lxxxi. 15 [16], lxxxiii. 16, 18 [17, 19]. Only l. has in the first verse Jehovah.

(6) Other Names of God which are frequent in these Psalms are 'El (אֵל), which, occurring in the whole Psalter sixty-four times, is found in the Psalms of Asaph alone sixteen times: and 'Elyōn (עֶלְיוֹן), "Most High," which occurs in these Poems eight times, and in the rest of the Psalter, in all, twenty-two times.

(7) Again, Jacob and Joseph are mentioned together as representatives of the whole nation, lxxvii. 15 [16], and Israel and Joseph, lxxx. 1 [2], lxxxi. 4, 5 [5, 6]; in the last two places Joseph stands in the parallelism, and therefore as synonymous with Israel.

(8) Other modes of expression there are, which, if not peculiar to these Psalms, occur in them most frequently, such as הוֹפִיעַ, *to shine forth*, l. 2, lxxx. 1 [2], only in xciv. 1, besides; זִיז שָׂדַי, *that which moveth in the field*, l. 11, and lxxx. 13 [14]; the peculiar form of the stat. constr. חַיְתוֹ, l. 10, lxxix. 2; the use of the verb נהג, to describe God's *leading* of His people, lxxx. 1 [2], lxxviii. (26) 52, elsewhere only xlviii. 14 [15], and the same thought lxxvii. 20 [21]; צֹאן מַרְעִית, lxxiv. 1, lxxix. 13; only twice besides in the Psalms; נָאָה, נָוֶה, *pasture*, lxxiv. 20, lxxix. 7, lxxxiii. 12 [13]. The verb רעה, *to feed a flock*, is also common in

these Psalms, see above (2). The verb שָׂרַף, *to burn*, which is found only three times in the Psalter, occurs in lxxiv. 8, lxxx. 16 [17]; שֵׁבֶט, in the sense of *tribe*, lxxiv. 2, lxxviii. 55, 68 (besides only in cv. 37, cxxii. 4). מַשּׁוּאוֹת, *destructions*, only lxxiii. 18, lxxiv. 3. מִקְדָּשׁ, *sanctuary*, lxxiii. 17, lxxiv. 7, lxxviii. 69, elsewhere only in lxviii. and xcviii.

There are, then, certain points of resemblance in all these Psalms sufficiently striking to have arrested the attention of transcribers, and to account for their having been ascribed to the same author. The selection, it is evident, must have rested on critical grounds—on the similarity of style, on the coincidence of the thoughts—and yet it is not a little remarkable that no attention seems to have been paid to the historical features of these Psalms. It is a manifest anachronism, as has been said, which would assign Psalms like the Seventy-fourth and Seventy-ninth, which speak of the destruction of the Sanctuary, to Asaph, the contemporary of David. Either the more ancient tradition ascribed some of these Psalms to Asaph, and the rest were conjecturally placed with them from their general resemblance to those which went by his name, or perhaps there may have been originally a small separate collection entitled "Psalms of Asaph," into which others, at a later period, may have crept. How easily this might have occurred we see from the whole history of hymnology. It has repeatedly happened that the hymns of one author have been ascribed to another, either from conjecture when the author was unknown, or from carelessness when his name might have been ascertained.

If we now turn to another principal group of Psalms inscribed with the name of their authors—those attributed to the sons of Korah—we shall again find them stamped by certain features of resemblance. This group consists of Psalms xlii.—xlix., lxxxiv., lxxxv., lxxxvii., lxxxviii.

Peculiarities of Psalms attributed to the Sons of Korah.

(1) As the Psalms of Asaph, for the most part, regard God as the JUDGE of the earth, so these Psalms delight to represent Him as KING Compare xliv. 4 [5], xlvii. 2 [3], 6, 7 [7, 8], lxxxiv. 3 [4], and even in xlv. 6 [7], the earthly

King is pourtrayed as the symbol and visible type of the heavenly, as may be seen by comparing xlv. 6 [7] with xlvii. 3 [4].

(2) These Psalms are decidedly Elohistic, though in five of them, viz. xlvi., xlvii., xlviii., lxxxiv., lxxxvii., the name Jehovah also occurs. In two of these Psalms, xlii. 2 [3], lxxxiv. 2 [3], God is called "the Living God" (אֵל חָי), and nowhere else in the Psalter. Another Name of God occurring several times in these Psalms, and but once beside in the Psalter (xxiv. 10), is "Jehovah of Hosts," xlvi. 7 [8], 11 [12], xlviii. 8 [9], lxxxiv. 1 [2], 3 [4], 12 [13], though we have in other Psalms "Adonai, Jehovah of Hosts," lxix. 6 [7]; "Jehovah Elohim (of) Hosts," lix. 5 [6], where see note, lxxx. 19 [20]; and "Jehovah God of Hosts."

(3) Jerusalem is represented as being ever under the watchful care and protection of God, xlvi., xlvii., xlviii., lxxxvii., and hence is called "the city of God," xlvi. 4 [5], xlviii. 8 [9], lxxxvii. 3; only once besides "the city of Jehovah," ci. 8.

(4) Other words and phrases characteristic of these Psalms link them with the Psalms of Asaph, where, however, they are of less frequent occurrence. Such are מַחֲשָׁךְ, lxxxviii. 6 [7], 18 [19], comp. lxxiv. 20 (besides only cxliii. 3); the plural of מִשְׁכָּן, "dwellings," or "tabernacles," xliii. 3, xlvi. 4 [5], xlix. 11 [12], lxxxiv. 1 [2], elsewhere only lxxviii. 28 (A Psalm of Asaph), and cxxxii. 5, 7. The noun פֶּלֶא, "wonder," occurs three times in the Psalms of Asaph, and twice in those of the sons of Korah; מִשְׁבָּרִים, "breakers," in xlii. 7 [8], lxxxviii. 7 [8], besides only in xciii. 4, and 2 Sam. xxii. 5. Psalms xlii. xliii., describe the same longing for the House of God, the same delight in visiting it, which are expressed in lxxxiv.

Two principal ideas stamp these Psalms: the one, the delight in the worship and service of Jehovah; the other, the thankful acknowledgement of God's protection vouchsafed to Jerusalem as the city of His choice.

Similarity between the two groups.

On the whole, there are many points of resemblance, not only between the Psalms belonging to each several group, but between the two groups themselves. Not so special and personal as most of those ascribed to David, and not so general as those of the later Books, inasmuch as they have some definite historical groundwork, they occupy a middle place between the two. The Korahite and Asaphite Psalms are, for the most part, national songs; either prayers for the nation in its distresses, or thanksgivings for deliverance vouchsafed: whilst the fact that so much is said in them of the Sanctuary, so much longing for its solemn services, so much joy and delight therein, lends no doubt confirmation to the hypothesis that they were written by members of Levitical families. All tends to show that some kind of criticism was exercised in the arrangement of these Poems. Possibly some tradition existed as to the style and manner of Korahite Psalms, for it is quite in accordance with the Oriental genius that a particular style of poetry should be perpetuated in the same family.

Historical notices in the Inscriptions.

III. The third class of notices is that which purports to give an account of the particular occasion for which a Psalm was composed. These seem, for the most part, nothing more than a kind of scholia, added by a later hand, though some of them may rest upon a genuine tradition.

The majority of them are questionable on the following grounds:—

Reasons for doubting them.

a. They occur only in the Psalms of David. But if David's singers copied his example so closely as Hengstenberg would persuade us, and David himself prefixed these notices to his own Psalms, how is it that we find none in the Psalms ascribed to Asaph, Heman, &c.? The fact that we find these notices in the Psalms of David exclusively is easily accounted for, because the history of David is so much better known than that of the other Psalmists; and hence it would be comparatively an easy thing to fit particular Psalms to particular occasions in his life.

b. Nearly all these notices refer to events which are recorded in the history more at length, and many of them are borrowed, almost word for word, from the historical books. The Inscription of Ps. xxxiv. is borrowed, but with some confusion, from 1 Sam. xxi. 14; that of Ps. lii. from 1 Sam. xxii. 9, &c.; that of Ps. liv. from 1 Sam. xxiii. 19; that of Ps. lvi. alludes to 1 Sam. xxi. 11—15 (but, as it deviates somewhat from the narrative there, may perhaps be taken from some independent and trustworthy source); that of Ps. lvii., which is obscure, possibly refers to 1 Sam. xxii, as also Ps. cxlii.

c. We can trace, in some instances, how the notice in the Inscription has been derived from words or allusions in the Psalm, even when it finds no support in the general tenour of the Psalm. Thus in Ps. xxxiv. the notice seems to have been derived from תִּתְהַלֵּל, ver. 3, and טַעֲמוּ, ver. 9, compared with 1 Sam. xxi. 14. The notice in Ps. lix., "when Saul sent, and they watched the house to put him to death," rests, apparently, on the allusions in ver. 6 [7], 10 [11], 14 [15].

d. The additions and deviations in the historical notices of the LXX. (comp. Pss. lxxi., xciii., xcvi., xcvii., cxliii., cxliv.) show how common it was for the collectors to adopt different traditions, or perhaps to follow mere conjecture.

e. The analogy of the Arabic Anthology of the Hamasa confirms the view above taken. The Inscriptions are not derived from the author, but, as Rückert in his translation has shown (Band i. 7, 13, &c.), are often merely guessed at from the contents, and that contrary to all probability.*

Some of these notices trustworthy.

Some of these historical notices, however, as I have said, are, beyond all reasonable doubt, ancient and trustworthy. Such are those chiefly in the First Book; as, for instance, those contained in the titles of Pss. iii., vii., and xviii., the last of which is further confirmed by its recurrence in that edition of the Psalm which is given in the history, 2 Sam. xxii. Much may also be said in favour of the notice in Ps. lx. This, though it alludes to the events mentioned in 2 Sam. viii. 13, 14 (comp. x. 16, and 1 Chron. xviii.), yet, as Ewald has observed, is clearly derived from other independent sources; the word הֵצָה is a rare and ancient word; and the Psalm itself, though in its present

* Stähelin, *Einleitung*, p. 398.

form apparently adapted to a later occasion, is, in part, as old as David, and therefore the Inscription may be as old as those of iii., vii., xviii.

The conclusion, then, at which we arrive here, is the same as in the case of the alleged authorship of certain Psalms. The Inscriptions cannot always be relied on. They are sometimes genuine, and really represent the most ancient tradition. At other times they are due to the caprice of later editors and collectors, the fruits of conjecture, or of dimmer and more uncertain traditions. In short, the Inscriptions of the Psalms are like the Subscriptions to the Epistles of the New Testament.* They are not of any necessary authority, and their value must be weighed and tested by the usual critical processes.

---

* Mr. Armfield, *Gradual Psalms,* chap. ii., finds fault with the comparison, because, as he says, "we have the very best evidence from without that they (the Subscriptions to the Epistles) are an interpolation," whereas we have no such evidence in the case of the Titles to the Psalms. He seems to have forgotten that our earliest MS. of the O. T. of which the date is certain is of the tenth century, whereas we have MSS. of the N. T. of the fourth, a century earlier than the date at which the Subscriptions were added. If the MSS. of the O. T. were of corresponding antiquity, we might in the same way be able to trace the addition of the Inscriptions. And this is rendered almost certain when we observe the variations of the LXX. and the Syriac, and when we further bear in mind that the *historical* Inscriptions are prefixed only to David's Psalms.

THE PSALMS

BOOK 1

Psalms 1—41

PSALM 1

THIS Psalm seems to have been placed first in the collection, because, from its general character and subject, it formed a suitable introduction to the rest. It treats of the blessedness of the righteous, and the misery of the wicked, topics which constantly recur in the Psalms, but it treats of them as if all experience pointed only in one direction. The moral problem which in other Psalms troubles the ancient poets of Israel, when they see the evil prospering and the good oppressed, has here no place. The poet rests calmly in the truth that it is well with the righteous. He is not vexed with those passionate questionings of heart which meet us in such Psalms as the 37th and 73d. Hence we may probably conclude that his lot was cast in happier and more peaceful times. The close of the Psalm, however, is, as Ewald remarks, truly prophetical, perpetually in force, and consequently descriptive of what is to be expected at all times in the course of the world's history.

In style the Psalm is simple and clear. In form it is little more than the expansion of a proverb.

The absence of any inscription, which is rare in the First Book, seems to indicate that this Psalm was from the first regarded in the light merely of an introduction (*προοίμιον βραχύ*, as Basil calls it), and perhaps as Ewald suggests, originally to some older and smaller collection. In some MSS. it is not numbered at all, being treated simply as a prologue or preface. This must have been a very early arrangement, as our present Second Psalm is quoted as the First (according to the best reading) in Acts xiii. 33, where the words, "Thou art my Son," &c., are cited as found *ἐν τῷ πρώτῳ ψαλμῷ*. In other MSS., again, the two Psalms appear as one. And accordingly, Albertus Magnus says, "Psalmus primus incipit a beatitudine, et terminatur in beatitudine," alluding to the "*Blessed* is the man," &c. i. 1, and "*Blessed* are all," &c. ii. 12. (So, too, the Jewish tradition, *Berachoth*, 9 *b*.) This last arrangement, however, is certainly wrong. There is no connexion of subject between the two Psalms, and in style and character they are totally unlike. They, may, however, be regarded as forming a double introduction to the Psalter, they embrace the two principal features of the ancient Revelation, they are the spiritual and poetical embodiment respectively of the Law and the Promise.

By some of the Fathers, and in some MSS. of the LXX., this Psalm has been ascribed to David, in accordance with the common practice of assigning to him all the Psalms which are not expressly said to have been written by other authors. But there is no historical or traditional basis for the statement, nor is it in itself probable. Perhaps the following considerations may help us to fix the date of the Psalm with some degree of probability. (1) It is earlier than the time of Jeremiah, for it is his habit to quote from, or allude to, earlier writers; and in xvii. 5—8, there is a manifest borrowing of the image employed in ver. 3 of this Psalm. (2) The word rendered "scorners," "mockers," ver. 1, occurs nowhere else in the whole Psalter, but is frequently applied in the earlier chapters of the Proverbs to those who set themselves to despise and scoff at religion. (See the definition of the word, Prov. xvi. 24.) This, and the sententious and somewhat proverbial form of the Psalm, might lead us even to ascribe it to Solomon himself. (3) The general doctrine of the poem, moreover, falls in with his reign, and with what may be gathered from the Proverbs as to the religious condition of the nation. It was a time when "wisdom uttered her voice," under the favour of power, and when the righteous were honoured; but it was also a time when, in the midst of abounding wealth and luxury, men disregarded the restraints of religion in their life (see chaps. i.—vii.), and even made an open scoff at its authority (i. 22). (4) The imagery of the Psalm is such as Solomon might naturally have employed. (See General Introduction, chap. iv. p. 76, note.) (5) If, as appears probable, Solomon made a collection of his father's poetry for the service of the Temple, he might have prefixed this Psalm by way of preface, and this circumstance would account for the absence of any inscription.

1 BLESSED is the man that hath not walked in the counsel
of the wicked,
Nor stood in the way of sinners,
Nor sat in the seat of the scorners;

1. BLESSED IS THE MAN, lit. "The blessedness (plur.) of the man,") cf. ii. 12, xli. 1 [2]). Not an exclamation, but the recognition of a fact. "The prophet seeing that such persons are few upon earth, breaks forth suddenly and says, *Blessed is the man.*"—*Luther.* The structure of the verse is very exact, the parallelism in each member

2 But in the Law of Jehovah is his delight,
And in His Law doth he meditate[a] day and night.

being carefully preserved; a kind of climax has also been noticed in the choice of expressions. Thus we have, first, three degrees of habit in the verbs "walked," "stood," "sat;" —next, three degrees of evil in the character: the "wicked," described as the passionate, or restless (cf. Is. lvii. 20, Job iii. 17); or perhaps, simply, as the unrighteous, the false; "the sinners," as the active, habitual doers of iniquity (from the Piel form of the verb, Gen. xiii. 13); "the scorners" (Prov. xxi. 24), who make an open scoff, and blaspheme: lastly, three degrees of openness in the evil doing, the "counsel" referring, apparently, to hidden designs (cf. Job xxi. 16, xxii. 18; Jer. vii. 24); "the way" to public life; "the seat" (so the LXX., as in 1 Sam. xx. 18, 25), or perhaps, "assembly") so the Syr., as cvii. 32, Jer. xv. 17), *consessus*, to a deliberate confederacy in wickedness. Calvin remarks: "Because it is difficult for us to separate ourselves altogether from the wicked with whom we are mixed up, the Prophet heaps up his words (*verborum congerie utitur*), in order to increase the force of his exhortation." And again, in the order both of the nouns and verbs, he sees a warning, "how men are wont to turn aside little by little from the right way." Similarly Grot.: "Tres hic gradus describuntur, male viventium, eorum qui incipiunt, eorum qui perstant, eorum qui plane jam in mala vita acquiescunt." Hupfeld, on the other hand, finds no climax in the three members of the verse, but regards them all as parallel and nearly equivalent expressions, merely poetic variations of the one thought, "Blessed is he who has no fellowship with the wicked in their doings," the parallelism being beautifully preserved by the use of three words to describe the wicked, three to describe their conduct, and three to denote intercourse and fellowship with them. So also Musculus gives the sense of the verse: "Beatum esse qui nec ullum, nec in ulla re, nec cum ullo reproborum hominum genere consortium habet."

2. In the former verse the righteous man is described negatively by that which he avoids, by that which he is not. Here his character is drawn on the positive side. And it is very remarkable that it should be summed up in the characteristic feature that he delights and meditates in the Law of Jehovah. This again seems to point to quiet and peaceable times, when a man lived "under his own vine and his own fig-tree, none making him afraid." The Law here meant is not so much Divine revelation generally (as in Is. i. 10, for instance) as the Law of Moses, the *Book* of the Law, as is plain from the manifest allusion to Josh. i. 8. (See also Deut. v. 31, xi. 18—20, xvii. 19; Ps. xl. 7, 8 [8, 9].)

HIS DELIGHT, the one word which describes the whole inner man, in striking contrast to the preceding amplification.

DOTH MEDITATE; a strict aorist, "is wont to meditate." The verb answers more nearly to the Latin *meditor* than any other word. Strictly, it means to utter any dull, confused sound: and hence it is employed of inward utterance, of the words a man speaks to himself; and also of giving open and loud expression to the thoughts. The emphasis laid on the Law is noticeable. "Repetitur denuo nomen legis ceu rei adeo caræ ac pretiosæ cujus vel solo nomine intime delectantur pii." — *Geier.* It is scarcely necessary to remark, that no merely outward observance of the Law is here meant. The man described is one who "keeps it with the whole heart," who "delights in it after the inner man." The Law here, moreover, is not to be taken in its most limited sense,

3 So is he like a tree planted by streams of water,
That bringeth forth its fruit in its season,
Whose leaf also doth not wither:
And all that he doeth he maketh to prosper.[b]

4 Not so are the wicked;
But (they are) like the chaff which the wind driveth away,
5 Therefore the wicked shall not stand in the judgement,
Nor sinners in the congregation of the righteous.

as apart from the promise which accompanied it. The very expressions, "his *delight*," and "meditates in it *day and night*," show clearly enough that the Law to such a man was more than a mere rule after which he was to frame his outward life, that it was the food and aliment of his spirit.

3. SO IS HE, or, "So shall he be." The pret. with the Vav either marks the consequence of his delight in the Law, or introduces a kind of apodosis to verse 1, an expansion of the "blessed" there; in which case we may simply render, "*he* shall be," &c.

The figure which follows possessed, for an Eastern mind, a vividness of which we can form but a faint conception. When all else was parched and sterile, the "brooks of water" and the "torrent-beds" had their bright strip of verdure (1 Kings xviii. 5). There the grass was freshest and greenest, and there the trees flourished most luxuriantly. (See the same figure used of outward prosperity, Job viii. 16, 17, Ezek. xix. 10, and also of the confidence and strength of the righteous, Ps. lii. 8 [10], xcii. 12 [13], Is. xliv. 4, Jer. xvii. 8, Ezek. xlvii. 12.)

STREAMS OF WATER, prop. "lesser streams or brooks," so called from their dividing themselves (*r.* פלג, *dividere*) into different branches, and not artificial canals divided and distributed by human labour. (LXX διέξοδους.) This is clear from other passages where the word, which is a poetical one, occurs (xlvi. 4 [5]; lxv. 9 [10], of the rain; Is. xxx. 25).

AND ALL, &c. A transition from the figure of the tree to the person who is compared to the tree. But apparently, the verbs are chosen so as to carry on the metaphor; for both of them would refer to the tree as well as to the man. See Critical Note.

4. NOT SO. A simple but emphatic contrast. The LXX., Vulg., and Syr. have repeated these words: "Not so are the wicked, not so." The wicked perish even more utterly than the dry and withered tree. They are as "the chaff." Again, far more striking as an Eastern image than among ourselves. In Is. xvii. 13, "chaff of the mountains;" because the threshing-floors were usually on high, exposed spots, where the wind would sweep over them the more freely. (See the same figure, Ps. xxxv. 5, Job xxi. 18, Is. xxix. 5, xli. 2; Hos. xiii. 3. Cf. Matt. iii. 12.)

5. THEREFORE, *i.e.* because they are in their very nature hollow, worthless, dry, bearing no fruit, &c.

IN THE JUDGEMENT. Primarily no doubt referring to the general course of God's righteous judgements, with an allusion to the forms of a human tribunal:—but reaching further to the final judgement. Chald.: "in the great day." Rashi and Qimchi, "in the day of judgement." The latter adds: "*i.e.* the day of death . . . for the righ-

6 For Jehovah knoweth the way of the righteous,
But the way of the wicked shall perish.

teous when they die shall have a resurrection, but the wicked shall have no resurrection, but their souls shall perish with their body in the day of their death."

CONGREGATION OF THE RIGHTEOUS, *i.e.* the true Israelites who are separated from the congregation of the evil-doers. (Cf. Ezek. xiii. 9.)

6. KNOWETH, *i.e.* regards with watchful care and love (xxxi. 7, cxliv. 3, Job xxiii. 10). The participle denotes that this is the *character* of Jehovah.

THE WAY, *i.e.* as in verse 1, "the life, the whole course of action."

SHALL PERISH, or, "perisheth," must perish from its very nature in the righteous judgement of God.

[a] יהגה. "The *imperfect*," says Hupfeld, "used to express the *present*, whereas in ver. 1 *perfects* are employed : for in Hebrew as in Arabic both tenses are used for the present ; not, however, quite arbitrarily, but with a nice distinction. Usually the *imperfect* is employed in general statements, in expressing what happens as a rule, without any definite mark of time, and when such statements include in a certain sense a promise in themselves [so that they have a future character as well as a present] ; *the perfect*, in definite assurances, in cases where a thing is supposed to have been in reality and for a long time existing, or when it stands in opposition to some consequence flowing therefrom ; a distinction partly, it is true, depending on the time and character of the utterance, and therefore one of which the limits are not to be strictly defined. In this place it is clear there must be some reason for change of tense. Evidently the *negative* side of the righteous man's character, his decided aversion from evil, is regarded as an already accomplished fact, and therefore put in the perfect ; the *positive* side, on the other hand, as that which is eternal (das ewige Moment), is put in the imperfect."

I would rather say, the perfect expresses the past resolve and conduct of which the effects still abide ; the imperfect or aorist, the character as it presents itself at any moment, irrespective of all question of time.

[b] עשה with פְּרִי, Jer. xvii. 8, and צלח, in like manner spoken of the growth of a tree (Ezek. xvii. 9, 10). It is uncertain whether the latter verb here is to be taken in its strict Hiph. signif., כֹּל being the obj. "all that he doeth he maketh to prosper" (as Gen. xxxix. 3) ; or whether the Hiph. should be taken in its neuter sense, "in whatsoever he doeth, he prospereth :" both constructions are equally admissible, and either is perhaps better than with the E. V. to make כֹּל the subject "whatsoever he doeth, shall prosper."

PSALM 2

THIS Psalm, like the last, is without any inscription, and it is probably owing to this circumstance that in a few MSS., four of Kennicott's and three of De Rossi's, the two Psalms are found written as one. But Qimchi observes, that in all correct MSS. a new Psalm begins here; but many of the Rabbis have said that the two Psalms are one, alleging that each division which was particularly dear to David, opens and closes with the same word, as in this instance with the word "Blessed," at the beginning of Ps. i. and at the end of Ps. ii. No two Psalms can possibly be more unlike in style and subject, and therefore it was not on any ground of internal connection that they were thus joined together. The First suggests, as we have seen, a time of profound peace. This rings with the tramp of gathering armies, and notes of lofty challenge addressed by the poet to the invaders of his country. It must have been written at a time when Jerusalem was threatened by a confederacy of hostile powers, and perhaps on the accession of a new monarch, the youth and inexperience of the king or the defenceless state of the kingdom having led them to anticipate an easy triumph.

It is plain, from the language which the poet puts into their mouth —"Let us break their bonds asunder," &c.—that the allies were vassal or tributary monarchs, who, having been subdued in former wars, or having in some other way tendered their allegiance, had seized this opportunity to assert their independence. We may suppose the song to have been written when the news of their approach reached Jerusalem. The poet encourages his countrymen by reminding them of the covenant made with David's house, and predicts for their enemies a disastrous overthrow. Their enterprise is in its very nature "a vain thing." It cannot but come to nought, because the king whom they would dethrone is the son and vicegerent of Jehovah Himself. The poet therefore counsels the rebels to return to their allegiance before it be too late.

It is quite impossible now to say what the event was which occasioned this poem. The older interpreters (especially the Jewish) referred it to David, and the attacks made upon him by the Philistines (2 Sam. v.). So Qimchi, who, however, strangely explains the "bonds" and "cords," not of the power which had hitherto held the insurgents in subjection, but of the confederation of the different tribes which had united to support David on his accession. Others, again (Ewald, Bleek), suppose Solomon to be the king spoken of.

But we hear of no gathering of hostile nations during any part of Solomon's reign, and the words of the poet are too large to apply to the weak attempt of the Philistines on David's accession. It would be better to connect the Psalm with the events mentioned in 2 Sam. x. There we find a confederacy of Syrians, Ammonites, and others, who had formerly been subdued (2 Sam. vii. 3, 12), and who were now making a last effort for their independence. Just about this time too (chap. vii. 14), the promise was given to which allusion seems to be made in ver. 7 of the Psalm.

Others (as Delitzsch) have found the groundwork of the poem in events connected with the earlier part of the reign of Ahaz. That monarch was threatened by the combined forces of Rezin and Pekah; and behind these, in the distant background, but visible to the eye of the Prophet, was the huge power of Assyria, which was destined to work such fearful ravages in Judæa. It was moreover at this crisis that Isaiah was sent to Ahaz with that very remarkable promise of deliverance which is recorded in the seventh chapter of his Book. In its general character, indeed, there is a considerable affinity between this Psalm and that part of the prophecy of Isaiah which speaks of Immanuel and Assyria. There, in like manner, the powers of the world are seen gathered against the house of David : and there a like challenge is given,—"Associate yourselves and be broken in pieces; gird yourselves and be broken in pieces; for God is with us." The objection to this view is, that Rezin and Pekah were not vassals, and did not *rebel.*

But though the poem was occasioned by some national event, we must not confine its application to that event, nor need we even suppose that the singer himself did not feel that his words went beyond their first occasion. He begins to speak of an earthly king, and his wars with the nations of the earth; but his words are too great to have all their meaning exhausted in David, or Solomon, or Ahaz, or any Jewish monarch. Or ever he is aware, the local and the temporal are swallowed up in the universal and the eternal. The king who sits on David's throne has become glorified and transfigured in the light of the Promise. The picture is half ideal, half actual. It concerns itself with the present, but with that only so far as it is typical of greater things to come. The true King, who to the Prophet's mind is to fulfil all his largest hopes, has taken the place of the visible and earthly king. The nations are not merely those who are now mustering for the battle, but whatsoever opposeth and exalteth itself against Jehovah and His Anointed.

Hence this Psalm is of the nature of a prophecy, and still waits for its final accomplishment. The first Christians saw a fulfilment of it in the banding together of Herod and Pontius Pilate against Jesus (Acts iv. 25—27). But this was not a literal one. Pontius Pilate was not a king: nor was it the heathen nations (גוים), but the Jews, who were the chief enemies of Christ when He appeared on earth. "*Ye*," says St. Peter, addressing the Jews, "have with wicked hands slain the Lord of Glory." Only, therefore, in a partial sense, rather perhaps in the way of application than anything else, did the words of this Psalm correspond to that event. But it may be said to have an ever-repeated fulfilment in the history of the Church, which is a history of God's kingdom upon earth, a kingdom which in all ages has the powers of the world arrayed against it, and in all ages with the same disastrous result to those who have risen "against the Lord, and against His Anointed." And so it shall be to the end, when, perhaps, that hostility will be manifested in some yet deadlier form, only to be overthrown for ever, that the kingdoms of this world may become the kingdom of our Lord and His Christ.

That the Messianic interpretation of this Psalm was the earliest, is admitted by the Jews themselves. Qimchi says, "Some interpret this Psalm of Gog and Magog, and 'the Anointed' is King Messiah, and so our Rabbis of blessed memory have expounded it; and the Psalm so expounded is clear; but it is more natural to suppose that David spake it concerning himself, as we have interpreted." R. Sol. Isaki (Rashi) makes the same statement as to the ancient interpretation, but with remarkable candour adds: "In order, however, to keep to the literal sense, and that we may be able to answer the heretics (*i.e.* Christians), it is better to explain it of David himself with reference to what is said 2 Sam. v. 17."

See Pococke, *Porta Mosis*, p. 306, &c.; and the remarkable passage from the Midrash Tillim, quoted by Raymundus Martinus, *Pug. Fid.*, Pars. III. Dist. i. cap. viii. § 14., p. 527, ed. Carpzov.

In form, the Psalm is dramatic, the action being carried on by different speakers, who successively take their parts. It consists of four strophes:—

I. The singer sees with astonishment the nations gathering together, and their Princes conspiring to cast off the yoke of Jehovah and His Anointed. Ver. 1—3.

II. Jehovah, sitting throned in heaven, mocks their designs, and confounds them with His word. Ver. 4—6.

III. The anointed king announces the Divine decree by which he rules, which assures him of victory in the struggle, and of boundless dominion. Ver. 7—9.

IV. The poet, in consequence of what he has seen, counsels the rebellious monarchs to submit themselves to the sway of their lawful sovereign. Ver. 10—12.

1 WHY have nations raged,
And (why do) peoples meditate a vain thing?
2 Kings of the earth set themselves,
And princes have taken counsel together
Against Jehovah and against His Anointed :—
3 " Let us break their bonds asunder,
And cast away their cords from us."

1. WHY—a question at once of wonder and horror. Looking with amazement on the gathering stir and tumult of the rebellion, nations in the full tide of insurrection, kings and princes placing themselves at the head of it, the loyal heart breaks forth with the question, Why this attempt to throw off the yoke of the true king? It is not a tyrant against whom they are leagued. It is Jehovah Himself who is assailed in the person of the king whom He has set on the throne. Such an enterprise cannot but fail. In its very nature it is "a vain thing." In this word, says Luther, is comprised the argument of nearly the whole Psalm. How can they succeed who set themselves against Jehovah and against His Christ? The abrupt question is in the true spirit of lyric poetry. So Horace, gazing with horror on the spectacle of civil strife, breaks forth : "Quo-quo scelesti ruitis? aut cur dexteris, Aptantur enses conditi?"

Why HAVE (pret.) they RAGED, or "gathered tumultuously" (Aq. ἐθορυβήθησαν, LXX. ἐφρύαξαν, cf. Acts iv. 25), i.e. *What is the reason* of their attempt? and why do they imagine (pres.), *i.e.* what is the design, the object they have before them? So Delitzsch explains (and I think rightly) the difference of tense in the two clauses.

A VAIN THING, lit. "vanity." The verb "meditate" is the same as in i. 2, where see note.

2. SET THEMSELVES—of assuming deliberately a hostile attitude, as of Goliath, 1 Sam. xvii. 16; of the angel who meets Balaam, Num. xxii. 22. This verb is in the *present;* for the singer sees, as it were, their hostile array before his eyes. The next is again in the *past*, "they *have* banded themselves," the conspiracy and confederacy having preceded the mustering of their hosts to the battle.

After the double parallelism with which the Psalm opens, there comes the single line which, in its majestic simplicity, at once reveals the design, and the hopelessness of the design, "Against Jehovah and against His Anointed."

Luther bids us observe how consolatory this truth is to the militant Church. For the rage of our enemies is not aimed at us, but at the Lord and His Christ. They can only reach us through him. "Sed ideo quoque sic ordinat verba ut pro nostra consolatione et exhortatione discamus, nunquam nos pati injuriam, quin prior et magis offendatur Deus quam nos, et tantam esse super nos Dei Patris curam, ut ante sentiat, indigniusque ferat nostram injuriam quam nos ipsi," &c.

3. But the singer not only sees the gathering host; he hears their menace of rebellion : "Let us burst their bonds asunder" (*i.e.* those of Jehovah and His Christ), &c. The metaphor is borrowed from restive animals which break the cords, and

4 He that is throned in the Heavens laughs :
The Lord hath them in derision.
5 Then He speaketh unto them in His wrath,
And in His sore displeasure terrifieth them :
6 —" But I have set[a] My King
On Zion, My holy mountain."

throw off the yoke. Cf. Is. x. 27, lviii. 6. The phrase occurs again, cvii. 14, and often in Jeremiah. "Legem Christi," says Luther, "quæ libertatis et suavitatis est, vincula et jugum appellant, servitutem et difficultatem arbitrati, rursus suam legem quæ vera est servitus et infirmitas libertatem et facilitatem esse credunt."

4—6. And now from all this wild tempest of confusion upon earth, from the trampling of gathering armies, and the pride of kingly captains, and their words of haughty menace, the poet turns his eye to heaven. There, on His everlasting throne, sits the Almighty King, in whose sight all nations and kings are but as a drop of the bucket. Luther, in his characteristic way, seizing on the eternal truth of the words, reminds us that " What is here written touching Christ, is an example for all Christians. For any man who sincerely desires to be a Christian, especially if, moreover, he be a teacher of the word, will have his Herods and Pilates, his princes, kings, nations, and people raging against him, meditating a vain thing, setting themselves up, and gathering together. And if men do not so trouble him, devils will, and finally his own conscience, at any rate when he comes to die. Then will he find it needful to remember this and such-like consolation, 'He that dwelleth in the heavens,' &c., and in this hope to stand firm, and on no account to give way."

HE THAT IS THRONED, &c. I have omitted in this edition the passage from the Mechilta, because it applies these words, not to the Messiah, but to the boasting of Pharaoh against the children of Israel. It will be found discussed with other Messianic passages in the Appendix to Vol. II. of this edition.

There is something very awful in the representation here given of God. First, as if in calm contempt, "He laughs ;" then there is the bitter derision which, in its effects, brings their counsels to nought, and baffles their purposes, " He mocks them :" lastly, with the thunder of His word He discomfits them. THEN, at last ; that is, after long patience, in the moment of their godless security, when their end seems almost gained.

5. The change in the rhythm of the original is worthy of notice ; it becomes full and sonorous, "donnerartig" as Delitzsch calls it, rolling like the thunder, and is rendered the more effective by its contrast with the quiet manner of ver. 4.

6. As the first strophe closed with the words of the rebels, so this with the words of Jehovah.

And in the words BUT I, we have the central truth of the Psalm. The "but" is to be explained as referring to an unexpressed "ye may plot," or some thought of the kind, in the mind of the speaker. It is God's own answer to them that oppose Him. I (the pronoun is emphatic in the Heb.), the King of heaven and earth, have set my own King, my Son and my vicegerent, on the throne. (Cf. 1 Sam. xvi. 1.)

ON ZION, not the place where the King was anointed, for that would hold neither of type (whether David or Solomon) nor of antitype : but as the seat of dominion, the centre from which His law goes forth, &c. Cf. cx. 2 ; and

7 I will tell[b] of the decree:
Jehovah said unto me: "Thou art my Son,
This day have I begotten thee:[c]
8 Ask of Me, and I will make the nations thine inheritance,
And the uttermost parts of the earth thy possession.
9 Thou shalt break them with a rod of iron;
Like a potter's vessel shalt thou dash them in pieces."

10 Now therefore, O ye kings, be wise!
Receive instruction, ye judges of the earth!

in the fact that His throne is on "the holy mountain," there is a kind of anticipative hint of the great truth which is first distinctly taught in the 110th Psalm, that the Anointed King should also be the Anointed Priest.

7. A sudden change of speakers takes place. The Son, the Anointed King, appears, and proclaims the Father's counsel concerning Him. He has received of Jehovah a decree—the new law of His kingdom. He reigns not by the will of man, but by the grace of God; not by right only as the Son of Jehovah, but by covenant and promise likewise. (See the stress laid on this Divine calling as fulfilled in Christ in Heb. v. 5.) This is true of the type in a primary sense, 2 Sam. vii. 14, "I will be his father, and he shall be my son" (with which compare Ps. lxxxix. 26 [27], "He shall call me, Thou art my Father," &c.). But the emphatic, "this day have I begotten thee," is true in its highest sense only of Him whom the Father sanctified, and sent into the world. (Compare the argument in Heb. i. 5.)

The expression, "I this day have begotten thee," can only mean, This day have I declared and manifested thee to be my Son, by investing thee with thy kingly dignity, and placing thee on thy throne. St. Paul teaches us to see the *fulfilment* of these words in Christ's resurrection from the dead. It was by *that* that He was declared to be (marked out as, in a distinct and peculiar sense, ὁρισθέντος) the Son of God. (Rom. i. 4; cf. Acts xiii. 33.) The day of Christ's coronation was the day of His resurrection. From henceforth He sits at the right hand of the Father, waiting till His enemies be made His footstool.

8. ASK OF ME. A poetical figure, by which is represented God's willingness to give to His Anointed the kingdoms of the world. The Father's love will withhold nothing from the Son. The iron sceptre is not only the symbol of an older and sterner dispensation. The Saviour is also the Judge. Even at His first coming it was said of Him, "whose fan is in His hand," &c., and He Himself, declared, "for judgement am I come into this world." And in the Apocalypse He appears as the King who makes war, and who should rule all nations with a rod of iron, chap. xix. 15 and xii. 5, and especially chap. ii. 27, where He gives a share in this His power and prerogative to all His true and faithful soldiers.

10—12. Finally, the poet, who has heard the words of Jehovah, and the words of His Anointed, seeks by wise counsel to dissuade the rebels from their mad enterprise.

10. NOW THEREFORE, or, "and now," drawing a conclusion from what precedes (Prov. v. 7, Is. xxviii. 22; cf. καὶ νῦν, 1 John ii. 28).

JUDGES OF THE EARTH, as in ver. 2, "kings of the earth," who

11 Serve Jehovah with fear,
And exult[d] with trembling !
12 Kiss the Son[e] lest He be angry
And ye perish in (your) way ;
For soon[f] is His wrath kindled :
Blessed are all they that find refuge in Him !

had placed themselves at the head of the insurrection.

LEARN WISDOM . . . . RECEIVE INSTRUCTION. Submit yourselves ; not only in a political sense, but also in a religious sense, become His true worshipers. In the Jewish mind the two ideas would never be dissociated.

12. KISS THE SON, *i.e.* Do homage to him : see 1 Sam. x. 1 ; cf. 1 Kings xix. 18, Hos. xiii. 2, Job xxxi. 27. LEST HE BE ANGRY. Who? not necessarily the Son. The subject of the verb may be Jehovah. Do homage to the Son or "proffer pure homage" (see more in critical note), lest He (*i.e.* Jehovah) be angry. And so afterwards, "Blessed are all they that find refuge in Him," *i.e.* in Jehovah. Still, there can be no objection to taking "the Son" as the subject.

It should be observed that two of the names given by the Jews themselves to the Hope of Israel were taken from this Psalm (and Dan. ix. 25), the Messiah, ver. 2, and the Son of God, ver. 7. Nathanael says to Jesus, σὺ εἶ ὁ υἱὸς τοῦ Θεοῦ, John i. 49, and both names are joined together by the High Priest, Matt. xxvi. 63, εἰ σὺ εἶ ὁ Χριστὸς ὁ υἱὸς τοῦ Θεοῦ. In like manner the name ὁ υἱὸς τοῦ ἀνθρώπου is taken from Ps. viii. 4, and Dan. vii. 13.

[a] נָסַכְתִּי, Ges. (*Thes.*) and Ew. (*in loc.*) render, "I have anointed," and this rendering is apparently supported both by the מָשִׁיחַ going before, and also by the derivative נָסִיךְ, "a prince." But the verb nowhere else occurs in this sense ; it means "to pour out," and then "to pour metals in a state of fusion into a mould :" hence it passes over into the meaning of *setting fast*, *establishing*, &c. So the Niph. Prov. viii. 23, and hence נָסִיךְ means not "one anointed," but "one appointed" to his office.

[b] אֲסַפְּרָה. The optat. form, "Let me tell," or "I would fain tell." For the construction with אֶל, see lxix. 27, similarly with אָמַר, Gen. xx. 2, Jer. xxvii. 19. חֹק in like manner without the art. Is. xxiv. 5. In the T. B. Succah., fol. 52*a*, the words are explained, "I will tell it for a decree, *i.e.* that it may be a statute, that the Messiah, the true Son of David, will certainly come." Qimchi : "These are the words of David, who says, 'I will make this announcement a statute and a law to myself ;' and what is the announcement ?—that the Lord said unto me, Thou art my Son, &c."

The LXX. and the Vulg. join this clause with the preceding verse (where they have the passive verb) by rendering 'אם as if it were a participle ; the LXX. and Jerome also repeat "Jehovah," making it first the genitive after חֹק and then the nom. to the following verb "said." Thus ver. 6 is the words of the king, ἐγὼ δὲ κατεστάθην βασιλεὺς ὑπ' αὐτοῦ . . . διαγγέλων τὸ πρόσταγμα κυρίου.

[c] יְלִדְתִּיךָ (instead of יְלַדְתִּיךָ). According to Gesen. from a form יָלֶד, as שְׁאֶלְתִּיו, 1 Sam. i. 20, from שָׁאֵל. (Gram. § 44, 2 Rem. 2.) But Hupf., who says truly that there is no trace of such a form in Hebrew, thinks that ĭ instead of ă is to be explained by the throwing forward of the tone, and compares the Hiph. הֲמִתִּיהוּ, where the tone is thrown forward, with הֵמַתָּ, where the ă remains, because the place of the tone is not altered.

[d] גִּילוּ, generally rendered "fear" or "tremble," because of the following בִּרְעָדָה, as if connected with גור, יגר, with the former of which, indeed, it is found parallel, Hos. x. 5. The LXX. however, ἀγαλλιᾶσθε αὐτῷ ἐν τρόμῳ. And this is the usual meaning of the verb. Nor is there any reason for departing from it here. "Rejoice" that ye are called to worship Jehovah, but rejoice with awe and holy fear. The older Versions generally paraphrase the word. Thus the Chald. "pray." Syr. "cleave to him." Arab. "praise him."

[e] נַשְּׁקוּ־בַר. The interpretation of these words has always been a difficulty. (1.) The Chald. has קבילו אלפנא, "receive instruction;" LXX. δράξασθε παιδείας. Vulg. *apprehendite disciplinam;* בַּר being thus, as in Arabic, "piety, obedience," &c. Hence Saadia, "Prepare yourselves with purity, that is sincerity, to obey him." (2.) Others have taken it as an adverb. Jerome (in his text) *Adorate pure.* Aq. καταφιλήσατε ἐκλεκτῶς. Symm. προσκυνήσατε καθαρῶς. (3.) Others, again, "the chosen one" (from ברר) without the article, as מֶלֶךְ, xxi. 1. (4.) Of the older Versions, only the Syriac has ܢܫܩܘ ܒܪܐ, "kiss the Son." Jerome however, in his *Apologia adv. Rufin.* lib. i. § 19, admits this as an alternative rendering. After observing, that he rendered the verb נשקו (the literal renderings of which in Greek and Latin would be καταφιλήσατε and *deosculamini*) by *adorate,* "worship," as conveying the true sense of the word, because they who worship are wont to kiss the hand and bow the head (quoting Job xxxi. 27 in proof); and after insisting on the ambiguity of the noun, which he says means not only "son," as in Barjona, Bartimæus, &c., but also "wheat," and "a bundle of ears of wheat," and "elect," and "pure," he thus defends himself from the charge of inconsistency: "In my little commentary, where there was an opportunity of discussing the matter, I had said *Adorate filium,* (but) in the body of the work (the translation), not to appear a violent interpreter and not to give occasion to Jewish calumny, I said *Adorate pure sive electe,* as Aquila and Symmachus had translated. What injury then is done to the faith of the Church, if the reader is instructed in how many different ways a verse is explained by the Jewish commentators (*apud Hebræos*)?"

Qimchi observes that בר may either be the same as the common Hebrew בן, as in Prov. xxxi. 2, or may mean "pure," as in the phrase "pure of heart." "If," he says, "we adopt the reading *son,* then the sense will be, 'kiss the son whom God hath called a son,' saying, 'Thou art my son;' and the verb must be explained by the custom of slaves kissing the hand of their masters. But if we adopt the reading *pure,* it means, 'What have I to do with you? for I am pure of heart, and there is no iniquity in me that you should come and fight against me; but it is your part to kiss me and to confess that I am king by the ordinance of God.' And it is possible to refer the word to a root meaning *to choose*, as in 'Choose ye (ברו) a man.'" Among the Jewish commentators, Aben Ezra and Maimon. (quoted in Benzev), who both refer to the בְּנִי above, render "Son." So also Mendelss. "dem Sohne huldiget;" and so Ges. and De Wette, who cannot be accused of any dogmatic bias in favour of their interpretation. The only objection to this, of any weight, is the Aram. form of the word בַּר, which occurs (except in the Chaldee of Daniel and Ezra) but once again, Prov. xxxi. 2, manifestly a later passage, and not free from other Chaldaisms. But to this it may be replied with Dr. Pusey (*Daniel*, p. 477) that the form *Bar* is in fact not Chaldee, but old Phœnician. Hupf. indeed alleges, besides, the absence of the article, and the change of subject in the following verse. The former, however, may be explained by poetic usage, and the latter is not uncommon in Hebrew. Del. observes that an Arabic grammarian would explain the absence of the article as equivalent to saying: "Kiss a son, and what a son!" Cf. Heb. i. 1, ἐν υἱῷ, "by a Son, not by any inferior being;" and לְמֶלֶךְ, Ps. xlv. 2.

It will be seen from the above renderings, that the verb has been taken in two different senses: (1) "to cleave, adhere to, lay hold of," &c.—a sense which is not supported by usage: and (2) "to kiss," *i.e.* according to the Eastern custom, to proffer homage and service. (Cf. 1 Sam. x. 1.) Gen. xli. 40 is probably to be explained in the same way (see Ges. *Thes.* p. 923). The word is also used of the worship paid to idols, 1 Kings xix. 18, Hos. xiii. 2. We must therefore either render (with the Syr.) "Do homage to the Son," or (with Jerome) "proffer pure homage, worship in purity." Both translations are admissible. Nor does it seem very important which we adopt, though the interpretation of this clause has sometimes been debated, as if the Messianic character of the Psalm depended upon it. But that must be determined by the general scope of the Psalm, not by a single phrase; not to mention that ver. 6, 7 are quite as emphatic as ver. 12.

f כִּמְעַט, either (1) "within a little," "almost," "all but," = *parum abest quin;* often with the perf. *parum aberat quin;* but also as here with the pres. 2 Sam. xix. 37; or (2) "quickly," "soon." Hupf. doubts this, but besides Job xxxii. 22, and Ps. lxxxi. 15, which admit this meaning better than the other, the phrase רֶגַע כִּמְעַט, Is. xxvi. 20, is decisive that כִּמְעַט may be used of *time;* and so it is best understood here.

PSALM 3

This and the following Psalm have several links of connection, are in the same strain of thought and feeling, and were probably composed under the same circumstances. From the inscription of this Psalm we learn what those circumstances were. It was written by

David when he fled from his son Absalom. Both Psalms, it has been conjectured, were composed on the same day; the one in the morning, the other in the evening of the day following that on which the king quitted Jerusalem. But it is far more probable that they were composed at a later time, written whilst the sense of the peril and the deliverance were still fresh in David's mind, written in the vivid recollection of all the events of that memorable day, but not written in the actual hurry and confusion of the flight. It has been urged, indeed, against this reference, that there is an absence of all allusion to Absalom, that the language is of the same general kind as that employed in other Psalms where the writer is surrounded by enemies, and that there is nothing to indicate that the author is a person of importance, much less a king. But we rarely find in any Psalm those clearly defined notes of time and those distinct personal allusions which lead us to connect it with one event rather than another. We need not, therefore, assume on this ground that the inscription is false. The titles may preserve a genuine ancient tradition, unless there be anything in the language of a Psalm which directly contravenes them; and there is certainly no word here which would warrant us in rejecting the inscription. The absence of any allusion to Absalom may be accounted for, in some measure at least, by the tender feeling of the father for his rebellious son. Or the mind of David may not have been suffered to dwell on so harassing a thought, in order that he might trust the more entirely in God as to the issue of the struggle. Even the recollection of his past sin, grievous as it was, and though he was now reaping the fruits of it, was not allowed to trouble him. His soul was at rest in the sense of God's forgiveness, and the Psalm which recalls the feelings of that eventful day breathes the same sense of inward peace. The words are the words of one who had often sought and found help from God (iii. 4, iv. 3); and who, even in this his sorest strait, calmly reposes, knowing that Jehovah is "his Glory and the Lifter-up of his head."

From ver. 5 we gather that the Psalm is, as has been said, a morning hymn. With returning day there comes back on the monarch's heart the recollection of the enemies who threaten him,—a nation up in arms against him, his own son heading the rebellion, his wisest and most trusted counsellor in the ranks of his foes (2 Sam. xv.—xvii.). Never, not even when hunted by Saul, had he found his position one of greater danger. The odds were overwhelmingly against him. This is a fact which he does not attempt to hide from himself: "How *many* are mine enemies;" "*Many* rise up against me;" "*Many* say to my soul;" "*Ten thousands* of the people have set themselves against me." Meanwhile where are his friends, his army, his counsellors? Not a word of allusion to any of them in the Psalm. Yet he is not crushed, he is not desponding. Enemies may be thick as the leaves of the forest, and earthly friends may be few, or uncertain, or far off. But there is One Friend who cannot fail him, and to Him David turns with a confidence and affection which lift him above all his fears. Never had he been more sensible of the reality and preciousness of the Divine protection. If he was surrounded by enemies, Jehovah was his shield. If Shimei and his crew turned his glory into shame, Jehovah was his Glory; if they sought to revile and degrade him, Jehovah was the Lifter-up of his head. Nor did the mere fact of distance from Jerusalem separate between him and his God. He had sent back the ark and the priests, for he would not endanger their safety, and he did not trust in them as a charm, and he knew that Jehovah could still hear him from "His holy mountain" (iii. 4), could still lift up the light of His countenance upon him, and put gladness in his heart (iv. 6, 7). Sustained by Jehovah, he had laid him down and slept in safety; trusting in the same mighty protection, he would lie down again to rest. Enemies might taunt (iii. 2) and friends might fail him, but the victory was Jehovah's, and He could break the teeth of the ungodly (iii. 7, 8).*

The Psalm may be devided into four strophes:—

I. The present danger and distress. Ver. 1, 2.

II. The recollection of mercy and help in times past. Ver. 3, 4.

III. As arising from this, the sense of peace and security even in the midst of the present danger. Ver. 5, 6.

IV. The prayer for help against enemies, and for blessings upon Israel. Ver. 7, 8.

[A PSALM OF DAVID, WHEN HE FLED FROM THE FACE OF HIS SON ABSALOM.]

1 JEHOVAH, how many are mine adversaries,
Many are they that rise up against me!

1. HOW MANY, &c.: nearly all Israel. Compare 2 Sam. xvi. 15, xvii. 1, 11—13, with xv. 18.

THAT RISE AGAINST ME. The very expression used twice by the Cushite who brings tidings to David

* In a very interesting paper on "The Revolt of Absalom" in *Good Words* for March, 1864, Mr. Plumptre has taken a similar view of these Psalms.

2 Many there be that say to my soul :
"There is no help[a] for him in God."—[Selah.]

3 But THOU, O Jehovah, art a shield about me ;
My Glory and the Lifter-up of my head.
4 With my voice[b] to Jehovah do I cry,
And He answereth me from His holy mountain.—[Selah.]

5 I laid me down, and slept ;
I awaked ; for Jehovah sustaineth me.

of the death of Absalom, and the defeat of the rebels. (2 Sam. xviii. 31, 32.)

2. TO MY SOUL, rather than "OF my soul," though this is implied : but they aim at, and strike to, his soul. He *feels* it, and feels how deadly the aim is. "My soul" here is not a mere periphrasis for the personal pronoun, any more than in xxxv. 3, "Say unto my soul, I am thy salvation."

NO HELP, or "salvation" (see the same noun in ver. 8 and the verb in ver. 7), *i.e.* God as well as man is against him, his destruction is certain, prayer itself will be of no avail. Hence the general name of God (Elohim) instead of Jehovah, which otherwise is characteristic of the Psalm. David was thinking perhaps of what Shimei had said : "The Lord hath returned upon thee all the blood of the house of Saul, in whose stead thou hast reigned ; and the Lord hath delivered the kingdom into the hand of Absalom thy son" (2 Sam. xvi. 8). This however is the common scoff of the ungodly, as they mock the trust of the righteous : xxii. 7, 8 [8, 9], xlii. 3 [4], 9 [10]. And not only enemies thus reproached, but friends seemed to despair. See on iv. 6.

3. BUT THOU. Emphatically opposed to all such assertions as that in ver. 2.

A SHIELD. Such God had declared Himself to be to Abraham in Gen. xv. 1, and that, it should be remembered, just after Abraham had returned from the battle with the kings. We cannot wonder that such a name of God should have had a peculiar preciousness for David. No man was ever harder pressed by enemies, and no man had ever more cause to rejoice in the thought that God was his shield.

MY GLORY AND LIFTER-UP, &c. ; primarily, perhaps, with reference to the kingly dignity which God had given him, but not to be confined to that, but to deliverance out of trouble, exaltation, &c. (Cf. xxvii. 5, 6 ; cx. 7.)

4. Expresses not a single act, but the habit of a life. Whenever I cry, God hears me from His holy hill, *i.e.* Zion, where was the ark of the covenant.

The Priests and Levites, when he left Jerusalem, would have carried the ark after him. But with that faith which can alone teach true resignation, he says, "Carry back the ark of God into the city : if I shall find favour in the eyes of Jehovah, He will bring me again, and show me both it and His habitation." To David the ark was no mere talisman. The presence and favour of Jehovah were not bound to the local symbol of His presence. "In the heart, not in the hands," was David's feeling. It was the very opposite of that superstitious impulse which led the Israelites to take the ark with them into battle, 1 Sam. iv. 3—6. (2 Sam. xv. 25.)

5. I LAID ME DOWN. The pron. is emphatic, as if he would say, "I, my very self, hunted and cursed

6 I will not be afraid of ten thousands of the people,
Which have set (themselves) against me round about.

7 Arise, O Jehovah! Help me, O my God!
For Thou hast smitten all mine enemies upon the cheek-bone;
Thou hast broken the teeth of the ungodly.

8 To Jehovah belongeth the victory.
Thy blessing be upon Thy people.—[Selah.]

by my enemies, have tasted the goodness of the Lord even in the night that is past."

The tenses require the rendering as given above. I laid me down —I went to sleep—I woke up again —for Jehovah sustaineth me (an aorist, as "I cry," in the last verse); His hand is my pillow.

6. Then from that thought there arose fresh confidence in his heart, "I will not be afraid of countless hosts," &c.

HAVE SET THEMSELVES. A military expression. (Cf. Is. xxii. 7; I Kings xx. 12, &c.) It is not necessary to supply an accus. such as "camp" or "battle." The word may be used intransitively.

7. HELP, or "save," see notes on ver. 2, 8.

FOR THOU HAST SMITTEN. An appeal to the past: O Thou that hast destroyed mine enemies on every side, ALL mine enemies, be they many, or be they few, rise up now for me against them that rise up against me. Or possibly, as in many other instances the perfects may anticipate the result, they express the sure confidence that God *will* crush his enemies, which he speaks of as an already accomplished fact.

It is impossible not to feel how appropriate this metaphor,—smiting on the cheek-bone, breaking the teeth, &c.—is in David's mouth. As he himself had smitten the bear and the lion when they came against him, so should God smite his enemies coming fierce and open-mouthed against him.

8 THE VICTORY, or, "THE help," or "salvation." The article is emphatic, and includes help and deliverance in all its fulness, as the preposition denotes that it belongs exclusively to, is at the entire disposal of, Jehovah.

Such is his confident, courageous answer to the timorous whispers of friends, and the mocking exultation of enemies. They said, "There is no help for him in God." He replies, To Jehovah belongeth help, help not in this strait only, but in all times and places.

Finally, how noble the prayer of the royal exile, asking not for himself alone, but for his poor, misguided subjects—"Let Thy blessing be upon Thy people," upon the whole nation, of whom David is the Father, as he is the King, not merely that portion of his subjects who remained true in their allegiance. What a glimpse this gives us of the greatness and generosity of that kingly heart! He is the type, as Delitzsch observes, of the true David who prayed for the people who crucified Him, "Father, forgive them."

THY BLESSING. "Benedictio Dei est Dei beneficentia."

[a] On the form יְשׁוּעָתָה, Hupfeld's note should be consulted. He maintains that the termination ָה, by which the original form (יְשׁוּעָה) is lengthened, is a remnant of the old accusatival termination, and in words of this kind denotes the acc. of purpose or aim; strictly, therefore, it is the

Lat. *saluti*, as עֶזְרָתָה, *auxilio*, xliv. 27, lxiii. 8, xciv. 17, = לְעֶזְרָה, and חָלִילָה לְּךָ = *religioni tibi sit.* And so also in lxxx. 3, לְכָה לִישֻׁעָתָה לָּנוּ, where, however, the accus. is rendered superfluous by the prep. לְ, as often (*e.g.* לְמַעְלָה, לִשְׁאֹלָה, בַּנֶּגְבָּה, &c.), the signification of the termination having been lost. The following dative לוֹ points to the same construction here, but in consequence of the בא׳, *in God*, the termination goes for nothing, and the noun is used as a nominative, as in Jon. ii. 10, and similar forms elsewhere.

[b] קוֹלִי אקרא. According to Hupf. a double subject of the person, and the active member or instrument, as often in the poets, xii. 3, xvii. 10, 13, 14, xxxii. 8, xliv. 3, &c.; and even in prose, Ex. vi. 3, 1 Sam. xxv. 26, 33. Gesen. on the other hand assumes an accus. of the instrument (§ 138, 3), quoting such passages as cix. 2, Prov. x. 4, Ezek. xi. 13, on which Hupf. remarks that in all these instances not only is there no pronominal suffix, but the noun stands with an adjective which describes the *manner* of the action, as elsewhere the *inf. absol.* or an *abstract* alone, whereas here we have a *concrete*. On "Selah," see the General Introduction.

PSALM 4

DAVID had said in the previous Psalm, "I laid me down and slept:" he says in this, "I will lay me down in peace, and sleep." These words evidently connect the Psalms together. That was a morning, this is an evening hymn. That was written with a deep sense of thankfulness for the undisturbed rest which had followed the most anxious, in some respects the dreariest, day of his life; this was written with a calm confidence, flowing directly from the previous experience. The interval between the two Psalms or the occasions to which they refer may only have been the interval between the morning and evening of the same day. The thoughts and turns of expression in the one are not unlike those in the other. As in the former he heard many saying to his soul, "There is no help for him in God" (ver. 2), so in this he hears many saying, "Who will show us any good?" (ver. 6). As in that he knew that, though at a distance from the Tabernacle, he was not at a distance from God, but would receive an answer to his prayer from the "holy mountain" (ver. 4), so in this, though the Priests have returned with the Ark to Jerusalem, he can look for "the light of Jehovah's countenance," which is better than the Urim and Thummim of the priestly ephod.

The Psalm opens with a short prayer, in which David's faith stays itself on his experience of past mercies. Then his thoughts run upon his enemies, on the curses of Shimei, on the treachery of Ahithophel. "O ye sons of men,"—thus he turns to address them, and the expression denotes persons of rank and importance,—"how long will ye turn my glory into shame?" How long will ye trample my honour as a king in the dust, refusing me the allegiance which is my due? How long will ye love vanity (or emptiness), and seek after lies? How is it that ye are bent on this mad enterprise, and persist in using the weapons of falsehood and slander to my prejudice? He reminds them that, in assailing him, they are assailing not him, but God, who chose him and appointed him to his office (ver. 3). "For them, if his words could reach them, as they were lying down to rest, in the pride of their successful plots, his counsel would be, 'Stand in awe, and sin not: commune with your own heart upon your bed, and be still.' Let the watches of the night be given to self-searching; let the voice of scorn and reviling be hushed in silence. Then, when that scrutiny and solemn awe have done their work, and repentance comes, 'offer the sacrifices of righteousness, and put your trust in the Lord.'"* Once more, David, ere he lies down to rest, lifts his eyes to Heaven. Many, in such circumstances, might be ready to despair: many, probably, among his own friends were then saying, "Who will show us any good?" David knows where true good is to be found. There is a Light which can "lighten his darkness," whether it be the darkness of night or the darkness of sorrow. The light of God's countenance lifted up upon him can fill his heart with greater joy than the joy of the threshing-floor or the vintage. And in that confidence he can lie down and take his rest, knowing that Jehovah Himself will keep him in the watches of the night.

It is worthy of notice that David does not cry to God for vengeance on his enemies, but earnestly seeks to bring them to a better mind. The strong feeling of injured innocence prompts no thought of revenge, but only the noble desire to teach those who have done the wrong a more excellent way. The monarch does not forget that he is a monarch; and with a monarch's heart, lifted here at least above the littleness of personal resentment, he tries to win over the subjects who have rebelled against him.

The Psalm may be said to fall into three unequal strophes:—

I. The cry directed to God. Ver. 1.

---

* See Mr. Plumptre's paper on "The Revolt of Absalom" in *Good Words* for March, 1864, p. 271.

II. The earnest warning addressed to his enemies, in two parts. Ver. 2—5.

III. The calm expression on the part of David of his peace and confidence in God. Ver. 6—8.

[FOR THE PRECENTOR. UPON STRINGED INSTRUMENTS.[a] A PSALM OF DAVID.]

1 WHEN I cry, answer me, O God of my righteousness!
Thou that in straitness hast made room for me:
Be gracious unto me, and hear my prayer.

2 Ye sons of men! how long shall my glory be (turned)[b] into shame?
(How long) will ye love vanity, will ye seek after lies?—[Selah.]

3 Know then, that Jehovah hath separated[c] for Himself one whom He loveth.[d]
Jehovah hearkeneth when I cry unto Him.

1. GOD OF MY RIGHTEOUSNESS, *i.e.* Thou who maintainest my right and my cause, asserting my righteousness against the slanders of my enemies. (Cf. lix. 10 [11].) But not to be confined to this: it also means who knowest the righteousness, the sincerity of my heart and life, and, moreover, art Thyself the ground and source of all righteousness in me. So Leighton: "Qui ipse justus es et justitiæ meæ patronus. *Justitiæ meæ*, id est, justæ tum causæ, tum vitæ."

The second clause of this verse is undoubtedly a relative clause, with the usual omission of the relative. It is certainly not to be taken (with De Wette) as imperative. On these two things he builds his plea, God's righteousness as pledged to himself, and God's goodness, as experienced either in past times, or in the present emergency.

2. SONS OF MEN. Generally "men of high degree," nobles, &c., as opposed to בְּנֵי אָדָם, "men of low degree," xlix. 2 [3], lxii. 9 [10]. So Qimchi understands by it men of high rank who had joined Absalom. And Luther translates, *liebe Herren*, and in the margin *Ihr grossen Hansen*. Some would see in it only a term of "ironical honour." Hupf. suggests that the expression thus nakedly used may rather denote human weakness, and that there is a sort of emphasis in the expression, "children of *men*," when the Psalm turns to them from *God;* but surely in that case another Hebrew word would have been employed: *'ish* is *vir*, not *homo*.

MY GLORY, *i.e.* personal honour, character, as in lxii. 7 [8], Job xix. 9; here, perhaps, my state and dignity as king, though it is frequently used in a more extended signification. (See on vii. 5.)

3. KNOW THEN. The conjunction here introduces a marked antithesis, as in ii. 6, iii. 3 [4]. Ye may seek to bring my glory to shame, *yet* know that it is one whom He loves (see critical note, and on xvi. 10) that God hath separated and chosen for Himself.

HATH SEPARATED, or "hath *marvellously* chosen;" for the notion of something wonderful is found in the root. David would naturally feel that his own career from the

4 Tremble and sin not :
Commune with your heart upon your bed, and be still.—
[Selah.]
5 Offer sacrifices of righteousness,
And put your trust in Jehovah.

6 There be many that say : "Who will show us (any) good ?"
Lift[e] Thou upon us the light of Thy countenance, O
Jehovah !
7 Thou hast put gladness in my heart,
More[f] than when their corn and their wine abound.

sheepfold to the throne was at every step an instance of this marvellous choice and separation.

ONE WHOM HE LOVETH, or "the godly man," *i.e.* His true worshiper. The word often occurs in the same sense as *pius* in Latin. (See more in the critical note.)

4. He passes on to wise and loving counsels. TREMBLE, *i.e.* before *God*, not before me, and sin not against *Him*. The verb expresses any sort of disquietude, or strong emotion, the agitation of anger as well as fear. Hence the rendering of the LXX. ὀργίζεσθε καὶ μὴ ἁμαρτάνετε, "Be ye angry and sin not," *i.e.* "do not suffer yourselves to sin in your anger," is certainly a possible rendering of the words, but not suitable here. St. Paul (Eph. iv. 26) uses the words as they stand in the Greek version, not, however, in the way of direct citation.

COMMUNE WITH, lit. *say (it) in your heart*, *i.e.* reflect, meditate on the truth I have already declared, ver. 3. Let the still hours of the night bring calmer and wiser thoughts with them.

5. OFFER SACRIFICES OF RIGHTEOUSNESS, or, RIGHTEOUS SACRIFICES, as in li. 19 [21]. The phrase occurs first in Deut. xxxiii. 19, and denotes either (*a*) sacrifices that God will accept, because they are offered not merely according to the ritual of the Law, but with clean hands and pure hearts (Is. xxix. 13) ; or (*b*) fitting sacrifices, such as past sin requires, in order to put it away. Thus, "draw nigh to God, and He will draw nigh to you." The advice to offer these sacrifices follows from the general exhortation in the previous verse to religious awe and reflection. Those who, like Absalom and his party, were in possession of Jerusalem, might "offer sacrifices" in the appointed place and with all legal observances, but the sacrifices would be of no worth unless offered in righteousness. "Offer them in a right spirit and trust in Jehovah Himself, and not merely in the offering and the lip-service."

6. THERE BE MANY THAT SAY. Not the enemies addressed before. The reference may be to the friends and companions of David, whose heart failed them in the day of trouble ; or more widely, to the general proneness of men to walk by sight rather than by faith.

But David has learnt a better lore. Though far from "the holy mountain," there still dwells in his heart the blessing wherewith the priests of Jehovah had there blessed His people. "Jehovah make His face to shine upon thee . . . Jehovah lift up His countenance upon thee, and give thee peace." To that remembered blessing his heart now gives the echo in the prayer, "Jehovah, lift Thou up the light of Thy countenance upon us . . . In peace I will lay me down," &c.

7. THEIR CORN AND THEIR WINE.

8 In peace, at once will I lay me down and sleep ;
For THOU, Jehovah, alone makest me to dwell in safety.

To whom does the pronoun refer? Hengstenberg and others have supposed the allusion to be to Zibah (2 Sam. xvi.), and the supply which he brought for David and his band. Others (as Ew. and Olsh.) think the pronoun is used indefinitely, as in lxv. 9 [10], "Thou preparest *their* corn," *i.e.* the corn of men in general. Hupfeld thinks the reference of the pronoun is to the "many" of the previous verse. They in their worldly-mindedness look for their happiness in the abundance of their earthly things. Hence when adversity threatens they begin to despond. David, on the other hand, has a source of joy, deeper and more unfailing because it flows from above. But perhaps David is thinking of his enemies. They have at their command all earthly means of support and enjoyment. He finds it difficult to collect supplies for himself and his army (2 Sam. xvi. 1, xvii. 26, &c.), yet God has given him a better joy than that of harvest or vintage.

For the comparison with the joy of harvest and vintage as the great occasions of festive mirth, see Is. ix. 3 [2], Jer. xlviii. 33.

Some have seen in this verse an answer to the prayer of the previous verse. David prays for the light of God's countenance ; the answer is given in this gladness of heart. But it is better to take the words, "Thou hast put," &c., as the record of a past as well as present experience, though it still remains true that the "light" is the source of the "gladness."

8. AT ONCE, *sc.* as soon as I lie down I sleep, not harassed by disturbing and anxious thoughts. For this meaning of the adverb, see cxli. 10, Is. xlii. 14.

THOU ALONE. This rendering is in accordance with the accentuation, with the order of the words and with the context, in which the contrast is implied that however others may fail, or oppose, God alone is sufficient ; and the sense may be supported by Deut. xxxii. 12. On the other hand, all the Ancient Versions, and many recent interpreters, refer the adverb to the speaker : "Thou makest me to dwell alone in safety ;" as in Jer. xlix. 31 the same word is used of a nation dwelling without bars or gates, *alone*, *i.e.* securely. Riehm says : "The thought that Jehovah is the only protection is without motive in the context; as it is not said that he lacked other protection, nor of the many that they sought protection elsewhere. [But in answer to this see ver. 6.] The two adverbs 'alone' and 'in safety' are parallel, and express a common idea as the two verbs in the first number."

Delitzsch remarks : "The iambics with which the Psalm closes are as the last sound of a cradle-song which dies away softly, and, as it were, falling to sleep itself. Dante is right : the sweetness of the music and harmony of the Hebrew Psalter has been lost in the Greek and Latin translations."

[a] See General Introduction, p. 88.

[b] For a similar construction, see xxxvii. 26, lxxiii. 19, Is. ix. 4.

[c] הִפְלָה. Many MSS. (37 of Kennic. and 28 De-Rossi) have הפלא, and the roots are no doubt closely allied. The idea of *separation* is the fundamental idea. (Cf. Exod. viii. 18, ix. 4.) To the form with א attaches more commonly the further idea of something "wonderful," something

out of the common course of things. (Is. xxix. 14.) But the same idea is also found with the form in ה. (xvii. 7, cxxxix. 14.)

[d] חָסִיד. (1.) The passive form of the word seems to denote "one who is the object of (the Divine) mercy," *i.e.* one who is in covenant with Jehovah, a true Israelite (see l. 5). Parallel with אֱמוּנִים, xii. 2, as חֶסֶד often is joined with אֱמֶת, "mercy and truth." (2.) It passes over sometimes apparently rather into an active signification, and means one who shows mercy or kindness to others (xviii. 26). In xliii. 1, לֹא חָסִיד, "the unmerciful." Hupfeld's note on this word should by all means be consulted.

[e] נְסָה, a doubly anomalous form for נְשָׂא, which is found in one MS. of Kenn. in the text.

[f] A pregnant brevity of construction. Fully, "a gladness greater than the gladness of the time when their corn and their wine are multiplied." There are therefore three ellipses: (1) of the *adjective* "greater," as lxii. 10, Job xi. 17, and often; (2) of the *noun* "gladness," as in Is. x. 10, Job xxxv. 2; (3) of the *relative*. This last ellipsis should, according to the accents, be supplied before the verb. Then the rendering would be, "more than the gladness of the season of their corn and wine, which are (or, when they are) increased." The Jewish interpreters, Ab. Ez., Kimchi, and others, avoid all ellipse, except that of the relative, by rendering מִן as a particle of time, "*since* their corn," &c. The LXX. *ἀπὸ κάρπου* (l. *καιροῦ*) *σίτου καὶ οἴνου . . . αὐτῶν ἐπληθύνθησαν*, thus making *men* the subject of the verb.

PSALM 5

LIKE Psalm III. this is a morning prayer. But the circumstances of the singer are different. He is not now fleeing from open enemies but he is in peril from the machinations of those who are secretly lying in wait for him (ver. 9, 10). He is not now an exile, but can still enter the house of the Lord and bow himself towards His holy dwelling-place (ver. 7).

Throughout the Psalm there breathes a strong feeling that God is pledged, by His very character as a righteous God, to defend and bless the righteous. And David (if the Psalm be his) speaks as if in the full consciousness of his own uprightness. Yet the words are not the words of a self-righteous boaster; for though no hypocrite or evil-doer, he confesses that it is only in the lovingkindness of God that he can enter His holy temple.

This last expression, "holy temple," it has been thought could not have been used by David, in whose time the Tabernacle was yet standing. But for the discussion of this question, see the Note on ver. 7.

The Psalm consists of three parts :—

I. An earnest entreaty that God would hearken to the sigh of his heart and the voice of his lips. Ver. 1—3.

II. Strophe A. The confidence of the righteous man in going to God as a God who hates iniquity. Ver. 4—7.

III. Strophe B. The prayer grounded on this confidence, (1) for guidance for himself : (2) for the destruction of his enemies : (3) for the protection and blessing of all those who, like himself, love the Lord. Ver. 8—12.

A kind of parallelism may be traced in the structure of the two strophes. The reason given in ver. 4 for the prayer corresponds to the reason given in ver. 9 : ver. 4—6 (the character of God) to ver. 10, where the Psalmist prays Him to *manifest* that character in righteous vengeance : ver. 7 (the individual believer) to ver. 11, 12 (the collective body).

[FOR THE PRECENTOR. WITH FLUTE ACCOMPANIMENT.[a] A PSALM OF DAVID.]

1 GIVE ear to my words, O Jehovah,
Consider my meditation.
2 Hearken unto the voice of my cry,[b] my King and my God,
For unto Thee do I pray.

1—3. The first Strophe or Introit. An earnest prayer to be heard. The thoughts are simple, but the language (ver. 1) carefully chosen. אֲמָרִים ("words") is a word peculiar to the poets and prophets : הַאֲזִין ("give ear") more common in poetry than prose : הָגִיג ("meditation") occurs only in two Psalms, here and xxxix 4. It is applied to a scarcely audible utterance, or a prayer like that of Hannah's, whose lips moved when her voice was not heard (*meditata murmura*). See i. 2. Then follows (ver. 3) the loud utterance, "the voice of my cry."

2. MY KING. The title is given to God, not merely in a general sense as Ruler of the world—as the Canaanites and others called their gods, Moloch and Milcom, or the Greeks addressed Zeus as ἄναξ and βασιλεύς—but with the distinct recognition of His theocratic

3 Jehovah, in the morning shalt Thou hear my voice,
In the morning will I set in order for Thee (my prayer)
and will watch.

4 For Thou art not a God that hath pleasure[c] in wickedness,
Evil cannot sojourn with[d] Thee.
5 Fools[e] cannot stand in Thy sight;
Thou hatest all workers of iniquity.
6 Thou destroyest them that speak lies;
The bloodthirsty and deceitful man doth Jehovah abhor.

relation to the people of Israel. The King of the nation is here also claimed by the individual as his king, the more emphatically, if the Psalm was written by David, by one who was himself a king. See the notes on xliv. 4, lxxiv. 12.

UNTO THEE, *i.e.* not to man or angel; to *Thee*, for thou wilt hear. (Cf. xvii. 6.)

3. IN THE MORNING. Emphatic. (Accus. of time, as lv. 18.)

I WILL SET (or "lay" IN ORDER) (viz. my prayer). The word is used of laying in order the wood (Lev. i. 7) and the victim (Lev. i. 8, vi. 12 [5]) for the sacrifices. One of the first duties of the priest, as soon as day dawned, was to lay the wood in order for the morning sacrifice (Lev. vi. 12 [5], Numb. xxviii. 4). So the Psalmist brings his offering, prepares himself as a spiritual sacrifice, and lays before God the fruit of his lips. (The idea is expressed at length in Ps. cxli. 2, "and the lifting up of my hands as the evening sacrifice.") And then he "watches," "looks out" (the same verb as in Hab. ii. 1), for an answer to his petition, as the priest might look (or as Elijah looked on Carmel) for the fire from heaven to descend and consume the victim.

4—7. Jehovah is a righteous God, and therefore He hateth and punisheth evil-doers, but will be merciful to him who worships Him aright.

4. The Psalmist expects to be heard, *for* only the righteous can approach a righteous God. "Ratiocinatur," says Calvin, "ab ipsius Dei naturâ."

"Evil (personified) cannot be a guest or friend of Thine; cannot tarry in Thy house," as xv. 1, lxi. 4 [5]; not merely however with a reference to the Temple, but to that spiritual abiding in the presence of God, and in the light of His countenance, which is the joy only of them that are true of heart. To the wicked the light of God's countenance is a consuming fire.

5. FOOLS, or perhaps rather, "the arrogant," "the vain-boasters," men who carry impiety to the height of madness. See Critical Note. CANNOT STAND, lit. "set themselves," the same word as in ii. 2. The allusion may be (1) to the judgement, "cannot stand before God's holiness and power as armed against them," as in Deut. vii. 24, ix. 2, &c.; or (2) to the privilege of nobles and others who stand in the presence of the King, cf. Prov. xxii. 29. So the angels are said to stand before God (Job i. 6, ii. 1).

WORKERS OF INIQUITY occurs frequently in Job and the Psalms as a description of the wicked, and has been adopted by our Lord in the N. T., οἱ ἐργαζόμενοι τὴν ἀνομίαν, Matt. vii. 23.

6. BLOODTHIRSTY . . . MAN, lit. "Man of bloods," the plur. being used of *bloodshed, murder*, as the plur. θάνατοι in Greek of *violent* death.

7 But as for me—in the multitude of Thy loving-kindness
will I enter Thy house;
I will bow myself towards Thy holy temple in Thy fear.
8 O Jehovah, lead me in Thy righteousness, because of
them that lie in wait[f] for me,
Make Thy way plain[g] before me;

7. TOWARDS. Reuss: "*In* thy holy temple;" but the other rendering is preferable. As the Psalm is a morning hymn, the Futures may be taken strictly, "I *will* enter," &c. But there is also something of the potential meaning about them: *sc.* the wicked *cannot* enter, but I *may* (and will) enter Thine house. The words בַּיִת (*bâyith*) and הֵיכָל (*heycal*) seem at first sight decisive against the Davidic authorship of the Psalm, as being only applicable to the Temple. But both words are applied to the sanctuary of Shiloh. The former is used of the Tabernacle, Josh. vi. 24, 2 Sam. xii. 20, as it is even of tents or moveable dwellings like those of the Patriarchs (Gen. xxvii. 15). Hupfeld thinks it need not refer here to the Temple at all, but may be used figuratively with reference to the verb "sojourn," ver. 4 [5], so that the meaning would be, Evil cannot find a welcome with Thee, but I may hope to be received by Thee as a guest and friend. But though, as was observed on ver. 4, and as appears from many other passages in the Psalms (see *e.g.* xxiii. and lxxxiv.), the two ideas of the earthly sanctuary and the spiritual enjoyment of God's Presence may not be very carefully distinguished by the writer, it is most natural to understand by the house of God the literal structure, whether tabernacle or temple; and this is confirmed by the parallelism in the next member of the verse. The other word הֵיכָל, which means properly a large building, "a palace" (cf. xi. 4), no doubt presents more difficulty. It is used of the sanctuary at Shiloh, 1 Sam. i. 9, iii. 3. But that seems to have been not a tabernacle, but a building of a more substantial kind. We read at any rate of posts and folding-doors (1 Sam. i. 9, iii. 15); whereas in the time of David, "the ark of the covenant of the Lord remained under curtains" (1 Chron. xvii. 1). And there is certainly no proof that הֵיכָל is ever used of this temporary structure. Still it is possible that the word, which had already been employed when speaking of the house in Shiloh, continued to be employed when only a tent was pitched for the ark (1 Chron. xv. 1). It might still be called a היכל, not because of its size (*r.* יכל=כול, כלל, *capax esse*), but because of its solemn dedication as the house of God, the palace of the Great King.

IN THE MULTITUDE OF THY LOVING-KINDNESS. The Psalmist has access to God not only because he is of a different *character* from those mentioned in ver. 7, but because the King of kings, of His grace and goodness, permits him to draw near. Therefore also he adds "in Thy fear." We see here the mingled feeling of confidence and liberty of access with solemn awe and deep humility which befits every true worshipper.

8—10. In the former part of the Psalm, David has placed himself in sharp contrast with "the workers of iniquity," with "them that speak lies," &c., and on this ground has claimed the protection and favour of Jehovah. Now he entreats more directly guidance for himself and the destruction of his enemies, as

9 For there is no faithfulness in their mouth ;[h]
Their inward part is a yawning gulf ;[i]
Their throat is an open sepulchre,
(While) they make smooth their tongue.
10 Punish[k] Thou them, O God :—
Let them fall through[l] their own counsels :
In[m] the multitude of their transgressions thrust them away ;
For they have rebelled against Thee.
11 And all who find refuge in Thee shall rejoice ;
For ever shall they shout for joy ;

false and treacherous men, like those whom he has already described and whom "Jehovah abhors."

8. LEAD ME (strictly, as a shepherd, cf. xxiii. 2, 3, xxxi. 3 [4]), used almost exclusively of *Divine* guidance, whether of the nation or of individuals.

IN THY RIGHTEOUSNESS. This may be understood (1) of God's own character. His righteousness itself is pledged to succour those who worship Him and seek His guidance ; cf. cxliii. 1. Or (2) it may mean "*the way* of God's righteousness" (cf. for instance, Prov. viii. 20, xii. 28), called *God's* righteousness, not only as pleasing to Him, but as coming from Him as its source, a righteousness of which He is the law and measure, as well as that which He has appointed for men to walk in. So δικαιοσύνη Θεοῦ in the N. T. means both God's own attribute of righteousness (as in Rom. iii. 5), and also the righteousness which He requires of men, and gives to men, Rom. i. 17, iii. 21, 22. Both senses seem to be blended in Rom. iii. 25, 26.

MAKE THY WAY. The way in which Thou wouldst have me to go, not any self-devised way of my own. This is to be preferred to the reading of the LXX., Vulg., and Arab.: "Make my way plain before Thy face."

PLAIN OF STRAIGHT, lit. "level" (cf. xxvii. 11, and Note on cxliii. 10), free from hindrances and temptations, lest I stumble and fall into the hand of my adversaries. The "straight way" may be either (morally) the path of purity, uprightness, &c.; or (physically) the path of safety, prosperity; or rather, both ideas are combined.

9. FOR. This gives the reason for the prayer, "Lead me because of them that lie in wait for me:" *for* their malice is such that I need Thy care and guidance. With them, mouth, heart, throat, and tongue are all instruments of evil.

NO FAITHFULNESS, lit. "nothing firm, settled."

The expressions point not to foreign oppressors, but evidently to ungodly men in the nation itself who had recourse to slander and treachery when they dared not use open violence. It is the opposition and the contest ever repeated between the Church and the world. Cf. Gal. iv. 29.

10. AGAINST THEE. The enemies of David are the enemies of David's God. "Whoso toucheth you, toucheth the apple of Mine eye." "Saul, Saul, why persecutest thou Me?"

11. AND ALL . . . . SHALL, or, SO SHALL ALL. For the cause of David is the cause of all who have David's heart and fear David's God. The overthrow of his enemies is the overthrow of the enemies of the Church. If one member suffer, all suffer ; if one triumph, all will be partakers in the triumph.

And Thou wilt defend them:
And they who love Thy Name shall exult in Thee.
12 For Thou, O Jehovah, dost bless the righteous,
With ſavour dost Thou compass him[n] as with a shield.

The verse might also be rendered, as in the E.V., Luther, Ewald, and in former editions of this work, in the optative:

"And let all who find refuge in Thee
rejoice;
Let them ever shout for joy;
And do Thou defend them:
And let them who love Thy Name
exult in Thee."

But ver. 11 seems not so much to carry on the wish, as to express the consequence which will certainly follow the fulfilment of the prayer in ver. 10.

AND THOU WILT DEFEND. This is almost equivalent to, "because Thou wilt (or, dost) defend," but the clauses, as is common in Hebrew, are simply linked together by the copula. The verb means strictly *to cover*, and the figure is either taken from the cherubim with outstretched wings covering the mercy-seat (hence of God, xci. 4); or from the *booth* or *tabernacle* (Heb. *succah*), used figuratively of God's house as a place of shelter and refuge from the world. See the expansion of the figure, Is. iv. 5, 6.

THY NAME. God's name is that whereby He makes Himself known: His revelation of Himself as a God of Love and Grace to His people.

12. FOR. If we take the preceding verse in an optative sense, this must be explained, let them rejoice, "for" this is an eternal truth, that Thou dost bless the righteous: or we may render, let them rejoice *that* Thou dost bless, &c.

SHIELD. The word denotes properly the large shield (Heb. *Tsinnah*, scutum) which covered the whole body; used of the shield of Goliath, 1 Sam. xvii. 7. For the difference between this and the other word used in iii. 3, see Smith's *Dict. of the Bible*, Art. ARMS.

[a] אֶל־נְחִילוֹת. LXX. ὑπὲρ τῆς κληρονομούσης, which is clearly wrong. נְחִילוֹת, sing. נְחִילָה = נְחִלָה (from the Niph. of חלל) is the name of a musical instrument, probably the same as חָלִיל, a hollow reed or flute. That this was in use in the Temple service is certain. See Is. xxx. 29, 1 Sam. x. 5, 1 Kings i. 40. Perhaps with אֶל, not עַל, because it was used as an accompaniment (so Lat. *canere ad*); but no stress can be laid on this, as the two prepositions are constantly interchanged.

[b] שַׁוְעִי only here, but doubtless from a noun שֶׁוַע, instead of the more usual שַׁוְעָה, from the root שׁוע, which only occurs in the Piel (connected with צוח, Æth. צוע, *to cry*). There is no need with Röd. in Ges. *Thes.* to take the word as inf. Piel with Dagesh omitted.

[c] חָפֵץ, as a verb most commonly, and in a stronger sense followed by בְּ = *delectari aliquo*, and used with reference both to persons and things; in a weaker sense with the accus. only of things (abstracts); and so here the part. or verbal adj. which in the sing. is always followed by the accus. as in xxxiv. 13, xxxv. 27, &c.; in the plur. it is sometimes in the stat. constr.]

d יָגֻרְךָ, the shortened form, in consequence of the drawing back of the accent, with accus. (as cxx. 5, Is. xxxiii. 14), instead of עִם, a construction which is common enough with verbs of dwelling, when there follows not only the *place* in which, but also the *persons* with whom, the dwelling is made, as here, and lvii. 5, lxviii. 19, cxx. 5, Gen. xxx. 20.

e הוֹלְלִים, a strong word, denoting fools who carry their folly to the height of madness. According to Hupfeld, the root-idea is that of *empty space* (as in German *Halle, Hölle*; hallen, *hohl* sein); then (1) to be *empty, hollow*, fig. *vain, foolish* = אלל (אליל), אהל, אול (אויל): so part. Qal. as here and fut. lxxvi. 5; trans. Po.; reflex. Hithpo.; (2) to *shout, call, boast* (comp. εὔχεσθαι and αὐχεῖν), = ילל ,אלל (also *to lament*); so in Piel and Hithp.; (3) to be *clear, shine*, especially Hiph. trans. According to Delitzsch, the primitive idea is that of *making a noise, shouting*, &c. See Note on lxxiii. 3.

f שׁוֹרְרָי. This is usually supposed to be for מְשׁוֹרְרַי, part. Pal. of שׁוּר, *observare*, as Jer. v. 26, Hos. xiii. 7, and so Aq. ἐφοδεύοντάς μου, and Jerome, *insidiatores meos*. See on the dropping of the מ, cxviii. Note e. But Hupf. regards it only as a kindred form of צֹרְרִים. Comp. שָׁוָה and צָוָה, שׁוַע and צוּחַ, &c.

g הושר, Kethîbh, to be read הוֹשַׁר. The Qeri הַיְשַׁר, as in Prov. iv. 25. In Gen. viii. 17, Is. xlv. 2, there are similar corrections of the Hiphil, but apparently without sufficient reason.

h בְּפִיהוּ. Sing. suff. for plur. by a common enallage of number, especially in the suff. of the third pers., not only in different clauses, but even in the same clause (see lxii. 5, Is. ii. 20, v. 23, Jer. xxxi. 15), to be explained by the fact that a class or species may be regarded either as many, or as one, or the sing. may be distributive *in ore uniuscujusque eorum*. The word is interposed between אֵין and its genitive, as in vi. 6, xxxii. 2. This is more usual with pronominal forms such as בּוֹ, לוֹ, Gen. xi. 30, Lev. xi. 10, 11, Is. i. 6. נְכוֹנָה is fem. part. Niphal of כּוּן, used here as a neuter.

i הַוּוֹת, a poetical word occurring only in Psalms, Proverbs, and Job, and mostly in plur. in the sense of "mischief wrought through human wickedness." It comes from a root הוה (cognate with אבה ,אוה, &c. root אב־הב ,או־הו) to *breathe*, prop. from *an open mouth*; hence it marks (1) the act, the open mouth, the yawning chasm (*hiatus, rictus oris*, χάω, *gap*), and (2) the feeling denoted thereby, the breathing, panting, and hence the eager desire, but always used in a bad sense of *evil* desire, as in lii. 7 [9] (see Note on lii. 2), and Prov. x. 13, xi. 6, Mic. vii. 3. The word occurs in the sing. and in a physical sense, only Job vi. 2, xxx. 13 (in both with Keri, היה), elsewhere only in plur. and with a moral meaning, but denoting not merely evil generally, but always evil or destruction *purposed* and *prepared*. So here, where the notion of a yawning abyss may be retained as supported by the parallelism, "no faithfulness," lit. "nothing firm," "no sure ground." See Hupfeld's note here.

k הַאֲשִׁימֵם. The Hiph. only here. In Qal the verb means *to incur guilt*, and then, by a natural transition, *to suffer* as guilty, *to be punished* (as in xxxiv. 21, 22 [22, 23], Hos. v. 15, x. 2, xiv. 1, with a double sense Jer. ii. 3, and elsewhere). Hence in Hiph. to *pronounce guilty*, *condemn*, *leave to punishment* (like הרשיע, as the opp. of הצדיק). So the LXX. κρῖνον αὐτούς. Jerome, *condemna*. This usage in Hebrew has a profound moral basis. Sin and chastisement, righteousness and the manifestation of that righteousness, are inseparable. The reward and the punishment *partake of the nature* of the things (or persons) rewarded and punished. Hence the same word means both guilt and punishment. Akin to this is the well-known use of the word *sin* for *sin-offering*.

[l] מִמּוֹ'. The prep. מִן is probably used here of the *cause*, as in Hos. xi. 6 (with the same word), *through* or *because* of their counsels. Others, however, as Ges., De W., Ew., render, "let them fall *from* their counsels;" and so in the 1st edit. of this work. So in Latin, *Excidere spe, excidere ausis*, and in Greek, πίπτειν ἀπὸ τῆς ἐλπίδος, Sir. xiv. 2. But it does not seem sufficiently justified by Hebrew usage, and I have therefore abandoned it. The other interpretation, too, accords better with the parallelism, " In the multitude of their transgressions."

[m] בְּרֹב. The prep. gives here not so much the *reason*, " on account of," as the *means by which*, and *the condition in which*, they are to be cast away. Delitzsch well compares John viii. 21, 24, "Ye shall die *in* your sins," ἐν ταῖς ἁμαρτίαις ὑμῶν.

[n] תַּעְטְרֶנּוּ. The verb is Qal. and not Hiph. as Ibn Ezra makes it, but he rightly explains the constr. as that of the verb act. with double accus. of the object (after the analogy of verbs of *covering*). The second accus., contrary to rule, is placed first; and not only so, but כַּצִּנָּה, which is in apposition with the second accus., is placed before instead of after it, so that there is a complete inversion of the usual order, which would be: תע' ר' כצ'

PSALM 6

THE first of the seven Penitential Psalms. (See Introduction, p. 24.)

In great peril from his enemies, and in great anguish of heart, David cries to God for mercy. In the malice of his enemies he sees the rod of God's chastisement; and therefore he makes his prayer to God for deliverance. The struggle has lasted so long, the grief is so bitter, that his health has given way, and he has been brought to the gates of the grave. But even whilst thus pouring out the anguish of his spirit, light and peace visit him, and he breaks forth into the joy of thanksgiving.

The Psalm is said to be a Psalm of David, and there is no reason to question this, although at the same time there is nothing in it to guide us to any peculiar circumstances of his life.

The Psalm falls into three strophes :—

I. (ver. 1—3) and II. (ver. 4—7) are both the outpouring of the heart in a cry for mercy, and in both it springs from the deep misery of the sufferer. But in II. this is dwelt upon more at length as a motive for deliverance.

III. The joyful assurance that already his prayer has been heard, and that all his enemies shall perish. Ver. 8—10.

Accordingly S. Schmid divides the Psalm into two parts, and says :—

"Preces hominis in angustia hostium et conscientiæ constituti : quam I. ut gravissimam describit et *deprecatur ;* ver. [2—8] 1—7. II. se auditum credens contra hostes gloriatur, ver. [9—11] 8—10."

[FOR THE PRECENTOR. UPON STRINGED INSTRUMENTS.[a] UPON THE OCTAVE.[b] A PSALM OF DAVID.]

1 JEHOVAH, in Thine anger rebuke me not ;
Neither in Thy hot displeasure chasten me.

1. ANGER .... DISPLEASURE. The prayer occurs again, in almost the same words, xxxviii. 1 [2]. All God's chastisements are not in anger. There is a fatherly correction of love. "As many as I love I rebuke and chasten," Rev. iii. 19. See also Ps. xciv. 12, cxviii. 17, 18 ; Prov. iii. 11, 12 ; and based upon this passage, Heb. xii. 3—11. Indeed the whole Book of Job is intended to correct the error that "God's chastisements are always an evidence of His displeasure." And the sufferings of Christ are a witness to the contrary ; for that "the Father loveth the Son" is eternally true.

Does the Psalmist then pray that God would chasten him indeed, but in love, not in anger? This is Luther's interpretation : "This he regards not, nay, will readily suffer that he be punished and chastened : but he begs that it may be done in mercy and goodness, not in anger and fury . . . he teaches us therefore that there are two rods of God ; one of mercy and goodness, another of anger and fury. Hence Jeremiah prays, chap. x. 24, 'O Lord, correct me, but with judgement ; not in Thine anger, lest Thou bring me to nothing.'" But though there is nothing against this view considered in itself, yet it does not harmonize with the context. David does not ask that the chastening may be a chastening of love, or that its severity may be mitigated, he asks that it may *altogether* cease. The chastisement has been so heavy, it has endured so long, and his own sense of sin is so grievous, that he begins to fear lest God should shut up His tender mercies in displeasure, and should even consume him in His wrath.

The meaning, says Calvin, is: "I

2 Be gracious unto me, O Jehovah, for I languish;[c]
Heal me, O Jehovah, for my bones are vexed.
3 My soul also is sore vexed;
But Thou, O Jehovah, how long?

4 Return, O Jehovah, deliver my soul:
O save me for Thy loving-kindness' sake.
5 For in death there is no remembrance of Thee:
In the unseen world[d] who shall give Thee thanks?

indeed confess that I deserve nothing but destruction: but because I could not endure the severity of Thy judgement, deal not with me after my deserts; yea rather, forgive the sins whereby I have provoked Thine anger against me."

2. MY BONES ARE VEXED, or "terrified." "Nec carnem nominat quæ tenerior est, sed ossium nomine intelligit præcipuum robur suum fuisse tremefactum."—*Calvin.*

3. MY SOUL. LXX. ἡ ψυχή μου ἐταράχθη σφόδρα, the words uttered by our Lord in John xii. 27.

BUT THOU, O JEHOVAH, HOW LONG? Deep and troubled emotion suffers him not to complete the sentence. Perhaps we may supply, "How long wilt Thou delay to have mercy upon me?" Cf. xc. 13. "Domine, quousque?" was Calvin's motto. The most intense grief in trouble, it is said, could never extort from him another word.

4. The beginning of this strophe is closely linked to the end of the last.

RETURN; for it seems to the sufferer as if God had been absent during his affliction. And there is no hope for him but in God. Therefore the repeated prayer, Do *Thou* be gracious unto me:—how long wilt *Thou* be absent? Return *Thou*, &c. And observe, not only "be gracious, *for I languish*," but "deliver me for *Thy loving-kindness' sake*." Any man may use the first argument: only one who has tasted that the Lord is gracious can use the last.

5. Exactly parallel to this is Hezekiah's language, Is. xxxviii. 18, "For the grave cannot praise Thee; Death cannot celebrate Thee; . . . The living, the living, he shall praise Thee." The argument here employed is no doubt characteristic of the Old Dispensation. They who then feared and loved God, nevertheless walked in shadows, and their hope was not yet full of immortality. Hence their earnest clinging to life, so different from St. Paul's "desire to depart," to which there is nothing parallel in the Old Testament. It was not that they dreaded annihilation, but rather a kind of disembodied existence apart from the Light of God's Presence. *Premature* death in particular seems to have been deprecated, as if it were a token of God's displeasure. "I said, O my God, take me not away in the midst of my days." So also Hezekiah prays, "Mine age is departed and is removed from me as a shepherd's tent: I have cut off like a weaver my life." As Calvin remarks, ". . . dicendum quod non simpliciter mortem sed iram Dei, et quidem non vulgarem, fuerit deprecatus." And further, the desire to continue in life is always connected with the desire to praise God. Cf. xxx. 9 [10], lxxxviii. 11—13, cxv. 17, and Is. xxxviii. 18, ff. The Old Testament saint pleaded with God for life, in order that that life might be consecrated to His service. And it is very touching to see how, with the weakness of man's heart trembling at dissolution, there mingles

6 I am weary with my groaning:
Every night make I my bed to swim,
I water my couch with my tears.
7 Mine eye wasteth away because of grief,
It waxeth old because of all mine adversaries.

8 Depart from me, all ye workers of iniquity,
For Jehovah hath heard the voice of my weeping;
9 Jehovah hath heard my supplication,
Jehovah will receive my prayer.
10 All mine enemies shall be ashamed and sore vexed;
They shall turn backward, they shall be ashamed suddenly.[c]

the child-like confidence which fears not to advance the plea that God's glory is concerned in granting its request.

"Through Christ not only has a change been wrought in men's *conceptions* of the unseen world, but a change has been partly wrought and partly made possible in the *condition* of the departed."—*Moll in Lange's Psalter*.

6, 7. A further description of his distress. The heart can make *all* known to God. Thoughts, and feelings, and acts that we should be ashamed to confess to our fellow men, we fear not to confess to Him. Nor is this exaggeration. "They who know only in some small degree," says Calvin, "what it is to wrestle with the fear of eternal death, will find in these words no exaggeration."

8—10. Mark the sudden change, as of sunrise upon night. Already the prayer and the weeping have been heard. Already Faith has triumphed. Already he can defy the enemies who have been maliciously anticipating his end, and tell them they shall be disappointed with a suddenness which only makes the disappointment more bitter.

8. WORKERS OF INIQUITY. See on v. 5.

9. HATH HEARD—WILL RECEIVE. The last is a consequence of the first, not a mere variation of tense. He *will* grant, for He *has* heard. The verb RECEIVE is used here in the sense of favourably accepting, as gifts, offerings, &c.

a See note on the Inscription of Ps. iv.

b עַל־הַשְּׁמִינִית. (Cf. Ps. xiii. 1, and 1 Chron. xv. 20, 21.) We read in this last passage of נבלים על עלמות (psalteries on Alamoth, Eng. Vers.) and כנרות על השמינית (harp on the Sheminith). Now if by Alamoth, maidens, we may understand "women's voices, *i.e.* sopranos," we may suppose "upon the Sheminith" or "octave," to mean that it was to be sung by men's voices.

c אֻמְלַל אָנִי. Many of the modern grammarians take this as Pret. Pul. 3d pers. Then in order to bring this into agreement with the pron. of the 1st pers. אָנִי, either (*a*) an ellipse of the relative is assumed: "one who languishes as I do,"—a construction which has no real parallel in such examples as הִנְנִי יִסַּד, Is. xxviii. 16 (see also Is. xxix. 14, xxxviii. 5), where הִנְנִי stands first, and the perf. as often takes the place of the future, which are commonly alleged as justifying it; or (*b*) the pron. אָנִי is supposed to stand for the afformative = אֻמְלַלְתִּי (Ges. § 44, 1 Not.). Ibn Ezra observes that R. Mosheh Hakkohen says that this is defective for אֻמְלַלְתִּי, as Lam. iii. 1, Is. xxxvii., and adopts the view himself. But the word can only be either an adj. = אֻמְלָל, Neh. iii. 34 (Qimchi, Ew. *Lehrb.*, § 157 *b*), or part. Palal, with loss of the מ for מְאֻמְלָל (which is not unusual in part. Pual), and the further shortening of Kametz into Pathach may readily be explained by the accentuation, the two words having, in fact, but one accent (*Merka mahpachatus*), as i. 3, ii. 7, though here, as in many other cases, the Makkeph is omitted.

[d] שְׁאֹל. The derivation of the word has been much disputed. The old etymology from שָׁאַל, *to ask*, as descriptive of the *insatiable* character of Hades (Prov. xxx. 15; comp. the *orcus rapax* of Catullus), is now generally abandoned. Most probably it is from a root שׁעל (with softening of the ע into א) not in use, the meaning of which is preserved in the noun שֹׁעַל, *the hollow palm*, מִשְׁעוֹל, *a hollow way*, so that Sheol would mean *the hollow* (subterranean) *place*. Cf. the German *Hölle* and *Höhle*, Gothic *halja*, English *hole* and *hell*. So Böttcher, Ewald, Maurer, Gesen. and others. Hupfeld, on the other hand, would connect the root with שׁוּל, שָׁלַל, שָׁלָה, נָשַׁל, in the sense of that which is *loose*, *lax*, *hanging down*, with the double notion of *sinking down* and *separation* (as in χάω, *hio*, χαλάω, &c.): hence in שְׁאֹל there is the notion both of *sinking*, *abyss*, *depth* (as in the poetic תַּחְתִּיּוֹת אֶרֶץ), and also that of *chasm*, *hollow*, *empty space*, as in the German *Hölle*, and in χάσμα, χάος. This view has been maintained at length by E. Scheid, *Cant. Hiskiæ*, p. 20 ff.; but I agree with Rödiger in Gesen. *Thes. s. v.* in thinking "nec minima quidem veri specie, quum *penduli*, *laxique* notio a notione inferni prorsus aliena sit."

[e] The Milel accent in the three last words makes the conclusion the more imposing. Observe, too, the play on the words *yashubhu*, *yebhoshu*.

PSALM 7

"SHALL not the Judge of all the earth do right?" might stand as the motto of this Psalm. In full reliance on God's righteousness, David appeals to Him to judge his cause. The righteous God cannot but save the righteous, and punish the wicked. This David believes to be the law of His moral government: and he applies it to his own case. His heart bears him witness that he has done no wrong to any man (ver. 3, 4), whereas his enemies have plotted unceasingly to take away his life. He therefore confidently anticipates his own deliverance and their overthrow (ver. 17, 18), as the manifestation of the righteous judgement of God.

According to the Inscription, this Psalm was written by David, and was occasioned by the words of Cush the Benjamite. There can be very little doubt that the Inscription in this instance preserves an ancient tradition. It is accepted by Ewald, as it is by the majority of critics, and the Psalm unquestionably bears every internal evidence of having been written by David. There is, however, more difficulty in fixing the precise circumstances under which he wrote it. Who Cush was we do not know. Some, as Thenius, would identify him with the Cushite (2 Sam. xviii., where the E. V. gives Cushi as a proper name), who brought the tidings of Absalom's death to the king. But the language of the Psalm does not harmonize with such a supposition. The Cushite was the bearer of heavy tidings, but there is no reason to suppose he was an enemy of David's, or he would not have been selected by Joab for such an errand. Others have conjectured that "Cush" is not a proper name, but merely a nickname or term of reproach, equivalent to "the black," "the blackamore," or "the negro," as describing, however, not the face, but the character. In this sense it has been applied to Shimei as the bitterest and most foul-mouthed of David's enemies. But the Psalm falls in far better with the persecution of Saul than with the flight from Absalom. Others, again, and in particular the Jewish commentators, think that the epithet designated Saul as the man of "black" heart. But this is not very probable; nor is it likely that David would have used such language as that of ver. 14—16 in reference to Saul. It is more probable that this Benjamite named Cush, belonging to Saul's tribe, was one of his adherents who took an active part against David, and was conspicuous among the calumniators of whom David complains to the king. His "words," it seems, were bitter and unscrupulous, words which kindled a fire of indignation in David's soul, and led him to repel the charges brought against him in the same eager and passionate way in which he protests his innocence to Saul.

The language is remarkably like the language which he addresses to Saul when he leaves the cave of Engedi. Compare, for instance, the words of ver. 3, 4:—

> If there be iniquity in my hands;
> If I have rewarded evil unto him that was at peace with me;
> Yea rather, I have rescued him that without cause is mine adversary:—

with his words in 1 Sam. xxiv. 11 [12], "Know thou and see that there is neither evil nor transgression in mine hand; and I have not sinned against thee; yet thou huntest my soul to take it;"—and with Saul's confession immediately afterwards (ver. 17 [18], "Thou art more righteous than I: for thou hast rewarded me good, whereas I have rewarded thee evil." "How forcible, read in this connection," it has been said, "is the singular reiteration in the narrative of the phrase 'my hand,' which occurs six times in four verses. The peculiarly abrupt introduction in ver. 4 of the clause 'I delivered him that without cause is mine enemy,' which completely dislocates the grammatical structure, is best accounted for by supposing that David's mind is still full of the temptation to stain his hand with Saul's blood, and is vividly conscious of the effort which he had made to overcome it. And the solemn invocation of destruction which he dares to address to Jehovah his God includes the familiar figure of himself as a fugitive before the hunters, which is found in the words already quoted, and which here as there stands in immediate connection with his assertion of clean hands." *

So again the solemn appeal to God's righteous judgement, the deep consciousness of his own integrity which was so fully admitted by Saul, are but the echo in the Psalm, only expressed in a lofty strain of poetry, of the same thought which is repeated with so much emphasis as he speaks to Saul on the hill-side: "Jehovah judge between me and thee, and Jehovah avenge me of thee: but mine hand shall not be upon thee. . . . Jehovah therefore be Judge, and judge between me and thee, and see and plead my cause, and do me justice at thy hand," ver. 12, 15 [13, 16].

We must look then to circumstances like those recorded in the 24th and 26th chapters of the First Book of Samuel, and to the reproaches of a Benjamite named Cush, a leading and unscrupulous partisan of Saul's, as having given occasion to the Psalm.

We have the following divisions :—

I. An Introduction, consisting (1) of an expression of confidence in God; and (2) of a prayer for deliverance from enemies. Ver. 1, 2.

II. A solemn protestation of innocence before God. Ver. 3—5.

III. An appeal to God as the righteous Judge of all the earth, to manifest in the most public manner (ver. 6, 7) His righteousness in

* Rev. A. Maclaren in *Sunday at Home* for 1871, p. 372, where the parallel is well worked out.

pronouncing sentence both upon the Psalmist himself (ver. 8) and upon his enemies (ver. 9.), with a confident assertion (ver. 10) as to the result. Ver. 6—10.

IV. A description of God's dealing with the wicked, (1) in the way of direct punishments, and (2) as leaving the wicked to be snared in his own devices. Ver. 11—16.

V. A short thanksgiving on review of the righteous judgement of God. Ver. 17.

[SHIGGAION [a] OF DAVID, WHICH HE SANG UNTO JEHOVAH, CONCERNING THE WORDS OF CUSH THE BENJAMITE.]

1 JEHOVAH, my God, in Thee have I found refuge.
Save me from all my pursuers, and deliver me!
2 Lest he tear my soul, like a lion,
Rending in pieces, while there is none to deliver.
3 Jehovah, my God, if I have done this;
If there be iniquity in my hands;
4 If I have rewarded evil unto him that was at peace with me:—
Yea rather I have rescued [b] him that without cause is mine adversary:—

1. With that word of Faith, Hope, and Love, "in Thee have I found refuge," David begins his prayer. Cf. xi. 1, xvi. 1, xxxi. 1, lxxi. 1. From that refuge, far safer than cave or rock or mountain fastness, he can watch his pursuers, thirsting for his blood.

MY PURSUERS. David being like a bird (xi. 1), "a partridge of the mountains," or like a roe or a gazelle chased by the lions.

2. The transition from the plural "pursuers," to the singular "lest he," &c. has been explained by the fact that some one of those enemies is prominently before the singer's mind. David was thinking, perhaps, of Saul, or of that Benjamite whose name appears in the Inscription. But such transitions are very common in Hebrew; often where no individual is meant the singular is used collectively, the many being now regarded as one. See on v. Note [h].

3. With a quick turn he protests passionately his innocence, his soul surging with emotion, his words broken by the vehemence of his feelings, as he thinks how unjustly he has been assailed. Again as in v. 1, "*my* God," IF I HAVE DONE THIS, *sc.* what follows, or rather "this thing that I am charged with." Under a deep sense of wrong, indignation choking him, he calls it "this," without stopping to explain. IF THERE BE INIQUITY. Comp. what David says to Saul, 1 Sam. xxiv. 12, xxvi. 18.

4. HIM THAT WAS AT PEACE WITH ME, cf. xli. 10, Jer. xxxviii. 22.

YEA RATHER, &c. The allusion may perhaps be to what is recorded 1 Sam. xxiv. 4—7.

5 Let the enemy pursue after [c] my soul and overtake (it);
Yea, let him tread down my life upon the earth,
And make my glory abide in the dust.—[Selah.]

6 Arise, O Jehovah, in Thine anger!
Lift up Thyself against the fierce wrath of mine adversaries;
Yea awake for me!—Thou hast commanded judgement—
7 And let the congregation of the people come about Thee,

5. The expressions may imply either the depth of humiliation and degradation, or absolute destruction.

MY GLORY may either mean (*a*) as in iv. 2 [3], Job xix. 9, "character, good name, honour, position," &c. and then to lay this in the dust will mean of course to degrade and to dishonour (as in many similar phrases, *e.g.* lxxiv. 7, lxxxix. 39, Job xvi. 15, xl. 13); or (*b*) as in xvi. 9, xxx. 12 [13], lvii. 8 [9], Gen. xlix. 6, "the soul" (so Ibn Ez.), as that which is noblest in man, that which most distinctly severs him from other creatures and links him to God,—a sense which here accords with the parallelism in the two previous members of the verse—and then THE DUST must mean "the grave," or "death," as in xxii. 15 [16], 29 [30]. The phrases "to tread down," "lay in the dust," may, however, still refer (Hengst. Hupf.) to a death of ignominy.

6—8. The rapid utterance of feeling has here again somewhat broken the poet's words. Hitherto he has protested his innocence; now in the full consciousness of that innocence he comes before the very judgement-seat of God, and demands the fullest and most public vindication. Then he sees as it were in a vision the judgement set: "Thou hast commanded judgement." Next, that sentence may be pronounced with due solemnity, he calls upon God to gather the nations round Him, and to seat Himself upon His judgement-throne. Lastly, he prays God, as the judge of all nations, to judge himself.

6. LIFT UP THYSELF, *i.e.* manifest Thyself in all Thy glory as the true and righteous Judge, cf. xciv. 2, Is. xxxiii. 10.

FIERCE WRATH. I have endeavoured by the epithet to express the plural as an intensive form, though it may also be used to denote the *many* acts in which the wrath was exhibited.

THOU HAST COMMANDED JUDGEMENT. I give this in accordance with the accents as an independent clause; but there may be an omission of the relative, "Thou who hast," &c. or of the casual conjunction, "Inasmuch as Thou hast," &c. The E. V. "Awake for me (to) the judgement (that) Thou hast commanded," takes the same view of the construction as the LXX., Syr., and Jerome. The "judgement" may either be generally that justice which God has ordained in His word,—Thou who art the source of justice, Thou who hast commanded men to practise justice, manifest that justice now; or it may refer to the particular act of judgement, mentioned in the next two verses.

7. Let there be a solemn, deliberate, and public vindication of my innocence. Mendelssohn renders freely:

"Versammle Völker um den Richterthron,
Und wende dich gen Himmel über sie."

And over it do Thou return on high.
8 Jehovah ministereth justice to the peoples;
Judge me, O Jehovah, according to my righteousness,
And according to my integrity be it done to me.[d]
9 O let the wickedness of the wicked come to an end,
And establish Thou the righteous!
For Thou that triest[e] the hearts and reins art a righteous God.
10 My shield is upon God,
Who saveth them that are upright of heart.

11 God is a righteous Judge,
And a God who is angry every day.
12 If (a man) will not turn, He whetteth His sword;
He hath bent His bow, and made it ready.

OVER IT, &c. God is represented as coming down to visit the earth, and to gather the nations before Him, and then as returning and sitting down above them on the judgement-seat.

The clause cannot mean that when God has delivered His judicial sentence, He is to return to His heavenly throne (Wordsworth). According to this explanation, the words "over it," *i.e.* the congregation of the people, are pointless, and moreover, the whole verse evidently describes the act of judgement, the crowd assembled to hear the sentence, and then the delivery of the sentence. The verb RETURN may mark that God *has resumed* the office of Judge, which for a time He had seemed to abandon; or it may be explained as above.

8. We may paraphrase: "O Thou who art the Judge of all *the world*, judge *me*."

MINISTERETH JUSTICE. The verb implies *ruling* as well as judging. For the difference between this verb and that in the next clause see note on lxxii. 2.

9. WICKEDNESS OF THE WICKED. Comp. 1 Sam. xxiv. 14, to which there may possibly be an allusion. The second clause of the verse does in fact (though not in form) give the reason for the prayer contained in the first clause. God is καρδιογνώστης, and being a God of knowledge is also a God of justice. He therefore both *can* and *will* requite each one according to his deserts.

10. A personal application to himself of the truth that God "establisheth the righteous." Lit. "My shield is upon God," *i.e.* my defence rests upon Him (as lxii. 7 [8], "my salvation rests upon God"), instead of the more usual form, "God is my shield."

11—16. God's dealing with the unrighteous vividly pourtrayed.

11. ANGRY, the same word as Nah. i. 2, 6.

12. God is long-suffering, but if a man (if the wicked) will not turn, He will punish him in his wickedness. He whetteth His sword (cf. Deut. xxxii. 41). The first members of this verse might however be rendered, in accordance with a well-known Hebrew idiom, "Surely He (*i.e.* Jehovah) will again whet His sword." And the first member of verse 13 will then be rendered: "He hath also prepared for Himself the weapons of death," &c.

13 Yea for that man He hath made ready the weapons of
death;
His arrows He maketh fiery (arrows).[f]
14 Lo, he travaileth with iniquity :—
He hath both conceived mischief and brought forth falsehood;
15 He hath digged a pit and hollowed it out;
And falleth[g] into the pitfall of his making.[h]
16 His mischief shall return upon his own head;
And his violent dealing shall come down upon his own
pate.
17 O let me give thanks to Jehovah according to His righteousness:
And let me sing praise to the Name of Jehovah Most
High.

13. YEA FOR (*i.e.* against) THAT MAN (the pron. is placed first as emphatic) He hath (already) aimed the instruments of death.

14. Not only the justice of God punishes, but the wickedness of the wicked effects his own destruction.

The three verbs, "he travaileth,—he hath conceived,—he hath brought forth," are not to be explained by an inversion of order in the first two. But the first verb (in the *fut.*) contains the general sentiment (strictly an aorist), which is then further broken up into two parts in the two perfects which follow. "He hath conceived mischief," "he hath brought forth falsehood," are the further extension of the first clause, "he travaileth with iniquity." Both the accents and the tenses point to this as the true interpretation.

15. HE HATH DIGGED A PIT, as a hunter to catch wild animals, but the loose treacherous soil gives way with him as he digs, or, in his haste to catch his prey, he does not notice the lightly-covered pitfall, and falls headlong into it.

16. Comp. 1 Sam. xxv. 39.

[a] שִׁגָּיוֹן, probably (from the root שׁגה, *errare*), a poem in *irregular* metre, a Dithyrambic Poem. "*Ode erratica, Dithyrambus*," Röd. Cf. Habak. iii. 1. The word is of the same form as הגיון, Higgaion, ix. 17, and Hupf. thinks of the same signification with substitution of שׁ for ה (שׁגה = הגה), so that it would be nothing more than "poem," "psalm" (as indeed the LXX. render it, ψαλμός). עַל־דִּבְרֵי may either mean *because of*, as in Deut. iv. 21, Jer. vii. 22, or literally, *on account of the words of*.

[b] ואחלצה צ׳ ר׳. The true interpretation of this clause is doubtful. It may be rendered: (1) "And (if) I have spoiled him that without cause," &c., in which case it forms one in the chain of suppositions which is denied; or (2) in a parenthesis: "Yea (rather) I have delivered him

that," &c., the clause then being antithetical to the two preceding. The objection to the first of these renderings is that the verb never occurs in the Piel in the sense of *spoiling*, but always in that of *delivering*. It is true it is found in that sense in the corresponding conjugation of the Syriac, and that the noun חֲלִיצָה means *exuviæ*. It is also true that the construction seems to flow more readily on this interpretation. On the other hand the sense is not very satisfactory: If I have rewarded evil to *my friend*, if I have spoiled him that *without cause is my adversary*. It is at least an anti-climax. On the whole, therefore, (2), which is the rendering of the Eng. Vers., and which is supported by the authority of Ibn Ezra and Qimchi among the ancients, and by such scholars as Ewald and Hupfeld among the moderns, is to be preferred.

Examples of similar parentheses with וְ, especially with the *fut. paragog.*, are to be found xl. 6, li. 18, lv. 13.

[c] יִרַדֹּף. A sort of hybrid form, half Kal. half Piel. The requirements of rhythm may possibly account for its introduction here. Or it may be a corrupted form יְרַדֵּף (like תִּמְלֹךְ, Jer. xxii. 5, יְצַחֶק, Gen. xxi. 6). See Gesen. § 114. 2; Ewald, § 224 *a*.

[d] עָלָי. We may either understand יְהִי, *sc.* "let it be done unto me:" or the expression may (like נַפְשִׁי עָלַי) = "my integrity *which is* in me," *quæ est penes me*.

[e] וּבֹחֵן. The sentence runs literally: "And a trier of the hearts and reins is the righteous God." This in fact gives the reason for the prayer and the hope expressed just before: so that the וְ is here equivalent to *for*, just as in the same participial construction, xxii. 29, lv. 20. We may, however, supply the pron. of the 2d person as virtually contained in the previous imperative, "For Thou that triest the hearts and reins art a righteous God:" or, "For Thou, O righteous God, triest," &c. Similar omissions of the pron. occur, of the 2d pers. in Hab. ii. 15, and of the 1st pers. in Hab. i. 5, in both of which cases it may be supplied from the suffix following. In the latter many would retain the 3d person.

[f] לְדֹלְקִים = זִקִּים (Lat. *malleoli*), arrows wrapped round with some inflammable material, which became ignited in their passage through the air, and set afire whatever they lighted upon. Sim. βέλη πεπυρωμένα. Eph. vi. 16.

[g] וַיִּפֹּל בְּשׁ׳ יִפְעָל. The verb as in ver. 13 [14]. Strictly a present: "which he is now in the act of making." But then we ought rather to read וְיִפֹּל, "and he shall fall." I have endeavoured to preserve in the translation something of the play upon sound in this passage.

[h] יִפְעָל. The change in tense is noticeable:—the act of preparing the arrows is described as going on = "whilst he makes his arrows fiery arrows." The succession of tenses in ver. 12, 13, is worthy of observation.

PSALM 8

This is the first of a number of Psalms which celebrate the praise of God in the phænomena of the natural world. The sun by day (Ps. xix.), the moon and the stars by night (Ps. viii.), the glory and the order of Creation (Ps. civ.), the terror of the thunder-storm and the earthquake (Ps. xxix.), are all dwelt upon in Hebrew verse, and are described with a force and animation, a magnificence of imagination and colouring, which have never been surpassed in the poetry of any nation.

But the Hebrew odes are never merely descriptive. There are pictures in them of extreme beauty and vividness, but the picture is never painted for its own sake. Nature is never regarded, whether in her aspect of terror or of grace, whether in her tumult or her repose, as an end in herself. The sense of God's presence of which the Psalmist is so profoundly conscious in his own spiritual life is that which gives its glory and its meaning to the natural world. There is a vivid realization of that presence as of a presence which fills the world, and from which there is no escape; there is a closeness to God, as of One who holds and compasses us about (Ps. cxxxix.), in the minds of the inspired minstrels of Israel, which, if it is characteristic of the Semitic races at large, is certainly in an emphatic degree characteristic of the Hebrews. The feeling lends its colouring to their poetry. Nature is full of God; Nature is the theatre of His glory. All admiration of Nature in a rightly tuned heart is a confession of that glory. To such a heart there can be no praise of Nature apart from the praise of God. All things are "of Him and through Him and to Him." The sun and the moon are His witnesses and heralds, the light is His robe, the clouds are His chariot, the thunder is His voice, the flashes of the lightning are His arrows and His spear. Apart from Him the universe is void and waste; He gives it its life and meaning.

This Eighth Psalm describes the impression produced on the heart of David as he gazed upon the heavens by night. In such a country as Palestine, in that clear Eastern atmosphere, "the moon and the stars" would appear with a splendour and a brilliancy of which we can scarcely conceive; and as he fixes his eyes upon them, awed and solemnized and yet attracted and inspired by the spectacle, he breaks forth into admiring acknowledgement of that God, who, as the

God of Israel, has set His glory so conspicuously in the heavens, that it is seen of all eyes and confessed even by the lisping tongues of children. They praise Him, and their scarcely articulate homage is a rebuke to wicked men who disregard or resist Him.

But as the Poet gazes on into the liquid depths of that starry sky there comes upon him with overwhelming force the sense of his own insignificance. In sight of all that vastness, before all that evidence of creative power, how insignificant is man! "What is man that Thou art mindful of him?" is the natural utterance of the heart—What is man, man in his frailty, his littleness, his sin? What in the sight of Him, who made those heavens and planted in them those glittering orbs? This is the first feeling, but it is immediately swallowed up in another,—the consciousness of man's true greatness, in nature all but Divine, of the seed-royal of the Second Adam, of highest lineage and dignity, crowned and sceptred as a king; "Thou hast put all things under his feet." This is the principal thought, not man's littleness, but his greatness. This subject is boldly but briefly handled, and then the Psalm is brought to a fitting close with the same ascription of praise with which it opened.

Nearly all critics are unanimous in regarding this as one of David's Psalms; there is more difference of opinion as to the time when it was composed. The Psalm furnishes us with no notes of time. But there are indications of another kind which may serve to guide us.

David, it may almost certainly be said, is still young; he has not yet been schooled by sorrow; he has not yielded to temptations which have darkened his heart; he has no personal enemies to contend with. The only enemies who for a moment cross his thought are the fierce and turbulent men who set themselves up against *God*, the revilers and contemners of His majesty, the men who *will not* behold His glory, plainly as it is manifested in Creation. It may be fanciful to see in the allusion to children and sucklings a reference to the youth of David, but there can be no doubt that the freshness of spirit, the joyousness of tone which pervade the Psalm, are such as would lead us naturally to associate it with his earlier years. It is undimmed by memories of sin, it bears no trace of struggle and anguish. There is a buoyant faith, there is the natural sense of wonder, there is joyful acknowledgement of God, there is the consciousness of man's high destiny as created in the image of God. The thought of man's royal prerogatives, of his kingly rule over creation, is no doubt derived from the early and simple record in the first chapter of Genesis, a record with which David must have been familiar. This Psalm has indeed been called the "lyric echo" of that chapter; a title, however, which might more aptly be given to the 104th Psalm. But this sovereignty of man is just one of those points on which, it has been truly remarked,* a high-souled youthful poet would most naturally dwell. There are touches in the Psalm which might even lead us to connect it with David's shepherd life. He may have written it while he was keeping "those few sheep in the wilderness," "far from men but near to God," whiling away the hours of his night-watch in contemplation of the heavens and in communion with his Maker. Nor do I see why such a supposition as to the origin of the Psalm should be described as "extremely improbable." † At the same time it must be admitted that the language of ver. 2 implies a larger acquaintance with the world than we can suppose David's life at Bethlehem to have furnished.

The conjecture that the Psalm was written after his combat with Goliath turns no doubt on a false interpretation of the Inscription, but it rests also partly on the contrast in ver. 2 between "children" and "the enemy." This reference, however, is scarcely now maintained by any critic of eminence.

One thing seems clear, that even if the Psalm were not written during David's shepherd life, it must at least have been written while the memory of that time was fresh in his heart, and before the bitter experience of his later years had bowed and saddened his spirit. Beyond this we cannot speak with anything like certainty.

The Messianic import of the Psalm is not of a direct kind. It is, however, necessarily implied in that mysterious relation of man to God and that kingship over the inferior creatures of which the Psalm speaks, for this rests upon the Incarnation. Man is what he is, because the Son of God has taken upon Him man's nature. Man is very near to God, higher than the angels, because the Christ is both God and Man. This is the profound truth on which the Messianic character of the Psalm depends. This truth is the key to its interpretation.

But it does not follow that David saw this distinctly. He takes what must in any case be the *religious* view of Creation, and of man's relation to God on the one hand, and to the inferior animals on the other. Some interpreters indeed have thought that David is describing, not man's actual position marred and broken by the Fall, but his original condition as created in the image of God. It is the ideal, it is the design and purpose of God, which for the moment hides from his sight the havoc and confusion which have been wrought

* By Mr. Maclaren, "Life of David in his Psalms," in *Sunday at Home* for 1871, p. 102.

† "Höchst unwahrscheinlich." Moll in Lange's *Bibelwerk*.

by sin, the broken sceptre and the discrowned king. Others, again, think that the whole Psalm is prophetic, or rather predictive. They conceive that it tells us what man shall be hereafter, redeemed and restored in the Second Adam to his rightful supremacy.

But the language of the Psalm, taken in its obvious sense, favours neither of these interpretations. David is manifestly speaking of the present. He sees the heavens witnessing for God; he sees man placed by God as ruler upon earth; he feels how high an honour has been put upon man; he marvels at God's grace and condescension. Man *is* king, however his authority may be questioned or defied.

When we turn to the New Testament, where verses of this Psalm are twice applied to Christ (besides our Lord's own quotation of ver. 2), we see at once the principle on which the quotations rest. It is precisely that which I have already laid down. The Incarnation explains it. In 1 Cor. xv. 27, St. Paul quotes with a slight change, using the third person instead of the second, the words of ver. 6, "Thou hast put all things under his feet," as describing accurately the complete subjection of the universe to Christ. The words may be true of man, but they are in their highest sense only true of Christ as the Great Head of mankind, and of man only in Him. Similarly the writer of the Epistle to the Hebrews (ii. 6—9) argues that the words "Thou hast put all things under his feet" have not yet been literally fulfilled of man, and declares that their proper fulfilment is to be seen only in Jesus, whom God had made "a little lower than the angels," * and had "crowned with glory and honour." He does

* That the quotation should be made so as to agree with the LXX. rather than the Hebrew is characteristic of the writer of the Epistle, and is in itself a matter of little moment; for as Calvin observes, "we know what liberty the Apostles allowed themselves in citing passages of Scripture; not indeed that they twisted them to a sense at variance with the true one, but because it was enough for them to indicate (*digito monstrare*) that their teaching was confirmed by the oracles of God. Wherefore, provided the main point was adhered to (*modo de summa re constaret*), they did not hesitate to alter a word here and there." But there is, as he points out, a greater difficulty than the mere substitution of "angels" for "God" in this quotation. For David is speaking of *man's greatness* as being little less than divine; the writer of the Epistle applies the passage to the *humiliation of Christ.* Now first, what is said of *man* is applied to *Christ*, because He is not only "the first-born of all creation," but also because He is the Second Head of the human race. All the riches of glory which the Father has bestowed upon Him in His human nature, He has bestowed on Him for our sakes. Out of His fulness we all receive. And if it be said that the exclamation of astonishment, "What is man that Thou art mindful of him?" cannot apply to Christ, the only-begotten Son of God, Calvin replies, that so far as the human nature of Christ is concerned, all that has been bestowed upon it has been bestowed freely, and that in this mirror the mercy of God is most brightly reflected, that a mortal man and a son of Adam is also

not make use of the Psalm as a direct prediction, but he shows that man's place in creation is his in Christ; his destiny as depicted in the Psalm is not, and cannot be, accomplished out of Christ. He is the true Lord of all. In Him man reigns, in Him man shall yet be restored to his rightful lordship, and shall really and completely be in the new world of Redemption (ἡ οἰκουμένη ἡ μέλλουσα) what now he is but very imperfectly, God's vicegerent, ruling a subject creation in peace and harmony and love.

[FOR THE PRECENTOR. UPON THE GITTITH.[a] A PSALM OF DAVID.]

1 JEHOVAH our Lord, how excellent is Thy name in all the earth,
Who hast set[b] Thy glory above the heavens!
2 Out of the mouth of children and sucklings Thou hast founded strength,

1. OUR LORD. For the first time in the Book of Psalms the personal feeling is lost sight of in the national. Jehovah is not the God of David only, but of Israel: fitting prelude to a Psalm which forgets the individual in the contemplation of God's glory in the universe. The thought which here appears is, in fact, the thought which is the key to the Book of Genesis, and indeed to the whole history of the Old Testament. The God who makes Himself known to Israel by His Name Jehovah, as their Redeemer, is the God who created the heavens and laid the foundations of the earth.

2. CHILDREN, not "babes," as the

---

the only Son of God, and the Lord of glory and the Head of the angels. As to the other point, that it is the *humiliation* and not the *greatness* which forms the point of the quotation in Heb. ii. 7, this, Calvin remarks, "is not an interpretation, but the writer turns to his own purpose (*ad suum institutum deflectit*) κατ' ἐπεξεργασίαν, what had been said in a different sense. In like manner St. Paul deals, in Rom. x. 6, with the words of Moses in Deut. xxx. 22. The Apostle therefore did not merely have an eye to David's meaning, but, in allusion to the two ideas of *humiliation* and *glory*, referred the one to the death, the other to the resurrection of Christ. Similarly, in quoting Ps. lxviii. 19 in Eph. iv. 8, St. Paul does not so much give an interpretation as with a pious turn apply the passage to the person of Christ (*pia deflexione ad Christi personam accommodat*)."

Still it is important to bear in mind that the writer of the Epistle does not set aside the reference to *man* in the Psalm. On the contrary he admits it, and bases his argument upon it. The Psalm speaks of man, tells us of the great things God had done for him, putting a crown on his head and a sceptre in his hand, and making him little less than the angels in glory and power. Now the author of the Epistle says, "All this has never been fully accomplished in man hitherto: the great idea and purpose of his creation has never been fulfilled but in the One Perfect Man, in Him who first stooped to put on human nature, and then was raised in that nature to lordship over all creation."

Because of Thine adversaries,
That Thou mightest still the enemy and the avenger.
3 When I see Thy heavens, the work of Thy fingers,
The moon and the stars which Thou hast ordained ;—
4 What is man, that Thou art mindful of him,
And the son of man, that Thou visitest him ?

E.V.; they are more advanced in age than the SUCKLINGS ; so that there is a kind of climax, " not children only, but sucklings." As Hebrew mothers did not wean their children till they were two, or even three years old, this is no mere figure of speech.

THOU HAST FOUNDED STRENGTH, *i.e.* Thou hast built up a bulwark, a defence, &c. The LXX. *κατηρτίσω αἶνον*, and Jerome, *fecisti laudem*, are clearly wrong : Aq. rightly, *ἐθεμελίωσας κράτος*. Cf. Jer. xvi. 19. Reuss, who renders "*sur la voix des enfants . . . tu fondes ta puissance*," notices the fine poetic effect of the paradox that God has established His power on that which is weakest.

When expositors introduce here the teaching of 1 Cor. i. 26-28, they depart from the simple language of the Psalm. David speaks *literally* of children. And so our Lord Himself applies the words, Matt. xxi. 16. Even the faith of a little child is bulwark enough against the folly of men of corrupt heart and perverted intellect, who can look upon the heavens and see there the glory of Newton or Laplace, but not the glory of God.

THE ENEMY AND THE AVENGER occurs again, xliv. 17. "Avenger" in modern English hardly conveys the sense of the Hebrew word ; it denotes " one who thirsts for or breathes revenge, one who is swift to avenge his own quarrel ;" *der Rache schnaubt*, as Mendelssohn renders it.

3. David has spoken generally of the glory of Jehovah, as seen in the earth and the heavens, and which is so conspicuous that even children can discern and acknowledge it ; he now passes to a particular instance of its manifestation, and one of the most impressive, and draws thence the lesson of God's marvellous condescension.

WHEN I SEE, *i,e.* "as often as I see" . . . (then the thought arises within me, or then I say) "What is man ?" &c. Cf. cxliv. 3, and for similar expressions as denoting a like sense of unworthiness, 1 Sam. xviii. 18, 2 Sam. vii. 18.

4. WHAT IS MAN. The first feeling is an overpowering sense of man's insignificance in presence of the vastness and splendour, the mysterious depth, and the exceeding glory of the heavens, as seen at night. " The vault of the sky arched at a vast and unknown distance over our heads ; the stars apparently infinite in number, each keeping its appointed place and course, and seeming to belong to a wide system of things which has no relation to the earth ; while man is but one among many millions of the earth's inhabitants ;—all this makes the contemplative spectator feel how exceedingly small a portion of the universe he is ; how little he must be in the eyes of an Intelligence which can embrace the whole." Add to this revelation of darkness the revelation of silence ; the man is alone ; the stir and noise of his own works, which in the light of day filled and absorbed him, are hushed and buried in darkness ; his importance is gone :—and "every person in every age and country will recognise as irresistibly natural the train of thought expressed by the Hebrew Psalmist." It is needless to remark, if this be the feeling of the untaught mind, how infinitely

5 And Thou hast made him little lower[c] than God,
And crownest him with glory and honour.
6 Thou makest him to have dominion over the works of Thy hands:
Thou hast put all things under his feet;

the impression must be deepened in one who looks upon the universe with the aid of astronomical discovery and theory. Such a person may well feel "lost, confounded, overwhelmed, with the vastness of the spectacle" . . . "the distance between him and the Creator appears to be increased beyond measure by this disclosure. It seems as if a single individual could have no chance and no claim for the regard of the Ruler of the whole." (Whewell, *Astr.*, &c. Bk. iii. ch. iii.)

MAN. The Hebrew word denotes man in his weakness and frailty (see ix. 19, 20), as in the next member SON OF MAN (son of Adam) refers also to his earthly nature as formed out of the ground.

5. But through God's marvellous condescension how *great* is man, little less than Divine in nature, and lord of all creation.

AND THOU HAST, &c., or, more freely, "And that having made him little less than divine, Thou crownest him," &c.

LITTLE LOWER, lit. "And Thou hast made him to want but little (or, to come short but little) of God."

LITTLE, *i.e.* in *degree*—whereas the βραχύ τι of the LXX. as applied to Christ may (possibly, though by no means certainly; see Alford on Heb. ii. 7) refer to *time*. "Thou madest Him for a little time lower," &c.

LITTLE LOWER THAN GOD, or "little less than divine." The LXX. ἠλάττωσας αὐτὸν βραχύ τι παρ' ἀγγέλους. And so of course in the Epistle to the Hebrews, which quotes the Alexandrian text. So also the Targum and the Jewish interpreters generally. And so the E.V. "than the angels." But there is obviously a reference in ver. 6 to Gen. i. 26, and therefore here doubtless an allusion to the creation of man in the image of God. Besides, the word Elohim (God) nowhere occurs in the sense of *angels*. The phrase is *sons of God*. On the other hand, Elohim expresses the abstract idea of Godhead, Divine nature, and so (without the article) that which is godlike, superhuman, Zech. xii. 8, and 1 Sam. xxviii. 13. Hence Hengst translates rightly: "Wenig unter göttlichen Stand erniedrigst du ihn." Cf. Cicero's "Homo mortalis Deus."

GLORY AND HONOUR, a common expression for the Divine majesty, and thence for the kingly as a reflection of the Divine. The former word etymologically means dignity, as that which is *weighty;* the latter represents the external show and splendour.

"Equidem non dubito," says Calvin, "quin præclaras dotes commendet, quæ declarent homines ad imaginem Dei formatos esse, et creatos ad spem beatæ vitæ et immortalis. Nam quod ratione præditi sunt, qua discernant inter bonum et malum, quod illis inditum est religionis semen, quod mutua est inter eos communicatio, sacris quibusdam vinculis astricta, quod inter eos viget honesti respectus et pudor, et legum moderatio; hæc non obscura sunt summæ et cœlestis sapientiæ signa."

6. Man is a king. God has put a crown upon his head, and not only so, but has given him a territory and subjects. "All things under his feet," with evident reference to the "let them have dominion" of Gen. i. 26. What David means by "all things" is then explained—beasts, birds, and fishes, which are in the same manner enumerated in Gen. i.

7 Sheep[d] and oxen, all of them,
Yea, and the beasts of the field,
8 The fowls of heaven and the fishes of the sea,
(And whatsoever) passeth[e] through the paths of the
seas.
9 Jehovah our Lord,
How excellent is Thy name in all the earth!

St. Paul, however, extends the meaning of the "all things" far beyond this. Jesus, as the true Lord of all, shall have a universal dominion. He must reign till He have put all enemies under His feet. But as yet we see not all things put under Him. Sin, and death, and hell are up in arms against Him, and these are yet to be subdued. Death, says the Apostle, is the last enemy which shall be destroyed. It is evident, then, that David's "all things" and Paul's "all things" are not the same. The one is thinking of the visible world, the other of the invisible. The one is praising God for His goodness to man in making him lord over beasts, and birds, and fishes; the other is thinking of a conflict with principalities and powers, which Christ conquers and which man can only conquer in Christ. The one speaks of that which is, the other of that which is to come.

9. The Psalm closes with the same expression of loving admiration with which it opened, but with added emphasis after the singer has told the tale of God's goodness to man: just as the repetition of a passage in music falls more sensibly on the ear, and touches the heart with quicker emotions, than the same passage when it first occurs.

A thousand years later other shepherds were keeping watch over their flocks by night on the same hills of Bethlehem, while the same stars looked down upon them from heaven. But a brighter glory than the glory of the stars shone round about them; and they knew better than David himself the meaning of David's words, "Lord, what is man that Thou art mindful of him?" For to them it was said by the angel, "Unto you is born this day, in the city of David, a Saviour, which is Christ the Lord."

---

[a] UPON THE GITTITH. The same inscription, lxxxi. lxxxiv. גִּתִּית (in form a fem. adj. from גַּת Gath, the well-known Philistine city of that name), either an *instrument*, which took its name from the city (so Chald.), as there was an Egyptian flute, and a Doric lyre; or a kind of measure or melody (as the Greeks had Lydian, Dorian, &c.).

[b] The word תְּנָה is very perplexing. (1) As it stands it can only be the imperat. of the verb נתן. And this would compel us to translate: "Which glory of Thine do Thou set in the heavens" (as Gesen. does). But this is against the whole scope of the Psalm. God's glory *is* in the heavens; David *sees it there*, and does not call upon God to make it manifest.

Kay retains the imperat. and says in his note: "*Lit.* 'who—oh set Thou;' or, 'whereas—oh set Thou.'" But this does not seem to justify his rendering in the text: "Who mightest have set Thy grandeur upon the heavens." (2) According to Delitzsch and others, תְּנָה is an irregular form of the inf. constr. after the analogy of רְדָה, Gen. xlvi. 3, verbs פ״נ and פ״י having a certain symmetry of formation. The rendering would then be: "Thou, the setting of whose glory is above the heavens." But the instance quoted is a solitary one, and, as Hupfeld remarks, the prep. accounts for the alteration there: מֵרְדָה instead of מֵרֶדֶת, with the usual interchange of trochaic and iambic forms, according to the requirements of the rhythm. (3) Others again, as Ewald, suppose תְּנָה to be a defective form for תָּנָה, and render: "Thou whose glory *is extended*," &c., תנה being supposed to be kindred with תנן, and the Indo-Germ. root *tan*, whence *τείνω*, *tendere*, &c. The root however does not occur in this sense, but in the sense *to sing*, *to praise*; whence it has been proposed to read תֻּנָּה, (Pual), "whose glory is praised." Other explanations are still less satisfactory. (4) Only one thing remains, viz. to suppose a corruption of the text, and read נָתַתָּה. This is the usual phrase, נָתַן הוֹד עַל. The older versions are divided: Chald. דיהבתא, Syr. ܕܝܗܒܬ, *qui dedisti*. Symm. ὃς ἔταξας. Jerome, "Qui posuisti gloriam tuam super cælos." LXX. ὅτι ἐπήρθη ἡ μεγαλοπρέπειά σου. Vulg. "Quoniam elevata est magnificentia tua." The Arab. follows the LXX. in giving the passive. The choice therefore seems to lie between (3) and (4). In Zunz's Bible the construction is carried on into the next verse: "Du, dessen Glanz über den Himmeln man verkündet, Hast aus dem Munde der Kinder und Saüglinge dir Sieg gegründet," &c. In the Arab. the construction is similar.

[c] וַתְּחַסְּרֵהוּ. The change in tense here (fut. consec.) takes us back to the original act, the creation of man, but only so as to mark that the Divine act abides in force. Hence we have 6 *a* perfect (fut. with וְ consec.), 6 *b* and 7 *a* present, 7 *b* perfect. Throughout David speaks of what man is in the present, though with a glance at the first creation. Hupf. was certainly wrong when in his 1st Ed. he translated all the verbs in ver. 5—7 as *preterites*, and supposed the Psalmist to be referring throughout to the original creation of man. In his 2nd Edition he has corrected this, and renders the tenses as past and present respectively.

[d] The language in ver. 7, 8 is highly poetical. צֹנֶה instead of the prosaic צאן, אֲלָפִים instead of בָּקָר, בַּהֲמוֹת שָׂדָי instead of חַיַּת הָאָרֶץ, and שָׂדָי instead of שָׂדֶה. Even צִפּוֹר שׁ׳ is instead of the more common עוֹף הַשׁ׳.

[e] עֹבֵר. The part. *sing.*, in apposition therefore (as a sort of neuter collective), not in agreement with דגי ה׳. So LXX. τὰ διαπορευόμενα. Œth. *quicquid* ambulat. "The paths of the seas," cf. the Homeric ὑγρὰ κέλευθα.

PSALM 9

A THANKSGIVING to God, the righteous Judge, who punishes the wicked and defends the cause of the oppressed. Throughout, with the exception of verse 13 (see note there), the Psalm is one continued strain of triumph. Hence, by many it has been regarded as a song of victory, composed perhaps by David at the conclusion of the Syro-Ammonite war, or after one of his victories over the Philistines.

From the times of the LXX. this Psalm has often been considered as forming one poem with the Psalm immediately following. This has arisen probably from the fact that the Tenth Psalm has no superscription, an uncommon thing in the First Book, as well as from the alphabetical arrangement, partially at least discernible in both Psalms, and certain phrases and turns of expression found in both and not found elsewhere. (See Critical Notes.) But this last circumstance only proves that the two Psalms are to be referred to the same author, not that they originally constituted one poem. And the alphabetical arrangement is exceedingly imperfect, especially in the Tenth Psalm; nor does it properly complete the defective portion of Psalm ix. Whereas, if we look to the general character of the two,—the first, all triumph and hope; the last, all prayer against the deeds of violence and blood, which the poet mourns over,—the Hebrew division must certainly be allowed to have much in its favour.

The strophical arrangement is as follows :—

I. (א) Resolve to praise Jehovah. Ver. 1, 2.

II. (ה, ג, ב) Reason for this : viz. His righteousness as manifested (*a*) personally. Ver. 3, 4. (*b*) generally. Ver. 5, 6.

III. (ו) Moreover, Jehovah is the only true and everlasting Judge (ver. 7, 8), and therefore not only the destroyer of the wicked, but the fortress of those that trust in Him. Ver. 9, 10.

IV. (ז) An exhortation to praise Jehovah because of this His righteousness. Ver. 11, 12.

V. (ח) Prayer that this righteousness may be manifested to the singer himself personally. Ver. 13, 14.

VI. (ט) The destruction of the nations, by being taken in their own devices, a witness to God's righteousness. Ver, 15, 16.

VII. (י) Further amplification of this destruction as contrasted with the hope of the poor. Ver. 17, 18.

VIII. (ק) A prayer that God would yet again declare the majesty of His righteousness, as He had already done in times past. Ver. 19, 20.

[FOR THE PRECENTOR. TO THE TUNE "DEATH OF THE SON."[a] A PSALM OF DAVID.]

א 1 I WILL give thanks unto Jehovah with my whole heart,
I will tell of all Thy wonderful works;
2 I will be glad and exult in Thee,
I will sing to Thy Name, O Thou Most High;

ב 3 Because[b] mine enemies are turned backward,
(Because) they stumble and perish at Thy presence.
4 For Thou hast maintained my right and my cause,
Thou hast sat down on (the) throne, a righteous Judge.
ג 5 Thou hast rebuked (the) nations, Thou hast destroyed the wicked;
Their name hast Thou blotted out for ever and ever.
ה 6 The enemy is cut off,—they are perpetual ruins;
And cities which Thou hast rooted out,—the very memorial of them is perished.

1, 2. In this first strophe each line begins with the first letter of the alphabet (א).

2. SING, rendered in our P.B.V. "sing psalms" (E.V. "sing praises"). The verb is from the same root as the noun *mizmor*, "psalm," and means both "to sing" and "to play."

4. MAINTAINED MY RIGHT, lit. "executed my judgement."

6. THE ENEMY IS CUT OFF. There can be no doubt that the sing. noun is here to be regarded as a collective, and so taken with the plural verb, cf. Is. xvi. 4, Prov. xxviii. 1, &c., and for the noun with art. preceding the verb as here, Judg. xx. 37. The construction is the same in that much misquoted and misinterpreted passage, Hag. ii. 7, "And the desirable things," *i.e.* delights, treasures, &c. (noun collect. sing.), "of all nations shall come," *i.e.* into the temple (verb plural). It is quite impossible, without doing violence to the plainest rules of grammar, to interpret that passage of the Messiah. The fact that the verb is in the plural settles the question. Besides, the context (v. 8), "Mine is the silver, and Mine the gold," &c. shows what the desirable things are.

THEY ARE RUINS; or rather, perhaps, SO AS TO BECOME RUINS FOR EVER, these words being a further predicate, enlarging the

ו 7 And Jehovah sitteth (as King) for ever,
He hath prepared His throne for judgement :
8 And He will judge the world in righteousness,
He will minister justice to the peoples in uprightness,
9 That so Jehovah may be a high tower to them that are crushed,[c]
A high tower in times of trouble.
10 And they that know Thy Name shall trust in Thee,
Because Thou hast not forsaken them that seek Thee, O Jehovah.

ז 11 Sing ye to Jehovah, who dwelleth in Zion,
Declare among the peoples His doings ;
12 For He that requireth blood remembereth them,
He hath not forgotten the cry of the afflicted.[d]

idea contained in the verb "cut off." May they not, however, be a predicate by anticipation of the sentence following?

THE VERY MEMORIAL, lit. "their memorial is perished—(even) they themselves." The pron. is thus repeated in order to produce the greatest possible emphasis (exactly parallel are Num. xiv. 32, Prov. xxiii. 15; see also 1 Sam. xx. 42, Prov. xxii. 19, Ezek. xxxiv. 11, Hag. i. 4). The antithesis which accounts for this emphasis is to be found in the following verse: "The enemy has been utterly annihilated whilst Jehovah remains King for ever."

8. HE (emphatically) and not any human judge: the world shall yet see a rule of *righteousness*.

JUDGE . . . MINISTER JUSTICE. On the difference between the two words, of which the latter is the more formal and technical, see note on lxxii. 2.

9. THAT SO, *i.e.* by virtue of His righteous exercise of judgement. MAY BE, or rather MAY BECOME, *i.e.* "prove Himself to be" a place of refuge and security.

10. WHO KNOW THY NAME. See notes on i. 6, v. 11. THEM THAT SEEK THEE, not to be paraphrased coldly, that honour Thee, worship Thee, &c. They who seek *God* seek *Him* for Himself; not like the worshippers of heathen deities, who ask for other things of their gods—wealth, honour, power, &c.

11. Jehovah dwells in Zion. There is the visible seat of His dominion—but that dominion extends to the whole earth—therefore "publish among the nations His doings." Jehovah is "the Dweller in Zion," since the ark was brought thither, lxxvii. 3.

12. REQUIRETH, or, "maketh inquisition for blood" (E.V.), *i.e.* "demandeth satisfaction for bloodshed." This is God's character, as opposed to the scoff of the wicked, "He *requireth* not," x. 4, 13 (where the same verb is used). Like the "Goël haddâm," the next of kin, who was bound to avenge the murder of his kinsman, so God *calls* the murderer *to account*, *requires satisfaction* at his hand, Gen. ix. 5, Deut. xviii. 19, and in a spiritual sense, Ezek. xxxiii. 6, 8, xxxiv. 10.

THEM, *i.e.* "the afflicted," in the next clause, the pronoun being placed first emphatically.

THE AFFLICTED. This seems at

ח 13 Be gracious [e] unto me, O Jehovah,
See mine affliction (which I suffer) from them that hate me,
O Thou that liftest me up from the gates of Death,
14 That so I may tell all Thy praise [f] in the gates of the daughter of Zion,
That I may exult in Thy saving help.

ט 15 The nations have sunk down in the pit that they made,
In the net which [g] they hid is their own foot taken.
16 Jehovah hath made Himself known, He hath executed judgement ;
In the work of his own hands is the wicked snared.[h]
[Higgaion—Selah.]

י 17 The wicked must return to the unseen world,
(Even) all the nations that forget God.
כ 18 For not for ever shall the poor be forgotten ;
The hope of the afflicted shall not perish eternally.

least the primary notion of the word and its kindred form, though they acquire also a moral signification, "the meek, the humble." The *afflicted* in the first instance would be the faithful part of the nation persecuted and oppressed by the ungodly and the powerful, and (2) the nation itself, trodden down by foreign tyrants. In either case it is they who through this very discipline learn meekness, submission, resignation, who "in patience possess their souls." In scarcely any instance is the primary meaning altogether in abeyance. In Num. xii. 3, where our Version has "Now the man Moses was very *meek*," &c. the other rendering, *afflicted*, is certainly more in harmony with the context. (See also Num. xi. 11—15, Deut. i. 12.) And so Luther: "Der Mann war *geplagt* vor allen Menschen."

13, 14. These two verses, according to Delitzsch, contain the cry of the afflicted. If we take them as the prayer of the singer himself, they disturb, he thinks, the unity of the Psalm, and interfere awkwardly with its general strain of triumph. But this sudden change of feeling is not uncommon in the Psalms, and the thought of God as the avenger of all the oppressed, naturally drew forth the prayer that He would look graciously upon the Psalmist himself.

14. IN THE GATES, &c. As the most public place of concourse, this being in the East, what the ἀγορά was to the Greeks, and the *forum* to the Romans.

17. MUST RETURN. Not "*be turned*," as E. V. The Biblical idea is that of a returning to the dust, taken from the original passage in Gen. iii. 19. Cf. Job xxx. 23, of a return to Sheol (*i.e.* Hades, the unseen world), as here and Ps. xc. 3: "Thou makest man return to destruction," expres-

19 Arise, O Jehovah, let not mortal man be strong,
Let the nations be judged in Thy sight.
20 Put them in fear,[i] O Jehovah ;
Let the nations know that they are but mortal men.
[Selah.]

sions only to be explained by the dimness which then hung over the grave and the life beyond it. The meaning is, that even now, before the eyes of men, God's righteousness shall be seen in cutting off the wicked by a sudden and premature end, and helping and exalting the righteous.

THE UNSEEN WORLD. E. V. "hell," which, now that the word has lost its original meaning and is used exclusively of the place of torment, is quite misleading.

19. ARISE. A solemn appeal to God to show Himself to be that which He is,—the Judge of the earth, with reference perhaps to Num. x. 35. Cf. Ps. iii. 8 ; vii. 7.

(1.) The following is a list of certain turns of expression characteristic of this and the next Psalm : the very peculiar phrase לְעִתּוֹת בַּצָּרָה, "in times of trouble," ix. [10] (see note), x. 1 ; דָּךְ, "the crushed," ix. 9 [10], x. 18 (only occurring besides lxxiv. 21) ; אֱנוֹשׁ (in this special sense), "mortal men," 19, 20 [20, 21], x. 18 ; שָׁכַח with עֲנָוִים, ix. [13], [19], x. 12, with לָנֶצַח, ix. [19], x. 11 ; זוּ, ix. [16], x. 2 ; עוֹלָם וָעֶד, ix. [6], x. 16 ; קוּמָה, ix. [20], x. 12 (concluding both Psalms). Both Psalms end with the same prayer against *weak* (*mortal*) *men ;* both anticipate the judgement and overthrow of the (heathen) nations, יִשָּׁפְטוּ גוֹיִם, ix. 19 [20], אָבְדוּ גוֹיִם, x. 16.

(2.) As regards the alphabetical arrangement it is exceedingly irregular. Ver. [2, 3] begin with א ; ver. [4] with ב ; ver. [6] with ג ; the letter ד is wanting, and ver. [7] begins with ה ; we have then four verses beginning with ו, and not till ver. [12] do we find ז ; ver. [14] ח : ver. [16] ט ; ver. [18] י ; ver. [19] כ. The alphabetical order ceases here, and does not reappear, unless the ל in x. 1 is part of the alphabetical arrangement, till ver. 12 of the next Psalm, where (the six intervening letters having been left out) we find ק, ר, ש, ת, concluding the Psalm.

An ingenious attempt to restore the alphabetical arrangement throughout has been made by Miss Evans, a learned lady, lately deceased.

[a] The title has been much discussed, but with little satisfactory result. The older Jewish commentators found in לַבֵּן a proper name. According to Qimchi, who adopts the view of his father Jos. Qimchi, the subject of the Psalm is Goliath, and the name of the author is one *Bên*, the Levitical singer mentioned 1 Chron. xv. 18. Others suppose Absalom to be meant, and render it "On the death of the Son." But it is better to take the prep. עַל in its usual meaning in such cases, as denoting "after the manner of ;" and the words which follow, as indicating some other poem beginning "Die for the son," or "Death of the son," to the music of which this was to be set.

[b] The older Versions, without exception, take the prep בְּ here as a prep. of *time*, = "when" or "whilst (*i.e.* now that) mine enemies," &c.; the Anglo-Saxon being the first, so far as I know, which takes it in a causative sense, "Forðam ðu gewhyrfdest," &c., Because, &c. But in any case this verse is connected immediately with the preceding, and clause (*b*) continues the construction in clause (*a*), the finite verb as usual taking the place of the inf. with the prep. (Ges. § 129, Rem. 2). Perhaps the temporal and causative meanings of the prep. may both be combined, as in the Lat. abl. absol.

[c] דַּךְ, lit. one who is crushed to powder (*r.* דכך = דכא, דקק). In בַּצָּרָה. the ב is not servile as Ges. asserts, but it is one word, from *r.* בצר, *coercuit*, formed from the Piel, as בַּקָּשָׁה from בִּקֵּשׁ, קַלָּסָה, &c. Literally it means therefore "the state of being shut up, cut off from resources," &c., and is kindred with בַּצֹּרֶת (Jer. xvii. 8), "drought," *cohibitio*, sc. *pluviæ*. Ewald would give the same meaning here.

[d] עֲנָוִים. So the Q'ri, as correction of the K'thibh עֲנִיִּים. Just the contrary ver. 19. See also x. 12. These seem quite arbitrary corrections. Generally it is supposed that עָנִי refers to external condition, "one who is bowed down, *i.e.* oppressed, afflicted;" עָנָו, to the inner spirit, "one who is meek, gentle," &c. (ταπεινός, πραΰς). But this distinction rests chiefly on the fact that the abstr. עֲנָוָה means "meekness," and that in the Targums עַנְיָא (= עָנִי) means "afflicted;" and עִנְוָן (= עָנָו) "meek." It is not clearly established by Biblical usage, for it is often impossible to say in the use of either word which meaning was uppermost in the writer's mind; the one passes indeed readily into the other, the afflicted being also the lowly of heart. (See more on these words in Hupfeld's note.)

[e] חָנְנֵנִי, an unusual form for חָנֵּנִי. According to another reading חַנְנֵנִי, which was the only reading known to Qimchi, who, however, makes it wrongly imper. Piel. It is imper. Kal from an intr. form חָנֵן.

[f] תהלתיך, a sing. noun with plur. suffix (as Ezek. xxxv. 11, שִׂנְאָתֶיךָ, and xvi. 51, 55, 61, אֲחוֹתַיִךְ; see also Is. xlvii. 13), but apparently a Massoretic freak, unless as Hitz. (Prov. vi. 3) suggests, the י was intended in the absence of vowels to mark the pausal forms of the noun with Segol. Qimchi maintains that this is a masc. plur., תהלתים, instead of the fem. The Cambridge MS. Add. 465 has simply תהלתך although the scribe had originally written a י. It is his own correction, as if he saw his mistake.

[g] זוּ, the old demonstrative form here used as a relative.

[h] נוֹקֵשׁ is clearly the part. Kal from a *r.* נקשׁ, *not* a Niph. for נוֹקַשׁ as if from יקשׁ.

[i] מורה, apparently incorrectly written for מורא, "fear," or perhaps a "terrible example." The LXX., Syr., and Vulg. seem to have read מוֹרֶה, and render accordingly, "set a teacher or master over them."

[k] אֱנוֹשׁ, used here and in the preceding verse to denote man in his frailty and impotence; hence the oxymoron, ver. 20, אַל יָעֹז אֱנוֹשׁ, "let not *weak* man carry himself as if he were *strong*."

PSALM 10

THE Psalmist calls upon God to chastise the unbridled insolence and scorn of the wicked. These have reached such a pitch, that it seems as if God winked at evil. Men are not only doing wickedness, but boasting of their wickedness, and finding that justice does not overtake them, are acting as if in the conviction that there is no God. The prosperity (ver. 5), security (ver. 6), insolence (ver. 4, 11), deceit (ver. 7), and violence (ver. 8—10) of these despisers of God is vividly pourtrayed. The Psalm concludes with the triumphant assertion of faith, that despite all seeming disorders, Jehovah *is* King, and that He does hear and answer the cry of the oppressed.

It is impossible to say to what period of Jewish history the Psalm is to be referred. The state of society which it supposes is peculiar. The violent oppressors belonged apparently to heathen nations, who had not yet been finally driven out of the land, but whose speedy destruction the poet anticipates (ver. 16). Compare Psalm ix. 15, 16 [16, 17]. In that Psalm, too, in a still more marked manner than in this, "the wicked" and "the (heathen) nations" are identified. See ver. 5 [6], 17 [18], 19, 20 [20, 21]. The only limit of time is that furnished by Psalm ix. 11 [12], 14 [15], from which it is certain that the Ark had already been placed on Mount Zion.

On the connection between these two Psalms see the Introduction and Notes to Psalm ix.

The Psalm consists of two principal divisions :—

I. The first contains a forcible description of the wicked in the ull maturity both of his impiety and of his power, together with a complaint to God against him. Ver. 1—11.

II. The second is an appeal to God to arise and show Himsel the avenger of the oppressed and the destroyer of the proud. Ver. 12—18.

I. 1 WHY, O Jehovah, standest Thou afar off?
(Why) hidest Thou (Thine eyes) in times of trouble?

1. STANDEST . . . AFAR OFF, *i.e.* like an idle passive spectator, unconcerned at the misery which he sees but refuses to relieve. See xxii. 2, 12, 20; xxxv. 22; xxxviii. 12, 22.

HIDEST, viz. "Thine eyes." So the ellipse is to be supplied. See

2 Through the pride of the wicked the afflicted is hotly
vexed;
They are taken in the devices they have imagined.
3 For the wicked boasteth of[a] his soul's desire,
And he blesseth the robber;[b] he despiseth Jehovah.
4 The wicked, such is his scornfulness, (saith) "He requireth not."
"There is no God," is the sum of his devices.
5 His ways are sure[c] at all times:
Thy judgements are far above out of his sight:

Is. i. 15. The same phrase is used of men who leave wickedness unpunished (Lev. xx. 4; 1 Sam. xii. 3), or who disregard the misery of others (Prov. xxviii. 27). LXX. ὑπεροράς.

IN TIMES OF TROUBLE. See on ix. 9 [10], Note[b].

2. THE AFFLICTED or "humble." See on ix. 12.

IS HOTLY VEXED, lit. "burns." LXX. ἐμπυρίζεται, Aq. ἐκκαίεται, Symm. φλέγεται. Hengstenberg explains this of *the indignation felt* by the oppressed against their persecutors, which, however, is hardly probable. It is more natural to understand it of the *suffering endured*, whether mental or bodily. Through the proud dealing of the wicked their victims are placed in the fire or furnace of affliction. The verb is intransitive; see vii. 13 [14].

The second clause of this verse is capable of two interpretations: either (1) they (*i.e.* the humble) are taken in the devices which the wicked have imagined; or (2) they (*i.e.* the wicked) are (or rather, *shall be*) taken in the devices which *they themselves* have imagined. In the former case we have the common change from the singular to the plural, "the afflicted" in the first clause meaning, of course, not an individual but a class.

3—10. The conduct of the wicked described as *the reason* of the singer's complaint. Hence introduced by "for."

3. Both members of this verse have been differently explained. The first may be rendered either (1) boasteth *of* his heart's desire; or (2) boasteth *after, according to*, &c.; or (3) giveth praise to his heart's desire (instead of praising Jehovah). This last is the interpretation of both Ewald and Hengstenberg, who refer to Hab. i. 11—16 in support of it. But on this, and the rendering of the second member, see Critical Note.

4. All the older versions render, "the wicked in (or, according to) his pride (lit. height of his nostril) will not inquire," viz. after God—never troubles himself, that is, whether God approves his conduct or not. But the other interpretation, which makes the words "He (*i.e.* God) will not require" the words of the evil-doer, accords better with the clause following, and also with the similar expression, ver. 13, "He hath said in his heart, Thou wilt not require."

THERE IS NO GOD: not that he is literally an atheist, but that the whole of his conduct, all his purposes and schemes, are carried on as if there were no God,—in a *practical* denial of His existence. See xiv. 1. Others render: "All his *thoughts* are, There is no God;" but the noun properly means *schemes, devices*, rather than *thoughts*.

5. FAR ABOVE, accusative used adverbially, as xcii. 9, Is. xxii. 16. The expression is just the opposite

As for all his adversaries, he puffeth [d] at them ;
6 He saith in his heart : "I cannot be moved ;
From one generation to another I shall have [e] no misfortune."
7 Of cursing is his mouth full, of deceit and oppression ;
Under his tongue is mischief and iniquity.
8 He sitteth in the lurking-places of the villages,
In secret corners doth he slay the innocent ;
His eyes are privily set against the helpless.[f]
9 He lurketh in his hiding-place, as a lion in his lair ;
He lurketh to catch the afflicted ;
He doth catch the afflicted, drawing him in his net.
10 So he is crushed,[f] sinks down and falls ;
The helpless [g] (perish) by means of his strength.[h]
11 He saith in his heart : "God hath forgotten ;
He hath hidden His face ; He will never see it."

to xviii. 22 [23], "all His judgements are before me;" whereas they are so far out of the sight of the wicked, that he acts as if they could never reach him. See Job xxii. 12, &c.

7. CURSING ; apparently, from what follows, "perjury" (though the word does not of itself mean this), reckless false swearing in order to effect his evil purposes. See lix. 12 [13], and Hos. iv. 2, in both which passages the same words "swearing and lying" occur together, as here "swearing and deceit."

UNDER HIS TONGUE,—not to be explained by a reference to the poison-bag of serpents, because the same phrase occurs also in a good sense, lxvi. 17, Cant. iv. 11. Just in the same sense, "*upon* the tongue," xv. 3, 2 Sam. xxiii. 2.

8—10. The crafty schemes of the wicked in order to entrap their victims.

8. VILLAGES. The word is explained, Lev. xxv. 31, to mean a collection of houses not enclosed within a wall. But it is doubtful whether the villages are mentioned because, from their defenceless state, it was easier there to plunder and kill; or whether by these villages are meant the haunts of the robbers themselves, the places *in which* they lurked, not *against which* they formed their designs ; nomad encampments of predatory Bedouins, who thence fell upon helpless travellers. This last seems more probable. Compare Gen. xxv. 16.

9. There is some confusion in the metaphors employed. The wicked is compared first to the lion watching for his prey, and then to the hunter taking wild animals in his net. Whereas, again in ver. 10 we seem to have the image of the wild beast crushing his prey.

10. For the explanation of this verse see Critical Notes.

11. A repetition of the statement in ver. 4, which at once puts in a more forcible light the character of these men, and lends greater earnestness to the prayer which follows. See for the same sentiment, Zeph. i. 12. In the last clause of the verse the verb is in the preterite : "He *hath* not seen it for ever,"

II. ק 12 Arise, O Jehovah! O God, lift up[i] Thine hand:
Forget not the afflicted.
13 Wherefore should the wicked despise God?
(Wherefore should he) say in his heart, "Thou wilt not require (it)"?
ר 14 Thou hast seen (it); for THOU considerest mischief and vexation,
That (men) may put[k] (the matter) into Thy hand.
The helpless[f] leaveth (it) to Thee:
Thou hast been the helper of the orphan.
ש 15 Break thou the arm of the wicked;
And as for the evil man, when his wickedness is sought for, let it no more be found.

which expanded="He hath not seen it—and He will not see it for ever."

12—18. Second principal division of the Psalm, in which the poet (1) cries earnestly to God for help and vengeance upon his enemies (12—15); and then (2) expresses his confidence that his prayer has been heard (16—18).

13. The argument is that God's honour is concerned in the reproach which is brought against it by the success of the wicked.

WHEREFORE SHOULD, &c. lit. "Wherefore hath the wicked despised God?" See xi. 3 (Heb.).

14. THOU HAST SEEN (IT). An emphatic energetic protest against the words immediately preceding, and also with a reference to the "He will never see," ver. 11, throwing back the word in the mouth of the wicked. (Cf. xxxv. 22.) There is a time coming, he feels assured, when all this disorder will be set right. God is not the passive spectator of human affairs which these men deem Him. He "considers" (*i.e.* regards with interest and sympathy) what is going on. See the same word, xxxiii. 13, lxxx. 15, Hab. i. 3, 13, and in many other passages. The helpless, therefore, may leave all to God;—and with the more confidence, because God *has been* the helper of those who, like the orphan, are deprived of human protectors. This appeal to past experience is always a ground of confidence. The road we are now travelling may be very dark, but let us look back, and on some spot which we have passed we shall see the light shining.

15. WHEN HIS WICKEDNESS, &c. Ordinarily such an expression might seem to denote a wish that his wickedness should be forgiven on repentance, but that clearly is not the sense here. The meaning must be, "Let the wicked and his wickedness disappear, so that even when sought for it cannot be found." "To seek and not find" is a proverbial expression, signifying that an object has utterly perished or disappeared, so as to leave no trace of its existence. See xxxvii. 36, Is. xli. 12. Cf. John vii. 34, Ζητήσετέ με, καὶ οὐχ εὑρήσετε. But what is the subject of the verbs? And are the verbs in the second or third person? If in the *second*, then two renderings are possible; (1) "Thou (Jehovah) shalt seek" (*i.e.* require so as to punish—which is the meaning of the same verb in ver. 4, 13), or rather, imperative: "Seek, *i.e.* punish his wickedness," (and) find

16 Jehovah is King for ever and ever:
The nations have perished out of His land.

ת 17 The desire of the afflicted hast Thou heard, O Jehovah;
Thou establishest their heart;
Thine ear hearkeneth (unto them),

18 That Thou mayest judge (the cause of) the orphan and the oppressed,
So that mortal man of the earth[1] may no more terrify.

nothing (more to punish); punish his wickedness, till it be clean gone; or (2) the second person is employed in a vague general sense, "Thou (*i.e.* anybody) shalt seek, &c." so that the sentence is equivalent to the impersonal "it shall be sought for," &c. So the LXX. ζητηθήσεται ἡ ἁμαρτία αὐτοῦ, καὶ οὐ μὴ εὑρεθῇ. Of these two explanations the last is certainly preferable, as preserving the proverbial character of the phrase, which is quite lost sight of in the other. A third, however, is possible. The verb may be in the *third* person, the noun, "his wickedness," being the subject (personified). The rendering would then be, "And as for the evil man" (according to the Massoretic punctuation this belongs to the second member of the verse), "let his wickedness seek him, and no more find him." But this, though not otherwise than forcible, seems somewhat artificial.

16. The triumph of faith, which, knowing that Jehovah is King, already sees by anticipation His righteous judgement executed. The bold plunderers who have so long infested the land are already swept away, says the singer, so sure is he of the issue. The land, which is Jehovah's land, must "be purged of all evil-doers," as once of the Canaanites, who were driven out. Israel may be "mightily oppressed," as by Sisera of old, but God will hear his cry, and give strength to his trembling heart (ver. 17), and so manifest His power that these tyrants who, with all their boasting, are but weak mortal men (ver. 18), shall no longer oppress His people.

[a] הִלֵּל with עַל apparently as in Ps. xliv. 9, with בְּ, "He maketh his boast *of*," &c. תַּאֲוַת נ׳ is then either abstract, "the desire itself," the boasting concerning which is the utmost height of wickedness (cf. Is. iii. 9); or, "the satisfaction of the desire:" or concrete, "the object of desire," as xxi. 3, lxxviii. 29, 30. The Syr. renders "he boasteth himself in," &c., LXX. ἐπαινεῖται, and Jerome, *laudabitur in*, but in some MSS. *laudabit desiderium*. But there is no other instance of this construction with עַל. Hupfeld, therefore, would render, "he boasts *according to* the desire," &c. *i.e.* he merely follows the promptings and suggestions of his heart, regardless of right or wrong. Cf. Is. xxvi. 8. But this is not very satisfactory, and הִלֵּל is never used absolutely like the Hithp. in the sense of boasting.

[b] Two questions have here to be decided. First, is בֹּצֵעַ the subject or the object of בֵּרֵךְ; and next, what is the meaning of בֵּרֵךְ? Some would render, "And the robber (or the covetous) curseth (and) despiseth

Jehovah." But Schultens on Job, p. 12, has proved that the verb ברך never has this meaning. At most it can only mean "to bid farewell to" (because at parting men blessed one another), and so "to renounce"—"And the robber renounceth and despiseth Jehovah." Hengst. however, who also makes בֹּצֵעַ the *subject*, retains the usual meaning of בֵּרֵךְ, and renders "he blesses [and yet] despises Jehovah;" *i.e.* he blesses Jehovah for his ill-gotten gains, and yet all the while despises Him. In support of this interpretation he refers to Zech. xi. 5, where the owners of the flock slay them and hold themselves not guilty, and they that sell them say, "Blessed be Jehovah, for I am rich." On the whole, however, it seems better to retain the same subject, as in the former member of the verse, viz. רָשָׁע, and to make בֹּצֵעַ the object of the verb. We then get, "he blesseth the robber," parallel to "he boasteth of (or, after) his heart's desire;" and the contrast, rendered more effective by the asyndeton, "He blesseth the robber—he despiseth Jehovah."

c יָחִילוּ, "are strong, sure, prosperous." Cf. Job xx. 21, and the noun חַיִל, "strength." The LXX. βεβηλοῦνται, evidently by a mistake connecting the word with the root חלל, חליל, *profanum*. Similar the Syr. ܚܝܼܠ, *profanæ sunt* viæ ejus, rendered by Dathe *solutæ sunt*. Jerome, *parturiunt*. Others give, "are crooked." But all these rest on mistaken interpretations of the root.

d יָפִיחַ, "puffeth," *i.e.* in scorn or contempt. See Mal. i. 13. So the Syr. ܡܫܝܛ, and Jerome *despicit*. Others, "bloweth upon them," *i.e.* He has only to blow and they wither. Hengst. compares Is. xl. 24, and the expression in Plautus, *Mil. Glor.* i. 1, 17, "Cujus tu legiones difflavisti spiritu quasi folia ventus." So Symm. ἐκφυσᾷ. Either of these renderings is admissible; but the first is the simpler, and more in accordance with the context, where the *pride* of the wicked man is the leading idea.

e אֲשֶׁר. The construction of this word has perplexed the interpreters. The Chald. has "from generation to generation I shall not be moved from doing evil." The Syr. "he meditates evil," following, however, perhaps a different text. The LXX. omit the relative altogether, and have merely ἄνευ κακοῦ. Jer. *sine malo*. Symm. οὐ γὰρ ἔσομαι ἐν κακώσει. The simplest way, perhaps, is to refer the relative to the words immediately preceding, דֹּר וָדֹר, "through generations which are free from evil." Others make אֲשֶׁר = בַּאֲשֶׁר, or עַל אֲשֶׁר, "inasmuch as, or because I am (or, shall be) free from misfortune." Hengst. will have it emphatic = "*I am one who* shall not," &c. which he attempts to defend by Is. viii. 20; where, however, אֲשֶׁר does not introduce the apodosis, as he asserts. According to Hitz. אֲשֶׁר depends upon אמר and introduces the direct discourse, as *e g.* 2 Sam. i. 4, only that, instead of standing at the beginning of the clause, it stands after other words, as in Zech. viii. 20, 23. "He hath said that from generation to generation," &c.

f ודכה = יִדְכֶּה, according to the Q'ri; which is then generally explained, "he crouches down the better to conceal himself; or, gathers himself together as if the better to make his spring." But there is no proof that the verb דכה ever has this meaning. In Qal it does not occur elsewhere. In Piel it means "to crush, to grind to fine powder." But retaining the K'thibh with other points we may read וְדָכֶה (so Gesen. and Hupf.) as an adjective with intransitive or passive meaning (like דַּךְ, ver. 18), "one who is crushed." Then we may render either "and crushed, he (the humble) sinks down;" or, "the crushed men, the oppressed, sink down." So Symm. ὁ δὲ θλασθεὶς καμφθήσεται. He may, however, have read יִדְכֶּה (taking it intransitively), and have meant merely to express the two Hebrew verbs by the participle and verb in Greek. The LXX. connect it with the foregoing verse, ἐν τῇ παγίδι αὐτοῦ ταπεινώσει αὐτόν. Jerome, *Et confractum subjiciet.*

g חֵלְכָה. The word occurs only in this Psalm: here and ver. 14, and again in the plural חֵלְכָּאִים, ver. 10. The Massoretic punctuation evidently intends us to take חֵלְכָה as = חֵילְךָ, from חיל with the suffix; "thy host," or "thy company" (the form in ver. 14 being pausal; where, in correct texts, we have a Segol חֵלְכָה, not a Tsere); and חֵלְכָּאִים, ver. 10, as two words, חֵיל כָּאִים, "the company of the afflicted, or terrified." But the punctuation is manifestly wrong. It is clear that we have the singular and plural forms of the same word. We must, therefore, assume an adjective, חָלְכָּה, formed after the analogy of חָפְשִׁי, but with the termination ־ָה (originally the Aramaic ־ָי) instead of ־ִי from a root חֵלֶךְ, "weakness, helplessness," which, though it does not occur in Heb. is found in Arab. حلك, "to be black," and so "to be miserable." For the introduction of the א in the plural, may be compared פְּתָאִים from פֶּתִי, and טְלָאִים from טְלִי, or טָלֶה.

The older Versions generally support this. They all render it as one word, "the poor," "the weak," &c. So Chald., Syr., Arab., though the Chald. fluctuates somewhat, using in ver. 8 לְמִסְכְּנַיָּא, and in ver. 10 עַנְיָא, whilst in ver. 14 it introduces the suffix עֲנָיָךְ. The LXX. use πένητες and πτωχοί. Aq. and Symm. ἀσθενεῖς.

h עֲצוּמָיו, rendered by many "his strong ones," and supposed to refer to the young of the lion, the metaphor already used being continued. Others again supply some noun, such as "claws" or "teeth." Ewald supposes the form to be dual, עֲצוּמַיִם, and translates "claws." But עֲצוּמִים may be an abstract plural noun, meaning "strength." So the Chald. interprets it by תקוף, and Jerome *viribus suis.*

i נְשָׂא, the fuller form, instead of שָׂא. Similarly, but with different though similar letters, נְסָה, iv. 7.

k לָתֵת בְּ׳. This is commonly explained by reference to Is. xlix. 16, עַל כַּפַּיִם חַקֹּתִיךְ, "I have graven thee upon the hands;" and the phrase is supposed to mean that God has so engraven all this evil-doing as it were on His hands, that He cannot forget it, and will therefore surely punish it. But the simple phrase נתן ביד cannot possibly mean "to engrave on the hand." It can only mean, either "to *take* into the hand," or "to *put* into the hand." The latter is the preferable rendering: "Thou considerest mischief and vexation, to put it (*i.e.* that men may put it, that it may be put) into Thy hand." And this agrees with what follows : "the helpless leaveth it to Thee." So LXX. τοῦ παραδοῦναι αὐτοὺς εἰς χεῖράς σου. Jerome, *Ut detur in manu tua.* And the Syr. "Thou waitest for it to be delivered into Thy hands." Calvin gives a similar turn to the passage, for he remarks : "Nostrum est patienter *quiescere* quamdiu in manu Dei reposita erit vindicta." But he explains לָתֵת בְּ׳, "That Thou mayest take (it) into Thy hand :" "*Ut ponas in manum*, quod nihil aliud quam serio et cum effectu cognoscere."

[1] The second clause of ver. 18 is capable of different interpretations, according as we join מִן הָאָרֶץ with the verb לַעֲרֹץ or with אֱנוֹשׁ. In the former case the rendering would be "that they (the wicked, or men generally, the subject not being determined) may no more terrify men out of the land," *i.e.* that the heathen persecutors may not drive out the Israelites from Canaan. But אֱנוֹשׁ is not used of the sufferers but of their tyrants (ix. 20), and we should expect עֲנָיִים, or some such word. In the latter case, אֱנוֹשׁ מִן הָ׳, "frail man of the earth," would seem to be an expression designedly chosen to pour contempt on the haughty plunderers described above. Similarly xvii. 14, מְתִים מֵחֶלֶד, "men of the world." Then the rendering will be, "That mortal man may no more terrify," or, taking ערץ not in the sense of "to terrify" but "to oppose, to resist," as in Is. xlvii. 12, "That mortal men, &c. may no more resist (Thee)." So the LXX. μεγαλαυχεῖν ; and then this clause would be exactly parallel to the אַל יָעֹז אֱנוֹשׁ, ix. 20. Perhaps, too, there is, as Calvin suggests, a tacit opposition between these men of the *earth* and the heaven where God dwells : "*E terra* tacitam continet antithesin inter humile terræ domicilium et cœlorum altitudinem. Unde enim ad oppugnandos Dei filios prodent ? E terra scilicet, perinde ac si vermiculi e terræ fissuris emergerent. Atqui hoc modo Deum ipsum impetunt, qui e cœlo auxilium servis suis promittit."

PSALM 11

The singer is in danger of his life ; and timorous and faint-hearted counsellors would fain persuade him to seek safety in flight. But, full of unshaken faith in God, he rejects their counsel, believing that Jehovah the righteous King, though He tries His servants, does not forsake them. Not the righteous, but the wicked have need to fear. The Psalm is so short and so general in its character, that it is not easy to say to what circumstances in David's life it should be referred. The choice seems, however, to lie between his persecution by Saul and the rebellion of his son Absalom. Delitzsch decides for the last, and thinks the counsel (ver. 1), "flee to your mountain," comes from the mouth of friends who were anxious to persuade the king to betake himself, as he had before done when hunted by Saul, to "the rocks of the wild goats" (1 Sam. xxiv. 3). It is in favour, to some extent, of this view that the expression in ver. 3, "when the foundations are destroyed," points to a time when lawful authority was subverted.

The Psalm consists of two strophes, which may be briefly characterized:—

I. The timid counsels of the faint-hearted. Ver. 1—3.

II. The answer of faith. Ver. 4—7.

The first strophe, however, it should be observed, opens with the calm assertion of confident trust, before we hear a word of expostulation with those whose advice the Psalmist rejects.

[FOR THE PRECENTOR. (A PSALM) OF DAVID.]

1 IN Jehovah have I found refuge:
How say ye to my soul:
"Flee ye [a] to your mountain, (like) a bird;

1. IN JEHOVAH — under the shadow of His wings (xxxvi. 7 [8]) —HAVE I FOUND REFUGE; I need no other refuge: how *can* ye say to me, &c.; my feet are on the true Rock, why should I look elsewhere for safety? This is the full force of the expression. There is moreover a force in the perfect, "I *have* found." It is an exclamation of joyful confidence in the thought that he *has* such a refuge, it is not yet to seek. The advice here given and which he repels is that of timid and desponding friends, who would persuade him that all is lost, and that the highest wisdom is to yield to circumstances, and to seek safety not in resistance but in flight. But in fact the voice which thus speaks is the voice of the natural heart, of the selfish and therefore shortsighted and cowardly instinct, which always asks first, not What is right? but, What is safe? The advice may be well meant, but it is unworthy. (Cf. iii. 3, iv. 6 [7].) This is the victory that overcometh the world, even our faith. But it is often a sorer trial for faith to have to withstand the pleadings of well-meaning friends than to arm itself against open enemies.

TO MY SOUL. Cf. iii. 2 [3]. "Significans pectus suum fuisse confixum probrosa illa rejectione."—*Calvin.*

FLEE YE, plural, because, though the words are aimed chiefly at David, and addressed to him ("to *my* soul"), yet his friends and partisans, who are involved in the same peril, are also included. (LIKE) A BIRD, or "like birds," the sing. being here collective, for the plural, as often.

TO YOUR MOUNTAIN. This partly perhaps follows the image of the bird, "which, when hunted on the plain, betakes itself to the woods and mountains" (De Wette); but the mountains, caves, and fastnesses of Palestine would be the natural hiding-place of persons in danger. (Cf. Jud. vi. 2, 1 Sam. xiii. 6, 1 Macc. ii. 28, Matt. xxiv. 16.) Hengst. sees an allusion to Gen. xix. 17, and Tholuck to the rocks

2 For lo! the wicked bend the bow,
They have aimed their arrow upon the string,
To shoot in the dark at them that are upright in heart.
3 When [b] the foundations are destroyed,
What can the righteous do?"

4 Jehovah is in His holy temple;
Jehovah,—His throne is in heaven:
His eyes behold, His eyelids try the children of men.
5 Jehovah trieth the righteous,
But the wicked and him that loveth violence doth His soul abhor.
6 May he rain upon the wicked snares,

in the wilderness of Judah to which David betook himself, 1 Sam. xxvi. 20; see also xxiii. 25—28, xxiv. 3.

2. Observe the change of tense: "they *are* bending; nay, they *have* already *armed*." The image here used of the bird pursued by the hunters reminds us of what David says to Saul, 1 Sam. xxvi. 20, "The king hath come to seek me, as when one hunteth a partridge in the mountains."

3. A further reason for the adoption of a timid policy. All is in hopeless disorder and confusion. THE FOUNDATIONS, or "pillars," may either mean the principal *persons* (such as magistrates and others in authority, cf. Is. xix. 10, and στύλοι of the Apostles, Gal. ii. 9), or the very principles of law and order (see lxxxii. 5, Ezek. xxx. 4.) which were now subverted.

4—7. The answer of Faith, the glance directed from earth to heaven, the full trust in the righteous and all-seeing Lord, the confidence that whatever the apparent confusion and disorder of the lower world, there is an Eye that sees and a Hand that directs all, that even the suffering of the righteous is part of a Divine purpose of love.

4. This verse might also be rendered:

Jehovah in His holy temple,
Jehovah (whose) throne (is) in heaven,—
His eyes behold, His eyelids try, &c.

In any case the emphasis rests upon the verbs in this last clause, which are the real predicates.

HOLY TEMPLE, or, PALACE, used not only of the Temple or Tabernacle in Jerusalem (see on v. 7), but also of the heavenly temple, xviii. 6 [7], xxix. 9, Is. vi., Hab. ii. 20, Mic. i. 2. Here the parallelism would rather favour the latter.

5. TRIETH. The same verb as in the previous verse, but used here in a more definite sense with reference to the result of the trial: puts them into the furnace (the word is used of the testing of metals), that they may come forth as pure gold. Cf. xvii. 3, Job xxiii. 10.

6. The figures in this verse are borrowed from the destruction of Sodom and Gomorrah.

MAY HE RAIN. We might rather have expected the future, "He will rain," as marking the certainty of the coming judgement. But the form is optative, and must therefore be

Fire and brimstone, and a burning wind,[c] as the portion of their cup.
7 For righteous is Jehovah, He loveth righteousness;
They that are upright shall behold His face.[d]

so rendered. David, who has just said that Jehovah abhors the wicked, thus places himself as it were on the Lord's side.

SNARES. The word presents some difficulty. It seems a harsh metaphor to speak of raining snares, especially in immediate juxtaposition with fire and brimstone. Still we must recollect that the Hebrew poets were not always careful to avoid incongruity of metaphor. We have immediately following a metaphor of an entirely different kind, "the portion of their cup." Ewald reads פַּחֲמֵי אֵשׁ, "coals of fire," and arranges the clauses as follow:—

"On the wicked He raineth coals of fire and brimstone;
A burning wind is the portion of their cup."

The first line gives, as he says, the image of a fiery rain from heaven, as in the overthrow from Sodom: the second, that of a poisonous Simûm, drunk in as it were from an envenomed cup; others again take the word SNARES as in apposition with the following nouns: "fire and brimstone as snares or nets," or, "in flakes, masses," this last sense of the word being derived from its use in Num. xvi. 38, where it means "thin plates."

7. Thus Faith kindles into Hope. Not only does David make Jehovah his refuge in calamity, but he can rejoice in the thought that he shall behold the face of God,—behold now the light of His countenance even in the midst of gloom and darkness. (Cf. iv. 7, xxi. 7.) Did his hope reach beyond this, and are we to suppose that here he looks forward to seeing God in the resurrection? We cannot tell. But see xvi. 11, xvii. 15. To us, however, his words may be the expression of a "hope full of immortality." "We know that our light affliction worketh out for us a far more exceeding and eternal weight of glory." We know that "when He shall appear . . . we shall see Him as He is."

[a] נודו. It is better to adopt the K'thibh in this case than the Q'ri, נודי, because of the plural suffix which follows. The correction to the sing. was made to suit the preceding נַפְשִׁי, but with the obvious disadvantage of clashing with the plur. suffix in הַרְכֶם. Nor can this be defended by Micah i. 11, עִבְרִי לָכֶם יוֹ' שׁ', because there the subject is *a city*, and the plur. therefore naturally refers to the *inhabitants*. צִפּוֹר, either with the particle of comparison omitted, as in xxii. 14, xlviii. 8, and elsewhere, or simple vocative, "ye birds," the persons themselves being so addressed (metaphor instead of comparison, as xii. 6 [7]). The accentuation of the three last words of the verse is very peculiar: Rebia geresh, Tiphcha finale (Tarcha) Silluk, instead of the usual accents after Athnach, viz. Tarcha, Munach, Silluk. But we find another instance of exactly the same kind in lxxiii. 9.

[b] The construction is unusual. כִּי, "when," in the protasis followed by a question in the apodosis with the verb in the *perfect*. The only other passage like it is Job xxxviii. 41, but there we have the *future* in the

apodosis. We have, however, כִּי followed by מה in Ps. viii. 4, 5, but without any verb expressed in the interrogative clause. The *perfect* here with the interrogation is remarkable. Lit. "What hath the righteous done?" *i.e.* what good has he effected by all his efforts? Or perhaps, hypothetically, "Quid *fecerit*, s. *efficeret* contra tantam insolentiam."

c The word זלעפה occurs Lament. v. 10, of hunger, and Ps. cxix. 53 as synonymous with קנאה. מְנָת, stat. construct. of מָנָה, for מְנַת; with Kametz, because = מְנָיַת as קְצָת = קְצָוֹת. The word occurs only as construct. See on xvi. note h.

d יָשָׁר, "the upright," singular, but in a collective sense, and therefore followed by a plural predicate (as ix. 7). The suffix ־ימו *may* be *singular* as well as *plural*, especially when used, as here, in reference to God.

PSALM 12

THIS, according to the title, is one of David's psalms; but there is nothing in the circumstances, so far as we know them, of his history, which can lead us to associate the Psalm with any particular period. Tholuck thinks it is aimed at persons by whom David was surrounded in the court of Saul. Others suppose that it was occasioned by the treachery of the Ziphites, 1 Sam. xxiii. 19, or the treachery of Ahithophel in Absalom's rebellion. But it is not one or two prominent individuals whose conduct forms the burden of the Psalmist's complaint. He is evidently smarting from the falseness and hypocrisy of the time. The defection which he deplores is a national defection. Like Elijah in the deserts, he feels himself alone. "there is not one godly man left: the true-hearted are cut off." A taint has spread through society (to use the modern expression, for which the Hebrew poet says, "this generation"). Falsehood is everywhere: truth nowhere. The heart of men is double; their lips are flattering lips (ver. 3). And whilst they utter slander, hypocrisy, and lies, they boast of their power; and not only give their tongues licence, but justify the licence: "Our lips are our own; who is lord over us?"

Now this utter hollowness and insincerity are very hard to bear. The few who, in the midst of the general corruption, still retain their integrity are persecuted, and sigh for deliverance. This deliverance is promised them in the form of a Divine interposition. The singer, filled with the Spirit of prophecy, consoles himself, and those afflicted like himself, not in his own words, but in the words of God (ver. 6). And then remembering how pure those words are, how unalterably true—not like the words of men which *seem* so fair, but *are* so false—he feels that there he can rest, calm in the conviction that, though the wicked walk on every side, Jehovah will save them that love Him from all their machinations (ver. 8).

Both the circumstances of the Psalmist and his prayer are very similar to what we find in the two immediately preceding Psalms. The belief here expressed as to the overthrow of the wicked (ver. 5—8 [6—9]) may be compared with xi. 5—7. In the latter passage that belief is based upon God's *character* as a righteous God. In this Psalm it rests apparently upon a special *promise*, but in fact upon God's *word*. But God's word teaches us what God's character is. The difference therefore is formal, not real.

The Psalm then consists of two principal divisions :—

I. A complaint. Ver. 1—4.

II. The answer to that complaint. Ver. 5—7.

These two principal sections may be further subdivided as follow :—

I. (1) The cry for help because
(*a*) good men are nowhere to be found ; and
(*b*) lies, and flattery, and insincerity prevail. Ver 1, 2.
(2) The prayer that flatterers and liars may be destroyed. Ver. 3, 4.

II. (3) God's promise of help in answer to the cry for help : and the Psalmist's Amen. Ver. 5, 6.
(4) The assurance and hope built upon the promise. Ver. 7, 8.

[FOR THE PRECENTOR. UPON THE OCTAVE.[a] (A PSALM) OF DAVID.]

1 SAVE, Jehovah, for the good man ceaseth,[b]
For the faithful fail[c] from among the children of men,

1. SAVE. More emphatic, because no object is expressed. Cf. cxvi. 1, where in like manner the verb "I love" stands without its object.

THE GOOD . . . THE FAITHFUL. The former (an adjective from the same root as the noun commonly rendered "loving-kindness") is either (1) one who is the object of God's loving-kindness, or (2) one who shows love to God or to man : it describes the good man both in his relation to God and in his relation to men. (See on iv. 3, note [d], and on xvi. 10.) The latter are those who are honest and true-hearted, lit. who are steadfast, unchanged by the evil influences around them; men that may be relied on (אמן, see Deut. xxxii. 21, *to be firm, stable*). Luther glosses : "Amens-

2 They speak vanity, every one with his neighbour;
With flattering lips and a double heart do they speak.
3 May Jehovah cut off[d] all flattering[e] lips,
(And) the tongue that speaketh great things,
4 Which say: "With our tongue we are strong,[f]
Our lips are our own: who is lord over us?"

5 "For the desolation of the afflicted,
For the deep sighing of the poor,
Now will I arise," saith Jehovah,
"I will set him in the safety for which he longeth."[g]

Leute," *Amen-folk*, i.e. those whose heart towards God and their neighbours is true and earnest, like the Amen of a prayer.

2. THEY SPEAK VANITY, *i.e.* emptiness, untruth (as xli. 7; cxliv. 8, 11).

EVERY ONE WITH HIS NEIGHBOUR. See the exact opposite of this enjoined, Eph. iv. 25, and the duty grounded on the fact that we are members one of another. But the word "neighbour" must not be pressed. "Neighbour" and "brother" are used in Hebrew without thinking of the exact relation implied in the words, where we should simply say "another."

WITH A DOUBLE HEART, lit. "with a heart and a heart;" *sc. altero quem proferunt, altero quem recondunt.* We have the opposite expression, 1 Chron. xii. 33; and in ver. 38 the parallel expressions to this last, "a perfect heart," "one heart."

3. The burning of a righteous indignation uttering itself in a fervent prayer for the uprooting of the whole kingdom of lies. "Querelæ imprecationem annectit." —*Calvin.*

3, 4. At first thought there seems to be a contradiction in speaking of *flattering* lips, and a tongue that speaketh *great*, i.e. proud words. But only at first thought. The men here described are evidently men occupying a high position, smooth and supple courtiers, perfect in the art of dissembling, yet glorying too in their power of saying what they list, however atrocious the falsehood or the calumny. So Calvin "Aulicos calumniatores perstringit, qui non modo suaviter se insinuant, sed grandiloqua mentiendi libidine obruunt miseros homines."

5. A remarkable instance of the close affinity between the Poet and the Prophet among the Hebrews. Each, though in different ways, was the teacher of that Eternal Truth which he received from God. And this, by the way, suggests to us what every true Poet should be. Broadly speaking, the difference lay here, that the Poet gave utterance to the longings, aspirations, fears, doubts, anxieties of *man's* heart; whereas the Prophet was commissioned to address himself directly to the people, as conveying to them the message *of God.* The one represented, so to speak, the human side of the truth—what man feels and is; the other the Divine —what God is and requires. The one speaks for man to God; the other for God to man. Here, however, David, instead of expressing his own feeling of confidence that God will answer him, seems as it were to hear God himself speaking ("Deum ipsum inducit loquentem," *Calvin*). See the prophetic counterpart of this, Is. xxxiii. 10.

NOW WILL I ARISE; emphat. as if after long silence and much forbearance, now at length, &c.

6 The words of Jehovah are pure[h] words,
(Like) silver fined in a furnace[i] in the earth, purified seven times.
7 Thou, O Jehovah, wilt keep them,
Thou wilt preserve them from this generation for ever.
8 The wicked walk to and fro on every side,
When a rabble[k] lifts itself up over the children of men.

6. The Poet dwells on the purity and perfect truth of God's promises, not only as opposed to all lying lips of men (though that, I believe, was in his mind), but also that he may thus more deeply print upon the heart of the afflicted the certain fulfilment of the promise. This emphatic assertion was rendered necessary by the wide-spread and apparently long-prevailing corruption. For those who were weak in faith might begin to doubt whether the truth of God itself had not failed.

7. The faith and hope which rest upon the fact just before stated, that the words of Jehovah are pure words.

THEM, *i.e.* "the afflicted and poor," in ver. 5. In the second clause, the pronoun in the Hebrew is in the singular used distributively, "him," i.e. each one of them.

THIS GENERATION, spoken of those who not only live in the same age, but are pervaded by the spirit of that age. So Is. liii. 8. Here, the world as opposed to the Church.

8. This verse is no doubt perplexing, as it seems to contradict the confidence expressed in ver. 7. Hupfeld therefore would either (1) interpret:—

(Though) the wicked walk about on every side,
(It is only) as when a rabble lifts itself up, &c.

i.e. their pride and insolence will be but for a short time; it will come to an end very soon, like the outbreak of a mob. Or (2) he would transpose verses 7 and 8 so as to make the confident assurance of preservation close the Psalm. Delitzsch, on the other hand, thinks that the heart having lifted itself up to the hope of the future, sinks again at the sight of the gloomy present. He calls the Psalm a ring, of which the oracle, ver. 5, is the precious stone. But this return to gloom and doubt is, I believe, without parallel at the conclusion of a Psalm.

[a] ON THE OCTAVE. See above, vi. 1.

[b] נמר, intransitive, as vii. 10.

[c] פסס, ἅπ. λεγ. Rashi observes that פסו is the same as אפסו, "have come to an end." Qimchi compares אפס דמים, 1 Sam. xvii. 1, with פס דמים, 1 Chron. xi. 13. אמונים, *not* the plur. abstr. from אֵמוּן (as the LXX. render ἀλήθειαι, Symm. πίστεις, &c.) but as the parallel חָסִיד shows, an adjective, "the true, the faithful." This is certain from the recurrence of the same parallelism, xxxi. 24 (see also 2 Sam. xx. 19, where the word occurs likewise as an adj.), as well as from the analogy of Micah vii. 2.

[d] יַכְרֵת, apoc. fut. in its proper opt. sense.

[e] חֲלָקוֹת, a plur. abstr. from חֶלְקָה (not from חָלָק, as Rosenm.). This may be accus. of the instrument according to Gesen. § 135, Rem. 3, or the ב *instrumenti* may be supplied from the next clause.

[f] לִלְשֹׁנֵנוּ, either (1) "over our tongue have we power," we can do with it as we like, so Hupf.; or (2) "*as to* our tongue (ל of reference) are we strong," the Hiph. in either case being = Qal. *Our lips are our own*, lit. "with us," *sc.* as allies (אֵת, as 2 Kings ix. 32). Cf. xxxviii. 10 [11], "The light of mine eyes is not with me," אֵין אִתִּי, *i.e.* it is gone—I can no longer make use of it.

[g] יפיח לו, either (1) "for which (*sc.* ישע) he panteth;" or (2) "that he may recover breath," לו being used in a reflective sense. פוח, to breathe hard, to pant (so Hab. ii. 3, "it panteth for the end," *i.e.* longeth for its accomplishment).

[h] טְהֹרוֹת, cf. Ps. xix. 9, 10. The image here expanded is hinted at elsewhere in the use of the word צרופה as applied to God's word, xviii. 31, cxix. 140, Prov. xxx. 5.

[i] עֲלִיל (prop. *officina*, r. עלל, *operari*), "furnace" for smelting of metals. It is difficult to say how לָאָרֶץ should be construed. Commonly, as describing the material of עֲלִיל, "in a furnace *of earth*." But אֶרֶץ is never used in this sense. Better therefore, "*belonging to* (*i.e.* fixed upon) the earth." Comp. in Schiller's *Glocke*:

> "Fest gemauert *in der Erden*
> Steht die Form aus Lehm gebrannt."

[k] זֻלּוּת (r. זלל, conn. with דלל, תלל, &c. to be *weak*, *languid*, *slack*, *worthless*) = Arab. ذُلّ *vilitas*, that which is contemptible and so vile, morally as well as socially. Abstr. for concr. Symm. οἱ εὐτελεῖς. Aq. εὐωνισμένοι. Jerome, *vilissimi*.

PSALM 13

IN this Psalm we see a servant of God long and sorely tried by the persecutions of unrelenting enemies, and, as it seems to himself, forgotten and forsaken of God, pouring out the agony of his soul in prayer. It is a long and weary struggle, it is a daily and hourly martyrdom; and wrestling with his despair, he can but cry (like the souls under the altar, Rev. vi. 10), How long? And then calmer words of prayer rise to his lips, ver. 3, 4. And at last Faith asserts her perfect victory (ver. 5). The rapid transition of feeling, from a depth of misery bordering on despair, to hope, and even joy, is very remarkable.

We have three strophes :—

I. The first is "the deep sighing" of a heart overwhelmed with the agony of its despair. Ver. 1, 2.

II. The calmer supplication succeeds, as if the very utterance of its grief had made the burden less. Ver. 3, 4.

III. Prayer kindles into hope, lighted up with something even of joy. Ver. 5.

[FOR THE PRECENTOR. A PSALM OF DAVID.]

1 HOW long, O Jehovah, wilt Thou forget me for ever?
How long wilt Thou hide Thy face from me?
2 How long must I take counsel in my soul,

1. It is quite unnecessary to point thus: "How long wilt Thou forget me? for ever?" as if there were two distinct questions. (See the same double question, lxxix. 5; lxxxix. 46 [47]). It is natural to a perturbed and doubting heart thus to express itself, in a confused and almost contradictory manner. In its despair it thinks "God hath forgotten me;" and yet out of the very midst of its despair there rises up the conviction,—"No, not for ever;" and then its hopelessness is changed to expostulation, "How long wilt Thou forget me?" We may, if we choose it, paraphrase, "How long wilt Thou *make as if* Thou wouldst forget me for ever?" God's anger, the hiding of His countenance, as Delitzsch observes, cannot but seem eternal to the soul which is conscious of it. Nevertheless Faith still cleaves to the Love which hides itself under the disguise of severity, and exclaims, "Though He slay me, yet will I trust in Him." "When we have long been crushed by sufferings, and no sign appears that God will succour us, the thought will force itself upon us, God hath forgotten me. For by nature we do not acknowledge that God cares for us in our afflictions; but by faith we lay hold of His invisible providence. So David, so far as he could judge from the actual state in which he was, seemed to himself forsaken of God. But at the same time, because the Light of Faith was his guide, he, with the eyes of his mind, looked through and beyond all else to the Grace of God, far as it might seem hidden from his sight"—*Calvin.* And Luther: "Does he not pourtray in fitting words that most bitter anguish of spirit, which feels that it has to do with a God alienated, hostile, implacable, inexorable, whose wrath is (like Himself) eternal? This is a state in which *Hope despairs, and yet Despair hopes* at the same time; and all that lives is 'the groaning that cannot be uttered,' wherewith the Holy Spirit maketh intercession for us, brooding over the waters shrouded in darkness, to use the expression in Gen. i. This no one understands who has not tasted it."

2. The "how long" four times repeated; for the long duration of the conflict is here the sting of the Poet's grief.

(Having) sorrow in my heart daily?[a]
How long shall mine enemy lift up himself against me?

3 Consider,—answer me, O Jehovah my God,
Lighten mine eyes, lest I sleep the (sleep of) death.
4 Lest mine enemy say: "I have prevailed against him;"[b]
(Lest) mine adversaries exult because I am moved.

5 But as for me—in Thy loving-kindness have I trusted;

HOW LONG MUST I TAKE COUNSEL? Lit. "put counsels or deliberations in my soul." See a similar use of the verb, Prov. xxvi. 24. This strikingly describes the helpless embarrassment of the sufferer. Plan after plan suggests itself, is resolved upon, and then abandoned in despondency as utterly unavailing. As Luther says: "His heart is like a raging sea, in which all sorts of counsels move up and down; he tries on all hands to find a hole through which he can make his escape; he thinks on various plans, and still is utterly at a loss what to advise." Well must David have understood what this was, when, hunted by Saul, he knew not where to betake himself, at one time seeking refuge among the Moabites, at another in the wilderness of Ziph; now an outlaw hiding himself in the cave of Adullam, and anon a captain in the service of the King of the Philistines; and amid all his projects, haunted by the mournful conviction, "I shall now one day perish by the hand of Saul." "Quanquam autem Dominus Spiritum consilii fidelibus se daturum promittit, non tamen semper ipsum in primo articulo suppeditat, sed quasi per flexuosas ambages ad tempus discurrere patitur, vel perplexos inter spinas hærere."—*Calvin*.

SORROW IN MY HEART. Not only parallel to, but flowing from "counsels in my soul," the burden of a heart saddened by its own thoughtfulness.

3. The lamentation now passes into prayer; and to the fourfold complaint of the first strophe answers the fourfold petition of the second, though the several members of the one do not exactly correspond to the several members of the other.

CONSIDER; "look upon me," opposed to the hiding of the face, 1 *b*. ANSWER ME, opposed to the forgetting, 1 *a*. First, look; then, hear and succour. "Thus," says Calvin, "does the Holy Ghost purposely accommodate the forms of prayer to our feelings." First, we must have the conviction that God sees us, and then we can cry to Him; first the assurance that He *is*, and then that He is the Rewarder of them that diligently seek Him.

LIGHTEN MINE EYES, said not of spiritual but of physical support, as is clear from what follows, "lest I sleep the sleep of death;" and also from the other passages where the same idiom occurs, 1 Sam. xiv. 27 and 29 (where the eyes of Jonathan are said to be enlightened, when, after being reduced to the extremity of faintness, he partakes of food), and Prov. xxix. 13. "Instaura lucem vitæ oculis obtenebrescentibus."—*Rud.*

Such is the fearfulness of the spiritual conflict, that it seems as if death only could be the end. He knew this who said: "My soul is exceeding sorrowful even unto death."

4. LEST MINE ENEMY SAY. Another reason why his prayer should be answered; not because he is an enemy, but because God's honour and God's cause upon earth are in peril. (Cf. v. 9.)

5. Supplication passes into the expression of a joyful confidence.

Let my heart exult in Thy salvation :
Let me sing [c] to Jehovah,
Because He hath dealt bountifully with me.[d]

Faith, strengthened by prayer, rises above the present with its sorrows, and sees what is not as though it were; and hopes yet to praise God with a song because of His goodness.

IN THY LOVING-KINDNESS, not in personal merit, nor in the justice of my cause.

"I have trusted—let me rejoice—let me sing—because of the experience I shall have that Jehovah *has dealt* bountifully with me."

"Whilst the thunder and the lightning are still raging around him, David sings his songs of praise, as Luther also says: 'While Satan rages and roars about him, he meanwhile sings quietly his little Psalm.'"—*Tholuck.*

With the two Iambics, *gamal àlái*, the Ps. ends, the very rhythm of the words conspiring as it were with the sense of peace in the singer's breast, and the waves of song, stirred so tumultuously at the beginning, sinking down into the breathless calm of an unruffled sea.

[a] יוֹמָם, elsewhere, "in the day," as opposed to לַיְלָה. And so the LXX., Aq., Th. ἡμέρας. Here, however, apparently = כָּל־יוֹם, as Symm. καθ' ἡμέραν. Similarly Ezek. xxx. 16, צָרֵי יוֹמָם, "daily adversaries," *i.e.* who *continually* assail.

[b] יְכָלְתִּיו = יָכֹלְתִּי לוֹ. Cf. cxxix. 2, Gen. xxxii. 26.

[c] אָשִׁירָה, "I fain would sing," 1 p. cohort. answering to יָגֵל, 3 p. jussive. אֲנִי, emphatic, as opposed to the enemies mentioned above. (Cf. iii. 6.)

[d] גָּמַל עָלָי, cf. cxvi. 7, cxix. 17, where the phrase occurs in the same sense.

PSALM 14

THE feeling expressed in this Psalm is in some measure the same which, as we have already seen, must have given occasion to the Twelfth Psalm. The singer, keenly alive to the evils of his time, sees everything in the blackest colours. The apostasy is so wide-spread that all are involved in it, except the small remnant (implied in ver. 4); and the world seems again ripe for judgement as in the days of Noah (ver. 2).

Both in this Psalm and in Psalm xii. the complaint is made that the wicked oppress and devour the righteous. In both, corruption has risen to its most gigantic height, but here the *doings* of bad men, there their *words*, form the chief subject of complaint.

In form the ode is dramatic, or quasi-dramatic. A great tragedy is enacting before the eyes of the poet. Sin is lifting itself up in Titanic madness against God, and God looks down upon its doings as once upon the builders of Babel. He sees utter apostasy (ver. 3); He speaks from heaven (ver. 4), and the evil-doers are confounded at the word of His mouth (ver. 5). "It would scarcely be possible," says Ewald, "for a great truth to be sketched in fewer or more striking outlines."

There is nothing in the Psalm which can lead us to fix its date or authorship precisely. The feeling is common enough at all times in men of earnest mind. Filled with a holy jealousy for God, no age seems to them so corrupt as their own, because they are engaged in perpetual and, as they are apt to think, hopeless encounter with its evils. Indeed, despair would be the result, did not the promise of the future lift them above the present (ver. 7).

Ver. 7 is not so decisive of a later date as has sometimes been supposed. For first, this might be a sort of liturgical doxology added to the original Psalm during the Exile; and next, it is not even certain that the reference is to the hope of return from the Babylonish captivity (see Note on this verse).

This Psalm (Jehovistic) appears again with some variations, especially in ver. 5, 6, as Psalm liii. (Elohistic). It is not certain which of the two may claim the merit of being the original poem. Its place in the collection may incline us to give this the preference. And the change in the Fifty-third might very well have been introduced to adapt it to the peculiar circumstances of the time.

The Psalm cannot be broken up into strophes; but the first verse answers to the third, and the second to the fourth.

In ver. 1, if we take the first member (*a*) as introductory, then the two remaining, (*b*) and (*c*), correspond to the two, (*a*) and (*b*), of ver. 3.

On the other hand, the idea in (*b*) of ver. 2 is expanded into two members (*a*) and (*b*) in ver. 4, whilst (*c*) in ver. 2 corresponds to (*c*) in ver. 4.

[FOR THE PRECENTOR. (A PSALM) OF DAVID.]

1 THE fool[a] hath said in his heart, There is no God.

1. THE FOOL. Thus the Bible ever speaks of those who have cast off the fear of God. They are those whose understanding is darkened; who, professing themselves to be wise, become fools. Such men, who make a boast of their reason and would fain walk by the light of their reason, prove how little their reason is worth. The epithet is the more cutting, because persons of this kind generally lay claim to more than ordinary discernment.

IN HIS HEART. Rather a prac-

Corrupt, abominable are they in their doing;[b]
There is none that doeth good.
2 Jehovah hath looked down from heaven upon the children of men,
To see if there be any that hath understanding,
That seeketh after God.[c]
3 They are all turned away, together they have become corrupt:
There is none that doeth good; no, not one.
4 "Have they no knowledge, all the workers of iniquity,

tical than a theoretical atheism; not so much a denial of the *being* of a God as a denial of His *moral government* of the world (cf. x. 5); and this evinced in actions rather than in words. The life shows what the thought of the heart is (as indeed immediately follows). "The fool" is not the philosophic atheist with his arguments ("subducta ratione vel formatis syllogismis," *Calvin*); but the man who by the *practice of wickedness* so stifles and corrupts within him the knowledge of God that he *virtually* acknowledges no God.

South, in his sermon on this verse (vol. iv. p. 19, Tegg's edit.), lays a stress on these words, as implying that the Atheist dare not avow his atheism, but only cherishes it within. But the occurrence of the phrase elsewhere, *e.g.* x. 6, 10, 13, does not justify this stress. Bacon (Essays, xvi. "Of Atheism,") draws another distinction: "It is not said, 'The fool hath thought in his heart,' so as he rather saith it by rote to himself as that he would have, than that he can thoroughly believe, or be persuaded of it; for none deny there is a God, but those for whom it maketh there were no God."

2, 3. God appears as Witness and Judge of what is done upon earth.

2. LOOKED DOWN. The word used strictly of looking out of a window, 2 Kings ix. 30; and again of God looking upon the earth, cii. 20. As "they have corrupted," reminds us of the Flood ("all flesh had corrupted his way on the earth," Gen. vi. 12), so this "looking down" of the Tower of Babel, Gen. xi. 5. (Cf. xviii. 21.)

3. NO, NOT ONE. "See," says Luther, "how many words he uses that he may comprehend all, excluding none. First he says *all*, then *together*, and then *no, not one*." This and the two previous verses are quoted freely by St. Paul (he does not adhere even to the LXX.) in Rom. iii. 10, &c., in proof of his position, that Jews as well as Gentiles are under sin. As his argument is at this point addressed particularly to the Jew, he reasons, not from the sense of sin or the voice of conscience, but from the Scriptures, whose authority the Jew acknowledged. The Jew would, of course, admit the inference as to the state of the Gentile world.

The rest of the quotations which follow the above in the Epistle to the Romans are brought together by the Apostle from different parts of the Old Testament. But in some MSS. of the LXX., in the Vulg., and both Arab. Syro-Arab. and Copto-Arab., and strangest of all in the Syro-Hex., they are found in the Psalm, having evidently been transferred hither from the Epistle. So also in our Prayer-Book Version, which, it should be remembered, is, in fact, Coverdale's (1535), and was made, not from the original, but mainly from the Latin and German.

4. God himself is introduced as speaking.

Who eat my people, (as) they eat bread,
(And) call not on Jehovah?"

5 There were they in great fear;
For God is in the generation of the righteous.

6 Though ye shame the counsel of the afflicted,
Yet Jehovah is his refuge.

7 Oh that the salvation of Israel were come out of Zion!
When Jehovah bringeth back the captivity[d] of His people,
Then may Jacob exult, then may Israel be glad.

NO KNOWLEDGE, used absolutely as in Is. i. 3. "Israel doth not know," is stupid like the brutes.

WHO EAT, lit. "who eating my people, eat bread;" who, so far from being conscious of their guilt, devour the righteous with the same unconsciousness with which they would take their accustomed meal. See the figure still further carried out, Mic. iii. 1—3. Cf. also for similar expressions, Jer. x. 21, Hos. vii. 7, in both of which passages the evil-doers are described (as here) as men who do not pray, "they call not upon Jehovah;" therefore are they so brutish. But see further on liii. 4.

MY PEOPLE. So, then, even in the worst times there is a remnant, the salt of the earth, "the righteous generation," as they are afterwards called.

5. THERE WERE THEY, &c., lit. "There did they fear a fear." THERE; when God thus speaks to them in the terribleness of Divine judgement. Calvin well explains: "Exprimitur pœnæ quam daturi sint certitudo, ac si eam digito monstraret."

By GENERATION we are not to understand merely contemporaries. Here, as often elsewhere, a moral meaning attaches to the word, and it denotes those who are of *the same spirit*, whether that be the spirit of the world (xii. 8) or the spirit which is of God (xxiv. 6; lxxiii. 15). In like manner γενεα is used in the N. T. to denote "the *race* with all its moral characteristics," not merely "the people now alive."

6. THOUGH YE SHAME, or, "ye may put to shame" (yet ye shall not succeed), for God, &c. The A.V. is clearly wrong in rendering, "Ye *have* shamed," as if the verb were in the past tense.

THE COUNSEL OF THE AFFLICTED, *i.e.* all that is done by those who bear the reproach of Christ to advance God's glory upon earth. The children of the world cannot bring all this to nought, for in fighting against the righteous they fight against God, who is in the midst of them.

7. This last verse looks certainly very much like a later liturgical addition (as ver. 18, 19 [20, 21] of Psalm li.). The exiles in Babylon hoped yet for deliverance from Zion. Jehovah, they believed, had not forsaken His holy mountain, though He had suffered them to be scattered among the heathen. Daniel, we know, in prayer turned himself towards Jerusalem (Dan. vi. 11). And it would be natural enough for a poet of that time to give utterance to the wish contained in this verse. It cannot, however, be denied, that the phrase, "to bring back the captivity," is used in other passages, metaphorically, of any deliverance from misery and restoration to prosperity. So of Job (xlii. 10), and so also Ezek. xvi. 53. It is better to adopt one of these explanations than to throw the whole Psalm as late as the Exile.

[a] The Hebrew is rich in epithets to describe different degrees of this infatuation. (1) פֶּתִי, *the simple*, one whose folly consists in being easily led; lit. one who is *open* (r. פתה) to the influence of others. (2) כְּסִיל, which denotes a grosser and almost brutish stupidity; such "hate knowledge," Prov. i. 22 (r. כסל, "to be fat," and then "sluggish"). (3) נָבָל, *the fool*, as one who is *flat*, *insipid* (r. נבל, "to wither"), without taste or discernment. (Cf. in the opposite sense טַעַם, which means properly "taste," and then "understanding;" just as in the Latin *sapere*, the transition is made from the bodily to the mental perception.) (4) אֱוִיל and הוֹלֵל, by which are denoted more outrageous forms of folly, amounting to madness. See on the latter word, v. 5, note [e]. For a fuller description of the נָבָל, see Is. xxxii. 6.

[b] עֲלִילָה, the suffix omitted, as often in poetry, but not a loosely appended accus. The Hiphil verbs, though frequently used absolutely, are here followed by the direct object; cf. Zeph. iii. 7, Gen. vi. 12. Lit. "they have made corrupt, they have made abominable (their) doing."

[c] אֵת. There is no departure here from the usual rule as to the use of אֵת, the Divine Name being of course considered as a proper name.

[d] שׁוּב שְׁבוּת. The Kal form seems to be used in this phrase in preference to the Hiph., for the sake of the alliteration. שׁוּב has occasionally elsewhere in Kal a transitive signification; cf. lxxxv. 2, 5, Nah. ii. 3. See also Ezek. xlvii. 7, בְּשׁוּבֵנִי, where, if the verb had been intrans., we should have had בְּשׁוּבִי, and, besides, the Hiph. וַיְשִׁבֵנִי immediately precedes, which shows that here, at least, שׁוּב = השׁיב, cf. Deut. xxv. 3.

PSALM 15

THIS Psalm is commonly supposed to have been written on the occasion of the removal of the Ark to Zion, and the consecration of the Tent, or Tabernacle there, 2 Sam. vi. 12—19. (Cf. 1 Chron. xv. 16.) The subject of the Psalm, and the occurrence of a similar question and answer in xxiv., which was certainly composed for that occasion, might indeed dispose us to adopt this view.

On the other hand, the name "holy mountain" (ver. 1), as applied to Zion, would rather suggest a later date. It was the removal of the Ark thither which made the mountain holy.

The form of the Psalm is very simple. Properly speaking, it has no strophes or divisions. It is a question (ver. 1), and an answer to the question (ver. 2—5). It teaches simply what is the condition of man's approach to God with acceptance. There is implied in it, no doubt, that all merely outward service is vain; but the Psalm can scarcely be said to be specially directed (like Psalm l.) against lip service and hypocritical worship. It describes rather the perfect character, the man who can draw near to God and live in His presence. Eleven particulars are enumerated in which this character is summed up. Hence in the Gemara (T. B. *Makkoth*, f. 24 *a*), it is said that David reduced the 613 commands of the Law given on Sinai to eleven; Isaiah (it is added) to six (xxxiii. 15); Micah to three (vi. 8); Amos (v. 4), or rather Habakkuk (ii. 4), to one (viz., trust in God).

[A (PSALM) OF DAVID.]

1 JEHOVAH, who may sojourn in Thy tabernacle?
Who may dwell on Thy holy mountain?
2 He that walketh perfectly,[a] and worketh righteousness,
And speaketh truth in his heart;

1. That this Psalm is no mirror for the self-righteous to see themselves in, is evident from its first word, JEHOVAH. It is in the presence of God and in the light of God that the singer draws his portrait of the godly man. In His sight neither the hypocrite nor the formalist can stand. And on this account, and not as a mere matter of form, does David direct his question to God. The answer is not to be considered as if coming from the heavenly oracle, but the Poet himself gives it, speaking by the light of the Spirit of God, as cast upon his own heart, upon the word of God, and upon the world about him. So the Anglo-Saxon Version paraphrases: "Then the Lord answered the prophet through inspiration of the Holy Ghost, and the prophet said: I know, yet I ask, who dwells there?" &c.

TABERNACLE . . . . HOLY MOUNTAIN. These words must not be explained away as mere figures of speech. TABERNACLE, or rather TENT, does not mean merely "dwelling," as when it is said, "The tabernacle of God shall be with men," nor can we with Venema interpret the HOLY MOUNTAIN as merely equivalent to a safe and indestructible abode. It always means Zion, and nothing else. But the Psalmist asks, Who is worthy to dwell, like Eli and Samuel of old, in the sacred courts; who is fitted for that close and constant communion with God which such a dwelling implies? for God's Presence and His Revelation of Himself were, under the Old Testament, connected with a certain *place*. And hence the love and ardent desire so constantly expressed for the place itself. (Cf. xxiii. 6; xxvi. 8; xxvii. 4, 5; lxxxiv. 1 [2], 5 [6], &c.) Of the two verbs, "sojourn" and "abide," the first denotes an occasional, the next a permanent, dwelling in a place. The first might be used of pilgrims coming up to Jerusalem; or of a guest lodging for a time at an inn, or in his friend's tent. But here they are apparently synonymous.

2, 3. The man with whom God will hold communion is now de-

3 (That) hath not slandered with his tongue,
Hath done no evil to his friend,
Nor taken up a reproach against his neighbour;
4 In whose eyes a vile person is contemned,[b]
But he honoureth them that fear Jehovah;
(Who) sweareth to (his own) hurt,[c] and changeth not;

scribed, first as to what he is (ver. 2), and then as to what he is not (ver. 3).

(*a*) He *is* a man (1) of whole heart and life; (2) who does the will of God; and (3) speaks the truth because he loves it: it dwells in his heart, and he speaks it there first, before he speaks it with his tongue. "It is a beautiful order," says Luther. "First the person must be acceptable by cleanness (alluding to the Vulg. translation, *qui ingreditur sine macula*); then the work by righteousness; then the word by truth. So God has regard to Abel (himself) first, and then to his gifts." "Pulcher ordo, primo persona grata requiritur per munditiam, deinde opus per justitiam, tandem verbum per veritatem. Sic respicit Deus ad Abel primum deinde et ad munera ejus." —*Oper. in Psalm.* ii. 326.

(*b*) He *is not* one who injures others either (1) by word; or (2) by deed; or (3) by listening to and propagating slander. This is, I think, the meaning of this last clause. It may be rendered either: "hath not received (*i.e.* from others) a reproach," &c. (That the verb will bear this meaning is certain. See Gesen. Thes. v. נשׂא.) Or, "hath not taken up;" *i.e.* has not stooped, so to speak, to pick up dirt out of the dunghill that he may cast it at his neighbour; or, "hath not lifted up," *i.e.* so as to place it like a burden upon his neighbour.

4, 5. Again, his character is further described by affirmations and negations.

(*a*) He *is* one who turns away from the evil and honours the good, who regards as inviolable the sanctity of an oath (not a casuist who sets himself to find a pretext for breaking his word, when it is inconvenient to keep it).

(*b*) He is *not* one who loves usury or takes bribes. The taking of usury is strictly forbidden in the Law (Exod. xxii. 25 [24]; Lev. xxv. 36, &c.), and denounced by the Prophets (Is. xxxiii. 15, "gain of oppressions;" Ezek. xviii. 8, 13, xxii. 12, &c.). Qimchi's casuistic distinction, that it is lawful for the Jew to take usury of strangers who are not kind to Israel, but not of his own people, is very significant; and, like too many Christian as well as Jewish interpretations of Scripture, framed to support a convenient and profitable practice.

Thus, in heart, in tongue, in actions, in his conduct as a member of society, he is alike free from reproach.

Such is the figure of stainless honour drawn by the pen of a Jewish poet. Christian chivalry has not dreamed of a brighter. We have need often and seriously to ponder it. For it shows us that faith in God and spotless integrity may not be sundered; that religion does not veil or excuse petty dishonesties; that love to God is only then worthy the name when it is the life and bond of every social virtue. Each line is, as it were, a touchstone to which we should bring ourselves. To speak truth in the heart—to take up no reproach against a neighbour—would not the Christian man be perfect (τέλειος) of whom this could be said? And that other trait in this divine cha-

5 Who hath not put out his money to usury,
Nor taken a reward against the innocent.
He that doeth these things shall never be moved.

racter, "who honoureth them that fear the Lord"—is there a surer test of our spiritual condition than this, that we love and honour men *because they love Christ?*

5. Instead of "he that doeth these things shall dwell in the house of Jehovah," &c., the answer is varied in form, "shall never be moved," which is, in fact, the same truth in another and larger form. Such a man may not take up his dwelling in the earthly courts of the Lord; but, at least, he shall so live in the presence of God, and under the care of God, that his feet shall be upon a rock.

The Epistle of St. James is the New Testament expansion of, and comment upon, this Psalm. For another treatment of the same subject in the Old, see Is. xxxiii. 13—16.

[a] הוֹלֵךְ תָּמִים occurs also Prov. xxviii. 18. Similar is הוֹלֵךְ צְדָקוֹת, Is. xxxiii. 15. We find also ה׳ בְּתָמִים, lxxxiv. 12. And more fully ה׳ בְּדֶרֶךְ תָּמִים, ci. 6, and הַיָּשָׁר הוֹלֵךְ, Mic. ii. 7. There can be no doubt, therefore, from a comparison of these passages, that the adj. תָּמִים is not a nom. predicate, but is an acc. defining the action of the verb, the adj. being here used as a neut. abstr., so that ה׳ ת׳ is lit. "one who walks perfectness, *i.e.* makes perfectness his way;" and so in Is. *l. c.* ה׳ צ׳, "one who makes righteousness his way." Hupf. will have it that תָּמִים is not an adj., but a neuter noun, after the analogy of רָכִיל (Jer. vi. 28, Ezek. xxii. 9).

[b] Verse 4 is difficult. In clause (*a*) the subject and the predicate are not clearly marked. Most take נִמְאָס as the subject, "*the reprobate* [see Jer. vi. 30] is despised in his eyes" (נ׳ ב׳); but, as Hupf. remarks, this is contrary to the accents, which make נִבְזֶה the subj. "The despised (contemptible) person is rejected in his eyes." For this use of נִבְזֶה cf. Mal. i. 7, ii. 9. Another rendering however is possible, and is perhaps the true one. We may take both נִבְזֶה and נִמְאָס as predicates, the suff. in בְּעֵינָיו as possessive, and render, "he (*i.e.* the subject of the Psalm) is despised and rejected in his own eyes," he thinks lowly of himself. The objection to this is, that נִמְאָס seems too strong a word to express merely a man's low opinion of himself.

[c] לְהָרַע, LXX. *τῷ πλήσιον αὐτοῦ*, and so Syr., Vulg., Arab., but then the Hebrew must have been לְרֵעֵהוּ. Nor can it stand for לָרַע, "to the evil," implying that even to the wicked he will keep his oath. The Chald. rightly, "so as to afflict himself." The word is inf. Hiph. of רעע for לְהָרֵעַ, and there is a reference, no doubt, to the formula in Lev. v. 4, לְהָרַע או לְהֵיטִיב, *i.e.* let the consequences be what they will (to himself of course), whether good or evil. In our Prayer-Book Version the rendering of the LXX. seems to have been combined with the true rendering of the Heb., "He that sweareth *unto his neighbour* and disappointeth him not, *though it were to his own hindrance.*" See another similar instance of combined readings in xxix. 1.

PSALM 16

FROM the opening words of this Psalm, "Keep me, O God; for in Thee have I found refuge," as well as from the conviction expressed in ver. 10, "Thou wilt not leave my soul to the unseen world," it has been conjectured that the Psalm was written by David in time of peril. But if so, the thought of peril is quite swallowed up in the consciousness of God's presence and love. The Psalm is bright with the uttterance of a happiness which nothing earthly can touch. It expresses the conviction of a life rather than of any sudden emergency. The living God himself is David's portion and inheritance (ver. 5, 6)—stands at his right hand (ver. 8)—is the joy of his heart now (ver. 9)—and we fill him with joy and gladness for evermore.

A comparison of the Psalm with 1 Sam. xxvi. 19 might suggest that it was written by David when he was in the wilderness of Ziph. "They have driven me out this day," he says, "from the inheritance of Jehovah, saying, "Go, serve other gods." The feeling that he was thus cut off from the service of Jehovah, and compelled to live amongst idolators, may have led him to write the words in ver. 4, 5 of the Psalm. And so again the consciousness that he was "driven out from abiding in the inheritance (נחלת) of Jehovah," might make him cleave the more stedfastly to the truth, that not the *land* of Jehovah, but *Jehovah himself* was his inheritance.

It is possible, however, that the contrast here brought out so strongly between the happiness to be found in the love of God, and the infatuation and misery of those who had taken some other to be the object of their worship, may have been suggested by the very position in which an Israelite *dwelling in the land* would be placed with reference to surrounding nations. "We very imperfectly imagine the force of such a contrast," says Isaac Taylor, "as it must have presented itself to an Israelite of the higher and brighter eras of Jewish history. . . . The great controversy of truth was maintained, single-handed, by the pastoral and agricultural tribes of Southern Syria, against all mankind beside. . . . It was a people simple in manners, and not distinguished either in art or science, against nations conspicuous in all that could give lustre and strength to empire. Abstract as well as mechanical philosophy, and the arts of luxury, and great experience in commerce, and much wisdom in government, together with the glories of conquest, contributed to recommend and illustrate the seductive idolatries of the mighty countries by which the clans of Judah, Ephraim, and Benjamin were hemmed in." After observing that the splendour and licentiousness of the idolatrous worship proved too often a snare to a large part of the Jewish people, and that this rendered the protest against it the more needful, he continues, "Nevertheless, though all visible recommendations were possessed by those gods 'of wood, and of stone, and of gold,' yet the poet-king of Israel, after looking to the south, the north, the east, could confidently revert to the heights of Zion and say, that the voice of joy and the acclamations of genuine and holy pleasure were heard in that 'Tabernacle of the righteous,' and nowhere else. . . . None could dare to affirm that it was JOY that dwelt in the temples of the demon-gods of Philistia, Phœnicia, Syria, Assyria, Egypt; or who would not have blushed to have said that perpetual PLEASURES filled the courts of Chemosh, of Ashtaroth, of Dagon, of Baal, of Mithri? What did the grove conceal? Lust—blood—imposture. What sounds shook the fane? Alternate screams of anguish, and the laughter of mad votaries. What was the priest? The teacher of every vice of which his god was the patron and the example.—What were the worshippers? The victims of every woe which superstition and sensuality can gender, and which cruelty can cherish.

"It was not then a blind national prejudice, any more than it was spiritual arrogancy, that made the prophet-poet and king of Israel exult in the distinction of his people. Rather it was a righteous scorn which made him exclaim, when he thought of the errors of the nations, 'Their drink-offerings of blood will I not offer, neither take their names into my lips.'"—*Saturday Evening*, pp. 303-6, Edit. 1855.

But a few words on the prophecy contained in the latter part of the Psalm. That we have here a prediction, and moreover a *conscious* prediction on the part of David, is distinctly affirmed by St. Peter, speaking under the immediate inspiration of the Holy Ghost (Acts ii. 30, 31). The language which he uses is very remarkable. Alleging ver. 8—11 in proof of the resurrection of Christ, he tells us that David here spoke as a prophet (προφήτης οὖν ὑπάρχων); that he *knew* that his great descendant would be the Messiah, and that God would place Him on his throne (εἰδὼς ὅτι ὅρκῳ ὤμοσεν αὐτῷ ὁ Θεὸς, ἐκ καρποῦ τῆς ὀσφύος αὐτοῦ [τὸ κατὰ σάρκα ἀναστήσειν τὸν Χριστὸν] καθίσαι ἐπὶ τοῦ θρόνου αὐτοῦ); and that he *foresaw* and spake of the resurrection of Christ (προϊδὼν ἐλάλησεν περὶ τῆς ἀναστάσεως τοῦ Χρ.). It is plain from all this—the προφήτης, the εἰδώς, the προϊδών—that, according to St. Peter's view, David not only uttered words which *might* be applied to Christ, but that he used prophetic, that is, inspired language, and knew himself that he was prophesying. But we may still allow a primary and lower reference of the words to David himself, without lessening their prophetic import; in some parts even an exclusive reference, for it is not necessary (and indeed seems scarcely possible) to refer the *whole* Psalm to Christ, because a part of it points to Him.

[A MICHTAM [a] OF DAVID.]

1 KEEP me, O God; for I have found refuge in Thee.
2 I have said [b] of Jehovah, "Thou art my Lord: [c]
I have no good beyond Thee," [d]—
3 Of the saints [e] who are in the land,
They are the excellent in whom is all my delight.
4 Their sorrows [f] shall be many who take another [g] (god) instead (of Jehovah)—

1—4. These verses express generally the principle that love to God and loyal trust in Him imply on the one hand union and fellowship with all who love Him; on the other, the most decided and open severance from all idolaters.

2. I HAVE NO GOOD BEYOND THEE. Lit. My good (my happiness), as in cvi. 5, Job ix. 25, is not beyond or beside Thee. (See Critical Note.) The "good" here spoken of is in contrast with the "sorrows" in ver. 4, and answers to the words, "my lot, my cup, my inheritance," in ver. 5, 6. For the sentiment, may be compared lxxiii. 25, "Whom have I in heaven but Thee?" &c. Hengstenberg observes that as "Thou art the Lord" is the soul's response to the words in Exod. xx. 2, "I am the Lord thy God;" so this, "Thou alone art my salvation" (or "I have no good beyond Thee"), is the response to the command, "Thou shalt have no other gods beside Me." This is the one grand thought which stamps the Psalm, "Thou, O Lord, art my portion, my help, my joy, my all in all."

3. THE SAINTS. In God's land there are others who, like David himself, cleave to God, and with these he claims fellowship. Or, "the saints" may be all Israel, set apart as a nation, and severed from the surrounding heathen. See the original designation of Israel to be "a kingdom of priests and a holy nation," Exod. xix. 6. See also Deut. vii. 6.

THE EXCELLENT, properly "the *outwardly* illustrious:" the root-meaning is that of "glitter, splendour," &c. But the same adj. is applied to the name of God in viii. 1 [2], and hence may contain the idea of a moral as well as of a merely outward glory. "Eadem causa præclaros vocat, vel magnificos, quia justitia et sanctitate in quibus relucet Spiritus ejus claritas, nihil pretiosius esse nobis debet."—*Calvin*.

4. THEIR SORROWS. This is opposed in the conviction of supreme and perfect blessedness in Jehovah, ver. 2; see also ver. 11.

WHO TAKE, *i.e.* in exchange, "acquire by barter." The word is properly used of obtaining a wife by the payment of a dowry, Exod. xxii. 16 [15]. (See Critical Note, or comp. Jer. ii. 11.)

ANOTHER, *i.e.* a false god (*das*

I will not pour out their drink-offerings of blood;
Neither will I take their names upon my lips.
5 Jehovah is the portion[h] of my allotment and of my cup:

Fremde, Zunz), or that which is not God (Is. xlii. 8, xlviii. 11), but purposely, perhaps, put in this indefinite form to signify "all besides God and against God that a man can make an idol of."

With such persons David will have nothing to do. He is joined to the saints, and he holds fast on Jehovah. With the utmost strength of abhorrence, he repudiates the worship, horrid and foul, of the surrounding idolaters.

THEIR DRINK-OFFERINGS OF BLOOD:—not offered with hands stained with innocent blood (Delitzsch); or loathsome as if they were of blood (Hupfeld), but as associated with bloody rites, *i.e.* such rites as those of Moloch and Chemosh, where the blood was the blood of human sacrifices. "In the Levitical ritual," says Prof. Robertson Smith, "libations had a very subordinate place; but in the idolatrous worship practised in Israel the drink-offering must have had higher importance, as appears from many references in the Prophets.... (Jer. xix. 13, xxxii. 29, xliv. 17, 18). The libation was supposed to be actually drunk by the gods (Deut. xxxii. 38).... It is natural therefore to suppose that libations of sacrificial blood are here alluded to." But, as he proceeds to remark, the Psalmist indicates that these bloody offerings were in their nature hideous and detestable, and therefore had in view not ordinary sacrifices, but the shedding of human blood in sacrifice (Hos. vi. 8, Is. lix. 3).

THEIR. The pronoun may refer to the idols implied in the word "another." Then "their drink-offerings" would mean those poured out in honour of them. But the pronoun seems to be used somewhat vaguely, first with reference to the idolaters, and then with reference to the idols. So deep is David's loathing of idolatry that he will not even pollute his lips by mentioning the names of false gods, in accordance with the command in Exod. xxiii. 13, "The name of other gods ye shall not mention; it shall not be heard in thy mouth." (Cf. Hos. ii. 17, Zech. xiii. 2.)

5. He now expresses more fully his own choice and resolve, enlarging upon what he had said in ver. 2.

THE PORTION OF MY ALLOTMENT, or "of my share," *i.e.* the portion assigned to me in the division of the territory. There is an allusion, probably, to the division of the Land of Canaan among the tribes, no part of which was assigned to the tribe of Levi, because, as was expressly declared, Jehovah would be their portion or share (חֵלֶק, Num. xviii. 20, the same word which occurs here), and the gifts consecrated to Jehovah the provision for their support: Deut. x. 9, xviii. 1, &c. In Jer. x. 16, Jehovah is said to be "the portion" of the whole nation, especially as contrasted with the idolatrous nations. But that which was true of the nation at large, and of the tribe of Levi in particular, was true in its deepest spiritual import of every believing Israelite. Hence the individual believer addresses God as his "portion," Ps. cxix. 57, cxlii. 5, and thus makes his own the great truth on which the national religious life was based. "What must not he possess," says Savonarola, "who possesses the Possessor of all?" In the words of St. Paul, "All things are yours, for ye are Christ's, and Christ is God's."

AND OF MY CUP. This also depends on the word "portion." See the same expression, "portion of the cup," xi. 6, but there used *in*

Thou maintainest[i] my lot.
6 The lines have fallen unto me in pleasant places,
Yea, I have a fair heritage.[k]
7 I will bless Jehovah who hath given me counsel:
Yea, in the night-seasons have my reins admonished me.
8 I have set Jehovah before me always;
Because He is at my right hand, I shall not be moved.

malam partem. The "cup" seems to be put by synecdoche for the whole meal. He thus speaks of God as the daily food by which he lives. See our Lord's words in John vi., and connect this with the expression of *trust* with which the Psalm opens.

THOU MAINTAINEST MY LOT, or, "holdest my lot in Thy hand." Therefore no creature can rob me of it. "Nor is the third comparison unnecessary," says Calvin, "for it often happens that the rightful owners are thrust out from their own possession, because there is none to defend them. But God hath given Himself to us as our inheritance in such wise, that by His aid we are ever maintained in the enjoyment thereof."

6. THE LINES HAVE FALLEN. In allusion to the ancient custom of marking out plots of land by measuring lines. See the same phrase, Josh. xvii. 5. The line was said to "fall" as being "thrown" by lot. See Micah ii. 5. But again, this is no earthly inheritance, but God's own gift of Himself.

I HAVE A FAIR HERITAGE, or, "mine inheritance pleaseth me well."

7. In the joyful remembrance that he has such a possession, he breaks forth into a strain of thanksgiving.

WHO HATH GIVEN ME COUNSEL, *i.e.* through whose grace I have been enabled to choose Him for my portion (ver. 5, 6). David confesses that he owes his blessedness to God. This is the Divine part: the next clause gives us the human.

MY REINS, here app. = "my heart." (See Job xix. 27, "my reins in my bosom.") "The reins are opposed to the mouth (Jer. xii. 2), as the heart to the lips (Is. xxix. 13)." "Reins and heart are the region of the inmost personal life (vii. 9, xxvi. 2, &c.), and embrace various functions, intellectual as well as emotional, for which we have distinctive words." God has led me to find my joy in Him, and now in the night-seasons, as the time most favourable to quiet thought, I meditate thereon. The heart itself is said to admonish, because it anxiously listens to the voice of God, and seeks to conform itself thereto. The meditation is of a directly practical kind, with a view to conduct. Luther, who interprets the words directly of Christ, explains them by a reference to Heb. v. 8 and Matt. xxvi. 41, and sees here the struggle between the flesh and the spirit. He says: "Dictum est supra Ps. vii. renes significare delectationes seu vim concupiscibilem, quæ tristitias odit, delicias ac quietem amat, quæ in omnibus hominibus etiam Christo facit, ut dura et amara sit passio et mors, quam spiritu consilii et fortitudinis oportet superari."

8. Further expression of his confidence. Not in the moment of peril only, but *at all times* has he his eye fixed upon God. AT MY RIGHT HAND. See cix. 31, cx. 5, cxxi. 5. God in David's eyes is no abstraction, but a Person, real, living, walking at his side.

9. MY HEART . . . MY GLORY (*i.e.* soul) . . . MY FLESH; in other words, the whole man. In like manner "soul," "heart," and "flesh," lxxxiv. 2 [3]; and "soul" and "flesh," lxiii.

9 Therefore hath my heart rejoiced, and my glory exulted;
Yea also my flesh shall dwell in safety;
10 For Thou wilt not leave my soul to the unseen world;
Thou wilt not suffer Thy beloved [l] to see the pit. [m]
11 Thou wilt make me know the path of life;

1 [2]; "heart" and "flesh," lxxiii. 26. So πνεῦμα, ψυχή, and σῶμα, 1 Thess. v. 23. FLESH, here as always, *the living body:* it never means *the corpse.* So also the phrase SHALL DWELL IN SAFETY must be understood of *this life.* (See Deut. xxxiii. 29 [28]: Ps. iv. 8 [9]; xxv. 13.) The rendering of the LXX. "shall dwell *in hope*," as if the reference were to the hope of a resurrection, is quite inadmissible. Hence these words as they stand in the Hebrew cannot be regarded as a prophecy that Christ's body should rest safely in the tomb. They are the expression of David's confidence that God would watch over his life, and preserve him from death. In this sense, of course, they are also applicable to our Lord.

10. TO THE UNSEEN WORLD. Not as in our Version, and in that of Luther and others, "*in* hell." David says nothing about what shall happen to him *after* death, but is expressing his conviction that God will not leave him to perish—will not give him up to be the prey of the grave, nor suffer him (as follows in the next clause) to see the pit. So too, in Acts ii. 27, St. Peter says, εἰς ᾅδου (or as Lachmann reads, ᾅδην). This was true in a different sense of Christ; for though He died, God did not leave Him to Hades, did not suffer His soul to *remain* there, or His body to rest in the grave. But that no stress can be laid upon the word "leave," that it means only "give over to," is plain from xxxvii. 33 (cf. xlix. 10 [11], Job xxxix. 14). The sense is in fact the same as in Ps. xlix. 15 [16]. See Umbreit, *Brief an die Römer*, S. 172.

THY BELOVED. I have ventured thus to render the word, because it may just as well mean "one who *has obtained favour* of the Lord," as one who *shows love* to God and love to men. See above on Ps. iv. 3 [4], note [c]. If we take it in the latter sense, we must render "Thy *pious*, or, Thy *godly* one," not "Thy *holy* one." The word חָסִיד (*châsid*) never means "holy." On the question whether this word is singular or plural, as also on the meaning of the phrase "to see the pit," or "to see destruction," see the Critical Note.

11. THE PATH OF LIFE. Not merely, that is, the life of the body. This is shown by the pleasure and the joy spoken of afterwards, which are to be found in God's Presence, and in communion with him. *Life*, in the only true sense, is union with God; and from that springs, of necessity, the idea of immortality. It seems impossible to suppose that David, who here expresses such a fulness of confidence in God, such a living personal relationship to Him, could have ever dreamed that such a relationship would end with death. In this Psalm, and in the next, there shines forth the bright hope of everlasting life. Why should men question this? Even the heathen struggled to believe that they should abide after death. Would they to whom God had revealed Himself, and who were bound to Him in a personal covenant, be left in greater darkness? Impossible. The argument which our Lord used with the Sadducees applies here with especial force—God is not the God of the dead, but of the living. They to whom God has made Himself known, they who are one with Him, cannot lose that Divine Life of which they are made partakers. Immortality

Fulness of joy is in Thy Presence,
Pleasures are at Thy right hand for evermore.

(and a Resurrection, see on xvii. 15) follows from the life of the spirit. And though probably there would be many fluctuations of belief (see above, note on vi. 5); though the spiritual eye would not be always equally clear; it seems impossible to doubt, when we read passages such as this, that there were times at least when the hope of a life beyond the grave did become distinct and palpable.

At the same time, in the utterance of this confident persuasion and hope, David was carried beyond himself. He spake as a prophet, *knowing* that God had promised of the fruit of his body to raise up Christ to sit on his throne. The hope of his own immortality was based upon, and bound up in, the Life of Him who was at once his Son and his Lord. What was true of David in the lower sense, was true in the fullest and highest sense of Christ; was only true of David, because it was true of Christ; and is only true of any of us in and through Him, according to His own words, "Because I live, ye shall live also." Briefly, then, it must be said that ver. 9—11, so far as they refer to David, express his confidence in God's protecting care in this life and his hope of a life to come. But as a prophecy of Christ they mean all that is drawn from them by St. Peter and St. Paul. In Christ's deliverance from the grave and His Resurrection, the whole fulness of their meaning is exhausted. See this well stated by Umbreit, *Brief an die Römer*, S. 172 ff. See also the Critical Notes.

For a very able and interesting discussion of the questions touched on in this Note I would refer my readers to Prof. Robertson Smith's Paper on this Psalm in the *Expositor* for Nov. 1876.

[a] מִכְתָּם. This occurs in the inscription of five other Psalms, lvi.—lx. The meaning of the word has been much questioned. The Rabbinical commentators connect it with כֶּתֶם, "gold," in the sense of "a golden or precious poem," like the term *χρυσᾶ ἔπη*, applied to the poems of Pythagoras for instance: and as in Arabic, the Moallakat are termed "golden." The LXX. *στηλογραφία*. Vulg. *tituli inscriptio.* Chald. גליפא תריצא, *sculptura recta*, as though it were engraven, marked, stamped with a peculiar impress; as, for instance, with peculiar words and turns of phrase, as Del. tries to show. Jer. *humilis et simplicis.* Aq. τοῦ ταπεινόφρονος καὶ ἁπλοῦ (Symm. ἀμώμου) τ. Δαυίδ. Others, again, connect כתם with כתב, so that *michtam* would merely be "a writing." But the meaning can be only a matter of conjecture.

Ver. 2, 3. The oldest interpreters as well as the latest have found these verses a stumbling-block in their path. I will subjoin the renderings of the principal Versions, before I proceed to the criticism of particular words. They may be arranged as follows: (1) The LXX. have *εἶπα τῷ Κυρίῳ, Κύριός μου εἶ σύ, ὅτι τῶν ἀγαθῶν μου οὐ χρείαν ἔχεις. τοῖς ἁγίοις τοῖς ἐν τῇ γῇ αὐτοῦ ἐθαυμάστωσε πάντα τὰ θελήματα αὐτοῦ ἐν αὐτοῖς.* This is closely followed (with the exception of one word) by the Vulg., "Dixi Domino; Deus meus es tu, quoniam bonorum meorum non eges. Sanctis qui sunt in terra ejus, mirificavit omnes voluntates meas in eis." The Arab. has, "I said to the Lord, Thou art my Lord, and indeed Thou needest not my good actions. He hath manifested among His saints His marvels in His land; and hath wrought in them all His pleasure." (2) The Syr., "I said to the Lord, Thou art my Lord, and my good (or happiness) is from Thee (ܘܛܳܒܬܝ ܡܢ ܠܘܳܬܟ ܗܝ): also to the saints who are in the land, and the illustrious in whom is all my delight" (which apparently means that the happiness of the saints is also from God). Similarly Jerome—

> "Dixi Domino, Dominus meus es tu:
> Bene mihi non est sine te.
> Sanctis qui in terra sunt, et magnificis,
> Omnis voluntas mea in eis."

It is doubtful, however, whether he intends to separate ver. 3 altogether from ver. 2. The dative *sanctis* may depend on *Dixi*. Symm. also renders טוֹבָתִי בַּל־עָלֶיךָ by ἀγαθόν μοι οὐκ ἔστιν ἄνευ σοῦ. With these the Chald. agrees in its interpretation of the latter clause of ver. 2, whilst in other respects it is peculiar: "Thou hast said, O my soul, before Jehovah, Thou art my God: surely my good is not given save of Thee. (As) for the saints that are in the land, they have made known the strength of my power from the beginning; and they that are glorious in good works, all my good will is in them." This is singular: still more singular is (3) the Anglo-Saxon paraphrase: "Have I not said to Thee, O Lord, that Thou art my God; seeing Thou hast given me all the good that I have, and Thou hast no need to take aught again from me? The Lord hath fulfilled all my will, and hath given me power to overcome the nations that were opposed to me, and to overthrow their idols, after mine own will." This widely departs in the last clause from the Lat. Vers. which accompanies it, and which is here the same as the Vulg. The former part is an expansion merely of the *bonorum meorum non indiges* of the Vulg.

We come now to the detailed criticism of the separate words.

[b] And first the word אָמַרְתְּ, according to the present punctuation of the verb, is 2 fem., and this has been defended by supposing, as the Chald. evidently does, an ellipse of נַפְשִׁי. But such an ellipse would be exceedingly harsh here, there being nothing whatever to indicate it. It is better to take אָמַרְתְּ as a defective reading with omission of the final ׳, for אָמַרְתִּי. This sort of writing ת for תי occurs in four other passages: cxl. 13, Job xlii. 2, 1 Kings viii. 48, Ezek. xvi. 59. The reading of two MSS. of De-Rossi's, אָמַרְתִּ, is wholly ungrammatical, and merely intended to indicate that the word is here in the first person. The omission of the ׳ may have been due to rapid pronunciation (Hitz.), or it may indicate an Aramaic form, or be analogous to 2 sing. fem. where the omission of the final ׳ has become constant.

[c] אֲדֹנָי. This form commonly denotes the Divine Name absolutely (without the suffix), "the Lord." But here it probably stands, as in xxxv. 23, as = אֲדֹנַי, "my Lord." So the LXX., Syr., and Vulg. take it.

[d] טוֹבָתִי בַּל־עָלֶיךָ, "my good, *i.e.* my happiness, the prosperity which I enjoy," &c. (not as Aq., "my *goodness* is not beyond Thee"). This, which is substantially the rendering of the Syr., Symm., and Jerome,

seems to be the best. It is doubtful, however, whether עַל should be rendered "besides," or "beyond." For the former, Exod. xx. 3, עַל פָּנָי, is usually quoted, though it is scarcely a strict parallel: for the latter, lxxxix. 8, Gen. xlix. 26. Rashi says "my happiness is not (incumbent) upon Thee—Thou art not bound to do me good," in which sense עַל occurs Ezra x. 12, Prov. vii. 14. But this does not suit the context. Qimchi (as his father's explanation), "my goodness does not reach (influence) Thee." Hupfeld suggests that בַּל may here mean "only," *non nisi*, "My happiness rests only upon Thee." But this seems questionable, and the difficulty might be avoided by a very slight emendation. We have only to read כָּל for בַּל, and then we get "My happiness rests wholly upon Thee." [Since writing the above, I find that this very natural correction is actually the reading of two MSS.]

[e] לִקְדוֹשִׁים. The great difficulty, no doubt, begins with this verse. And the first question is, Does the verse form a complete whole in itself, or is it connected with the preceding, or with the following verse? Those who regard it as containing an independent proposition, render: (1) "As for the holy ones who are in the land, and the noble, all my delight is in them." But the objections to this are, first, that this use of ל before the *subject* is questionable, though it has been defended by Is. xxxii. 1. And next, that no satisfactory example can be alleged of the use of the stat. constr. for the absol.: אַדִּירֵי כ׳ ח׳ ב׳ is a relative clause with the common omission of the relative. Other instances of the use of the stat. constr. before the relative clause are עַם לֹא יָדַעְתִּי, xviii. 44; שְׂפַת ל׳ י׳, lxxxi. 6. See also lvi. 4, xc. 15 (a double example), Job xviii. 21, Is. xxix. 1. Or (2) "As for the saints, &c. . . . they are the excellent, in whom is all my delight," the וְ in וְאַדִּירֵי thus introducing the apodosis. But the וְ could scarcely thus stand alone, and we should certainly expect the demonstrative pronoun in the second clause. Accordingly Delitzsch transfers the וְ to the beginning of the verse (וְלִקְדוֹשִׁים), and makes the demonstr. הֵמָּה being the apodosis. He also (as many others do) makes the ל in this verse co-ordinate with the ל in ver. 2. "I said to (or, of) Jehovah," . . . "I said to the saints, &c. they are the noble in whom is all my delight;" *i.e.* I love God, and I love His saints, and I keep aloof from all idolaters. Others again, supposing the ל as above to depend on אָמַרְתִּי, carry on the constr. into the next verse, "I said to the saints, that are in the land, and the excellent, &c. . . . their sorrows shall be multiplied." Ewald renders, "As for the saints that are in the land, and the noble who have all my love—Many are their gods, they take strange gods instead [of the true God]—they whose bloody drink-offerings I cannot offer, nor take their names upon my lips." He supposes the poet *in exile* to be contrasting his own lot, happy as he was, even in a far land, because Jehovah was with him, with the lot of those who, though "called to be saints," as belonging to the chosen people, had renounced their privileges, and had become worshippers of idols. But (1) the allusion to "the land" does not compel us to suppose that the Psalmist himself was an exile. (2) Those who had become idolaters would hardly still be called קְדוֹשִׁים; and (3) the construction is somewhat awkward when thus carried on from

ver. 3 into ver. 4. On the whole, however, it seems more satisfactory to connect this verse with the preceding. We have, then, still a choice of renderings: (*a*) we may repeat בַּל־עָלֶיךָ from the preceding verse, "There is nothing beyond Thee to the saints who," &c. (So Mendelssohn.) (*b*) We may take לְ in the sense of "belonging to," "joining myself to;" and the passage would mean, "I have no good beyond Thee, belonging as I do to the fellowship of the saints, and the noble in whom," &c. And some such meaning seems to be favoured by the context; for it is evident that it is the design of the Psalmist to contrast his own happy lot, and that of others who, like himself, had found their happiness in Jehovah, with the miserable condition of those "whose sorrows were increased," because they went after other gods. (*c*) We may take לק' as depending on אָמַרְתְּ, and make the apodosis begin with המה, and either with Del. transfer the וְ from וְאַדִּירֵי to the beginning of ver. 3, or strike it out altogether as having crept in by mistake. Then the rendering will be as given in the text in this (4th) edition. In previous editions I adopted explanation (*b*).

f עַצְּבוֹתָם. The first clause of this verse has again been very differently interpreted. The LXX. ἐπληθύνθησαν αἱ ἀσθένειαι αὐτῶν, μετὰ ταῦτα ἐτάχυναν, which is followed by the Vulg. and Arab. The Syr. also renders עַצְּבוֹתָם by ܟܐܒܝܗܘܢ, "their sorrows." On the other hand, the Chald., Jerome and Theod. (see Montef.'s note) take עַצְּ' to mean "their idols." The Chald.: "They multiply their idols, and afterwards hasten to offer their gifts." Jerome: "Multiplicabantur idola eorum post tergum sequentium." So far as the etymology goes, the word עצ' might no doubt mean either "idols" or "sorrows," but *in this form* it only occurs in the latter sense, cxlvii. 3, Job ix. 28, whereas the form עֲצַבִּים is used exclusively of idols.

g אַחֵר, "another," *i.e.* a false god—not only in plur. with אֱלֹהִים (Exod. xx. 3, xxiii. 13, &c.), but in sing. and absolutely, Is. xlii. 8, xlviii. 11.

מָהָרוּ, *not* "they hasten," which is the meaning of the verb only in the Piel. In Qal it signifies "to buy" (Exod. xxii. 15): here, according to the original meaning of the root, "to exchange, to barter." Cf. המיר in the same sense, cvi. 20, Hos. iv. 7, Jer. ii. 11.

h מְנָת, stat. constr. of מָנָה, with ā instead of ă, owing to the omission of the radical י or ו. The proper stat. constr. of מָנָה would be מְנַיַת, whence מְנָת and (to mark the omission of the י) מְנָת. The י appears in the plur. מְנָיוֹת, Neh. xii. 57, for which we have א in the alt. form, v. 44, מְנָאוֹת. This, which is beyond all doubt the true explanation of the appearance of the long vowel instead of the short, is due to Hupfeld. See his note on Ps. xi. 6, where the same form occurs. Fürst (Concord. in v. פִּנָּת) explains these forms and similar nouns as formed by the addition of ת to the fem. termination א ָ.

i תּוֹמִיךְ. App. a fut. Hiph. from a root ימך, which Schultens assumes and supposes to be kindred with an Arab. root ومك, *amplum esse*, "Thou enlargest my lot." But no such verb exists either in Heb. or Arab. It is better, therefore, to take it as = תּוֹמֵךְ, (the י having crept in, and the Chirek consequently having been written by mistake under the מ), part. Qal of תמך, which means both "to hold in the hand" (Amos i. 5, Prov. xxxi. 19), and "to support with the hand" (xvii. 5, xli. 13, &c.). No other exactly analogous form occurs, but there is a similar introduction of י in the form סֹבֵיב, 2 Kings viii. 21.

k נַחֲלָת for נַחֲלָתִי, parallel with גּוֹרָלִי above. Sim. זִמְרָת, Exod. xv. 2 (after עָזִּי; see the same phrase repeated, Is. xii. 2, Ps. cxviii. 14); or it may be for נַחֲלָה, as עֶזְרָת for עֶזְרָה, lx. 13, cviii. 13. See also similar forms, cxxxii. 4, Num. xi. 32, Jonah iv. 7. The LXX. and the Syr. support the former explanation, as they express the pronoun: the Chald. and Jerome ("hæreditas speciosissima mea est") the latter. Either, therefore, (1) "my inheritance pleases me well" or (2) "it is an inheritance which pleases me well" (lit. is fair for me, or in my estimation). Comp. civ. 34, יֶעֱרַב עָלָיו, "may it please Him, be sweet for Him."

l חסידיך. Does this stand for חֲסִידֶיךָ, "thy beloved ones" (plur.), or are we to adopt the correction of the Massoretes, who give חֲסִידְךָ as the Q'ri? The plur. has found favour with most of the modern critics (except Delitzsch and Stier); but the weight of critical authority is decidedly in favour of the sing. All the ancient Versions, without exception, have the singular. So also have St. Peter (Acts ii. 27) and St. Paul (xiii. 35). Further, the singular is found in the Babylon Talmud, *'Erubin* 19*a*, the Midrash Tehillim, the Yalqut Shime'oni (*in loco*, § 66) and many of the Rabbinical writers. It is also the reading of 269 MSS. (being more than half of the existing number); whilst in seven others the י is added by a later hand, and in four it is crossed out. Moreover, among these are the oldest and best MSS. On the other hand, in those in which the K'thîbh stands, it is with the punctuation of the singular, and often with the marginal annotation י יתיר, "the Yod is superfluous." Against all this it is in vain to urge that the plur., as the more difficult reading, ought to be retained. The plur. certainly *might* stand, for the Psalmist had already spoken of other "saints in the land," as well as of himself, and the change of number is not more abrupt than the אֵלֵינוּ in xl. 6. Nor would this overthrow the reference to Christ. That which is true of the members, is true in its highest sense of the head, and is only true of the members because they are joined to the head. But the weight of evidence clearly supports the singular, and this must have been felt from the earliest times; for it would have been to the interest of the Jews to have retained only the K'thibh.

m שַׁחַת. This is rendered here by the LXX. διαφθοράν, though elsewhere they give other equivalents. In vii. 16, xciv. 13, Prov. xxvi. 27, they have *βόθρος*: all the other ancient interpreters, without exception, give the meaning of "corruption," in this passage. But to this it has been objected, that the word elsewhere means either "a pit," or "the grave," and that such must be its meaning, because it is formed from the r. שׁוח, "to sink down," not from r. שחת, "to destroy." Only one passage can be alleged, viz. Job xvii. 14, where שַׁחַת seems to require the rendering "corruption," and that because of the parallelism with the word "worm."

Hence Winer's Simonis gives in that one passage the signification *corruptio, putredo.* (And so does Prof. R. Smith, regarding it as a distinct word from a different root, being in that passage masc., the other word being always fem.—a distinction which seems very doubtful, as the pron. אַתָּה may be attracted into the gender of the immediately preceding noun אָבִי.) But, as Ges. (*Thes.* v. שׁוח) remarks, "grave" may be the parallel to "worm," as well as "corruption." He, however, admits the meaning "destruction" in Job xxxiii. 18, 22, 30; "*exitium, interitus* (hoc etiam ex foveæ vel ipsius sepulcri imagine ductum)." What, then, it may be asked, becomes of St. Paul's argument (Acts xiii. 35—37), that "David did see *corruption*, whereas He whom God raised up saw no *corruption*"? It is not essentially shaken. In the first place, even if we follow the LXX., we ought to translate, "David did see *destruction*," &c.; for διαφθορά means "destruction," not "corruption" (see their rendering of ix. 15, xxxv. 7; and in the next, if we adhere to the Hebrew, "David did *see the grave*, but He (Christ) . . . . did not *see the grave*," the argument is still true, if only we take the phrase "to see the grave," in its proper acceptation of dying as men generally do,—dying and abiding in death. So the expression occurs Ps. xlix. 9 [10]. Cf. lxxxix. 48 [49], "see death." Christ did not see the grave in the same sense as David did; for He could not be holden of it. That this is the true meaning of "seeing the grave," is further established by the use of the opp. phrase, "seeing life," *i.e.* abiding, remaining alive. This is substantially the interpretation of Hengstenberg (stigmatized by Dr. Pusey, *Daniel*, p. 501, as an "unhappy compromise"), and of Umbreit, *Brief an die Römer*, S. 174, who, though he admits that שַׁחַת may mean "corruption," denies any direct prediction here of the resurrection of Christ.

PSALM 17

In this Psalm, a servant of God, conscious of his own uprightness, and surrounded by enemies, prays to be kept from the evil world, and from evil men who persecute him; and then from the dark present looks forward with joy to the bright future.

Every tried and tempted servant of God may find in it the touchstone whereby to prove himself; the sure refuge whither to betake himself; the hope which is the anchor of the soul, and which entereth within the veil. The Psalm may be, as the inscription states, a Psalm of David; and if so, we may probably attribute its composition to the time of Saul's persecution.

It may be divided into three strophes :—

I. The Psalmist's confidence in his appeal to God. Ver. 1—5.

(*a*) This is based upon the righteousness of his cause, and the absence of all hypocrisy in his prayer. Ver. 1, 2.

(*b*) The consciousness of this integrity further declared, and that even on the closest scrutiny. Both heart (ver. 3) and life (ver. 4, 5) are free from reproach, notwithstanding the evil by which he is surrounded.

II. Prayer to be kept in the evil world. Ver. 6—12.

(*a*) The appeal now lies to God's marvellous loving-kindness and tender affection, that he may be protected against his enemies.

(*b*) The description of their bitterness (ver. 9), their pride (ver. 10), and their relentless persecution (ver. 11, 12) is then given.

III. The spirit of the world, and the spirit which is of God. Ver. 13—15.

(*a*) Prayer that the sword of Jehovah may overtake his enemies.

(*b*) And then the broad contrast, not without its consolation: their portion, at the best, is for this life, and then perishes; mine is in the Presence and the Vision of God, and therefore cannot be taken from me.

[A PRAYER OF DAVID.]

I. 1 HEAR, O Jehovah, righteousness;
 Hearken to my cry;
Give ear to my prayer
 Which (is uttered) by no deceitful lips.
2 From Thy presence let my judgement go forth;
 Thine eyes behold uprightness!
3 Thou hast proved my heart;
 Thou hast visited (me) by night;

1. Not only a righteous cause, but a righteous prayer, offered in all sincerity, with no hypocritical reserve or pretence, are urged as motives why God should hear him. Calvin remarks on the importance of joining prayer to the testimony of a good conscience, lest we defraud God of His honour by not committing all judgement to Him.

2. In this verse both verbs may be either *presents* or *optatives*. Hence we may render, (1) "Let my sentence . . . may Thine eyes behold," &c.; so the LXX., Syr., Vulg., and Arab.: or (2) "Thy sentence goes forth . . . . Thine eyes behold," &c.: or (3) the first verb may be opt., and the second present, which is Hupfeld's rendering; and so also Stier and Mendelssohn.

3. This has given offence to some as an over-bold assertion of innocence. Hence the Jewish interpreters supposed it to have been written by David before his fall. Others, as Zunz, make the sentence conditional. "Prüfst du mein Herz . . . . — dass du nichts fändest!

Thou hast tried me (and) findest no evil thought [a]
in me,
Neither doth my mouth transgress.
4 As for [b] the doings of men,—by the word of Thy lips
I have kept (me from) the ways of the destroyer:
5 Holding fast [c] with my goings in Thy paths,
My footsteps have not been moved.

II. 6 As for me—I have called upon Thee, for Thou
answerest me, O God:
Incline Thine ear unto me; hear my speech.

Hab' ich Böses gesonnen, dass es nicht gehe über meinen Mund!" But it is not absolute innocence which the Psalmist here asserts: he is not indulging in self-righteous boasting, but appealing to God as knowing his uprightness of heart and honesty of purpose. Calvin gives the sense very well: "Tu, Domine, qui creando omnes cordis mei sensus tenes, sicuti tuum est probare homines, optime nosti *me non esse duplicem nec quicquam fraudis intus alere.*"

HAST PROVED—HAST TRIED—both words used of the testing of metals, and especially the latter, which means properly to melt in the fire, so as to separate the dross from the ore.

BY NIGHT, as the season of quiet thought and self-examination. Comp. iv. 4 [5], xvi. 7.

The latter half of this verse might be rendered with Delitzsch, "Thou hast tried me and findest nothing: Have I entertained an evil thought? —it shall not pass my mouth," for (1) the accent in זמתי is not conclusive against it (see Critical Note), and (2) עבר by itself does not seem to be used in the sense of *to transgress* or *sin*.

4. THE DOINGS OF MEN, *i.e.* the common course of action of worldly men. "Men" = the great mass of men (opposed to the "doings of Jehovah," xxviii. 5), and here contrasted with "the word of God." Comp. the expression "after the manner of men" (Hos. vi. 7, Job xxxi. 33). Whatever men in general may do or say, I have but one guide and rule of action, viz. Thy word. This is the first mention of the opposition to which he was exposed, and of that contrast which comes out more clearly in the next strophe, and which is completed in the last.

I HAVE KEPT (ME FROM), lit. "I have watched, observed," but here evidently with the further notion of watching so as to avoid: and so rightly Symm. ἐγὼ ἐφυλαξάμην ὁδοὺς παραβάτου. The pron. is emphatic, as again ver. 6, and may be explained both by the strong sense on the one hand of the Psalmist's uprightness and consequent relation to God, and on the other as a tacit opposition to the enemies spoken of ver. 9, 10. He seems anxious, as it were, to place himself in his distinct and proper character before God, and to isolate himself from the wicked.

5. See Job xxiii. 11, Ps. xli. 12 [13].

6—12. The prayer to be kept in the evil world. The earnest, affectionate cleaving to God, the prayer to be hidden in the shadow of His wings, is proof enough that the former part of the Psalm is no merely self-righteous boast.

7 Show Thy marvellous[d] loving-kindnesses, O Thou that
savest those who find refuge (in Thee)
From them that lift themselves up against Thy right
hand.
8 Keep me as the apple—as the pupil—of an eye,
Hide me in the shadow of Thy wings,
9 Because of the wicked who would destroy me,
(Because of) mine enemies who eagerly compass me
about.
10 (In) their fat have they enclosed (themselves),
With their mouth they speak proudly.
11 Whithersoever we go, have they now surrounded us;

7. SHOW, &c., lit. "make wonderful," *i.e.* exhibit in a marked manner Thy loving-kindness, which looks at first sight as if David expected a special miracle to be wrought in his favour. Hence Calvin excuses the prayer by the greatness of the strait and peril which drove him to ask for this extraordinary deliverance. But the truth is, that the notion contained in the verb only expresses the general *well-known* character of God's loving-kindness, which is always wonderful (so De Muys, "exsere omnem *illam* mirificam tuam clementiam"), and this David desires to experience as others have experienced it before him, as follows.

THOSE WHO FIND REFUGE, absol. as Prov. xiv. 26; comp. οἱ καταφυγόντες, Heb. vi. 18.

8. Both the images in this verse, alike expressive of the affection of the Psalmist and of his deep sense of God's tender care and love to him, are borrowed from the beautiful passage in Deut. xxxii. 10, 11. For the former, see also Zech. ii. 8. The latter occurs frequently. In the New Testament our Lord uses the still more tender image of the hen gathering her brood under her wings (Matt. xxiii. 37).

9. EAGERLY, lit. "with the soul," *i.e.* with the longing desire to destroy me. (So the Chald. "with the desire of their souls.") Others, "my enemies against the soul" (so the Syr. "enemies of my soul"), *i.e.* "my deadly enemies;" but this is harsh, especially with the omission of the pronoun (we should expect it to be expressed), and the former is supported by xxvii. 12, xli. 2 [3], where the word "soul" is used in the same way.

10. IN THEIR FAT, &c. lit. "Their fat have they shut up." This may refer both to the outward condition and the state of heart. These men led a luxurious and selfish life (as is further said, ver. 14), in consequence of which they had become proud and unfeeling. For this double meaning of "fatness," comp. on the one hand Deut. xxxii. 15, Job xv. 27, and on the other, Ps. cxix. 70, Isa. vi. 10. Others render, "they have closed their *heart*" (see for this meaning of the word, Ges. *Thes.* in v., and Hupfeld in his *Comm.*), *i.e.* they have no feeling of compassion, like κλείειν τὰ σπλάγχνα, 1 John iii. 17, and so Theodoret, ἀποκλείσαντες εὐσπλαγχνίαν = εὔνοιαν καὶ φιλαδελφίαν.

11. WHITHERSOEVER WE GO, lit. "*Our steps*, have they now surrounded *us*," there being thus a double object of the verb, viz. the person and the part of the person,

Their eyes do they set to cast (us) down to the
earth,
12 Like as a lion that is greedy to ravin,
And as a young lion lurking in (his) lair.

III. 13 Arise, O Jehovah, go forth to meet him, cast him
down;
Deliver my soul from the wicked, by Thy sword.
14 From men, O Jehovah, by Thy hand,—from men of
the world,[e]
Whose portion is in (this) life, and whose belly Thou
fillest with Thy treasures,
Who are satisfied with sons, and leave their substance
to their children.

just as in iii. 7 [8], "Thou hast smitten all *mine enemies* on the *cheek-bone*."

TO CAST DOWN, in same sense as in xviii. 9 [10], lxii. 4 [5]. No object is expressed. We may supply "us," or, "our steps," from the first hemistich; cf. lxxxiii. 2, or more widely, "whatever comes in their way."

12. LIKE AS A LION, lit. "his likeness is (that of) a lion," where the sing. may be distributive, viz. each of them is as a lion; or one particular enemy, as leader of the rest, may be present to his mind.

13. If the enemy be thus fierce and powerful, the more need for a powerful protector. The image is a common one in the Psalms, but may have been suggested in the first instance by David's personal experience. See note on iii. 7 [8].

GO FORTH TO MEET HIM, just as David himself went forth, to meet first the lion and the bear, and afterwards the champion of Gath.

BY THY SWORD, and in ver. 14, BY THY HAND. These words are accusatives further defining the action of the verbs: they denote the *instrument with which* the deliverance was to be effected, and are not in apposition with the nouns after which they are placed. David does not here regard the wicked as the sword of God, as Isaiah (x. 5) does the Assyrian as the rod of His anger—a thought which would be quite at variance with the whole scope of the Psalm—but calls upon God to destroy them.

14. MEN OF THE WORLD. The word here used for "world" (*cheled*) denotes the transitory nature of the world as a thing of *time*. Men of the world are those who have made it their home, and who, together with the world and the lust thereof, are passing away. (Comp. "men of the earth," Ps. x. 18.) In the New Testament they are the *κόσμος* of St. John, and the *υἱοὶ τοῦ αἰῶνος τούτου*, Luke xvi. 8. Being thus worldly-minded, they have *their portion* in life, *i.e.* in the brief years of their existence upon earth. (For this absolute use of the word LIFE, see Eccl. vi. 12, ix. 9.) Then this love of the world is opposed to the love of the Father, not the present to the future, so much as the temporal to the eternal, the world to God. The contrast to "their portion in this life" is to be found in xvi. 5, "Jehovah is my portion;" and in ver. 15 of this

15 As for me—in righteousness let me behold Thy face;

Psalm. On the one side, the Outward, the Transitory, the Unreal: on the other, the Inward, the Abiding, the True. We have here a view of the *world* and of *life* very remarkable for the Old Testament —a kind of anticipation of the contrast between the flesh and the spirit which St. Paul gives us, or the love of the world and of God, of which St. John speaks.

15. Worldly men have their *satisfaction* in this life, in treasures, in children; David hopes to be *satisfied* with the likeness, or rather real, manifest *bodily form* (תְּמוּנָה) of God. The personal pron. stands emphatically at the beginning of the verse, in order to mark the contrast between his own feelings and those of the men of the world. He hopes (as Job also does, xix. 26, 27) to see God. (The parall. of the next clause shows that this must mean more than merely "to enjoy His favour, the light of His countenance," &c. as in xi. 7.) There is an allusion probably to such a manifestation of God as that made to Moses, Numb. xii. 8, where God declares that with Moses He will speak "mouth to mouth, even apparently, and not in dark speeches; and the similitude (rather *form*, the same word as here) of Jehovah shall he behold."

WHEN I AWAKE. How are we to understand these words? (1) Certainly not "when I wake up from sleep," as Ewald and others explain, because of the reference to the night in ver. 3. This would give a lean and hungry sense indeed. Why should David expect a clear vision of God, and especially of His form, on the following morning, or on the morning of any day, more than at any other time? (2) Nor again does he mean by "waking," a deliverance from the present night of sorrow and suffering, as though he would say, This my sorrow shall pass away, and then I shall see God as my deliverer (which may perhaps be the meaning of the hope which Job expresses, chap. xix.). So Calvin explains the "waking" of which David speaks, "ut tantundem valeat ac respirare a tristitia," and supposes him to have been so worn out by his afflictions as to have fallen into a kind of sleep or lethargy. But this seems an inadequate explanation. The night might be used as a figure of suffering, but the sufferer would scarcely be said to *sleep* in his suffering, and then to awake out of it. I cannot doubt that the reference is to "the waking from the sleep of death," and therefore to a resurrection. In opposition to this interpretation, it is commonly asserted that the truth of a resurrection had not yet been revealed, and that, consequently, if we find the doctrine here, the Ps. must be of later date, after the Exile. (So De Wette.) But this is mere assertion. First, as regards the use of the figure. "Waking" from death occurs in 2 Kings iv. 31. Death is spoken of as a sleep from which there is no awaking; Job xiv. 12, Jer. li. 39. Next, Is. xxvi. 19, "Awake—ye that sleep in the dust," plainly refers to the resurrection. (Hence critics who think this truth *could not* be known before the Exile, are obliged to suppose that this chapter was written *after* that time.) Again, why should not David have attained, in some degree, to the knowledge of a truth, which in later times was so clearly revealed as it was to Ezekiel (who makes use of it as the image of the resurrection of Israel, xxxvii. 1—14) and to Daniel (xii. 2)? Is it astonishing that a truth should first appear somewhat dimly expressed, and afterwards shine with a greater brightness? Is it strange that a conviction should be possessed and uttered by one man ages before it becomes the common heritage of all? May there not be even now truths slumbering in the Bible which have not yet been fully

Let me be satisfied, when I awake, with Thine image.

grasped by Christian men? In all times there are men whom God takes into a nearer communion with Himself, and who attain to an insight and an utterance beyond that of the dull unripe world.

[a] זַמֹּתִי. This looks like 1 perf. of זמם, and so perhaps it was taken by the Chald., which, however, seems to fluctuate in its rendering; but this is not in accordance with the accent, which is on the *last syllable.* [Del. however refers to Deut. xxxii. 41, Is. xliv. 16, as containing examples of a similar accentuation of the perfect.] Nor is it a noun with suff. from זַמָּה = זִמָּה (Ges. *Lex.*), but an *infinitive* of verb ע״ע, like חַלּוֹת, שַׁמּוֹת, חַנּוֹת, with the fem. termination וֹת־, borrowed from verbs ל״ה. According to the Massoretic punctuation, it is to be joined to the words following. Hence many render, "my thought varies not from (lit. passes not by יַעֲבָר) my mouth," *i.e.* I do not think one thing, and say another: others taking פִּי as subj. not as obj., "my mouth goes not beyond my thought," *i.e.* I do not say more than I think. But זמם and זִמָּה commonly refer to *evil* thoughts and devices (see x. 4). Hence it would be better to render, "No evil thought of mine passes over my mouth." But it seems best, following most of the older Vers., to connect זַמֹּתִי with the preceding words. So the LXX. οὐχ εὑρέθη ἐν ἐμοὶ ἀδικία. So too the Syr., Chald. (altern.), Arab., and Æth., but *not* Jerome (as Hupfeld asserts), at least not in the best MSS., which have "cogitatio mea utinam non transisset os meum;" others, however, read "non invenisti cogitationes meas."

[b] לִפְעֻלּוֹת א׳. The לְ is here either the prep. of general reference, "with regard to," or the לְ of *time*, as in xxxii. 6, לְשֵׁטֶף (Hupf.), or *condition*, as in lxix. 22 (Del.). But neither of these instances is exactly parallel to that in the text. Many of the older interpreters join these words with the preceding verse. The LXX. ὅπως ἂν μὴ λαλήσῃ τὸ στόμα μου τὰ ἔργα τῶν ἀνθρώπων. Vulg. "non loquatur os meum opera hominum." Syr. "Nor have the works of men passed over my mouth in the discourse of [my] lips."

[c] תָּמֹךְ. The infin. absol. perhaps used for the finite verb (not for the imperat., which is against the connection, and moreover would require a fut. instead of a pret. in the next member); and either for the 1st pers. sing., or for 3d pers. plur., "I have held with my goings," or, "my goings have held." Or the infin. may be (as Hupf. suggests) like the Lat. gerund in *-do*, the first member of this verse being connected either with the last of ver. 4, "I have kept me . . . . by holding fast," &c., or with the one immediately following, "By holding fast, my footsteps have not moved." See the same constr. in xxxv. 15, 16.

[d] הַפְלֵה, prop. "separate," "set apart," but with the further idea of something that is *wonderful* or *miraculous* = הַפְלֵא. Comp. Ex. xxxiii. 16, and Ps. cxxxix. 14, and see above, note on iv. 4. See the same phrase in xxxi. 22, הִפְלִיא חַסְדּוֹ. The LXX. θαυμάστωσον τὰ ἐλέη σου. In the same way the idea contained in the verb passes over to the noun in Is. xxviii. 29, הִ׳ עֵצָה.

ᵉ חֶלֶד = עוֹלָם, *αἰών*, *ævum*, prop. "time," "life-time," xxxix. 6, lxxxix. 48 (אֲנִי מֶה חָלֶד, *ego quantilli sim ævi*), Job xi. 17 (*life* itself); then, that which is subject to time, *the world* (comp. the later uses of עוֹלָם, *αἰών*, and *sæculum*), as in xlix. 2, ח '', "inhabitants of the *world*." The root signif. may be that of *transitoriness*, the same as חדל by mere transposition of letters, or it may be connected with the Syr. ܚܠܕ, "to creep, to crawl," whence in Heb. חֹלֶד, and words from the same root in Syr. and Arab. mean "a mole." The idea therefore of חֶלֶד is that of time as *slowly creeping on*. In Arab. خلد is "to grow gradually old."

PSALM 18

In this magnificent hymn the Royal Poet sketches in a few grand outlines the tale of his life—the record of his marvellous deliverances and of the victories which Jehovah had given him—the record, too, of his own heart, the truth of its affection towards God, and the integrity of purpose by which it had ever been influenced. Throughout that singularly chequered life, hunted as he had been by Saul before he came to the throne, and harassed perpetually after he became king by rivals who disputed his authority and endeavoured to steal away the hearts of his people—compelled to fly for his life before his own son, and engaged afterwards in long and fierce wars with foreign nations—one thing had never forsaken him, the love and the presence of Jehovah. By His help he had subdued every enemy, and now, in his old age, looking back with devout thankfulness on the past, he sings this great song of praise to the God of his life. With a heart full of love he will tell *how* Jehovah delivered him, and then there rises before the eye of his mind the whole force and magnitude of the peril from which he had escaped. So much the more wonderful appears the deliverance, which accordingly he represents in a bold poetical figure, as a stooping of the Most High from heaven to save him—who comes, as He came of old to Sinai, with all the terror and gloom of earthquake, and tempest, and thick darkness. But God delivers those only who trust in Him, and who are like Him. There must be an inner life of communion with God, if man will know His mercy. Hence David passes on to that covenant relationship in which He had stood to God. He had ever been a true Israelite, and therefore God, the true God of Israel, had dealt with him accordingly. And thus it is at the last that the servant of

Jehovah finds his reward. Jehovah, to whom he had ever looked, did not forsake him, but girded him with strength to the battle, and made even distant nations the vassals of his sway.

The hymn concludes as it had opened, with a joyful thanksgiving to Jehovah, who had done so great things for him.

The inscription, which informs us that this hymn was composed towards the close of David's life, is confirmed by the fact that we have the same account given of its composition in 2 Sam. xxii., where this hymn is also found, though with a number of variations. The internal evidence, too, points in the same direction; for we learn from ver. 34 [35] and 43 [44] that the Poet is both warrior and king; and every part of the description suits the events and circumstances of David's life better than those of any other monarch.

The Psalm consists of three principal divisions or strophes, together with an introduction and conclusion :—

I. Introduction, setting forth all that Jehovah is to the Psalmist. Ver. 1—3.

II. Strophe I. The record of David's sufferings and peril, and the mighty deliverance by which he was rescued. Ver. 4—19.

III. Strophe II. The reason for this deliverance as based upon the character of God and the principles of His moral government. Ver. 20—30.

IV. Strophe III. The blessings which he had received in his life; his own preservation and that of his race (ver. 28); help and strength in battle, rule over all enemies. Ver. 31—45.

V. Conclusion, consisting of a joyful thanksgiving and acknowledgement of all God's mercies. Ver. 46—50.

[FOR THE PRECENTOR. (A PSALM) OF DAVID, THE SERVANT OF JEHOVAH, WHO SPAKE UNTO JEHOVAH THE WORDS OF THIS SONG, IN THE DAY THAT JEHOVAH DELIVERED HIM OUT OF THE HAND OF ALL HIS ENEMIES, AND OUT OF THE HAND OF SAUL: AND HE SAID :]

1 FERVENTLY do I love Thee, O Jehovah, my strength.

SERVANT OF JEHOVAH. Also in the inscr. of Ps. xxxvi., and, in the mouth of God, "my servant," lxxxix. 3 [4], 20 [21], as 2 Sam. iii. 18, vii. 5. David is so called in a special sense as one put in office, and commissioned by God. The same title is applied also to Moses, Joshua, the Prophets, the Angels, &c., as sent by God to do His work. It is strictly an *official* designation, but is never applied by any person to himself. In this it differs from the δοῦλος Θεοῦ (Χριστοῦ) of the New Testament. (Philip. i. 1; Tit. i. 1.)

1—3. Looking back upon his

2 Jehovah is my stronghold and my fortress, and my
Deliverer,
My God is my rock wherein I find refuge,
My shield and the horn of my salvation, my high tower.
3 I will call upon Jehovah who is worthy to be praised,[a]
So shall I be saved from mine enemies.

4 The bands of death compassed me,

eventful life, a life full of peril and full of mercy, David pours out his heart, first in the expression of strong and tender love (רחם, the verb in Qal, and in this meaning, occurs only here) to his God; and then in the attempt to set forth in some measure, by employing one figure after another, all that God had been to him during the days of his pilgrimage.

The images, which are most of them of a martial character, are borrowed from the experience of David's life, and the perpetual struggles in which he was engaged. Some of them were suggested by the natural configuration of Palestine. Amid the "rocks" and "fastnesses" of his native land, and the "high tower" perched on some inaccessible crag, he, with his band of outlaws, had often found a safe hiding place from the wrath of Saul.

The "shield" and the "horn" seem to stand respectively for all weapons of *defence* and *offence*. The shield, as covering the body; the horn, as a symbol of strength in attack (itself an image, borrowed from animals who push with their horns). Comp. Deut. xxxiii. 17; 1 Kings xxii. 11. The image is very common in the Psalter. For a like crowding together of metaphors in address to God, see the opening of Pss. xxxi. lxxi.

3. I WILL CALL. The futures in this verse do not express a present resolution, but are either (1) *aorists*, and mark the constant habit of his past life = "it has ever been my wont to call upon Jehovah, and He has saved me," a statement which is then further expanded in what follows: or (2) they may express the conviction of faith = "whenever I cry, I shall be delivered." (See note on iii. 4 [5].) Then follows the record of his past experience, which gives the reason both for his *love* of Jehovah, and his prayer to Him.

4—6. As he looks back on the past, he gathers into one all the perils to which he had been exposed, all the sufferings which he had endured, and so measures them not by the depth or intensity of any one, but by their aggregated volume and pressure. It was as if they had risen and swelled above him wave upon wave; he had been as a swimmer, beaten and buffeted to and fro till his strength was spent, and it had like to have gone hard with him for his life. He was sinking (comp. xxx. 3 [4]; xxxii. 6; xl. 2 [3]; lxix. 1, 2 [2, 3]), and, like Jonah, seemed beyond reach of succour (Jon. ii. 4, 6, 7):—or, varying the figure, he had been taken in the toils, which Death, like a mighty hunter, had cast about him (ver. 5). But even in this his uttermost strait he was not beyond the reach of God's arm. Neither the depths of the sea nor the gates of Death can resist Jehovah's power. Therefore, when from the lowest depths the prayer goes up to Jehovah in heaven, He reaches forth His hand from the highest heaven to the uttermost abyss, and plucks His servant from the jaws of Death.

4. THE BANDS OR "CORDS." LXX. ὠδῖνες θανάτου (cf. Acts ii. 24), "the pains or pangs of Death;" a possible meaning, but not so suit-

And the floods of ungodliness[b] made me afraid.[c]
5 The bands of hell surrounded me,
The snares of death came upon me.
6 In my distress I called upon Jehovah,
And unto my God did I cry:
He heard my voice out of His temple,
And my cry before Him came unto His ears.
7 Then the earth was moved and did quake,

able here to the context, where Death is represented, as in the next verse, as a hunter (cf. xci. 3). But in Sam. the word employed means "billows," or lit. "breakers," instead of "bands."

5. HELL, *lit.* "Sheol," "the unseen world," or here = "the grave."

6. TEMPLE, *i.e.* not the temple, or tabernacle (see v. 7 [8]), on Mount Zion, but the Temple in heaven, wherein God especially manifests His glory, and where He is worshipt by the heavenly hosts—a place which is both temple and palace. See xi. 4, xxix. 9.

All the verbs in this verse are imperfect, expressing habit. It might be rendered: "In my distress I would call upon Jehovah, and unto my God would I cry; He would hear my voice out of His temple; and my cry before Him would come unto His ears."

On the constant interchange of the preterite with the imperfect or aorist in this Psalm, see more in the critical notes.

7—19. The deliverance is now pictured as a magnificent theophany. God comes to rescue His servant as He came of old to Sinai, and all nature is moved at His coming. Similar descriptions of the Divine manifestation, and of the effects produced by it, occur lxviii. 7, 8 [8, 9], lxxvii. 14—20 [15—21], Ex. xix. Judg. v. 4, Am. ix. 5, Micah i. 3, Hab. iii.; but the image is nowhere so fully carried out as here. David's deliverance was of course not really accompanied by such convulsions of nature, by earthquake and fire and tempest, but his deliverance, or rather his manifold deliverances, gathered into one, as he thinks of them, appear to him as marvellous a proof of the Divine Power, as verily effected by the immediate presence and finger of God, as if He had come down in visible form to accomplish them.

The image is carefully sustained throughout. First, we have the earthquake, and then, as preluding the storm and as herald of God's wrath, the blaze of the lightning (ver. 7, 8). Next, the thick gathering of clouds, which seem to touch and envelope the earth; the wind, and the darkness, which shrouds Jehovah riding on the cherubim (9—11). Lastly, the full outburst of the storm, the clouds parting before the presence and glory of Jehovah, and pouring upon the earth the burden with which they were heavy—the thunder, and the lightning, and the hail,—the weapons of Jehovah by which, on the one hand He discomfits His enemies, and, on the other, lays bare the depths of the sea and the very foundations of the world, that He may save His servant who trusts in Him (12—16).

The image with which the description opened in ver. 4, of a sinking, drowning man, is resumed in ver. 16, and thus completes the whole. In ver. 17—19 the figure is dropped, and the language falls into a lower key.

7. The earthquake. In Sam., instead of foundations of the mountains, "foundations of heaven," by

And the foundations of the mountains began to tremble,
And were moved to and fro because He was wroth.
8 There went up a smoke in His nostrils,
And a fire out of His mouth devoured,
Coals were kindled by it.
9 And He bowed the heavens, and came down,
And thick darkness was under His feet.
10 And He rode upon a cherub and did fly,
And came flying upon the wings of the wind.
11 He made [d] darkness His secret place, His pavilion round about Him,
Dark gloom of waters, thick clouds of the skies.

which probably the mountains are meant, which elsewhere are compared to pillars which bear up the heaven (Job xxvi. 11).

8. The swift approach of the storm is vividly described. The *smoke* and the *fire* are symbols of the Divine wrath before which all creation must tremble (see ver. 7): here they are the clouds and the lightning of the storm, probably as seen about the mountain summits and in the distance.

IN HIS NOSTRILS. Some have taken offence at the apparent coarseness of the figure, and would therefore render, "in His anger." But the other is more in accordance with the parallelism, "out of His mouth," in the next clause, and may be defended by "the blasting of the breath of Thy nostrils," ver. 15. Cf. Deut. xxix. 19 [E.V. 20]: "The anger of Jehovah . . . shall smoke against that man."

9. HE BOWED THE HEAVENS, which, with their dark masses of low hanging clouds, seemed almost to touch the earth. Comp. cxliv. 5 and Is. lxiii. 9.

10. AND HE RODE. In the midst of the storm, though hidden, is Jehovah Himself. The wrath of the elements is no blind power, but is guided and controlled by Him.

UPON A CHERUB; or, perhaps, rather a collective noun, and so used for the plural. The cherubim are, as it were, the living chariot of Jehovah, and in their form, being compounded of a man, a bull, a lion, and an eagle (see Ezek. i. and x.), seem to symbolize the powers of nature. As to the etymology of the word "cherub," we are still quite in the dark. It remains what Bähr calls it, a *crux interpretum.* But there can be little doubt that the cherubim—the *living* creatures of Ezekiel—were emphatically the representatives of the life of the creature, and that in its most perfect form The four animals of which the cherub is composed belong to the highest class of organized beings, so that the old Jewish proverb (T. B. *Chagigah*, 13^b) says: "Four things are chiefest in the world. The lion among beasts, the bull among cattle, the eagle among birds, and man among all (creatures); but God is the Most High over all." See Bähr, *Symbol d. Mos. Cult.* i. pp. 311, 340, &c.; Herder, *Geist d. Heb. Poes.* i. 1, 6, &c. There is evidently a connection between this and the heathen symbols, such, for instance, as they appear on the Assyrian monuments. Compare, too, the description in the *Prometheus* of Æschylus, of the approach of Oceanus, who comes τὸν πτερυγωκῆ τόνδ' οἰωνὸν γνώμῃ στομίων ἄτερ εὐθύνων.

12 At the brightness that was before Him, His thick clouds passed,[e]—
Hail-stones and coals of fire.
13 Jehovah also thundered in the heavens,
And the Highest gave His voice,
Hail-stones and coals of fire.
14 And He sent forth His arrows, and scattered them,
And lightnings innumerable,[f] and discomfited them.
15 Then the channels of water were seen,
And the foundations of the world were discovered,
At Thy rebuke, O Jehovah,
At the blasting of the breath of Thy nostrils.
16 He sent from above; He took me,
He drew me out of many waters,
17 He delivered me from my strong enemy,
And from them that hated me; for they were too strong for me.
18 They came upon me in the day of my calamity,
But Jehovah was my stay.
19 And He brought me forth into a large place,
He delivered me, because He delighted in me.

20 Jehovah rewarded me according to my righteousness,
According to the cleanness of my hands did He recompense me.
21 For I have kept the ways of Jehovah,
And have not wickedly departed from my God.
22 For all His judgements are before me,
And His statutes do I not put away from me.

12. AT THE BRIGHTNESS, &c., *i.e.* the reflection of His glory, which seems to pierce and part the clouds, which then discharge the hail, the lightning, and the thunder. The repetition of the words, "hailstones and coals of fire," adds much to the force of the description: "Hail is rare in Palestine, but often the more terrible and destructive when it does fall. Comp. Job xxxviii. 22, Josh. x. 11."—*Ewald.*

20—30. Next follows the reason for this deliverance—the first hint of which had already been given in the preceding verse in the words, "because He delighted in me." God deals with men according as He sees their heart to be towards Him. Those who walk before Him

23 I have also been perfect with Him,
And have kept myself from iniquity.
24 Therefore Jehovah recompensed me according to my righteousness;
According to the cleanness of my hands in His eyesight.
25 With the good Thou wilt show Thyself good,
With a perfect man Thou wilt show Thyself perfect.
26 With the pure Thou wilt show Thyself pure,
And with the perverse Thou wilt show Thyself froward.
27 For THOU savest the afflicted people,
And bringest down high looks.

in simplicity and uprightness of heart may expect His succour. And David here, as in the last Psalm, asserts not his freedom from sin, but the consciousness of his own integrity. Some, indeed, have seen in the language a too boastful spirit, and therefore would refer this Psalm, as well as the last, to the time before David's fall. Bunsen even thinks that the self-righteous feeling here betrayed laid him open to temptation, and was the first step in his departure from God. But such a notion has no support from the general tenour of the Psalm, which everywhere breathes a spirit of confidence and trust in God, as far removed as possible from the spirit of self-righteousness. The words are, in truth, words of childlike, open-hearted simplicity, not of arrogant boastfulness. Some allowance, too, must perhaps be made for the fact that under the Old Covenant the knowledge of sin was more superficial than it is under the New. Yet St. Paul does not hesitate to say: "I have lived in all good conscience before God unto this day;" and a man may call himself a miserable sinner, and yet be more of a Pharisee than one who asserts his own righteousness. [It may, however, be fairly doubted whether David would have used such language as this after his fall; and although the Psalm is placed in 2 Sam. at the end of David's history, it does not follow that it was *written* at the close of his life. The special mention of Saul in the inscription would rather favour an earlier time, perhaps the "rest" mentioned in 2 Sam. vii. 1.]

23. The language seems very strong, but is really to be explained (by a reference to the preceding and the following verse) of the desire and intention of the heart, and the earnest endeavour to avoid all known sin. Compare with this, David's testimony concerning himself, 1 Sam. xxvi. 23, 24; the testimony of God, 1 Kings xiv. 8; and the testimony of the history, 1 Kings xv. 5.

26. THOU WILT SHOW THYSELF FROWARD. The expression seems rough and harsh, but is no doubt designedly employed in contrast with what goes before. The meaning is—him who is perverse God gives up to follow his own perverse way, till it brings him to destruction. (See lxxxi. 12 [13], and Rom. i. 28.) It is also, of course, true, that to the perverse heart God Himself appears perverse. The wicked man thinks that God is "altogether such an one as himself;" but this idea is not so prominent here as the other.

The Chaldee Paraphrase gives Abraham, Isaac, and Jacob as examples of "the good" or "pious," the "perfect" and the "pure," re-

28 For THOU givest light to my lamp,
Jehovah my God maketh my darkness to be bright.
29 For by Thee I can rush against[g] a troop;
And by my God I can leap over a wall.
30 As for God—His way is perfect;
The word of Jehovah is tried;
He is a shield to all who find refuge in Him.

31 For who is God but Jehovah,
And who is a rock save our God?
32 The God who girdeth me with strength,
And maketh my way perfect;
33 Who maketh my feet like hinds' feet,
And setteth me on my high places;
34 Who traineth my hands for war,
So that mine arms can bend[h] a bow of brass.

spectively; and Pharaoh and the Egyptians as "the perverse," "whom, because they imagined evil devices against Thy people, Thou didst confound in their devices."

28. MY LAMP. Still more forcibly in Sam. "Thou, O Jehovah, art my lamp." The lamp lighted in the house is the image at once of *prosperity* and *continuance* of life and happiness. See cxxxii. 17, and of the house of David, 1 Kings xi. 36, xv. 4; 2 Kings viii. 19. So, on the other hand, the extinction of the royal race is compared to the quenching of the lamp, 2 Sam. xxi. 17.

29 FOR. Co-ordinate with the "for" in the two previous verses.

30. TRIED, *i.e.* like metal purified in the fire; in God's promise there is no admixture of alloy: see xii. 6 [7].

31—45. For this, the third principal division of the Psalm, the way has already been prepared in ver. 28—30, as descriptive both of what God is and of the help which He had vouchsafed to His servant. David now dwells in a strain of triumph on the victories and successes which God had given him. We see, therefore, how Strophes I. and III. are connected with Strophe II. The central thought is the relation in which David stands to God. Before the holy God he has walked in his integrity (ver. 20—27); and therefore on the one hand God delivered him from his peril (4—19), and on the other made him victorious over all enemies (31—45).

31. The reference is to Deut. xxxii. 4, 15, 18, &c.

32. MAKETH MY WAY PERFECT, correlative to "His way is perfect," ver. 30.

33. ON MY HIGH PLACES, *i.e.* the mountain strongholds which I have seized (as in taking the stronghold of Zion itself). On the occupation of these military positions would depend the possession of the whole country.

34. In the preceding verse the comparison with the hind denoted the extraordinary swiftness, which, whether for attack or escape, was considered a great excellence in the warriors of ancient times. Here, the bending of a bow of brass (or bronze rather, χαλκός, which seems to have been tempered and rendered

35 And Thou hast given me the shield of Thy salvation,
And Thy right hand hath holden me up,
And Thy graciousness hath made me great.
36 Thou hast made room for my footsteps under me,
That mine ankles have not slipped.
37 I pursued mine enemies and overtook them,
Neither did I turn again, until they were consumed.
38 I have smitten them, that they were not able to rise,
They are fallen under my feet.
39 For Thou hast girded me with strength to the battle;
Thou hast bowed down under me those that rose up against me,
40 Mine enemies also Thou hast made to turn their backs before me,
So that I destroyed them that hate me.
41 They cried,—but there was none to save them,—
Even unto Jehovah, but He answered them not.
42 And I beat them small as the dust before the wind,
Like the mire of the streets I emptied them out.
43 Thou hast delivered me from the strivings of the people;
Thou hast made me Head over the nations:
A people that I know not, serve me.
44 At the hearing of the ear, they obeyed me,[i]
The sons of the alien came crouching unto me.

pliable like steel with us) indicates his great strength (comp. Job xx. 24). In Homer, Ulysses leaves behind him at Ithaca a bow which no one but himself could bend.

35. Yet it is not the bow of brass which has been David's protection, but Jehovah's shield covered him; Jehovah's right hand held him up; Jehovah's wonderful condescension (by which he was taken from the sheepfolds to be king) made him great; Jehovah made room for him to stand, and subdued those that rose up against him.

THY GRACIOUSNESS, lit. "meekness," "lowliness," a very remarkable word as applied to God, and just one of those links connecting the Divine with the human, which in the Old Testament so strikingly foreshadow an incarnation. [It is easy to exclaim against anthropomorphisms, but they speak to the heart, which is never touched by cold philosophic abstractions.]

41. The cry extorted in terror, and not coming from an upright heart (ver. 24, &c.), is not heard. See the opposite, ver. 6.

44. AT THE HEARING OF THE EAR, *i.e.* even at a distance, without seeing me, as soon as they heard my command. (See Job xlii. 5.)

OBEYED, or "shall obey." (See Critical Note.)

45 The sons of the alien faded away,
They came trembling out of their fortresses.

46 Jehovah liveth, and blessed is my Rock,
And exalted the God of my salvation ;
47 (Even) the God who giveth me vengeance,
And (who) subdued peoples under me.
48 Thou art He that deliverest me from mine enemies ;
Yea, Thou liftest me up above those that rise against me ;
Thou hast delivered me from men of violence.
49 Therefore will I give thanks unto Thee, O Jehovah, among the nations ;
And to Thy Name will I sing praises :

CAME CROUCHING, lit. "lied unto me," so descriptive of the *abject, fawning* submission of the Oriental. Cf. lxvi. 3 (where see note), lxxxi. 15 [16], "feigned submission."

45. FADED AWAY, *i.e.* before the victorious might of David, like plants scorched and shriveled before the hot blast of the simoom (Is. xl. 7).

CAME TREMBLING (lit. trembled out of, &c.), *i.e.* in order to give in their submission and to implore the clemency and protection of the conqueror (Micah vii. 17). The verbs in this and the preceding verse *may* be rendered as *futures*, as in the E.V., and then they will express David's sure hope, based upon the past, of the final subjugation of all his enemies.

FASTNESSES, lit. places in which they had shut themselves up.

46—50. The hymn now concludes with the praise of Jehovah, who had done so great things for David and for his seed. And as Jehovah has not only placed him on the throne of Jerusalem, but has given him dominion over foreign nations, he will proclaim amongst these also the Name and the praises of his God. Here we have the first utterance of a hope, which in later times became clear and distinct, that the heathen should learn to fear and worship Jehovah. The Chald. Paraphrast on ver. 31 [32] gives a remarkable prominence to this expectation. After applying ver. 27, 28 [28, 29] to the deliverance of Israel from captivity (" Thou wilt light the lamp of Israel which has been put out in captivity," &c.), he thus expands ver. 31 [32]:—Because of the wonder and the redemption which Thou wilt accomplish for Thine Anointed, and for the remnant of Thy people which shall be left, all peoples, nations, and tongues shall praise (Thee), and shall say, "There is no God but Jehovah ; for there is none but Thou only ;" and Thy people shall say, "There is none strong save our God."

49. St. Paul quotes this verse Rom. xv. 9, as well as Deut. xxxii. 43, and Ps. cxvii. 1, as proof that the salvation of Christ belonged, in the purpose of God, to the Gentiles as well as the Jews. The Psalm therefore looks beyond David. David and David's rule over the nations are but a type and image of Christ, and of that spiritual kingdom which He came to establish. "Nec enim dubium est," says Luther, "Davidis bella et victorias Christi passionem et resurrectionem figurasse." At the same time he admits that it is very doubtful how far the Psalm

50 Who giveth great delivearnce to His King;
And showeth loving-kindness to His Anointed,
To David and his seed for evermore.

applies to Christ, and how far to David, "nec ipse hactenus certus factus sum utra intelligentia sit germana et propria ut citra periculum non queam hic versari." It would be well if the modesty of this great man were found in those who, having neither his faith nor his learning, pronounce their confident decisions on such questions.

a מְהֻלָּל. This word, by most of the older translators, is taken in an active sense, as if they read מְהַלֵּל. The LXX. *αἰνῶν ἐπικαλέσομαι, κ.τ.λ.* Vulg. *Laudans.* Chald. "In a hymn of praise do I utter my prayer." The Syr. joins it as an epithet to מִשְׂגַּבִּי in the previous verse, "my glorious refuge." Strictly it means "who is praised." So Jerome, *Laudatum invocabo Dominum.* But it may also mean "worthy to be praised," "glorious," as the one great object of praise, after the analogy of נוֹרָא, נֶחְמָד. Ewald takes it as a predicate: "Worthy to be praised is Jehovah, do I cry."

b בְּלִיַּעַל, "Belial," lit. "worthlessness" (fr. בְּלִי and יַעַל, fut. of עלה, in the sense of the cogn. root, Hiph. הוֹעִיל, "to profit, to be of service.") Here used perhaps of *physical* rather than of moral evil, from the parallelism with Death and Sheol. The older interpreters generally take it in the moral sense = "wickedness." So the LXX., *χείμαῤῥοι ἀνομίας*, as a designation of David's enemies, the abstract being put for the concrete. Finally, many give the word a personal meaning, and understand by it the Evil One, Satan (as Βελιάλ, 2 Cor. vi. 15). So Jerome, *torrentes diaboli*, a meaning, however, which is certainly later than the Old Testament. At any rate, *physical* evil can hardly be excluded here. Comp. xli. 9; Nahum i. 11. The E. V. never renders the word as a proper name except in the Historical Books, in the phrases "sons of Belial," "daughters of Belial;" everywhere else the word is translated. The LXX. never render it as a proper name.

c יְבַעֲתוּנִי, "began to terrify," or "were terrifying me." The verb must refer to the past because of the pret. אֲפָפוּנִי, going before. But the constant interchange of the preterites and futures (so called) in this Psalm is remarkable, and in many cases very perplexing. The context sometimes determines, as here, that the fut. must be taken as an imperf. or aorist, the time being, in fact, conditioned by the preterite preceding: So in ver. 7 (Heb.) אֶקְרָא must mean "I was wont to cry," . . . יִשְׁמַע, "he would ever hear," &c. (The text in Sam. has וַיִּשְׁמַע.) And then the *consequence* of this hearing is marked by the ו consec. at the beginning of ver. 8, וַתִּגְעַשׁ. Again, יִרְגָּזוּ must of necessity refer to the same time as the preceding verbs with the ו consec. Precisely in the same way in ver. 14 we have וַיַּרְעֵם, followed by יִתֵּן, where this last may be rendered "kept giving," as referring to the *repeated* crash of the thunders. The continued use of the futures, however, in ver. 17, 18, 19, is more noticeable. They do not alternate here, as in the previous instances, with preterites, or futures with ו consec. Yet they can only refer to past time, and then not to repeated action, but to *the* deliverance which was the result of the Theophany. In verses 26—29 (in the Eng. Vers. 25—28) the futures are strict aorists, denoting habit. In ver. 30, they may either be futures proper, or—which seems to me better—have a sort of potential meaning.

In verses 38, 39, 43, 44—46, there is again considerable doubt as to the proper rendering of the futures. Most of the old Verss. here give the strict *future* meaning. So the Chald., except in ver. 43. The LXX. in 38, 39, and 43, 44. Jerome in 37, 38, and 42—46. The Syr. in the whole passage, 38—46; even where the fut. with ו consec. occurs in ver. 40, and the pret. in ver. 41. The English Version adopts the fut. only in the last member of ver. 44, and in ver. 45, 46 (in the English Vers. 43—45). Hupfeld also contends for the *future*, beginning at ver. 38. He thinks that we have not mere narration, but a general expression of confidence for all future time, based upon and flowing out of the deliverance already accomplished. (This is, no doubt, somewhat confirmed by the fact, that in 2 Sam. we have the optat. form, אֶרְדְּפָה, in the parallel passage.) Others, as Ewald, Hengstenberg, &c., take the futures here as *presents.* I incline, however (with Maurer), to think that the reference of the verbs is still to the past, and I would explain them as aorists, of repeated past action, though it is quite possible that David, here transferring himself into the past, might use these futures as proper futures, *speaking from the past,* and not from the present.

[d] יָשֵׁת. In 2 Sam. וַיָּשֶׁת, the historic tense, which seems almost necessary. יָשֵׁת may, however, stand, as introducing a subordinate explanatory clause,—"whilst He made," &c.

[e] This has been differently interpreted: (1) "At the brightness that was before Him, His thick clouds passed away—or, separated themselves—(so that) hail and coals of fire (issued from them);" (2) . . . "His clouds went forth, viz. hail and coals of fire." So Vat., "e splendido conspectu ejus *egrediuntur* nubes in quibus generantur fulmina," &c.; (3) "Out of the brightness before Him, there passed through His clouds hailstones," &c., *i.e.* the lightning coming from the brightness of God's Presence, (and accompanied by hail) burst through the clouds. Hupfeld decides for (3) as the only one consistent with grammar. It must be admitted that in (1) the ellipsis is somewhat harsh, yet not more so, perhaps, than is consistent with the boldness of lyric poetry, and the *sense* is certainly the most satisfactory. In (2) the apposition is weak, and it is not natural to speak of the clouds as coming forth from the brightness before Jehovah.

[f] רָב. Many (after Qimchi) render, "he shot out," referring to Gen. xlix. 23. The LXX., ἐπλήθυνε. Syr., ܐܣܓܝ. Jerome, *multiplicavit.* It may, however, be an adverb, "in abundance," subjoined to the noun instead of an adj, as מעט commonly is. So app. the Chald., who express it by an adj., וברקין סגיאין.

[g] אָרֻץ. This has been taken by Ewald and others as a fut. from רצץ (instead of אָרֹץ), as in Is. xlii. 4, Eccl. xii. 6. But it is better to take it as fut. of רוץ (in 2 Sam. we have the fuller form). The verb is used of

hostile attack, lix. 5, Joel ii. 7; and with prep., עַל and אֶל, Job xv. 26, xvi. 14, Dan. viii. 6. Here with the acc. after the analogy of verbs of motion. Cf. Job vi. 4, with iii. 25, xv. 21.

h נִחֲתָה, not (as Qimchi, *Lib. Rad.*) Niph. of חתת, "is broken," but Piel of נחת, "to press down, and so to bend," fem. sing. with plur. subj. as Gen. xlix. 22, Joel i. 20, Zech. vi. 14.

i יִשָּׁמְעוּ. The Niph. (instead of the Qal, which is more usual) must = Hithp. *Showed themselves obedient*, as Dan. vi. 27. Cf. for the same use of the Niph. Exod. xiv. 4, Numb. xx. 13, Is. v. 16.

A comparison of the two texts leads to the conclusion that in almost every instance where they differ, that of 2 Sam. is inferior to the other. In two instances only does it preserve readings of any importance: (1) חַשְׁרַת, 2 Sam. xxii. 12 (instead of חֶשְׁכַת in the Psalm), a ἅπ. λεγ. "a gathering, collection," of waters; the root is not found in Heb. but there is a kindred root in Arab. حشر, "to collect" (comp. also Heb. קשׁר); and (2) in ver. 16, אֲפִיקֵי יָם, "channels of the sea," is perhaps the original expression. In ver. 5 מִשְׁבְּרֵי (text of Sam.) seems preferable, as avoiding the repetition of חֶבְלֵי; and so מַיִם is used with the same verb אֲפָפוּנִי, "the waters took hold on me," Jon. ii. 6. In many cases the variations seem to have arisen from the licence of popular expressions creeping into the text. In ver. 27 the forms תִּתַּבָּר and תִּתַּפָּל are completely in defiance of all grammar.

PSALM 19

THIS Psalm consists of two distinct parts, in which are contrasted God's Revelation of Himself in Nature, and His Revelation of Himself in His Word. It speaks first of His glory as seen in the Heavens, and then of His glory as manifested in His Law.

It may have been written perhaps in the first flush of an Eastern sunrise, when the sun was seen "going forth as a bridegroom out of his chamber, and rejoicing as a mighty man to run his course." The song breathes all the life and freshness, all the gladness and glory, of the morning. The devout singer looks out, first, on the works of God's fingers, and sees all creation bearing its constant though silent testimony to its Maker; and then he turns himself with a feeling of deep satisfaction to that yet clearer and better witness concerning Him to be found in the inspired Scriptures. Thus he begins the day; thus he prepares himself for the duties that await him, for the temptations that may assail, and the sorrows that may gather as a cloud about him. He has made trial of the preciousness of that word. He knows its deep, hallowing, soul-sustaining power. He knows that it is full of life and healing. But he knows also that it is a word that searches and tries the heart, that reveals the holiness of God, and the sinfulness of man ; and therefore he bows himself in prayer, saying, " As for errors,—who can understand them ? Cleanse Thou me from secret faults."

The difference of style observable between the two parts of the Psalm, and the abruptness of the transition from one part to the other, have led some critics to the conclusion that these did not originally constitute one Poem. Thus Ewald speaks of the former half as a beautiful torso—a splendid but unfinished fragment of the time of David, to which some later bard subjoined the praise of the Law. But it is not absolutely necessary to adopt such a supposition. No doubt there is a very considerable difference between the sustained lyric movement of verses 1—6, and the regular didactic rhythm of the latter half of the Psalm. But it may fairly be argued that the nature of the subject influenced the change in style. The apparent suddenness of transition, too, though it cannot be denied, may not only be accounted for by the nature of lyric poetry, but was probably the result of design in order to give more force to the contrast. That such *is* the effect it is impossible not to feel.

This is one of the Psalms appointed by the Church to be read in her service on the Festival of the Nativity. But the selection surely does not rest on any of those merely external and superficial points of connection which are commonly supposed to have guided it. Thus, for instance, it has been said that the Psalm speaks of the glory of the natural sun as seen in the heavens, and the Church celebrates on that day the rising of "the Sun of righteousness" upon the earth. Or again, St. Paul illustrates the diffusion of the Gospel throughout the world by words borrowed from the Psalm (Rom. x. 18), and hence it may be naturally associated with the Incarnation which led to that diffusion. But it is obvious that, if this quotation influenced the selection, the Psalm would far more appropriately have been appointed for Ascension Day or Whitsunday.*

No, it is with a far profounder wisdom that the Church puts this Psalm into our lips on Christmas Day. What is the great truth which the Church brings before us so prominently on that day ? Not only the Incarnation, but the truth that in the Incarnate Jesus

---

* "In the Latin Church this Psalm is appointed for use also on the festivals of the Ascension and of Trinity Sunday ; so likewise it was in the Sarum Use ; and in the Gregorian Use it is appointed for the Annunciation."—*Wordsworth.*

we have the perfect Revelation of God. It is the Word who was with God and was God, who being in the bosom of the Father declared the Father, who as on that day became flesh. And what does the Psalm speak of, but two other imperfect and partial and preparatory Revelations of God, His Revelation in Nature and His Revelation in His written word? Thus we are led step by step from the first and lowest Revelation in the natural world, to the Revelation in the written word, and then beyond and above these to the one great, perfect, all-embracing, all-completing, Revelation in His Son. The Gospel and Epistle for the Day give the true explanation of the choice of this Psalm. It begins, and they finish, the cycle of Divine Revelation to man.

The strophical arrangement of the Psalm is as follows :—

I. The Glory of God in Creation. Ver. 1—6.

(1) The witness of the heavens to God as their Creator (ver. 1).

(2) The nature of the witness as continuous (ver. 2), though not audible (ver. 3); and universal (ver. 4 *a*, *b*).

(3) The witness especially of the sun, who, as the most glorious of the heavenly bodies ("dux et princeps et moderator luminum reliquorum"), is chiefest herald of God's praise (ver. 4 *c*—6).

II. The Glory of God in His Word. Ver. 7—14.

(1) The excellence and power (ver. 7—9), and the exceeding preciousness (ver. 10, 11), of the Law of Jehovah.

(2) The prayer of the servant of Jehovah in the light of that Law, to be kept from unconscious errors, as well as from open transgressions (ver. 12, 13), from sins of the lip, and sins of the heart (ver. 14).

[FOR THE PRECENTOR (A PSALM) OF DAVID.]

I. 1. THE heavens are telling the glory of God;
And the work of His hands doth the firmament declare.

1. The Psalm opens with the impression produced on the Poet's mind by the magnificence and the order of Creation. Of the two clauses of this verse, the first states the *fact* that the heavens publish God's glory; the second explains *how* this is done, viz. by testifying that He has made them. Comp. viii. 1 [2], 3 [4], Rom. i. 20, Acts xiv. 17. This is the true meaning of the heavens and their pomp. That splendour which fills their arch, that beauty which so attracts the eye, that everlasting order by which Day and Night follow in sweet

2 Day unto day poureth forth speech :
And night unto night revealeth knowledge.
3 There is no speech, and there are no words,
Their voice is not heard :[a]
4 Through the whole earth hath their line[b] gone forth,
And their words unto the ends of the world.
For the sun hath He set a tabernacle in them ;

vicissitude—these things are not the offspring of Chance ; they are not the evolution of some blind spirit enchained within the mass which it vivifies ; much less are they the work of some evil power whose kingdom and whose triumph are to be seen in the material universe. *God* created them, and they show forth *His* glory. *His* fingers fashioned them. He clothed them with light as with a garment, and put the sun in the midst of them to show forth His praise.

2. To the personification of the Heavens succeeds that of Day and Night. The words may either be rendered as in the text, or, "one day after another," "day after day, night after night," &c. This verse expresses not so much the progressive character, as the never-failing continuance of the testimony. There is no pause, no change in the stately procession; none of them thrusts or breaks his ranks; for ever they abide the same.

3. THEIR VOICE IS NOT HEARD, lit. "is inaudible." This seems to be a kind of correction or explanation of the bold figure which had ascribed language to the heavens. They have a language, but not one that can be classed with any of the dialects of earth. They have a voice, but one that speaks not to the ear, but to the devout and understanding heart. The sense is very well expressed in the well-known paraphrase of Addison:—

"What though *in solemn silence* all
Move round this dark terrestrial ball,
* * * *
In *reason's ear* they all rejoice,
And utter forth a glorious voice,"
&c.

4. Once more, this testimony is not only full, and clear, and unbroken, it is universal. Everywhere the heavens span and compass the earth, and everywhere they preach the same divine sermon. If no fire of love to God burned in any heart of man, still He would not have left Himself without a witness in yon blue vault and those shining orbs. St. Paul, Rom. x. 18, quotes the former part of this verse in illustration of the progress of the Gospel. "Faith," he says, "cometh by hearing," and then asks, "Have they (*i.e.*, the nations at large) not heard?" Yea, rather, so widely has the Gospel been preached, that its progress may be described in the words in which the Psalmist tells of God's revelation of Himself in Nature. The one has now become co-extensive with the other. The *præconium cœlorum* is not more universal than the *præconium evangelii*. The older interpreters, not perceiving the drift of the Apostle's quotation, supposed that his authority compelled them to give an allegorical explanation of the former part of this Psalm, and therefore took the heavens as a figure of the Church, and the Sun as a figure of the Gospel. Luther, too, contrary to his wont, adopts here this strange fancy, instead of adhering to the literal meaning of the text.

IN THEM, *i.e.* in the heavens, hath God set a tent or pavilion, &c. In like manner a tabernacle or pavilion

5 And he is like a bridegroom that goeth forth out of
his chamber ;
He rejoiceth as a mighty man to run (his) course.
6 From (one) end of the heaven is his going forth,
And his circuit as far as the (other) ends thereof,
Neither is anything hid from his heat.

is ascribed to the sun, Hab. iii. 11. But it is doubtful whether the heavens themselves are the royal pavilion—" tentorium augustale et prætorium . . . . sol tanquam rex cœlorum," as Venema says (and so also Stier) ; or whether the sun is supposed to issue from a tent when he rises, and return to it when he sets. The former certainly accords best with the passage in Habakkuk.

5, 6. Nothing can be more striking than the figures in which the freshness and gladness of the young morning, and the strength of the sun's onward march, are described. "The morning light," says Delitzsch, " has in it a freshness and cheerfulness, a renewed youth. Therefore the morning sun is compared to a bridegroom, the desire of whose heart is satisfied, who stands as it were at the beginning of a new life, and in whose youthful countenance the joy of the wedding-day still shines."

7. But the singer turns from God's Revelation of Himself in Nature, to His Revelation of Himself in His written word. He turns from that which was the common property of all, to that which was the special privilege of the Jew. In accordance with this change of subject is the difference in the use of the Divine Names. " The word of Nature declares to us God (אֵל, 'El) ; the word of Scripture, Jehovah (יהוה) : the one God's creative might and majesty, the other His counsel and will."—*Del.* " For it is written," says Bacon, " *Cœli enarrant gloriam Dei;* but it is not written, *Cœli enarrant voluntatem Dei*, but of that it is said, *Ad legem et testimonium, si non fecerint secundum verbum istud,*" &c. (Adv. of Learning, Book II.) The transition to this new subject is no doubt somewhat abrupt, but this only renders the contrast the more forcibly striking. There is a quick rebound of the heart as it were from the world of Nature, beautiful and glorious as it is, to that which is far more beautiful and more glorious, the word of Revelation. But despite the seeming abruptness, there is a point of connection between the two portions of the Psalm. What the sun is in the natural world, that the Law is in the spiritual : the one quickens and cherishes all animal life—nothing being hid from his heat ; the other quickens and cherishes the life of the soul.

7—10. It would be difficult to find a more perfect example of Hebrew parallelism. In ver. 7, 8, we have in each member of each verse the Law of Jehovah described, first, by means of a simple attribute setting forth its inherent character; and then subjoined, without a copula, what it is in its effects upon the heart and spirit of men. The second division, too, of each member is constructed in both verses exactly on the same principle : it consists, that is, of an active participle in the stat. constr. followed by the object of its action. Thus to " perfect " in one clause, answers " sure " in the next : to " restoring the soul," " making wise the simple," and so on. In ver. 9 the parallelism is no less strictly observed, but it is thrown into a different form, the latter half of each member being now a further predicate of the *nature* of the Law considered in

7 The law of Jehovah is perfect, restoring the soul;
The testimony of Jehovah is sure, making wise the simple.
8 The precepts of Jehovah are right, rejoicing the heart;
The commandment of Jehovah is pure, enlightening the eyes.

itself, not in its *effects*. In ver. 10 we have not the effects of the Law, as before, but its preciousness and sweetness set forth; and here again there is the most exact parallelism between the two members of the verse.

7. THE LAW . . . . THE TESTIMONY. These are the collective terms embracing the whole body of "statutes," "judgements," &c. afterwards mentioned: "totum illud doctrinæ corpus," as Calvin says, "ex quo constat vera religio et pietas." This revelation has the name of "testimony," as testifying, bearing witness of, God's character both in His good will towards those who obey Him, and in His displeasure against transgressors, especially in the latter sense. It is, as Harless says, "the word of God, testifying of Himself, and affirming what He is, in opposition to the apostasy of man." (*Ethik*, § 14, Anm.) See Deut. xxxi. 26, 27. Hence the force of its connection with the ark and the mercy-seat (כַּפֹּרֶת), Exod. xxv. 16, xxvi. 34, Lev. xvi. 13; the symbol of God's righteous severity against sin being hidden beneath the symbol of His grace and mercy. With affectionate tenderness the sacred Poet lavishes his epithets of admiration upon this word of God. In its nature he declares it to be perfect, sure, right, pure, standing fast for ever, the very truth itself, righteous altogether. These epithets mark it as reflecting the holiness of God (pure, righteous, &c.), as being in its nature worthy of all reliance, as that which cannot be set aside or tampered with. It is no leaden rule that may be bent and twisted by the unsteady hand of human caprice to suit its own selfish purposes; but *the truth* that we may believe it, *pure* that it may lift us out of our sin, *standing fast for ever* that we may find in it at all times the same unerring guide.

Next we have its marvellous effects declared.

RESTORING THE SOUL, *i.e.* it calls it back from its wanderings by reminding it of its ingratitude, by setting before it its high destiny, by bringing it to its true Shepherd and Guardian.

MAKING WISE THE SIMPLE. It gives to each one who studies it with *open*, unprejudiced, candid mind, that divine wisdom whereby he attains to salvation. Comp. 2 Tim. iii. 15, "the sacred scriptures which are able to make thee wise (σοφίσαι) unto salvation." The purposes for which Scripture is there said to be profitable should be compared with what is said here.

THE SIMPLE, lit. "the open" (r. פתח, *patere*, to be open), not here "the foolish," as often in Proverbs, but he who is ready to become a fool, that he may be wise, who has the true child-like spirit (Matt. xi. 25, 1 Cor. i. 27) which best fits him to become a disciple in the school of God.

8. RIGHT, *i.e.* straight, as opposed to the crooked ways of man.

REJOICING THE HEART, filling it with joy in God, by manifesting Him as the portion of the soul, and so lifting it above the joys as well as the sorrows of earth.

ENLIGHTENING THE EYES. According to the expressive Hebrew idiom, it is to the soul what food is to the worn and fainting body. It

9 The fear of Jehovah is clean, standing fast for ever;
The judgements of Jehovah are truth, they are righteous altogether.
10 More to be desired are they than gold, yea than much fine gold;
Sweeter also than honey and the dropping of the honeycomb.
11 Moreover thy servant is enlightened[c] by them,
In keeping of them there is great reward.

12 As for errors,—who can perceive (them)?
From secret (faults) do Thou pronounce me innocent,
13 Also from presumptuous (sins)[d] keep Thy servant back;
Let them not have dominion over me;
Then shall I be perfect,[e]
And innocent from great transgression.

is what the honey which he found in the wood was to Jonathan, when he returned wearied and exhausted from the pursuit of his enemies. Cf. cxix. 18, Acts xxvi. 18, Eph. i. 18.

9. THE FEAR OF JEHOVAH. Another name for the Law, but as contemplated not so much in its outward aspect, as in its working on the heart. Not the religious feeling itself is here meant, but the Law as intended to evoke and guide that religious feeling, and therefore identified with it: "doctrina quæ præscribit quomodo Deum timere oporteat."—*Calvin.*

11. Personal experience of the blessedness of obeying God's Law, inasmuch as it brings with it both *enlightenment* and *reward.*

12. But with all this affection for God's word, there is mingled awe and reverence. That word lays a man bare to himself. It judges him: it shows him what is in him, convinces him how much there is that needs to be purged, how far even one who loves it is from a perfect obedience. It is at once a copy of the will of God, and a mirror of the heart of man. Hence it calls forth the penitent confession, "As for errors, who can understand them?" and the prayer both to be absolved—"*pronounce* me free" (like the New Testament δικαιοῦν)—and to be kept from sin; first for pardon, and then for sanctification.

ERRORS, only here sins both of ignorance and infirmity, those which are done unintentionally and unconsciously; "For we are entangled in so many nets and snares of Satan, that none of us can perceive the hundredth part of the evils that cleave to him."—*Calvin.*

SECRET (FAULTS), lit. things hidden, *i.e.* not only from others, but from our own hearts, through inobservance, through a too ready forgetfulness of them when observed, through the habit of self-deception, or even through their being wilfully cherished.

PRONOUNCE ME INNOCENT, or perhaps, "clear me," or "acquit me," as the E.V. renders in other passages.

13. PRESUMPTUOUS (SINS). This neuter sense of the word seems required by the context. (See Critical Note.) These are sins done with a high hand; see Numb. xv. 27—31.

14 Let the words of my mouth and the meditation of my
heart be acceptable before Thee,
O Jehovah, my Rock and my Redeemer!

Against these he prays that they may not get the full mastery over him. This completes the climax, which begins with involuntary, and advances to hidden, presumptuous, and at length ruling sins, which leave a man their hopeless slave.

14. BE ACCEPTABLE, the usual formula applied to God's acceptance of sacrifices offered to Him (Lev. i. 3, 4, &c.). Prayer to God is the sacrifice of the heart and of the lips. Comp. Hos. xiv. 2, "So will we offer our lips as calves."

The name of Jehovah is repeated for the seventh time. The epithets "my Rock," "my Redeemer," have here a peculiar force. For He is my strength in keeping the Law; my Redeemer as delivering me from the guilt and the power of sin.

[a] The rendering given in the text is that of Qimchi, who has been followed by Hengstenberg and Hupfeld. Qimchi says: "Their words are not like the words of the children of men, but the work which they perform that is their words." The second clause would be more literally rendered, "their voice is an inaudible one." Delitzsch objects to this that such a meaning would require a Vau adversative, = "but," or "but yet," in the next verse, and that the sense moreover is flat and in contradiction to what had been said before: he accordingly renders (following Vitringa): "It is not a speech, and it is not words, The voice (sound) whereof is inaudible;" *i.e.* the utterance of the heavens is in discourse, that all can catch, in words that all can understand, one that is φανερόν, Rom. i. 19. But would not this require לֹא instead of אַיִן?

The rendering of our own version, which is that of Luther, Calvin, and others, "There is no speech or language, but their voice is heard among them" (*i.e.* all nations hear their tidings), must be rejected: first, because אֹמֶר does not mean "a language," but only "speech, utterance," as in ver. 2; it must have been לָשׁוֹן or שָׂפָה (Gen. xi. 1): and next, because בְּלִי is here construed with a participle, not with a finite verb. "Without their voice being heard," must have been בְּלִי נִשְׁמַע (Gen. xxxi. 20) or בְּלִי יִשָּׁמַע (Job xli. 18, Hos. viii. 7). With the participle בְּלִי has the same effect as the Greek *a privat.* See 2 Sam. xii. 1.

[b] קַו, prop. "a line, plummet-line" (as used in building, Zech. i. 16, or in pulling down, Is. xxxiv. 11, al.), also "a measuring line" (for marking out the extent of a city, Jer. xxxi. 39, where it is also used with יצא, Ezek. xlvii. 3). Hence, as the Heaven seems to measure and mark out the earth (whence the term horizon or boundary), here "their line, or boundary." Others interpret "their writings or characters," as in Is. xxviii. 10, "line upon line." Others, again, "their sound." So LXX. *φθογγός*. Cf. Rom. x. 18. Symm. *ἦχος*. Jerome and Vulg. *sonus*. Others, again, connect it with the Arab. قوى, and render "*intensio*," *sc.* vocis, like τόνος fr. τείνω.

The last member of the verse, in which the Sun is introduced, more naturally begins a new strophe. The suffixes "their," "in them," &c., all refer to "the heavens," ver. 2.

[c] נִזְהָר, "enlightened" (from the root signif. *to shine, be bright*), hence "instructed," "taught," as P. B. V. The LXX. seem to have read שׁוֹמֵר אֹתָם as they render φυλάσσει αὐτά. Vulg. *custodit ea.*

[d] זֵדִים. In form this word no doubt is masc., and would naturally be explained after the analogy of גֵּר, לֵץ, &c., "proud, bold, transgressors," as the word is translated everywhere else; but this sense is quite at variance with the context. Hence the neuter sense is preferable. Comp. סֵטִים, ci. 3, Hos. v. 2. So Qimchi and Rashi explain it by זְדוֹנוֹת, and the Rabb. use of בְּזָדוֹן, as opposed to בִּשְׁגָגָה, points the same way. Aq. or Symm. (see Field's Hex.) ἀπὸ τῶν ὑπερηφάνων. Mich., *prohæretica peccata.* Calvin, *superbiæ.* So also amongst more modern commentators, Stier and Delitzsch.

[e] אֵיתָם. Fut. Qal for אֵתַם, the י having been incorrectly inserted (as a *scriptio plena*), from תמם, like תֵּיעָשֶׂה, Exod. xxv. 31.

PSALM 20

THIS is evidently a liturgical Psalm, and was intended originally, it would seem, to be sung on behalf of a king who was about to go forth to war against his enemies. The structure of the Psalm, and the change from the plural to the singular, render it probable that it was chanted in alternate measure by the congregation and the Priest or Levite who led the choir. As the king stands within the sanctuary offering his sacrifice, the whole assembled crowd of worshipers in the spacious courts lift up their voices in the prayer, that Jehovah would graciously accept those sacrifices, and send him help and victory in the battle.

For what special occasion the Psalm was first composed, it is of course now quite impossible to say. Some, following the Syriac translator, would refer it to the time of David's war with the Syrians and Ammonites (2 Sam. x.); but obviously it would apply to other circumstances equally well. From the way in which the king is spoken of in the third person, the Rabbinical and other later commentators have concluded that the Psalm was not written by David himself, but by some other poet in his honour. Calvin, however, argues that there is no absurdity in supposing David to be the author, provided we recollect that he is here speaking in his prophetical character, and instructing the Church how to pray for the safety of that kingdom which God has set up.

The Psalm has no doubt a prophetical aspect, from the fact that the Jewish king was by virtue of his office a type of Christ. Luther, indeed, observes: "This Psalm almost all expound of Christ. But such an exposition appears to me to be too far-fetched to be called literal (*remotior quam ut literalis dici possit*). Accordingly, in its more simple and evident meaning, I think it to be a kind of general litany for magistrates and those who are placed in high office, for whom the Apostle also (1 Tim. ii.) bids us first of all pray, that we may lead a quiet and peaceable life." Calvin, however, is right in saying that inasmuch as this kingdom differed from all other kingdoms, because God had determined to govern and defend His people by the hand of David and of his seed, therefore we ought to recognise under the type of the temporal kingdom that better rule on which the joy and happiness of the Church depend.

The Psalm consists of three parts :—

I. The prayer of the congregation. This was probably chanted by the Levites, whilst the smoke of the sacrifices ascended towards heaven. Ver. 1—5.

II. Either the king himself, strengthened and encouraged by the prayer of the congregation, or more probably one of the Levites, now takes up the strain, gives utterance to his faith in God, and already in spirit sees his enemies, great and powerful as they were, broken and overthrown. Ver. 6—8.

III. The congregation once more respond, and taking up the words of the king or the Levite (ver. 6), change them into a prayer for the king, adding also a petition that their prayer may be heard. Ver. 9.

[TO THE PRECENTOR. A PSALM OF DAVID.]

The congregation led by the Levites.

1 JEHOVAH answer thee in the day of distress,
The Name of the God of Jacob defend thee.
2 Send thee help from the sanctuary,
And uphold thee out of Zion !
3 Remember all thine offerings ;

Ver. 1—4. The futures are all optative, the prayers and wishes of the people accompanying the offering of the sacrifice.

1. THE NAME OF THE GOD OF JACOB (see above, Ps. v. 11 [12]), Al-sheikh sees a reference to Gen. xxxv. 3, where Jacob says, "I will make there (at Bethel) an altar unto God, who *answered me in the day of my distress*, and was with me in the way which I went."

2. SEND THEE HELP, lit. send "thy help."

SET THEE UP ON HIGH, cf. lxix. 29 [30] xci. 14, *i.e.* as in a fortress where no enemy can do thee harm, or on a rock at the foot of which the waves fret and dash themselves in impotent fury.

3. The king offers, as was usual, before going into battle (1 Sam. xiii. 19, &c.), his whole burnt-sacrifices (עוֹלָה), together with the bloodless

And graciously accept [a] thy burnt sacrifice. [Selah.]
4 Give thee according to thy heart's desire ;
And fulfil all thy counsel !
5 So will we shout for joy because of thy salvation,
And in the Name of our God will we wave our banners.[b]
Jehovah fulfil all thy petitions.

The King or a Levite.

6 Now know I that Jehovah saveth His Anointed ;
He will answer him from His holy heaven

offering (מִנְחָה) of fine flour, mixed with oil and frankincense. To this last the verb "*remember*" is peculiarly applicable. For the priest was to take a handful of it, and burn it as a "*memorial*" (אַזְכָּרָה, *μνημόσυνον*, cf. Acts x. 4) upon the altar, to be an offering made by fire of a sweet savour unto the Lord, Lev. ii. 2.

GRACIOUSLY ACCEPT, lit. "make fat" (xxiii. 5), but here in a declarative sense, "regard as fat," and so "receive as fat," *i.e.* as worthy to be offered, the fattest of the flock being chosen for sacrifice.

Very excellent are Luther's remarks here, and capable of wide application. After observing that the sacrifices of the Old Law are done away in Christ, he continues, "Notwithstanding at the present day others as well as David may use this Psalm in prayer, for as the person, the circumstances, the time and place are all different in the New Law, so likewise is the sacrifice ; but one faith and one spirit abide through all ages, and amid all diversities of places, works, persons. The external varies, the internal remains ever the same."—*Operat. in Ps.* xix. [xx.]

4. THY COUNSEL, *i.e.* all thy plans and measures in the war.

5. The form of the verb here (with ה paragog.) marks the conclusion following from, the resolve based upon, what goes before, yet still as a prayer or wish. Rather "so *may* we shout for joy" (*i.e.* do Thou grant this as the result) than "so *will* we," &c.

THY SALVATION, or, "victory." This *may* mean "the help and victory vouchsafed by God to the king," as in xxi. 5 ; but Thrupp observes : "The almost instinctive dependence of the Israelites upon their king, as the man who should save them (cf. 1 Sam. x. 27), fully justifies us in interpreting the expression *thy salvation*, ver. 5, in its most natural sense, not as the salvation bestowed by God upon the king, but as that wrought by the king for his people."

6. The second division of the Psalm. The offering of the sacrifices had, we may suppose, been concluded ; and now, after a pause of some duration, a single voice (probably of one of the Levites) is heard, declaring that the sacrifice has been graciously received, and thence drawing an augury of success.

The hope suddenly changes into certainty, *Now know I*, that Jehovah *hath* saved, *hath* given the victory. The singer speaks in the full assurance of faith, that the prayer is heard, and as if he already saw the victory gained.

The prayer had been (ver. 1, 2) that God would hear and send help from the *earthly* sanctuary or Zion. Now the answer is said to come from His holy *heaven*. For if God then condescended to dwell in visible glory among men, yet He would teach His people that He is not

With the strength of the salvation of His right hand.
7 Some of chariots and some of horses,
But *we* will make mention of the Name of Jehovah our God.
8 *They* have bowed down and fallen,
But *we* have risen and stood upright.

The people and Levites.

9 O Jehovah, save the king!
May He answer us when we cry (unto Him)!

limited by the bounds of time and space. He is not like the gods of the heathen, the god of one city or country. He sends help out of Zion, but the heaven of heavens cannot contain Him. (See the recognition of this truth in Solomon's prayer, 1 Kings viii. 27, &c.) Calvin sees expressed in the earthly sanctuary made by hands the grace and condescension of God to His people; in the heavenly, His infinite power, greatness, and majesty.

STRENGTH OF THE SALVATION, or, "saving" or "victorious strength."

7. SOME OF CHARIOTS, *i.e.* make mention of chariots, the verb being supplied from the next member, and the construction being precisely the same. Others, as the E.V. supply another verb: "some *trust* in chariots," &c. According to the Law, Israel was forbidden to maintain a standing army. See the directions concerning the king, Deut. xvii. 16. This law, however, does not seem to have been observed, at least in later times. Solomon at any rate gathered together chariots and horsemen, 1 Kings x. 26—29.

With the sentiment here expressed, comp. David's words to Goliath, 1 Sam. xvii. 45, and Ps. xxxiii. 16, &c. Similar language is common in the Prophets. The basis of it all is to be found in the Law, Deut. xx. 2—4, xxxii. 30.

8. Again preterites of confidence, describing what shall be in the war, as what already is accomplished. "Great certainly is the Faith," says Luther, "which hath such courage by remembering the name of the Lord. Soldiers in our day are wont, when they go into battle, to recall to mind the brave exploits of their fathers, or former victories, and the like, wherewith to warm and stir their hearts. But let our princes remember the Name of God, wherein all salvation and victory do stand."

9. After the solo, the Chorus again take up the strain.

O JEHOVAH, SAVE THE KING, &c. Such is the rendering of the LXX., which is also followed by the Vulg., *Domine, salvum fac regem*, whence our "God save the King." According to the Massoretic punctuation, on the other hand, the rendering would be, "Save, O Jehovah; May the King answer us," &c. This last is adopted by Delitzsch [but not in his 2nd edit.], who, however, understands by the king, Jehovah, (referring to xlviii. 2 [3],) which is quite unnecessary, and only introduces confusion into the Psalm. The king is "the Anointed" of ver. 6. See also note on ver. 5.

[a] יְדַשְּׁנֶה, Piel with termination ֶה for ָה, optative, as in 1 Sam. xxviii. 15.

[b] נִדְגֹּל. "We will set up," or rather, "wave our banners." Mendelss. "lassen wehen unser Siegspanier." The LXX. apparently read נְגַדֵּל, as they render *μεγαλυνθησόμεθα*.

PSALM 21

THE last Psalm was a litany before the king went forth to battle. This is apparently a Te Deum on his return. In that the people cried, "Jehovah give thee according to thy heart's desire:" in this they thank God who has heard their prayer, "The wish of his heart hast Thou given him."

Hupfeld's objection to this view of the Psalm, viz. that the latter part of it speaks of *future* victories, and that therefore, if composed for any special occasion at all, it was more likely intended as a hymn on going into battle, is surely of no force. What singer in writing an Ode of Thanksgiving for the past, would not utter a hope for the future? The victory which he celebrated was, he would believe, but one in a long series of brilliant successes which Jehovah would vouchsafe to the arms of His Anointed. He could not but augur a glorious future from a glorious past.

Again, it has been said that the expression in ver. 3, "Thou puttest a crown of gold upon his head," makes it more probable that the Psalm was composed on the occasion of a coronation, (though some think the allusion is to the crown of the king of Rabbah which David took, and "it was set upon his head," 2 Sam. xii. 30,) and ver 4, "He asked life of thee," &c., seems to intimate that *long life*, and not victory over enemies, was the subject of the wish and request mentioned in ver. 3. On the other hand, the *past* tenses in ver. 2 and 4 compel us to suppose that the monarch had already reigned for some time, and so exclude the idea of a coronation. See further in the note to ver. 3.

The Psalm was evidently sung in the Temple, either by the whole congregation, or by a choir of Levites. Like the last, it is Messianic, and in the same sense. Each Jewish monarch was but a feeble type of Israel's true King; and all the hopes and aspirations of pious hearts, however they might have for their *immediate* object the then reigning monarch, whether David himself or one of David's children, still looked beyond these to Him who should be David's Lord as well as his Son.

The Targum renders מֶלֶךְ, "king," in ver. 1, by מלך משיחא, "King Messiah;" and Rashi observes: "Our old doctors interpreted this Psalm of King Messiah, but in order to meet the Schismatics (*i.e.* the Christians) it is better to understand it of David himself."

It falls into two strophes:—

I. A Prayer to Jehovah on behalf of the king. Here we have the gladness of the king ascribed (1) to what Jehovah has done, is doing, and will do in his behalf; and (2) to the fact that the king *trusteth* in Jehovah. Ver. 1—7.

II. Good wishes and words of happy augury addressed to the king himself, who is assured of victory over all his enemies Ver. 8—12.

[FOR THE PRECENTOR. A PSALM OF DAVID.]

1 JEHOVAH, in Thy strength shall the king be glad,
And in Thy salvation how greatly shall he exult!
2 The wish of his heart hast Thou granted him;
And the desire[a] of his lips hast Thou not refused. [Selah.]
3 For Thou comest to meet him with blessings of prosperity,
Thou puttest a crown of fine gold upon his head.
4 He asked life of Thee:—Thou gavest (it) him,
Length of days, for ever and ever.

1, 2. Introduction. Jehovah has answered the prayer of the king, and so filled him with joy.

1. STRENGTH . . . SALVATION (or, SAVING HELP), words used especially of strength and succour vouchsafed in battle. The former may either = מָעֹז (as viii. 2 [3], xxviii. 8), "a bulwark, defence," &c., or it may mean "the Divine strength as imparted to the king, and manifested by him in the war" (as lxviii. 28 [29]).

Ver. 3—6. The manner in which the king's prayer has been answered.

The blessings vouchsafed to him. BLESSINGS OF PROSPERITY, *i.e.* blessings which bring and consist in prosperity; cf. Prov. xxiv. 25.

The verbs in 3, 5, 6 are best rendered as *presents* (not with Calv. and others as *futures*, and certainly not with Hupf. as *preterites*). In each case they are employed to represent the result or consequence of the past action denoted by the preterites immediately going before. The singer looks on as it were and sees the petition granted before his eyes. "Thou *hast not refused* his request—for Thou *comest* to meet him with blessings," &c.

A CROWN OF FINE GOLD. I see no reason to suppose a reference either to David's first coronation, or to his taking the crown of the king of Rabbah, 2 Sam. xii. 30. "Thou puttest a crown of fine gold upon his head" may only mean, "Thou givest him kingly dignity and presence." The parallelism with the first member of the ver. "Thou comest to meet him," &c. would lead us rather, I think, to understand this member as a poetical figure, than as the literal assertion of an historical fact.

4. FOR EVER AND EVER. There is no difficulty in this expression even as applied to David. It was usual to pray that the king might live for ever (1 Kings i. 31, Neh. ii. 3, &c.), and a like anticipation of an endless life occurs in other Psalms (xxiii. 6, lxi. 6 [7], xci. 16). The Chald., the older Rabbinical, and other commentators have been led

5 Great is his glory through Thy salvation ;
Honour and majesty dost Thou lay upon him.
6 For Thou makest him (full of) blessings for ever ;
Thou dost gladden him with joy in Thy presence.
7 For the king trusteth in Jehovah,
And through the mercy of the Most High he shall not be moved.

(*To the King.*)

8 Thy hand shall find [b] all thine enemies,
Thy right hand shall find out them that hate thee,
9 Thou shalt make them as a furnace of fire in the time of thy wrathfulness :

by the form of expression here and ver. 6, which they supposed to be inapplicable to any earthly monarch, to refer the Psalm to the Messiah. Still, this would not exclude a primary reference to David, although we know that whatever was true of the glory, and dignity, and length of life of David as king of Israel, is far truer in its spiritual and eternal sense of Christ the Son of David.

5. SALVATION, see on ver. 1 and xx. 5.

6. Lit. "*Thou makest him blessings*," i.e. blessed himself and the bearer of blessing to others. Comp. Gen. xii. 2, Is. xix. 24, Ezek. xxxiv. 26. For the expression, JOY IN THY PRESENCE, comp. xvi. 11.

7. A reason why the blessing is vouchsafed. It is a blessing given to faith. The king trusts not in himself, not in chariots or horses, but in the Most High. This verse does, it is true, prepare the way for what follows, but it is not to be regarded (with Hengst. and Delitzsch) as the beginning of a new strophe. It most appropriately closes the strophe which begins with the words "In *Thy* strength," &c.

Nothing is more common in the Psalms than for a new strophe to begin by a resumption of the thought with which the strophe immediately preceding concludes. The king who was spoken of in the 3d pers. at the beginning of the Psalm is here again also spoken of in the 3d person. And thus a preparation is made for the transition to a direct address, with which the next strophe opens.

8. The hope passing into a prophecy that in every battle the king will be victorious over his enemies.

9. THOU SHALT MAKE THEM AS A FURNACE OF FIRE. This is capable of two interpretations : (1) we may take the word "as a furnace" as the accus., in apposition with the pron. suffix, so that it will be equivalent to "as if they were in a furnace," or by a metonymy the furnace may be put for the fuel which it consumes (as lxxxiii. 14, "Thou wilt make them . . . as the fire which consumeth the wood," instead of "as the wood which the fire consumes;" see also Zech. xii. 6). (2) "As a furnace" may here be nominative, and so not his enemies, but the king himself be compared to a furnace. "Thou shalt do with them, as a furnace would, viz. consume them." There is a similar ambiguity in the reference of the image in xxxix. 11 [12].

IN THE TIME OF THY WRATHFULNESS, lit. "of thy countenance," here, as turned in anger upon his enemies, or the word may mean simply, "presence." Hupfeld argues

Jehovah in His anger shall consume them ;
And a fire shall devour them.
10 Their fruit shalt thou destroy from the earth,
And their seed from among the children of men.
11 For they intended [c] evil against thee ;
They imagined a mischievous device—which they cannot perform.
12 For thou shalt make them turn their back : [d]
On thy strings thou shalt make ready (thine arrows) against the face of them.
13 Be Thou exalted, Jehovah, in Thy strength ;
So will we hymn and praise Thy might.

that this phrase can only be employed of God, not of any human monarch, and consequently interprets the whole of this second division of the Psalm as a prayer to God. But the word is used of the presence of a king, 2 Sam. xvii. 11 (where E. V. has, "that thou go to battle in *thine own person;*" lit. "thy *face* or *presence* goeth"), and we find the same sentiment Prov. xvi. 14, xix. 12.

Observe the rhythmical structure; two long lines, (ver. 9, (*a*) and (*b*),) followed by two short ones (ver. 10, (*a*) and (*b*).) The first describe the *process* of destruction, the last its *consummation.*

10. THEIR FRUIT=children, posterity, &c. Lam. ii. 20, Hosea ix. 16; more fully "fruit of the womb," cxxvii. 3, cxxxii. 11.

13. The singer has done with his good wishes and prophecies for the king. Now he turns to the Giver of victory, and prays Him to manifest Himself in all His power and glory, that His people may ever acknowledge Him as the only source of their strength.

[a] אֲרֶשֶׁת. The word occurs only here : no doubt connected with ירשׁ, רושׁ ; lit. *to be empty*, hence *to want, desire*, &c. (Arab. ورش, *avidum esse.*) The LXX. rightly render δέησις.

[b] מצא לְ in clause (*a*), as Is. x. 10, and מצא with acc. in (*b*), as 1 Sam. xxiii. 17. The difference seems to be that the former means "*to reach after,*" *to aim at;*" the latter, "*to find out, attain to.*" But see cxxxv. 10, 11, where the verb הרג is followed both by the accus. and the prep. without any difference of meaning.

[c] כִּי gives the reason for this destruction of the king's enemies. Or perhaps logically the perfects are concessive, "for *though* they have intended, &c. . . . yet they can effect nothing." נָטוּ עָלֶיךָ, either they have *spread* against thee evil (like a net, Lat. *tendere insidias*) : or they have *bent* against thee, &c. (like a bow, Lat. *tendere arcum*).

[d] Turn the back, lit. "the shoulder," שית שכם = נתן עורף, xviii. 41. תְּכוֹנֵן, "Thou shalt aim" (*sc.* thine arrows), as xi. 2, *et al.*

PSALM 22

In the midst of enemies who are thirsting for his life, and in anguish of mind almost bordering on despair, a sufferer cries to God for help. There is perhaps no Psalm in which the sense of loneliness is so utter, none in which the peril is so imminent; for "the parting of the raiment" is only the last act of indignity before he is put to death.

The Psalm which has the nearest resemblance to this is the 69th; but there is this observable difference between the two, that in this Psalm we hear only the accents of lamentable complaint, the cry of suffering and of sorrow, whilst in that the complaint of the sufferer turns finally into bitter imprecation upon his enemies.

According to the Inscription, this is one of David's Psalms. We know, however, of no circumstances in his life to which it can possibly be referred. In none of his persecutions by Saul was he ever reduced to such straits as those here described. Nor is Calvin's explanation satisfactory, when he suggests that David gathers up into one view the whole history of his past sufferings and persecutions. There is a distinctness in the enumeration of circumstances, as in ver. 18, 19, which connects the Psalm evidently with some particular occasion.

The older Jewish interpreters felt the difficulty, and thought that the sorrows of Israel in exile were the subject of the singer's complaint. Qimchi, citing this opinion, thinks that by "the hind of the dawn" is meant the congregation of Israel in their *present* dispersion: Rashi, that David here prophesied of the exile in Babylon. They were led to this view, no doubt, in some measure by the high hopes entertained in the latter part of the Psalm of the conversion of all nations to the faith and worship of Jehovah, hopes which could not, it seemed to them, be the fruit of an *individual's* suffering. Without adopting this view to the full extent, it is so far worthy of consideration that it points to what is probably the correct view, viz. that the Psalm was composed by one of the exiles during the Babylonish captivity. And though the feelings and expressions are clearly individual, not national, yet they are the feelings and expressions of one who suffers not merely as an individual, but so to speak in a representative character.

Naturally, one who was made the scoff and derision of the heathen, and the object of their worst cruelty, would cling to the thought that he suffered not only as an individual, but as one of the chosen of

God. The bitterness of his grief was that God—so it seemed—had forsaken him : the joy born out of that grief was that he should yet praise God for His saving health in the midst of his brethren (delivered like himself out of the hands of their oppressors) and that thus, and as a consequence of this deliverance, all the kindreds of the nations should worship before the Lord.

And we must not narrow the application of the Psalm to the circumstances of the original sufferer. It has evidently a far higher reference. It looks forward to Christ. It is a foreshadowing of Him and of His passion : and arguing from the analogy of the 16th Psalm, we might even say a conscious foreshadowing. He who thus suffered, and prayed, and hoped in the land of his captivity, might have seen by the eye of Faith that Another far mightier than he must also suffer, and be set at naught of the heathen, and rejected of men, that through Him salvation might come to the Gentiles. This truth of a suffering Messiah seems, indeed, to have been taught more clearly towards the latter days of the nation's history ; and surely it was most fitting that at the very time when the nation itself was shown how, through its own sufferings in exile, the heathen were to be claimed for Jehovah, it should also learn how, through the sufferings of the Great Deliverer, all its hopes would be fulfilled. Thus the history of Israel was fashioned to be typical of the history of Redemption, as well as that of the individual Israelite to be typical of Christ.

The references in the New Testament to this Psalm, as fulfilled in Christ, are many. The first words of it were uttered by Jesus on the cross, Matt. xxvii. 46. The scorn of the passers-by, and the shaking of the head in ver. 7, have their counterpart in the story of the crucifixion, Matt. xxvii. 39. The words of ver. 8 are found in Matt. xxvii. 43 : the intense thirst, "my tongue cleaveth to my jaws," of ver. 15 in John xix. 28 ; the parting of the garments, &c. ver. 18, in John xix. 23 ; the piercing (if that is a correct rendering ; see note on the ver.) of the hands and feet in ver. 16, in the nailing to the cross. Similarly we are justified in interpreting the latter part of the Psalm of the fruit of Christ's Passion and Resurrection by the way in which ver. 22 is quoted, Heb. ii. 11, &c.

Dr. Binnie, who holds the Psalm to be not typical but directly prophetical, remarks : " In one respect the Psalm stands alone in the Scriptures, and indeed in all religious literature. It is a cry out of the depths,—the sorrowful prayer of One who is not only persecuted by man, but seems to himself, for the time, to be utterly forsaken of his God. Yet there is no confession of sin, no penitent sorrow, no trace of compunction or remorse. This distinguishes the Psalm, quite unequivocally, not only from ordinary psalms of complaint, but from those in which Christ speaks in the person of David his type. The complaints found in them are never unaccompanied with confession of sin. If David, or any other ancient saint, had written the 22nd Psalm, as the expression of his own griefs and hopes, there would certainly have been audible in it some note of penitence."—*The Psalms*, pp. 190, 191.

The remark is of value, but the inference based on it is refuted by reference to the 44th Psalm, where in like manner there is not only the sorrowful complaint without any confession of sin, but the strong sense and assertion of righteousness.

This Psalm "as we learn from Augustine, was sung in the North African congregations at the Easter celebration of the Lord's Supper. More than fourteen centuries have passed since the Vandals drowned those songs in blood; but a stranger who happens to look in upon a Scottish congregation on a Communion Sabbath, will be likely enough to find the Psalm turned to the same holy and solemn use."—*The Psalms, their History*, &c., by W. Binnie, D.D. pp. 172, 173.

According to the Rabbinical Tradition mentioned by Rashi and Qimchi, the Psalm "is spoken concerning Esther and the Israel of her time;" and is appointed in the Synagogue for the Feast of Purim.

The Psalm consists of two parts :—

I. Complaint and Prayer. Ver. 1—21.

II. Vows and Hopes. Ver. 22—31.

Each of these principal divisions admits of its subdivision. For we have—

I. First, the pouring out of the heart's sorrow, with one of the tenderest appeals to God's compassionate Love that ever trembled on human lips (ver. 2—11); and next, the earnest entreaty for help, because of the greatness and nearness of the peril (ver. 12—22). The peril so near, and God so far off—this is the thought which colours all, both complaint and prayer.

II. In the second part, again, we have, first, the vows of thanksgiving for deliverance, and the praising of God's Name in the "midst of the congregation" (ver. 23—27). Next, the confident hope that God's kingdom shall be set up in all the earth, and that all, great and low, shall submit themselves to Him (ver. 28—32).

According to a different and more general arrangement, the Psalm consists of three parts :—

I. Complaint. Ver. 1—10.

II. Prayer. Ver. 11—21.

III. Expression of Hope. Ver. 22—31.

[FOR THE PRECENTOR. TO THE MELODY "THE HIND OF THE DAWN." A PSALM OF DAVID.]

I. 1 MY God, my God, why hast Thou forsaken me?
(Why art Thou) far from helping me, (and from) the words of my roaring?
2 O my God, I cry in the day-time, but Thou answerest not,
And in the night season, and keep not silence:
3 And Thou art Holy, throned above the praises of Israel.

1. WHY? Not the "why" of impatience or despair, not the sinful questioning of one whose heart rebels against his chastening, but rather the cry of a lost child who cannot understand why his father has left him, and who longs to see his father's face again.

It is the question of faith as well as of an anguish that cannot be told. For he who asks "why," nevertheless calls God "*my* God," and repeats the appropriating word again and again with the very emphasis of Faith. Indeed, such a question can only be asked by one whom God has taken into covenant with Himself, and to whom he has vouchsafed His promises.

What these words were in the lips of the Holy One of God, heart of man may not conceive. For a moment in that last agony, the Perfect Man was *alone*, alone with the sin of the world. But it is going beyond Scripture to say that a sense of God's wrath extorted that cry. For to the last breath He was the well-beloved of the Father, and the repeated "My God," "My God," is a witness even then to His confidence in the Father's Love. Stier says with great truth: "Neither could the damned in hell so call to God and ask, nor could Christ have done so if He were really to be considered here as suffering in their place." Our Lord uses the Aramaic word *σαβαχθανί* (which the Chald. paraph. gives שְׁבַקְתַּנִי) instead of the Hebrew.

There is some doubt as to the rendering of the latter part of the verse. The LXX. are clearly wrong, *μακρὰν ἀπὸ τῆς σωτηρίας μου οἱ λόγοι τῶν παραπτωμάτων μου.* Jerome has "longe a salute mea verba rugitus mei." "Far from my help are the words of my roaring," *i.e.* there is a great gulf between my cry for help, and the obtaining of that help. Rashi and others repeat the prep. with the second noun, "Why art Thou far from my help (and) from the words of my roaring?" A third interpretation is also possible, "My God, &c. . . . . Why art Thou far from my help? are the words of my roaring." Mendelss.: "Warum sind meine Klagen so fern von Hilfe?"

2. Again "*my* God." And this verse further explains the "why" of the first verse. It is as if he said, "I cannot understand this darkness. It is not that I have forgotten Thee. Day and night I cry—*to me* (לִי) there is no silence."

3. "Yea, moreover, *Thou* art Holy [or, the Holy One]. Thou canst not have changed. The history of the past, too, witnesses to Thy faithfulness: our *fathers* trusted in Thee, and Thou didst deliver them. But *I*—ah! I am not worthy of Thy help. I am but a worm, not a man. It is not that I have ceased to seek Thee: it is not that

4 In Thee our fathers trusted ;
They trusted, and Thou didst rescue them :
5 Unto Thee did they cry and were delivered,
In Thee they trusted and were not ashamed.
6 But as for me—I am a worm, not a man,
A reproach of men, and despised of the people.
7 All they that see me, laugh me to scorn,
They shoot out the lip, they shake the head, (saying,)

Thou hast ceased to be Holy : it is not that Thou canst not help, for Thou hast helped others :—why, then, hast Thou forsaken me ?" It is impossible to describe the sadness, the humility, the tenderness, the longing of this complaint.

HOLY. Does it seem strange that the heart in its darkness and sorrow should find comfort in this attribute of God ? No, for God's holiness is but another aspect of His faithfulness and mercy. And in that remarkable Name, "the Holy One *of Israel*," we are taught that He who is the *Holy* God is also the God who has made a covenant with His chosen. It would be impossible for an Israelite to think of God's holiness without thinking also of that covenant relationship. "Be ye holy ; for I the Lord your God am holy," were the words in which Israel was reminded of their relation to God. (See especially Lev. xix. 2 [1].) We see something of this feeling in such passages as lxxxix. 15—18 [16—19], and xcix. 5—9 ; Hos. xi. 8, 9 ; Is. xli. 14, xlvii. 4.

THRONED ABOVE THE PRAISES, &c., or *inhabiting the praises*, apparently with allusion to the phrase "dwelling between the cherubim," 1 Sam. iv. 4 ; 2 Sam. vi. 2 ; cf. lxxx. 1 [2], xcix. 1 ; but describing in a more spiritual manner the dwelling of Jehovah in His temple. THE PRAISES (plur.), with reference to the many acts of deliverance and redemption which had from time to time called forth a thankful remembrance. There is perhaps an allusion to Exod. xv. 11, 12.

The reading of the P.B.V. :

And Thou continuest holy,
O thou Worship of Israel,

follows Qimchi, who takes the participle, not in the sense of "throned upon" (or "inhabiting" as the A.V.), but in the other sense which it often has of "abiding." He explains : "Thou that abidest holy for ever, hast often been (the object of) the praises of Israel, who have sung praises to Thee for Thy deliverance."

4, 5. Thrice "they trusted," and only once "they cried."

5. UNTO THEE. Emphatic : "and not to other gods."—*Qimchi*.

6. Every word of this verse finds its echo in Isaiah. There Israel is "a worm," xli. 14. And there "the servant of Jehovah" is one whose "visage is so marred that he is not like a man," lii. 14. See, also, Is. xlix. 7, l. 6, and liii. 3, where "not belonging to men"="not a man," here.

7. St. Luke, in his account of our Lord's crucifixion (xxiii. 35), has used the verb employed by the LXX. who render here, ἐξεμυκτήρισάν με.

SHOOT OUT THE LIP. Cf. xxxv. 21, Job xvi. 10.

SHAKE THE HEAD—clearly not as an expression of compassion, but of malicious joy. Cf. cix. 25, xliv.

8 "Cast[b] (thyself) upon Jehovah—let Him rescue him,
Let Him deliver him, seeing He delighteth in him."
9 For Thou art He that took me[c] out of the womb,
Thou didst make me trust, (when I was) on my mother's breasts.
10 On Thee was I cast from the womb,
From my mother's belly THOU art my God.

II. 11 Be not far from me; for trouble is hard at hand,
For there is none to help me.
12 Many bulls have come about me:
Bashan's strong ones have beset me round.
13 They have gaped upon me with their mouth,
(As) a ravening and roaring lion.
14 Like water am I poured out,
And all my bones are out of joint;
My heart is become like wax,
It melteth in the midst of my body.
15 My strength is dried up like a potsherd,
And my tongue cleaveth to my jaws;
And Thou wilt lay me[a] in the dust of death.

14 [15], lxiv. 8 [9], where see Note. See also Matt. xxvii. 39.

8. LET HIM. Perhaps, with still bitterer scorn, in the future,

He will rescue him,
He will deliver him, &c.

HE DELIGHTETH, *i.e.* either God in the man, or the man in God.

9. Faith turns the mockery of his enemies into an argument of deliverance. They mock my trust in Thee—yea, I do trust in Thee; for Thou art He, &c.

In the first strophe the scorn and derision—in this the violence of his enemies—is the great subject of complaint.

11. Be not *far* (with reference to ver. 1), for trouble is *near*.

12. BASHAN'S STRONG ONES, or "Mighty bulls of Bashan." The sense is given by the LXX., *ταῦροι πίονες*, who are in the habit of rendering Bashan (as if allied to) דָּשֵׁן, *dashēn*, "fat," and not the name of a country) by *πίων*, see on lxviii. 15 [16]. The land of Bashan was celebrated for its fat pastures (cf. Deut. xxxii. 14, and Amos iv. 1; Ezek. xxxix. 18), extending from Jabbok to Mount Hermon, and eastward to the extreme boundary of Palestine.

14. After speaking of the violence of his tormentors, he passes on to speak of the effects of their violence upon himself. I AM POURED OUT. Thus he describes the utter melting away of all strength of body and courage of heart, in his fear and pain. Cf. Lam. ii. 11.

MY BONES ARE OUT OF JOINT. Lit. "have separated themselves," as of a man stretched upon the rack.

BODY so in P.B.V. Lit. "bowels."

15. AND THOU WILT LAY ME. Death must be the end, and it is Thy doing. Thou slayest me. So

16 For dogs are come about me,
The assembly of evil-doers have enclosed me,
Piercing [d] my hands and my feet.
17 I can tell all my bones:
They stare, they look upon me.
18 They part my garments among them,
And upon my vesture do they cast lots.
19 But Thou, O Jehovah, be not far (from me);
O my Strength, haste Thee to help me.
20 Deliver my soul from the sword,

does the soul turn from seeing only the instruments of God's punishment, to God who employs those instruments. Even in the extremity of its forsakenness it still sees God above all.

We are reminded of Peter's words, "Him, being delivered according to the determinate counsel and foreknowledge of God, ye have taken and with wicked hands have crucified and slain."

16. FOR DOGS ARE COME ABOUT ME. The enemies are still compared to savage animals, but the figure is somewhat different: "dogs" not only as fierce, but as unclean. Almost the only trait of bitterness in the Psalm. We must remember that these dogs are the savage wild dogs of the East, 1 Kings xiv. 11; Ps. lix. 6 [7], 14, 15 [15, 16].

PIERCING MY HANDS AND MY FEET. The Massoretic punctuation, if adhered to, would require the rendering, "Like a lion, (coming about) my hands and my feet." And it derives some support from the mention of the dog and the lion together, in the same way, in vers. 20, 21. But see more on this in the Critical Note.

17. I CAN TELL. Before: "all my bones are out of joint." Hence it would seem that the body was racked by some violent torture; not merely emaciated by starvation and suffering. And thus in his utter misery he is a gazing-stock to them that hate him: "they look upon me," *i.e.* with malicious satisfaction at my sufferings.

18. And now follows the last act of indignity, perpetrated as it were in sight of his death: his very clothes are stript from him, and are shared as plunder among his foes. This passage clearly cannot apply to David. On the other hand, there is nothing to lead us to suppose that we have here naked prediction. There is no change in the speaker. He continues to speak of *his own* sufferings. Why may not some Jew in exile have really suffered such things, and so have prefigured in history the sufferings of Christ? If Daniel was cast to the lions, and the Three Children into the furnace, others may have been exposed to other forms of death not less terrible. Whether, however, we take the Psalm as typical or predictive, in any case it is a prophecy of Christ and of His sufferings on the cross. All this was fulfilled to the letter in Him. See John xix. 23, &c.

19. Again the anxious prayer, "Be not far." First, Why art Thou far from helping me (ver. 1); then, Be not far from me . . . for there is none to help. Now with yet greater emphasis, as in the last extremity, But *Thou* (emphatic, as he turns from his persecutors and his sufferings, to fix his eyes upon his God), O Jehovah, be not far: O my Strength, *haste* Thee to help me.

20. MY ONLY ONE, or, as English Version, *my darling*. From the

My only one from the power of the dog.
21 Save me from the lion's mouth,
And from the horns of the wild oxen [e]—Thou hast answered me.

III. 22 So will I tell Thy name to my brethren,
In the midst of the congregation will I praise Thee: (saying,)
23 "Ye that fear Jehovah praise Him,
All ye the seed of Jacob glorify Him,
And stand in awe of Him, all ye the seed of Israel!
24 For He hath not despised nor abhorred the affliction of the afflicted,
Neither hath He hid His face from him;

parallelism = *my soul, my life.* In similar connection, xxxv. 17. The LXX. in both places, *τὴν μονογενῆ μου*, Vulg. *unicam meam.* It occurs besides, Judges xi. 34, of Jephthah's daughter (see Gen. xxii. 2; Prov. iv. 3). *The life* is so called either because man has but *one* life, or because it is the most precious of all things. Comp. Homer's *φίλον κῆρ*, and Plato's *τιμιοτάτη (ψυχή)*. Jerome renders *solitariam*, i.e. forsaken: which may be defended by xxv. 16, lxviii. 6 [7], but the other is preferable.

FROM THE POWER (Heb. hand) of the dog. Similarly "from the hand of the lion and the bear," 1 Sam. xvii. 37; "from the hand of the flame," Is. xlvii. 14.

21. THOU HAST ANSWERED ME. Are we to take this strictly as a pret. or as an imperative? It certainly *may be* the latter. (Ew. Gr. § 346 *b*, Ges. § 126, 6, *c*.) Here perhaps it is better to take it as a strict past, *Thou* HAST *answered me*, God's answer of peace and deliverance having come to the soul in the midst of its uttermost distress. "From the horns of the wild oxen —Thou hast heard and delivered me" (opp. to ver. 3, "Thou hearest not"). Before it had been "Thou answerest not,"—now at the most critical moment Faith asserts her victory, "Thou hast answered." See the same sudden transition, the same quick assurance that prayer has been heard, vi. 2, xx. 7, xxvi. 12, xxviii. 6, xxxi. 22. The vows and thanksgivings which follow are a consequence of this assurance.

22. SO or THEREFORE WILL I TELL. (Obs. the form with ה paragog. as marking a consequence from what precedes.) "*My brethren = the congregation = ye that fear Jehovah,*" ver. 23, *i.e.* the whole nation of Israel, as follows. In ver. 23 the singer calls upon the Church (קָהָל = *ἐκκλησία*) to praise God. In ver. 24 he gives the reason for this exhortation; the experience, viz. of God's mercy, and truth, and condescension, chiefly to himself, though not to the exclusion of others. For God is not like the proud ones of the earth. He does not *despise* the afflicted.

24. THE AFFLICTION OF THE AFFLICTED. The same word is used with Messianic reference, Is. liii. 4, 7; Zech. ix. 9.

NEITHER HATH HE HID (cf. x. 1, xiii. 1 [2] . . . WHEN HE CRIED HE HEARD. What a contrast to ver. 1, 2! Very remarkable is this confident acknowledgement of God's goodness in hearing prayer.

And when he cried unto Him, He heard."
25 From Thee is my praise in the great congregation;
My vows will I pay before them that fear Him.
26 The afflicted shall eat and be satisfied;
They shall praise Jehovah that seek Him:
May your heart live for ever!
27 All the ends of the earth shall remember and turn unto Jehovah,
And all the families of the nations shall worship before Thee.
28 For Jehovah's is the kingdom;
And He ruleth among the nations.
29 All the fat ones of the earth have eaten and worshipt,
Before Him shall all they that go down [f] into the dust bend the knee,

25. He has spoken to the congregation: he turns again to the Giver of his salvation, who has thus suffered him to praise Him in the great congregation.

FROM THEE, not merely OF THEE, which might mean that God was the object only of his praise. He is both source and object. It is God Himself who has put this great subject of praise into his heart and into his mouth. The will and the power to praise as well as the deliverance come from Him. Comp. cxviii. 23, where the construction is precisely the same, "from Jehovah is this."

MY VOWS, thank-offerings vowed in his trouble. The flesh of the sacrifice in such cases was to be eaten (Lev. vii. 16): hence the account of the banquet which follows, "they shall eat and be satisfied."

26. MAY YOUR HEART LIVE. This would have sounded more natural to our ears if it had been, "Their heart shall live (be strong, rejoice, &c.) for ever." This abrupt transition, however, from narration in the third person to address in the second, is not unusual in Hebrew. See the next verse, and Zech. xiv. 5. "The Lord my God shall come, and all the saints with *Thee*," instead of "with *Him*."

That the thank-offering and the meal which follows it are to be conceived of after a spiritual and not after a ritual manner, is clear from the high anticipations of the next verse.

27. For all the ends of the earth, all the families of the nations, are to acknowledge the God of Israel as the true King of the earth. He *is* the Ruler of the world, and His kingdom shall be visibly set up, and His lordship confessed.

29. The poet again returns to the figure of the banquet, and uses here the past tenses instead of the future, as is very usual with the Prophets, because in vision he already beheld his hopes fulfilled. Hence he speaks of what *is to be* as if it already *were*. All "the fat ones of the earth" (the rich and mighty) as well as the poor, "who cannot keep his soul alive," *i.e.* who is so poor that he has not the bare means of subsistence, shall sit down together at that banquet in the kingdom of heaven. (The same banquet which is spoken of Is. xxv. 6.)

THEY THAT GO DOWN INTO THE DUST. Here not literally "the

And whosoever cannot keep his soul alive.[g]
30 A seed shall serve Him;
It shall be told to the generation (to come)[h] concerning the Lord.
31 They shall come, they shall declare His righteousness
To a people that shall be born, that He hath done (it).

dead," as in the expression "they that go down into the pit," &c., but rather they who are "*ready* to go down," whose misery is so great that they are at the point to die.

30. A SEED. The P.B.V. following the Vulg. has "my seed;" the LXX. "his seed." IT SHALL BE TOLD, *i.e.* they shall hear of Him and of His saving help.

31. THEY, *i.e.* this new generation, this church which the Lord has planted.

HIS RIGHTEOUSNESS not only as manifested in the deliverance of His righteous servant, but as manifested in all His great work of salvation, both in the suffering and in the exaltation of Christ, and also in providing the feast for all who will partake thereof.

In the latter part of the Psalm,—from the words "Thou hast answered me" (ver. 21) to the last word, "He hath done it,"—the heart lifts itself up on the wings of Faith, and the prophet sees visions ever brighter and brighter opening before his gaze.

First, he will praise God in the congregation of Israel, and make known His name to his brethren. Then, all nations shall come and sit down at the banquet of fat things, and worship before the Lord. Lastly, to future ages also shall God's righteousness be declared. This hope of the conversion of other nations to the faith of God's elect, was in an especial manner characteristic of the period of the return from the Babylonish captivity. The prophecies of Zechariah are full of it; and so are many of the Psalms which probably date from that period.

It is impossible not to feel how far such hopes must have extended beyond the personal fortunes of the singer, or any results that he could possibly have anticipated from his own sufferings. If even in those sufferings he was but a feeble type of the Great Sufferer who should give His life for the world, certainly in the thanksgiving for his deliverance, and the results of that deliverance, there must have been but a very faint foreshadowing of the joy set before Him who endured the Cross, and who saw of the travail of His soul and was satisfied. Unnatural as I cannot help thinking that interpretation is, which assumes that the Psalmist himself never felt the sorrows which he describes, nor the thankfulness which he utters, but only put himself into the place of the Messiah who was to come,—I hold that to be a far worse error which sees here no foreshadowing of Christ at all. Indeed, the coincidence between the sufferings of the Psalmist and the sufferings of Christ is so remarkable, that it is very surprising that any one should deny or question the relation between the type and the antitype.

[a] UPON THE HIND OF THE DAWN. The LXX. render *ὑπὲρ τῆς ἀντιλήψεως τῆς ἑωθινῆς*, Vulg. *pro susceptione matutina*, renderings which are based on a confusion between אילת and אילות, which occurs ver. 20 (Heb.). Theodoret, adopting this, gives as an explanation *ἀντ. ἑωθ. ἡ τοῦ σωτῆρος ἡμῶν ἐπιφάνεια.* Rashi says that it is the name of a musical instrument, but that another account refers it to the congregation

of Israel. Qimchi interprets it of Israel in exile, "a hind fair as the morning-dawn" (Song of Sol. ii. 7, vi. 10). Luther and others, of "a hind early chased," with reference to our Lord, as having been brought in the early morning before the Council. Jerome, "pro cervo matutino," which he explains, "Ipse (Christus) et non alius quasi mane et aurora paratus est nobis." The Midrash refers to Song of Sol. ii. 8, and the Targ. sees an allusion to "the morning-sacrifice," which was offered so soon as the watchman on the pinnacle of the Temple cried ברק ברקאי (T. B. *Yomah*, 28[b]), "the rays of the morning do lighten." The most natural view of the words, however, is that first given by Aben-Ezra, according to whom, "the hind of the morn" are the first words of some other song, to the music of which this was to be sung. The prep. עַל occurs in this sense in the inscriptions of other Psalms, as ix., lvi., lx., &c. The phrase itself seems to have arisen from comparing the rays of the early sun shooting above the horizon to the horns of the hind. Hence the Arabian poets, too, speak of the morning or sunrising as "the horns of the dawn."

[b] גֹּל is neither inf. abs. (as קֹב, Num. xxiii. 25), nor 3 pret. after the analogy of אוֹר and בּוֹשׁ, but imperat, as xxxvii. 5, Prov. xvi. 3. Lit. "roll," viz. thy burden, or thyself, upon Jehovah. The abrupt transition from the 2d to the 3d pers. is too common to occasion any difficulty. The LXX., it is true, have ἤλπισεν ἐπὶ Κύριον; and similarly in the words of the mockers under the cross, πέποιθεν ἐπὶ τὸν θεόν. Matt. xxiii. 47. According to Qimchi גֹּל is an adjective of the same form as חֹם and תֹּם, and means "one who turns his ways, his petitions, and his prayers to God."

[c] גֹחִי (part. of גוח) = גָּחִי. This form of the part. of verbs ע״ו is found in other instances, and not only in the case of intrans., but also of trans. verbs (cf. לוֹט, Is. xxv. 7; Zech. x. 5). See Gesen. Gram. § 72, Remark 1. This verb occurs intrans. Job xxxviii. 8, "breaking forth," *i.e.* from the womb; trans., Micah iv. 10. Others take גֹחִי as the infin., "my breaking forth," *i.e.* the author, cause, &c. of my breaking forth. So Rosenm.: "*Tu* τὸ *prodire meum*, i.e. auctor proditus mei ex utero, per metonymiam effectus," &c. But such a metonymy is harsh and grammatically unnecessary.

[d] כארי. There is scarcely any passage of the Old Testament, the true reading and interpretation of which have given rise to so much discussion. The grounds for a critical conclusion are furnished, first, by the MSS.; and secondly, by the Ancient Versions.

I. The MSS., almost without exception, have (1) the present Massoretic reading, *i.e.* either כָּאֲרִי or כַּאֲרִי, "like a lion." The Targ. in the Antwerp Polyglot has נכתין אידי ורגלי, with a various reading, "post נכתין add. in aliis היך כאריה (or היך אריה)," and with this addition it is found in Walton's Polyglot. (2) In only two genuine Jewish MSS. do we find כארו. But in one of these (Kenn. 39) it would seem that the י has been altered by a later hand into ו, and the other (De-Rossi, 337) has כארִו., a union of both readings. Jacob Ben Chayyim, however, in the Massora finalis, says that he had found כארו as the K'thîbh, and כארי as the Q'ri in good MSS., and this is supported by the Massora Magna on

Numb. xxiv. 9. (3) For כרו there is still less to be said. It is only found in three late MSS., and in two of these on the margin; and is generally attributed to Christians, as it is by Joseph and David Qimchi. In the Bereshith Rabba of R. Moses Hadarshan, however, if we are to credit R. Martini (*Pug. Fid.* fol. 244), it is ascribed to the *Tikkun Sopherim.*

II. On the other hand, the Ancient Versions are all in favour of a verb, though they attach to it different significations: (1) "They pierced, bored through" (the root כאר being regarded as a cognate form of כור and כרה). So the LXX. ὤρυξαν, Syr. ܒܙܥܘ, Arab. نقبوا, Vulg. *foderunt.* (2) "They bound." So Aq. in his 2d edition, ἐπέδησαν (s. συνεπόδισαν), Symm., ὡς ζητοῦντες δῆσαι, and Jerome, who in some MSS. has *vinxerunt,* in others *fixerunt.* In this case the word must have been associated with the Arab. root كار, "to gather together," and so "to bind," &c. (3) "They put to shame." Aq. 1st ed. perhaps ᾔσχυναν (if the reading is correct), no doubt because he supposed it to be cognate with Aram. and Talmudic כאור and כער; cf. the Syr. ܟܐܪ, *pudefecit.* But as regards interpretation (2), it may be observed it is very doubtful whether the Arabic root can properly mean "to bind," as Gesen., De Wette, and Winer maintain. In the Kamus it is said that the verb كار in the 2d conjug. means "to dig the earth," and with acc. of the pers. is equivalent to طعن, "to pierce through." (See this fully discussed in Reinke's note.) As regards (3), the Syr. ܟܐܪ means "to put to shame in the way of rebuke and reproach," not of bodily wounding or disfiguring, as Aquila probably understood it. Field remarks that the rendering of the LXX. in the Syro-Hex. ܒܙܥܘ is the equivalent of the Greek ἔτρησαν, ἔτρωσαν, ἔρρηξαν, διέρρηξαν, but never, unless he is mistaken, of ὤρυξαν.

III. How is this direct opposition between the apparent reading of the MSS. and the interpretations of the Versions to be reconciled? This can only be done by neglecting the Massoretic *punctuation,* whilst we retain the reading כארי. This word, with different vowels, may be a participle instead of a noun, and we may thus obtain the required verbal meaning. It will then be a plur. constr., and should be either written כֹּאֲרֵי, if we assume a form כאר, or כָּארֵי, if, as is probable, the root is כור, the א being introduced as in קאם, Hos. x. 14; רָאֲמָה, Zech. xiv. 10. (See Gesen. § 71, A. 1.) Others would retain the Massoretic punctuation, and regard כָּאֲרִי as an imperfect plural absol., with termination ־ִי instead of ־ִים. The existence of such an apocopated plur. is recognized both by Gesen. § 86, *b,* and Ew. § 177, *a,* but the examples are questionable, and we should then have *two* unusual forms combined in the same word.

It seems probable, therefore, that the Massoretic interpretation ought to be given up, especially as "like a lion" is not very forcible, and leaves the structure of the sentence incomplete, although the verb may certainly be supplied from the first clause, "like a lion have they come about my hands and my feet" (see *e.g.* x. 10); but unless we accept this, we are left to follow the Versions in rendering either "piercing, transfixing," or, "binding my hands and my feet."

IV. It may be observed that the Massoreth on Is. xxxviii. 13 says, that the form כארי occurs in two different senses (בתרי לשוני) there and here, but it does not say what the meaning is here. The Targum (which, according to Jahn, is as late as the 7th, or 8th, century) combines both meanings, and gives נכתין היך כאריא, *mordentes sicut leo.* And Abraham of Zante, in his Paraphrase in rhyme (quoted by Delitzsch), גם כארי ידי ורגלי אסרו. "Like a lion (*i.e.* as men bind a lion) they have bound my hands and my feet."

e רֵמִים, an abbrev. form of רְאֵמִים, xxix. 6, "wild oxen," which still are found in herds on the east of the Jordan. LXX., μονοκερώτων; Jerome, *unicornium*, whence the rendering of E. V.

יוֹרְדֵי, "*ready* to go down." Comp. אוֹבֵד (Prov. xxxi. 6), "one who is ready to perish."

g וְנַפְשׁוֹ לֹ׳ ח׳, a relative clause (with the common omission of the relat.) instead of the part. here necessary (comp. xxxvii. 21, lxxviii. 39), because לא cannot stand before the part. or inf. For חִיָּה נ׳, comp. Ezek. xviii. 27. Lit. "and he who *hath* not (hitherto), and so *cannot* keep his soul alive."

h לַדּוֹר, "to *the* generation," *i.e.* the future one = לדור א׳ (xlviii. 14). So, too, even without the article, lxxi. 18. The article here, I think, necessitates this interpretation, which, moreover, agrees with what follows as to the continuance and propagation of this testimony concerning the Lord. (For this use of ל see the Lexicons.) Delitzsch renders: "A seed, which shall serve Him, shall be reckoned to the Lord for the generation" (*i.e.* which peculiarly belongs to, and serves Him), and refers to Ps. lxxxvii. 5 for a similar use of יְסַפֵּר, "counted as in a census." But the other is preferable.

PSALM 23

THIS Psalm breathes throughout a spirit of the calmest and most assured trust in God: it speaks of a peace so deep, a serenity so profound, that even the thought of the shadow of death cannot trouble it. Perhaps there is no Psalm in which the absence of all doubt, misgiving, fear, anxiety, is so remarkable; and certainly no image could have been devised more beautifully descriptive of rest and safety and trustful happiness, than that of the sheep lying down in the deep, rich meadow-grass, beside the living stream, under the care of a tender and watchful shepherd. This feeling of confidence is expressed in three different ways: first, "I cannot (or, shall not) want;" next, "I will fear no evil;" lastly, "I will dwell in the house of Jehovah for ever."

On the other hand, God's care for the soul is represented under a twofold image. First, Jehovah is the true shepherd, ver. 1, 2. Next, He is the bountiful host, ver. 5, who exercises princely hospitality towards His guests. But there is no marked transition from the one to the other. In ver. 3, 4, the figure of the *shepherd* is gradually lost in the representation of Jehovah as the faithful *guide* of His people, and so the way is prepared for the introduction of the next image, which occupies the rest of the Psalm. But the one thought, the one feeling which gives unity to the Psalm, is the thought, the feeling of trust in God. "This," says Mr. Stopford Brooke, of this Psalm, "enters into all the images and their ideas. This it is which harmonises all its contrasts, mellows all its changes, and unites into one whole the quiet contemplation of the first verses, the gloom of the fourth, the triumph of the fifth, and the combined retrospect and prophecy of the last; David's spirit of trust in God pervades the whole."

It is unnecessary to refer this Psalm to any particular period of David's history. As the outpouring of a heart which has found perfect rest in God, it was most probably written in advanced years, after a long experience of God's goodness. Its language is coloured by the reminiscences of his past life. His own shepherd experience no doubt suggested the image of the former part; and in the latter we may perhaps trace a recollection, more or less distinct, of the circumstances mentioned 2 Sam. xvii. 27—29, when, on David's coming to Mahanaim, during Absalom's rebellion, he and his party were succoured and refreshed in their faintness and weariness, through the kindness of Barzillai and other friends who supplied their wants.

The simplicity of diction which has led some persons to the conclusion that the Psalm was written in early youth, may be otherwise accounted for, as Mr. Stopford Brooke has remarked. Referring the Psalm to David's sojourn at Mahanaim, he accounts for it by the bitter grief of David at the rebellion of his son. "One of the most remarkable effects of intense grief," he observes, "is that it brings back to us the simplicity of childhood." But in any case the simplicity of diction so perfectly in harmony with the thoughts and images of the Psalm, might be looked for more naturally in mature years, than in the fervid glow and rush of early enthusiasm, struggling to express itself, and breaking into bold thoughts and rough forms of language.

[A PSALM OF DAVID.]

1 JEHOVAH is my Shepherd, I shall not want.

1. MY SHEPHERD. Faith appropriates God. The image, natural amongst a nation of shepherds, is first employed by Jacob, Gen. xlviii. 15, "The God which feedeth me," lit. "my Shepherd;" xlix. 24. There

2 In pastures[a] of grass He maketh me to lie down;
Beside waters of rest doth He guide me.

as here, God is the Shepherd of the *individual*, cf. Ps. cxix. 176, still more frequently of His *people;* lxxviii. 52, lxxx. 1 [2]; Micah vii. 14; Is. lxiii. 13, and especially Ezek. xxxiv.: most beautifully and touchingly in Is. xl. 11. So in the New Testament of Christ, John x. 1—16, xxi. 15—17; Heb. xiii. 20; 1 Pet. ii. 25, v. 4. To understand all the force of this image, we must remember what the Syrian shepherd was, how very unlike our modern western shepherd. "Beneath the burning skies and the clear starry night of Palestine," says F. W. Robertson, "there grows up between the shepherd and his flock a union of attachment and tenderness. It is the country where, at any moment, sheep are liable to be swept away by some mountain torrent, or carried off by hill-robbers, or torn by wolves. At any moment their protector may have to save them by personal hazard." It is the country, too, we may add, of long, scorching summer days, and intense and parching drought, when the fresh herbage and the living stream are beyond all price, and the shepherd's care and skill must be taxed to provide for his flock. "And thus there grows up between the man and the dumb creatures he protects, a kind of friendship. . . . Alone in those vast solitudes, with no human being near, the shepherd and the sheep feel a life in common. Differences disappear, the vast interval between the man and the brute: the single point of union is felt strongly. One is the love of the protector; the other the love of the grateful life: and so between lives so distant there is woven by night and day, by summer suns and winter frosts, a living network of sympathy. The greater and the less mingle their being together: they feel each other. 'The shepherd knows his sheep, and is known of them.'"

Again, on our Lord's appropriation of the figure to Himself, the same writer says with much force and beauty, "'I am the Good Shepherd.' In the dry and merciless logic of a commentary, trying laboriously to find out minute points of ingenious resemblance in which Christ is like a shepherd, the glory and the tenderness of this sentence are dried up. But try to feel, by imagining what the lonely Syrian shepherd must feel towards the helpless things which are the companions of his daily life, for whose safety he stands in jeopardy every hour, and whose value is measurable to him, not by price, but by his own jeopardy, and then we have reached some notion of the love which Jesus meant to represent, that Eternal Tenderness which bends over us — infinitely lower though we be in nature—and knows the name of each, and the trials of each, and thinks for each with a separate solicitude, and gave Himself for each with a Sacrifice as special, and a Love as personal, as if in the whole world's wilderness were none other but that one." (*Sermons*, 2d Series, pp. 286, &c.)

I SHALL NOT WANT, or, perhaps, "I cannot want," as describing not only the present experience, but as expressing confidence for all time to come. Observe the absolute, *I shall not want*, stronger than in xxxiv. 10 [11], or Deut. ii. 6, or viii. 9. These words are the key-note of the Psalm. David speaks them out of the fulness of his own experience. As he had watched over, and provided for, and tended his flock, leading them to the greenest pastures, and finding for them the water which in that country was so scarce, and guarding them by night from beasts of prey, so he felt his God would provide for and watch over him.

2. WATERS OF REST or "refresh-

3 He restoreth my soul;
    He leadeth me in the paths of righteousness,
  For His Name's sake.
4 Yea, though I walk through the valley of the shadow of
      death,[b]
    I will fear no evil, for Thou art with me:
      Thy rod and Thy staff—they comfort me.

ment." (Not "still waters," as in the very different phrase, Is. viii. 6.) LXX. rightly ὕδατα ἀναπαύσεως.

3, 4. The image of the shepherd is here partially lost in the use of proper, instead of figurative terms.

3. RESTORETH. "He does not *only* give us comfort; that would weaken character. He gives us power; for the true comforter is the strengthener in pain, not the remover of pain."--*Stopford Brooke.*

3. PATHS OF RIGHTEOUSNESS. This can hardly mean only "straight paths," as opposed to crooked; *i.e.* as Ibn Ezra explains it, "He will not make me go over hills and valleys, but on smooth, level ground." There is rather a blending of the natural image with its spiritual counterpart. It makes some difference, no doubt, whether, we suppose the Psalmist to be speaking here only of God's *providential* care in giving him "the blessings of this life," or whether we suppose him to refer also to God's dealings in grace: apparently he is speaking chiefly of the former, but certainly not exclusively; and, indeed, what truly devout mind would be careful to separate the two? The God of providence is the God of grace, and who can tell where the one ends, and the other begins? Providence runs up into grace, and grace loses itself in providence. Hence he adds,

FOR HIS NAME'S SAKE—not for my deserving, but out of His own goodness, for the manifestation of His own glory, and the furtherance of His kingdom upon earth.

4. This consciousness of Divine protection is his support, not only in quiet times, but even when dangers threaten. "Even though I should be called upon to walk," &c.

VALLEY, or, rather, "deep cleft," or "ravine;" horrid with frowning rocks and long deathly shadows growing deeper and more chilling as the sun sank.

SHADOW OF DEATH, or simply "dark shadow." (See Critical Note.)

THEY,—emphatic, because they are *Thy* rod and *Thy* staff. Calvin: "Neque tamen se omni metu vacuum esse jactavit David, sed tantum fore superiorem, ut intrepide, quocumque deductus fuerit a pastore suo, pergat: quod ex contextu melius patet. Primo dicit: *non timebo malum:* sed causam mox reddens, aperte fatetur se in baculi pastoralis respectu quærere timoris remedium. Quorsum enim consolatio ista, nisi quia metus eum solicitat?"

It matters little, Stier observes, in which order the connection in ver. 2—4 is taken. "Either the soul begins with the certainty of the present consolation, and the secret, inner refreshment in the paths of righteousness where the Lord leads, in order thence to derive confidence for the rest of the way, or it looks forward at once, in hope, ver. 2 [supposing the verbs there to be rendered as *futures* instead of *presents*], to the *future rest* in the pastures, and by the waters of eternal life, in order that thence a light may fall on the dark valley of its present pilgrimage. For to comprehend both fulfilment and foretaste in one consolation, which shall be

5 Thou preparest a table before me,
In the presence of my foes :
Thou hast anointed my head with oil,
My cup runneth over.
6 Surely goodness and loving-kindness shall follow me all the days of my life,
And I shall dwell[c] in the house of Jehovah for length of days.

suitable to each varied feeling and circumstance, is the purpose of the Spirit in this Psalm, which cannot be exhausted by any merely one-sided interpretation."

5, 6. A guest at a royal banquet. God is even more than a shepherd who provides for the wants of his sheep. He is a king who lavishes his bounty in rich provision for his guests. This is an image also adopted by our Lord in His parables. (Matt. xxii. 1, &c.)

5. PREPARE A TABLE, the common formula for furnishing a meal, Prov. ix. 2 ; Is. xxi. 5 ; Ezek. xxiii. 41.

IN THE PRESENCE OF MY FOES, *i.e.* who look on, but cannot harm me. The addition of this remark would intimate that we have more here than merely a figure. Some recollection of the past seems to break out which probably suggested it.

On the anointing the head, which was customary at banquets, comp. xcii. 10 [11].

6. I SHALL DWELL IN THE HOUSE OF JEHOVAH FOR LENGTH OF DAYS. What did the Psalmist mean by this ? The house of Jehovah might refer primarily to the tabernacle, as later to the temple. And if so, that to which he looked forward was access to God in His sanctuary, and the blessedness of communion with Him there. But is there no more than this ? no anticipation of a more perfect and abiding blessedness in the everlasting sanctuary above ? To us the language seems to bear such a meaning. It may not have done so to David. To him it was enough that he was the sheep for whom the Divine Shepherd cared, the guest for whom the Divine Host provided. He was thinking, perhaps, of this life more than of the next. Calvin, however, remarks : "*Habitabo in domo Jovæ.* Hac clausula aperte demonstrat, se in terrenis voluptatibus aut commodis minime subsistere, sed scopum sibi in cœlo figere ad quem omnia referat."

[a] נְאוֹת only occurring in the plural, and in poetry. (A sing. constr. נְוַת only in Job viii. 6 ; for in lxviii. 13, the same form is an adjective ; and a plur. constr. נְוֹת, only Zeph. ii. 6.) It probably means "meadows, pastures : " this at least seems the most suitable in passages like lxv. 13 ; Joel i. 19, ii. 22 ; Amos i. 2, &c. In other places, however, it means "habitations," as lxxiv. 20 ; Jer. xxv. 37, from a root נאה, נוה, "to sit, to rest." Hence some would interpret it here "resting-places," but the former, which is supported by usage, is preferable.

[b] צַלְמָוֶת. Hupfeld, following earlier authorities referred to by Abulwalid and Qimchi, objects to this being regarded as a compound word, "shadow of death," because, as he justly observes, such compound forms

are extremely rare in Hebrew, except in proper names, and the general signification of "darkness" is all that is required. He therefore supposes that it ought to be pointed צַלְמוּת, formed from צֶלֶם, "shadow, darkness," &c. after the analogy of מַלְכוּת, יַלְדוּת, &c.

[c] שַׁבְתִּי, according to the present punctuation, can only be pret. of שׁוּב, and then שׁוּב בְּ would be for שׁוּב וּבוֹא בְּ. Others take it as a defective writing for יָשַׁבְתִּי. It is better, however, to regard it as the inf. with suff., from ישׁב, שַׁבְתִּי being for שִׁבְתִּי ; cf. xxvii. 4.

PSALM 24

THIS grand choral Hymn was in all probability composed and sung on the occasion of the removal of the Ark from the house of Obed-Edom, to the city of David on Mount Zion (2 Sam. vi.). It was a day of solemn gladness and triumph. No long period had elapsed since David had wrested the stronghold of Zion from the last remnant of the hill-tribes of the Canaanites which lingered in Palestine. Henceforth this mountain-city, deemed by its ancient inhabitants impregnable, was selected by the conqueror as the seat of the royal residence, and the centre of religious worship; and thither, after having subdued his enemies, he determined to bring the Ark, which, for nearly fifty years, had been left neglected at Kirjath-Jearim. It is difficult for us to conceive the feelings which would be awakened in the hearts of the people by such an event, feelings of the most exalted and fervent patriotism, as well as of the deepest religious enthusiasm. The land was now indeed their own land; the king of their choice reigned over them; the most sacred emblem of Jehovah's presence and blessing was to be fixed in a central and permanent abode. The first attempt to remove the Ark had indeed miscarried, and the death of Uzzah, on that occasion, had filled the heart even of David with dismay: he feared to bring the symbol of so awful a presence to his city. But the blessing which had descended on the house of Obed-Edom, during the three months for which the Ark remained there, reassured him. His purpose, so hastily broken off by the judgement upon Uzzah, was resumed; and king, and priests, and people, the elders of Israel, and the captains over thousands (1 Chron. xv. 2), in solemn procession, and with all the accompaniments of music and song, conducted the Ark to its resting-place on the holy mountain. It was then that this majestic anthem rose to heaven: "Jehovah's is the earth, and the fulness thereof," and the gates of that grey old fortress were bid to lift themselves up, as being too narrow to admit the King of Glory.

It seems quite evident that the Psalm was intended to be sung in antiphonal measure, voice answering to voice, and chorus to chorus. Seven choirs of singers and musicians, so Josephus tells us, preceded the Ark on this occasion, as the king commanded, he himself playing upon the harp, and dancing before Jehovah with all his might.

We may suppose the whole congregation, as they wound in festal procession up the sacred hill, to have begun the solemn strain: "Jehovah's is the earth, and the fulness thereof," &c. (ver. 1, 2). Then one choir, or it may have been only a single voice, asked the question in ver. 3, "Who shall ascend into the hill of Jehovah?" &c., and was answered by another choir, or another voice, in ver. 4, "He that is clean of hands," &c.; whilst both finally united in ver. 5, 6, "He shall receive a blessing," &c. After this prelude, the singing ceased for a time (as the *Selah* seems to indicate), and the musical instruments only were heard. In the second part, a band of Priests and Levites heading the procession have already passed within the gates, as representatives of the holy nation. And whilst the rest of the vast assembly, as it still ascends, bursts forth with the magnificent choral hymn, "Lift up your heads, O ye gates," &c., the company from within reply, "Who is the King of Glory?" who thus demands admittance; and again the answer peals back from the choir without as with a voice of many waters, "Jehovah of Hosts, He is the King of Glory."

There is no reason to conclude, with Ewald, that in this Psalm the fragments of two ancient compositions have been united. The opening of the Psalm, which claims for Jehovah universal dominion, is quite in keeping with its close. The feeling thus expressed is remarkably characteristic of the great Hebrew Poets and Prophets. Jehovah is to them, indeed, the covenant God of Israel, but He is also the Lord of heaven and earth. And the verses which declare the characters of His true worshipers, were not only most fitting at such a season, but may perhaps have been suggested by the death of Uzzah, or at any rate would have received a force of sanction from that event, which reminded all who witnessed it, in so awful a manner, of the holiness of Him who had stooped to make His dwelling among them.

The Psalm, then, consists of two principal divisions:—

I. The preparation for the entry of Jehovah into His holy mountain. Ver. 1—6.

II. The entry itself. Ver. 7—10.

[A PSALM OF DAVID.]

I. 1 JEHOVAH'S is the earth, and the fulness thereof;
The world, and they that dwell therein:
2 For HE hath founded it upon (the) seas,
And upon (the) streams doth He make it fast.

3 "Who shall ascend into the mountain of Jehovah?
And who shall stand in His holy place?"
4 "He that is clean of hands and pure of heart,
Who hath not lifted up his soul [a] unto vanity,
And hath not sworn deceitfully."—

5 "He shall receive a blessing from Jehovah,

1, 2. Jehovah, the God of Israel, is also Creator of the world, and therefore, of right, Lord of the world and all its inhabitants. He is no merely local or national deity, like the gods of the heathen (see the same idea, xxxiii., and comp. l. 12, lxxxix. 11 [12]; see also Jonah i. 9, and Is. xxxvii. 16); the more marvellous therefore, and the more worthy to be praised, are His condescension and grace in having chosen Zion for His dwelling-place.

2. SEAS—STREAMS. The reference is no doubt to the account of the creation, in Genesis, the dry land having emerged from the water, and seeming to rest upon it. (Comp. cxxxvi. 6, Prov. viii. 29.) It would, however, be quite out of place to suppose that in such language we have the expression of any theory, whether popular or scientific, as to the structure of the earth's surface: Job says (xxvi. 7), "He hangeth the earth upon nothing." Such expressions are manifestly poetical. (See Job xxxviii. 6.)

It may be mentioned as a curiosity of Romish interpretation, that the Vulgate *super maria*, "upon the seas," was converted into *super Maria*, "upon (the Virgin) Mary." See Selnecker's Commentary as referred to in Delitzsch.

3—6. The moral conditions which are necessary for all true approach to God in His sanctuary. The Psalm passes as usual from the general to the particular, from God's relation to all mankind as their Creator, to His especial relation to His chosen people in the midst of whom He has manifested His presence. The *Almighty* God is also the *Holy* God. His people therefore must be holy. This part of the Psalm is almost a repetition of Ps. xv. 1, &c. See also Is. xxxiii. 14, 15.

4. LIFTED UP HIS SOUL. In Deut. xxiv. 15, the same phrase is rendered in the E. V., "setteth his heart upon."

UNTO VANITY, *i.e.* either (1) the perishing things of earth, Job xv. 31; or (2) falsehood, Job xxxi. 5, which signification passes over into a wider one of moral evil in general, cxix. 37; or (3) false gods, idols, xxxi. 6 [7]. It may be taken here in the widest sense of all that the human heart puts in the place of God.

5. We are here told in other words (as at the close of Ps. xv.) who is thus worthy to enter the holy place.

And righteousness from the God of his salvation.
6 This is the generation of them that seek after Him,
That seek Thy face, [O God of] Jacob!" [Selah.]

II. 7 "Lift up your heads, O ye gates;
And be ye lift up, ye everlasting doors,
That the King of Glory may come in."

8 "Who, then,[b] is the King of Glory?"

"Jehovah, strong and mighty;
Jehovah, mighty in battle."

9 "Lift up your heads, O ye gates,
Yea, lift them up, ye everlasting doors,
That the King of Glory may come in!"

A BLESSING, such as Abraham's seed might look for (Gen. xv. 6).

RIGHTEOUSNESS, not in the New Testament sense of justification, but in the Old Testament acceptation of inward and outward holiness; but still even this regarded as a *gift* from the God of his *salvation.* For this connection between *salvation* and *righteousness,* see the note on lxxiv. 15, and cf. cxxxii. 9, 16, and especially the prophecy of Isaiah, xlv. 22, 24, xlvi. 13, l. 5, lvi. 1.

6. THIS IS THE GENERATION OF THEM, *i.e.* Such are they, this is their character.

As the text at present stands, in the Heb. "That seek thy face, Jacob," the only way of explaining it is by taking the word "Jacob" as in apposition with "the generation that seek Thy face." The meaning would then be, "This is the generation that inquire after God, and seek His face, viz. Jacob," *i.e.* the true Israel, those who worship in spirit and in truth. But this seems harsh, and the word אֱלֹהֵי may have slipt out of the text, as may be inferred from the renderings of the LXX. and Syriac. I have therefore adopted this view.

7—10. The entry of Jehovah as the King of Glory into His sanctuary. The festal procession has now reached the gates of the city of Zion. "The singers go before, the minstrels follow after," and in the midst of these is the Ark, "whose name is called by the name of the Lord of Hosts, that dwelleth between the cherubim" (2 Sam. vi. 2); so that the entry of the Ark is the entry of Jehovah Himself into Zion (Num. x. 35). By a sublime figure the poet bids "the everlasting gates" of that grey old fortress be lifted up; for the greatest and most glorious of all kings is He who now enters in, to claim it for Himself. David had taken the stronghold from the hands of the Jebusites. But not David, but Jehovah, is the true King of Zion. The gates are termed "gates of old," or "everlasting," as being of a hoar antiquity, possibly also with the hopeful anticipation that they would abide for ever.

This Psalm is no doubt prophetic or rather typical in its character. It has been appointed by the Church as one of the Psalms for Ascension Day; and most fitly, in its Christian application, celebrates the return of Christ as the King of

10 "Who, then, is that King of Glory?"

"Jehovah of Hosts,
He is the King of Glory." [Selah.]

Glory to His heavenly throne, and the inauguration of that dominion which He thence exercises in the world. It will be fully accomplished when the doors of all hearts, all temples, and all kingdoms, shall be thrown wide before Him; when He shall be acknowledged upon earth as He is acknowledged in heaven.

[a] The reading fluctuates between נַפְשִׁי and נַפְשׁוֹ. The former has been supposed by some of the Rabbinical commentators to be equivalent to the personal pronoun אֹתִי, referring to God (cf. Jer. l. 14, Amos vi. 8), or rather to be equivalent to שְׁמִי in Exod. xx. 7, where the same phrase נשא לשוא occurs. But such an expression as "who hath not taken up Me, or My soul in vain," spoken of God would be extremely harsh; and moreover God is nowhere introduced in the Psalm as speaking in the first person.

[b] זֶה, not "Who is this," &c., but זֶה is employed adverbially in interrogations, as making the interrogation more emphatic. German, *Wer denn?* In a still stronger form below, ver. 10, מי הוא זה. Cf. Jer. xxx. 21. So again in 1 Kings xviii. 7, "Is it thou (not as in E. V., Art thou that), my lord Elijah?"

PSALM 25

This is an acrostic or alphabetical Psalm, the first verse beginning with the first letter of the Hebrew alphabet, and the other letters following in order at the beginning of each successive verse. The order indeed is not perfectly observed: for according to the present text the second verse begins with א, Aleph, instead of ב, Beth; the letter ו, Vau, is altogether omitted; ר, Resh, is repeated ver. 18, 19, whereas the former verse should have begun with ק, Koph. And a last verse, added to make up the number 22, commences with, פ Pe. This peculiarity, as well as the omission of the ו, Vau, in its proper place, occurs also in the 34th, another alphabetical Psalm. Indeed, the last verse of these two Psalms not only begins with the same letter but with the same *word*, פדה, "redeem." Here the prayer is that God would *redeem* Israel; there it is said that Jehovah *redeems* the soul of His servants.* This looks like design. It would seem to indicate that

* Lagarde's notion that in the two first words of this last verse the writer conceals his own name has little to recommend it. I have noticed it elsewhere.

the same person was author of both poems, and that the condition of the people was the same at the time they were written. We have no means of fixing what that time was, but they probably both belong to the later period of the history—perhaps to the time of the Exile. Other Psalms which are constructed on a similar principle are the 37th, the 111th, 112th, 119th, and 145th. The general character of all these Psalms is didactic, and it is probable that this artificial arrangement was intended to be an assistance to the memory.

The Psalm hardly admits of formal division. It is a prayer for instruction and forgiveness.

The recurrence of certain expressions, such as "waiting" and "being ashamed" (ver. 2, 3, 5, 20, 21); "affliction" and "afflicted" (ver. 9 *bis*, 16, 18); the prayer for "instruction" (ver. 4, 5, 8, 9, 12, 14), together with earnest entreaty for "forgiveness" (ver. 7, 11, 18), gives a peculiar character to the Psalm. Its prevailing thought is that God is the teacher of the afflicted, and the guide of the erring: and this is constantly repeated either in the way of statement or of prayer.

[(A PSALM) OF DAVID.]

I. 1 א UNTO Thee, O Jehovah, do I lift up my soul.
2 א O my God, in Thee have I trusted;
Let me not be ashamed,
Let not mine enemies triumph over me.
3 ג Yea, none that wait [a] on Thee shall be ashamed;
They shall be ashamed who are faithless [b] without cause.[c]

4 ד Thy ways, O Jehovah, make me to know;
Teach me Thy paths:
5 ה Lead me in Thy truth, and teach me;

1. UNTO THEE, emphat., not to any false god, or to any human deliverer. Similarly ver. 2, 5.

2. This ver. begins with an א instead of a ב, as it should do, according to the acrostic arrangement. Possibly the first two words of the ver. have been transposed. At any rate we must not (with Ewald and others) refer אֱלֹהַי to the former verse.

3. The writer passes from the optative with אַל (μή), ver. 2, to the future with לֹא (οὔ). He here expresses not so much a general truth as his own individual conviction, and includes tacitly himself in the number of those who thus hope. The LXX. are mistaken in returning, in the second clause of the verse, to the optative. For the sentiment, cf. Rom. v. 5, ἡ δὲ ἐλπὶς οὐ καταισχύνει.

5. LEAD ME IN THY TRUTH, more lit. "Cause me to walk in Thy truth," *i.e.* let me ever live in

For Thou art the God of my salvation:
On Thee [d] do I wait all the day.

6 ז Remember Thy tender mercies, O Jehovah, and Thy loving-kindnesses,
For they have been ever of old.

7 ח The sins of my youth and my transgressions remember not;
According to Thy loving-kindness remember THOU me
For Thy goodness' sake, O Jehovah.

II. 8 ט Good and upright is Jehovah,
Therefore doth He teach sinners in the way.

9 י He leadeth [e] the afflicted in judgement,
And teacheth the afflicted His way!

10 כ All the paths of Jehovah are loving-kindness and truth,
To them that keep His covenant and His testimonies.

11 ל For Thy Name's sake, O Jehovah,
Pardon [f] mine iniquity, for it is great.

the experience of it, that I may not be like the faithless ones who are put to shame. So Calvin: "Postulat ut Deus servum in fide promissionum retineat, i.e. sibi patefieri quam verax et fidelis Deus sit in promissis suis, promissa Dei penitus cordi suo insculpi." Rightly, for the Hebrew word here employed means *truth* not as apprehended by man, but as an attribute of God. Comp. xxvi. 3, lxxxvi. 11.

6. Comp. Gen. viii. 1, ix. 15, xix. 29, &c. An appeal to the unchangeableness of God's nature, as well as a calling to mind of past mercies. But sin is that which shuts out God's mercy, and hence the prayer for forgiveness in the next verse.

6, 7. "Tender mercies," "loving-kindnesses," "loving-kindness," "goodness." How the soul dwells on these attributes of God, and cleaves to them when it is troubled with the sad recollection of "the sins of its youth," and its "transgressions!"

8, 9. Again an appeal to God's attributes as the ground of His dealings with man.

8. SINNERS, here apparently with reference to the etymology of the word, those that "have erred and strayed" from the way.

9. THE AFFLICTED, see on ix. 12.

10. LOVING-KINDNESS (or grace) AND TRUTH, the χάρις καὶ ἀλήθεια of John i. 17. These paths—the ways in which He leads His people—"are loving-kindness, for the salvation of men is the end thereof, and truth, for they give proof at every step of the certainty of His promises. Grace is their Alpha, and truth their Omega."—*Delitzsch.*

11. Again a prayer for forgiveness, that the grace and truth (ver. 10) may be manifested to his soul.

12 מ What man is he that feareth Jehovah?
Him doth He teach the way that he should choose.
13 נ His soul shall dwell at ease,
And his seed shall inherit the land.
14 ס The secret[g] of Jehovah is for them that fear Him,
And His covenant doth He make them know.

15 ע Mine eyes are ever towards Jehovah,
For He shall pluck my feet out of the net.
16 פ Turn Thee unto me, and be gracious to me,
For I am desolate and afflicted.
17 צ My heart is (full of) troubles: O set it at liberty,[h]
And bring me forth out of my distresses.

18 ר Look upon my affliction and my trouble,
And forgive all my sins.
19 ר Look upon mine enemies; for they are many,
And they hate me with cruel hatred.
20 ש O keep my soul, and deliver me.
Let me not be ashamed; for I have found refuge in Thee.
21 ת Let perfectness and uprightness preserve me;
For I wait on Thee.

The mention of the keeping of the covenant (ver. 10) suggests the thought of manifold failure, and the consequent need of pardon.

12. WHAT MAN IS HE? or simply, "Whosoever he is that feareth," &c.; see xxxiv. 12 [13].

THE WAY THAT HE SHOULD CHOOSE, *i.e.* the best way. So Luther (whom Ewald follows), *den besten Weg*.

13. SHALL DWELL, lit. "pass the night," but used in the more extended sense, as in xlix. 12 [13], xci. 1, Prov. xix. 23.

AT EASE, lit. "in prosperity."

SHALL INHERIT THE LAND. Cf. Exod. xx. 12, Lev. xxvi. 3, Deut. iv. 1, &c.

14. SECRET. As God said, Gen. xviii. 17, "Shall I hide from Abraham that thing which I do?" Or the word may mean "close and intimate communion," in which God makes Himself known to the soul. See lv. 14 [15], Prov. iii. 22, Job xxix. 4. God alone possesses the truth, for He is the truth, and therefore He alone can impart it, and He imparts it only to them that fear Him.

15. PLUCK, lit. "bring forth," the same word as in ver. 17.

22 פ Redeem Israel, O God,
Out of all his troubles.

22. This last verse, which contains a prayer for the whole congregation, was perhaps added in order to adapt the Psalm to liturgical use. (Cf. li. 18, 19 [20, 21].) The name of God is here Elohim, whereas throughout the rest of the Psalm it is Jehovah.

[a] קֹוֶיךָ. Part. Qal (the fin. verb being Piel), occurring, however, only in st. constr. or with suff., which seems to rest on the constr. of the verb with the accus. (ver. 5, 21) as well as with לְ, or rather perhaps on the affinity between the part. and the noun. Sim. קָם is more common in plur. with suff., than with the prep. עַל, which the verb requires.

[b] הַבּוֹגְדִים. LXX. *οἱ ἀνομοῦντες διακενῆς*. Aq., *οἱ ἀθετοῦντες*. Sym., *οἱ ἀθ. εἰκῆ*. S′. *ἀποστατοῦντες*. בֹּגֵד, "one who acts treacherously," whether against God (lxxviii. 57, Jer. iii. 20, &c.) or man (Judges ix. 23, Job vi. 5, Mal. ii. 14, &c.), often opp. in the Proverbs, to צַדִּיק, and rendered by the LXX. *παράνομος*, used by the prophets of plunderers and oppressors (Is. xxi. 2, xxiv. 16, Hab. i. 13).

[c] רֵיקָם, either "without cause," or, as qualifying the preceding word, "vainly, emptily." Cf. בֹּגְדֵי אָוֶן, lix. 6; שָׂטֵי כָזָב, xl. 5. So Luther, *die losen Verächter.*

[d] Some of Kennicott's and De-Rossi's MSS. read ואותך, making a fresh verse begin here. This would restore the alphabetical arrangement (see Introd. to the Psalm). The LXX., Syr., Arab., and Vulg. seem also to have had this reading.

[e] יַדְרֵךְ, properly an optative, though nearly all commentators take it as fut. or pres. But the ver. might very well be rendered as a prayer. "May He lead," &c.

[f] וְסָלַחְתָּ. This is one of the most remarkable instances of the use of the pret. with Vau emphatic, for the imperative. Usually where this is the case, an imperat. has gone before. But not so here, and this should have been noticed by Gesen., when he classed this amongst examples of the ordinary constr., § 124, 6. a.

[g] So Symm. renders *ὁμιλία*; while Aq. has *ἀπόρρητον*, and Theod. *μυστήριον*. The LXX. have *κραταίωμα*, as if they read יְסוֹד instead of סוֹד. And in Rabb. literature the words are sometimes used interchangeably.

The second clause may be rendered in three ways: (1) "That He may make them know His covenant." (2) "And His covenant is for their instruction." (3) "And His covenant He doth (or will) make them know." The last rendering is in accordance with the not uncommon substitution of the inf. with לְ, for the fut. Cf. Is. xxi. 1, xxxviii. 20, Prov. ix. 8. Gesen. § 129, Rem. 1; and see on lxii. note [g].

[h] הרחיבו. The older translators generally have taken this in an intr. or pass. sense, as E. V. But the verb nowhere else occurs, except in a trans.

sense. As the text now stands, we can only render, "Distresses have enlarged my heart," *i.e.* have made room for themselves, as it were, that they might come in and fill it; or have rushed in like a flood of water, swelling the stream till it overflows its banks, and so spreads itself over a wider surface. So Bakius: "fecerunt latitudinem quaquaversum undiquaque, metaphora sumta ab aquis subito per omnes campos se diffundentibus." Unless, indeed, we take the word in the same meaning as in cxix. 32, where to enlarge the heart = to open it to instruction. But that sense is scarcely suitable here. Most modern editors read הרחיב וממצוקתי (imperat.), instead of הרחיבו מ׳. The rendering then is: "My heart is troubles (*i.e.* is nothing but troubles, is full of troubles), O set it at liberty! And out of my distresses," &c.

PSALM 26

THIS Psalm has some points of resemblance, both in thought and expression, to the last. Both open with the same declaration of trust in God (xxv. 2, xxvi. 1); in both there is the same prayer that God would redeem (xxv. 22, and xxvi. 11) and be gracious (xxv. 16, xxvi. 11) to His servants. Other points of contact may be found in xxv. 21, xxvi. 11, and xxv. 5, xxvi. 3. There is, however, this marked difference between the two, that there are wanting, in this Psalm, those touching confessions of sinfulness and pleadings for forgiveness which in the other are thrice repeated. Here is only the avowal of conscious uprightness, an avowal solemnly made as in the sight of the Searcher of hearts, and deriving, no doubt, much of its intensity and almost impassioned force, from the desire, on the part of the singer, to declare his entire separation from, and aversion to, the vain and evil men by whom he is surrounded.

The Psalm furnishes no direct evidence as to its date, but it may have been composed during Absalom's rebellion. His partisans may especially be hinted at in the "vain men" and "dissemblers" of ver. 4, who had only recently been unmasked; for Absalom, it is said, "had stolen the hearts of the men of Israel."

The Psalm scarcely admits of any strophical division. The flow of thought is natural and unbroken throughout. The singer begins by appealing to God as the witness of his sincerity and uprightness, ver. 1—3. He then passes on to state how this sincerity has manifested itself, in complete separation from the wicked on the one hand, ver. 4, 5; and on the other, by the love of God's house and worship, ver. 6—8. Hereupon follows, first, a prayer that he who is thus upright (ver. 11) should not be involved in the lot of the wicked, but, on the contrary, experience God's redeeming love and grace, ver. 9—11; and next, the confident sense of security which is the very answer to his prayer, together with the resolve expressed, to declare, in the most public manner, his thankfulness to God, ver. 12.

[(A PSALM) OF DAVID.]

1 JUDGE me, O Jehovah,
For I have walked in my integrity,
And in Jehovah have I trusted without wavering.[a]
2 Prove me, O Jehovah, and try me,
Purify [b] my reins and my heart:
3 For Thy loving-kindness is before mine eyes,
And my conversation hath been in Thy truth.
4 I have not sat with vain persons,
Neither do I go in with dissemblers;

1. JUDGE ME, *i.e.* vindicate my cause, so that my innocency may be made manifest:—do me justice (as vii. 8 [9], xxxv. 24).

INTEGRITY, not moral perfection, but uprightness of heart, conscious sincerity of intention, is meant (see Gen. xx. 5, 1 Kings xxii. 34); and this, as resting on that unwavering trust in God which follows.

2. PROVE . . . . PURIFY. Words used of the testing of metals, the last especially of trying and refining them by means of smelting, xii. 6 [7], lxvi. 10. The REINS, as the seat of the lower animal passions (but also the seat of counsel, xvi. 7); the HEART, as comprising not only the higher affections, but also the will and the conscience. He thus desires to keep nothing back; he will submit himself to the searching flame of the Great Refiner, that all dross of self-deception may be purged away.

3. This verse gives the reason for the foregoing prayer.

LOVING-KINDNESS . . . . TRUTH. See above on xxv. 10.

MY CONVERSATION HATH BEEN, lit. "I have walked to and fro in Thy truth." The verb is used like the Hellen. περιπατεῖν, of the general conduct and behavour.

We have here again those strong assertions of conscious innocence, united even with an appeal to the searching scrutiny of God Himself, which we have noticed in other Psalms. (See xvii. 3, xviii. 20—24.) The explanations given on those passages will apply here. It is clear, on the one hand, that this is no Pharisaic boast. The trust in God, the eye fixed on His loving-kindness, the prayer to be proved and tried, could not proceed from a Pharisee. On the other hand, it must always be borne in mind, that the full depth and iniquity of sin was not disclosed to the saints of the Old Test. Sin could only appear to be sin in all its blackness and malignity, when it was brought into the full light of the Cross of Christ. And it is only as any man grasps that cross, that he can bear to look into the pollution which cleaves to his nature.

4. VAIN PERSONS, or, "men of

5 I hate the congregation of evil-doers,
And with the wicked do I not sit.
6 I wash my hands in innocency,
That so I may compass Thine altar, O Jehovah,
7 To make the voice of thanksgiving to be heard,[c]
And to tell of all Thy wondrous works.
8 Jehovah, I love the habitation of Thine house,
And the place where Thy glory dwelleth.
9 Gather not my soul with sinners,
Nor my life with bloody men;
10 In whose hand are wicked devices,
And whose right hand is full of bribes;—

vanity," as Job xi. 11. On this word "vanity" see note on xxiv. 4. It signifies all the emptiness of the creature apart from God, "the chaotic void of estrangement from God, the terrible Nay into which man perverts the divinely ordained Yea of his being."—*Delitzsch.*

6. I WASH MY HANDS. Here of course only a figurative expression, though the action itself was often symbolical (Deut. xxi. 6, Matt. xxvii. 24), after the fashion of the East, where it is common to address the eye as well as the ear. The figure is borrowed apparently from Exod. xxx. 17—21, where Aaron and his sons are commanded to wash their hands and feet, before they approach to do service at the altar.

THAT SO I MAY COMPASS. The form of the verb requires this rendering. It is the cohortative, not the simple future. It may, however, here be used rather in an optative sense: "And so may I compass—so may I not be considered unworthy to compass—Thine altar." So Olshausen, who is followed by Delitzsch. This compassing, or going round the altar, was, it would seem from this passage, a part of the ritual of Divine worship, and was performed with the accompaniment of music and singing, as may be gathered from the next verse. If so, it is remarkable that no such custom is provided for in the Law, or alluded to in the history. That the notice of such a custom should have been preserved in a Psalm may readily be accounted for, from the fact that the Psalms were most of them intended for liturgical use. But could David hope to be permitted thus to join with the Priests and Levites in near approach to the altar? Delitzsch replies, that as the Priests represented all Israel, whatever acts of worship they performed, each Israelite might be said to perform in them; and that thus David, having the priestly heart, might use also the priestly expression. But Moses (xcix. 6), Samuel, David, Solomon, all took a prominent part in public worship; so that we need not shrink from taking the passage in its literal and obvious meaning.

7. TO MAKE, or, confining the construction as before, "that I may make, &c. . . . . and may tell, &c."

8. I LOVE, &c., the antithesis to ver. 5, "I hate the congregation of evil-doers."

9. Thus he would have God judge him (ver. 1), *i.e.* declare what he is, by separating him from the wicked.

10. WICKED DEVICES. The Heb. is in the singular "a wicked de-

11 Whilst as for me, I walk in mine integrity:
Redeem me and be gracious unto me.
12 My foot standeth upon even ground:
Among the congregations will I bless Jehovah.

vice," but this may be used collectively, like the word "bribe" in the next line.

11. Asserting again the integrity of his own character, in opposition to the violence and unscrupulousness of his enemies, he makes on this ground a fresh appeal to God for deliverance from their devices.

12. His prayer has been heard. He is safe. He stands on the open, level table-land, where he has room to move, and where his enemies cannot hem him in, and therefore he fulfils the resolve made before (ver. 7), and publicly pours out his thanksgivings to God.

[a] לֹא אֶמְעָד, a subjoined adverbial clause, "without being moved," like לֹא יֵדָע, xxxv. 8, and not a distinct and independent assertion.

[b] צְרוּפָה. So the K'thibh is to be read, according to similar forms in Is. xxxii. 11. See also Judges ix. 8, 12; 1 Sam. xxviii. 8.

[c] לַשְׁמִיעַ for לְהַשְׁמִיעַ. Cf. Is. xxiii. 11. It may be here used without any object expressed, as in 1 Chron. xv. 19, 2 Chron. v. 13, "to sing aloud." In Ps. lxvi. 8, קוֹל is the direct object of the verb; but in 2 Chron. v. 13, it seems to be used as the accus. of the instrument "with one voice." So here, the prep. may be used to mark the instrument; or perhaps we may take בְּקוֹל as itself the object of the verb (for the construction with the prep., see Ezek. xxvii. 30), and render, "to make the voice of thanksgiving to be heard."

PSALM 27

THIS Psalm, like the last, and the one which follows, may very probably be referred to the time of Absalom's rebellion. All alike are characterised by the affectionate remembrance of God's sanctuary, as of one who was debarred from the privilege of constant and uninterrupted access to it. This feeling, however, is most vivid, this yearning after the service and ordinances of His Tabernacle is most intense, in this Psalm. It seems as if all other desires of the heart were concentrated and swallowed up in this one: "One thing have I desired." The feeling of calm unshaken confidence in God, in the former part of the Psalm, reminds one of Psalm iii., which may undoubtedly be referred to the same circumstances.

The Psalm consists of two parts. The first (ver. 1—6) is an expression of the most assured confidence in Jehovah, whatever enemies may threaten. The second (ver. 7—14) is an earnest cry for help and comfort in present need, out of which the soul rises again to hopeful trust in God.

As still further subdivision we have—

I. The Psalmist's confidence in God :

A 1. As his refuge against all fear (ver. 1) :
2. As his protection in times past (ver. 2) ;
3. As his hope at all times.

B Further expression of that confidence in the longing to abide ever in the house of Jehovah (ver. 4).
1. For there will he find safety (ver. 5) ;
2. And so may confidently hope for victory over his enemies (ver. 6).

II. The Psalmist's prayer in time of need :

A Forsake me not !
1. For I plead thy word (ver. 8).
2. I am Thy servant whom Thou hast saved (ver. 9).
3. I am desolate and forsaken (ver. 10).

B But deliver me,
1. By showing me Thy way ;
2. By saving me from my enemies.

C I know in whom I have believed.
Therefore 1. My trust in Him still supports me (ver. 13).
2. Let me trust Him evermore.

[A PSALM OF DAVID.]

I. 1 JEHOVAH is my Light and my Salvation :
Whom shall I fear ?
Jehovah is the defence of my life :
Of whom shall I be afraid ?

1—3. The fearlessness of the man who has made Jehovah his confidence.

1. MY LIGHT, MY SALVATION . . . THE DEFENCE (or bulwark) OF MY LIFE. This, says Calvin, is the triple shield which he opposes to all the different terrors which threaten him. MY LIGHT—the only instance of the direct application of this name to God in the Old Test. But see xviii. 28 [29], xxxvi. 9, lxxxiv. 11 [12], and Deut. xxx. 20, " He is thy Life."

2 When the evil-doers came near unto me
To eat up my flesh—
My adversaries and mine enemies to (do) *me* (harm),
They themselves stumbled and fell.
3 Though a host should encamp against me,
My heart will not be afraid :
Though there rise up war against me,
For all this do I trust.
4 One thing have I asked of Jehovah,
That will I seek after :
That I may dwell in the house of Jehovah
All the days of my life ;
To behold the beauty of Jehovah.

2. This verse may be regarded, with most commentators, as recording David's past experience of God's protection. Stier, however, sees in it the confidence of Faith with regard to the present and the future, David being so sure of the defeat of his enemies, that he speaks of it as already accomplished : "When mine enemies come upon me, &c. . . . they *have* stumbled and fallen," *i.e.* such is their inevitable fate.

TO EAT UP MY FLESH, an image taken from wild beasts ; see Job xix. 22.

TO (DO) ME (HARM). The use of the pronoun here is not pleonastic, but emphatic, and is evidently put in immediate and designed opposition to the pron. "they," referring to his enemies, which follows.

3. A HOST. Lit. "though a CAMP should encamp against me," but the English idiom would hardly admit of such a rendering.

FOR ALL THIS. So the same expression is rightly rendered in the E.V. of Lev. xxvi. 27. The fuller form occurs lxxviii. 32, Job i. 22. Cocc., rightly, *hoc non obstante*, "in spite of this," and Mendelssohn, "Auch dann (even then, even in this case), bleib' ich getrost." The Rabb. commentators, as Rashi and Ibn Ezra, explain, "In this," viz. that the Lord is my light, &c., ver. 1, "do I trust." Rosenm. refers the pronoun "this" to the war mentioned just before, "even in the battle itself," *in ipsa pugna*. But the first rendering is more forcible.

4. Such happiness had he experienced in the service of God in His tabernacle, such peace and joy had he found there, that there, if it might have been, he would have chosen always to remain. For there God vouchsafed to dwell ; there He manifested His immediate Presence ; there David seemed, as it were, to abide under the very shadow of the Almighty. The supreme blessedness of a life entirely devoted, like that of the priests, to the service of God, seems often to have forced itself upon the minds of the holy Psalmists (see xv., xxiii., lxv., lxxxiv., &c., and note on xxvi. 6), and upon none more than upon that of David, who was compelled so often to wander at a distance from the sanctuary. There is the same feeling here of the perfect security and abounding happiness of such a dwelling-place as in Psalm xxiii. 6. Indeed the two Psalms have much in common.

BEAUTY, apparently with reference to the ordinances of the sanctuary, the worship as there con-

And to look with pleasure upon His temple.
5 For He shall keep me privily in His tabernacle in the day of evil;
He shall hide me in the hiding-place of His tent;
On a rock shall He lift me up on high.
6 And now shall my head be lifted up above mine enemies round about me:
So will I offer in His tent sacrifices of shouting,
So will I sing, yea I will make melody unto Jehovah.

II. 7 Hear, O Jehovah, when I cry with my voice,
Be gracious also unto me and answer me.

ducted, &c. (So Luther: "die schönen Gottesdienste des Herrn.") But of course not to be confined merely to the external glory of the tabernacle, but to be understood chiefly of that glory which is unveiled to the eye of faith. Others, however, explain the word here, as in xc. 17, in the sense of "kindness," "loving favour." (Del. "Freundlichkeit.") Our English word "favour" is perhaps the nearest equivalent to the Hebrew word, as expressing at once beauty of person (E.V. of Prov. xxxi. 30) and kindness shown to others.

CONSIDER, or "look with pleasure upon." The verb denotes "to look at a thing earnestly," to "mark," "survey it with care," &c., so as to take pleasure in it; see Lev. xiii. 36, Prov. xx. 25, and comp. Ps. xlviii. 12 [13], which expresses at length the same thing. The LXX. ἐπισκέπτεσθαι τὸν ναὸν αὐτοῦ. E.V., "to inquire in his temple." Leeser (apparently adopting a wrong derivation): "to be every morning early in His temple."

TEMPLE here, as is evident from what follows, applied to the tabernacle. (See note on Ps. v. 7.) But I have retained the word, as it is employed by our translators, in 1 Sam. iii. 3, to denote the building at Shiloh.

5. TABERNACLE or "covert," see lxxvi. 2 [3], and note there. Mr. George Grove notices "a curious progression in the mention of the Temple in this and the following verses. (1) the house; (2) the sanctuary (?) *hêycal;* (3) the tabernacle or covert, *sōkh* (i.q. *sukkah*); (4) the tent; and lastly (5) the rock protruding (?) from the floor, like the rock of the Sakrah at present, on which, when David was mounted, he was out of reach, and could burst into a secure hurrah." He suggests that "the rock may be the rock of Araunah's threshing-floor."

5. The tent here spoken of was not the Mosaic tabernacle of the congregation—for that remained at Gibeon till Solomon removed it to the Temple (see 2 Chron. i. 3, 4)—but the tent which David erected for the Ark, when he removed it to Zion (2 Sam. vi. 17).

6. SACRIFICES OF SHOUTING: Vulg. *vociferationes*, LXX. ἀλαλαγμοῦ, a stronger form of expression than the usual "sacrifices of thanksgiving," and equivalent to "sacrifices accompanied with the loud and glad expression of thankfulness," with perhaps an allusion to Num. x. 10.

7. The triumphant strain of confidence now gives way to one of sad and earnest entreaty. Is it (as Calv.) that the Psalmist sought in the former part of the Psalm to comfort himself with the review of God's unfailing strength and protection, that he might with the more

8 To Thee hath my heart said: "Seek ye My face—"
"Thy face, Jehovah, will I seek."
9 Hide not Thy face from me;
Put not Thy servant away in anger:
Thou hast been my help; cast me not away,
Neither forsake me, O God of my salvation.
10 For my father and my mother (may) have forsaken me;
But Jehovah taketh me up.
11 Teach me Thy way, O Jehovah,
And lead me in an even path,
Because of them that lie in wait for me.
12 Give me not over into the will of mine adversaries;
For false witnesses have risen up against me,
And they that breathe out [a] violence.

reason utter his prayer for help? Or is it not rather, that even whilst he is thus strengthening himself in his God, a sudden blast of temptation sweeps over his soul, freezing the current of life,—some fear lest he should be forsaken, some thought of the craft and malice of his enemies,—till now the danger which threatens him is as prominent an object as the salvation and defence were before?

8. The words SEEK YE MY FACE are the words of God, which the servant of God here, as it were, takes from His mouth, that so laying them before God, he may make his appeal the more irresistible. Thou hast said, "Seek ye My face:" my heart makes those words its own, and builds upon them its resolve. It takes them up and repeats them, "Seek ye My face." It first claims thus Thine own gracious words, O Lord, and then its echo to those words is, "Thy face, Lord, will I seek." The P. B. V. gives the sense, "My heart hath talked of Thee." Such is the soul's dialogue with itself, when it would comfort itself in God. We are reminded of that touching scene in the Gospel history, where another, a woman of Canaan, in like manner overcomes the Saviour with His own words: "Yea, Lord, yet the dogs eat of the crumbs," &c.

Another possible rendering is: "To thee, O my heart, hath He said," &c. But the usual form in Heb. of self-address is "O my soul."

10. Some have supposed that the allusion in this verse is to the time of Saul's persecution, when David was compelled to separate from his parents, and leave them under the protection of the king of Moab, 1 Sam. xxii. 3. But, as Delitzsch observes, he left them, not they him. It is better therefore to understand the expression hypothetically: "(Though) my father and my mother may have forsaken me," *i.e.* though my condition be helpless and friendless as that of a child deserted of his parents, there is One who watches over me and will take me to His bosom. See Is. lxiii. 16, xlix. 15. The phrase has, as De Wette says, somewhat of a proverbial character.

TAKETH ME UP. The verb is here used in the same sense as in Deut. xxii. 2, Josh. xx. 4, "receives me under His care and protection," or perhaps, as Stier suggests,

13 Oh did I not[b] believe to see the goodness of Jehovah
In the land of the living!—
14 Wait on Jehovah,
Be of good courage, and let thine heart be strong;
Wait, I say, on Jehovah.

"adopts me as His child;" see xxii. 10 [11].

13. An instance of aposiopesis. Our Version gives the sense very well in supplying "I had fainted;" but the words refer to the present, not to the past. The holy singer feels now, at this moment, when the false and violent men are before his mind, how helpless he would be, did he not trust and hope in his God: "There were an end of me—or what would become of me, did I not believe," &c.

14. See the same expression xxxi. 24.

[a] יְפֵחַ, stat. constr. of a verbal adjective, יָפֵחַ (= יָפִיחַ), and formed undoubtedly from the future of the verb. The plural does not occur. The sing. is here used in a collective sense.

[b] לוּלֵא. See similar instances of aposiopesis with an omitted apodosis after לוּ, Gen. l. 15, and after לוּלֵי, with the apodosis introduced with כִּי, Gen. xxxi. 42, xliii. 10, 1 Sam. xxv. 34, 2 Sam. ii. 27; and see also Num. xxii. 33. The preterite after לוּלֵא may have either a pluperfect meaning, as Gen. xlii. 10, Ps. cxxiv. 1, or an imperf., as Deut. xxxii. 29, where an imperf. (fut.) follows, and so here.

PSALM 28

After earnestly beseeching God to hear him (ver. 1, 2), the Psalmist prays that he may not be involved in the evil doings of the wicked (ver. 3); and that they may receive righteous punishment (ver. 4, 5). He thanks God that He has heard his prayer (ver. 6, 7), and, acknowledging Him as the Saviour both of king and people (ver. 8), entreats Him to help, and bless, and feed His heritage for ever (ver. 9).

The structure of the Psalm is based on the common principle of dipodia, or strophes of two verses; the only exception being in the central one, which consists of three verses.

Hitzig thinks that Jeremiah, and Ewald suggests that Josiah, may have been the author of the Psalm. But these are guesses which have little to recommend them: and there is no valid reason why we should reject the traditional title which gives the Psalm to David.

Like the two preceding Psalms, it might very well have been composed at the time of Absalom's rebellion. Verses 2 and 3 bear a close resemblance to Ps. xxvi. 8, 9.

[(A PSALM) OF DAVID.]

1 UNTO Thee, O Jehovah, do I cry;
O my Rock, hold not Thy peace from me!
Lest if Thou keep silence from me,
I become like [a] them that go down into the pit.
2 Hear the voice of my supplications when I cry unto Thee,
When I lift up my hands toward the innermost place [b] of Thy sanctuary.
3 Draw me not away with the wicked,
And with the workers of iniquity;
Who speak peace with their neighbours,
But wickedness is in their hearts.
4 Give them according to their work,
And according to the wickedness of their doings;
According to the operation of their hands give them,
Requite them that they have deserved;

1, 2. The earnestness of the cry is to be measured not only by the greatness of the peril which threatened, but by the faith which cleaves to God, knowing that in *Him only* is there help. HOLD NOT THY PEACE FROM ME: IF THOU BE SILENT (or dumb) FROM ME. The prep. in both cases, used with something of a pregnant meaning, = "Turn not away from me in silence." The expression is often applied to God, with reference to prayer which seems to remain unanswered: see xxxv. 21, xxix. 12 [13], lxxxiii. 1 [2], cix. 1, &c., for the one verb; and Is. lxii. 1, 6, lxiv. 12, 13, for the other.

3. DRAW ME NOT AWAY, viz. to destruction with them, as in Ezek. xxxii. 20. See also Job xxiv. 22. The same sentiment above, xxvi. 9.

WHO SPEAK PEACE, &c. Perhaps the same as the "dissemblers," in xxvi. 4. We might almost suppose a reference to the arts by which Absalom secretly undermined David's authority, and "stole away the hearts" of the people, before he broke out into open rebellion. But the prayer which follows in the next verse David would not have offered against Absalom. The aiders and abettors of the rebellion may, however, have been in his mind.

4. The second petition is for the destruction of his enemies, as the first was for his own preservation.

GIVE THEM: of a judicial act, Hos. ix. 14. With the language of this and the next verse, comp. Is. i. 16, iii. 8—11, v. 19. I have spoken elsewhere of these prayers for vengeance upon the wicked, which sometimes meet us in the Psalms. (See note at the end of Psalm xxxv.) In this instance certainly there is no trace of the expression of personal animosity and the mere desire of revenge. It is rather an appeal

5 For they have no regard to the works of Jehovah,
Nor to the operation of His hands:
(Therefore) shall He break them down, and not build them up.
6 Blessed be Jehovah,
For He hath heard the voice of my supplications.
7 Jehovah is my Strength and my Shield;
In Him hath my heart trusted, and I am helped;
Therefore doth my heart exult.
And with my song will I praise Him.
8 Jehovah is their strength,
And He is the saving defence of His Anointed.
9 O save Thy people and bless Thine inheritance:
Feed them also, and bear them up for ever.

to God's justice to deal with the righteous and the wicked according to their deserts. See Calvin's excellent remarks upon the passage, who warns us against praying for the destruction of the wicked, unless we can first lay aside all passionate and vindictive feelings.

5. The reason why God's judgement should overtake the wicked, not their malice against the Psalmist, but their disregard of the Most High. See x. 4, and Is. v. 12, 19. The works of Jehovah, and the operation of His hands, are in manifest opposition to those of the wicked in ver. 4.

SHALL HE DESTROY. Thus the Psalmist's prayer passes into the expression of confidence that God will so deal with them; a confidence based upon the very attributes of God. And thus the way is paved for the thanksgiving which immediately follows.

6. In his own heart he has already received the answer to his prayer. He knows that God will fulfil his petitions, and therefore breaks out in the glad certainty of faith, "Blessed be Jehovah," &c. The certainty that prayer is heard, anticipates its visible fulfilment.

7. The two preterites mark that the *trust* and the *help* belong to one and the same time, whilst the *joy* which follows from the help is expressed by the verb in the fut. consec., which here may be = a present (as in Job xiv. 2). All three verbs may, however, be rendered strictly as perfects.

WITH MY SONG, lit. *out of* my song; the song being, as it were, the source from which the praise flowed.

8. THEIR STRENGTH: the pron. thus emphatically mentioned before the word "people," to which it refers in the last verse. See a similar instance in ix. 12 [13], lxxxvii. 1.

SAVING DEFENCE, lit. "stronghold of salvations." First the people, then himself their monarch, but not David the man, but David the king as anointed of God, and chosen to feed His people.

9. *Thy* PEOPLE, *Thine* INHERITANCE. In those words are his plea with God. It is impossible not to see in these tender, loving words, "feed them and bear them," the heart of the shepherd-king. Feed them, O Thou true Shepherd of Israel (lxxx. 1, [2]): bear them, carry them in Thine arms (Is. lxiii. 9, xl. 11). The reference may be to Deut. i. 31; xxxii. 11. Compare with this the conclusion of Ps. iii.

[a] וְנִמְשַׁלְתִּי. This depends on פֶּן, although the accent is on the penultimate, not on the last syllable, which is its proper accentuation as *perf. consec.* following the *future.* There are, however, occasional exceptions to this rule (see Deut. viii. 12—14, Prov. xxx. 9), so that this need not have been classed as a license by Ewald, § 234 *c.* It is to be explained on a principle of attraction, the second clause being, as is usual in Hebrew, coordinate with, instead of being subordinated to, the first (comp. xxvii. 10). The *perf.* marks the consequence which then *would take place* if the condition implied in the previous future were fulfilled (*e.g.* Gen. iii. 22, Is. vi. 10). This is especially the constr. where the conditional clause is repeated. See Exod. xxxiv. 12—15, Jos. vi. 18, and Deut. xxv. 3. The following are the constructions of פֶּן when a sentence of more than one member depends upon it : (1) *fut.* and *perf.*, the last either with the tone of the *perf. consec.*, as for instance, Exod. xxxiv. 15, or without it, as here, and in the examples given above. (2) *fut.* and *fut.* as Deut. xx. 6, Ps. ii. 12, Jer. li. 46, in which case the second future denotes a consequence immediately springing from the first, the first being assumed as certain. (3) *fut.* and *perf.* without *Vau consec.* (4) Even *perf.* and *fut. consec.*, as 2 Kings ii. 16.

[b] דְּבִיר. Elsewhere only in the books of Kings and Chron. (See 1 Kings vi. 5, 19—22 ; 2 Chron. iii. 16, iv. 20, &c.) The adytum, or innermost part of the Sanctuary, where was the Ark of the Covenant : not however so called because thence answers and oracles were given, as if from the root דָּבַר, as the Rabbis explain, and as Aq. and Symm. render χρηματιστήριον, and Jerome, *oraculum ;* but connected no doubt with the Arab. دبر, *pone fuit,* دُبْر, *pars postica.* Hence also the Talmud. בדובר, which Baal Aruch explains *retrorsum,* but is written as two words in the Talmud (*Berachoth,* 6 [b]), and is explained by Rashi, "one who believes in a double (דו) principle (בר)."

PSALM 29

THIS Psalm is a magnificent description of a thunder-storm. Its mighty march from north to south, the desolation and terror which it causes, the peal of the thunder, the flash of the lightning, even the gathering fury and lull of the elements, are vividly depicted.

The Psalm consists of five parts ; a prelude, the body of the poem in three divisions, and a conclusion. The structure* of the whole is highly artificial, and elaborated with a symmetry of which no more

* This was first fully explained by Ewald in his *Jahrbücher,* viii. 68—73, to whose masterly analysis I am here indebted.

perfect specimen exists in Hebrew. But this evidently artificial mode of composition is no check to the force and fire of the Poet's genius, which kindles, and glows, and sweeps along with all the freedom and majesty of the storm; the whole Psalm being one continued strain of triumphant exultation.

I. In the prelude, the singer lifts our thoughts at once from earth to heaven, by calling on the angels who stand around the throne of God to praise Him who manifests His glory in the thunder and lightning which He sends upon the earth. Ver. 1, 2.

II. Then follows the description of the storm in the three strophes which constitute the main body of the Poem. These are so constructed, that the first (ver. 3, 4) gives us the beginning of the storm, the low, faint, muttering thunder in the distant heavens; the next (ver. 5—7) describes the storm at its height, when it crashes the cedars, and shakes the mountains; the last (ver. 8, 9) tells how it passes on over the plain country to the forest of Kadesh in the south, where it dies away.

But not only the arrrangement of the three strophes, but the structure of each separate strophe, contributes in a very striking degree to the whole effect of the Poem. Each consists of five members, and each begins with a fresh burst, and closes with a lull in the tempest.

i. Thus, in the first strophe, we hear the first yet distant sound of the thunder in the words, "The voice of Jehovah is upon the waters." In the next two clauses, "The God of glory thundereth; Jehovah is upon many waters," the long loud peal grows more distinct, whilst ver. 4 again is pitched in a lower key, as if telling us of a pause in the storm.

ii. In the next strophe we have again, (*a*) first, the renewed fury of the tempest, as, coming nearer yet, it falls on the glory of Lebanon and breaks her cedars in its might: "The voice of Jehovah breaketh the cedars," &c. (*b*) Next, gathering with a wilder intensity of wrath, it bursts upon the mountain peaks, roaring amid their rocks and shattering them, and making the everlasting hills themselves to tremble as with the throes of an earthquake, so that "Lebanon and Sirion skip like young buffaloes." (*c*) Lastly, we hear it sinking down in the line which describes the flashing of the forked lightning: "The voice of Jehovah cleaveth the flames of fire." Ver. 5—7.

iii. Again the same structure is observable. One long peal after another has rolled and reverberated along the sky, and now the storm, in its jubilant strength, sweeps the whole land from north to south. (*a*) Again it is up in its majesty: "The voice of Jehovah maketh the wilderness to tremble." (*b*) Again its last fury is poured out upon the wilderness of Kadesh. The very hinds bow themselves in travail-pangs, and the forest is torn open and laid bare, as the hurricane drives through it in its path. (*c*) And again the tempest is stilled, but this time its voice is hushed and lost for ever in the music and songs of the heavenly host: "In His temple all that are therein cry, Glory." Ver. 8, 9.

III. The conclusion consists, like the prelude, of two verses, each of two members. And here we are beautifully reminded that Jehovah, whom the angels praise, and who both *rules* and *stills* the elements in their wildest uproar, is the same Jehovah who gives *strength* and *peace* to His people. Ver. 10, 11.

It is further observable, in proof of the evidently artificial structure of the whole, that each of the three central strophes has the same characteristic double line :—

(1) The voice of Jehovah is upon the waters,
Jehovah is upon many waters.
(2) The voice of Jehovah breaketh the cedars,
Yea Jehovah breaketh the cedars of Lebanon.
(3) The voice of Jehovah maketh the wilderness to tremble,
Jehovah maketh the wilderness of Kadesh to tremble.

In each of these instances, we have first, "The voice of Jehovah," and then "Jehovah," and in each the second line is an amplification or strengthening of the first. It is further to be noticed that the expression "voice of Jehovah" occurs *seven* times in the *three* principal divisions of the Psalm, thus reminding us of the ἑπτὰ βρονταί, "the seven thunders," of the Apocalypse.

According to the tradition preserved in the inscription of the LXX., ἐξοδίου (al. ἐξόδου) σκηνῆς, it would seem that in the Second Temple this Psalm was sung on the Shemini 'Azereth, the last day (ἐξόδιον, Lev. xxiii. 36) of the Feast of Tabernacles. In the modern Ashkenazic (*i.e.* German, Polish, and Dutch) synagogues, however, this Psalm stands in the Jewish liturgy, to be used on the first day of Pentecost (Shebuoth); in the Sephardic (Spanish, Portuguese, Greek, &c.) the 68th Psalm is recited on that day.

[A PSALM OF DAVID.]

1 GIVE unto Jehovah, O ye sons of God,[a]
Give unto Jehovah glory and strength.

1. SONS OF GOD, or perhaps, simply "godlike ones," *i.e.* "the angels," so called also in other passages, or we may render "sons of the mighty." See this more fully discussed in the Critical Note.

2 Give unto Jehovah the glory due to His Name.
    Worship Jehovah in holy attire.

3 The voice of Jehovah is upon the waters,
    The God of glory thundereth;
  Jehovah is upon many waters;
4   The voice of Jehovah is in might,
    The voice of Jehovah is in majesty.

5 The voice of Jehovah breaketh the cedars,
    Yea Jehovah breaketh the cedars of Lebanon;
6 And He maketh them to skip like a calf,
    Lebanon and Sirion like the young of the wild ox:
7 The voice of Jehovah cleaveth flames of fire.

8 The voice of Jehovah maketh the wilderness to tremble,
    Jehovah maketh the wilderness of Kadesh to tremble.

2. IN HOLY ATTIRE, Mendelss. "heilig geschmückt," LXX. Syr. and others "holy sanctuary." Perhaps we may keep "beauty of holiness" as covering both ideas; heaven being thought of as one great temple, and all the worshipers therein as clothed in priestly garments, and doing perpetual service. In the earthly temple, in like manner, Priests and Levites arrayed themselves on occasions of solemn pomp. Cf. 2 Chron. xx. 21, where E.V. has "beauty of holiness," Ps. cx. 3, where see note.

3. THE WATERS. This may either refer to the Mediterranean sea, from which the storm comes up (as J. D. Michaelis), or to "the waters above the firmament," the dense lowering masses of the storm-cloud charged with water. Probably the latter. See xviii. 11 [12].

4. IN MIGHT—IN MAJESTY. The attributes of God as displayed in the storm. The expression is more forcible than if adjectives denoting these qualities ("mighty," "majestic") had been used. Comp. *ἐν ἐξουσίᾳ*, Luke iv. 32; *ἐν ἰσχύϊ*, (rec.) Apoc. xviii. 2.

6. SIRION, *i.e.* Anti-Lebanon, acc. to Deut. iii. 9, the Sidonian name of Hermon. The force of the tempest bursts on these mountains, and is accompanied perhaps by an earthquake, though we need not press what may be only a strong poetical figure.

7. With every thunder-peal comes the terrible forked lightning, so striking in tropical and Eastern lands. Its vivid, zigzag, serpent-like flash is given in a few words.

CLEAVETH FLAMES OF FIRE, *i.e.* parts the blaze of the lightning, so as to give it the forked appearance.

8. KADESH, in the south of Palestine, thus indicating the course taken by the storm. It sweeps the land from north to south. "The geographical notices of its situation," says Stanley, speaking of Kadesh, "are unfortunately too slight to be of much service. Yet thus much they fix, that it was 'in the wilderness of Zin,' that it was 'on the edge of the border of Edom,' that it was near Mount Hor, that it was at the southern point to which the territory of Judah afterwards reached." He then gives reasons for identifying Kadesh with Petra. Travelling in

9 The voice of Jehovah boweth the hinds in travail-pangs,
And strippeth the forests (bare) :—
And in His temple all that is therein uttereth "Glory."

10 Jehovah sate throned above the Flood :
Yea Jehovah sitteth throned a King for ever.
11 Jehovah giveth strength to His people ;
Jehovah blesseth His people with peace.

the direction it did, the storm would first reach the 'Arabah, and then pass on to the acacias, and palms, and vegetation which clothe the rocks of sandstone in the neighbourhood of Petra. See Stanley's interesting account of his journey in the opposite direction, from Petra to Palestine through the 'Arabah. (*Sinai and Palestine*, p. 94, &c.)

9. IN TRAVAIL-PANGS. This is a phenomenon which is also noticed and recorded as a fact by Arabian poets.

ALL THAT IS THEREIN, lit. "all of it."

10. ABOVE, or more literally "at," so the Chald. paraphrases—"The Lord sat in the generation of the deluge."

FLOOD, *i.e.* the Deluge. The word here employed occurs nowhere else, except in the story of the Flood (Gen. vi.—xi.), and therefore refers, I cannot help thinking, to that great act of judgement, and not merely to a recent inundation caused by the storm, the mountain-torrents having been swollen by the rain, and having flooded the country. This might have happened. But the selection of so peculiar a word (מַבּוּל, "flood"), as well as the fact than the verb is in the past tense, "*sate* throned," makes the other more probable.

Very beautiful is the conclusion of the Psalm. If, in His heavenly temple above, all that are therein ascribe "glory" to God, upon earth too He has manifested that glory. He sat as King when He sent the flood of water to destroy the earth. He sits now, and for ever will sit, as King. As then He saved the righteous man from death, so now He watches over His people : for Jehovah is the God of Israel. It was He who, when the storm waxed strong, gave it its strength : it was He who, when it was hushed, spread over earth, and sea, and sky, the sweet sabbath stillness of peace. And He whose almighty power was seen in the march of the tempest, whose voice was heard in its wildest uproar, and whose words stilled its fiercest war, shall He not give both strength and peace ? Yea, Jehovah, who is strong and mighty, will give His own strength to His people ; and He who is the Prince of Peace will bless His people with peace. Thus the Psalm begins, as Delitzsch says, with a *Gloria in excelsis*, and ends with a *Pax in terris*.

[a] בְּנֵי אֵלִים, "*sons of God*," not the mighty upon earth, as בְּנֵי עֶלְיוֹן, lxxxii. 6, but the *angels*, who are called elsewhere (as Job ii. 1) "sons of God." The word אֵלִים, however, is difficult, though it occurs in the same phrase, lxxxix. 7. It is never found by itself meaning "God" = אֱלֹהִים, but always "the gods," Exod. xv. 11, Dan. xi. 36. It would seem therefore as if the word "sons" were here used after the Hebrew idiom, somewhat vaguely : as בְּנֵי אֶבְיוֹן, "sons of the poor," *i.e.* poor persons, so here ב׳ א׳, "sons of the gods," may only mean, "godlike beings." The Chald. explains

it "angels." The Syr. takes the words as the acc., and renders "young rams." The LXX. and Vulg. followed by our P.B.V. curiously combine both interpretations. The former has ἐνέγκατε τῷ κυρίῳ υἱοὶ θεοῦ, ἐ. τ. κ. υἱοὺς κριῶν. The latter, *Afferte Domino, filii Dei, afferte Domino filios arietum.* Mendelssohn takes אֵלִים as = אֵילִים, and interprets, "sons of the great ones," in the sense of אֵילֵי מוֹאָב, the mighty men, or princes of Moab, Exod. xv. 15, and some MSS. have here אֵילִים. Others understand "the children of Israel" as "sons of the mighty," *i.e.* Abraham, Isaac, and Jacob.

PSALM 30

THIS Psalm was composed after recovery from a sickness which had very nearly proved fatal. The singer begins with an ascription of praise to God for His great goodness, and calls upon all who, like himself, had known the loving kindness of Jehovah (חֲסִידָיו), to join him in his thanksgiving. Thence he passes (ver. 6) to a recital of his own experience, his pleading with God in his affliction, and God's answer to his prayer.

According to the inscription, the Psalm was composed "at the dedication of the house." But what house? Some would understand the dedication of the spot on which the Temple afterwards stood, and which David purchased of Araunah (2 Sam. xxiv., 1 Chron. xxi.). This spot, it is true, together with the altar erected there, might be called "the house of Jehovah" (as it is 1 Chron. xxii. 1), or absolutely "the house," even before the Temple was built. But if the Psalm were written for this occasion, it could not have been written by David, as he himself did not fall sick in the time of the pestilence (2 Sam. xxiv. 17).

Others conjecture that by "the dedication of the house," is meant a purification and reconsecration of David's palace which Absalom had defiled (2 Sam. xx. 3). But חֲנֻכָּה, "dedication," according to J. H. Mich., is only used of the original dedication of an object, never of its reconsecration. And besides, the Psalm speaks not of escape from enemies, but of recovery from sickness.

But perhaps, if the inscription is trustworthy, it refers to the house which David built in his new city of Zion, and the building of which he seems to have regarded as a pledge of the security and prosperity of his kingdom (2 Sam. v. 11, 12). We must, however, still suppose that he had suffered just before from a sickness, about which the history is silent.

The Psalm is used by the Jews to this day on the Festival of the

Chanucah, or re-dedication of the Temple after it had been defiled by Antiochus Epiphanes.

It consists of two principal divisions:—

I. A thanksgiving on recovery. Ver. 1—5.

(1) An ascription of praise. Ver. 1. The reason, viz. that God had brought him back to life from the gates of death. Ver. 2, 3.

(2) An exhortation to others to unite with him in praise. The reason, because God keepeth not His anger for ever. Ver. 4, 5.

II. A recital of the Psalmist's experience during his sickness. Ver. 6—12.

(1) The sudden change by which he had been brought low. Ver. 6, 7.

(2) His prayer in his sickness. Ver. 8—10.

(3) The answer to his prayer and thanksgiving thereupon. Ver. 11, 12.

[A PSALM OF DAVID. A SONG AT THE DEDICATION [a] OF THE HOUSE.]

I. 1 I WILL extol Thee, O Jehovah, for Thou hast lifted me up,
And hast not made mine enemies to rejoice over me.
2 O Jehovah, my God,
I cried unto Thee, and Thou hast healed me.
3 O Jehovah, Thou hast brought up my soul from the unseen world:
Thou hast kept me alive, that I should not be of them that go down [b] into the pit.
4 Sing praises unto Jehovah, O ye beloved of His,
And give thanks to His holy name:

I. Thanksgiving, ver. 1—5.

1. THOU HAST LIFTED ME UP, lit. "Thou hast drawn me up" (*i.e.*) as a bucket is drawn up out of a well). It has been inferred from this expression, that the Psalm was written by Jeremiah when he was taken up out of the dungeon. But this is turning poetry into prose. The word is clearly metaphorical.

3. KEPT ME ALIVE. So the verb is used in xxii. 29 [30]; see also Exod. i. 17, 22.

4. BELOVED, more literally, "who have obtained mercy of Him" (as Hupfeld), or, "ye His godly ones;" but see note on xvi. 10.

HIS HOLY NAME, lit. "His holy memorial," with reference, no doubt, to the passage, Exod. iii. 15, "This is my name for ever, and this is my *memorial* to all generations." God's

5 For His anger is but for a moment,
His favour for a life long[c]:
At even, weeping may come in for a night,
But with the morning is a shout of joy.

II. 6 And as for me—I had said, in my prosperity,
"I shall not be moved for ever."
7 Thou, O Jehovah, by Thy favour hadst made my mountain to stand strong:
Thou didst hide Thy face:—I became troubled.

Name is His revelation of Himself, in all His various attributes of Love, Wisdom, Power, Holiness, Truth, Righteousness. God's memorial is that great history of redemption which was, so to speak, the setting up of a monument to His glory, on which all these attributes were inscribed.

5. A reason why God's saints should praise Him, because He manifests Himself to them in love, not in wrath, or if in wrath, but for a moment. Love rules over all. The literal rendering of the verse is: "For in His anger is (but) a moment, in His favour a life: in the evening, weeping may come in to pass the night; but with the morning (there is) a shout of joy." The parallelism is preserved in each member: "anger—favour;" "a moment—a life;" "weeping—joy." The only objection to this rendering is that the Heb. word for "life" does not elsewhere denote the duration of life. See Critical Note.

We must not repeat the verb "pass the night," with the second clause. Weeping is described in the first under the image of a wayfarer who comes in at evening to lodge for the night. (Jer. xiv. 8.) The suddenness and surprise of gladness, on the other hand, in the morning, are beautifully represented by the simple לַבֹּקֶר רִנָּה, "at dawn, a shout of joy," without a verb. Just as the sun in Eastern lands, without any long prelude of twilight to announce his coming, leaps as it were in a moment above the horizon, so does the light of God's love dispel in a moment the long night and darkness of sorrow. See the beautiful parallel, Is. liv. 7, 8.

II. The recital of his experience. Ver. 6—12.

6. AND AS FOR ME. The pronoun with the conjunction, thus at the beginning of a clause, is always emphatic, and generally stands in opposition to something going before, either expressed or understood. Here there is a tacit opposition between the Psalmist's present and his former experience. Now he had learnt through the lesson of suffering to trust in God. Before that suffering came, he had begun to trust in himself. "I seemed so strong, so secure, I began to think within myself, I shall never be moved; Thou hadst made my mountain so strong. And then, Thou didst hide Thy face, and I was troubled." Obs. that the last three clauses follow one another without a copula, "Thou hadst made," &c., "Thou didst hide," &c., "I became," &c., as if to mark how rapidly the one followed upon the other. The security was followed, as its necessary consequence, by the hiding of God's countenance, and this by terror of spirit.

7. HADST MADE STRONG, lit. "Thou didst make strength to stand to my mountain:" or perhaps "Thou didst place a fortress upon my mountain." The language is clearly figurative, though the em-

8 (Then) to Thee, O Jehovah, did I begin to cry,[d]
Yea to Jehovah I made supplication : (saying,)
9 "What profit is there in my blood, when I go down to the pit ?
Shall the dust give thanks to Thee ? shall *it* declare Thy truth ?
10 Hear, O Jehovah, and be gracious unto me ;
O Jehovah, be Thou my helper."
11 (And) Thou didst turn for me my mourning into dancing :
Thou didst put off my sackcloth, and girdedst me with gladness ;
12 To the end that (my) glory[e] should sing praise to Thee, and not be silent.
O Jehovah, my God, I will give thanks unto Thee for ever.

blem no doubt is borrowed from the stronghold of Zion. So Calv., "fortunas meas ita stabiliveras ut firmissimi montis instar haberent."

9. He now gives us the words of his prayer.

WHAT PROFIT? (quid lucri? τί ὄφελος). The earnest prayer for life, so frequent with the Old Testament saints who walked in shadows, and who only now and then caught a glimpse of the world beyond the grave. Their faith and hope were in God, and therefore could not be bounded by things temporal ; but we must remember that the promises made to them were mostly of a temporal character, and that life and immortality were not yet brought to light. In seasons of despondency, therefore, the abode of the dead (Sheol) seemed dark and cheerless: and there was not only a natural but even a religious recoil from death, because in this life only could men praise God. In the land of forgetfulness no Psalms could be sung. Hezekiah's thanksgiving, Is. xxxviii., and many expressions in the Book of Job, which last seems to have been in the Psalmist's mind, are in the same strain. The truth seems to be, that whilst *the Faith* of the Old Testament saints *in God* was strong and childlike, their *Hope of Immortality* was at best but dim and wavering, brightening perhaps for a moment, when the heart was rejoicing in God as its portion, and then again almost dying away.

11. How his prayer was heard. This is described by its *effects* upon himself. (A return to the past tenses, as in ver. 6.) The copula (which I have inserted in the translation, to mark the connection more clearly) is omitted in the Heb., because the answer to the prayer is regarded as simultaneous with the prayer itself. Comp. Jer. xxxi. 13, Lam. v. 15. The sackcloth of his humiliation God had taken off from him, and had clothed him with the garment of praise. (Is. lxi. 3.) How should he do otherwise than praise God for ever for His goodness ?

[a] The first Psalm which is called שִׁיר, and the only one in this book, חֲנֻכָּה, "dedication." LXX., ἐγκαινισμός. Various ceremonies of dedica-

tion are mentioned : of the sanctuary, Exod. xl. ; of the altar, Num. vii. 10, &c. ; of a house, Deut. xx. 5 ; of Solomon's temple, 1 Kings viii. 63 ; of the new walls of Jerusalem, Neh. xii. 27. This Ps. is still the Ps. "of dedication" in the Jewish ritual (see Tract. *Sopherim*. c. 18, § 2). For the origin of the feast, see 1 Macc. iv. 52, &c.

[b] The Q'ri מִיָּרְדִי, = *ita ut non descenderem*, is ungrammatical in form ; for an inf., יְרֹד instead of רֶדֶת, nowhere occurs (though we find a similar anomalous infin., יָסְדִי, Job xxxviii. 4). There can be no doubt that the K'thibh מִיּוֹרְדֵי is right ; see xxviii. 1. So the LXX., *ἔσωσάς με ἀπὸ τῶν καταβαινόντων εἰς λάκκον.*

[c] חַיִּים seems here to be used of *duration* of life (Hupf. Del.), though it would be difficult to support the usage. Hence the rendering of the E.V. may certainly be defended (though it injures the parallelism), "In His favour is life." The LXX. *ὅτι ὀργὴ ἐν τῷ θυμῷ αὐτοῦ, καὶ ζωὴ ἐν τῷ θελήματι αὐτοῦ* ; Vulg. "Quoniam ira in indignatione ejus, et vita in voluntate ejus ;" Syr. "Rebuke is in His anger, life in His favour" ;—all giving a different meaning to רֶגַע.

[d] The futures here are properly *imperfects* (or what Hupf. terms *relative preterites*, and what the Arabs call "the present in the past"). אקרא, *sc.* Then when I was in trouble *I began to call*, &c. Or we may suppose the poet to throw himself back into the past, and speak from the past, in which case we may keep the strict future, as describing his resolve at the time, and supply the ellipse, "Then I thought," or "Then I said I will call," &c., *ἐν τοῖς κακοῖς γενόμενος ἔλεγον, πρὸς σέ, Κύριε, βοήσω*, Symm.

[e] כָּבוֹד, app. for כְּבוֹדִי, "my glory" = my soul. LXX., *ἡ δόξα μου.* But Jerome, *ut laudet te gloria*. Aq. Symm. and Theod. in like manner omit the pronoun. The Chald., taking it as abstr. for concr., כבוד = נכבדים, renders "the nobles of the world." The Syr. as accus. after the verb, "therefore will I sing to Thee glory," and changing the third pers. of the verb into the first. This last interpret. has very much in its favour, for it is remarkable, that of the older Versions, the LXX. alone have the pronoun. But it requires a change in both the verbs יזמר and ידם, into אזמר and אדם. However, the 3d pers. may be used impersonally "that one may sing glory to Thee, ascribe glory to Thee, in his song," &c.

PSALM 31

A Psalm in which earnest prayer for deliverance from trouble is kindled and animated throughout by a lively trust and hope in God. This Psalm may be compared throughout with Psalms ix. and xxvii. and especially with the latter, with which it has many points of resemblance.

It consists of three principal divisions :—

I. The singer prays God to be gracious to him in his trouble, expressing at the same time his trust in Him, who in times past had been his deliverer. Ver. 1—8.

II. He pours out before God the story of his sufferings and his sorrows, beseeching Him again to lift upon him the light of His countenance, and to put his enemies to shame. Ver. 9—18.

III. He concludes with praise and thanksgiving to God for His goodness to all who trust in Him, and particularly to himself, and calls upon all the righteous to love the Lord. Ver. 19—24.

The older interpreters, for the most part, supposed the Psalm to have been composed by David when he fled from Saul into the wilderness of Maon (1 Sam. xxiii. 24). The chief support for this view was found in the use of בְּחָפְזִי (ver. 23, Heb.), compared with נֶחְפָּז (1 Sam. xxiii. 26). But this, in any case, would be far too slight a ground to rest upon, not to mention that the noun here is clearly used in a different sense from the verb there (see note on the word).

In some of its expressions the Psalm is not unlike Psalms vi., xxxviii., xxxix. On the whole, however, it reminds us more of some parts of Jeremiah than of any other of the Old Testament writings. In its tender and plaintive character it resembles Lament. iii. The phrase מָגוֹר מִסָּבִיב, "Fear on every side" (ver. 13 [14]), occurs no less than six times in Jeremiah; and the first member of the same verse is repeated word for word in Jer. xx. 10. Hence Ewald and Hitzig have concluded that the Psalm was written by Jeremiah. Two other suppositions are, however, admissible, viz. either that the Prophet, with whom this may have been a favourite Psalm, borrowed from the Psalmist, or that the Psalmist (who may have been one of the later poets) borrowed from the Prophet.

On other grounds there is no reason why the Psalm should not be David's. It breathes throughout his rare tenderness of spirit, as well as his faith and courage. The figures of the stronghold and the rock so often repeated, ver. 2—4, are most suitable in his mouth (comp. Ps. xviii.), and so are the expressions in ver. 8 and ver. 21.

[FOR THE PRECENTOR. A PSALM OF DAVID.]

I. 1 IN Thee, O Jehovah, have I made my refuge,
Let me never be ashamed;
In Thy righteousness rescue me.

Ver. 1—3 are found with slight variation in lxxi. 1—3.

1. NOT . . . FOR EVER = "never:" *not* as Hengst. and others interpret. "Though I am put to shame *now*, yet let not that shame last for ever," Ps. xxx. 5 [6].

IN THY RIGHTEOUSNESS. See iv. 1 [2], v. 8 [9].

2 Incline Thine ear unto me,
Make haste to deliver me
Be Thou to me a strong rock,
A house of fortresses to save me.
3 For Thou art my rock and my fortress,
And for Thy Name's sake Thou wilt lead me and guide me;
4 Thou wilt bring me forth out of the net they have laid privily for me,
For THOU art my stronghold.
5 Into Thy hand I commend my spirit:

2. The figures here employed are the same as in xviii.

STRONG ROCK, lit. "a rock of stronghold," *i.e.* not a rock with a castle upon it, but "a rock which is itself a stronghold."

A HOUSE OF FORTRESSES; a poetical expression = a fortified place.

3. FOR THOU ART, &c. "*Be* to me a rock, &c., *for* Thou *art* my rock." This has been called illogical. But is it so illogical as it seems? The Psalmist prays, "Be Thou to me," or rather, "become to me, *prove Thyself to be*, my rock and house of defence; for I *know* that Thou, and Thou only, art my refuge." This is the logic of the heart, if not of the intellect; the logic, it may be added, of every prayer of faith.

The word "rock" here is different from that in v. 2, and denotes a precipitous rock, or crag.

FOR THY NAME'S SAKE . . . LEAD ME AND GUIDE ME, exactly as in xxiii. 2, 3. The futures here and in the next verse are not to be rendered as imperatives. They express the strong hope and confidence that it will be done according to his faith and his prayer.

5. INTO THY HAND, &c. Upon the expression of confidence in the Power and Faithfulness of God follows the expression of the singer's resolve. *My spirit* (*ruach*) more than my *soul* or *life* (*nephesh*). It is not only from sickness and death, but from sin and all ghostly enemies, that the man of God would be kept, and therefore he commends to God, not his body or his bodily life alone, but the life of his spirit, which is more precious (comp. Is. xxxviii. 16, "life of my spirit").

I COMMEND (παρατίθεμαι), *i. e.* place as a *deposit*, entrust.

With these words our Lord breathed out His life, Luke xxiii. 46, as He had before used words from another Psalm in His agony on the cross. The first words were from a Psalm (the 22nd) which, typically at least, foreshadowed His sufferings; whereas, this is not in the same way predictive. But the Holy One of God, in that last hour of mortal agony, chose these words of one of His servants, to express the solemn surrender of His life. And in so doing he gave them a new interpretation. The Jewish singer only meant by them that he put himself and all his hopes into the hand of God. Jesus meant by them, that *by His own act*, *of His own free will*, He gave up His spirit, and therewith His life, to the Father. (Obs. how the Evangelists carefully choose their expressions, ἀφῆκεν τὸ πνεῦμα, Matt.; παρέδωκεν τὸ πν., John.) And they who have died with their Lord, have died with the same words on their lips. These were the last words of Bernard, of Huss, of Jerome of Prague, of Luther, Melanchthon, and many others. "Blessed are they," says Luther, "who die not

Thou hast redeemed me, Jehovah, Thou God of Truth.
6 I hate [a] them that observe lying vanities;
But as for me—in Jehovah do I trust.
7 Let me exult and be glad in Thy loving-kindness,
For Thou hast seen my affliction,
Thou hast known my soul in adversities,
8 And hast not shut me up into the hand of the enemy;
Thou hast set my feet in a large room.

II. 9 Be gracious unto me, O Jehovah, for I am in trouble:
Mine eye is consumed with vexation,—my soul and my body.
10 For my life is spent with sorrow,
And my years with sighing:
My strength hath failed because of mine iniquity,
And my bones are consumed, because of all my adversaries.
11 I am become a reproach to my neighbours exceedingly,[b]
And a fear to mine acquaintance:

only *for* the Lord, as martyrs; not only *in* the Lord, as all believers; but likewise *with* the Lord, as breathing forth their lives in these words, 'Into Thy hand I commend my spirit.'" The words are used by all dying Israelites to this day.

THOU HAST REDEEMED ME. This gives the reason why he entrusts his spirit to God. (It may be rendered as a relative clause, Thou who hast, &c.) It is = "Thou *hast been*, and Thou *art*, my Redeemer;" and further, there is implied, "because Thou changest not, I confidently anticipate redemption from this present calamity." The past continuing up to the present moment (strict perfect), is in the singer's mind a pledge of the future, especially because God is the GOD OF TRUTH, as opposed to the lying vanities (in the next verse), *i.e.* all false objects of trust, here perhaps especially *false gods*. Comp. 2 Chr. xv. 3. [In Deut. xxxii. 4, אֵל אֱמוּנָה, not very different, except that אֱמֶת here refers rather to the Being and Nature of God, who is the absolutely true, אֱמוּנָה, to His dealings with His creatures, in which His *faithfulness* is shown.]

7. HAST SEEN, &c., cf. Exod. iii. 7. HAST KNOWN. See note on i. 6.

8. SHUT ME UP, cf. 1 Sam. xxiii. 11; Deut. xxxii. 30.

A LARGE ROOM, as in xviii. 19[20].

9—13. The prayer of the Psalmist now bases itself upon the greatness of his suffering.

10. BECAUSE OF MINE INIQUITY. See how the eye is turned within, as well as without upon his enemies. Suffering does its work when it leads us to commune with our own hearts, and to discover the evils which are hidden there.

They that did see me in the streets fled from me.
12 I have been forgotten as a dead man out of mind;
I am become like a broken vessel.
13 For I have heard the slander of many,
Terror on every side;
Whilst they took their counsel together against me,
They devised to take away my life.
14 But as for me, I have trusted in Thee, O Jehovah;
I said, "Thou art my God."
15 My times are in Thy hand:
Deliver me from the hand of mine enemies, and from them that persecute me.
16 Make Thy face to shine upon Thy servant;
O save me in Thy loving-kindness!
17 O Jehovah, let me not be ashamed, for I have called upon Thee:
Let the wicked be ashamed, let them be put to silence [c] in the grave;
18 Let the lying lips become dumb,
Which speak stoutly against the righteous,
With pride and contempt.

III. 19 O how great is Thy goodness,

12. OUT OF MIND, lit. "out of heart;" sim. "out of the mouth," Deut. xxxi. 21.

13. FOR, not as giving the reason of his comparison of himself to a broken vessel, but as a further explanation of "because of all mine adversaries," ver. 10. From the effects he goes back to the cause. The verbs are in the pret., because this state of things had lasted long. The first two members of the verse occur again, word for word, Jer. xx. 10, and the phrase, "terror round about," Jer. vi. 25, xx. 3, 4, xlvi. 5, xlix. 29; Lam. ii. 22.

14—18. Again wonderful words of trust, out of which flow his petitions, "Thou art my God." Mighty strength of faith when a man, conscious of his own sinfulness (ver. 10), and with a world in arms against him, yea, forsaken of his own friends (ver. 11), can still turn to God and say, Thou art my God.

15. MY TIMES, *i.e.* all my life with its "sundry and manifold changes," its joys and sorrows, its hopes and conflicts, are not the sport of chance, or the creatures of a blind fate, but are in Thy hand, O Thou living, personal Redeemer. On this confidence are grounded the petitions which follow, and the hopes expressed, ver. 18. The second of the petitions, ver. 16, is borrowed from the sacerdotal benediction, Num. vi. 25. Comp. Ps. iv. 6 [7].

19—24. "His well-grounded hope now brings triumphant certainty, and this breaks forth in glad acknowledgement of God's goodness

Which Thou hast laid up for them that fear Thee,
Which Thou hast wrought for them that find refuge in Thee,
In the presence of the sons of men.
20 Thou hidest them in the hiding-place of Thy presence from the conspiracies of men;
Thou keepest them privily in a tabernacle from the strife of tongues.
21 Blessed be Jehovah,
That He hath showed me His marvellous loving-kindness in a fenced city:
22 As for me—I had said in my confusion,
"I am cut off from the sight of Thine eyes."
Yet surely Thou didst hear the voice of my supplications
When I cried unto Thee.
23 O love Jehovah, all ye beloved of His!
Jehovah preserveth the faithful,
And plentifully rewardeth the proud doer.

to the righteous, and an exhortation to all to wait on Him in unshaken confidence of heart."

19. THOU HAST LAID UP, lit. "hidden," or "kept privily," the same word as in ver. 20. God's loving-kindness and God's saints are both "hidden," "laid up," as treasures; comp. xvii. 14, and "the hidden manna," Rev. ii. 17. This is the love of God manifested to the soul in secret; the next clause tells of its open manifestation, "Thou hast wrought."

Compare with the language of this and the next verse the very similar passage xxvii. 5.

20. THE HIDING-PLACE OF THY PRESENCE, or "of Thy countenance:" elsewhere, of God's tabernacle, xxvii. 4 [5]; or of His wings, lxi. 5, or of His shadow, xci. 1. But this is the most striking figure of all: to be hidden in the light of God's face, hidden in that splendour where His power is hidden (Hab. iii. 4); what an image at once of safety and blessedness! Milton's striking expression, "Dark with excess of bright," explains how it is possible to be *hidden* in *light*.

21. David now turns to his own experience. HATH SHOWED ME, &c. Mendelss. "Wunderbar bewies er seine Güte mir." But what is the fenced or fortified city? I incline to think there is an historical reference in the words. Possibly Ziklag may be meant (as Del. suggests). Most, however, understand it metaph.=with Thee I am *as if* I were in a fortified place.

22. IN MY CONFUSION (*in stupore meo*, Jerome; ἐκπλήξει, Symm.; *in trepidatione mea*, Calv.).

I AM CUT OFF—so did his faith begin to waver, and yet in the midst of this confusion he betook himself to prayer. "Nec obstat," says Calvin, "carnis infirmitas quo minus (sancti) etiam fere dejecti indefessos Deo athletas se præbeant."

23. And now because God had

24 Be of good courage, and let your heart be strong,
All ye that hope in Jehovah.

heard his prayer of faith, and been better to him than his unbelief, he calls upon all to whom God has been gracious to love Him.

24. ALL YE THAT HOPE. (The Psalm ends nearly as Psalm xxvii.) Hope and waiting are marks peculiarly of the Old Testament dispensation. It is true even in the New, one apostle writes, "We are saved by hope." And another says, "It doth not yet appear what we shall be:" but he adds what no believer in the day of types and shadows could have said, "We *know* that when He shall appear, we shall be like Him, for we shall see Him as He is." Wonderful indeed is the hopeful trust of the saints of old in God, when we remember that they did not know Him as God manifest in the flesh.

[a] שָׂנֵאתִי. The LXX., Syr., Arab. (and in some MSS. Jerome), have here the second pers., "*Thou* hatest." And this has been adopted by Ewald, Hitzig, and others, because of the opposition in the following וַאֲנִי, "but as for me." The opposition, however, may be in thought between himself and those who adhere to false gods. הַשֹּׁמְרִים, lit. "who keep," or as the P. B. V., "hold of," hence "who follow, obey," &c. (cf. the similar use of the Latin *observare*, Virg. Georg. iv. 212), as in Hosea iv. 10 (E. V. "take heed"), Prov. xxvii. 18 (E. V. "wait on"). In Jonah ii. 9 we have the same phrase, but with *Piel* instead of *Qal*.

[b] This verse is difficult. According to the Massoretic text it stands: "Because of all mine adversaries I am become a reproach, and to my neighbours exceedingly, and a terror to mine acquaintance," &c. But this reads lamely. The word מְאֹד comes in very awkwardly even if we repeat הָיִיתִי חֶרְפָּה with the second member. Hence Ewald joins the words מִכָּל צֹרְרַי with the previous verse; and this completes the parallelism in ver. 11, and is on the whole satisfactory, except that the וְ in וְלִשְׁכֵנַי is not well accounted for. It is true that most commentators, while retaining the present division of the verse, take the וְ here to be = "even;" "*etiam* vicinis meis," Calv.; "*selbst* meinen Nachbarn Schmach," Mendelss. But the passages generally quoted in support of this meaning of the conjunction are, as Hupf. has shown, not to the point. It does occur in the sense of "and that," *idque* (Ges. Thes.); a sense, however, which does not suit here. Del., after J. H. Mich., supposes מְאֹד in this place to be a noun meaning "a burden," formed from a root אוד, cogn. with the Arab. root أَوْدٌ, *onus*. Then the verse would read, "Because of, &c. . . . I am become a reproach to my neighbours, a burden," &c.

[c] יִדְּמוּ may either be fut. Qal. for יִדְּמוּ (Ges. § 67), or Niph. for יִדַּמּוּ, "shall be silent, or be made silent to Sheol," *i.e.* shall be reduced to silence by being laid in the grave.

PSALM 32

THIS is the second of the Seven Penitential Psalms, as they are called, "which," says Selnecker, "St. Augustine used often to read with weeping heart and eyes, and which, before his death, he had written on the wall over against his sick-bed, that he might exercise himself therein, and find comfort therein in his sickness." St. Augustine's own words, "intelligentia prima est ut te noris peccatorem," might stand as its motto.

Beginning with the recital of his own experience, David here turns it into instruction and warning for others. He had long struggled with the sense of his sin, had long been crushed to the earth with his burden, because he would not humble himself before God; but God had given him again the heart of a child. He had gone to his Father with the penitent confession, "I have sinned;" and as in the parable, the Father's heart moved towards his prodigal son when he was yet a long way off, so David found that his Father was ready to forgive —"I said, I will confess," and "Thou tookest away the guilt of my sin."

There can be little doubt, I think, that this Psalm was composed after Nathan came to him. Psalm li. was the confession of his great sin and the prayer for forgiveness. This Psalm is the record of the confession made and the forgiveness obtained, and the conscious blessedness of his position as a son restored to his Father's house. There was a shelter for him there now—"Thou art my hiding-place." There was joy and gladness on his return—"Thou shalt compass me about with songs of deliverance." And here he carries out the resolve of Psalm li., "Then will I teach transgressors Thy way, and sinners shall be converted unto Thee."

The instruction of the Psalm may be summed up in the words of Prov. xxviii. 13, or in those of 1 John i. 8, 9.

[A MASKIL[a] OF DAVID.]

I. 1 BLESSED is he whose transgression is taken away,
whose sin is covered:

1, 2. Sin is here (as in Ex. xxxiv. 7) spoken of under three appellations, so as to include the whole idea of sin in all its manifestations: First, as "transgression" (פֶּשַׁע) or departure from God, and open

2 Blessed is the man to whom Jehovah reckoneth not
iniquity,
And in whose spirit there is no guile.
3 For (while) I kept silence, my bones waxed old
Through my roaring all the day long.

defection from His covenant; or as Donne says in his sermon on this Psalm, "It is a malicious and a forcible opposition to God: it is when this Herod and this Pilate (this body and this soul of ours) are made friends and agreed, that they may concur to the crucifying of Christ." Secondly, as "a coming short of the mark" (חֲטָאָה), a deflection from an aim, a *not* doing of our duty (see the original meaning of the root, Judg. xx. 16, where the Benjamites are said not to *miss* the mark by a hair's breadth). Thirdly, as including in the idea of wrongdoing, the guilt, and also the punishment (עָוֹן).

And there is a threefold blessedness. The man is one who has his transgression *taken away* (lit. who is *lightened of the burden* of sin), comp. Exod. xxxiv. 7, John i. 29; who has his sin *covered*, so that he is in God's sight as one who has not done the sin, cf. lxxxv. 2 [3], and Is. xxxviii. 17, xliii. 25, xliv. 22;—for as Donne says, "Our merciful God, when He sees us under this mantle, this covering, Christ spread upon His church, conceals His knowledge of our sins and suffers them not to reflect upon our consciences, in a consternation thereof;"—he is also one to whom *iniquity is not reckoned* (ver. 2), which, according to St. Paul's interpretation, Romans iv. 6—9, is equivalent to saying that he is one whose faith is reckoned for righteousness. The non-reckoning of iniquity, and the reckoning of righteousness, are convertible terms: and the righteousness so reckoned is faith, or a righteousness without works. But God only thus forgives and justifies one who, with all truth and sincerity of heart, confesses his sin, making no reservation, no excuses, no attempts still to hold fast and hide some darling lust, as De Muis says: "qui non peccat animo pœnitendi, aut non pœnitet animo peccandi." "As the prophet David's principal purpose in this text is, according to the interpretation of St. Paul, to derive all the blessedness of man from God: so it is also to put some conditions in man, comprehended in this, *That there be no guile in his spirit.* . . . He that makes half repentance, makes none." (The clause may be a relative clause, or may be taken conditionally, as Seb. Schmid, "modo non sit in spiritu ejus dolus.") The two things are, at any rate, "connected as conspiring to the blessedness of the man (as Leighton says), viz. the free remission of sin, and the inner cleansing of the heart."

No guile: no falseness, that is, either to himself or to God. Of this guilelessness Leighton remarks, "Nothing is more pleasing to God, who seeth the heart, nothing more like to God; and therefore is it most pleasing to Him, because it is most like Him."—*Meditat. Ethico-Crit.* in Ps. xxxii.

3. For, as explaining how he had come to know what he had just before said. David had felt the need of this guileless spirit, *for* he had "kept silence," had striven but too long to smother the sense of his guilt, which was meanwhile like a smouldering fire within him. Afraid to confess his sin to himself, afraid to confess it to God, he could not still escape the goading and pricking of his conscience, and hence his misery.

My bones; see vi. 2 [3], and cf. Job xiii. 28.

Through my roaring, *i.e.* the

4 For day and night Thy hand was heavy [b] upon me ;
My moisture was turned into the drought of summer. [Selah.]

5 (I said) I would acknowledge [c] my sin unto Thee,
And mine iniquity did I not cover,
I said, "I will confess my transgressions unto Jehovah,"
And THOU didst take away the iniquity of my sin. [Selah.]

II. 6 For this cause let every godly man pray to Thee

cry extorted from the anguish of his spirit so long as he KEPT SILENCE, *i.e.* refused to confess his sin. "Sin is a serpent, and he that covers sin does but keep it warm, that it may sting the more fiercely, and disperse the venom and malignity thereof the more effectually."—*Donne.* This "roaring" brought him no relief, because "deerat adhuc vox illa, cui semper resonant viscera paterna, vox filii revertentis et errores confitentis."—*Leighton.*

4. FOR (this gives the reason of his roaring) God's hand was heavy upon him (cf. 1 Samuel v. 6, 11 ; Job xxiii. 2 ; Ps. xxxviii. 2 [3]), and that hand is "premens gravissima, sublevans suavissima et potentissima."

MY MOISTURE, *i.e.* the juices of life. By the inward anguish in the struggle not to confess, these were turned (as it were) into the drought of summer. "He would not be humbled by the confession of his sin, and therefore he was humbled by the weight of God's hand." Thus, in his attempt to spare himself, he was guilty of the worst cruelty to himself ; "sub specie parcendi vere sibi crudelis est." Cf. cii. 3 [4], where the particle of comparison is supplied. In Job xxx. 30, it is omitted as here. Symm. ὡς καῦσος θερινόν.

5. The end of the struggle—confession, and so forgiveness and peace. God covers sin, but man must not cover his sin before God. "If we confess our sins, He is faithful and just to forgive us our sins." (1 John i. 9.) The former part of this verse contains the *resolve,* "I would acknowledge," &c. ; the second, the *expression* of the resolve, "I said," &c. (See more in Critical Note.)

AND THOU. The pronoun is emphatic : it was *God's* doing. To *Him* he made his confession : *He* forgave. The same words are used here of sin and its forgiveness as in ver. 1. The confession and the taking away are described as simultaneous. "Vox nondum est in ore," says Augustine, "et vulnus sanatur in corde." And Leighton : "Quam sit proclivis et facilis ad veniam misericordiarum Pater, tanto clarius elucescit, quod vel ad primam confessionis vocem emissam, imo vel propositum interius conceptum, emittitur extemplo e curia cœlesti remissio, seu indulgentia plenissima, Dixi confitebor et tu condonasti," &c.

INIQUITY OF MY SIN. Many, after Symmachus and Qimchi, have supposed this to be equivalent to "my very great sin ;" but perhaps the word here and above (ver. 2), rendered "iniquity," might better be rendered "guilt," a meaning which it often has.

6. And now because of the grace thus vouchsafed to every repentant

In a time when Thou mayest be found ;
(So) surely [d] when the great waters overflow,
They shall not reach unto him.
7 Thou art my hiding-place ;
Thou wilt preserve me from trouble ;
Thou wilt compass me about with songs [e] of deliverance. [Selah.]

III. 8 I will instruct thee and teach thee in the way thou shouldest go,
I will counsel thee with mine eye upon thee.[f]
9 Be ye not as horse, (or) as mule without understanding,

sinner, David would encourage all the godly to seek Him who deals so graciously with sinners.

IN A TIME WHEN THOU MAYEST BE FOUND, lit. "in a time of finding," no object being expressed. The object may either be Jehovah Himself (as Is. lv. 6 ; comp. Deut. iv. 29, Jer. xxix. 13), or more generally "grace and forgiveness," as in the common phrase "to find grace." See also lxix. 13 [14] ; Is. xlix. 8. The LXX. render ἐν εὐθέτῳ καιρῷ. It has been well remarked, "Aptissimum inveniendi tempus, quando invenit homo cor suum præparatum ad revertendum Deumque quærendum." He who thus seeks Jehovah when He may be found shall not be swept away when His judgements are let loose like a flood of waters upon the earth.

7. David's own joyful experience of this safety, of which he is speaking to others. Scarcely has he held out the hope to others, when he turns with a happy trustfulness to God—

THOU ART MY HIDING-PLACE. He would be hidden in God. St. Paul could scarcely say more, "Our life is hid with Christ in God."

COMPASS ME ABOUT, *i.e.* give me abundant cause, turn where I may, to praise Thee. God will do this, and so be the *author* as well as the *object* of his praise. Comp. xxii. 25 [26], "*From* Thee comes my praise."

8. Out of his past and present experience he will now counsel others, and especially those who are still impenitent ; and the tenour of his counsel is, that they should not, like brutes, resist and refuse submission till they are forced into it, but that they should willingly come with repentance and confession to God.

The transition here to the direct form of address in the first person is certainly abrupt. Some have supposed that these are the words of God ; but perhaps David himself speaks with something of a father's warning.

I WILL INSTRUCT, &c. Comp. for this word ci. 2 ("behave myself wisely," E.V.) with Prov. i. 3 ; and for "teaching in the way," xxv. 8, 12, with Prov. iv. 11.

I WILL COUNSEL, &c. Mendels. "Ich rathe dir ; mein Auge *schaut* auf dich."

The guidance with the eye is a gentle guidance. A look is enough, as opposed to that bit and bridle which the mulish nature requires. "Thus Christ counselled Peter with his eye, Luke xxii. 61."—*Ainsworth.*

9. Then follows the warning against a brutish and stubborn im-

Whose trapping[g] is with bit and bridle to hold them,
Or else they will not come nigh unto thee.[h]
10 Many are the sorrows of the wicked,
But whoso trusteth in Jehovah, loving-kindness compasseth him about.
11 Rejoice in Jehovah, and exult, O ye righteous,
And shout for joy, all ye that are upright in heart.

penitence, with the not unfrequent comparison of men to the lower animals (comp. Is. i. 3, Jer. viii. 6).—James iii. 3.

10. The usual contrast between the lot of the ungodly and that of the righteous, as the sum of all that has been said, and as a great religious axiom.

[a] מַשְׂכִּיל. LXX. συνέσεως, εἰς σύνεσιν, and hence by many explained, "giving instruction," "a didactic poem." But this is a meaning often not applicable, as, for instance, xlv., where it is also found, nor in xlvii. 7 [8], where זַמְּרוּ מ׳ must mean "play skilfully." Hence it probably denotes "a skilfully constructed or choice poem;" "ein feines Lied," as Ewald renders it. See more in the General Introduction.

[b] תִּכְבַּד. The fut. here seems to be equivalent either to an aorist or an imperfect, and denotes either the frequent blow, or the continued blow.

[c] אוֹדִיעֲךָ. The use of the *fut.* here again presents some difficulty. It evidently refers to past time, as Hupfeld says, and hence he calls it a relative preterite. But I cannot see why it may not be designedly employed not to express the past *action*, but the past *resolve*, the sentence being somewhat elliptical: "(Then I thought, then I resolved) I would acknowledge." Comp. a similar instance in xxx. 8. It may be indeed, as Hupf. suggests in his critical note (p. 177), that the אָמַרְתִּי of the following clause has been misplaced, and should stand before אוֹדִיעֲךָ at the beginning of the verse (as in lxxiii. 15, where it ought to stand, he thinks, before ver. 13), but then it must be repeated before אוֹדֶה. At any rate, the two futures correspond to one another as expressing the *resolve*, first as conceived, then as uttered; and the two preterites as marking the consequence in each case. אוֹדֶה only in this sense, besides, Prov xxviii. 13, with עַל in the Hithp., Neh. i. 6, ix. 2.

[d] רַק. Here used in strong assertion. It means primarily "thin," then "simple, absolute." Thence it passes into the meaning of "only," "nothing else but," and hence, as the strongest restrictive particle, is used in affirmations; for that which so takes place that nothing else takes place, does *assuredly* take place. It is a particle not only of restriction and exception, but of opposition (1 Kings viii. 18, xv. 5) and strong affirmation (1 Kings xxi. 25, Prov. xiii. 10, Gen. xx. 11.)

[e] רָנֵּי is a plural construct. formed from the infinitive רֹן (Job xxxviii. 7), used as a substantive, like רִבֵּי from רֹב, חֻקֵּי from חֹק.

[f] אִיעֲצָה. Evidently this is a *constructio prægnans*. The Chald. explains it: "I will counsel thee and keep mine eye upon thee," some such verb as שׂוּם being supplied before עֵינִי. It is, however, unnecessary to do this. The words "mine eye upon thee" may be merely subjoined as a further explanation of *the manner in which* the counsel would be given. This is better than to connect עָלֶיךָ with אִיעֲצָה, "I will consult upon, or concerning, thee, *i.e.* for thy good;" עֵינִי, "with mine eye," being then equivalent to "watching thee with mine eye." Hupfeld contends that עֵינִי is not an *accus.* of the instrument, but that we have here an instance of a *double subject* of the person and the instrument, as in iii. 5: he also explains the use of the prep. עַל, as arising from the idea of "watching" in the verb: "I will counsel (thee), *watching over thee* (עָלֶיךָ) with mine eye."

[g] עֶדְיוֹ, harness, or trappings (from עדה, "to put on"). Ewald, following the older versions (LXX. *ἐν χαλινῷ καὶ κημῷ τὰς σιαγόνας αὐτῶν ἄγξαι τῶν μὴ ἐγγιζόντων πρὸς σέ*, and Jerome, "in camo et fræno maxillas eorum constringe qui non approximant ad te"), takes עֶדְיוֹ in the sense of "jaw," connecting it with the Arab. خَدّ, "cheek." The sentence is a relative one: "(Whose) trapping (consists) in bit and bridle to hold (them)."

[h] בַּל קְרוֹב, lit. "not approaching, or, there is no approaching, to thee." An asyndeton. We must supply "because," *i.e.* otherwise, and without force, they will not come nigh to men. This is the only instance in which בַּל stands before the inf. or noun, elsewhere it is always בְּלִי.

PSALM 33

God is the God of Creation, of Providence, of Grace. This is, in a few words, the Psalmist's theme. Jehovah created the world (ver. 6, ff.). Jehovah governs the world (ver. 10, ff.); and all nations and kings, whether they acknowledge Him or not, are but instruments in His hand. Jehovah especially reveals Himself in mercy and love to His own chosen people (ver. 18, ff). The key-note of this last sentiment is already struck in ver. 12.

This is one of the few Psalms in the First Book which in the Hebrew is without an inscription.

The Psalm consists of the following divisions:—

I. An introduction, in which the singer calls on the righteous to praise Jehovah with all manner of music. Ver. 1—3.

Then follow the reasons why He is worthy to be praised.

II. (1) First, because He is Good and Faithful (ver. 4, 5); and next (2), because by His word all things were created. Ver. 4—9.

III. Because He is the All-wise (ver. 10, 11), All-seeing (ver. 13—15), and Almighty (ver. 16, 17) Ruler of Nations. Ver. 10—17.

IV. Lastly, because He watches over (ver. 18), preserves (ver. 19), and protects (ver. 20) all those that fear Him and trust in His Holy Name. Ver. 18—21.

The Psalm concludes with a short petition, that it may be done unto Israel according to his hope.

1 SHOUT for joy, O ye righteous, in Jehovah;
For the upright, praise is comely.
2 Give thanks to Jehovah with a harp,
Upon a ten-stringed lute play unto Him.
3 Sing unto Him a new song,
Play skilfully on the strings with a loud noise.

4 For the word of Jehovah is upright:
And all that He doeth is faithfulness.
5 He loveth righteousness and judgement:
The earth is full of the loving-kindness of Jehovah.
6 By the word of Jehovah were the heavens made;
And all the host of them by the breath of His mouth.

3. A NEW SONG, not here one which has new marvels of God's Power and Grace for its theme, as in xl. 3 [4], xcviii. 1 (comp. ᾠδὴ καινή, Rev. xiv. 3), but rather one which springs freshly from a thankful and rejoicing heart; one which seeks to put an old theme in a new light.

4, 5. First the *moral* attributes of God are mentioned as a reason why the righteous should praise Him. See the same attributes enumerated in xxxvi. 5, 6 [6, 7], with the same reference to God's providential care of His creatures. Comp. lxxxix. 14 [15].

6. From the present proofs of God's love in the earth, the thoughts of the sacred Poet naturally go back to the creation of all things.

And as he had before declared what the "word" and "work" of Jehovah are in their essential characters (ver. 4), so now he describes further the operation of that word, and the work which results therefrom.

BY THE WORD, explained further ver. 9, the creative fiat as in Gen. 1.

THE BREATH OF HIS MOUTH, apparently almost the same thing as "the word" before. So in Is. xi. 4, "the breath of His lips," is used of the sentence of judgement which thence issues. (So Calvin.) It can

7 He gathereth the waters of the sea together as an heap;
He layeth up the depths in storehouses.
8 Let all the earth fear before Jehovah;
Let all the inhabitants of the world stand in awe of Him.
9 For He said, and it was:
He commanded and it stood fast.

10 Jehovah hath brought to naught the counsel of the nations;
He hath made the thoughts of the peoples of none effect.
11 The counsel of Jehovah standeth fast for ever,
The thoughts of His heart to all generations.
12 Blessed is the nation whose God is Jehovah,
The people whom He hath chosen for His own inheritance.

hardly be understood here of the Spirit of God who moved over the chaotic mass as the great Source of Life in Creation, at any rate not in the personal sense, which is quite precluded by the addition "of His mouth." The two expressions are designedly employed in the parallelism "word" and "breath of His mouth," to indicate that it was *only* by the utterance of His will and not by any work or effort that God created all things. This is further explained in ver. 9.

7. The heaven and the sea are mentioned as the theatre of God's almighty power, as the earth before of His loving-kindness; and thus the Universe is summed up.

AS AN HEAP, a figure I think manifestly suggested by the appearance of the waves of the sea. The expression may have been borrowed from Josh. iii. 13—16, and Exod. xv. 8. Clericus finds the point of the comparison (the *tertium comparationis*) in the fact that the sea is shut in by its shores as the heaps of corn (Is. xvii. 11) are by the walls of the granary in which they are stored. This he thinks is confirmed by the parallelism in the next member of the verse which repeats the same idea in a different form. Both expressions would thus refer to the original act of creation, when the waters were "gathered together" that the dry land might appear.

9. A manifest reference to Gen. i. 3: "And God said, Let Light be, and Light was."

10, 11. After speaking of God's power in creation, the Psalmist goes on to speak of His providence as ordering the world. As Calvin says, "Postquam breviter attigit mundi creationem ad institutum sermonem redit, quotidianos scilicet eventus certos esse providentiæ testes.' There is a manifest antithesis between "the counsels and the thoughts" of men which Jehovah *brings to naught*, and "the counsels and thoughts" of Jehovah which *abide for ever*.

12. This verse already anticipates what is said more fully verses 18—20, and here we have the doctrine

13 From heaven hath Jehovah looked,
He hath seen all the children of men.
14 From the place of His dwelling He hath looked down
Upon all the inhabitants of the earth,
15 (Even) He who fashioneth their hearts together,
Who considereth all their works.
16 A king doth not triumph by a great host,
A mighty man is not delivered by great strength.
17 A horse is a vain thing for victory,
Neither can he deliver any by his great power.

18 Behold, the eye of Jehovah is upon them that fear Him,
Upon them that hope in His loving-kindness,

of God's universal Providence looked at in its special application to the chosen people, as often: see Ps. xxiv. 1. It is, however, immediately connected with the preceding verse; for the fact that Jehovah's counsels stand fast for ever is a matter of consolation for the people whose God He is (cxlvii. 19, 20), and whom He hath chosen for His own inheritance (xlvii. 4 [5]). Similarly Calvin: "Apte hîc versus cohæret cum proximo: quia parum prodesset quod de perpetuitate consilii Dei dictum fuit tenere, nisi ad nos pertineret."

13—15. The Omnipresence and Omniscience of God. He not only observes men's doings, but knows their hearts as having created them. This is implied in ver. 15. As Calvin well puts it: "Ab ipsa autem creatione ratiocinatur; . . . etsi flexuosos quisque recessus in animo suo occultet, ut mire alii ab aliis differant, ac in tanta varietate confusa sit caligo, Dei tamen oculos non perstringi neque offuscari, quin idoneus sit operis sui cognitor." (Comp. Is. xxix. 15, 16, and see the fuller statement of the truth, Ps. xciv. 8 ff.)

16, 17. The weakness and insufficiency of all human *power* however great, as before of all human *intellect*. "King, and mighty man, and horse" (*i.e.* war-horse, as elsewhere, "chariot and horse"), are selected as types of earthly power in all its greatness.

TRIUMPH or, "gain the victory." See on next verse.

17. VICTORY. The word (יְשׁוּעָה) does not necessarily mean "salvation," "deliverance," &c. It occurs in the sense of "victory," Habak. iii. 8, and the verb in ver. 16 of this Ps. and in xliv. 3 [4].

18. UPON: more literally, "towards."

18—22. HOPE—TARRY—TRUST—HOPE. This attitude of hope and trust is the attitude of the Church in all ages, for she is not yet made perfect; but the Jewish Church was in a special sense the Church of the Future, and therefore also in a special manner a waiting and hoping Church. The whole history of Israel may, indeed, be summed up in

19 To deliver their soul from death,
And to keep them alive in famine.
20 Our soul hath tarried for Jehovah;
He is our Help and our Shield,
21 For in Him our heart rejoiceth,
Because we have trusted in His Holy Name.
22 Let Thy loving-kindness, O Jehovah, be upon us,
According as we have hoped in Thee.

Jacob's dying words: "I have waited for Thy salvation, O Lord." The Hebrew language has accordingly several words which express this hoping, forward-looking attitude. Besides the two words here, there is the more common word which occurs three times in Ps. xxv. (see note on ver. 3), twice in xxvii. 14, and often elsewhere.

PSALM 34

This is, like the last, a Psalm in which God's providence and moral government of the world are the subject of grateful acknowledgement. His guardian care of the righteous is more especially celebrated, and applied to the individual circumstances of the Psalmist.

This is one of the alphabetical Psalms, on which see the Introduction to Psalm xxv. The order of the Hebrew alphabet is preserved, except that there is no verse* beginning with the letter ו (Vau). The number of verses, however, is made to correspond with the number of letters in the alphabet, notwithstanding this omission, by means of a verse added at the end, which begins (as is also the case in Psalm xxv.) with the word פדה, " redeem."

No value can be attached to the superscription with its historical reference, because while it is borrowed from 1 Sam. xxi. 13 [14], Abimelech is substituted for Achish, which looks like a confusion with the narrative in Gen. xx. xxi.; and further, the contents of the Psalm do not very readily, or naturally, harmonise with the supposed circumstances.

The contents of the Psalm may generally be distributed into pairs of verses. But the alphabetical order of course precludes anything

* It may be noticed, however, that the second member of ver. 5 begins with Vau, which preserves the alphabetical order, though not the balance of the verses.

like very close connection. The principal thought of the Psalm is God's care of the afflicted, and this appears repeated in different forms.

The closest connection is between ver. 12—15, which contain one consecutive piece of instruction.

[A PSALM OF DAVID, WHEN HE CHANGED HIS BEHAVIOUR BEFORE ABIMELECH; WHO DROVE HIM AWAY, AND HE DEPARTED.]

א 1 I WILL bless Jehovah at all times,
Continually shall His praise be in my mouth.
ב 2 In Jehovah shall my soul make her boast:
The afflicted shall hear thereof and be glad.
ג 3 O magnify Jehovah with me,
And let us exalt His name together.
ד 4 I sought Jehovah, and He answered me,
And delivered me out of all my fears.
ה 5 They looked unto Him, and were lightened;
And may their faces not be confounded.
ז 6 This afflicted man called, and Jehovah heard,
And saved him out of all his troubles.
ח 7 The angel of Jehovah encampeth round about them that fear Him,
And setteth them free.

5. THEY LOOKED, viz. "the afflicted," mentioned in ver. 2; or it may only mean generally "men looked;" others, *i.e.* besides myself, have in like manner experienced God's loving-kindness.

WERE LIGHTENED, *i.e.* were bright with gladness because He heard them, reflecting as it were the Light of His countenance; comp. iv. 6 [7]. The verb is clearly to be taken in this sense here as in Is. lx. 5. In its more common acceptation it means "to flow" (whence *nāhār*, "a stream," and *n' hārāh*, "light"). The connection between the two ideas is obvious.

AND MAY, &c., lit. "And their faces—may they not be put to the blush?" The use of the negative אַל here seems to require an optative rendering.

Delitzsch translates the verse:

"Hinblickend auf Ihn wird man licht,
Und solcher Antlitz darf erröthen nicht."

And Hengstenberg very well explains the use of אַל (= μή = *ne*) by saying, that "it signifies a shuddering at their being put to shame as though it were something monstrous." But see on cxxi. 3.

7. THE ANGEL. Not apparently here used of any particular angel, as "the Angel of the Covenant," or "the Captain of the Lord's host," but rather in a collective sense, "troops of angels."

ט 8 O taste and see that Jehovah is good!
Blessed is the man that findeth refuge in Him.

י 9 O fear Jehovah, ye His saints!
For there is no want to them that fear Him.

כ 10 Young lions have lacked and suffered hunger,
But they that seek Jehovah shall not want any (good thing).

ל 11 Come, ye children, hearken unto me,
I will teach you the fear of Jehovah:

מ 12 What man is he that desireth life,
That loveth (many) days that he may see good?

נ 13 Keep thy tongue from evil,
And thy lips from speaking guile;

ס 14 Depart from evil and do good,
Seek peace and pursue it.

ע 15 The eyes of Jehovah are towards the righteous,
And His ears (are open) unto their cry.

פ 16 The face of Jehovah is against the evil-doers,
To cut off the remembrance of them from the earth.

צ 17 They cried, and Jehovah heard,
And delivered them out of all their troubles.

ק 18 Jehovah is nigh unto them that are of a broken heart,
And saveth such as are of a contrite spirit.

ר 19 Many are the sufferings of the righteous,
But out of all of them doth Jehovah deliver him.

SETTETH THEM FREE. Ainsworth, "releaseth them."

8. O TASTE AND SEE. Comp. γεύσασθαι, Heb. vi. 5; 1 Pet. ii. 3. "Nisi gustaveris," says St. Bernard, "non videbis. Gustate, inquit, et videte, quoniam suavis est Dominus. Manna absconditum est, nomen novum est, quod nemo scit nisi qui accepit. Non illud eruditio, sed unctio docet, nec scientia sed conscientia comprehendit."

10. YOUNG LIONS. Instead of this the LXX. have πλούσιοι.

11. A form of address common in the Proverbs. See chapters i.—ix. Similar is the use of τέκνα by St. John in his Epistles.

13. On this taming of the tongue —of which so much is said in the proverbs of all nations—see xv. 2. 3, xxxix. 1—3 [2—4], cxli. 3; Prov. iv. 24, xiii. 3, xxi. 23; James iii. 2 ff.

17. THEY, *i.e.* the righteous, mentioned ver. 15, and again ver. 19, which is supplied by all the Versions. See on this position of the pronoun the note on ix. 12.

ש 20 He preserveth all his bones;
Not one of them is broken.
ת 21 Evil shall slay the wicked,
And they that hate the righteous shall be punished.
פ 22 Jehovah redeemeth the soul of His servants,
And all they that find refuge in Him shall not be punished.

21. BE PUNISHED, or "condemned," or "held guilty." See note [k] on Ps. v. 10.

PSALM 35

THIS Psalm, if it be, as the inscription tells us, a Psalm of David, must have been composed either during his persecution by Saul, or during the revolt of Absalom. It is usual to connect it with his words in 1 Sam. xxiv. 15 [16], "Jehovah therefore be judge, and judge between thee and me, and see, and plead my cause (the same expression as in ver. 1 of the Psalm), and deliver me by His judgement out of thine hand." Its peculiar feature is that the enemies on whom the Poet imprecates the righteous judgements of God, are men who had formerly been his friends, men for whom he had prayed in their sorrow "with a brother's heart," and who now requited his love with ungrateful hatred. Such an enemy Saul may have been; but we never find any trace of bitterness in David's feelings towards Saul. The generous enemy whose heart smote him because he had cut off Saul's skirt, and who always recognised in Saul the Lord's anointed, would never have called down the judgements of God upon his head. It seems to me, therefore, more probable that the aiders and abettors of Absalom's conspiracy, men like Ahithophel and his associates, are aimed at in the Poet's burning words. But all this, and even the authorship itself, must be matter of mere conjecture.

The Psalm falls into three principal divisions; each of which closes with a thanksgiving.

I. Ver. 1—10. 1. Cry to God to come forth as a champion armed for his defence (1—3).

2. Prayer for the confusion and destruction of his enemies (4—8).

3. Thankful acknowledgement of God's deliverance (9, 10).

II. Ver. 11—18. 1. Contrast between the love and good-will which he had shown to his enemies, and the bitter hatred with which they had requited him (11—16).

2. Appeal to God against them, with vows of thanksgiving (17, 18).

III. Ver. 19—28. 1. Prayer that they may not triumph, with description of their craft and wickedness (19—21).

2. Again a prayer that God would appear to vindicate his cause and put them to confusion (22—26).

3. The joy of all the righteous and of the singer, because God executeth judgement upon the ungodly (27, 28).

[(A PSALM) OF DAVID.]

I. 1 CONTEND,[a] O Jehovah, with them that contend with me:
Fight[b] Thou against them that fight against me.
2 Lay hold of shield and buckler,
And arise up as my helper.
3 Draw out[c] also the spear and battle-axe[d]
Against them that pursue me;
Say unto my soul, I am thy salvation.
4 Let them be ashamed and brought to dishonour that seek after my soul;
Let them be turned back and put to confusion that devise my hurt.
5 Let them be as the chaff before the wind,
And the angel of Jehovah thrusting[e] (them).

2. An amplification of the figure occurring already in the Pentateuch, where God is spoken of as a man of war, Exod. xv. 3, Deut. xxxii. 41. The bold anthropomorphic working out of the figure is, however, remarkable. It shows the earnest desire in the Poet's mind to realize the fact that God not only taught his fingers to fight, but mixed in the battle, fighting as it were by his side, and assuring him of victory.

4. LET THEM BE DRIVEN BACK. Very similar words occur ver. 26, Cf. also xl. 14 [15], and lxx. 2, 3 [3, 4].

5. AS THE CHAFF. See i. 4, and comp. xviii. 42 [43], lxxxiii. 13 [14].

THE ANGEL OF JEHOVAH, here perhaps, as in the last Psalm, not to be understood of any particular angel. Delitzsch supposes the Angel of Israel to be meant, "who took off Pharaoh's chariot wheels, so that they drave them heavily."

6 Let their way be darkness and exceeding slipperiness,[f]
And the angel of Jehovah pursuing them.
7 For without cause have they hid for me their net in a pit;[g]
Without cause have they digged (a pit) for my soul.
8 Let destruction come upon him at unawares,[h]
And let his net that he hath hidden catch himself;
Into that very destruction[i] let him fall.
9 So shall my soul exult in Jehovah,
It shall be joyful in His salvation.
10 All my bones shall say,
"Jehovah, who is like unto Thee?
Who deliverest the afflicted from him that is too strong for him,
Yea the afflicted and the poor from him that spoileth him."

II. 11 Violent witnesses rise up,
They ask of me things that I know not,
12 They reward me evil for good;
My soul is bereaved.
13 But as for me, when they were sick, my clothing was sackcloth;
I afflicted my soul with fasting,
And my prayer—may it return into my own bosom.

7. A common metaphor borrowed from the artifices employed for taking wild beasts. See more in Critical Note.

11. VIOLENT, *i.e.* unscrupulous or "malicious" witnesses, *μάρτυρες ἄδικοι*, LXX. See Exod. xxiii. 1.

ASK OF ME, or "question me concerning."

12. Very touching are the words "My soul is bereaved," I am alone in the world. I, who have ever sought to help the friendless and comfort the afflicted, and who prayed so earnestly for others, am forsaken of all.

13. AND MY PRAYER, &c. These words have been very differently rendered. (1) Some, as Ewald and Delitzsch, understand them as referring to the posture of prayer, *sc.* I prayed with my head bowed on my breast; an interpretation which they support by 1 Kings xviii. 42, where, however, it is not said that Elijah prayed, nor was this, so far as we know, a customary posture in prayer, not to mention that the prayer is said not "to fall upon," but "to return to," the bosom. Such an interpretation, I confess, seems to me almost ludi-

14 As though it had been my friend, my brother, so did
I behave myself;
As one who sorroweth for a mother, I bowed down
mourning.
15 But when I halted, they rejoiced and gathered themselves together,
They gathered themselves together, smiting [k] (me)
when I knew it not.
They did tear (me) and ceased not;
16 With them that are profane in their outlandish
mouthings,[l]
Gnashings upon me with their teeth.
17 O Lord, how long wilt Thou see (this)?
Bring back my soul from their destructions,[m]
My only one from the lions.
18 I will give Thee thanks in the great congregation,
I will praise Thee among much [n] people.

crous, and quite out of place here. It is like the Jewish interpretation of Is. xxvi. 2, quoted by Stanley on 1 Cor. xiv. 16. In any case this would be a singular way of expressing the attitude of prayer: we should have expected, "with head bowed on my breast," or something of the kind. (2) Others take them as referring to the inward act of prayer, "in sinu precari;" but again this is a sense which does not lie in the Hebrew words. (3) Better, "was repeated again and again," uttered with increasing fervour. (4) "My prayer returned (or *shall*, *must* return) into my bosom," according to the usual signification of this and similar phrases (lxxix. 12, Is. lxv. 6, 7, &c.), would mean, as Hupf. remarks, "This was all the return I had for my prayer, that they requited me evil for good." He thinks there is something sarcastic in the expression. This, however, is doubtful. I prefer rendering: "And my prayer—may it return into mine own bosom." The prayer I offered for them is a prayer I might have offered for myself. So true a prayer was it, so full of love, that I could wish nothing more than that the blessings I asked for them should be vouchsafed to me. This passage was apparently understood thus by the LXX., who have the imperative ἀποστραφήτω. This agrees, too, with what follows, "As though for my friend or my brother," &c. It may perhaps be illustrated by reference to Matt. x. 13, Luke x. 6.

14. MOURNING, *i.e.* with all the outward signs of sorrow, especially the garments (as the word particularly denotes), perhaps also the untrimmed beard, unwashed face, &c., which were tokens of Oriental mourning. Comp. xxxviii. 6 [7], Job i. 20, v. 11, &c.

15, 16. The cruel requital of all this affection and sympathy.

16. On the interpretation of this difficult verse see the Critical Note.

17. MY ONLY ONE. See note on xxii. 20.

18. CONGREGATION, or "assem-

III. 19 Let not them that are mine enemies falsely [o] rejoice over me,
Neither let them that hate me without a cause wink with the eye,
20 For not peace do they speak,
But against them that are quiet [p] in the land they devise words of deceit.
21 Yea, they opened their mouth wide against me;
They said, Aha, aha, our eye hath seen (it).
22 Thou hast seen, O Jehovah : keep not silence;
O Lord, be not far from me.

bly," or "church," the Greek equivalent being ἐκκλησία.

22. THOU HAST SEEN, with reference to the "our eye HATH SEEN" in the preceding verse.

This latter part of the Psalm is on the whole calmer than the former, as if the spirit had found rest in pouring out its complaints. Though the singer again calls for confusion on his enemies, the expressions are not so apparently vindictive as at the beginning of the Psalm. Comp. ver. 25, 26, with ver. 4—6.

But how are we to account for such prayers for vengeance at all? We find them chiefly in four Psalms, the 7th, 35th, 69th, and 109th, and the imprecations in these form a terrible climax. In the last, no less than thirty anathemas have been counted. Are these the mere outbursts of passionate and unsanctified feeling, or are they the legitimate expression of a righteous indignation? Are they to be excused as being animated by the "spirit of Elias," a spirit not unholy indeed, but far removed from the meekness and gentleness of Christ; or are they stereotyped forms in which the spirit of Christian devotion may utter itself? Are they Jewish only, or may they be Christian also? An uninstructed fastidiousness, it is well known, has made many persons recoil from reading these Psalms at all. Many have found their lips falter when they have been called to join in using them in the congregation, and have either uttered them with bated breath and doubting heart, or have interpreted them in a sense widely at variance with the letter. Some have tried to reconcile them with a more enlightened conscience, by regarding such words not as the expression of a wish, but as the utterance of a prediction; but the Hebrew optative, which is distinct enough from the simple future, absolutely forbids this expedient. Others again would see in them expressions which may lawfully be used in the soul's wrestling against spiritual enemies. And finally, some would defend them as utterances of righteous zeal for God's honour, and remind us that if we do not sympathize with such zeal, it may be not because our religion is more pure, but because our hearts are colder.

Now the real source of the difficulty lies in our not observing and bearing in mind the essential difference between the Old Testament and the New. The older dispensation was in every sense a sterner one than the new. The spirit of Elias, though not an evil spirit, was not the spirit of Christ. (Luke ix. 55.) "The Son of Man came not to destroy men's lives, but to save them." And through Him His disciples are made partakers of the

23 Arouse Thyself and awake to my judgement,
My God and my Lord [q] to my cause.

same spirit. But this was not the spirit of the older economy. The Jewish nation had been trained in a sterner school. It had been steeled and hardened by the discipline which had pledged it to a war of extermination with idolaters, and however necessary such a discipline might be, it would not tend to foster the gentler virtues; it is conceivable how even a righteous man, under it, feeling it to be his bounden duty to root out evil wherever he saw it, and identifying, as he did, his own enemies with the enemies of Jehovah, might use language which to us appears unnecessarily vindictive. To men so trained and taught, what we call "religious toleration" was a thing not only wrong, but absolutely inconceivable.

It may be quite true that we find revenge forbidden as directly in the Old Testament as in the New, as, for instance, in Lev. xix. 18, "Thou shalt not avenge," &c., though even there there is a limitation "against the children of thy people." And it may be no less true that we find instances of imprecation in the New, as when St. Paul says (2 Tim. iv. 14), "Alexander the coppersmith did me much evil: the Lord reward him according to his works:" [if we accept the optative of the Textus Rec., though the future ἀποδώσει, for which there is good authority, slightly softens the passage:] or when he exclaims, Acts xxiii. 3, "God shall smite thee, thou whited wall," or, "If any man love not the Lord Jesus Christ, let him be anathema." But even these expressions are very different from the varied, deliberate, carefully constructed, detailed anathemas of the Psalms. And our Lord's denunciations, to which Hengstenberg refers, are in no way parallel. They are not curses upon individuals, but in fact solemn utterances of the great truth, "Except ye repent, ye shall all likewise perish." But after all, whatever may be said of particular passages, the general tone which runs through the two covenants is unquestionably different. To deny this is not to honour Moses, but to dishonour Christ. (Matt. v. 43, xix. 8.) On the other hand we must not forget that these imprecations are not the passionate longing for personal revenge. The singer undoubtedly sees in his enemies the enemies of God and His Church. They that are not with him are against God. And because the zeal of God's house ever consumes him, he prays that all the doers of iniquity may be rooted out. The indignation therefore is righteous, though it may appear to us wrongly directed, or excessive in its utterance.

Once more, the very fact that a dark cloud hid God s judgement in the world to come from the view of the Old Testament saints, may be alleged in excuse of this their desire to see Him take vengeance on His enemies here. How deeply the problem of God's righteousness exercised their minds, is abundantly evident from numerous places in the Psalms. They longed to see that righteousness manifested. It could be manifested, they thought, only in the evident exaltation of the righteous, and the evident destruction of the wicked here. Hence, with their eye always fixed on temporal recompense, they could even wish and pray for the destruction of the ungodly. The awful things of the world to come were to a great extent hid from their eyes. Could they have seen these, then surely their prayer would have been, not "Let the angel of the Lord persecute them;" "Blot them out of Thy book;" but rather with Him who hung on the cross: "Father, forgive them; for they know not what they do."

24 Judge me according to Thy righteousness, O Jehovah
my God,
And let them not rejoice over me.
25 Let them not say in their heart, 'Aha, so would we
have [r] it;'
Let them not say, 'We have swallowed him up.'
26 Let them be ashamed and put to confusion together
That rejoice at my hurt;
Let them be clothed with shame and dishonour
That magnify themselves against me.
27 Let them shout for joy and be glad
That have pleasure in my righteousness,
And let them say alway, 'Jehovah be magnified,
Who hath pleasure in the prosperity of His servant.'
28 So shall my tongue talk of Thy righteousness,
(Of) Thy praise all the day long.

[a] רִיב, properly used of a suit in a court of justice: here, however, of a decision by force of arms. Instead of the more common form ריבה ריבי, we have here ר' את יריבי, אֵת being here the prep., as Is. xlix. 25.

[b] לחם. Qal instead of Niph. Cf. lvi. 2, 3.

מָגֵן, the buckler or smaller shield. צִנָּה, the large shield which covered the whole person; both mentioned to convey the idea of defence of all kinds. See v. 13, and cf. 1 Kings x. 16.

בְּעֶזְרָתִי, "in my help," *i.e.* as my helper, in that character, cf. Ex. xviii. 4, Prov. iii. 26. So also Ex. vi. 3, בְּאֵל שַׁדָּי, "in the character of the Almighty God." The ב is the so-called *Beth Essentiæ*, used to introduce the predicate. (Gesen. § 154, 3*a*.) Possibly xxxi. 22 is to be explained in the same way, "in a strong city," *i.e.* in such a character God has been to me, Himself like a fortified city.

[c] הָרֵק, "draw out," properly from a sheath (as a sword). But there is no evidence that spears were so carried. It may therefore be used in a wider and more general sense, as Abraham is said to "draw out" his trained men, Gen. xiv. 14.

[d] סְגֹר. There is no reason, as far as the constr. is concerned, why we should not (with the older translators generally) take this as the imper. of the verb, with an ellipse of דֶּרֶךְ. The word is used absol. Is. xxii. 22. So the LXX. *σύγκλεισον*, Targ. טְרוֹק. There is force, however, in Hupf.'s objection that לִקְרַאת indicates the going forth *to meet* an enemy, an attack, and not merely the passive resistance implied in the expression "bar the

way." Hence he, Ew., and others, following the hint of Qimchi (שם כלי מכלי מלחמה), take the word as a noun = σάγαρις, "battle-axe" (a Persian and Scythian weapon mentioned by Herod. and Xen.), Armen. *sacr*, and this interpretation is further favoured by the accents.

[e] דֹּחֶה . . . . רֹדְפָם. Hupfeld suggests, with much reason, that these words have changed places. We want the suffix with the first, and moreover דֹּחֶה, "thrusting," does not agree with the figure of the chaff.

[f] חֲלַקְלַקּוֹת, an emphat. form by reduplication for the simpler חלקות, lxxiii. 18, as in Jer. xxiii. 12.

[g] שַׁחַת רִשְׁתָּם, "pit of their net," *i.e.* a pit lightly covered over, and with a net concealed in it, in order to take wild animals. But it is not improbable that the text is wrong, and that שַׁחַת belongs to the second clause of the verse. The Verss., however, support the existing text.

[h] לֹא יֵדָע, a sort of adverbial clause, *improviso*, "at unawares" (Aq. rightly οὐ γινώσκοντι), as Prov. v. 6, Is. xlvii. 11; though probably the relat. is understood. Comp. לֹא יַחְמֹל, "pitilessly," Is. xxx. 14.

[i] בְּשׁוֹאָה יִ׳ בּ׳. I see no reason why we should not render as the Eng. Vers. does, following all the older translators. The pron. is placed in app. with the noun by way of emphasis (see ix. 7), and the word שׁוֹאָה refers to the previous clause, "the net which he hath hidden:" so that it is not necessary to supply the ellipse with the Syr., "in foveam quam foderunt cadant." Others render, "with a violent overthrow, a crash, let him fall into it (*i.e.* the net)." So Ewald explains: "Im Ungewitter das ihn dabei treffen soll."

[k] נֵכִים, ἅπ. λεγ., from a form נֵכֶה, like גֵּאֶה, רֵעֶה. The meaning, however, is doubtful. LXX. μάστιγες, so also the Syr. and Vulg. But Symm. better, πλῆκται, and Jerome, *percutientes*. The Chald. paraphrases, "the wicked who smite me with their words." Qimchi gave the word a passive sense, "the smitten," *i.e.* poor, miserable, worthless beings; whence "the abjects" of our Vers. But it is better to take it as active, "smiters," *i.e.* either in a literal sense, as denoting the violence of his enemies; or figuratively, as referring to their malicious use of their tongues.

וְלֹא יָדַעְתִּי may either mean, "And I was innocent," or like the לֹא יֵדָע above, ver. 8, "without my being aware of it."

[l] בחנפי ל׳ מ׳. Very difficult. The word מָעוֹג, in 1 Kings xvii. 12, the only other passage where it occurs, means "a cake." Hence ל׳ מ׳ is interpreted by Gesen. and others to mean, hangers-on at the tables of the rich (lit. "cake-mockers"), whose business it was, by witticisms and buffoonery, to make entertainment for the guests, and who got their dinner in return, like the Gr. ψωμοκόλακες, κνισσοκόλακες, and the Mediæv. Lat. *buccellarii*. Then the words would mean, "amongst the profanest (חנף never means 'hypocritical,' Gataker, *Adverss. Miscc.* c. 22) parasites," or as our Version, "mockers in feasts." But לַעֲגֵי, in the only other passage where it occurs (Is. xxviii. 11), means "stammerings," or rather

"barbarisms," or the confused, unintelligible speaking of foreigners (it is quite unnecessary to make the word an adj. as Ges. does). That this is the meaning in Is. xxviii. is clear from the parallel לָשׁוֹן אַחֶרֶת. Comp. Is. xxxiii. 19, עַם נִלְעַג לָשׁוֹן parallel with עַם עִמְקֵי שָׂפָה. And it is remarkable that none of the Ancient Versions here give מָעוֹג, the signif. "cake." They all evidently take לַעֲגֵי מ׳ together, in the general sense of "mockery," or the like. LXX. *ἐξεμυκτήρισάν με μυκτηρισμόν*. Symm. *ἐν ὑποκρίσει, φθέγμασι πεπλασμένοις*. Jerome: *in simulatione verborum fictorum*. Chald. "with derisive words of flattery." It is better, therefore, to refer מָעוֹג to the root עוג, in the sense "to turn, twist," &c. Cf. Talmud. לשן עגה, of a foreign language. Thus the rendering would be, "with the profane in their foreign stammerings," or, "amongst profane, foreign, barbarous stammerers."

With regard to the constr. of חַנְפֵי, that must depend on the meaning we attach to לַעֲגֵי. If this be an adjective, then the first adj. prefixed in *stat. constr.* must have a partitive, and according to the Heb. idiom, a superlative signif., "Among the profane (*i.e.* the profanest) of foreign mockers, or feast-mockers." Cf. Prov. xiv. 1, Ezek. vii. 24, Micah vii. 4. If on the other hand לַעֲגֵי be a noun, then ל׳ מ׳ may be considered as one word, and depend immediately upon the adj. "Among those who are profane in their barbarous stammerings, outlandish mouthings, &c.;" or, keeping the play upon words in the Hebrew, we might render ל׳ מ׳, "who jabber gibberish," as has been suggested to me by a friend.

[m] שׁאיהם, a form occurring only here, app. a masc. plur. from the fem. שׁואה, ver. 8.

[n] עָצוּם, "numerous," as in Gen. xviii. 18, Deut. ix. 14.

[o] שֶׁקֶר, "falsely," *i.e.* without any just cause, clearly parallel to חִנָּם, which follows.

[p] רִגְעֵי א׳, adj., as from רָגֵעַ, not found elsewhere, but nouns from the same root occur Is. xxviii. 12, Jer. vi. 16.

[q] אֲדֹנָי, with the Kametz as in xvi. 2, though there the sense does not absolutely require "*my* Lord." According to the Massoreth ואדני occurs three times.

[r] נפשׁנו, lit. "It is our pleasure, our desire." Comp. אֹיְבַי בְּנֶפֶשׁ, xvii. 9.

PSALM 36

THIS Psalm is not so distinct in its features that we can assign it to any particular occasion in the life of David, or associate it with any definite period of Jewish history. It has, as De Wette has remarked, some points of resemblance with xii. and xiv., but there is no reason to conclude, as he does, that the wicked who are here described are heathen oppressors.

The Psalm opens with a striking picture of what a wicked man is, who abandons himself, without check or remorse, to the inspirations of his own evil heart. Ver. 1—4.

Next, as if oppressed and terrified with the picture which he has drawn of secure and thoughtful wickedness, the holy Psalmist turns with a quick revulsion of feeling to Him whose Love and Truth are at all times a sure defence. Here he pours out all the fulness of his heart. Words seem to fail him as there rise before him, in all their length and breadth, the loving-kindness, the faithfulness, the righteousness of Jehovah. Ver. 5—9.

Lastly, with his heart full of what God is, he prays that God would show His loving-kindness and His righteousness to those who, like himself, were upright in heart, and would defeat the designs of the wicked. He concludes with the confident acknowledgment that his prayer had been heard. Ver. 10—12.

[FOR THE PRECENTOR. (A PSALM) OF THE SERVANT OF JEHOVAH, OF DAVID.]

1 THE wicked hath an oracle of transgression in his heart,[a]
There is no fear of God before his eyes.
2 For He flattereth him in his eyes,
To find out his iniquity, (and) to hate (it).[b]
3 The words of his mouth are wickedness and deceit;
He hath left off to behave himself wisely to do good.

1. IN HIS HEART. The evidence of the older Versions (with the exception of the Chald. and Symm.) is in favour of this reading. Transgression is personified, and is represented as uttering its counsels to the wicked man, and finding the same ready obedience in his heart, as the voice of God Himself in that of the good man. (The word נְאֻם, "utterance" or "oracle," is everywhere else used of a *Divine* utterance.) Hence there is no fear of God before his eyes; nay, so blinded is he by his own evil heart, that he thinks God to be verily such an one as himself. In his eyes, *i.e.* in his opinion or belief, God flatters him or deals smoothly with him, with respect to finding out his iniquity, so as to punish it, and show His abhorrence of it. Such seems to be the general scope of the passage, but its interpretation is very doubtful. See a full discussion in the Critical Note.

Ver. 1—4 describe generally the character of the ungodly: first, the sin of his heart (ver. 1, 2); then the sin of his lips (ver. 3); lastly, the sin of his hands, the evil schemes which he devises and executes (ver. 4): thought, word, and deed, as in xvii. 3, 4.

As there is a climax in the whole description of the evil man, so especially is there a progress from bad to worse in ver. 3, 4. (1) He hath *left off* to do good; (2) on his bed he *meditates* evil (iv. 4, Micah ii. 1);

4 Wickedness doth he devise upon his bed,
He setteth himself in a way that is not good,
He abhorreth not evil.

5 O Jehovah, high as the heavens is Thy loving-kindness,
Thy faithfulness (reacheth) unto the clouds:
6 Thy righteousness is like the mountains of God,
Thy judgements are a great deep.
Man and beast dost Thou preserve, O Jehovah.

(3) he resolutely *sets himself* to do evil; (4) his very conscience is hardened, so that he does evil without repugnance or misgiving.

4. UPON HIS BED. "Nocte cum maxime scilicet vacet animus, tempus est, ut ad se homo redeat et meliora cogitet, si etiam toto die male vixisset.'—*Rosenmüller*. And Calvin remarks: "Reprobos consilia male agendi intus coquere dicit, atque ita quamvis nulla se illecebra objiciat, nullum eos incitet malum exemplum, sibi ipsis esse scelerum autores ac magistros absque alieno impulsu."

HE ABHORRETH NOT, *i.e.* is far enough from rejecting any instrument, however sinful, for attaining his purposes.

5—9. The transition from this description of the wicked to the praise of God's goodness and faithfulness, is certainly very abrupt; and we can feel no surprise that Hupfeld should be inclined to doubt an original connection between the two portions of the Psalm. Yet may we not account for the abruptness here, by a very natural recoil of feeling? No good man can ever delight to pourtray the workings of a heart alienated from God. If the evil he sees around him force him for a time to trace it to its hidden source, or watch its outward development, with the more joy and thankfulness will he find refuge (see ver. 7) from its hideous shadow in the faithfulness and goodness of God.

5. Words seem to fail him when he would speak of the loving-kindness, the faithfulness, the righteousness of God. (See the same attributes associated in like manner in xxiii. 4, 5, and there also in connection with God's providential care of His creatures.) The universe itself is too little to set forth their greatness. (Comp. ciii. 11; Eph. iii. 18.)

HIGH AS, lit. "in the heavens."

6. MOUNTAINS OF GOD (so "cedars of God," lxxx. 10 [11]) . . . . A GREAT DEEP (cf. Rom. xi. 33, ὡς ἀνεξερεύνητα τὰ κρίματα αὐτοῦ): —the mightiest things in creation, whether in the height above, or in the depth beneath. Not, however, are "mountains of God" to be considered as only = "highest mountains;" but, like "the trees of Jehovah," civ. 16, which are explained as "the cedars of Lebanon which He hath planted" (comp. Numb. xxiv. 6); and "the river of God," lxv. 9 [10], *i.e.* the rain which He sends down upon earth; so here the mountains are spoken of as the work of His hand. So too in Gen. xiii. 10, "the garden of Jehovah" is not merely "a very fair garden," but the garden of Eden which He Himself planted. The phrases, "to God," "to Jehovah" (לֵאלֹהִים, לַיהוָֹה), are different, as in these the preposition "to" = "in the sight of," or "before;" and so in the New Testament ἀστεῖος τῷ Θεῷ, Acts vii. 20, is "fair before God," not "divinely fair," or "exceeding fair."

7 How precious is Thy loving-kindness, O God!
And the children of men in the shadow of Thy wings find refuge;
8 They are abundantly satisfied with the fatness of Thy house,
And Thou makest them drink of the brook of Thy pleasures;
9 For with Thee is the Fountain of Life;
In Thy Light do we see Light.
10 O continue Thy loving-kindness unto them that know Thee,
And Thy righteousness to the upright in heart.
11 Let not the foot of pride come against me,
Neither let the hand of the wicked drive me away.

7. The remembrance of God's goodness, faithfulness, and righteousness, and of His care both of man and beast, makes the singer to burst forth in holy ecstasy: "How precious is Thy loving-kindness, O God." This preciousness (comp. cxxxix. 17) is then further enlarged upon. God is viewed as the gracious Host who provides for all who come to His house and His table. See the same figure, xxiii. 5, xxxiv. 8 [9]. Here the *loving-kindness* of God is the great subject of praise, because in this His *faithfulness* (in fulfilling His promises) and His *righteousness* manifested in rewarding the righteous (as well as in the punishment of the wicked) may be included. In the same way when St. John says, "God is Love," it is because Love in fact embraces and implies all other of the Divine attributes.

CHILDREN OF MEN, purposely the most general expression that could be employed, every one who feels his weakness and his sinfulness, and with that feeling seeks refuge in God.

SHADOW OF THY WINGS. See on xvii. 8.

8. FATNESS OF THY HOUSE, *i.e.* generally the rich provision made (comp. Job xxxvi. 16, and Ps. xxiii. 5). If there is an allusion to the Temple, as Hupfeld thinks, "fatness" would = "fat sacrifices," and men would be regarded as the priests in the house, after the analogy of Jer. xxxi. 14.

9. These are some of the most wonderful words in the Old Testament. Their fulness of meaning no commentary can ever exhaust. They are, in fact, the kernel and the anticipation of much of the profoundest teaching of St. John.

THE FOUNTAIN OF LIFE, *i.e.* of all life, both animal and spiritual. God only has Life in Himself, Life underived, as our Lord says, John v. 29.

IN THY LIGHT. Comp. Dan. ii. 12, "The light dwelleth with Him;" and 1 John i. 5—7. Out of God all is darkness. The creature is darkness, our own hearts and consciences are darkness, our duties are darkness, our deeds are darkness (John iii. 19, 20), the very order and constitution of the world, yea the word of God itself, except as seen in His Light, is darkness.

10. LOVING-KINDNESS. For the third time he dwells on this attribute of God, and again associates it, as in ver. 5, 6, with the "righteousness" of God.

11. DRIVE ME AWAY, lit. "make

12 There have the workers of iniquity fallen ;
They are thrust down, and are not able to rise.

me to wander," *sc.* from the temple and the land; see 1 Kings xxi. 8.

12. THERE, pointing as it were to the scene. The field on which God's righteous judgement has been manifested in the overthrow of the wicked is before his eyes. "David quasi e sublimi fidei specula procul aspicit eorum interitum, nec minus secure de eo pronuntiat, quam si prope instaret."—*Calvin.*

[a] לִבִּי, "*my* heart." So the text at present stands in the Hebrew, and in accordance with this reading two renderings have been usual of the former part of the verse: (1) "That which Transgression saith to the wicked is within my heart, *i.e.* forms the subject of my present meditation." So apparently the Chald., and so Calv., Ros., Delitzsch, and others. The objection to this is, that the revelation which Transgression is thus supposed to make to the wicked does not follow after all, but only a description of that transgression and its effects. (2) "An utterance concerning the transgression of the wicked is within my heart." So Symm., φησὶ περὶ ἀσυνθεσίας τοῦ ἀσεβοῦς ἔνδοθεν ἡ καρδία μου. So Ges., De Wette, Stier, and others. If the last rendering could be defended by the usage of נְאֻם in other passages, it would at once remove all difficulty. But נְאֻם, *effatum*, *oraculum*, is never followed by the object or subject of the utterance, but always by the author or person *from* whom the utterance proceeds. It would be permitted therefore by usage to say, "The utterance of Transgression" (*i.e.* which Transgression makes, Transgression being personified), but it would not be permitted by usage to say: "An utterance concerning transgression, &c."

There can be very little doubt that we ought to read לִבּוֹ, instead of לִבִּי, a reading which is supported by the LXX., Vulg., Syr., Arab., and Jerome, and which is found even in some MSS. Then the rendering will be, "The wicked hath an oracle of transgression within his heart, *i.e.* his wickedness is to him a source of evil counsel, evil designs," &c. The only objection to this is the antachrestic use of נְאֻם, which everywhere else is spoken of a Divine utterance, and this may be balanced against the difficulty above mentioned of rendering, "A saying concerning transgression," as in either case we have an unusual mode of expression, so that the rendering, "That which God saith concerning the transgression of the wicked is within my heart," may perhaps, after all, be defensible.

It has also been suggested to take נְאֻם by itself as a description, or title, of the Psalm: "A Divine oracle. The transgression of the wicked is in my heart," *i.e.* "I am pondering it, that I may tell of it to others."

[b] This second verse is still more perplexing than the first; for first, what is the subject of הֶחֱלִיק? Is it transgression which flatters the sinner, or is it the sinner who flatters himself in his own eyes, or who deals smoothly, hypocritically towards God, in *His* sight? or is it God, who in his (the sinner's) eyes, *i.e.* in his opinion, flatters, or deals gently

with him? And next, what is the meaning of לִמְצֹא עֲוֺנוֹ, and of the subordinated infinitive לִשְׂנֹא? Now in the first place, בְּעֵינָיו in this clause ought to correspond with בְּעֵינָיו above; "in his eyes," *i.e.* in the eyes of the sinner, according to his belief. (So in a passage, generally misunderstood, in the Proverbs, i. 17, "Surely in the eyes (in the opinion) of every bird, the net is spread in vain.") Next, the phrase לִמְצֹא ע׳ occurs elsewhere of the *punishment* of iniquity, Gen. xliv. 16, Hos. xii. 9. (Hence Ibn. Ezra has rendered, "He flattereth himself in his own eyes, till God find out his iniquity and hate it:" and our A. V. "till his iniquity be found to be hateful.") Rashi apparently takes פשׁע as the subject of החליק, "Transgression flatters him." Lastly, לִשְׂנֹא is evidently a merely subordinated infinitive, further describing למ׳ ע׳, as below, in like manner, "to be wise, to do good." There can be very little doubt, then, that if מצא ע׳ means "to find out, so as to punish sin," the subject of the verb הֶחֱלִיק must be אֱלֹהִים, "God hath dealt smoothly with him, as he thinks, with reference (לְ, as often) to finding out," &c.

Ewald and Stier, however, both take מצא ע׳ in the sense of "reaching, attaining to his wickedness," *i.e.* gaining the evil objects he has in view (and so Qimchi, who refers to 1 Sam. xx. 21, 36, where, however, the verb is not followed by עָוֹן). Ewald renders: "It flattereth him in his eyes, to accomplish his iniquity, to hate," *i.e.* so as to gratify his hatred. And similarly Gesen. "ut odium foveat:" but this, it seems to me, is to give too much prominence to the manifestly subordinate verb לִשְׂנֹא. On the whole, therefore, I am inclined to explain: For He (God) seems to deal smoothly with the sinner in his own opinion, so far as the punishment and hatred of his sin is concerned. So in the main Hofmann and Hupfeld, except that the last connects the second clause of the verse with the words, "There is no fear of God before his eyes," treating the first clause as parenthetical.

I subjoin the renderings of the Ancient Versions:

The Chaldee: "Wickedness saith to the sinner, in the midst of my heart, there is no fear of God before his eyes. For he flattereth him (ליה, not therefore "blanditur *sibi*," as in the Polyglot) in his eyes, to discover sins, to hate instruction." Syr.: "The transgressor meditates wickedness in his heart, because there is no fear of God before his eyes. Because it is hateful in his eyes to forsake his sins and to hate them." LXX.: "*φησὶν ὁ παράνομος τοῦ ἁμαρτάνειν ἐν ἑαυτῷ· οὐκ ἔστι φόβος Θεοῦ ἀπέναντι τῶν ὀφθαλμῶν αὐτοῦ. ὅτι ἐδόλωσεν ἐνώπιον αὐτοῦ τοῦ εὑρεῖν τὴν ἀνομίαν αὐτοῦ καὶ μισῆσαι.*" Jerome: "Dixit scelus impii in medio cordis ejus: Non est timor Dei ante oculos ejus. Quia dolose egit adversus eum in oculis suis: Ut inveniret iniquitatem ejus ad odiendum." Arab. (in the Par. and Lond. Polyglot): "He that opposeth the law saith that he will sin within himself, and there is no fear of God before his eyes, because he hath dealt treacherously in his sight, after he discovered his sin and hated it." Sym. *ὅτι ἐξολισθαίνειν τὰ περὶ αὐτοῦ δοκεῖ, τοῦ εὑρεθῆναι τὴν ἀδικίαν αὐτοῦ εἰς τὸ μισηθῆναι αὐτήν*, which is in favour of the interpretation I have given.

PSALM 37

A Psalm wherein the righteousness of God's providence is vindicated in His administration of the world. The Psalmist's own heart had no doubt at one time been shaken by the apparent successes and triumphs of the ungodly, for it is a common temptation to distrust God when we see "the ungodly in great prosperity." The advice which the Psalmist gives is "to wait," "to trust in the Lord," to look at the end, and to observe how even in this life God manifests His righteousness, in rewarding the godly and punishing the wicked. This sentiment is repeated in various forms, and with much beauty of expression. The Psalm has something of a proverbial character about it, owing no doubt in some measure to the fact that the writer chose to fetter himself by an acrostical arrangement: for this is one of the Alphabetical Psalms, like Psalms xxv. and xxxiv.

The structure of the Psalm is exceedingly regular. With few exceptions, the separate portions, as marked by the letters of the alphabet, consist of four members.

Tertullian calls the Psalm *providentiæ speculum:* Isidore, *potio contra murmur:* Luther, *vestis piorum cui adscriptum: Hic sanctorum patientia est.*

[(A PSALM) OF DAVID.]

1 א FRET not thyself because of the evil-doers,
Be not envious because of the workers of iniquity.
2 For they shall soon be cut down like the grass,[a]
And like the green herb shall they wither.
3 ב Trust thou in Jehovah, and do good:
Dwell in the land, and enjoy safety.[b]
4 Delight thyself also in Jehovah,
And He shall give thee the petitions of thy heart.

1. The whole verse is to be found almost word for word, Prov. xxiv. 19; the latter part of it also, Prov. iii. 31, xxiii. 17, xxiv. 1. Comp. lxxiii. 3. The phrase "workers of iniquity" differs in the Hebrew from the phrase commonly employed elsewhere, *e.g.* xxxvi. 12 [13].

3. Trust in God is the true antidote for the fretfulness and envy which are before forbidden.

DWELL IN THE LAND—for the promises to Israel, and Israel's glory as a nation, were bound up with the land.

4. DELIGHT THYSELF in Him, and so thou wilt choose and love

5 ג Cast thy way on Jehovah,
And trust in Him ; and He will bring (it) to pass.
6 Yea He will bring forth thy righteousness as the light,
And thy judgement as the noon-day.
7 ד Hold thee still for Jehovah, and hope in Him ;
Fret not thyself because of him who prospereth in his way,
Because of the man who bringeth wicked devices to pass.
8 ה Cease from anger and let go wrath ;
Fret not thyself, only to do evil.
9 For evil-doers shall be cut off ;
But they that wait on Jehovah, *they* shall possess the land.
10 ו Yea, yet but a little while and the wicked is not,
And thou shalt diligently consider his place and he is not (there).
11 But the meek shall possess the land.
And shall delight themselves in the abundance o peace.
12 ז The wicked deviseth evil against the righteous,
And gnashed upon him with his teeth.

that which He chooses and loves: therefore He will give thee thy heart's desires.

5. CAST, or ROLL. Cf. xxii. 8 [9], and St. Peter's πᾶσαν τὴν μέριμναν ὑμῶν ἐπιῤῥίψαντες ἐπ' αὐτόν, 1 Pet. v. 7.

6. HE WILL BRING FORTH, *sc.* like the sun going forth (יצא) in the morning. Cf. Jer. li. 10.

7. HOLD THEE STILL (so well rendered in our Prayer Book Vers.), lit. Be silent for or unto Him, *i.e.* with reference to Him, and His will (E.V. "Rest in ;" Gen. "Wait patiently upon)." A word expressive of that calm resignation which leaves itself absolutely in the hands of God. This hushed, bowed temper of spirit best befits us. Here is the best cure for dissatisfaction with the present, and for anxiety about the future, that we leave both in the hands of God. Here is our highest wisdom even for the life of our spirits, that we stay ourselves not upon outward acts or inward impulses, but on Him who worketh in us both to will and to do of His own good pleasure.

8 ONLY TO DO EVIL, *i.e.* nothing but evil can come of it. (So Calv. "fieri aliter non posse quin ad peccandum impellat.")

10. IS NOT (THERE) or, "is no more."

11. THE MEEK. See on ix. 12.

THE LAND. Cf. xxv. 13, and Matt. v. 5, where, however, the range is wider, "shall inherit *the earth.*"

13 The Lord laugheth at him,
For He hath seen that his day is coming.
14 ח The wicked have drawn the sword,
They have also bent their bow,
That they may cast down the afflicted and the poor,
That they may slay them that are upright in (their) way.
15 Their sword shall enter into their own heart,
And their bows shall be broken.
16 ט Better is a little that the righteous man hath,
Than the riches of many wicked.
17 For the arms of the wicked shall be broken,
But Jehovah upholdeth the righteous.
18 י Jehovah knoweth the days of the perfect,
And their inheritance shall be for ever.
19 They shall not be ashamed in the evil time,
And in the days of famine they shall be satisfied.
20 כ But the wicked shall perish,
And the enemies of Jehovah shall be as the glory of the pastures:
They consume—in smoke they consume away.
21 ל The wicked borroweth, and payeth not again;
But the righteous is gracious, and giveth.

13. LAUGHETH, cf. ii. 4.

HIS DAY, cf. cxxxvii. 7; Job xviii. 20; Jer. l. 27, 31; Obad. 12.

16. See a similar sentiment, Prov. xv. 16.

18. KNOWETH THE DAYS, *i.e.* watcheth over, careth for, lovingly orders all that befalls them. See the same use of the verb, i. 6, xxxi. 7 [8], compared with 15 [16], "My times are in Thy hand."

20. THE GLORY OF THE PASTURES or meadows (*not* of the flocks, cf. lxv. 13 [14], Is. xxx. 23), *i.e.* the grass and flowers.

IN SMOKE THEY CONSUME, &c. This is generally supposed to refer to the preceding figure, the grass being conceived of as cut down and heaped together, and set on fire. But this is not necessary: two *distinct* figures are employed, the first that of the glory of the grass fading away naturally; the next taken from objects destroyed by fire. From not observing this, probably came the other rendering, "like the fat of lambs," viz. which was consumed on the altars, and so ascended in smoke.

21, 22. The blessing and the curse of God, as seen in the different lots of the righteous and the wicked. The wicked, through God's curse resting on him, is reduced to poverty, so that he is compelled to borrow, and cannot pay; whereas, the righteous hath even abundance not only for his own wants, but for the wants of others. It is the

22 For they that are blessed of Him shall possess the land
And they that are cursed of Him shall be cut off.
23 מ From Jehovah is it that a man's goings are established,
So that He hath pleasure in his way.
24 Though he fall, he shall not be utterly cast down,
For Jehovah upholdeth his hand.
25 נ I have been young, and (now) am old ;
Yet have I not seen the righteous forsaken,
Nor his seed begging bread.
26 All the day long is he gracious and lendeth,
And his seed is blessed.
27 ס Depart from evil, and do good ;
So (shalt thou) dwell for evermore.
28 For Jehovah loveth judgement,
And forsaketh not His beloved.
[? ע] For ever [c] they are preserved ;
But the seed of the wicked is cut off.
29 The righteous shall possess the land,
And dwell therein for ever.
30 The mouth of the righteous uttereth wisdom,
And his tongue speaketh judgement.
31 The Law of his God is in his heart :
None of his steps shall slide.
32 צ The wicked lieth in wait for the righteous,
And seeketh (occasion) to slay him.

promise, Deut. xv. 6, xxviii. 12, 44, turned into a proverb.

23. He that would walk securely, and so as to please the Lord, must trust in the Lord to guide him. (Cf. Prov. xx. 24, and xvi. 9.) The sentiment is put in a general form, but the righteous man, as he appears in the Psalm ("der Mann wie er sein soll"), is meant, as is clear from the next verse. The second clause is ambiguous. It may be "And he the man hath pleasure in His (God's) way."

25. On this Bakius observes: "Promissiones corporales intelligendæ sunt cum exceptione crucis et castigationis." But it should be remembered that temporal rewards were distinctly held out to the Old Testament saint, and he accepted them as a proof of God's righteous dealing even in this world.

26. See above, ver. 21, and comp. cxii. 5. The promise in Deut., quoted in the note on ver. 21, no doubt it was which made this characteristic of *lending* so prominent.

30. UTTERETH, or "talketh of," lit. "meditateth." The word is used both of thought and utterance. See note on i. 2.

31. The Law within is the guiding principle which directs his steps.

33 Jehovah will not leave him in his hand,
Nor condemn him when he is judged.
34 ק Wait on Jehovah and keep His way,
So shall He exalt thee to possess the land :
When the wicked are cut off thou shalt see (it).
35 ר I have seen a wicked man full of violence,
And spreading himself like a green tree in its native soil ;
36 Yet he passed away, and lo he was not :
And I sought him, but he could not be found.
37 ש Observe the perfect (man), and behold the upright,
That the man of peace hath a posterity ;
38 But the transgressors are destroyed together ;
The posterity of the wicked is cut off.
39 ת The salvation also of the righteous is of Jehovah,
Their fortress in the time of trouble.
40 And Jehovah helpeth them and rescueth them,
He rescueth them from the wicked, and saveth them,
Because they have found refuge in Him.

33. Men may condemn, but God acquits. Here, as in 1 Cor. iv. 3, the righteous judgement of the Great Judge is opposed to the ἀνακρίνειν of human judgement (ἡμέρα). So Tertullian : "Si condemnamur a mundo, absolvimur a Deo."

34. WAIT ON JEHOVAH. Keep thine eye fixed on Him (cf. ἀποβλέπειν, Heb. xii. 2) despite the prosperity of the wicked, and the persecutions which thou sufferest.

THOU SHALT SEE IT, or thou shalt look upon it with satisfaction.

35. FULL OF VIOLENCE or inspiring terror. The adjective occurs in Jer. xx. 11, as an epithet of God.

A TREE IN ITS NATIVE SOIL (one word in Hebrew, well rendered by Jerome, *indigenam*), one that has never been transplanted or disturbed, that has therefore struck its roots deep, and shot out with luxuriant strength.

36. HE PASSED. Others note LXX. render "I passed." Or the third person may be used impersonally "one passed by."

37. HATH A POSTERITY. As opposed to the wicked in the next clause, whose posterity is cut off. Then it would be = "Thou shalt see thy children's children and peace upon Israel." Others render "a residue;" and others understand by the word "the future," the end that yet awaits him. Cf. Prov. xxiv. 14, and in ver. 19 of the same chapter, a quotation from ver. 1 of this Psalm. Cf. Jer. xxix. 11.

40. He *delivereth* them ; because they *trust* in Him. The whole lesson of the Psalm lies in these words.

[a] יִמָּלוּ, fut. Qal of מָלַל = אמל, in the sense, "they wither away," the form being pausal for יִמְּלוּ, as Job xxiv. 24. (Ges. § 67.) But it may perhaps be fut. Niph. for יִמַּלוּ, נמל.

[b] רְעֵה אֱמוּנָה. These words have been very variously rendered. The Chald. has חֲסַן בְּהֵימָנוּתָא, *fortis esto in fide.* LXX., ποιμανθήσῃ ἐπὶ τῷ πλούτῳ αὐτῆς. So too the Vulg., *pasceris in divitiis ejus.* Symm., ποιμαίνου διηνεκῶς. But Jerome, *pascere fide.* Syr., ܘܒܥܝ ܗܝܡܢܘܬܐ, *quære fidem.* Aq., νέμου πίστιν. Luther, "nähre dich redlich." Diodati, "vi pasturerai in confidanza." Zunz and Delitzsch, "pflege Treue." Ewald, "geniessend Sicherheit." The Hebrew, indeed, is capable of several interpretations, both the verb and the noun admitting of different renderings: (1) Cherish confidence (*sc.* in God), cf. Hab. ii. 4; and so Maurer explains, *sta in fide Jovæ.* (2) Cherish or delight in truth and faithfulness, &c. towards men (so Gesen., *delectare veritate*). (3) Enjoy, or delight in, security, אֱמוּנָה being taken in the same sense as in Is. xxxiii. 6. The verb רעה, with accus. of pers. "to be a friend of," Prov. xii. 20, with accus. of thing, "to have pleasure in," Prov. xv. 14. Or (4) if רעה is taken abs. in the sense of feeding, we must render: "Feed in security" (Horsley), or "feed, *i.e.* live, in faith" (Hammond); for the constr. see Is. xxx. 23.

The second member of this verse, though the words are imperat., has something of a future colouring, = Trust in Jehovah and do good, *so shalt* thou dwell in the land and enjoy safety. For "dwelling in the land" is everywhere *promised* as a special blessing, xxv. 13, Deut. xxxiii. 28, &c. Comp. vers. 9, 11, 22, 29, 34, of this Psalm. All the Ancient Versions, it is true, take this clause, "dwell in the land," as a proper imperative, but that the imperative in certain cases may stand for the future is certain (Ges. § 127). It depends, however, on the meaning we give to רְעֵה א׳, whether we take these as strict imperatives, or as imperatives with a future meaning. If we render "cherish faithfulness," then, as this is clearly an exhortation, so must the preceding imperative be; "dwell in the land," *i.e.* regard it as a duty, occupy there the position in which God has placed you as a member of the Theocracy, and be thankful that He has so placed you, and accordingly "cherish faithfulness, or confidence, in Him."

[c] Up to this point the alphabetical arrangement has been strictly preserved. Here, apparently, the ע has dropped out. The structure of the Psalm is, on the whole, so regular, that there can be no doubt that the ע strophe should begin with the second distich of this verse. We should then have the ס and the ע strophes, each consisting of a tetrastich. Hence Ewald supposes the words עֹשֵׂי טוֹב to have dropped out. Others would supply עַוָּלִים, which occurs several times in Job (Hitz. עָרִיצִים), and read נִשְׁמָדוּ instead of נִשְׁמָרוּ, which finds some support in the LXX., ἄνομοι δὲ (B. ἄμωμοι) ἐκδιωχθήσονται, καὶ σπέρμα ἀσεβῶν ἐξολοθρευθήσεται, and Symm.

ἄνομοι ἐξαρθήσονται. But עֲוִילִים or עֲוָלִים is not a word which occurs in the Psalms, and עָרִיצִים is too special a word for the context. Delitzsch, I believe, is right in suggesting that the ל in לְעוֹלָם goes for nothing, and that the ע of עולם is the acrostic letter, just as in ver. 39 the ת strophe begins with וּתְשׁוּעַת, where the ו goes for nothing.

PSALM 38

THIS Psalm tells the story of a bitter suffering. The suffering is both in body and in mind. The body is wasted by a cruel and loathsome disease, and the mind is full of anguish, arising partly from a deep sense of sin, and partly from the fear of relentless, and now rejoicing enemies. Body and mind, in such circumstances act and react upon one another. Mental anguish impairs the strength of the body; and bodily suffering and weakness make us less able to face with steady and resolute courage the horrors which crowd upon the mind.

To add to his distress, the sufferer is deserted even of his friends. They to whose kind offices he might naturally have looked at such a time, they who had been his friends in his health and prosperity, and who might now have watched by his sick bed, and spoken words of comfort to him in his sorrow, turned coldly away and left him alone with his grief. A burning fever consumed him (ver. 7), his heart beat hotly, his eyes failed him, the bitter remembrance of his sin was with him : there was the consciousness and the fear of God's displeasure, and as if this were not enough, there was, besides all this, the utter loneliness, never so hard to bear as in such a season of bodily and mental prostration; the weary couch never so weary as when no hand is there to smooth it; the pain of the disease far more acutely felt, because none offered sympathy; the terrors of conscience and of the imagination aggravated, because they had to be endured in solitude. Suffering seems here to have reached its height. But out of the very midst of the furnace the sufferer can say, "Lord, before Thee is all my desire—in Thee, O Jehovah, have I hoped;" can cry with all the earnestness of a faith purified by affliction, "Leave me not, be not far from me, O Lord, my Salvation."

The Psalm may be said to consist of three principal parts, each of which opens with an address to God. Each of these contains an appeal to God's mercy—each rests it on different grounds.

The first of these is based on the *greatness* of the suffering. Ver. 1—8.

The second on the *patience* of the sufferer, as well as on the suffering. Ver. 9—14.

The third on the fear lest, through his fate, wicked men should have an occasion of triumph. Ver. 15—22.

[A PSALM OF DAVID. TO BRING TO REMEMBRANCE.[a]]

1 O JEHOVAH, in Thy wrath [b] rebuke me not,
Neither in Thy hot displeasure chasten me.
2 For Thine arrows stick fast [c] in me,
And Thy hand presseth upon me.
3 There is no soundness in my flesh because of Thine indignation;
There is no health in my bones because of my sin.
4 For mine iniquities have passed over my head;
Like a heavy burden, they are too heavy for me.
5 My wounds stink, they are corrupt,
Because of my foolishness.

1. See note on vi. 1, where very nearly the same words occur. Most of what has been said on that Psalm is applicable here, and need not be repeated. Bakius interprets: "Corripe sane per legem, castiga per crucem, millies promerui, negare non possum; sed castiga, quæso, me ex amore ut pater, non ex furore et fervore ut judex; ne punias justitiæ rigore, sed misericordiæ dulcore."

2. There is here, and in what follows, as Calvin observes, a tacit appeal to God's promises. Why is it that the saint of God thus sets forth all his sufferings, but because he knows that his God will not lay on him a punishment heavier than he can bear? It is not therefore merely as a complaint, but as an appeal to the mercy of God, that he tells all his woe. There is a yet further appeal in the recognition of God's hand. "*Thine* arrows . . . . *Thy* hand." It is this conviction that God has inflicted the chastisement, that leads him to seek the remedy from the same source.

PRESSETH UPON ME, lit. hath lighted upon me.

3. NO SOUNDNESS. Comp. Is. i. 6.

NO HEALTH, or "wholeness." Such is the proper and original meaning of the word שָׁלוֹם (*shālōm*), *integritas*, "peace" being the derived meaning, peace only there properly existing, where all is *complete* and entire, nothing wanting.

4. HAVE PASSED. A metaphor, as often, from waves passing over the head. Comp. xviii. 16 [17], lxix. 2 [3], 15 [16].

5. FOOLISHNESS. His sin, as seen now in its true light, showing itself to be folly, for all sin is self-destruction. "Hoc sensu," says Calvin, "David de stultitia sua loquitur: ac si diceret se fuisse mente alienatum, et instar pecudis abreptum, et circumactum bruto impetu, dum neg-

6 I am bent, I am bowed down sore,
All the day long have I gone mourning ;
7 For my loins are full of burning,
And there is no soundness in my flesh.
8 I am benumbed and sore broken,
I have roared by reason of the unrest of my heart.
9 Lord, before Thee is all my desire,
And my deep sighing is not hid from Thee.
10 My heart throbbeth,[d] my strength hath failed me,
And the light of mine eyes—even that [e] is gone from me.
11 My friends and my companions stand aloof from my plague,
And my kinsmen have stood afar off.
12 They also that seek after my soul, lay snares,
And they that strive to do me evil speak mischievous things,
And meditate deceits all the day long.

lecto Deo suas cupiditates secutus est." This confession of his sin is, in fact, at the same time, a confession of the justice of his punishment.

WOUNDS as of stripes. ARE CORRUPT or "putrefied."

6. I AM BENT, properly, as writhing with pain, as Is. xxi. 3.

MOURNING, or rather, "as a mourner." See on xxxv. 14.

8. I AM BENUMBED, lit. I have become deadly cold, cold as a corpse; possibly with reference to the burning inflammation in the previous verse, as marking the alternations in the fever-fit.

9. The one gleam of comfort and refreshment in his misery; the one bright ray which lights up the darkness; the one thought which sustains him, that he may "unburden himself of all his griefs in the bosom of God." We have but to read the first fourteen verses, without this verse, to see how much blacker the night of suffering grows.

11. Up to this point he has spoken of his suffering as arising from his own state both of body and mind. He describes now its aggravation from the conduct of others; first of friends who deserted him, and next of enemies who plotted against him. And this aggravation of his misery is again a fresh argument with God, —an argument borrowed, as Calvin reminds us, from the word of God, and one intended for our use. He remarks : "Si nos deficiunt omnia mundi præsidia, alii nos fraudant justis officiis, alii nihil quam cædem nostram spirant ; veniat nobis in mentem, non frustra hoc inter precandum Deo proponi, cujus proprium est succurrere miseris, perfide desertos ac proditos in suam tutelam suscipere, compescere improbos," &c.

MY PLAGUE, lit. "my blow," a word always used of punishment as inflicted by God.

12. MISCHIEVOUS THINGS, lit. "a yawning gulf of destruction," as

13 But as for me, as a deaf man, I could not hear,
And (I was) as a dumb man that openeth not his mouth.
14 Yea, I was as a man that heareth not,
And (as one) in whose mouth are no replies.
15 For in Thee, O Jehovah, have I hoped;
Thou wilt answer (for me), O Lord my God.
16 For I said,—Lest they rejoice over me,
(Lest)[f] when my foot slippeth, they magnify themselves against me;
17 For as for me, I am ready to halt,
And my pain is ever before me;
18 For I must confess my iniquity,
I am in heaviness because of my sin;

though they would swallow me up. See on v. 9, Critical Note.

14. NO REPLIES, not here "reproofs" or "rebukes," but answers, in self-vindication, to the calumnies of his enemies. "Arguments," as the word is rendered in the A.V. of Job xxiii. 4.

Calvin sees two reasons for this comparison of himself to a dumb man: first, that he was *compelled* by the injustice of his enemies to be silent; they would not suffer him to speak: and next, his own patient submission to the will of God. But I think the last only is prominent here. It was not that David could not, but that he would not, answer. Comp. Rom. xii. 19. In this, he was the type of a greater Sufferer in a more august agony (Is. liii. 7; 1 Pet. ii. 23).

16. I SAID, *i.e.* within myself.

LEST, with the usual ellipsis of some verb, such as "I fear," but again addressed as an argument to God; the argument being, that His honour is concerned in upholding His servant, lest the wicked should triumph. Therefore, too, he leaves it to God to answer, lest by answering himself he should give occasion to the enemy to blaspheme.

17. PAIN or "suffering," arising not only from the outward persecution, but also from the inward sense of sin, or the "pain" may refer to the "plague" in ver. 11.

18. FOR. The conjunction recurs here for the fourth time in verses 15—18. But it is hardly used in so loose a manner as Hupfeld and others suppose. It seems in each case to supply a link in the train of thought. In ver. 15 it gives the reason why David made no reply to his enemies, *for* God, he felt, would answer for him. In ver. 16 it gives the reason why he would have God answer—*for* he feared that if he took the matter into his own hand, his enemies would have occasion to triumph. In ver. 17 the *for* gives a further reason why this was probable, viz., his own weakness; and in ver. 18, the reason for the weakness, with another *for*, is found in his sin which he has to confess, whilst, on the other hand (ver. 19), his enemies are full of strength, and numerous as they are strong. This, I believe, is the connection between the different verses.

I AM IN HEAVINESS, LXX. μεριμνήσω, "I will be *careful*" or "anxious." Ges. *solicitus.*

19 And mine enemies are vigorous [g] (and) strong,
And they are many that hate me without cause;
20 And requiting evil for good,
They withstand me because I follow [h] that which is good.
21 Leave me not, O Jehovah;
My God be not far from me.
22 Haste (Thee) to help me,
O Lord, my Salvation,

19. VIGOROUS, lit. "alive," in full lusty life, as opposed to the state of quasi-death in which the Psalmist is.

21, 22. With this conclusion of the Psalm compare the similar expressions, xxii. 11 [12], 19 [20], xxxv. 22, xl. 13 [14], &c.

[a] לְהַזְכִּיר, found also in the superscription of Psalm lxx., "to bring to remembrance," *i.e.* either as a memorial of suffering and deliverance, or, "to bring me into remembrance *with God.*" So the Chald., "to bring a good remembrance upon man;" Rashi, "to remind the sufferer to pray to God;" similarly, Ges., Hengst. The last explains it of complaints and prayers, as opposed to praises and thanksgivings, with reference to 1 Chron. xvi. 4. There is perhaps an allusion to the אַזְכָּרָה (see xx. 4, and Is. lxvi. 3), or offering of incense, the smoke of which went up for a memorial before God.

[b] קֶצֶף is wrath, as *an outburst of passion;* חֵמָה, as *a burning glow;* זַעַם, as *a foaming up.*

[c] נִחֲתוּ, "have sunk down, entered deep." Niph. of the form נחת, which immediately follows in the Qal, unless, indeed, this is only a false punctuation for נָחֲתוּ, used intransitively.

[d] סְחַרְחַר, Pealal, as descriptive of the rapid pulsations of the heart in a state of fever: but according to Hupfeld the form is not intensive, but diminutive, the pulsations being *less* in proportion to their rapidity.

[e] גַּם הֵם. This is not a fresh nominative, but is in apposition with עֵינַי, as the pronoun sometimes is with a *casus obliquus,* and therefore a genitive = *et ipsorum,* "The light of my eyes, even of them, I say, is not with me." Gesen. § 121, 3. Vulg. *et lumen oculorum meorum, et ipsum.*

[f] On the construction of פֶּן, as covering both the verbs in this verse, see note [a], on xxviii. 1.

[g] חַיִּים. For this Houbigant would read חִנָּם, and he is followed by Hupfeld, Ewald, and others. No doubt this answers to שֶׁקֶר in the next clause, and is a common form of expression. But the other reading is at least as old as the LXX., *οἱ δὲ ἐχθροί μου ζῶσι καὶ κεκραταίωνται ὑπὲρ ἐμέ.*

[h] רדופי. The Q'rî is רָדְפִי, as xxvi. 2, צָרְפָה instead of צְרוֹפָה. (Comp. the future form, Is. xviii. 4.) But the K'thîbh might stand here רָדוֹפִי, as the last word but one has sometimes the pausal form, when the last word is a monosyllable (Deut. xxxii. 37), or has the tone on the penultimate (Josh. xiii. 9).

PSALM 39

"THE most beautiful," says Ewald, "of all elegies in the Psalter." It is the sorrowful complaint of a heart, not yet subdued to a perfect resignation, but jealous with a godly jealousy, lest it should bring dishonour upon its God, and longing for light from Heaven to scatter its doubts. The holy singer had long pent up his feelings; and though busy thoughts were stirring within him, he would not give them utterance. He could not bare his bosom to the rude gaze of an unsympathising world. And he feared lest, while telling his perplexities, some word might drop from his lips which would give the wicked an occasion to speak evil against his God. (This feeling is one, the expression of which we have already had in the preceding Psalm.) And when at last, unable to repress his strong emotion, he speaks, it is to God and not to man. It is as one who feels how hopeless the problem of life is, except as seen in the light of God. It is with the deep conviction of personal frailty (ver. 6) and sinfulness (ver. 9), as well as of the frailty and sinfulness of all men. It is with the touching sadness of one who cannot be comforted. And yet the weeping eye is raised to heaven, and amidst all his grief and perplexity, notwithstanding all that is so dark and cheerless in the world, pilgrim and stranger as he is, the Psalmist can still say, "My hope is in Thee." Ver. 7.

The Psalm consists properly of two parts:—

I. A preface descriptive of the circumstances under which it was composed. Ver. 1—3.

II. The expression of the Psalmist's feelings at the time. Ver. 4—13.

This latter part, however, may be again subdivided into three sections, the first two of which close with the refrain and the Selah.

(1) A prayer to be taught rightly concerning the vanity of life. Ver. 4, 5.

(2) A confession of that vanity—a cleaving to God, and an acknowledgement that sin deserves chastisement. Ver. 6—11.

(3) A further prayer that God would hear him, because he is but a stranger, and his days few upon earth. Ver. 12, 13.

[FOR THE PRECENTOR. FOR JEDUTHUN.[a] A PSALM OF DAVID.]

1 I SAID, Let me keep (watch over) my ways,
That I sin not with my tongue:
Let me keep a bridle upon my mouth,
While the wicked is yet before me.
2 I remained dumb in silence;
I held my peace, and had no comfort,[b]
And my sorrow was stirred.
3 My heart was hot within me;
While I was musing a fire kindled;
(Then) spake I with my tongue:
4 O Jehovah, make me to know mine end,
And the measure of my days what it is,
Let me know how frail[c] I am.

1. I SAID, *i.e.* I thought, I formed this resolution. (Comp. xxxviii. 16 [17].) And the resolution was not to sin with his tongue. He feared lest his complaint should be misinterpreted as murmuring against God. But the sadness of his heart prevails against his resolution; the more the feeling was checked the more hotly it burned (comp. Jer. xx. 9), till at last it could be restrained no longer.

Mozley (*Sermons*, p. 256, 1st ed.) understands this of the determination of the Psalmist to repress his judgement concerning the ungodly. "He had deep thoughts about the world, but they must not be uttered." . . . "He repressed himself; and all repression is difficult and grievous when a man is full of some truth. But he saw that the condition of things here was such that it would not admit of the unqualified divulgement of such truth as this." And he proceeds to remark on the great "strength not only of self-control, but of actual feeling and passion," shown in such a temper of mind. But however true these remarks may be in themselves, this can hardly be the meaning of the Psalmist. He does not repress his judgement upon the wicked, but fears to utter what they will misunderstand, as looking like complaints of God.

4. Herder supposes that the words which the Psalmist "spake with his tongue" are not given, but that, instead of this, he turns to God with the prayer to be taught resignation. Delitzsch takes the same view. But this I am persuaded is not the most natural interpretation. The words that he "spake with his tongue" are those which follow to the end of the Psalm. The introduction is merely the record of that inward struggle out of which the Psalm itself arose. And the words that he does speak are directed to God in prayer for teaching, not to man in complaints.

But in what relation does the prayer which follows stand to the perplexity which gave birth to it? Why does he ask, MAKE ME KNOW MINE END? It is not (as Hengst. supposes) an expression of impatience, "I am weary of this suffer-

5 Behold, Thou hast made my days as hand-breadths,
And my life-time is as nothing before Thee:
Surely every man, at his best estate, is nothing but a breath. [Selah.]

6 Surely as a shadow doth a man walk to and fro;
Surely for a breath are they disquieted:
He heapeth up (treasures), and knoweth not who shall gather them.
7 And now what have I waited for, O Lord?
My hope is in Thee.

ing: tell me when my life shall end, and so my suffering end;" nor is it an expostulation with God (as Qimchi and Calv.), as if he would say, "See how short my life is; is such a life long enough for all Thou layest upon me?" Such interpretations are at variance with the tone of sad resignation which breathes through the Psalm. It is rather this: "Make me rightly to know and estimate the shortness and uncertainty of human life, that so, instead of suffering myself to be perplexed with all that I see around me, I may cast myself the more entirely upon Thee," as indeed follows, "And now, Lord, what wait I for?" The prayer in xc. 12 is somewhat similar, though it stands there in a different connection.

5. LIFE-TIME. On this word see xvii. 14, note [e].

AT HIS BEST ESTATE, lit. "standing fast," *i.e.* however firmly established he may be.

A BREATH. Such is the literal meaning of the word "a mere vapour" (Jam. iv. 14). The same word occurs Prov. xxi. 6, "a vanity tossed to and fro," E.V., or perhaps rather "a breath that is driven away." In xc. 9, a different word is used; see note there.

6. With this verse, as is evident both from the refrain at the end of the last, and the Selah, a new strophe or division of the Psalm begins. Hence Delitzsch divides wrongly when he makes this verse close a strophe. Nothing is more usual than the resumption, in a fresh strophe, of a sentiment which has occurred before.

AS A SHADOW. The preposition is what is called the *Beth essentiæ*, which serves to introduce the predicate. See on xxxv. note [b], xxxvii. 20.

WALK TO AND FRO, or "come and go," *va e viene*, as Diodati, with an exact appreciation of the Hebrew, renders it.

ARE THEY DISQUIETED, lit. "do they make a noise, or commotion." All the fret and stir, all the eager clamour and rivalry of men, as they elbow and jostle one another to obtain wealth and rank, and the enjoyments of life, are but a breath. Comp. Jam. iv. 13, 14, where, after describing the busy scene, the buyers and sellers thronging the market-place, and full of the thought of their trade and of their speculations for the year, he solemnly asks, "For what is your life? For it is a vapour (ἀτμίς) which appeareth for a little while, and then vanisheth away."

7. AND NOW, turning away, as it were, with a sense of relief from the sad contemplation of man's fleeting, transitory life, to fix the eye of his heart on Him who abideth for ever. We seem almost to hear the deep sigh with which the words are uttered. It is remarkable that even

8 From all my transgressions deliver me;
Make me not a reproach of the fool.
9 I was dumb,—I could not open my mouth;
Because Thou didst it.
10 Turn aside Thy stroke from me,
I am (even) consumed by the blow of Thine hand.
11 (When) with rebukes for iniquity Thou hast chastened man,
Like the moth Thou makest his beauty to melt away.[d]
Surely every man is (but) a breath. [Selah.]

here it is on God Himself, not on a life to come, that his hope sustains itself.

"Although not expressly assured of a future life of blessedness, his faith, even in the midst of death, lays hold on Jehovah as the Living One, and as the God of the living. It is just this which, as Hengstenberg also here observes, is so heroic in the Old Testament faith, that in the midst of the riddles of the present, and in view of a future, losing itself in a night of gloom, it casts itself absolutely and without hesitation into the arms of God."—*Delitzsch.*

Calvin, who says that the Psalm consists partly of true prayers, and partly of hasty complaints, observes that it is here that David begins truly to pray.

8. FROM ALL MY TRANSGRESSIONS. He now strikes at once at the root of all his sufferings and all his perplexities. "Pergit in contextu piæ sanctæque precationis. Neque enim jam rapitur doloris impetu, ut cum Deo expostulet, sed reum se coram Deo suppliciter statuens, ad misericordiam ejus confugit: quia dum se a sceleribus eripi postulat, Deo justitiæ laudem adscribens, miseriæ quam sustinet culpam in se suscipit: neque unius tantum peccati se accusat, sed fatetur multiplici reatu se esse obstrictum."—*Calvin.*

MAKE ME NOT A REPROACH—said, it would seem, with reference to the temptation which had assailed him before, to give utterance to his disquietude even in the presence of the ungodly. But the connection is difficult, and it may only mean, "Do not so chasten me that fools will rejoice at my suffering."

9. I WAS DUMB. This clearly refers to the resolve and conduct described in ver. 1, 2. It does not introduce the expression of a fresh resolve, as many have supposed.

I COULD NOT OPEN; or simply as a subordinate clause to the preceding, "without opening my mouth." He thus reiterates before God how careful he had been to avoid giving offence by any hasty word; alleges the reason for this, because he felt that his suffering was God's doing; and urges it as a motive with God in the entreaty which follows.

Qimchi explains this verse with reference to the preceding, thus: I could not complain of man, for it was God's doing: I could not complain of God, for it was because of my sin.

10. BLOW, lit. "attack, conflict;" the word only occurs here—parallel with STROKE, which precedes. For this last word, see on xxxviii. 11 [12]. The pron. "I" expressed is emphatic, and implies a tacit contrast between his own weakness and the power of God, whose hand was laid upon him.

11. This verse contains a further

12 Hear my prayer, O Jehovah,
And give ear unto my cry;
At my weeping be not silent:
For I am a stranger with Thee,
A sojourner, as all my fathers (were).
13 Look away from me, that I may recover strength,
Before I go hence, and be no more.

reason why God should take away His stroke.

LIKE THE MOTH. This may either mean (1) that man's beauty is like the moth, frail and perishing (cf. Job iv. 19, "crushed before the moth," xxvii. 18); or (2) the action of God upon man may be compared to the silent, secret, yet sure, effect of the moth in fretting a garment, as in our P.B.V., where the words are paraphrased, "like as a moth fretting a garment." This last may be supported by Hos. v. 12, "I will be to Ephraim as a moth."

12. The Psalm closes with a yet more earnest appeal to God's pitying mercy, based still on that very transitoriness of life which is the burden of the whole.

A STRANGER, A SOJOURNER. LXX. *πάροικος καὶ παρεπίδημος*, as 1 Pet. ii. 11, *ξένος καὶ παρεπίδημος*, Heb. xi. 13, borrowed from Gen. xxiii. 4. Comp. the confession of David, 1 Chron. xxix. 15, "For we are strangers with Thee, and sojourners, as all our fathers (were). As a shadow are our days upon the earth, and there is no hope (here)." A STRANGER (גֵּר), "one who is but a passing guest:" A SOJOURNER, "one who settles for a time in a country, but is not a native of it."

AS ALL MY FATHERS: as the patriarchs had been in the land which was theirs only by promise. He himself, he felt, and all men were on the earth, what Abraham was in the land of promise: he could not call one foot of it his own. Comp. also Lev. xxv. 23.

13. The last verse is borrowed from Job vii. 19, x. 20, 21. See also Job vii. 8, ix. 27, xiv. 6.

LOOK AWAY, *i.e.* keep not thine eye fixed upon me in anger; it answers to "Turn aside Thy stroke," in ver. 10.

THAT I MAY RECOVER STRENGTH, prop. applied to the countenance, "that I may become cheerful," "Dass ich mich erheitere."—*Del.*

[a] ידותון,—found also in the inscriptions to Pss. lxii. and lxxvii.,—the name of one of David's three choir-masters, as we learn from 1 Chron. xvi. 41, 42, xxv. 1—6. See also 2 Chron. v. 12. In 2 Chron. xxxv. 15 he is called "the king's seer," and was probably the same person as Ethan, 1 Chron. xv.

According to the K'thîbh, the form here is ידיתון, as also lxxvii. 1, 1 Chron. xvi. 38, Neh. xi. 17, to be explained by the constant and ready interchange of יְ and וּ. The Keri, however, is more in analogy with other forms, such as זְבוּלוּן, יְשֻׁרוּן.

[b] מִטּוֹב. This has been very differently explained. The Chald., Aq., and the older interpreters generally, as the E. V., "I was silent even from good," taking the "good" however in different senses, such as "the law,"

"the praise of God," or such "good words" as might have been a reply to his adversaries. This, however, is not defensible. מִן, after the verb of silence, can only allow, as Hupfeld rightly maintains, of one of two interpretations, either, (1) "*far from* good," *i.e.* without comfort, joy, or the like, comp. Job xxviii. 4; or, (2) as the negative consequence of the silence (טוֹב being an infin. for מִטּוֹב לִי), "so that it was not well with me," or, "without its being well with me," parallel with what follows, "and my sorrow was stirred."

[c] מֶה־חָדֵל. The LXX. τί ὑστερῶ, Vulg. *quid desit mihi*, i.e. "how much of my life yet remains;" Chald. "when I cease to be in the world," חָדֵל is lit. "that which ceases, or has an end," and so transitory, frail, &c. Hence it is not necessary to correct with Hupf. ' מֶה־חֶלֶד, *quantilli sim ævi*, as lxxxix. 48. There can be no doubt that there is a confusion of the two words in Is. xxxviii. 11, where for חָדֶל we must read חָלֶד.

[d] וַתֶּמֶס, fut. apoc. Hiph. of מסה (Ges. § 75, Rem. 16), following the *perfect conditional.* But see on lviii. 8 [9], Critical Note.

חֲמוּדוֹ is properly a part. pass. (like נֶחְמָד), with suff., and means strictly "that which is lovely, precious, &c." as Job xx. 20, Is. xliv. 9; here "beauty, loveliness."

PSALM 40

THIS Psalm consists of two parts. The first (ver. 1—10) tells the story of God's mercies in a former time of trouble; the second (ver. 11—18) is a cry for the like help and deliverance, now that fresh calamities are come. The singer, looking back to the past, tells how he had been brought into the deepest abyss of misery; he had been like one falling into a pit, or sinking in a deep morass, where there was no resting-place for his feet; but God of His great mercy had heard him when he cried, had delivered him from his trouble, had set his feet on a rock, and established his goings (ver. 3): and not only had He done this, but He had also given him a heart and a tongue to praise Him (ver. 3). Then follows the expression of his feelings at the time. Here, after speaking of the blessedness of trusting in Jehovah, and of the wonders of His goodness, not only to the singer himself, but to all Israel (comp. lxxiii. 1), he further declares what had been the great lesson of his affliction,—how he had learnt that there was a better sacrifice than that of bulls and goats, even the sacrifice of an obedient will; and how, moreover, he had found that this truth which God had opened his ears to receive (ver. 6) was in most perfect harmony with the truth taught in the written law (ver. 7);

and lastly, how, constrained by a sense of gratitude, he had published to "the great congregation" the loving-kindness and truth of the Lord.

In the second division of the Psalm, he pleads the past, and his own conduct in the past, as a ground for renewed mercies being vouchsafed to him, now that he is in fresh trouble, bowed down by the burden of his sins (ver. 9), and cruelly pursued by his enemies (ver. 14). Thrice he prays earnestly for himself (ver. 11, 13, 17); the last time, faith having vanquished in the struggle, there mingles with the cry for help the touching expression of confidence in God: "But as for me, miserable and helpless though I be, the Lord thinketh upon me." With these personal petitions are joined others against the malice of his enemies (14, 15), and intercession on behalf of all those who, like himself, love and seek Jehovah.

This second part, or rather the portion of it from ver. 13 to ver. 17, appears again, in an independent form, as Psalm lxx. But it is, I think, almost certain, that the Psalm in its present form is the original, and the latter verses were subsequently detached and slightly altered, in order to form a distinct poem. In proof of this, it may be observed, (1) that the two parts of the Psalm are always found united in all ancient Versions and MSS.; (2) that the differences of language which occur in Psalm lxx. are more easily explicable, on the supposition that it was detached from Psalm xl., than on the opposite hypothesis; (3) that there is a play in the second half of the Psalm on words already occurring in the first half, which shows an original connection between them. (See more in the notes here, and on Ps. lxx.)

Whether David was the author of this Psalm is a question which we can hardly hope now to decide. There are expressions in it not unlike those which we find in Psalms unquestionably his: but we cannot pretend to point to any circumstances in his life to which it undoubtedly refers. Ewald thinks that the prominence given to the roll of the book in ver. 7 is an indication that it was written about the time of Josiah's reformation, and shortly after the discovery of the Book of the Law in the Temple. This, however, is one of those external coincidences of which too much may easily be made.

With regard to the predictive character of the Psalm, and the reference of one portion of it in the Epistle to the Hebrews to Christ, something will be found on that subject in the notes on ver. 6, as well as in chap. iii. of the General Introduction. The great principle of a *typical* predictiveness in all Jewish history is the most satisfactory principle of interpretation in this and in all similar cases.

The first division of the Psalm consists of ten, and the second of seven verses.

I. The first may again be subdivided into two strophes, consisting of five verses each. Here, ver. 1—5 declare what God had done; ver. 6—10, what return the Psalmist had made. (1) In the former strophe, ver. 1—3 speak of the Divine aid as vouchsafed to the individual; ver. 4, 5, as extended to all His people. (2) In the latter we have, first, the thanksgiving of *act*, ver. 6—8; and then the thanksgiving of *word*, ver. 9, 10.

II. The second part has also its subdivisions, though not so clearly marked. We may either regard it as consisting of two strophes, the first of three verses (ver. 11—13); and the second of four (ver. 14—17); or we may distribute it into three parts, ver. 11, 12, ver. 13—15, ver. 16, 17. According to the last division we have, first, the appeal to God based on the greatness of the Psalmist's personal sufferings; and next, as directed against the power of his enemies: and finally, the confident hope in God's care and love which never fails those that seek Him.

[FOR THE PRECENTOR. A PSALM OF DAVID.]

1 TRULY I had waited upon Jehovah,
And He inclined unto me, and heard my cry;
2 And He brought me up out of the pit of destruction,[a]
Out of the miry swamp,
And set my feet upon a rock,
(And) made my footsteps firm;

1, 2. He tells how Jehovah had rewarded his trust by answering his prayer, and how He had rescued him from imminent destruction.

1. TRULY I HAD WAITED, or "I did indeed wait," as implying there was such a thing as an opposite temper of mind, and that this had been carefully avoided. This use of the infinitive absol. with the finite verb may serve to assert a fact strongly in opposition to some other fact implied or expressed; and not only to emphasize the idea contained in the verb itself. The latter usage *may* have been intended here: and if so, the *long-continued, patient* waiting will be the prominent notion. In the former case, the waiting as opposed to the not waiting; in the latter, the nature of the waiting itself, is described.

2. The deliverance. The metaphor of the pit may be used either with reference to a pitfall for wild beasts, as vii. 15 [16], or a dungeon, such as that into which Jeremiah was cast (Jer. xxxviii. 6), and which would often have a damp and miry bottom.

MIRY SWAMP, lit. "mire of mud," an almost pleonastic expression; comp. lxix. 2 [3]. The expressions are clearly metaphorical. This I mention, because some expositors have maintained that the Psalm was written by Jeremiah, and that the reference is to the literal pit, or dungeon, into which he was cast. If so, where, asks Maurer, was the rock on which his feet were placed?

MADE MY FOOTSTEPS FIRM, *i.e.* did not merely bring me into a place of safety and there leave

3 And He put a new song in my mouth,
(Even) praise unto our God :—
Many shall see (it) and fear,
And shall put their trust in Jehovah :—
4 Blessed is the man who hath made Jehovah his trust,
And hath not turned to the proud,[b] and to such as go aside falsely.[c]

5 Thou hast greatly multiplied,[d] O Jehovah my God,
Thy wonders, and Thy thoughts towards us;
They cannot be set in order unto Thee :
Would I declare them, and speak of them,
They are more than I can tell.

me, but provided for my future security.

3. A NEW SONG, *i.e.* one celebrating with all the power of a recent gratitude a new and signal act of deliverance. The old forms, the customary expressions, the well-known hymns were not enough. See on xxxiii. 3. So Calvin: "*Novum* ponit pro singulari et exquisito: sicuti genus liberationis non vulgare erat, sed æterna memoria dignum." Ewald thinks that there follows, partly a reminiscence, and partly the very words of this new song, as it had been sung at the time of the deliverance. The words "praise unto our God" are, he supposes, a reminiscence, the Psalm having probably begun, "Praise ye Jehovah." So too the words, "many shall see it and fear,"&c., may have appeared in the song in the form of an exhortation: "see it and fear, and put your trust," &c. Finally, the words of verses 4, 5 are, according to him, words of the former song quoted in this. I was at one time disposed myself to regard the latter part of ver. 3, "Many shall see . . . trust in Jehovah," as parenthetical, and ver. 4—10 as the very words of the new song. But such a supposition is perhaps unnecessary. The train of thought is sufficiently clear without having recourse to it.

4. HIS TRUST, *i.e.* object of trust, as lxv. 5 [6], Is. xv. 5, and elsewhere. This obviously is a continuation of the last clause of the preceding verse. "Many shall trust in Jehovah, and blessed are they who do so." The next verse again gives the reason for this trust, the manifold and marvellous deliverances which God had ever vouchsafed to Israel.

HATH NOT TURNED, a word used especially of apostasy from the true God to idols, as Lev. xix. 4, Deut. xxix. 18 [17], Hos. iii. 1, and often.

5. THOU HAST GREATLY MULTIPLIED, &c. lit. "many hast Thou made Thy wonders," &c. Three different renderings of the former part of this verse are possible.

(1) "Thou hast multiplied Thy wonders and Thy thoughts to usward:—There is none that can be compared unto Thee—Would I declare," &c. (2) "Thou hast multiplied,"&c. (as before) . . . "It is not possible to set them in order unto Thee, &c." (3) "Thou hast multiplied Thy wonders; and Thy thoughts towards us, it is not possible to set in order," &c. See more in the Critical Note. Similarly in the latter part of the verse, there is a choice as to the way in which we connect the clause, "Would I declare them," &c. with what goes before, or with what follows: "They

6 In sacrifice and offering Thou hast not delighted,
—Mine ears hast Thou opened,—
Burnt-offering and sin-offering hast Thou not required.

cannot be set in order, would I declare them," or "Would I declare . . . they are more," &c.

6. He proceeds now to declare the great truth which God had taught him, and which it would seem he had learnt in his affliction, that God desires the sacrifice of the will rather than the sacrifice of slain beasts.

We may perhaps paraphrase ver. 5—8 as follows: My heart is full to overflowing with the thought of Thy goodness. How can I express, how can I acknowledge it? Once I should have thought sacrifices and offerings a proper and sufficient acknowledgement. Now I feel how inadequate these are; for Thou hast taught me the truth; my deaf unwilling ears didst Thou open, that I might understand that a willing heart was the best offering I could render. Then, being thus taught of Thee, I said, Lo I come, presenting myself before Thee, not with a dead and formal service, but with myself as a living sacrifice. The truth here inculcated is stated fully in Ps. l., and is often insisted on by the Prophets. Comp. 1 Sam. xv. 22, Ps. li. 16 [18], lxix. 30, 31 [31, 32], Is. i. 11, Jer. vii. 21, &c.; Hos. vi. 6, Mic. vi. 6—8.

SACRIFICE, properly of slain beasts. OFFERING, *i.e.* the bloodless offering of fine flour, &c. BURNT-OFFERING, the object of which was to obtain the Divine favour; whereas that of the SIN-OFFERING was to make propitiation. But the four are here mentioned only with a view to express in the largest way *all manner of sacrifices*.

MINE EARS HAST THOU OPENED, lit. "Ears hast Thou dug (or pierced) for me;" "given me open ears." This is a parenthetical clause, which has been variously explained. (1) Aq. ὠτία δὲ ἔσκαψάς μοι. Symm. ὠτία δὲ κατεσκεύασάς μοι. Theod. and Gr. 5 and 6, ὠτία κατηρτίσω μοι. Jerome, *aures fodisti mihi.* Syr. "ears hast Thou pierced for me." Vulg. *aures perfecisti mihi.* The same sense was probably designed by these different interpretations, Aquila and Jerome giving the literal rendering, whilst the others exhibit the meaning = "Thou hast so constructed my ears that they have an open passage through which Thy instructions can reach me," or as Rud. explains, "meatus aurium mearum aperuisti mihi, et aptasti ut pateant tibi." (Comp. Cic. *Tusc. Quæst.* i. 20, ". . . viæ quasi sunt . . . ad aures . . . a sede animæ perforatæ. Foramina illa quæ patent ad animum a corpore, callidissimo artificio natura fabricata est." Hence, "Thou hast dug (or constructed) ears for me," would be equivalent to saying, "Thou hast given me ears to hear;" that which is literally true of the structure of the bodily ear being here transferred in a figure to the *spiritual* ear, as is evident from the context. (So in the parallel phrases "eyes to see," "a heart to understand," &c. Is. vi. 9, 10; Deut. xxix. 4 [3], &c.)

(2) Others again take the expression here, "to dig the ears," as = "to pierce the ear," in the same sense as the phrases "to *open* the ear," Is. xlviii. 8, l. 4, 5, "to *uncover* the ear," 1 Sam. ix. 15, xx. 2, 12, 13, Job xxxiii. 16, and many other passages, as implying a Divine communication, a supernatural impartation of knowledge. Then, "ears hast Thou pierced for me" would mean, "This truth hast Thou revealed to me;" which comes to very much the same thing as the last, "This hast Thou enabled me to receive and understand." It is not a sufficient objection to these interpretations that the verb כרה means only "to dig," not "to pierce." See on xxii., note [d].

(3) The Rabbinical commenta-

7 Then said I, "Lo, I come;
—In the roll of the Book it is prescribed to me,—

tors, for the most part, interpret the phrase to mean, "Thou hast made me obedient," the connection between hearing and obedience being common enough, with reference to 1 Sam. xv. 22, "to obey (lit. hear) is better than sacrifice," and Jer. vii. 22.

(4) There is certainly no allusion to the custom of nailing the ear of the slave to the door-post as a symbol of perpetual servitude and obedience (Exod. xxi. 6). For this, the technical word רצע is used; only *one* ear was thus pierced; and the allusion would be far-fetched and quite out of place here,—*coacta argutia*, as Calvin calls it.

(5) The LXX. have the singular reading σῶμα δὲ κατηρτίσω μοι, "a body hast Thou prepared me." [All the other Greek versions (and even some MSS. of the LXX.) have ὠτία, and the Vulg., which is translated from the LXX., *aures*.] This reading, which appears also in Heb. x. 5, 7, where this passage is quoted, is commonly supposed to have arisen from a corruption of **ΩTIA** into **CΩMA**; the **C** being repeated from the previous **HΘEΛHCAC** and the **TI** being changed into **M.** But it is more probable that the LXX. intended to give a paraphrase rather than a literal rendering of the passage. An old Scholion supposes the writer of the Epistle to the Hebrews to have made the change himself purposely (πρὸς οἰκεῖον σκόπον τούτῳ χρησάμενος). And Calvin almost intimates that this might have been the case: "*Corporis* vocem ad suum propositum deflexit." Grotius suggests that the word σῶμα may even have found its way from the Epistle into the MSS. of the Alexandrine Version, the like to which has certainly happened in other instances: see on xiv. 3. Bengel says, that the writer of the Epistle merely interprets the Psalmist as putting the part, "the ears," for the whole, "the body."

It should be noted, however, that this change in a word, considerable as undoubtedly it is, is not such as very materially to affect the argument in the Epistle to the Hebrews, where the purpose of the writer is not so much to insist on the fact that our Lord's sacrifice was the sacrifice of a human body—that was already implied in His "coming into the world," His incarnation,—but that it was the offering of an obedient will. It should also further be observed, that the words are not quoted as a prophecy which was fulfilled in Christ, but the writer finds words which once expressed the devotion of a true Israelite to be far more strikingly expressive, indeed, in their highest sense, only truly expressive, of the perfect obedience of the Son of God. All true words of God's saints of old, all high and holy aspirations, however true and excellent in their mouths, went far beyond themselves, and found their perfect consummation only in Him who was the Perfect Man. (This view of these and like Messianic passages will be found enlarged upon, and fully justified, in the General Introduction.)

7. LO, I COME, *i.e.* to appear before Thee; a phrase used to indicate the coming of an inferior into the presence of a superior, or of a slave before his master, Num. xxii. 38, 2 Sam. xix. 21:—as in the similar expression "behold, here I am,"—generally expressive of willingness.

IN THE ROLL OF THE BOOK. Another parenthetical clause, corresponding to the former, "Mine ears hast Thou opened," that which Thou hast taught me is that which is contained in Thy Law; I find

8 To do Thy pleasure, O my God, I delight,
Yea Thy Law is in my inmost heart."
9 I have published righteousness in the great congregation:
Lo, I would not refrain my lips,
O Jehovah, THOU knowest,
10 I have not hid Thy righteousness within my heart.
Thy faithfulness and Thy salvation have I uttered,
I have not concealed Thy loving-kindness and Thy truth
From the great congregation.

there the same truth which Thy Spirit hath already written on my heart. The BOOK is the Book of the Law of Moses. The ROLL shows that it was written upon parchment; this is a word common enough in Jer. and Ezek.

IT IS PRESCRIBED TO ME, or laid upon me as a duty, exactly in the same sense as the words occur 2 Kings xxii. 13, where, on the discovery of the Book of the Law, it is said, "Great is the wrath of Jehovah—because our fathers hearkened not to the words of this Book, to do according to all which is prescribed to us;" where our Version has, "which is written *concerning* us," just as in this passage it has, "it is written *of* me," in this following the interpretation of the LXX. περὶ ἐμοῦ; an interpretation which is adopted in the Epistle to the Hebrews.

Ewald, Delitzsch, and others, strangely enough render, "Lo, I come *with* the roll of the Book," &c. as if the Psalmist actually took the roll of the Pentateuch (or of Deuteronomy, a copy of which the king in particular was commanded to have, Deut. xvii. 14—20) with him into the Temple. What the propriety or significance of such an act could be, I am at a loss to imagine. They then explain the prep. עַל differently. Ew. "für mich," "*for* me." Del. "über mich," "*concerning* me," *i.e.* as prescribing to me my duties as a king. De Wette, "Lo, I come with the roll of the Book written upon me," *i.e.* upon my heart, referring to Jer. xxxi. 33, Prov. iii. 3. But first it seems very doubtful if עָלָי, "upon me," could stand thus nakedly for "upon my heart" (xlii. 4 [5] is not strictly parallel, as "my soul" follows): secondly, though the *Law* might be said to be written on his heart, to say that the *roll* of the Book was written upon his heart, would be a very different and a very harsh expression.

8. TO DO THY PLEASURE (or will). These words would seem naturally to depend on the foregoing, "Lo, I come," and so they are twice cited in Heb. x. 7, 9. Instead of that, however, a new verb is supplied, "I delight."

IN MY INMOST HEART (lit. "in the midst of my bowels," as the seat of the affections), written there on its "fleshy tables," and not merely in the Book. Comp. xxxvii. 31, Deut. vi. 6, and see the prophetic promises that so it should be with the whole nation (Jer. xxxi. 33, Is. li. 7).

9. But not obedience only, but thanksgiving also shall form a part of his grateful acknowledgement of God's goodness; he will both do the will and speak the praises of Jehovah. This last, too, is better than sacrifice, l. 14, 15, 23.

On the enumeration of the various attributes of God, see above, xxxiv. 5—7.

9, 10. I HAVE PUBLISHED . . . I WOULD NOT REFRAIN . . . I HAVE NOT HID . . . I HAVE UTTERED . . . I HAVE NOT CONCEALED: words are heaped upon words to express the

11 Thou, O Jehovah, wilt not refrain Thy tender compassion from me;
Let Thy loving-kindness and Thy truth alway defend me.
12 For evils have come about me without number;
My iniquities have overtaken me that I cannot see:
They are more than the hairs of my head,
And my heart hath failed me.

13 Be pleased, O Jehovah, to deliver me;
O Jehovah, haste Thee to help me,
14 Let them be ashamed and confounded together
That seek after my life to destroy it!
Let them be turned backward, and brought to dishonour,
That delight in my hurt!

eager forwardness of a heart burning to show forth its gratitude. No elaborate description could so well have given us the likeness of one whose "life was a thanksgiving."

11. The Psalmist turns to earnest entreaty. Apparently, therefore, he has recalled a former deliverance, in order to comfort himself therewith in his present sorrow, and pleads his conduct in the past as a ground for fresh mercies. THOU WILT NOT REFRAIN, with evident reference to the I WOULD NOT REFRAIN, ver. 9. Again, THY LOVING-KINDNESS AND THY TRUTH, with like reference to the preceding verse, "As I have not concealed them from others, so let them ever defend me."

12. MY INIQUITIES. This verse is quite decisive as to the question which has been raised respecting the Messianic interpretation of the Psalm. It is quite impossible to refer such words as these to Christ; and when expositors choose to say that "my iniquities" mean "the iniquities laid upon me," they are doing violence most unjustifiably to the plain words of the text. Such interpreters can hardly find fault with Romanists for adding to the Word of God.

FAILED, lit. "forsaken."

13. From this verse to the end appears in a separate form as Ps. lxx., where consult the notes for the variations, &c. Hupfeld maintains that Ps. lxx. is the original which has been appended here; but then, in order to support this hypothesis, he is obliged to make Ps. xl. end with ver. 11, feeling, no doubt, that with ver. 12 the conclusion would be lame and imperfect. But it is, on the face of it, improbable that Ps. lxx. should have been joined on here by means of an intercalated verse. It is more likely that the latter part of this Psalm was detached and altered by a later writer, who felt, perhaps, that he could not so well use the former part in his own case.

BE PLEASED (omitted in Ps. lxx.), here used apparently with reference to "Thy *pleasure*," ver. 8.

The whole of the conclusion of this Psalm reminds us of the conclusion of Ps. xxxv.

15 Let them be struck dumb as a reward of their shame,
That say unto me, Aha, Aha!
16 Let all those that seek Thee rejoice and be glad in Thee!
Let such as love Thy salvation say alway,
"Jehovah be magnified."
17 And as for me,—afflicted and poor, the Lord thinketh upon me.
Thou art my Help and my Deliverer:
O my God, make no long tarrying.

[a] מִבּוֹר שָׁאוֹן. LXX. ἐκ λάκκου ταλαιπωρίας. Others, "pit of roaring (waves)." And שָׁאוֹן no doubt generally occurs in this sense (1) of the noise of waters, as lxv. 7 [8], Is. xvii. 12, 13, and then of the noise of multitudes; but in Jer. xlvi. 17, it can only mean "destruction" (abstr. for concr.). This must likewise be the meaning here, for waters do not rage in a pit or cistern. Hence it is allied to other words from the same root as שְׁאֵת, *interitus*, Lament. iii. 47, and שְׁאִיָּה, *ruinæ*, Is. xxiv. 12.

[b] רְהָבִים. The plur. only occurs here. Most take the words as an adjective from a sing. רָהָב, which does not exist, and this agrees with the following שָׂטֵי כָזָב. The Targ. סוּרְבָּנַיָּא. The LXX. εἰς ματαιότητας, and Jerome also renders it as a noun, *superbiæ*, plur. for sing., as is common with abstr. nouns. The sing. רַהַב is used as a name of Egypt, to denote its *noisy, boastful* reliance upon its own strength, a reliance therefore which could only be shamefully disappointed.

[c] שָׂטֵי, another ἅπ. λεγ. part. plur. constr. of a form שׂוּט not in use instead of שׂטה. Most take the following כָזָב as the object to which this deflection is made, "who incline to lies," (like יוֹרְדֵי בוֹר, "who go down to the pit,") *i.e.* who have recourse to some false and deceitful object of help. But as Hupf. justly remarks, ירד, like בוא, עלה, &c., always takes the accusat. of direction after it, and שׂטים does not mean merely "those who incline themselves," but "those who turn aside," *i.e.* apostates. Hence he takes כָזָב as a qualifying word, explaining the *nature* of the apostasy, "lying apostates," like בֹּגְדֵי אָוֶן, in lix. 6. LXX. μανίας ψευδεῖς. Vulg. *insanias falsas*. Jerome, *pompas mendacii*.

[d] The connection of the different clauses of this verse is somewhat doubtful. Symm. πάμπολλα ἐποίησας . . . τεράστιά σου καὶ τοὺς διαλογισμούς σου τοὺς ὑπὲρ ἡμῶν. Jerome, *Multa fecisti . . . mirabilia tua et cogitationes tuas pro nobis*. The LXX., on the other hand, connect the last words with what follows: καὶ τοῖς διαλογισμοῖς σου οὐκ ἔστι τις ὁμοιωθήσεταί σοι. Much depends on how we render the words, אֵין עֲרֹךְ אֵלֶיךָ. (1) These may be rendered, "there is none (lit. nothing) that can be put in comparison of Thee." ערך with לְ, as lxxxix. 7. Comp. Is. xl. 18. So the LXX. and Syr. They will then stand in a parenthesis, and we must join "Thy

marvellous works and Thy thoughts" (*i.e.* purposes whence the works spring), as objects alike of the verb עָשִׂיתָ. But (2) ערך may also mean "to set forth" (see note on v. 3 [4]). "There is no laying forth of them unto Thee," *i.e.* as follows in the parallelism, they are beyond enumeration. So the Chald., and so Symm., *οὐκ ἔστιν ἐκθέσθαι ἐπὶ σοῦ*, and Jerome, *non invenio ordinem coram te.* Similarly Qimchi, Calv., Ros., Stier, &c. And again, these words may either stand in a parenthesis, or, following the constr. (not the sense) of the LXX., be joined with what follows, "And Thy thoughts which are to uswards, there is no setting forth unto Thee." רַבּוֹת is clearly the predicate.

PSALM 41

THIS Psalm seems to have been written in a season of recovery from sickness, and under a deep sense of the hypocrisy and ingratitude of false friends, who came to the Psalmist pretending to condole with him in his sickness, whilst in reality they hated him in their hearts and wished for his death. In this respect the Psalm has some resemblance to Ps. xxxviii., except that there the sufferer is deserted by his friends, and has to complain of their coldness rather than of their treachery.

The Psalm opens with a eulogy pronounced on those who know how to feel for and show compassion to the miserable and the suffering. This is evidently designed in order to condemn more forcibly, by way of contrast, the opposite line of conduct which is the subject of complaint. The Psalmist's own experience of the baseness and hollowness of the men who surrounded him made him only appreciate more sensibly the great value of faithful sympathizing friends in a season of affliction. Ewald throws the whole of what follows into the past. He supposes the sacred Poet to be recalling his own feelings, the words of his enemies, and his prayers on that occasion; and that in his suffering he had learnt a great truth, viz. that the merciful should obtain mercy, and the unsympathising and the hard-hearted meet with the destruction they deserve. But, as Hupfeld observes, the Psalm only pronounces a blessing on the compassionate, it says nothing of the fate of the unfeeling; the sentiment expressed can hardly be called a great truth; and it is forced and unnatural to suppose that the whole passage, ver. 4—11, is a narrative of some long past event. The danger is one, as is evident from ver. 10, which is not yet past. The period is one of convalescence, but of not yet established health. Compare verses 3, 5, 6, 8, 10.

The Psalm consists of three parts:—

I. A blessing on those who with watchful love and compassion are ever ready to succour the needy and the distressed. Such men shall themselves experience the favour and loving-kindness of Jehovah when they are laid on a bed of sickness. Ver. 1—3.

II. The Psalmist himself had found no sympathy. On the contrary, although (as I think is implied in the former part of the Psalm) he had ever been ready to sympathize with others, he found, now that he was himself in pain and suffering, the utter hollowness of those who in brighter hours had called themselves his friends. (One is reminded of the complaint of Job, chaps. xxix. xxx.) Even the most trusted counsellor, the most honoured guest, had treacherously turned against him. Ver. 4—9.

III. A prayer that being restored to health, of God's mercy, he may be permitted to chastise his enemies; and an expression of his confidence that God will not suffer his enemies to triumph, but will, as in times past, so now also deliver him. Ver. 10—12.

[FOR THE PRECENTOR. (A PSALM) OF DAVID.]

1 BLESSED is he that considereth [a] the miserable:
In the day of evil Jehovah will deliver him.
2 Jehovah will keep him, and save him alive;
He shall be blessed [b] in the land:
And give Thou not him over to the will of his enemies!

1—3. It is not easy to decide whether the verbs here should be taken as simple *futures* or *presents*, or whether they should be rendered as *optatives*. The last clause of ver. 2, "and give Thou not," &c., [where obs. the negat. אַל], favours the latter construction. This is also supported by the LXX., who, though they give the fut. in ver. 1, ῥύσεται have rendered all the verbs in ver. 2 and the first member of ver. 3 in the opt. On the other hand, it may be said that the perf. in the latter clause of ver. 3, "Thou hast changed," requires the preceding verbs to be either *presents* or *futures:* and further, in other instances where a Psalm begins with אַשְׁרֵי, "blessed," &c., there follows a description of the blessedness itself, an enumeration of the particulars in which that blessedness consists. Comp. the opening of Pss. i. xxxii., cxii., cxix., cxxviii.

1. THE MISERABLE, or "the suffering:" the word is one of wide meaning, and is used of the poor (as in Exod. xxx. 15), of the lean and weak in body (as Gen. xli. 19), of the sick in mind (as 2 Sam. xiii. 4).

2. IN THE LAND. On this Calvin remarks: "It might indeed appear absurd, that he promises himself a happy life in the world, for our condition were hard indeed if a better lot did not await us elsewhere: but

3 Jehovah will support him upon the couch of languishing :
All his bed hast Thou changed in his sickness.
4 As for me—I said : " Jehovah, be gracious unto me ;
Heal my soul, for I have sinned against Thee."
5 Mine enemies say evil of me :
" When will he die and his name have perished ? "
6 And if he come to see (me), he speaketh vanity,
His heart gathereth iniquity to itself;
(When) he goeth abroad, he speaketh (it).
7 Together against me do all that hate me whisper;
Against me do they devise evil for me :
8 " Some shocking thing (they say) is poured out[c] upon him,

because many had despaired of his recovery, he expressly says that he shall still survive, and that not without manifest tokens of God's grace :—words which by no means exclude the hope of a better life." The expression is, of course, due to that prominence given to temporal reward which was characteristic of the Old Testament.

3. HIS BED. The word above rendered "couch" means more strictly the bed itself, whereas this denotes rather the keeping the bed in sickness.

HAST THOU CHANGED. Many understand this of the refreshment and ease given to the sufferer by the smoothing of the pillow, &c. ; and hence the E. V., "Thou wilt *make* all his bed," &c. But the meaning rather is : "it is no longer a sick bed, for Thou hast healed him of his disease." The past tense expresses here a common experience, not a single circumstance, as J. H. Mich. rightly explains, "Ut *vertisti*, ita et in posterum *vertes* melius."

4—9. The hypocrisy of his pretended friends described. Their conduct is precisely the opposite of that which he has just before commended. They come to visit him indeed, but not from motives of compassion, but with the secret hope that they may see him perish.

4. AS FOR ME—I SAID. The pron. is emphatic, and marks both the transition from the previous eulogy of the compassionate man to the Poet's personal feelings and desires, and also the opposition to the "enemies" in the next verse.

FOR I HAVE SINNED, *i.e.* It is my sin which has brought this suffering on me : but obs. the prayer is, "Pardon my sin," not "take away my suffering." These words absolutely forbid an application of the whole Psalm to Christ.

5. SAY EVIL OF ME; or "say there is evil to me," or "I am in an evil plight."

HAVE PERISHED. Fut. perf., which has been observed by Diodati (though generally overlooked) : " E quando *sarà perito* il suo nome ? "

6. IF HE COME. Sing. not impersonal, but because the Psalmist has in mind some individual whose hostility was peculiarly active. Here again Diodati shows his accuracy. " E se *alcun di loro* viene," &c. "To see" = " to visit in sickness," as 2 Sam. xiii. 5, 2 Kings viii. 29. Symm., ἐπισκοπῆσαι, or ἐπισκέψασθαι. Three things are mentioned of them : a lying mouth, an evil heart, a love of slander.

8. SOME SHOCKING THING, Heb. "thing of Belial," which may mean

And (now that) he lieth, he shall rise up no more."
9 Yea mine old familiar friend, whom I trusted,
Who did eat of my bread,
Hath lifted up his heel against me.

10 But Thou, O Jehovah, be gracious unto me,
And raise me up, that I may requite them :

either physical or moral evil. See xviii. 4 [5], note[b]. But the latter signification is the more common. Here the same form of expression occurs as in ci. 3 ; cf. Deut. xv. 9, in both of which passages *moral* evil is meant. Perhaps, however, "a thing of Belial" is = a punishment which comes for evil-doing, a moral cause with a physical result. So Rashi.

9. WHO DID EAT OF MY BREAD. The Oriental feeling as to the sacredness of hospitality would stamp such conduct with peculiar blackness. If David wrote the Psalm, the ingratitude was the worse, because of the *honour* conferred on one who was admitted to the king's table. (2 Sam. ix. 10 ff., 1 Kings xviii. 19.)

Part of this verse is quoted by our Lord in John xiii. 18 as applicable to the treacherous conduct of Judas, but with the significant omission of the words "mine own familiar friend *whom I trusted;*" for our Lord knew what was in Judas from the beginning, and therefore did not trust him. Nothing can be more decisive both as to the way in which quotations were made, and also as to the proper interpretation of the apparently strong phrase ἵνα ἡ γραφὴ πληρωθῇ with which the quotation is introduced. First, it is plain that *particular expressions* in a Psalm may be applicable to events which befel our Lord, whilst the whole Psalm is not in like manner applicable. And next it is evident that "the Scripture is fulfilled" not merely when a prediction receives its accomplishment, but when words descriptive of certain circumstances in the life of the O. T. saints find a still fuller and truer realization—one not foreseen by the Psalmist, yet one no less designed of God—in the circumstances of our Lord's earthly life. This will be peculiarly the case here if Ahithophel be meant ; for as David was in much of his life a type of Christ, so the treachery of his trusted counsellor would be a foreshadowing of the treachery of Judas.

The rendering in John xiii. ὁ τρώγων μετ' ἐμοῦ τὸν ἄρτον, ἐπῆρεν ἐπ' ἐμὲ τὴν πτέρναν αὐτοῦ, is independent of the LXX., who have here more literally, ἐμεγάλυνεν ἐπ' ἐμὲ πτερνισμόν. The Heb. phrase is "hath *made great* his heel," which may either mean "he has lifted it on high, so as to trample on the object of attack," or "has given a hard violent blow with it."

10. THAT I MAY REQUITE THEM. Such a wish cannot be reconciled with our better Christian conscience. We find a purer and nobler tone of feeling in vii. 4 [5] ; and Ṣaadia would here supply, "good instead of evil," which however is plainly not the meaning of the Psalmist. Calov's attempt to turn the edge of the words is worse : "Hinc constat, non Davidem, qui ipsi etiam Simei condonavit, sed Christum, cujus est vindicta, hæc loqui." The true explanation of such expressions is, I believe, that given in a note on xxxv. Delitzsch, however, defends the wish here by saying that such a wish was justifiable in David as a lawful king who had been dethroned by rebellious subjects, and one which by the help

11 By this I know that Thou delightest in me,
That mine enemy doth not shout over me.
12 And as for me,—in mine integrity Thou hast upheld me
And settest me before Thy face for ever.

---

13 Blessed be Jehovah, the God of Israel,
From everlasting and to everlasting.
Amen, and Amen!

of God he actually accomplished when he crushed the rebellion of Absalom.

13. This last verse is no part of the original Psalm, but is merely a later doxology appended here when the Psalms were collected in order to mark the conclusion of the First Book. Similar doxologies occur at the end of the three following Books.

[a] הִשְׂכִּיל may either mean "to consider," "regard," *i.e.* look with an eye of compassion upon; comp. Neh. viii. 13, and with עַל, Prov. xvi. 20, with לְ, Prov. xxi. 11, 12: or it may mean "to deal wisely," *i.e.* with the true wisdom of righteousness; cf. Ps. xiv. 2, where the wise man = the man who loves God. The LXX. give the first of these meanings, *ὁ συνιῶν ’πὶ πτωχόν.* A scholiast, the last, *ὁ ἐννοῶν ἃ προσῆκε περὶ τῶν πενήτων.* Verss. and Commentt. are divided between these two meanings. Vulg. *qui intelligit super egenum et pauperem.* Luther, "der sich des Dürftigen annimmt." Diodati, "che si porta saviamente inverso 'l povero e misero." Mendels. "der für den Armen sorgt." Hupf. "der achtsam (fromm) ist gegen den Schwachen (Bedrängten)."

[b] יְאֻשַּׁר, to be preferred to the Q'ri וְאֻשַּׁר, which seems to have arisen from an attempt to supply the conj. Either (1), Pual of אִשֵּׁר, "to pronounce happy." (Symm. *μακαριστὸς ἔσται*), "he shall be pronounced happy," or simply as echoing אַשְׁרֵי, ver. 2, "shall be happy," as in Prov. iii. 18, the only other place where the word occurs: or (2), from אִשֵּׁר, "to lead in the right way;" so J. H. Mich. "feliciter in via salutis dirigetur." אל ת, a sudden transition from the description of the good man's lot to a prayer on his behalf. See note on xxxvi. 5. On נֶפֶשׁ in this sense, see xxvii. 12.

[c] יצוק, Part. Pual fr. יצק, occurring also 1 Kings vii. 24, 30; Job xli. 15, 16. Perhaps the same figure as in Jer. xlii. 18. "Is poured out," *i.e.* so as to cover him and penetrate his whole body, like metal poured into a mould which fills and adheres to every part. E. V. "cleaveth fast unto him," as if from root צוק.

THE PSALMS

BOOK 2

Psalms 42—62

The Second Book of the Psalms differs from the first by one distinguishing characteristic,—its use of the Divine Name. In the First, God is spoken of and addressed as Jehovah; in the Second, as Elohim, the latter name being that which, in our Version, is rendered "God." According to the computation given by Delitzsch, Jehovah occurs 272 times in the First Book, and Elohim but 15 times; whereas in the Second, Elohim occurs 164 times, and Jehovah only 30 times. There is also another observable difference between the two Books. In the First, all those Psalms which have any inscription at all, are expressly assigned to David as their author; whereas in the Second, we find a whole series attributed to some of the Levitical singers. These inscriptions will be found noticed in their places. With regard to the meaning of the Divine Names, and their peculiar and characteristic occurrence, it may suffice to refer to the articles JEHOVAH, GENESIS, and PENTATEUCH, in Smith's *Dictionary of the Bible*.

PSALM 42

THIS Psalm, though its date and authorship are uncertain, leaves us in no doubt as to the locality in which it was written. The Sacred Poet was in the land beyond the Jordan, near the mountain ridges of Hermon (ver. 6), in that land which was "emphatically the land of exile—the refuge of exiles." Many expositors are of opinion that the Psalm was written by David on the occasion of his flight from his son Absalom, when, as we read 2 Sam. xvii. 24 &c., having crossed the fords of the Jordan near Jericho, he ascended the eastern height and took refuge at Mahanaim. It was at this spot, consecrated in patriarchal times by the vision of the Hosts of God to Jacob,—this "sanctuary of the trans-Jordanic region,"—that the exiled monarch stationed himself, whilst the people that were with him spread themselves in the neighbouring wilderness. The words of the Psalm are supposed to describe his sense of the greatness of his loss as debarred from all access to the sanctuary of God in Zion. But there are expressions in it which are clearly not applicable to David's circumstances at the time. David was not amongst enemies who would mock him for his trust in Jehovah (xlii. 3, 10); on the contrary, he was surrounded by friends who were full of devotedness to his person and who possessed the same religious faith with himself (2 Sam. xvii. 27—29). David could hardly say at such a time, "I go mourning all the day because of the oppression of the enemy" (xlii. 9, xliii. 2), however bitterly he might feel the unnatural conduct of his son and the alienation of his subjects. Hence Paulus, who has been followed by De Wette, Maurer, and others, conjectured that the Psalm is the lamentation of a Priest, who either in the time of Jeroboam was shut out from all access to the Temple, or who was among those who were carried away by the Chaldæans after the capture of Jerusalem, and who from these hills looked back on Western Palestine—his "last sigh" before it vanished for ever from his sight. Vaihinger supposes it to have been written by one of the Levites who was banished by Athaliah. Ewald thinks that the words may have been those of King Jehoiakim himself, when in the hand of his captors, who perhaps halted somewhere in this neighbourhood for a night, on their return to Assyria. But the general tone of the Psalm is rather that of one looking for *speedy* restoration to his native land, than of one carried away into enduring captivity in Babylon.

"From these heights [beyond Jordan]," says Stanley, "Abner in his flight from the Philistines, and David in his flight from Absalom, and the Israelites on their way to Babylon, and the Christian Jews of Pella, caught the last glimpse of their familiar mountains. There is one plaintive strain which sums up all these feelings,—the 42d Psalm. Its date and authorship are uncertain; but the place is, beyond doubt, the trans-Jordanic hills, which always behold, as they are always beheld from, Western Palestine. As before the eyes of the exile the 'gazelle' of the forests of Gilead panted after the fresh streams of water which there descend to the Jordan, so his soul panted after God, from whose outward presence he was shut out. The river with its winding rapids, 'deep calling to deep,' lay between him and his home. All that he could now do was to remember the past, as he stood 'in the land of Jordan,' as he saw the peaks of 'Hermon,' as he found himself on the eastern heights of Mizar, which reminded him of his banishment and solitude. As we began, so we end this brief account of the Peræan hills. They are the 'Pisgah' of the earlier history: to the later history they occupy the pathetic relation that has been immortalized in the name of the long ridge from which the first and the last view of Granada is obtained; they are the 'last sigh' of the Israelite exile."—*Sinai and Palestine*, chap. viii. § 6.

There are good grounds for concluding that this Psalm and the next constituted originally but one Poem. The internal evidence favours this hypothesis. Besides the refrain at the end of xliii., which is the same as that which occurs twice in xlii. (ver. 5 [6], and 11 [12]), there is the remarkable coincidence of thought and language in xliii. 2 and xlii. 9 [10]. The longing, too, for the sanctuary in xliii. 3, 4, with the hope again to visit it, may be compared with the regret to which it answers in xlii. 4 [5]. Nor is external evidence wanting which points the same way. Thirty-seven of Kennicott's MSS. and nine of De-Rossi's have but one Psalm instead of two. The LXX., it is true, make a distinct Psalm of the 43d. But, according to a Midrash which reckons 147 Psalms in all, these two must be reckoned as one, as well as Psalms ix. x., and xxxii. xxxiii.

On the other hand, there can be no doubt that each Psalm is complete in itself; and it is conceivable that, though originally existing as one Poem, the present arrangement might have been adopted, the better to suit the purposes either of personal or liturgical use. The language of the 43d Psalm, it is obvious, might be used by those who were not in the circumstances indicated in the 42d. We have traces of a similar separation in Ps. xl., the latter part of which appears in a detached form as Ps. lxx., and probably for the same reason.

Assuming, then, that the two Psalms are in fact one, the whole may be divided into three strophes, each consisting of five verses, and each closing with the same words.

I. The first expresses the longing of the soul after God and the service of His sanctuary (xlii. 1, 2); the deep sorrow occasioned by the taunts of scoffing enemies (ver. 3); the attempt to find comfort in the recollection of past occasions of spiritual blessing (ver. 4). The expostulation at the close forms a refrain with which the two following strophes are also concluded (ver. 5).

II. The sense of distance from God and of the loss of His Presence oppresses the soul yet more (ver. 6, 7); yet still there is the effort to rise out of this despondency (ver. 8); but again the enemies who reproach and who triumph occupy the foreground, while God seems to have forgotten, and His help to be far off (ver. 9). The expostulatory refrain recurs as at the end of the first strophe.

III. The tone here is throughout more hopeful. First there is the appeal to God's justice (xliii. 1); then the ground of that appeal (ver. 2 *a*); then a further expostulation (ver. 2 *b*, *c*); then the prayer for Divine light and truth (ver. 3); and lastly, the confident hope of restoration to the land, and of being permitted again to join in the services of the sanctuary (ver. 4). The refrain as before (ver. 5).

[TO THE PRECENTOR. A MASKIL, OF THE SONS OF KORAH.[a]]

I. 1 Like as a hart which panteth [b] after the water-brooks,
So panteth my soul after Thee, O God.
2 My soul is athirst for God, for the Living God:

2. MY SOUL IS ATHIRST. The figure occurs again lxiii. 1 [2]. Comp. xxxvi. 8, 9 [9, 10], and Is. xli. 17, lv. 1, Jer. ii. 13. Of this thirst Robertson beautifully says: "There is a desire in the human heart best described as the cravings of infinitude. We are so made that nothing which has limits satisfies. . . . Man's destiny is to be not dissatisfied, but for ever unsatisfied. . . . Infinite goodness—a beauty beyond what eye hath seen or heart imagined, a justice which shall have no flaw and a righteousness which shall have no blemish—to crave for that, is to be 'athirst for God.'" (*Sermons*, 2nd Series, pp. 120, 121.)

THE LIVING GOD. Comp. lxxxiv. 2 [3], not only as opposed to the gods of the heathen, nor as Stier suggests (and as the old Latin paraphrast, *fontem vivum*, and the A.-S. *se libbenda wylle*), with an allusion to the expression "living waters;" but in opposition to all

When shall I come, and appear before God?
3 My tears have been my food day and night,
While they say unto me continually, "Where is thy God?"
4 These things would I remember,[c] and pour out my soul in me,[d]—

dead abstractions, all vague head-notions, as the Living Person, the Source and Fountain of all life, loving and loved in return, as xxxvi. 9 [10]. Again I cannot deny myself the pleasure of quoting from Robertson: "What we want is, we shall find, not infinitude, but a boundless *One;* not to feel that love is the *law* of this universe, but to feel One whose name is Love. For else, if in this world of order there be no One in whose bosom that order is centred, and of whose Being it is the expression: in this world of manifold contrivance no Personal Affection which gave to the skies their trembling tenderness and to the snow its purity: then order, affection, contrivance, wisdom, are only horrible abstractions, and we are in the dreary universe alone. . . . It is a dark moment when the sense of that personality is lost; more terrible than the doubt of immortality. For of the two—eternity without a personal God, or God for seventy years without immortality—no one after David's heart would hesitate. 'Give me God for life to know and be known by Him.' No thought is more hideous than that of an eternity without Him."

Calvin interprets this longing for God, as a longing for His sanctuary and its ordinances. "Clamavit igitur David ad Deum . . quia ab externo cultu erat exclusus, quod vinculum est sacræ cum Deo conjunctionis: non quod per se Deo nos ceremoniæ concilient, sed quia pietatis sunt exercitia, quibus carere non sustinet nostra infirmitas. Itaque a sanctuario exulans David, non aliter anxius est quam si a Deo ipso esset alienatus." And this is no doubt supported by the expression which follows:

WHEN SHALL I . . . APPEAR BEFORE GOD? For this is a phrase commonly used of going to the sanctuary or temple, lxxxiv. 7 [8]; Ex. xxiii. 17; and still more often "before *the face of* God," Ex. xxxiv. 24; Deut. xvi. 16, xxxi. 11; 1 Sam. i. 22. Here the verb is construed with the simple accus. without a preposition, as in Ex. xxiii. 15; Is. i. 12. But the longing for the sanctuary was because God's Presence was there peculiarly manifested.

3. MY TEARS HAVE BEEN, &c. *i.e.* they have been my daily portion, like my daily meal. See lxxx. 5 [6], cii. 9 [10], and Job iii. 24. Comp. Plaut. *Asinar.* "pro cibo habes te verberari." Ovid. *Metam.* x. 288, "Cura dolorque animi lacrimæque alimenta fuere."

WHERE IS THY GOD? The bitterest of all taunts, see lxxix. 10, cxv. 2; Joel ii. 17; Micah vii. 10, and comp. xxii. 8 [9], with Matt. xxvii. 43. "This is ever the way in religious perplexity: the unsympathizing world taunts or misunderstands. In spiritual grief they ask, Why is he not like others? In bereavements they call your deep sorrow unbelief. In misfortune they comfort you, like Job's friends, by calling it a visitation . . . they call you an infidel, though your soul be crying after God. Specially in that dark and awful hour, 'Eloi, Eloi,' *He* called on God: they said, 'Let be, let us see whether Elias will come to save Him.'"—*Robertson.*

4. THESE THINGS WOULD I REMEMBER, or, "let me remember,"

How I passed with the festal throng,[e]
How I led them in procession[f] to the House of God,
With the voice of loud song and thanksgiving,—a multitude keeping holy-day.
5 Why art thou bowed down, O my soul,
And (why) art thou disquieted within me?
Hope in God; for I shall yet give Him thanks,

"fain would I remember." In such a recollection there would be mingled feelings of bitterness and consolation. No doubt the thought of those happy days in which he had travelled with the festal caravan to the holy city, would make him feel more intensely his present loneliness, but it would also be a kind of solace in his sorrow, or, as Delitzsch terms it, "a bitter-sweet remembrance."

THESE THINGS, viz. what follows, how I once led the rejoicing multitudes in procession to the house of God. On the construction, see Critical Note.

WITH THE VOICE OF LOUD SONG, &c. These pilgrim caravans went up to Jerusalem with all the accompaniments of music and song (see 2 Sam. vi. 5, and the beautiful little collection of pilgrim songs preserved in Psalms cxx.—cxxxiv., which were inspired by and adapted to such occasions).

A MULTITUDE (a word occurring with the same reference, 2 Sam. vi. 19), in apposition with the THRONG mentioned above: KEEPING HOLY-DAY, or festival; the word is used absolutely, as in Exod. xxiii. 14.

5. WHY ART THOU BOWED DOWN? lit. "Why bowest thou thyself down?" The verb only occurs here and in the next Psalm, in this reflexive form (Hithpael). "David here presents himself to us," says Calvin, "divided into two parts." It is the struggle between the spirit of faith and the spirit of dejection, between the higher nature and the lower, between the spirit and the flesh. The true I speaks; the faith which is born of God rebukes the depression and gloom of his natural infirmity.

DISQUIETED, a word used elsewhere of the raging and roaring of the sea (as xlvi. 3 [4]): His soul is tossed and agitated like an angry sea.

HOPE. "Distinguish between the *feelings* of faith that God is present, and the *hope* of faith that He will be so. . . . There are hours in which physical derangement darkens the windows of the soul; days in which shattered nerves make life simply endurance: months and years in which intellectual difficulties, pressing for solution, shut out God. Then faith must be replaced by hope. 'What I do thou knowest not now; but thou shalt know hereafter.' 'Clouds and darkness are round about Him: *but* Righteousness and Truth are the habitation of His Throne.' 'My soul, hope thou,'" &c.—*Robertson.*

IN GOD. "This hope was in *God.* The mistake we make," says Robertson, "is to look for a source of comfort in ourselves: self-contemplation instead of gazing upon God;" and then, after showing that it is impossible to derive consolation from our own *feelings*, because they are so variable, or from our own *acts*, because in a low state no man can judge of these aright, and warning us that besides, whilst engaged in this self-inspection, we lose time in remorse, he continues, "When we gaze on God, then first the chance of consolation dawns. He is not affected by our mutability: our changes do not alter Him. When we are restless, He remains serene and calm: when we

(Who is) the health of my countenance and my
God.[g]

II. 6 [My God,] my soul is bowed down within me :
Therefore do I remember Thee from the land of
Jordan,
And (from) the Hermons, from the mountain of
Mizar.

are low, selfish, mean, or dispirited, He is still the unalterable I AM, the same yesterday, to-day, and for ever, in whom is no variableness, neither shadow of turning. What God is in Himself, not what we may chance to feel Him in this or that moment to be, that is our hope. 'My soul, hope thou in GOD.'"

I SHALL YET GIVE HIM THANKS, *i.e.* I shall do again as I have done before. Once I went . . . with the voice of song and *thanksgiving*, ver. 4., . . . and again I shall *give* Him *thanks*.

(WHO IS) THE HEALTH, &c. According to the present Hebrew text, the rendering would be : "For the health of His countenance." But see Critical Note.

6. The first division of the Psalm ends with the expostulation addressed to the soul in its despondency, "Why art thou cast down?" and with an effort to rise into a brighter region of hope. But the gloom is too deep to be so soon dispersed. Therefore this second strophe opens with the complaint, "My soul is bowed down."

Throughout this second portion of the Psalm, the constant fluctuations, the alternations of despondency and hope, are very remarkable. "My soul is cast down,—therefore will I remember Thee. All Thy waves and Thy billows are gone over me,—Jehovah will command His loving-kindness. I will pray unto God,—though my prayer be nothing but the outpouring of my complaint. God is my Rock,—even whilst I say, Why hast Thou forgotten me?"

MY SOUL IS BOWED DOWN. The rendering of the LXX. here, ἡ ψυχή μου ἐταράχθη, and that in the previous verse, of the words, Why art thou cast down, &c., τί περίλυπος εἶ ἡ ψυχή μου, are both appropriated by our Lord ; the former in John xii. 27, the latter in Matt. xxvi. 38.

THEREFORE DO I REMEMBER, in that strange land so much the more. Comp. the prayer of Jonah, ii. 8.

THE LAND OF JORDAN, *i.e.* as mentioned in the Introduction, the country east of the Jordan, which had this special designation.

THE HERMONS, or the peaks or ridges of Hermon, the plural being used either because of the *two* peaks of the mountain (Wilson, *Land of the Bible*, ii. 161), or perhaps with reference to the whole range of its snowy heights.

MIZAR, apparently the name of some one of the lesser peaks of the same mountain range, though the particular peak cannot now be identified. The older translators generally supposed the word to be used merely as an appellative, in its literal sense, of "littleness" or "contempt" (comp. the play on the word "Zoar," from the same root, Gen. xix. 20), as if the Sacred Poet were anxious to express how little in his eyes seemed even that giant range, with all its snows and forests, compared with the true greatness and dignity of the holy hill of Zion : as Rosenm. explains, "religionis studio ita ardebat ut sorderent ei præ monte Sion omnia." But the objection to such an interpretation is, that the Hebrew Poets do not seek to depreciate the greater mountains of Hermon and Bashan, in comparison with Zion, but rather

7 Deep calleth unto deep at the voice of Thy cataracts ;
All Thy breakers and Thy billows have passed over me.
8 (Yet) in the day-time will Jehovah command His loving-kindness ;
And in the night His song shall be with me,
A prayer unto the God of my life.
9 So will I say unto God my Rock, "Why hast Thou forgotten me ?
Why go I mourning because of the oppression of the enemy ?"

to raise Zion to a level, or to exalt it above these. Hengstenberg supposes that the name of "contempt" designates not the particular mountain, but the whole trans-Jordanic territory.

7. DEEP CALLETH UNTO DEEP. An image borrowed, Stanley thinks (see the passage quoted in the Introduction to this Psalm), from the winding rapids of the Jordan : Delitzsch, from the rushing mountain torrents which dashed and foamed before his eyes. But so common an image as that in which sorrows and calamities are compared to floods and waves (see xviii. 16 [17]), need not have been suggested by any external object then immediately present. Besides, the word "deep" is properly used only of "the sea" or of "the great subterranean reservoir of waters" (Gen. vii. 11), and probably it is used in this last sense even in Ezek. xxxi. 4, 15, where the cedars of Lebanon are supposed to be nourished by it. One vast body of water seems to summon another, as if on purpose to swallow him up. Comp. Eur. *Suppl.* 614, *δίκα δίκαν κάλεσσε καὶ φόνος φόνον.*

AT THE VOICE OF, *i.e.* accompanied by the sound of, &c. THY CATARACTS, or waterfalls ; such seems to be the meaning here. LXX. *καταρράκται.* The only other place where the word occurs is 2 Sam. v. 8, where it is in the singular, and is rendered in the E.V. "the gutter," but probably means rather "the watercourse." Hence it would appear that, like many other words (נַחַל for instance), it might denote both the bed or channel itself, and the water in the channel. (Comp. צַנְתָּר, Zech. iv. 12).

BREAKERS . . . BILLOWS. The first, from the verb שׁבר (*shābhar*), "shiver, break," with the same idea in Hebrew as in English, of the waves *breaking* on the shore ; the last of the waves as *rolling*.

8. WILL COMMAND. Clearly not to be referred to the past, as Ibn Ezra and others have supposed. It is a bright ray of hope which gleams upon the singer in the midst of his present despondency. God will command,—send, that is, like a divine Iris, or heavenly messenger, His loving-kindness. So xliii. 3, "Send Thy Light and Thy Truth," &c.

IN THE NIGHT, not to be emphasized, as if intended in opposition to IN THE DAY, but day and night are used poetically to describe the *continuance* of the action.

HIS SONG, comp. Job xxxv. 10.

9. SO WILL I SAY. The resolve which follows (expressed by the optative form of the verb), based on this his hope in the goodness of God.

MOURNING, or rather, "as a mourner," "in mourning attire." See on xxxv. 14.

10 As though they would break[h] my bones, mine enemies
reproach me,
While they say unto me all day long, "Where is
thy God?"
11 Why art thou bowed down, O my soul,
And (why) art thou disquieted in me?
Hope in God; for I shall yet give Him thanks,
(Who is) the health of my countenance, and my God.

PSALM 43

III. 1 JUDGE me, O God,
And plead my cause against a cruel nation;
From the man of deceit and wrong rescue me
2 For Thou art the God of my strength:
Why hast Thou cast me off,
Why go I to and fro mourning because of the
oppression of the enemy?
3 O send forth Thy Light and Thy Truth; let *them*
lead me,
Let them bring me to Thy holy mountain, and to
Thy tabernacles.
4 So will I come unto the altar of God,
Unto God my exceeding joy:

1. JUDGE ME, *i.e.* "show the justice of my cause," "pronounce sentence for me," as often elsewhere. AGAINST, lit. "from." A brief form of expression for the fuller "Plead my cause, so as to deliver me from."

UNGODLY, lit. "not godly," or perhaps "not-good," if the adjective be taken here as in xii. 1 [2], in its active sense; hence "cruel," "unmerciful."

2. The question is repeated from xlii. 9 [10], but in a stronger form. Not "Why hast Thou forgotten?" but "Why hast Thou cast off?"

3. The one object of his heart's desire is to be restored to the house of God.

LIGHT and TRUTH (instead of the more usual Loving-kindness and Truth)—these shall be to him, so he hopes, as angels of God, who shall lead him by the hand, till they bring him to the holy mountain, to the tabernacle, and to the altar, there to offer his thank-offerings. Or possibly there may be an allusion to the Urim and Thummim, as the symbol of Light and Truth. See the article "Urim and Thummim," by Prof. Plumptre, in Smith's *Dict. of the Bible.*

TABERNACLES. The plural may denote the *several parts* of the building; but see on lxxxiv. 1.

4. GOD MY EXCEEDING JOY, lit. "God the joy of my exultation."

Yea, upon the harp will I praise Thee, O God, my God.
5 Why art Thou bowed down, O my soul,
And why art thou disquieted in me?
Hope in God; for I shall yet give Him thanks,
(Who is) the health of my countenance, and my God.

[a] מַשְׂכִּיל. See on Ps. xxxii. note [a].

לִבְנֵי קֹרַח. These words are first found in the inscription of this and the six following Psalms. Jebb supposes this title to denote not the authors of the Psalms, but the Levitical singers and musicians *for* whom they were composed. He would, therefore, take the לְ not as in לְדָוִד, but as in לַמְנַצֵּחַ. It is more natural, however, to consider the לְ here as expressive of authorship; and so the LXX. τοῖς υἱοῖς Κορέ, as in other Psalms, τῷ Δαυίδ. It is remarkable that the inscription should assume this anonymous character, mentioning not the individual singer, but only the family to which he belonged; especially when, as Delitzsch has remarked, we have in the inscriptions of other Psalms (as, for instance, lxxiii.—lxxxiii.) the individual לְאָסָף, instead of the family לִבְנֵי־גֵרְשֹׁם, or the like. This may be owing to some circumstance with which we are unacquainted. These Levitical singers may have been like the Bardic families or colleges in other nations, especially those living in mountain regions. All may have made poetry and music their profession, and only in rare cases did an individual, perhaps like Asaph, acquire great personal reputation. The "Korah" whose "sons" are here spoken of, is the Levite who headed the insurrection against Moses and Aaron in the wilderness (Numb. xvi.). We find his descendants existing as a powerful Levitical family in the time of David, at least if they are to be identified, as is probable, with the Korahites mentioned in 1 Chron. xii. 6, who, like our own warlike bishops of former times, seem to have known how to doff the priestly vestment for the soldier's armour, and whose hand could wield the sword as well as strike the harp. These Korahites were a part of the band who acknowledged David as their chief at Ziklag; warriors "whose faces," it is said, "were like the faces of lions, and who were (for speed) like gazelles upon the mountains." According to 1 Chron. ix. 17, the Korahites were, in David's time, keepers of the threshold of the Tabernacle; and still earlier, in the time of Moses, watchmen at the entrance of the camp of the Levites. In 1 Chron. xxvi. 1—19, we find two branches of this family associated with that of Merari, as guardians of the doors of the Temple. There is probably an allusion to this their office in Ps. lxxxiv. 11. But the Korahites were also celebrated musicians and singers, 1 Chron. vi. 16—33, where Heman, one of the three famous musicians of the time, is said to be a Korahite (comp. 1 Chron. xxv.). The musical reputation of the family continued in the time of Jehoshaphat, 2 Chron. xx. 19, where we have the peculiar doubly plural form בְּנֵי הַקָּרְחִים, "sons of the Korahites."

[b] תַּעֲרֹג. We have three points to consider with reference to this verb: (1) its meaning, (2) its gender, (3) its construction in the sentence.

(1) The word only occurs here and Joel i. 20, where it is spoken of "the beasts of the field." The older interpreters seem to have guessed at the meaning of the word, as they explain it differently in the two passages. Here the LXX. have ἐπιποθεῖ; similarly the Chald. מְרַגֵּג. Jerome renders: "Sicut areola præparata ad irrigationes aquarum: sic anima mea præparata (h. desiderat) ad te, Deus." In Joel i. 20, the LXX. have ἀνέβλεψαν, Chald. מְסַבְּרָא, Jerome, *suspexerunt*, but he has there the remarkable gloss, *quasi area sitiens imbrem*, which seems to have been borrowed from this Psalm, and looks as if he wished to explain both the verb and the preposit. אֶל, by this rendering; the *suspexerunt* referring to the latter, and the *sitiens*, &c. to the former. The Rabbinical commentators, following the lead of the Syr., suppose the word to describe the peculiar cry of the stag, as געה does the lowing of the ox, and שׁאג the roar of the lion. The word, however, is probably cognate in root with the Arab. عرج, which means (not as Gesen. *ascendere*, and hence with the prepos. *desiderare, appetere*, but) *inclinare, flectere*. Comp. عرج, *ad occasum vergere*, II. V. *intentum esse, instare*, &c. So Hupfeld. It is evident from the passage in Joel, as well as from this, that the word is used properly of the *longing* of animals for *water*. It is said there, "that the water-brooks are dried up;" it expresses therefore the *panting* of the stag in the burning heat of the steppes, or perhaps when hard pressed by the hunters. The Gr. ὀρέγεσθαι is apparently a kindred root.

(2) The verb is fem. though the noun אַיָּל is properly masc. The irregularity is best explained by regarding אַיָּל as a collect. or epicœne noun (like שׁוֹר, חֲמוֹר).

(3) As regards the construction, כְּ is usually taken here as a *conjunction*, as a matter of course, as if it were = כַּאֲשֶׁר, "*as* a hart panteth." Its normal use as a particle of comparison is certainly as a preposition; so that it belongs only to the noun to which it is prefixed. The accentuation, too, commonly restricts it to the noun, and separates it from the following verbal clause, which must consequently be a relative clause. So here, כא' ת' will be, "As a hart *which* panteth." Hupfeld, indeed, maintains that כְּ can be used as a conjunction, and gives several passages in which he says such a construction is necessary, xc. 5, cxxv. 1, Is. liii. 7, xi. 11. In all these passages the ordinary construction of כְּ as a prep. is not only admissible, but preferable.

[c] אֶזְכְּרָה, optative. Two constructions are possible: either that of the E. V., "When I remember these things, then I pour out my soul in me: *for*," &c., in which case the paragogic form is used both in protasis and apodosis, and the apodosis is introduced by וְ. So Ewald. (Comp. the use of ה paragog. in the protasis xl. 6). Or, the second clause may be parenthetical. "Fain would I remember these things—and (in the remembrance) pour out my soul—*how*," &c. In this case כִּי depends on the verb אֶזְכְּרָה, and, in fact, explains אֵלֶּה. Hence Mendelssohn paraphrases:

"Ueber mich ergiesst sich meine Seele, wenn ich denke wie ich mit Gefolg," &c.

[d] עָלַי, lit. "upon me," "with me," *penes me*, as (besides vers. 6, 7, 12, in this and ver. 5 in the next Ps.) in cxlii. 4, cxliii. 4, where it is parallel with בְּתוֹכִי. Comp. Job xxx. 16.

[e] סָךְ, only occurring here, but kindred with סֹךְ, סֻכָּה (Chald. סַךְ), properly *a thicket*, and so any dense interwoven mass; here, the densely-crowded caravan of pilgrims to the Holy City. The LXX. ἐν τόπῳ σκηνῆς θαυμαστῆς, supposing the Tabernacle to be meant, and so the Ethiop., but Rashi rightly גדודי בני אדם.

[f] אֶדַּדֵּם, Hithp., of a r. דדה, not in use, for אֶתְדַּדֶּה; occurs only here and Is. xxxviii. 15, "to move slowly," here of the slow march of the procession, but the pronom. suffix with the Hithp. is an anomaly, as the suffix must then = לָהֶם or עִמָּהֶם; the Hithp. cannot have the transitive meaning "to lead." Hence, either the suffix should be omitted; or we should point אֲדַדֵּם, Piel. The Piel דִּדָּה is found in the Talmud, and means there "to lead children and young animals." This verb and the preceding אֶעֱבֹר are both proper imperfects, as expressing a past habit.

[g] According to the present Hebrew text, יְשׁוּעוֹת פָּנָיו, we must render with the E. V., "for the help of His countenance" (so the Chald. "the redemption which comes from before Him"); or with Ibn Ezra, "His countenance or presence is salvation." But in both the other instances of the refrain, ver. 11 [12], and xliii. 5, the reading is י׳ פָּנַי וֵאלֹהָי, and this may have been the case originally here, as the next verse now begins with אֱלֹהַי. The alteration is extremely slight—the removal merely of the ו from the end of the one word to the beginning of the next; פָּנַי וֵאלֹהָי instead of פָּנָיו : אֱלֹהַי. Hengst. argues, on the other hand, that slight variations are of constant occurrence in the refrains of other Psalms—xlix. 13, 21; lvi. 5, 11; lix. 10, 18—and thinks that the address to God is necessary at the beginning of the next verse. It is, I think, more natural, notwithstanding Hupfeld's remark to the contrary, that the next verse should contain a direct address to God. In xliii. 1, we have in like manner a direct address after the refrain. In this case the reading may have been originally י׳ פ׳ וֵאלֹהָי : אֱלֹהַי, and the repetition of the word may have occasioned first its omission at the end of ver. 5 [6], and then the alteration of the text.

[h] רֶצַח בּ׳, "a breaking *in* my bones," instead of "a breaking *of*," &c. The first בְּ before רֶצַח (lit. "consisting in") serves here, in some measure, to introduce a comparison, comp. xxxvii. 20. Hence, "With a breaking in my bones,"—"like a shattering blow, crushing the very bones, is the taunt of the foe." Comp. lxix. 21. רֶצַח is, properly, "breaking,"—as in Ezek. xxi. 27, and the verb in Ps. lxii. 4, in both of which passages it is used of the breaking down of walls; LXX. καταθλᾶσθαι—not "murder," as Symm. ὡς σφαγὴν διὰ τῶν ὀστέων μου; Luther, "als Mord;" nor as in E. V. "as with a sword."

PSALM 44

THERE is scarcely any Psalm which seems at first sight to furnish a more decided clue to the probable date of its composition than this, and yet leaves us, after all, in so much uncertainty. The notes of time are apparently three.

1. The conquest of Palestine was looked back upon as distant, "the times of old."

2. The period was a period of great national distress; the people were hard pressed by enemies.

3. All this had come on them *not* as a judgement for national sin: hence the age must have been one when the nation was holding fast to the worship of Jehovah and eschewing idolatry.

This last circumstance is so peculiar, that we might expect it to decide the question.

Now we know of no period of Jewish history previous to the Exile, when the assertion would be true that the people had not forgotten God, nor "stretched out their hands to any strange god." Hence many interpreters refer the Psalm to the times of the Maccabees, and the persecution of Antiochus Epiphanes (2 Macc. v. 11—23). The nation was then free from the taint of idolatry, and it suffered cruelly. So far as the internal evidence goes, it is unquestionably in favour of this period. But the history of the Canon is said to be against it. Gesenius and others have argued, that Psalms composed at so late a date would not have been received into the Canon, which was finally settled in the time of Ezra and Nehemiah. This, however, is an entire mistake. The formation of the Canon was a slow and gradual work, extending over a very considerable period of time, and cannot be said to have been finally completed before the age of the Maccabees. See the able article on the Canon by Prof. Westcott in Dr. Smith's *Dict. of the Bible.*

Some, as De Wette (in his last edition) and Tholuck, refer the Psalm to the time immediately preceding the Exile, after Josiah's reforms; others, to the Exile itself, or the interval between the rebuilding of the Temple and Nehemiah's arrival in Jerusalem.

Others again, as Hengstenberg, Keil, and Delitzsch, suppose the Psalm to have been written in the time of David; and to have been occasioned by an invasion of the Edomites into the land which was left defenceless during the time that David was engaged in his wars with the Syrians (2 Sam. viii. 13, where, no doubt, אֱדֹם *Edom*, LXX. τὴν Ἰδουμαίαν, should be read, instead of אֲרָם, *Aram*, or Syria), and hence the fearful vengeance which he took upon them; see ver. 14, and comp. 1 Kings xi. 15. They refer Psalm lx. to the same occasion, —to the time, that is, which elapsed between the Edomite invasion, when some Israelites were carried away (hence the complaint, "Thou hast scattered us among the heathen") and the retribution which was executed by Joab. But this is obviously an improbable view. The language of the Psalm is altogether too large to be applied to a sudden attack. It describes a more serious and lasting calamity.

Calvin says with perfect truth that, if anything is clear, it is that the Psalm was written by any one rather than by David. The complaints which it contains, he observes, are most suitable to the wretched and calamitous time when the cruel tyranny of Antiochus was exercised without check; or we may extend it more widely, inasmuch as almost any time after the return from the Exile was a time of trouble and rebuke.

This Psalm, if not composed in the time of the Maccabees, was, we are told, used daily in the liturgy of that time. Each day the Levites ascended the pulpit (דוכן) and cried aloud, "Awake, why sleepest Thou, O Jehovah?" These Levitical Muezzin were termed "wakers" (מְעֹרְרִים). John Hyrcanus put an end to this custom, saying, "Doth God sleep? Hath not the Scripture said, 'The Keeper of Israel slumbereth not, nor sleepeth'? It was only in reference to a time when Israel was in trouble, and the nations in rest and prosperity, that it was said, 'Awake, why sleepest Thou, O Jehovah?'" (See Delitzsch, i. 342, note 2.)

The Psalm consists of four principal divisions:—

I. The Sacred Poet calls to mind the great deeds which God had wrought for His people in the days of old. God alone, he confesses, had given them possession of the land of Canaan, and had driven out their enemies before them. Remembering this, they had ever made their boast in His Name, and would still continue to praise Him. Ver. 1—8.

II Most painful is the contrast of the present with the past. God has forgotten His people. He has given them over into the hand of enemies, who hate, and insult, and slay them. God goes not forth now with their armies, as He had done when He brought them into Canaan: they are scattered among the heathen and sold for nought. Ver. 9—16.

III. And yet this cannot be a chastisement for their transgressions; for they have not forgotten God, but, on the contrary, die the death of martyrs for His truth. Ver. 17—22.

IV. Therefore he prays that God the Saviour of His people, and the Giver of Victory, would again be favourable unto them, as of old, and redeem them from their enemies. Ver. 23—26.

[FOR THE PRECENTOR. OF THE SONS OF KORAH. A MASKIL.]

I. 1 O GOD, with our ears we have heard,
Our fathers have told us,
A work which Thou didst work in their days,
In the days of old.
2 Thou, with Thine own hand, didst dispossess (the) nations.
And didst plant *them* in:

1. The Psalm opens with a glance at the past history of the nation, and the acknowledgement that from the first, every victory which they had won, had been won, not by their own strength, but by the immediate hand of God. This was, it might be said, the perpetual lesson of their history. They did not rise upon their Egyptian masters, but God bowed the heart of the monarch and the people by His signs and wonders, till they thrust them out in haste. At the Red Sea they did not turn to fight with the chariots and the horsemen of Pharaoh: they were but to *stand still*, and see the victory of Jehovah. When they came to Canaan, their first exploit was not a feat of arms; for Jericho fell by a miracle. The Roman army, by the lake Regillus, attributed its victory to the two mysterious horsemen who, on their white horses, led the charge. The Jewish host with a better faith believed that in every battle an invisible Captain led them, and knew that, whenever they conquered their enemies, it was because an invisible arm gave them the victory.

OUR FATHERS HAVE TOLD US, in accordance with the duty so often impressed upon the minds of the people, to perpetuate from generation to generation "the mighty acts" of Jehovah, on their behalf. See Exod. x. 2, and comp. xii. 26, &c., xiii. 8, 14; Deut. vi. 20; Judges vi. 13.

A WORK; emphat. as in lxiv. 9, [10], xcv. 9. The same phrase, "to work a work," "do a deed," occurs with like meaning in Hab. i. 5. It seems to be employed here collectively, gathering up in one the deliverance from Egypt, the guidance through the wilderness, and the settlement in Canaan.

As regards the construction, this may either be an independent clause, or it may be a relative clause, with the common omission of the relat., "Our fathers have told us a work (which) Thou didst," &c.

2. THINE HAND. It is simplest, I think, to take this as the accus. of the instrument, as is usual in Hebrew, though Hupfeld contends for a double subject: "Thou, Thy hand," as Is. xlv. 12, "I, my hands," and as he also explains, Ps. iii. 4 [5], "my voice, I cry."

DIDST PLANT *them* IN . . . DIDST SPREAD *them* ABROAD. In each

Thou didst afflict (the) peoples,
And cause *them* to spread abroad.
3 For not by their own sword gat they the land in possession,
Neither did their own arm give them the victory;
But Thy right hand, and Thine arm, and the Light of Thy countenance,
Because Thou hadst a favour unto them.
4 Thou, even Thou Thyself[a] art my King, O God;
Command the victories of Jacob.
5 Through Thee shall we push down our adversaries;
In Thy Name shall we tread them under that rise up against us.

case the pronoun refers to "our fathers," who are thus emphatically contrasted with the "nations" and "peoples" who were dispossessed. The figure is taken from the planting and growth of a vine, and is carried out in Ps. lxxx. It first occurs in Exod. xv. 17, "Thou wilt *plant* them in the mountain of Thine inheritance." Comp. 2 Sam. vii. 10, and Ps. lxxx. 8 [9]. For the other verb, "Thou didst spread them abroad" (like the roots and branches of a tree), comp. lxxx. 11 [12], Jer. xvii. 8, Ezek. xvii. 6. "Veteres incolas terræ Chanaan comparat arboribus, quia longa possessione illic radices egerant. Subita igitur quæ contigit mutatio perinde fuit ac si quis revulsis arboribus in earum locum alias substituat."—*Calvin.*

3. FOR, a more emphatic insisting upon the truth that God's power alone had achieved all.

GIVE THEM THE VICTORY. Such seems here, and generally in this Psalm, to be the force of the word usually rendered "save," "help." See above, xxxiii. 17. Not very unlike is the use of σωτηρία sometimes in the N. T. Cf. for instance 1 Pet. i. 5, where, as Alford remarks, it has more than a negative idea. So in the next verse, "the victories of Jacob" = "the salvation of Jacob" liii. 6.

The RIGHT HAND and the ARM, as emblems of *power:* the LIGHT OF THY COUNTENANCE, as the manifestation of God's *grace;* the last further explained by "because Thou hadst a favour," &c. Comp. Deut. iv. 37.

4—8. Application of this acknowledged truth to the present and to the future.

4. MY KING, apparently with a personal application to himself, the Poet individually claiming his own place in the covenant between God and His people. The singular fluctuates with the plural in the Psalm; see ver. 6 and 15, where the individual is again prominent.

COMMAND, in Thy royal majesty, as an act of sovereign authority.

5. PUSH DOWN, in the sense of butting, an image taken from horned cattle, and of common occurrence in the Old Testament, borrowed, in the first instance, it would seem, from the fat buffalos in the pastures of Bashan. See Deut. xxxiii. 17. Comp. also Ps. lxxv. 4 [5], 10 [11] Ezek. xxxiv. 21; Dan. viii. 4; 1 Kings xxii. 11.

TREAD UNDER, as lx. 12 [14],

6 For not in my bow do I trust,
And my sword cannot give me the victory :
7 But THOU hast given us the victory over our adversaries,
And hast put to shame them that hate us.
8 In God have we made our boast [b] all the day long,
And to Thy Name will we for ever give thanks.
[Selah.]

II. 9 But [c] Thou hast cast (us) off, and put us to confusion,
And goest not forth with our hosts.
10 Thou makest us to turn back from (the) adversary,
And they which hate us have spoiled for themselves :
11 Thou makest us like sheep (appointed for) food,
And Thou hast scattered us among the nations.
12 Thou sellest Thy people for nought,

Is. xiv. 19, 25, lxiii. 6. The verbs in this verse are strictly aorists of repeated action.

6. The same contrast here and in the next verse as before in ver. 3.

8. The past experience of God's saving might is the reason that they praise and thank Him.

9—16. The painful contrast in the experience of the present, to all the warrant of the past, and all the hopes which had sprung from the past.

9. THOU HAST CAST OFF (the obj. omitted, as in ver. 23 [24], and in lxxvii. 7 [8], lxxxix. 38 [39], preterite, expressing the completed action, whilst the following future (or present) "goest forth" expresses the *consequence* of the action. Comp. xlvi. 6 [7], "He uttered His voice (past action) ; the earth melteth (consequence)."

GOEST NOT FORTH, *i.e.* as leader of the army (see Jud. iv. 14, 2 Sam. v. 24), as once visibly with the pillar of a cloud, and the pillar of fire before the host in the desert. This verse occurs almost word for word in Ps. lx., with which, and lxxxix., this Psalm has many points of resemblance.

10. FOR THEMSELVES. "At their own will ;" as Calvin well explains : "quod hostes pro arbitrio et sine ulla repugnantia quasi suam prædam diripuerint."

11. MAKEST US LIKE. See the same construction in Is. xli. 2, Ezek. xvi. 7.

HAST SCATTERED. This may perhaps refer to the Babylonish captivity. De Wette, however, who in the first edition of his Commentary thought this and the next verse most applicable to the time of Antiochus Epiphanes, quotes 2 Macc. v. 11—23, where we are informed that Antiochus Epiphanes, on his return from Egypt, carried Jerusalem by storm, slew in three days 40,000 Jews, and had as many more sold as captives. Hence, according to him, the allusion in the following verse.

12. THOU SELLEST. This need not be explained literally of an historical fact (see note on last verse):

And hast not increased (Thy wealth) by their price.
13 Thou makest us a reproach to our neighbours,
A scorn and a derision to them that are round about us.
14 Thou makest us a proverb among the nations,
A shaking of the head among the peoples.
15 All the day is my confusion before me;
And the shame of my face hath covered me;
16 Because of the voice of him that reproacheth and blasphemeth,
Because of the enemy and the avenger.

it is a figure expressive of God's giving up His people into *slavery* to their enemies, just as, on the other hand, their deliverance is described as *redemption*, *ransoming*. The figure, Hupfeld thinks, is borrowed from the right of the father to sell his children as slaves: but the Jewish law gave him no such right, the case mentioned in Exod. xxi. 7 being altogether exceptional. We have the same figure in Deut. xxxii. 30, Judges ii. 14, iii. 8, and in many other passages.

FOR NOUGHT, lit. "for not-riches," *i.e.* for that which is the very opposite of riches, a mere nothing. Comp. for similar composition of nouns with the negative, Is. x. 15, "not-wood," *i.e.* something the very opposite of wood; Ps. xxii. 6 [7], "not-man," &c., and for the idea, Is. lii. 3, Jer. xv. 13.

HAST NOT INCREASED, *i.e.* hast gained nothing. The verb is used absol., as the Hiph. in Prov. xxii. 16, "he that oppresseth the poor to *make himself rich*." Eccl. ii. 9, "I added to my wealth." This verse is almost an expostulation with God. An earthly ruler might sell men like cattle to increase his own wealth, but God cannot be richer by such merchandise. Calvin's remark, however, is of importance, as bearing on all this attributing of their calamities to God: "We must observe, however, that God is represented as the author of these calamities, not by way of reproaching Him (*non obstrependi causa*), but that the faithful may with the more confidence seek the remedy from the Hand which hath smitten and wounded."

13. THEM THAT ARE ROUND ABOUT US (lit. "our surroundings," lxxix. 4, comp. lxxx. 6 [7]), *i.e.* nations like the Philistines, Edomites, Moabites, and Ammonites, the bitterest enemies of the Jews, whose insulting mockery in the day of their triumph is often the subject of complaint in the later Prophets.

14. A PROVERB (*māshāl*) or "byword," often used of words uttered in mockery. Comp. lxix. 11 [12], Is. xiv. 4, possibly also the verb, Num. xxi. 27 ("they that speak in proverbs," E.V.), where the taunting Amorite song is quoted.

SHAKING OF THE HEAD. See on xxii. 7 [8].

15. THE SHAME, &c. This rendering is favoured by the accent (Tiphcha conj.), the shame seen in the face being regarded as a mantle enveloping the whole man, the construction being the same as in xlix. 6, "the iniquity of my heels compasseth me about," where see note; but the grammatical construction may be that of the double object, "shame hath covered me as to my face." The meaning here is evident from the simpler phrase in lxix. 7 [8.]

16. THE AVENGER. See on viii. 2 [3].

III. 17 All this is come upon us, and yet we have not forgotten Thee,
Neither have we dealt falsely in Thy covenant;
18 Our heart is not turned back,
Neither hath our step declined from Thy path,
19 That [d] Thou hast crushed us in the place of jackals,
And covered us with the shadow of death.

17—22. A complaint that all these calamities have come upon them without any fault or demerit on the part of the nation. Such a complaint is doubly remarkable. First, because as an assertion of *national* innocence and faithfulness to God's covenant it is without parallel in the Old Testament, and next, because it wears the air of a reproach cast upon the righteousness of God, in permitting the chastisement.

(1) We often find an *individual* declaring that he suffers unjustly for the sake of God, and appealing to God to do him right, because of his innocence. Comp. lxix. 7 [8], "*For Thy sake*," &c., and Jer. xv. 15, Is. lxvi. 5, &c. But here the whole nation is said to have adhered steadfastly to God, and, because of this steadfastness, to have brought upon themselves persecution. The expression, "For Thy sake," has been supposed to indicate that the persecution was a religious one, that the sufferers were martyrs for their faith: and hence it has been inferred that the Psalm was written in the time of the Maccabees, the only time in which the nation, as a nation, so suffered. The national abjuration of idolatry, verse 20, seems also to show that the date of the Psalm must be subsequent to the Exile. It is not certain, indeed, that the words of verse 22 refer to *religious persecution*. The language would hold good of all sufferings endured *in the service of God* (as Hupfeld observes, referring to 1 Sam. xvii. 45, Is. x. 9 ff., xxxvi. 18 ff., xxxvii. 4, 10 ff.). But we know of no earlier period in Jewish history when it could be said with truth of the nation at large, "Our heart is not turned back, neither have our steps declined from Thy path."

(2) It is on the ground of this national adherence to the covenant, that the Psalmist expostulates with God, who has given them over into the hand of their enemies. Such chastisement appears to him unmerited. There is nothing apparently in the conduct of the nation at large to call for it. God seems pledged by His very faithfulness to take away the rod. Such an expostulation, however, it is clear, can only be defended as coming from a saint under the Old Testament dispensation. No nation, no Church now could, in the eyes of any of its members, be so pure, that chastisement laid upon it would seem undeserved or unneeded. The work of the Spirit has given a deeper view of sin, has shown how much hidden corruption may consist with the open profession of godliness, and has taught us to confess national guilt in every national punishment.

17. IS COME UPON US. The construction is the same as in xxxv. 8, xxxvi. 11 [12]. Comp. Jud. vi. 13.

18. The negative must be repeated with the second clause of the verse from the first.

19. PLACE OF JACKALS, or "howling creatures." A dreary, waste, howling wilderness, commonly described by the Prophets as inhabited by such creatures (Aq. ἐν τόπῳ ἀοικήτῳ). See the similar expression, "a dwelling of jackals," used with a like figurative meaning, Jer. ix. 10, x. 22, &c.

20 If we had forgotten the Name of our God,
And stretched out our hands to any strange god,
21 Would not God search this out?
For He knoweth the secrets of the heart.
22 But for Thy sake are we slain all the day long;
We are counted as sheep for the slaughter.

IV. 23 Up, why sleepest Thou, O Lord?
Awake, cast not off for ever.
24 Wherefore hidest Thou Thy face?
Why forgettest Thou our affliction (and) our oppression?
25 For our soul is bowed down to the dust;
Our body cleaveth to the earth.
26 Do Thou arise, to be a help unto us!
And redeem us, for Thy loving-kindness' sake.

20. STRETCHED OUT, or "spread forth," *i.e.* in prayer. Comp. cxliii. 6, and see xxviii. 2.

21. This solemn appeal to God's omniscience shows the honest conviction of the national integrity, while it is an indication at the same time that the sense of sin was comparatively superficial.

22. BUT, or perhaps, "nay," FOR THY SAKE. This passage is cited by St. Paul, Rom. viii. 36, apparently from the LXX., in illustration of the fact, that the Church of God has in all ages been a persecuted Church. But there is this remarkable difference between the tone of the Psalmist and the tone of the Apostle. The former cannot understand the chastening, complains that God's heavy hand has been laid without cause upon His people: the latter can rejoice in persecutions also, and exclaim, "Nay, in all these things we are more than conquerors, through Him that loved us."

23. AWAKE, &c. See vii. 6 [7].

25. IS BOWED DOWN. Cf. xlii. 5 [6]. CLEAVETH TO THE EARTH, alluding to the custom of mourners sitting down in dust and ashes. See xxxv. 14.

[a] אַתָּה־הוּא. The pronoun of the third person is thus subjoined to the pronouns of the first or second person, in order to render them emphatic, like *αὐτός* in Greek. So the LXX. here, *σὺ εἶ αὐτὸς ὁ βασιλεύς μου.* Comp. Is. xliii. 25, אָנֹכִי אָנֹכִי הוּא מֹחֶה וגו׳; 2 Sam. vii. 28, אַתָּה־הוּא הָאֱלֹהִים. In cii. 28, and Deut. xxxii. 39, to which Hupf. (1st edit.) refers, the construction is different, הוּא being there the predicate. Calvin renders, "Tu ipse rex meus," and remarks: "Hoc valet (meo judicio) demonstrativum הוּא: ac si Propheta longam beneficiorum Dei seriem in prima redemptione contexeret; ut appareat, Deum qui semel redemptor fuerat populi sui non dissimilem fuisse erga posteros. Nisi forte emphatice positum sit asserendi causa, ut omnibus aliis exclusis et valere jussis Deum unum salutis suæ præsidem celebrent."

[b] הִלֵּל with בְּ, of the object, as elsewhere Hithp., "to make one's boast of a thing." Cf. the noun תְּהִלָּה with בְּ, in like manner, lxxi. 6. In lvi. 5, 11, the construction is different.

[c] אַף, a particle which may be used not only in advancing from a minor to a major proposition, but also to introduce a contrast, as lviii. 3, lxviii. 17, Job xiv. 3. Comp. Ew. § 341 *b*.

[d] כִּי, Rosenm. renders *quando*. Del. *und doch*, but explains that he does this merely for the sake of perspicuity, and that he considers it = *quod*. Hupfeld also rejects the meaning *when*, and says: "The particle introduces the reason of what goes before; the fact, on which the reproach rests, *weil* or *dass* (in Greek, γάρ), [it would have been better to say ὅτι,] as Gen. xx. 9, 10, 'In what have I sinned, that,' &c., 'What hast thou seen that,' &c., and xxi. 7, xxxi. 15, xl. 15, Ex. iii. 11 ('Who am I that,' &c., as Num. xvi. 11, &c.), Num. xi. 12, 13, Is. vii. 13, xxxvii. 19, 20." Many of these and other passages are also given by Gesenius, *Thes.* p. 679. But not to mention that it is not an indifferent matter whether כִּי here means "because" (*weil*), or "that" (*dass*),—for in the former case it would be implied that the chastisement had *not led to* apostasy; in the latter, that the chastisement was *not on account of* apostasy,—I cannot satisfy myself that the passages quoted are strictly parallel, the form of the sentence being in nearly every instance interrogative (except in Hos. i. 6, quoted by Gesen. "I will no more have compassion on the house of Israel *that* I should forgive them," and Gen. xl. 15), and כִּי in every instance depending *immediately* on the interrogative, or a verb in the primary clause. [In Is. xxxvii. 19, 20, the construction is quite different.] However, Gen. xl. 15, "Neither have I done anything *that* they should," &c. is a sufficiently near parallel to justify the rendering *that* here. Otherwise we might retain the usual signification of *for*, and regard ver. 19 as conveying a further reason for the complaint made. It will then belong to those cases respecting which Gesen. remarks (*loc. cit.*): "Nonnunquam vis causalis particulæ non statim in oculos incurrit, sententiarum tamen nexu accuratius perpenso revera in ea inest." See Exod. xiii. 17, where (and in two other passages, Ps. xlix. 19, cxvi. 10) Gesen. wrongly gives the meaning *etsi*.

PSALM 45

THIS Psalm is evidently a Marriage-song composed for some day of royal espousals. It celebrates the nuptials of a Jewish king with a princess, apparently of foreign extraction: but in honour of what particular king it was written, is matter of conjecture. The older and perhaps the more common interpretation refers it to Solomon's nuptials with the daughter of Pharaoh, king of Egypt. Hupfeld thinks that the princess here celebrated was not an Egyptian, but a daughter of Hiram, king of Tyre; and accordingly, in ver. 12 [13], he renders the words, "daughter of Tyre," in the vocative, as if the Poet were there addressing the new Queen. The history (1 Kings xi. 1, &c.), he observes, mentions *Zidonian* (=Tyrian, Is. xxiii. 12) princesses among Solomon's foreign wives. Hitzig refers the Psalm to the marriage of Ahab with Jezebel, daughter of Ethbaal, "King of the Zidonians" (1 Kings xvi. 31), and sees an allusion to Ahab's ivory house (1 Kings xxii. 39) in ver. 8 [9]. Delitzsch thinks Joram, "the son of Jehoshaphat, the second Solomon of the Jewish history," is the king mentioned in the Psalm, and Athaliah the queen. This accounts, he says, for the use of the word שֵׁגָל (*shégal*), as applied to the queen-consort, which occurs elsewhere as a Chaldee (Dan. v. 2) or Persian (Neh. ii. 6) title; and which would be more of a North Palestine than a Jewish word. For Athaliah was of Tyrian origin, and of the royal family of Israel. Hence the peculiar significance of the exhortation to forget "her father's house:" and hence, too, the homage demanded especially of Tyre. Moreover, Jehoshaphat seems to have had something of Solomon's passion for foreign trade (though he was unsuccessful in it), which explains, according to Delitzsch, the allusions to gold and ivory; or perhaps the "ivory palaces" may refer to the "ivory house" of Ahab, who was Athaliah's father (1 Kings xxii. 39, comp. Amos iii. 15). Finally, some commentators have supposed the Psalm to have been written in honour of a Persian king's bridal, because of the Persian title given to the queen, because the Tyrians bring tribute, and because the "princes in all lands" (ver. 16 [17]) applies best to Persian satraps. But these reasons are of no weight at all, as may be gathered from what has been already observed; and, on the face of it, it is extremely improbable that such an ode as this should have been inspired by the harem of a Persian monarch.

On the whole, the general character of the Psalm, describing as it does the majesty and persuasive eloquence of the king, the splendour of his appearance and of his palace, and the hopes which he raised for the future, is such as to make it more justly applicable to Solomon than to any other of the Jewish monarchs, so far as we are acquainted with their fortunes. Nor is it necessarily an objection to this view, that the monarch in the Psalm is spoken of as a warrior, whilst Solomon was peculiarly "a man of peace." Something must be allowed to poetry. An extended dominion would naturally be associated with ideas of conquest. And, with the recollection of the father's exploits fresh in his mind, the Poet could not but regard warlike virtues as essential to the glory of the son. Besides, Solomon himself does not seem to have been deficient in military spirit. Either in person or by his captains he carried his arms far to the east, and conquered the district Hamath Zobah, lying near the Euphrates. He took pains to strengthen the fortifications of various towns in his dominions, as well as the "Millo" or citadel of Jerusalem, and added largely to the army which he already possessed, by the introduction of a new kind of force, consisting of chariots and horses, and amounting, we are told, to 1,400 chariots and 12,000 horsemen. Why should not the Poet say, addressing such a king, "Gird thee with the sword upon thy thigh—in thy majesty ride forth and prosper"?

But "a greater than Solomon is here." Evident as it is that much of the language of the Poem is only properly applicable to the circumstances of the royal nuptials which occasioned it, it is no less evident that much of it greatly transcends them. The outward glory of Solomon was but a type and a foreshadowing of a better glory to be revealed. Israel's true king was not David or Solomon, but One of whom they, at the best, were only faint and transient images. A righteous One was yet to come who should indeed rule in truth and equity, who should fulfil all the hopes which one human monarch after another, however fair the promise of his reign, had disappointed, and whose kingdom, because it was a righteous kingdom, should endure for ever. Such a ruler would indeed be the vicegerent of God. In such an one, and by such an one, God would reign. He would be of the seed of David, and yet more glorious than all his fellows; human, and yet above men. It was because of this wonderfully close and real relation between God and man—a relation which the true king would visibly symbolize—that the Psalmist could address him as God. In him God and Man would in some mysterious manner meet. This perhaps he did see; more than this he could not see. The mystery of the Incarnation was not yet revealed. But David knew that God had made man to be but little short of divine (Ps. viii. 5 [6]). And he and others, full of hopes, the very greatness of which made them indistinct, uttered them in words that went far beyond themselves.

The mistake so commonly made in interpreting this Psalm and the Song of Solomon, is to suppose that we have in them *allegories*, every part of which is to find its appropriate spiritual interpretation. The earthly fact has, *as a whole*, its spiritual counterpart. For Christ speaks of Himself as "the Bridegroom," and of the Church as His "bride," and of the kingdom of God under the figure of a marriage-feast. (Matt. xxii. 1, &c., xxv. and ix. 15. See also Ephes. v. 32,

2 Cor. xi. 2, and Rev. xix. 7, xxi. 2.) The same figure also occurs in the Old Testament. God speaks of Himself as the bridegroom of the Jewish *people* (Is. liv. 5, Jer. iii. 1, Ezek. xvi. 8, Hos. i. ii.), though never, observe, of an *individual*, as the Mystics are wont to speak. But this Psalm is not an *allegory*. It is the actual celebration of a circumstance in Jewish history, and derives its higher meaning from the fact that all Jewish history is typical.

The Messianic interpretation of the Psalm is the most ancient. The Chaldee paraphrast on ver. 2 [3] writes: "Thy beauty, O King, Messiah, is greater than that of the sons of men." And even the later Jews take the same view. Ibn Ezra says: "This Psalm treats either of David or of his son Messiah, for that is His name, Ezek. xxxiv. 24, 'And David My servant shall be their prince for ever.'"

In the Epistle to the Hebrews (i. 8, 9) the writer rests upon this Psalm, among others, his argument for the Divine Nature of Christ.

The Psalm consists of two principal divisions, and a brief conclusion in the shape of auguries for the future.

I. The praise of the royal bridegroom. His more than human beauty, his persuasive eloquence, his might and prowess in war, his Divine Majesty, and the righteousness of his sway, are extolled. Ver. 1—9.

II. The description of the royal bride, her gold-inwoven garments, the virgins who follow in her train, the music and songs of the bridal procession. Ver. 10—15.

III. Anticipations and hopes expressed for the children by the marriage, who shall perpetuate the dynasty of the monarch, so that his name shall be famous for ever. Ver. 16, 17.

[FOR THE PRECENTOR. "ON THE LILIES."[a] OF THE SONS OF KORAH. A MASKIL. A SONG OF LOVE.]

1 MY heart is overflowing with a goodly matter;
I speak; my work[b] is for a King:

1. This verse is a kind of preface of a very unusual kind in Hebrew poetry, in which the singer tells how great his subject, and how full his heart is of it.

IS OVERFLOWING, lit. boils or bubbles up (the word only occurs here, though the noun formed from it occurs Lev. ii. 7, vii. 9), his heart being stirred within him by the greatness of his subject (Symm. ἐκινήθη ἡ καρδία μου). The metaphor may be taken either from boiling water, or from a fountain bubbling up from its source. (See Stanley, *Jewish Church*, i. 435.) And that which inspires him is A GOODLY MATTER (*ein feines Lied*,

My tongue is the pen of a ready writer.
2 Fair, fair[c] art Thou beyond the children of men ;
Grace is shed upon Thy lips :
Therefore[d] hath God blessed Thee for ever.
3 Gird Thy sword upon the thigh, O mighty One,
Thy glory and Thy majesty.
4 Yea in Thy majesty ride on prosperously
On behalf[e] of truth and righteous meekness ;[f]
And let Thy right hand teach Thee terrible things.

Luther), a subject worthy of his highest efforts (cf. Is. lii. 7, Zech. i. 13).

I SPEAK—*sc.* it is thus that I begin. MY WORK, *i.e.* my poem (Theod. ποίημα), the work or creation of my imagination, is for a king, is dedicated to and inspired by him.

FOR A KING. I see no reason to supply the article which is wanting in the Hebrew, though interpreters, ancient and modern, with one consent render, "*the* King." The absence of the article only makes it more emphatic. It is a King—not a meaner person who is the object of my song. Comp. ἐν υἱῷ, Heb. i. 1.

2. The *beauty* of the monarch first calls forth the Poet's praise (Is. xxxiii. 17), and then his *persuasive* eloquence (Eccl. x. 12). Cf. Cic. *Clar. Orat.* lix. 15, "suadelam sessitasse in labris ejus." Calvin observes, it were more kingly for kings to win their subjects' hearts by gracious words, than to rule them by brute force. So, too, of the Great Antitype, the true King, we read that men wondered at the gracious words (the λόγοι τῆς χάριτος, Luke iv. 22) that proceeded out of His lips : for the Lord had given Him the tongue of the learned, that He might know how to speak a word in season to them that were weary (Is. l. 4).

THEREFORE, *i.e.* beholding this beauty and this grace, do I conclude that God hath blessed thee for ever. Such gifts are the proof of God's good-will towards thee.

3. But the king is not only fair to look at, and gracious of speech, but he is mighty in battle. The nations shall fall under him. Nevertheless, "in righteousness doth he make war," to uphold truth, and to avenge the oppressed. Instead, however, of directly celebrating his prowess, the singer calls on the king to go forth to battle, and predicts his victory.

THY GLORY AND THY MAJESTY, a second accusative, not in apposition with "Thy sword," but dependent on the verb "gird on," in the first clause.

4. YEA IN THY MAJESTY : repeated for the sake of emphasis. Hupfeld, with utter want of poetic feeling, would reject the words as a useless repetition.

RIDE ON PROSPEROUSLY, lit. "make thy way, ride on," the first verb being used adverbially, to add force to the other (Ges. § 142, obs. 1), "make thy way," *i.e.* either lit. "pass through" the ranks of the enemy, and overcome all obstacles, or metaph. "be successful :" RIDE, either in the war-chariot (1 Kings xxii.), or on the war-horse, as in the Apocalyptic vision, xix. 11.

ON BEHALF OF, *i.e.* in order to assert and uphold, &c. ; so the LXX. ἕνεκεν ἀληθείας. Luth. *der Wahrheit zu gut.* This is the very loftiest conception of kingly might. The wars which such a king wages are not to acquire territory or renown.

5 Thine arrows are sharp ;—peoples fall under Thee ;
(They are sharp) in the heart of the King's enemies.
6 Thy throne, O God,[g] is for ever and ever;
A sceptre of uprightness is the sceptre of Thy kingdom.

6. THY THRONE, O GOD. I have retained the vocative, which is the rendering of all the ancient Versions ; and so the passage is quoted in Heb. i. 8. This rendering seems indeed at first sight to be at variance with the first and historical application of the Psalm. Can Solomon, or any Jewish king, be thus directly addressed as God? We find the title given to rulers, kings, or judges, lxxxii. 6, 7, " I said, ye are *gods*," (see our Lord's comment, John x. 35) ; Exod. xxi. 6. Calvin, indeed, objects that *Elohim* is only thus used when more than one person is meant, or with some restriction, as when Moses is said to be made a God (*Elohim*) unto Pharaoh (Exod. vii. 1). But the word is evidently used of one person in 1 Sam. xxviii. 13, as is plain from Saul's question, " What form is *he* of?" though our Version renders, "I saw *gods* ascending." Calvin, however, admits the first application to Solomon, only observing, that, "though he is called *God*, because God hath stamped some mark of His glory upon kings, yet so high a title must go beyond any mere man." It is one of the indications, as he rightly remarks, that the Poet is thinking of a greater King, and a more illustrious kingdom ("canticum hoc altius quam ad umbratile regnum spectare"). The difficulty is to understand how far the writer himself saw the purport of his own words. That they have a meaning which is only fully realized in Christ, and that God designed this fulfilment, I unhesitatingly admit. But on the other hand, it is impossible to suppose that the mystery of the Incarnation was distinctly revealed, and clearly understood, under the Old Testament dispensation. God does not thus make haste with men. I conclude, therefore, that in the use of such language the Psalmist was carried beyond himself, and that he was led to employ it by a twofold conviction in his mind, the conviction that God was the King of Israel, combined with the conviction that the Messiah, the true King, who was to be in reality what others were but in figure, was the son of David. In this sense I subscribe to Calvin's statement : " Itaque non dubium est quin Divina Christi majestas hic notetur." Again, he beautifully observes : " Jam vero notare operæ pretium est, sermonem hic de Christo haberi quatenus Deus est manifestatus in carne. Etsi enim Deus vocatur, quia Sermo est a Patre genitus ante secula, hic tamen statuitur in persona Mediatoris : unde et paulo post Deo subjicitur. Et certe si ad Divinam ejus naturam restringas quod dicitur de æterno ejus regno, peribit nobis inæstimabilis fructus quem ex hac doctrina percipimus : dum intelligimus quatenus caput est Ecclesiæ, et salutis nostræ custos ac præses, non regnare ad tempus, sed æterno imperio potiri, quia hinc nobis solida tam in vita quam in morte securitas. Clare etiam ex proximo contextu patet, Christum nobis Mediatorem proponi, quia unctus a Deo suo proponitur, et quidem præ sociis. Id autem in æternum Dei Sermonem non competit sed in Christum carne indutum, in qua et servus Dei est, et frater noster."

A SCEPTRE OF UPRIGHTNESS, and in the next verse, " Thou hast loved righteousness." Not only is righteousness the kingliest of all virtues, but it is the necessary basis of a throne and a kingdom which are to endure for ever.

7 Thou hast loved righteousness and hated wickedness,
Therefore God, (even) Thy God hath anointed Thee
With the oil of gladness above Thy fellows.
8 Myrrh and aloes (and) cassia are all Thy garments;
Out of ivory palaces music [h] hath made Thee glad.
9 Kings' daughters are among Thy beloved,[i]
The queen-consort stands at Thy right-hand in gold of
Ophir.

10 Hearken, O daughter, and see, and incline thine ear:

7. But this Divine King is nevertheless a distinct person from God Himself. GOD, EVEN THY GOD, peculiar to this Book of the Psalms, instead of "*Jehovah* Thy God." See xliii. 4, l. 7, lxvii. 6 [7]. It is contrary to all usage to render the first noun as a vocative, "O God, Thy God hath," &c. See more in Critical Note.

WITH THE OIL OF GLADNESS. Scarcely therefore is this the act of coronation, the anointing to His office (cf. lxxxix. 20 [21], with Acts x. 38), but rather the meaning is, that this king is, as it were, the very personification of gladness, beyond all the kings upon earth.

FELLOWS may either mean "other kings," or the friends who escorted him at his marriage, παρανύμφιοι.

8. The song of loves here reaches its culminating point in the description of the king. It has pourtrayed the king as man, as warrior, as godlike ruler; now it pictures him as bridegroom on the day of his espousals. (Compare with this the vision of the Apocalypse, where the "King of kings" goes forth to war, followed by the armies in heaven, after which there follows "the marriage of the Lamb," Rev. xix. 7, &c.)

MYRRH AND ALOES (AND) CASSIA. (Cf. Prov. vii. 17.) The royal garments are so filled with perfumes, that they seem to be nothing but perfumes.

And the marriage procession is accompanied by music. (See Critical Note.)

9. KINGS' DAUGHTERS; other wives and concubines of the monarch. Such, as Calvin observes, is the evident meaning of the words, although, as polygamy had only the permission, not the sanction, of God, it may seem strange that this should be mentioned as a feature in the splendour of the monarch. But polygamy was practised even by the best of kings; and the Psalmist is describing the magnificence of an Oriental court, such as it actually existed before his eyes, not drawing a picture of what ought to be in a perfect state of things. "In summa, quam liberaliter Deus rerum omnium abundantiam in Solomonem effuderit, hic narratur. Quod autem sibi coacervavit multas uxores, nec frugalem modum in splendore adhibuit, hoc est quasi accidentale."—*Calvin.*

THE QUEEN-CONSORT (*shēgāl*), the distinguishing title of the newly-married princess; a word occurring, except here, only in the later books.

STANDS, lit. "hath placed herself," "taken her position."

AT THY RIGHT HAND, as the place of honour; so Bathsheba, as queen-mother, sits at the right hand of Solomon, 1 Kings ii. 19.

10. The sacred Poet now turns to address the Bride. He bids her forget her father's house, and devote herself in reverent affection to

Forget also thine own people and thy father's house;
11 That the King may desire[k] thy beauty;
For He is thy lord, and do thou bow thyself down before Him.
12 And the daughter of Tyre (shall come) with a gift:
The rich among the people shall entreat thy favour.
13 All glorious[l] is the King's daughter in the inner palace,
Of thread of gold is her clothing.

her new lord, promising her at the same time that rich gifts shall be poured out at her feet.

O DAUGHTER (like "my son," in the Book of Proverbs), a common Oriental style of address, when the person who employed it, either from age or authority, or as divinely commissioned, had a right to give instruction, such as a father might give to his child.

11. THY LORD. Cf. Gen. xviii. 12.

12. Maurer has, I believe, rightly explained the construction, when he says that the two clauses of this verse must each have a word supplied from the other. He renders "*Et Tyrii muneribus* adulantur tibi; *Tibi adulantur* muneribus *ditissimi quique populi.*"

The "seek thy favour" of the second clause must be supplied with the first; the "with a gift" with the second. The "daughter of Tyre" is then a mere personification of the people of Tyre, according to the well-known Hebrew idiom, "daughter of Zion," &c. According to this explanation, there is no force in Hupfeld's objection, that, as a personification, it cannot be construed with a *plural;* for the verb may be *supplied* in the *singular* in the first clause, though it stands in the plural in the second. He further objects that Tyre was never subject to the Israelites. But gifts might be brought by nations that were not tributary, as Hiram gave large presents to Solomon. The Tyrians are mentioned only as one nation among many. Hupfeld himself (following Jerome, *et o filia fortissimi*) renders, "And, O daughter of Tyre," the princess herself being a Tyrian, and, as a king's daughter, a representative, as it were, of the people, so that she might be termed a *daughter* of her people. And Maurer admits the possibility of this rendering: "*Et o filia Tyri, muneribus adulantur tibi ditiores populi* (Judaici), te Tyriam, virginem peregrinam, quam ad nos adduxit rex, oblatis muneribus venerantur ditissimi quique novæ quam nacta es patriæ." The strongest objection to this view lies, I think, in the conjunction "and" prefixed, which is never prefixed to a vocative, except to join it to a vocative preceding. Riehm refers to vi. 4, as an instance to the contrary, but there the conjunction is prefixed to the pronoun, and the sentence is elliptical.

THE RICH AMONG THE PEOPLE, or, "the richest of the people;" so in the same construction, Is. xxix. 19, "the poorest of men."

ENTREAT THY FAVOUR, lit. smooth, or stroke, thy face (*demulcere faciem*, Ges.), Job xi. 19, "make suit unto," Prov. xix. 6, and used often of imploring the favour of God.

13. A description of the magnificent appearance presented by the queen, as she stands, or perhaps sits, beside the king on the throne, arrayed in her royal and bridal apparel *in the inner apartments of the palace*—the presence-chamber where the throne was placed. Her arrival there is anticipated in this verse, as the bridal procession is

14 On tapestry of divers colours[m] is she conducted unto the King:
The virgins in her train, (that be) her companions,
Are brought unto Thee.
15 They are conducted with great joy and exultation;
They enter into the King's palace.

16 Instead of Thy fathers, shall be Thy children,
Whom Thou shalt set as princes in all the earth.
17 Let me (then) make Thy name known through all generations;
Therefore shall the peoples give Thee thanks[n] for ever and ever.

subsequently described; unless, as Maurer suggests, this was not the king's palace but some other, where the bride was first lodged, and whence she was conducted to the king.

IN THE INNER PALACE (not "within," as E.V., whence the common interpretation, that the bride, the Church, must be pure within; the LXX. ἔσωθεν and the Vulg. *ab intus* are ambiguous), ἐν τοῖς ἐνωπίοις, the further wall of the house, which was over against the principal entrance, and where the throne stood.

14, 15. The bridal procession described. The bride walks in Oriental fashion on the richly woven carpets spread for her feet, accompanied by her maidens, and a festive band with music, dancing, &c.

14. TAPESTRY OF DIVERS COLOURS, or perhaps, "embroidered carpets."

15. GREAT JOY, lit. "joys," the plural denoting fulness and manifoldness: see on lxviii. 35.

16. After having thus dwelt on the personal graces of the royal pair, the magnificence of their attire, and the splendour of their retinue, the Poet again addresses the King, and concludes with congratulations and hopes expressed as to the issue of the marriage. The monarch cannot trace his descent from a long line of kings, but his children shall be better to him than royal ancestry. They shall be made princes in all the earth—or perhaps in all the *land*. Comp. Solomon's princes, 1 Kings iv. 2, and Rehoboam's sons, 2 Chron. xi. 23.

This verse and those immediately preceding are, to my mind, evidence sufficient that this Psalm cannot, as a whole, be regarded as prophetical of the Messiah. It is only by doing violence to language that the spiritual sense is extracted; and it seems to me far wiser to acknowledge at once the mixed character of such Psalms as this. It does speak, no doubt, of One who is higher than the kings of earth, but it does so under earthly images. It is typical, partially, yet not altogether. ("Necesse non est singula membra curiose ad Christum aptari."—*Calvin.*) The Sacred Poet sees the earthly king and the human marriage before his eyes, but, whilst he strikes his harp to celebrate these, a vision of a higher glory streams in upon him. Thus the earthly and the heavenly mingle. The Divine penetrates, hallows, goes beyond the human; but the human is there. See farther in Introduction and notes to Ps. cx.

[a] *On*, or *after the manner of*, *lilies*. See the same inscription Ps. lxix. and lxxx., and a similar one, Ps. lx. Some suppose an instrument shaped like a lily to be meant (but *not* one of six strings, as if derived from שֵׁשׁ, which grammar forbids); others take עַל in the usual sense, "after the manner of," and suppose the reference to be to the measure according to which the Psalm was to be sung. Others again, metaphorically, "concerning her who is like the lilies," connecting it with the rest of the title "a song of loves," or, "of sweet, delightful things." Aq. (more abstract) ᾆσμα προσφιλίας, with which the μέλος προσφιλές of Theocritus has been compared. On Maskîl, see xxxii. note [a].

[b] אֹמֵר אָנִי. It is doubtful whether this should be taken with what follows, or as an independent clause. The older Versions all render, "I am speaking my works," &c. LXX. λέγω τὰ ἔργα μου τῷ βασιλεῖ. Theod. ἐξαγγελῶ τὰ ποιήματά μου. But the accents separate the clauses, "I am speaking :—my work is (or, may it be) for," &c. מַעֲשַׂי is sing. not plur., the inflexion being that of a word with 3 rad. ה (or י). See Gesen. § 93, Rem. 9.

[c] יָפְיָפִיתָ. A passive, by reduplication of the first two radicals (of יפה, ground form יפי), of which there is no other instance; formed according to Ew. § 131 g., from an act. יְפֵיפִית, Pealal (Gesen. § 55, 3). Hupf. however thinks, that according to the analogy of יְפֵה־פִיָּה (or as some MSS. יְפֵיפִיָּה adj. dimin.), Jer. xlvi. 20, and such forms as סְחַרְחַר, xxxviii. 11; חֲמַרְמַר, Lam. i. 20; we ought to punctuate יְפֵיפִיתָ; but he objects that, as these are diminutives, such a form would not be applicable here. Hence, as the ancient Versions have two words—LXX. ὡραῖος κάλλει, Aq. κάλλει ἐκαλλιώθης, Symm. κάλλει καλὸς εἶ, Jerome, *decore pulchrior es*—he thinks the original reading may have been יָפְיִ or יָפֹה, before יָפִיתָ, but prefers reading simply יָפִיתָ. As regards the Versions, they may have merely endeavoured thus to express by periphrasis the reduplicated form. And as regards the diminutive, Gesenius observes that this is employed in all languages to express affection or praise, and instances the Spanish *bonito*, *bonitino*. (*Thes*. p. 612.)

[d] עַל־כֵּן, "therefore," it never means anything else: though it has been usual to take it here as standing for עַל־כֵּן אֲשֶׁר, "because;" the sense, apparently, requiring this rendering. It may however be explained as in the note—"therefore," *i.e.* because one good gift of God draws another after it.

[e] עַל־דְּבַר; because רְכַב, "ride," does not occur elsewhere absolutely; some join it with עַל־דְּבַר, and render (with the Syr. and Joseph Qimchi), "ride upon the word of truth," &c., the truth itself being compared to the horse or chariot. And Calvin remarks, "Aptissime has virtutes vehiculis comparat, quæ Regem in sublime attollant." Hupfeld, adhering to the more usual meaning of עַל דְּבַר, "because of," regards "the truth" and "meekness," &c. as the attributes of the monarch himself: "because of thy truth," &c.

f עַנְוָה צֶדֶק. How are we to account for the juxtaposition of these two words without a copula? Perhaps it is an asyndeton, such as occurs below, ver. 9, "myrrh and aloes (and) cassia." But עַנְוָה seems to be a sort of middle form between the abs. עֲנָוָה and constr. עַנְוַת, so that instead of the first noun being in constr. it is in very close apposition with the other, "a meekness which is also righteousness."

g אֱלֹהִים. But few modern interpreters take this word as a vocative. They explain either (1) Thy throne of God, *i.e.* thy throne Divine—as Solomon's throne is called the throne of Jehovah, 1 Chron. xxix. 23, cf. xxviii. 5—thy thronė which God has given thee, and which He evermore protects, is, or stands fast, for ever (cf. 2 Sam. vii., Ps. lxxxix.). The pron. suff. with the noun in constr. is defended by such examples as מַחֲסִי עֹז, lxxi. 7; אֹיְבִי עָז, 2 Sam. xxii. 18; מָעֻזִּי חָיִל, *ib.* 33; מִדּוֹ בַד, Lev. vi. 3; דַּרְכֵּךְ זִמָּה, Ezek. xvi. 27; מַרְכְּבֹתֶיךָ יְשׁוּעָה, Hab. iii. 8. But it is of importance to observe, that in all these instances, the noun with the suffix may be explained as being in *apposition* (not in construction) with the noun following: "my refuge which is strength;" "his garment which is linen," &c.; but it would be absurd to say, "Thy throne which is God." The constructions therefore are not identical.

(2) Thy throne is (a throne) of God (כִּסֵּא being repeated before אֱלֹהִים, the constr. being as in יְהוָֹה צְבָאוֹת, הָאָרוֹן הַבְּרִית, &c.). So Ibn Ezra, and Ewald, who objects to לְעוֹלָם ו' as a predicate, but see Lam. v. 19.

(3) "Thy throne is God" (like "God is my rock," &c.), Döderlein; which is also the rendering of the "Improved Version" of the N. T. published by the Unitarian Society, in Heb. i. 8, but which is, to say the least of it, very harsh and unnatural, and very different from the examples which are supposed to justify it, such as "God is our dwelling-place," "God is my rock, my shield," &c. Dr. Hort has, however, recently maintained that this is the most probable rendering of the words as they stand in the Greek of Heb. i. 8, *ὁ θρόνος σου ὁ θεὸς εἰς τὸν αἰῶνα [τοῦ αἰῶνος]*. He observes that there is no philological difficulty in the way of the rendering (the separation of "thy throne" from "for ever and ever," having a parallel, *e.g.* in Ps. lxxiii. 26); and that it is made almost certain by that reading of the second clause which appears to him to have the support of the best MSS., viz. *καὶ ἡ ῥάβδος τῆς εὐθύτητος ῥάβδος τῆς βασιλείας αὐτοῦ* (א B); though the LXX. following the Hebrew have *σου*, a rendering which has other support. No doubt, if the reading *αὐτοῦ* is correct, the first clause must be rendered "God is thy throne," &c., otherwise *αὐτοῦ* has no antecedent. But even retaining *σου*, Dr. Hort still contends for this rendering. For in the second clause it will be observed the place of subject and predicate is inverted in the Greek: "And the sceptre of uprightness is the sceptre of thy [his] kingdom." "'The sceptre of uprightness,' then, can only be a periphrasis for 'God's sceptre,' the pre-eminent sceptre of uprightness; and the affirmation must be that God's sceptre does itself rule the kingdom of the king addressed." But Dr. Hort admits that with *σου* there is some awkwardness of language: "We should not expect to find God's sceptre described as *a* sceptre of the

king's kingdom, or the attribution of a Divine character transferred from the grammatical predicate to the grammatical subject. When σου is replaced by αὐτοῦ everything falls into its right place . . . . the statement is that the king's sceptre is a sceptre of God's own kingdom, even as his throne is God Himself." He thinks that a passing sentence in Jerome's exposition of this Psalm (*Ep.* 65 *ad Princ.* c. 13), shows that the identification of ὁ θεός with the throne, not the king, obtained at least some acceptance in its theological application in ancient times: 'quanquam enim Pater in Filio et Filius in Patre, et *alter utrum sibi et habitator et thronus sint*, tamen in hoc loco ad regem qui Deus est sermo dirigitur.'" It must be observed, however, that this rendering turns entirely upon the Greek text of the Ep. to the Hebrews. Aq. has the vocative expressly, θεέ. Symm. clearly intends ὁ θεός to be a vocative when he renders, ὁ θρόνος σου, ὁ θεός, αἰώνιος καὶ ἔτι. The LXX. and Theod. (ὁ θρόνος σου, ὁ θεός, εἰς, κ.τ.λ.) are ambiguous, but may be said almost certainly to have intended ὁ θεός as a vocative (see below), and the LXX. have not the inversion of predicate and subject in the second clause, which is found in א B in the Ep. to the Hebrews; nor has any ancient Version a trace of αὐτοῦ for σου. Jerome, commenting on the passage (*Ep.* 65 *u.s.*) says: "Aquila ELOIM verbum Hebraicum non nominativo casu sed vocativo interpretatur, dicens θεέ, et nos propter intelligentiam *Dee* posuimus [this, however, is not in any MS. of Jerome's text, which runs, *Sedes tua Deus in seculum seculi*], quod Latina lingua non recipit; ne quis perverse putet Deum dilecti et amantissimi et Regis bis Patrem nominari." And commenting afterwards on ver. 7, he contends for the vocative there likewise, "Quod sequitur, *Unxit te, Deus, Deus tuus*, primum nomen Dei vocativo casu intelligendum est, sequens nominativo. Quod satis miror, cur Aquila non ut cœperat in primo versiculo, vocativo casu interpretatus sit, sed nominativo." I may add that Saadia, who paraphrases "God shall establish thy throne for ever," &c., must have supposed the construction to be that of the nominative and not the vocative.

The truth is, Dr. Hort attaches far too much importance to the two MSS. א B, and, so far as the Hebrew is concerned, does not allow sufficient weight, I think, to such a passage as 1 Sam. xxviii. 13, or to our Lord's words in Joh. x. 35, commenting on Ps. lxxxii. 6, 7.

Dr. Pusey (*Daniel*, pp. 471-4) has discussed the construction here with learning and bitterness.

[h] מִנִּי. A difficult word. It has been taken (1) as a repetition of the מִן preceding (in its poetical form), in which case we must render, "out of ivory palaces, whence they gladden thee" (but this is a very harsh construction, inasmuch as the prep. thus stands alone, though it may be parallelled by the repetition of כְּעַל, Is. lix. 18); or perhaps it is better, with the LXX., to carry on the constr. into the next verse, ἐξ ὧν ηὔφρανάν σε θυγατέρες βασιλέων ἐν τῇ τιμῇ σου. So also the ancient Lat. Vers. published by Thorpe, "Ex quibus te delectaverunt filiæ regum in honore tuo." And Jerome, "Quibus lætificaverunt te filiæ," &c. We find this form of the prep. in xliv. 11, lxxxviii. 10, and elsewhere, but there it is followed by its case.

Or (2) to mean a district of *Armenia* (as in Jer. li. 27), "ivory of the land of Minni, or Armenia." So the Chaldee: a rendering to which one would incline, because of its simplicity, if there were any evidence that Armenia was celebrated for its ivory. (Or the Minnæi, a people of Southern Arabia, who, according to Diod. iii. 47, had houses adorned with ivory.)

Or (3) as an apoc. plur. for מִנִּים, "viols," "stringed instruments," cl. 4. But the existence of such an apoc. plur. is disputable (see xxii. 17, 2 Sam. xxii. 44, and comp. the apoc. dual יָדַי, Ezek. xiii. 18). But Maurer suggests that מִנִּי may either be = *fides mea*, or = *fidicen*, the singular being in this last case put collectively for the plural. So Ges. *Thes.* "fides (*i.e.* concentus musici) exhilarant te, and Reuss: "des concerts te réjouissent."

i בִּיקְּרוֹתֶיךָ. Both the meaning and the form are subjects of debate. יָקָר means *precious, costly*, and so *dear, beloved* (Prov. vi. 26, comp. Jer. xxxi. 20); hence, here, "thy beloved ones," *i.e.* the ladies of the harem. Hengst. renders *deine herrlichen*, *i.e.* as magnificently appareled. Others "in thy precious things," *i.e.* arrayed in the ornaments and costly apparel presented her by the king. Or, "*among* thy precious things, or treasures." As regards the form, the reading received is that of Ben-Naphtali, instead of that of Ben-Asher, בְּיִקְּרוֹתֶיךָ (though the Jews, as a rule, prefer the reading of the latter to that of the former). In Prov. xxx. 17, is the exactly anal. form לִיקְּהַת (יִקְּהַת, Gen. xlix. 10): similar are וִילְלַת, Jer. xxv. 36; כִּיתְרוֹן, Eccl. ii. 13, where the orthography of Ben-Naphtali is also followed. In this case the Dagesh is merely euphonic. Saadia, Rashi, and others, however, derive the word, not from יקר, but from בָּקַר, making the י merely a *mater lectionis* after the analogy of מִשְׁפָּה, Is. xlii. 24. See the whole question fully discussed in Hupfeld's note, and comp. Ew. § 53 c, and Luzzatto, *Gramm. della Lingua Ebraica*, § 193.

k וְיִתְאָו. Fut. apoc. here introducing the apodosis, as the foregoing clause with the verb in the *imperative* may be considered as equivalent to a *conditional* clause, "If thou forget, &c., then, so will the king delight himself in," &c.

l כָּל־כְּבוּדָּה, lit. "all-glory," "nothing but glory." Comp. כָּל־כָּבוֹד, Is. iv. 5; and Ps. xxxix. 6, כָּל־הֶבֶל, "nothing but a breath." The form is incorrectly written for כְּבֻדָּה (arising from the later fluctuation between lengthening the vowel and doubling the consonant), either adj., as Ezek. xxiii. 41, or subst., as Jud. xviii. 21. Here the last, because it is joined with כָּל.—*Hupfeld.*

m לִרְקָמוֹת. Most understand this of "variegated or embroidered garments" (Jud. v. 30, Ezek. xvi. 18, xxvi. 16, in the last passage spoken of the robes of princes). But I think Maurer is right in rendering *In stragulis versicoloribus.* He observes that the dress of the bride has already been mentioned twice, ver. 9 [10], and 13 [14]; and that the prep. לְ is not used of motion to a place, but of rest in a place. It is used of walking *on*, or *over*, Hab. i. 6. The very instances which Hupfeld quotes in support of the other interpretation לָבֶטַח, לָחוּץ, are most decidedly in favour of Maurer's rendering. Reuss too has : "sur des tapis diaprés." I would compare Æsch. *Agam.* 881-883 :—

> δμωαὶ, τί μέλλεθ', αἷς ἐπέσταλται τέλος
> πέδον κελεύθου στρωννύναι πετάσμασιν ;
> εὐθὺς γενέσθω πορφυρόστρωτος πόρος.

and 896 :

> ἐν ποικίλοις . . . . . κάλλεσιν
> βαίνειν.

[n] יְהוֹדוּךָ, the fuller form for יוֹדוּךָ ; see on lxxxi. 5 [6], and cxvi. 6, note [c].

PSALM 46

THIS and the two following Psalms are hymns of triumph, composed on the occasion of some great deliverance. I am inclined to think that they all celebrate the same event, the sudden and miraculous destruction of the army of Sennacherib under the walls of Jerusalem. That proud host had swept the land. City after city had fallen into the power of the conqueror. The career of Sennacherib and his captains had been one uninterrupted success. The capital itself alone held out, and even there the enfeebled garrison seemed little likely to make a successful resistance. The swollen river had, in the language of the prophet, overflowed all his channels, and risen even to the neck. It was at this crisis that deliverance came. When there were no succours to be expected, when neither king nor army could help the city, God helped her. He, the Lord of Hosts, was in the midst of her, keeping watch over her walls and defending her towers. His Angel went forth at dead of night and smote the host of the Assyrians, and when men awoke in the morning, there reigned in that vast camp the silence and the stillness of death. Such a deliverance must have filled the whole nation with wonder and joy. The old days of Moses and David would seem to have returned. The hopes of Prophets, so great and so glowing, yet so often apparently defeated, seemed now nearer to their accomplishment. The times were at hand when Jerusalem should be indeed the joy of the whole earth, when all nations should acknowledge Jehovah as their King. Her towers, her palaces, the temple of her God, stood in all their beauty, saved by a miracle from the spoiler's hand. God had made Himself known there as a sure refuge, and henceforth His Name would be acknowledged in the earth.

We should expect to find such a deliverance celebrated by songs of thanksgiving and triumph. We should expect to find in these songs some indications of the particular events which they were intended to commemorate. Accordingly we do find, especially in this Psalm, and in the 48th, certain expressions which are most natural and most intelligible, on the supposition that they were written at this time. In this Psalm there occur, moreover, very remarkable coincidences, both of thought and expression, with those prophecies of Isaiah which were uttered in prospect of the Assyrian invasion. The prophet had compared the Assyrian army about to come, to a mighty river, the Nile or the Euphrates, overflowing its banks, carrying desolation far and wide, rising till it had submerged all but the most prominent objects. The Psalmist employs a like image when he compares the enemies of his country to an angry sea, its waves roaring, and the mountains trembling at the swelling thereof. Isaiah had described the peace and safety of Jerusalem, weak and defenceless as she seemed to all eyes but the eye of Faith, under the emblem of her own gently-flowing stream of Siloam (viii. 6). The Poet also sings the praises of that stream, whose channels make glad the city of God. Thus each has recourse to similar metaphors, and each heightens their effect by contrast. Again the Prophet had assured the house of David that it had a better defence than that of chariots and horses; had laughed to scorn the power of the enemy, saying, "Associate yourselves, and ye shall be broken in pieces . . . take counsel together, and ye shall come to nought . . . . for GOD IS WITH US" (*Immanu 'El*); and had symbolized the promised deliverance by the birth of the child, *Immanuel*. The ever-recurring thought of the Psalm is, "God is our refuge and defence;" "God is in the midst" of the Holy City; Jehovah (God) of Hosts IS WITH US (*Immanu*). The burden alike of Prophecy and Psalm is IMMANUEL, GOD WITH US.

Delitzsch (following Hengstenberg) refers this and the two following Psalms to the victory of Jehoshaphat over the allied forces of the Moabites, Ammonites, and Edomites, recorded in 2 Chron. xx., but he admits how thoroughly this Psalm is conceived in the spirit, and coloured by the language, of Isaiah. He compares it more particularly with Is. xxxiii., and remarks that the principal idea of the Psalm appears in Is. xxxiii. 2 (referring to Is. xxv. 4, in proof of the similarity of language between the Psalmist and the Prophet); that its concluding address resembles Is. xxxiii. 13, and that the image of the stream in ver. 4 of the Psalm is repeated, but in a bolder form, in ver. 21 of the same chapter. The "I will be exalted" in ver. 10 of the Psalm is to be found in Is. xxxiii. 10, whilst the hope that war shall cease throughout the world is in harmony with the bright picture of universal peace which the Prophet draws (chap. ii.). According to the view of Delitzsch, however, the Prophet copies the Psalmist, and " Ps. xlvi. is not an echo but a prelude of Is. xxxiii."

Luther's noble hymn, " Ein' feste Burg ist unser Gott," is based upon this Psalm.

The Psalm consists of three strophes, the conclusion of each being marked by the Selah, and that of the last two by the refrain.

I. In the first, God is magnified as the one sure defence at all times. Those with whom God dwells can never fear, whatever perils may threaten. Ver. 1—3.

II. The peace of Zion is secured by the abiding presence of God in her; and the discomfiture of all her foes is certain. Ver. 4—7.

III. God has manifested but even now His saving might, in the great deliverance which He has wrought. His arm has been made bare, His voice has been heard, He is exalted in the earth. Ver. 8—11.

[FOR THE PRECENTOR. OF THE SONS OF KORAH. UPON 'ALAMOTH.[a] A SONG.]

I. 1 GOD is unto us a refuge and stronghold,
A very present help in trouble.
2 Therefore do we not fear, though (the) earth be changed.[b]
And though (the) mountains be moved into the heart of (the) seas;

1—3. First Strophe. The safety and security of the people of God, even when the earth itself and the strong foundations of the earth are shaken. The revolutions and commotions of the political world are here described by images borrowed from the convulsions of the natural world, the earthquake which makes the mountains to tremble, the roaring of the seas, &c. See below, ver. 6, where the figure is dropt.

A VERY PRESENT HELP, &c., lit. "a help in trouble is He very surely found."

2. THOUGH THE MOUNTAINS, &c. The strongest figure that could be employed, the mountains being regarded as the great pillars of the earth. See xviii. 7 [8], lxxv. 3 [4], lxxxii. 5, Job ix. 6.

INTO, not "*in* the heart," as Jerome, *in corde maris*, but as the Vulg., rightly, *transferentur in cor maris*.

HEART OF THE SEAS. So "heart of heaven," Deut. iv. 11; "heart of the oak," 2 Sam. xviii. 14.

For the general sentiment of the verse, comp. Horace, *Od.* iii. 3, " Si

3 Though the waters thereof[c] roar, though they be
troubled,
Though the mountains quake with the swelling
thereof. [Selah.]

II. 4 A stream (there is) whose channels make glad the city
of God,
The holy place[d] of the dwellings of the Most High.
5 God is in the midst of her; she shall not be moved;
God shall help her, when the morning dawns.
6 Nations roared; kingdoms were moved;

fractus illabatur orbis, Impavidum ferient ruinæ."

3. The first strophe does not close with the refrain, as the second (ver. 7) and the third (ver. 11) do. There is no reason for inferring, with Hupfeld, an error in the text. We must not expect to find the same regularity in these early lyrics, that we should in a modern ballad. Besides, there is a sufficient reason for the omission of the refrain here. It may have been purposely omitted, in order to bring into more striking contrast the roaring waves of the troubled sea, and the gentle, peaceful flow of the brook of Siloam, in the next verse. This contrast, as has been said, may have been suggested by the figures employed in the prophecy of Isaiah. Another contrast, the same in spirit, though the image is different, occurs in the same Prophet. On the one side, the Assyrian, in the day of his might, is compared to the forest of Lebanon in all the pride of its branching cedars: and on the other, the Saviour of Israel to the slender shoot, springing from the stem of Jesse (Is. x. 33, 34, xi. 1). The division of the chapters here has most unhappily marred the effect of this contrast, which is very striking, and which is conceived in the truest spirit of poetry.

SWELLING, or "pride."

4—7. The peace and tranquillity of the city of God, whilst all is uproar and confusion without her walls.

4. A STREAM. The one never-failing stream of water with which Jerusalem was supplied, and which, in its gentle, undisturbed, refreshing flow, was an image of the peace and blessing which the Holy City enjoyed under the protection of her God. (See Stanley, *Sinai and Palestine*, p. 181.) The probable allusion to Is. viii. 6 has been already remarked on, and the metaphor may have been borrowed designedly, as Calvin suggests, "that the faithful might learn that, without any aid from the world, the grace of God alone was sufficient for them.... Therefore, though the help of God may but trickle to us, as it were, in slender streams, we should enjoy a deeper tranquillity than if all the power of the world were heaped up all at once for our help."

5. SHE SHALL NOT BE MOVED. The antithesis to this follows in the next verse, "Kingdoms were moved."

WHEN THE MORNING DAWNS, lit. "At the turning of the morning," as Exod. xiv. 27, Jud. xix. 26, and the same phrase of the evening, Gen. xxiv. 63; not "early," as E.V., Ros., and others, nor "every morning," as Calvin, De Wette, but in the morning of redemption and triumph, as opposed to the night of disaster and sorrow. See note on xxx. 5 [6].

6. There is a manifest reference to verses 2, 3, though the figure

He uttered His voice,[e]—the earth melteth.
7 Jehovah (God of) Hosts is with us;
A high tower unto us is the God of Jacob. [Selah.]

III. 8 Come, behold the deeds of Jehovah,[f]
Who hath done terrible things[g] in the earth;
9 (Who) stilleth wars unto the end of the earth,
Who breaketh (the) bow and cutteth (the) spear in sunder.
(And) burneth (the) chariots in the fire.
10 "Cease ye, and know that I am God,
I am exalted among the nations, I am exalted upon the earth."

there employed is now dropt, except so far as we are reminded of it by the use of the same verbs, "roared," "were moved," words which are employed in other passages, both of natural and political convulsions.

The absence of any copula in the verse adds much to the force of the description. The preterites are not hypothetical (as Delitzsch explains). Each act of the drama is, so to speak, before the eyes of the Poet.

UTTERED HIS VOICE, *i.e.* in thunder (past tense), on which the melting of the earth (present tense) is described as following immediately (without a copula). The thunder (called also in xxix. "the voice of Jehovah") is the symbol of the Divine judgement. Comp. xviii. 13 [14], and especially as explaining this passage, lxxvi. 8 [9].

7. JEHOVAH (GOD OF) HOSTS. The name first occurs in the mouth of Hannah, 1 Sam. i. 11, and is applied to God as the Great King whom all created powers, the armies both in heaven and in earth, obey. To this Name the Psalmist immediately subjoins another, "the God of Jacob," the covenant God of His people. Thus we are reminded, as Calvin remarks, of the double prop on which our faith rests; the infinite power whereby He can subdue the universe unto Himself, and the fatherly love which He has revealed in His word. Where these two are joined together, our faith may trample on all enemies. The Talmud says that this verse should never depart from the mouth of an Israelite.

8—11. The application of the general truth of God s Presence and help to the particular circumstances of the nation at the present crisis. Hence "Come, behold." Comp. lxvi. 5.

9. STILLETH. The participle expresses the *continuance* of the action. Who not only does so now, but will do so evermore, till His kingdom of peace shall be set up in all the earth. This hope, however, is not prominent here, as it is in Mic. iv. 3, Is. ii. 4, and ix. 5 [4]. "For every greave of the greaved (warrior) in the battle-tumult, and the (soldier's) cloak rolled in blood, shall be for burning, and fuel of fire" (where our Version has most unhappily marred the sense, by inserting "but this"), on which follows the reign of peace of the Messiah.

10. CEASE YE. The verb is used absolutely here, as in 1 Sam. xv. 16, "stay, and I will tell thee," but, strictly speaking, the expression is elliptical, Lit. "Let your hand sink down," *i.e.* cease your efforts.

God Himself here "utters His

11 Jehovah (God of) Hosts is with us ;
A high tower unto us is the God of Jacob. [Selah.]

voice," as sole Judge and Arbiter of the world. (So the A.-S. paraphrase supplies "Then God answered and said by the Prophet.") What are all the fret and stir of armies, and captains of armies, and kings and kingdoms, in His sight, who is the Ruler and the Judge of all !

[a] עַל־עֲלָמוֹת. See on vi. note [a]. Not as Böttcher, *De Inferis*, p. 192, *ad voces puberes*, "to be sung by tenor voice," but *ad voces puellarum ;* as Perret-Gentil, *chant avec voix de femmes*, and Armand de Mestral still more exactly, *en soprano.* In lxviii. 26, maidens playing on the timbrels accompany the Ark. They may also, like Miriam, have joined in the singing, and taken their several parts.

[b] בְּהָמִיר. The inf. may here be impers., as xlii. 3 [4], Gen. xxv. 26, Exod. ix. 16, with a passive idea, "when one changes" being = "when it is changed." אֶרֶץ would then be accus., as in the passages quoted in Gen. and Exod. ; but perhaps it is better, with Gesen. (§ 133, 2) and Hupfeld to take אֶרֶץ here as the subject in the nominative, "when the earth changes." According to the latter, the Hiph. is here used in a passive sense, instead of the Niph. or Hoph., which are not in use. But the Hiph. may perhaps be explained as expressing a *state* or *condition*, Gesen. § 53, 2.

[c] מֵימָיו. The sing. suffix in this word and in בְּגַאֲוָתוֹ can only refer to יַמִּים, which is merely a plural of poetic amplification. In the same way cvii. 25, גַּלָּיו refers to מַיִם רַבִּים, ver. 23. Comp., as applied to the sea, גֵּאוּת, lxxxix. 10. The futures in this verse carry on the construction of the previous verse. This transition from the infin. constr. to the finite verb is very usual. Others take the futures as concessive, a new sentence beginning here. So Maurer, *Fremant, æstuent aquæ ejus ! Contremiscant*, &c. (nihil timebimus, or something of the kind, being supplied). Hupfeld rejects both explanations, and thinks that this verse forms the protasis of a sentence which in the present text stands incomplete ; the apodosis he finds in the refrain, which he thinks ought to stand here before the Selah, as in ver. 7, 11. But see on ver. 3.

[d] קְדֹשׁ, either with transposed vowel for קֹדֶשׁ (see the same form as a noun lxv. 5, and Is. lvii. 15, and comp. גְּדֹל, Exod. xv. 16, and so Symm. τὸ ἅγιον τῆς κατασκηνώσεως), or adj., agreeing with "City of God," *i.e.* "holy in (or, because of) the dwellings," &c.

[e] נָתַן בְּקוֹלוֹ. This constr. of the verb with the prep. occurs also lxviii. 34, Jer. xii. 1. Gesen. explains it as elliptical = *edere* (strepitum, fremitum) *voce*, and compares the similar phrases "to shake the head," and "*with* the head," "to gnash the teeth," and "*with* the teeth" (§ 135, 1, Rem. 3, note). Hupfeld denies any ellipse, and thinks that נתן itself means "to sound :" which, however, is a meaning confined to the Piel ; comp. תַּנָּה and תַּנִּים, "jackals," lit. "howlers."

[f] יהוה. For this many MSS. (32 Kenn., 46 De-Rossi) have אלהים which would be more in accordance with the Elohistic character of the Psalm. The variation is as old as the Talmud [Babli], Del. observes. Norzi (*i.e.* R. Shelomoh Yedidyah of Norcia) inclines to it, and Biesenthal adopts it in his Edit. of the Psalter. Comp. lxvi. 5. Hupfeld's note (1st Edit.), by mistake, refers to the preceding verse. He is wrong in saying that the Chald. favours the reading א׳.

[g] שַׁמּוֹת, plur., here only instead of the sing. שַׁמָּה, unites the two meanings of "desolation" and "wonder, astonishment" (as the verb also does), either of which is suitable here. The first is that usually adopted. Jerome, *solitudines*, and so Calv., Ros., and others. The second, "astonishing, *i.e.* terrible things," is preferred by Ewald and Hupf., following the LXX. (*τέρατα*) and the Syriac. The A.-S. also has "and his *wundru* þe he wyrcd."

PSALM 47

A Hymn of triumph, in which the singer calls upon all the nations of the earth to praise Jehovah as their King, and joyfully anticipates the time when they shall all become one body with the people of the God of Abraham. In this sense the Psalm may be called Messianic, a prophecy of the final triumph of God's kingdom upon earth. The older Christian expositors, for the most part, suppose it to have been written, like Psalm xxiv., on the occasion of the removal of the Ark to Mount Zion (2 Sam. vi.), and to be a prophecy of the Ascension of Christ, and of His kingly rule, as sitting at the right hand of the Father. The Rabbinical interpreters regard the Psalm as Messianic.

By Venema, Hengstenberg, and Delitzsch, it has been referred, like the last, to the victory of Jehoshaphat over the Moabites, Ammonites, Edomites, and Arabians, 2 Chron. xx. Hengst. relies especially on the fact that the sons of the Korahites are said to have been present with the army on that occasion, ver. 19, and supposes this Psalm to be alluded to, ver. 26. R. Mosheh Hakkohen thinks it was composed in Babylon; Ewald places it after the Exile, on the return of Jehovah into His temple, and in consequence of the hopes then kindled of the conversion of the nations to the God of Israel. Eichhorn, who connects Psalms xlvi. and xlviii. with the defeat of Sennacherib, considers this Psalm to belong to David's time: it alludes, he thinks, to the final subjugation of the Canaanites, when the Jebusites were driven out of their stronghold, and celebrates the bringing up of the Ark to the City of David. He is of opinion, however, that the Psalm was not written by David, but either by a contemporary, or by a later Poet, who transferred himself in imagination into those times.

I see no reason, however, why the Psalm should not have been composed, like the 46th and 48th, after the defeat of Sennacherib; and Hupfeld is, I think, right in calling it "a lyrical expansion of the idea prominent in xlvi. 10 [11], that Jehovah is high exalted above the nations, and the great King over all the earth."

We have two strophes, the end of the first being marked by the Selah; but the subject of both is in fact the same, the second, ver. 5—10, being only a lyrical variation of the first, ver. 1—4. The chief difference is, that what is expressed as a wish or hope in the first part (ver. 3, 4), viz. that God would make the nations the inheritance of Israel, is in the second (ver. 8, 9) regarded as already accomplished.

Very probably this Psalm, like the 24th, was sung in choral antiphonies, one company of Levites beginning with the words "O clap your hands," &c. (ver. 1, 2), and another answering "He subdueth," &c. (ver. 3, 4). Then, again, the first company would take up the words, "God is gone up," &c. and would sing ver. 5, 6. The antichoir would respond in ver. 7 and 8; and finally both would unite in ver. 9, 10.*

[FOR THE PRECENTOR. OF THE SONS OF KORAH. A PSALM.]

1 O ALL ye peoples clap (the) hand;
O shout unto God with the voice of triumph!
2 For Jehovah, Most High, is terrible,
A great King over all the earth.
3 He subdueth peoples under us,
And nations under our feet!

1, 2. The nations called upon to do homage to Jehovah. Cf. Ps. lxvi. 1.

1. CLAP (THE) HAND . . . SHOUT, as demonstrations of joy, in solemn, festal procession. We have the former at the coronation of a new king, 2 Kings xi. 12, and so here the nations are to rejoice before their new monarch. See also 1 Sam. x. 25, and comp. Num. xxiii. 21, "the shout of a king."

TRIUMPH, lit. "singing" or "joyful song."

3, 4. There is considerable difficulty in satisfactorily explaining these verses. They seem, at first sight, to refer to the past—to the destruction of the Canaanites, and the establishment of Israel in the promised inheritance. So the LXX. *ὑπέταξε λαοὺς ἡμῖν . . . ἐξελέξατο ἡμῖν τὴν κληρονομίαν αὐτοῦ.* Jerome, *con-*

* In the Ashkenazic synagogues, this Psalm is recited *seven* times before the blowing of the ram's horn trumpet on New Year's Day. In all other synagogues, *once* on the same occasion.

4 He chooseth for us our inheritance,
The excellency of Jacob whom He loveth! [Selah.]

5 God is gone up with a shout,
Jehovah with the voice of a trumpet.

6 Make melody to God, make melody;
Make melody to our King, make melody!

7 For God is King of all the earth;
Make melody in skilful strains.

gregavit (Vulg. *subjecit*) . . . *Elegit*, &c. Calv. *ordinavit*. . . . *subjecit*. Luther makes the first verb *fut.*, "Er wird . . . zwingen," and the second *pres.*, "Er erwählet." Our own Version renders both as *future*. Hupfeld translates both as *optatives*, and, in the case of the first verb, this seems required by the form (but see Is. l. 9), "May He subdue, &c. . . . May He choose (them) for us (as) our inheritance, (as) the pride of Jacob," &c. According to this view, "the inheritance" cannot refer to the Holy Land immediately, but to the nations who are to be gathered in; they are to be the heritage of Israel, just as in ii. 8, "I will make the heathen Thine inheritance" (the same word as here). There is, however, a difficulty still, even with this explanation. The word "choose" is not the word we should expect. It sounds awkward to say, "May He *choose*," &c., instead of "May He *make* the nations our inheritance." Hence Hupf. proposes to read יַרְחֵב, "May He make wide, enlarge," &c., but there is no support for such a conjecture, either in MSS. or Versions. I am inclined therefore, with Ewald, Hengst., and Bunsen, to take both verbs as *presents* (which the previous context seems to require), either as referring to a recent act of God, or (as Delitzsch) to a continued act—"God is ever choosing Israel's inheritance anew, inasmuch as He shows Himself to be the true and mighty Protector thereof." The *present* may be used, as in civ. 2, where the act of creation is spoken of as present, because its results are present. Comp. Is. xiv. 1, where Israel's restoration is described as another choosing.

4. THE EXCELLENCY. In the sense of that by which as God's gift, Jacob excels every other people (cf. cxxxv. 4). Others, "the pride." Apparently the Holy Land is so styled here; probably also in Amos vi. 8 (where "his palaces," and "the city," stand in the parallelism), and perhaps in viii. 7, though not apparently in Nahum ii. 3. The Holy Land is so called, as the glorious possession wherein Jacob prides himself, because it is the gift of God's love and favour.

5. GOD IS GONE UP. An expression taken from the entry of the ark into the city of David, 2 Sam. vi. 15. Here God is said to ascend His royal Throne either in heaven, or in Zion, as entering it at the head of the triumphal procession. Cf. lxviii. 18 [19], and ix. 4 [5], vii. 6 [7].

WITH A SHOUT (A.-S. "with winsome song"). See note on ver. 1.

6. SING PSALMS. The word means both *to sing* and *to play*. The LXX., rightly, ψάλατε. Hupf. *Singet*. Del. *Harfnet*.

7. This verse contains the great subject of the Psalm, the reason why all nations are called to unite in this festal joy.

SING PSALMS, or "sing and play."

IN SKILFUL STRAINS, lit. "a skilful song," a song either fine in its structure, or beautiful in its melody. See xxxii. note[a]. Hup-

8 God is King over (the) nations;
God sitteth upon His holy throne.
9 The princes of (the) peoples are gathered together,
(To be) a people[a] of the God of Abraham:
10 For to God (belong) the shields of the earth;
Very high is He exalted.

feld, *ein Lied* (e.g. *eine Lehre*); Delitzsch, *Oden* (the ode being, he says, something of a reflective character, between a purely subjective song, and an objective hymn). But these renderings rest upon a mistaken notion as to the meaning of the root. LXX. *συνετῶς*, Jerome, *erudite*, rightly as regards the sense.

8. Is King, lit. "hath become King," has asserted and is exercising His sovereignty. Calvin, "regnum obtinuit," because, as he says, "verbum sub tempore præterito continuum actum designat;" and so in the next clause, "hath taken His seat."

9. The prayer is answered, the hope is accomplished. The princes of the nations are gathered together, are come in one body, as it were, on a day of solemn coronation, to do homage as vassals to their liege Lord and King, cii. 22 [23], Is. lxvi. 18, and cf. Is. xiv. 1.

10. Shields of the earth, *i.e.* Princes as the defenders and champions of their people. See the same figure Hos. iv. 18.

They are incorporated with the Jews, they are one people. Hence we might perhaps render, "to be the people," the noun being defined by the following genitive. But Mendelss. "zu einem Volke."

[a] עַם א׳. These words can only be in apposition with the foregoing. The older translators (except Symm. and Chald.) not seeing this, render as if the reading were עִם, instead of עַם. So also Qimchi and Ewald. Others, as Ros., understood the prep. אֶל or לְ before עַם, but possibly עם has dropt out. De Wette 3, and Hengst. explain the constr. as accus. of direction. But it is much simpler to take it as above, in appos. to נְדִיבֵי ע׳. Ibn Ezra, להיות עם לאל א׳.

PSALM 48

This Psalm, there is every reason to suppose, was composed on the same occasion as the two preceding, It celebrates God's protecting care of Jerusalem, and especially the deliverance of the city from the army of Sennacherib (2 Kings xviii. 19, Is. xxxvi. &c.), as may be inferred from the many verbal coincidences which present themselves, on a comparison of the Psalm with the prophecies of Isaiah relating to the Assyrian invasion (chaps. viii., xxviii., xxix. 1—7, xxxiii.). See the introduction to Psalm xlvi.

From ver. 9 it may be inferred that the Psalm was intended to be sung in the Temple-service. Hupfeld says that the Rabbinical commentators refer this like the preceding Psalms, to the times of the Messiah, and the struggle with Gog and Magog, which was to issue in the everlasting glory of Jerusalem. Qimchi says so, but not Rashi or Ibn Ezra.

It consists of three parts or strophes.

I. An Introduction which, after an ascription of praise to God, describes the glory (ver. 2) and the security (ver. 3) of Zion, as the city in which God had made Himself known. Ver. 1—3.

II. The defeat of the enemy. Because God thus dwells in Zion, and loves Zion, she has been saved out of the hand of the Assyrian. That mighty host, led by its kingly captains, did but look upon the city, and were confounded, as in a moment, broken as with the east wind, which breaks the ships of Tarshish, melting away "like snow in the glance of the Lord." Ver. 4—8.

III. Thanksgiving to God, whose praise is not only in Zion, but in all the earth: the Poet would have His great goodness in delivering His people remembered in all time to come. Ver. 9—14.

[A SONG. A PSALM. OF THE SONS OF KORAH.[a]]

1 GREAT is Jehovah, and highly to be praised,
In the city of our God, in His holy mountain.
2 Beautiful in elevation,[b] the joy of the whole earth,

1—3. It is because Zion is the city of *God*, that she so far surpasses all other cities in beauty and renown. It is the Glory of His Presence which makes her glorious: the strength of His Presence which makes her safe.

1. GREATLY TO BE PRAISED. See xviii., note[a]. Comp. xcvi. 4, cxlv. 3.

THE CITY OF OUR GOD, as again in ver. 8. Comp. xlvi. 4 [5].

2. BEAUTIFUL IN ELEVATION, or "rising aloft in beauty." This is precisely one of the most striking features in the topography of Jerusalem. "Its elevation," says Stanley, "is remarkable, occasioned not from its being on the summit of one of the numerous hills of Judæa, like most of the towns and villages, but because it is on the edge of one of the highest table-lands in the country. Hebron, indeed, is higher still, by some hundred feet; and from the south, accordingly, the approach to Jerusalem is by a slight descent. But from every other side the ascent is perpetual; and to the traveller, approaching Jerusalem from the west or east, it must have always presented the appearance, beyond any other capital of the then known world—we may add, beyond any important city that has ever existed on the earth—of a mountain city: breathing, as compared with the sultry plains of the Jordan or of the coast, a mountain air, enthroned, as compared with Jericho or Damascus, Gaza or Tyre, on a mountain fastness."—*Sinai and Palestine*, pp. 170, 171.

THE JOY OF THE WHOLE EARTH.

Is the mountain of Zion, the sides of the north,
The city of the great King.

Most recent interpreters render, "a joy of the whole *land*," a rendering which I am satisfied does not do justice to the largeness of the sacred Poet's conceptions. In a Psalm where the range of anticipation is so wide, and in which God's name is declared to be known to the ends of the earth, we must understand the language employed, in its broadest, not in its narrowest sense. Comp. Lam. ii. 15. Is not this the city which they called the crown of beauty, "a joy of the whole earth?" and Is. lx. 15, "a joy of many generations."

THE SIDES OF THE NORTH. It is not very clear what is meant by this expression here. In other passages, it denotes "the furthest north," "the extremest regions of the north," as in Ezek. xxxviii. 6, 15, xxxix. 2, where it is used of the land of God. In Is. xiv. 13 (the only place, besides those mentioned, where it occurs), it seems to describe the locality of the Assyrian Olympus, or mount of the gods. Hence Ewald, Hitzig, and Hengstenberg suppose that the Psalmist, borrowing here a figure from the Assyrian mythology, intends to represent Zion as holding the same position in Israel, which Merû or Alborg would have amongst the Asiatics, or Olympus amongst the Greeks. Ewald even suggests that, in consequence of the Assyrian invasion, the expression may have become familiar to Jewish writers, in the same way as Olympus is to Christian writers. But surely this is a most extravagant supposition. The affectation of embodying a piece of Pagan mythology in a sacred hymn, in order to express a sacred idea, could never have occurred to men animated by such strong religious and patriotic sentiments as the Hebrew poets of old. In Is. xiv. 13, it must be remembered, the case is widely different, as the expression is there put into the mouth of the king of Assyria himself. But for a Jew to speak of Zion, the holy mountain, as if it were no more than some mountain of heathen fable, would have been nothing short of profanity.

One thing is clear, that by "the sides of the north" is indicated, in some sense or other, the typography of the Holy City. The question is, to what particular part of it the words refer? (1) Now Jerusalem itself did not lie on the north, but on the south side of the elevated table-land mentioned in a preceding note. But the *Temple* did lie north, *i.e.* north-east of the city; and as the Temple was, in a peculiar sense, the dwelling-place of God, the Psalmist may have intended to designate this when he spoke of "the sides of the north," the expression being sufficiently accurate for the purposes of poetry. Hence we have the Holy City regarded from three different points of view, viz. "the mount Zion" (the city of David), "the sides of the north" (Mount Moriah and the Temple), "the City of the Great King" (Jerusalem proper, comp. Matt. v. 35). (2) If, however, Zion be the peak now levelled on the *north* of the Temple Mount, as Fergusson (*Essay*, p. 55 ff.) and Thrupp (*Antient Jerusalem*, p. 17 ff.) suppose, "the mount Zion (on) the sides of the north" may be the true rendering here. And this, too, might peculiarly be called "beautiful for elevation," as it was the highest point of the whole plateau, and that which would most readily strike the eye. (3) Another reason may be suggested why the north should be especially mentioned, because an enemy approaching like the Assyrians, would obtain their first view of the city on that side.

Dr. Kay: "'In the recesses of the north,' the mountain rising in a mass to the north as the spectator views it from the south."

3 God in her palaces
Hath made Himself known as a high tower.

4 For lo! the kings were assembled,
They passed by together :
5 They saw (it); then [c] they were amazed;
They were terrified, they were utterly confounded.
6 Trembling took hold upon them there,
Pangs as upon a woman in travail :

3. HATH MADE HIMSELF KNOWN, especially by the great act of deliverance recently accomplished, a description of which immediately follows.

4. There follows, in a few lines, a striking picture of the advance of the hostile army, and of its sudden destruction. Compare with this the wonderfully graphic description of the same march in Is. x. 28—34.

THE KINGS. The mention of "kings" in the plural does not prove that the Psalm cannot be referred to the Assyrian invasion. They were perhaps satraps, or petty kings (comp. Judges v. 3, 19), dependent upon Sennacherib. In his Annals, as lately deciphered, he speaks of setting up tributary kings or viceroys in Chaldæa, Phœnicia, and Philistia, after conquering those countries. Cf. Is. x. 8. Calvin and others, who refer the Psalm to the time of Ahaz, suppose Pekah and Rezin to be meant. Hengstenberg and Delitzsch think that "the kings" are those of Moab, Ammon, and Edom, who united to attack Jehoshaphat, and that it is their discomfiture which is the subject of the Psalm. But the battle at Tekoa would surely not have been described as the deliverance of Jerusalem.

WERE ASSEMBLED. The word is used of a formal confederation as of the Canaanite kings, Josh. xi. 5.

THEY PASSED BY TOGETHER: spoken of the marching of an army in battle array. Comp. Is. x. 29, &c. But it might also be rendered, "They vanished, disappeared at once, or altogether." For this meaning of the verb see xxxvii. 36. If so, this verse expresses in its two clauses, briefly, the gathering and the destruction of the hosts, and then these two ideas are expanded in what follows.

5. THEY SAW (IT), viz. the Holy City. The pronoun is very emphatic, as if to make prominent the hostile forces. Jebb: "they themselves." The force of the description in this verse, as in the last, is much increased by the way in which the verbs follow one another without a copula. Calvin well illustrates it by Cæsar's *veni, vidi, vici*. A succession of scenes is thus flashed upon the eye. Each word is a picture. First, we have the mustering of the hosts; then their march; then, their first sight of the city; then their astonishment, their dismay, their wild panic and flight.

WERE UTTERLY CONFOUNDED. So Symm. *ἐξεπλάγησαν*, LXX. *ἐσαλεύθησαν*. But it may mean "were driven to flight," as Gesenius and Hupfeld here take it.

6, 7. This confusion and terror are now further pourtrayed under two images: the first, that of a travailing woman, a common one in the Old Testament, and found also in the New; and the second, in which the defeat of Sennacherib's army is compared to the wreck and dispersion of a navy in a storm. The image in this case is presented with lyric vividness, as if the Poet

7 (Thou brakest them as) with the east wind
Thou breakest the ships of Tarshish.
8 As we have heard, so have we seen
In the city of Jehovah of Hosts, in the city of our God;
God will establish it for ever. [Selah.]

9 We have thought,[d] O God, on Thy loving-kindness
In the midst of Thy temple.
10 As is Thy Name, O God, so is Thy praise to the ends
of the earth!
Full of righteousness is Thy right hand.

were himself looking on the scene. It is a comparison, without any particle of comparison to introduce it.

But there are two ways of rendering ver. 7, according as the verb is 2 pers. masc., or 3 pers. fem.; for it may be either. If the first, then God is the subject. "(Thou, O God, brakest them as) thou brakest the ships of Tarshish," &c. So the LXX. συντρίβεις, Symm. κατεάξεις. So also Calv., J. H. Mich., Hengst., Hupf. And there is a certain lyric force and animation in this sudden apostrophe to God, which inclines me to give it the preference. If the second, then the rendering will be, "They were broken as with the east wind, which breaketh," &c. So Ewald and De Wette. Ewald renders: "durch des Ostens-Sturm der zertrümmert Tarschisch-Schiffe." Diodati's translation gives the sense most exactly: "(Furono rotte come) per lo vento Orientale (che) rompe le navi di Tarsis."

For the image, as descriptive of the irresistible power of God, compare Is. xxvii. 8, Amos iv. 9, Jonah iv. 8, Jer. xviii. 17, and see 1 Kings x. 22, where ships of Tarshish denote the strongest and largest ships. Comp. the "afflavit Deus, et dissipantur" of our own history. Macaulay: "Their ranks were broken as the clouds break with a Biscay gale." In Is. xxxiii. the Assyrian power is also compared to a gallant ship.

8. This marvellous deliverance is but a fresh proof, in our own experience, of that wonder-working Love which in the days of old has so often manifested itself in Israel. The things which our fathers have told us, we have now witnessed with our own eyes. (Comp. xliv. 1.) And therefore, also, the present is regarded as a pledge for the future: "God will establish it—make it stand firm—for ever," as lxxxvii. 5.

9—14. The next portion of the Psalm consists of the grateful celebration of that which God had done for Zion.

9. WE HAVE THOUGHT, *i.e.* pondered, considered in that deep, still, heartfelt gratitude, whence issue the loud praises of the tongue. IN THY TEMPLE, either as the place in which the congregation met to acknowledge God's loving-kindness, or as the place in which He had *manifested* His loving-kindness. Calvin: "locum ubi invocaretur sedem virtutis et gloriæ suæ fore."

10. AS IS THY NAME, SO IS, or, as others, "So let Thy praise be," *i.e.* Mayest Thou be praised according to the greatness of thy Name, God's Name being here that Name which He had got Himself in Israel, by His manifold mighty acts on their behalf.

11 Let the mountain of Zion be glad,
Let the daughters of Judah rejoice,
Because of Thy judgements.
12 Compass Zion, and go round about her ;
Tell the towers thereof,
13 Consider her bulwarks,[e] mark well her palaces,
That ye may tell it to the generations following,
14 For such is God, our God, for ever and ever ;

11. The verbs may either be taken as optatives, as above, or as simple presents. " The mountain of Zion *rejoices*," &c. Comp. xcvii. 8.

THE DAUGHTERS OF JUDAH, not here literally " the maidens of Judah," though it was usual for these to take a prominent part in the celebration of every victory, with songs and dances ; but, as the parallelism with "the mountain of Zion" would indicate, the various cities and villages of Judah which had suffered from the invasion. The metaphor is common in prose as well as in poetry.

12. The glad sense of freedom, the shout of deliverance, are no less noticeable in this verse than the strong patriotic feeling which breathes in it.

The horrors of the siege are at an end. No hostile army lies before the walls, and shuts the besieged within the gates. Therefore it is that the sacred Poet, kindling with emotion, as he looks with all the pride and all the deep affection of a true patriot on the towers of Zion, which still stand in their beauty, unscathed by the spoiler's hand, calls upon all her inhabitants to go forth, now that they can do so freely, to look upon her beauty, to gaze with affection upon her bulwarks, to consider one by one her palaces.

13. MARK WELL. The word occurs only here, lit. " divide," *i.e.* mark them one by one, in a poetical and a figurative sense, answering to the "tell her towers" before. Symm. *διαμετρήσατε τὰ βασίλεια αὐτῆς*. L. de Dieu gives it a more literal turn : " dividite palatia, *h.e.* obambulate inter palatia ejus, secando omnes palatiorum vias, quo omnia possitis commode intueri."

Still, in thus calling on them to admire the material glory of their city, the Poet would not have them do so only that they may take pride in her strength and her stateliness, but that they may tell to the generations to come who that God is whose hand has saved her.

14. FOR SUCH IS GOD, or, "for this is," &c. Comp. for the same position of the demonstr., lxviii. 8 [9], Exod. xxxii. 1, Joshua ix. 12, 13. Or it may be used still less definitely in the sense of " here " (like the Greek *ὅδε*), as civ. 25, 26, Is. xxiii. 13. See note on xxiv. 10.

It is interesting to compare with these words of the Jewish Poet a similar burst of patriotic sentiment from the lips of a Grecian orator. *Καὶ οἵδε μέν*, says Pericles, *τοιοίδε ἐγένοντο· τοὺς δὲ λοιποὺς χρὴ ἀσφαλεστέραν μὲν εὔχεσθαι, ἀτολμοτέραν δὲ μηδὲν ἀξιοῦν τὴν ἐς τοὺς πολεμίους διάνοιαν ἔχειν, σκοποῦντας μὴ λόγῳ μόνῳ τὴν ὠφέλειαν . . . ἀλλὰ μᾶλλον τὴν τῆς πόλεως δύναμιν καθ' ἡμέραν ἔργῳ θεωμένους καὶ ἐραστὰς γιγνομένους αὐτῆς, κ.τ.λ.* It is needless to observe how exactly these last words correspond to those of the Psalmist : " Mark well her bulwarks," &c. Indeed, Arnold, in his note on the passage in Thucydides (ii. 43), well observes, that "the words *ἔργῳ θεωμένους* might furnish matter for an oration or a poem. They mean, 'Look at our temples, and the statues which embellish them ; go

He will be our Guide unto death.[f]

down to Piræus, observe the long walls, visit the arsenals, and the docks of our three hundred ships; frequent our theatres, and appreciate the surpassing excellence of our poets, and the taste and splendour of our scenic representations; walk through the markets, observe them filled with the productions of every part of the world; and listen to the sound of so many dialects and foreign languages, which strike your ears in the streets of our city, the resort of the whole world.'" But with the same strong love of country, with the same enthusiastic admiration of her present grandeur, the same fond recollection of her glory in times past, there is a very striking difference of spirit. The Greek thinks only of the men who achieved that glory, and who embellished the city of their birth, and whose right hand gave them the victory; the Jew traces all the glory of his land, and all the success of her children, immediately to God. With the one all is of man, with the other all is of God.

[a] לִבְנֵי ק׳. See on xlii. note [a].

[b] יְפֵה נוֹף, "beautiful of elevation," *i.e.* a beautiful summit. נוֹף occurs only here, and has no doubt been rightly explained by Reland and Schultens, by reference to the Arab. نَوْفٌ, "height." See Ges. *Thes.* in v.

[c] כֵּן. There is no need to supply the correlative in the protasis before רָאוּ. The word is used here as a particle of time, to denote immediate consequence (like the Greek οὕτως), as in 1 Sam. ix. 13, Hos. iv. 7, where, however, כְּ stands in the protasis. But in English more vividly it would be omitted.

[d] דִּמִּינוּ. The word has been variously rendered. The LXX. ὑπελάβομεν. Symm. εἰκάσαμεν. Jerome *æstimavimus.* Calvin *expectavimus.* But the root is apparently cognate with זמם, and signifies the quiet, thoughtful consideration of a thing; the forming an idea in the mind (cf. l. 21), as in Latin, *sibi informare.* Hence "we have formed an idea, so to speak, corresponding to the greatness of Thy goodness," as Hupf. explains.

[e] לחילה. This ought clearly to be לְחֵילָהּ, with mappik, as in Zech. ix. 4.

[f] על מות. Many MSS. (as in ix. 1) and early Edd. read עלמות, one word, but in different senses: either (1) עֲלָמוֹת, "youth." So the Chald. "as in days of youth," which Luther follows; and this has been explained as = "in youthful strength:" or (2), "in a hidden manner, mysteriously." Others would defend the present reading, by rendering not "*unto* death," which gives but a poor sense, especially in relation to the general tenour of the Psalm, but "*beyond* death." So Mendelss. "über den Tod," Cocc., &c., following the Syr., which has ܠܥܠ ܡܢ ܡܘܬܐ, *desuper vel supra mortem*, and Aq. ἀθανασίᾳ. Stier tries to support this by Ps. xxiii. 5, lxviii. 21, and Is. xxv. 6—10. But not a single passage has been adduced in which the prep. עַל has this meaning.

Others read עוֹלָמֹת (cod. 157 Kenn.), *for ever*, as LXX. *εἰς τοὺς αἰῶνας*, and so Symm., Menach., Ibn Ez., but the fem. plur. does not occur elsewhere; otherwise this gives the best sense. עַל־מוּת, however, may be only like ע׳ מ׳ לַבֵּן, ix. 1, intended to mark the measure to which the song was to be sung; and then it either stands exceptionally at the end, instead of the beginning of the Psalm, as a similar notation does in Hab. iii. 19; or it belongs to the title of the next Psalm, in which case the conclusion of this Psalm is imperfect.

PSALM 49

THIS Psalm is not inaptly described in the ancient Latin Version of the Psalms (published with the Anglo-Saxon Paraphrase by Thorpe) as, *Vox Ecclesiæ super Lazaro et divite purpurato.* It is designed as a vindication of the ways of God in sight of the different fortunes of the righteous and the wicked in this world. It is no mere common-place on the shortness of life and the uncertainty of riches. It is no philosophical dissertation, which bids us bear up bravely in our perils and sufferings, telling us that virtue is its own reward. It goes at once to the root of the matter. It shows us not only the vanity of riches, but the end of those who "boast themselves in their riches." It comforts the righteous in their oppression and affliction, not merely by the assurance that they shall finally triumph over the wicked, but by the more glorious hope of life everlasting with God. Here is the true ground of consolation, that God will not only not forsake those who trust in Him in this life, but that He will take them to Himself. It is this doctrine specially enunciated, which gives the Psalm its distinctive character, and which leads the Psalmist himself to claim for it so attentive a hearing.

The Psalm consists of three parts.

I. First: An Introduction, in which the whole world is called upon to listen to the words of the Poet, and in which he further declares that he speaks by Divine inspiration. Ver. 1—4.

Then follows the main body of the Poem, in two principal divisions, marked by the refrain, which closes each. Ver. 5—12, and ver. 13—20.

II. The former of these contains, generally, a description of men prosperous and rich, whose riches puff them up with pride, and with the foolish imagination that they can secure for themselves an immortality upon earth; but who are so far from being able to save themselves or others from death by their riches, that they are no better than the beasts that perish. Ver. 5—12.

III. The remainder of the Psalm deals chiefly with the consolation to be derived from the end of the righteous, as contrasted with the end of the worldly. Ver. 13—20.

Others divide the Psalm differently, and consider ver. 5—15 to contain one consecutive piece of instruction as to the several lots of the worldly and the faithful, and ver. 16—20, the application of the instruction, by way of consolation, to those who are in suffering and poverty, and to whom the prosperity of these men is a stumbling-block.

It should be remarked, that the rich men of the Psalm are not described as "the wicked," "the ungodly," "the violent," &c. as in other Psalms. Only one hint is given in the word "iniquity" (ver. 5), that they are evil men. But this seems to be designed, as in our Lord's parable of the rich man and Lazarus, to show that the selfish, proud, boastful use of riches, the mere luxuriousness of wealth, apart from violence or unscrupulousness of conduct, is evil, and finds its end in the outer darkness.

[FOR THE PRECENTOR. OF THE SONS OF KORAH.[a] A PSALM.]

1 HEAR ye this, all ye peoples,
Give ear all ye inhabitants of the world,
2 Both low and high,
Rich and poor together!

1—4. Introduction and announcement of the Psalmist's purpose.

The opening is solemn and formal, like that of the Prophets. Comp. Micah i. 2, 1 Kings xxii. 28, with Deut. xxxii 1, Is. i. 2, Ps. l. 1. "Quoniam Psalmus hic, a quocunque fuerit compositus, unum ex præcipuis cœlestis philosophiæ capitibus continet, non abs re tam splendidis verbis auctor præfatur, de rebus magnis et reconditis sibi fore sermonem, quo sibi attentionem conciliet."—*Calvin.*

1. THE WORLD; the term here used is that which indicates its temporary, fleeting character: see xvii. note[e]. Two things are implied in this verse: first, that the doctrine of the Psalm concerns all; and next, that it is one which men are apt to neglect, and to the consideration of which, therefore, they need to be roused.

2. LOW AND HIGH, lit. sons of (common) men, and sons of (great) men, cf. Ps. lxii. 9, the two names for *man* here used answering very nearly to the distinction between ἄνθρωπος and ἀνήρ, and between *homo* and *vir*. The older versions, however, see no antithesis here,

3 My mouth shall speak wisdom,
And the meditation of my heart is understanding;
4 I will incline mine ear to a parable.
I will open my dark saying upon the harp.

5 Why should I fear in the days of evil,
(When) iniquity at my heels compasseth me about? [b]

but take the phrase as = "all and every." So Symm. ἥ τε ἀνθρωπότης, προσέτι δὲ καὶ υἱοὶ ἑκάστου ἀνδρός. Jerome, *Tam filii Adam quam filii singulorum.* RICH AND POOR, between whom the instruction of the Psalm is divided, its lessons being a warning to the one, and a consolation to the other.

3. WISDOM . . . UNDERSTANDING. In the Heb. these words are plural, but apparently not so used with any intensification of meaning. The plural in these and like words is very common in the Proverbs: i. 20, ix. 1, xiv. 1, xxiv. 7. In the second clause of the verse I have supplied the copula "is;" for, notwithstanding Hupfeld's remark to the contrary, I cannot think it a natural construction to repeat the verb from the first clause: "The meditation of my heart shall speak understanding."

4. I WILL INCLINE MINE EAR, as one who listens patiently for the Divine revelation. The inspiration of the Poet, as well as that of the Prophet, is from above. He cannot speak of his own heart; he must hear what God the Lord will say. The *inclining* of the ear is the act significant of ready obedience on the part of man; the *revealing* or uncovering the ear (as it were, by drawing away the long hair which hung over it) denotes the imparting of supernatural knowledge, heavenly wisdom, and the like, on the part of God, Is. l. 5. Similarly, Wordsworth, speaking of a maiden whose soul is filled, and whose very features are moulded by the inspiration caught from the world of Nature:

"... she shall *lean her ear*
In many a secret place,
Where rivulets dance their wayward round,
And beauty born of murmuring sound
Shall pass into her face."

Diodati supposes that the metaphor is borrowed from musicians, who incline the ear when they tune their instruments, in order to ascertain that each note is true. It is because he has thus listened to receive a message from above, that the Poet can call upon all nations to hear him. He who would be a true teacher of the things of God must first incline his ear to hear, before he can open his lips to speak.

A PARABLE, a truth cast in a weighty, sententious (and frequently, as here, an antithetical) form; as a RIDDLE is one clothed in metaphor, &c. Comp. lxxviii. 2, Prov. i. 6. Both words, however, are used of profound and important truths. The very expression, "I will open," shows that it is not the design of the Poet to express himself in a dark, obscure manner.

5. WHY SHOULD I FEAR. The consolatory result at which he has arrived, after looking at the world, and weighing in the balance those whose fortune seems fair and prosperous, is placed first, before he tells the tale, as in xxxvii. 1, lxxiii. 1.

THE DAYS OF EVIL, not merely a time of misfortune, as the parallelism shows, but the time in which evil men bear sway.

(WHEN) INIQUITY, &c. lit. "when the iniquity of my heels compasseth me about." Comp. xliv. 15 [16], "the shame of my face covereth me," instead of "shame covereth my face."

6 They that trust [c] in their wealth,
And in the greatness of their riches make their boast,
7 None (of them) can by any means redeem another,[d]
Nor give to God a ransom for him;
8 And too costly is the redemption of their soul,
And it must be let alone [e] for ever,—
9 That he should still live continually,
That he should not see the grave.
10 For [f] he must see (it):
Wise men must die;
Together the fool and the brutish person must perish,
And leave their wealth for others.

Diodati correctly: "quando l'iniquità che m' è alle calcagna m' intornierà." Calvin quotes the French saying, *poursuivre jusqu'aux talons*, and remarks, "Fateor eum de hostibus loqui, sed iniquas eorum persequutiones calcaneo suo hærere dicit, quia potentia prævaleant, et quasi talos pede prementes, immineant ad ipsum premendum." Or, perhaps, Iniquity is supposed to be lying, like a serpent in his path, ready to fasten on the heel, as the most exposed and vulnerable part. See more in the Critical Note.

7. ANOTHER, lit. "a brother," the word, however, being employed in the widest sense, as in Lev. xxv. 48, and often. The sentiment is expressed in its most general form, but with a tacit opposition. Man cannot redeem man from death: God only can do this.

On the legal redemption of life, see Exod. xxi. 30, xxx. 12, Num. xxxv. 31, 32.

8. SOUL, *i.e.* as is evident from the whole scope of the contest here, "life." It is much to be regretted that superficial readers of the Psalm so often give a totally false meaning to this and the preceding verse. The passage has been alleged to prove that our Lord, as the Redeemer of man, must be God as well as man. The doctrine is most true, but it is not in the Psalm, nor is there the remotest allusion to it. All that is here taught is, that no wealth can save a man from death, because the life of men is not in their own hands, or in that of their fellows, but only in the hand of God, who cannot be bribed. There is a kind of solemn irony in the idea of the richest of men offering all his riches to God, to escape death.

IT MUST BE LET ALONE, or, "one must let that alone" (as P.B.V.).

9. THAT HE SHOULD LIVE. This is dependent on the last clause of ver. 7, "Nor give to God a ransom for him, that he should live," &c., verse 8 being parenthetical. Others connect it with the last clause of ver. 8, and render: "And he must give up (all hope) for ever, that he shall live continually," &c. But see note.[e]

10. FOR HE MUST SEE IT. In support of this rendering see such passages as x. 11, 14, xxxv. 21, 22, Is. xxvi. 11.

WISE MEN, not simply meaning that their wisdom cannot save them, but that their utmost wisdom will not lead them to make so profitable a use of their wealth as thereby to escape the grave. DIE.... PERISH: the words seem purposely chosen to denote the end respectively of the *wise* and the *brutish*.

11 Their inward thought[g] is that their houses shall be for ever,
Their dwelling-places to many generations:
They have called (their) lands after their own names.[h]
12 But man, (being) in honour, abideth not,
He is like to the beasts that are destroyed.

13 This their way is their folly,
And after them men approve their sayings. [Selah.]
14 Like a flock they are gathered to the unseen world;[i]

11. AFTER THEIR OWN NAMES. Thus hoping to build for themselves an immortality upon earth.

12. IN HONOUR. These words belong to the subject "man," not to the verb following. Man (being) in honour, or "for all his honour," notwithstanding all the magnificence of his position and his wealth, abideth not,—lit. does not pass the night, is not so secure in his position even as a wayfarer, who turns in for a night's lodging at the inn.

ARE DESTROYED, lit. "are reduced to silence," the eternal silence of death. The clause is a relative one. Others, however, refer this verb to "man," as the subject. So Calvin: "similis factus est jumentis: intereunt." They (*i.e.* men) perish. But the sudden transition from the singular to the plural is harsh: and, on the other hand, the omission of the relative is common enough. Delitzsch, better, considers both "men" and "beasts" to be the subject of the verb.

13. This verse is evidently closely connected with ver. 11, and hence Hupfeld would transpose it with ver. 12. It is, as he says, naturally connected by the train of thought with ver. 11, and indeed carries on and completes the picture, by showing how these rich men have their example followed even after their death. The very expression, "*This* their way," &c., is a summing up of what had been just said. And the *Selah*, standing as it now does, at the end of ver. 13 [14], instead of standing, as it naturally would, after the refrain, ver. 12, seems to intimate that there has been some disarrangement.

THIS THEIR WAY. Both the meaning and the construction of this clause are doubtful. It may mean (1) "This their way (*i.e.* manner of life, course of conduct) is their folly:" or (2) "This their prosperous condition is, (or, becomes) their infatuation (blind confidence);" for *kĕsĕl* may mean "a stupid security or presumptuous confidence, foolhardiness," as well as "folly." As regards the construction, it may be as above, or the clause may consist of two independent sentences: "This is their way; they have confidence;" or, as Mendels. "Dies ist ihr Thun: sich selber Thorheit;" or finally, the latter part of it may be a relative sentence (as Ewald takes it): "This is the way of those who are foolish." כֶּסֶל is rendered *confidence* in almost every instance in E.V.

APPROVE THEIR SAYINGS, lit. "find pleasure in their mouth." Their example and their words survive them. Their maxims are the maxims which find favour and currency in the world. Ewald carries on the construction from the previous verse:

"This is the way of those who have folly,
And of those after them who delight to speak in like manner."

14. A further description of the end of these rich fools. They perish like cattle (ver. 12): they are laid in the grave; they descend to Hades (*Shĕōl*, the world of spirits), and

Death is their shepherd:
(And the upright have dominion over them in the morning,)
And their beauty [k] shall the unseen world consume,
That it have no more dwelling-place.[l]
15 But God will redeem my soul from the power of the unseen world:
For He shall take me. [Selah.]

there they are like a flock of sheep, with Death for their shepherd, their beauty and their glory gone.

IS THEIR SHEPHERD, *i.e.* feeds them (not feeds *on* them, as the E.V.), tends them. LXX. θάνατος ποιμανεῖ αὐτούς. Symm. νεμήσει αὐτούς. Jerome, *pascet eos.* They have been like a flock fed to the full in fat pastures during the day: they are now like a flock which the shepherd, when night comes, puts into the fold.

HAVE DOMINION, or, have trampled upon them, putting their feet, as it were, upon the neck of prostrate foes. LXX. κατακυριεύσουσιν. Stated as a past fact, because the destruction of the wicked is also regarded as already accomplished (the pret. is used in the first clause of the verse).

IN THE MORNING. Apparently the morning of deliverance is meant, after the night of misery and suffering which they have experienced at the hand of their oppressors. The Patristric and other expositors understand it of the morning of the resurrection, and the kingdom and dominion which the saints shall then share with Christ. But see on ver. 15.

15. The lot of the righteous is now contrasted with that of the wicked, but with a personal application to the Psalmist himself, "God shall redeem my soul."

BUT, or, "only," as an exception to the general lot of men, such as those before described.

FROM THE POWER OF THE UNSEEN WORLD, lit. "from the hand of Sheōl," *i.e.* the grave and Hades.

FOR HE SHALL TAKE ME. This short half-verse is, as Böttcher remarks, the more weighty, from its very shortness. The same expression occurs again lxxiii. 24, "Thou shalt take me," the original of both being Gen. v. 24, where it is used of the translation of Enoch, "He was not; for God *took* him."

We have, then, in this passage again (comp. xvi. 11, xvii. 15), the strong hope of eternal life with God, if not the hope of a resurrection. In the preceding verse, in the very midst of the gloomy picture which the Psalmist draws of the end of the ungodly, there breaks forth one morning-ray of light, the bright anticipation of the final triumph of the good over the evil. This is the inextinguishable hope which animates the Church of the Old Testament, as well as that of the New. Righteousness *shall* eventually, must in its very nature, reign upon the earth. The wicked shall find their end in Sheol (see ix. 17 [18]), and the righteous shall trample on their graves. This, and not more than this, seems to have been the meaning originally of the Psalmist, in the words, "And the righteous have dominion over them in the morning." But now that he comes to speak of himself, and his own personal relation to God, he rises into a higher strain. He who knows and loves God has the life of God, and can never perish. That life must survive even the shock of death. "God," says the Psalmist, "shall

16 Be not thou afraid when a man groweth rich,
When the glory of his house is increased :
17 For when he dieth he can take nothing (away),
His glory cannot descend after him :
18 For (though) while he liveth he blesseth his soul,
And men praise thee because thou doest good to thyself.
19 He shall go to the generation of his fathers,
Who nevermore see the light.
20 Man, (being) in honour, and having no understanding,
Is like to the beasts (that) are destroyed.

redeem my soul from the hand of Hades, for He shall take me," as He took Enoch, and as He took Elijah to Himself. We are not, of course, to suppose that the Sacred Poet himself expected to be taken up alive to heaven ; but those great facts of former ages were God's witnesses to man of his immortality, and of the reality of a life with Him beyond this world. It is a hope based on facts like these which here shines forth. It is a hope, not a revealed certainty. It rests on no distinct promise : it has not assumed the definite form of a doctrine. But it was enough to raise, to cheer, to encourage those who saw ungodliness prospering in this world. The end of the wicked, after all, was a thick darkness that had never been penetrated : the end of the righteous, life with God. (See the same contrast in xvii. 15, and note there.)

16. Having encouraged himself with this hope, he now turns to encourage others.

18. BLESSETH HIS SOUL, *i.e.* pronounces himself a happy man, "counteth himself happy," P.B.V. Comp. Deut. xxix. 19 [18], "blesseth himself in his heart," and the address of the rich man to his soul, Luke xii. 19, "Soul, thou hast much goods laid up for many years."

The second clause of the verse is parenthetical, and the sentiment is a general one : "when thou (*i.e.* any one) doest good," &c. Symm. ἐπαινέσουσί σε ἐὰν καλῶς ποιήσης σεαυτῷ.

19. HE SHALL GO. According to the present text, "*it* shall go," *i.e.* the soul (ver. 18), which is the only subject, if the verb here is in the 3d pers. fem. Some expositors, however, alleging that such an expression is not used of the *soul*, would take the verb here as 2d pers. masc., "thou shalt come," as if the rich man were addressed : but this involves the exceeding harshness of a return, immediately after, to the 3d pers., "*Thou* shalt come to the generation of *his* fathers." It is better, therefore, with all the older Versions, to render, "*he* shall come," instead of "it shall come," though it is not certain that they had the masc. instead of the fem. verb ; for they may have only paraphrased.

20. The Psalm concludes with the refrain, as at ver. 12, but with the alteration of one word. Instead of "abideth not," we have now, "and hath no understanding," or rather as a sort of adverbial clause, "and without understanding." There is consequently a fresh idea here. There the statement is, that men in general are like dumb cattle ; here, that only if they possess not the true wisdom, they perish like the brutes.

[a] See on xlii. note [a].

[b] עֲוֺן עֲקֵבַי, "the iniquity of my heels," LXX. ἀνομία τῆς πτέρνης μου, Symm. ἀν. τῶν ἰχνέων μου, Jerome, *iniquitas calcanei mei*, the heels being taken as = "steps," and "the iniquity of my steps" meaning "my errors," which are said to compass a man about, because they bring punishment upon him. But עָקֵב is not used like אָשׁוּר in a moral sense, but always as that which is the object of attack, the vulnerable part of the man. (Comp. Gen. iii. 15.) Hence most modern interpreters derive עֲקֵבַי from an adj. עָקֵב, "a supplanter," one who, as it were, trips another up by the heel (as perhaps the Syr. "my enemies"). But such a form does not occur elsewhere, and it is unnecessary to introduce it here; nor need we punctuate עָוֺן, as Hupfeld proposes. "The iniquity of my heels" is the iniquity which attacks them, lies in wait for them, like a serpent in the path; and the construction may be defended and explained by reference to xliv. 15 [16], as mentioned in the note on ver. 5. The second member of this verse may depend logically on בִּימֵי in the first, "in the days when," &c.

[c] הַבֹּטְחִים. The subj. of the following clause, where it is resumed and expanded in אָח and אִישׁ, and a transition is made from the constr. with the partic. to that with the fin. verb (Ges. § 134, 2, Rem. 2). Those who take עֲקֵבַי to mean "supplanters," carry on the construction into this verse, "my supplanters who trust," &c.

[d] אָח, the accus. placed first in the sentence: lit. "a brother can a man not redeem." [Delitzsch, however, takes it as nom. "a brother, *i.e.* one who is only of the same flesh and blood, cannot redeem a man."] אָח stands without the suffix, instead of אָחִיו, as occurs in similar instances, Ezek. v. 10, xviii. 18, Mic. vii. 6, Mal. i. 6. There is no reason, with Ewald and others, to read אַךְ and יִפָּדֶה, "surely a man cannot be redeemed."

The position of the negative before both tenses of the verb (instead of coming, as is more common, between the infin. and the fut. פ׳ לֹא י׳) is noticeable. Comp. Gen. iii. 4, Amos ix. 8 (Ges. § 131, 3, Rem. 1).

[e] וְחָדַל. The subject of this verb is clearly פִּדְיוֹן, "It (the redemption of the soul) hath ceased for ever," *i.e.* there is an end of it, it must be given up. So Ew. "dass es fehlet auf immer." Gesen. and others take the verb here in its active signification, "He (*i.e.* the person who would redeem) has given it up;" but חדל in this sense is always followed by the prep. מִן, and the construction of the sentence is rendered less simple.

[f] כִּי. The particle here confirms the preceding negation, by introducing the opposite = "yea, rather (or, for, on the contrary), see (it) he must." Comp. 1 Kings xxi. 15. There is no need to supply any new object to יִרְאֶה, or to carry on the construction, as in our Version, "For he seeth that wise men," &c.

[g] קִרְבָּם· The Chald., LXX., and Syr. evidently read קִבְרָם, "their grave (graves) are their houses for ever" (comp. Eccl. xii. 5, where the grave is

called "the long home" of man), which gives a good sense, and is the simplest reading: but the other is defensible; nor is there any reason to render, with Hupfeld, "Their inward hearts are their houses," &c. *i.e.* their houses fill all their thoughts (as in xlv. 8 [9], "myrrh are all thy garments," instead of "all thy garments are full of myrrh").

[h] קָרְאוּ ב׳. This has been rendered, "men call upon their names (*i.e.* praise them), upon the earth (or, far and wide)." So Ewald, "sie die hochgepriesen waren überall!" But ק׳ בְּשֵׁם does not mean "to praise," but to "call on, invoke," &c., and is always used of Jehovah, and the plur. אֲדָמוֹת cannot = אֶרֶץ; it means "lands," as in the parall. we have "houses." We have no instance of an exactly parallel construction, but the meaning is sufficiently clear, and has been given by the older interpreters, LXX. and Th. ἐπεκαλέσαντο τὰ ὀνόματα αὐτῶν ἐπὶ τῶν γαιῶν αὐτῶν. Jerome, *vocaverunt nominibus suis terras suas.*

[i] שַׁתּוּ for שָׁתוּ, from שִׁית, as if from שתת, as lxxiii. 9: no definite subject need be supplied. "They (indef.) lay or place them," = they are laid: שַׁתַּנִי is used in the same sense, lxxxviii. 7. I have translated "gathered," because of the prep. לְ following, and because of the comparison with a flock. Or, it may be "they are set, marshalled, *for* the grave." In Ps. iii. שָׁתוּ "have set themselves."

[k] צִירָם (as Is. xlv. 16) or צוּרם, "their form (*i.e.* not merely the *bodily* form, but the whole outward show of the man) is for the consumption of Sheōl," *i.e.* is destined to be consumed by Sheōl (Ges. § 132, 3, Rem. 1). Symm. τὸ δὲ κρατερὸν αὐτῶν παλαιώσει ᾅδης. Jerome, *figura eorum conteretur in inferno.*

[l] מִזְּבֻל לוֹ, either "out of (*i.e.* from) its dwelling," or "*without* its dwelling," *i.e.* so that it has no dwelling more, מִן being used in its negative sense; the latter is preferable here. The English prep. "out of" has the same ambiguity, as it may mean either "from," or "without."

PSALM 50

This Psalm furnishes us with no evidence as to the time of its composition, but in elegance and sublimity of language, in force and dignity, it is worthy of the best days of Hebrew poetry. It is a magnificent exposition of the true nature of that service and worship which God requires from man. It rebukes the folly which thinks that religion is a matter of sacrifices and gifts, and declares that obedience and thanksgiving are the true fulfilling of the Law. It condemns alike a prevalent formalism and a prevalent hypocrisy.

How needful it was to insist upon such truths we learn from the whole history of Israel, and the perpetual and indignant remonstrances of the Prophets. The tendency to substitute the outward act for the inward, the sacrifices of bulls and goats for the sacrifice of thanksgiving, was deeply ingrained in the nation, till at last it issued in Pharisaism, and wore its most hideous aspect on that day of solemn Passover, when the sacrifices of the Law were offered by those whose hands were stained with the greatest crime which the world has seen.

The Psalm thus inculcates at length the same doctrine which we find in briefer lines in Psalms xl. 6—8 [7—9], li. 17 [18], lxix. 30, &c. [31, &c.], and which is implied in xv. and xxiv. 1—6. In its general tone and character it is essentially prophetic. It consists of three principal parts :—

I. A magnificent exordium, in which the whole scene of judgement is described. As formerly, at the *giving* of the Law on Sinai, so now God is represented as appearing in Zion for *the explanation* of it, and for judgement against its transgressors. Ver. 1—6.

II. From His judgement-seat God solemnly rebukes the errors and delusions which prevailed as to the nature of His service. He reminds His people of the peculiar relation in which they stand to Him, and asks if they can believe that sacrifices, merely as sacrifices, can be of any value to Him who has all creatures at His command. Thanksgiving and prayer are the sacrifices in which He delights, and these will best avail in the day of trouble. Ver. 7—15.

III. But there were those in Israel who not only exalted the outward service unduly, but who made its punctual observance a cloke for, and a makeweight against, their iniquity. The first evil, indeed, of superstitious formalism, naturally engendered this still deadlier evil of conscious hypocrisy. Against this, sentence is now pronounced; and again the truth, already enunciated, is repeated, that the love of a grateful heart is the sacrifice which is truly pleasing to God. Ver. 16—23.

In verses 8—15, Hengstenberg remarks, that prevailing errors as to the *First* Table of the Law, the worship of God, are condemned. In verses 16—21, the discourse turns to the *Second* Table. Here those are reproved who have the Law of God constantly in their mouths, and at the same time wickedly transgress it in their behaviour towards their neighbour.

[A PSALM OF ASAPH.[a]]

I. 1 THE God of gods, Jehovah, hath spoken
And called the earth, from the rising of the sun to the setting thereof.
2 Out of Zion, the perfection of beauty,
God hath shined forth.
3 Our God cometh, and surely will not [b] keep silence!
A fire devoureth before Him,

1—6. The Psalm opens with a description of God's coming to judge His people. He comes now to Zion, as once He came to Sinai. He comes with all the gloom and terrors of thunder, and lightning, and storm. He summons before His judgement-seat those whom He has taken into covenant with Himself; and at the same time as exercising universal dominion, He calls heaven and earth to be His witnesses against them.

1. THE GOD OF GODS. So Mendels. "der Götter Gott." So also, Hupf. Zunz; Wellbeloved, and Leeser, "the God of gods." So the Gen. Vers. This is, there can be no doubt, the proper rendering of the words *El Elohim;* as the LXX. Θεὸς θεῶν, and not as Aq., Symm., Th., ἰσχυρὸς θέός: still less have we here three distinct names of God, *El*, *Elohim*, *Jehovah*, as Delitzsch and Hengstenberg suppose, and as the Massoretic accentuation would imply. These three names of God occur in the same way in Josh. xxii. 22, where they are twice repeated, and where they are in like manner separated by the accents. This is the only use of the name Jehovah in the Psalm, which is in accordance with the general Elohistic character of the Second Book; but the adjunct, "God of gods," is certainly remarkable. The peculiar use of the Divine Names in the Psalms, and in the historical Books, is however too large a question to be satisfactorily discussed in a note.

HATH SPOKEN, and in the next verse HATH SHINED, the preterites being employed because, as Ewald explains, the whole scene had first presented itself in a concrete form, the more imposing, because it was thus presented to the Poet's eye; and though afterwards, in order to narrate the vision, it would be necessary for him to arrange in detail and in order the several parts, still he would naturally go back to the first impression of the whole upon him, and so describe the scene as *past*.

THE EARTH, as afterwards "the heaven and the earth," are summoned as witnesses of the solemn act of judgement, and as lending grandeur to the whole awful scene —borrowed, as Is. i. 2, from Deut. xxxii. 1.

2. THE PERFECTION OF BEAUTY. Mendels. "die Krone der Schönheit." Comp. xlviii. 2 [3]. The same expression is applied to Zion also in Lament. ii. 15. In 1 Macc. ii. 12, the Temple is called ἡ καλλονη ἡμῶν. Zion would be so called, as possessing the Sanctuary, whether Tabernacle or Temple. "Ten measures of beauty," say the Rabbis, "hath God bestowed upon the world, and nine of these fall to the lot of Jerusalem."

HATH SHINED. Comp. lxxx. 1 [2], Deut. xxxiii. 2.

3. God is seen coming, the devouring fire and the mighty tempest being the accompaniments of His Presence, and the symbols of the judgement which He will execute.

And round about Him a tempest rageth.
4 He calleth to the heavens from above,
And to the earth that He may judge His people.
5 "Gather unto Me, My beloved,
They that have made a covenant with Me by sacrifice."
6 And the heavens have declared His righteousness,
For God is Judge Himself. [Selah.]

II. 7 "Hear, O my people, and I will speak;
O Israel, and I will testify against thee:

See the more elaborate working out of the same image in xviii. 7—15 [8—16]. Comp. xcvii. 2—6.

A TEMPEST RAGETH, lit. "it is tempestuous exceedingly," the verb being used impersonally. The P.B.V. well "a mighty tempest is stirred up."

5. All nature having been summoned as witness to the awful scene, God now speaks.

GATHER, &c. To whom are these words addressed? Many suppose, to the angels, as the ministers of God's will. But it is unnecessary to make the expression more definite than it is in the Psalm.

MY BELOVED, not "My *saints*," as E. V., but "those who have obtained favour, grace, in My sight" (the whole nation being so called, "non ut omnibus promiscue reddat veræ pietatis testimonium, sed ut melius ad finem vocationis suæ attendant"), or as is explained in the parallel, "those whom I have taken into covenant with Myself." See note on xvi. 10. God has made Himself known to Israel; He has given them His Law and His Covenant; and He comes now to judge them, to see whether they have kept His Law, whether they have been faithful to His Covenant.

BY SACRIFICE, lit. "upon sacrifice," as that by means of which the covenant was sealed, Exod. xxiv. 8.

6. This verse is quasi-parenthetical. It states the fact that God having called to the heavens, the heavens *have* announced the righteousness of God (the verb is in the *historic* tense, and cannot be rendered as a *future*, as so many interpreters render it), a prelude, as it were, to the solemn judgement which follows. Comp. xcvii. 6.

FOR GOD IS JUDGE. God is now about to act as Judge Himself, the participle being, as often, rather a future than a present participle. Others, "*That* God is Judge;" but this rendering of the particle does not harmonize so well with the preceding clause, where the object of the verb, viz. "His righteousness," is already given. If there were no such object, the sentence would stand: "the heavens have declared *that* God," &c.; but as it is, the reason is given why God's *righteousness* is declared; *for*, &c.

7. Then judgement opens. The whole nation is called before the bar of its Judge, who is "God" (the God of the world), and "*thy* God" (the God of Israel). Calvin: "Nam quum Deus sim, compescere omnem proterviam debebat majestas mea, ut ad vocem meam sileret omnis caro. Inter vos autem quibus me patefeci in Deum eo plus obsequii merebar."

AND I WILL SPEAK, or, "*that I may* speak," and in the next clause, "that I may testify," the paragogic form of the verb denoting a purpose.

TESTIFY AGAINST THEE, or perhaps "conjure thee," "solemnly warn thee," or "testify unto thee,"

God, (even) thy God, am I.
8 Not because of thy sacrifices do I reprove thee,
Yea, thy burnt-offerings are always before Me.
9 I would not take a bullock out of thine house,
Nor he-goats out of thy folds;
10 For Mine is every beast [c] of the forest,
(And) the cattle upon the mountains by thousands.
11 I know every bird of the mountains,
And that which moveth in the field is with Me.

see lxxxi. 8; but this Divine testimony generally implies rebuke. Ewald, "dass ich ermahne dich;" Maurer, *Ut te graviter horter.*

GOD, (EVEN) THY GOD, in an Elohistic Psalm, instead of "Jehovah, thy God" (see xlv. 7 [8]), with reference probably to the Mosaic formula, as at the beginning of the Decalogue, Exod. xx. 2. Compare the shorter formula, "I am Jehovah," Ex. vi. 2, 6—8, which is so often repeated in the solemn enactment of different laws in the Book of Leviticus. It is the utterance both of the Lawgiver and of the Judge.

8. The reason for this act of judgement is given. First, negatively. It is not because the people had neglected the externals of the Law, or had forgotten to offer the sacrifices appointed by the Law. They had brought them; but they had brought them as if the act were everything, and as if the meaning of the act, and the spirit in which it was done, were nothing. But God demands no service for its own sake, but only as the expression of an obedient will. A thankful heart is more than all burnt-offerings.

The Prophets are full of the like sentiments. Thus, in Isaiah, God expostulates, "To what purpose is the multitude of your sacrifices unto Me? I am full of the burnt-offerings of rams," &c. (i. 12; compare also lviii. and lxvi. 3); Micah asks, "Will Jehovah be pleased with thousands of rams?" &c. (vi. 6—8); Hosea testifies, "I will have mercy and not sacrifice." And so deep-rooted was this tendency in the people to exaggerate the importance of the dead work, to bring the sacrifice of the dumb animal instead of the sacrifice of the heart, that Jeremiah carries the opposition between sacrifices and obedience even to the extreme of a paradox. "For I spake not unto your fathers, and I commanded them not, in the day that I brought them up out of the land of Egypt, concerning burnt-offering and sacrifice; but this thing I commanded them, saying, Hear My voice," &c. (vii. 22, 23).

SACRIFICES, *i.e.* peace-offerings, often joined with BURNT-OFFERINGS, as li. 17 [18]. See also xl. 6 [7], the two being mentioned probably as representing and including all manner of sacrifices.

The following verses, 9—13, are in a strain of lofty irony, in which the gross stupidity which could suppose that the flesh and blood of the victims were of themselves acceptable to God, is finely exposed.

10. CATTLE. The word is most commonly used of *tame* animals, but here generally of large herds of grazing cattle.

BY THOUSANDS, lit. "on the mountains of a thousand," *i.e.* where a thousand are; or, where they are by thousands.

11. THAT WHICH MOVETH, or "roameth," where however it is very difficult to render it thus. Mendels. "Was sich im Felde regt." Comp. lxxx. 13 [14]. The

12 If I were hungry, I would not tell thee;
For mine is the world and the fulness thereof.
13 Should I eat the flesh of bulls,
Or drink the blood of he-goats?
14 Sacrifice unto God thanksgiving,
And pay Thy vows unto the Most High,
15 And call upon Me in the day of distress,
I will deliver thee, and thou shalt glorify Me."

III. 16 But unto the wicked saith God:
"What hast thou to do to rehearse My statutes,
And that thou shouldest take My covenant into thy mouth?
17 Whereas for thee, thou hatest instruction,
And hast cast My words behind thee;
18 When thou sawest a thief, thou foundest pleasure in him,
And with adulterers (has been) thy portion;

exact meaning of the Heb. word is doubtful. Ewald (2nd Ed.) renders it, "fruit of the field," but the above is the interpretation of Gesen. (*Thes.* in v.), and is the one commonly adopted. In his 3rd Ed. Ewald has *Brut.*

14. There follows now, positively, what God requires. The sacrifices which He would have are thanksgiving, and the prayer of faith in the time of trouble. Comp. li. 18 [19].

Under the name of *thanksgiving* and *prayer* all the rest of religion is comprehended, as Calvin truly observes: "Nec vero ordinem invertit, a Dei laude incipiens. Videri quidem posset hæc ratio esse præpostera, quum invocatio gratiarum actionem præcedat: sed quia hinc orandi principium ducitur, quum adscribitur Deo justus ac debitus honor, atque hæc etiam fidei rudimenta sunt, Deum quærere tanquam unicum bonorum omnium fontem, non temere Propheta laudem in primo gradu locavit."

THY VOWS. See note on xxii. 25. Comp. cxvi. 13.

16. The former part of the Divine sentence was directed against those who attached undue importance to the external acts of religion. What follows is directed against those who make use of the outward observances of religion as a mask and cloke under which they may hide their iniquities. First, formalists, and next, hypocrites are condemned. With this and the following verses, comp. Rom. ii. 17—24.

TO TELL, *i.e.* "to number," "to count up," as if with a view to their more punctual observance.

17. WHEREAS FOR THEE. The pronoun is emphatic, and is thus placed, to mark the strong contrast between such a character and the Law which he professes to understand. Comp. Is. i. 15.

18. FOUNDEST PLEASURE IN HIM, *i.e.* in his society; in intercourse with him, &c. Comp. Job xxxiv. 9. The transgression of three commandments of the Decalogue is specified, in the same way as in Rom. ii. 17, &c., by way of example.

19 Thy mouth thou hast let loose in wickedness,
And thy tongue frameth deceit;
20 Thou sittest (and) speakest against thy brother,
Against thy mother's son thou givest a thrust.
21 These things hast thou done, and (because) I kept silence,
Thou thoughtest I was altogether such[d] an one as thyself;
(But) I will reprove thee, and lay (the matter) in order before thine eyes."
22 Consider, now, this, O ye that forget God,
Lest I tear (you), and there be none to deliver.
23 Whoso sacrificeth thanksgiving glorifieth me,[e]

19. FRAMETH, lit. "weaveth." Comp. Lat. *texere fraudes*, &c.

20. THOU SITTEST, *i.e.* in company with others who slander and speak evil. (See i. 1.)

THY MOTHER'S SON, stronger than "thy brother," and intended to mark the *unnatural* blackness of such conduct.

GIVEST A THRUST (the noun occurs only here); or, perhaps (as the LXX. ἐτίθεις σκάνδαλον), "puttest a stumbling-block." Others, however, take the word here in the sense of "shame, reproach," and this suits the parallelism better, "thou uttered slander."

21. And because the sinner is allowed to go on long unpunished, he waxes confident by his impunity, and imagines that God is like himself, and that good and evil are things indifferent; not that he *says* so in words, but his conduct shows his ignorance both of the exceeding sinfulness of sin, and of the truth and righteousness of God.

KEPT SILENCE, *i.e.* did not manifest My abhorrence of sin by signal vengeance on the ungodly. "Hoc ludibrium Dei," says Calvin, "gravissime exagitat (Propheta), quod eum sceleribus favere existiment. Neque enim atrociore contumelia potest effici, quam dum justitia sua spoliatur."

But the long-suffering of God cannot always be abused. The time comes when the sinner is made to feel that God is a righteous Judge.

I WILL LAY IN ORDER—the whole sin in all its evil course, its poisonous root, and its deadly branches, shall be put before the man. The sin that he did and would not look at, God shall make him look upon. The sin which he thought he could hide from God, or which, with strange infatuation, he supposed God took no notice of, shall be proclaimed upon the housetops. "Sic enim interpretor verbum *ordinare*, quod Deus distincto ordine catologum omnium scelerum proponet, quem (velint, nolent) legere et agnoscere cogantur."

23. This third great division of the Psalm concludes with the assertion of the same truth as the second. The lesson of the Psalm for all who pervert the Law of God, whether to purposes of superstition or hypocrisy, is the same: God desires the heart and the will of man as the true sacrifice.

SACRIFICETH THANKSGIVING, as above, ver. 14. The verb is

And whoso prepareth (his) way,[f]
I will shew him the salvation of God.

designedly employed, in order to mark the nature of the *sacrifice* which God will have: slay not victims, bring not animals, but bring thanksgiving as sacrifices. The E.V. with its rendering, "*Offereth* praise," loses sight of the distinct reference to the Mosaic sacrifices, which are not indeed absolutely superseded—the time had not yet come for this—but are put in their true place. The very great prominence again given to thanksgiving, is worthy of our careful notice. There is no duty so commonly forgotten. God showers down His benefits upon us with both hands, large and free, and we receive them as a matter of course, and never consider Whose Love has bestowed them; and thus, in our unthankfulness, we rob God of His honour.

Further, as thanksgiving is thus dwelt upon because it is so commonly forgotten, so it is also put as the sum of religion because it, in fact, includes all else. Faith, and prayer, and self-denial, and the endurance of the cross, and all holy exercises, are, as Calvin observes, comprised in this one grace. For it is by faith only that we are sensible of God's goodness; therefore he who is truly of a thankful spirit has faith; he who is thankful triumphs over his earthly trials; he who is thankful is accomplishing man's highest end, inasmuch as in all things He gives glory to God.

The instruction of the Psalm abides: it has not lost its force. The sacraments and ordinances of the Christian Church may become to us what sacrifice and offering were to the Jews, a mere *opus operatum;* a man may give all his goods to feed the poor, and yet have no love; a man may be punctual in his attendance at all holy ordinances, and yet cherish iniquity in his heart, and, upon occasion, secretly practise it. Hence the Psalm is truly prophetical; that is, universal in its character. It deals with "the sinners and the hypocrites in Zion," but it reaches to all men, in all places, to the end of time.

[a] לְאָסָף. This is the first Psalm, and the only one in this Book, ascribed to Asaph. In the Third Book of the Psalter, eleven Psalms, lxxiii.—lxxxiii., have his name prefixed to them. He was one of the three choir-leaders or chief singers appointed under the direction of David to preside over his great choral company of Levites, the other two being Heman and Ethan (or Jeduthun). Comp. 1 Chron. xv. 16, &c., with xxv. 1, &c. Their special instruments of music were cymbals of brass, 1 Chron. xv. 19, with which, and with harps and psalteries, they were said to prophesy, xxv. 1. On the occasion of bringing up the Ark to Jerusalem, David delivered "to Asaph and his brethren" the Psalm which had been composed to celebrate that event, 1 Chron. xvi. 7; and in the division of the Levitical services which became necessary, as the Tabernacle still remained at Gibeon, Asaph and his company were selected "to minister before the Ark of Jehovah, and to record, and to thank and praise Jehovah the God of Israel," 1 Chron. xvi. 4, 5. In later times, Asaph was ranked with David as one of the famous singers of Israel. Comp. Neh. xii. 46, with 2 Chron. xxix. 30.

[b] וְאַל־יֶחֱרַשׁ. The optative seems to be required by the form of the negative (אַל = μή) with the second verb. Still, it must be confessed that

the abrupt introduction of a wish here disturbs the flow of the language, and this is not obviated even if, with Hupfeld, we suppose this to be a common formula, in which God is called upon to manifest Himself. Ewald renders, "Heran kommt unser Gott und *darf* nicht schweigen." Bunsen, ". . . *mag* nicht." Delitzsch, "kommen wird . . . und *kann* nicht schweigen." He explains the negative as being used subjectively to express the conviction of the writer's mind, = *nequaquam silebit.* Maurer remarks, "Non sine quadam elegantia in media adventantis Dei descriptione 'וְאַל י *neque est quod sileat* dicit." The nearest parallels to this use of the negative are to be found in xxxiv. 5 [6] (where see note) and xli. 3.

[c] חַיְתוֹ. The older form of the stat. constr. for חַיַּת. See lxxix. 2, civ. 11, 20, Is. lvi. 9, all imitating the earliest instance in Gen. i. 24. This old case-ending is either in וֹ or in יְ. See on cxiii. note [a], cxiv. note [b], and Ewald, § 211, b. 2 (Eng. Transl. 406).

[d] הֱיוֹת, constr. infin., instead of the absolute before the finite verb. The sentence is in the *oratio obliqua*, as ix. 21, x. 13, xvii. 3, Gen. xii. 13. (Ges. § 155, 4*c*.) Hence also in Eccles. x. 4, the rendering: "he saith to every one that he is a fool," is perfectly correct, notwithstanding the omission of the כִּי.

[e] יְכַבְּדָנְנִי. Pausal form, as if from a termination ־ָנְנִי, instead of ־ֶנִּי, or ־ֵנִי, but without parallel elsewhere, apparently formed after the plural epenthetic form, like יְקְרָאֻנְנִי, Prov. i. 28. Comp. viii. 17, Hos. v. 15. (Gesen. § 58, 4.)

[f] שָׂם. The LXX. read שָׁם, καὶ ἐκεῖ ὁδὸς ᾗ δείξω αὐτῷ τὸ σωτήριον Θεοῦ. But the present reading is ancient. Jerome renders: *qui ordinat viam.* Böttcher explains: *viam faciens, h. e.* recta incedere (*lege agere*) *parans.* It may be a question, however, with which of the two preceding clauses the words שָׂם דֶּרֶךְ should be joined. Del. takes them with the last: "He that offereth thanks, honoureth me aright, and prepareth a way where I may show him the salvation of God."

PSALM 51

THIS Psalm is the expression of a deep and unfeigned repentance. It is a prayer, first, for forgiveness, with a humble confession of sinful deeds springing from a sinful nature as their bitter root; and then for renewal and sanctification through the Holy Ghost; together with vows of thankfulness for God's great mercy to the sinner, and holy resolutions for the future.

It is the first of a series of Psalms, li.—lxv., which, in the Second Book of the Psalter, are ascribed to David; and, according to the title, was written by him after his great sin, when the words of the Prophet Nathan roused his conscience from its uneasy slumber. Before that, we cannot doubt, remorse had been busy with him. Before that he had felt his misery, had fought against it, but had refused to confess his sin. But the home-thrust, "Thou art the man," pierced him to the heart, and this Psalm is but the fuller record of the confession, "I have sinned," which the history mentions so briefly.

So profound a conviction of sin, so deep and unfeigned a penitence, so true a confession, a heart so tender, so contrite, a desire so fervent for renewal, a trust so humble, so filial in the forgiving love of God, are what we find nowhere else in the Old Testament, but what we might surely expect from "the man after God's own heart." This Psalm, indeed, and the 32nd, justify the title thus given him. In them we see the true man. Great as had been his sin, it was not the sin of a hardened nature, of the merely selfish sensualist, of the despot to whom all men were but as tools to minister to his pleasures and his crimes. And therefore, when the Prophet comes to him, he turns to God with a real sorrow, and God meets him, as the father in the parable meets his erring son, with a free forgiveness.

Many objections have been raised by modern literary scepticism to the genuineness of the title.

1. It has been said that the Psalm could not have been written by David, because the prayer in ver. 18, "Build Thou the walls of Jerusalem," could only have been uttered at a time when those walls lay in ruins, and therefore either during or shortly after the Babylonish captivity.

But to this objection two different replies have been given. (1) That the expression is merely figurative, and that David, conscious how grievously he had imperilled by his sin the safety of his kingdom, here prays God to uphold and protect it. (2) That the last two verses of the Psalm are a later addition, made perhaps after the Exile, like the doxologies for instance at the close of xli. and lxxii. This is most probable. See note on ver. 18.

2. It has been argued that many of the expressions in the Psalm are unsuitable in David's mouth.

(*a*) David, it is said, when Nathan came to him, in 2 Sam. xii., at once confessed his sin and received the announcement of pardon, whereas here he seeks pardon. But God's forgiveness is not always received fully and at once by one who has greatly sinned. See more in note on ver. 9.

(*b*) David could not have said "Against *Thee only* have I sinned." "Such language," says Reuss, "would be very strange in the mouth of a man who had treacherously slain a faithful servant and dishonoured his wife:" his sins were obviously against man as well as against God.—For the answer to this objection see note on ver. 4.

(*c*) The Psalmist prays not for forgiveness of some one heinous sin, but of many, and for the renewal of his whole nature.—But he who sees sin in its true light will see it in its hidden source and in its manifold evil fruits.

(*d*) The knowledge of sin in its deep-seated innate depravity, its clinging taint, is a knowledge not to be expected so early as the time of David,—which is a merely arbitrary assertion.

I see then no ground for departing from the constant and reasonable belief of the Church, that the Psalm was written by David under the circumstances indicated in the title.*

It consists of three principal divisions :—

I. The prayer for forgiveness. Ver. 1—8.

II. The prayer for renewal. Ver. 9—12.

III. The holy resolutions of one who has experienced the forgiving love and the sanctifying grace of God. Ver. 13—19.

The Psalm concludes with a prayer for Zion and the utterance of a hope that the time will come when God will be honoured with "sacrifices of righteousness."

[FOR THE PRECENTOR. A PSALM OF DAVID, WHEN NATHAN THE PROPHET CAME TO HIM AFTER HE HAD GONE IN UNTO BATHSHEBA.]

I. 1. BE gracious unto me, O God, according to Thy loving-
kindness,

1, 2. The prayer for forgiveness.

1. ACCORDING TO THY LOVING-KINDNESS. In all godly sorrow there is hope. Sorrow without hope may be remorse or despair, but it is not repentance. Hence the true penitent always looks to the loving-kindness of God, even at

* I feel it a duty to protest against the extravagant view of Reuss, who says: "We hear in this Psalm the voice of the *people* of Israel, lamenting its former errors, and confessing that it can only obtain pardon and its restoration, as a consequence, by the grace of God, and not by bloody rites. It is the people, which, groaning under foreign tyranny, can express its fear of murder, that is, of annihilation, and which, in the perspective of its reconciliation with Jehovah, recognises also its providential mission of propagating the true religion, which is one of the great ideas developed in the second part of Isaiah." The power of misinterpretation could go no further.

According unto the greatness of Thy tender mercies
blot out my transgressions:
2 Wash me thoroughly [a] from mine iniquity,

the very time when he feels most deeply how he has sinned against it. The cry on his lips is "My *Father*," even when he confesses, "I am no more worthy to be called Thy son."

THE GREATNESS, &c. It is in this that David seeks the ground of forgiveness, not in himself. Comp. xxv. 6, 7. The deep sense of the *greatness* of his own sin makes him feel the need of a *great* mercy.

BLOT OUT. The forgiveness of sins is expressed by the use of two figures. The first, that of *blotting out*, "making that which is done as if it had not been done," is capable of two explanations: either (1) it refers to *erasing* from a book or tablet what has been written therein, as Ex. xxxii. 32, Num. v. 23, comp. Ps. lxix. 28 [29], in which case sin must here be regarded as a *debt* entered against the debtor, and so cancelled by being blotted out; or (2) it may mean, in a more general sense, the *wiping away* of a thing, and so its entire removal, as in 2 Kings xxi. 13, it is said, "I will *wipe* (the same word as here) Jerusalem as a man wipeth a dish." And in Is. xliv. 22, "I will blot out *as a cloud* thy sins," *i.e.* take them away as a cloud is swept away by the wind from the face of heaven.

MY TRANSGRESSIONS. The use of the plural has been variously explained. Some suppose that the several sins of adultery and murder are thus denoted. So Calvin: "Multiplex ejus culpa erat, quod adulterio adjunxerat perfidiam et crudelitatem: nec unum hominem modo prodiderat vel paucos, sed totum exercitum, pro salute Ecclesiæ Dei pugnantem." But this is too superficial a view. No sin ever stands alone: each single transgression is the mother of many transgressions: each is a root of bitterness whence spring many bitter branches, so that we cannot confess one sin without confessing many.

On the various words used here and in the next verse, TRANSGRESSIONS . . . INIQUITY . . . SIN, see note on xxxii. 1.

2. WASH ME. This is the second figure employed to denote the working of God's forgiveness for which David prays. How is it to be understood? Does it refer only, like the first (the blotting out of sin), to the act of forgiveness, or does it denote the cleansing and purifying of the sinner's soul, the sanctification of the spirit?

The verb כַּבֵּס, "to wash," is used of the washing of dirty spotted garments, like the Greek πλύνω (as distinct from רָחַץ = λούω, which is used of washing the body); and the figure is commonly employed in reference to the putting away of sin. See Is. i. 16; Jer. ii. 22, iv. 14; Mal. iii. 2, 3. So far as the figure itself is concerned it might certainly be symbolical, as all outward washing was, of inward purification. On the other hand, the prayer here is for *forgiveness* of sins—that the burden of guilt may be taken away, and afterwards, in ver. 10 ff, comes the prayer for renewal and sanctification. The verb in the next clause also, "cleanse me," though a word of more general use, is specially applied to the priest who "*pronounces* clean" the leper, a declarative act. Comp. Lev. xiii. 6, 34. But we must not expect in the O. T., and least of all in *prayers*, sharply defined and accurate statements of doctrine. Stier, who understands the "washing" here of sanctification, says, with perfect truth, that justification and sanctification, though distinct, are always closely connected in Scripture. God does not *declare* righteous without *making* righteous.

THOROUGHLY or perhaps "many

And from my sin make me clean.
3 For I know my transgressions,
And my sin is ever before me.
4 Against Thee—against Thee only have I sinned,

times," as Calvin says: "minime ambiguum est quin clare asserat non leves esse suas sordes, ut modica lotione elui queant, sed tenaciter hærere, immo esse profundas, ut iteratis lotionibus ad eas purgandas opus sit."

3. FOR. This particle expresses, not the reason why God should forgive him, but the reason why *he asks* for forgiveness; namely, his own sense and acknowledgement of his sin. Those, however, who adopt the first sense, regard the confession of sin not as the meritorious cause of forgiveness, but rather as its indispensable condition (comp. xxxii. 5, Prov. xxviii. 13). So Luther: "That little word *for* must be understood so as not to imply that his sins must be forgiven him because he had confessed them; for sin is always sin, and deserving of punishment, whether it is confessed or not; still confession of sin is of importance on this account, that God will be gracious to none but to those who confess their sin."

I KNOW. There is no need to render with the E.V. "I acknowledge," though no doubt the *confession* of sin is implied. That however is not here prominent, but rather that discernment of sin and of its true nature which leads to a confession of it. In xxxii. 5, "I will confess unto Thee" is lit. "I will *make* Thee know."

IS EVER BEFORE ME. Comp. xxxii. 3, 4. Luther says: "That is, my sin plagues me, gives me no rest, no peace; whether I eat or drink, sleep or wake, I am always in terror of God's wrath and judgement." But surely here, not the terror of God's wrath and judgement, but the deep sorrow for despite done to God's love and goodness, is the feeling uppermost. David dreads not punishment, but separation from God.

4. Then follows an acknowledgement of the double evil of sin: first, in its aim, and next in its source; first, as done against God, and then as springing from a corrupt nature.

AGAINST THEE ONLY. This language has perplexed commentators, who cannot understand how it could come from the mouth of David, who had been guilty of sins which were so directly against *men* as well as against God. The sin against Bathsheba whom he had tempted, the sin against Uriah whom he had slain by the sword of another, the sin against his own family which he had polluted, and against his kingdom which he had weakened,—were not all these sins against men? They were. And yet he says, Against *Thee only* have I sinned.

(1) Some expositors, as Arnobius, Cassiodorus, Nichol. de Lyra (and Patristic and Romish divines generally), account for this by saying that David here speaks as king, and that as king he was responsible to no human authority, but only to God. But though, as holding a despotic power, he could not be *tried* or *punished* by his subjects, the wrong done, and therefore the sin was the same whether done by a prince or by a private person.

(2) Others suppose that David means to say that his sin was *known only to God.* So Qimchi and Maldonatus, "tibi soli, *h. e.* secreto, nemine conscio," referring to 2 Sam. xii. 12, "For thou didst it *secretly;*" or as Geier, "in defiance of God;" "audacter ac proterve, omni reverentia erga tuos occulos vel te omnipræsentem Deum seposita." But such an interpreta-

And that which is evil in Thine eyes have I done;

tion falls far short of the whole deep meaning of the passage.

(3) Calvin approaches more nearly to the truth. He observes: "I think the words are equivalent to his saying, Lord, though the whole world should acquit me, yet for me it is more than enough that I feel that Thou art my Judge, that conscience summons me and drags me to Thy bar: so that men's excuses for me are of no avail, whether they spare me, or whether to flatter me they make light of my crime, or try to assuage my grief with soothing words. He intimates therefore that he has his eyes and all his senses fixed upon God, and consequently does not care what men think or say. But whoever is thus crushed, yea overwhelmed by the weight of God's judgement, needs no other accuser, because God alone is more than a thousand others."

To this might be added that all human judges can only regard wrong actions as *crimes*: God alone takes cognizance of them as *sins*.

(4) But true as all this is, it scarcely reaches the whole truth.

First, then, the words are to be explained by David's *deep conviction* of sin *as sin*. For the moment all else is swallowed up in that. Face to face with God, he sees nothing else, can think of nothing else, but His presence forgotten, His holiness outraged, His love scorned. Therefore he must confess and be forgiven by God before he could even think of the wrong done to his neighbour.

But secondly, this deep feeling of the penitent heart, of the heart which loves God above all things, has its root in the very relation in which God stands to His creatures. All sin, *as sin*, is and must be against God. All wrong done to our neighbour is wrong done to one created in the image of God; all tempting of our neighbour to evil is taking the part of Satan against God, and, so far as in us lies, defeating God's good purpose of grace towards him. All wounding of another, whether in person or property, in body or soul, is a sin against the goodness of God. Hence the Apostle says (1 Cor. viii. 12), "But when ye sin so against the brethren, and wound their weak conscience, ye sin against Christ." In like manner, all love to our neighbour is love to God whom we love in him. On this principle we shall be judged: "Inasmuch as ye have done it to the least of these, ye have done it unto Me." It is not therefore enough to explain these words of David, "Against Thee *only*," by saying that they are the expression of his *own deep sense* ("die Innigkeit des Gefühls," De Wette, Hupf.) of his guilt and the dishonour done to God. That feeling rested upon the eternal truth of which it was the expression, a truth on which, as Hengstenberg observes, the Decalogue itself is based: "Thou must honour and love God in Himself, in those who represent Him on earth (Deut. v. 12), in all who bear His image (ver. 13, 14). Comp. *Beitr.* iii. 604. The love of God appears constantly in Deuteronomy as the ἓν καὶ πᾶν, as the one thing which of necessity carries along with it the fulfilment of the whole Law; as for instance in chaps. x. xii. Earlier still, in Gen. ix. 6, the punishment of murder is grounded on this, that man bears God's image." "How must David have trembled," says the same commentator, "how must he have been seized with shame and grief, when he referred everything to God, when in Uriah he saw only the image of God, the Holy One, who deeply resented that injury,—the gracious and compassionate One, to whom he owed such infinitely rich benefits, who had lifted him up from the dust of humiliation, had so often delivered him, and had also given

That Thou mightest be just in Thy speaking,[b]
(That) Thou mightest be pure in Thy judging.
5 Behold, in iniquity I was brought forth,

him the promise of so glorious a future!"

THAT. Strictly speaking, "in order that," which would imply that the sin was done in order that God's justice might shine the more conspicuously thereby; and this would seem of course to make God the author of sin. Hence some, as Ab. Ezra, would connect the conjunction (לְמַעַן, "in order that") not with the words immediately preceding, but with the acknowledgement in ver. 3. Nor can I see any objection to such a connection of the clauses. Others again take the conjunction here in the sense of "so that," as marking the *consequence* (ἐκβατικῶς), not the *purpose* of the action preceding = "I have sinned, and the result of my sin has been that Thy righteousness and holiness have been manifested," &c. This interpretation, according to the grammarians, inevitably falls to pieces against the hard inexorable canon that "the conjunction always means *in order that;*" in the same way as ἵνα in the N. T. Winer however (*Gram. d. N. T. Sprach-Idioms*), gives the right explanation of the usage of both conjunctions. He shows that their employment is due to a different metaphysical conception on the part of the Biblical writers from that which we are in the habit of forming as to the nature of the Divine government. They drew no sharp accurate line between events as the consequence of the Divine order, and events as following from the Divine purpose. To them all was ordained and designed of God. Even sin itself in all its manifestations, though the whole guilt of it rested with man, did not flow uncontrolled, but only in channels hewn for it by God, and to subserve His purposes. Hence, God is said to have hardened Pharaoh's heart, to have put a lying spirit in the mouth of the prophets, to do evil as well as good in the city, and the like. We must not expect therefore that the Hebrew mind, profoundly impressed as it was with the great phenomena of the universe, and beholding in each the immediate finger of God, but altogether averse from philosophical speculation, should have exactly defined for itself the distinction between an action viewed as the *consequence*, and the same action viewed as the *end* of another action. The mind which holds the simple fundamental truth that all is of God, may also hold, almost as a matter of course, that all is *designed* of God. That from such a view, where the conscience is not healthy, a perilous misconception may arise, is clear from the way in which St. Paul argues upon this very passage in Rom. iii. 4, 5, where he refutes the possible perversion that men are at liberty to sin because thereby God's righteousness is commended. But, after all, there is perhaps no need to press the exact signification of the particle here. The conjunction, which properly expresses purpose, here denotes rather consequence, as in other passages, xxx. 12 [13], Exod. xi. 9, Deut. xxix. 18, Is. xliv. 9, Hosea viii. 4.

IN THY SPEAKING, *i.e.* as is evident from the parallelism, "when Thou givest sentence."

IN THY JUDGING. The LXX., ἐν τῷ κρίνεσθαί σε (quoted thus in Rom. iii. 4), "When Thou contendest." There is not the slightest reason for rendering the Greek as a passive, "when Thou art judged," *i.e.* when the justice of Thy dealings is called in question in having suffered Thine own servant so grievously to fall.

5. Sin is now regarded in its source. From my very earliest

And in sin did my mother conceive me.
6 Behold, Thou delightest in truth in the inward parts,[c]
And in the hidden part Thou wilt make me to know wisdom.
7 Thou wilt purge me with hyssop, that I may be clean ;

being, from the hour when I was conceived, sin has been with me. Sinfulness consists not merely in so many several sinful acts, but in a sinful and corrupt nature. The depth of the abyss of sin is here opened before the eyes of the penitent with a distinctness of which the instances are comparatively few in the O. T. (Comp. however Job xiv. 4, Gen. viii. 21.) Manifestly not in extenuation, but in aggravation of his sin does David thus speak ("ad amplificandam malorum suorum gravitatem a peccato originali ducit exordium," Calvin). "He lays on himself the blame of a tainted nature, instead of that of a single fault : not a murder only, but of a murderous nature. 'Conceived in sin.' From first moments up till then, he saw sin—sin—sin : nothing but sin."—*F. W. Robertson.* Luther says : "If a man will speak and teach aright of sin, he must consider it in its depth, and show from what *root* it and all that is godless springs, and not apply the term merely to sins that have been committed. For from this error, that men know not and understand not what sin is, arises the other error that they know not nor understand what grace is. . . . According to this Psalm, then, we must say that all is sin which is born of father and mother, and from so evil a root nothing good can grow before God." And Calvin : "Here at length he confesses himself guilty, not of one sin only or of many, but he rises to the fountain-head, (acknowledging) that from his mother's womb he has brought nothing with him but sin, and that by nature he is altogether corrupt and as it were smeared over with vices. . . . And of a truth we do not thoroughly acknowledge our sins unless we condemn our whole nature as corrupt."

Stier says : "Men may say what they will, the doctrine of original sin is contained in this passage ;" and so it is, precisely in that sense in which the doctrine is alone true, viz. that sinfulness is innate, that corrupt parents can only have corrupt children. The taint is, and must be, propagated. The later ecclesiastical development of the doctrine, involving the imputation of Adam's sin, and the fiction of a covenant made with Adam in the name of his descendants, is repugnant to reason and has no foundation in Scripture, as Mr. Birks has shown with remarkable force and clearness in his *Difficulties of Belief, &c.* The heathen view of this innate corruption was widely different, because the thought of God did not enter into it. See Cic. *Tusc.* iii. 1, and Marc. Aurel. lib. xi. c. 18.

BEHOLD. The word is used to indicate the attainment of a new and higher knowledge (comp. Job iv. 18, xv. 15, xxv. 5), as if it had come with something of surprise on the mind, or were seen with a new brightness. The repetition of the word at the beginning of the next verse marks the connection and correlation of the two. On the one hand, lo ! I have seen sin as I never saw it before. On the other, lo ! I have learnt that truth is what Thou desirest in the secret heart.

6. TRUTH. Uprightness of heart : that very uprightness and integrity which David and other O. T. saints assert elsewhere, but in which, now under deep conviction of his sinfulness, he feels himself to be so deficient.

7. THOU SHALT PURGE ME. The

Thou wilt wash me, that I may be whiter than snow.
8 Thou wilt make me to hear joy and gladness,

LXX. and Jerome take the verbs in this verse and the next as futures, and so also Ewald, though the majority of modern commentators, with the E. V., take them as imperatives. Both Hengstenberg and Hupfeld argue that they must be imperatives (or optatives) because of the imperative in ver. 9; but surely the very fact that we have a change in the mood of the verb there should lead us not to confound the two. Besides, the notion that the verbs in this verse must be imperative proceeds partly from a total misconception as to the true structure of the Psalm, the first division of which ends not with ver. 6, but with ver. 8, according to a principle which has never yet been sufficiently recognized, viz. that some of the thoughts of one strophe are constantly resumed, with some modification, in another. The use of the future here, as well as the meaning of the verb, has been most happily explained by Donne in his Sermon on this verse (Sermon lxii.): "How soon and to what a height came David here! He makes his petition, his first petition, with that confidence, as that it hath scarce the nature of a petition: for it is in the original: *Thou wilt purge me, Thou wilt wash me,* Thou hadst a gracious will and purpose to do it, before Thou didst infuse the will and the desire in me to petition it. Nay, this word may well be translated not only *Thou wilt*, but by the other denotation of the future, *Thou shalt, Thou shalt purge me, Thou shalt wash me;* Lord, I do but remember Thee of Thy debt, of that which Thy gracious promise hath made Thy debt, to show mercy to every penitent sinner. And then, as the word implies confidence and acceleration, infallibility and expedition too, that as soon as I can ask I am sure to be heard; so does it imply a totality, an entireness, a fulness in the work; for the root of the word is *peccare*, to sin, for purging is a purging of peccant humours; but in this conjugation [the Piel] . . . it hath a privative signification; . . . and if in our language that were a word in use, it might be translated, Thou shalt un-sin me." I am sorry that want of space prevents my quoting the beautiful passage in the same sermon, in which Donne dwells on the truth that *God* Himself alone can thus purge the sinner, *Domine Tu.* It will be found in vol. iii. p. 91, of Alford's edition of his Works.

WITH HYSSOP. In allusion to the lustration enjoined by the Mosaic ritual of the leper (Lev. xiv. 4 ff.) and those who had defiled themselves by contact with a dead body (Num. xix. 6 ff. 18 ff.), the hyssop being dipped in the blood of the bird which had been killed, and so used to sprinkle the person who was to be cleansed. This is certainly a remarkable instance of the manner in which the symbolism of the Mosaic Law was understood by a pious Jew. David evidently sees that the outward lustration is a sign of a better cleansing; another proof of that profound spiritual insight which throughout the Psalm is so striking, and which almost justifies St. Augustine's saying, *Sunt quibus expedit cadere.*

THOU SHALT WASH ME. Again in allusion to a further ceremony of purification enjoined by the Law, the washing, namely, of the clothes, and the bathing of the body of the defiled person. WHITER THAN SNOW. Comp. Is. i. 18.

8. THOU SHALT MAKE ME TO HEAR: not said with reference to God's announcement of forgiveness by the Prophet Nathan, or as made in His word, but rather with reference to those public festivals in which the whole congregation would unite in praising God, and in which David hoped now, as a

(That) the bones which Thou hast crushed may
rejoice.

II. 9 Hide Thy face from my sins,
And blot out all my iniquities.
10 A clean heart create for me, O God,
And renew a steadfast spirit within me.
11 Cast me not away from Thy presence,
And take not Thy Holy Spirit from me.

forgiven sinner, to take his own part. He would be one of those who, with a heart full of thankfulness, would openly testify that thankfulness.

THE BONES: not merely, as Hupfeld says, instead of the heart, but as constituting the strength and framework of the body, the crushing of the bones being a very strong figure, denoting the most complete prostration mental and bodily: see vi. 2 [2].

9. The second division of the Psalm begins here with the renewed prayer for forgiveness. From the confident assurance of the last two verses, that God would do that which he asked, David now passes to earnest pleading with God. This is surely what is to be found in all true prayer; it will be marked by fluctuations of feeling; its order will be the order of need, not the order of the intellect. Again, David asks for forgiveness first, and then for renewal. "For though God fully and completely (in solidum) forgives," says Calvin, "still the narrowness of our faith does not take in so large a goodness on His part, but it must flow down to us gradually and drop by drop (necesse est ut paulatim distillet)."

HIDE THY FACE, *i.e.* Thy face of wrath; do not look upon them in anger, or so as to bring me into judgement. In the more common use of the phrase, God is said to "hide His face" in displeasure, the face of God generally signifying His favour.

10. After the prayer for forgiveness there follows now the prayer for renewal and sanctification.

A CLEAN HEART, as the necessary condition of communion with God. Comp. xxiv. 4 and Matt. x. 8.

CREATE. A word always used strictly of the creative power of God. The whole spiritual being of the man had, as it were, fallen into a chaos. The pure heart and the childlike feeling of confidence could only return as a new creation, *καινὴ κτίσις*. Comp. Ephes. ii. 10, iv. 24. With this prayer compare the promise in Jer. xxiv. 7; Ezek. xi. 19, xxxvi. 26.

A STEADFAST SPIRIT; one, that is, firm in faith, not easily swayed hither and thither through its own weakness or by blasts of temptation, and therefore also firm and constant in obedience. Jerome, rightly, *spiritum stabilem*: it is more than the *πνεῦμα εὐθές* of the LXX., the *spiritum rectum* of the Vulg., and "the right spirit" of the E. V.

11. CAST ME NOT AWAY. Stier sees an allusion partly to the exclusion of the leper from the congregation (Lev. xiii. 46), and partly to the rejection of Saul (1 Sam. xvi. 13, 14); but the expressions employed in both cases are different. The phrase, as it occurs 2 Kings xiii. 23, xvii. 20, xxiv. 20, Jer. vii. 15, refers to the rejection of the nation of Israel from the favour of God.

TAKE NOT THY HOLY SPIRIT FROM ME. Calvin infers from this that the Spirit had not been alto-

12 Restore unto me the joy of Thy salvation,
And uphold me with a willing spirit.

III. 13 So will I teach transgressors Thy ways,

gether taken away from David, and hence draws the consolatory conclusion, that the faith of the elect cannot finally fail. The Lutherans, on the other hand, supposing a total loss, and deeming a total renewal necessary, insert the word "again,"—"Take not (again) Thy Holy Spirit from me." But the words do not justify either interpretation. The petition expresses rather the holy fear of the man who has his eyes open to the depth and iniquity of sin, *lest at any moment* he should be left without the succour of that Divine Spirit, who was the only source in him of every good thought, of every earnest desire, of every constant resolution. It is the cry of one who knows, as he never knew before, the weakness of his own nature, and the strength of temptation, and the need of Divine help; and to whom therefore nothing seems so dreadful as that God should withdraw His Spirit. At the same time we need not hesitate to admit that such a prayer in the lips of David could not mean all that it means now to a Christian. David could hardly have understood by the Holy Spirit a Divine Person, nor could he have been made partaker of the Spirit in the same sense that Christians are; for not till Jesus was glorified was the Spirit given in all His light and power, in all His quickening, sanctifying grace. But we see in such prayers how marvellously the words of Scripture are adapted to our necessities; how, used at first as it were by children, they still express the maturest feelings of our Christian manhood, and, as in this instance, have even become permanently fixed in our Christian liturgies.

12. The first clause of the verse again puts, as a petition, that which in ver. 8 is the utterance of a confident hope and trust.

WITH A WILLING SPIRIT, or, "a free, or 'noble' spirit." Comp. Ex. xxxv. 5, 22, "willing of heart." The meaning "noble," and the use of the word as a subst. "a prince," are apparently derived from this. Hence, the LXX. ἡγεμονικῷ πνεύματι. Vulg. *spiritu principali.* Jerome, *potenti spiritu.* The expression here, as well as the similar expression in ver. 10, "a steadfast spirit," refers *immediately* to the spirit of man, but to that spirit as influenced and guided by the Spirit of God. That mechanical distinction which is sometimes made in theology is not made in Scripture. The use of πνεῦμα in the New Testament is exactly analogous. See the notes of Alford and Ellicott on πνεῦμα δειλίας, in 2 Tim. i. 7; and comp. Rom. viii. 15, Gal. iv. 6. Luther somewhere strikingly illustrates this close and intimate union of the Spirit of God with the spirit of man, by saying that the latter, under the influence of the former, is like water heated by fire.

13. With a conscience set free from guilt, with a heart renewed by the Spirit of God, and full of thankfulness for God's great mercy, he cannot keep silent, but will seek to turn other sinners to God. The 32d Psalm, which was probably written after this (see Introduction to that Psalm), shows us how this resolution was kept.

SO WILL I TEACH, or, "So let me teach." The form is optative, and expresses that which he desires to do, as an evidence of his gratitude, and as knowing how greatly his sin must have been a stumbling-block to others. Terrible had been the fruit of his sin, not only in the wasting of his own soul, but in the injury done to others. Terrible was his punishment in witnessing this; and therefore the more anxious is he, though he cannot undo his own

And sinners shall return unto Thee.
14 Deliver me from blood-guiltiness, O God, thou God
of my salvation;
My tongue shall sing aloud of Thy righteousness.
15 O Lord, open Thou my lips,
And my mouth shall show forth Thy praise.
16 For Thou delightest not in sacrifice, else would I give it;
In burnt-offering Thou hast no pleasure:
17 The sacrifices of God are a broken spirit,

sin, to heal the breach, and repair the evil of sin in other souls.

THY WAYS, *i.e.* the ways of God's commandments in which he would have men walk. Comp. xviii. 21 [22].

14. BLOOD-GUILTINESS, literally, "bloods," the plural of this word being used to denote blood *shed*, murder. Comp. Gen. iv. 10, "The voice of thy brother's blood," &c. Here, too, the blood of Uriah, whom he had slain, seems to cry against David for punishment. See 2 Sam. ix. 10. Reuss renders this, "save me from murder," *i.e.* from being murdered, a rendering wholly against Hebrew idiom. See Exod. xxii. 1; Deut. xix. 10.

The repetition of the Divine Name which follows is not due to emphasis (as Calvin thinks), but is a peculiarity of this Book of the Psalter. See note on xlv. 7.

THY RIGHTEOUSNESS. Why is this attribute of God especially mentioned as the subject of praise? Surely not in that vague sense in which Hupfeld puts it, "as the principle of God's government," but with especial reference to the forgiveness of sins. The righteousness of God is that attribute according to which He gives to every one his own, to those who with repentance and faith turn to Him, the forgiveness which they ask, and which He has *promised* to bestow. Hence St. John says, "If we confess our sins, He is faithful and *just* (or *righteous*) to forgive us our sins."

15. OPEN MY LIPS. His lips had been sealed by sin, but God, by His free forgiveness, would give him fresh cause of rejoicing, and so would open them. Calvin compares xl. 4, where the Psalmist says that God had put a new song in his mouth. David thus prays God to be gracious, that he may be the loud herald of that grace to others, "My mouth shall declare," &c.

16. FOR, as expressing the reason why he will offer to God the *spiritual* offering of thanksgiving, a grateful heart and grateful lips.

ELSE WOULD I, or possibly, "that I should," as in margin of the Eng. Vers.

SACRIFICE . . . . BURNT OFFERING. In what sense God is said to reject them is clear from xl. 6 [7], l. 7 [8], where see notes. The Rabbinical interpreters suppose *sin-offerings* to be meant, and think that these are here set aside because for a sin like David's, done with a high hand, no sacrifice, but only repentance, could avail. But the words here employed in reference to sacrifices are never used of sin-offerings, but always of *thank-offerings*, and this sense is plainly required by the context.

17. THE SACRIFICES OF GOD, *i.e.* those in which He really has pleasure, are A BROKEN HEART. Another evidence of a deep sense of sin, and of a tender conscience. When speaking of *thankfulness*, we might have expected him to say, "a *joyful* heart, or a thankful heart," but instead of that he says,

A broken and contrite heart, O God, Thou wilt not
despise.

18 Do good in Thy good pleasure unto Zion ;
Build Thou the walls of Jerusalem,
19 Then Thou shalt delight in sacrifices of righteousness,
In burnt-offering and whole burnt-offering ;
Then shall they offer up bullocks upon Thine altar.

"a contrite heart." For the joy of forgiveness does not banish sorrow and contrition for sin : this will still continue. And the deeper the sense of sin, and the truer the sorrow for it, the more heartfelt also will be the thankfulness for pardon and reconciliation. The tender, humble, broken heart is therefore the best thank-offering.

18, 19. The Psalm concludes with a prayer (not as before for the individual) for the nation at large.

After carefully weighing all that has been urged by Hengstenberg and others in support of the genuineness of these verses, I cannot think that they formed any part of the Psalm as originally written. To me, they bear evident marks of having been added at a date subsequent to the Exile. [Otherwise, the whole Psalm must be of that date.] The prayer, "build Thou the walls of Jerusalem," is certainly most naturally explicable with reference to the ruinous condition of the city after the Captivity. Some suppose, indeed, that the walls were not yet completed in David's time, or that the allusion is to the walls of the Temple ; others, that the expression is used in a figurative sense of God's protection and favour, as vouchsafed to the people (see the Introduction to the Psalm), but these are not natural or satisfactory interpretations. Again, ver. 19 seems to have been added expressly to correct wrong inferences which might possibly have been drawn from verses 16, 17, as to the worth of sacrifices as enjoined by the Law. We need not, indeed, push this so far as to suppose that the last verses *contradict* the sentiment of the former part of the Psalm. For as the sacrifice in which God delights not (ver. 16) means one not offered with a true heart, so those sacrifices in which it is said He will delight when the walls of Jerusalem are built, are expressly said to be sacrifices of righteousness, offered therefore with right motives ; still there is, I think, a difference of *importance* attached to the ceremonial sacrifice, in the two passages.

On these grounds, then, I regard the two concluding verses as having been added shortly after the return from the Exile, a time when every effort was made to rouse the people whose heart had grown cold to a sense of the value of the Temple services, and the appointed worship of Jehovah. On this point I have said more in an article on the Prophet Zechariah, in Smith's *Dict. of the Bible.*

19. SACRIFICES OF RIGHTEOUSNESS, *i.e.* such as God would accept, because offered in righteousness, from a heart right with God, and not merely in external compliance with the Law. See note on iv. 7 [8].

[a] הַרְבֵּה. The Qeri הֶרֶב is imper. apoc. Hiphil for הַרְבֵּה, as הֶרֶף, xxxvii. 8, for הַרְפֵּה, and consequently the constr. is that of the double imperative, without the copula (Gesen. § 142, 3 *b*). Hence the K'thîbh is usually supposed to be the full form of the imperative. It may, however, be the

infin. absol. used adverbially, like הֵיטֵב (Gesen. § 128, 2). So Hengst., Hitz., and Hupf.

[b] בְּדַבְּרֶךָ. Apparently Inf. Qal after the analogy of בְּשָׁפְטֶךָ, but not occurring elsewhere, this verb being found in the Qal only in the participle.

[c] טֻחוֹת, only here and Job xxxviii. 36, not as the Chald. and Rabb. "the reins," as if so called from טוּח, "to cover, to smear," the reins being covered with fat; but as the older translators, LXX. ἄδηλα, Jerome, *abscondita*, "the hidden depths of the heart," which agrees with the parallelism. J. H. Mich. *in intimis animi recessibus.* Comp. ἐν τῷ κρυπτῷ, Rom. ii. 29.

PSALM 52

THIS Psalm is not a prayer or complaint addressed to God against the oppression of the wicked; it is a stern upbraiding addressed to the man who, unscrupulous in the exercise of his power, and proud of his wealth (ver. 9), finds his delight in all the arts of the practised liar. It is a lofty challenge, a defiance conceived in the spirit of David when he went forth to meet the champion of Gath. The calm courage of faith breathes in every word. There is no fear, no trembling, no doubt, as to the end which will come upon the tyrant. How vain is his boast in presence of the loving-kindness of God, which protects His people; in presence of the power of God, which uproots the oppressor! Such is briefly the purport of the Psalm. Whether it was really composed by David on the occasion to which the title refers it, may be a matter of doubt. We know too little of Doeg to be able to say if the description in verses 1—4 applies to him or not. Nor, in fact, does the title intimate that he is the subject of the Psalm. It only points out the occasion on which the Psalm was written, and Saul's name is mentioned in it as well as Doeg's. So far Hengstenberg is right. But I cannot see any force in the arguments with which he endeavours to show that the Psalm is aimed at Saul. He says: (1) The address, "Thou mighty man," is more suitable to Saul, to whom David, in his lamentation, 2 Sam. i. 19, gives the same epithet, than to Doeg, the chief herdsman of the royal flocks, who was so far from being a hero, that he was famous for nothing but the cowardly massacre of the priests, a deed which Saul's *warriors* refused to perform. (2) The reproach of lying, in ver. 1—3, does not apply to Doeg. So far as the history informs us, Doeg simply reports the *fact* that Ahimelech had received David, whereas it is Saul who falsely accuses David and the priests of plotting together against him, 1 Sam. xxii. 17. (3) Doeg would not be described as a man who trusted in the abundance of his riches, whereas Saul might, 1 Sam. xxii. 7. (4) David would not have been so incensed against Doeg, who was nothing but the tool of Saul, but his indignation would naturally have been directed against Saul, who commanded the slaughter of the priests.

But all these arguments show rather that Doeg is *not* the person against whom the Psalm is directed, than that Saul *is*. Neither the might, nor the lying, nor the trust in riches, is peculiarly applicable to Saul. Nor can we imagine that these features of his character would have been selected for animadversion at such a time, but rather the inhuman barbarity which could conceive of such an outrage, the insolent contempt of all justice which it displayed.

Whilst, therefore, the faith and courage which breathe in this Psalm are such as to incline me to think that it was written by David, and whilst there may even be an allusion, in ver. 8 (see note there), to the sanctuary at Nob, I see little reason on other grounds for maintaining the accuracy of the inscription.

The Psalm scarcely admits of any formal strophical division, but the arrangement is clear and natural.

The first verse states briefly the subject of the whole : the folly, namely, of boasting in wickedness when God's loving-kindness is the sure and abiding defence of those against whom that wickedness is directed. Then follow :—

First, a description of the evil-doer, who, in this instance, is pourtrayed as an habitual and practised liar. Ver. 2—4.

Next, a denouncing of God's judgement against him. Ver. 5.

Then, the exultation of the righteous at his overthrow. Ver. 6, 7.

And lastly, the confidence and security of the Sacred Poet himself and his thankfulness to God for His goodness to him. Ver. 8, 9.

[FOR THE PRECENTOR. A MASKIL OF DAVID, WHEN DOEG THE EDOMITE CAME AND TOLD SAUL, AND SAID TO HIM, DAVID CAME INTO THE HOUSE OF AHIMELECH.]

1 WHY boasteth thou thyself in wickedness, O mighty
man ?—

1. O MIGHTY MAN. So the E.V., whilst the Prayer-book Version has, more pointedly, "O tyrant," and the LXX. ὁ δυνατὸς ἀνομίαν. The word

The loving-kindness of God (endureth) continually,
2 Destruction doth thy tongue devise,
Like a sharp razor, working guile.
3 Thou lovest evil rather than good,
Falsehood rather than to speak righteousness. [Selah.]
4 Thou lovest all devouring words,
O thou deceitful tongue!

evidently occurs here in a bad sense; though this is the only instance of such usage. Elsewhere it is used of a hero, of one who shows his prowess and his valour in war, &c. Hence Hengst. and Del. would retain the same meaning here. But the word means strictly, one who exercises power, might, &c., and the connection must determine how that power is exercised. The root occurs *in malam partem* in several places, Jer. ix. 2, xxiii. 10; Job xv. 25, xxxvi. 9. With this "boasting" (see x. 3) of the mighty man there is then put, in brief but forcible contrast, the "loving-kindness of God," as that in which the Psalmist himself found his hope and confidence, and that which indeed rendered all such boasting vain.

CONTINUALLY, lit. "all the day," as xlii. 3 [4], xliv. 8 [9].

2—4. It is remarkable that there follows, not the description of the bold bad man, ruling all around him by brute force, and crushing others into submission at his will, but that of one who gains his evil end by means chiefly of unblushing, deliberate falsehood.

2. DESTRUCTION (properly, "a yawning gulf," as in v. 9 [10], where see note), the plural form, of which the singular occurs in ver. 7, in a different signification, "evil desire."

SHARP, lit. "whetted." Similarly, in other passages, the tongue is compared to a sharp sword, spears and arrows, &c.

WORKING GUILE, as ci. 7, does not refer to the sharp razor (as Qimchi and others), as if that were a deceitful instrument (as we find "a deceitful bow," lxxviii. 57), one which wounds him who uses it, or cuts where it should not, but to the tongue, or rather, as the participle is masc., and the noun, "tongue," fem., to the man himself, who is, as it were, identified with the tongue which he employs, as again ver. 4, though it is not necessary to render, "O thou that workest," &c. LXX. *ὡσεὶ ξυρὸν ἠκ. ἐποίησας δόλον.*

3. RIGHTEOUSNESS, here opposed to FALSEHOOD, because by this, not only *speaking* the lie, but false *conduct* is meant, the opposite of which, therefore, is not *truth* merely, but *righteousness.*

4. DEVOURING WORDS, literally, "words of swallowing up," which accords exactly with the figures employed in v. 9 [10], "their mouth is a yawning gulf," &c., and so the LXX. well, *ῥήματα καταποντισμοῦ.*

O THOU DECEITFUL TONGUE! So the E.V., and so Ewald, Maurer, and many others, and I see no objection to taking this as a vocative, the tongue here being, so to speak, identified with the man, because the tongue is *the* member with which he works his mischief. The LXX., Syr., and Jerome (alt.) take it as an accusative, in apposition with "the devouring words" of the preceding clause, and De Wette asks how "a tongue" can be said "to love"? But, with the explanation given above, there is no difficulty, and we have the same identification of the tongue and the man in ver. 2.

5 God also shall break thee down for ever.
He shall seize thee, and pluck thee out of (thy) tent,
And root thee out of the land of the living. [Selah.]
6 And (the) righteous shall see (it) and fear,
And over him shall they laugh (saying):
7 Behold the man, who maketh not God his stronghold,

5. Now comes, in short and powerful contrast to the unscrupulous violence, deceit, and falsehood of the proud oppressor, the righteous judgment of God. The most forcible expressions are employed to describe his utter overthrow and uprooting.

ALSO, *i.e.*, "in like manner," "as thout hast done, so shall it be done to thee." The law of the Divine dealings is a law of retribution.

BREAK THEE DOWN, *i.e.* as a house is broken to pieces and laid in ruins.

SEIZE THEE, prop. as coals are taken with the tongs or the shovel. So in the other three passages where it occurs.

OUT OF (THY) TENT. Some suppose the herdsman's tent of Doeg to be meant: others, the Tabernacle; as if the phrase, "to pluck or tear away from the Tabernacle," were equivalent to "destroying from the congregation," &c. [Hupfeld very harshly, as it seems to me, renders, "will tear thee away, that that there be no tent," *i.e.* as he explains, "will tear away thy tent," which he endeavours to defend by Prov. xv. 25, where, however, the construction is different, as, though the same verb occurs, it governs the direct object, and is not used, as here, with the preposition.]

6. SHALL SEE (IT) AND FEAR. They shall witness it with that solemn awe which must be felt by all who understand aright the judgements of God. But mingled with this fear there will be joy,—joy that the wicked one is overthrown, joy that God has executed His righteous judgement.

OVER HIM, over the wicked man thus cast down, THEY SHALL LAUGH. Such exultation, to our modern sensibilities, seems shocking, because we can hardly conceive of it, apart from the gratification of personal vindictiveness. But there is such a thing as a righteous hatred, as a righteous scorn. There is such a thing as a shout of righteous joy at the downfall of the tyrant and the oppressor, at the triumph of righteousness and truth over wrong and falsehood. This is very different from imprecating the judgements of God on the heads of the ungodly. No such imprecation occurs in this Psalm, nor is there in it any trace of personal animosity. The explanation, therefore, which has been given in the notes on xxxv. 22, xli. 10, does not apply here. Indeed, even in the New Testament, we find the exultation at the overthrow of proud and luxurious wickedness. "Rejoice over her," it is said, at the fall of Babylon, as seen in the Apocalypse, "thou heaven, and ye holy apostles and prophets; for God hath avenged you on her," Rev. xviii. 20. See also xix. 1—3, where the same strain of holy triumph is repeated.

The manifest difference between such a strain of sentiment and the expression of a merely personal hatred, has been entirely overlooked by Hupfeld, in his haste to condemn Hengstenberg. A *malicious* joy over a prostrate foe is condemned in direct terms in the Old Testament. See Prov. xxiv. 17, Job xxxi. 29, and compare 2 Sam. i. 19 ff.

7. The words in which the righteous express their triumph, pointing, as it were, to the fallen oppressor, and the lesson to be

But hath trusted in the greatness of his riches,
(And) is strong in his evil desire.
8 But as for me,—I am like a green olive-tree, in the house of God;
I have trusted in the loving-kindness of God, (and will do so) for ever and ever.
9 I will give Thee thanks for ever, for Thou hast done (it).
And I will wait on Thy name,[a] for it is good,
In the presence of Thy beloved.

learnt from his overthrow. His trust was in his riches (comp. xlix. 6 [7], Prov. x. 15, xviii. 11), and his strength in his evil desire (see note on ver. 2), not in God.

8. In strong contrast to such a man is the character and the hope of the Psalmist himself. The tyrant shall be like a tree rooted up (ver. 5): I, he says, shall be like a tree ever green and ever flourishing. Both images are common in the Psalms. Comp. i. 3, xxxvii. 35, xliv. 2 [3], cxxviii. 3, and especially xcii. 12, 13 [13, 14]; the olive-tree is here specially selected as a type of gladness and fruitfulness; comp. Jer. xi. 16. Hupfeld finds the figure perplexing, because he says no trees grew even in the courts of the Temple. But not to mention that trees may have been planted in the Temple area (see on xcii. 13), there is no need, surely, to put such an interpretation upon the words. The olive is not said to be *in the house of God*, any more than in the use of a similar figure in cxxviii. 3, the olive-plants are supposed to be round about the table. Just as there it is said, "Thy children about thy table are like olive-plants," so here: "I, in the house of God, am like an olive," *i.e.* whilst permitted daily access to His sanctuary and presence, I may compare myself to that tree which, in its greenness and fruitfulness, is an apt emblem of joy. This is obviously the form of the comparison, as in fact is indicated by the accents. Bishop Colenso (Part II. pp. 274, 284) has very ingeniously suggested a particular reason for this comparison here. Assuming the correctness of the title of the Psalm, there would at this time be a sanctuary at Nob, a "house of God," or tabernacle for Divine worship. Nob was the northern summit of Olivet, a mountain which derived its name from the olives and oliveyards with which it was once clothed. And hence the connection in the Psalmist's mind between "the house of God" and "the olive." Bishop Colenso refers to Stanley's *Sinai and Palestine*, p. 187.

9. THOU HAST DONE. Absolutely, as in xxii. 31 [32], xxxviii 5; the past tense, expressing the *conviction* of faith that his prayer has already been answered.

THY BELOVED. See xvi. 10, and note there; and for the vow of a *public* thanksgiving, xxii. 25 [26].

[a] אֲקַוֶּה. Hupfeld doubts the correctness of the reading, because everywhere else with the word שֵׁם, verbs of *praising* and the like are used, such as אוֹדֶה, אֲהַלְלָה, אֲזַמְּרָה, and also because the expression, "before Thy beloved," implies that the action of the verb is something that

appeals to the senses. He suggests that אֲסַפְּרָה may be the word. But a writer is not bound to adopt only current phrases; and though the expression, I will *wait upon* Thy name, *in the presence of*, &c., may not be strictly correct, yet all languages furnish instances of such inaccuracies even in classical writers.

PSALM 53

THIS Psalm is only another version of the Fourteenth Psalm, from which it differs in two particulars: first, in its use of the Name of God, which here is Elohim instead of Jehovah, a peculiarity which is characteristic of all the Psalms in the Second Book: next, in the remarkable deviation, ver. 5 [6], from the language of the parallel passage, ver. 5, 6, of Psalm xiv. This deviation is remarkable, because, whilst there is a material difference in the *sense* of the two passages, very many of the same or similar *letters* occur in both. Hence it has been supposed that the one text may have been copied from a partially defaced and illegible MS. of the other, the lacunæ having been conjecturally filled up by the transcriber; or that the text, having been corrupted through carelessness, or perhaps at first preserved orally, rather than in writing, attempts were made to correct it, and hence the variations which now exist. But neither supposition is satisfactory. There seems to have been an intentional alteration, with a view of adapting the Psalm to different circumstances. Perhaps, as Bunsen suggests, a later poet may have wished to apply Psalm xiv. to the events of his own time, when Israel was threatened by foreign enemies, and thus have sought to encourage the people to hope for deliverance, by reminding them of God's help vouchsafed in former times of trouble. In this case, verses 4, 5 [5, 6] must be taken as referring to the past, not to the future.

That of the two texts Ps. xiv. is the original, appears to me almost certain. Whilst there is some abruptness in both, the sixth verse here is unquestionably more disjointed and less obviously connected with the subject of the Psalm than the corresponding passage in Ps. xiv. Dr. Colenso's theory, as to the use of the Divine Names, obliges him to assume that this is the earlier form of the Poem; but the language of ver. 5 [6] is decidedly opposed to the theory, and so also is the tradition, as old as the formation of the Canon, which, by assigning to Ps. xiv. its place in the First Book, manifestly regarded it as the original work.

The Introduction and Notes to Psalm xiv. may be consulted here. In some few instances only, where it seemed desirable, additional notes have been introduced, and especially where this text differs from the other.

[FOR THE PRECENTOR. UPON MACHALATH.[a] A MASKIL OF DAVID.]

1 THE fool hath said in his heart, There is no God.
Corrupt and abominable are they in (their) iniquity.
There is none that doeth good.
2 God hath looked down from heaven upon the children of men,
To see if there is any that hath understanding,
That seeketh after God.
3 Every one of them is gone back, together they have become corrupt,
There is none that doeth good, no not one.

4 " Have the workers of iniquity no knowledge,
(Who) eat my people (as though) they ate bread,

1. CORRUPT, &c. Lit. "They have corrupted and made abominable." This passage differs from the parallel one in xiv., first, in the introduction of the copula—which is unnecessary, and of itself a sign of a later text; and in the substitution, not very happy, of "iniquity" (*gnāvel*) for "doing" (*gnalīlah*), though this last may be compared with the very similar expression in Ezek. xvi. 52, "Thy sins, which thou hast made abominable."

3. THEY HAVE BECOME CORRUPT. A different verb from that employed in ver. 1, and one therefore for which a different equivalent should be found in our language; perhaps "tainted" would convey the idea. It is used strictly of *physical* corruption (the Arabic cognate in conj. viii. being used of milk which turns sour), but here, as in Job xv. 16, transferred to moral corruption.

4. HAVE, &c. . . . NO KNOWLEDGE? According to this rendering, the interrogative must cover the whole clause, and the negative belonged strictly to the verb = Do they not know, *i.e.* Are they so senseless, so without understanding? Other renderings, however, are possible :—

(1) "Do they not know, acknowledge," *i.e.* God, whom, according to ver. 1, they deny—parallel with "They call not upon God." as in lxxix. 6, Jer. x. 25. Or,

(2) "Do they not know" absolutely., *i.e.* show that they have knowledge, exercise their reason, &c., as lxxiii. 22, lxxxii. 5. The older Verss. take the word thus absolutely, but render it as a future. LXX. οὐχὶ γνώσονται; Jerome and Vulg. *Nonne cognoscent?*

(3) Hupfeld renders, "Haben sie es nicht erfahren?" *i.e.* "Have they not gained knowledge," by experience of the past, sufficient to deter them from their madness?

WHO EAT, &c. These words

(And) call not upon God ?"
5 There were they in great terror, (where) no terror was,
For God hath scattered [b] the bones of him that encampeth against thee.[c]
Thou hast put (them) to shame ; for God hath rejected them.

6 Oh that the salvation of Israel were come out of Zion !
When God bringeth back the captivity of His people,
(Then) shall Jacob exult, (then) shall Israel be glad.

are very difficult, and are again capable of a different interpretation from that given in the note on xiv. As is there said, the literal rendering is, " Eating my people, they have eaten bread, they have not called on Jehovah." This may be explained, " Whilst they devour my people (comp. Jer. x. 25, Lam. ii. 16), they have eaten bread, &c. *i.e.* in the midst of their cruel destruction of Israel, they have gone on in their brutal security, eating and drinking, quite regardless of God, or of any reverence for His Name."

I am now inclined, however, with L. de Dieu, to refer the words, " Who eat my people," to the first member of the verse : " Have the workers of iniquity, who devour my people, no knowledge ? They eat bread (they live their careless life of self-enjoyment), they call not upon Jehovah (do not acknowledge or fear Him)."

5. THERE, as if pointing to the scene ; see on lxvi. 6.

WHERE NO TERROR WAS. These words are not in Ps. xiv. and are somewhat difficult to explain. Do they mean no terror *within*, or terror *without ?* Taken with what follows, and supposing the Psalm to have been adapted to some such occasion as the destruction of Sennacherib's army, they might mean, " suddenly, in the midst of their proud security, when *they were free from all apprehension*, they were smitten with terror." Others understand it of *external* occasion of terror. They were seized with a sudden panic, where there was really *no object to occasion alarm.* The words may perhaps be a later gloss. As we do not know for what occasion the alteration was made in the text, their interpretion must remain obscure. The other variations of the present text will be found in the Critical Note.

HATH SCATTERED, *i.e.*, on the field of battle, or around the walls of the city, there to whiten in the sun and rain (comp. cxli. 7, Ezek. vi. 5. Jer. viii. 2), instead of being interred.

[a] עַל מַחֲלַת. The words occur again in the title of Ps. lxxxviii., with the addition of לְעַנּוֹת (from עָנָה, "to sing," Is. xxvii. 2). What they mean is uncertain. מַחֲלָה is "sickness," and as the word is here in the stat. constr., it would seem as if we had only part of a sentence, the rest being understood. עַל would then, as usual, denote "after the manner of," and מַחֲלַת be the first word of the song to whose melody this was to be set. It might, perhaps, begin, as Delitzsch suggests, מַחֲלַת לֵב, or something of

the kind. The word may, however, be in the stat. absol., with the rarer feminine termination *ath.* Comp. נְגִינַת, lxi. 1. Possibly it may mean that the Psalm was to be sung in a sad, mournful tone, as the addition of the verb in lxxxviii. 1, and the whole character of that Psalm, which is the darkest in the Psalter, seem to imply.

[b] The variations here from Ps. xiv. are as follow: פזר corresponds to בדור, עצמות חנך to עצת עני, הבישתה to תבישו, and מאסם to מחסהו. There is, therefore, a great similarity of *letters*, in the two texts, though the *words* and the *sense* are widely different.

[c] חֹנָךְ, pausal form, and with omission of the prepos. instead of חֹנֶה עָלֶיךָ, on the same principle as קָמַי, for instance, stands for קָמִים עָלַי; or perhaps the verb of *encamping* may follow the construction of verbs of dwelling, and so take the accusative directly after it.

PSALM 54

THIS Psalm, like several others of the Psalms ascribed to David in the Second Book, refers, according to the title, to the time of his persecution by Saul. The particular occasion was this. David had taken refuge with six hundred men in the fastness of Keilah; but, warned by Abiathar the son of Ahimelech, that the men of Keilah were not to be trusted, he escaped into the wilderness of Ziph. Here, however, he was very near falling into the hands of the Ziphites, who would have betrayed him to Saul, when happily an irruption of the Philistines into the country compelled the king to desist from his pursuit, and to turn his arms in another direction. See 1 Sam. xxiii. 19, and the additional particulars furnished by the later annalist, 1 Sam. xxvi. 1, from which sources the title is borrowed.

The language of the Psalm is, however, of so general a character, that it might have been composed under almost any circumstances of peril. Even the epithet "strangers" applied to the Psalmist's enemies, ver. 3 [5], does not necessarily refer to foreign enemies, as De Wette supposes. See note on the verse.

The Psalm consists of two principal divisions:—

I. A prayer to God to hear and to judge the cause of His servant, together with the reason for this prayer in the violence and unscrupulousness of the enemies who beset him. Ver. 1—3.

II. The confident assurance that God will hear his prayer, and the promise and vow of thanksgiving for God's goodness which is thus anticipated. Ver. 4—7.

[FOR THE PRECENTOR. WITH STRINGED INSTRUMENTS.[a] A MASKIL OF DAVID; WHEN THE ZIPHITES CAME AND SAID TO SAUL, DOTH NOT DAVID HIDE HIMSELF WITH US?]

1 O GOD, by Thy Name save me,
And in Thy might judge my cause.
2 O God, hear my prayer;
Give ear to the words of my mouth.
3 For strangers [b] have risen up against me,
And violent men have sought after my soul;
They have not set God before them. [Selah.]

4 Behold, God is my Helper,
The Lord is the Upholder of my soul.
5 He will requite [c] the evil to mine adversaries:
Destroy Thou them in Thy truth.

1. BY THY NAME. See above on xx. 1.

3. STRANGERS . . . . . VIOLENT MEN. (Cf. lxxxvi. 14.) Supposing the inscription of the Psalm to be correct, the enemies thus spoken of would be the Ziphites. As they belonged to Judah, the word *strangers* seems to be used with special bitterness. But the epithet would seem still more applicable to the men of Keilah, whom David had rescued from the Philistines, and who so basely requited his generous assistance.

Their hostility to David probably was the result rather of a selfish regard to their own interests than of any affection or loyalty to Saul. They could never have doubted on which side lay justice and right: but because they were wicked men, "who did not set God before them," they took pleasure in hunting down one whose only fault was that he was the king's enemy. The word "strangers" may mean only enemies, the idea of a foreigner, one of another country, passing over readily into the idea of an enemy, just as in Latin *hostis* meant originally nothing more than *hospes*. Here, however, the epithet may be employed to denote the savageness and cruelty of these men, as Calvin: "mihi videtur immanem eorum barbariem perstringere." So Mendels. "Barbaren." Rosenm. refers to Job xix. 13, "de propinquis suis;" but there it is the verb, "they are *become* strangers to." See Num. xvi. 40 [xvii. 5].

4. But though *men* were against him, David knew that God was with him.

THE UPHOLDER OF MY SOUL. Lit. "among them," or "with them that uphold my soul." But this would not convey the meaning of the Psalmist. For God is not to him one out of many helpers, but the only true helper. The use of

6 With free will will I sacrifice unto Thee,
I will give thanks to Thy Name, O Jehovah, for it is good.
7 For out of all distress hath He delivered me,
And mine eye hath seen (its desire) upon mine enemies.

the plural denotes the *class* or *category* of upholders, in which God is, though of course without placing Him on a level with human helpers. See the same grammatical figure in cxviii. 7, Judges xi. 35.

6. WITH FREE WILL, or, with glad, willing heart, as the expression occurs in Num. xv. 3, and (without the preposition) in Hosea xiv. 5. This explains the motive of the sacrifice. The offering would be a literal offering, as appointed by the Law, but it would be brought with all the cheerfulness and love of a thankful heart, not under the compulsion of a vow, or in mere slavish compliance with an established ritual. Hupfeld suggests that the word (נְדָבָה) here may mean not "free will," but "free will offering," because of the verb "sacrifice" which accompanies it. But, he remarks, the verb is not construed with the prep. as here, but takes the accusative of the thing offered. And I see no reason for departing from the interpretation which has the support of all the ancient Versions and is generally received.

THY NAME . . . FOR IT IS GOOD. With reference to ver. 1, "By *Thy Name* save me."

It is possible that in the next verse the Name of God is the subject of the verb, so that we may render "IT hath delivered me." If so, this passage (and Is. xxx. 27) would come very near the later Rabbinic usage, according to which "the Name" (הַשֵּׁם) is constantly put for God Himself. The original passage is Lev. xxiv. 11.

7. The perfects in this verse denote not that the deliverance is already accomplished, but the confidence of faith that it will be, and give the reason for the thanksgiving of the preceding verse.

MINE EYE HATH SEEN. See note on xli. 10.

[a] For the title, see notes on the titles of iv. and xxxii.

[b] זָרִים. Instead of this, many of Kennicott's and De-Rossi's MSS. have זֵדִים, which was the reading also of the Chald., and was probably borrowed from lxxxvi. 14.

[c] יָשׁוּב. "The evil shall return." This is one of the very few instances in which the Q'ri seems preferable to the K'thîbh.

PSALM 55

As this Psalm is, in the title, ascribed to David, and as it contains a bitter complaint of the faithlessness of a trusted friend, it has been commonly supposed to refer to the desertion and treachery of Ahithophel in Absalom's rebellion. We know too little of Ahithophel to be able to say whether he was the close personal friend of the king, as well as his councillor of state. But the prayer of David, 2 Sam. xv. 31, when he was told that Ahithophel was among the conspirators, "O Lord, I pray Thee turn the counsel of Ahithophel into foolishness," is very different from the general tone of this Psalm. Here throughout, there is a sense of personal wrong; the treachery is without excuse. And if Blunt is right in supposing that Bathsheba was the granddaughter of Ahithophel (*Undesigned Coincidences*, p. 147), and that he, in revenge for the insult to his family, had espoused the cause of Absalom, David could hardly complain of his desertion. His own conscience must have told him how well-merited it was. He could scarcely upbraid the man whom he had so wronged with treachery to himself, though he might pray that his counsel should not prosper. There is another objection to the view that Ahithophel is aimed at in the Psalm. The writer of the Psalm is evidently *in the city* (no doubt Jerusalem is meant, comp. ver. 14), surrounded by evil men, but especially cognizant of the perfidy of his trusted friend. If David, therefore, wrote the Psalm, he must have written it before he left Jerusalem, and the treachery of Ahithophel must have been already unmasked. But, according to 2 Sam. xv. 30, it was not till David had begun his flight that he was told that Ahithophel had joined the conspirators. The Psalm seems, therefore, to have been composed under other circumstances, and to be directed at some person of whom we know nothing beyond what the Psalm itself tells us. Hitzig thinks it was written by Jeremiah, and discovers certain similarities of expression between the Prophet and the Psalmist to justify his view. According to him, Pashur is the friend whose treachery is stigmatized. Ewald supposes the Psalm to have been written during the last century before the Captivity, the discord and confusion of the city, as here described, according best with that period; and he infers from ver. 10 [11], that the city was in a state of siege. This interpretation of the verse, however, is doubtful. See note on the verse. Such conjectures, after all, are of little value. One thing only is certain, and that is, that whoever the hollow friend may have been, who knew so well to cloke his treacherous designs,—who, with war in his heart, could use words smoother than oil,—his perfidy was very deeply felt, and very bitterly resented by the man who here records it. At one moment sadness, at another indignation prevails. In his sadness the Psalmist would flee away, and so escape the suffering and the recollection of his wrong. In his burning indignation at the black perfidy of which he had been made the victim, he would have the earth open her mouth and swallow up the faithless friend, together with all his accomplices.

The abruptness in many parts of the Psalm is to be accounted for, to a great extent, by the strong emotion under which it was written; and the transposition of verses, in order to soften this abruptness, is a violent remedy to apply, especially to these ancient compositions, which are so commonly wanting in anything like regularity of structure.

The Psalm consists of three principal divisions:—

I. The first contains the earnest appeal to God against his enemies, the expression of his suffering, and the horror of mind which has come upon him, together with the longing to escape from the hostility to which he was exposed, and the evil he was compelled to witness. Ver. 1—8.

II. In the next his tone changes. The portentous wickedness which has filled the whole city, and, worse even than this, the perfidy of the man he had trusted, rouse his indignation, and he prays that all the counsels of the wicked may be brought to naught, and that they themselves may go down alive into the grave. Ver. 9—15.

III. The last strophe is altogether in a calmer strain. It opens and closes with the confession of trust in God, and though the figure of the traitor again comes prominently into view, it does not provoke the same burning imprecation as before. Instead of this, the Psalmist rests calmly confident that the righteous shall never be moved, and that the bloodthirsty and deceitful man shall speedily be cut off. Ver. 16—23.

[FOR THE PRECENTOR. ON STRINGED INSTRUMENTS.[a] A MASKIL OF DAVID.]

I. 1 GIVE ear, O God, to my prayer,
And hide not Thyself from my supplication.
2 Hearken unto me, and answer me;

I am tossed to and fro [b] in my complaint, and must groan,[c]
3 Because of the voice of the enemy,
Because of the oppression [d] of the wicked;
For they cast [e] iniquity upon me,
And in anger do they persecute me.

4 My heart is sore pained within me,
And the terrors of death have fallen upon me:
5 Fear and trembling come upon me,
And horror hath overwhelmed me.
6 And I said: Oh that I had wings like the dove,
Then would I fly (away) and be at rest;
7 Lo, then would I flee afar off,
I would lodge in the wilderness: [Selah.]
8 I would haste to find me a place of shelter
From stormy [f] wind (and) from tempest.

2. I AM TOSSED TO AND FRO, or, "I wander in my thoughts," "am distracted." Cf. the Homeric Διvεύεσκ' ἀλύων, Il. Ω. 12.

3. PERSECUTE ME, or, "are adversaries unto me." See the same root in cix. 6, 20, 29.

4. SORE PAINED, lit. "writhes," as in travail-pangs.

5. HORROR. The word so rendered is of comparatively rare occurrence. The LXX. here explain it by σκότος. Aq. εἰλίνδησις. Symm. φρίκη. It is to be found only in three other places: Job xxi. 6, Is. xxi. 4, Ezek. vii. 18.

6. BE AT REST, lit. "dwell, abide," *i.e.* have some fixed and settled place of abode, where I should be free from persecution, instead of leading a wandering life, exposed to peril, and at the mercy of my enemies. The verb seems to have a like force in Prov. vii. 11, Nah. iii. 18. So the LXX. πετασθήσομαι καὶ καταπαύσω. It would, however, be possible to adhere to the literal rendering of the word: "Then would I fly away and dwell (somewhere)." Symm. πετασθῆναι καὶ ἑδρασθῆναι.

8. This verse will admit of a different rendering in both its clauses:

I would hasten my escape
Swifter than stormy wind, (and) than tempest.

In the first clause the word *miphlâ* (occurring only here) may mean, according to its form, either the escape itself (Aq. and Theod. διασωσμόν, Symm. ἔκφυξιν), or the place to which the escape is made. And, in the second, the prepos. may mean either "from," or be used in comparison, as it often is. Maurer, Hupfeld, and others think that a comparison is here implied, to mark the exceeding swiftness of the flight, which would be more rapid than that of the storm (as Virgil has, *ocior Euro*). And Drusius says: "Nubes et venti celerrime feruntur; sed nihil celerius vento, e depressa nube contorto. Hinc proverbium: *turbine* celerius, quo rei festinatæ summa celeritas significatur." But I agree with

II. 9 Confound, O Lord, divide their tongues;
For I have seen violence and strife in the city:
10 Day and night, they go about it upon the walls thereof;
Iniquity also and mischief are in the midst of it.
11 Destruction is in the midst of it;
Deceit and guile depart not from the market-place thereof.
12 —For it is not an enemy that reproacheth me;

Bunsen in thinking such a comparison here extremely unsuitable. In fact, not only the swift flight, and the distant flight, but the flight to a shelter *from* the storm, is what the context seems to require. (Comp. lxxxiii. 15 [16], Jer. xxiii. 19, xxx. 23.) And so all the older Versions: Aq. and Theod. ἀπὸ πνεύματος λαιλαπώδους, ἀπὸ λαίλαπος. Symm. ἀπὸ πνεύματος ἐπαίροντος λαίλαπος. Jerome, *a spiritu tempestatis et turbinis.*

9. The tone of sadness and melancholy now gives way to one of hot and passionate indignation. He would have escaped if he could from that city of sinners, who vexed his righteous soul from day to day with their ungodly deeds; but as he could not do this, he would gladly see God's judgements executed upon them. The sudden outburst of these fervent, impetuous feelings, gives an irregularity to the whole Poem. But this is natural; and there is no need to suppose that its parts have been disarranged, and that the order should be restored by placing verses 12—14, and 20, 21, immediately after verse 5.

CONFOUND, or, "frustrate" (as in Is. xix. 3, "I will frustrate, or, bring to naught, its counsel"); lit. "swallow up." The LXX. καταπόντισον. It is not certain whether this verb, as well as the following, has "their tongues" for its object. According to the accents, the two clauses are distinct, and with the first some other object must be supplied, "Confound or destroy (them, *i.e.* the enemy)."

DIVIDE. Comp. Gen. x. 25, xi. 1—9, to which there may possibly be an allusion.

10. THEY GO ABOUT, *i.e.* most probably "the wicked," mentioned ver. 3, who are the subject, and hardly "violence and strife" (ver. 9) personified, as the ancient Versions render, and as the Rabbinical commentators generally suppose (and with which we may compare Virgil's

"... ubique
Luctus, ubique Pavor et plurima
Mortis imago").

The figure may perhaps be borrowed from sentinels keeping their watch upon the walls; others think, from besiegers watching the walls in order to find some weak point. In the former case we must render "*upon*," in the latter "*round about* the walls." But neither figure need be pressed. The *walls* in this clause of the verse are parallel to *the interior* of the city in the next clause, so that the whole city may be represented in *all its parts* to be full of wickedness.

11. DESTRUCTION. See on v. 9, note[i], and xxxviii. 12 [13].

MARKET, or "broad place" (πλατεῖα); the square or market-place near the gates, where was the general place of concourse. See on ix. 14 [15].

12. FOR gives a special reason for the prayer in ver. 9, his eye

Then I might bear it:
Neither is it one who hateth me, that hath magnified himself against me;
Then I would hide myself from him.
13 But thou art a man, mine equal,[g]
My companion and my well-known friend;
14 We were wont to take sweet counsel together,
To walk to the house of God among the (festal) crowd.[h]
15 Let death come suddenly[i] upon them;
Let them go down to the unseen world alive;
For wickedness is in their dwelling, in the midst of them.

falling upon one in particular among the crowd of enemies and evil-doers. This is a sufficient explanation of the use of the particle, which is often employed rather with reference to something in the *mind* of the speaker, than in direct logical sequence.

THEN I MIGHT BEAR IT—the verb with the copula in a subjoined sentence, as in li. 17 [18], "then (else) would I give it."

13 MINE EQUAL, lit. "according to my estimation," *i.e.* the estimation or worth which I put upon him. But such a sense does not apply here. It must rather mean "of the same rank and position as myself." LXX. ἰσόψυχε. Symm. ὁμοιότροπος. Jerome, *unanimis*, as understanding it rather of similarity of mind and character than of rank. See more in the Critical Note.

COMPANION. In Prov. xvi. 28, xvii. 9, the same word is rendered in the A.V. "chief (or, very) friends." Here, as in Prov. ii. 17, Jer. iii. 4, Mic. vii. 5, the A.V. has "guide."

14. WE WERE WONT, &c. The verb is in the imperfect (or future, as it is commonly called). Lit. "we were wont to make (our) counsel, or confidential intercourse, sweet." The word which is here rendered "counsel," is rendered "secret" in xxv. 14, where see note. In both passages the meaning "close intimate intercourse," would be suitable. Symm. and Aq. have respectively the same rendering here, as there, of the word. This clause speaks of private intimacy, the next of association in public acts, and especially in the great festivals and processions to the Temple.

THE CROWD, here the festal caravan; comp. xlii. 4 [5], lxiv. 3.

15. Again indignation at the blackness of this treachery, so far worse to be endured than any open enmity. To have trusted, and to find his trust betrayed; to have been one with a man in public and in private, bound to him by personal ties, and by the ties of religion, and then to find honour, faith, affection, all cast to the winds—this it was that seemed so terrible, this it was that called for the withering curse. Thus the second strophe ends as it began, ver. 9, with imprecations upon the wicked; the intervening stanzas, in describing the faithlessness of the trusted friend, giving the reason for this anathema.

LET THEM GO DOWN. Comp. ix. 17 [18]. ALIVE, as Prov. i. 12.

III. 16 As for me—unto God do I cry,
And Jehovah saveth me :
17 Evening, and morning, and at noon do I complain and groan,
And He hath heard my voice.
18 He hath redeemed my soul, in peace, from the war that was upon me ;
For there were many against me.
19 God shall hear (me) and humble them,[k]
—For He sitteth (as King) of old—[Selah.]
(Even them) who have no changes,[l] and who fear not God.

There may possibly be an allusion to the fate of Korah and his company. Num. xvi. 30, &c.

16. AS FOR ME. The pronoun emphatic, in opposition to the conduct of his enemies.

DO I CRY. The use of the past tenses in the second member of ver. 17 and the first of ver. 18 seem to show that the Psalmist refers to a continued past experience.

17. EVENING AND MORNING, &c. The three principal parts of the day are mentioned probably as marking special times set apart for prayer, not merely as a poetical expression for "the whole day," "at all times," "without ceasing." Comp. v. 3 [4], lxxxviii. 1 [2], 13 [14], xcii. 2 [3]. Hence Herzfeld, who at one time argued that Daniel's prayer three times a day "pointed to a time when religious ideas had penetrated from India into the neighbouring countries to the west," was compelled by this passage to admit that the practice was of much earlier date among the Jews.—*Gesch. d. V. Isr.* ii. 185, 191.

COMPLAIN AND GROAN, the same words as in ver. 2.

18. IN PEACE, as denoting the end of the redemption, the condition in which he was placed thereby.

MANY. Perhaps more literally, With many (or, in great numbers) were they against me. But the prep. serves here, as elsewhere, to introduce the predicate. Comp. liv. 4 [6]. AGAINST ME, lit. "*with* me;" but the prep. must be understood according to the context, whether it implies *help* or *opposition*. Comp. xciv. 16. In fact, its use is just that of the equivalent prep. in English and in other languages. To fight *with* = to fight *against*. To be angry *with* = to be angry *against*, &c.; the notions of *addition* and *opposition* being always closely connected.

19. An obscure verse. The first clause runs in the Hebrew, "God will hear and answer them," which, however, gives no very suitable sense, unless we suppose the sentence to be ironical. I have therefore followed the LXX. εἰσακούσεται ὁ Θεὸς καὶ ταπεινώσει αὐτούς (and Jerome, *humiliabit eos*), a rendering which requires only a slight change in the vowel points. The second clause, "And He sitteth," or, "even He who sitteth," &c. may be quasi-parenthetical. But the introduction of the *Selah* into the middle of the verse is very unusual, and not easily accounted for; and the third clause beginning with the relative is by no means clear. Who are they who have no changes? Apparently, those whom God is said to humble or chastise. And what is the meaning of the word "changes," as here used? Many understand it of a moral change; "who are without change of heart or reformation."

20 He hath put forth his hands against them that were
at peace with him:
He hath broken his covenant.
21 Smooth as butter[m] itself is his mouth;
But his heart is war:
Softer are his words than oil;
Yet are they drawn swords.
22 Cast thy burden[n] upon Jehovah,
And He shall sustain thee:
He shall never suffer the righteous to be moved.
23 But Thou, O God, shalt bring them down into the pit
of destruction:
Bloody and deceitful men shall not live out half
their days;
But as for me, I trust in Thee.

But the word never occurs in this sense. It means, properly, "a change," in the sense of *succession;* as of garments, of troops relieving guard, servants leaving work, and the like. Hence it would rather mean in a moral sense: "They who have no cessation in their course (by being relieved guard, for instance), who always continue and persevere in their evil life." Calvin and others understand it of *change of fortune*, i.e. "who are always prosperous;" but this, again, is not supported by usage. See more in the Critical Note.

20. The individual traitor (who had once been the trusted friend) is again prominent. And hence Hupfeld would place this and the next verse immediately after ver. 14.

BROKEN, lit. "profaned." See lxxxix. 39 [40], where the word is applied to the crown.

HIS COVENANT. Apparently not a particular covenant solemnly made, as that between David and Jonathan, but figuratively, the covenant implied in a close friendship, of itself a holy bond, the breaking of which is a profanity.

21. SMOOTH, &c. Lit. "smooth are the creaminesses of his mouth," or as Ewald well renders, "Glatt sind die Butterlippen seines Mundes." His words drop from his lips like cream, or butter.

YET THEY. The pronoun is emphatic. *They*, those very words so smooth and so fair.

22. THY BURDEN. The word occurs only here. But there are similar expressions in xxxvii. 5, "thy way;" and Prov. xvi. 3, "thy doing." See also xxii. 8 [9]. The LXX. render, ἐπίρριψον ἐπὶ Κύριον τὴν μέριμνάν σου, which is evidently before the mind of St. Peter in 1 Pet. v. 7.

23. THEM, *i.e.* "the bloody and deceitful men" in the next clause, the pronoun being placed first as in many other instances. See on ix. 12.

[a] See note on title of Ps. iv.

[b] אָרִיד, from a verb רִיד (the Qal, not Hiphil from רוּד), which occurs in three other passages, Gen. xxvii. 40, Jer. ii. 31, Hos. xii. 1. The meaning assigned to it by the older Verss. and the Rabb. is different in different

places. Here the LXX. have ἐλυπήθην. Symm. κατηνέχθην προσλαλῶν ἐμαυτῷ. Chald. אֶתְרַעַם, *murmuro*. Later commentators follow Schultens and Schröder in referring it to the Arab. root راد, *vagari, discurrere*. Properly, it signifies to wander restlessly, especially as homeless, without fixed abode, &c. This is probably the meaning in Gen. xxvii. 40, "when thou wanderest," *i.e.* becomest a free nomad people (not as in the E.V., "when thou shalt have the dominion"). Here it is used of the restless tossing to and fro of the mind, filled and distracted with cares and anxieties.

c אָהִימָה, from a form הום, kindred with המה, המם: properly used of any deep confused sound; as the noise of a multitude, Micah ii. 12, as also the kindred roots are, of the roaring of the sea, the growl of a bear, &c. LXX. ἐταράχθην. Symm. συνεχύθην. Chald. וְאַרְגּוּשׁ. The optat. or cohortative conveys the notion of "must," "am obliged to," &c. Ewald, § 228, *a*.

d עָקַת. The word only occurs here, but is common in Aram. from a root עוק, which is also found in Hebrew, Amos ii. 13, and the deriv. מוּעָקָה, lxvi. 11.

e יָמִיטוּ. The Hiph. occurs only here and cxl. 10, K'thîbh, lit. "they cause to move, set in motion," as it were, a stone which they would bring down upon his head. So Symm. ἐπέρριψαν κατ' ἐμοῦ. LXX. ἐξέκλιναν ἐπ' ἐμέ.

f סֹעָה occurs nowhere else. Rashi refers it to the root נסע, *to move away;* A. Schultens, who is followed by Gesen., would connect it with the Arab. سعى. Hupfeld rejects the word, and thinks it is a mistake for סוּפָה, which occurs with סַעַר, lxxxiii. 16, and in several other places.

g כְּעֶרְכִּי. The easiest way of explaining this, as Hupfeld says, is by taking עֵרֶךְ here, as in Ex. xl. 23, Jud. xvii. 10, to mean "rank, order." So Calvin: *secundum ordinem meum*. Others explain it by reference to the phrase אִישׁ כְּעֶרְכּוֹ, 2 Kings xii. 5, xxiii. 35, &c., "each one as he is valued, or assessed," "every one according to his taxation" (as the latter passage is rendered in the E. V.). Hence here, "a man who is assessed as I am," and therefore, "of the same rank," &c. But the idea of equality is, in fact, in the root itself. Comp. Is. xl. 18, and see note on Ps. xl. 5.

h רֶגֶשׁ only here, but the form רִגְשָׁה occurs lxiv. 3, where there is the same antithesis as here with סוֹד. The word is used of public festal processions, = הָמוֹן and סָךְ, xlii. 5.

i יְשִׁימוֹת, "Desolations," from ישם, kindred with שׁמם; but according to the Q'ri, which is more probable, יַשִּׁי (יַשִּׁיא) מָוֶת, "let Death deceive," *i.e.* let Death come deceitfully, unawares upon them, steal upon them,—the notion of *coming* lying not in the verb, but in the prep. עַל. This last is the reading of the majority of the MSS., and amongst them, of the best Spanish MSS. (De-Rossi). Symm. αἰφνιδίως θάνατος ἐπέλθοι αὐτοῖς. The LXX. ἐλθέτω θάνατος ἐπ' αὐτούς. Cocceius, "Exactorem aget mors super eos."

[k] יַעֲנֵם. There is manifestly some error in the text. Either the punctuation of the word, or the suffix, is wrong. Hupfeld observes, that after the verb שמע we should naturally expect ענה, in the sense "to answer," this being the usual collocation of the two verbs "hear and answer;" but in that case the suffix must be wrong. It should be יַעֲנֵנִי, "God will hear and answer *me*." This seems an easy correction, but it occasions another difficulty; the relative, אֲשֶׁר, in the last member of the verse, with the *plural* suffix following, and the plural verb, has now nothing to refer to. And accordingly, Hupf. transposes the last clause of this verse to the end of ver. 15 [16]. "Wickedness is in the midst of them Who have no changes," &c. But we may retain the suffix and slightly alter the punctuation, יְעַנֵּם, and this is the reading which the older Versions seem to have had, the verb ענה in the Piel having the meaning "to chastise, afflict," &c. The words that follow, וְיֹשֵׁב קֶדֶם, are then, in a measure, parenthetical; the וְ is here explanatory, = והוא, as in vii. 9 [10], xxii. 28 [29]. "And it is He," or, "for He," &c. The verb ישב is used here of God's session as Judge or King; comp. xxix. 9 [10]. Similarly in Latin, *sedere*, Phædr. i. 10, 6, and *Consedere duces*, of judges on the bench, Ov. *Met.* xiii. 1. Comp. Juv. *Sat.* vii. 115.

[l] חֲלִיפוֹת. The usual interpretations of this word have already been given in the note on the verse in which it occurs. But, it must be confessed, the sense is in no case very satisfactory, whichever way we take it. Hence A. Schultens would refer the word to an Arab. root حِلْف "covenant," "oath," and also "faithfulness" in keeping the same. The meaning would then be, "men to whom oaths are of no account," or, "men who have no faithfulness." Aq. has οἷς οὐκ εἰσὶν ἀλλαγαὶ αὐτοῖς. Symm. οὐ γὰρ ἀλλάσσονται. And another Greek translator, ὅτι ὁ δόλος (perhaps he read אָוֶן, but Field suggests ὅτι οὐδ' ὅλως) ἀντάλλαγμα αὐτοῖς. LXX. οὐ γάρ ἐστιν αὐτοῖς ἀντάλλαγμα.

[m] מַחֲמָאוֹת, a plural noun formed with מ from the simpler חֶמְאָה, after the analogy of such forms as מַעֲרַמִּים, מַחֲמַדִּים, and מַחֲמֻדִּים (from חָמוּד), מַטְעַמִּים, מַשְׁמַנִּים, and the like; not, however, plur. absol., but constr. (notwithstanding the Kametz), as is usual in words whose 3d radical is Aleph, as, for instance, מוֹצָאֵי, מִקְרָאֵי, &c., and even in other forms (Ges. *Lehrg.* § 130, Obs. 1). Ewald well, "Butterlippen," and other German translators, "Butterworte." The reading מֵחֲמָאוֹת in the comparative sense, "(smoother) *than* butter," which is that of the Chald., Symm., and Jerome, in order to suit the parallelism מִשֶּׁמֶן, introduces a double anomaly, (1) the incorrect plural חֲמָאוֹת, and (2) a plural verb with a singular nominative, פִּיו. It would be far better to read, with Dathe, מֵחֶמְאָה.

[n] יְהָבְךָ, only here. In the Talmud the word has the meaning "burden," and so it is commonly taken here from יָהָב or יְהָב. Hupf. thinks it is the perfect of the verb, with omission of the relative, "(that which) He, *i.e.* God, hath given thee."

PSALM 56

THE complaint of one who, though hard pressed by enemies, nevertheless trusts in God, rests in His promises, flees to Him for succour, and renders thanks for His mercy. Throughout, his confidence never forsakes him. Indeed we see here the victory rather than the struggle of Faith. Hence the refrain, with which the first and second parts conclude, "In God will I praise His word. . . . What can flesh (man) do unto me?"

According to the inscription, it was composed when David was detained in Gath by the Philistines. But on neither occasion when he visited Gath does the history inform us of any such detention. (1 Sam. xxi. 11—16, and xxvii.—xxix.) Hengstenberg, indeed, and Delitzsch suppose that some seizure or imprisonment is implied in the words he "feigned himself mad *in their hands;*" and the expression at the beginning of chap. xxii., "David therefore departed thence, and *escaped* to the cave of Adullam," may imply that he had been subjected to some confinement. Hupfeld concludes, from the absence of anything in the history corresponding to the title of the Psalm, that the title is not to be trusted. Yet it is perhaps more likely on this very account that it rests upon some ancient tradition. A modern compiler would have endeavoured to make the title square better with the history.

The Psalm falls naturally into three divisions :—

The first and second scarcely differ in their subject-matter. They each contain a cry for help against enemies, and an expression of confidence in God; the second, however, being somewhat more emphatic than the first. The first consists of ver. 1—4; the second of ver. 5—11. The Psalm then concludes (ver. 12, 13) with words of devout thankfulness.

[FOR THE PRECENTOR. TO THE TUNE OF "THE SILENT DOVE IN FAR-OFF LANDS."[a] A MICHTAM OF DAVID, WHEN THE PHILISTINES LAID HOLD ON HIM IN GATH.]

1 BE gracious unto me, O God, for man would swallow
me up:

1. MAN. The word used denotes man in his weakness and frailty as contrasted with God in His power and majesty.

All the day long he, fighting, oppresseth me.
2 Mine adversaries would swallow (me) up all the day long;
For many are they that fight proudly against me.
3 In the day that I am afraid,
I put my trust in Thee.
4 In God do I praise His word:
In God have I put my trust; I am not afraid;
What can flesh do unto me?

WOULD SWALLOW ME UP, lit. Hath panted after me, with open mouth ready to devour me, like a wild beast, thirsting for my blood. Cf. Job vii. 2, "longeth as with open mouth for the shadow." The verb is repeated in the next verse, but without any object expressed.

2. PROUDLY, lit. "on high," an accusative used adverbially, and not a vocative, "O Thou Most High," as Aq., Jerome, the Chald. and others. There is no need to understand the word so even in xcii. 8 [9]. In Micah vi. 6 it does not stand alone: God is there mentioned by name: "to God on high."

3. IN THE DAY, &c. (As regards the construction, this is an accus. of time placed in constr. with the finite verb instead of the infinitive, as again ver. 9 [10].) Hupfeld thinks it a manifest contradiction to say, "In the day that I *fear* I *trust*;" but there is no contradiction except to the narrow understanding exercising its narrowest faculty of vision. It is not even necessary to explain: "In the day when I have reason to fear, or when terror assails me," &c. Fear and trust may co-exist. Faith may vanquish the rising fear, or, with Peter sinking in the sea through fear of the winds and the waves, may only have strength to cry, Lord, save me, I perish. Trust in God does not make us cease to be men and to have the feelings of men; but it gives a better than any stoical calmness; it lifts the man who is trembling in himself above the fear which assails him; in the very midst of fear it listens to the voice which says, Fear not, for I am with thee. "Assuredly," says Calvin, "this is the true test and proof of our faith; when fears harass us, so far as our fleshly nature is concerned (*pro sensu carnis*), but do not overthrow and unsettle our minds. It seems, indeed, as if *fear* and *hope* were feelings too contrary the one to the other to dwell in the same heart; but experience shows that Hope there in fact really reigns where some portion of the heart is possessed by Fear. For when the mind is calm and tranquil, Hope is not exercised, yea rather is as it were hushed to sleep; but then, and not till then, does she put forth all her strength, when the mind has been cast down by cares and she lifts it up, when it has been saddened and disturbed and she calms it, when it has been smitten with fear and she sustains and props it."

4. IN GOD, or perhaps "*through* God" (comp. lx. 13 [14]), *i.e.* by His help, trusting in Him, do I praise.

HIS WORD, *i.e.* His promise. God Himself gives me to know ever anew the truth of His promise, and therefore I make my boast of it. The promise of God, true and precious as it is, is nothing in itself, but only in God who makes it true and precious to our souls.

I DO NOT FEAR, or "I *cannot* fear;" for such may be the force of the tense. "But how can David thus all at once have put off all

5 All the day long they wrest my words :
All their thoughts are against me for evil.
6 They gather together, they lie in wait,[b] they watch my steps,
As [c] they have hoped (to take away) my life.
7 Shall they escape [d] because of iniquity ?
In anger bring down the peoples, O God.
8 THOU tellest my wandering ;

weakness, so that he who but a moment before was in dread of death, now courageously tramples upon his enemies ? I answer that this confidence is no proof that he was rid of all fear, as if he were like a man placed beyond the reach of every weapon (*extra telorum jactum positus*), and could quietly smile at all perils ; but because he was so far from yielding to fear that he rose victoriously above it, and by holding up the shield of hope and so driving back all apprehensions was defended by a sure and certain salvation (*munitus esset certa salute*), he might well break forth with the holy boast, *Because I hope in God I will not fear*."—*Calvin*.

5. The second strophe contains a fuller description of the attacks and evil designs of his enemies, and a cry to God to take vengeance upon them.

THEY WREST MY WORDS, *i.e.* they twist and pervert them, give them a wrong meaning, purposely misrepresent me. The expression, however, may perhaps be taken in a wider sense. "My words" may be="my circumstances :" all that concerns me, all that I say and do, they twist, turn it into an occasion of bitterness and *sorrow* to me (comp. the noun "sorrows," xvi. 3 [4], from the same root). *My circumstances* may then be almost a periphrasis for *me*, and the phrase mean, "They torment me, occasion me sorrow," &c.

6. THEY. The pronoun stands here emphatically.

MY STEPS, lit. "my heels," the heels being the part exposed to any person coming from behind, or to an enemy lying like a serpent in the path. See on xlix. 5 [6]. Comp. lxxxix. 51 [52], Job xviii. 9.

7. This verse gives vent to the stronger feelings of the heart, in the prayer that those who have banded themselves in a treacherous conspiracy against the peace and life of the Psalmist may be overthrown.

SHALL THEY ESCAPE, &c. Such seems the only possible rendering of the text as it at present stands. But by a very slight change in a single consonant we should have the meaning : "Requite them according to (their) iniquity." See more in Critical Note.

THE PEOPLES. Instead of saying "mine enemies," his eye takes a wider range. These men are only a few out of many ungodly, and therefore he appeals to God as the Judge of the world to root out all ungodliness everywhere. Comp. lix. 5 [6], 8 [9], and see on vii. 7 [8].

8. As in the last Psalm we noticed the sudden transition from sadness to anger, from a tone of weariness and despondency to one of stern indignation, so here we have the contrary. For a moment the Psalmist prays for destruction upon his adversaries ; then he turns, with words of touching entreaty, to God.

MY WANDERING, perhaps "my flight, or exile." Others understand, "my (inward) restlessness." The word, however, may mean "complaint," "lamentation," &c. Comp.

O put [e] Thou my tears into Thy bottle,[f]
Are they not in Thy book?
9 Then shall mine enemies be turned backward, when I call (upon Thee):
This [g] I know, that God is for me.
10 In God do I praise (His) word: [h]
In Jehovah do I praise (His) word.
11 In God have I put my trust; I am not afraid:
What can man do unto me?
12 Upon me, O God, are Thy vows;

Job ii. 11. The word is in the singular number, perhaps, as Calvin suggests, in order to express "his whole wandering life, as though he would term it one continuous exile."

The tone here is changed. The Sacred Poet turns from man to God with that tender personal affection which is so striking both in this Psalm and in the next, and which makes one willing to believe that these are, as the titles tell us, Psalms of David. He knows that each day of his wandering, each nook in which he has found shelter, each step that he has taken, every artifice by which he has baffled his foes,—all have been numbered by his Heavenly Keeper. Yea, no tear that he has shed, when his eye has been raised to heaven in prayer, has fallen to the ground. He asks God to gather them all in His bottle, and trusts that He will note them in His book. Comp. cxxxix. 16, lxix. 28 [29], Exod. xxxii. 32, Mal. iii. 16, in which the figure of the book occurs.

The BOTTLE is the skin-bottle which in Eastern lands is used for keeping water, milk, wine, &c. In this he prays God by a bold figure to treasure his tears. The prayer is, no doubt, abrupt, coming as it does between the double expression of confidence: "Thou hast numbered," &c. "Are they not," &c. But there is no reason on this account to render, "My tears *are put*," &c. Such a turn of the sentence may seem less harsh; but I confess I cannot understand that kind of criticism which will allow no play to the emotions of the heart, and which would bind the spirit of prayer in the withes of the rhetoricians. This verse has been beautifully imitated in P. Gerhardt's Hymn (quoted by Hupfeld):

"Du zählst wie oft ein Christe wein',
Und was sein Kummer sei;
Kein stilles Thränlein ist so klein,
Du hebst und legst es bei."

10. The refrain is varied from ver. 4, by the emphatic repetition of the first clause, with the substitution however in its repeated form of *Jehovah* for *Elohim*. Calvin thus explains the repetition: "Though to-day God may have seemed to depart from me, because He has withdrawn His aid, still I will rest in His word. Should the same thing happen to-morrow, or the next day, I will persist in the same praise of it." He goes on to urge the importance of learning to be thus content with the bare word (*nudo verbo contenti*) in all our trials. "For though God ever furnishes believers with manifold subjects of praise and boasting in the benefits He bestows, still they can scarcely take three steps unless they have learned to lean only on the word."

12. THY VOWS, *i.e.* the vows

I will pay thanksgivings unto Thee.
13 For Thou hast delivered my soul from Death :
Hast Thou not (delivered also) my feet from stumbling
That I may walk before God in the Light of Life ?

which I have vowed to Thee (the only instance, however, in which the pronoun refers to God instead of to the person who makes the vow). ARE UPON ME, *i.e.* it is incumbent upon me to pay them, because the condition of deliverance upon which I vowed has been fulfilled. Cf. Prov. vii. 14.

13. The verb from the first clause of this verse must be repeated with the second, where the change to the question ("Hast Thou not," &c.) is characteristic of the writer. See ver. 8 [9].

FROM STUMBLING, lit. "from a thrust or blow."

THAT I MAY WALK, lit. "walk to and fro," as expressive of the general habit of the life.

IN THE LIGHT OF LIFE, or "in the light of the living," *i.e.* as a living man (as in Job xxxiii. 30). Comp. xxvii. 13 and the parallel passage cxvi. 8, 9, where, however, it is "land of the living."

[a] עַל יוֹנַת א׳ ר׳. The inscription is obscure. Some suppose that it is intended to describe David's situation as a wanderer in a strange country ; he being like the *dove* in his innocence, *silent* in his patience and defencelessness, and among the *distant* ones or strangers, *i.e.* the Philistines. But the prep. עַל probably here, as in the inscriptions of other Psalms, denotes merely the tune or melody of some song beginning with the words "Silent dove," &c., after the measure of which this was to be sung. See on the inscription of xxii. The word רְחֹקִים is a plur. abstr. as in lxv. 6. יָם ר׳, "the far-off sea." For אֵלֶם Bochart (*Hieroz.* ii. 1) would punctuate אֵלִם, as if written defectively for אֵלִים, "terebinths," "the dove of the distant terebinths." On Michtam, see xvi. note [a].

[b] יצפינו. The K'ri is יִצְפּוֹנוּ Kal (the וֹ being only inserted to mark the conjugation as distinct from the Hiphil), but the correction is unnecessary. The Hiphil may be used as in Ex. ii. 3, Job xiv. 13, without a causative signification, and there is no need to supply an object, as if it were = "they hide *nets*," or "they put in ambush *liers-in-wait*." Symm. takes this and the preceding verb יָגוּרוּ together, and the one as modifying the other adverbially, *συνήγοντο λάθρα*, and Jerome, *congregabuntur abscondite.* On the meaning of גור, see Gesen. *Thes.* and comp. lv. 16, where Aq., Symm., and Jerome give the same signification to the noun.

[c] כַּאֲשֶׁר. Not *because* (though such a meaning may be defended by Num. xxvii. 14), nor *when*, nor *as if* (as Ewald takes it, in which case the imperf. or the infin. with כְּ would follow), but simply *as.* They are now lying in wait for me, *as* they have done in times past. Both the grammar—for the verb is in the past tense—and the accentuation, according to which the Athnach stands at the end of the clause with the two imperfects, show that this is the construction, as Hupfeld rightly observes.

[d] פְּלֶט־לָמוֹ. As these words stand, there are two interpretations grammatically possible. Either they are a question, "Is there escape to them (can they escape) because of iniquity?" or they express the opinion of the wicked, "they escape (as they think) because of iniquity." But both interpretations are harsh. Mendels. renders: "Umsonst sei ihr Entrinnen." He takes אָוֶן in its original meaning of "nothingness," and עַל אָוֶן as signifying "for nothing," *i.e.* "in vain," as other adverbial ideas are expressed by the same prep. עַל שֶׁקֶר, "falsely," Lev. v. 22. (See other examples in Ges.. *Thes.* p. 1028.) And so app. the LXX. ὑπὲρ τοῦ μηθενὸς σώσεις αὐτούς. The sense so obtained, "They lie in wait for me, but they themselves shall not (or let them not) escape," is unobjectionable; but there is no proof that אָוֶן can be used in the alleged sense. It is therefore better, with Ew. and Hupf., to read פַּלֵּם, a very trifling alteration, "weigh out to them," *i.e.* "requite them on account of (their) iniquity." Ibn. Ez. "Rescue me from them."

[e] שִׂימָה. This, according to the accentuation, is imperative. Some, however, who think this sudden transition to the form of entreaty in the middle of the verse not easy to be accounted for, would accentuate שִׂימָה as part. pass. fem. of שִׂים, "My tears *are put*," &c. The part. occurs Num. xxiv. 21, 1 Sam. ix. 24, and in the K'thîbh, 2 Sam. xiii. 32. But this is unnecessary. The LXX. seem to have had a different text, τὴν ζωήν μου ἐξήγγειλά σοι, ἔθου τὰ δάκρυά μου ἐνώπιόν σου, ὡς καὶ ἐν τῇ ἐπαγγελίᾳ σου. Symm. renders the first clause τὰ ἔνδον μου ἐξηρίθμησας, and the second like the LXX., except ἔνδον for ἐνώπιον. Jerome has, *Secretiora mea numerasti*, *Pone lacrymam meam in conspectu tuo: sed non in narratione tua.* All seem to have been puzzled.

[f] בְּנֹאדֶךָ. The LXX., Syr., and Jerome render this as if it were בְּנֶגְדֶּךָ. Hupf. and Olsh. would get rid of the next clause הֲלֹא ב' as a gloss, but the question only repeats, in a more emphatic form, the conviction expressed before in the first member of the verse. The word סִפְרָה occurs only here. The older interpreters for the most part, except the Syr., render it not "book" = סֵפֶר, but "numbering," "reckoning," &c., and perhaps "register" would be the best equivalent.

[g] זֶה, used here apparently with a neuter meaning, instead of זאת, as in 1 Kings xvii. 24. In what follows, אֱלֹהִים לִי, the prep. is used as in cxxiv. 1, 2, "for me," *i.e.* on my side.

[h] דָּבָר, instead of דְּבָרוֹ in ver. 4 [5], used here absolutely without either the article or the pron. suffix, probably because its meaning was sufficiently fixed and intelligible, especially as having already occurred in the Psalm. Aq., Symm., and Jerome, who all express the pronoun (αὐτοῦ) in the former instance, omit it here, and have simply ῥῆμα, λόγον, *verbum.* The repetition of the clause with Jehovah is also supported by the united testimony of the ancient Versions, and need not therefore be treated as a gloss.

PSALM 57

THIS Psalm is in many respects like the last, and, like that, was probably written by David.

Both Psalms open with the same cry to God for mercy; both are written in circumstances of no common peril (lvi. 1, 2, 5, 6, lvii. 4, 6); both are full of the same lofty trust in God, and courage in the midst of danger (lvi. 3, 4, 9—11, lvii. 1—3, 7), and of the same joy and thankfulness in the assurance of deliverance (lvi. 12, 13, lvi. 7—9). Both have even the same peculiar and characteristic expression by which the enemy is described as one ready *to swallow up* the Psalmist (lvi. 1, 2 [2, 3], and lvii. 3 [4]), and both have a double refrain at the conclusion of the two principal divisions of the Psalm. But this Psalm is written in a still more triumphant strain of holy confidence than the last, and closes with a shout of exultation,

According to the title, it was written by David "when he fled from Saul, in the cave;" or as the LXX. render it, "*into* the cave." The history tells us of two occasions on which David found refuge in a cave. The one cave was that of Adullam, situate in the face of the cliffs which skirt the low valley of the Philistines, 1 Sam. xxii.; the other was that of En-gedi, one of the numerous caves in the limestone rock, among the "alps" or high pastures of the district on the western bank of the Dead Sea. Hengstenberg thinks the former is meant, because the connection between this and the preceding Psalm is so close, and because, being alike in character and form, and following one another in the Psalter, they may reasonably be referred to the same time. Now Psalm lvi. was written, according to the inscription, in Gath, and therefore this was probably composed immediately afterwards when David hid himself in the cave of Adullam. Tholuck, on the other hand, decides for En-gedi. But this is a question which must be left. There is nothing in the Psalm either for or against the title.

The Psalm consists of two parts, the conclusion of each being marked by the refrain :—

I. The first contains a cry to God for mercy, together with an expression of confidence in Him in the midst of enemies and dangers. Ver. 1—5.

II. The second repeats briefly the story of the Psalmist's persecutions, and then concludes with a triumphant acknowledgement of God's goodness. Ver. 6—9.

[FOR THE PRECENTOR. "DESTROY NOT."[a] A MICHTAM OF DAVID WHEN HE FLED FROM SAUL, IN THE CAVE.]

I. 1 BE gracious unto me, O God, be gracious unto me,
For in Thee hath my soul found refuge ;[b]
And in the shadow of Thy wings will I find refuge,
Until the destruction[c] be overpast.
2 I will call upon God Most High,
Upon the God who conferreth benefits[d] upon me.
3 He shall send from heaven and save me,
—(Though) he that would swallow me up hath reproached,[e] [Selah]—
God shall send His loving-kindness and truth.
4 As for my life—in the midst of lions must I lie,[f]
(Among) those who are ready[g] to devour, (even) the children of men,
Whose teeth are spears and arrows,

Ver. 1—5. The cleaving of the soul to God, and the trust in His power and mercy despite all perils.

1. IN THE SHADOW OF THY WINGS. This exceedingly striking image may have been suggested by Deut. xxxii. 11. See above on Ps. xvii. 8. Still more tender is the N.T. figure, Matt. xxiii. 57. Perhaps there is nothing more remarkable in the Psalms than this ever-recurring expression of a tender personal affection on the part of the sacred Poets to God. There is no parallel to this in the whole range of heathen literature. Monsters to be feared and propitiated were the deities of paganism, but what heathen ever loved his god? The apotheosis of man's lusts could only produce a worship of servility and fear.

The change of tense in the repeated use of the verb gives a force and beauty to the passage which is quite lost sight of when both are rendered as presents (as Ewald does). The Psalmist looks back to the past and forward to the future: In Thee hath my soul found refuge; in Thee I will find refuge.

3. HE SHALL SEND. The verb may be used here absolutely, as in xviii. 16 [17]; or perhaps the object may be "His loving-kindness and truth," the verb being repeated emphatically in the third member of the verse, the construction being somewhat broken by the position of the second member (see Critical Note). For the sentiment, comp. xliii. 3.

HE THAT WOULD SWALLOW ME UP. The same word which occurs in lvi. 1, 2 [2, 3], and one of the links connecting the two Psalms.

And their tongue a sharp sword.
5 Be thou exalted above the heavens, O God,
(And) Thy glory above all the earth.

II. 6 They prepared a net for my steps;
My soul was bowed down.[h]
They digged before me a pit;
They fell into the midst thereof (themselves). [Selah.]
7 My heart is steadfast, O God, my heart is steadfast;
I will sing and make melody.
8 Awake up, my glory; awake harp, and lute;
I will wake the morning-dawn.[i]
9 I will give thanks unto Thee among the peoples, O LORD,
I will play unto Thee among the nations.
10 For great unto the heavens is Thy loving-kindness,
And unto the clouds Thy truth.
11 Be Thou exalted above the heavens, O God,
(And) Thy glory above all the earth.

4. A SHARP SWORD. Cf. lv. 21 [22], lix. 7 [8], lxiv. 3 [4], Prov. xxx. 14.

5. BE THOU EXALTED, i.e. *manifest* Thy glory and Thy majesty in the exercise of Thy universal dominion both in heaven and in earth. For this manifestation David prays; that this will be, he rests assured, and this is his comfort when enemies assail. God's deliverance of those who trust in Him is bound up with His glory; for the wicked strike not only at the righteous, but at God Himself in them. The prayer, therefore, for God's exaltation is at the same time a prayer for his own deliverance, but it is—may we not say?—a less selfish and a nobler prayer.

7. MY HEART IS STEADFAST, *i.e.* in the confidence of faith. The adjective is the same as in li. 10 [12]. So Symm. renders ἑδραία, whereas the LXX. have ἑτοίμη, which has been followed by the E.V. and is no doubt admissible (see xxxviii. 17 [18]).

8. I WILL WAKE THE MORNING-DAWN. The figure is at once bold and beautiful. My song shall itself awake the morning. Hengst. compares Ovid, *Met.* xi. 597: "Non vigil ales ibi cristati cantibus oris Evocat auroram."

11. "Greater words of prayer than these," says Delitzsch most truly, "never came from human lips. Heaven and earth have, as they imply, a mutually interwoven history, and the blessed, glorious end of this is in the sunrise of the Divine glory over both."

The latter part of this Psalm is repeated at the beginning of cviii. where see notes.

[a] אַל תַּשְׁחֵת. The conjectures as to the meaning of these words here are various, and as unsatisfactory as they are various. Perhaps they were

the opening words of some other poem, to the measure and melody of which this was to be sung. (Ew. *Poet. B.* i. 173.) Maurer suggests that the prayer of Moses in Deut. ix. 26 may be meant; and Hengst. thinks this is a watchword of David, based on the same passage, "Destroy not Thy people," &c.

On Michtam, see xvi. note [a].

[b] חֲסָיָה. 3 fem. as if from a form חסי = חסה. See Gesen. § 75, Rem. 4.

[c] הַוּוֹת י׳. A fem. plur. with a verb sing. masc. On this enallage of number, see Gesen. § 147 *a*. Some suppose that the singular verb is used distributively, "until every one of the destructions is overpast," but even then the difficulty of the gender remains. Why is the verb masculine?

[d] גֹּמֵר עָלָי, lit. "who accomplisheth concerning me," *i.e.* who fulfilleth His good pleasure, or what He hath promised, or what I desire, for me. The verb גמר occurs only in the Psalms, and may also be used intransitively as in vii. 10, xii. 2. But it seems almost certain that it stands here for the cognate form גמל (the interchange of *l* and *r* being common enough), which occurs constantly with עַל, xiii. 6, cxvi. 7, 12, cxlii. 8, and in a good sense means "to benefit." So the LXX. here, τὸν εὐεργετήσαντά με, "my Benefactor."

[e] חֵרֵף שֹׁאֲפִי. The older translators make God the subject of the verb: "He hath brought reproach upon, put to shame, him that would devour me," &c. But this is contrary to all usage, according to which men are said to reproach one another and to reproach God, but God is nowhere said to reproach men. It is clear, then, that שֹׁאֲפִי is the subject of the verb חֵרֵף. But is this clause to be connected with the preceding or the following? Some would connect it as a relative clause with the foregoing: God shall . . . . save me, even He whom my persecutor (the man who would swallow me up) hath reproached. It is however, I think, on the whole better, notwithstanding the Selah, to connect this with what follows, taking the preterite חֵרֵף as concessive: He that would swallow me up (see note on lvi. 1) hath reproached (me), i.e. *though* he has, &c. The Selah in the middle of the verse is very unusual. See lv. 19 [20].

[f] אֶשְׁכְּבָה. It seems impossible to explain satisfactorily the use of the paragogic (optative) form of the verb here. It is commonly rendered as a present, as in the E. V. "I lie," but in defiance of grammar. Olsh. and others take "let me lie," here = "I am ready to lie," as an expression of bold resolve based on trust in God: but this does not cohere with the rest of the verse. Hupfeld suggests that the form here may be used to denote *external* compulsion (as the same form expresses an *internal* necessity in verbs of *lamenting*, *exulting*, &c.) = "I *must* lie." Comp. the use of the paragog. form in Is. xxxviii. 10, Jer. iii. 25, iv. 21, vi. 10. He would, however, read שָׁכְבָה to agree with the nom. נַפְשִׁי. On the other hand, for the same constr. of נַפְשִׁי prefixed to the verb in the first pers., comp. Is. xxvi. 9.

[g] לֹהֲטִים, not as the Chald. and Rabb. "set on fire," "flaming," &c. (a meaning which they seem to have derived from the constant use of the

root with words denoting fire, flame, &c.), but "devouring," "consuming." Aq. ἐν μέσῳ λεαινῶν κοιμηθήσομαι λάβρων. Theod. μετὰ ἀναλισκόντων. Symm. has ἐν μέσῳ λεόντων εὐθαρσῶν ἐκοιμήθην μεταξὺ φλεγόντων, where εὐθαρσῶν may have been intended, as Mr. Bensly suggests (adopted by Field) to bring out the force of the form אֶשְׁכְּבָה. See note [f]. Jerome, "In medio leonum *dormivit* ferocientium." [He would seem, therefore, to have forestalled Hupfeld's emendation; see note [f].] So civ. 4, אֵשׁ לֹהֵט, "a devouring fire," and in the verb in the Piel, lxxxiii. 15, cvi. 18, Is. xlii. 25, Joel i. 19, ii. 3. Properly the root means, like other similar roots (comp. לוע), "to lick," and then "to devour," "to swallow," &c. As regards the construction, this cannot agree with לְבָאִים, as Aq., and Jerome, which is forbidden by the position of the verb between the noun and the participle, but either לֹהֲטִים must be governed by the prep. בְּתוֹךְ, "in the midst of them that devour, (even) the sons of men;" as Symm., Theodor. (see above); or it must be the predicate to ב׳ א׳, "the sons of men devour." This last, though against the accents, is perhaps the simplest construction.

[h] כָּפַף. The word occurs everywhere else in a transitive meaning. Hence Böttcher would explain: It (viz. the crafty design of my foes) hath bowed down my soul. Others make the enemy himself (sing. for plur.) the subject: "He hath," &c. But it is better perhaps to assume an indefinite subject: "One hath bowed down my soul" = "My soul is bowed down."

[i] שָׁחַר. The words may be rendered as in E. V. "I will wake early" (lit. "at the dawn"); for the verb, though Hiphil, is used intransitively, as in lxxiii. 20 (in fact this is the normal use of this verb); and although שַׁחַר is never used elsewhere to denote a part of time, yet it may perhaps follow the analogy of words like בֹּקֶר, לַיְלָה, &c. See on cxxvii. note [d].

PSALM 58

THIS Psalm is a bold protest against unrighteous judges. It opens with an indignant expostulation on their deliberate perversion of justice, whilst they pretend to uphold it. It lays bare their character and that of those whom they favour, as men thoroughly, habitually, by their very nature, currupt. And finally, because they are thus beyond all hope of correction or amendment, it calls upon God to rob them of their power and to bring all their counsels to nought.

The Psalm abounds in bold and striking images, and is remarkable for a nervous force of expression. The title ascribes it to David, but without assigning it to any particular occasion in his life. Various guesses have been made as to the time of its composition, but the Psalm furnishes us with no data for any certain or even probable conclusion.

It consists of three principal divisions :—

I. The forcible picture of unrighteousness in the seat of judgement. Ver. 1—5.

II. The swift punishment which is about to overtake these unjust judges, and for which the Psalmist prays. Ver. 6—9.

III. Lastly, the joy of those who shall behold their overthrow, and who shall acknowledge that, however the name of justice may have been profaned by human judges who abuse their office, there is, nevertheless, a righteous Judge in the earth. Ver. 10, 11.

[FOR THE PRECENTOR. "DESTROY NOT."[a] A MICHTAM OF DAVID.]

I. 1 Do ye of a truth in silence[b] speak righteousness?
Do ye with uprightness judge the children of men?
2 Nay, rather, in heart ye work iniquities;
In the earth ye weigh out the violence of your hands.
3 The wicked are estranged[c] from the womb,
They go astray from their birth, speaking lies.

1. IN SILENCE. They are *dumb* when they ought to speak, as afterwards they are said to be *deaf* when they ought to hear.

The second member of the verse may be rendered, "Do ye judge uprightly, O ye children of men?" See more in Critical Note.

2. IN THE EARTH, *i.e.* openly, in your public administration; opposed to the "in heart," before.

YE WEIGH OUT; said sarcastically. Ye pretend indeed to hold the balance of justice, and nicely to weigh out to each his just award, but violence is the weight with which ye adjust the scales. Aq. διασταθμίζετε.

3. Those to whom the indignant question has been put cannot answer, being condemned by their own consciences, and therefore the Poet goes on at once, abandoning the form of address, to give a further description of their character in the third person. Or possibly the description may apply, not to the unrighteous judges, but to the evil-doers whom they countenance and support. (So Hupfeld.)

FROM THEIR BIRTH, lit. "from the belly." See on li. 5 [7]. The

4 Their poison is like the poison of a serpent:
(They are) like a deaf adder which stoppeth her ear,
5 Which hearkeneth not to the voice of enchanters,
(To) the charmer, charming never so wisely.

II. 6 O God, break their teeth in their mouths,
The jaw-teeth of the young lions wrench out, O Jehovah.
7 Let them melt,[d] as water that runneth apace;
(When) they shoot their arrows,[e] let them be as though cut off.[f]

object, however, here, is clearly not to insist upon the general truth of an innate depravity, but rather to mark the special character of these wicked men as men whose *whole life* has been one continuous unchecked career of wickedness—bold, habitual, hardened transgressors, whose maturity in vice is what might be expected from their early depravity.

4, 5. Their wickedness is desperate, for they are like the adder, which the subtlest charmer cannot tame. The ADDER is mentioned as peculiarly dangerous. (Comp. xci. 13, Job xx. 14, 16, Deut. xxxii. 33, Is xi. 8.) The serpent-charmers, a class of men so well known in the East, are spoken of also Jer. viii. 17, Eccles. x. 11. For instances of the exercise of this art, which is still in vogue, see Lane's *Modern Egyptians*, vol. ii. chap. 20; Hengst. *Egypt and the Books of Moses*, p. 99 (Transl.), and especially the very full account, with references to authorities, both ancient and modern, given by Knobel, on Exod. vii. 11, pp. 60, 61.

5. OF ENCHANTERS, properly "whisperers." Symm. *ψιθυριζόντων*; the allusion is probably to the hissing sound by which the enchanters endeavoured to draw out the serpents from their retreats.

A CHARMER, &c. lit. "one charming (with) charms," &c. (Deut. xviii. 11). Symm. *ἐπαστοῦ τε ἐπῳδαῖς σεσοφισμένου*. Aq. *ἐπαειδεῖν ἐπαοιδὴν σεσοφισμένου*.

NEVER SO WISELY, lit. ("though) he be made wise, *i.e.* well versed in his art." (Comp. Is. iii. 3.) For a like use of the participle, comp. xxxix. 5 [6]. "At his best estate," lit. "though standing never so fast."

6. There is an abrupt change in the image employed. As these men are incorrigible in their wickedness, as they cannot be tamed, the Psalmist prays God to destroy their power for mischief; but instead of continuing the figure of the serpent-charmer, who robs the serpent of his poison, he suddenly represents them as young lions, whose teeth he would see broken that they may no longer devour. (Comp. iii. 7 [8], Job iv. 10.)

7. Then in a series of bold figures he draws further the picture of the destruction which he would fain see come upon them.

The first is taken from water running away, and so wasted and lost (comp. 2 Sam. xiv. 14): the next from arrows shot, but with their points broken off and blunted, so that they fail to inflict a wound.

(WHEN) THEY SHOOT, lit. "(When) he shooteth," the verb being in the singular. Either the singular is here used distributively = "when any one of them (the wicked) shooteth;" or, perhaps more

8 (Let them be) as a snail,[g] (which) melteth away[h] (as) it goeth,
(Like) the untimely birth of a woman, (as those who) have not beheld[i] the sun.
9 Before your pots[k] can feel (the fire of) thorns,
Both green and burning, they shall be whirled away.

III. 10 The righteous shall rejoice that he hath beheld (the) vengeance,
He shall wash his footsteps in the blood of the wicked;
11 So that men shall say, Surely there is a reward for the righteous,
Surely there is a God that judgeth in the earth.

generally, "when one shooteth," is merely the impersonal put, according to the Hebrew idiom, for the passive="When their arrows are shot." Hitz. "Let him shoot his arrows, when they are blunted." Others, because the verb is in the singular, render as if God were the subject. "When He, *i.e.* God, shoots His arrows (at them), immediately they shall be cut down." But this is unnecessary. See more in Critical Note.

8. (WHICH) MELTETH AWAY (AS) IT GOETH, lit. "which goeth in melting" (or slime), the noun being in the accus. as describing the nature of the action, and the allusion being to the slimy trail which the snail leaves behind it, so that *it seems* to waste away. Evidently this is nothing more than a poetical hyperbole, and need not be explained therefore as a popular error or a mistake in natural history.

HAVE NOT BEHELD THE SUN. Comp. Job iii. 16.

9. The general sense of this difficult verse seems to be this: As a sudden whirlwind in the desert sweeps away the thorns which have been gathered for cooking, almost as soon as they have been set on fire, and before the caldron has grown hot (comp. Eccles. vii. 6), so shall the wicked, and all their yet incomplete designs, be swept away by the wrath of God. For the explanation of the separate words, see Critical Note.

10. On the satisfaction here expressed in the prospect of vengeance on the ungodly, see on lii. 6 [8]. Comp. lxviii. 23 [24], Deut. xxxii. 42, 43. This terrible vengeance was such as was not uncommonly practised in the wars of those times.

11. A REWARD, lit. "fruit." Comp. Is. iii. 10, Prov. i. 31.

THERE IS A GOD, or, perhaps, "there is a Deity," the word Elohim being here construed with a plural participle (Ges. § 112, Rem. 3), and therefore not used so much in the personal sense, as in contrast to those false judges who call themselves "gods," but are not. This verse refers evidently to ver. 1, 2, whether we adopt the reading "O ye gods" there, or not. Ewald translates here: "Gibt es doch Götter richtend auf der Erde;" Delitzsch: "Ja es gibt eine Gottheit richtend," &c.; and Bunsen: "Es gibt doch eine göttliche Gerechtigkeit auf Erden."

[a] See lvii. note [a].

[b] אֵלֶם. The word, according to its present punctuation, means "dumbness," "silence," as in the title to lvi., the only other place where it occurs, א׳ י׳, "the dumb, or silent dove." If we adhere to this reading, the construction will be that of the accusative used adverbially; "in silence," "silently," *i.e.* if ye keep silence (as the Chald. takes it), &c. Gesen. and others would render, "Do ye indeed decree dumb justice?" *i.e.* do ye really at length decree justice, which has so long seemed dumb? But א׳ צ׳, "dumbness of righteousness," cannot mean "dumb righteousness." This would be expressed by צ׳ א׳, "righteousness of dumbness." Rashi takes אֵלֶם as the predicate, "Is the righteousness which ye should speak really dumb (in your mouth)?" Others, very harshly, would make two clauses: "Are ye really dumb? Do ye speak?" &c. Qimchi would give to אֵלֶם the meaning of "band" (from אלם, *to bind*), and has been followed by Calvin and others, and the E. V. "O congregation." Mendels., J. D. Mich., Ewald, and others, would change the punctuation and read אֵלִם, defective for אֵלִים (as in Ex. xv. 11), "O ye gods," a term applied to the judges who are here addressed, a meaning which is defended by Ex. xxi. 6, xxii. 7, 8, Ps. lxxxii. (See note on ver. 1 of that Psalm.) Neither the LXX. nor the Syr. expresses the word at all, and it may possibly have arisen from the preceding אֻמְנָם. The question with אֻמְנָם expects a negative answer, *num vere?* as in Num. xxii. 37, 1 Kings viii. 27. Hence the answer with אַף = *imo vero*, or as Calvin, *quin potius*.

[c] זֹרוּ instead of זָרוּ, as בֹּאוּ, Jer. xxvii. 18 (Ges. § 72, Rem. 1).

[d] יִמָּאֲסוּ, as from a form מאס, instead of מסס, as also in Job vii. 5, instead of יִמַּסּוּ. The following לָמוֹ is used with a reflexive shade of meaning (as in the Latin, *suo* sibi *gladio*), which cannot be conveyed in English.

[e] יִדְרֹךְ חִצָּו. The verb, which is properly used of the *bending of the bow*, is here applied *to the shooting of the arrow*. For the K'thîbh, חצו, the Q'ri has חִצָּיו, on which Hupf. strangely observes, that if God be the subject of the preceding verb, it must be read חִצּוֹ. But why may it not be said that God shoots His arrows as well as His arrow? The instances of this defective writing in the case of plur. nouns with the suffix are very numerous, especially in the Historical Books.

[f] כְּמוֹ. The particle has been strangely misinterpreted. The LXX. *ἕως οὗ ἀσθενήσουσιν*. Jerome, "donec conterantur." Syr. "*until* they be consumed." Delitzsch would here take כְּמוֹ (which in Gen. xix. 15 means "so soon as") as meaning "immediately," and refers to Is. xxvi. 18, where, however, it may be rendered "as though," which is its signification here. יִתְמֹלָלוּ, either Hithpal. from מול (so Gesen.) or Hithpo. from מלל.

[g] שַׁבְּלוּל (with *Dag. dirimens* for שַׁבְלוּל) is properly "the slug." So Qimchi, following the Chald. Aq. has *ὁμοίως γῆς ἐντέρῳ*, "like a worm," and so Jerome, *quasi vermis*. LXX. and Theod. render it by *κηρός*, "wax" (and so the Syr.), and they are followed by Ewald. Rashi says that the word has been taken by some in the sense of "slug."

[h] תֶּמֶס, here a noun, and not (as in xxxix. 10 [11]) fut. apoc. Hiph. of מסה (as Del., "as a slug which thou squashest"). On the constr. see Ges. § 138, Rem. 1.

[i] חָזוּ, the plur. verb, while the preceding נֵפֶל is singular. Possibly the noun may here be used as a collective or noun of multitude = "those untimely born." Otherwise this clause must be elliptical, and the particle of comparison be repeated here as well as before נ׳ א׳. The latter is, I think, preferable, and so Del. and Bunsen. אֵשֶׁת, which is probably stat. constr., stands here as in Deut. xxi. 11, 1 Sam. xxviii. 7, as absol.

[k] This verse has been very differently rendered. A careful criticism of the words may help us to decide as to its meaning.

(1) סִירֹתֵיכֶם. The word סִיר may mean either *a thorn*, or *a pot*, or *vessel for cooking*. A distinction, however, is observed in the plur. of this word, the masc. being always used of *thorns*, and the fem. of *pots* (except in Amos iv. 2, where it is used of *fish-hooks*, perhaps as resembling thorns).

(2) יָבִינוּ, "perceive, are sensible of, *i.e.* feel the effect of," is used here like other verbs, which properly imply a *living* agent, of things without life. Comp. Judges xvi. 9; Jer. xvii. 8; Job vi. 30, xiv. 9, xxx. 1.

(3) אָטָד, the *rhamnus* or *blackthorn*, here apparently put for a fire composed of such thorns.

(4) חַי, "living." In 1 Sam. ii. 15, the adj. is used of *raw, uncooked* meat, and some would so understand it here of the meat in the cooking vessel; but as this has not been mentioned, it seems better to refer it to אָטָד, in the sense of *fresh, green*, the thorn which has not yet been parched by the fire, the opposite to which is.

(5) חָרוֹן (prop. *a burning*, or *brand*), here used of the *burning* thorn; that which has already caught the fire, or, as others, *dry*. Symm. ὀλόξηρον. Those who interpret חַי of the *raw* flesh, explain this of the *cooked* meat. חָרוֹן, however, is not here used as an adj., but like other words in וֹן־, as an accus. expressing state, condition, &c. "*in burning*." Others, again, render it *wrath*.

(6) כְּמוֹ . . . כְּמוֹ, the two particles evidently answer to one other, = *sive* . . . . *sive*, or, *as well* . . . . *as*. Elsewhere it is only repeated with suffixes, and, in formulæ like the present, the double כְּ is used instead. Hence some have taken the first כְּמוֹ as a particle of time, and חַי as a verb: "whilst it (the thorn) is still living, before it has been cut down, that is, and used for the fire, (it shall be) as if wrath (חָרוֹן) swept it away like a whirlwind."

On the impers. יִשְׂעָרֶנּוּ, "one shall whirl it (*i.e.* the thorns, אָטָד) away," for the passive, "they shall be whirled away," comp. note on ver. 7.

The older Verss. for the most part take סִירֹת in the sense of *thorns*, and do not take the כְּמוֹ . . . . כְּמוֹ as correlative (except the Vulg.). The LXX. πρὸ τοῦ συνιέναι τὰς ἀκάνθας ὑμῶν τὴν ῥάμνον ὡσεὶ ζῶντας ὡσεὶ ἐν ὀργῇ καταπίεται ὑμᾶς. Symm. πρὶν ἢ αὐξηθῶσιν αἱ ἄκανθαι ὑμῶν ὥστε γενέσθαι ῥάμνος, ἔτι ζῶντα ὡς ὀλόξηρον λαῖλαψ ἀρεῖ. Jerome, "Antequam crescant spinæ vestræ in rhamnum, quasi viventes, quasi in ira tempestas rapiet eos."

PSALM 59

THIS Psalm, which in tone, colouring, and expression, has much in common with the four preceding Psalms, is said in the title to have been composed by David when Saul's emissaries watched him in his own house. The history is given in 1 Sam. xix. 11—18. Saul commanded the men whom he sent to surround the house, and to kill David if he attempted to leave it. They were baffled by Michal's artifice; but from that hour Saul's hatred of him never slumbered, and he never ceased to persecute him and to hunt him down like a wild beast. It is quite consistent with David's character that he should commemorate in his songs such a crisis in his life. But the internal evidence lends little confirmation to the accuracy of the title. The allusions in verses 6 and 14 are obviously not applicable to Saul's emissaries; they could not possibly be described as making their rounds every evening, as a patrol, through the city, uttering oaths and curses, howling like dogs, and wandering about seeking for food; and it is not easy to see why they should be spoken of as sinning through every word of their lips, or how their destruction could be an evidence that God ruled in Jacob and unto the end of the earth. The third verse seems to have suggested the reference of the Inscription; but there is no other support for it in the Psalm, and all that seems certain is, that the Psalm was called forth by some attack upon the life of its author.

From the internal evidence, it is extremely difficult to construct any plausible hypothesis as to the time and circumstances of the writer. He is an innocent man (ver. 3) exposed to the machinations of enemies, who are described, it is true, as bloodthirsty men, but who seem to have employed stratagem rather than violence to effect their purpose, and who in particular used their tongues as their principal weapon; "swords are in their lips" (ver. 7): their mouth is full of cursing and lying: they sin in every word they utter (ver. 12); such is the picture drawn of them. These enemies, moreover, are *in the city;* they go about it (ver. 6, 14; comp. lv. 10 [11]); they patrol it at night; they howl like unclean dogs seeking their garbage; their curse is to wander about for bread. And finally, they are men whose overthrow will make the name of the God of Jacob famed throughout the world. Who can these enemies be? The allusions to "the nations," in verses 5, 8, would seem to imply that they are foreign oppressors. On the other hand, it seems strange in that case that they should be described as exercising their power by means of falsehood and reckless and malicious charges rather than by the strong hand of the conqueror. It may be possible (see note on verses 5, 8) to explain these allusions otherwise. But unless we accept some such explanation as is there suggested, the only period to which the Psalm seems at all applicable is that which followed Nehemiah's return to Jerusalem; the only enemies who could answer the double condition of being foreigners and bloodthirsty men, and yet seeking to do mischief by their tongues, would be men like Sanballat the Horonite, and Tobiah the Ammonite, and Geshem the Arabian. Comp. with the Psalm Neh. ii. 10, 19; iv. 1—20.

Reuss escapes partly from the embarrassment occasioned by the peculiar features of the Psalm which I have enumerated, by regarding it as the expression not of individual, but of national circumstances. It is the nation which asserts its innocence (as in Ps. xliv.). "The Psalmist calls God *our* shield, the God of *Israel*, the King of *Jacob*; it is therefore in the name of a believing people that he speaks, it is their sentiments that he wishes to express." Reuss fixes no date for the Psalm beyond saying that it is a late Psalm, as one evidence of which he cites the name *Sabaoth* as a name of God (ver. 5, which he renders, "Jahaweh God, Sabaoth," referring to Rom. ix. 29, James v. 4). On this peculiar form of the Divine Name, see note on ver. 5. It only occurs again in Psalms lxxx., lxxxiv.

De Wette thinks it is a lamentation of the people in the time of the Exile; Hitzig, that it was written by Hezekiah when shut up in Jerusalem by the Assyrians; Ewald, that it is the work of one of the last kings of Judah when besieged by a multitude of heathen enemies in league with the Chaldæans. But it is certain the Psalm does not describe a state of siege.

The structure of the Psalm is highly artificial. It has a double refrain. Ver. 6 [7] answers to ver. 14 [15], each opening a strophe or stanza; ver. 9 [10] to ver. 17 [18], each concluding a strophe in like manner. Besides this, separate words and phrases correspond: the "And *Thou*" (emphatic), ver. 5 [6], 8 [9], with "and *I*," ver. 16 [17]; "all nations," 5 [6], 8 [9], with "the ends of the earth," ver. 13 [14]; "they wander about," ver. 11 [12], and 15 [16].

The Psalm consists of two principal divisions, ver. 1—9 and ver. 10—17. Each of these again falls into two lesser strophes; the first, in each case, closing with Selah, and the last, in each case, opening with a similar verse, and closing with the refrain.

I. (1) A cry to God for help against enemies; a description of their persevering malice; an assertion of the Psalmist's own innocence, and the confiding of his cause to God as the Judge. Ver. 1—5.

(2) A further account of the machinations of the wicked: the confident assurance of their discomfiture, and an expression of trust in God. Ver. 6—9.

II. (1) This part opens with a renewed expression of trust in God, especially with reference to the issue of the struggle with his enemies; repeats the story of their malice, and also the prayer for their punishment, in such wise that God may be acknowledged as the Judge of the earth. Ver. 10—13.

(2) It closes with the curse upon the wicked, and with joyful acknowledgement of God's goodness to the Psalmist. Ver. 14—17.

[FOR THE PRECENTOR. "DESTROY NOT." A MICHTAM [a] OF DAVID WHEN SAUL SENT, AND THEY WATCHED THE HOUSE TO PUT HIM TO DEATH.]

I. (1) 1 DELIVER me from mine enemies, O my God!
Set me on high from them that rise up against me.
2 Deliver me from the workers of iniquity,
And save me from blood-thirsty men.
3 For lo, they have woven plots for my soul,
They gather themselves together against me in their strength,
Not for [b] my transgression, and not for any sin of mine, O Jehovah!
4 Without guilt (of mine) do they run and set themselves;

3. THEY HAVE WOVEN. The *perfect* as describing the past plotting and deliberation, whilst the present result is expressed by the verb in the *present* tense, "They gather," &c.

IN THEIR STRENGTH, lit. "strong," but the adj. is here not, I think, a fresh subject, "strong (or violent) ones gather," &c. as it is usually rendered, but rather a predicate, the subject having been already expressed in ver. 2.

NOT FOR MY TRANSGRESSION, &c., lit. "Without my transgression and without my sin."

4. RUN AND SET THEMSELVES. The words are military terms: for the first, see xviii. 29 [30] (according to one interpretation), Job xv. 26, xvi. 14; the other denotes the marshalling in order, the array of

Awake, then, to meet me, and see!
5 Yea, do THOU, O Jehovah, God (of) hosts,[c] God of Israel,
Rouse Thyself to visit all the nations!
Spare not any of them that are faithless in (their) iniquity. [Selah.]

(2) 6 They return at evening, they howl like a dog,
And make their round about (the) city.

troops, with a view to the execution of a determined plan. Or as Hengstenberg explains, a metaphor borrowed from an attacking host, which, getting a firm footing on the walls of a beleaguered city, is ready to rush in over them, or through them as already broken, into the city.

TO MEET ME, *i.e.* to help me: comp. ver. 10 [11], and see vii. 6 [7]. The phrase is elsewhere used in the opposite sense, xxxv. 2 [3].

5. THOU. The pronoun is emphatic, the heart turning to God as the sure defence against its fierce and cruel enemies.

JEHOVAH GOD or "Jehovah Elohim" (cf. lxxii. 18), the name of God, which is characteristic of the section, Gen. ii. 4—iii. 23. Joined, as here, with Sabaoth (hosts), it occurs besides lxxx. 4 [5], 19 [20], lxxxiv. [8, 9]. In calling Jehovah *the God of Hosts*, the Psalmist sets forth, as Calvin observes, His boundless power; in adding *the God of Israel*, the peculiar regard which He has for His own children and the Church. (See more in Critical Note.)

ALL THE NATIONS, *i.e.* heathen nations, but it is difficult to determine why they are particularly mentioned here. Some suppose that the Psalmist was living among heathens (see Introduction to the Psalm); others, that the term "nations" is here improperly applied to those Israelites who, in their godlessness, were no better than heathen. But the expression, "*all* nations," is against the first view, and the second is wholly unsupported by usage. It is more probable that the language is intended to denote that God is the *universal* Judge. "The nations," to an Israelite, would be the embodiment of all that opposed itself to God; and in appealing to God to punish them, he would, in fact, be appealing to Him to punish all evil wherever manifested. The special judgement would follow from the universal, and be an instance of it. Even for the vindication of his personal innocence, we find one Psalmist (vii. 6—8 [7—9]) calling upon God to assemble all nations to His judgement-seat.

Such expressions seem to us exaggerated, partly because of the comparative coldness of the Western mind, and partly because it is very difficult for us to conceive of the feelings of a true Israelite, to whom the whole outer heathen world was a world lying under the heavy wrath of God, and to whom the greater part even of Israel itself seemed corrupt and apostate. An intensity both of privilege and also of suffering thus attached to the "small remnant," which it is necessary to remember if we would understand the strong language of Psalmists and Prophets.

FAITHLESS IN (THEIR) INIQUITY, or iniquitous traitors. Ewald renders: *alle sündliche Räuber*, "all sinful *robbers*," taking the other meaning of the participle. See xxv. note.[b]

6. He compares his enemies to the gaunt, hungry, half-starved, half-wild dogs which, to this day,

7 Lo, they belch out with their mouth,
Swords are in their lips ;
For who (they think) doth hear ?
8 But THOU, O Jehovah, dost laugh at them,
Thou mockest at all (the) nations.
9 O my strength,[d] on Thee will I wait,
For God is my high tower.

II. (1) 10 My God with His loving-kindness [e] shall come to meet me,

in the East, prowl in troops about the cities and villages, without a master, looking for the offal and carrion which are their food, wherever they can find it. Comp. xxii. 16 [17] ; 1 Kings xiv. 11 ; 2 Kings ix. 36.

AT EVENING, *i.e.* every evening, the evening being the time when these animals usually assemble : or denoting, as Calvin thinks, their insatiable cruelty, "for he says that they return at evening, not because they rest at other times, but because they are never tired in their wickedness. If all day long they get nothing, the evening will find them still running about the city." Comp. lv. 10 [11], Cant. iii. 2.

7. THEY BELCH OUT. Such seems here to be the force of the word as given by the E. V. Properly it means "to gush out," as water ; see the same word in xix. 2 [3], "Day unto day *poureth forth* speech." Comp. xciv. 4, Prov. xv. 2, 28. Symm. ἀποβλύζουσι.

8. BUT THOU. These men with their murderous thoughts, whose very words are swords (comp. lii. 2 [4], lv. 21 [22], lvii. 4 [5]), and who feel so secure in their bloodthirsty designs that they think God hearkens not, and will not punish, shall learn their mistake. *Thou*, O God, *Thou* whom they forget, wilt laugh them to scorn, as Thou dost all throughout the world who oppose Thee. Hence he says,

ALL NATIONS, taking the widest view, and therefore including those who are here the prominent enemies. See above on ver. 5 : or, as Calvin explains, though they should in numbers equal the whole world, yet they and their power would all be mocked. Comp. ii. 4, xxxvii. 13.

9. O MY STRENGTH. The Massoretic reading, "*his* strength," gives no satisfactory sense, though various attempts have been made to defend it. See Critical Note.

"David here ascends the watch-tower of faith, whence he can look down calmly on the violent assaults of his foes, fully assured that they can do nothing but by the permission of God."—*Calvin.*

10. MY GOD, &c. According to the Massoretic correction the reading would be, "The God of my loving-kindness, *i.e.* my gracious, merciful God, shall come to meet me." This is a favourite passage with Augustine in his arguments against the Pelagians. He often alleges it in proof of the doctrine that the grace of God precedes all merit of man. And here he observes : "Quid in me invenisti nisi sola peccata? . . . Antequam aliquid boni ego faciam, *misericordia ejus præveniet me.* Quid hic respondebit infelix Pelagius?" But, as Calvin very justly remarks, this may be a pious, but it is not a fair use of the passage (pie quidem, sed nimis argute).

SHALL COME TO MEET ME, as in xxi. 3 [4].

The prayer that follows is a very fearful one. The Psalmist would

God shall make me see (my desire) upon them
that lie in wait for me.
11 Slay them not, lest my people forget (it),
Make them reel by Thy power, and cast them
down,
O Lord, our shield!
12 Their mouth sinneth through every word of their
lips,
And so[f] let them be taken in their pride;
And because of (their) cursing and of lying
which they speak.
13 Consume (them) in wrath, consume (them), that they
be no more,
That men may know that God ruleth in Jacob
Unto the ends of the earth. [Selah.]

not have his enemies crushed in a moment by the heavy hand of God, but he would see them come to a lingering end; he would have God take them, as it were, in their own infatuation; he would see them reel and stagger in the intoxication of their own pride, and under the strong buffeting of God's hand, a spectacle and a warning to all, before they are finally cast down; he would watch their course as they are carried, blind with passion, to the summit, thence to be hurled headlong over the precipice. Comp. with this curse, 2 Sam. iii. 29, and 1 Sam. ii. 36.

11. MAKE THEM REEL, lit. "make them wander," which many take literally and not metaphorically. So Hengst. who compares the curse on Cain, Gen. iv. 12, and Numb. xxxii. 13, Ps. cix. 10.

OUR SHIELD, as in iii. 3 [4], xviii. 2 [3]. xxviii. 7.

12. THEIR MOUTH SINNETH, &c. lit. "The word of their lips is the sin of their mouth," *i.e.* every word of their mouth is sin. But the addition, "of their lips," seems weak and unnecessary, so that perhaps Ewald's rendering is better:

"The sin of their mouth, the word
of their lips—
Oh let them be taken in their
pride," &c.

(See Critical Note.)

13. CONSUME THEM. This does not contradict the previous imprecation. He would have his enemies destroyed at last, but only *after* they had been, by a protracted miserable existence, a warning to men of God's righteous severity.

GOD, and not Saul (if the allusion be to him), or any other whatsoever.

UNTO THE ENDS OF THE EARTH. This may mean that God, sitting in Jacob, having there His throne, exercises thence a universal dominion. But, according to the accent, these words should rather be connected with the words "that men may know." So Calvin: "David indicates a singular kind of punishment, one the fame of which would reach even the most distant nations." And so Hengst., who refers to David's words to Goliath, 1 Sam. xvii. 46, "And all the earth shall know that there is a God in Israel."

(2) 14 And they shall return at evening, they shall howl like a dog,
And make their round about (the) city;
15 As for them, they shall wander about for food,
Without being satisfied must they pass the night.[g]
16 But as for me, I will sing of Thy strength,
Yea I will shout aloud, in the morning, of Thy loving-kindness.
17 For Thou hast been a high tower for me,
And a refuge in the day when I was in distress.
18 O my strength, unto Thee let me sing,
For God is my high tower, the God of my loving-kindness.

14. This verse repeats what was said in ver. 6, but the language of ver. 15 shows plainly that a different turn is given here to the expression. There, the conduct of his enemies is described; here, their punishment. They came about him like dogs; like dogs shall they be treated. Their sin becomes its own curse. They come with their mouth wide open, ready to devour, but they shall find nothing to satisfy their hunger; they shall remain lean, hungry, savage, as they came. So Calvin: "There is an allusion to what he had before said concerning their ravenous hunger. For he does not now repeat the words in the same sense in which he had employed them before, but ironically says that they shall be hungry in another way. Before, he complained that they barked like dogs, because they were urged by an insatiable desire to do mischief; but now he mocks at their wicked attempts, and says that, after they have wearied themselves all day long, they shall fail of their object." This seems to be the meaning here, though some interpreters think there is no variation in the sense of the two verses 6 and 14, and either understand both as describing the present conduct of David's enemies (as Delitzsch), "they return," &c., or both as optative, said with a kind of defiance, "let them return," &c.

15. THEY SHALL WANDER ABOUT: the same verb as in ver. 11, so that perhaps the same rendering should be preserved in both places: either there, "make them wander," or here, "they shall reel." The Massoretic change of punctuation here is made for the sake of uniformity, to have the Hiph. in both verses, but obviously a neuter, not an active, meaning is required here. The Qal should therefore be retained.

16. IN THE MORNING, here apparently = "every fresh morning," parallel to "in the evening," ver. 6, 14.

17. The refrain occurs as at the end of the second strophe, ver. 9, but with slight variations, which have already been noticed there.

[a] See above on lvii. note [a].

[b] לֹא stands here for בְּלֹא, Ew. § 286 *g.* in the same sense as בְּלִי ע׳, which follows. In the next verse יְרִיצוּן is the energetic future, as expressing the

readiness and willingness of the action, and יְכּוֹנָנוּ the Hithp. with Dagesh supplying the place of the characteristic ת. For similar forms see Prov. xxvi. 26, Lev. xiii. 55, and Deut. xxi. 8 (Nithp.).

[c] י׳ א׳ צְבָאוֹת. The juxtaposition is peculiar; it occurs again lxxx. 5, 20, lxxxiv. 9. We should expect the constr. אֱלֹהֵי instead of the absol., but it seems to be formed upon the analogy of יהוה צ׳, the name יהוה אלהים being considered as one word. There is, however, still no doubt an ellipse as in י׳ צ׳, and the full expression would be, as Ibn Ezra (on lxxx. 5) remarks, י׳ א׳ אֱלֹהֵי צ׳.

[d] עֻזּוֹ. By the suff. of the 3rd pers. some suppose Saul to be meant. Hengst. "the ideal person of the wicked,"—either a nom. abs. "as to his strength," or "because of his strength, let me," &c., or as an accus., "his strength will I keep for Thee," *i.e.* however he may boast of his strength, I will remain quiet and leave it to Thee; or as Hengst., "Conscious of my own weakness, I will put his strength into Thy hands that Thou mayest deal with it." But these and other renderings only show how hopeless the reading is. We must therefore read עֻזִּי here as in ver. 17 [18], a reading which is supported by some MSS. of Kenn. and De-R., the LXX., and Jerome; but there is no need to change the verb אֶשְׁמֹרָה, as variations in the refrain are common enough. שׁמר here with אֶל seems to be used in nearly the same sense as in xxxi. 6 [7] (where see note [a]), "regard, honour, wait upon," &c. with the accus. Hupf. defends its use by 1 Sam. xxvi. 15, 16, where it is true the prep. follows, but the verb has a different meaning, "to keep watch over."

[e] The K'thîbh חסדו seems to require the reading אֱלֹהֵי חַסְדּוֹ, which yields a very satisfactory sense (as in text); and there is no reason, consequently, for the Q'ri א׳ חַסְדִּי, "God of *my* loving-kindness," *i.e.* my gracious God, which was probably adopted here from ver. 18, and has the oldest Versions against it. The LXX. *ὁ Θεός μου τὸ ἔλεος αὐτοῦ προφθάσει με*. And the Syr. "O God, Thy goodness shall prevent me."

[f] וְיִלָּכְדוּ. This may either be an opt. "and so let them," &c., or may carry on the description "and they are taken." According to Ewald's rendering (see note on the verse) the וְ stands emphatically before the verb, as in xxv. 11. In the next clause, מִן cannot mean *of, concerning*, but *because of, on account of*. Why Hupf. should object to this, as making מִן equivalent in meaning to בְּ, I cannot understand. Surely to say "let them be taken *in* their pride and *because of* their lies" is not to reduce the two prepositions to the same meaning. His own rendering, "out of cursing and out of lies do they speak" (as the source or motive of their discourse), has nothing to recommend it. The relat. is understood before יְסַפֵּרוּ, which has here the general sense of *speaking*, as in lxiv. 6, lxix. 27, &c.

[g] אִם לֹא י׳ ו׳. "If they are not satisfied, so must they pass the night," the opposite to the promise given to the righteous, Prov. xix. 23. Instead of the imperf. (fut.) we should expect here, as Hupf. remarks, either the

perf. or the participle, "not satisfied," as in Prov. xix. 23; but this last seems here to be resolved by אם with the imperf. (fut.) in the sense of *though*—"though they are not, or, without being satisfied;" or the fut. may be the fut. perf., as Calvin: "quamvis non fuerint saturati, cogentur tamen ire cubitum." The ו in וַיָּלִינוּ introduces the apodosis. Ew. takes אם לא in the sense of *assuredly, verily,* and renders:

> They will reel to their food,
> Verily they shall satisfy themselves—and remain,

i.e. lie dead, after having drunk of the cup of wrath which God puts into their hands. This he thinks is said sarcastically.

PSALM 60

ACCORDING to the title, this Psalm was composed in memory of Joab's victory over the Edomites in the Valley of Salt. Nothing is said in the scanty record in 2 Sam. viii. of the circumstances which led to this war; but it is probable that whilst David was engaged in his first Syrian campaign, the Edomites turned the opportunity to good account, and threatened, if they did not actually invade, Palestine. The king, therefore, was compelled hastily to detach Joab and some part of his forces to meet these new enemies. Whether they had not yet crossed the frontier, or whether they were on their way back from a successful raid into Hebrew territory, as has been conjectured, we do not know; but a severe battle was fought in the Valley of Salt, near the southern extremity of the Dead Sea, in which the Edomites were defeated with great slaughter. This battle decided the fate of the Edomites; they never rallied after it, and Joab overran the whole country. After the fashion of Eastern conquerors, he almost exterminated the male population, garrisoned the principal cities with Hebrew troops, and reduced the people to a state of vassalage. It was in the interval between the first great battle and the final subjugation of the country that this Psalm, as Hengstenberg and others suppose, was written. It seems to acknowledge a partial success, and to anticipate a greater: "Who *will* conduct me into the fortified city (or cities)? Who *hath* led me unto Edom?" Further, the Psalm speaks of the Moabites and Philistines as recently vanquished enemies, and from 2 Sam. viii. we know that they had been completely subdued by David shortly before his Syrian campaign. Lastly, it supposes the unity of the kingdom; Judah being the ruling tribe, and Ephraim at the same time maintaining a high and honourable position, without dissension and without rivalry; and this was the case only during the reigns of David and Solomon.

So far, no doubt, the contents of the Psalm agree very well with the statement made in the title as to the date of its composition. On the other hand, it opens with a wail of lamentation, which implies that the arms of Israel had met with some terrible reverses, or that the state had been shaken by intestine disorders. But we have no record in the history of any such catastrophe at the time. On the contrary, David seems to have been at the very height of his glory and to have been everywhere victorious. Bishop Colenso indeed argues that David's forces may on some occasions have been defeated, and yet that such defeats would not be mentioned in the rapid summary of his exploits in 2 Sam. viii.; and Hengstenberg thinks that the lamentation of the Psalmist has reference to an invasion of the Edomites into Judæa during David's absence in Syria, and that the terrible vengeance upon Edom was in consequence of the excesses which they had then committed. But the language of verses 1—3 points to some loss more serious and more permanent than a hasty invasion, or an occasional defeat; and if so, it is surprising that the history should pass it over in silence. Again, the union between Judah and Ephraim (ver. 7) is represented rather as a matter of hope and promise than as already accomplished. And, in like manner, all that is said of Moab, Edom, and Philistia, may refer to the future, not to the past. (See notes on verses 7, 8.)

To say the least, therefore, it is not certain that the Psalm belongs to the age of David. In its lamentations over past disasters it bears considerable resemblance to Psalm xliv., but is so different from it in style that it cannot have been written by the same author, nor does it seem to belong to the same period. Psalm xliv. is clearly the later Psalm, and may have been partly based upon this. "The fact is," says Reuss, "that the known history of David contains absolutely nothing which can explain our text." He thinks it refers probably to some disaster in the time of the Maccabees.

Ewald thinks that the Psalm in its present form is to be referred to a time after the Captivity, but that "the words from ver. 6 [8] as far as the first words of ver. 10 [12], 'Hast not Thou, O God?' are borrowed from an older, and no doubt Davidic, song. . . . The dissimilarity strikes the eye at the first glance." The *old* passage, according to him, was composed by David in the latter part of his life, when he was threatened by the Philistines (comp. 2 Sam. v. 17, &c.

xxiii. 9, &c.): he had besought counsel and strength from Jehovah in the sanctuary, and he here records the cheering answer which he received. The later poet, Ewald says, feeling how suitable such an oracle was to his own times, though the enemies which he had to fear were not *Philistines*, but other heathen nations, adopted it without alteration, merely adding a new introduction and a new conclusion in his own words, to make the whole more suitable to the times in which he lived.

The Psalm consists of three strophes:—

I. A lamentation over past disasters, with a cry for help. Ver. 1—5.

II. The appeal to God's word and promise as the sufficient pledge that the prayer which precedes will be answered. Ver. 6—8.

III. The triumphant hope and anticipation of victory as springing out of and resting upon the Divine oracles. Ver. 9—12.

[FOR THE PRECENTOR. UPON "THE LILY OF THE TESTIMONY." A MICHTAM OF DAVID. FOR TEACHING. WHEN HE FOUGHT WITH ARAM OF THE TWO RIVERS (MESOPOTAMIA) AND ARAM OF ZOBAH; AND JOAB RETURNED AND SMOTE EDOM IN THE VALLEY OF SALT (TO THE NUMBER OF) TWELVE THOUSAND MEN.]

I. 1 O GOD, Thou hast cast us off, Thou hast broken us;
Thou hast been angry; restore us again.[b]
2 Thou hast made the land to tremble, Thou hast cleaved it;
Heal the breaches thereof, for it hath tottered.

1. THOU HAST CAST US OFF. The same word as in xliv. 9 [10]. It is also used of an individual in xliii. 2.

THOU HAST BROKEN US. The word is employed of the defeat of an army whose ranks have been broken, 2 Sam. v. 20, where the comparison is made of water breaking through a dam. In Judges xxi. 15 it is said of the destruction of the tribe of Benjamin, that "Jehovah had made *a breach* (*Perez*) in the tribes of Israel," a great gap being left as it were in the goodly phalanx which the twelve tribes presented. Primarily, no doubt, the root is used of the breaking down of a wall, as lxxx. 12 [13], lxxxix. 40 [41]. And hence it is applied to the breaking down and overthrowing of armies and nations, as here and in the passages cited above, and also of individuals, as in the judgement upon Uzzah, 2 Sam. vi. 8. Cf. Job xvi. 14.

2. The metaphor is borrowed apparently from the action of an earthquake, which has split asunder the ground and torn it into rifts and chasms. In like manner there has been a violent disorganization of

3 Thou hast showed Thy people a hard thing,
Thou hast made us drink infatuation [c] (as) wine.
4 Thou hast given a banner to them that fear Thee,
That they may muster [d] (around it) from before the bow,[e] [Selah.]
5 That Thy beloved may be delivered:
Save with Thy right hand, and answer us.

the body politic. Hupfeld infers from the words "heal the *breaches* thereof" that the image (as in the previous verse) is that of a building or wall broken down, an image frequently employed in the O. T., and one which in Is. xxx. 13, Jer. vi. 14 is applied to the overthrow of the nation. But both figures may have been in the Psalmist's mind; the "trembling" of the land denoting the earthquake, and the second member of the verse referring to its effects in broken buildings and tottering walls. Whether the "cleaving" here spoken of is to be understood of the actual disruption of the kingdom and the separation of the tribes is not certain. In any case, however, verses 2 and 3 are more readily understood of internal political disorganization than of the terror produced by hostile invasion.

3. THOU HAST SHOWED, lit. "made to *see*," *i.e.* made to *feel* or experience, the verb of *sight* being used, as in Greek, of the senses generally. A HARD THING, a heavy fate; the same word as in 1 Sam. xx. 10, 1 Kings xii. 13.

INFATUATION, or "bewilderment," lit. "reeling, staggering," as the effects of intoxication. This infatuation is the wine which God has made them drink, the two words being in apposition with one another: the rendering of the E.V., "the wine *of* astonishment," is grammatically impossible (see Critical Note). The same figure occurs lxxv. 8 [9], Is. li. 17, 22, Jer. xiii. 13, xxv 15, xlix. 12, and in many other passages. It denotes not merely a Divine punishment, but that kind of punishment which comes of men's own desperate indulgence of their pride, folly, passions. When men *will* drink presumptuously of the cup of their own wickedness, God forces it as it were into their hands, till they have drained the very dregs as the cup of His wrath. Thus God punishes evil with greater evil, pride with presumptuous pride, folly with more desperate folly. As is usual in the O. T. this, though sin as well as curse, is ascribed directly to God, as is the hardening of Pharaoh's heart, the sending of the evil spirit into Saul, and of a lying spirit into the false prophets. See note on li. 4.

4. A BANNER. The standard was raised as a signal for war, round which they were to rally. (Comp. Is. v. 26, xiii. 2.) The fact that God had given them such a banner, that he had Himself reared it in the midst of them, was a ground of hope, and also of prayer, "Save with Thy right hand," &c. Notwithstanding the *Selah*, the construction might be carried on into the next verse; the words "That Thy beloved," &c. depending not upon the prayer which follows, but upon the words "Thou hast given a banner," or perhaps on the whole sentence in ver. 4. But see more in Critical Note.

5. THY BELOVED (plural) the same word as in Deut. xxxiii. 12, and in the name Jedidiah given to Solomon.

ANSWER US. According to the Massoretic correction, "Answer *me*," which however seems to be unnecessary.

II. 6 God hath spoken in His holiness:
Let me exult, let me portion out Shechem,
And the valley of Succoth let me measure.

6. Having thus encouraged himself and his people with the assurance of God's favour and the hope of deliverance, he now turns to the promises on which those hopes rested. "Nam utcunque Deus innumeris gratiæ suæ exemplis nos obruat, nulla tamen vigebit eorum notitia, nisi præfulgente verbo."—*Calvin.*

GOD HATH SPOKEN IN HIS HOLINESS, almost equivalent to "hath *promised by* His holiness." Comp. lxxxix. 35 [36], "One thing have I sworn by My holiness." Amos iv. 2. The LXX. have ἐν τῷ ἁγίῳ αὐτοῦ. Jerome, *In sanctuario suo*, and so Luther, "In His sanctuary," as if the allusion were to an oracle shortly before received; and Delitzsch suggests that in the war with Edom, David may have received an oracle from the High Priest by means of the Urim and Thummim, which assured him of the safety of the Holy Land, and of his victory over the bordering tribes. But, as he admits, the promise in 2 Sam. vii. 9 is quite sufficient to meet the occasion. Hengst. thinks that Gen. xlix., Numb. xxiv., Deut. xxxiii. may also have been in the Psalmist's mind. "We need not suppose," says Reuss, who regards the Ps. as Maccabean, "that we have here the textual copy of an ancient oracle. It is the *résumé* of the national hopes, the expression of the dominant idea of the prophets, the restoration of the kingdom of David."

In the words that follow, "Let me exult," &c., to the end of ver. 8 [10], there is some doubt who is the speaker. According to Hupf., Bunsen, and Olsh. it is God. Ewald is of the same opinion, except that he takes the first words, "Let me exult," as the words of the Psalmist himself, parenthetically—which is favoured by the accent—and the rest as the utterance of the Divine oracle. Hengst. thinks that the people, and Del., following the older interpreters, that the king is the speaker. This last seems to me the most probable view, though it is possible that by a bold figure God himself may be supposed to speak as an earthly warrior, and as the leader of the hosts of His people through whom they achieve the victory. He, as their true King and captain, identifies Himself with them, and hence speaks not only of their success, but of their joy as His own.

LET ME EXULT, or the paragogic form may be rendered as in E. V. "I will exult therefore, I will," &c.

PORTION OUT . . . . MEASURE, in allusion to the assigning the different portoins (κλῆροι) of the conquered territory, as by Joshua on the conquest of Canaan. Here, however, the figure is borrowed from the original conquest of the country and applied to its reconstitution, not by means of a redistribution of territory, but by a fresh political organization, which should give new life to the whole country, and be as it were the beginning of a new state.

SHECHEM and SUCCOTH are probably selected as famous names in ancient times; Ros. and others think they are intended to mark, the one the cis-Jordanic, and the other the trans-Jordanic region, and so to embrace the whole land which Israel claimed on both sides the river as his inheritance. Succoth was the first place at which Jacob halted when, on his return from Mesopotamia, he descended from the mountains of Gilead, and it received its name from the "booths" or "huts" which he then built there. (Comp. Gen. xxxiii. 16, 18, with Judg. viii. 5—17, whence it appears that Succoth lay between

7 Mine is Gilead, and mine is Manasseh,
Ephraim also is the defence of my head;
Judah is my sceptre.
8 Moab is my wash-pot;

Peniel, near the ford of the Jabbok, and Shechem.) Shechem in the heart of Palestine was the next station, and there he found a permanent home: it became afterwards the chief city of the tribe of Ephraim, and for a time the capital of the northern kingdom. But it seems doubtful whether Succoth was on the east of the Jordan. Jerome, indeed (*Quæst. in Gen.* xxxiii. 16), places it there, and the fact that it was allotted to the tribe of Gad (Josh. xiii. 27) renders this probable. On the other hand, Robinson (*B. R.* iii. 309, &c.) and Van de Velde (*Syr. and Pal.* ii. 343) identify it with a place called *Sâkût*, on the western bank of the river. "Until the position of Succoth is more exactly ascertained, it is impossible to say what was the valley of Succoth." (See Mr. Grove's article, SUCCOTH, in the *Dict. of the Bible.*) Why this valley should be mentioned at all, it is hard to say, except it be from its old association with Shechem in the history of Jacob, Gen. xxxiii. Instead of Succoth, Aq. has *κοιλάδα συσκιασμῶν*, and the LXX. *τὴν κοιλάδα τῶν σκηνῶν*.

7. This verse has reference both to the geographical and to the political division of the Holy Land. Geographically, Gilead and Manasseh denote the Israelitish territory east of the Jordan, as Ephraim and Judah represent Western Palestine. Politically, the two last-mentioned tribes were the most important, the one in the north, and the other in the south; and thus the whole land and nation are in fact summed up.

THE DEFENCE OF MY HEAD, the strong and warlike tribe of Ephraim being to the state what the helmet is to the warriors in battle; or perhaps, "the *strength* of my head," the allusion being to Deut. xxxiii. 17, "His horns are as the horns of a buffalo: with them he shall push the nations."

MY SCEPTRE, or "bâton of command." The reference is to Gen. xlix. 10, where, as well as in Numb. xxi. 18, the parallelism seems to require this meaning. But the other rendering, "My Lawgiver," may be defended by Deut. xxxiii. 21, Is. xxxiii. 22, and has the support of the Ancient Versions. Symm. *προτάσσων ὁ ἐμός*. LXX. *βασιλεύς μόυ*. Jerome, *legifer meus*. Vulg. *rex meus*.

8. But the Psalmist anticipates not the constitution only of the kingdom in its integrity and its firm consolidation by the union of the various tribes, but the extension of the kingdom also by the subjugation of neighbouring nations. Those nations are chiefly mentioned which had been from the earliest times the enemies, and the bitterest enemies, of Israel. The order in which they are mentioned is from the east, and thence along the south to the west. None of them was ever completely subjugated, though David greatly reduced them and humbled their power, 2 Sam. viii., but triumph over them forms part of the promise of later Prophets. See especially Is. xi. 14, where it is promised in connection with the union of Ephraim and Judah.

The expressions which follow, indicating the subjugation of Moab and Edom, are decidedly contemptuous.

MY WASH-POT, expressive of the state of ignominious bondage to which the Moabites would be reduced. The vessel used for washing the feet is meant, as a dishonourable vessel. (Comp. Herod. ii. 172.) This meaning is perhaps

To Edom will I cast my shoe.
Because of me, O Philistia, cry aloud.

III. 9 Who will conduct me into the fortified city?
Who hath led me unto Edom?
10 Hast not THOU, O God, cast us off?
And wilt not Thou, O God, go forth with our hosts?
11 O give us help [f] from (the) adversary,

intended to be conveyed by the rendering of one of the Greek translators, λεκάνη τῆς καταπατήσεώς μου.

WILL I CAST MY SHOE. Edom is regarded as the slave to whom the master throws his shoes to be taken away or to be cleaned. Comp. Matt. iii. 11, and for the construction, 1 Kings xix. 19. The expression is not used of taking possession of property, for in Ruth iv. 7 the kinsman does not throw his shoe, but takes it off and gives it; and so far from the action being symbolical of taking possession, it is symbolical of giving up one's right. There is thus a connection between the two figures; Moab is the vessel in which he washes his feet; Edom the slave to whom he casts his shoe which he had just drawn off.

CRY ALOUD. I have left the word in its ambiguity. As it is elsewhere used of a shout of rejoicing and triumph, it has been explained either (1) ironically, as by Qimchi, "Triumph if thou canst, it is rather for me to triumph now;" so in the Marg. of our A. V.; or (2) of the forced homage, the shout of welcome and gratulation extorted by the victor from the vanquished. (Comp. ii. 11, xviii. 44 [45].) Ewald and others understand it of the cry of fear and sorrow, a sense which the Hiph. of the verb has, Micah iv. 9, Is. xvi. 4. In the parallel passage in cviii. 10 we have the easier reading, "Over Philistia will I shout aloud," *i.e.* in triumph, which Hupfeld would adopt here.

This Hithp. form of the verb occurs again only in the Ps. cvii.; and in lxv.

9. The application of these Divine promises to the present condition of the nation.

WHO WILL CONDUCT ME, as the expression of a wish apparently = "Oh for one to conduct me!"

THE FORTIFIED CITY. Comp. xxxi. 21 [22]. Although the article is wanting, still some particular city may be meant, the absence of the article being not uncommon in poetry. Hengstenberg thinks that "the wonderful rock-built city of Petra" (comp. 2 Kings xiv. 7), others that Rabbath Ammon or Rabbath Moab. is meant; Calvin, that the noun is used collectively of fortified cities generally.

WHO HATH LED ME. The change of tense is not easily accounted for. Hengst. understands it as "the pret. of *faith*, which anticipates the future, and so represents the matter to itself as if God had already led forth. Del. *quis perduxerit me*, referring to xi. 3. Others take this second question as an answer to the first, "Who *will* bring?" &c. "He who hath brought me unto Edom." But see introduction to the Psalm.

10. HAST NOT THOU, &c. This might also be rendered "Wilt not" (or, Is it not) Thou, O God, (*who*) has cast us off, and goest not forth," &c., the reference being to ver. 1, there being an ellipse of the relative after the personal pronoun. (So Symm., the LXX., Vulg., Jerome.) But in cviii. 11 [12], where the passage is repeated, it is without the pronoun, and consequently the relative cannot be understood. See also xliv. 9 [10].

For vain is the salvation of man.
12 Through God shall we do valiantly;
And it is HE (who) shall tread down our adversaries.

As rendered above the meaning will be, Hast thou in the past rejected us, and wilt Thou not in the future change Thy dealing towards us and go forth? &c. But the second clause may only mark the consequence of the first: Hast Thou not, &c. . . . and goest not forth, *i.e.* so that Thou goest not forth, &c. Or, as Kay: Alas, Thou goest not forth, reading the second clause as if uttered with a sigh.

12. DO VALIANTLY. Comp. cxviii. 16 and Numb. xxiv. 18.

[a] עַל שׁוּשַׁן עֵדוּת. In the great darkness which envelops this and other inscriptions it is impossible to explain the words satisfactorily, but they most probably denote the measure or melody to which the Psalm was to be set. See on xlv. note [a]. For Michtam, see on xvi. note [a].

לְלַמֵּד, "to teach," *i.e.* intimating that it was to be taught to the people, perhaps with reference to Deut. xxxi. 19. See also 2 Sam. i. 18.

בְּהַצּוֹתוֹ, "when he warred with," or perhaps, as Hengst., "when he laid waste," from the meaning of the Qal in Jer. iv. 7. LXX. ἐνεπύρισε. א׳ נ׳, Aram of the two rivers, *i.e.* Mesopotamia, not mentioned in 2 Sam. viii., but in David's *second* Syrian expedition (2 Sam. x.) the kings of Mesopotamia are described as vassals of the king of Zobah, and would therefore as a matter of course be engaged in both wars. The exact position of Aram of Zobah is uncertain, but it is usually supposed to lie between the Euphrates and Orontes (see Winer, *Bibl. R. W. B*).

וַיָּשָׁב. "When Joab *returned* and smote" (not "*again* smote") on his way back, *i.e.* from the expedition against Zobah, as is said 2 Sam. viii. 13. There however *David* himself, and in 1 Chron. xviii. 12, *Abishai*, is said to have been in command of the forces; on which discrepancy Mich. remarks, "David as king, Joab as commander-in-chief, Abishai as sent by his brother on this particular expedition, defeated the enemy."

בְּגֵיא מֶלַח. The Valley of Salt, according to Robinson (iii. p. 25), is a low marshy tract, impregnated with salt, south of the Dead Sea, and so named from the neighbouring salt-mountain on the western shore of the sea. In 2 Kings xiv. 7, the Edomites are said to have been defeated there by Amaziah with a loss of 10,000 men. There is a discrepancy here in the title, when compared with the accounts in Samuel and Chronicles, as to the number of the slain, which in those Books is estimated at 18,000, whether arising from a confusion in the numbers שנים and שמנה, or in any other way, it is impossible now to say.

[b] תְּשׁוֹבֵב לָנוּ. The ל may perhaps be used, as in the later Hebrew more especially, to mark the object. It is possible, however, that the object is to be understood; "restore *to us* (Thy favour, or salvation, or the like)." Hupf. would supply the object from the preceding verb, "Appease *Thine anger* towards us," referring to the phrase השיב אף, "to let go, to appease anger," and to the similar passage, Is. xii. 1. If however it is necessary

to assume any object, the simplest way is to find it in the verb, תְּשׁוֹבֵב being = "give restoration, or refreshment," to us; as in lxxii. 4, יוֹשִׁיעַ, לִבְנֵי א׳, "He shall give salvation to," &c. The verb here in the fut. is nearly equivalent to the imperative, though there is implied in it not only entreaty, but a confidence that the prayer will be granted, so that it might be rendered "Thou wilt restore us." See a similar instance in lxi. 2 [3].

c יַיִן תַּרְעֵלָה. The two nouns are in appos. and must be rendered accordingly. It is out of the question to assume that the stat. abs. is here used for the constr. There is no proof that the one ever stands for the other. The first noun is immediately subjoined to the verb as more closely defining its action: "Thou hast given us to drink infatuation, or bewilderment, as men drink wine." So Hupf. explains the construction, referring to lxxx. 6, "Thou hast made them feed upon weeping like bread;" 1 Kings xxii. 27, "Feed him with affliction as bread, and with affliction as water" (וּמַיִם לַחַץ not וּמֵי ל׳); Is. xxx. 20. But the apposition is capable of being explained in another way; for the second noun may in fact be a predicate further defining the first: "Thou hast given us wine to drink which is (not wine but) bewilderment." Luther gives the sense very well: "Du hast uns einen Trunk Wein gegeben, dass wir taumelten." תַּרְעֵלָה, lit. *staggering* as from intoxication. Comp. Is. li. 17, "cup of staggering," here however applied to confusion and stupor of mind, the helplessness, the bewilderment, the giddiness, which made them so easily beaten down before their enemies. As Calvin, *vinum stuporis, vertiginis*, which he explains, "potio quæ mentes sensu et intelligentia privat." The ancient interpreters were perplexed with the word. The LXX. *οἶνον κατανύξεως.* Aq. *καρώσεως.* Symm. (who is nearer the mark) *σάλου.* The Chald. לְוָט, *cursing.* Syr. ܚܡܪܐ ܠܡܪܬܐ, *wine in the dregs.* Jerome, *vino consopiente.*

d לְהִתְנוֹסֵס. This may either be Hithpal. from נוּס—so Gesen. takes it, "to betake themselves to flight," but this does not occur elsewhere—or Hithpo. from נסס, "to lift themselves up," so Zunz: "sich zu erheben," the participle of this last form occurs Zech. ix. 16. But the Targ. on that passage refers מִתְנוֹסְסוֹת, not to the אַבְנֵי נֵזֶר, but to the people flocking homewards. With the word נֵס, "banner," immediately preceding, the verb would seem to be used here in its reflexive conjugation, as a denom. verb from נֵס, in the sense of "gathering round the banner." According to the first rendering, the sense would be, "Thou hast given a banner to them that fear Thee, not as a presage of victory, but rather of defeat, only that Thy people may flee before the archers of the enemy." This, it is said, is required by the context, which speaks only of disaster and defeat. But I do not see why a transition should not be made in these words to the prayer which follows. Why may not the Psalmist find encouragement in the thought that God had given to His people a banner to which they may flock, a standard round which they may range themselves, and base upon this fact his prayer: "That Thy beloved may be delivered, Save," &c.? For the position of the *Selah*, comp. lvii. 4.

[e] מִפְּנֵי קֹשֶׁט. This has been rendered "because of the truth," *i.e.* on behalf of it, in order to defend it; as Maurer, *dimicaturi pro sacris avitis.* The word קֹשֶׁט does indeed occur parallel with אֱמֶת, Prov. xxii. 21, and the Chald. קְשׁוֹט in the same sense, Dan. ii. 47, iv. 34. And Aq. has here *βεβαιότητος*. But מִפְּנֵי cannot mean "because of, for the sake of," like עַל דְּבַר, בַּעֲבוּר, &c. Delitzsch indeed argues that it has the sense of *propter*, not only in later Hebrew, as Neh. v. 15, but in earlier, as in Deut. xxviii. 20, but neither passage is really in point. In the one "*because of* the fear of God," and in the other "*because of* the wickedness of your doings," the prep. really = "owing to;" but here "*because of* the truth" does not mean "*owing to* the truth," but *for the sake of it.* Maurer with no better success appeals to Is. x. 27. He suggests, indeed, another explanation, taking קֹשֶׁט in the sense of *fides,*—"*Propter fidem,* ut promissa tua impleres, *i.e.* tu ipse ut solveres promissum de exilio nos reduxisti" (he supposes the Psalm to have been written after the Exile). But it is far better, following the LXX., Syr., Ar., Æth., Symm., Jerome, Vulg., to take קֹשֶׁט here as = קֶשֶׁת. The interchange of the ת and ט may be seen in the Syr. ܩܫܛܐ and the Chald. קוּשְׁטָא, and the prep. will then retain its usual signification (comp. Is. xxxi. 8). The rendering of the Syr. transl. (who must have read לֹא יָנוּסוּ) gives really the best sense: "Thou has given to them that fear Thee a banner, that they should *not* flee from before the bow."

[f] עֶזְרָת. On the form of this word with termination *ath*, see on xvi. note [k].

PSALM 61

THE title of this Psalm ascribes it to David but does not say under what circumstances it was composed (though according to the Syriac Version it was when Jonathan revealed to him Saul's design to slay him). There is no reason to doubt that David was the author, and the language of ver. 2 renders it probable that it was written when he was shut out from the sanctuary, and therefore either during his persecution by Saul or during the rebellion of Absalom. Ver. 4 makes the latter the more probable occasion. At a time when the Tabernacle had itself no settled resting-place, the wish to dwell and abide in it, as Delitzsch has rightly remarked, is not so natural as afterwards, when the Ark was fixed on Mount Zion.

Again, if, as is most probable, the king spoken of in ver. 6 is David—Bishop Colenso's suggestion that Saul is meant is violently improbable—then it is clear that the Psalm must have been written after he was king, and therefore in his flight from Absalom and on the other side of the Jordan. Or if it be thought that David would not thus speak of himself in the third person, the Psalm may still have been composed under the same circumstances, by one of the friends who accompanied him.

It consists of two principal divisions, ver. 1—5 and ver. 6—8. But these again admit of sub-divisions.

I. First, we have the usual introduction. Ver. 1.
Then, the prayer, and the ground on which it rests. Ver. 2, 3.
Then, the ardent wish to dwell in the sanctuary of God, accompanied by the reason for such a wish. Ver. 4, 5.

II. Hopes expressed concerning the king. Ver. 6, 7.
Finally, the usual conclusion, the vow of grateful praise. Ver. 8.

[FOR THE PRECENTOR. ON A STRINGED INSTRUMENT.[a] (A PSALM) OF DAVID].

I. 1 HEAR my cry, O God,
Attend unto my prayer.
2 From the end of the earth unto Thee do I call, when my heart is overwhelmed :
To a rock which is too high for me, Thou wilt lead me.
3 For Thou hast been a refuge for me,

2. FROM THE END OF THE EARTH. A strong hyperbolical expression by which the sacred Poet would describe his own *sense* of his distance from the sanctuary, or from the Holy Land. Comp. Is. v. 26. The feeling is that which is expressed in xlii. 6 [7], and other Psalms.

IS OVERWHELMED, or "fainteth." The verb means literally "to cover," as in lxxiii. 6, title of lii. ; hence "to cover one's face in sorrow," and then as here, "to be overwhelmed with distress."

TO A ROCK, lit. "*Upon* a rock," the full construction being, "Thou wilt lead me to and place me upon," &c. (Lee, *Heb. Gram.* § 230, 8.) The rock is a place of security (comp. xl. 2 [3]), but it is one which he cannot reach by his own unaided effort, "che è troppo alta da salirvi da me." Diodati.

THOU WILT LEAD ME. The words may be either thus rendered as an expression of confidence (future), or as a prayer (imperative) See on lx. 1 [3]. There is the same ambiguity in ver. 6.

3. This appeal to God is now based, as commonly in the Psalms, on the past experience of His mercy.

A strong tower from the face of (the) enemy.
4 Let me sojourn in Thy tabernacle for ever,
Let me find refuge in the hiding-place of Thy wings. [Selah.]
5 For Thou, O God, hast hearkened to my vows,
Thou hast given (me) the possession [b] of them that fear Thy Name.

II. 6 Thou wilt grant the King a long life,
His years (wilt Thou make) as many generations.
7 He shall sit (on his throne) for ever before God.
Loving-kindness and truth do Thou appoint [c] to preserve him.
8 So let me sing of Thy Name for ever,
That I may pay my vows day by day.

A STRONG TOWER, as in Judg. ix. 51, Prov. xviii. 10, "The name of Jehovah is a strong tower."

4. LET ME SOJOURN. Or, "I will sojourn therefore." See notes on xv. 1, xxvii. 4.

IN THY TABERNACLE, or "tent." The expression would hardly have been employed after the Temple was built, and hence it is almost certain that the Psalm belongs to the time of David. See xv. 1.

FOR EVER, lit. "(for) ages." Comp. xxiii. 6.

THY WINGS. The figure is borrowed, as the parallelism shows, from the outstretched wings of the Cherubim over the Mercy-seat. See lvii. 1 [2].

5. THE POSSESSION. Primarily this would be the land of Canaan, and then it would include all blessings, temporal and spiritual, which were in fact implied and comprised in the possession of the land.

6. THOU WILT GRANT, &c., lit. "Days to the King's days wilt Thou add." The king, according to the Targum, is the King Messiah. The eternal duration of the kingdom here anticipated no doubt led to this interpretation. But in the original sense of the passage, not merely an individual monarch, but the *dynasty*, the whole royal house of David may be meant. But see note on xxi. 4.

The king is spoken of in the third person, but the Psalm may nevertheless have been written by David himself.

Others take this and the next verse as a prayer: "O prolong the days. . . May his years be. . . May he sit, &c." Mendelss. makes v. 7 dependent, "that he may sit upon his throne."

7. HE SHALL SIT. The verb may only signify "He shall *abide, dwell*," but when spoken of kings and judges it is commonly employed in the more formal and solemn sense of sitting on the throne, the judgement-seat, &c., as in ix. 7., xxix. 10, &c.

[a] עַל־נְגִינַת. Qimchi observes, "although the noun is with a Pathach, it is not in the constr. state, and there are many like instances." So too Del. considers it a feminine ending in *ath*, somewhat rare in Hebrew, but

the usual one in Phœnician." Comp. חָכְמַת, Is. xxxiii. 6. Otherwise we must read נְגִינוֹת, as in the title of Psalm iv.

b יְרֻשַּׁת. The older Versions all render, "Thou hast given a heritage to them that fear Thy name." And so Maurer, but not Ewald, as Hupfeld asserts, who stigmatizes the rendering as ungrammatical. But surely that depends on how far we press the meaning of נָתַתָּה. It may be rendered, "Thou hast *appointed* (not necessarily *given*) the possession *of* them that fear," &c., which comes to the same thing as "Thou hast given a possession to them," &c.

c מַן, apoc. imperat. Piel of מנה. (For similar forms see cxix. 18, Lev. vi. 2.) The Chald. renders it, "from the Lord of the world," and therefore perhaps read מִן יְהוָֹה. The LXX., Syr., and Arab. take the word as an interrogative pronoun, which it is in Aram., but not in Hebrew.

PSALM 62

THIS Psalm and the 39th are Psalms which, though very different in their subject, yet are so similar in the phraseology which they employ, that there can be no doubt that they were written by the same author. Ewald supposes, from the 11th [12th] verse of this Psalm, that he was a Prophet, and one of the great supporters of true religion in the struggle with the corrupt men of his time. We see him here, he says, contending with men, his fellow-citizens, who, upheld and favoured by a worldly power which was just starting into fresh life, endeavoured for this very reason to drag him down into the dust, because they could not endure his spiritual greatness and superiority. Long had they attacked him; now they felt sure of his overthrow. But, strong in his trust in God, though assailed and threatened afresh, the divine Poet places himself in calm resignation in the hands of the one true Redeemer, and not only finds in Him, rest, refreshment, strength for himself, but is also enabled to encourage, enlighten and comfort others.

Scarcely anywhere do we find faith in God more nobly asserted, more victoriously triumphant; the vanity of man, of human strength and riches, more clearly confessed; courage in the midst of peril more calm and more unshaken, than in this Psalm, which is as forcible in its conception and its language, as it is remarkable for the vigorous and cheerful piety which it breathes.

Donne, in his sermon on ver. 9, says that Athanasius "observes in the Psalm a summary abridgment of all : for of this Psalm he says in general, *Adversus insidiantes*, Against all attempts upon thy body, thy state, thy soul, thy fame, temptations, tribulations, machinations, defamations, say this Psalm . . . . not that therein David puts himself to weigh particular temptations and tribulations, but that he puts every man, in every trial, to put himself wholly upon God, and to know, that if man cannot help him in this world, nothing can ; and for man, *Surely men of low degree are vanity, and men of high degree are a lie : to be laid in the balance they are altogether lighter than vanity.*" —*Sermon* lxv. ; Works, vol. iii p. 137, Alford's Edition.

The Psalm consists of three strophes of four verses each. The first two express the blessedness and security of trust in God when enemies assail, ver. 1—4 and ver. 5—8. The last places in forcible contrast with this the folly of reliance on man, ver. 9—12.

[FOR THE PRECENTOR. AFTER THE MANNER OF JEDUTHUN.[a] A PSALM OF DAVID.]

I. 1 ONLY upon God my soul (waiteth in) silence,[b]
From Him (cometh) my salvation.[c]
2 Only He is my rock and my salvation,

1 ONLY. The particle may be so rendered as restrictive ; or, *surely*, as affirmative. It occurs no less than six times in the Psalm. In xxxix. 5, 6 [6, 7], it is repeated three times in three successive lines, one of the indications that the two Psalms are by the same author. Our translators have rendered it differently in different verses of this Psalm : in ver. 1, *truly ;* in vers. 2, 4, 5, 6, *only ;* in ver. 9, *surely* : but it is better to keep the same word throughout, at least in the same Psalm. If we render *only*, the meaning will be here that God exclusively is the object of trust ; if *surely*, that this truth, that God is his salvation, has come home to the Psalmist with a more lively conviction, with a more blessed certainty, than ever. Hupfeld thinks that in ver. 4, [5] the rendering *surely* is necessary, and therefore that this is to be prefered throughout ; on the other hand, in ver. 5 [6], *only* is certainly more suitable.

The first line of the verse rendered literally is, "Only unto God my soul is silence," (Cf. Lam. iii. 25), *i.e.* is hushed into perfect resignation before Him, simply trusting in His Love, and leaving all that concerns me to the disposal of His fatherly will. "It is," says Calvin, "that settled submission, when the faithful rest in the promises of God, give place to His word, obey His rule, and keep down every murmur of passion in their hearts." But this, as he also remarks most truly, is the result, not of one only, but of many struggles with the temptations of Satan.

2. MY SALVATION. The repetition of the word is not without meaning. Not only does his salvation *come from* God, but God *is* his

My high tower, (so that) I cannot be greatly[c]
moved.
3 How long will ye set [d] upon a man,
Will ye all of you break (him) down,[e]
As (though he were) a bowing wall, a tottering
fence ?[f]
4 Only from his dignity have they taken counsel to
thrust him down,
They (who) have pleasure in lies,
(Who) bless (each one) with his mouth, and curse
inwardly. [Selah.]

II. 5 Only upon God (wait) in silence, O my soul,
For from Him is my hope.
6 Only He is my rock and my salvation,

salvation. The Being on whom he waits, the loving Person in whom he trusts, the God whose arms compass him about is to him all that is comprehended in that great word salvation. He heaps these epithets upon God, says Calvin, that he may use them as so many shields against the assaults of Satan.

3. Having thus strengthened himself in his God, the Psalmist turns to address his enemies. The form of the address is very similar to that in iv. 2 [3]. There, they are men who would turn his glory (*i.e.* his kingly dignity) into shame, as here they would thrust him down from his high place. There too, as here, they have pleasure in lies. But here the circumstance "that they bless with their mouth, but curse inwardly," points to men who had worn the courtier's mask of a smooth hypocrisy, in order to conceal the better their designs against his life and honour, but who had thrown it off, as soon as they found that they could do so with safety. When he was in peril, when he seemed to be already tottering to his fall, like a wall shaking and giving way, then they were ready to finish the work by thrusting him down altogether.

4. EACH ONE WITH HIS MOUTH. As the pronominal suffix is singular, it must be thus rendered distributively. Comp. Is. ii. 20, v. 23.

5. WAIT IN SILENCE. The first strophe opens with the expression of his resignation ; this, with the exhortation to resignation. But this is no contradiction. The life of man's spirit cannot always preserve the same even tenour. The heart of man is like the sea ; however calm and smooth it may seem, a light air will ruffle its surface. The resignation, the trust in God, the peace, the rest which have come after long struggle and much prayer, may too easily be broken. And hence, when these have been attained, we need to exhort ourselves to them in renewed measure.

FOR FROM HIM IS MY HOPE. "He never disappoints the patient abiding of His children. There is laid up, he says, a sure reward for my silence, and therefore will I restrain myself, lest my haste should hinder the course of my salvation." —*Calvin*.

6, 7. Still further he strengthens

My high tower (so that) I cannot be moved.
7 Upon God (resteth) my salvation and my glory;
The rock of my strength, my refuge, is in God.
8 Trust in Him, at all times, O people;
Pour out your hearts before Him.
God is a refuge for us. [Selah.]

III. 9 Only a breath are men of low degree, men of high degree a lie;
In the balances they will kick the beam,[g] lighter than a breath altogether.

himself in God, and again heaps up one expression upon another, that he may, as it were, feel how safe and sure the ground is under him, how little reason he has to be disquieted, whatever man may do unto him. (See note on ver. 2.) Then having thus encouraged himself, he turns to encourage others.

On these reiterated names of God, Donne beautifully observes, in the Sermon before quoted: "Twice in this Psalm hath he repeated this, in the second and in the sixth verse, *He is my rock, and my salvation, and my defence*, and (as it is enlarged in the seventh verse) *my refuge and my glory*. If my *refuge*, what enemy can pursue me? If my *defence*, what temptation shall wound me? If my *rock*, what storm shall shake me? If my *salvation*, what melancholy shall deject me? If my *glory*, what calumny shall defame me? . . . . Let him that is pursued with any particular temptation, invest God, as God is a *refuge*, a sanctuary. Let him that is buffeted with the messengers of Satan, battered with his own concupiscence, receive God, as God is his *defence* and target. Let him that is shaked with perplexities in his understanding, or scruples in his conscience, lay hold upon God, as God is his *rock* and his anchor. Let him that hath any diffident jealousy or suspicion of the free and full mercy of God, apprehend God, as God is his *salvation;* and him that walks in the ingloriousness and contempt of the world, contemplate God as his *glory*. Any of these notions is enough to any man, but God is all these, and all else that all souls can think, to every man."—*Works*, vol. iii. pp. 154, 155.

7. UPON GOD. Comp. vii. 10[11], "My shield is upon God."

8. O PEOPLE. This may either mean men generally, or the people of Israel in particular; or if the Psalm be David's, it may refer to his immediate followers. The word is used in this sense of *retainers*, *followers*, &c., Judg. iii. 18, 1 Kings xix. 21. These he exhorts to faith and prayer, that, like himself, they may learn the lesson of patience; and as in ver. 7 he had claimed God as his own refuge, now he assures them that He is their refuge as well—God is a refuge for *us*.

9. In vivid contrast to that sure help and refuge which are to be found in God, the Psalmist now places the weakness and worthlessness of man's strength and man's resources.

LIGHTER THAN, or, "they are all vanity together."

A BREATH. Symm. ἀτμός. Comp. with this and the next verse, note on xxxix. 5, 6, and the passage there quoted from St. James.

10 Trust not in oppression, and in robbery be not vain;
When wealth increaseth, set not (your) heart (thereon).
11 Once hath God spoken; twice have I heard this;
That power (belongeth) unto God.
12 And to Thee, O Lord, (belongeth) loving-kindness,
For THOU rewardest every man according to his work.

MEN OF LOW DEGREE, &c., lit. "sons of (common) men, sons of (great) men." Comp. xlix. 2 [3].

10. BE NOT VAIN, *i.e.* put not a foolish trust in. The verb is a very expressive one, from the same root as the word rendered "breath" above. Comp. Jer. ii. 5.

INCREASETH, lit., "germinates," "sprouts."

11. In conclusion, the sacred Poet solemnly confirms his previous exhortation by an appeal to God's revelation.

ONCE . . . TWICE, *i.e.* many times. Comp. Job xxxiii. 14, xl. 5. (The LXX. δύο ταῦτα, "These two things" have I heard, viz., that strength and that loving-kindness belong unto God.) This is the substance of the revelation, that God is both a God of power and a God of love. If we need strength, we shall find it not in man, who is but as a fleeting vapour, but in God, who is Almighty. If we covet a reward, let us seek it not in robbery or in riches, but from the loving hand of Him who rewardeth every man according to his work. (Comp. Rom. ii. 6.) This is the only truly worthy representation of God. Power without Love is brutality, and Love without Power is weakness. Power is the strong foundation of Love, and Love is the beauty and the crown of Power.

[a] יְדוּתוּן. See xxxix. note [a]. The prep. עַל here makes it doubtful whether the *person* of that name be meant. Hence Rashi supposes it to be the name of a musical instrument, and Mendels. that it was invented by Jeduthun, and so called after his name.

[b] דּוּמִיָּה. Some, as Ges. and Stier, take the word as an adj., after the analogy of בּוֹכִיָּה, פּוֹרִיָּה, but then it ought to be דּוֹמִיָּה. It is better therefore to take it here as a subst. (as it is in xxii. 3, xxxix. 3, and lxv. 2) the form having the same analogy to דּוּמָה, as עֲלִילִיָּה, Jer. xxxii. 19, to עֲלִילָה; but I do not see that it is necessary to consider it an accus. abs., as Hupf. does, *in Schweigen*, much less is there any ellipse of בְּ, as others suppose; the noun is forcibly put in apposition with נַפְשִׁי, "my soul is silence," *i.e.* is hushed in absolute resignation, waiting upon God. Comp. cix. 4, וַאֲנִי תְפִלָּה, "but I am prayer," *i.e.* give myself only to prayer.

[c] רַבָּה. An adv., as perhaps Job xxxi. 34, and as רַבַּת, lxv. 10, and elsewhere. Rashi, Qimchi and others take it as an adj., supplying a noun מוֹטָה, from the verb אָמוֹט.

[d] תְּהוֹתְתוּ occurs nowhere else. The old attempts to derive it from אתה and from הַוּוֹת (as Qimchi explains תחשבו הוות, whence the E. V. *devise mischief*) are contrary to every rule of language, and, as Del. observes, could only belong to the childhood of Hebrew grammar. Most probably the root is kindred with the Arab. هتّ, هتهت, prop. *to speak in a rapid, broken, disorderly manner*, and then *to break*, &c. The Chald. renders, "will ye be tumultuous?" The Syr. "are ye incited or provoked?" The LXX. ἐπιτίθεσθε. Vulg. *irruitis.* Aq. ἐπιβουλεύετε. Jerome, *insidiamini* (and so Rashi, Ibn Ezra, and Qimchi, "plot against"). Symm. ματαιοπονήσετε.

[e] תְּרָצְחוּ. According to the reading of Ben-Asher, which is followed by the Western Jews, this is for the Pual, תְּרָצְּחוּ, which is given by Baer in his text. So Ab.-Ez. and Qimchi, and so the E. V. The reading of Ben-Naphtali, which is adopted by the Eastern Jews, is the Piel, תְּרַצְּחוּ, and this is expressed by most of the ancient Versions. The LXX. φονεύετε. Vulg. *interficitis.* Similarly the Syr. and Ethiop. The reading of the text without the Dagesh, and with the vowel Kametz, is peculiar. The Kametz cannot be explained as compensating for the absence of the Dagesh (as Ew. § 83, *c*, and Luzzatto, § 417, suppose), because there is no Metheg. Hence it must be read *t'rots'chu*, which would make it a Poel form, like *m'loshni*, ci. 5.

As regards the meaning of the word, רצח signifies commonly *to slay*, but here it seems to be used in the original sense of the root *to break down.* Comp. the noun רֶצַח in this sense in xlii. 11.

[f] גָּדֵר הַדְּחוּיָה. As the noun is elsewhere masc., and the art. prefixed to the part. when the noun is indefinite (though not contrary to grammatical rule) is unnecessary, and deviates from the constr. in the parall. קִיר נ', it is perhaps better to read (with Olsh., Hupf., and Del.) גְּדֵרָה דְּחוּיָה.

[g] לַעֲלוֹת. The infin. constr. with ל is used here for the imperf. (according to Ges. § 132, 3, Rem. 1), or, as Del. more exactly puts it, serves to express the future periphrastically. See xv. 14 [15], note [g], xlix. 15. Hab. i. 17. It marks intention, purpose, &c. Our own idiom is similar in such phrases as, He is *for going*, &c. So here, "(When laid) in the balances (they are) ascending," *i.e.* will certainly go up, kick the beam. Hupfeld contends that עלה does not refer to the *going up* of the lighter scale of the balance, but to the *putting* (*up*) *into the balance* of the object to be weighed. The verb נשׂא is so used, *e.g.* Job vi. 2, and see Ges. *Thes.* in v. Hence he would explain, "when they are *laid* in, or *weighed* in the balance." לַעֲלוֹת, he observes, may be taken, as often, as a gerund: "*beim Aufsteigen* (ascendendo) d. i. indem sie aufgelegt werden." And so he renders: "*Auf Wagschalen gehoben, sind sie leichter,*" &c. This is no doubt a possible rendering, but the reasons he gives for rejecting the other are strangely weak: they are (1) that the dual is used, whereas only *one scale* of the balance goes up; (2) that in what follows there is no meaning, without doing violence to the accents, or arbitrarily supplying something,

and even then only an artificial meaning. But in answer to (1) it is sufficient to say, that the Hebrew has no singular to express one scale of the balance; and in answer to (2), that only the same word of comparison is supplied which Hupf. himself is obliged to supply when he renders, "sie sind *leichter* als ein Hauch." The deviation from the accents is not of any great moment, but it may be avoided by taking the two clauses separately:

In the balances they ascend;
(They are lighter) than a breath altogether.

The last clause, moreover, need not be rendered as comparative; מֵהֶבֶל may mean, "*of*, i.e. consisting of, a breath," or "*of* nothing," "breath-like." Comp. Is. xl. 17, xli. 24, where there is a similar ambiguity, though Is. xliv. 11 is, as Del. remarks, in favour of the last rendering. So also Symm. *αὐτοὶ ματαιοῦνται ὁμοῦ.* LXX. *ψευδεῖς οἱ υἱοὶ τῶν ἀνθρώπων ἐν ζυγοῖς τοῦ ἀδικῆσαι, αὐτοὶ ἐκ ματαιότητος ἐπιτοαυτό.*

PSALM 63

THIS is unquestionably one of the most beautiful and touching Psalms in the whole Psalter. Donne says of it: "As the whole book of Psalms is *oleum effusum* (as the Spouse speaks of the name of Christ), an ointment poured out upon all sorts of sores, a cerecloth that supples all bruises, a balm that searches all wounds; so are there some certain Psalms that are imperial Psalms, that command over all affections, and spread themselves over all occasions,—catholic, universal Psalms, that apply themselves to all necessities. This is one of those; for of those constitutions which are called Apostolical, one is, that the Church should meet every day to sing this Psalm. And, accordingly, St. Chrysostom testifies, 'That it was decreed and ordained by the primitive fathers, that no day should pass without the public singing of this Psalm.'" And again, he observes that "the spirit and soul of the whole Book of Psalms is contracted into this Psalm."—*Sermon* lxvi.; Works, vol. iii. pp. 156, 157.

In many respects the Psalm bears a striking resemblance to Ps. lxi., and both Ewald and Maurer observe that the two must clearly be referred to the same circumstances and the same author. That the author was David I see no reason to doubt. Characterized as it is by an exquisite tenderness and a deep personal affection towards God, and yet not wanting, withal, in energy and even a certain abruptness of expression, it bears all the marks of his poetry. According to the inscription, it was written in the wilderness of Judah, which would seem to intimate that it was written during his persecution by Saul (comp. 1 Sam. xxii. 5; see also xxiii. 14, 15, 24, 25, xxiv. 2). But against this is verse 11, where David, as in lxi., speaks of himself in the third person, and speaks of himself as king. Hence it is more probable that the Psalm was composed when he was on the other side of the Jordan, in his flight from Absalom. The very tenderness and depth of feeling which characterize it, and which it has in common with xlii., are what might be looked for in a heart sorely wounded and tried in its natural affections, and therefore cleaving with the more intense, devoted love to Him, of whom it could say, "Thou hast been my help, Therefore in the shadow of Thy wings will I shout for joy."

It is remarkable that in this Psalm, as in the last, there is no petition. There is gladness, there is praise, there is the most exalted communion with God, there is longing for His Presence as the highest of all blessings; but there is not one word of asking for temporal, or even for spiritual good.

The Psalm consists of two principal divisions :—

I. The longing of the heart for God, and the joy of the heart in communion with Him. Ver. 1—8.

II. The anticipated destruction of his enemies, and his own triumph in consequence. Ver. 9—11.

[A PSALM OF DAVID. WHEN HE WAS IN THE WILDERNESS OF JUDAH.[a]]

I. 1 O GOD, Thou art my God, earnestly do I seek Thee;
My soul thirsteth for Thee, my flesh pineth[b] for Thee,

1. I SEEK THEE, not as the E.V. *Early* will I seek Thee." The noun which signifies "the dawn, the early morning," and the verb "to seek," are both from the same root, and are both to be referred to the same primitive idea. The meaning of the root is *to break in*, and hence this in the verb passes into the signification of *seeking* (earnestly), and in the noun *the dawn* is so called as that which *breaks in* upon the darkness.

MY FLESH, *i.e.* "my body," answering to "my soul" in the parall., and so describing the whole man. Comp. xvi. 8 [9]. So again, lxxxiv. 2 [3], "My heart and my flesh cry out for the living God." In that intense worship in which every thought, feeling, desire, affection are centred in the One true Object of Love, body and soul both take their part. It is as a living man, every pulse of his being filled with the love of God, that he responds to that love. And when he cries out "O God, Thou art my God," this is not merely an appropriation of God as the God of his worship

In a dry and weary [c] land where no water is.
2 So [d] have I gazed upon Thee in the sanctuary,
To see Thy power and Thy glory;
3 For Thy loving-kindness is better than life;
My lips shall praise Thee.
4 So will I bless Thee, while I live,
In Thy Name will I lift up my hands.

and trust: it is the *heart of flesh* stretching out *its human affections* towards Him who has a personal affection for His creature, and whose loving-kindness it knows to be better than life.

IN A DRY AND WEARY LAND. Some understand this literally, as describing the wilderness of Judah in which David was, according to the title of the Psalm. Others suppose that the language is figurative, and expresses the spiritual thirst and weariness of one who is shut out from God's Presence in the Sanctuary. (In this last case a comparison is implied, with the not uncommon omission of the particle of comparison: Symm. has ὡς ἐν γῇ, κ.τ.λ.; see on xlviii. 7 [8].) There can be no doubt that the last is the true interpretation. Nevertheless, the figure may perhaps have been suggested by the natural objects which immediately surrounded the Psalmist, as afterwards the allusion to the jackals, ver. 10.

2. So; that is, with the same ardent desire, or, such views have I had in past time of Thy glory, &c. See Critical Note.

TO SEE or, "beholding."

THY POWER AND THY GLORY. The special manifestation of these attributes was in the Holy Place. Comp. lxxviii. 61, where God is said to have given His power and His beauty (= glory here) into the adversary's hand, when the Ark was taken: see also 1 Sam. iv. 21, where *the glory* of God in like manner is identified with the Ark.

3. FOR. According to some, the particle gives the reason for the longing, ver. 1. According to others, it refers immediately to the last clause of ver. 2. "To see Thy power and Thy glory, *for* Thy loving-kindness," &c., this third attribute of God being inseparable from the other two, so that they who see His power and glory, see His loving-kindness also. But as ver. 2 is quasi-parenthetical, I think the first explanation of the use of the particle the more probable. Hupfeld would transpose the clauses again, as in the preceding verse: My lips shall praise Thee, For, &c. And so Mendelss. But this is hardly necessary. The rendering of our own Version, "Because Thy loving-kindness," &c. "My lips shall praise Thee," may be defended; see Gen. iii. 14, 17, where in like manner the causal sentence with כִּי *because*, precedes.

LIFE, in all the fulness of its earthly meaning. Life, and all the blessings of life, as they are commonly enjoyed (as Calvin, "omnia media quibus statum suum tuentur homines, terrena subsidia"). Comp. xvii. 13 [14]; Jer. viii. 3.

4. So, *i.e.* either with the same yearning affection, with the same heart of love and thanksgiving; or, *accordingly, consequently* (because of Thy loving-kindness), as in lxi. 8 [9]. There is no reason to take the *So* in this verse as answering to the *So* in ver. 2. The connection between the first four verses is not very exact, but may be traced as follows: My soul longeth for Thee (ver. 1). With the same longing with which I now desire to see Thee, I once did see Thee in Thy

5 As with marrow and fatness shall my soul be satisfied,
And with lips of joyful songs my mouth shall praise (Thee).
6 When [e] I have remembered Thee upon my bed,
In the night-watches I meditate upon Thee.
7 For Thou hast been a help unto me,
And in the shadow of Thy wings will I sing for joy.
8 My soul hath followed hard after Thee,
Thy right hand hath upholden me.

sanctuary (ver. 2). This longing is because of Thy loving-kindness, which is more precious than all else (ver. 3). Accordingly, I will praise Thee all my life long (ver. 4).

WHILE I LIVE, lit. "in, during, my life;" not as Hengst. "when brought back to life, or to salvation."

IN THY NAME, see xx. 1 [2], 5 [6], liv. 1 [3]. On the lifting up of the hands, as the gesture of prayer, see xxviii. 2.

5. AS WITH MARROW AND FATNESS, an image borrowed from a rich and splendid banquet. Comp. xxii. 26 [27], 29 [30], xxiii. 5, 6. Hupfeld, following J. H. Mich., thinks that the reference is immediately to the sacrificial meal which accompanied the thank-offering, here used as an image of thanksgiving (comp. l. 13 [14], liv. 6 [8], &c.), and that the comparison is between his delight in rendering thanksgiving to God, and the enjoyment of the fat of the sacrifices. But the simpler explanation is the more probable. Comp. Deut. xxxii. 14, Is. xxv. 6, Jer. xxxi. 14.

LIPS OF JOYFUL SHOUTING, or lips of singing.

6. WHEN I HAVE REMEMBERED . . . I MEDITATE. The heart having begun to occupy itself with the thought of God and His goodness, recalling all His loving-kindness in past times, continues to dwell upon it through the hours of the night. Others would connect this verse with the preceding, thus, "My lips shall praise Thee, when I remember Thee, &c.; when I meditate, making the two clauses of this verse co-ordinate.

IN THE NIGHT-WATCHES, *i.e.* the whole night through. According to the O. T. division, there were three watches. (Comp. Lament. ii. 19, Judg. vii. 19, Ex. xiv. 24.) According to the Roman reckoning, which we find in the N. T., four.

7. On this verse Donne remarks: "Now as the spirit and soul of the whole Book of Psalms is contracted into this Psalm, so is the spirit and soul of the whole Psalm contracted into this verse."—*Sermon* lxvi. vol. iii. p. 157. It embraces, as he observes, the "whole compass of time, past, present, and future;" David, in the present distress, finding support in the past, and from that sure ground looking forward with confidence and joy to the future.

IN THE SHADOW OF THY WINGS. Comp. xvii. 8, xxxvi. 7 [8], lvii. 1 [2], lxi. 4 [5]. That which David "promises himself, is not an immunity from all powerful enemies, nor a sword of revenge upon those enemies [but see ver. 10]; it is not that he shall have no adversary, nor that the adversary shall be able to do him no harm, but that he should have a refreshing, a respiration, *in velamento alarum*, under the shadow of God's wings."—*Donne*, p. 170.

8. The verse describes the mutual

II. 9 But *they* to (their own) destruction [f] seek my soul;
They shall go into the lower parts of the earth,
10 They shall be given over [g] to the power of the sword,
A portion for jackals shall they become.
11 But the king shall rejoice in God:
Every one that sweareth by Him shall boast himself;
For the mouth of them that speak falsehood shall be stopped.

relation of the soul and God. The soul follows after God and cleaves to Him (the expression in the Hebrew is literally, "my soul hath cleaved after Thee," so that the two ideas of following and cleaving are mingled); and God, on the other hand, stays and upholds the soul with His right hand. Out of that Hand of Power and Love neither man nor devil can pluck it.

9. Upon our modern feelings and thoughts this and the next verse seem, perhaps, somewhat to jar. We pass all at once into a different atmosphere. We have come down, as it were, from the mount of holy aspirations, into the common every-day world, where human enemies are struggling, and human passions are strong. Yet this very transition, harsh as it is, gives us a wonderful sense of reality. In some respects, it brings the Psalm nearer to our own level. The man who has been pouring out the fervent affection of his heart towards God is no mystic or recluse, lost in ecstatic contemplation, but one who is fighting a battle with foes of flesh and blood, and who hopes to see their malice defeated, their power crushed, and their carcases left to be the prey of jackals in the wilderness. What may be called the human force of character remains even amid thoughts whose impassioned earnestness is not of this world, and whose strain of intensely exalted spiritual fervour is such as but very few can reach.

BUT THEY. The pronoun used emphatically, as placing his enemies in sharp contrast with himself.

INTO THE LOWER PARTS OF THE EARTH. The expression seems here to denote Sheōl or Hades. The sentiment is the same as in ix. 17 [18], lv. 15 [16]. In cxxxix. 15 it denotes merely "darkness, obscurity." In Is. xliv. 23 it seems to mean little more than the earth, as opposed to the heavens. The LXX. *εἰς τὰ κατώτατα τῆς γῆς*. Comp. Eph. iv. 9.

11. THE KING. See Introduction to the Psalm, and comp. lxi. 6 [7].

EVERY ONE THAT SWEARETH BY HIM, *i.e.* every one to whom God is the object of religious fear, and trust, and worship (comp. Deut. vi. 13, Is. xix. 18, xlv. 23, lxv. 16, Am. viii. 14), the Psalmist himself, and his friends and companions. Those on the other hand who, because they have no fear of God, seek to prevail by lies, shall be confounded.

[a] מִדְבַּר יה׳. "The wilderness of Judah." Here, and here only, *Midbar* appears to be synonymous with *Arabah*. See Smith's *Dict. of the Bible*, i. 1156 *b*. The Chaldee, Aq., and Symm. follow the Hebrew text here, but the LXX. have Ἰδουμαίας, and they are followed by the Arab. and Ethiop., Jerome and the Vulg. Bellarmine tries to reconcile this by supposing that the wilderness of Idumæa was the larger name, comprehending the whole region, of which a part was called "the wilderness of

Judah." The difficulty attaching to the Inscription, however, is, that David was in the wilderness of Judah, so far as we know, only when he fled from Saul, whereas the Psalm must clearly be referred (see Introduction) to the time of Absalom's rebellion. Tholuck (who refers to Robinson, ii. p. 495) observes that this wilderness extends along the western shore of the Dead Sea, and higher up along the west bank of the Jordan. Here David halted, waiting for news from Jerusalem, before he crossed the river, probably by the same ford, near Gilgal, by which he afterwards returned from Mahanaim.

[b] כָּמַהּ. The word occurs nowhere else in the Bible. It may, however, be explained by the Syr. ܟܡܗ, which Castell explains, *caligine offusus est, excæcavit*, and the Arab. كمه, "to become dark, as the eye through blindness, the mind from faintness," &c. See Gesen. *Thes.* in v.

[c] עָיֵף, adj. masc. instead of fem. (to agree with אֶרֶץ), as in the parall. passages, cxliii. 6, Is. xxxii. 2. Similarly in other cases where two adjectives come together, the nearer agrees with the noun fem., and the more distant remains in the masc. gender. Comp. 1 Kings xix.11, רוּחַ גְּדוֹלָה וְחָזָק, 1 Sam. xv. 9, Is. xiv. 9, and even in the predicate, Is. xxxiii. 9 (Ges. § 147, Rem. 1). The difficulty however here is, that צִיָּה is prop. a noun, not an adj. Hence some (as Ven. and Del. 2d ed.) would refer עָיֵף to בְּשָׂרִי ; others, as Schm. and Hengst., to the subject, as a relative sentence *ubi lapsus sum* (conf. lxviii. 10, וְנִלְאָה).

[d] כֵּן. The use of this particle here is full of difficulty. *So*, how? To what does it refer? (1) Ewald : *So*, namely, as his God, has the Poet seen Him before in the splendour of the Temple, acknowledging and praising His glory and majesty; and *so* as his God, does he still ever bless Him, the כֵּן in ver. 4 [5] thus answering to the other, and לִרְאוֹת having a gerundial sense (*videndo*) : he renders,

> "So hab' ich dich im Heiligthum geschaut
> Erblickend deine Macht und Herrlichkeit."

(2) Oetinger : even so, *i.e.* with the same thirsty longing, have I gazed upon Thee in the sanctuary. Very similarly Calvin : "particulæ *sic* non leve pondus inest, acsi diceret : Quamvis in hac solitudine nihil nisi triste et horridum appareat, ut ipsa loci asperitas possit obtenebrare oculos ; ego tamen in gloriæ et virtutis tuæ intuitu me exerceo, perinde acsi in Sanctuario essem."

(3) Others, again, as Diod., Thol., take the particle *So* as introducing the reason of his intense longing based on past experience. "My soul longeth for Thee, so (*i.e.* in such beauty and glory) have I seen Thee in times past in the sanctuary." See the same use of כֵּן, as giving a reason, in Is. lii. 14.

(4) Luther supposes the particle *So* to describe the condition in which the Psalmist is, *sc.* being in this dreary waste, thus at a distance from the sanctuary, and renders the following perf. as a present, "Daselbst sehe

ich nach dir in deinem Heiligthum, wollte gerne schauen." This, at any rate, is better than to take it with others (as Ges.), as a future or optative, which is contrary to the plainest grammatical rules.

(5) Perhaps we may, with the E. V., transpose the clauses of the verse. לִרְאוֹת then depends upon the verbs in ver. 1 [2], and כֵּן must be rendered *so as* = כַּאֲשֶׁר. So also Rashi, Mendels., Zunz, and Hupfeld, the last of whom further supposes that a like transposition of clauses has taken place in all the following verses, to the end of ver. 8 [9]; an arrangement which certainly obviates some of the grammatical difficulties of the passage.

On the whole, I incline to the interpretation, "*So*, i.e. as I now long after Thee, and desire to see Thee, in the same way have I gazed at Thee in the sanctuary, in order to see Thy majesty," &c. The use of כֵּן in cxxvii. 2, is, it seems to me, very similar (see note there).

[e] אִם, here used as a particle of time, followed by the perf. as frequently, xli. 7, xciv. 18, Amos vii. 2, &c. Some, however (as Del. 1st ed.), would make this clause co-ordinate with the following, and so render אֶהְגֶּה also as a past, *meditabar*. In his 2d ed. Del. has the present: "wenn ich dein gedenke . . . . sinn' ich." Others, again, would connect the clause with אִם, with the preceding verse. I think it better, however, to regard the first clause as the protasis, and the second as the apodosis. Symm., well, *ἀναμιμνησκόμενός σου ἐπὶ τῆς στρωμνῆς μου, καθ' ἑκάστην φυλακὴν ἐμελέτων σε.*

[f] וְהֵמָּה לְשׁוֹאָה. The pron. with the וְ prefixed is used, as commonly, with an emphatic meaning, and may of itself denote the Psalmist's enemies, without any further description of them, the sense being clear enough from the context. It would be possible, however, to render, "But *they* (shall be) for destruction (or, doomed to destruction), *who* seek my soul," the relat. being understood in the usual way. The rendering, "They who seek my soul to destroy it," is objectionable, as inverting the order of the words in the Hebrew. The LXX. express לְשׁוֹאָה by *εἰς μάτην*, and therefore, perhaps, read לַשָּׁוְא, though Hupf. considers the one as the fem. form only of the other. שׁוֹאָה means, properly, *a downfall with a crash*. Comp. xxxv. 17.

[g] יַגִּירֻהוּ, lit. "they shall pour him out," which = "he shall be poured out," the act. verb being used with indefinite subject instead of the passive. See note on lviii. 7 [8]. The suffix of the pron. is used in the sing., as often, instead of the plur. (see v. 10, vii. 3), and may perhaps be explained distributively: "*Every one of them* shall be poured out, *i.e.* given over." On מְנָת see xi. note [c]; xvi. note [h].

PSALM 64

THIS Psalm contains a stirring and vigorous picture of the plotting by which evil men were aiming at the Psalmist's life. It opens, as is usual in such Psalms, with a cry to God against their machinations; it describes at length the methods they take to accomplish their purposes; and it concludes with a confident prediction of their sudden and utter overthrow. We have already observed a similar strain of feeling in other Psalms, such as the 52d, 57th, 58th, and 59th. In all these we find allusions to the mischief done by *the tongue* of the wicked: in the last three the same figures are employed, the tongue, and its words, being compared to arrows and swords. Comp. lxiv. 3, 4 [4, 5] with lvii. 4 [5], lviii. 7 [8], lix. 7 [8].

The Psalm is said to be David's, and Ewald observes that it so nearly resembles Psalm vii. that one might be tempted to ascribe it to David, did not a careful comparison contradict such a supposition. But where there is this admitted resemblance, the minute criticism may very well be distrusted, and the title suffered to stand.

The Psalm is regular in its structure, but scarcely admits of strophical division. We have, however, after the introductory petition in ver. 1, 2,

I. The description of the wicked and their devices. Ver. 3—6.

II. The destruction which shall assuredly come upon them, and which shall fill the righteous with joy. Ver. 7—10.

[FOR THE PRECENTOR. A PSALM OF DAVID.]

1 HEAR my voice, O God, in my complaint,
From terror of (the) enemy preserve my life.
2 Hide me from the conspiracy of evil-doers,
From the raging of (the) workers of iniquity;

2. CONSPIRACY. This word denotes any kind of familiar intercourse, but generally *secret* converse, plotting, &c. (see on xxv. note [g]); whereas the word RAGING, in the parallelism, means properly, a noisy, tumultuous assemblage. Jerome, *a tumultu*. The noun is from the

3 Who have sharpened their tongue, like a sword,
(Who) have aimed their arrow, (even) a bitter word,
4 That they may shoot in (their) lurking-places at (the) perfect:
Suddenly do they shoot at him and fear not.
5 They strengthen themselves in an evil purpose;
They reckon how they may lay snares privily;
They say, Who shall observe them?
6 They devise iniquities;
They have perfected [a] the device devised (by them);
And the inward part of each (of them) and the heart is deep.

same root, as the verb "raged" in ii. 1. Comp. lv. 14 [15].

3. HAVE AIMED. The verb is used commonly of bending the bow, but is transferred also to the aiming of the arrow; see lviii. 7 [8]. For the figures employed, comp. lii. 3 [4].

4. AND FEAR NOT, *i.e.* without scruple or remorse, having no fear of God, who takes vengeance on the wicked (comp. lv. 19 [20]). There is a play in the Hebrew on the two words, "shoot" and "fear."

5, 6. These verses carry on the picture of the plots of these evil men, and especially describe their resolute persistence in their schemes, their confidence of success, and the depth and subtlety of their designs.

5. THEY STRENGTHEN THEMSELVES, or, "they harden themselves," lit. "They strengthen for themselves an evil thing (word)," *i.e.* they take every means to secure their object, follow it up resolutely, &c. So Reuss: "ils assurent leur mauvaise cause."

THEY RECKON; each part of their evil plot being, as it were, carefully gone over and enumerated. See the same word in like sense, lix. 12 [13], lxix. 26 [27].

THEY SAY, *i.e.* within themselves, they think, as the word is often used in such phrases; for the fuller expression see x. 6.

WHO SHALL OBSERVE THEM? The question is an indirect one, for which the Syr. substitutes the direct, "Who shall observe *us?*" The pron. *them* refers to the speakers, not to the snares. The prep. with the pronoun is not merely instead of the accus., but marks more distinctly the *aim* of the verb. Lit. "Who shall see (look) *at* them," as 1 Sam. xvi. 7.

6. THEY DEVISE or, "they search out." And the next clause may be rendered, if the present reading is correct: "We have accomplished (say they) a diligent search."

THEY HAVE PERFECTED. This word is grammatically difficult of explanation. See Critical Note.

AND THE INWARD PART, or, "inward thought," as in xlix. 11, &c. This last clause is added loosely, as a further explanation of the character of the men. Tholuck, who supposes the Psalm to have been written by David at the court of Saul, when he became aware of the plots by which others were seeking to injure him and traduce him to the king, sees in this clause the expression of amazement which fills the mind of the upright, honest youth, when he first becomes aware of the deep duplicity and treachery of the aspirants to royal favour, by whom he was surrounded.

7 But God hath shot at them with an arrow;
Suddenly have their wounds come.
8 And He hath made them stumble, (with) their own tongue against them; [b]
And all that look upon them shake the head.
9 And all men have feared,
And they have declared God's doing,
And His work have they considered.
10 The righteous rejoiceth in Jehovah, and hath found refuge in Him;
And all the upright in heart boast themselves.

7. The Divine judgement is now painted as if actually fulfilling itself before the very eyes of the Psalmist. Hence the verbs are in the past tense, by which a certain dramatic effect is produced, which is lost when they are rendered in the future. So vividly is the Divine judgement anticipated, that it is *as if* already accomplished.

The first clause might stand thus, according to the accents: "But God hath shot at them with a sudden arrow," or the verse might be divided as follows:

"But God hath shot at them:
(With) a sudden arrow have been their wounds."

But the first of these methods of punctuation leaves the second clause strangely bare. The second has the support of the LXX., Symm., Aq. &c. But the punctuation I have adopted, which is that of our A.V. Ew. and Del., is, on the whole, the best. The arrow of God (comp. vii. 12 [13], xxxviii. 2 [3]) thus answers to the arrow of the wicked, ver. 3.

8. HE HATH MADE, &c. So with a slight change of the vowel-points; or, with the present reading, "they have been made to stumble." SHAKE THE HEAD. For this meaning of the verb, comp. Jer. xviii. 16, xlviii. 27; for the gesture, as one of malicious triumph in looking upon suffering, &c., see xxii. 7 [8].

[a] תַּמְנוּ. This, as it stands, can only be for תַּמֹּנוּ, plur. pret. of תמם, and must either be (1) the triumphant assertion of the wicked, glorying in the success of their plans: "They devise iniquities (saying), We have accomplished the device (we had) devised" [or, if תמם be intrans. "we are ready (with) the device," &c., or, as Hitz. "wir sind fertig; herrlich ausgedacht"]; or (2) which is still more hard and abrupt, the complaint of the righteous, "We are cut off," *i.e.* without the help of God, by the devices of these men. The same form, without the connecting long vowel, and consequently with the Dagesh dropt, occurs Numb. xvii. 28 [13 E.V.], Jer. xliv. 18, and (with Kametz) Lam. iii. 22. In the first two of these passages it is certainly 1 pers. plur., and it *may be* so in the last, as it is rendered in the E. V., "It is of the Lord's mercies that *we* are not consumed." But there, as here, the 3d pers. is preferable: the difficulty, however, is to account for the form תַּמְנוּ, instead of תַּמּוּ. Some, as Qimchi

and Buxt., suppose the נ to stand instead of the doubling of the מ, and would defend its position as standing *after* instead of *before* the consonant which ought to be doubled, by reference to מְעֻזְנֶיהָ for מָעֻזֶּיהָ, Is. xxiii. 11. It is better, however, either to read תַּמּוּ, *they have perfected*, or, with many MSS. טָמְנוּ, *they have hidden* (*i.e.* in their heart), and so Rashi, Luth., Ven., Död., Schnurr.

b וַיַּכְשִׁילֻהוּ. Qimchi explains: "And they shall make it, viz. their tongue, fall upon themselves." For this position of the pronom. suffix in anticipation of the proper object, the noun, he refers to Exod. ii. 6, Job xxxiii. 20. But in this case the suff. ought to be fem., as the noun (*tongue*) is. The suff., if the reading is correct, can only refer to the enemies, the sing. standing for the plur. by a not unfrequent enallage of number (see on lxii. 4 [5]). Then the act. verb in 3 pers. plur. is used impersonally for the passive (comp. lxiii. 11, xlix. note [i]): "they (*i.e.* men) make them fall," = "they are made to fall," and the subjoined clause need not be considered, contrary to the accents, as an independent clause, but may describe further the manner of their fall: "And they have been (shall be) made to fall (with) their own tongue (turned) against themselves." This gives a good sense, and describes their punishment as a righteous retribution. I prefer, however, by a very slight alteration, to read וַיַּכְשִׁלֵהוּ, the subject being God: "And He hath made them (lit. "him") stumble," &c. Reuss arranges the clauses differently:

Mais Dieu va leur lancer sa flèche :
Soudain ils sentiront les coups qui les renverseront :
Leurs calomnies retomberont sur eux.

PSALM 65

We can hardly doubt that this beautiful Psalm, "marked by the brilliant vivacity of its poetic colouring," was composed on the occasion of an abundant harvest, and was intended to be sung as a hymn of thanksgiving by the whole congregation gathered before God in Zion. From the allusions in verses 7, 8, it would seem that the time was one of great political convulsions, of a shaking of nations and kingdoms, in the midst of which God had manifested His goodness to His people. The Psalm connects together these two great concurrent instances of God's protecting care and love. He had given peace to Zion when her enemies were raging around her. He had crowned her with the year of His goodness when drought and famine seemed to threaten. "The Hearer of prayer" had heard the petitions of His people, when they met to confess their sins and to make known their need before Him; and now it was but fitting that they should gather again within His courts, there to thank Him for His mercy, and to show forth all His praise.

This twofold character of the Psalm is best explained by referring it to the time immediately subsequent to the destruction of the Assyrian army before Jerusalem. An abundant harvest, it had been promised, Is. xxxvii. 30, should follow that event; and the fields so lately trampled beneath the feet of the invader seemed now, with their waving crops, to sing and shout for joy.

The title of the Psalm assigns it to David, but it is impossible to read it and not to feel that it bears every evidence of a later date. So strong indeed is this evidence, that even Delitzsch, who is usually a strenuous supporter of the Inscriptions, abandons the tradition here, and with Ewald thinks that the Psalm was written about the time of Sennacherib's overthrow (*i.e.* about 712 B.C.).

The Psalm consists of three strophes :—

I. The opening is an expression of the thoughts and feelings with which the congregation may fitly approach God, now that they come to thank Him for His goodness. Ver. 1—4.

II. Then follows the celebration of the mighty acts of Jehovah, both in the world of nature and also among the nations, so that His name is known and acknowledged to the ends of the earth. Ver. 5—8.

III. Lastly, the special thanksgiving which is called forth by the refreshing rain which God has sent, and the rich and glorious harvest which is already waving and ripening before their eyes. Ver. 9—13.

The difference between the first and last strophe in the mode of expression is striking. In the first, there is a certain abruptness. The thoughts follow one another, not indeed altogether without order, but without anything like formal cohesion. In the last, on the other hand, the language flows with the thoughts. The bright harvest-scene is before the eyes of the inspired singer. He stands looking on the fields white already to the harvest, and his soul within him rejoices in their glorious promise. The Poet and the world without him are at one accord. The fulness of joy in his heart, as he sees how his God has poured blessing upon the land, passes as it were by a contagion of sunny gladness into the inanimate creation, and the very cornfields seem to him to shout together, yea to sing for joy.

[FOR THE PRECENTOR. A PSALM OF DAVID. A SONG.]

I. 1 FOR Thee praise waiteth,[a] O God, in Zion;
And unto Thee is (the) vow paid.
2 O Thou that hearest prayer,
Unto Thee doth all flesh come.
3 Iniquities [b] have prevailed against me,

1—4. In these verses, whilst the meaning of the separate sentences is clear, it is not equally easy to trace the line of thought. I believe it to be this: In Zion God is known, there He is praised and worshipt. He is the hearer of prayer; that is His very character, and therefore all flesh comes to Him. All who feel their weakness, all who need help and grace, seek it at His hand. It is true that they who thus come, come with the burden of sin upon them: their iniquities rise up in all their strength and might, and would thrust them away from the presence of the Holy One. But He Himself, in the plenitude of His mercy, covers those iniquities, will not look upon them, and so suffers sinners to approach Him. And how blessed are they who, reconciled and pardoned, are thus suffered to draw nigh. Of that blessedness may we ourselves be partakers, may we be filled and satisfied therewith.

1. WAITETH, lit. "is silent," the word being used apparently metaphorically, in the sense of *resting*, and so of *waiting*. So Diodati, "laude t' aspetta in Sion." The meaning is, as Calvin observes, that God is so gracious to His people that He supplies them every day with fresh subject for praise. Others, however, explain it of the silence of the heart in devotion, "there is silence before Thee (and) praise." See Critical Note.

IS (THE) VOW PAID. The noun in the singular here is used collectively, and may be considered as equivalent to a plural. The verb is manifestly a present, stating the actual fact.

2. O THOU THAT HEAREST PRAYER. This is the very character of God. "He describes not what has once happened, but clothes God with this everlasting attribute (*perpetuo ornatu*), as though he said, God can no more be deaf to the prayers of His people than He can deny Himself."—*Calvin.*

UNTO THEE DOTH ALL FLESH COME. By *flesh* is meant man in his weakness and need, but the word scarcely includes here (as Hengst. and Hupf.) other animals. It is clear, however, that the privilege of access to God is not intended to be confined merely to the Israelites, or so general an expression would not have been chosen. It is again, as in the last verses, the statement of a fact, true generally, true so far as men pray at all. Tholuck carries this so far as to say that even prayers offered in blindness to other gods yet reach the true God (see a similar remark in R. Cecil, *Remains*, ii. 517), and supposes these to be contrasted with the prayer offered to God in Zion.

Calvin and others, who render the verbs in the future, see here a prophecy of Christ's kingdom, and of the conversion of the heathen, as in Is. xlv. 23, 24. But the general tenour of the Psalm does not support this view.

3. INIQUITIES, lit. "things (or words) of iniquities," perhaps not

(But) as for our transgressions, THOU coverest them.
4 Blessed [c] is he whom Thou choosest,
And bringest near that he may dwell in Thy courts!
Oh let us, then, be satisfied [d] with the blessing of Thine house,
The holy [e] place of Thy temple.

II. 5 With terrible things [f] in righteousness dost Thou answer us, O God of our salvation,

merely pleonastic, but intended (as Del.) to mark the several parts of the object more distinctly.

HAVE PREVAILED, lit. "have been too strong for me." Comp. xl. 12 [13]. It is the remembrance of this which brings up before the mind the one great obstacle to approach to God: the next line telling us how that obstacle is removed. Calvin well explains: "Although our iniquities, as they deserve repulse, would cast us far from Thy sight, yet because Thou showest Thyself ready to be reconciled, they will not prevent the course of our prayers." Comp. Is. lix. 1, 2.

AGAINST ME. The pronoun of the first pers. sing. comes in somewhat abruptly. Del. thinks that the whole congregation here speak as one man. It is more probable that the Psalmist makes a personal application to himself of that which was true of all, putting his own guilt however in the first place, as Daniel also confessed his own sins first (Dan. ix. 20), and then those of the people.

THOU COVEREST, or "forgivest," lit. "makest atonement for." See on xxxii. 1. The pronoun is emphatic, as though to express the conviction that God and God alone could do this.

Reuss softens the abruptness by connecting the two clauses of the verse thus: "Quand le poids des péchés nous accable, c'est toi qui pardonnes nos transgressions."

4. BLESSED. See notes on xv. 1, xxvii. 4. This blessedness is here felt especially as vouchsafed to God's *chosen*, as the privilege of Israel rather than of other nations ("Blessed is he whom Thou choosest"), and also as flowing from the *forgiving* love of God, who covers the transgressions which else would separate from Him even His chosen.

OH LET US BE SATISFIED. "For all that God's grace offers us we can give no better thanks than that we hunger and thirst after it, and that the poor empty soul be satisfied therewith."—*Delitzsch.*

HOLY PLACE OF THY TEMPLE, or perhaps, "with the holiness of Thy temple."

5. The Psalmist now approaches more nearly to his main subject: and first, he declares God's wonders on behalf of His people, wonders so great and so signal that all the earth has been made to know that there is a God in Israel.

TERRIBLE THINGS (as elsewhere, "great things," "wondrous things"), commonly used of God's great acts wrought in behalf of Israel, especially in their deliverance out of Egypt. (Deut. x. 21; 2 Sam. vii. 23; Ps. cvi. 22, cxlv. 4, &c.)

DOST THOU ANSWER US (not fut. "Thou *wilt* answer us," but), now, as at all times, when our need is sore, IN RIGHTEOUSNESS (comp. Is. xlii. 6), that being the very foundation of God's moral government of the world, and that righteousness being manifested in the salvation of His people as in the overthrow

Thou that art the trust of all the ends of the earth,
and of the sea, afar off:
6 Who setteth fast (the) mountains by His strength,
Being girded about with might;
7 (Who) stilleth the roaring of (the) seas,
The roaring of their waves,
And the tumult of the nations.
8 Therefore they that dwell in the ends [g] (of the earth)
are afraid at Thy signs;

of their enemies; a cloud and darkness to these, but a light and defence to those.

TRUST. "The meaning is," says Venema, "that God is the most certain help and defence of men, whether He be acknowledged by them and trusted in or not." Tholuck thinks that the congregation, "lifting up their hearts to the survey of God's wondrous works, declare the conviction that whatever of blessing and of consolation all the nations of the earth receive, issues from this source only, wherein is involved the confession, that all prayers of the heathen also, however perverted their ideas of the Deity may be, still in reality mount to the throne of the God of Israel." (See above on ver. 2.) He then refers to the testimony of the Prophet Amos (ix. 7), that the same fatherly Hand which led Israel out of Egypt had also guided and blessed heathen nations. But here, as in ver. 2, it is the *claim* of God to be thus recognized and trusted in which is asserted. God is the hearer of the prayers of all. He is the only object of trust, even though all do not pray to Him or trust in Him. As Luther well says: "One may run over the wide world, even to its utmost extremity, yet Thou art the only foundation on which the trust of a man's heart can rest." At the same time, there is an anticipation of a universal recognition and worship, such as could not but spring up in the hearts of those who were met together on such an occasion as this, to record God's wonderful works. In Ps. lxvii. this anticipation becomes more nearly predictive.

AFAR OFF. The word is properly an adj., and may, as Hupf. takes it, belong to the noun "ends," the construction being "the distant ends of the earth and sea." Comp. Is. xxvii. 15. He refers to lxiv. 7, Is. lxvi. 19, as compared with v. 26, viii. 9, xxxiii. 17. And so Diodati: "confidanza di tutte l'estremità le più lontane della terra e del mare." And so Reuss. But according to the accent the construction is "sea of the distant ones," *i.e.* the dwellers on distant coasts and islands.

6, 7. Mountains and seas are not to be understood figuratively, but literally, the statement being that the same God who stills the earthquake and hushes the storm gives peace also to contending kingdoms and nations. Both in the natural and the political world He rules. The *sea* and the *nations* are mentioned together, the one being so often used as an image of the other. See xlvi.

8. THEREFORE. I have thus rendered the *Vau consec.* as marking the consequence. Lit. "and (accordingly) they have feared."

SIGNS. In like manner σημεῖον is used in the N. T. of miracles as "tokens and indications of the near presence and working of God" (Trench). Or as Basil says: ἔστι

Thou makest the outgoings[h] of the morning and
evening to sing for joy.

III. 9 Thou hast visited the earth, and made it overflow,[i]
Thou greatly enrichest it with the brook of God,
which is full of water;
Thou preparest their corn,
For so dost Thou prepare the earth.

σημεῖον πρᾶγμα φανερὸν κεκρυμμένου τινὸς καὶ ἀφανοῦς ἐν ἑαυτῷ τὴν δήλωσιν ἔχον. Calvin: "opera Dei insignia, quibus gloriæ suæ notas insculpsit;" and then observing that all God's works, those which appear to us the most ordinary or the least, do still manifest Him, he adds, "miraculis κατ' ἐξοχὴν tribuitur hoc nomen, quia illic clarius refulget Dei majestas."

OUTGOINGS, or rather *the places* where morning and evening have their birth ("les lieux d'où surgissent l'aube et le crépuscule," Perret-Gentil; "portals," Kay), the East and West; the meaning being, that all things, the inanimate as well as the animate creatures, from the rising to the setting of the sun, break forth into songs of joy before God.

Briefly, verses 5—8 may be summed up thus: the whole wide world, its mountains and its seas, and all the dwellers in the world from one end of it to the other, are in the hand of God, wait upon Him, and He makes all to rejoice.

9. With this verse begins the special subject of thanksgiving, the thanksgiving for the harvest. It is manifest, from the use of the *perfect tenses* in ver. 9, 11, 13, that this is not merely a general acknowledgement of God's goodness in bringing the fruits of the earth to maturity, but has reference to a particular season.

THOU HAST VISITED THE EARTH, or perhaps "the land." Comp. Jer. xxvii. 22. On this Arnd. (quoted by Hengst.) says: "The Holy Spirit makes use of a homely word when, in describing the fertilizing genial rain, he terms it a visiting of the earth. When a visit is made by rich and affectionate friends, they do not come empty, but bring with them a blessing or good gift to testify their favour and love. Thus, although God is over all, and fills heaven and earth, He does not at all times leave traces or marks of His presence. But when in time of drought He gives a gracious fertilizing shower, it is as if He paid us a visit, and brought along with Him a great blessing, that we might mark His love and goodness."

THE BROOK OF GOD, not as the Chald. "reservoir," and others "the clouds," but rather "the rain." The Arabs have the same expression. Schultens quotes from *Hist. Tamerl.*, p. 82, the Arabic proverb: "When the river of God comes, the river Isa (in Bagdad) ceases." It is the heavenly stream as opposed to earthly streams; called a *brook* or *channel* (it is rather rivulet than river; Mendelss. has Brünnlein), (see on i. 3) with reference to the irrigation of the land by means of such. It is full of water, whereas the wells which men dig, the channels which they cut, dry up and cease to flow.

It is uncertain as regards the construction whether "the brook of God" is a second object of the verb as rendered above, or whether it is the subject of a fresh clause, "The brook of God is full of water."

SO, *i.e.* by sending the rain. The present tenses are employed here to express that this God does not in one year only, but every year.

10 Thou waterest[k] the furrows thereof abundantly,
Thou settlest the ridges thereof;
With showers of rain Thou makest it soft;
Thou blessest the springing thereof.
11 Thou hast crowned the year with Thy goodness,[l]
And Thy tracks drop fatness;
12 The pastures of the wilderness drop (therewith),
And with gladness the hills gird themselves.
13 The meadows are clothed with flocks,
The valleys also are covered over with corn:
They shout for joy together, yea they sing.

THE EARTH. The Hebrew has only the pronoun "it," but this is hardly intelligible in English.

The pronominal suffixes THEIR and IT are used somewhat freely, the first referring to *men* (as the dwellers in the earth), and the last to the *earth* itself.

The repetition of the verb *prepare* seems designed to mark that all is God's doing. He prepares the earth, and so prepares the corn.

10. WATEREST ABUNDANTLY, soakest, drenchest, givest to drink to the full. Jer. xxxi. 14, "satiate;" Prov. vii 18.

SETTLEST, lit. "pressest down," describing vividly the effect of a rich and abundant rain. The same word is used of *bending* a bow in xviii. 34 [35], where see note. The *ridges* are the lines of earth thrown up by the action of the plough between the *furrows*.

SPRINGING. The word means "a bud," or "fresh shoot." It is rendered "bud" by the Gen.-Vers. here and by our A. V. in Is. lxi. Reuss: "ses jeunes pousses."

11. WITH THY GOODNESS. I have so rendered somewhat doubtfully, because no exactly parallel construction supports the translation (see Critical Note). The other rendering, "Thou hast crowned the year of Thy goodness," gives no bad sense. The year of God's goodness would mean the year in which it had been emphatically displayed (comp. Is. lxi. 2); and this might be said to be crowned with the harvest.

THY TRACKS, prop. *marks of the chariot-wheels*. Comp. xviii. 10 [11], Deut. xxxiii. 26, Is. lxvi. 15.

12. THE PASTURES OF THE WILDERNESS. Comp. Job xxxviii. 26, 27. But the wilderness does not mean a bare desert, as the word "pastures" shows; it is merely contrasted with the cultivated arable land.

13. THE MEADOWS. See on xxxvii. 20. Is. xxx. 23.

THEY SHOUT TOGETHER, striving, as it were, and vying with one another in their gladness; as the reflexive form of the verb denotes. Ewald and Del. strangely introduce a new subject here—men, or all creatures, shout, &c. But nothing can be more beautiful, or more truly poetical, than the figure by which the valleys waving with corn are said themselves to shout and sing.

[a] דֻּמִיָּה has been variously interpreted. The LXX. σοὶ πρέπει ὕμνος; Jerome, *Tibi decet hymnus*, "Praise is comely for Thee;" and so the older Versions generally, as if they read דֹּומִיָּה (as the Rabb. commenta-

tors punctuate the same word in lxii. 2), part. of דמה, "to be like, suitable." This has been adopted also by Hitz. and Ewald. But retaining the present punctuation, דּוּמִיָּה, "silence," "silent resignation," explanations differ. (1) Some, as Gei., De Wette, Ges., suppose an asyndeton: "For Thee there is silence, (and) praise," *i.e.* Thou art worshipt both with the heart's stillness and with the words of men's lips [or with *resignation* (in sorrow) and with thanksgiving (in joy)]. (2) Others, as Qim., Calv., Cocc., &c. "Praise waiteth for Thee." (3) Luth., Hengst., Del.: "Praise (is given) to Thee (in) silence," *i.e.* in the deep stillness of the heart's devotion, as opposed to the loud, noisy service of heathen worshipers. Of these, either (2) or (3) seems preferable. דּוּמִיָּה is clearly a predicate; and the constr. in lxii. 2 is quite parallel, "My soul waiteth (is silent) for God," *i.e.* yields itself to Him in quiet resignation.

[b] דִּבְרֵי ע׳, perhaps not merely pleonastic, but, as Delitzsch suggests, enumerative, denoting the variety of circumstances, &c. (See xxxv. 20, cv. 27, cxlv. 5, and 1 Sam. x. 2, 2 Sam. xi. 18.) Comp. the somewhat similar use of the Greek χρῆμα, χρήματα. It would be possible, however, to render: "iniquitous words."

[c] אַשְׁרֵי, with relat. omitted as lxxi. 18, lxxxi. 6, &c. יִשְׁכֹּן in the next clause is a subordinate clause marking the *purpose*. (Ew. § 337 *b*.)

[d] נִשְׂבְּעָה, not fut. but either opt. or possibly conjunct., "that we may be satisfied," though this does not suit the connection so well.

[e] קְדֹשׁ (instead of קֹדֶשׁ). See xlvi. note [d].

[f] נוֹרָאוֹת, not an adv. as cxxxix. 14, but a second accus. after the verb תַּעֲנֵנוּ, which is here a pres. or rather an aorist, as denoting an action continued and repeated.

[g] קַצְוֵי from קְצָת, properly stat. constr. for קְצָוֹת from קְצָוָה, fem. of קֶצֶו, or rather קְצוּ. (Hupf.)

[h] מוֹצָאֵי, "the places whence the morning and evening go forth," *i.e.* the East and West. Strictly speaking, the expression can refer only to the *morning* (יצא being always used of the rising sun), but by zeugma, or attraction, the word is made here to refer also to the *evening*. Ewald gives somewhat similar expressions from the poets of Arabia and India. Zunz, in his translation, avoids the difficulty by rendering, "des Morgens Aufgang, und den Abend machst du jubeln." He thus makes מוֹצָאֵי depend only on בֹּקֶר, and not on עֶרֶב.

[i] תְּשֹׁקְקֶהָ, from שׁוּק cognate with שׁקה, "Thou makest overflow, waterest," &c. in the same sense as the Hiph., Joel ii. 24, iv. 13. In תַּעְשְׁרֶנָּה we have a shortened form of the Hiph. (Ges. § 53, 3, Rem. 4.) Or perhaps, as Ibn Ez.: "Makest it to desire." Cf. נֶפֶשׁ שֹׁקֵקָה, "A longing soul."

[k] רַוֵּה and נַחֵת are, according to the existing punctuation, imperatives. But the sense thus obtained is awkward, and very few of later commentators have defended it. Most regard them as infinitives absolute (רַוֵּה

being for רַוֹּה; cf. Ex. xxii. 22, 1 Sam. iii. 12, Jer. xiv. 19, &c.), denoting *the manner in which* this preparation of the earth took place, "watering the furrows," &c. It is better perhaps to consider them as standing instead of the finite verb. (Ges. § 131, 4 *b*.) Hupfeld would however alter the punctuation, and read רִוָּה, נִחֵת, 3d pers. pret., in which case we should only have a not uncommon transition from the second person to the third.

1 שְׁנַת טוֹבָתֶךָ, lit. "the year *of* Thy goodness," and so the older interpreters understood it (in the same sense as "the year of grace," Is. lxi. 2), *i.e.* the year in which that goodness has been peculiarly manifested. The other rendering, "Thou hast crowned the year *with* Thy goodness," is undoubtedly preferable, so far as the sense is concerned, but the construction, in point of grammar, is questionable. Hupfeld indeed refers to xlix. 6, and Böttcher to xc. 12, as instances of a similar attraction, but neither the one nor the other is exactly parallel.

PSALM 66

The Poet celebrates God's great deeds on behalf of His people, and calls upon all nations to join in thanksgiving to Him. From the language of verses 8—12, the Psalm would seem to have been composed on the occasion of some special deliverance, but the expressions used are too general to lead to any certain conclusion as to the time when it was written. Some have supposed that the allusion is to the defeat of the Assyrians under Sennacherib (so Ven., Köst., Hengst., Del., Thol., the last even supposing it to have been written by King Hezekiah); others, to the return from the Babylonish Captivity (Flam., De W. Ew.); others again, to the times of the Maccabees (Hitz., Olsh.); Qimchi, to the final ingathering of Israel. But not a single critic of any name has ventured to place this Psalm earlier than the times of Hezekiah. Bp. Colenso, indeed, in order to support his theory as to the Elohistic Psalms, is obliged to suppose that it may have been written in the time of David. But, not to mention that the whole character and style of the Psalm are against such a supposition, it is obvious that the language of verses 8—12 is not applicable to the age of David. Here, as in Psalms xlvi. and xlviii., we have Psalms, beyond all reasonable doubt, as late as the times of Hezekiah, in which God is addressed by the name Elohim, and not by the name Jehovah.

In ver. 13, there is a sudden and remarkable change from the use of the plural to the use of the singular. Some would explain this on the principle that the people are personified, and therefore speak in the singular. This, however, is very unnatural; no probable reason can be given for such a personification. It is far more likely that the Sacred Poet, after having spoken for the whole congregation, speaks for himself as one of that congregation, declaring with thanksgiving God's goodness to himself, felt and acknowledged by himself, as well as to all Israel. In fact, as the Psalm was clearly intended for the public worship of the Temple, the former part was probably designed to be sung by the whole choir of Levites and the latter by a single voice.

Ewald thinks that ver. 13—20 formed originally a distinct poem; but the similar turn of expression in ver. 5 and ver. 16, and the abruptness of ver. 13, considered as the beginning of a Psalm, are against this view, which otherwise is plausible.

The Psalm consists of five strophes, three of them being distinguished by the Selah at the close:—

I. The exhortation addressed to the whole world to give glory to God. Ver. 1—4.

II. The recounting of God's great acts on behalf of His people in times past. Ver. 5—7.

III. The wonderful deliverance recently vouchsafed. Ver. 8—12.

IV. The Psalmist himself promises to bring large offerings to God in grateful acknowledgement of His goodness. Ver. 13—15.

V. He calls upon all to hear the story of God's mercy to himself, and especially of His answer to his prayer. Ver. 16—20.

[FOR THE PRECENTOR. A SONG. A PSALM.[a]]

I. 1 SHOUT unto God, all the earth!
2 Sing the glory of His Name,
Ascribe (to Him) glory, (in) His praise.

1. ALL THE EARTH, used with a plural verb, as in Deut. ix. 28, the inhabitants being of course meant, as again in ver. 4 of this Psalm.

2. ASCRIBE, &c. lit. "Make glory His praise," *i.e.* in giving Him praise ascribe to Him that glory which is His; or, "make His praise glory," *i.e.* to be glorious, as

3 Say unto God, " How terrible is Thy work ![b]
Because of the greatness of Thy strength do Thine
enemies feign allegiance unto Thee.
4 All the earth boweth down unto Thee and singeth
to Thee;
They sing Thy Name." [Selah.]

II. 5 Come and see the great acts of God:
Terrible (He is) in His doing concerning the
children of men.
6 He turned the sea into dry land,
They passed through the river on foot:—
There let us rejoice[c] in Him!

E.V. The two nouns are in apposition with one another. Comp. Joshua vii. 19, Is. xlii. 12.

3. SAY UNTO GOD. He now gives the reason why God should be praised, and he would have this acknowledgement addressed directly to God, in order to stir and rouse the hearts of those who uttered it the more effectually: "for nothing so compels us to a due reverence towards God, as when we place ourselves before His face." —*Calvin.*

HOW TERRIBLE. Comp. the song of the heavenly harpers, Rev. xv. 3.

FEIGN ALLEGIANCE, *i.e.* do so in a forced and reluctant manner, though they would willingly withdraw their necks from the yoke if they could. Or, as in xviii. 44, " come crouching." Lit. " *lie* unto Thee," whence the P.B.V. "shall be found liars unto Thee." The E.V. has here, and in xviii. 44 [45], where the same word occurs, " shall submit themselves," and in the margin in both places "yield feigned obedience," which is doubtless the true rendering.

There is perhaps a tacit comparison implied. If even His enemies must render a forced and tardy and hypocritical submission, what should they do to whom He has manifested Himself in love?

4. BOWETH DOWN. It is unnecessary to render the verbs as futures of prediction. Faith boldly brings the future into the present, and sees that as already accomplished which is so in the purpose and will of God. Not Zion only, but the whole earth is the temple of God, wherein His praises are sung.

5. COME AND SEE. Comp. xlvi. 8 [9]. The dull hearts of men must be roused, their attention excited; the exhortation implying also that *fresh* acts of God's power and grace are to be beheld.

" Come and see," in imagination and thought; " There," ver. 6, in thought as we look upon it.

6. Faith makes the past as well as the future her own. The God who has now wrought wonders for His people is the same who once led them dryshod through the Red Sea and through the Jordan. Those miracles of the past recur in the present. That ancient story is not the record merely of a bygone age, but is daily new, daily repeats itself to those who have eyes open to see and hearts open to perceive. Hence the Psalmist says:

THERE LET US REJOICE IN HIM. *There*, pointing as it were to the field in which God had made bare His arm, and where the past history

7 Ruling in His might for ever,
His eyes keep watch upon the nations;
As for the rebellious—let them not exalt themselves.[d]
[Selah.]

III. 8 Bless our God, O ye peoples,
And make the voice of His praise to be heard.
9 Who putteth our soul in life,
And hath not suffered our foot to be moved.
10 For Thou hast proved us, O God,
Thou hast fined us, as silver is fined.
11 Thou broughtest us into the net,
Thou didst put a heavy burden on our loins.
12 Thou madest men to ride over our head;
We came into fire and into water:—
But Thou hast brought us out into abundance.[e]

IV. 13 I will come into Thy house with burnt-offerings,
I will pay Thee my vows,

had been repeated in the present, *there* let us rejoice in Him. (See more in Critical Note.)

7. KEEP WATCH or "spy out." All the attempts of the nations against Israel are not unobserved of God: hence the warning which follows.

THE REBELLIOUS, *i.e.* the heathen nations who threaten Israel, and so lift themselves up against God.

8. Again he calls upon all nations to bless God for His wonderful deliverance vouchsafed to His people. Then he describes their oppression.

9. WHO PUTTETH OUR SOUL IN LIFE. The expression denotes the being rescued from imminent peril, like the phrase "bringing up from the gates of death," &c.

10. The suffering of Israel is now described by a series of figures, the first of which marks *God's purpose* in the affliction.

THOU DIDST PROVE, &c. Comp. xii. 6 [7], xvii. 2 [3].

11. THE NET. Probably here and in Ezek. xii. 13, this is the meaning of the word. It occurs, however, often in the sense of *a hold*, or *strong, fortified place*, as in 1 Sam. xxii. 4, xxiv. 23, &c. Hence many take it here to mean *prison, siege*, &c. So Aq. *ἐν ὀχυρώματι*, Symm. *ἐντὸς πολιορκίας*. Jerome, *in obsidionem*. Similarly, Luther and Hupfeld. They had been like wild animals taken by the hunter in the toils, or like beasts of burden on whose loins a heavy load was laid (an image of servitude); they had been, as it were, cast down and trampled upon by the horse-hoofs and chariot-wheels of their triumphant and savage enemies.

13. We have now the *personal* acknowledgement of God's mercy, first, in the announcement on the part of the Psalmist of the offerings which he is about to bring, and which he had vowed in his trouble; and then, in the record of God's dealing with his soul, which had called forth his thankfulness.

14 Which my lips openly uttered,
And my mouth spake when I was in distress.
15 Burnt-offerings of fatlings will I offer to Thee
With the incense of rams;
I will sacrifice bullocks with he-goats. [Selah.]

V. 16 Come, hear, and I will tell, all ye that fear God,
What he hath done for my soul.
17 I called unto Him with my mouth,
And He was extolled [f] with my tongue.
18 If I had seen iniquity in my heart,
The Lord would not hear me.
19 But God hath heard,
He hath attended to the voice of my prayer.
20 Blessed be God who hath not turned away my prayer,
Nor His loving-kindness from me.

14. OPENLY UTTERED, lit. "opened," used in like manner of vows, Judges xi. 35.

15. INCENSE, *i.e.* evidently the steam and smoke of the burnt sacrifices ascending in a cloud, the word being used, as Hupf. observes, in its root-meaning. Comp. the Hiph. of the verb, *to make a smoke*, and hence *to burn*, &c. The enumeration of the various kinds of offerings may be (as Hengst.) an expression of his zeal and devotion, or as denoting that he considered no offerings too large or too costly.

17. HE WAS EXTOLLED, lit. "extolling was under my tongue." See Critical Note, and comp. x. 7.

18. IF I HAD SEEN, *i.e.* probably, if I had been conscious of iniquity in my heart, the assertion being that of freedom from anything like purposed deceit, as in xvii. 1, xxxii. 2; or the phrase may mean, as the English Version takes it, "If I had *regarded* iniquity," *i.e.* looked upon it with pleasure and satisfaction. Comp. for this use of the verb (with the accus.) Job xxxi. 26, Habak. i. 13, Prov. xxiii. 31. For the general sentiment of the passage, comp. Job xxvii. 8, 9; Is. i. 15, lix. 2, 3; John ix. 31; 1 John iii. 21. See South's Sermon on this verse, vol. iv. p. 118.

FROM ME, lit. from being with me so as to accompany me.

[a] שִׁיר מִזְמוֹר. The juxtaposition of the words is peculiar, without any name of the author following, as it does in the titles of xlviii., lxv., lxviii. In the title of lxvii. we have a similar instance, only the order is reversed, מ׳ שׁ׳, as also in lxviii. Hupfeld connects the two words together, taking the one as in constr. with the other: here, Song of a Psalm or Psalm-Song, and in lxvii. Psalm of a Song, or Song-Psalm. The difference between the two words will be found noticed in the General Introduction.

[b] מַעֲשֶׂיךָ. This is commonly supposed to be a plural form, and therefore to be dependent (either as genitive or accusative) on נוֹרָא, "terrible *in* Thy works," as in ver. 5, "terrible in His doing." But 'מ may be singular. See on xlix., note [b]. (Ew. *Lehrb.* § 256 *b.*)

[c] נִשְׂמְחָה. Notwithstanding the optat. form of the word, almost all interpreters, ancient and modern, with one consent render this as a past tense: "There *did* we rejoice," it being supposed that this sense is required by the connection. Hupf. endeavours to defend it as a relative pret., like יַעַבְרוּ, which precedes. But יַעַבְרוּ is merely the simple fut., and this, of course, constantly stands after the pret. as a relative pret. (see for instance li. 7); but not a single instance can be alleged where the optat. form is thus used. Hupf. refers, indeed, to the use of the simple fut. with אָז in a past sense, and the paragog. fut. with עַד, lxxiii. 17 (a passage, however, which may be otherwise interpreted), and with the Vau consec.—all constructions widely differing from this. But if we choose to determine what a writer *must* say, instead of endeavouring to understand what he *does* say, we shall probably disregard grammar. What is he speaking of? He bids all men come and look upon God's mighty acts: those acts are typified by two; the passage of the Red Sea and the passage of the Jordan. Then, turning to the congregation, he says, *There* (looking in thought on those wonderful works) let us rejoice in God, who is still the same God who delivered our fathers. Comp. the use of the particle שָׁם in xxxvi. 12 [13], where see note. Delitzsch, in his first edition, maintained the grammatical rendering, though he supposes the drying up of the sea and the rivers to be spoken figuratively of the deliverance which had just been vouchsafed, and which might be compared to those of old, and שָׁם to point to the state of freedom into which they had been brought. He renders (1st ed.): "Allda wolln wir freun uns seiner." In his 2d ed. he has: "Allda freuten wir uns seiner."

[d] יָרִימוּ, Hiph. according to the K'thîbh, and we must understand *the head* or *the horn* (see iii. 4), לָמוֹ being used as a *dat. commodi* "for themselves, for their own advancement," &c.

[e] רְוָיָה, lit. "overflow," "superfluity;" comp. xxiii. 5. It is unnecessary to correct רְוָחָה, though Symm. has εὐρυχωρία, and this is supported by the Chald. Hupf. thinks that the other Ancient Versions are in favour of the same reading. LXX. ἀναψυχήν, another, ἀνάψαυσιν, Jerome, *refrigerium;* but they more probably connected the root with the idea of *moisture*, and so of refreshment.

[f] רוֹמָם. Not a verb, as Symm. in the 3d pers. ὑψώθη, and the LXX. and Jerome in the 1st pers., but a noun (of the same form as עוֹלָל, &c.) prop. inf. Pal. for רוֹמֵם; the plur. occurs cxlix. 6, "high praises." For the fem. form (common in Syr.) of the same inf. comp. Is. xxxiii. 3.

PSALM 67

THIS Psalm, which, like the last, is anonymous, and which is evidently much later than the age of David, may have been composed either in the time of Hezekiah, when great hopes began to be entertained of God's purposes towards the nation, or at a time subsequent to the return from the Exile, when those hopes were so signally revived. The Psalm is not, properly speaking, a prophecy, if by that be understood a prediction: it is rather the fervent expression of a well-grounded hope. It is the joyful outpouring of a heart which longs to see the God and King of Israel acknowledged and worshipt as the God and King of the world.

The Psalm, which was clearly designed for liturgical use, and may have been written, like the 65th, at the time of the gathering in of the harvest (see ver. 6), opens with words borrowed from the blessing of the High Priest in Numb. vi. 24—26, a fact of which Bp. Colenso takes no notice in his remarks on the Psalm. The passage in Numbers, according to him, was probably written by a disciple of Samuel's, contemporary with David, who first introduced the name of Jehovah. On that hypothesis the Psalm is earlier than the passage in Numbers: indeed, Bp. Colenso thinks it "may have been written by David." The supposition is without foundation. If anything is plain, it is that the Psalmist *alludes to* the blessing of the High Priest, not that this is *an expansion* of the words of the Psalm. That a Psalm designed for the Temple service should be built upon the solemn Priestly Blessing so often heard in the Temple, a Blessing thrice repeated (comp. ver. 1, 6, 7), is natural and easily explicable. That the Psalm should have suggested the formula of the Blessing is extremely improbable. Besides, in three other Psalms we have allusions to the same formula, iv. 6 [7], xxxi. 16 [17], and the thrice-repeated refrain in lxxx. Who can believe that the Blessing was composed out of these passages? Psalm lxxx. was written long after David's time, and it is evident that all the expressions in the Psalms are borrowed from the one original in Numbers. The only conclusion is, that a later writer uses deliberately the name Elohim instead of the name Jehovah. The Psalm is marked by the refrain, ver. 3 and 5, but has no strophical division properly so called.

[FOR THE PRECENTOR. ON STRINGED INSTRUMENTS. A PSALM. A SONG.]

1 GOD be gracious unto us, and bless us,
(And) cause His face to shine among us. [Selah.]
2 That Thy way may be known upon earth,
Thy salvation among all nations.
3 Let the peoples give thanks to Thee, O God,
Let all the peoples give thanks unto Thee!
4 Oh, let the nations be glad and sing for joy,
For Thou judgest the peoples uprightly,
And guidest the nations upon earth. [Selah.]
5 Let the peoples give thanks to Thee, O God,
Let all the peoples give thanks to Thee!

1. Borrowed, as has already been observed, from the High Priest's blessing, Numb. vi. 24—26, but with some variations, and with the Divine Name Elohim instead of Jehovah.

AMONG US, lit. "*with* us," as accompanying and guiding us, instead of "upon us," as in Numb. vi. 25.

2. THAT THY WAY MAY BE KNOWN. The infin. is used impersonally. Lit. "to know," *i.e.* that men may know. God's goodness manifested in Israel would lead to a recognition of Him among the heathen as the Lord of all. Comp. ix. 11 [12]. God's *way* is His purpose of grace, His salvation as vouchsafed first to Israel and afterwards to the world.

3—5. The only real difficulty in interpreting this Psalm is in determining how the tenses are used. In ver. 1 all are agreed that there is the expression of a wish, and that the verbs there are consequently optatives. But from ver. 3 onwards, interpretations vary. Some render these verbs as optatives, others as presents, others again as futures. But in so short a Psalm, opening with a wish, and, as the majority of critics are agreed, concluding with a wish, it seems to me most probable that we have the expression of a wish throughout.

Ewald, Hupfeld, and Bunsen take the verbs here as *presents:* "Es danken dir," &c. Calvin, Diodati, Hengstenberg, and Delitzsch as futures: "Loben werden," &c. Tholuck and Zunz: "Loben (preisen) müssen." Of the older Versions, the LXX., Vulg., Jerome, have throughout these verses the optative (and Symm. in ver. 4, where Aq. has the future); and so Stier, and the E. V.

LET ALL, &c., lit. "Let the peoples, all of them," and so again in ver. 5.

4. FOR THOU JUDGEST. Ewald and Tholuck, "*That* Thou judgest;" and Zunz, "*When* Thou judgest."

GUIDEST. The E. V. gives the general sense by rendering "govern." The verb is the same as in xxiii. 3, God being the great Shepherd of all nations. The object of the verb is repeated

6 (The) land hath given her increase:
May God, (even) our own God, bless us!
7 May God bless us,
And all the ends of the earth fear Him!

pleonastically by means of the pronoun, lit. "the nations upon earth Thou leadest them."

6. HATH GIVEN. The verb is in the past tense, and would seem to refer to a recent harvest, or to a year of plenty. Many, however (as the E. V.), understand this as the prophetic past, which is often used instead of a future. Others, again, as Ewald and Zunz, render it as a present. The expression occurs again in lxxxv. 12 [13], in Lev. xxvi. 4 (where the pret., it is true, has a fut. signification, but only because it stands with ו in the apodosis of the sentence), and Ezek. xxxiv. 27. The passage in Lev. is the original passage, this Psalm claiming the fulfilment of the promise.

7. The Psalm closes with the same hope and longing for the blessing of God with which it opened. Del. here again renders the verbs in the future (as in the E. V.), and Zunz and Reuss in the present. But such renderings are against the general character of the Psalm.

PSALM 68

THE subject of this grand hymn is the entry of God into His Sanctuary on Zion. This is described under figures borrowed from the triumph of an earthly conqueror, who, after having vanquished his enemies, and taken possession of their country, marches in solemn procession at the head of his troops, to occupy the city which he has selected as his capital and the seat of empire. God is represented, first as advancing at the head of the Israelites through the desert; then as leading them victoriously into Canaan; and finally as fixing His royal abode on Zion, whence He reigns in the majesty of universal dominion, acknowledged and feared by all the nations of the earth. Such is, briefly, an outline of the Psalm.

The methods of interpreting it, however, are various.

I. The Fathers, and most of the older theologians, hold the Psalm to be Messianic. Christ and the great facts of His history, especially His resurrection and ascension, and dominion at the right hand of the Father, and the victory of the Church over the world, are by them supposed to be here foreshadowed, in accordance with St. Paul's citation of the Psalm in Ephes. iv. 8—11.

i. By many of them, indeed, the Psalm is regarded as a direct prophecy of Christ and His Kingdom, and devoid altogether of any reference to events occurring at the time it was written. Thus they explain its several portions as describing the advent of Christ (ver. 1—6); His doctrine (ver. 7—16); His triumphant ascent into heaven (ver. 17, 18); and His dominion and kingdom (ver. 19—35).

ii. Others more reasonably maintain a first reference to the historical circumstances of the time, and then apply the Psalm, either in whole or in part, typically to Christ. Thus, Calvin sees in verses 17, 18, a prefiguring, in the historical event of the Ark entering into Zion, of Christ's ascension into heaven. More recently, Stier has interpreted the whole Psalm in this double sense, and has drawn out carefully the parallel throughout between the type and the antitype. Even Hupfeld, though he sets aside altogether the force of the quotation in Ephes. iv. 8, &c., as being without sufficient ground in the meaning of the words as they stand in the Psalm, admits that in a certain sense the Messianic interpretation may be justified, inasmuch as the Second Part of the Psalm speaks of the subjection of all nations to the kingdom of God.

II. But even those who contend that the Psalm is to be explained, in the first instance, by a reference to the circumstances under which it was composed, are very much divided in their opinions.

i. The majority of interpreters suppose it to have been written at the time when the Ark was removed from the house of Obed-Edom to Mount Zion, 2 Sam. vi. This view, says Hupfeld, though not adopting it himself, "gives incontestably the best sense; in fact, it is the only one which suits, not only the selection of Zion, in preference to Sinai and the heights of Basan, and the historical retrospective glance at the earlier leading of God from Sinai onwards, as introductory to the triumphal entry, but also the lofty utterances and prospects connected with it."

ii. Others again, from the martial character of the Psalm, conceive that it was written at the successful termination of some war, when the Ark, which had accompanied the army to battle, was brought back to the holy mountain. "Why," says De Wette, "do we find so much about victory, the scattering of enemies, the leading away of captives, &c., unless some victory were the occasion on which the Psalm was written?" Similarly Hengstenberg argues that the whole character of the Psalm is in favour of this view. "God is spoken of in it as the Lord of battle and of victory; the 18th verse announces the great fact which is celebrated; and the epithets applied to Benjamin and Judah in ver. 27 are given with reference to the military prowess of those tribes. Besides all this, the close imitation of the song of Deborah, in a main part of this poem, is not without its significance." The glories of the present were to the Psalmist a repetition of the glories of the past. The shout of victory was ringing in his ears, and, almost in his own despite, the old battle-songs of his nation mingled themselves with the Poet's verse.

iii. Still the question remains, *What* victory is here commemorated? Of those who refer the Psalm to David's time, some (as Cler. and Ros.) think that it was composed after David's victory over the Syrians and Edomites, 2 Sam. viii. Others, after that over the Syrians and Ammonites, 2 Sam. xi. xii. So Böttch., Thol., and Hengst., the last arguing that, from ver. 1 and 24 of the Psalm, the Ark of the Covenant must have been in the field, and that it may be inferred from 2 Sam. xi. 11, that this was the case in the war with the Ammonites. Others, again, as Calvin and Ladvocat, suppose that David's victories generally, rather than any particular one, are commemorated.

iv. Another class of commentators hold that later victories are here alluded to, because of the mention of the Temple (ver. 29); either that of Jehoshaphat and Jehoram over Moab and Edom, 2 Kings iii. (so Hitzig); or that of Hezekiah over the Assyrians (so Qimchi); or finally, even those of the Maccabees, after the consecration of the Temple, 1 Macc. v.

v. Others find in the Psalm not so much the celebration of a particular historical event, as the expression of a general idea, clothed in a lyrical form. Thus, for instance, according to J. D. Mich., the holy places, the different sanctuaries of God, Sinai, Bashan, Zion (or Heaven); according to Herder, the victories of God (comparing "Thy goings," ver. 25, with the same expression, Habak. iii. 6), with an application to the removal of the Ark to Zion, which he considers to be the occasion of the Psalm, are the subjects here treated of. Similarly Reuss * terms it a festal hymn, in which

---

* I only know his work by Hupfeld's description of it. The title is, "Der 68 Psalm, ein Denkmal exegetischer Noth und Kunst zu Ehren unserer ganzen Zunft." Jena, 1851. It professes to have collected and exhibited the opinions of no less than 400 interpreters, and, according to Hupfeld, "is written with much humour, full of points and antitheses in the grouping, and very amusing to read." But the very title shows the nature of the work, and it can scarcely be regarded as a serious contribution to the *history* of interpretation. In his recent commentary, however, he has given an admirable translation of the Psalm, bringing out very happily in this, and in his comment, the force and structure of the whole. But he still maintains the late date of the Psalm, referring it to "the wars of Antiochus III. and his sons against the Macedonian kings of Egypt." "The *monster of the reeds*, the crocodile, is the

are expressed the general feelings, recollections, hopes of the nation, in its oppressed condition under the Seleucidæ and Ptolemies (220—170 B.C.).

vi. Gesenius, Ewald, and Hupfeld all refer the Psalm to the return from the Babylonish Captivity. Ewald expressly connects it with the dedication of the Second Temple, for which he thinks it was written, and when it was probably sung. Both he and Hupfeld consider that the second occupation of Canaan is described under figures borrowed from the first. But the latter sees in the language of the Psalm rather the promise than the accomplishment of the return from Babylon. The march of God with His people through the Arabian wilderness is, he says, made use of by the Poet as a type and pledge of their speedy deliverance and restoration to their own land. He thus states his opinion: "We have in this Psalm the hope or promise of the return of the Jewish nation from the Babylonish Captivity, and the establishment of the kingdom of God upon Zion in a state of great power, as it is announced in the Pseudo-Isaiah, and in close connection with that announcement, perhaps by the very same author, in the form of a lyrical utterance, such as often occurs here and there in separate outbursts, and in the midst of the prophetical discourses of the Pseudo-Isaiah, but is here moulded into a perfect hymn, the most glowing, the most spirited, and the most powerful which exists in the whole Psalter. It describes the Restoration according to the well-known type, as a new victorious march of God through the desert to Canaan, and a second choosing and occupation of Zion as His royal residence, with all the features of a triumphal entry (*pompa*), and the consequent homage and submission which He receives."

Olshausen, as usual, puts the Psalm in the Maccabean period, and supposes it to have been written when the tidings came of the result of the war between Ptolemy Philometer and Alexander Balas, 1 Macc. xi.

It will be seen from this bare enumeration that there is the greatest difference of opinion both as to the occasion for which, and the period at which, the Psalm was written: some (as Ges., Ew., Hupf., Olsh., Reuss) regarding it as one of the later, or even of the very latest of Hebrew poems; and others (as Böttch, De Wette, Hitz.) classing it with the very earliest. One set of critics sees in it every

---

symbol of Egypt; the *herd of the bulls* is the symbol of the power which was mistress of the Lebanon and the plains of Mesopotamia: in a word, these are the two empires of the Ptolemies and the Seleucidæ, contending, not with national armies, but with mercenaries who have no other object but plunder."

evidence of antiquity and originality; another sees in it every mark of a late age, and a great absence of originality. All, however, combine in praising its vigour, its life, its splendour; all recognize in it the work of a poet of no ordinary genius.

III. It remains for us to consider how far the allusions in the Psalm itself may help us to determine its age, and the occasion for which it was composed.

First, then, it is clear that the great central idea of the Psalm is the choice of Zion as the dwelling-place of Jehovah. To this all leads; from this all flows.

Secondly, this fact of itself would lead us to fix upon the age of David as the most probable time for the composition of the Psalm, and the removal of the Ark to Zion as the most probable occasion. Nor is this set aside by the reference to the "Temple" in ver. 28, inasmuch as the word here usually rendered *Temple* is a word also applied to the Tabernacle (see note on Psalm v. 7) at Shiloh.

Thirdly, the mention of the four tribes, Benjamin, Judah, Zebulun, and Naphtali, as representatives of the Southern and Northern kingdoms respectively, seems more natural then, than at any latter period. There does not appear to be in ver. 27 any prophetic anticipation of a restoration of the kingdom, and the reunion of the tribes as of old, such as Hupfeld is obliged to assume. "After the Captivity," says Hengstenberg, "there could be no such thing as the distinct tribes of Zebulun and Naphtali, with their princes."

Fourthly, the peculiar manner in which the tribe of Benjamin is introduced, as "little Benjamin their ruler," does not seem suitable to post-Exile times, but is very naturally to be explained at a time shortly subsequent to the death of Saul. The tribe which had been the royal tribe, and had so lately enjoyed the pre-eminence in Israel, might still be honoured with the title of "ruler."

Fifthly, Egypt and Ethiopia are mentioned evidently as the great nations of the world, then occupying the most prominent position. It would seem, then, that the Psalm must have been written before the great Asiatic monarchies, the Assyrian especially, had become formidable. Hupfeld, indeed, argues that an anticipation of the conquest of Egypt and Ethiopia is not suitable to the age of David, but there is nothing in the language of the Psalm which implies such an anticipation of conquest. All that is implied is, that the Name of the God of Israel would be reverenced even by these nations, regarded as the representatives of the heathen world, and that they would bring their gifts in homage to Jerusalem. That which really weakens the argument drawn from the mention of these nations is, that they also occupy the same prominent position in the writings of the later Isaiah.

So far then as the historical allusions of the Psalm are concerned, the evidence is, on the whole, in favour of the age of David rather than of a much later period.

But an argument for the later date has been built upon the language and general character of the Psalm. Both Ewald and Hupfeld insist upon the fact, that so much of the Psalm is borrowed from passages in the older poetical literature of the nation, in proof that it is neither original nor ancient. They also lay particular stress upon the points of resemblance between its ideas and expressions and those of the later Isaiah. Thus they compare ver. 4 [5], "cast up a highway," &c., with Is. xl. 3, lvii. 14, lxii. 10; the description of the procession, &c., with Is. xl. 9, lii. 7; the restoration of the exiles, in the expression of *bringing home*, ver. 6 [7], with Is. lviii. 7; God's leading of His people, and His care of them, ver. 7—10 [8—11], with Is. xxxv., xli. 17, &c., xliii, 16, &c.; the shout of the festal procession, ver. 3 [4], with Is. xxxv. 10, li. 11, lii. 1, 8, &c.; the looking of the nations on God's doings, ver. 24 [25], with Is. xl. 5, xxxv. 2, lii. 10; the references to Egypt and Cush (Ethiopia), ver. 29 [30], &c., with Is. xliii. 3, xlv. 14, lx. 5, &c.

But with the exception of the first two instances, the alleged similarities of expression are not very close, and are no proof of imitation in the Psalmist. The more manifest quotations from Numbers x., and from the song of Deborah, are of course reconcilable with the hypothesis of an earlier date. On the other hand, the general ruggedness and abruptness of the style are hardly compatible with the post-Exile theory. De Wette's canon applies here; "The more difficult, the more rugged in the style, the more nervous, vigorous, and compressed in the thoughts, the older a Psalm is; on the contrary, the easier and the more flowing in the style, the more transparent, regular, and smooth in the contents, the later it is." (Introd. to Comm. IV.) See also Renan, *Job*, p. xxxvii. If this be true, there can be little doubt of the antiquity of the Psalm.*

---

* It will be seen that so far I agree with Bishop Colenso as to the probable date of the Psalm. But his theory as to its *composition* appears to me extravagant and utterly untenable. He supposes that Samuel invented the story of the Exodus, that he communicated this invented story to the Priests and Levites, and that in the course of thirty or forty years they had so persuaded the nation of its truth, that it could be introduced into a hymn to be sung at a great religious festival. He further argues that the passage in Numbers x. must have been borrowed from

Even Ewald admits that there have been incorporated in it, to all appearance, important fragments of an earlier poem now lost, which was probably intended to celebrate the removal of the Ark to Zion.

The general structure of the Psalm, notwithstanding all the difficulties which beset many portions of it, is clear and well defined It consists of the following divisions (which rest on the common principle of pairs of verses) :—

I. An introduction which, with true lyric animation, sets before us the victorious march of God, the deliverance He has accomplished for His people, and the loud exultation to which they are called in consequence. Ver. 1—6.

II. Then follows a glance at the former history—the journey of

---

the Psalm, not the Psalm from the history : but the reasons he alleges are devoid of all cogency. He says :—

"Surely if the *Psalmist* drew his language from so sacred a book as the Pentateuch, according to the ordinary view, must have been, he would not have changed the name from Jehovah to Elohim."

Ans. Here obviously the question, what the Pentateuch is, according to the ordinary view, has nothing to do with the matter. The question is, On what principle these changes in the use of the Divine Names rest, and why one is preferred to the other? We have already seen that in two recensions of the same Psalm (xiv. liii.) there is every reason to suppose that the one which contains the name *Jehovah* is the earlier. Indeed, in the later books of the Bible there is a general disposition to use Elohim in preference to Jehovah.

Again : —"The Name Jehovah, if it had really originated in the way described in the Pentateuch, would have been the very name required for this Psalm, considering its character, as the Name of the Covenant God of Israel."

Ans. We are quite in the dark on this subject. Besides, the object might have been in such a Psalm as this, to represent God not only in His relation to Israel ("His Name is Jah"), but as the God of all the earth, and hence most fittingly the nations are called upon to "sing praises to Elohim."

As to the *older* grammatical forms which the Bishop asserts occur in the Psalm, as compared with the forms of the same words in the passage in Numbers, there is no proof that they are older, but quite the reverse. Thus, for instance, in Gen. iii. 24 we have הַכְּרֻבִים, and in 1 Kings vi. 23 כְּרוּבִים, this last being, according to the Bishop's theory, the older word. Nay, we have in the same narrative in Gen. xxiv. the two forms of the same word אוּלַי in ver. 5, and אֻלַי ver. 39.

Again, in Gen. xiv. 10, one of the very oldest portions of the Hebrew Scriptures, we have וַיָּנֻסוּ, which is the usual mode of writing, till we come to the *later* books; see 2 Kings vii. 7 (where, however, we have *both* forms) and 1 Chron. xix. 14, 15.

As regards the form אוֹיְבָיו, we have in this very Psalm the other (alleged later) form מֵאֹיְבִים, ver. 24.

Israel through the wilderness, under the immediate guidance and care of God. Ver. 7—10.

III. The triumphant occupation of the land of Canaan, and the flight of the hostile kings. Ver. 11—14.

IV. The choice of Zion as the abode of God, and His solemn entry into it. Ver. 15—18.

V. The Psalmist contemplating the glorious results of this abode of God in Zion, calls upon all Israel to praise Him, chiefly because He will punish all the enemies of His people. Ver. 19—23.

VI. The next strophe reverts to a description of the triumphal procession. Ver. 24—27.

VII. The hope is expressed that all the nations of the world shall acknowledge and submit themselves to Jehovah who dwelleth in Zion. Ver. 28—31.

VIII. The Psalm closes with a summons to all the kingdoms of the earth to praise God. Ver. 32—35.

[FOR THE PRECENTOR. A PSALM OF DAVID. A SONG.]

I. 1 LET God arise, let His enemies be scattered,
And let them that hate Him flee before Him.
2 As smoke is driven away, do Thou drive (them) away;[a]

1. As the last Psalm opened with a reference to the High Priest's blessing, Numb. vi. 24, so this opens with a reference to the watchword, Numb. x. 35, with which the Ark was wont to set forward during the journeys in the wilderness. "Rise up, O Jehovah, and let Thine enemies be scattered; and let them that hate Thee flee before Thy face." There are two variations here from the original formula: first, the use of the third person optative (for the future should not be rendered, with Hengst. and others, as a present), instead of the imperative; and secondly, the substitution of Elohim for Jehovah, as the name of God, which is characteristic of the Psalm, and accounts for its place in the Second Book. With regard to the former, Böttcher truly remarks, that the formula with the imperative, "Arise," &c. is certainly historically older than our Psalm [and not, as Bishop Colenso and others would maintain, the Psalm more ancient than the passage in Numbers], and that it must have originated with the more ancient custom; comp. Numb. xxxi. 6, Joshua vi. 4, 1 Sam. iv. 4, 2 Sam. xi. 11.

"I cannot doubt," says Calvin, "that Moses dictated this form of prayer for all ages, in order that the faithful, relying on the Ark of the covenant as the visible symbol of God's presence, might rest sure that they would be safe."

2. The figures here employed occur elsewhere; comp. xxxvii. 20, xcvii. 5, Hosea xiii. 3, and Micah i. 4. They describe forcibly the real weakness, the easy and instantaneous overthrow, of the strongest

As wax melteth before the fire,
(So) let the wicked perish from before the face of God,
3 But let the righteous rejoice, let them exult before God.
And let them be glad with joy.

4 Sing unto God, play (on the harp) to His Name,
Cast up a highway for Him who rideth through the deserts:[b]
Jah is His Name,[c] and exult ye before Him.
5 A Father of the fatherless, and a Judge of the widows,

earthly power when arrayed against God. Hupfeld, and Herder before him, as it seems to me without reason, suppose them to have been "borrowed from the pillar of smoke and fire above the Ark."

In the last member of this verse, and the first of the next, Hengstenberg sees a reference to the conclusion of the song of Deborah: "So let all Thine enemies perish, O Lord, but let them that love Him be as the sun when he goeth forth in his might."

Others take ver. 2, 3 as a comment upon the quotation in ver. 1, and hence render the verbs in these verses as futures ("Thou shalt drive . . . the wicked shall perish," &c.) or as presents (Thou drivest).

3. THE RIGHTEOUS. Here, Israel as a nation regarded in its ideal character, and as placed in contrast with its heathen oppressors, "the wicked." Comp. Habak. ii. 4.

4. The first part of the Introduction ends with the last verse, and perhaps a second chorus here takes up the strain.

CAST UP A HIGHWAY; the figure being borrowed from the custom of Eastern monarchs, who sent heralds and pioneers before them to make all the necessary preparations—to remove obstructions, &c. along the route which they intended to follow. Great military roads were mostly the work of the Romans, and were almost unknown before the Persian and Grecian periods. Comp. Is. xl. 3, lvii. 14, lxii. 10, where the same verb, or the noun formed from it, occurs.

WHO RIDETH, said perhaps with allusion to the cherubim on which Jehovah was borne (xviii. 10 [11]), God Himself being the Leader and Captain of His people, riding as it were at their head, as an earthly captain might lead his army, riding on a war-horse.

THE DESERTS, or "sandy steppes" (as in Is. xl. 3), such as those on both sides of the Jordan over against Jericho, and the Arabian deserts to the south and east. The allusion is, in the first instance, to the journey of the Israelites through the wilderness, or Arabah, though, supposing the Psalm to be post-exile, there would be a further reference to the deserts lying between Babylon and Palestine. The word cannot mean *heavens*, as the Targ. and Talmud (led astray, probably, by the similar figure in Deut. xxxiii. 26); nor *the West*, as the LXX. and the Vulg. render it. The former is found in our P. B. V., "magnify Him that rideth upon the heavens, as it were upon a horse," which is the more remarkable, as that Version usually follows the Vulg. and the German. Here it departs from both. The words "as it were upon a horse," were added, I presume, as a further explanation of the verb "rideth." I can discover nothing answering to them in any of the Ancient Versions.

5. The character and attributes of God, and His gracious dealings

Is God in His holy habitation.
6 God maketh the solitary to dwell in a home;
He bringeth forth (the) prisoners into prosperity: [d]
Only the rebellious abide in a land of drought.

II. 7 O God, when Thou wentest forth before Thy people,
When Thou marchedst through the wilderness, [Selah]

with His people, are now alleged as the reason why He should be praised. The "fatherless" and the "widows" are mentioned as examples of those who most need succour and protection. As Arndt says: "The meaning of the Holy Ghost is, that God the Lord is a gracious, friendly God and King, whose first, highest, and principal work it is to give most attention to the *miserabiles personæ*, that is, to those persons who ought to be most pitied, because they are helpless and comfortless. Great potentates in the world do not act thus; they respect the noblest and richest in the land, the men who may adorn their court, and strengthen their power and authority. But the highest glory of God is to compassionate the miserable." God is both the loving *Father* and the righteous *Judge;* and the several classes of the lonely, the destitute, the oppressed, the captives, are mentioned as so many instances of those who have experienced both His care and His righteousness, in order that from these the conclusion may be drawn in all similar cases. Hengstenberg compares Hos. xiv. 4, "With Thee the fatherless findeth mercy;" and therefore all who need mercy.

IN HIS HOLY HABITATION, *i.e.* heaven, not the earthly sanctuary (comp. xi. 4), "in opposition to the earth, as the seat of unrighteousness and coldness of heart." (Hengst.)

6. THE SOLITARY...THE PRISONERS. Those who hold that the Psalm was written subsequently to the Babylonish Captivity, see in these words an allusion to the actual circumstances of Israel during the Exile. But it is more natural to suppose that these are mentioned as other particular examples, like the orphan and the widow, of God's fatherly care.

TO DWELL IN A HOME, or "to keep house," cxiii. 9.

ONLY, here almost = *but.* It may be explained, "it is not otherwise than thus." Comp. lviii. 11 [12]. THE REBELLIOUS; all enemies of God, whether heathen, or those who in Israel itself were disobedient. Aq. ἀφιστάμενοι. Symm. ἀπειθεῖς.

7. The proper theme of the Psalm now opens with allusions to the great triumphal march of God at the head of His people through the wilderness, and in their occupation of the land of Canaan.

The words of this and the next verse are borrowed, with some variations, from the song of Deborah, Judges v. 4, 5, and this again rests on passages such as Deut. xxxiii. 2 and Ex. xix, 16, &c. Comp. Habak. iii. The reference is first to the terrors of the Theophany on Sinai, and the glorious Majesty of God as there seen.

WENTEST FORTH...MARCHEDST, words used especially of going forth to battle, God being regarded as the Captain of His people. Comp. xliv. 9 [10], lxxxi. 5 [6]; Numb. xxvii. 17, 21; Habak. iii. 13; Zech. xiv. 3.

THE WILDERNESS (or "waste," *y'shīmon*, not *midbar*, which last may mean only uncultivated land, pasture-ground), often applied to the Arabian desert, as lxxviii. 40, cvi. 14. Comp. Deut. xxxii. 10; Is. xliii. 19, 20.

Throughout their whole march

8 The earth shook, the heavens also dropped before God,
Yon Sinai before God, the God of Israel.
9 With a bountiful rain Thou didst sprinkle Thine inheritance, [e] O God,
And when it was weary, THOU didst refresh it;
10 Thy creatures dwelt therein;

God's Presence and Glory were manifested, but never so awfully as when He came down on Sinai, to give His Law to His people. Then all nature was moved at His coming; then "so terrible was the sight, that Moses said, I exceedingly fear and quake" (Heb. xii. 21). Hence it is that the great prominence is given to *this* manifestation of God. And hence He is here called "the God of Israel," because from Sinai dates God's covenant relation to Israel, as Delitzsch observes.

8. YON SINAI (the demonstrative pron. prefixed, as in xlviii. 14 [15]). Some verb must be supplied, "shook," "was moved," from the first member of the verse. The original passage, Judges, v. 5, contains the full expression.

9. A BOUNTIFUL RAIN, lit. either "a rain of free-willingness," which has hence been interpreted to mean, rain as a gift of free grace (so Calv.), or "a rain of liberality," *i.e.* as a liberal, bountiful gift (see note on liv. 6 [8]). The early interpreters understand this rain spiritually of the outpouring of the Holy Ghost. Others, again, figuratively of the various gifts and benefits with which God visited His people in the wilderness. Those who take the word in its more literal sense, are divided in their interpretation; some, as J. D. Mich. and Herder, supposing a literal rain to be meant (the former, a rain which fell at the giving of the Law), and which changed the barrenness of the desert into verdure and fruitfulness; others, that the reference is to the manna, which is said in lxxviii. 24 to have been *rained* from heaven. To me it seems certain that the expression is used figuratively of refreshment and blessing; this appears, indeed, to be required by the following clause: "And when it was weary," &c.

THOU DIDST SPRINKLE. The verb is the aorist of repeated past action, and is construed with the double accusative. See Critical Note.

AND WHEN IT WAS WEARY, lit. "and weary (it was), and Thou," &c.

REFRESH, literally, "confirm," "strengthen."

10. THY CREATURES. I have left the word in the ambiguity of the original. Three different interpretations have been given of it.

(1) If the *rain* spoken of in ver. 9 be *the manna* (Exod. xvi. 4, "I will rain bread from heaven for you," Ps. lxxviii. 24), then *the creatures* here spoken of may be *the quails;* "Thy living creatures settled therein" (*i.e.* in Thine inheritance, among Thy people, comp. lxxviii. 28, "in the midst of the camp"); with which the rest of the verse corresponds, "Thou preparedst (them, as food, see the same verb, lxv. 9 [10], lxxviii. 20) for the afflicted" (*i.e.* Thy people in their distress). The LXX. by their rendering τὰ ζῷά σου seem to have taken the word in this sense.

(2) Others take the word here in the meaning "host" (as in 2 Sam. xxiii. 11, 13, where it is used of *an army*), *i.e.* the congregation, or people of Israel.

(3) But it may also mean Israel in another sense, viz. as compared to *a flock*, a favourite image in the Psalms. So Delitzsch (who refers to lxxiv. 19), "Thy afflicted creatures," which, however, might be rendered in accordance with (2), "the congregation of Thy afflicted

Thou preparedst in Thy goodness for the afflicted,
O God.

III. 11 The Lord giveth (the) word:
The women who publish the tidings are a great host.
12 " Kings of hosts do flee, do flee,[f]
And she that tarrieth at home divideth the spoil.

ones." The difficulty in the last two interpretations lies, no doubt, in the feminine pronoun, בָּהּ, *in* it, or *therein*. There is no noun to which it can immediately refer. Hence it has been supposed either (*a*) to denote *the land of Canaan*, as the well-known beloved land which needed no special designation (as Del.); comp. the use of the fem. pron. in ver. 14 [15], and see note there; but according to this, the settlement in the land is mentioned before the description of its occupation, which follows, ver. 11, &c. Or, (*b*) the wilderness mentioned ver. 7, which is then said in the next clause to have been *prepared* by fertilizing rains, &c., or by the manna which was showered upon them. This last explanation, viz. that when God's people dwelt in the wilderness, God prepared it for their abode, gives on the whole the best sense.

THOU PREPAREST. The word may be used here absolutely, = "Thou preparest a table," as in 1 Chron. xii. 39, and it need not be rendered as a past, as referring to the provision in the wilderness; rather, that is one of *many repeated instances* of God's care; and we have consequently the statement of a general truth.

11. The sacred Poet now passes to the actual occupation of the Holy Land.

THE LORD (ADONAI) GIVETH (THE) WORD. The noun "word" (which is found only in poetry) is used in lxxvii. 8 [9], of the "word of *promise*;" in Habak. iii. 9, apparently of the "word of *power*," or "word of victory." Perhaps both meanings may be combined here. It is in virtue of God's word of promise that Israel takes possession of Canaan; it is by His word of power that the enemies of Israel are discomfited. "God speaks— and the victory is won." Others (as Ewald, Fürst, &c.) render "song of victory," God Himself putting this into the mouths of the women, who came forth with timbrels and dances to meet the victorious army on its return.

THE WOMEN. The participle is in the feminine, and the allusion is to the custom above mentioned. The deliverance of Israel from Pharaoh's host, the overthrow of Sisera, and David's victory over Goliath, were all thus celebrated. Comp. Exod. xv. 20; Judges v. 1, 12; 1 Sam. xviii. 6; 2 Sam. i. 20.

12. This and the next two verses wear the air of being a fragment of one of those ancient battle-songs, sung by the women after the defeat of the foe. The fact that they have thus been torn from their original context accounts for the great obscurity which hangs over them. It is indeed almost hopeless now to understand the allusions.

KINGS OF HOSTS, not those defeated by Moses, as the kings of the Amorites (Ros. and others), but, as the reference to the song o Deborah clearly shows, the Canaanitish kings, Judg. v. 19, and vii. 26, where observe also the repetition of the verb. Bunsen, however, suggests that there may rather be an allusion to Joshua x.

SHE THAT TARRIETH AT HOME; the mistress of the household, so called as keeping house, whilst her husband goes forth to battle: an expression peculiarly in conformity

13 Will[g] ye lie among the sheep-folds,
(As) the wings of a dove that is covered with silver,
And her feathers with yellow gold ?—

with Eastern customs. Similar is the phrase "women in the tent," Judges, v. 24. De Wette compares οἰκουρός, Eurip. *Hec.* 1261.

DIVIDETH THE SPOIL, not merely (as Hupf.) "receives her portion of the spoil," but rather "distributes among her daughters and handmaidens, &c. the share of the spoil" which her husband has brought home. Hence the mother of Sisera is represented as anticipating the share of the spoil which would fall to her lot, Judg. v. 30, "one coloured garment, two pieces of embroidery as spoil for my neck" (so, with a very slight correction, the passage should probably be rendered).

13. WILL YE LIE, or "When ye lie, &c. . . . it is (or, ye are) as the wings, &c." Scarcely two commentators will be found to agree as to the interpretation of this and the next verse. The only point on which there can be said to be anything like a consensus, is in the explanation of the figure in ver. 13. Nearly all see, in the dove and the glittering of her wings in the sunshine, an emblem of prosperity and peace, though some suppose that the allusion is to the bright armour of the warriors, glittering in the sunshine. Cf. the same figure in Soph. *Antig.* 114, λευκῆς χιόνος πτέρυγι στεγανός.* I will mention some of the interpretations of the more celebrated critics.

J. D. Mich. renders: "Lie not among the drinking-troughs, (among) the doves' wings covered with silver," &c. He supposes the words to be addressed to the two tribes and a half, whose territory lay on the other side of the Jordan, and who were rich in flocks and herds: They are exhorted not to indulge their natural inclination for the shepherd's life, but to join their brethren in the invasion of Canaan.

De Wette: "When ye lie among the stalls of the cattle (*i.e.* in the indolent repose of a country life), there are doves' wings covered with silver," &c. (a figurative expression denoting the rich ornaments of silver and gold taken from the spoil, with which the women decorated themselves). Similarly, Rosenm., only that he supplies before the second clause: "*Then shall ye be as* the wings of a dove," &c.

Ewald, who says there is evidently an opposition between 13 and 14, explains the whole passage as follows: "When ye (Israelitish men, for it is the women who sing) rest between the sheep-folds, *i.e.* lazily stretched at length on pleasant, grassy spots by the water-side (Judges v. 16, Gen. xlix. 14), consequently when ye have peace, as now after the conclusion of the war, *so are the wings of the doves covered with silver*, &c. (in allusion to the glittering of the plumage in the sunshine); *but when God scatters kings* in the hard battle, *then the snow falls in it* (the same land) *darkly;* i.e. then sends the same God dark snow (and hail) for the destruction of the enemies who assail His sanctuary (Job xxxviii. 22, &c.), as has been shown just before." Thus, Ewald finds a contrast between peace and sunshine on the one hand, and war and stormy weather on the other. But it is fatal to this view that hail is not mentioned at all, and that snow is not used elsewhere as an image of darkness or destruction.

Herder (*Geist der Heb. Poes.* ii.

* So Mr. Plumptre, in a spirited translation of this Psalm:
"The hosts their might display,
Like silver dove with wings of golden glow."

14 When the Almighty scatters kings therein,
(It is as when) there is snow in Zalmon."

69, 70) thinks that all is said by way of taunt, borrowed from the song of Deborah. Deborah reproached the unwarlike tribes, to whom the bleating of the flocks was sweeter than the clashing of arms and the din of battle ; here they are taunted, because, in their cowardice, they kept aloof from the war, tending their cattle, and admiring the bright plumage of their doves, whilst a woman, the inhabitant of a house, Deborah, divided the spoil. Hence he renders, "Why rest ye there among the troughs?" (an ironical question.) "The feathers of the doves are, no doubt, bright as silver. And her wings sparkle like yellow gold!" (said sarcastically of the occupations and conversation of men who thought more of their doves than of the freedom of their country.) In the same way he supposes their effeminacy to be lashed in what follows : "When the Almighty scattered kings, snow fell upon Zalmon;" *i.e.* it was in rough, and stormy, and wintry weather that Deborah went forth to her battle and her victory ; but the recreant tribes, seeing snow lying even upon the comparatively low hill of Zalmon, in the south, argued how far worse it must be in the north, and thus refused to join the army. This view has been adopted by Hupfeld. But Bunsen justly remarks, that it would be very extraordinary if the only portion of the song of the women here quoted should be that which was aimed in biting taunt against their own countrymen, not that which described most vividly the glorious victory which had been won.

According to Hengstenberg, the Israelites, to whom the address is directed, are described figuratively as the wings of the doves, &c., or they are *like* doves whose wings glitter with silver and gold. The allusion is to the play of colours on the wings of the dove in sunshine. This denotes the peaceful, and, at the same time, *splendid* condition enjoyed by Israel, in the lap of prosperity. The same idea is carried out in the second figure, that of the *snow*, an image of the bright gleam of heaven which fell on the darkened land on the prosperous termination of the war ;—when the Lord scatters kings, the light of prosperity illuminates the darkness of the land, just as dark Zalmon becomes white when covered with snow. He observes that snow is generally used as an image of brightness and purity. Comp. li. 7 [9], Is. i. 18, Mark ix. 3 (with Matt. xvii. 2), Rev. i. 14. Zalmon is a hill mentioned in Judges ix. 48, situated in the neighbourhood of Shechem, and covered with a thick wood, so that, as Luther says, "it might be called in German a *Schwartzwald*, or dark forest, the dark or black mountain." This, on the whole, is preferable to any of the other interpretations. It has the merit of simplicity, and it yields a fairly satisfactory sense. I would venture, however, to suggest another explanation of ver. 14. It seems to me, as Ewald has remarked, that this verse is rather in opposition to the preceding, than a continuation of the same idea. The first describes the sunshine of peace ; the second the storm of war. May not then the comparison of the snow refer to the *scattering* of the kings? May not those kings and their armies, broken and scattered far and wide over the land, be aptly compared to the white patches or the thick flakes of snow, lying in broken masses over the dark boughs of the forest? "When the Almighty scattered kings in the land, it was like a fall of snow on (darkly-wooded) Zalmon." The comparison becomes still more strikingly apt, when we remember how the arms, and armour, and rich spoil, dashed here and there in the wild disorder of the flight,

IV. 15 A mountain of God is the mountain of Bashan,
A mountain of (many) summits [h] is the mountain of Bashan.

would *glitter* like snow in the sunshine.*

The interpretation of Gesenius and others, "the land was snow-white with the bones of the slain in (or near) Zalmon," is forced and unnatural. It drags in an idea which is not suggested by the figure of the *snow*, but only by the general one of *whiteness;* and, further, the mention of the bones bleached and whitening of the battle-field, could only be possible at a time long subsequent to the victory.

14. THEREIN, *i.e.* in the land, implied, though not expressed, in what goes before ; comp. the same mode of expression in Is. viii. 21 : or perhaps, in Zalmon ; for the pronoun is thus frequently anticipative of the noun : "It was like snow in Zalmon, when the Almighty scattered kings there."

THERE IS SNOW, or "it snoweth." Or omitting all comparison, it would be quite possible to render the second clause, "It snowed in Zalmon."

ZALMON, or "the dark mountain," probably as already remarked, the hill mentioned in Judges ix. 48, the only other passage where the word occurs. Böttcher supposes that some other loftier mountain belonging to the Basanitic range is meant. Others, that the noun is here not a proper name, but signifies "darkness, gloom," &c. I have retained here the orthography adopted by our translators in Judges ix., the Z representing the same Hebrew letter as in Zion, Zoar, &c.

15. The end of all this manifestation of God's power on behalf of His chosen, of all these splendid victories, is the occupation of the Holy Land. He has given it to His people, that He may abide and reign in the midst of them. He has chosen, not the lofty range of Bashan, but the more lowly Zion for His seat : and to this new Sanctuary He comes from Sinai, attended by "an innumerable company of angels."

A MOUNTAIN OF GOD (not merely "a high mountain," see on xxxvi. 6 [7]). The huge range of Bashan, with its rocky pillars and sharp pinnacles (its "many summits,"—not, like Thabor, a single cone, but a wide-spreading mountain with "many cones"), is so termed, as if bearing witness in a special manner, by its strong massive formation, to the power of him who created it. (The basalt, or *basanites* of the ancients, has been supposed to take its name from Bashan, where it is found.) This stood in the most striking contrast to the limestone formation and unimposing character of the hills of Central Palestine. These bold mountain masses, rising in dark majesty, and producing the impression of everlasting strength, stand on one side, while on the other is placed the small and ap-

* Since writing the above note, I have discovered that Delitzsch also associates the image of the snow with the dispersed army, but finds the point of the comparison, not in the dispersion, but only in the *bright shining* of the scattered armour and spoils. He refers, as Böttcher had already done before him, to Homer's comparison of the gathering of the Achæans from their ships, with lance and helmet and plume glittering in the sunlight (λαμπρὸν γανόωσαι), to the thickly-falling snow-shower (ταρφειαὶ νιφάδες)—*Il.* xix. 357, &c. ; comp. xii. 258, &c. Böttcher says that he once heard the remark made in a town near Leipzig, of a large body of students who were approaching, "They come like snow from the mountain" (Sie kommen wie geschneit vom Berge), and that this first threw light for him on this passage in the Psalm.

16 Why look ye enviously,[i] ye mountains of many summits,
Upon the mountain which God hath desired to dwell in?
Yea, Jehovah will abide (therein) for ever.
17 The chariots of God are twice ten thousand,[k] are thousands upon thousands,
The Lord among them (hath come from)[l] Sinai into His sanctuary.
18 Thou hast ascended up on high,
Thou hast led captives captive,

parently insignificant Zion, having no greatness or strength in itself, but great and strong nevertheless in the immediate and glorious Presence of God; and hence the former seem to look with envy upon the latter, at seeing it thus elevated to a height to which it had no natural claim. Comp. xlviii. 2 [3], Is. ii. 2. Others again suppose that Bashan is styled a "mountain of God" as an ancient seat of religious worship. So Hupf., who quotes J. D. Mich., "Neque illi Libani Basanisque fastigio suæ defuerunt religiones."

16. According to the accents the rendering would be: "Why look ye enviously (or jealously . .)? The mountain which God hath desired to dwell in, surely Jehovah will abide (therein) for ever." Or "This mountain hath God desired to dwell in. Yea, Jehovah, &c."

17. In solemn triumph, at the head of armies of angels, and like a victor who leads trains of captives and spoils in long array, God enters His sanctuary in Zion.

CHARIOTS (the sing. used collectively), *i.e.* war-chariots (comp. xx. 7 [8]); carrying out the image, as in Habak. iii. 8, 15. The angelic hosts are evidently meant. Comp. 2 Kings vi. 17.

TWICE TEN THOUSANDS, lit. "two myriads." Comp. Deut. xxxiii. 2 (where the angels are spoken of as "holy myriads"); Dan. vii. 10. These angels may be meant also in Numb. x. 36 (the passage borrowed in ver. 1, and perhaps alluded to here), "Return of Jehovah, with the myriads of the thousands of Israel."

THOUSANDS UPON THOUSANDS, lit. "thousands of repetition."

(HATH COME FROM) SINAI. For a defence of this rendering, see Critical Note. The rendering of the E.V. "*As* is Sinai, in the holy place," is grammatically wrong; and still worse is the P. B. V., "as in the holy place of Sinai."

18. THOU HAST ASCENDED. Comp. xlvii. 5 [6]. Whither? Not, I think, as many interpreters explain, into heaven; for though that is the meaning of the passage in its N. T. application (see below), it is not, apparently, the primary meaning. Here, as we have seen, the triumphant procession winds its way up the sacred hill of Zion. The ascent, therefore, can be none other than the ascent of the Ark into the tabernacle, or temple there.

ON HIGH. See for this, as applied to Zion, Jer. xxxi. 12, Ezek. xvii. 23, xx. 40. Hofmann (*Schriftb.* II. i. 484) denies that either *heaven* or *Zion* is intended by this expression, but that general exaltation of God which is spoken of in the similar passages, xlvii. 5 [6], xii. 13 [14]. The closest resemblance is found, he remarks, in vii. 7. [8]. And God is said to ascend in triumph over His vanquished foes. Similarly Calvin, although admitting the typical sense.

CAPTIVES, lit. *a captivity*, i.e. a number of captives; the image being still carefully preserved of the victor,

Thou hast taken gifts amongst men : [m]
Yea, with the rebellious (also) shall Jah God abide. [n]

with his long train of captives following him in the triumph. The rendering of the E. V., "Thou hast led captivity captive," is ambiguous, as it might mean, "Thou hast led captive those who have led others captive," which, however, is not the meaning of the Heb. phrase (comp. Judges v. 12).

GIFTS, *i.e.* tribute from the vanquished ; or rather, perhaps from all those who submit themselves to His sway.

AMONGST MEN. This is the literal rendering (not "*for* men," *i.e.* to let them go free, nor *of* men, they themselves being the gifts, for the history of David knows nothing of "prisoners who were sent as gifts to the sanctuary," nor of "proselytes, who, as it were, gave themselves as gifts to God," as Hengst. remarks), and, in the context in which it stands, is, of course, very nearly the same as "*from* men."

THE REBELLIOUS. This completes the picture of the triumph. *All*—even those nations which hold out the longest in their stubborn resistance, and refuse to submit themselves to the Great Victor—must finally acknowledge His sway. All shall be united in one kingdom, and God the Lord shall reign in the midst of them. This is the great prophetic idea which recurs so often in the writings of Psalmists and Prophets. God is the King of all the earth ; and, in spite of all opposition, His kingdom shall be set up, and on the throne of that kingdom, His Son, His Anointed (the Messiah, the Christ), shall reign. Hence it is that St. Paul (Eph. iv. 9) applies this verse to the Resurrection and triumphant Ascension of Christ. It is true that in so doing he has departed from the Heb. and from the LXX. The latter have : ἀναβὰς εἰς ὕψος ᾐχμαλώτευσας αἰχμαλωσίαν, ἔλαβες δόματα ἐν ἀνθρώπῳ, καὶ γὰρ ἀπειθοῦντες τοῦ κατασκηνῶσαι. The first clause of this—the only part of it which is intelligible—the Apostle retains, except that he substitutes the 3d per. ᾐχμαλώτευσεν, for the 2d ; but for the second clause he has : καὶ ἔδωκε δόματα τοῖς ἀνθρώποις, "and gave gifts unto men." Hence he is giving, not a translation, but an interpretation of the Hebrew. For the verb לקח, "to take," never means "to give," and the meaning for which Eadie contends (and which Alford thinks substantiated), "Thou receivedst in order to give," cannot be maintained here. The examples, Gen. xv. 9, xviii. 5, xxvii. 13, xlii. 16, Exod. xxvii. 20, 1 Kings xvii. 10, are not in point. In all those instances the verb may be rendered (as it commonly is in the E.V.) "fetch." But it would be impossible to say, "Thou hast fetched gifts among men." It must at least be "*for* men" (לָאָדָם), and then, "Thou hast given gifts *to* men" would be an equivalent expression to "Thou hast taken gifts *for* men." We cannot, therefore, argue from the meaning of the word, but we may from the scope of the passage. The truth is, that the Apostle sees in the literal O.T. fact a higher spiritual significance. The ascent of the Ark, in which God was present, into Zion, prefigured the ascent of Christ into heaven. As God came down to fight for His people, so Christ had descended to this earth for the salvation of men. As, on the return of the Ark, the captives and the spoil appeared in the procession, so on the return of Christ in triumph to heaven (Col. ii. 15) He led captive sin and death and hell and all evil powers. As God had *taken* tribute among men, which He, however, as the victorious monarch of Israel, had given to Israel, so Christ also had taken gifts among men (in His human nature and through His work on earth)

V. 19 Blessed be the Lord,
Who day by day beareth our burden,[o]
(Even) the God (who is) our salvation. [Selah.]

20 Our God is a God of deliverances,
And to Jehovah the Lord (belong) the means of escape from death.[p]
21 But God will smite the head of His enemies,
The hairy scalp which goeth on still in his trespasses.
22 The Lord hath said: "From Bashan will I bring again,
I will bring (them) again from the depths of the sea,

which He now, as ascended Lord, gave to men. The Apostle sees that when a king takes, he takes to give, and therefore substitutes the one word for the other, without at all putting the one word as the *translation* of the other. He seizes the idea and represents it in its true fulfilment. Calvin has some excellent remarks on the principle of interpretation to be followed here.

19. The description of the great triumphal procession is here suddenly broken off with an ascription of praise to God as the Protector and Avenger of His people, and is not again resumed till ver. 24.

BEARETH OUR BURDEN. The majesty of God and the tenderness of God are thus ever associated in Holy Scripture. The same God who came once in awful glory to Sinai, and who now, accompanied by myriads of angels, enters into His sanctuary in Zion, is the God who bears the burden which is too heavy for us (or, perhaps, "who bears *us*," *i.e.* carries us as a shepherd when he finds the lost sheep lays it upon his shoulder). See Critical Note.

20. MEANS OF ESCAPE FROM DEATH, lit. "for death," or "with reference to death." As Calvin observes, "With God are wonderful and various and secret methods, whereby He raises His children from death to life. . . . Even when He has suffered them to be in a manner swallowed up, He certainly furnishes marvellous means of escape," &c. Hupf. compares the use of ἔκβασις in 1 Cor. x. 13, and of πόρος in Classical writers, Æsch. *Prom.* 59. δεινὸς κἀξ ἀμηχάνων εὑρεῖν πόρους. Aristoph. *Eq.* 756 (769) κἀκ τῶν ἀμηχάνων πόρους εὐμηχάνους πορίζων.

Ainsworth: "issues or passages, that is, ways and means of death, or to death, meaning that He hath many ways of bringing His enemies to death, and to deliver His people out of it: for 'He hath the keys of death,' Rev. i. 18, Cf. Deut. xxxii. 39." So "issues of life," Prov. iv. 23.

21. The reverse of the previous truth: God will take terrible vengeance on His enemies.

THE HAIRY SCALP, personified, *i.e.* the proud, bold, wilful, secure sinner, the thick head of hair being an image of youthful vigour and pride (as in the case of Samson and Absalom). Similarly in Greek, κομᾶν, *to wear long hair*, is used metaphorically in the signification *to plume oneself*, *to be proud*, &c. Comp. Is. xxii. 12.

22. I WILL BRING AGAIN. No object is supplied, but it is evident from the context that not Israel, as the older Commentators generally supposed, but the enemies of Israel are meant. God will bring these back, wherever they may have fled in the hope of safety, and give them up to the vengeance of Israel

23 That thou mayest wash thy foot in blood,
That the tongue of thy dogs may have its portion from the enemy." q

VI. 24 They have seen Thy goings, O God,
The goings of my God, my King, into the sanctuary.
25 The singers went before, the players on stringed instruments followed after,
In the midst of the maidens playing with the timbrels:
26 " In the congregations bless ye God,
(Bless) the Lord, (ye that are) of the fountain of Israel."

From Bashan in *the east*, and from the sea in *the west*, from *the heights* of the mountains, and from *the depths* of the sea (one or both of these antitheses may be designed), they shall be brought back. The passage which really throws light upon this is the similar passage (first pointed out by Geier) in Amos ix. 1—3: "He that escapeth of them shall not be delivered. Though they dig into Sheōl, thence shall My hand take them; though they climb up into heaven, thence will I bring them down. And though they hide themselves in the top of Carmel, I will search and take them out thence; and though they be hid from My sight in the bottom of the sea, thence will I command," &c.

23. THAT THOU MAYEST WASH. So it seems almost certain we ought to read with the change of one letter (*tirchaz*), instead of the present text (*timchaz*). This change is supported by the similar passage, lviii. 10 [11], and by the LXX. ὅπως ἂν βαφῇ, and the Vulg. *ut intingatur pes tuus.* Hengst. and Del. endeavour to defend the received text by rendering, "That thou mayest dash (them) (with) thy foot in blood." But this is harsh and unnecessary. Others—"That Thou mayest dash Thy foot in blood."

24. The picture of the triumphal procession to the sanctuary is now resumed.

THEY HAVE SEEN, *i.e.* men in general have seen (hence equivalent to a passive, "Thy goings have been seen," as the LXX. ἐθεωρήθησαν). Hupfeld, however, supplies "the nations," *i.e.* the hostile nations, as the subject, and explains the "goings of God" of the various acts already celebrated in the Psalm.

THY GOINGS, here not the march of God against His enemies, as in lxxvii. 13 [14], Hab. iii. 6, but, as is plain from the context, His solemn entry into the sanctuary. Here we have the visible, as before, ver. 17, the invisible part of the spectacle.

25. PLAYING WITH THE TIMBRELS, or "beating the tambourine." Comp. Exod. xv. 20; Judges xi. 34.

26. The words of this verse may be a sudden outburst of feeling on the part of the Poet himself (comp. Judges v. 9), or, perhaps, the words sung by the chorus of maidens.

IN THE CONGREGATIONS. The masc. of the same plural noun occurs xxvi. 12. In both cases the plural may only denote *fulness*, *extension*, &c. (Gesen. § 108, 2*a*), so that it may mean only "in full assembly." Böttcher compares the Latin *comitia* (of men), and *comitium* (of the place).

THE FOUNTAIN OF ISRAEL. The

27 There was little Benjamin their ruler,[r]
The princes of Judah, their company,[s]
The princes of Zebulun, (and) the princes of Naphtali.

VII. 28 Thy God[t] hath commanded thy strength:
Strengthen,[u] O God, that which Thou hast wrought for us from Thy temple.[x]

29 Up to Jerusalem shall kings bring presents unto Thee.

30 Rebuke the beast of the reeds,

Patriarch, Israel, is the fountain from which the whole nation has issued as a stream. Comp. Is. xlviii. 1, li. 1. Others, who render "from the fountain," &c., suppose Zion to be meant as in a later Ps., "Bless ye God out of Zion."

27. Four of the tribes are mentioned by name as taking part in the procession, these four being representatives of the rest, Benjamin and Judah of the Southern kingdom, and Zebulun and Naphtali of the Northern. The last two are especially named with reference to the part which they played in the war against Sisera, and the position they occupy in the song of Deborah (Judges v. 18). The ancient commentators strangely enough see in the mention of these tribes an allusion to, or rather a prophecy of, the birthplace of the Apostles, and in Benjamin of the Apostle Paul, whom Tertullian, in reference to this Psalm, styles *parvus Benjamin*.

LITTLE BENJAMIN. So called, either because their ancestor was the *youngest* son of Jacob (LXX. νεώτερος, Gen. xliii. 33), or because it was in reality the smallest tribe, 1 Sam. ix. 21. It is called THEIR RULER, because from that tribe came Israel's first king; hardly, as Del. and Köst., because the Temple, according to the promise, Deut. xxxiii. 12, and the division of the land, Joshua xviii. 16, lay within the borders of their territory. Hupfeld considers the dominion thus attributed to this tribe "only a prophetic idea of the restoration, which often (especially in Isaiah) is set forth as an inversion of things, according to which the last shall be first and the first last."

THEIR COMPANY, or *crowd*, Judah being the largest and most numerous of the tribes. See Critical Note.

28. The Psalmist now turns in prayer to that God who has ascended into His holy habitation, beseeching Him thence to manifest His power in the subjugation of all enemies; he beholds the nations bringing tribute to Him as to their sovereign; and finally calls upon them to join in loud praise and worship of Him who rules in heaven, and who is the God of Israel.

THY GOD. According to the present text, there is here an abrupt address to Israel. But we should probably read (with many of the Ancient Verss.), "O God, command Thy strength." Comp. the similar expressions in xlii. 8 [9], xliv. 4 [5]. See Critical Notes.

FROM THY TEMPLE (or, perhaps, *tabernacle*, see note on Ps. v. 7). This should, probably, be detached from the next verse. See Critical Note.

30. In ver. 29 the voluntary submission of foreign powers is described. Here the prayer is that God would compel to submission those who oppose themselves.

REBUKE, as in ix. 5 [6].

THE BEAST OF THE REED, evidently a symbolical description of Egypt. Either the crocodile (called elsewhere *Leviathan*, lxxvi. 14, comp. Job. xl. 24, and *tannîn*, lxxiv. 13, Is.

The herd of bulls, with the calves of the peoples :
Trampling under foot[y] those that have pleasure in silver,[z]
Disperse Thou the peoples that delight in wars.
31 The rich ones[aa] shall come out of Egypt ;
Cush shall quickly stretch forth her hands unto God.

VII. 32 O ye kingdoms of the earth, sing unto God,

li. 9, parall. with Rahab, *i.e.* Egypt) is meant ; or the hippopotamus, in Job. xl. 15, called *behemoth*, and said there (ver. 21) to be "among the lotus, in the covert of the reeds :" (the reeds of the Nile are mentioned also in Is. xix. 6, xxxv. 7.) Probably the former, as the latter does not occur as a symbol of Egypt. Gesen. (on Is. xxvii. 1) supposes the beast of the reed, *i.e.* "the dragon, the crocodile," to be a symbol of Babylon. Lowth (*Præl.*) and Schnurrer think that the lion is meant as a symbol of Syria, lions making their haunts in the thick reeds by the rivers of Mesopotamia, and also by the Jordan, Jer. xlix. 19. Ewald also says, "The lion or the tiger, *i.e.* the great king." Egypt is selected as an example of the nations of the world, being at this time, no doubt, the leading power. See Pusey's *Daniel*, p. 68.

The E.V. "company of the spearmen" (the margin gives the true sense) follows Ibn Ezra, Qimchi, Ar., Mont., Pisc., Vat., Calvin ("genus armaturæ acsi diceret lancearios"). The word rendered *company* is the same which in ver. 10 is rendered *congregation* (in both, properly, *living* creature). Ibn Ez. refers to ver. 10 to justify his interpretation, and observes that "spears are long like a reed."

BULLS, lit. "strong ones." See on xxii. 12 [13]. These are the leaders of the nations, kings and captains, whereas the CALVES are explained by the addition of THE PEOPLES, as the nations themselves.

TRAMPLING UNDER FOOT. The participle refers to God, not to the calves. Hence some would change it into the imperative, "Trample under foot." According to the received text, this would stand : "(Rebuke) those that prostrate themselves (sing. for plur.) with pieces (or bars) of silver," or, "so that they prostrate themselves with pieces of silver." This last, which is followed by the E.V., is the interpretation of Ibn Ezra, but it does not seem grammatically defensible. On this, and the rest of the verse, see the Critical Note. The general sense is sufficiently clear. The Psalmist anticipates the entire subjection of all the princes and nations of the earth to the God who has now seated Himself on His throne in Zion.

31. Egypt and Ethiopia are mentioned as examples (as Tyre, xlv. 12 [13], see note there) of the most wealthy and powerful nations, who will bring their treasures and pour out their gifts before God. Comp. Is. xliii. 3, xlv. 14, lx. 5, &c.

SHALL QUICKLY STRETCH FORTH, lit. "shall make to run." The allusion is to stretching out the hands, not in prayer, but in the offering of gifts. Others understand it as a sign of submission like the Latin *dare manus.* The verb is in the feminine, Cush, or Ethiopia, being, as is usual with names of countries, regarded as fem. ; but, by a confusion not unusual in Heb., we have the suffix of the masc. pronoun, "*his* hands," instead of "*her* hands."

32. The remaining verses of the Psalm are, in fact, prophetic. Standing in the midst of that future glory,

Play (on the harp) to the Lord. [Selah.]
33 To Him[bb] who rideth on the heaven of heavens (which are) of old :—
Lo, He uttereth His voice, a voice of strength.
34 Ascribe ye strength unto God,
Whose majesty is over Israel and whose strength is in the clouds.
35 Terrible (art Thou), O God, from Thy sanctuaries, Thou God of Israel ;
He giveth strength and much power unto the people.
Blessed be God.

which he anticipates so vividly that it seems already to be present, the Psalmist calls upon all the kingdoms of the world to praise God, whose glory is in heaven, but who has also chosen Zion, there to dwell, and to manifest His glory, as He manifests it in heaven.

33. THE HEAVEN OF HEAVENS, *i.e.* the highest heavens (comp. Deut. x. 14, 1 Kings viii. 27), said to be "of old" with reference to their creation (comp. cii. 25 [26]) ; and on this throning of God in the heavens, whilst at the same time He appears as the Redeemer and Protector of His people upon earth, see Deut. xxxiii. 26.

HIS VOICE. Comp. xlvi. 6 [7], and xxix. 3, &c., where the thunder is so called ; God's thunder being the utterance of His power.

35. FROM THY SANCTUARIES. So cx. 2, "Jehovah shall send the rod of thy strength *out of* Zion," as the seat of God's dominion, as the centre *from which* He exercises His power. The plural, as lxxiii. 17, Jer. li. 51, Ezek. xxi. 7 (comp. Ps. lxxxiv. 1 [2], cxxxii. 5, 7), as expressing the *various parts* of the one sanctuary.

HE GIVETH STRENGTH. Comp. xxix. 11, Is. xl. 29. The word "strength" is repeated for the fourth time in five lines.

MUCH POWER. I have so rendered in order to express the *plural* noun : lit. "powers." It occurs nowhere else.

[a] הִנְדֹּף, a peculiar form ; inf. constr. instead of הִנָּדֵף, and apparently written thus because of the similarity of sound with the following תִּנְדֹּף. This last, as it stands, is 2d masc. (the נ being expressed as in Is. lviii. 3, Jer. iii. 5), though Ewald would make it a 3d fem. in an intransitive sense. This, I must think, would be preferable, were it supported by usage. But as the Kal is transitive, a different punctuation might be adopted, כְּהִנָּדֵף . . . תִּנָּדֵף, "as smoke is utterly driven away" (עָשָׁן being then here fem). The LXX., Syr., Chald., Ar., Vulg., seem to have read יִנָּדֵף, making "the wicked" the subject.

[b] בָּעֲרָבוֹת. The plur. form of the word may be used here poetically for the sing. which occurs in the parallel passage Is. xl. 3, or it may be employed purposely, the object of the Psalmist being not to speak of God's march only through *the 'Arabah* properly so called,—through the

desert tract, that is, "which extends along the valley of the Jordan from the Dead Sea to the Lake of Gennesareth, now called by the Arabs El-Ghor,"—but through all the desert regions by which He led His people. In Deut. i. 1 and ii. 8, the 'Arabah, is the valley between the Dead Sea and the Gulf of Akaba, which is called Wadey el 'Arabah. The plural of the word is used of the country of Moab and the district about Jericho (Deut. xxxiv. 1, 8, and Joshua iv. 13, &c.), and generally of the tract east of the Jordan, 2 Sam. xv. 28 (K'ri). But the word has been strangely misinterpreted. The LXX. ἐπὶ δυσμῶν, as in 2 Sam. iv. 7, from ערב (II. Ges.), *to grow dark*, comp. the Arab. غرب, *to set* (of the sun), and so the Syr.; but Chald. and the Rabb. *the heavens* or *the clouds* (according to Mendelss. the highest heavens are so called as having no stars, and so being waste; he renders *Æther-wüste*); Luther, "Der da *sanft* herfahret," deriving it from ערב (I. Ges.), *to be sweet, pleasant.*

[c] יָהּ apocop. from יָהוֹ, and this again apoc. from יְהוָה. It occurs first in Exod. xv. 2. Hence borrowed here, cxviii. 14, and Is. xii. 2, and elsewhere in the formula הַלְלוּ יָהּ. The בְּ prefixed is the so-called *Beth essentiæ*. See above, xxxv. note [b], and comp. liv. 6. Ges. § 154, Rem. 3, יְחִידִים. The LXX. μονοτρόπους. Theod. μοναχούς. Comp. xxv. 16 and Is. lviii. 7, *the lonely*, *the destitute*, who are here said to be brought back to a house (as exiles, wanderers, &c. restored to their home): others understand it of the *childless* who are blessed with a family, as cxiii. 9.

[d] כּוֹשָׁרוֹת, only here: rendered by the LXX. ἐν ἀνδρείᾳ, and Theod. ἐν εὐθύτησιν. Symm. better εἰς ἀπόλυσιν, and the Syr. "*into prosperity*." Comp. כִּשְׁרוֹן, Eccl. ii. 21, from כשר syn. with אשר, ישר; according to Hupf. a *later* Aramaic form for this last; hence properly "the *right* condition," and so "freedom, prosperity," &c. The Syriac transl. employs here a word from the same root.

[e] תָּנִיף. The Hiph. is here construed with double accus. (like the Qal, Prov. vii. 17). "The imperf. is the relat. pret. with reference to the situation in ver. 8" (Hupf.), or simply the aor. of repeated past action. נַחֲלָתְךָ (by which we are to understand the *people* not the *land*) is certainly the object of this verb, and is not to be joined (according to the accents) with וְנִלְאָה, which follows. This would necessitate the rendering: "Thine inheritance, even when (or, and that when) it was weary," &c. וְ epexeget., as in 1 Sam. xxviii. 3, Amos iii. 11, iv. 10. But this is without point. The participle is here used without the art. hypothetically, Ew. § 341 *b*. On נְדָבוֹת (plur. for sing., as cx. 3) see on liv. 6 [8]. The construction as given above is that of the LXX. βροχὴν ἑκούσιαν ἀφοριεῖς τῇ κληρονομίᾳ σου.

[f] יִדּוֹדוּן. The ancient Versions wrongly derived this from ידד, *to love*, hence LXX. τοῦ ἀγαπητοῦ, Symm. ἀγαπητοὶ ἐγένοντο, as explained by Syr. and Jerome in the sense of being friends, and so joined in alliance. It is the fut. energet. from נדד, as the Rabb. rightly give it. It seems to have been the fate of almost every word in this Psalm to have been misunderstood. Even the following נְוַת was derived from נאה, *to be beautiful*, whereas it is the fem. of the adj. נָוֶה, as Jer. vi. 2.

[8] In the interpretation of this and the next verse two questions have to be considered: first, the meaning of the separate words, and then the construction of the sentences.

First, as regards the words. שְׁפַתַּיִם occurs also Ezek. xl. 43. (1) According to the Rabb. *pots, dirty vessels.* They explain the passage thus: Though ye lie now in dirt and squalor and wretchedness among the pots, yet ye shall be as the wings of a dove, &c. *i.e.* bright and beautiful. Ye have been in gloom and misery; ye shall be in peace and prosperity. (2) Others (following Rashi תחומיכם, and Jerome, *terminos*) understand *boundaries,* which they explain either (as Luth. and Gei.) of the *ranks* of battle, in which the army, with the light dancing on its plumes and lances, is compared to the dove; or (as Böttch., Stier, and Hengst.) of the boundaries of fields, &c., the allusion being to shepherd life or country life in general. The LXX. κλῆροι. (3) According to J. D. Mich. the word denotes *drinking-troughs* (from the Arab. سَقَتَ, *to drink,* comp. Judges v. 11). (4) But there can be little doubt that it should rather be rendered, like the kindred word מִשְׁפְּתַיִם, Gen. xlix. 14, Judges v. 16, *sheep-folds, hurdles,* from שפת, *to set, place.* (So the E. V. has *sheep-folds* in the last passage, whereas in the first it has *panniers.*) According to (2), (3), (4), the allusion is to a quiet, indolent country life; the strong men who should have furnished recruits for the army being content with their usual rustic occupations, busying themselves with their cattle, &c.

פָּרֵשׂ commonly both in Qal and Piel means *to spread abroad,* and hence the LXX. ἐν τῷ διαστέλλειν τὸν ἐπουράνιον βασιλεῖς (Th. ἐπ' αὐτῆς) χιονωθήσονται ἐν Σελμών. And so Stier understands it of the appointment of the heads of the tribes and princes throughout the country: but in Zech. ii. 10, *to scatter,* and so the Niph. Ezech. xvii. 21, and this meaning is clearly preferable here.

תַּשְׁלֵג, 3 fem. Hiph. in a neut. sense (Böttcher makes it 2 masc. "Thou, O God, makest it snow," &c.), either *it snows,* or *snowed* (according to analogy of other verbs, though this verb does not occur in that sense), or *it was white as snow.* Gesen. § 53, 2. The voluntative form is to be explained here by its use in the apodosis when the protasis is hypothetical. It denotes the consequence which will happen, supposing something else happens. Gesen. § 128, 2.

צַלְמוֹן. In the only other passage where the word occurs, the name of a mountain near Shechem, Judg. ix. 48. Some (as Böttcher) suppose another lofty peak of he Bashan range to be meant, and this may be supported by the remarkable reading of the Alex. MS. in Judg. ix. ὄρος ἑρμών; and others, as Theod., the Chald. ("shadow of death"), and the Rabb., and Luther, take it is an appell. = צֶלֶם, *shadow, gloom,* &c. "When the kings (13) were scattered, then that victory was like light, brightness in the darkness." And so recently Reuss, "Et l'éclat de la neige remplace l'obscurité," admitting, however, the doubtfulness of the explanation.

Secondly, as regards the construction. אִם may (1) introduce the protasis, as a particle of condition (*if*), or of time (*when*), and then the apodosis may begin at כַּנְפֵי י׳, as Hengst. takes it and Del., "*Though* ye lie (or, *when* ye lie), &c. . . . ye are (or, ye shall be as) the wings of a dove," &c. Or (2) אִם may be used, as in formulæ of swearing, to express a negative. So J. D. Mich. "Lie *not* among," &c. Or (3) as an interrogative, "Will ye lie," &c. (so Hupf. and Böttch.), implying *surely ye will not,* comp. 1 Kings i. 27, Micah iv. 9, Job vi. 12, in which case the particle of comparison only need be supplied in the next clause, "*As* the wings," &c. [or the interrogative force of the particle may be explained by taking it in its usual conditional sense, and supposing an ellipse: "*If* ye lie—what then, what will happen?" &c. Comp. Is. xxix. 16.].

נֶחְפָּה, part. fem. Niph. which *may* be predicate to כַּנְפֵי (comp. 1 Sam. iv. 15, Micah iv. 11, Ew. § 317 *a*), but may also refer to יוֹנָה.

בָּהּ. The reference of the pron. is obscure. It is commonly rendered *in it*, or *because of it*, and the reference is assumed to be to the Holy Land, as in ver. 11 [E. V. 10] and Is. viii. 21, in both of which passages the pron. is so used; but it must be confessed that there is something singular in this vague reference to an idea scarcely implied even in the context. (2) It may be better, perhaps, to take the pron. as referring by anticipation to the following צַלְמוֹן, as in ix. 12 [13]. (3) Others refer the pron. to *the dove*, as well as the verb תַּשְׁלֵג following: "On her (*i.e.* the dove) it was white as snow," alluding to the brilliancy of the plumage. Or, she, the dove or the people, was white as snow. (4) Böttcher takes the pron. in a neut. sense, and the verb תַּשְׁלֵג, as remarked above, as 2 pers. masc., and the prep. בְּ in בְּפָרֵשׂ as marking not the time but the manner of the action: "With the scattering of kings, O Almighty, *therewith* (בָּהּ) Thou makest snow fall upon Zalmon," which he explains to mean that God so discomfited the kings, so scattered them and their armies in wild disarray over the heights of one of the Bashan range, that it looked like a thick fall of snow. Symm.: ὁπότε κατεμέριζεν ὁ ἱκανὸς βασιλεύειν αὐτήν, ὡς χιονισθεῖσα ἦν Σελμών.

h גַּבְנֻנִּים, from a sing. גַּבְנֹן, which however does not occur, usually regarded as an abstract quadriliteral noun, and compared with נַאֲפוּף and similar forms; but these, as Hupf. observes, are not parallel instances, inasmuch as they do not double their last radical. He considers the termination ןֹ here to be the same as ־וֹן, which, as well as ןָ (and םָ, ־ם formed from a nunnated accusative termination הָ), commonly appears as an adjectival termination, and sometimes also in substantives. It might be regarded as a denom. abstr. subst. (like אַלְמוֹן, *widowhood*, for אַלְמָן); but here, again, there is no doubling of the last radical. Hence he decides that the word is an adj.: (1) because of the doubling of the final consonant as in שַׁאֲנָן, רַעֲנָן, and ־ם in חַרְטֻמִּים, עֵירֻמִּים; (2) because in ver. 17 [16, E. V.] it is clearly an adj. agreeing with הָרִים; (3) because in Chald. the adj. גַּבְנוּן, *tumidus, superciliosus*, occurs. Hence הר־ג׳ (though the noun is in the constr.) is not to be explained *mons gibbositatis*, "a mountain of many-peakedness" (if such a word may be coined), but either "a mountain of many-peaked (mountains)," or else הַר must be taken collectively as = הָרִים. It is remarkable that the older Verss., while they give Zalmon, do not give Bashan here as a proper name. LXX. ὄρος Θεοῦ, ὄρος πῖον, ὄρος τετυρωμένον, ὄρος πῖον. (So in xxii. 13 they render שָׁן by the same adj. ταῦροι πίονες.) Symm. ὄρος εὐτροφίας, ὄρος ὑψηλότατον, ὄρος εὐτροφίας. Jerome, *mons Dei, mons pinguis: mons excelsus, mons pinguis.*

[i] תְּרַצְּדוּן. The word occurs only here, and has been wrongly translated by the Chald. and others as = רקד, *to hop.* The other ancient Versions are nearer the mark. LXX. ὑπολαμβάνετε; Aq. Th. ἐρίζετε; Symm. περισπουδάζετε; Jerome, *contenditis;* Vulg. *suspicamini;* R. Mosheh Haddarshan, quoted by Rashi, "watch," or "lie in wait." The verb is to be explained by the cogn. Arab. root رصد, *oculis intentis, insidiose, observare,* "to watch jealously." The N. T. synonyms are παρατηρεῖν, ἐνεδρεύειν.

[k] רִבֹּתַיִם, dual of רִבּוֹת, which is either (1) a noun abstr. = רִבּוֹת, and so *two myriads;* or (2) a plur. contracted from רִבֹּאוֹת, Ezra ii. 69, in which case it would be (as a plur. with dual termination added) "*two series* of myriads," as חומותים, "the double line of walls," לוחתים, "the double series of planks of a ship."

In אַלְפֵי שִׁנְאָן, lit. "thousands of repetition," we have another ἅπ. λεγ. שִׁנְאָן = שִׁנְיָן. The Targ. and Saad. render "thousands of *angels.*" LXX. χιλιάδες εὐθηνούντων; Jerome, *millia abundantium,* as if it were שאנן. Comp. Dan. vii. 10, Numb. x. 36.

[l] אֲדֹנָי בָם סִינַי בַּקֹּדֶשׁ. This gives no satisfactory sense. "Grammatically," says Hupfeld, "it could only mean: *The Lord is* or *was among them* (the myriads of the angelic host), or *with them* (as lx. 12), or *rides* (*rode*) *upon them* (the chariots) *to Sinai into the sanctuary* (as ver. 25), or *with holiness* (majesty), which would be a glance back at the theophany on Sinai; according to the older translators and Hengst. with reference to the tradition of the giving of the Law by the mediation of angels, Gal. iii. 19, Heb. ii. 2, which is supposed to rest on Deut. xxxiii. 2, where however we have only the usual representation of God in the O. T. as accompanied by angels, without special reference to the giving of the Law. But this does not suit the context, according to which only an application or comparison of Sinai with the present abode of God is in place, as has been felt by the Rabb. and almost all interpreters, who have consequently inserted the particle of comparison, '*as* on Sinai,' which however is grammatically inadmissible. Hence the more recent interpreters generally follow L. de Dieu, 'Sinai is (now) in the sanctuary (on Zion);' Sinai as it were having become appellative: either (as L. de Dieu) for the theophany or glory of God among the angelic host on Sinai, which is now to be seen in the sanctuary on Zion; or more simply, according to Schnurrer, Sinai stands by meton. for the abode of God which is now transferred to Zion (see the classical parallels quoted in Merrick's *Annot. on the Psalms;* Mart. 4, 60, 'In medio Tibure Sardinia est;' Juv. *Sat.* iii. 62, 'Jampridem Syrus in Tiberim defluxit Orontes;' Themist. *Orat.* 31, μετελήλυθεν ὁ Ἑλικὼν εἰς τὸν Βόσπορον; and the well-

known, 'Hic Rhodus,' &c., and similar instances in all languages) : in either case the idea being that Zion is a second Sinai. ["It (Zion) is a Sinai in holiness."] But suitable as the sense would be, this would be a strange way of expressing it ; for not only is the *now* wanting, but also the name of the new sanctuary, and הַקֹּדֶשׁ alone could scarcely form an opposition to Sinai. Probably the reading is wrong, and we ought to read בָּא מִסִּינַי for בָּם סִינַי, *hath come from Sinai into the sanctuary* (קֹדֶשׁ with the article in this connection being intelligible enough as meaning Zion). So Pott., Köst., Maur., Olsh., as an allusion to Deut. xxxiii. 2, where the same phrase occurs." I accept this emendation in part, but I think the gap is larger ; we cannot dispense with בָּם, without which this sentence stands abrupt and dissevered from the rest. Supposing the text to have stood originally אדני בם [בא מ]סיני, it is easy to see how the letters between brackets, from their similarity to those immediately preceding, might have slipt out altogether. I am glad to find that Reuss follows me here :

> " Le Seigneur avec des myriades
> Du Sinai vient au sanctuaire."

[m] בָּאָדָם, "*among* men," as the region in which, instead of "*from* men," as the persons from whom, the gifts were taken : or, as Hengst. "among men" = upon earth, in opp. to heaven. J. D. Mich. renders "*consisting* of men," *i.e.* who have thus become the servants of God (with reference to Ephes. iv. 11, &c.). So Böttch.—who supposes prisoners taken in war and devoted to the service of the Temple (*nethinim*)—and De W., who thinks that proselytes are meant. The rendering of the Ap. in Ephes. may be perhaps a free rendering of the passage, ἔδωκε δόματα τοῖς ἀνθρώποις ; but it is remarkable that the Chald. has the same, יְהַבְתָּא לְהוֹן מַתְּנָן לִבְנֵי נָשָׁא. As the Targum on the Psalms is manifestly composite, some portions being much earlier than others, this rendering *may* have been earlier than the time of the Apostle.

[n] וְאַף סֹרְרִים. With what are these words to be connected ? Many take them with the previous verse, and regard them as dependent either upon שָׁבִיתָ, or upon לָקַחְתָּ, repeating the prep. בְּ before ס׳, "and even among the rebellious Thou hast taken gifts" (so Del.). But in this case the rest of the sentence, לִשְׁכֹּן י׳ א׳, stands very lamely, "that Jah Elohim may dwell," *i.e.* as Del. explains, "on Zion," or as J. D. Mich. "among them." Others would connect this last clause with the words "Thou hast ascended." So Lee (*Heb. Gram.* § 241, 18, "*Thou, O Lord God, hast ascended up on high* (there) *to dwell; Thou hast taken captivity captive; Thou hast received gifts for man* (*i.e.* mankind), *nay even* (for) *the rebellious ones.*" This, however, is an unnecessary transposition. The inf. constr. לִשְׁכֹּן here takes the place of the fut. act. or pass. See on lxii. note [g] : either, "the rebellious shall dwell with Jah," so Hupf. who takes יָהּ as the accus. after the verb *of dwelling*, as v. 5, lxxx. 2 ; or, as seems to me preferable, "the rebellious (shall be) for the dwelling of Jah," *i.e.* "Jah shall dwell among them." We thus get the proper force of the particle וְאַף, "*yea, even* the rebellious, those who would not willingly

bring gifts, must nevertheless yield." LXX. καὶ γὰρ ἀπειθοῦντες τοῦ κατασκηνῶσαι.

[o] יַעֲמָס־. This verb (like נשׂא and סבל) seems to combine the two meanings, (1) *to put a burden upon another*, and (2) *to bear a burden.* In the former sense it is always construed with עַל. Of those who adopt (1), some, as Calv., and the E. V., take it in a good sense, "who daily loadeth us (with benefits);" others, as L. de Dieu, De W., Reuss, make יַעֲמָס־לָנוּ the protasis to what follows, "If any lay a burden upon us, (still) God is," &c.; others, again, as Gei., take הָאֵל as the subject, "He who lays (or laid) a burden upon us is the God who is also our salvation," *i.e.* this burden was a discipline and so a means of blessing. But these constructions are harsh, and (2) seems preferable. Comp. Is. xlvi. 1, 3, Zech. xii. 3. Then לָנוּ either stands here (according to later usage) for the accus., as Hupf. takes it, "schleppt uns" (and so Jerome, *portavit nos*); or, which is better, retains its proper force as a dat. commodi, "Who beareth for us (our burden)." So Ew. and Del., and De Wette says of this rendering, "besser vielleicht."

[p] לַמָּוֶת תּוֹצָאוֹת, lit. "means of escape *for* death," or *with reference to* i.e. *against* or *from* death." So Ew. explains, "God gives to Israel the means to escape from death." Similarly De W., "Vom Tode Rettung;" Zunz, "Ausgänge vom Tode." And the E. V., "issues from death." (2) Others, "goings forth *to* death," *i.e.* God has means of leading the enemy to death. So Symm. αἱ εἰς θάνατον ἔξοδοι, and so Rashi and Qimchi. The LXX., Jerome, Calv., render "*of* death."

[q] מִנֵּהוּ. This has been commonly taken as = מִמֶּנּוּ, either (1) distributively, *of every one* of them (the enemies), which involves however a very harsh ellipse, "that the tongue of thy dogs (may drink the blood) of the enemies, of every one of them;" so Symm., ὅπως . . . . λάψῃ ἡ γλ. τ. κ. σ. ἀπὸ ἑκάστου τῶν ἐχθρῶν σου: or (2) "*of it*," i.e. the blood. So Calv. and the E. V., "the tongue of thy dogs *in the same*," and app. the LXX. παρ' αὐτοῦ. Others, "The tongue of thy dogs, from the enemy, even from them," or, "even from it (the blood)." According to Rashi we have the verb מִנָּה (as in Job vii. 3, Jonah ii. 1, Dan. i. 10): "the tongue of thy dogs hath made it (the blood) of the enemies its food," lit. hath prepared it. But it would be better then, as Hupf. observes, to make לְשׁוֹן the dat., "He hath given it as a portion to the tongue of thy dogs." Simonis, however, is probably right in referring מִנֵּהוּ to a noun מֵן, *portion*, and so I have rendered in the text. So too in the Arab. Vers. of R. Yapheth: *pars ejus.* It is unnecessary therefore with Olsh. to read מְנָתוֹ, as in lxiii. 11.

[r] רֹדֵם cannot be referred to רדם, but to רדה. It is the part. with the suff., with *Tsere* instead of Kametz, and construed with the accus. instead of the more usual בְּ. The suff. refers not to the enemy, "their subduer" (as Hengst.), but "their (Israel's) ruler." The Syr. ܒܫܠܝܐ, *in rest*, or *tranquillity*.

[s] רִגְמָתָם. Qimchi derives the word from רגם, *to stone*, as though the meaning were *their heap*, i.e. "the princes of Judah (with) the heap (or crowd) of the common people." But the verb רגם is always used of *stoning* as a punishment appointed by the Law, and the noun could hardly therefore mean *a heap* of stones, and so *a crowd*. Either, therefore, we must suppose the root signification of רגם to be that of the Arab. رَكَم, *congerere*, or we must conclude that we have here a false reading for רִגְשָׁתָם (comp. lxiv. 3 and lv. 15). The מ and the שׁ are very similar in the old Hebrew character. Hengst., who always defends the Massoretic text at the expense of any interpretation however far-fetched, renders the word *stoning*, and observes: "Judah is called the *stoning* of the enemies, in allusion to *David*, who put to death by a stone Goliath, the representative of the might of the world"!

[t] צִוָּה אֱלֹהֶיךָ, *Thy God* (O Israel) *hath commanded*. This sudden address to Israel introduces confusion, and disturbs the parallelism. It is therefore better to read with all the older Verss. צַוֵּה אֱלֹהִים.

[u] עוּזָּה, incorrectly for עֻזָּה, and this for עֻזָּה. By the LXX. δυνάμωσον, Symm. ἐνίσχυσον, taken transitively. And so Calv. and the E. V. *strengthen*. But elsewhere עזז is always intrans., *to be strong*, *to show oneself strong*. But then it is difficult to explain the pron. זוּ, which must in this case be accus., "show Thyself strong *in that which* Thou hast wrought." This gives no satisfactory sense. It should rather be "in that which Thou *wilt* work." Others, again, take זוּ as the nom., "*Thou who* hast," &c. (but can זוּ be used as referring to the person as the agent?), but not Ewald (as Hupf. asserts), who renders, "Glänzend mach', Gott, was du uns bereitet." He therefore takes the verb as transitive, and this on the whole is perhaps best. Eccl. vii. 19.

[x] מֵהֵיכָלֶךָ. This cannot be rendered as the E. V. "*Because of* Thy temple" (although Symm. has διὰ τὸν ναόν σου). It can only mean "*From* Thy temple," and manifestly belongs to the preceding verse, as indeed is confirmed by the pausal form of the word. The following עַל יְ׳, "*up to* Jerusalem," is not to be connected with this, but with the verb יוֹבִילוּ.

[y] מִתְרַפֵּס. This is commonly rendered *submitting*, or *prostrating themselves* (the Hiph. of רפס, *calcare*, meaning *se calcandum præbere=prosternere*, which is defended by Prov. vi. 3). But why should the Psalmist pray, *Rebuke* the beast of the reeds (*i.e.* Egypt), &c. whilst they prostrate themselves? If already prostrate, they would not need the rebuke. Hence it has been attempted to render this, *ut supplex veniat* (Flam.), and the E. V. "till every one submit himself;" but this is grammatically indefensible. The truth is, that the meaning commonly assigned to the verb is wrong. The Hithp. has here the force of the Greek middle, *to trample under foot for oneself*, and so it should be rendered in Prov. vi. 3. Then the part must be taken, not with the nouns immediately preceding, but as a predicate of God (as in text and as it is in the Arab. Vers. published by Bargès). Hupf. indeed says that the part. cannot be connected with anything going before, and would correct הִתְרַפֵּס imperat. as afterwards בַּזֵּר instead of בִּזַּר. But this seems unnecessary. [Bunsen, I

find, retains the participle.] Symm. has the right sense of the part. though with a wrong construction, συνόδῳ παμμεγεθῶν . . . . τοῖς διαλακτίζουσι. The part. may perhaps be taken with the animals, "rushing on, trampling like a herd."

[z] בְּרַצֵּי פ׳, "with bars of silver." If the interpretation given above of מִתְרַפֵּס is correct, it is clear that the received punctuation here cannot be defended, and there can be little doubt that we should point בְּרֹצֵי, "(trampling) *on them who have pleasure in silver.*" This is supported by R. Yapheth's rendering, "conculcatus *ob studium* argenti," which shows that he connected it with the root רצה. Four MSS. read the word without Dagesh, and the older Verss. do not seem to have had the present reading. Symm. τοὺς εὐδοκήτους ὡς δοκιμὴν ἀργυρίου. LXX. τοὺς δεδοκιμασμένους τῷ ἀργυρίῳ. Jerome, *in vitulis populorum calcitrantium contra rotas argenteas.* The Syr. for מת׳ ב׳ כ׳ has "who are clothed with silver."

[aa] חַשְׁמַנִּים, a quadrilit. not occurring elsewhere, but apparently the same as מִשְׁמַנִּים, lxxviii. 31, lit. *fat ones,* i.e. "great men, princes," &c., as the Rabb. Hence, "Hasmoneans" = priest-princes. A Cardinal is to this day called חשמן. On the other hand, the LXX. have πρέσβεις, and the Syr. "ambassadors." It is either formed, Hupf. says, from שמן with prosthetic ח (as elsewhere א and ה)—but where is there any parallel to this?—or from the Arab. خشم, with the termination ָן, which is more probable. Mich. *Hasmoneans,* i.e. inhabitants of the Egyptian province Aschmunim. The Chald. has חוסמנא, the name of a province.

[bb] סֶלָה. Hupf. finds the Selah here out of place (though there are other instances, see lx. 6), as disturbing the construction, and ingeniously suggests that the reading should be סֹלּוּ לָרֹכֵב. As the text now stands the prep. לְ is out of place, unless with Schn. we connect לָר׳ with שִׁירוּ לֵא.

PSALM 69

WHEN and by whom this Psalm was written, we have no very certain clue to guide us; except that the closing verses point to a time of national disaster, and that the hopes there expressed are such as might naturally have been uttered on the return from the captivity in Babylon. All that is certain from the general tenour of the Psalm is, that it was written under circumstances of great and unmerited suffering, by one who was persecuted for righteousness' sake. The zeal which he had shown for the service and honour of God had provoked the hostility of bad men against him, and made him the object of their unholy mockery. In the former part of the Psalm we have the fact of this persecution detailed, in the form of a humble complaint to God, together with an earnest prayer for deliverance. In the latter part there is a marked change of feeling. The sad, humble, subdued, entreating tone in which he had spoken, turns suddenly into a strong outburst of indignant execration. One curse is heaped upon another, till the whole terrible series is completed in the prayer that those who have persecuted and mocked God's afflicted servant may have their names blotted out from His Book of Life.

In some of its features this Psalm bears much resemblance to Psalms xxxv. and cix. In all three Psalms there is the same deep sense of grievous wrong, of innocence unjustly persecuted, and in all alike the same burning indignation is poured in a hot lava-stream of anathemas upon the persecutors. (See note on xxxv. 22.)

In other respects there are points of coincidence between this and the Fortieth Psalm, which seem to justify the conclusion that the two were written by the same person. In each the Sacred Poet describes his affliction as a sinking in the deep mire (xl. 2 [3], lxix. 2 [3]) in the one we have "they that hate me without a cause are more than the hairs of my head," lxix. 4 [5]; in the other, "mine iniquities . . . . are more than the hairs of my head," xl. 12 [13]; in both there is the same hope that the triumphant issue of the suffering endured will be a subject of joy to the righteous and the strengthening of their faith, xl. 3 [4], 16 [17], lxix. 6 [7], 32 [33]. This last passage, again, bears a striking resemblance to xxii. 26 [27], so that Hitzig considers it certain that the Twenty-second Psalm must also be ascribed to the same author.* That author he supposes to be Jeremiah. Seiler, and others before him, had thrown out the same suggestion with regard to Psalms xl. and lxix. The grounds on which this view rests are: (1) the character of the suffering, which was occasioned by zeal for God's house, the humility of the sufferer, and the scorn with which he was treated, all of which correspond with what we read in Jer. xv. 15—18; (2) the murderous hate of the men of Anathoth towards Jeremiah, xi. 18—23, which may be compared with the complaint of the Psalmist, ver. 8 [9]; (3) the close of the Psalm, ver. 34—36 [35—37], which is, as it were, a summary of what Jeremiah foretold in his Book of Restoration, xxx.—xxxiii.; (4) the peculiar nature of Jeremiah's suffering, who was cast by the princes into the dungeon or cistern of Malchiah, where he sank down in the mire. To this the Prophet is supposed to allude in Lam. iii. 53—58, and, according to Hitzig, this Psalm was his prayer whilst he lay in the cistern or pit (comp. ver. 15). Delitzsch, in his

* In this Ewald differs from him, though he admits that xl. and lxix. are by the same author, but he adds several other Psalms to the list, xxv., xxxiv., xxxviii., li., lxx., lxxi.. lxxxviii., cix.

Introduction to the Psalm, thinks this far from improbable; indeed, he inclines strongly to Hitzig's view, and confesses that the Psalm can be explained much more satisfactorily on the supposition that Jeremiah, than on the supposition that David, was the author; adding, at the same time, that he has not the courage to pronounce the inscription false. When he comes to the end of his commentary on the Psalm, after again arguing that the last verses present no difficulty if we suppose them to have been written by the Prophet, he with strange inconsistency turns round and says: "Considering the relation of the New Testament to this Psalm, we hold fast to the Inscription, (A Psalm) of David."

Yet if any inference can be drawn from style and language, if criticism have any testing power, it would hardly be too much to say that this Psalm could not have been written by David. Moreover, to what possible circumstances in David's life could verses 11, 12, and 21 refer, or what meaning could verse 35 have in his mouth? The fact that it is cited as his in Rom. xi. 9 proves nothing for "David" there means nothing more than the Book of Psalms.

This has usually been regarded as a Messianic Psalm. No portion of the Old Testament Scriptures is more frequently quoted in the New, with the exception of Psalm xxii. When Jesus drives the buyers and sellers from the Temple, John ii. 17, His disciples are reminded of the words of ver. 9*a*. When it is said, John xv. 25, that the enemies of Jesus hated Him without a cause, and this is looked upon as a fulfilment of Scripture, the reference is probably to ver. 4 (though it may be also to xxxv. 19). To Him, and the reproach which He endured for the sake of God, St. Paul (Rom. xv. 3) refers the words of this Psalm, ver. 9*b*, "the reproaches of them that reproached Thee are fallen upon Me. In ver. 12 we have a foreshadowing of the mockery of our Lord by the soldiers in the prætorium, Matt. xxvii. 27—30; in ver. 21, the giving of the vinegar and the gall find their counterpart in the scenes of the Crucifixion, Matt. xxvii. 34. In John xix. 28 there is an allusion, probably, to ver. 21 of this Psalm (and to xxii. 15). The imprecation in ver. 25 is said, in Acts i. 20, to have been fulfilled in the case of Judas Iscariot, though, as the words of the Psalm are plural, the citation is evidently made with some freedom. According to Rom. xi. 9, 10, the rejection of Israel may best be described in the words of ver. 22, 23.

It will be observed that many of these quotations are made generally, by way of illustration and application, rather than as prophecies which have received fulfilment. Enough, however, remains to justify the Messianic sense of the Psalm, provided our interpretation be fair and sober. The broad principle laid down in the Introduction to the Twenty-second Psalm applies here. The history of Prophets and holy men of old is a typical history. They were, it may be said, representative men, suffering and hoping, not for themselves only, but for the nation whom they represented. In their sufferings, they were feeble and transient images of the Great Sufferer, who by His sufferings accomplished man's Redemption: their hopes could never be fully realized but in the issue of His work, nor their aspirations be truly uttered save by His mouth. But confessions of sinfulness and imprecations of vengeance, mingling with these better hopes and aspirations, are a beacon to guide us in our interpretation. They teach us that the Psalm is not a prediction; that the Psalmist does not put himself in the place of the Messiah to come. They show us that here, as indeed in all Scripture, two streams, the human and the Divine, flow on in the same channel. They seem designed to remind us that if Prophets and Minstrels of old were types of the Great Teacher of the Church, yet that they were so only in some respects, and not altogether. They bear witness to the imperfection of those by whom God spake in time past unto the fathers, in many portions and in many ways, even whilst they point to Him who is the Living Word, the perfect Revelation of the Father.

The Psalm consists of two principal divisions, each of eighteen verses. These, however, again admit of subdivision as follows:—

I. (1) The lamentation, which declares the miserable condition of the Psalmist. Ver. 1—4.

(2) The fuller account of his persecutions, especial prominence being given to the fact that his sufferings are *for the sake of God and of His house*, and the reproach to which he is exposed in consequence. Ver. 5—12.

(3) The prayer to God for deliverance, urged both upon the ground of his great misery and of God's great mercy. Ver. 13—18.

II. (1) He turns back, and again dwells upon the malice and cruelty of his enemies. Ver. 19—21.

(2) And then, roused by the recollection of his wrongs, conscious that he is on the side of God and of truth, and that he has been treated with shameful injustice, he calls for God's worst vengeance upon his enemies. Ver. 22—28.

(3) Lastly, we have the threefold expression of joy: first, as regards God's deliverance of himself, and his own acknowledgement of that mercy (ver. 29—31); then, as regards the encouragement hereby given to all the righteous (ver. 32, 33); and, finally, in prospect that God will save Zion, and build up the cities of Judah (ver. 34—36).

[FOR THE PRECENTOR. "UPON LILIES."[a] (A PSALM) OF DAVID.]

1 SAVE me, O God,
For the waters have come in unto (my) soul.
2 I have sunk in the mud of the abyss, where there is no standing-place.
I have come into the depths of the waters,
And a flood hath overwhelmed me.
3 I am weary with my calling, my throat is parched,
Mine eyes have failed, whilst I wait for my God.
4 More than the hairs of my head are they that hate me without cause,
Strong are (they that are) my destroyers,[b] mine enemies without reason :—

Ver. 1—4. These contain the cry for help, and the description of the Psalmist's miserable condition.

1. THE WATERS, frequently occurring as an image of extreme danger, as in xviii. 4 [5] and 16 [17], xxxii. 6, xlii. 7 [8], and often.

UNTO (MY) SOUL, expressive of a peril threatening the life, as in Jer. iv. 10, Jonah ii. 6. Calvin, however, thinks that *soul* is put for *heart*, and that the expression denotes that the waters had not only covered him, but had forced their way down his throat.

2. MUD OF THE ABYSS, perhaps not simply "deep mud," as the similar expression in xl. 2 [3], "mire of mud," for in ver. 15 "the abyss" occurs alone, as parallel with "flood of waters." The word FLOOD in these two verses is the well-known Shibboleth which the Ephraimites were unable to pronounce, Judg. xii. 6. It occurs again, Is. xxvii. 12, "flood of the river."

3. IS PARCHED, or "dried up," lit. "is made hot," "burned," as in cii. 3 [4], where it is said of the bones (comp. Job xxx. 30). See xxii. 15 [16].

WHILST I WAIT. The part. is in apposition with the subject contained in the pronominal suffix, as Hupfeld rightly explains the construction. It was an example, says Calvin, of a rare and wonderful patience, to wait upon God in so deplorable a condition, and adds, "when he speaks of his throat being parched, this is not as though he had left off praying, but rather intimates, that though his bodily strength failed, the power of his faith did not give way."

4. MORE THAN THE HAIRS. Comp. xl. 12 [13].

WITHOUT CAUSE, as in xxxv. 19, xxxviii. 19 [20]. To this passage, probably, allusion is made by our Lord, John xv. 25 : *ὅτι ἐμίσησάν* (LXX. *οἱ μισοῦντες*) *με δωρεάν*, words which He introduces with *ἵνα πληρωθῇ ὁ λόγος ὁ γεγραμμένος ἐν τῷ νόμῳ αὐτῶν*. The manner of citation plainly shows how we are to understand *ἵνα πληρωθῇ*; what was true, in some sense, even of the suffering Israelite under the law, was still more true of Him in whom was no sin, and whom, therefore, His enemies did indeed hate without cause.

MY DESTROYERS. So the text at

That which I did not rob, then must I restore.

5 O God, THOU knowest [c] my foolishness,
And my guiltiness hath not been hid from Thee.
6 Let not them that wait on Thee be ashamed through me,
O Lord, Jehovah (God of) hosts.
Let not them be confounded, through me, that seek Thee,
O God of Israel.
7 For Thy sake I have borne reproach,

present stands, but various attempts have been made to correct it. See Critical Note.

THAT WHICH I DID NOT ROB, &c. The expression seems to be proverbial. It is equivalent to saying, "I am treated as guilty though I am innocent." Comp. Jer. xv. 10, and the similar complaint in Ps. xxxv. 11.

THEN MUST I RESTORE. The particle of time seems to be used here almost instead of the demonstrative pronoun, = "What I did not rob, *that* I must restore;" Job ix. 30, 31. The particle may be used, as Hupfeld explains, to mark the consequence which *then* immediately follows from the robbery, or, as I think more likely, to mark the consequence of the calumnies of his enemies. The P. B. V. gives the sense very well: "I paid them the things that I never took."

5. Then follows the appeal to God from the unrighteousness of men. The manner in which this appeal is made is, however, unusual. Generally speaking, under such circumstances, we find a strong assertion of the integrity and innocence of the sufferer, and a complaint that he suffers unjustly: here, on the contrary, we find him appealing to God's knowledge of his *foolishness* and his *transgressions*. The passage presents a great difficulty to Augustine in his attempt to explain the whole Psalm as a prophecy of Christ; and he escapes from the difficulty by saying that the words apply to the members of Christ and not to the Head. Some would explain this: Thou knowest exactly what the *extent* of my foolishness is, and that I am not so guilty as others would represent me, "Thou knowest *what* my foolishness, &c. is." Calvin understands the words ironically: Death hypothetically; "Thou *wouldest* know," &c., *i.e.* if I were really guilty. Ewald takes *foolishness* here to mean *the consequences* of folly and sin, *i.e.* the punishment of them, and renders, "Thou knowest my punishment, and my sufferings are not hid," &c. And Hupfeld inclines to the same view. But all such interpretations are far-fetched. We have here, as in xl. 12 [13], a confession of sinfulness, a confession that that sinfulness has brought upon him the punishment from which he now suffers. With this confession he turns to God, who knows him far better than he knows himself. "God, *Thou* knowest." He does not attempt to assert that he is innocent, but only that his enemies are unjust and malicious in their attacks. And then he urges his appeal for mercy on the ground that others who trust in God will be put to shame, if His servant is left to perish.

GUILTINESS. Heb. "guiltinesses."

7. FOR THY SAKE. Another reason urged why God should rescue him from his enemies. It is true he is a sinner, it is true he suffers for his sin; nevertheless the men who have injured him have injured him unjustly. It is Jehovah him-

Confusion hath covered my face.
8 I am become estranged from my brethren,
And an alien to my mother's sons.
9 For zeal for Thine house hath consumed me,
And the reproaches of them that reproach Thee are fallen upon me.
10 And I wept (and) my soul fasted,[d]
And it became (a subject of) reproaches for me.
11 I made sackcloth also my clothing,
And I became a proverb unto them :

self, and the people of Jehovah (see last verse), who are reproached in him: it is Jehovah's honour and the honour of His house and worship which are at stake. See note on xliv. 17—22.

The complaint is very similar to the one made in xliv. 13 [14], &c. Compare particularly the expressions, "for Thy sake," "confusion hath covered my face," "I became a proverb," the only difference being that there they are spoken of the nation, here of the individual. An exact parallel is to be found in Jer. xv. 15, "know that for Thy sake I have suffered rebuke."

8. Even his own nearest of kin are estranged from him on this account. Comp. the similar complaints, xxvii. 10, xxxi. 11 [12], xxxviii. 11 [12].

9. ZEAL FOR THINE HOUSE. Perhaps, for the state of neglect in which it was, or for the profanation of the sanctuary, though the phrase *may* only mean zeal for God's service and worship. (So Hupfeld.) Still, I think, this expression is only to be accounted for on the supposition that the Temple was standing.

HATH CONSUMED, lit. "eaten." Comp. cxix. 139. Similar expressions with respect to the Prophets will be found, Jer. vi. 11, xv. 17, xx. 9, xxiii. 9, Ezek. iii. 14. This, which was true in various imperfect degrees of these servants of God of old, was in a far higher sense true of the Only-begotten Son, who could say, I seek not mine own glory. Hence, when He purged the Temple, the disciples could not help thinking of these words of the Psalm, as finding their best application in Him. (John ii. 17.)

UPON ME, as upon all God's true prophets (comp. Jer. i. 6—8, Ezek. ii. 6, 7), and above all upon the Great Prophet of the Church, as St. Paul reminds us, quoting these words, Rom. xv. 3.

10. MY SOUL FASTED, lit. "was in fasting," (on the construction see Critical Note), and in the next verse SACKCLOTH, symbols of deep sorrow, and of repentance. Comp. xxxv. 13. But it has been disputed whether they denote, (1) humiliation for his own sin, and outward tokens of his suffering; or (2) sorrow for the despite done to God's honour and house; or (3) whether the Psalmist appears here in a representative character, sorrowing for the sins of his people, shedding tears for those who had no tears to shed for themselves, fasting for those who were living in pleasure in the earth and were wanton, putting sackcloth on his loins for those who saw not the judgments of God. It is most probable, I think, that a public expression of sorrow is meant, and that this was called forth by the general neglect of religion (ver. 9): and then this public protest against ungodliness was turned into ridi-

12 They that sit in the gate talk of me,[e]
And the songs of them that drink strong drink (are concerning me).

13 But as for me—my prayer is unto Thee, O Jehovah, in a time of favour:[f]
O God, in the greatness of Thy loving-kindness, answer me with the truth of Thy salvation.
14 Deliver me from (the) mire, that I sink not;
Let me be rescued from my haters, and from the depths of the waters.
15 Let not a flood of waters overwhelm me,
Neither let the abyss swallow me up,
And let not the pit shut her mouth upon me.
16 Answer me, O Jehovah, for Thy loving-kindness is good;

cule by those against whom it was directed (ver. 11, 12).

12. IN THE GATE, as the place of public resort. See note on ix. 14 [15].

TALK OF ME. The verb is used in poetry, and may mean here either to *converse* generally, or *to sing songs*, as in cv. 2, cxlv. 5.

AND THE SONGS, &c. . . . ARE CONCERNING ME, lit. "And I am (the subject of) the songs, &c." Comp. the use of the singular in Job xxx. 9, Lam. iii. 14, 63, Ezek. xxxiii. 32. In every boisterous company of drunkards he is the butt of their unholy merriment.

13. BUT AS FOR ME. The pronoun, as usual, emphatic; in order to mark the contrast between his own conduct and that of such men; and a nom. absol. as in xxxv. 13, Gen. xvii. 4.

FAVOUR, or "of good pleasure." The same expression occurs in Is. xlix. 8. Comp. Ps. xxxii. 6. The right distribution of the clauses of this verse is doubtful. The arrangement I have adopted is that of Delitzsch, and is in accordance with the accents. Ewald joins the words "in a time of favour," &c. with what follows. Hupfeld and Bunsen make the first principal division of the verse after the word "loving-kindness."

14. This and the next verse answer to verses 1, 2, almost the same expressions being employed, there in describing the lamentable condition of the Psalmist, here in pleading for deliverance from that condition.

15. THE PIT. The Hebrew word (בְּאֵר *B'er*) is commonly rendered in the E. V. "well," but here and lv. 23 [24], and Prov. xxiii. 27, rightly "pit" (= Heb. בּוֹר *Bor*). It means properly, (see App. to Stanley's *Sinai and Palestine*, p. 512,) "a dug pit, usually with water at the bottom" (except Gen. xiv. 10, where it is used of the natural pits of bitumen). These wells, as is evident from numerous vestiges of them still remaining, had "a broad margin of masonry round the mouth, and often a stone filling up the orifice." This explains the prayer, "Let not the pit *shut her mouth* upon me." Such a person would have been buried alive.

16. GOOD, *i.e.* either *sweet, comforting*, as in lxiii. 3 [4], or *gracious*, χρηστός. Comp. cix. 21. This appeal to God's tender mercy, remarks

According to the greatness of Thy tender mercies turn
unto me;
17 And hide not Thy face from Thy servant,
For I am in distress; answer me speedily.
18 Draw nigh unto my soul, ransom it;
Because of mine enemies, redeem me.

19 THOU knowest my reproach, and my shame, and my
confusion;
Before Thee are all my adversaries.
20 Reproach hath broken my heart, and I am full of
heaviness,[g]
And I waited for sympathy, and there was none;
And for comforters, and have not found (them).
21 And they gave me gall for my food,

Calvin, "shows how great was the strait of the holy Prophet . . . and of a truth it is a very difficult matter to be sure that God is gracious while He is angry, and near while He is far off."

19. The second principal division of the Psalm opens with a renewed appeal to God. Comp. ver. 5 and ver. 13. There is a repetition of what had been said already, ver. 4, 7, 9, &c., together with the additional aggravation mentioned in ver. 21.

THOU KNOWEST. In the certainty that all his sorrows, fears, sicknesses, reproach, sufferings, are known to God, the Psalmist again finds his consolation.

20. FULL OF HEAVINESS, or "sick," or "faint." Perhaps here used in reference to the mind rather than the body. The word does not occur in this form elsewhere, but we have the cognate root, Jer. xv. 18, xvii. 16, and in other passages.

SYMPATHY. This is the only place in the psalter where the word is found. Properly speaking it is not a noun, but a verb in the infin. Hence the periphrasis in the E. V. "I looked for some to take pity," or, as in the marg., "to lament with." The word *sympathy* has nowhere been employed by our translators, but it exactly conveys the force of the Hebrew word, inasmuch as it is used of sympathy in joy as well as in sorrow; see Job xlii. 11, where our Version renders "and they bemoaned him:" "and they sympathized with him" would have been better. They would not *bemoan* him on his restoration to health and prosperity. This word also is used several times by Jeremiah, xv. 5, xvi. 5, xlviii. 17.

21. THEY GAVE ME FOR MY FOOD. I have adopted this rendering because it seems best to accord with the parallelism in the next verse; the preposition בְּ is the so-called *Beth essentiæ*, and introduces the predicate. And so the E. V. has understood the construction: "*for* my meat," and the P. B. V. "to eat" following Luther, "zu essen." According to the usual construction of the verb with the prep. the rendering would be, "they put gall *into* my food;" and so Ewald takes it, and the older Versions generally. And the Gen. Vers. has "in my meat." Delitzsch, who adopted this in his first edition, has altered it in his second edition, and now renders "als Speise." The word translated FOOD occurs only here, but see

And when I was thirsty they gave me vinegar to drink.

22 Let their table before them become a snare,

the kindred form, 2 Sam xiii. 5, 7, 10.

GALL. What is the exact meaning of the word (Heb. ראשׁ, *rosh*) it is difficult to say. Both Symm. and the LXX. have χολή, and Jerome, *fel;* the Syr. *bitternesses, bitter things.* According to Hosea x. 4, it is a plant "growing in the furrows of the field," and there the E. V. renders it by "hemlock." In Deut. xxix. 17, [18 E. V.], Lam. iii. 19, it is joined with "wormwood." Gesen. referring to Deut. xxxii. 32, supposes some berry-bearing plant to be meant, and conjectures that it may be the "poppy." And this Mr. Houghton (Smith's *Dict. of the Bible,* App. GALL) thinks most probable, where all is uncertain. Hengstenberg suggests it may mean only "something very bitter," and not of necessity any particular root or plant.

WHEN I WAS THIRSTY, lit. "for my thirst."

VINEGAR or "sour wine;" the Greek translators, ὄξος and the Latin, *acetum.* St. Matthew, who never forgets the foreshadowings of the O. T., alludes, there can be no doubt, to this verse of the Psalm, when he mentions, in his narrative of the Crucifixion (xxvii. 34), that the Roman soldiers offered our Lord "vinegar mingled with gall" (ὄξος [οἶνον] μετὰ χολῆς μεμιγμένον), just before He was nailed to the cross. St. Mark, on the other hand, in his narrative (xv. 23) speaks of "wine mingled with myrrh" (οἶνος ἐσμυρνισμένος). Dean Alford, in his note on the former passage, seems to think that the two potions could not be the same, though he admits that οἶνος might mean the same as ὄξος, *sour wine.* But Mr. Houghton has observed (in the article before referred to) that "the wine mingled with myrrh" "was probably a mere ordinary beverage of the Romans, who were in the habit of seasoning their various wines, which, as they contained little alcohol, soon turned sour, with various spices, drugs, &c." and if so, then the *same* potion may be described by St. Matthew, and the words "with gall" may either denote generally the bitter nature of the draught, or some bitter substance may have been purposely added by way of mockery. It has been usually assumed that this drink was given to criminals to stupefy, and deaden pain; but it does not seem that myrrh has any of the properties of an anodyne.

If, however, St. Matthew and St. Mark admit of such reconciliation (though were no reconciliation possible it need not startle us), the allusion to this Psalm in St. John presents another difficulty. This Evangelist (xix. 28) tells us that Jesus, in order that the Scripture might be accomplished, said, "I thirst." But this was not before our Lord was crucified, but at the last, only just before He gave up the ghost. It is clear, therefore, that he and St. Matthew, though both acknowledging a fulfilment of the Psalm in our Lord's crucifixion, associate that fulfilment with two different circumstances. But we are not, therefore, compelled to conclude, as Hupfeld does, that there is no fulfilment at all. The Psalm is truly typical, and *its whole meaning* is exhausted not in the one circumstance only, but in both.

22. The imprecations which follow can only be perplexing to those who, having adopted a hard mechanical theory of prophecy, feel themselves compelled to understand every part of the Psalm as equally predictive of our Lord; or to those who persistently refuse to acknowledge the difference between the Old Testament and the New. If we go on the broad ground of a typical foreshadowing of Christ in the person of some saint of old, then we shall not be obliged to

And when they are in peace (let it be) a trap.
23 Let their eyes be darkened that they see not,
And make their loins constantly to shake.
24 Pour out upon them Thine indignation,
And let the burning of Thine anger overtake them.
25 Let their encampment be desolate,

assume that *all* his words are words such as our Lord could use. And if we remember what our Lord himself has taught us, that the spirit of Elijah—the greatest of the O. T. Prophets—is very different from the spirit of Christ, then we shall not be offended at language in the mouth of a saint under the Old Dispensation which we do not find sanctioned under the New. See more on this subject in the note on xxxv. 22.

THEIR TABLE, said with reference to ver. 21. They had given him gall and vinegar for his food: let their food, their table, with all its sumptuousness and all its luxury, become a snare to take them. It has been spread for their enjoyment; let it turn to their destruction. Comp. xxiii. 5. Or perhaps the meaning may be: Let them be like persons who while sitting at their meals "in peace," in security, unarmed, and unsuspecting, are suddenly surprised by their enemies. Their "table becomes a snare," as exposing them to certain destruction.

WHEN THEY ARE IN PEACE, lit. "to (them) in peace, or in security." It denotes that kind of security which is the very gate of destruction. Comp. 1 Thess. v. 3. The LXX. render the second clause of the verse **καὶ εἰς ἀνταπόδοσιν** (as if they read in their text לְשִׁלּוּמִים, "for retributions"), **καὶ εἰς σκάνδαλον.** Jerome, "in retributione eorum ad corruendum." Indeed, all the older Verss. give a similar interpretation. Rashi takes the word (*sh'lomim*), which is an adjective, as the plur. of the noun used for the sing., and renders "when they look for peace;" and so Calv., who however supposes an omission of the relative: "quæ ad pacem sunt (pacifica eorum), et quæcunque illis in vitam et prosperam commoditatem destinata erunt, Deus convertat in exitium." He has been followed by the E. V., "And that which should have been for their welfare." The Gen. Vers. "and their prosperity their ruin." The Apostle, citing this passage in Rom. xi. 9 (εἰς παγίδα, καὶ εἰς θήραν, καὶ εἰς σκάνδαλον, καὶ εἰς ἀνταπόδομα αὐτοῖς), follows neither the Hebrew nor the LXX., but either quotes from memory or gives a free rendering of his own. His application of the words is also remarkable, for he quotes them in illustration of his position that a judicial blindness has fallen upon the nation of Israel at large, from which only "the elect" had been exempted. To discuss the principle of this illustration, would be to discuss the whole question of citations in the New Testament from the Old—a subject much too large to be satisfactorily investigated in a note.

23. The darkening of the eyes denotes weakness and perplexity, as the enlightening of the eyes (see on xix. 8) denotes renewed vigour and strength. Similarly, the shaking of the loins is expressive of terror and dismay and feebleness. (Nah. ii. 10 [11], Dan. v. 6.) Or the first may mean the depriving of reason and understanding; the second, the taking away of all strength for action.

25. THEIR ENCAMPMENT. LXX. ἔπαυλις. Prop. "the moveable village of nomadic tribes," who usually pitch their tents in a circle. See Gen. xxv. 16, where *tīrah* is

In their tents let there be no dweller.
26 For him whom THOU hast smitten have they persecuted,
And of the pain of Thy wounded ones do they tell.
27 Add iniquity unto their iniquity,
And let them not come into Thy righteousness.
28 Let them be blotted out from the book of life,
And with the righteous let them not be written.

joined with *châtsär*, the former being the moveable and the latter the stationary village, as Tuch (*in loc.*) rightly explains. The expression is of course used here figuratively, in accordance with "tents" in the parallelism.

26. The reason for the imprecation is given, because of the unpitying cruelty which delighted in adding to the pain and affliction of one whom God had already brought low. His very suffering might have moved them to compassion. Comp. Job xix. 21, 22. The plural in the second clause of the verse, THY WOUNDED ONES (comp. Is. lxvi. 16, Jer. xxv. 33), passes from the individual instance to the general conduct of these men, but implies at the same time that there are some few others exposed to the like treatment with himself.

DO THEY TELL, as if they *counted* one by one every blow that fell upon him, every cry that he had uttered, only to turn it into mockery (comp. lix. 12 [13], lxiv. 5 [6]). The verb is followed here by the prep. (אֶל) as in ii. 7; it is the aorist (fut.) of repeated action.

27. ADD INIQUITY, &c. *i.e.* let it all stand against them in Thy book; one sin after another, as committed, not being blotted out, but only swelling the fearful reckoning. Comp. Jer. xviii. 23. This swelling of the catalogue of guilt is in fact swelling the punishment, but there is no need to render (as French and Skinner do), "Give them punishment upon punishment."

COME INTO, *i.e.* "be partakers of" (as Ezek. xvi. 7).

THY RIGHTEOUSNESS, that righteousness which God gives and which alone is accepted in His sight.

28. BOOK OF LIFE, or "of the living" (as the LXX., Luth., Calv., the E. V.), called in Exod. xxxii. 32, "the book of God." Comp. Is. iv. 3; Dan. xii. 1. See also Luke x. 20; Phil. iv. 3; Rev. iii. 5, xiii. 8. The figure is borrowed from the civil lists or register in which the names of citizens were enrolled (Jer. xxii. 32, Ezek. xiii. 9). To be blotted out of this denotes exclusion from all the blessings and privileges of the theocracy, and therefore from all hope of salvation, as is evident from the next clause: "let them not be written with *the righteous*;" the righteous being the true Israelites, as in Habak. ii. 4. This is the most terrible imprecation of all, though but the necessary consequence of that obstinate impenitence before supposed. Calvin, who supposes God's eternal counsel of salvation to be meant by *the book of life*, is obliged to explain away the obvious meaning of the words, and argues that, inasmuch as God's purpose cannot be changed, the expression is merely adapted to human notions. They, he says, who have once been written in that book cannot be really blotted out; but because God's counsel is secret to us, those may be said to be "blotted out of His book," whom He *openly* excludes from his Church. It is this open rejection therefore which is here meant, and the expression is equivalent to saying: "Do not reckon them in the number of Thy people, neither let them be gathered with Thy

29 But as for me—(I am) afflicted and in pain:
Thy salvation, O God, shall set me up on high.
30 Let me praise the Name of God with a song,
And magnify it with thanksgiving.
31 And it shall please Jehovah better than an ox,
(Than) a bullock with horns (and) hoofs.
32 The afflicted have seen (it), and rejoice:
Ye that seek God,—let your heart live.
33 For Jehovah hearkeneth to (the) poor,
And His prisoners He hath not despised.
34 Let heaven and earth praise Him,
The seas and all that swarmeth therein.
35 For God will save Zion, and build the cities of Judah,
And (men) shall dwell there, and possess it.

Church." To such straits is the ablest of commentators driven, when he has resigned himself to the fetters of an inexorable logic.

29. The Psalm closes with joyful hopes and vows of thanksgiving for God's mercy, in this respect resembling Psalm xxii. In this joy and thanksgiving all other righteous sufferers shall share. And finally Zion and the cities of Judah shall be rebuilt, amid the universal jubilee of all creation.

BUT AS FOR ME, placing himself emphatically in contrast to those who had been the object of his imprecation.

31. WITH HORNS (AND) HOOFS, lit. "showing horns, showing hoofs." The epithets are not merely otiose, as Hupfeld asserts. The first is mentioned in order to mark that the animal was not under three years old, and therefore of the proper age according to the Law; the last as intimating that it belonged to the class of clean four-footed animals, parting the hoof, Lev. xi.; and the meaning is, that the most perfect and valuable of the sacrifices ordained by the Law was not to be compared to the sacrifice of a grateful heart. See notes on l., li.

32. LET YOUR HEART LIVE. Comp. the same expression xxii. 26 [27].

33. This joyful certainty of his own deliverance, this joyful hope that others afflicted like himself will rejoice together with him, rests upon the known character of God, upon the universal experience of His goodness.

HIS PRISONERS, *i.e.* those of His people who have been led into captivity in Babylon.

34. In remembrance of this he calls upon the universe to praise God.

35. The conclusion of the Psalm is not unlike Is. lxv. 9. If the Psalm was written, as seems not improbable, by Jeremiah, there is no reason why these verses may not have formed part of the original text. Indeed, there is but little pretence for regarding them as a later liturgical addition, made at the time of the Exile. They are not so easily separable from the context as the close of Ps. xiv. for instance, or that of li. This Delitzsch himself admits. Yet for those who maintain that David was the author this is the only tenable ground. Such words could have no meaning in David's mouth.

36 And the seed of His servants shall inherit it,
And they that love His Name shall abide therein.

[a] עַל שׁוֹ. See on xlv. note [a].

[b] מַצְמִיתַי. Hupf. objects to the word because it means properly "my *destroyers*," whereas here it can only mean "my adversaries." He observes that the Syr., probably feeling the difficulty, must have changed it into מֵעַצְמוֹתַי, as they render "more than my bones;" and some sort of comparison, he argues, is required by the parallelism and indicated by the verb עָצְמוּ, which in the similar passage, xl. 13, is also followed by מִן expressing a comparison. [Riehm adds (2d Ed.), "cf. however Lam. iii. 53."] Hare (who is followed by Lowth and Merrick) conjectures מִצַּמָּתִי, "more than the *locks of my hair;*" but צַמָּה means not *a lock of hair*, but *a veil.* Hupf. himself conjectures מִצַּמַּרְתִּי from צַמֶּרֶת, *a fleece*, used also of the *foliage* of trees, but he confesses there is no proof that it was ever used of human hair. None of these conjectures is satisfactory.

[c] לְאִוַּלְתִּי. This construction of the prep. לְ with the verb ידע occurs nowhere else, but we find it in the case of similar verbs, such as בין, *to consider*, זכר, *to remember*, &c.

[d] בַצּוֹם נַפְשִׁי. It is impossible to translate this, as the Chald. and others do, "in the fasting of my soul," because the first noun has the art. and therefore is not in the stat. constr. Either, therefore, נַפְשִׁי is a second nominative: "I, *i.e.* my soul, wept in fasting" (comp. iii. 4 [5], "my voice, I cry," Jer. xiii. 17), or perhaps a remote object of the action of the verb with a pregnant construction. So Mendelss. and Del., "Ich verwein', im Fasten, meine Seele." Ewald regards נַפְשִׁי as simply subordinated to the verb (not, as Phillips says, as having a pronominal sense), and renders, "da weinte ich tief, fastend," *i.e.* I wept in my very soul. The LXX. *καὶ συνέκαμψα ἐν νηστείᾳ τὴν ψυχήν μου*, in accordance with which Hupf. would read וָאֲעַנֶּה instead of וָאֶבְכֶּה, "and *I afflicted* my soul with fasting," which there can be no doubt is the usual expression.

[e] יָשִׂיחוּ. The word is a poetical one, and expresses almost any kind of utterance, whether of speech or song, whether sad (as in lv. 3) or merry, and even sarcastic, as here. It is construed with the accus. in Prov. vi. 22. The construction of the second clause of the verse has been differently explained. The simplest way seems to repeat this verb, making נְגִינוֹת its subject: "the songs of the drunkards talk of me;" but according to the analogy of Job xxx. 9, Lam. iii. 14, we should rather supply הָיִיתִי, or וָאֱהִי, or simply the pronoun אֲנִי, as in Lam. iii. 63, "And I am (the subject of) the songs," &c. (the plur. as lxxiii. 22).

[f] עֵת רָצוֹן. This is simply the accus. of time. There is no ellipse of בְּ. Hengstenberg strangely denies that עֵת is ever used as an accus. of time, and therefore renders, contrary to the accents, and to the destruction of all rhythm and even tolerable sense, "But I pray to

Thee, O Jehovah! A time of favour, O God, through the abundance of Thy mercy!" But even if no other instance of this use of עֵת could be alleged, it might be amply defended by the use of analogous words like יוֹם, לַיְלָה, &c. We have, however, this very usage in Jer. li. 33, Ezek. xxvii. 34.

[g] אָנוּשָׁה, "I am sick unto death," fut. Qal of נושׁ, which occurs only here, cognate with אנשׁ. Lee, however (Gram. 189 *b*), would make it fut. of אנשׁ for אֶאֱנוּשָׁה, and would explain the form with *Shurek* by such instances as יִשְׁפּוּטוּ, Exod. xviii. 26; תִּשְׁמוּר, Prov. xiv. 3.

PSALM 70

THIS Psalm is a repetition, with some variations, of the last five verses of Psalm xl. Besides the difference in the use of the Divine Names, there are some other divergencies which will be found discussed in the Critical Notes. I see no reason to abandon the opinion which I have expressed in the note on xl. 13, that this Psalm formed originally a part of Psalm xl., and was subsequently detached and altered for a special occasion.

[FOR THE PRECENTOR. (A PSALM) OF DAVID. TO BRING TO REMEMBRANCE.[a]]

1 O GOD, (make haste) to deliver me;[b]
O Jehovah, to help me make haste.
2 Let them be ashamed and confounded
That seek after my soul;
Let them be turned backward and brought to dishonour
That wish me evil.
3 Let them return[c] as a reward of their shame,

1. O GOD, instead of O JEHOVAH, xl. 13 [14], and the verb BE PLEASED, omitted here, which is expressed there.

TO HELP ME, lit. "to my help."

2. CONFOUNDED or, "put to the blush:" in xl. 14 [15] there is added, TOGETHER, and at the end of the next member of the verse, TO DESTROY IT.

THAT WISH ME EVIL, lit. "that delight in my evil, *i.e.* my misfortune."

3. LET THEM RETURN. In xl. 15 [16] we have the far stronger expression, LET THEM BE STRUCK

Who say, Aha! Aha!
4 Let all those that seek Thee be glad and rejoice in Thee,
And let them that love Thy salvation say alway,
"God be magnified."
5 And as for me, afflicted and poor,
O God, make haste unto me! [d]
My help and my Deliverer art Thou;
O Jehovah, make no long tarrying!

DUMB, *i.e.* with amazement. See more in Critical Note.

AS A REWARD OF THEIR SHAME, lit. "upon the heel of their shame," and hence "as a consequence of retribution," &c. and as a prep. simply "on account of."

4. GOD (*Elohim*), in xl. 16 [17) Jehovah.

5. O GOD, MAKE HASTE UNTO ME! For this we have in xl. 17 [18], "the Lord thinketh upon me" (*Adonai* instead of *Elohim*); and afterwards "O my God," instead of "O Jehovah."

[a] לְהַזְכִּיר. On this title, see Ps. xxxviii. note [a].

[b] לְהַצִּילֵנִי. This must depend here on חוּשָׁה in the second clause of the verse (a construction of which, according to Delitzsch, there is no other example in the Psalter); unless, indeed, we take the infin. with לְ to be used for the future (see xlix. note [k]). On the other hand, in xl. 13 [14], the infin. depends on רְצֵה. This, again, is an unusual construction, as רצה elsewhere occurs only with the accus. or בְּ, once with עִם and always in the sense *to take pleasure in*, not, as here, *to be pleased*.

[c] יָשׁוּבוּ. Hupfeld, who argues for Ps. lxx. as the original, finds this reading preferable to the much more forcible יָשֹׁמּוּ, in xl. 15 [16]. He alleges that it is more in accordance with the context and with analogy, and refers to the similar expression in ver. 2 (xl. 15), "let them be *turned backward*." But the only passage which he can quote in defence of such a meaning for the verb שׁוּב is vi. 11. I have myself so rendered יָשֻׁבוּ there, "let them be turned backward," where it certainly stands in a very similar connection with בּוֹשׁ; but after carefully examining the various uses of the verb שׁוּב, I am persuaded it cannot mean *to be turned back*, but only *to return*. "Let them return," *i.e.* re infecta; but it is obvious that here this is a comparatively weak expression, and it seems to me that the person who detached this portion of Ps. xl. and slightly altered it, may very probably have borrowed this form of expression from vi. 11.

[d] אֱלֹהִים חוּשָׁה־לִּי (comp. cxli. 1), for which, in the other version, we have אֲדֹנָי יַחֲשָׁב־לִי, "*The Lord thinketh of me*," i.e. careth for me. So the LXX. φροντιεῖ μου, and Jerome, *solicitus erit pro me*, understood it. Hupfeld objects that the passages which Gesen. quotes, Is. xiii. 17, xxxiii. 8, liii. 3, in support of this meaning of חשב, are not in point, because in

every one of them the negative precedes, and לֹא חִ׳ means *nihili facere;* but he omits to notice that Gesen. also quotes Mal. iii. 16, לְחֹשְׁבֵי שְׁמוֹ, "those who *think upon* or *regard* His Name," where we have the meaning required here, the only difference being that there the verb is followed by the accus. and here by the prep. לְ.

PSALM 71

THIS Psalm is without any Inscription in the Hebrew. In the LXX. its title is "(A Psalm) of David, of the sons of Jonadab, and of those who were first led captive," a curiously composite title, which contains a contradiction in itself. It may, however, have been intended to denote that, in the opinion of the translators, the Psalm was Davidic in origin, and, at the same time, to record the tradition that it was a favourite Psalm with the Rechabites, and the earlier exiles.

On two points, only, do we gather any certain information from the Psalm itself. First, it is evident that it was written by one already past the meridian of life, and verging upon old age. And, secondly, it borrows so largely from other Psalms, the 22d, 31st, 35th, and 40th, some of them, probably, Psalms written long after the time of David, that it must be regarded as one of the later specimens of Hebrew poetry.

Other evidence of an internal kind renders it not improbable that the Psalm was written by Jeremiah. It would apply obviously to his circumstances. His life had been a life of extraordinary perils and extraordinary deliverances. He had been consecrated from his birth, and even before his birth, to his office (Jer. i. 5, compared with ver. 6 of the Psalm). He had discharged that office for more than thirty years, and might, therefore, be verging on old age in the reign of Zedekiah. The prominent position which he occupied for so long a period before princes and people harmonizes well with the language of the Psalm in verses 7 and 21. Finally, the style and general character of the poetry are not unlike those of Jeremiah. There is the same plaintive elegiac strain which we find in his writings, and the same disposition to borrow from earlier poets.

All this falls in very well with the tradition which has been preserved by the LXX. A Psalm written by Jeremiah would very naturally have a peculiar value in the eyes of the Rechabites whom the Prophet mentions so honourably, and in the eyes of the first exiles who had so often listened to the words of his lips. In the allusion to national troubles in ver. 20, Ewald finds evidence that the Psalm belongs to the times of the Exile. But the language there is too vague to be conclusive.

The Psalm can hardly be said to have any regular strophical form.

It has first an introduction. Ver. 1—3.

Then follow two main divisions. The first of these tells the story of *the past*, recounts God's goodness and the Psalmist's trust, and concludes with a prayer for the overthrow of his enemies. Ver. 4—13.

The next looks forward to *the future*, anticipates deliverance, promises thanksgiving, and sees the prayer for the overthrow of his enemies answered. Ver. 14—24.

Verses 13 and 24 correspond to one another almost in the manner of a refrain.

1 In Thee, O Jehovah, have I found refuge,
Let me not be ashamed for ever,
2 In Thy righteousness deliver me and rescue me;
Incline Thine ear unto me, and save me.
3 Be Thou to me a rock of habitation,[a] (to which) I may alway come;
Thou hast given commandment to save me;
For Thou art my rock and my fortress.

I. 4 O my God, rescue me from the hand of the wicked,
From the grasp of the evil-doer and the violent.

1—3. The opening of the Psalm is borrowed, with slight verbal alterations, from the opening of xxxi.

3. (TO WHICH) I MAY ALWAY COME, *i.e.* where I may always find safety when danger threatens.

THOU HAST GIVEN COMMANDMENT. This might be rendered as a relative clause: "Thou who hast," &c.; but it certainly cannot be rendered as an imperative, "Give commandment." Nor is it necessary to suppose that the command is given to the Angels; for, as Calvin long ago observed, God has innumerable means of imparting help and protection, and He may be said to command deliverance when He shows it in some open and signal manner; "quoties favorem suum palam exerit aliquo signo, et nunc solo nutu, nunc per homines vel alias creaturas exequitur, quod apud se statuit." Comp. xliv. 4 [5], lxviii. 28 [29].

ROCK (Heb. *Sela'*). Not the same word as that used before (which is *tsur*), but apparently the two words are used without any difference of meaning.

4. EVIL-DOER, or "him that

5 For THOU, O Lord, Jehovah! art my hope,
Thou art my trust from my youth up.
6 Upon Thee have I been holden up from the womb,
From my mother's bowels Thou art my benefactor,[b]
Of Thee is my praise alway.
7 I am become as a wonder unto many,
But Thou art my strong refuge.[c]

dealeth perversely." The verb occurs only once besides, Is. xxvi. 10.

5. MY HOPE. Comp. Jer. xvii. 13, where God is called "the Hope of Israel." So in the New Test. Christ is called ἡ ἐλπὶς ἡμῶν, 1 Tim. i. 1.

6. HAVE I BEEN HOLDEN UP (in the passage which has here been imitated, xxii. 10 [11], "I have been cast"), an expression wonderfully descriptive of what faith is, and of what God is to those who trust in Him. He is a father who bears them in His arms and carries them in His bosom; they are as children who lean all their weight upon Him, and find their sweetest rest in His supporting hand. This is the very idea of faith, according to its Hebrew signification. When it is said in Gen. xv. 6, that "Abraham believed God," it means literally, "*he leaned upon God*" (though the root there is different, it is the same which in the Qal conjugation means *to bear* or *carry a child*, Num. xi. 12, and in Is. xlix. 23 is used of a *nursing father*). But the Psalmist speaks here, not mainly of his own trust in God, but rather of his experience of God's loving care and protection.

MY BENEFACTOR. (See Critical Note.) Calvin, who renders "a visceribus matris meæ tu extractor meus," sees here a reference to God's goodness even *before* his birth, and has some admirable remarks on our forgetfulness of God's wonders to us both before and at our birth. In the mouth of Jeremiah, if, as we have conjectured, the Psalm was written by him, such words have a peculiar interest, for they refer, no doubt, to that word of Jehovah which came unto him, saying, "Before I formed thee in the belly I knew thee; and before thou camest forth from the womb I sanctified thee." (Jer. i. 5.)

OF THEE, lit. "*in* Thee," God being the great object of his praise, and the construction being the same as that with the verb in xliv. 8 [9], where see note[b].

7. A WONDER. Commentators are divided in their interpretation of the word. Some understand it in a good sense, "a marvel of God's protecting care and love, which had been vouchsafed to him even in the extremest perils." (So Ges., De W.) Others suppose him to mean, that because of the greatness of the sufferings and calamities which had befallen him, he had been, as it were, a portent, a prodigy. So Calvin: "quod propter urgentes miserias quibus opprimebatur, passim fuerit detestabilis. . . . *Portenti* vero nomine, non vulgaris calamitas exprimitur." But perhaps it is better, with Delitzsch, to understand it as applying to his whole wonderful life of trials and blessings, of perils and deliverances, such as did not ordinarily fall to the lot of man. It is implied, at the same time, that his life was a public life, such as that of a Prophet, or leading man amongst his people, or it would not have attracted the notice and excited the wonder of "many."

8 My mouth is filled with Thy praise,
With Thine honour all the day long.

9 Cast me not away in the time of old age,
When my strength faileth forsake me not.
10 For mine enemies have said of me—
And they that watch for my soul have taken counsel together,
11 Saying :—God hath forsaken him,
Pursue and seize him, for there is none to deliver.
12 O God, be not far from me;
O my God, haste Thee to help me!
13 Let them be ashamed, let them be consumed,
That withstand my soul;
Let them be covered with reproach and confusion.
That seek to do me evil.

II. 14 But as for me—I will alway hope,
And will praise Thee more and more.
15 My mouth shall tell of Thy righteousness,

8. IS FILLED. It is, I think, best to take the verb here as a present, describing the immediate and natural consequence of all that care and love which in the previous verses he had celebrated.

9. This review of the past leads him to look forward to the future, and especially to the season of old age, which already, it would seem, was creeping upon him.

10. HAVE SAID OF ME. The preposition may be so rendered : "with respect to me;" or simply "*to* me;" as, "*to* my soul," iii. 2 [3], where see note. *What* they say is given in ver. 11, the intervening words being parenthetical. The repetition of the verb at the beginning of the next verse, SAYING, is unnecessary, as Delitzsch remarks, and a sign of later age. Comp. cv. 11, cxix. 82. In the 1st ed. of his com. he connected the preposition לִי, "*of* me," or "*to* me," not with the verb, but with the noun immediately preceding : lit. "mine enemies to me," the pronoun being repeated pleonastically, as in xxv. 2, xxvii. 2.

HAVE TAKEN COUNSEL TOGETHER, as lxxxiii. 3 [4], 5 [6]. Comp. ii. 2.

12. This and the next verse are composed of phrases borrowed from other Psalms, xxii. 11 [12], 19 [20], xxxviii. 21, 22 [22, 23], xl. 13 [14].

13. TO DO ME EVIL, lit. "my evil," or hurt, as in lxx. 2.

14. AND WILL PRAISE, &c. lit. "And will add to all Thy praise;" but I have preferred adopting the more idiomatic rendering of the E. V.

15. RIGHTEOUSNESS. The word (צְדָקָה) has, most unfortunately, been rendered here and in the next verse, by French and Skinner, "mercy," to the grievous marring of the whole passage. In the O. T. I am persuaded it never means anything but *righteousness*, least of all when spoken of God. It is true that Gesenius gives the meaning *benignitas, misericordia* in

(And) of Thy salvation all the day;
For I know no numbers (thereof).
16 I will come with the mighty deeds of the Lord Jehovah;
I will make mention of Thy righteousness, (even) of Thine only.
17 O God, Thou hast taught me from my youth;
And hitherto do I declare Thy wondrous works.

xxiv. 5, Prov. xi. 4, and *liberalitas* in Prov. x. 2, Mic. vi. 5, but it is quite unnecessary in any of these passages to depart from the usual signification. In his smaller Lexicon he gives *deliverance, prosperity*, as its equivalent (in the Thesaurus he has *salus*) in a multitude of passages in Isaiah, where it occurs as here, parallel with *salvation* (יְשׁוּעָה), and again classes Ps. xxiv. 5 (where *righteousness* answers to *blessing* in the parallelism) under this head. But it would be the merest tautology to render the word, *salus, salvation*, in many of the passages cited. Is. xlv. 8, xlvi. 13 [xlviii. 18, *peace* in the parallelism], li. 6, 8 [liv. 17], lvi. 1 [lvii. 12, "*Thy works*" in the parall.], lix. [9], 17, lxi. 10, 11. In all the references not inclosed in brackets we have *salvation* as the parallel to righteousness, and therefore it is obvious the one word does not stand for the other. Still less can the word *righteousness* mean only *temporal prosperity*. This mistake on the part of Gesenius is due to his not perceiving the real theological relation between the two. God's salvation stands to His righteousness in the relation of effect to cause. God has pledged Himself to save those who put their trust in Him, and as a righteous God He cannot deny Himself. This seems to be the connection between the two words in this Psalm. In Isaiah, *righteousness* is regarded, not merely as an attribute of God, but as imparted to man (almost in the sense of justification), and so, in fact, constituting his true salvation.

In the Talmud and in Rabbinical writers no doubt the word is used in the sense of *mercy, good deeds*, and even of *almsgiving*, which explains the curious various readings δικαιοσύνην and ἐλεημοσύνην in Matt. vi. 1, but this is a later usage.

NO NUMBERS (the Hebrew word occurs only here). God's righteousness and God's salvation are infinitely beyond all man's power to calculate or to repeat. Comp. xl. 5 [6], cxxxix. 17.

16. I WILL COME WITH, &c. *i.e.* "I will come (into the Temple, probably, comp. lxvi. 13) with all the great and mighty deeds which God has done on my behalf as my subject of grateful praise." That this is the meaning is plain from the parallelism in the next clause. The rendering of French and Skinner, "I will *dwell upon* the mighty deeds," &c., is indefensible.

OF THINE ONLY, lit. "of Thee alone."

17. AND HITHERTO. The Hebrew phrase occurs only here in the Psalter, elsewhere it is found usually in prose.

DO I DECLARE. I have thought it best to render the verb in the present, but it seems to be almost equivalent, with the particles preceding, to "I have declared and will declare." It has been proposed to arrange the clauses thus:

Thou hast taught me from my youth
and to the present time:
I will declare, &c. . . . unto old age
and hoariness.

But this is extremely harsh and unrhythmical, and, moreover, quite unnecessary.

18 Yea also unto old age and hoary hairs, O God, forsake
me not,
Till I declare Thine arm to (the next) generation,
Thy might unto all that are to come,
19 And Thy righteousness, O God, which is very high:
Thou who hast done great things,
O God, who is like unto Thee!
20 (Thou) who hast showed us distresses many and sore,
Thou wilt quicken us again,
And from the depths of the earth Thou wilt lift us
up again.
21 Do Thou increase my greatness,
And turn (Thyself and) comfort me.

18. THINE ARM. Comp. Is. lii. 10, liii. 1, Ezek. iv. 7.

TO (THE NEXT) GENERATION, lit. "to a generation," but here used absolutely for the following generation, as in xxii. 30 [31]: the meaning is evident from the parall. in the next clause, from which indeed "to come" may be supplied here.

19. AND THY RIGHTEOUSNESS. The construction is continued from ver. 18. Delitzsch, indeed, in his 1st ed. carried it still further, and made verses 19, 20, 21, all depend on the verb "I declare" in verse 18: "Till I declare . . . Thy might and Thy righteousness, &c. . . . *that* Thou hast done great things, &c. *That* Thou hast showed, &c."

20. US. The sudden transition to the plural here seems to have given offence to the Massoretes, or their predecessors, who consequently changed it in the Q'ri to the singular. But these fluctuations between singular and plural are not unusual in the Psalms, and there is no reason why, in the recital of God's dealings, the Psalmist should not speak of them with reference to the nation at large, as well as to himself in particular. On THOU HAST SHOWED, see lx. 3 [5].

THE DEPTHS OF THE EARTH. A figurative expression, like "the gates of death," denoting the extremest peril. Comp. lxix. 2 [3], 14 [15]. The word DEPTHS is the same word as in xxxiii. 7, "He layeth up the depths in storehouses" (it is the plur. of the word which occurs in Gen. i. 2), and means the vast collection of waters in the seas. God is said to bring back His people to life, who had been, as it were, drowned in the depths of the waters.

21. DO THOU INCREASE, or, "mayest Thou increase." This rendering seems necessitated by the apocopated form of the verb, unless, indeed, we make the verse (with Del.) depend on the verb in ver. 18, "I declare . . . that Thou increasedst," &c.

MY GREATNESS. An unusual expression. The word is used of the majesty of God, cxlv. 3, 6; of kings, Esth. i. 4; and of princes, vi. 3, x. 2; and its use here, therefore, would seem to imply that the Poet was a person of considerable position and influence.

TURN THYSELF. The verb seems here to be employed almost in the same adverbial sense as the twice-repeated "again" (lit. "Thou wilt return"), in ver. 20. Our translators adopted the other meaning of the verb, viz. "*to compass about*," and so got the rendering, "Thou

22 Also *I* will praise Thee with a lute, (even) Thy truth,
O my God;
I will play to Thee upon a harp, O Thou Holy One
of Israel.
23 My lips shall shout for joy, for I will play unto Thee,
And my soul which Thou hast redeemed;
24 Also my tongue all the day shall talk of Thy righteousness,
For they are ashamed, for they are put to confusion,
that seek to do me evil.

comfortest me *on every side*," lit. "Thou compassest, Thou comfortest, me."

22. WITH A LUTE, lit. "with an instrument of a lute, or *nabla*."

HOLY ONE OF ISRAEL. This name of God occurs in the Psalms only in two other places, lxxviii. 41, lxxxix. 18 [19], these last two being according to Delitzsch, older Psalms than this. In Isaiah this Name of God occurs thirty times, in Habakkuk once, in Jeremiah (who may have adopted it from Isaiah) twice, l. 29, li. 5.

[a] צוּר־מָעוֹן instead of צ׳ מָעוֹז, in xxxi. 3, and which the Chald. and many MSS. have here. The LXX. perhaps had the same reading, and omitted צִוִּיתָ, which follows: γενοῦ μοι εἰς Θεὸν ὑπερασπιστήν, καὶ εἰς τόπον ὀχυρὸν τοῦ σῶσαί με. The insertion of καί does not prove that they read וּמָעוֹן (as Davidson); they took צוּר as a proper name of God, and מָעוֹן as a distinct word. The words לָבוֹא תָּמִיד צִוִּיתָ look, as Hupf. remarks, as if they were formed out of the fragments of לְבֵית מְצוּדוֹת in xxxi. 3, and צִוִּיתָ seems to have been put in to form a support for the following לְהוֹשִׁיעֵנִי.

[b] גוֹזִי instead of גֹּחִי, in xxii. 10. This has been rendered, "Thou who bringest me forth," as if it were the participle transitive of גוז; but the form in *o* is usually intransitive, though this is not always the case. See on xxii. note [c]. (In xc. 10 גָּז is probably the preterite, not the participle.) Hence others, as Hengst., would take the form here, as well as in xxii. 10, as infin., "my bringing forth," *i.e.* the agent in bringing me forth. And so Maur. "*transire meum*, i.e. ejus auctor per metonym." But perhaps it is better, following Schult., *Animadv. Phil.*, to derive the word from a root גזה (cognate with the Arab. جَزَا *retribuere*), signifying *to distribute, to requite, to reward*. Hence גֹּזֶה would mean literally, *one who dispenses*, ταμίας, and so *provides, takes care*, &c. The LXX. σκεπαστής, Vulg. *protector meus*. So Ges., Ew., Hupf., Zunz. But Del. prefers the meaning *abscindere*, and explains it: *Thou art He that separatest, loosest me* (mein Entbinder) *from*, &c.

[c] מַחֲסִי־עֹז. This is commonly cited as an instance in which a noun with the pronom. suff. is placed in construction with the following noun. But all the instances usually alleged in proof of such construction may be explained on the principle of apposition: here, "my refuge which is strength." See on xlv. note [g].

PSALM 72

Two Psalms only in the entire compass of the Psalter, this and the 127th, bear the name of Solomon. Apart from the question whether these particular Psalms are rightly attributed to him or not, the fact is worthy of notice, as it shows us that tradition, which has shed so many glories round the name of Solomon, did not suppose him to have inherited his father's taste for religious poetry and music, or it would not have failed to add this to his many other accomplishments.

Calvin, indeed, and others, have conjectured that the inscription even here does not denote that Solomon was the author. They appeal to ver. 20, which tells us that this was the last prayer of David, and they urge that accordingly the title must signify "*For* Solomon," not "*of* Solomon." (And so the LXX. have *εἰς Σαλωμών.*) Calvin observes: "After carefully weighing all, I incline to the view that David uttered this prayer as he was dying, and that it was put into the form of a Psalm by his son, that the memory thereof might never perish. . . But as Solomon took the argument from his father, and only clothed it in the garb of poetry, we may regard David as the principal author."

But ver. 20, taken to the letter, would rather imply that all the Psalms in this Book were written by David, whereas the inscriptions themselves contradict this, not to mention that the verse itself is manifestly a later addition. And in all other instances where the name of an author is prefixed to a Psalm, it is prefixed with the same preposition which is here employed. The inscription, beyond all doubt, means to say that the Psalm is Solomon's. Nor do I see any reason for rejecting the tradition thus conveyed to us. Hupfeld indeed asserts that the Psalm bears evident traces of belonging to a later time than that of Solomon, but he brings forward no proof of his assertion. Delitzsch, on the other hand, contends that we find here the marks both of Solomon's style and of Solomon's time; that the expressions are arranged for the most part in distichs, like the

Proverbs, that the character of the poetry is reflective, that it is rich in images borrowed from the world of nature. Besides this, the allusion to Sheba and to Tarshish, and even the extent of dominion which it is hoped would be given to the king, all harmonize with the reign of Solomon better than of any other Jewish monarch. Delitzsch conjectures that he may have composed the Psalm shortly after his accession, and have designed it as a prayer to be offered for himself, as the inheritor of David's throne and David's promises, in the public services of the Temple. At the same time he admits, as all the soundest expositors have done, that the hopes and aspirations here expressed—so grand and so far-reaching, that they are little less than prophecies—find their fulfilment in One greater than Solomon. "These promises were realized in Solomon, but only typically. They expect, therefore, after Solomon their final realization, and that in the Son of David whom the Prophets of the later kingdom foretell."

Solomon, then, may have uttered such a prayer, may have uttered it for himself, and yet may have felt how far he was, how far any human monarch must be, from approaching to the great ideal which rose, in all its majesty, before his mind. Whether he uttered it, as Delitzsch supposes, at the beginning of his reign, is more doubtful. The allusions to Sheba and Tarshish would seem to imply a somewhat later date. But be this as it may, we have here another instance of the way in which prophecy rooted itself in the Jewish soil, how it looked first to the Present and then to the Future, first to the Type and then to the Antitype. Calvin observes most justly, and the observation bears upon the interpretation of all the Messianic Psalms : "They who will have this to be simply a prediction of the kingdom of Christ seem to twist the words very violently. And besides, we should always take care not to give the Jews good reason for reproaching us, as if we were determined by mere force of sophistry to apply to Christ (*sophistice ad Christum trahere*) what does not directly refer to Him."

The Targum, however, paraphrases the first verse of the Psalm thus : "O God, give Thy judgments to the King Messiah, and Thy justice to the Son of King David."

And the Midrash Tehillim gives as one explanation, "This is the King Messiah, for it is said, And a stem shall go forth from the root of Jesse."

The Psalm is, like the second, the twentieth, twenty first, and forty-fifth, a Royal Psalm.

It has no regular strophical division, but consists of the following parts :—

I. The prayer that the reign of the king may be a reign of righteousness, peace, and prosperity, and that it may endure for ever. Ver. 1—7.

II. That his dominion may know no bounds, save those of the world itself. Ver. 8—11.

III. Then follows the reason why such a dominion should be granted him. He is worthy to receive riches, and honour, and glory, and might, for he is a righteous saviour of the poor and the afflicted. Ver. 12—15.

IV. Lastly, the prayer is repeated both for prosperity and for an everlasting and a universal dominion. Ver. 16, 17.

[(A PSALM) OF SOLOMON.]

1 O GOD, give Thy judgements unto the king,

1. The prayer is that God would give His righteousness to the king, that so he may rule and judge righteously and his righteous government produce righteousness, and therefore peace, among the people.

The difference between the JUDGEMENTS of God in the first clause, and the RIGHTEOUSNESS of God in the second, is this: the former refers to *the several decisions* which the king may be called upon to pronounce, and the prayer is that these may be so in accordance with the will of God, that they may be as if uttered by His mouth; the second refers to the inner mind and spirit, the wisdom and discernment, which should be the reflex of the Divine mind.

This is the very idea of justice, as Hengstenberg observes, when the decisions of the earthly judge are in perfect accordance with those of the heavenly: but this can only be when there rests upon the former "the Spirit of the Lord, the spirit of wisdom and understanding, the spirit of knowledge, and of the fear of the Lord." To One only was this Spirit given without measure. In One only was this idea realized. Solomon, it is true, prayed (1 Kings iii. 9) that God would give him an understanding, or rather *obedient* heart (לֵב שֹׁמֵעַ), that he might judge his people; and of him we read (1 Kings iii. 28), "And all Israel heard of the judgement which the king had judged, and they feared before the king, for they saw that the wisdom of God was in him to do judgement;" and to him the Queen of Sheba said (1 Kings x. 9), "Because Jehovah loved Israel for ever, therefore made He thee king to do judgement and righteousness." But Solomon did not fulfil the hope of this prayer. The righteous judge became the oppressor of his people, the wise king the weak, foolish, despicable voluptuary: God brake in pieces, before the eyes of His people, the frail earthly type, that He might lead them to wait for Him who was "higher than the kings of the earth," and who would "not judge after the sight of His eyes, neither decide after the hearing of His ears, but would judge with righteousness the weak, and decide with uprightness for the afflicted of the earth."

The Talmudic saying is very striking, and worth quoting here:

And Thy righteousness to the king's son.
2 May he decide the cause of Thy people with righteousness,
And of Thine afflicted with judgement.
3 May the mountains bring forth peace unto the people,
And the hills in righteousness!

"Every judge who judgeth a judgement of truth truly, maketh the Divine Glory (the Shechinah) to dwell in Israel."—T. B. *Synh.* 7a.

THE KING. This and the following, THE KING'S SON, are both without the article, which may be accounted for partly by the licence of poetry, and partly by the fact that the noun (*melech*), as a name of office, is sufficiently definite in itself.

THE KING'S SON. The stress laid upon this is in accordance with Oriental usage. That the king was of royal ancestry was mentioned on coins, public monuments, and the like. See Is. xix. 11.

2. DECIDE THE CAUSE, as in liv. 1 [3]; or "minister justice," as in ix. 8. The word (*dîn*) is a different word from that in ver. 4 rendered "judge" (*shâphat*). The root of the first signifies *to govern, to rule;* the root of the second, *to be erect, upright.* But both verbs are used in the general sense of *governing:* for the first see 1 Sam. ii. 10, Zech. iii. 7; for the second, 1 Sam. viii. 20, and elsewhere, and the name of Judges given to the leaders of Israel from Joshua to Samuel: both are also used with reference to the double aspect of justice, as defending the oppressed and innocent, and punishing the evil. The main difference between the two, as might be inferred from their respective derivation, is, that the first is the more formal and technical word. Hence the later *Bêth Dîn*, "house of judgement," *i.e.* court, consistory, &c. (Gr. δικαστήριον), a name given also to the great Sanhedrim.

There has been much question as to the manner in which the tenses are employed here, and in the next verses. Are they optative, or future (predicting what shall be hereafter), or conjunctive, as standing in a dependent clause, and marking the consequence of the preceding wish, with a not uncommon omission of the conjunction? To render them as futures, as the E. V. and as Hengst. do, is clearly wrong, because at the beginning of verses 8, 16, 17 we have the apocopated forms which are optatives. We must therefore render all as optatives, or some as optatives, some as conjunctives: Hupfeld and Zunz keep the optative throughout, and Delitzsch to the end of ver. 8. Ewald has the conjunctive in verses 2, 3.

Mendelss. Dass er richte, "that he may judge;" or we may render, "then shall he decide," &c.

3. The mountains and hills are mentioned as being the great characteristic features of a country like Palestine. Comp. Joel iii. 18: "The mountains shall drop down new wine, and the hills shall flow with milk." See Smith's *Dict. of the Bible*, art. "Palestine," § 26.

BRING FORTH. The verb which is here used figuratively is used literally Ezek. xvii. 8, "to bring forth fruit." It is quite unnecessary therefore to render, as French and Skinner, "shall lift up."

PEACE. This is ever represented in Scripture as the fruit of righteousness, and as the great blessing of the times of the Messiah. The king of righteousness is also king of peace. Comp. Is. ii. 4, ix. 5, 6, xi. 9, lxv. 25, Micah iv. 3, Zech. ix. 10.

IN RIGHTEOUSNESS. For the third time this is mentioned as that attribute which, beyond all others, stamps the king and his rule over

4 May He judge the afflicted of the people,
Save the sons of the poor,
And crush the oppressor!
5 (So that) they fear Thee as long as the sun (endureth),
And before the moon unto all generations.

his people. As regards the construction, this word in fact belongs to both clauses of the verse. "May the mountains and the hills bring forth peace in (or, through) righteousness," or the preposition may be the *Bêth essentiæ*, as it is called. To render, as Delitzsch does, "in abundance," besides giving to *ts'dâkâh* an unheard-of meaning, mars the whole point of the passage. He tries to defend this meaning by saying that the word denotes the righteousness of grace, as well as of punishment, and then passes through the idea of *clemency*, ἐλεημοσύνη [so the LXX. sometimes render it], into that of *bountifulness*, for which he quotes Joel ii. 23 (a passage, the sense of which is doubtful) and Ps. xxiv. 5, where it stands parallel with *blessing*. But that this is not in point, see note on lxxi. 15.

4. SONS OF THE POOR, *i.e.* merely "poor persons," in accordance with the usual Hebrew idiom.

5. (SO THAT) THEY FEAR THEE. It is doubtful whether the address is to *God*, or to *the king*. The change from the third person to the second, and *vice versâ*, is so common in Hebrew (see on xxii. 26), that the person addressed, so far as the construction is concerned, may certainly be the king. Nor is the extended duration of his reign implied in the words, "as long as the sun," &c., against this view, even if we suppose the words to be addressed originally to a human monarch. For the Jewish monarch was ruler in a theocratic kingdom, which by its very nature was destined to endure for ever. Comp. ver. 7, 17, and lxxxix. 4 [5], 28 [29], &c., 36 [37], &c.; and if in those passages the throne and the race of the monarch are the object of hope, whereas here the hopes of the Psalmist centre in his *person*, still this also finds its parallel in xxi. 4 [5], "He asked life of Thee: Thou gavest (it) him, Length of days for ever and ever" (see note there). Still I think, considering that the Psalm opens with a prayer addressed to God, it is better to suppose that God is also addressed here; and then the clause will be conjunctive, and mark the consequence of the king's righteous rule.

The SUN and the MOON are mentioned here, and again ver. 7, and in lxxxix. 37 [38], as witnesses to an everlasting order, and as it were figures of eternity, things fixed and unchangeable, compared with the fleeting, dying generations of men, as Jer. xxxi. 35, xxxiii. 20; though, as compared with God, themselves subject to decay and destruction, cii. 26 [27], &c. Is. li. 6, comp. Job xiv. 18.

AS LONG AS THE SUN, lit. "*with* the sun." Comp. Dan. iii. 33 [E. V. iv. 3], "*with* generation and generation."

BEFORE THE MOON, or, "in the presence of the moon," *i.e.* as long as the moon shines, "so long as she turns her face to the earth." In Job viii. 16 the use of the preposition is similar; "He is green *before* the sun," though the phrase means there not "as long as the sun shines," but rather "in the sunshine," "under the influence of the warmth and light of the sun." Classical parallels have been quoted. Ovid, *Amor.* i. 16, "Cum sole et luna semper Aratus erit." *Theogn.* 252, καὶ ἐσσομένοισιν ἀοιδὴ Ἔσσῃ ὁμῶς ὄφρ' ἂν γῆ τε καὶ ἠέλιος.

6 Let him be as rain coming down upon the mown grass,
As showers that water[a] the earth.
7 Let the righteous flourish in his days,
And abundance of peace, till there be no more moon.

8 And let him have dominion from sea to sea,

6. LET HIM BE, &c., lit. "let him come down as rain," the verb which belongs strictly to the figure being applied improperly to the subject.

The gracious influence of the monarch, and of his righteous sway, is strikingly compared to the bountiful shower which freshens the withered herbage, and changes the brown, bare, parched, dusty surface, as by a touch of magic, into one mass of verdure and bloom. We have the same figure in Deut. xxxii. 2, Job xxix. 22, 23, and Prov. xvi. 15. But the most striking parallel is in the last words of David, 2 Sam. xxiii. 4, where it is said of one who ruleth righteously and in the fear of God among men, that he is

Like the light of the morning when the sun ariseth,
A morning without clouds;—
From the sunshine, from the rain, the green grass (sprouteth) from the earth.

THE MOWN GRASS, lit. "that which is shorn," whether *fleece* or *meadow*. In the former sense it occurs Judg. vi. 37, and so the older translators all take it. (Aq. ἐπὶ κουράν, LXX. and others ἐπὶ πόκον, Jerome and Vulg. *in vellus*), probably with the idea that the reign of the monarch would be accompanied by signal tokens of the Divine favour and blessing, like the dew upon Gideon's fleece: in the latter sense, the word is found Amos vii. 1 (where the E. V. has "mowings"); and this is indisputably its meaning here, as the parallelism shows. The *mown* meadow is particularly mentioned, because the roots of the grass would be most exposed to the summer heat, after the crop had been gathered in, and the effect would be most striking in the shooting of the young green blade after the shower. "Striking image," says Dr. Pusey, "of a world, in all appearance, hopelessly dead, but with a hidden capacity for receiving life! ver. 7." —*Daniel*, p. 480, note.

THAT WATER THE EARTH, lit. "a watering of the earth," the word being a noun, in apposition with the preceding "showers." (See Critical Note.)

7. FLOURISH, lit. "shoot," "bud forth," &c., the figure which describes the effects of the rain being thus carried on. Comp. xcii. 7 [8], 12 [13]. All these sentences, Calvin observes, depend on the first verse. "Therefore that the righteous may flourish, and the people be prosperous, David prays that the king may be clothed with righteousness and judgement. It was Solomon's office, indeed, to defend the righteous; but it is Christ's work to make men righteous, because He not only gives to each one his right, but by His Spirit fashions anew their minds. And thus He brings back again righteousness, which else would be banished from the world."

TILL THERE BE NO MORE MOON. See a similar expression in Job xiv. 12.

8. In verses 5—7 the prayer and the hope are that this kingdom should endure for ever: in verses 8—11 that it should know no limits but those of the earth itself.

FROM SEA TO SEA. "From the Mediterranean, their Western boundary, to the encircling sea beyond Asia's utmost verge; and from their Eastern boundary, *the river*, the Euphrates, *unto the ends*

And from the River to the ends of the earth.
9 Before him let the inhabitants of the wilderness [b] bow,
And let his enemies lick the dust.
10 Let the kings of Tarshish and the isles render gifts,
Let the kings of Sheba and Saba offer presents.

of the earth." (Pusey, *Daniel*, p. 480.) But perhaps we have only a poetical expression, not to be construed into the prose of geography, or to be explained (as by Rashi and others) as indicating the extent of territory laid down in Exod. xxiii. 31; "I will set thy bounds from the Red Sea even unto the sea of the Philistines, and from the desert unto the River." There *may* be an allusion to that passage (comp. Gen. xv. 18), but if so, it is expanded and idealized, as the expression "unto the ends of the earth" (as in ii. 8) shows. The RIVER is, doubtless, the Euphrates, and it seems probable, therefore, that the Poet had in his eye the actual extent of the kingdom to which Solomon succeeded, who reigned "over all kingdoms from the river Euphrates to the border of Egypt," and that he thus anticipated a dominion co-extensive with the world. Comp. the Messianic passage, Zech. ix. 10, "He shall speak (command, or enjoin) peace to the nations (as in verses 3, 7 here), and His dominion shall be from sea to sea, and from the River to the ends of the earth."

10. TARSHISH, in all probability the same as the Greek Ταρτησσός, a great naval mart, and, according to Arrian, a colony of the Phœnicians, in the south of Spain. It traded with Tyre in silver, iron, tin, and lead (Ezek. xxvii. 12). Tarshish and the isles, "the empires on the shores of the Mediterranean," are here mentioned as representatives of all the great maritime and commercial countries of the world. [It is worth notice as evidence that the different books were translated by different men, that the LXX. render Tarshish by Θάρσεις in Gen. x. 4, but in Isaiah and Ezekiel, where the word occurs, substitute "Carthage," and "the Carthaginians."] See Smith's *Dict. of the Bible*.

RENDER GIFTS or "tribute." The verb is used in the same way 2 Kings iii. 4, and (with the same noun) xvii. 3; comp. Ezek. xxvii. 15. Qimchi explains it of *the repeated bringing* of tribute, a regular yearly or periodical payment; and so Ges., Ros., and others. But this idea is not contained in the verb (used as an auxiliary in the Qal the construction is different.) Hengst. explains "*return* a gift," *i.e.* as a grateful acknowledgement for the benefits they have received. But Hupfeld rightly observes that the notion of *return*, which the verb expresses, is found in all languages in a similar association. He compares the Latin *reditus*, and the French [and English] *revenue*.

SHEBA, the great South Arabian kingdom, so called after Sheba, one of the sons of Joktan, Gen. x. 28. The mention of this, as well as of Tarshish above, harmonizes very well with the opinion that this Psalm was composed either by or for Solomon. The Queen of Sheba, who came to visit Solomon (1 Kings x. 1), was queen of Sheba in Arabia, and not of Seba, the Cushite kingdom of Ethiopia, as Josephus and some of the Rabbinical writers would make out. The kingdom of Sheba embraced the greater part of the Yemen, or Arabia Felix. See Mr. R. S. Poole's article in Smith's *Dict. of the Bible*, ii. 1231.

SABA, in E. V. "Seba," first mentioned as among the sons of Cush, Gen. x. 7, and joined with Egypt and Cush (E. V. Ethiopia) in Is. xliii. 3, "a nation of Africa, bordering on or included in Cush,

11 Yea, let all kings bow themselves down before him,
Let all nations serve him.

12 For he delivereth the poor when he crieth,
And the afflicted, who hath no helper;
13 He hath pity upon the miserable and poor,
And the souls of the poor he saveth;
14 From deceit and from violence he ransometh their soul,
And precious [c] is their blood in his eyes,
15 So that they live, and give him of the gold of Sheba,

and in Solomon's time independent, and of political importance." According to Josephus, Seba was the ancient name of the Ethiopian island and city of Meroe (*A. J.* ii. 10, § 2), and this must at least have formed part of any ancient Ethiopian kingdom. (See Mr. Poole as above, ii. 1189.)

PRESENTS. The word, like the preceding "gifts," is a singular noun collective: it only occurs once again, Ezek. xxvii. 15.

The whole verse is in accordance with what we read of Solomon, 1 Kings v. 1, x. 10, 25.

12. FOR HE DELIVERETH. The reason is given why all kings and nations should thus do homage to him who sits on David's throne. He has merited such submission by the exercise of every royal virtue, by the justice and the mercy of his sway, by his deep sympathy with, and compassion for, the poor, by the protection which he extends to them against the ministers of fraud and violence. It is not that he merely covers with the shadow of his throne all neighbouring nations, and is acknowledged as their political head, but that the bright example which he sets, the Majesty of Righteousness enthroned in his person, compels all to bow before him.

The verse occurs almost word for word in Job xxix. 12, whence it is perhaps borrowed.

14. PRECIOUS IS THEIR BLOOD. He will not see it spilt on the ground, without avenging it. Comp. cxvi. 15, 1 Sam. xxvi. 21, 2 Kings i. 13.

15. Besides the Divine reward which he has merited, the king shall receive also the grateful acknowledgement of those whom he has protected and saved from death.

Although the verbs here are in the singular, the subject of them must be, not the king, but "the poor," mentioned before, who in ver. 12, 13, are spoken of in the singular number. The apocopated form of the verb with the conjunction denotes a consequence from what precedes (as in xlix. 9 [10], where the very same words occur). Precious is their blood in his sight, so that by his powerful aid they are saved from death, and being also by his goodness made rich, they offer to him the costliest gifts they can bring. The older Versions make "the king" the subject of the first verb ("and he shall live," or, "and let him live"), and take the others impersonally ("and one shall give him," *i.e.* there shall be given him, &c.). And so Luth., Calv., and the E. V. And so French and Skinner, in defiance of grammar, render,

He shall live and prosper,
And unto him shall be given of
the gold of Sheba.

Delitzsch makes "the poor" the subject of the first verb, and "the king" of the second: "that he (the poor) should be saved alive, and

And pray for him alway,
(And) bless him all the day.

16 Let there be abundance [d] of corn in the land,
(So that) on the top of the mountains the fruit thereof rustles like Lebanon,

that the king should give him," &c. But this, in itself harsh, is rendered harsher, because in the next clause it is evident that "the poor" is again the subject, who pray for the king and bless him.

GOLD OF SHEBA, the offerer being, it is supposed, a native of Sheba. See on ver. 10.

AND PRAY FOR HIM. The rendering of the P.B.V., "prayer shall be made ever *unto* him," is quite indefensible. The preposition never occurs in this sense. But the *exclusive* Messianic interpretation seemed to require it. The LXX. περὶ αὐτοῦ Vulg. *de ipso*. Augustine, however, who here, as in Ps. lxix., supposes not Christ only, but Christ and the Church to be spoken of, explains the prayer as made, not for Christ Himself, but for the kingdom of Christ. "When we pray *for Him*, we pray for the Church, which is His body." But this I confess appears to me a style of exposition which is very arbitrary, and one that only leads to endless confusion and perplexity. Dr. Pusey, on the other hand, renders, "And He (the king) shall pray for him (the poor) continually." "The words," he says, "anticipate the revelation by St. Paul, 'He ever liveth to make intercession for them.' (Heb. vii. 26: add Rom. viii. 34.) The words cannot be rendered, as in the P.B.V., 'prayer shall be made ever *unto* Him:' on the other hand, the idiom is used exclusively of the intercession of one nearer to God for one less near." He then gives the instances of Abraham interceding for Abimelech, Gen. xx. 7; Moses for Aaron, after the sin of the calf, Deut. ix. 20; Samuel for the people, 1 Sam. vii. 5, xii. 19—23; the prophet for Jeroboam, 1 Kings xiii. 6; of Jeremiah, at Zedekiah's request, Jer. xxxvii. 3 (comp. also Jer. xlii. 2, 20, vii. 16, xi. 14, xiv. 11, xxix. 7); of Job for his friends, Job xlii. 10. "These are all the cases in which the Concordances, at least, give the idiom. The verb occurs with other prepositions, Job xlii. 8 and 1 Sam. ii. 25."

16. The verbs are again optatives in form, and must be taken as the expression of a wish. The wish, however, here is also a hope. Extraordinary fruitfulness of the soil, and an extraordinary increase of population, are anticipated, as in Is. iv. 1, xxvii. 6, Zech. ii. 4, x. 10.

ON THE TOP OF THE MOUNTAINS: not mentioned (as something extraordinary) because the mountains were usually the least fruitful parts of the land, but because they were the most prominent (see ver. 3). The idea is that the whole country should be one bright sunny picture of gladness and fertility, the corn-fields being seen not only in the valleys, but rising, terrace above terrace, along the mountain-sides, till they reach their summits. The rustling of the corn-fields in the wind is compared to the rustling of the cedars of Lebanon, so thick shall the corn stand, so rich shall be the harvest.

I have departed here from the accents, though at the risk of differing from all other editors. The common division of the verse is: Let there be abundance of corn in the land on the top of the mountains: Let the fruit thereof rustle, &c. But, thus, the point is lost or at least obscured. This would seem to imply that there was to be no corn anywhere but on the mountains, whereas the object is to make the

And let (men) spring forth from the city like the
herbs of the earth.
17 Let his Name be for ever!
Before the sun let his Name be continued,[e]
And let men bless themselves in him;

corn-fields *on the mountains* a principal feature; and there especially would they be exposed to the action of the wind, and so be compared to Lebanon. I also take the verb (יִרְעַשׁ, *rustles*) as subjoined to, not co-ordinate with, the previous verb.

LET (MEN) SPRING FORTH. Comp. xcii. 7 [8], Job v. 25, Is. xxvii. 6. FROM THE CITY, as the dwelling-place of men. Comp. Numb. xxiv. 19.

17. BE CONTINUED, lit. "be propagated," continued in his offspring (comp. xlv. 16 [17]), *i.e.* taking the verb as a passive; or if it be active, "ever make fresh shoots." Or, as Dr. Pusey: "*His Name shall propagate*, gaining, generation after generation, a fresh accession of offspring." The verb occurs nowhere else, but the noun is found in Gen. xxi. 23, Job xviii. 19 (where Lee's note may be consulted), Is. xiv. 22, and means always *offspring*.

BLESS THEMSELVES IN HIM. The same reflexive form of the verb occurs in Gen. xxii. 18, xxvi. 4, whereas in xviii. 18 the passive is employed, "and in him all the nations of the earth shall be blessed." Gesen., indeed, would retain the reflexive sense in the last instance (and it is certain that the Niphal has sometimes a middle force): Phillips, on the other hand, would take all as passives; but, in spite of the grammarians, I do not believe that a Hithpael is ever used as a strict passive: the reflexive sense is always discernible, even where the idiom of our language does not allow us to retain it in a translation. The meaning seems to be, that the king shall be to them the very type and living image of all blessing, so that they can wish for nothing higher or more glorious than that his blessedness should flow forth upon them. There is so much truth in the note with which Delitzsch concludes his commentary on this Psalm, that, though it is rather long, I will quote it: "Solomon," he says, "was in truth a righteous, gracious, God-fearing Prince: he established and even extended the kingdom, he ruled over innumerable people, exalted in wisdom and riches above all the kings of the earth; his time was the most happy, the richest in peace and joy which Israel ever knew. The words of the Psalm were all fulfilled in him, even to the mere particular of the universal dominion which is wished for him. But the end of his reign was not like the beginning and the middle of it. The fair, the glorious, the pure image of the Messiah which he had exhibited, waxed pale. In the time of David and Solomon, the hope of believers, which was attached to the kingdom of David, had not yet fully broken with the present. That time, with few exceptions, knew as yet no other Messiah than the anointed of God, who was David or Solomon himself. When however the kingdom, in the person of these its two most glorious representatives, had proved itself unable to bring to perfection the idea of the Messiah or the Anointed of God; and when the line of kings who followed thoroughly disappointed the hope which clung to the kingdom of the present; and when, though here and there, as under Hezekiah, that hope blazed up for a moment, it was finally extinguished, and men were driven from the present to look to the future,—then, and not till then, did there come a decisive break between the Messianic hope and the existing

Let all nations call him happy!

---

18 Blessed be Jehovah, God, the God of Israel,
Who alone doeth wondrous things!
19 And blessed be His glorious Name for ever,
And let all the earth[f] be filled with His glory!
Amen and Amen.

state of things: the image of the Messiah was now painted on the pure sky of the Future (though of the immediate Future), in colours furnished by the unfulfilment of the older prophecy, and the contradiction between the existing kingdom and its idea; it became more and more, so to speak, something superearthly, superhuman, extending into the future, the invisible refuge and the invisible aim of a faith despairing of the present, and thereby rendered more spiritual and more heavenly (comp. the Messianic image as described in colours borrowed from our Psalm, Is. xi., Mic. v. 3, 6 [E. V. 4, 7], Zech. ix. 9, 10). Rightly to understand this, we must free ourselves from the prejudice that the centre of the Old Testament gospel (Heils-Verkündigung) lay in the prophecy of the Messiah. Where is the Messiah set forth as the Redeemer of the world? The Redeemer of the world is Jehovah. The coming (*Parusia*) of Jehovah is the centre of the Old Testament gospel. How this unfolded itself may be made clear by means of a comparison. The Old Testament, in relation to the Day of the New Testament, is Night. In this Night there rise in opposite directions two stars of Promise. The one describes its path from above downwards: it is the promise of Jehovah, who is about to come. The other describes its path from below upwards: it is the hope which rests on the seed of David, the prophecy of the Son of David, uttered at first in tones wholly human, and only earthly. These two stars meet at last, they mingle so as to form but one, the Night vanishes, and it is Day. This one Star is Jesus Christ, Jehovah and David's Son in one person, the King of Israel and at the same time the Redeemer of the world; in a word, the God-man, blessed be He!"

The only part of the above note from which I dissent is the too favourable picture given of Solomon and his reign. This seems to me as much too favourable as that drawn by Mr. Plumptre, in Smith's *Dict. of the Bible* [SOLOMON], seems too dark.

18, 19. These verses are a later doxology, appended here to mark the close of the Second Book of the Psalter. Similar doxologies occur at the end of all the other books (see at the end of Ps. xli.). This approaches the nearest, as Delitzsch has observed, to the regular liturgical *Berachah*, or blessing; for it contains what is required in that, *the Name* of Jehovah, *the Amen*, and the mention of *the kingdom*, though this last is only implied in "the Name of *His Glory*," and it is not expressly said "the Name of the Glory of His Kingdom," as it is, for instance, in the Berachah, at the pronouncing of which, on the Day of Atonement, the people fell on their faces, so often as the Name of Jehovah passed over the lips of the High Priest.

18. JEHOVAH, GOD, see on lix. 5 [6].

WHO ALONE DOETH WONDROUS THINGS. Comp. cxxxvi. 4, and Job ix. 8, 10.

19. HIS GLORIOUS NAME, or "the Name of His Glory." Comp. Neh. ix. 5; and with the concluding words of the verse, Num. xiv. 21.

The repeated AMEN, with the

20 Ended are the Prayers of
David the Son of Jesse.

conjunction, is in the Old Test. peculiar to these doxologies in the Psalter.

The characteristic difference between the two books of the Psalter, and the use of the Divine Names, is preserved even in their concluding doxologies. In the First, God is spoken of as "*Jehovah*, the God of Israel;" here as "*Jehovah Elohim*, the God of Israel."

20. This verse, again (with which may be compared Job xxxi. 40), does not belong originally either to the Psalm or to the Doxology, though perhaps older than the last. Augustine, indeed, took it as the inscription of the next Psalm, remarking: "tot habemus Psalmos, in quorum titulis scriptum est nomen David; nusquam est additum *filii Jesse* nisi in hoc loco." It is remarkable that the elder Qimchi treated the words as an integral portion of the Psalter. He says: "When all shall have been fulfilled, so that Israel, brought back from exile, shall have been restored to their land, and the Messiah, the son of David, rules over them, then will they need no more atonement, and deliverance, and blessing, for they will possess all, and then will be ended the prayers of David the son of Jesse" (quoted by Delitzsch).

As several Psalms bearing the name of David occur in the later Books of the Psalter, it is evident that this notice, "ended are the Prayers of David," &c., must have been placed originally at the end of a smaller collection of Psalms, which was supposed to comprise those only which were known as his, or which at least belonged to his time. It does not prove that all the Psalms of the first two Books were regarded as David's, or that he wrote none of those which in the latter Books go by his name.

[a] זַרְזִיף. The word occurs only here, and is in form a quadrilit. noun formed from the Aram. זרף. A deriv. in Syr. has the meaning of *heavy rain*, and a similar root occurs in Arab. In the Talmud Babli, *Jom.* 87a, the word occurs in the sense of *droppings*, זרזיפי דמיא, "droppings of water." The noun stands in apposition with the preceding רְבִיבִים. So Ew.: "Wie Regenschauer, Sättigung der Erde." So too the older Verss. seem to have understood it. But Hupf. finds this apposition "intolerably harsh," and thinks the sense requires a verb, and would therefore correct יְזַרְזֵף or יַזְרִיף.

[b] צִיִּים. According to Hupf. the word everywhere else is used, not of men, but of wild beasts inhabiting the wilderness, even in lxxiv. 14, Is. xxiii. 13. He denies therefore that the nomad inhabitants of the steppes can be meant by the word, and with Olsh. would correct צָרִים, *adversaries*, which he considers the parall. also requires. But there is no reason why צִיִּים should not be a comprehensive term, denoting all inhabitants of the wilderness, whether man or beast. The Greek Verss. and Jerome all render the word "Ethiopians." The Syr. has "the islands," and if any change were necessary, I should incline to this, אִיִּים, as in ver. 10.

[c] יֵיקַר. The radical *Yod* is retained, as in אֵילְכָה, Micah i. 8, and the verb is followed precisely as in xlix. 10, by וִיחִי as a conjunctive, marking

the purpose or object of יְיַקֵר. Hupfeld, however, is inclined to take the optative form here as hypothetic, or as a condition of what follows: "and when he lives, then he gives," &c.

d פִּסַּת, only here; probably meaning "abundance" (so the Syr. and Rashi), lit. "spreading abroad," referred by the Jewish lexicographers to פסס = פּשׂה (used of the *spreading* of the leprosy); comp. Aram. פסא, "to spread, so as to cover a wide surface;" and the Arab. فشا, and also فشّ, to which last this Dageshed form comes nearest. Qimchi and others, connecting it apparently with פַּס, *a piece, an end*, render *a handful.* And so Calv., Hengst., Stier, and the E. V., an interpretation which rests on the false notion that the mountains are spoken of as the least fruitful portion of the country.

In the Midrash Koheleth, on Eccl. i. 9, we read, in reference to this verse: "R. Berechia said in the name of R. Isaac, As was the First Goël, so shall be the Last. . . . . The First Goël made the manna to descend, for it is said, *Behold, I will rain bread upon you from heaven.* (Ex. xvi. 4.) So also the Last Goël makes the manna to descend, for it is said, *There shall be an abundance of corn upon the earth.*"

e ינין. For this, the Hiphil, the Q'ri substitutes the Niphal יִנּוֹן, which the E. V. (according to its rule) has followed. On this Dr. Pusey (*Daniel*, p. 481, note 16) remarks: "It is a mere substitution for the bold image of the text. Yet it must be an old correction, since it supplies one of the names of the Messiah," in proof of which he quotes from Schöttgen, *de Messia* ad loc.: "Bereshith Rabba, cap. i., 'Six things' (*seven* are counted in Pirqe derabb Eli'ezer, cap. iii., T. B., Pesachim, 54a; Nedarim, 39b; Midrash Tehillim, on xciii. 2 [see in Mart. *Pug. Fid.* f. 335]; and Midrash Mishle, on viii. 9), were before the foundation of the world, and were named before their birth, and among them the name of the Messiah, *Before the sun, Yinnon is His Name.* [See in Mart. f. 334.] Echa Rabbathi, on i. 16, f. 59, 3, and T. B. Synhedrin, 98b, 'They who are of the school of Jannai said, that "the name of the Messiah is Yinnon" from this place.' Midrash Mishle, on xix. 21, f. 57, 1, 'The name of the Messiah is Yinnon,' also quoting it." Dr. P. adds: "In the Bereshith R. l. c. and Midr. Till. l. c. it is explained actively [as in the K'thîbh], yet the pass. form seems to have crept in, 'Why is his name called ינון? Because he shall give birth to (ינין) those who sleep in the dust of the earth.'" [I have corrected the references throughout in the above passage from Schöttgen.]

f אֶת־כָּל ה׳. On אֵת with the subject of the passive verb, see Ges. § 143, 1 *a*.

CONTENTS

VOLUME TWO

THE PSALMS, continued

THE PSALMS

BOOK 3

Psalms 73—89

PSALM 73

THERE are some questions which never lose their interest, some problems of which it may be said, that they are ever old and yet ever new. Not the least anxious of such questions are those which deal with God's moral government of the world. They lie close to man's heart, and are ever asking and pressing for solution. They may differ in different times, they may assume various forms; but perhaps no man ever looked thoughtfully on the world as it is without seeing much that was hard to reconcile with a belief in the love and wisdom of God.

One form of this moral difficulty pressed heavily upon the pious Jew under the Old Dispensation. It was this: Why should good men suffer, and bad men prosper? This difficulty was aggravated, we must remember, by what seemed to be the manifest contradiction between the express teaching of his Law, and the observed facts of human experience. The Law told him that God was a righteous Judge, meting out to men in this world the due recompense of their deeds. The course of the world, where those who had cast off the fear of God were rich and powerful, made him ready to question this truth, and was a serious stumbling-block to his faith. And further, "the Hebrew mind had never risen to the conception of universal law, but was accustomed to regard all visible phenomena as the immediate result of a free Sovereign Will. Direct interposition, even arbitrary interference, was no difficulty to the Jew, to whom Jehovah was the absolute Sovereign of the world, not acting, so far as he could see, according to any established order."* Hence it seemed to him inexplicable that the world of life should not reflect perfectly, as in a mirror, the righteousness of God.

This is the perplexity which appears in this Psalm, as it does in the 37th, and also in the Book of Job. Substantially it is the same problem: but it is met differently. In the 37th Psalm the advice given is to wait, to trust in Jehovah, and to rest assured that in the end the seeming disorder will be set right even *in this world.* The wicked will perish, the enemies of Jehovah be cut off, and the

* For some valuable suggestions on this Psalm I am indebted to a friend, the Rev. J. G. Mould.

righteous will be preserved from evil, and inherit the land. Thus God suffers wickedness *for a time*, only the more signally to manifest His righteousness in overthrowing it. That is the first, the simplest, the most obvious solution of the difficulty. In the Book of Job, where the sorrow and the perplexity are the darkest, where the question lies upon the heart, "heavy as lead, and deep almost as life," the sufferer finds no such consolation. As a Gentile, he has no need to reconcile his experience with the sanctions of the Pentateuch. But he has to do that which is not less hard, he has to reconcile it with a life's knowledge of God, and a life's love of God. He searches his heart, he lays bare his life, he is conscious of no transgression, and he cannot understand why chastisement should be laid upon him, whilst the most daring offenders against the Majesty of God escape with impunity. Sometimes with a bitterness that cannot be repressed, sometimes with a sorrow hushing itself into resignation, he still turns to God, he would fain stand before His judgement-seat, plead with Him his cause, and receive a righteous sentence. But Job does not find the solution of the Psalmist. He is driven to feel that all this is a mystery. God will not give an account of any of His matters. "I go forward, but He is not there; and backward, but I cannot perceive Him" (Job xxiii.). And when Jehovah appears at the end of the Book, it is to show the folly of man, who would presume to think that, short-sighted and ignorant as he is, he can fathom the counsels of the Most High. He appears, not to lift the veil of mystery, but to teach the need of humiliation and the blessedness of faith.*

In this Psalm, again, a different conclusion is arrived at. In part it is the same as that which has already met us in Psalm xxxvii., in part it is far higher. The Psalmist here is not content merely with visible retribution in this world. He sees it indeed in the case of the ungodly. When he was tempted to envy their lot, when he had all but yielded to the sophistry of those who would have persuaded him to be even as they, the temptation was subdued by the reflection that such prosperity came to an end as sudden as it was terrible. But he does not place over against this, on the other side, an earthly portion of honour and happiness for the just. Their portion is in

---

* There is a difficulty, no doubt, in reconciling this solution, or rather non-solution of the problem, with that which is given subsequently in the historical conclusion of the Book. There we find Job recompensed *in this life* for all his sufferings. If the historical parts of the Book are by the same author as the dialogue (as Ewald maintains), then we must suppose that when Job is brought to confess his own vileness, and his own ignorance and presumption, then, and not till then, does God reward him with temporal prosperity.

God. He is the stay and the satisfaction of their hearts now. He will take them to Himself and to glory hereafter. This conviction it is which finally chases away the shadows of doubt, and brings light and peace into his soul. And this conviction is the more remarkable, because it is reached in spite of the distinct promise made of temporal recompense to piety, and in the absence of a full and definite Revelation with regard to the life to come. In the clear light of another world and its certain recompenses, such perplexities either vanish or lose much of their sharpness. When we confess that God's righteousness has a larger theatre for its display than this world and the years of man, we need not draw hasty conclusions from "the slight whisper" of His ways which reaches us here.

It is an interesting question suggested by this Psalm, but one which can only be touched on here, how far there is anything in common between doubts, such as those which perplexed the ancient Hebrews, and those by which modern thinkers are harassed.* There are some persons, who now, as of old, are troubled by the moral aspect of the world. To some, this perplexity is even aggravated by the disclosures of Revelation. And men of pious minds have been shaken to their inmost centre by the appalling prospect of the everlasting punishment of the wicked. But the difficulties which are, properly speaking, modern difficulties, are of another kind. They are, at least in their source, speculative rather than moral. The observed uniformity of nature, the indissoluble chain of cause and effect, the absolute certainty of the laws by which all visible phenomena are governed, these are now the stumbling-blocks even to devout minds. How, it is asked, can we reconcile these things with the belief in a Personal God, or at least with an ever-active Personal Will? Had the world ever a Maker? or, if it had, does He still control and guide it? Knowing as we do that the order of cause and effect is ever the same, how can we accept miracles or Divine interpositions of any kind? What avails prayer, when every event

* This point has been touched on by Dr. A. S. Farrar in his "Bampton Lectures," a work which, for breadth and depth of learning, has few parallels in modern English literature, and which combines in no common degree the spirit of a sound faith and a true philosophy. Dr. Farrar says: "It is deeply interesting to observe, not merely that the difficulties concerning Providence felt by Job refer to the very subjects which painfully perplex the modern mind, but also that the friends of Job exhibit the instinctive tendency which is observed in modern times to denounce his doubt as sin, not less than to attribute his trials to evil as the direct cause. These two books of Scripture [Job and Ecclesiastes], together with the seventy-third Psalm, have an increasing religious importance as the world grows older. The things written aforetime were written for our learning."—*Lecture* I. p. 7, note.

that happens has been ordained from eternity? How can any words of man interrupt the march of the Universe? Ships are wrecked and harvests are blighted, and famine and pestilence walk the earth, not because men have forgotten to pray, but in accordance with the unerring laws which storm, and blight, and disease obey. Such are some of the thoughts—the birth, it may be said, of modern science—which haunt and vex men now.

Difficulties like these are not touched upon in Scripture. But the spirit in which all difficulties, all doubts should be met, is the same. If the answer lies in a region above and beyond us, our true wisdom is to wait in humble dependence upon God, in active fulfilment of what we can see to be our duty, till the day dawn and the shadows flee away. And it is this which Scripture teaches us in this Psalm, in Job, and in that other Book, which is such a wonderful record of a doubting self-tormenting spirit, the Book of Ecclesiastes. It has been said that the Book of Job and the 73rd Psalm "crush free thought." * It would have been truer to say that they teach us that there are heights which we cannot reach, depths which the intellect of man cannot fathom; that God's ways are past finding out; that difficulties, perplexities, sorrows, are best healed and forgotten in the Light which streams from His throne, in the Love which by His Spirit is shed abroad in the heart.

But the Psalm teaches us also a lesson of forbearance towards the doubter. It is a lesson perhaps just now peculiarly needed. Christian sympathy is felt, Christian charity is extended toward every form of misery, whether mental or bodily, except toward that which is often the acutest of all, the anguish of doubt. Here it seems as if coldness, suspicion, even denunciation, were justifiable. And yet doubt, even to the verge of scepticism, as is plain from this Psalm, may be no proof of a bad and corrupt heart; it may rather be the evidence of an honest one. Doubt may spring from the very depth and earnestness of a man's faith. In the case of the Psalmist, as in the case of Job, that which lay at the bottom of the doubt, that which made it a thing so full of anguish, was the deep-rooted conviction of the righteousness of God. Unbelief does not doubt, faith doubts.† And God permits the doubt in His truest and noblest

---

* Quinet, *Œuvres,* tome i. c. 5, § 4.

† The expression has been criticised as paradoxical, but the following admirable passages, which I have met with since the first edition of this work was published, may justify my language. They are quoted by Archbishop Whately in his *Annotations on Bacon's Essays*, pp. 358, 359. The first is from a writer in the *Edinburgh Review* for January, 1847, on "The Genius of Pascal": "So little inconsistent with a *habit* of intelligent faith are such transient invasions of doubt, or such diminished

servants, as our Lord did in the case of Thomas, that He may thereby plant their feet the more firmly on the rock of His own everlasting truth. There is, perhaps, no Psalm in which Faith asserts itself so triumphantly, cleaves to God with such words of lofty hope and affection, and that precisely because in no other instance has the fire been so searching, the test of faith so severe. It may be well to remember this when we see a noble soul compassed about with darkness, yet struggling to the light, lest we "vex one whom God has smitten, and tell of the pain of His wounded ones" (Ps. lxix. 26).

The Psalm consists of two parts :—

I. The Psalmist tells the story of the doubts which had assailed him, the temptation to which he had nearly succumbed. Ver. 1—14.

II. He confesses the sinfulness of these doubts, and explains how he had been enabled to overcome them. Ver. 15—28.

These principal portions have their further subdivisions (which are in the main those given by Hupfeld) :—

I. *a.* First we have, by way of introduction, the conviction to which his struggle with doubt brought him, ver. 1 ; then the general statement of his offence, ver. 2, 3.

b. The reason of which is more fully explained to be the prosperity of the wicked, ver. 4, 5 ; and their insolence and pride in consequence, ver. 6—11.

c. The comfortless conclusion which he had thence drawn, ver. 12—14.

---

perceptions of the evidence of truth, that it may even be said that it is only those who have in some measure experienced them, who can be said in the highest sense to believe at all. He who has never had a doubt, who believes what he believes for reasons which he thinks as irrefragable (if that be possible) as those of a mathematical demonstration, ought not to be said so much to *believe* as to *know ;* his belief is to him knowledge, and his mind stands in the same relation to it, however erroneous and absurd that belief may be. It is rather he who believes — not indeed without the exercise of his reason, but without the full satisfaction of his reason—with a knowledge and appreciation of formidable objections—it is this man who may most truly be said intelligently to believe."

The other is from a short poem by Bishop Hinds :

" Yet so it is ; belief springs still
In souls that nurture doubt ;
And we must go to Him, who will
The baneful weed cast out.

" Did never thorns thy path beset?
Beware—be not deceived ;
He who has never doubted yet
Has never yet believed.'

II. *a.* By way of transition, he tells how he had been led to acknowledge the impiety of this conclusion, and how, seeking for a deeper, truer view, he had come to the sanctuary of God, ver. 15—17, where he had learned the *sudden* and *fearful* end of the wicked, ver. 18—20, and consequently the *folly* of his own speculation.

b. Thus recovering from the almost fatal shock which his faith had received, he returns to a sense of his true position. God holds him by his right hand, God guides him for the present, and will bring him to a glorious end, ver. 23, 24; hence he rejoices in the thought that God is his great and only possession, ver. 25, 26.

c. The general conclusion, that departure from God is death and destruction; that in His presence and in nearness to Him are to be found joy and safety, ver. 27, 28.

[A PSALM OF ASAPH.[a]]

1 SURELY[b] God is good to Israel,
(Even) to such as are of a pure heart.
2 But as for me, my feet were almost gone,[c]

1. SURELY. This particle, which occurs twice again in this Psalm, is rendered differently in each case by the E. V.; here *truly*, in ver. 13 *verily*, in ver. 18 *surely:* but one rendering should be kept throughout. The Welsh more correctly has, *yn ddïau* (ver. 1), *dïau* (ver. 13, 18). The word has been already discussed in the note on lxii. 1, where we have seen it is capable of two meanings. Here it is used affirmatively, and expresses the satisfaction with which the conclusion has been arrived at, after all the anxious questionings and debatings through which the Psalmist has passed: "Yes, it is so; after all, God is good, notwithstanding all my doubts." It thus implies at the same time a tacit opposition to a different view of the case, such as that which is described afterwards. "Fresh from the conflict, he somewhat abruptly opens the Psalm with the confident enunciation of the truth, of which victory over doubt had now made him more, and more intelligently, sure than ever, that God is good to Israel, even to such as are of a clean heart."—*Essential Coherence of the Old and New Testament*, by my brother, the Rev. T. T. Perowne, p. 85, to which I may, perhaps, be permitted to refer for a clear and satisfactory view of the whole Psalm.

It is of importance to remark that the result of the conflict is stated before the conflict itself is described. There is no parade of doubt merely as doubt. He states *first*, and in the most natural way, the *final* conviction of his heart.

ISRAEL. The next clause limits this, and reminds us that "they are not all Israel, which are of Israel." To the true Israel God is Love; to them "all things work together for good."

OF A PURE HEART, lit. "pure of heart," as in xxiv. 4. Comp. Matt. v. 8.

2. BUT AS FOR ME. The pronoun is emphatic. He places himself, with shame and sorrow, almost in opposition to that Israel of God

My steps had well-nigh slipt.
3 For I was envious at the arrogant,
When I saw the prosperity of the wicked.
4 For they have no bands in their death,[d]
And their strength [e] (continueth) firm.
5 They are not in trouble as (other) men,

of which he had just spoken. He has in view the happiness of those who had felt no doubt. Calvin somewhat differently explains : Even I, with all my knowledge and advantages, I who ought to have known better.

GONE, lit. "inclined," not so much in the sense of being bent under him, as rather of being turned aside, out of the way, as in Numb. xx. 17, 2 Sam. ii. 19, 21, &c. The verb in the next clause expresses the giving way from weakness, fear, &c., HAD . . . SLIPT, lit. "were poured out" like water.

3. ENVIOUS, as in xxxvii. 1, Prov. xxiii. 17, wishing that his lot were like theirs who seemed to be the favourites of heaven. Calvin quotes the story of Dionysius the Less, who, having sacrilegiously plundered a temple, and having sailed safely home, said : "Do you see that the gods smile upon sacrilege ?" The prosperity and impunity of the wicked invite others to follow their example.

THE ARROGANT. The word denotes those whose pride and infatuation amounts almost to madness. It is difficult to find an exact equivalent in English. Gesenius renders it by *superbi*, *insolentes*, and J. D. Michaelis by *stolide gloriosi*, "vain boasters." It occurs in v. 5 [6], where see note [d], and again in lxxv. 4 [5]. The LXX., in all these instances, render vaguely, ἄνομοι, παράνομοι.

4. BANDS. This word "bands," or "tight cords," or "fetters," occurs only once besides, Is. lviii. 6. I have now [2nd Edit.] adopted the simplest and most straightforward rendering of the words, "They have no bands in their death" (lit. *at* or *for* their death, *i.e.* when they die), because the objection brought against it, that such a meaning is at variance with the general scope of the Psalm, the object of which is not to represent the *end* of the ungodly as happy (the very reverse is asserted ver. 17, &c.), but to describe the general prosperity of their *lives*, no longer appears to me to be valid. For we must remember that the Psalmist is describing here not the fact, but *what seemed to him* to be the fact, in a state of mind which he confesses to have been unhealthy. Comp. Job xxi. 13, and see the note on ver. 18 of this Psalm. Otherwise it would be possible to render [as in 1st Edit.], "For no bands (of suffering) (bring them) to their death." No fetters are, so to speak, laid upon their limbs, so that they should be delivered over bound to their great enemy. They are not beset with sorrows, sufferings, miseries, which by impairing health and strength bring them to death. This sense has been very well given in the P.B.V., which follows Luther :—

"For they are in no peril of death,
But are lusty and strong."

5. The literal rendering of this verse would be :—

"In the trouble of man they are not,
And with mankind they are not plagued."

The first word used to express *man* is that which denotes man in his frailty and weakness. See on ix. 19, 20, note [1]; x. 18, note [1]. The other is the most general term, Adam, man as made of the dust of the

Neither are they plagued like (other) folk.
6 Therefore pride is as a chain [f] about their neck;
Violence covereth [g] them as a garment.
7 Their eye [h] goeth forth from fatness;
The imaginations of (their) heart overflow.
8 They scoff [i] and speak wickedly,
Of oppression loftily do they speak.
9 They have set their mouth in the heavens,
And their tongue walketh [k] through the earth.
10 Therefore his people are turned [l] after them,

earth. These men seem exempt not only from the frailties and infirmities of men, but even from the common lot of men. They appear almost to be tempered and moulded of a finer clay than ordinary human nature.

PLAGUED, lit. "smitten," *i.e.* of God; a word used especially of Divine chastisement. Comp. Is. liii. 4.

6. IS AS A CHAIN ABOUT THEIR NECK, or "hath encircled their neck." See for the same figure, Prov. i. 9, iii. 22. The neck (the *collum resupinum*) is regarded as the seat of pride: comp. lxxv. 5 [6], Is. iii. 16.

7. FROM FATNESS, *i.e.* from a sleek countenance, conveying in itself the impression of worldly ease and enjoyment. The whole figure is highly expressive. It is a picture of that proud satisfaction which so often shines in the eyes of well-to-do men of the world.

OVERFLOW. The metaphor is from a swollen river which rises above its banks. The verb is used absolutely, as in Hab. i. 11, "Then (his) spirit swells and overflows," where the same figure is employed in describing the pride and insolence of the Chaldæans. See also Is. viii. 8. This is better than, with the E. V., to take the verb as transitive, "They have more than heart could wish" (lit. they have exceeded the imaginations of the heart); the two clauses of the verse correspond, the proud look being an index of the proud heart; these being followed, in the next verse, by the proud spirit.

8. According to the Massoretic punctuation, the verse would be arranged thus:—

"They scoff and speak wickedly of oppression,
Loftily do they speak."

But the LXX. arrange the clauses as in the text and render the latter, *ἀδικίαν εἰς τὸ ὕψος ἐλάλησαν*, and so Aq. *συκοφαντίαν ἐξ ὕψους λαλοῦντες.*

LOFTILY, or "from on high," not "against the Most High," as the P. B. V. See note on lvi. 2.

9. IN THE HEAVENS, not "against the heavens." The stature of these men seems to swell till it reaches heaven. Thence they issue their proud commands, the whole earth being the theatre of their action.

10. THEREFORE. This, as Mendelssohn has observed, is co-ordinate with the "therefore" in ver. 6. Both depend on the statement in ver. 4, 5. Because the wicked have no bands, &c., therefore pride compasseth them, &c., and therefore others are induced to follow their example.

HIS PEOPLE. This is capable of two interpretations. (1) In accordance with a common Hebrew idiom, there may be an abrupt transition from the plural to the singular, an individual being now substituted for the mass. "*His* people," in this

And at the full stream would slake their thirst:[m]
11 And they say: "How doth God know?
And is there knowledge in the Most High?"
12 Lo, these are the wicked,
And (these men), ever prosperous, have increased wealth.

sense, are the crowd who attach themselves to *one and another* of these prosperous sinners, that they may share *his* prosperity, and then "*his* people" is equivalent to "*their* people," the crowd which follows them. (2) The pronoun may refer to God. So the Chald. "they (the wicked) turn upon His (God's) people to punish them;" and the LXX. ὁ λαος μου, Vulg. *populus meus*. But with this reference of the pronoun we may explain: Even His people, forsaking Him, are led away by the evil example, just as the Psalmist confesses he himself was.

AFTER THEM, lit. "thither," *i.e. to* the persons before described, and, as is implied, *away from* God. The next clause of the verse is more difficult of explanation. The E. V. by its rendering, "And waters of a full (cup) are wrung out to them," probably means us to understand that the people of God, when they turn hither, *i.e.* to the consideration of the prosperity of the wicked, are filled with sorrow, drink as it were the cup of tears; the image being the same as in lxxx. 5 [6]. The P. B. V. comes nearer to the mark:—

"Therefore fall the people unto them,
And thereout suck they no small advantage,"—

only that apparently in the second clause the pronoun *they* refers, not to the people, but to the wicked mentioned before. Whereas it is the people, the crowd of hangers-on, who gather like sheep to the water-trough, who suck this advantage, such as it is, as the reward of their apostasy.

AND AT THE FULL STREAM, &c., lit. "and fulness of water is drained by them;" *i.e.* broad and deep are the waters of sinful pleasures, which they, in their infatuation, drink.

11. AND THEY SAY. The reference of the pronoun has again been disputed. Mostly it is referred to those just spoken of, who have been led astray by the prosperity of the wicked to follow them. Hupfeld thinks it is the wicked themselves (of ver. 3) who thus speak, and certainly the boldness of the language employed, which questions the very being of a God, is more natural in the mouth of those whose long prosperity and long security have made them unmindful of His providence.

But much depends on the view we take of the next three verses. Do these continue the speech, or are they the reflection of the Poet himself? The former is the view of Ewald, Stier, Delitzsch, and others. In this case the words must be throughout the words of those who have been tempted and led astray by the untroubled happiness of the wicked. They adopt their practically atheistical principles; they ask, "How doth God know," &c.; they point, with a triumph not unmingled with bitterness, at their success: Lo, these are the ungodly, whose sudden and utter overthrow we have been taught to expect; they come to the conclusion that the fear of God is in vain, for it does not save a man from suffering and disappointment, and thus they justify their choice. It is certainly in favour of this view that ver. 15 seems naturally to introduce the reflections of the Psalmist himself, who had almost been carried away by the same sophistry. On the other hand,

13 Surely in vain have I cleansed my heart,
And washed my hands in innocency,
14 And have been plagued all the day long,
And chastened every morning.
15 If I had said,[n] "I will utter (words) like these,"[o]
Lo, I should have been faithless to the generation of
Thy children.
16 And when I pondered[p] it that I might know this,
It was a trouble in mine eyes;
17 Until I went into the sanctuary of God

Hengstenberg and Hupfeld suppose the reflections of the Psalmist to begin at ver. 12. Verses 13, 14 will then describe the temptation which pressed upon him, the thoughts which forced themselves into his mind, and which, as verses 15, 16 show, he only with difficulty repressed. He did utter his disappointment, he was gliding on to something worse, to the atheistic language of ver. 11, when he checks himself as in ver. 15. In favour of this interpretation it may be urged, that the LXX. have introduced a *καὶ εἶπα* at the beginning of ver. 13.

I confess that, while inclining to the former, I feel it difficult to decide between these two views; and the decision must after all rest upon a certain feeling and instinct, rather than upon critical grounds.

15. IF I HAD SAID, *i.e.* to myself (as the verb is constantly used); if I had given way to the temptation to utter thoughts and misgivings like these. "The Hebrew Psalmist," it has been well said, "instead of telling his painful misgivings, harboured them in God's presence till he found the solution. The delicacy exhibited in forbearing unnecessarily to shake the faith of others, is a measure of the disinterestedness of the doubter."—FARRAR, *Bampton Lectures*, p. 27.

I WILL UTTER (WORDS) LIKE THESE, or, "I will recount the matter thus."

THE GENERATION OF THY CHILDREN. As in xiv. 5, "the generation of the righteous." So the people at large are called, Deut. xiv. 1; Hos. ii. 1. Here, however, the true Israel, "the clean of heart," are meant. But the *individual* is not called a son of God under the Old Testament, except officially, as in ii. 7.

16. I PONDERED. See the same use of the verb in lxxvii. 5 [6], "the days of old;" Prov. xvi. 9, "one's way." THAT I MIGHT KNOW, *i.e.* reconcile all that I saw with the great fact of God's moral government.

A TROUBLE, or a weariness, as of a great burden laid upon me (comp. Eccles. viii. 17). Thought could not solve the problem. The brain grew wearier, and the heart heavier. Light and peace come to us, not by thinking, but by faith. "In Thy Light we shall see Light." God Himself was the Teacher.

17. THE SANCTUARY is the place of His teaching; not heaven, "the world of angels and spirits," as Qimchi and others, but the Temple, as the place of His special manifestation, not only by Urim and Thummim, but in direct answer to prayer. There, in some hour of fervent, secret prayer, like that of Hannah (1 Sam. i. 13, comp. Luke xviii. 10), or perhaps in some solemn service—it may have been (who can tell?) through the words of some inspired Psalm—a conviction of the truth broke upon him. The word

(Until) I considered their latter end.
18 Surely in slippery places dost Thou set them,
Thou hast cast them down to ruin.[q]
19 How are they brought to desolation as in a moment!

SANCTUARY is in the plural, which is used here, as in xliii. 3, lxviii. 35 [36], for the singular.

18. The conclusion is remarkable. That which dispels the Psalmist's doubts, and restores his faith, is the end of the ungodly in this world,—their sudden reverses, their terrible overthrow in the very bosom of their prosperity. Hitherto he has not taken notice of this fact as he ought : he has been so dazzled with the prosperity of the wicked, that he has forgotten by what appalling judgements God vindicates His righteousness. He does not follow them into the next world. His eye cannot see beyond the grave. Even the great horror of an evil conscience is scarcely, in his view, a part of their punishment, unless the expression "because of terrors," in ver. 19, may be supposed to point that way, which, however, is very doubtful. But this *Théodicée* was the only one then known, and is in fact based upon the Law, which, resting upon temporal sanctions, justified the expectation of visible retribution in this world. The judges of Israel were appointed as the vice-gerents of God, to execute this retribution (Deut. i. 17). Hence the deep-rooted conviction on this point, even in the minds of the godly. It was not till a later period, and especially till after the Exile, that the judgement after death was clearly recognised. Comp. Mal. iii. 13, &c.

It is singular that in Job xxi. 13 (comp. ix. 23) it is reckoned as an element in the good fortune of the wicked, that they die not by a lingering disease, but suddenly; but it may be that Job, perplexed and eager to make everything tell on his side, which his friends would urge against him, is determined not to admit their inference from the facts of Divine Providence. Otherwise this passage of Job supports the obvious rendering of ver. 4, "They do not die by lingering diseases, but easily," this being the mistaken view afterwards corrected.

"We come to the conclusion," it has been well said, "that in the case of the wicked this Psalm does not plainly and undeniably teach that punishment awaits them after death; but only that in estimating their condition it is necessary, in order to vindicate the justice of God, to take in their whole career, and set over against their great prosperity the sudden and fearful reverses and destruction which they not unfrequently encounter. But in turning to the other side of the comparison, the case of the righteous, we are not met by the thought, that as the prosperity of the wicked is but the preparation for their ruin, so the adversity of the godly is but an introduction to worldly wealth and honour. That thought is not foreign to the Old Testament writers (see Psalm xxxvii. 9—11). But it is not so much as hinted at here. The daily chastening may continue, flesh and heart may fail, but God is good to Israel notwithstanding. He is their portion, their guide, their help, while they live, and He will take them to His glorious presence when they die. 'Nevertheless I am continually with Thee,' &c. The New Testament has nothing higher or more spiritual than this."—*Essential Coherence*, &c., pp. 86, 87.

19. This verse, taken in connection with ver. 27, seems almost to point, as Ewald has remarked, to some particular instance of the Divine judgement which had recently been witnessed.

They are come to an end, they are cut off because of
terrors.[r]

20 As a dream when one awaketh,
(So), O Lord, when Thou arousest Thyself,[s] dost Thou
despise their image.

21 For my heart grew bitter,
And I was pricked in my reins ;

22 So brutish was I myself and ignorant,
I became a very beast[t] before Thee.

23 And yet as for me,—I am always with Thee,

20. AS A DREAM, the unreality of which is only seen when a man awakes. Comp. xc. 5 ; Job xx. 8.

The first member of this verse is apparently connected by the LXX., and perhaps by Symm., with what goes before, "they are cut off as a dream," &c.

WHEN THOU AROUSEST THYSELF. The verb in Hebrew is a different one from that in the previous clause, although in the E.V. both are in this passage rendered by the same word. In xxxv. 23, where the two verbs also occur together, our translators have employed two different words to express them, and I have thought it best to do so here. The figure is carried on. When God thus awakes to judgement, the image, the shadow, of the wicked passes from Him as a dream from the mind of a sleeper. He "despises" it, as a man in his waking moments thinks lightly of some horrible dream.

21. FOR. There is no reason to depart from this, the common meaning of the particle. (See Critical Note.) It explains the whole of the previous struggle. I was tempted to think thus, *for* I brooded over these difficulties till I became no better than the dumb cattle. So it ever is. Man does not show wisdom when he wearies himself to no purpose with the moral and speculative problems which beset him. His highest wisdom is to stay himself upon God.

22. SO BRUTISH, lit. "And I myself (the pronoun is emphatic) was brutish." Comp. Prov. xxx. 2, 3.

A VERY BEAST. The noun is in the plural, which is here used in a superlative or emphatic sense (see note on lxviii. 35), so that we need not render "like the beasts," still less "like Behemoth" as though some particular beast were meant.

23. The words that follow, in their exquisite beauty, need not comment or interpretation, but a heart in unison with them. They lift us up above the world, above doubts, and fears, and perplexities into a higher and holier atmosphere: we breathe the air of heaven. The man who can truly use these words is not one who has "crushed free thought," but one who has seen all his doubts swallowed up in the full light of God's Love. "Though all else in heaven and earth should fail, the one true everlasting Friend abides."—*Ewald.*

It strangely mars the force of such a passage to limit its application to this life. To render the words of ver. 24 as Grotius and others do, "Thou shalt receive me with honour" (in allusion to David as placed on the throne), or "bring me to honour," *i.e.* in this world, is to rob the whole passage of its Divine significance. The verb "Thou shalt take me," is the same

Thou hast holden my right hand ;
24 Thou wilt guide me in Thy counsel,
And afterward Thou wilt take me to glory.[u]
25 Whom have I in heaven (but Thee)?
And there is none upon earth in whom I delight beside Thee.
26 (Though) my flesh and my heart fail,
(Yet) God is the rock of my heart and my portion for ever.
27 For behold they that are far from Thee must perish ;
Thou hast destroyed every one that goeth a-whoring from Thee.
28 But as for me, it is good for me to draw near unto God ;
I have made in the Lord Jehovah my refuge,
That I may tell of all Thy works.

as that employed in xlix. 15 (where see note), and Gen. v. 24, to which last passage there is doubtless an allusion in both places in the Psalms. But this Psalm is an advance on Ps. xlix.

The great difference, though with essential points of contact, between the hope of the life to come, as pourtrayed even in such a passage as this, and what we read in the New Testament, will best be understood by comparing the language here with St. Paul's language in the 4th and 5th chapters of the Second Epistle to the Corinthians, and the 1st chapter of the Epistle to the Philippians, ver. 21—23.

THOU HAST HOLDEN ; either implying that thus he had been saved from falling altogether, when his feet were almost gone (ver. 2), or perhaps rather as stating more broadly the ground of his abiding communion with God, at all times and under all circumstances. Comp. lxiii. 8 [9].

24. THOU WILT GUIDE ME. "With confidence he commits himself to the Divine guidance, though he does not see clearly the mystery of the Divine purpose (counsel) in that guidance."—*Delitzsch.* It is because he has forgotten to look to that counsel, and to trust in that counsel, that his faith has received so startling a shack.

TAKE ME TO GLORY. Others, "receive me with glory." (See Critical Note.)

25. BUT THEE, or "beside Thee," lit. "*with* Thee." These words are to be supplied from the next clause, a word or a phrase belonging to two clauses being commonly in Hebrew expressed only in one.

THERE IS NONE, &c., lit. "I have no delight (in any) upon the earth."

26. FAIL, lit. "have failed," *i.e.* "may have failed," the preterite being here used hypothetically.

27. The figure is very common. Israel is the spouse of God, and idolatry is the breaking of the marriage vow. But here it seems to be used, not merely of idolatry, but of departure from God such as that described in ver. 10.

28. At the end of this verse the LXX. add, "in the gates of the daughter of Zion," whence it has passed through the Vulgate, intc our Prayer-Book Version.

[a] See Psalm l. note [a], and General Introduction, vol. i. pp. 94, 97.

[b] אַךְ *surely*, or as it may be rendered, with Mendels. and others, even more pointedly, *nevertheless*. The exact force of the particle here has been best explained by Calvin : "Quod autem abruptum facit exordium, notare operæ pretium est, antequam in hanc vocem erumperet David, inter dubias et pugnantes sententias æstuasse. Nam ut strenuus athleta seipsum exercuerat in pugnis difficillimis : postquam vero diu multumque sudavit, discussis impiis imaginationibus, constituit Deum *tamen* servis suis esse propitium, et salutis eorum fidum esse custodem. Ita subest antithesis inter pravas imaginationes quas suggesserat Satan, et hoc veræ pietatis testimonium quo nunc se confirmat : *acsi malediceret carnis suæ sensui* qui dubitationem admiserat de providentia Dei. Nunc tenemus quam emphatica sit exclamatio . . . quasi ex inferis emergeret, pleno spiritu jactare quam adeptus erat victoriam." This has been seen also by some of the older interpreters (Symmachus, πλήν ; Jerome, *attamen*), as well as by the Rabbinical and other expositors. In like manner we have in Latin writers passages beginning with a *nam* or *at*, where something is implied as already existing in the mind of the writer, though not expressed.

[c] נטוי. "The K'thîbh is part. pass. sing., either absol. with the accus. following, or in the stat. constr. נְטוּי, with the gen., either construction of the part. pass. being admissible. Comp. 2 Sam. xv. 32 with 2 Sam. xiii. 31 ; Ezek. ix. 2 with 11 (Ges. § 132). For this the Q'ri very unnecessarily substitutes 3 pl. perf. נָטָיוּ, but in the full form, which would only be suitable in pause. In the same way the following שפכה, which is no doubt שֻׁפְּכָה, 3 fem. sing., with the plur. noun אֲשֻׁרַי (a not uncommon construction, as in xxxvii. 31, see Ges. § 143, 3), has been just as unnecessarily corrected in the K'ri to שֻׁפְּכוּ. It is, however, possible that the punctuation, רַגְלַי and אֲשֻׁרַי, as plur. depends on the Q'ri of the verbs, and that these words in the K'thîbh are meant to be singular (as xliv. 19, Job xxxi. 7). So Cler., Hasse, and others."—*Hupfeld*.

[d] לְמוֹתָם. This, as it stands, must mean "*for*, or *at*, or *belonging to*, their death," *i.e.* when they die. So the E.V. "in their death," and so the Welsh : "yn eu marwolaeth." But this, it has been said, does not fall in with the general scope of the passage, where not the death but the life of the wicked is described as one that seems enviable. Hence Hupfeld would render, "till their death," and refers to the use of the prep. in Is. vii. 15 to justify this interpretation ; but there לְדַעְתּוֹ means not "*till* he knows," but "*when* he knows," as both Ewald and Knobel take it ; and Drechsler, on the passage, has clearly shown, in opposition to Gesenius, that the prep. לְ is in no instance used to mark duration of time up to a certain point, and therefore never means *until*. Bates, quoted by Horsley, proposed to make of לְמוֹתָם two words, לָמוֹ תָּם, joining לָמוֹ with the first clause, "they have no bonds," and תָּם, as an adjective, with what follows, "*souna* and fat is their body." This has been adopted by Strut, Fry, &c., and by Ewald, who defends this sense of תָּם (which is

nowhere used of physical, but always of moral, soundness), by the use of the noun תֹּם in Job xxi. 23 [Delitzsch refers to the similar use of תָּמִים, xviii. 33, Prov. i. 12, but the first of these seems doubtful]. Mendelssohn supposes למותם to be for לִימוֹתָם, and renders: "Kein Knotten hemmt ihrer Tage Lauf;" the figure being that of the thread of life, which, if it becomes knotted and entangled, is liable to be broken. But retaining the reading of the present Massoretic text, two interpretations are possible: (1) "They have no fetters for their death," which may either mean, if we take *fetters* (as in Is. lviii. 6, the only other passage in which the word occurs) in the literal sense, "they are not delivered over bound to death;" or, if we take it metaphorically, "they have no sufferings, diseases," &c., which bring them to death. So Hulsius: "*Nulla sunt ipsis ligamenta ad mortem eorum, i.e.* nullis calamitatibus, nullis morbis sunt obnoxii; morbi sunt mortis ligamenta quod in mortis potestatem homines conjiciant." And Delitzsch, in his first Edition: "Denn keine Qualen gibts, daran sie stürben." (2) "They have no fetters (*i.e.* troubles, cares, sufferings) in their death." In this case the Psalmist is stating here by anticipation, not his *present* conviction as to the death of the wicked, but the view which he *once* took of it, in a mood of mind which he afterwards discovered to be wrong. So Aq. *οὐκ εἰσὶ δυσπάθειαι τῷ θανάτῳ αὐτῶν.* It is of importance to observe, however, that Symm. and Jerome seem to have had a different reading. The former has: *ὅτι οὐκ ἐνεθυμοῦντο περὶ θανάτου αὐτῶν*, the latter: "*quod non cogitaverint de morte sua.*" Did they read אֵין חֲשָׁבִים? Or did they intend to explain the present text in this sense, "They have no troubles, anxious reflections, &c. with reference to their death?" The Syr. also here, as indeed throughout the Psalm, differs from the Heb. It has ܠܝܬ ܣܘܦܐ, "*there is no end* to their death," the exact meaning of which is not very clear. The rendering of the LXX. is equally obscure: *οὐκ ἔστιν ἀνάνευσις ἐν τῷ θανάτῳ αὐτῶν.* With all this variation in the ancient Versions, they agree in one respect, they all have the word *death.* But for this, I should be disposed to accept the alteration of the text proposed above, as the simplest solution of the difficulty. Delitzsch has now (in his 2d Edit.) accepted this, and renders: Denn keine Qualen leiden sie, gesund und mastig ist ihr Wanst.

e אוּלָם, from the noun אוּל, *strength* (connected with אֱיָלוּת, אֵל, &c., from the root אול), with the suffix, and occurring only here (an alleged plur. form, 2 Kings xxiv. 15, is doubtful). Symm. and others of the ancient interpreters, supposed it to be the noun אוּלָם, meaning *vestibule, portico*, &c., and hence the rendering of Symm., *στερεὰ ἦν τὰ πρόπυλα αὐτῶν*, and Jerome, *vestibula.* The LXX. have *καὶ στερέωμα ἐν τῇ μάστιγι αὐτῶν.* The Syr. ܘܣܓܝܐܐ ܗܝ ܫܛܝܘܬܗܘܢ, "and great is their folly," seems to have read by a confusion of letters וְרַבָּה אִוַּלְתָּם, but the variations of the Syr. in this Ps., as in the 56th, are very numerous.

f עֲנָקַתְמוֹ, a denominative from עֲנָק, *a necklace*, and occurring in the Qal only here.

[g] יַעֲטָף. The second clause of this verse will admit of four renderings: (1) שִׁית may be in constr. with חָמָס (comp. Is. lix. 7), "a clothing of violence," and לָמוֹ, the object of the verb (which is the construction of other verbs of *clothing*, comp. כִּסָּה לְ, Is. ix. 9); (2) שִׁית may be the predicate (which the accent *Rebia Geresh* would indicate), "violence covereth them as a garment;" (3) לָמוֹ may belong to חָמָס, and the object of the verb be understood, "their violence covereth (them) as a garment" [this rendering is most in accordance with the accents]; (4) By an enallage of number, sing. for plur., "they cover (themselves) with their own violence as with a garment." So the LXX. περιεβάλοντο ἀδικίαν, Symm. ὑπερηφανίαν ἠμφιάσαντο, and Jerome, *Circumdederunt sibi iniquitatem.*

[h] עֵינֵמוֹ [or עֵינֵימוֹ, which is found in some MSS. the dual noun being with the sing. verb. Stier, indeed, maintains that this is the only correct form, as ֵמוֹ is not used with a singular noun, but we have אֵינֵימוֹ in ver. 5, which is only a plena scriptio for אֵינֵמוֹ, אַיִן having no plural], lit. "their eye goeth forth (looks out proudly) from fatness (*i.e.* a sleek countenance)." Comp. Job xv. 27. Aq. ἐξῆλθον ἀπὸ στέατος ὀφθαλμοὶ αὐτῶν, and Symm. προέπιπτον ἀπὸ λιπαρότητος (al. ἐξῄεσαν ἀπὸ λίπους) οἱ ὀφθ. αὐτ., take 'עי as plural. Ewald, Hupfeld, and others, following the LXX. ἐξελεύσεται ὡς ἐκ στέατος ἡ ἀδικία αὐτῶν, would read עֲוֹנָמוֹ, "their iniquity," or without changing the word, would take עין here to stand for עון, as in Zech. v. 6, and the Q'ri in Hos. x. 10. (And so the Syr. ܥܘܠܗܘܢ.) They also take חֵלֶב, as in xvii. 10, in the sense of *heart*, or as Ewald renders, *aus feistem Innern*, the word *fatness* denoting *a stupid, insensible heart.* And so Ges. *Thes.* in v.

[i] יָמִיקוּ. The word occurs only here. It is doubtless to be connected with the Aramaic מֵיק, Eng. *mock.* Comp. the Greek, μῦκος, μυκτήρ, *the nose*, as expressing scorn; μυκτηρίζω, &c. So Symm., καταμωκώμενοι, and Jerome, *irriserunt.* The Chald., Rabb., and others, wrongly connected the word with מקק, either (1) trans. "they make to melt, *i.e.* afflict, others;" or as the P. B. V., "they corrupt other;" or (2) "they melt away, *i.e.* they are dissolute, corrupt," &c.

[k] תִּהֲלַךְ, as in Ex. ix. 23, for תֵּלֵךְ, though it looks almost like an abbreviated Hithpael, a form which would be peculiarly suitable here in its common meaning, *grassari.* שַׁתּוּ in the first clause of the verse is for שָׁתוּ, as in xlix. 15, and with the tone on the ult. The perfect, followed by the future, shows that the second clause is subordinated to the first: "*They have set*, &c., *whilst* their tongue goeth," &c. The construction is the same as in ver. 3.

[l] ישיב. If we retain the K'thîbh, we must assume that the sing. is here put for the plur., the subject being virtually the same as that of the plur. verbs in ver. 7, 8, only that now these prosperous sinners are regarded singly, not collectively. "He, *i.e.* one and another of these proud, ungodly men, makes his people (those whom he draws after him) turn hither, *i.e.* copy his example;" or, more generally, "one turns his people," which is equivalent to the passive, "his people are turned." Hence the

Q'ri, according to which עַמּוֹ is the subject, is unnecessary. Phillips, who adopts the Q'ri, refers the suffix to Jehovah. *His* people, *i.e.* the people of God. And so the Chald., and Abulwalid, and the LXX. who have ὁ λαός μου.

m יִמָּצוּ, from the root מצה, *to wring out*, *to drain*. The verb is several times used with שתה, *to drink*, in order to convey the idea of draining to the dregs. So in lxxv. 9, Is. li. 17, Ezek. xxiii. 34. It is used of *wringing* out (*a*) the dew from the fleece, in Judg. vi. 38; (*b*) the blood of the sacrifices, Lev. i. 15, v. 9. Our Version has everywhere employed *wring out* as the equivalent, except in Ezek., where it has *suck out*. Mendelssohn renders :—

> Bethöret folgt ihm das Volk in ganzen Haufen,
> Strömt ihm, wie Wasserfluthen, nach.

In the Biur, "waters to the full" is explained to mean "the waters of a full river, which rush along with strength," and to be used as a figure or comparison; "so the men of their generation run after them;" and יִמָּצוּ is said to be for יִמָּצְאוּ, the א being dropt, as in Num. xi. 11, and Ezek. xxviii. 16. So this word was taken, too, by the older interpreters. The LXX. ἡμέραι (reading יְמֵי) πλήρεις ἐνευρεθήσονται ἐν αὐτοῖς. Sym. καὶ διαδοχὴ πλήρης εὑρεθήσεται ἐν αὐτοῖς. Jerome, *quis* (מִי) *plenus invenietur in eis*.

n אָמַרְתִּי. The word, Hupfeld thinks, is out of place. What is the meaning, he asks, "If I had said (or thought, *i.e.* said to myself) let me declare thus"? Not the forming the purpose to speak so, but the speaking so itself, would have been the treachery against the children of God. And therefore he would transpose the word either before the particle אִם, "I said (thought) if I should declare thus," &c., or to the beginning of ver. 13. See on xxxii. note c. But is it not possible that אָמַרְתִּי may stand parenthetically: "If (methought) I should declare thus"?

o כְּמוֹ. If the reading be correct, this word must here stand as an abverb, in the sense *so, thus* = כֵּן, a meaning, however, in which it never occurs anywhere else. [Maurer, however, contends for this as the primary meaning, כְּ being abbreviated from כֵּן and מוֹ = מָה, indefinite, *quidquam;* hence the compound כְּמוֹ means *tale quid.*] Some would punctuate כָּמוֹ, and suppose it to stand for כָּהֶם, *like them* (the persons mentioned before), or *like these things* (such words as those just repeated), but this form, again, is never found. Ewald would read כְּמוֹהֵנָּה, and supposes the הֵנָּה to have been dropt out because of the following הִנֵּה, and we must either adopt this supposition, or with Ges., Hupf., and Del. conclude that the word כְּמוֹ is here used abnormally as an adverb, as the older interpreters take it. LXX. εἰ ἔλεγον, διηγήσομαι οὕτως. Aq. (perhaps Symm.), Theod., εἰ ἐ. δ. τοιαῦτα. Del. compares the elliptical use of the prep. כְּעַל, Is. lix. 18, and the absolute use in Hos. vii. 16, xi. 7.

p וָאֲחַשְּׁבָה. The punctuation of the ו with Pathach here, instead of Qametz, appears to be arbitrary. Delitzsch, indeed, draws a distinction, and says that with וְ the word would mean *et cogitavi*, whereas with וָ it means *et cogitabam* (or, which would be unsuitable here, *et cogitare volo*). But in other passages where this last form occurs, as lxix. 21; Judg. vi. 9; Job xxx. 26, it is joined either with another verb in the fut., with וְ, or with a verb in the pret., without any mark of difference of time. There is more force in what Del. says as to the cohortative form of the fut., which often serves, without a particle of condition, to introduce the protasis. (See on xlii. note [c].) So here we might render, "And *when* (or *if*) I thought to understand," &c., καὶ εἰ ἐλογιζόμην, as Aq. and Theod.

In the next clause it is unimportant whether we adopt the K'thîbh הִיא, or the Q'ri הוּא. The former may refer more immediately to the preceding זאת, and the latter to the whole preceding sentence, but either must be taken equally in a neuter sense.

[q] מַשּׁוּאוֹת occurs again only in lxxiv. 3. It is related, as Hupf. remarks, to such forms as מְשׁוֹאָה, and the like, but is not to be derived from שׁאה, as if it were for מַשְׁאוּאוֹת, "an impossible form," but from a root נשׁא, with the common interchange of letters in weak stems. (See next note.) The LXX. κατέβαλες αὐτοὺς ἐν τῷ ἐπαρθῆναι, connecting the word with the root נשׁא.

[r] בַּלָּהוֹת. The noun is apparently by transposition of letters for בֶּהָלָה. It occurs once in the sing. in Is. xvii. 14, elsewhere only in Job and Ezekiel, and there always in the plur.

[s] בָּעִיר. So far as the grammatical form goes, this might mean *in the city*, as the ancient interpreters understood (whence our P. B. V., but in defiance of grammar, "Thou shalt make their image vanish *out of the city*"). But the sense is not suitable. The word is evidently a contracted form of the Hiphil infin. for בְּהָעִיר, and is used intransitively, as in xxxv. 23. For other instances of this contracted infin. see Jer. xxxix. 7; 2 Chron. xxxi. 10; Prov. xxiv. 17.

[t] כִּי. According to Hupfeld, this introduces the protasis "*when* my heart," &c., the apodosis beginning with וְ in ver. 22, and the imperfects (futures) being relative preterites. Similarly Ewald. But I know of no instance by which such a construction can be defended. Commonly when כִּי introduces the protasis, followed by a verb in the future, that tense is used in its proper *future* (not its *imperfect*) meaning. Comp. lxxv. 3; 2 Chron. vi. 28. Delitzsch, feeling this, supposes that the Psalmist is speaking, not of the past, but of a possible return of his temptation, and renders, *si exacerbaretur animus meus atque in renibus meis pungerer*, "if my mind should grow bitter, &c. . . . then I should be," &c. But I cannot see why, if כִּי be taken simply as a conjunction, (LXX., Aq., ὅτι) *for*, and not as governing the clause, the verbs may not be regarded as imperfects, describing continued past action. The first verb means, properly, "to turn acid" (lit. "make itself acid"). Flam. *acescere*, Calv. *acidum esse instar fermenti*. Perhaps Aq. meant this by his rendering ἐτυροῦτο. The second is also strictly a reflexive, "to prick

oneself." Both verbs, misunderstood by the ancient interpreters, were first rightly explained by Rashi.

[u] כָּבוֹד ת'. The Hebrew will admit of the rendering, "Thou wilt receive me *with* glory" (accus. of instrument). So the LXX. *μετὰ δόξης προσελάβου με.* Symm. takes 'כ as the nominative, and the verb as in the 3d pers., *καὶ ὕστερον τιμὴ διεδέξατό με.* Contrary to the accents, others would take אַחַר as a prep. (referring to Zech. ii. 12, which is not really analogous): "Thou leadest me *after* glory," *i.e.* as my aim (Ew. Hitz.), or "*in the train of* glory" (Hengst.). But the other interpretation, "*to* glory," *i.e.* "to the everlasting glory of God's presence," is far better. אחר is an adverb, as in Gen. x. 18, xxx. 21, Prov. xx. 17, and many other places. On the use of the verb לקח in this sense, see xlix. 16. The whole context is in favour of the rendering "to glory."

PSALM 74

THIS Psalm and the Seventy-ninth both refer to the same calamity, and were, it may reasonably be conjectured, written by the same author. Both Psalms deplore the rejection of the nation, the occupation of Jerusalem by a foreign army, and the profanation of the Sanctuary: but the Seventy-fourth dwells chiefly on the destruction of the Temple; the Seventy-ninth on the terrible slaughter of the inhabitants of Jerusalem. Assuming that both Psalms refer to the same event, we have to choose between two periods of Jewish history, and only two, to which the language of the sacred Poet could reasonably refer. The description might apply either to the invasion of Nebuchadnezzar, or to the insolent oppression of Antiochus Epiphanes; and with one or other of these two occasions it has been usually connected.

That no presumption can be raised against the latter of these dates from the history of the Canon, I have already shown in the General Introduction to Vol. I. pp. 17—19, and in the Introduction to Ps. xliv.; and there are, more particularly in this Psalm, some expressions which are most readily explained on the supposition that it was composed in the time of the Maccabees.

(*a*) One of these is the complaint (ver. 9), "There is no prophet any more." It is difficult to understand how such a complaint could have been uttered when Jeremiah and Ezekiel were both living; or with what truth it could be added, "Neither is there any among us who knoweth how long," when Jeremiah had distinctly foretold that the duration of the Captivity should be seventy years (Jer. xxv. 11, xxix. 10).* On the other hand, such words are perfectly natural in the mouth of a poet of the Maccabean age. For 250 years, from the death of Malachi, the voice of Prophecy had been silent. During that long interval, no inspired messenger had appeared to declare and to interpret the will of God to His people. And how keenly sensible they were of the greatness of their loss in this respect, we learn from the frequent allusions to it in the First Book of Maccabees (iv. 46, ix. 27, xiv. 41). The language of this Psalm, then, is but the expression of what we know to have been the national feeling at that time.

(*b*) Another feature of this Psalm is the description of the profanation of the Sanctuary, and the erection there of the signs (ver. 4), the military standards or religious emblems, of the heathen. The Book of Maccabees presents the same picture. There we read that Antiochus, on his return from the second Egyptian campaign, "entered proudly into the Sanctuary, and took away the golden altar, and the candlestick of light, and all the vessels thereof" (i. 21). Two years later, the king sent a division of his army against Jerusalem, which fell upon the city and having made a great slaughter of the inhabitants, plundered it, set it on fire, pulled down the houses and walls, and carried away captive women, and children, and cattle. A strong garrison was placed in the city of David, the sanctuary was polluted, and the sabbaths and festival days profaned. The abomination of desolation was set up on the altar, and sacrifice offered "on the idol altar, which was upon the altar of God." (1 Macc. i. 30—53. See also ii. 8—12, iii. 48—51.)

On the other hand it has been urged, that there is nothing in the language of the Psalm inconsistent with the supposition that it refers to the Chaldean invasion. The desolation of Jerusalem and the profanation of the sanctuary are described in terms quite as suitable to that event. Indeed, one part of the description, "They have cast Thy sanctuary into the fire," ver. 7, it is argued, would only hold good of the destruction of the temple of the Chaldeans. Antiochus Epiphanes plundered the temple, but did not burn it. On the contrary, we are particularly informed that not the temple itself, but the gates of the temple (1 Macc. iv. 38; 2 Macc. viii. 33) and the porch of the temple (2 Macc. i. 8), were burned, nor is the

* It has been suggested to me by a friend, that this complaint would not be unsuitable to the time of Esar-haddon's invasion (2 Chron. xxxiii. 11). That period was singularly barren in prophets.

complete destruction of the whole building implied in the same way as it is in the Psalm.

It has also been contended that even the complaint of the cessation of prophecy is not absolutely at variance with the older date, provided we suppose that the Psalm was written during the Exile, when both Jeremiah and Ezekiel had ceased to prophesy, and before Daniel entered upon his office. (So Delitzsch; and Calvin admits this to be possible). Tholuck, however, observes that ver. 10, 18, 23, lead us to infer that the Chaldean army was still in the land, and even in Jerusalem itself, and therefore that the Psalm must have been written when Jeremiah had already been carried away in chains to Ramah, on his way to Babylon (Jer. xl. 1). He suggests further, that these words (and the same may be said of the words which immediately follow, "Neither is there any among us who knoweth," &c.) need not be taken in their exact literal meaning. The deep sorrow of the poet would lead him to paint the picture in colours darker and gloomier than the reality. Seventy years—who could hope to see the end of that weary length of captivity?—who knew if the end would ever come? Such was the language of despondency. To one who refused to be comforted, the end promised was as though it were not.

Further, both Jeremiah and Ezekiel, it has been observed, indulge in a similar strain. Thus the former sings: "Her gates are sunk into the ground; He hath destroyed and broken her bars: her king and her princes are among the Gentiles: the Law is no more; *her prophets also find no vision from Jehovah*" (Lam. ii. 9). And the latter threatens: "Then shall they seek a vision of the prophet: but the law shall perish from the priest, and counsel from the ancients" (Ezek. vii. 26). Neither of these passages, however, so absolutely denies the existence of a prophet as that in the Psalm. One other expression in the Psalm, ver. 3, "Lift up Thy feet to the everlasting ruins," seems, it must be confessed, most suitable in the mouth of an exile during the Babylonish captivity.

The relation both of this Psalm and the Seventy-ninth to the writings of Jeremiah, presents another difficulty. Jeremiah x. 25 is almost word for word the same as Ps. lxxix. 6, 7. Again, Lam. ii. 2 resembles lxxiv. 7, and Lam. ii. 7 is very similar to lxxiv. 4; and, as we have already seen, there is at least a point of connexion between lxxiv. 9 and Lam. ii. 9; besides these, other minor similarities may be observed, on a comparison of the Psalmist with the Prophet. Now we know that it is the habit of Jeremiah to quote largely and frequently from other writers, and in particular from the Psalms and the Prophets. But on either of the hypotheses above mentioned, as to the date of our two Psalms, the writer of these must have imitated the language of Jeremiah. This is, of course, quite possible. A similar problem, and a very interesting one, arises out of the relation of Jeremiah to the later chapters of Isaiah xl.—lxvi. That one of the two writers was familiar with the other, is beyond a doubt.

On the whole, I am inclined to think that this Psalm may be most naturally explained by events that took place in the time of the Maccabees. If, in any particular, the language seems too strong as applied to that time—as, for instance, the description of the burning of the temple—this may be as readily explained by poetic exaggeration, as ver. 9 is so explained by those who hold the opposite view. Or perhaps, as Calvin suggests, the writer, overcome by the mournful spectacle before his eyes, could not but carry back his thoughts to the earlier catastrophe, and thence borrowed some images, blending in his imagination the two calamities in one.

The Psalm does not consist of any regular system of strophes.

It opens with a cry of complaint, and a prayer that God would remember His people in their desolation. Ver. 1—3.

It then pictures the triumph of the enemy, the destruction of the sanctuary, and the loss of Divine counsel in the day of peril. Ver. 4—9.

Then again there is an appeal to God for help (Ver. 10, 11), and a calling to mind of God's past wonders on behalf of His people, and of His Almighty power as seen in the world of Nature. Ver. 12—17.

And finally, based upon this, a prayer that God would not suffer reproach to be brought upon His own Name, by the triumph of the heathen over His people. Ver. 22, 23.

[A MASCHIL OF ASAPH.[a]]

1 O GOD, why hast Thou cast (us) off for ever,
(Why) doth Thine anger smoke against the sheep of Thy pasture?

1. HAST THOU CAST OFF. See note on xliv. 9. The object here may be supplied from the next clause, viz. "the sheep of Thy pasture."

WHY DOTH THINE ANGER SMOKE. For the figure, compare xviii. 8 [9], where see note. There is a change in the tenses, the preterite in the first clause being used to denote *the act* of casting off, the future (present) here to denote the continuance of the same. See on xliv. 9.

SHEEP OF THY PASTURE; a favourite figure in those Psalms which are ascribed to Asaph. (See

2 Remember Thy congregation which Thou hast purchased of old,
Which Thou hast ransomed to be [b] the tribe of Thine inheritance,
(And) the mount Zion wherein Thou hast dwelt.

Introduction, Vol. I. p. 97.) It is found also in Jer. xxiii. 1. The name contains in itself an appeal to the compassion and tender care of the shepherd. Can the shepherd slay his sheep?

2. THOU HAST PURCHASED . . . THOU HAST RANSOMED. Both verbs contain in themselves a reason why God should remember His people. The first verb (*kanah*) may mean only *to get*, *to acquire*, the idea of a price paid for the acquisition being not necessarily contained in the word. So Gen. iv. 1, "I have *gotten* a man with (the help of) Jehovah:" Gen. xiv. 22, "the most High God, *possessor* of heaven and earth;" Prov. viii. 22, "Jehovah *possessed* me in the beginning of His way." And Jerome renders here *possedisti* and the LXX. ἐκτήσω. Exactly analogous is the use of the Greek περιποιεῖσθαι: Acts xx. 28, "The church of God which He purchased (acquired) with His own blood." 1 Tim. iii. 13: "Purchase (acquire) to themselves a good degree." Comp. Eph. i. 14, and 1 Thess. v. 9, where see Vaughan's note. The second verb (*ga-al*, to *ransom*, whence *goël*,) from a root meaning *to loosen* [see Fürst's Concord.], is the technical word for every kind of redemption under the Law, whether of fields (Lev. xxv. 25), tithes (Lev. xxvii. 31, 33), or slaves (Lev. xxv. 48, 49). The next of kin was called Goël, because on him devolved the duty of redeeming land which his poor relation had been compelled to sell (Lev. xxv. 25), and also because on him fell the obligation of redeeming, demanding satisfaction for, the murder of a kinsman. (Num. xxxv. 12, 19, and often.)

A third word is common in Hebrew, *padah*, which means properly *to separate*, and then *to loosen*, and so *to redeem*, as in Deut. ix 26, "Thine inheritance which Thou hast redeemed." This word is also employed, but more rarely, in the technical sense of the redemption of the first-born of animals for instance (Ex. xiii. 13, xxxiv. 20). Both this and the verb *ga-al* are frequently used of the deliverance from Egypt and from Babylon.

OF OLD, as in xliv. 2, with reference, doubtless, to the deliverance from Egyptian bondage.

THE TRIBE. Such is, apparently, the meaning of the word here, the whole nation being regarded, not as many tribes, but as one tribe, probably in reference to other nations. The same expression occurs besides only in Jeremiah x. 16, and li. 19, whereas in Isaiah lxiii. 17 we have the plural form, "*the tribes of Thine inheritance*." The E. V. has here "*rod* of thine inheritance," and so Luther, Calvin, and others, and the word frequently means *rod*, *staff* (as in xxiii. 4), *sceptre* (as in xlv. 6 [7]), &c., but here it is usually explained to mean *measuring-rod*, and so *the portion measured out*—a meaning, however, in which the word never occurs. Jerome explains it by *sceptre*, and so Theophylact, δηλοῖ δὲ ἡ ῥάβδος τὴν βασιλείαν.

The CONGREGATION represents the people in their religious aspect, THE TRIBE in their national and political aspect, or as distinct from other nations (Del.) cf. Jer. x. 16, li. 19, with Is. lxiii. 17. The two great facts, the redemption from Egypt, and God's dwelling in the midst of them, the one of which was preparatory to the other, seem here, as in the Sixty-eighth Psalm, to sum up all their history.

3 Lift up Thy feet unto the everlasting ruins! [c]
The enemy hath laid waste all in the sanctuary;
4 Thine adversaries have roared in the midst of Thine assembly; [d]
They have set up their signs as signs.

3. LIFT UP THY FEET (lit. *footsteps,* the word being a poetical one), *i.e.* "come speedily to visit those ruins which seem as though they would never be repaired." A similar phrase (though the words in the original are different) occurs in Gen. xxix. 1, where it is said of Jacob, that after his vision, "he lifted up his feet," a phrase "which in Eastern language still signifies to walk quickly, to reach out, to be in good earnest, not to hesitate."—Kitto, *Bible Illustrations*, i. 305.

EVERLASTING, the same word as in ver. 1, "for ever," *i.e.* which seem to human impatience, *looking forward*, as if they would never be built again. In Is. lxi. 4, "the everlasting ruins," (where, however, the Hebrew words are different) are so called, *looking back* on the long past continuance of the desolation.

IN THE SANCTUARY. This is his greatest grief. His country has been laid waste with fire and sword, his friends slain or carried into captivity, but there is no thought so full of pain as this, that the holy and beautiful house wherein his fathers worshipt has been plundered and desecrated by a heathen soldiery. Instead of the psalms, and hymns, and sacred anthems which once echoed within those walls, has been heard the brutal shout of the fierce invaders, roaring like lions (such is the meaning of the word in the next verse) over their prey. Heathen emblems, military and religious, have displaced the emblems of Jehovah. The magnificent carved work of the temple, such as the Cherubim, and the palms, and the pillars, with pomegranates and lily-work (1 Kings vi. 15, &c., if the allusion be to the first temple) which adorned it, have been hewed down as remorselessly as a man would cut down so much wood in the forest. And then that splendid pile, so full of sacred memories, so dear to the heart of every true Israelite, has been set on fire, and left to perish in the flames. Such is the scene as it passes again before the eyes of his mind.

4. THINE ASSEMBLY, *i.e.* here evidently "a place of assembly," a word originally applied to the Mosaic tabernacle, and afterwards to the great national festivals. Here it would seem the temple is meant. Comp. Lam. ii. 6, where the word occurs in both senses. "He hath destroyed *His assembly* (or temple; E.V. *His places of assembly*) . . . He hath caused to be forgotten *solemn feast*, and sabbath," &c. It comes from a root signifying to *fix* to *establish*, &c., and hence is used both of a fixed time (see on lxxv. 2) and a fixed place.

THEIR SIGNS. An emphasis lies on the pronoun, comp. ver. 9. I have retained the literal rendering, together with the ambiguity of the original. These were either military ensigns, standards, trophies, and the like (as in Num. ii. 2 ff.), the temple having been turned into a barrack; or, religious emblems, heathen rites and ceremonies, perhaps even idols, by which the temple and altar of Jehovah were profaned. (In this last sense the words would aptly describe the state of things under Antiochus Epiphanes. Comp. 1 Macc. i. 54 and 59, "Now the five-and-twentieth day of the month they did sacrifice upon the idol altar, which was upon the altar of God." Again in chap. iii. 48, it is said that "the heathen had sought to paint the likeness of their images" in the book of the

5 It seems[e] as though one lifted up on high
Axes against the thickets of the wood:
6 And now the carved work thereof[f] altogether
With hatchet and hammers they break down.
7 They have set Thy sanctuary on fire;
They have profaned the dwelling-place of Thy Name
(even) unto the earth.
8 They have said in their heart: "Let us make havoc[g]
of them altogether."
They have burnt up all the houses[h] of God in the land.

Law.) This last sense is further confirmed by the use of the word in ver. 9. But both meanings may be combined, the word *sign* being here used in its most general sense of all symbols of a foreign power of whatever kind. So Geier, "ita ut accipiatur pro indicio potestatis alienæ, quæ est tum politica, tum religiosa : ita namque hostes mutaverant quoque signa priora, quibus tum Dei, tum magistratus proprii jurisdictio ac veneratio designabatur."

5. This verse has been completely misunderstood by our translators, who have here followed Calvin, as well as by nearly all the older interpreters. It does not describe the preparation once made for building the temple, by hewing down cedars in the forest of Lebanon, but it compares the scene of ruin in the interior, the destruction of the carved work, &c., to the wide gap made in some stately forest by the blows of the woodman's axe. See the use of the same figure, Jer. xlvi. 22. Buchanan's paraphrase gives the true meaning :—

Ædis ruentis it fragor :
Quales sub altis murmurant quercus jugis
Cæsæ bipenni quum ruunt.

IT SEEMS, lit. "it is known, makes itself known, appears," &c., as in Gen. xli. 21 ; Ex. xxi. 36, xxxiii. 16. Or possibly, "he, *i.e.* the enemy, makes himself known as one who lifts up," &c.

7. THEY HAVE SET ON FIRE, lit. "They have cast into the fire." Hupfeld compares the German, "in Brand legen, stecken," and the French, "mettre à feu."

THEY HAVE PROFANED . . . UNTO THE EARTH, *i.e.* "by casting it to the earth," as the expression is filled up in the E. V., but in the P. B. V. the English idiom is made to adapt itself to the Hebrew, and this I have followed. We have a similar construction in lxxxix. 39 [40], "Thou hast defiled his crown to the earth," *i.e.* by casting it to the earth. For the fuller expression, on the other hand, see Lam. ii. 2.

8. ALL THE HOUSES OF GOD IN THE LAND, lit. "all the assemblies," which must here mean "places of assembly," as in ver. 4, and Lam. ii. 6. The work of devastation does not stop short with the temple. The plain meaning of the words is that there were many other places for religious worship in the land besides the temple, and that these, as well as the temple, were destroyed. All attempts to get rid of this meaning are utterly futile. It is assumed that this Psalm refers to the Chaldean invasion, and as we hear of no synagogues or legalized holy places before the Exile, therefore it is said the temple must be meant, the plural being here used for the singular. It is quite true

9 Our signs we see not; there is no prophet any more,
Neither is there with us any who knoweth how long.

that we have other plural forms applied to the temple. Thus in xliii. 3, "Thy tabernacles," lxxii. 17, "the sanctuaries of God," the plural being used to denote the several parts, courts, chambers, &c., of the one building. But it is not only the plural word that we have here, but the far wider phrase, "*all* the places of assembly *in the land*." Hupfeld tries to escape from this difficulty by saying that all the previous different names of the sanctuary are finally comprised in one—that one house which may be called "all the houses of God," because it represents and is the substitute for all; and he attempts to defend this by Is. iv. 5, where, however, "every dwelling-place," and "her assemblies," are expressly confined to "Mount Zion." Mendelssohn has a similar explanation, except that he supposes the expression to be used from the point of view of the enemy: "They say in their heart, that by destroying this house, we shall destroy all the assemblies of God together:" Israel having but one sanctuary, while all other nations build houses of assembly for their gods in every city and district. But all this is the merest trifling, and it is surprising that commentators of unquestioned ability should have recourse to such strained interpretations. Such interpretations are unnecessary, even on the assumption that this Psalm refers to the Chaldean invasion. Before that time synagogues are not mentioned, it is true, nor indeed are they in the Books of the Maccabees; still it is scarcely credible that even before the Exile there were no houses of God, no places for religious worship, except the temple in Jerusalem. Without holding, as Vitringa surmised and as others have thought, that sacred places, such as those consecrated by the patriarchs and others, in earlier times—Ramah, Bethel, Gilgal, Shiloh—are meant, or "the high places" (see 2 Chr. xxxiii. 17; comp. 1 Kings xviii. 30, from which it appears that in [? before] Elijah's time there was an altar of Jehovah on Mount Carmel), there must have been buildings where it was customary to meet, especially on the Sabbath (which in Lev. xxiii. 3 is called "an holy convocation'), and to pray, turning towards Jerusalem. There must surely have been some public worship beyond the limits of the family, and if so, places, houses, for its celebration. If, however, the Psalm be of the age of the Maccabees, there is no difficulty, for before that time, there can be little doubt, synagogues were established. Our translators would seem, by their rendering "synagogues," to have regarded this as a Maccabean Psalm. See more in Critical Note.

9. OUR SIGNS, *i.e.* the sign of God's dominion and presence in the midst of us. Taken in connexion with what immediately follows, "There is no prophet," &c., these may mean miraculous signs, in which sense the word frequently occurs. Or it may only denote here religious emblems, which were displaced to make room for the signs of the heathen. See ver. 4.

NO PROPHET. Such a complaint seems most suitable to the time of the Maccabees, when, in fact, the complaint was frequent. See Introduction to the Psalm.

Stier draws attention to the emphatic way in which the lament here closes: no signs—religion destroyed and rooted out: no prophet —to announce approaching consolation, or to begin the work of restoration; none of us all therefore knows how long this sad state of things shall last. The latter expression refers, not to the prophet (as Hupfeld), but to the mass of the people.

10 How long, O God, shall the adversary reproach?
Shall the enemy despise Thy name for ever?
11 Why withdrawest Thou Thy hand, even Thy right hand?
(Pluck it out) from the midst of Thy bosom, consume
(them)!
12 Surely God is my King of old,
Working deliverances in the midst of the earth;
13 THOU didst divide the sea through Thy strength,
Thou brakest the heads of the monsters upon the
waters.

10. Taking up that word, How long? the Psalmist turns with it to God, beseeching Him not to suffer this reproach to be cast upon His Name. Twice the same appeal is made, see verses 18 and 22. This holy jealousy for the honour of God, as bound up with His people's deliverance, is characteristic of the Old Testament. The feeling is strikingly exemplified in the prayers of Moses, Ex. xxxii. 12, 13; Num. xiv. 13—16; Deut. ix. 28, comp. xxxii. 27.

11. WHY WITHDRAWEST THOU, lit. "Why makest Thou to return," *i.e.* into Thy bosom. See Ex. iv. 7, where the full expression occurs: it denotes, of course, a state of inactivity, the hand being enveloped in the ample folds of the Eastern robe.

(PLUCK IT OUT.) It seems necessary to supply the ellipse in this way. The construction is a pregnant one, similar to that which we have already had in ver. 7. For the absolute use of the verb, CONSUME, comp. lix. 13 [14]. It may either be rendered as above, or perhaps as Meyer, Stier, and others, "Make an end," *i.e.* of this state of things.

12. SURELY, or, "and yet," in spite of this seeming inactivity. The appeal rests, first, on the fact that God has already manifested His power in signal instances on behalf of His people, and next, on the dominion of God as Creator and absolute Ruler of the universe.

MY KING, expressive of the strong personal feeling of the Psalmist. See note on xliv. 4, and comp. Hab. i. 12, where in like manner the Prophet claims his own covenant relation to God, whilst speaking as the representative of the people, "Art Thou not for everlasting, O Jehovah my God, my Holy one?—we shall not die."

13—15. Special instances of God's wonder-working power in the passage of the Red Sea, in bringing water from the rock, and in the passage of the Jordan.

13. THE MONSTERS. (Symmachus, τῶν κητῶν, the *whales*). A symbolical description of the Egyptians. Comp. Is. li. 9, and Ezek. xxix. 3, where Pharaoh is called the "monster which is in the sea." The E.V. has in all these places, "dragon" as the equivalent word. Here the LXX. have δράκων, to express both this word and *Leviathan* in the next clause. The same Hebrew word, *tannin*, is employed again cxlviii. 7, and also Gen. i. 21 (where it is rendered *whales*), to denote huge sea-monsters, lit. creatures *extended*, *stretched out*, hence serpents, crocodiles, &c. Perhaps the crocodile (as in the next verse *Leviathan*) is meant here as emblematic of Egypt. The head of the monster has been smitten, and the huge unwieldy carcase lies floating on the waters.

The plural HEADS has been sup-

14 THOU didst crush the heads of Leviathan,
That Thou mightest give him as food to the people
inhabiting the wilderness.[i]
15 THOU didst cleave fountain and brook ;
THOU driedst up everflowing rivers.
16 Thine is the day, Thine also is the night,
THOU hast established the light and the sun.
17 THOU hast set all the borders of the earth:

posed to refer to Pharaoh and his princes, as in next ver., but it may be only poetic amplification.

14. LEVIATHAN, *i.e.* the crocodile, as in Job xl. 25 (xli. 1. E. V.). In what sense is this said to be given as food to the people inhabiting the wilderness? Bochart, who is followed by Hengstenberg and others, supposes that the allusion is to the Ichthyophagi who, according to Agatherides, fed on the sea-monsters which were thrown up on their shores. Comp. Herod. ii. 69. Similarly, the LXX. render λαοῖς τοῖς Αἰθίοψι. Others, again, think that by the people inhabiting the wilderness are meant the Israelites, to whom the Egyptians, are said, figuratively, to be given as food, *i.e.* as plunder. But by far the simplest way is to understand the passage as meaning that the corpses of the Egyptians were cast upon the shore, and so became the prey of the wild beast, which are here called a *people* inhabiting the wilderness, as in Prov. xxx. 25, 26, the ants and the conies are called "a people." Comp. also Joel i. 6, Zeph. ii. 14.

INHABITING THE WILDERNESS. On this word see on lxxii. note.[b]

15. THOU DIDST CLEAVE FOUNTAIN, &c. Another instance of a pregnant construction : for "Thou didst cleave the rock, whence fountain and brook issued forth." Comp. lxxviii. 15 ; Hab. iii. 9. The reference, is, no doubt, to Exod. xvii. 6.

THOU DRIEDST UP. The same word is used, Josh. ii. 10, of the Red Sea, and iv. 23, v. 1, of the Jordan.

EVERFLOWING RIVERS, literally "streams of constant flow." The same word occurs in Exod. xiv. 27, "The sea returned to its *constant flow*, its usual current." See also Deut. xxi 4 ; Amos v. 24. Here the Jordan is meant, the plural being used, not to denote the several streams by which it is fed (as Qimchi), but merely by way of poetic amplification. Aq. ποταμοὺς στερεούς. Sym. π. ἀρχαίους.

16. From the wonders wrought by God on behalf of His people in their history, the Poet rises to the wider view of His ever-continued, ever-displayed power and majesty in the world of nature. The miracle does not lead him to forget God's power and goodness in that which is not miraculous. The one is rather a witness to, and an instance of, the other.

LIGHT, or rather "luminary," corresponding to the Greek φωστήρ (which Aquila employs here). It is the same word which occurs in Gen. i. 14, 16, and is there rendered "lights.". The singular is used collectively for the plural, all the heavenly bodies being meant, and then of these the sun is named as chief. In the same way we have, as Hupfeld remarks, Judah and Jerusalem, Ephraim and Samaria, and so the Greeks say, Ἕλληνές τε καὶ Ἀθηναῖοι, and the like.

17. THE BORDERS OF THE EARTH, *i.e.* not those merely by which the land is divided from the sea (Gen. i. 9, comp. Prov. viii. 29 ;

Thou hast formed summer and winter.
18 Remember this, how the enemy hath reproached Jehovah,
And how a foolish people have despised Thy Name.
19 O give not the soul of Thy turtle-dove to the wild beast,[k]
The life of Thine afflicted forget not for ever.
20 Look upon the covenant,
For the dark places of the land are full of the habitations of violence.
21 O let not the oppressed turn back confounded,

Job xxxviii. 8, &c.), but all the boundary lines by which order is preserved, as those of the seasons, those of the nations, Deut. xxxii. 8 ; Acts xvii. 26, &c.

SUMMER AND WINTER, as before, DAY AND NIGHT, as marking the everlasting order of the world, and perhaps with reference to Gen. viii. 22. The literal rendering is, "Summer and winter—Thou has formed them." This verb is used of the fashioning of men and the animals, Gen. ii. 7, 19, from the dust, and here it is applied to the seasons, as in Is. xlv. 7, to "the light and the darkness," as creatures of God's hand.

18. REMEMBER. The petition recurs (comp. ver. 2) with renewed force after the Psalmist has comforted himself with the recollection of God's Almighty Power, as both ruling the history of Israel, and giving laws to the material universe.

A FOOLISH PEOPLE, *i.e.* the heathen oppressors of Israel, whether Chaldean or Syrian. In ver. 22, again, we have the same word, "the foolish (man)." There the Targum has, "a foolish king," which has been supposed to mean Antiochus Epiphanes, though it might of course refer to Nebuchadnezzar. The same Chaldee word (טַפְּשָׁא *tiphsha*) is in the Targum on Deut. xxxii. 21 the equivalent of the same Hebrew word, where again the reference is to a heathen nation employed as the instrument of Israel's chastisement. In Lev. xxvi. 41, it is equivalent to the Hebrew *uncircumcised.* In Ecclus. l. 26, the Samaritans are called "that foolish people."

20. LOOK UPON THE COVENANT. The appeal lies to that, not to anything in the Psalmist himself, or in his people. "This," says Tholuck, "is the everlasting refuge of the saints of God, even in the greatest dangers. And even if they have broken it, can the unbelief of men make the truth of God of none effect?" The covenant is that made first with Abraham, and then renewed with him and with the fathers. Comp. lxxviii. 10; Is. lxiv. 8.

THE DARK PLACES, or, "darknesses." The word occurs elsewhere of the darkness of the grave, lxxxviii. 6 [7], cxliii. 3 ; Lam. iii. 6, and hence it may be used here in a figurative sense, merely as expressing, generally, *misery, gloom,* &c., or as Delitzsch explains (who understands the Psalm of the Chaldean invasion), "Turn where we may, the darkened land is full of abodes of tyranny and oppression." It seems most probable, however, that those spots are meant which were the best fitted for scenes of violence and murder—the haunts of robbers, who there lay in wait for their victims. The banditti would speedily become numerous in a country where law and order were at an end. Com. x. 8.

21. THE OPPRESSED, lit. "the crushed :" TURN BACK, as in vi. 10 [11], or, perhaps, simply "re-

Let the afflicted and the poor praise Thy name!
22 Arise, O God, plead Thine own cause;
Remember how the foolish man reproacheth Thee all the day long.
23 Forget not the voice of Thine adversaries,
The tumult of them that rise against Thee which goeth up for ever.

turn" (the usual meaning of the verb), *i.e.* from his approach and entreaty to Thee.

22. REMEMBER HOW, &c.: lit. "Remember Thy reproach from a foolish man all the day." See note on ver. 18.

23. GOETH UP, *i.e.* which ascends to heaven, crying aloud for vengeance.

[a] On Maschil, see above on xxxii. note [a], and General Introduction, Vol. I. p. 86; on Asaph, see l. note [a], and General Introduction, Vol. I. p. 97.

[b] שֵׁבֶט נח׳. These words seem to be a predicate, the relative being supplied before גָּאַלְתָּ. So Ewald: "Hast erlöst zum Stamme," &c. Mendelss. renders somewhat differently, as if שֵׁבֶט depended on זְכֹר, and נח׳ were the predicate: "(Denke), Des Stammes, dir zum Eigenthum, befrei't." But in the Biur, the explanation of Ibn Ezra is quoted: "to be a tribe on the mountain of Thine inheritance," which is substantially the same view of the construction as that I have given. Delitzsch (1st Edit.) takes this clause as parenthetical, and says that the relative form of expression is here given up, though the next clause depends on זְכֹר, but in his 2d Edit. renders as in text.

[c] מַשּׁוּאוֹת. On the form and derivation of this word see on lxxiii. note [q].

[d] מוֹעֲדֶךָ. A large number of MSS. and editions have the plur. מוֹעֲדֶיךָ, as in ver. 8. The Chald., Qimchi, and others, have also adopted it, and it is in itself admissible, even if the temple be meant. See note on ver. 8.

[e] יִוָּדַע. *It is known*, and so *it appears*, see note on ver. 5. This word puzzled all the ancient interpreters. The Chald. omits it altogether, but gives the true sense of the passage, which all the others have missed. As regards the construction, either this and the next verse describe, as in a parenthesis, the scene of destruction, and hence the verbs are *presents*, giving more vividness to the narration; or perhaps the two verses may be taken as protasis and apodosis. *As . . . so now* (וְעַתָּה). כְּמֵבִיא, lit. *as one causing to come in*, or perhaps *as one bringing*. So Ges. *Thes. in v.* בוא, comp. Job xii. 6. In סְבָךְ, the vowel is Qametz, not Qametz-Khatuph, as Sol. Yedidyah of Norcia calls it. Comp. כְּתָב־הַדָּת, Esth. iv. 8.

[f] פִּתּוּחֶיהָ, *carved wood-work*, as in 1 Kings vi. 29. The fem. suff. cannot refer immediately to any of the preceding nouns. It seems to be

used here as a neut., in an indefinite sense, referring generally to the "sanctuary" and "assembly" mentioned before.

[g] נִינָם. Qimchi first rightly explained this as 1 plur. fut. Qal. of ינה (elsewhere, except in the Part., occurring only in Hiph.), with suff. ◌ָם, instead of ◌ֵם, as נִירָם, Num. xxi. 30.

[h] מוֹעֲדֵי־אֵל. The word מוֹעֵד, as has been remarked, may be used either of a fixed *place* of meeting (hence the Tabernacle was called אֹהֶל מ׳, *tent of meeting*, *i.e.* where God met the people) or of a fixed *time*, and so of the festivals, as in Lev. xxiii. 2, 4, 37. The ancient interpreters were divided as to the signification here. Aq. has ἐνέπρησαν πάσας τὰς συναγωγάς. On the other hand, Sym. πάσας τὰς συνταγὰς τοῦ Θεοῦ. Theod. πάντας καιρούς. And the LXX., who put the words into the mouth of the enemy, render, δεῦτε, καταπαύσωμεν (πάσας) τὰς ἑορτὰς τοῦ Κυρίου ἀπὸ τῆς γῆς. The sixth translator in the Hexapla (Montf.) has κατακαύσωμεν, which may have been the original reading of the LXX., as Jerome (in his Ep. to Sunnia and Fretela) contends. It might easily have been altered to avoid the awkwardness of saying, "Let us *burn up* all the *feasts*." Jerome translates the LXX. *Quiescere faciamus omnes dies festos Dei in terra;* but his own rendering of the Hebrew is *Incenderunt omnes solennitates Dei in terra.*

[i] לְעָם לְצִיִּים. This is grammatically indefensible. If the two nouns are in apposition, then the first cannot be in the stat. constr. It must be לְעָם. But more probably the second ל has been inserted by mistake before צִיִּים. See a similar instance in Is. xxxii. 1. The LXX. λαοῖς τοῖς Αἰθίοψιν. Aq. τοῖς ἐξελευσομένοις. Theod. (λαῷ) τῷ ἐσχάτῳ. E′ (λαῷ) τῷ ἐξεληλυθότι.

[k] לְחַיַּת. According to the accents, this word is not to be joined with what follows; hence many regard it as the constr. state put for the absol. But there is no instance of such usage. Others would supply שָׂדֶה or some such word, *beast of* (*the field*). It is better to regard it as an instance of a feminine noun terminating in its absolute state, in *-ath* instead of *-âh*. See on lxi. note [a], and Qimchi's remark there quoted. It is, then, doubtful whether we should take חַיַּת in the sense of *wild beasts*, or in the sense of *host* (sc. of enemies). Delitzsch contends that the latter is required, because in the very next clause it occurs in this sense, "*the congregation* or *host* of Thine afflicted." Comp. lxviii. 10 [11], and note there.

Others would connect לְחַיַּת נֶפֶשׁ together, taking נֶפֶשׁ in the sense of *eagerness*, as in xvii. 9 (where see note). Hence ל׳ נ׳ would either mean *to the eager host* (sc. of enemies)—so Ges., Maur., and others—or, *to the eager* (fierce, devouring) *wild beast.*

Hupfeld thinks the difficulty at once got over by the simple remedy of transposition, אַל תִּתֵּן לְנֶפֶשׁ חַיַּת ת׳, "Give not to rage (to the fierce will of the enemy) *the life* of Thy turtle-dove." He tries to defend this absolute use of נֶפֶשׁ in the sense of *fierce desire*, by reference to xxvii. 12, xli. 2 [3], where the word, however, occurs with a genitive ("will of mine enemies"), which he thinks may be supplied here from the context. In the next clause he keeps the same meaning of 'ח, "*the life* of Thine afflicted."

None of these explanations is satisfactory, though there can be no doubt as to the general sense of the passage. All the ancient Versions have misunderstood תּוֹרֶךָ. The Chald. either read תּוֹרָתֶךָ, as it paraphrases, "the souls of them that teach Thy Law," or perhaps gave this as a midrashic interpretation. Sym. (ψυχὴν) ἣν ἐδίδαξας τὸν νόμον. Jerome, *animam eruditam lege tua*. Others, apparently, as the LXX., Syr., Arab., and Ethiop., read תּוֹדָךְ, "the soul (which) confesseth, or giveth thanks, to Thee." All agree in rendering the first part of the sentence alike, "Give not to the wild beasts," except the Syr., which has ܠܡܘܬܐ, 'ne des *fractioni*" (Dathe); but why not *prædæ?* as in Is. v. 29. Does not this point to a reading הַוָּה or הַוּוֹת, and may not the copyist have fallen into the error by his eye catching חַ in the next line?

PSALM 75

THE Psalm celebrates in prophetic strain the righteous judgement of God. The voice of God Himself from heaven declares His righteousness, announces to the world that He is not, as human impatience has ever been wont to deem, regardless of wrong and suffering, but that He only waits for the moment which to His infinite wisdom seems best, that He may chastise the insolence of evildoers.

There are no clearly marked historical allusions in the Psalm. It seems, however, not improbable, as has been conjectured by many commentators (Ewald, Tholuck, Delitzsch, &c.), that it may refer to the time of the Assyrian invasion, either as celebrating, or immediately anticipating, the defeat of Sennacherib. Like Ps. xlvi. it bears some resemblance to the prophecies of Isaiah uttered at that time. But there is, as Ewald has observed, a difference in the manner in which the Prophet and the Psalmist treats his subject. The Prophet adds thought to thought and scene to scene; he expands, enlarges upon, diversifies his theme. He sees in this one act of righteous judgement the prelude to many others. He threatens not the Assyrian only, but other nations who lift themselves up. The Poet, on the other hand, seizes upon the one truth, the single thought of God's righteous judgement as manifested in this instance, and strives to present it to others with the same force and vividness with which it has filled his own mind. He too is a Prophet, a Prophet who has heard the word of God (ver. 2, &c.) and seen the vision of the Most High, but a Prophet, as it were, under narrower conditions and for a more limited purpose.

The close resemblance between many of the expressions in this Psalm and parts of the song of Hannah in 1 Sam. ii. is very noticeable.

The Psalm opens with the ascription of praise which God's wonders now and in all past time have called forth, ver. 1.

It passes then to the prophetic announcement of the truth which has been uttered from heaven and echoed with triumph upon earth, of God's righteous judgement, ver. 2—8.

Finally, it concludes with a determination to publish the praise of Jehovah for ever, whilst the same prophetic strain of triumph is heard, as in one last echo, repeating itself, ver. 9, 10.

[FOR THE PRECENTOR. (TO THE MELODY) "DESTROY NOT."[a] A PSALM OF ASAPH, A SONG.]

1 WE give thanks to Thee, O God, we give thanks;
And (that) Thy name is near Thy wondrous works have told.

Ver. 1, 2. The connexion between these verses is not, at first sight, very obvious. It may, perhaps, be traced as follows. First, the Psalmist blends in one the past and the present. God has been, and is now, the object of Israel's praise; as He has both in the past and in the present displayed His wonders on their behalf. (Hence the use of the perfect tense lit. "We have given thanks," &c.) Then he abruptly cites the words of God, words whose fulfilment he had just witnessed, or whose approaching fulfilment he saw in the spirit of prophecy; words that were themselves an exemplification of the truth that God is near, despite the madness of men and the disorders of the world.

AND (THAT) THY NAME IS NEAR. The construction of this member of the verse is doubtful. It may be rendered in two separate clauses: "And Thy Name is near: they (*i.e.* men, or our fathers, as in xliv. 1, [2], lxxviii. 3) have told of Thy wonders" (so Ewald). But it is, perhaps, better to connect the two clauses, as our translators have done. Luther and Mendelssohn, and, more recently, Hupfeld and Bunsen, have taken the same view.

THY NAME IS NEAR, not "near in our mouth," *i.e.* as the great object of praise (as Hengstenberg and others explain it, referring to Jer. xii. 2, a passage which is totally different), but near in presence, near in self-manifestation, near in love and power, near in succour and

2 "When the set time is come,
I myself will judge uprightly.
3 (Though) the earth and all the inhabitants thereof are melting,
I myself have set up the pillars of it. [Selah.]

blessing. So in Deut. iv. 7, "What nation is there that hath God so *near* unto them?" Comp. xlviii. lxxvi. l., "His name is great in Israel," and see xxxiv. 18 [19], cxlv. 18, and the note on xx. 2.

2. God is abruptly introduced as the speaker, as in xlvi. 10 [11]. The oracle is thus given as from the mouth of God Himself, to those who may be in doubt or perplexity because their lot is cast in troublous times.

WHEN THE SET TIME IS COME, lit. "When I shall have taken (reached) the set time," *i.e.* the time appointed in the Divine counsels. The thread of time is ever running, as it were, from the spindle, but at the critical moment God's hand arrests it. (For this strong sense of the verb *take*, see xviii. 16 [17] and comp. καιρὸς δεκτός, εὐπρόσδεκτος of 2 Cor. vi. 2.) God is ever the righteous Judge, but He executes His sentence, not according to man's impatient expectations, but at the exact instant which He has Himself chosen. The words are an answer to all such misgivings as those in lxxiii. 3, as well as a rebuke to all hasty and over-zealous reformers, who would pull up the tares with the wheat rather than wait for the harvest.

SET TIME. The Hebrew word (*mo'ed*) has also the signification *assembly*, *congregation*, which our translators have adopted here, and which is common in the phrase "tabernacle of the *congregation*," &c. The root-idea is that of something *fixed*, whether time or place (and hence persons gathered in a place). See note on lxxiv. 4. The former sense is clearly preferable here. Comp. cii. 13 [14] (where the E.V. has correctly "set time" instead of "congregation" as here); Hab. ii. 3, "the appointed time," *i.e.* for the accomplishment of the vision. And so also Dan. viii. 19, xi. 27, 35. The proper rendering is given by the LXX. ὅταν λάβω καιρόν. Jerome and the Vulgate, *cum accepero tempus*. Symmachus, apparently, led the way with the other interpretation, ὅταν λάβω τὴν συναγωγήν. The "congregation" would, of course, mean all who are assembled to behold the solemn act of judgement, as in vii. 7 [8], l. 5.

I MYSELF. The pronoun is emphatic. The Greek Version known as the Fifth renders it still more emphatically: "I am; I prepared the pillars thereof for ever" (ἐγὼ εἰμὶ, ἡτοίμασα τοὺς στύλους αὐτῆς ἀεί). The same prominence is given to the pronoun in the second member of the next verse.

3. Such a critical moment is the present. The world itself seems "utterly broken down and clean dissolved" (Is. xxiv. 19, 20), but He who once built it up like a stately palace, still stays its pillars with His hand. The natural framework and the moral framework are here identified. To the poet's eye, the world of nature and the world of man are not two, but one. The words of Hannah's song (1 Sam. ii. 8) furnish an exact parallel. "For the pillars of the earth are Jehovah's, and He hath set the world upon them,"—language which, as the context shows, has a moral application.

HAVE SET UP, lit. "poised, balanced." A word properly used of fixing a thing by weight or measure. Comp. Job xxviii. 25; Is. xl. 12, 13.

4 I said unto the arrogant, Deal not arrogantly;
And to the wicked, Lift not up the horn,
5 Lift not up your horn on high,
Speak (not) with a stiff neck." [b]
6 For not from the East, and not from the West,
And not from the wilderness (cometh) lifting up.[c]
7 No, God is Judge;
He putteth down one, and lifteth up another.
8 For there is a cup in the hand of Jehovah.

4. I SAID. Ewald and others suppose the Divine utterance to end with the previous verse. This is possible; for the Poet, speaking as a Prophet, may thus triumph in the revelation which has just been made, and turn it into a defiance of the proud. At the same time, as there is no indication of any change of speaker, it is better to regard this and the next verse as a continuation of the Divine oracle.

UNTO THE ARROGANT, &c., or "Unto the madmen, Deal not madly," — the same words as in lxxiii. 3, where see references.

5. WITH A STIFF NECK. Here, again, there is evidently an allusion to the words of Hannah's song. 1 Sam. ii. 3.

6. FOR. The Poet himself speaks, taking up and applying to himself and to others the Divine sentence which he had just been commissioned to deliver. Glory and power come not from any earthly source, though a man should seek it in every quarter of the globe, but only from God, who lifteth up and casteth down, according to His own righteous sentence. Again, an allusion to 1 Sam. ii. 6.

FROM THE WILDERNESS, *i.e.* the South, the great wilderness lying in that direction. Thus three quarters are mentioned, the North only being omitted. This may be accounted for, supposing the Psalm to refer to Sennacherib, by the fact that the Assyrian army approached from the North; and therefore it would be natural to look in all directions but that for assistance to repel the invader.

LIFTING UP. The word is evidently an emphatic word in the Psalm; it is the same which occurs in ver. 4 and 5, and again in ver. 7 and ver. 10. I have, therefore, given the same rendering of it throughout. The rendering of the E. V. "promotion," besides losing sight of the manifestly designed repetition of the same word, is peculiarly unfortunate in conveying a wrong idea. "Lifting up," in its Hebrew sense, does not mean "promotion," as we commonly understand it, but deliverance from trouble; safety; victory. The image, in particular, of lifting up the head or the horn (the last, borrowed from wild beasts, such as buffaloes, &c., in which the horn is the symbol of strength), denotes courage, strength, victory over enemies. See iii. 3 [4], xviii. 2 [3], xxvii. 6. For other interpretations of this verse, see Critical Note.

8. The solemn act of judgement. God puts the cup of His wrath to the lips of the wicked, and holds it there till they have drained it to the uttermost. It is the same figure which we have already had in lx. 3 [5]. In the Prophets it occurs frequently. Is. li. 17—23 (comp. xix. 14); Hab. ii. 15, 16; Ezek. xxiii. 32, &c.; Jerem. xxv. 27; xlviii. 26; xlix. 12; and, in the form of a symbolical action, xxv. 15; Obad. i. 16, &c.

And the wine foameth,[d] it is full of mixture;
And He poureth out of the same:
Surely the dregs thereof, all the wicked of the earth
Shall drain (them) out in drinking (them).
9 But as for me, I will declare for ever,
I will sing praises to the God of Jacob.
10 And all the horns of the wicked will I cut off,
(But) the horns of the righteous shall be lifted up.

FOAMETH, *i.e.* as it is poured into the cup from the wine-jar, as is expressed in the next member of the verse.

MIXTURE, *i.e.* the aromatic herbs, &c., which were put into the wine to make it more intoxicating. See the article WINE in Smith's *Dict. of the Bible*.

POURETH OUT, *i.e.* from the wine-jar into the cup.

OF THE SAME, the wine; the DREGS THEREOF are the dregs of the cup. (See Critical Note.)

9. BUT AS FOR ME—placing himself and the congregation of Israel in opposition to the proud oppressors — I will be the everlasting herald of this great and memorable act. This is the true *Non omnis moriar*.

10. Triumphantly in this last verse he claims, for himself and for the Church, a share in the signal act of deliverance. That which God threatens (ver. 4, 5), He accomplishes by the hand of His servants. Every horn of worldly power must fall before Him. Comp. Rev. ii. 26, 27.

Ewald sees an emphasis in the word *all*, repeated ver. 8 and here. The punishment is, as yet, only begun. Some only have drunk of that deadly wine, but the cup is large, and *all* the wicked must drain it.

[a] See above on l. note [a]; lvii. note [a], and General Introduction, Vol. I. pp. 89, 97.

[b] עָתָק. Delitzsch and others take this, not as an adj. qualifying the preceding noun, but as immediately dependent on the verb of speaking, which is, in fact, its usual construction. So in 1 Sam. ii. 3; Ps. xxxi. 19, xciv. 4. In this case בְּצַוָּאר must be taken absolutely; "with the neck," meaning "with a proud stiff neck," a mode of expression which it is supposed may be defended by Job xv. 26, "he runneth against Him with the neck," where, however, as Hupfeld remarks, the phrase seems only equivalent to our expression "with the head."

[c] מִמִּדְבַּר הָרִים. This reading is supported by most of the MSS. and Edd., and can only be translated from "the wilderness of the mountains" (Sym. ἀπὸ ἐρήμου ὀρέων. LXX. ἀπὸ ἐρήμων ὀρέων), which is usually explained to mean the Arabian desert, so called because it is walled in by the mountains of Idumea. "The desert of the mountains" is, then, a mode of describing the South, and, according to Hengst., the allusion is to Egypt, as the great Southern power which was the hope of Israel in the Assyrian invasion. According to this reading, there is an aposiopesis. Not from the East, &c., and not from the wilderness of mountains—

[cometh judgement (Hengst.) or lifting up (Del.)]. But it is far better to read, מִמִּדְבָּר (absol. instead of constr.) and to take הָרִים as the Hiph. Inf. used as a noun, *lifting up*, like הָבִין, xxxii. 9. Qimchi testifies that in his time (end of the 12th and beginning of the 13th century) this was the reading of the best MSS. (it is still found in several), and the Midrash expressly says that *harim* means *harim* (*i.e.* mountains) everywhere but in this passage. The whole scope of the Psalm, where so much is said of "lifting up," confirms this view. Ewald also adopts the reading מִדְבָּר, but supplies the copula before הָרִים, which he takes in its usual signification "mountains," *i.e.* Lebanon, &c. as descriptive of the North. Thus he completes the four quarters, as the Chald. has done also, only inverting the order and understanding the North by the desert and the South by the mountains.

[d] יַיִן חָמַר. It seems doubtful whether יַיִן is here accusat. or nominat. So far as the constr. is concerned, it may be the former: "It (*i.e.* the cup) foameth with wine." The objection to this is that the verb is in the masc., whereas כּוֹס is, in almost every instance, fem., and the suffix in שְׁמָרֶיהָ would seem to show that it is fem. here. To this Hupf. replies: (1) that in Jer. xxv. 15, כּוֹס is masc. (and therefore a noun of common gender), and (2) that the fem. suffix here refers to מֶסֶךְ and not to כּוֹס.

The LXX. (*ποτήριον*) . . . *οἴνου ἀκράτου πλῆρες κεράσματος*. Sym. *καὶ οἶνος ἄκρατος πληρῶν ἐκχυθείς*.

מָלֵא is a verb followed by the accus. See lxv. 10.

PSALM 76

THIS is one of several Psalms which, as has been remarked in the Introduction to Psalm xlvi., were composed in celebration of the miraculous overthrow of Sennacherib's army. From the days of Israel's first occupation of the land, when God went forth with their hosts, giving the victory by signs and wonders from heaven, no deliverance so signal had been witnessed. Hence it roused in an extraordinary degree the religious fervour of the nation, and called forth loud songs of thanksgiving. Like Psalms xlvi., xlvii., xlviii., this is an ode of victory over the Assyrians. It tells of Zion's glory and Zion's safety (to which there may be an allusion in the name *Salem*), because God has chosen it for His dwelling-place. It tells of the discomfiture of that proud army, whose might was weakness itself when arrayed against the might of Jehovah. It tells how the warriors sank into their last sleep before the walls of the city, not beaten down before a human enemy, not slain by any earthly arm, but at the rebuke of the God of Jacob. And then the Poet looks beyond the immediate scene. He beholds in this great deliverance, not the power only, but the righteousness of God. It is God's solemn act of judgement. It is His voice speaking from Heaven and filling the earth. And the lesson which this act of judgement teaches is, the folly of man who would measure his impotent wrath against the Majesty of God; and the wisdom of submission to Him who is the only worthy object of fear.

The internal evidence points so clearly to the occasion for which the Psalm was written, that the LXX. have inscribed it, πρὸς τὸν Ἀσσύριον, and this reference has, with few exceptions, been recognized by commentators, ancient and modern.

The Psalm consists of four strophes, each of which is comprised in three verses.

I. The first celebrates Jerusalem and Zion as the abode of God, and the place where He has manifested His power, ver. 1—3.

II. The second describes in a forcible and animated manner the sudden destruction of the beleaguering army, ver. 4—6.

III. The third dwells on that event as a solemn, far-reaching act of judgement, conveying its lesson to the world, ver. 7—9.

IV. The last tells what that lesson is, counseling submission to Him whose power and whose righteousness have so wonderfully made themselves known, ver. 10—12.

[FOR THE PRECENTOR, WITH STRINGED INSTRUMENTS.[a] A PSALM OF ASAPH. A SONG.]

1 IN Judah is God known,
His name is great in Israel.

1—3. The whole emphasis of this first strophe consists in the prominence given to the particular locality where God has manifested His power. It is on the same field where He has so often gotten to Himself glory. It is in Judah, in Salem, in Zion. It is *there* (ver. 3, the word is peculiarly emphatic) that He hath dashed in pieces the might of the foe.

1. IS KNOWN, or perhaps more exactly, "maketh Himself known," as xlviii. 3 [4], *i.e.* by the present deliverance which he has wrought. The participle expresses present action.

IN ISRAEL. According to Hupfeld, Israel is here mentioned in the parallelism merely for the sake of the poetry, although Judah only is meant. He accounts for such usage by saying that "Judah and Israel" was a common phrase to denote the whole nation. But if the date assigned to the Psalm be correct, there may be a special reason for the mention of Israel. Hezekiah was the first monarch who made any attempt to restore the ancient unity of the tribes. After the fall of Samaria, and the deportation of the inhabitants of the northern kingdom by Esar-had-

2 In Salem also hath been His tabernacle,
And His dwelling-place in Zion.

don, Israel, *i.e.* the ten tribes, had no longer a national existence. And yet we read that Hezekiah, on his accession, after purifying the Temple, and restoring the worship of God, "sent to all *Israel and Judah*, and wrote letters also to *Ephraim and Manasseh*, that they should come to the house of the Lord at Jerusalem, to keep the passover unto the Lord God of *Israel*." (2 Chron. xxx. 1.) A study of the whole chapter will show what importance was attached to this union of Israel with Judah, at the time, and will explain, as it seems to me, the mention of both together in the Psalm.

2. SALEM. The LXX. render ἐν εἰρήνῃ, and the Vulg. *in pace:* but the word is evidently a proper name. "It seems to be agreed on all hands," says Mr. Grove, "that Salem is here employed for Jerusalem, but whether as a mere abbreviation, to suit some exigency of the poetry and point the allusion to the *peace* which the city enjoyed through the protection of God [this is Ewald's view], or whether, after a well-known habit of poets, it is an antique name preferred to the more modern and familiar one, is a question not yet decided. The latter is the opinion of the Jewish commentators, but it is grounded on their belief that the Salem of Melchizedek was the city which afterwards became Jerusalem. This is to beg the question." He shows that this was the general belief, up to the time of Jerome, of Christians as well as Jews. But Jerome places the Salem of Melchizedek near Scythopolis, and identifies it with the Salim of John the Baptist. The narrative in Genesis does not mark the return route of Abraham, so as to furnish any data for fixing the locality of Salem. It is probable that Abraham "would equally pass by both Scythopolis and Jerusalem." On the other hand, the distance of Sodom from the former place (80 miles), renders it unlikely that the king of Sodom should have gone so far to meet Abraham, and makes it more possible that the interview took place after his return; and this "is, so far, in favour of Salem being Jerusalem." Mr. Grove, who has discussed the whole question with his usual learning and ability, throws out the suggestion that the antithesis in ver. 1, between "Judah" and "Israel" may "imply that some sacred place in the northern kingdom is contrasted with Zion, the sanctuary of the south. And if there were in the Bible any sanction to the identification of Salem with Shechem [according to a tradition of Eupolemus, which he has quoted], the passage might be taken as referring to the continued relation of God to the kingdom of Israel." Although there is no "identification of Salem with Shechem," there is mention of a Salem, a city of Shechem, Gen. xxxiii. 18. But see note on ver. 1. Salem and Zion denote the lower and upper city respectively.

HIS TABERNACLE, lit. "booth," as made of *interwoven* or interlacing boughs of trees, &c. (So the feast of *tabernacles* is the feast of *booths* or huts.) The name may have been used of any temporary structure, and so of the Tabernacle, and then, as here, of the Temple. Comp. xxvii. 5, and Lam. ii. 6.

But I am inclined to prefer another meaning here, and one more in accordance with the context. The word may signify a dense thicket, the lair of wild beasts. (It occurs in this sense in x. 9, "like a lion in his *lair*.") In ver. 4 it is said, "Thou art glorious from the mountains of *prey*." May not God be here likened to a lion couching in his *lair*, and going forth from those mountains to destroy? This seems almost certain, when we find

3 There[b] brake He the arrows[c] of (the) bow,
Shield, and sword, and battle. [Selah.]

4 Glorious [d] art Thou, excellent
From the mountains of prey.
5 The stout-hearted have been spoiled,[e]
They have sunk into their sleep,

that the word in the parallel "His dwelling," is also used in civ. 22 of the *den* of lions; "the lions roaring after their *prey*, &c. . . . lay them down in their *dens*." The same word occurs in the same sense in Am. iii. 4. Then we should render: "In Salem is His covert, and His lair in Zion." Dean Stanley, I find, takes the same view, *Sinai and Pal.* p. 177, note 2. As regards the figure itself, Jehovah is said in other passages to *roar* (as a lion), Hos. xi., 10, and Joel iii. 16 [iv. 16], cf. Jerem. xxv. 30. He is here, as it were, identified with "the lion of the tribe of Judah."

3. THERE. Emphatically pointing to the spot where the great deliverance had been accomplished. Comp. for this use xxxvi. 12 [13], lxvi. 6, and for the general sense of the verse xlvi. 9 [10]:

"Who stilleth wars to the end of the earth,
Who breaketh the bow and cutteth the spear in sunder,
And burneth the chariots in the fire."

ARROWS OF THE BOW, lit. "fiery shafts, or lightnings of the bow," the arrows being so called, from their rapid flight, and their glittering in the air: or possibly with an allusion to the burning arrows employed in ancient warfare. See on vii. note [c].

4. There is no comparison, as in the E.V., "*more* glorious *than* the mountains of prey," though the Hebrew would admit of such a rendering (see an instance of the same ambiguity in the use of the preposition, lv. 8 [9], and note there), and it has been adopted by many commentators. They suppose that the Assyrian power is tacitly compared either to a lion going forth to ravin (comp. the fuller picture in Nah. ii. 11—13 [Heb. 12—14]), or to robbers issuing from their strongholds in the mountains. And thus the power of God is said to be "more excellent" than the power of Assyria, whether regarded as that of a lion, or as that of armed banditti. But such a comparison is flat and tame, and the rendering given in the text, which is that of all the Greek translators and of Jerome, is far preferable. See note on ver. 2. God goes forth victoriously from Zion to crush his foes.

"The promise," Tholuck says, "is fulfilled:—

'I will break the Assyrian in my land,
And upon my mountains tread him under foot.' (Is. xiv. 25.)

Yea, upon the mountains of Jerusalem they themselves must become a prey, who had hoped there to gather the prey." The plural, MOUNTAINS, either used in the wider sense, as in the passage just quoted from Isaiah, or possibly of Zion only, as in lxxxvii. 1, cxxxiii. 3. The great prominence always given to the *mountains* of their native land, both by Psalmists and Prophets, is a further confirmation of the view that the mountains of Palestine, not those of Assyria, are here meant. See Mr. Grove's admirable article, PALESTINE, § 26, in *Dict. of the Bible*.

5. THEY HAVE SUNK INTO THEIR SLEEP. (Comp. 2 Kings xix. 35.) The verb (which is of a different root from the noun "sleep") ex-

And none of the men of valour have found their hands.
6 At Thy rebuke, O God of Jacob,
Both chariot and horse are cast into a dead sleep.

7 Thou, even Thou, art to be feared,
And who can stand before Thee when once Thou art angry?
8 From heaven Thou didst cause judgement to be heard;
The earth feared and was still,
9 When God arose to judgement,
To save all the afflicted of the earth. [Selah.]

presses the languor and lassitude by which a man is overpowered, and so falls asleep. In all other passages where it occurs, the E.V. renders it by *slumber*. See, for instance, cxxi. 3, 4; Is. v. 27, &c. and comp. Nah. iii. 18, "Thy shepherds *slumber*, O King of Assyria," where the word is used, as here, of the sleep of death. A third word is employed in the next verse.

HAVE FOUND THEIR HANDS finely expresses the helplessness and bewilderment of those proud warriors who but a short while before had raised their hands in scornful defiance against Jerusalem (see Is. x. 32). The idiom is apparently similar to our common expression "*losing* heart." (Comp. 2 Sam. vii. 27, to "*find* heart.") Hupfeld thinks that this rendering is not supported by usage, and would render "have found nothing, *i.e.* achieved, affected nothing, with their hands." But this is hypercritical. The Rabbis have the phrase, "he has not found his hands and his feet in the *Beth ham-Midrash*" (the school of allegorical interpretation), when they wish to describe an ignorant, incompetent person.

6. ARE CAST INTO A DEAD SLEEP. In the Heb. this is but one word (a participle, denoting present condition). It is used of a profound slumber, either (1) natural, or (2) supernatural, the sleep into which God casts men. Comp. Jud. iv. 21; Dan. x. 9, and the noun from the same root, Gen. ii. 21; 1 Sam. xxvi. 12.

CHARIOT AND HORSE, *i.e.* of course the riders in chariots and on horses (as the ancient Versions paraphrase). The figure is so obvious, that it might be left to explain itself, were it not for the strange prosaic misunderstanding of Hengstenberg, who supposes that the chariot is said to sleep, because it has ceased to rattle.

Byron's animated lines on the destruction of Sennacherib, which may have been partly suggested by this Psalm, will occur to every reader:—

"And there lay the steed with his nostril all wide,
But through it there rolled not the breath of his pride:
And the foam of his gasping lay white on the turf,
And cold as the spray of the rock-beating surf.
And there lay the rider distorted and pale,
With the dew on his brow, and the rust on his mail."

7. WHEN ONCE THOU ART ANGRY, lit, "from the time of Thine anger." See a similar form of expression, Ruth ii. 7; Jer. xliv. 18.

8. As in the last Psalm, God is spoken of as the Judge (this is a

10 For the wrath of man must praise Thee,
With the remainder of wrath Thou girdest Thyself.[f]
11 Vow and pay unto Jehovah your God ;
Let all that are round about Him bring presents unto Him who ought to be feared.
12 He cutteth off the spirit of princes :
He is to be feared by the kings of the earth.

peculiar feature in the Psalms ascribed to Asaph) ; and, as in that, He speaks from heaven, terrifying His enemies with the thunder of His word. Comp. lxxv. 2, 3, 7, 8 [3, 4, 8, 9]. The train of thought in that Psalm has certainly sufficient in common with the train of thought in this to justify us in assigning both to the same period.

10. WITH THE REMAINDER OF WRATH, &c. The meaning is not very clear. Whose wrath is here meant? that of man, or that of God? Some understand the latter, and explain the verse thus: All the wrath of men, every attempt that they make to defeat the will of God, does but turn to their own discomfiture, and His glory ; and after all their efforts, He has a store, a residue, of wrath to pour out upon them as punishment. But the objection to this is, that in the previous clause the wrath spoken of is that of man : and it is better to retain the same subject in both clauses. Then we have :—

(*a*) Man's wrath does but praise God.

(*b*) With the remainder of man's wrath, his last impotent efforts to assert his own power, God girds Himself, puts it on, so to speak, as an ornament—clothes Himself therewith to His own glory.

Thus the parallelism of the two clauses is strictly preserved.

The word WRATH is in the plural, denoting either wrath of every kind, or wrath in its intensity. See note on lxviii. 35 [36], and for a like use of the plural (1 Sam. ii. 3), where "a God of knowledge" is lit. "a God of knowledges."

11. This is the end. God has wrought His terrible act of judgement—but the first of a long series of judgements to be executed on the nations, unless by timely submission they acknowledge Him as their King. See the similar exhortation in ii. 11.

VOW AND PAY. See on xxii. 25 [26], BRING PRESENTS, comp. lxviii. 29 [30].

ALL THAT ARE ROUND ABOUT, *i.e.* the heathen nations, who are to bring presents in token of homage, as in lxviii. 30.

UNTO HIM WHO OUGHT TO BE FEARED, lit. "to the fear," *i.e.* the proper object of fear. See the same use of the word in Is. viii. 12. In like manner God is called "the Fear of Isaac" in Gen. xxxi. 42, 53 (though there the word is different).

12. This verse, or at least the first clause of it, reminds us of the last verse of the preceding Psalm, which closes in a similar strain.

HE CUTTETH OFF, like a vinedresser, who prunes away the rank boughs, or cuts off the ripe clusters of the vine. Comp. Is. xviii. 5, where the same image is employed by the Prophet at the same time, Jud. viii. 2, xx. 45 ; Jer. vi. 9, li. 33 ; Joel iii. 13, [iv. 13] ; Rev. xiv. 15.

[a] בִּנְגִינֹת. See on iv. note [a], and General Introduction, Vol. I. p. 87. On Asaph, see l. note [a].

[b] שָׁמָּה here used apparently as = שָׁם. Hupfeld refers to its use in the common phrase אֲשֶׁר אִוָּעֵד לָכֶם שָׁמָּה (Ex. xxix. 42, al.), "where I meet

with you;" but surely there *motion to a place* is implied = "*whither I go* to meet you." More in point is Ezek. xlviii. 35, *Jehovah shammah*, "Jehovah is *there*. See also cxxii. 5; Is. xxxiv. 15 (where שָׁם occurs in the parall.); Jer. xviii. 2; 1 Chron. iv. 41. "The Semitic accus. has a wide signification, and denotes not only the *whither* (and *how long*), but also the *where* (*when* and *how*), so that, for instance, פֶּתַח in the accus., and פֶּתְחָה, mean *before*, or *at the door*, as שַׁעְרָה, *at the gate*. Again, the accusative ending ־ָה, is only met with in a partial and fragmentary manner; and in dying out seems to have lost much of its original meaning. Finally, of this particular word neither the Arab. nor Aram. has the simple form, but only the accus. form in the same sense." The above is from Hupfeld.

c רִשְׁפֵי ק׳. The word רֶשֶׁף denotes any hot, glowing substance. Hence Cant. viii. 6, רִשְׁפֵּי אֵשׁ (where observe the Dagesh, which is wanting here), "*coals* of fire;" Job v. 7, בְּנֵי ר׳, "sons of *burning*," or, *a firebrand*, interpreted by many to mean *sparks*. In Hab. iii. 6, the word is used of *a burning fever*.

d נָאוֹר, a Niphal form from אוֹר (which, like בּוֹשׁ, טוֹב, is intrans.), and therefore questionable; for יֵאוֹר, in 2 Sam. ii. 32, is not fut. Niph., but Qal, like יֵבוֹשׁ, as Hupf. observes. He therefore thinks that perhaps נוֹרָא should be read; comp. ver. 8, 13, and so Theod. φοβερός. Sym., however, has ἐπιφανής, the LXX. φωτίζεις, Aq. φωτισμός, and Jerome, *Lumen*. As regards the construction of מִן in the next hemistich all the Greek versions render it by ἀπό. Jerome has *a montibus captivitatis*.

e אֶשְׁתּוֹלְלוּ, lit. *have suffered themselves to be plundered* (an Aramaic form instead of הִשְׁתּ׳. Comp. אֶתְחַבַּר, 2 Chron. xx. 35; אֶגְאָלְתִּי, Is. lxiii. 3). This is an instance, according to Hupf., of the passive use of the Hithpael. He quotes other instances given by Gesen. and Ewald, of an alleged similar use. But in every one of these examples, the reflexive meaning may be retained; and in fact it is retained, in most cases, by syme one of the translators or commentators. Here, for instance, Phillips says: "*They have been plundered*, or they have exposed themselves to plunder, agreeably to Abu'l Walid, who has taken the verb in a reciprocal, and not in a passive sense: *they have* despised themselves, *i.e.* they have cast away their weapons." So in Jud. xx. 15, 17, Zunz has "*stellten sich zur Musterung*" and in xxi. 9, "*liess sich mustern*." (Indeed it is quite astonishing that the Hithp., in these instances, should have been regarded as a passive.) In Micah vi. 16, he renders "*halten sich*." On Eccl. viii. 10, Preston remarks: "The verb יִשְׁתַּכְּחוּ, being in the Hithp., expresses that their quiet and unostentatious lives cause them to be forgotten, 'that they sink of themselves into oblivion.'". In Is. lix. 15, מִשְׁתּוֹלֵל (the same verb that we have here) is rightly rendered in the E. V. "maketh himself a prey." In Prov. xxxi. 30, *gets to herself prasie*, and in Lam. iv. 1, *pour themselves out* (inanimate things, by a common figure, having life attributed to them); in 1 Sam. iii. 14, *shall not make atonement for itself*, lit. *shall not cover itself*, are the proper renderings of the several Hithpaels. There is no necessity, I am satisfied, in any case, to lose sight of this strict reflexive meaning of the conjugation, though it may be more convenient in another language to employ the passive, just as in rendering the German phrase, "davon *findet sich* keine Spur," in English, we may say, "No trace of it *is found;*" yet it would be absurd to maintain that the German reflexive is here used as a passive. Ewald, indeed, limits this pass. use of the Hithp. to rare cases, and to the later books chiefly, and only gives the two passages from Micah and Ecclesiastes, as illustrating it (*Lehrb. d. H. S.* § 124 *c.* p. 284, 6te Auf.); but even in these the proper reflexive force is retained. The rendering is merely a question of idiom.

[f] תַּחְגֹּר. There is no reason for departing from the ordinary meaning of the root. (Jerome, *accingeris*, and so apparently the Chald. and Sym. λείψανον θυμῶν περιζώσει.) Comp. Is. lix. 17, &c. Qimchi gives this sense in his commentary, but in his *Michlol* he explains it by תאסור, *restrain* (as it is found in a passage of the Mishnah, and in accordance with the signif. of the cognate roots in Arab. and Syr.). The LXX. again have ἑορτάσει σοι, and must therefore have read תְּחָגֶּךָּ, *shall hold festival to Thee*, answering to the parall. *shall praise Thee.* This Ewald adopts, observing: "Ver. 11 contains a very lofty thought. The only object with which Jehovah judges and punishes is, that even the most furious transgressors may at last attain to wisdom and to the praise of Jehovah; and though many fall under His chastisements, at least the remainder, taught by these terrible examples, will be saved. Or to put it in a shorter and more emphatic form: The wrath of man itself will praise Thee, being suddenly changed to its opposite, and as it were against its will.

PSALM 77

THIS Psalm is the record, first, of a sorrow long and painfully questioning with itself, full of doubts and fears, trying in vain to find in itself, or in the past, a light for the present; and then of the triumph over that sorrow by the recollection of God's love and power, as manifested in the early history of Israel. By whom the Psalm was written, or to what period of the history it is to be referred, it is now impossible to say. The manner in which, towards the close, the passage of the Red Sea is dwelt upon, has led many to conclude that it was written by one of the exiles during the Babylonish captivity. Those two memorable events, the deliverance from Babylon, and the deliverance from Egypt, were always associated in the minds of the Jews, the one being regarded, in fact, as the pledge of the other. This, however, in itself, is not decisive. At any time of great national depression, the thoughts of the true-hearted in

Israel would naturally revert to God's first great act of redeeming love: and other Psalms (the 78th, the 80th, the 81st), evidently not written during the Exile, look back to the Exodus, and the wonders of God's hand displayed then, and in the journey through the wilderness. Besides, an inference of a positive kind, in favour of an earlier date, has been drawn from the relation of this Psalm to the Prophecy of Habakkuk. Delitzsch, in his commentary on the Prophet, has traced carefully the coincidences in thought and expression between Hab. iii. 10—15, and verses 16—20 [17—21] of the Psalm. Among the various arguments by which he endeavours to establish the priority of the Psalm, two seem to be of weight; first, that the Prophet throughout his ode is in the habit of quoting from the Psalms; and secondly, that with his eye on the future, he arrays all the images of terror and magnificence which are suggested by the past, in order to describe with more imposing pomp the approaching advent of Jehovah; whereas the Psalmist is not looking to the future, but dwelling on the past: hence it is far more probable that the Prophet imitates the Psalmist, than that the Psalmist borrows from the Prophet. Supposing this to be satisfactorily established, we might reasonably infer that this Psalm was not written later than the reign of Josiah. But on the other hand, as Hupfeld has pointed out, the mode of expression in Habakkuk, as compared with that here employed, would lead us to an exactly opposite conclusion. (1) The figure in Hab. iii. 10, "The *mountains* saw Thee, they were afraid (lit. in pangs or throes)," is more natural and correct than the use of the same figure as applied in the Psalm to the *waters* (ver. 16 [17]). (2) The phrase, "the overflowing of the waters," in Hab. iii. 10, is more simple and natural than the corresponding phrase in ver. 17 [18] of the Psalm, as I have remarked in the Critical Note on that verse, the verbal form here employed occurring nowhere else. Hence it is most likely that the latter was a designed alteration in copying from the former. (3) That the lightning should be termed the "arrows" of God in Habakkuk, is quite in keeping with the martial character and figures of the whole passage. In the Psalm, on the other hand, the figure seems more out of place.

There is some force, no doubt, in this argument. There is less, I think, in that which Hupfeld urges, on the ground of the apparent want of connexion between the "lyric episode," ver. 16—19 [17—20], and the rest of the Psalm. It is true that the rhythm of this portion is different, being in three members instead of in two; and that here the strophe consists of four verses [or five], whereas the preceding strophes consist of three. But these are of themselves unimportant variations. Nor do I see that ver. 20 [21] is naturally connected with ver. 15 [16]. On the contrary, it is far more striking (see note) in its present position. As to the objection that a single instance of God's deliverance is so enlarged upon, is made to occupy so prominent a place, that is surely quite in accordance with the true genius of lyric poetry; not to mention that it was the one great act from which the whole history dated, and which has left its stamp on all the literature of the people.

But whenever, and by whomsoever, the Psalm may have been written, it clearly is individual, not national. It utterly destroys all the beauty, all the tenderness and depth of feeling in the opening portion, if we suppose that the people are introduced speaking in the first person.* The allusions to the national history may indeed show that the season was a season of national distress, and that the sweet singer was himself bowed down by the burden of the time, and oppressed by woes which he had no power to alleviate; but it is his own sorrow, not the sorrows of others, under which he sighs, and of which he has left the pathetic record.

The Psalm falls naturally into two principal parts: the first, verses 1—9, containing the expression of the Psalmist's sorrow and disquietude; the second, verses 10—20, telling how he rose above them.

Of these, again, the former half consists of strophes of three verses, 1—3, 4—6, 7—9, the end of the first and third being marked by the Selah. The latter may also be divided into three strophes, the first two only being of three verses each, 10—12, 13—15 (the second having the Selah), and the last consisting of five, 15—20.

[FOR THE PRECENTOR. AFTER THE MANNER OF JEDUTHUN.[a] A PSALM OF ASAPH.]

1 WITH my voice unto God let me cry,[b]
With my voice unto God, and may He give ear unto me.[c]

1. AND MAY HE GIVE EAR, or more literally, in the form of an address to God, "And do Thou give ear." The constant interchange of

* It is much to be regretted that the author of the Art. PSALMS in *Dict. of the Bible* (vol. ii. p. 957), should have committed himself to the theory that all the Psalms ascribed to the Levitical singers are of necessity national. He has thus been obliged to give a most strained and unnatural interpretation to many of them. Thus, for instance, he holds that this Psalm is "the lamentation of the Jewish Church for the terrible political calamity . . . . whereby the inhabitants of the northern kingdom were carried into captivity, and Joseph lost, the second time, to Jacob." And still more strangely, of the 73d Psalm, that "though couched in the first person singular, (it) is really a prayer of the Jewish faithful against the Assyrian invaders." (*Ib.* p. 959.) This is, I must think, an entire misunderstanding of a very striking Psalm.

2 In the day of my distress I sought the Lord;
My hand was stretched out in the night and failed not,
My soul refused to be comforted.
3 I would remember God, and must sigh,[d]
I would commune (with myself), and my spirit is overwhelmed. [Selah.]

4 Thou hast held mine eyes waking;[e]
I am so troubled that I cannot speak.
5 I have considered the days of old,
The years of ages (past);

tenses in the first six verses lends vividness to the expression of the Psalmist's feelings. Sometimes, as in ver. 2, 4, 5, we have the past tenses in narration, and then alternating with these, the paragogic future or optative, as in ver. 1, 3, 6, expressing purpose, resolve, and the like. And thus are marked the fluctuating emotions of the mind, ever passing from the mere statement of fact to the utterance of feelings and desires.

2, 3. These verses show both the reality and earnestness of the prayer, and the strong faith of the Psalmist. It is no occasional petition hastily put up, but a struggle, like that of Jacob, through the livelong night. It is even a sorer conflict, for he has not found the blessing as Jacob did. He cannot be comforted. He would think of God, but even that thought brings him no strength: he looks within, and his sorrow deepens.

2. WAS STRETCHED OUT, lit. "poured out" like water, 2 Sam. xiv. 14; or as the eye is said to be poured out or dissolved in tears, Lam. iii. 49; here apparently applied to the hand stretched out in prayer. "The stretched-out, weak and powerless hand," says Hengstenberg, "conveys the picture of a relaxation of the whole body." Or there may be a confusion of metaphor, that being said of the hand which could only properly be said of the eye (so the Targum substitutes the latter for the former). Rashi explains *my hand* to mean *the hand*, or blow, *laid upon me*, and hence came the singular rendering of the E. V., *my sore ran*, &c.

AND FAILED NOT (or it may be rendered as an adverbial clause, *without intermission*. Sym. ἐκτέτατο διηνεκῶς), lit. "and grew not cold," like a corpse; "became not weary," used, like the last verb, of tears. Comp. Lam. ii. 18, "Let tears run down like a river day and night: give thyself *no rest*;" and iii. 49, "Mine eye trickled down (the word rendered above *was stretched out*), and ceaseth not, without any *intermission*." The words *rest* and *intermission* are derivatives from the verb here employed, and are applied to tears, perhaps as *frozen* at their source.

REFUSED. Comp. Gen. xxxvii. 35, where the same is said of Jacob when he received the tidings of Joseph's death.

3. MUST SIGH, or "groan." It is the word used of the *roaring* of the sea, xlvi. 3 [4]. See Rom. viii. 26 (στεναγμοῖς ἀλαλήτοις.) "St. Paul teaches us that it is the Holy Ghost who in such sighs makes intercession for believers with God."—*Tholuck*.

4. I CANNOT SPEAK. Silence and thought succeed to the uttered

6 I would call to remembrance my song in the night,
I would commune with my heart,—and my spirit hath made diligent search:
7 "Will the Lord cast off for ever?
And will He be favourable no more?
8 Hath His loving-kindness come to an end for ever?
Hath (His) promise failed to all generations?
9 Hath God forgotten to be gracious?
Hath He shut up in anger His tender mercies?" [Selah.]

10 Then I said: This is my sorrow,[f]
That the right hand of the Highest hath changed.

prayer. But the heart still prays on in secret, though the mouth is silent.

6. MY SONG, properly, a song sung to a stringed instrument, as the harp. He would console himself with the recollection of a happier past. Such recollections, as Tholuck remarks, may hush the storm of the soul, may give a man courage to say to himself, Thou art His, He cannot forsake thee. But such recollections may also be made the very instruments of Satan's temptations, when the soul asks, Why is it not always thus? and so falls into the sad and desponding thoughts which follow in the next verses.

IN THE NIGHT. This repeated mention of the night (see ver. 2) shows that he was one who loved the stillness and the solitude of night for meditation and prayer. (Comp. xvi. 7, xvii. 3; Is. xxvi. 9.)

8. God's loving-kindness and God's promise (or, *word*, as in lxviii. 11 [12], and Hab. iii. 9) are the two props of his faith.

9. IN ANGER HIS TENDER MERCIES. The words are evidently placed with design in juxtaposition, in order to heighten the contrast. Comp. Hab. iii. 2, "In wrath remember mercy," where there is the same juxtaposition in the Hebrew.

10. All this that I have been asking myself, and saddening myself with asking, seems impossible, and yet it is this very change which perplexes me.

MY SORROW, or perhaps "my sickness," *i.e.* as Calvin explains, a disease which is only for a time, and to which, therefore, I should patiently submit. Comp. Jer. x. 19. Others, "my infirmity," *i.e.* the weakness of my own spirit, which leads me to take this gloomy view, and which I must resist.

THAT THE RIGHT HAND, &c., lit. "the changing of the right hand." This fact, that it is no more with him as in days past, it is which fills him with grief. And then in the next verse he recovers himself, and passes from self-contemplation to record God's wonders for His people. But another rendering is possible. The word *changing* (*sh'noth*) may mean *years* (as it does in ver. 5): "The years of the right hand," &c., and the whole verse might be understood thus:—

"Then I thought: This is my sadness,—
The years of the right hand of the Most High."

i.e. the very recollection of those years, and God's help vouchsafed in times past, does but increase my present gloom.

The E. V. connects this second clause with the following verse, and repeats the verb from that verse. See more in Critical Note.

11 (But) I will celebrate the deeds of Jah,
For I will call to remembrance Thy wonders of old;
12 Yea, I will meditate on all Thy work,
And commune with myself of Thy doings.
13 O God, Thy way is holy!
Who is a great God as (our) God?
14 Thou, even Thou, art the God that doest wonders,
Thou hast made known Thy strength among the peoples.
15 Thou hast with (Thine) arm redeemed Thy people,
The sons of Jacob and Joseph. [Selah.]

11. With this verse the change of feeling begins. Hitherto he has looked too much within, has sought too much to read the mystery of God's dealings by the light of his own experience merely. Hence the despondency, when he contrasts the gloomy present with the far brighter and happier past. He cannot believe that God has indeed forgotten to be gracious, that He has indeed changed His very nature; but that he may be re-assured and satisfied on this point, his eye must take a wider range than that of his own narrow experience. There lies before him the great history of his people. There recurs especially the one great deliverance never to be forgotten, the type and the pledge of all deliverances, whether of the nation or of the individual. On this he lays hold, by this he sustains his sinking faith. Calvin says: "Jam animosius contra tentationes exsurgit Propheta quæ fere ad opprimendam ejus fidem prævaluerant. Nam recordatio hæc operum Dei ab ea cujus ante meminit [ver. 5] differt: quia tunc eminus intuebatur Dei beneficia, quæ lenire vel minuere dolorem nondum poterant. Hic vero arripit quasi certa testimonia perpetuæ gratiæ, et ideo vehementiæ causa sententiam repetit."

THY WONDERS. The word is in the singular (though the Ancient Versions and many MSS. have the plural) here, and also in ver. 14. So also in the next verse THY WORK, because the one great wonder, the one great work in which all others were included, is before his thoughts. Comp. Hab. iii. 2, "Revive Thy *work*."

13. IS HOLY, lit. "is in holiness," not as others, "in the sanctuary," for the Psalmist, though speaking generally of God's redeeming love and power, is evidently thinking chiefly of the deliverance from Egypt, on which he afterwards dwells. In this and the next verse there is an allusion to Exod. xv. 11, "Who is like unto Thee, O Jehovah, among the gods? Who is like Thee, glorious in holiness, fearful in praises, doing wonders?" (where the noun, as here, is singular.)

15. THOU HAST REDEEMED, a word especially applied to the deliverance from Egyptian bondage. See note on lxxiv. 2. "The word 'Redemption,' which has now a sense far holier and higher," says Dean Stanley, "first entered into the circle of religious ideas at the time when God '*redeemed* His people from the house of bondage.'"—*Jewish Church*, Lec. V. p. 127.

JOSEPH, mentioned here apparently as the father of Ephraim (comp. lxxviii. 67), and so as representing the kingdom of Israel (as lxxx. 1 [2], lxxxi. 5 [6]); perhaps this special mention of Joseph may indicate that the Psalmist himself belonged to the northern kingdom.

16 The waters saw Thee, O God, the waters saw Thee, they
were troubled[f];
Yea, the depths also trembled;
17 The clouds poured out[g] water; the skies thundered;
Yea, Thine arrows went abroad;
18 The voice of Thy thunders rolled along,[h]
The lightnings gave shine unto the world:
The earth trembled and shook.

19 Thy way was[i] in the sea,
And Thy paths[k] in the mighty waters:
And Thy footsteps were not known.

16—20. There follows now a description of the manner in which the redemption (ver. 15) was accomplished in the passage of the Red Sea. In verses 17, 18, the rain, the thunder and lightning, and the earthquake, are features of the scene not mentioned in the history in Exodus, though Tholuck sees an allusion to a storm in Exod. xiv. 24. Both Philo (*V. M.* i. 32) and Josephus (*Ant.* ii. 16 § 3) add this circumstance in their narrative of the event. "The Passage, as thus described," says Dean Stanley, "was effected, not in the calmness and clearness of daylight, but in the depth of midnight, amidst the roar of the hurricane, which caused the sea to go back—amidst a darkness lit up only by the broad glare of the lightning, as the Lord looked out of the thick darkness of the cloud." He then quotes these verses of the Psalm. (*Jewish Church*, pp. 127-8.) This is one of those instances in which we obtain valuable incidental additions, by means of the Psalmists and Prophets, to the earlier narratives. See Mr. Grove's Article on OREB, in Smith's *Dict. of the Bible.*

16. SAW THEE. Comp. cxiv. 3, where both the Red Sea and the Jordan are mentioned, a passage which Hupfeld thinks is the original from which both this and Hab. iii. 10 are copied.

WERE TROUBLED, lit. "were in pain," as of travail. The same expression is used of the mountains in Hab. iii. 10: "The mountains saw Thee, they were in pain;" where the verb seems more aptly to describe the throes of the earthquake, by which the mountains are shaken.

17. The way is made by means of tempest and hurricane.

POURED OUT. Comp. Hab. iii. 10 (where the noun is from the same root): "*the overflowing* of the waters." E.V. In the same way the lightning is spoken of as "the arrows" of God, in Hab. iii. 11.

18. ROLLED ALONG, lit. "was in the rolling," with allusion to God's chariot; or perhaps "in the whirlwind" or "rolling cloud." See Critical Note.

GAVE SHINE. I have adopted here the Prayer-Book Version of the same words in xcvii. 4 (its rendering in this place is less correct), in preference to that of the E. V., "*the lightnings lightened*," (1) because the verb and the noun are from entirely different roots; (2) because the idiomatic "*gave* shine" is an exact equivalent of the Hebrew.

19. THY FOOTSTEPS WERE NOT KNOWN. "We know not, they knew not, by what precise means the deliverance was wrought: we know not by what precise track through the gulf the passage was effected.

20 Thou leddest Thy people like sheep
By the hand of Moses and Aaron.

We know not, and we need not know; the obscurity, the mystery here, as elsewhere, was part of the lesson. . . . All that we see distinctly is, that through this dark and terrible night, with the enemy pressing close behind, and the driving sea on either side, He led His people like sheep by the hand of Moses and Aaron."—STANLEY, *Jewish Church*, p. 128.

20. This verse stands in beautiful and touching contrast with the last. In that we have pourtrayed the majesty, the power, the unsearchable mystery of God's ways; in this, His tender and loving care for His people, as that of a shepherd for His flock. See for a like contrast, Is. xl. 10—12, li. 15, 16, lvii. 15.

So ends the Psalm. Nor can I see in such a close that abruptness which has led some commentators to suppose that the Psalm was never finished. The one great example is given, and that is enough. All is included in that; and the troubled, desponding spirit has found peace and rest in the view of God's redemption. "He loses himself, as it were, in the joyful recollection." (De Wette.) So may every sorrowful spirit now find peace and rest in looking, not to itself, not even to God's dealings with itself, but to the cross of Christ.

[a] עַל יְדוּתוּן, see on xxxix. note [a], and General Introduction, Vol. I. p. 89.

[b] וְאֶצְעָקָה. The use of the conjunction here may be explained by supposing in the previous clause an ellipse = "my voice (is directed) to God, *and* I would fain cry." Hupf. assumes a double subject, as in iii. 5, cxlii. 2, though it is sufficient in these instances to take קוֹלִי as accus. of the instrument.

The paragogic ה shows that the verb is an optative. The same form recurs ver. 4, 7, 12, 13. Alternating as it does with the perfects, it well describes the strong emotions of the Psalmist's mind. This nice distinction of tenses has been too often completely overlooked.

[c] וְהַאֲזִין, not the infin., but the imperat, *And do Thou give ear to me*, by a somewhat abrupt transition. Ewald and others would soften this harshness by taking it as the preterite, with change of vowels, for הֶאֱזִין. And in this they are supported by the LXX. *καὶ ἡ φωνή μου πρὸς τὸν Θεὸν, καὶ προσέσχε μοι*, and Sym. *καὶ βοήσαντός μου πρὸς τὸν Θεὸν, παρέσχε τὰς ἀκοὰς αὐτοῦ*. But the preterite with the וְ may be equivalent to a future, and I have rendered accordingly.

[d] The double paragogic form may be taken here as marking protasis and apodosis. "*When* I remember, *then* I sigh," &c. (so Ewald): or as in the text. See on xlii. 5, note [c], and lv. 3, 18.

[e] שְׁמֻרוֹת, only here. It may be either for, (1) אַשְׁמֻרוֹת, *the night-watches*. Comp. for the sense lxiii. 7; and then, "Thou hast held the night-watches of mine eyes," = "Thou hast held mine eyes in the night-watches." Or (2) *the eyelids* (so called as *guards*, *keepers* of the eye, as R. Mosheh Hakkohen explains), as the Chald., Ges., De Wette, &c. the meaning being, Thou hast held them so that I could not close them in sleep. Or (3) it may be the part. pass., as a predicate to the noun *eyes* = *watchful*, *waking*.

[1] חַלּוֹתִי, with the accent drawn back, because of the tone on the following monosyllable. This is either (1), as Qimchi takes it, an infin. (like חֲנוֹת, ver. 10), from חלל, meaning lit. *my wounding*, and so *my suffering*. Comp. for this use of the verb, cix. 22 (so Ewald). Or (2), infin. Piel of חלה, *my sickness*, lit. "that which makes me sick." See the same verb in the Piel, Deut. xxix. 21, "the diseases wherewith Jehovah *hath made it sick*." Hiph., Is. liii. 10. This seems to be supported by the parallel passage Jer. x. 19, "And I said, Surely this is my sickness (זֶה חֳלִי) and I will bear it," *i.e.* God has laid His hand upon me, and I will resign myself to His chastisement. Here, too, there is a similar expression of resignation. Or (3), the verb has been supposed to occur here in the same sense as in the phrase חִלָּה פְּנֵי פ׳, *to entreat the favour of any one.* Hence it has been rendered *my supplication.* But the objection to that is, that here the phrase is incomplete, the noun being wanting, whereas the verb by itself never means *to supplicate.*

There is another word in this verse which presents a difficulty.

שְׁנוֹת. This is capable of two meanings. Either it is (1), infin. constr. of the verb שׁנה, *to change*, in a neuter sense = *to be changed* (the verb in Qal. is never used transitively); or (2), the plur. constr. of the noun שָׁנָה, *a year* (as in ver. 6). According to these different renderings of these two words, the passage has been very differently interpreted. Even the Chald. gives two explanations :—

(*a*) "This is my *infirmity* (מַרְעוּתִי); the strength of the right hand of the Highest *is changed* (אִשְׁתַּנִּין)." (*b*) Another Targum: "This is my *supplication* (בָּעוּתִי), (that) *the year* of the end (should come) from the Right Hand."

The LXX. νῦν ἠρξάμην (a meaning which חלה has only in the Hiph.), αὕτη ἡ ἀλλοίωσις τῆς δεξιᾶς τοῦ ὑψίστου.

Of more modern interpretations the following may be mentioned. Mendelssohn: "*Flehen steht bei mir; ändern in des Höchsten Macht*," which is ingenious; but even admitting that חל׳ can mean *flehen*, שׁנ׳ cannot be transitive. The same objection applies to Luther's translation: "*Ich muss das leiden; die rechte Hand des Höchsten kann alles ändern.*" Zunz has: "*Das ist mein Flehen—die Jahre der R. d. Höchsten!*" which certainly gives a very good sense: "This is what I long and pray for—those years of God's right hand in which He exhibited His grace and power." *The right hand of God* cannot mean, as some would take it, "His chastening hand," it must mean "His supporting hand." It would be possible, however, to render, "This it is which saddens me,—the years of the right Hand," &c. *i.e.* the remembrance of God's power and grace in past times, as compared with my present lot. And this falls in with the previous complaint: "Hath God forgotten," &c. On the whole, however, the rendering of J. H. Mich. is to be preferred: "*meine Krankheit* (*i.e.* the misery of my spirit) *ist das: dass die R. des H. sich geändert habe.*" So also Hupfeld. And Maurer well explains: "*quod ægrum me facit hoc est*, hæc est mea calamitas: *quod se mutavit*, non amplius ut olim parata est ad juvandum *dextera Altissimi.*" He then supports interpretation (2) of חלותי and observes of שׁנה, "*mutari* in deterius, ut Thren iv. 1, in fide : Prov. xxiv. 21 ; Mal. iii. 6, quo posteriore loco in contrarium hæc leguntur haud nihil lucis accendentia huic quem tractamus loco : *ego, Jova, non mutor, ideoque vos, filii Jacobi, non periistis.*" Not unlike this is the rendering of Aq., ἀῤῥωστία μου, αὕτη ἀλλοίωσις δ. ὑ. (except that he must have understood 'חל of bodily infirmity, not of mental suffering). Theod. and the Quinta, ὠδῖνές (μου) εἰσιν, ἀλλοίωσις δ. ὑ.

In this instance the E. V. and the P. B. V. coincide, the latter not following here either the Vulg. or the German. Our translators have copied Ibn. Ez. and Qimchi, in supplying the verb *I will remember*, from the next verse. In so doing, they have followed the Q'ri, whereas the K'thîbh, אַזְכִּיר, *I will celebrate*, is preferable, as it avoids the tautology with אֶזְכְּרָה in the next verse.

[g] זֹרְמוּ, only here, sometimes regarded as a Poel, but better as a Pual, the construction being that of the accus. מַיִם, with the pass., "the clouds were poured forth (in, or with) water." (Phillips, indeed, would make 'מ the subject, and suggests an ellipse of the prep. מִן, *from* the clouds, but I am not aware of any instance of such an ellipse.) Cf. 'זֶרֶם מ, Hab. iii. 11, which, certainly, looks like the original expression. In חֲצָצֶיךָ we have the expanded poet. form, instead of הִצֶּיךָ (comp. עֲמָמֵי, הֲרָרֵי, &c.), perhaps chosen to express the zig-zag flash of the lightning. The verb in the Hithp. fut. is also expressive : "kept going hither and thither."

[h] גַּלְגַּל, properly, *a wheel.* (1) Some, following Qimchi, understand it of *the globe* or *sphere* of heaven. So Luther and the E. V., and with this has been compared the difficult and doubtful expression τροχὸς τῆς γενέσεως, in James iii. 6. (2) J. D. Mich. and others render it *whirlwind.* So Ewald, *im Wirbel.* In lxxxiii. 14, it means "a whirling mass," or perhaps "a dust-storm." It is better, therefore, to take the word here in the sense of *rolling*, a sense to which it might easily pass from that of *wheel*, and which its etymology confirms. The *rolling* will be that of the chariots of God. Comp. Hab. iii. 8 ; Joel ii. 5. Or possibly *the wheel* may stand by metonymy for the *chariot.*

[i] The omission of the copula, here and in the previous verse, where the reference is clearly to the past, is rare. See a similar instance in Jer. vii. 12 : לְכוּ־נָא אֶל מְקוֹמִי אֲשֶׁר בְּשִׁילוֹ, "Go to my place which *was* in Shiloh."

[k] שְׁבִילֶיךָ. So the K'thîbh in the plur., as in Jer. xviii. 15, the only other place where it occurs. The Q'ri is an unnecessary correction.

PSALM 78

In this, the longest of the historical Psalms, the history of Israel is briefly recapitulated, from the time of the Exodus to the final union of the tribes under David, and the establishment of the kingdom in his family. This appeal to the past is made evidently with a purpose. The Psalmist comes forward as a prophet to rebuke the sin, the ingratitude, the rebellion of his people. This he does by showing them the present in the light of the past. God had wrought wonders in behalf of their fathers of old; God had redeemed them from Egypt, led them through the wilderness, brought them to His holy mountain. But the history of their nation had been at once a history of wonders and a history of rebellions. Miracle had followed on miracle to win them; chastisement had succeeded to chastisement to deter them; but the miracle was forgotten, the chastisement produced but a temporary reformation. They had ever been "a faithless and stubborn generation." It is evident, from his opening words, that the Psalmist was anxious to bring out sharply and clearly the lessons with which the past teemed. He saw that his people were in danger of forgetting those lessons. He saw in that history, instruction, warning, reproof, for the age in which he lived.

It is, however, remarkable that another and more special purpose appears in the Psalm. If the whole nation is rebuked, the rebuke falls heaviest upon Ephraim. Ephraim is singled out as the leader in the earlier apostasy of the people, as the very type of a faithless and recreant spirit (ver. 12). The rejection of Ephraim and the choice of Judah are dwelt upon at the close in a tone of satisfaction and triumph, as the fulfilment of the purpose of God. It is scarcely possible, therefore, to resist the conclusion, that the Psalm was written after the defection of the Ten Tribes, and that it was designed either to curb the pride of the northern kingdom, or to address a warning to Judah, based on the example of Ephraim.

Various conjectures have been hazarded as to the time when the Psalm was written. Hengstenberg, who is determined, at the risk of any absurdity, to maintain the authority of the Inscription, which gives this Psalm to Asaph, is obliged to place it in the reign of David. He says that the object of the Psalmist is "to warn the people against a possible revolt from David, and from the sanctuary

---

* On this Psalm see Isaac Taylor, *Spirit of the Hebrew Poetry*, p. 154.

in Zion; he cannot therefore have composed the Psalm after this event had taken place." But if the Psalmist had any such object in view, he seems most effectually to have disguised it. Indeed, Hengstenberg is obliged to admit that he does "not once name the disruption which he is anxious to prevent, and makes no express mention whatever of any inclination to this, which might exist at the time;" and tries to account for this singular reticence by supposing that "it was of importance not to irritate, for fear of increasing the dissatisfaction." But could any more effectual mode of irritation have been devised, than first to exhibit Ephraim as chief in transgression (ver. 12), and then to commemorate in tones of triumph the degradation of that tribe from its ancient supremacy, and the exaltation of the rival tribe of Judah in its place? Was this a method likely to heal those heart-burnings and animosities which even David had failed altogether to allay? When Hengstenberg therefore adds that, "to deny that the Psalm belongs to the time of David manifests utter ignorance of its contents," we can only say that the facts point to an exactly opposite conclusion.

Ewald, with equal dogmatism, and equal improbability, places the Psalm as late as the fifth century B.C., in the time of Ezra and Nehemiah. According to him, it was composed in a spirit of strong antagonism to the Samaritans, "the new Ephraim," in whom the Poet sees the old Ephraim revived. In this spirit he reviews the ancient history of his nation: "what would happen if Ephraim were the centre, he infers from the misfortunes of the period between Joshua and Saul, when the ark of the covenant was yet in Shiloh, which belonged to that tribe, whereas the true worship of Jehovah was only firmly established in Zion under David . . . The history itself was a witness that rest and faith could not be found in Ephraim." But so arbitrary a treatment of the Psalm as this may at once be dismissed. Where is the proof that the Samaritans were ever regarded as the successors and legitimate representatives of Ephraim? Or what trace is there in the Psalm of any such feeling as that which Ewald supposes to have influenced the writer?

The Psalm itself furnishes us with the following data for a conclusion.

(1) It is clear from the concluding verses that it was written after David was established on the throne; from ver. 69 it might even be inferred after the Temple had been built. (2) The manner in which these events are spoken of leads naturally to the inference that they were of no very recent occurrence; men do not so speak of events within their own memory. (3) The sharp contrast between Ephraim and Judah, the rejection of Shiloh and the choice of Zion,

are an indication, not of a smouldering animosity, but of an open and long-existing separation.

But at this point two hypotheses become possible.

(*a*) On the one hand, the Psalmist's object may have been, by holding up the example of Ephraim, to warn Judah against a like falling away, not from the house of David, but from the God of their fathers. In this case we must suppose that a particular prominence is given to the conduct of Ephraim, in the past history, though the whole nation was guilty, in order to prepare the way for what is said of Ephraim's subsequent rejection (see note on ver. 9). Such a warning might be compared to that of Jeremiah at the time of the Chaldean invasion (chap. vii.).

(*b*) On the other hand, the Psalmist's design may have been not so much to warn Judah, as to rebuke Ephraim. Hence it is that whilst speaking of the past history of *all* Israel he mentions only Ephraim by name. Though all the burden of guilt in that mournful past did not rest exclusively upon them, yet it is with them only that he is concerned. Hence it is, too, that he dwells with so much pride and satisfaction on the transference of the sanctuary from Shiloh to Zion. That haughty tribe, strong in numbers and in power, might boast that it had recovered its ancient ascendency. Ten out of the twelve tribes might be lost to David's house. But God's presence and favour were not with the ten, but with the two. His sanctuary was not in Shiloh, but in Zion. He had chosen to be the ruler of His people, no scion of the thousands of Ephraim, but the shepherd stripling of the tribe of Judah.

On the whole, I confess that the tone of triumph with which the Psalm concludes seems to me to favour the last hypothesis, though I fear I must also add that I am unsupported in this view by other commentators.

The Psalm has no regular strophical division. Groups of four verses frequently occur, and the general structure may be said to rest on the common principle of pairs of verses. Here and there certain expressions recur, such as "They tempted and provoked the Most High;" "When God heard this, He was wroth," &c., which, as Hupfeld says, give a kind of epic character to the Psalm. In the review of the past history, the narrative is not given in bare chronological order, but is rather combined in two principal masses. In the first of these the Psalmist but mentions the "wonders in Egypt," and passes on to detail the events in the wilderness. Then, having set forth all God's marvellous works there, and all the rebellion of Israel, he begins the history again. He will paint more fully those "signs in Egypt," which were of themselves so wonderful a proof of

God's Redeeming Love, he will show more convincingly Israel's ingratitude, and having done this, he pursues the narrative, passing lightly now over the march through the wilderness, touching on the history in the time of the Judges, and bringing it down to the days of David, in whose election God had again magnified His grace.

[A MASCHIL OF ASAPH.[a]]

1 GIVE ear, O my people, to my law,
Incline your ear to the words of my mouth.
2 I would open my mouth in a parable,
I would utter dark sayings of old.

1—4. The Introduction, announcing the Psalmist's purpose. He will recall the past, that it may act as a warning to the present, and that the wholesome lessons which it teaches may be perpetuated in the future. In the following four verses he declares that such commemoration of God's wonders is the very destiny of Israel. For this end did He give them His law, and the lively oracles of His mouth.

1. MY PEOPLE. This does not imply that God or the Messiah is the speaker. The Prophet, speaking in the name and by the authority of God, as His inspired messenger, thus addresses the nation. The opening of the Psalm is similar to that of Ps. xlix. See also Deut. xxxii. 1; Is. i. 2.

MY LAW, here evidently used in its wider sense of *instruction* generally, as often in the Book of Proverbs. It is the teaching of a Prophet (Matt. xiii. 35), and in that sense a law—a law of life to those who hear it.

2. I WOULD OPEN. The form of the tense expresses the wish, resolve, &c. The sentence is very similar to that in xlix. 4 [5]. The two words PARABLE and DARK SAYINGS are the same which occur in that passage, where see note. The former (*mashal*) etymologically signifies *a comparison*, the placing of two objects in their due relation, whether of likeness or unlikeness; hence it is used of gnomic sentences, proverbs, parables, and indeed of poetical discourse generally (see Numbers xxi. 27, *hammosh'lîm*, "the ballad-singers"), as being based on the principle of parallelism, or of antithesis. The latter means, properly, either (1) *a sharp* or *pointed saying;* or (2) *a perplexed saying, a riddle.* (For a discussion of these words, see Delitzsch on Habak. ii. 6, and in *Gesch. der Jüd. Poesie,* S. 196, 199.) Having said so much on the meaning of these words, we have two further questions to consider.

(*a*) In what sense is the early history of Israel, which forms the subject of the Poem, called here a "parable" and "dark sayings"? Does the Psalmist merely announce his purpose of treating that history in *language of poetry* (we have seen that the word "parable" may be almost equivalent to "poetry"), or does he mean more? Does he mean that he has a *moral end* in setting forth that history? that under it truths are veiled which have a significance and an application to present circumstances for those who can read them aright? Probably, though we can hardly say certainly, the last.

(*b*) How are we to understand the quotation made by St. Matthew of this passage, who sees a fulfilment of it in the parables spoken by our Lord (Matt. xiii. 34, 35)? It cannot be supposed for a moment that these words were a prediction of our Lord's mode of teaching, or that He Himself is here the speaker.

3 (The things) which [b] we have heard and known.
And our fathers have told us,
4 We will not hide (them) from their children;
Telling to the generation to come the praises of Jehovah,
And His strength and His wonderful works that He hath done.

5 For He established a testimony in Jacob,
And appointed a law in Israel,
Which He commanded our fathers
To make known unto their children;
6 To the intent that the generation to come might know (them),
(Even) the children which should be born,
Who should rise up, and tell (them) to their children;
7 That they might put their confidence in God,
And not forget the doings of God,
But keep His commandments;
8 And might not be as their fathers,
A stubborn and rebellious generation,
A generation that was not steadfast in heart,
And whose spirit was not faithful towards God.

But here, as elsewhere, that which the Old Testament Prophet says of himself, finds its fittest expression, its highest realization, in the Great Prophet of the kingdom of heaven.

Citatur hic locus a Matthæo, et *accommodatur* ad Christi personam. . . . In hac igitur parte quum similis Prophetæ fuerit, quia de sublimibus mysteriis concionatus est in altiore dicendi forma, apposite transfertur ad ejus personam quod Propheta de se affirmat."—CALVIN. St. Matthew's quotation runs, *ὅπως πληρωθῇ τὸ ῥηθὲν διὰ τοῦ προφήτου λέγοντος, Ἀνοίξω ἐν παραβολαῖς τὸ στόμα μου, ἐρεύξομαι κεκρυμμένα ἀπὸ καταβολῆς.* The LXX. have in the latter clause: *φθέγξομαι προβλήματα ἀπ᾽ ἀρχῆς.*

4. WE WILL NOT HIDE. Comp. Job xv. 18, where it is used in like manner of the faithful transmission of truths received. All truth known is a sacred trust, given to us, not for ourselves alone, but that we may hand on the torch to others.

5. The very object with which God gave HIS LAW and HIS TESTIMONY (see on these words, note on xix. 7) was, that they might be preserved, not in writing only, but by oral communication and transmission, that they might be a living power in the people. See the commands in Ex. x. 2, xii. 26, 27, xiii. 8—10, 14, 15; Deut. iv. 9, vi. 20, &c.

8. THAT WAS NOT STEADFAST IN HEART, lit. "that did not establish its heart," was ever wavering in its allegiance. This sense is most in accordance with the parallelism; though perhaps the rendering of the E.V., "that set not their heart aright," *i.e.* towards God, might be

9 The children of Ephraim, being equipped [c] as archers,
Turned back in the day of battle.

defended : comp. 1 Sam. vii. 3 ; Job xi. 13.

9. THE CHILDREN OF EPHRAIM. An example of that "stubborn and perverse generation" mentioned ver. 8. But why are "the children of Ephraim" mentioned, and what particular sin of theirs is here alluded to? (1) We must not be led astray by the expression "equipped as archers," &c., to look for some defeats of the tribe in battle (as the Chald., the Rabb. (referring to 1 Chr. vii. 20—22), Schnurrer, and others do), for it is not a *chastisement*, but a *sin* which is spoken of. Hence the description of their carrying bows and turning back must be a figure employed in the same sense as that of "the deceitful bow," ver. 57. (2) The allusion cannot be to the separation of Ephraim and the other tribes from Judah (as Venema, De Wette, &c. explain), because it is the earlier history of the nation in the wilderness which is here before the Poet's eyes. (3) Nothing is gained by introducing the particle of comparison (so Luther, Rosenmüller, &c.), as in the P.B.V., "*like as* the children of Eph.," &c., for such a comparison rests upon nothing. (4) Nor can "the children of Ephraim" here stand merely for the whole nation, as has sometimes been maintained by referring to lxxx. 2 [3], and lxxxi. 5 [6] ; for in ver. 67 the distinction between Ephraim and Judah is marked. (5) It would seem, then, that *their* treacherous conduct is here specially stigmatized, in order, as it were, to sound the note of that rejection on which the Psalmist afterwards dwells, ver. 67. Ephraim had been, after the settlement in Canaan, the most numerous and the most powerful of the tribes. Shiloh, the religious capital of the nation, and Shehcem, the gathering-place of the tribes (Josh. xxiv. 1 ; Jud. ix. 2 ; 1 Kings xii. 1), were both within its borders. During the time of the Judges it seems to have asserted a kind of supremacy over the rest. Possibly the Psalmist is thinking of this. Having their rejection in view, he remembers their ancient position, and regards them as leaders of the people, and, morally, leaders in their sin. It is true this could only apply to their history in the land of Canaan. During the wanderings in the wilderness, with which a large part of the Psalm is occupied, the tribe of Ephraim, so far from holding a leading position, was the smallest of all, except Simeon. It may be, however, that the Psalmist forgets or neglects this circumstance, and only thinks of the tribe as the rival of Judah in later times, and the leader in the revolt. But see the remarks in the introduction to the Psalm.

A different interpretation is given in the article EPHRAIM in Smith's *Dict. of the Bible*. Hupfeld would expunge the words "the children of Ephraim" as a gloss, but it is difficult to see how such a gloss could have crept in.

EQUIPPED AS ARCHERS. This and the next clause are designed apparently to express, in a figure, the faithlessness of the Ephraimites. They are like archers who, fully equipped for war, at the critical moment when they should use their weapons, afraid to meet the shock of battle, wheel round and fly in disorder.

TURNED BACK. Comp. Jud. xx. 39, 41. Panic-struck, when they were expected to be of service; hardly (as Maurer suggests) pretending flight, like the Thracian archers, in order to take the enemy at greater advantage. In any case, the image is one of faithlessness. The next verse is an explanation of the figure.

The following paraphrase is given in the *Catena Aurea* (from Aug. Cassiod. and the Glossa Ord.).

10 They kept not the covenant of God,
And refused to walk in His Law;
11 And they forgat His doings,
And His wonderful works which He had showed them.
12 In the sight of their fathers He did wonders,
In the land of Egypt, in the field of Zoan.
13 He clave the sea, and caused them to pass through,
And made the waters to stand as an heap.
14 And He led them with the cloud in the day-time,
And all the night through with a light of fire.
15 He clave [d] rocks in the wilderness,

"The children of Ephraim taking aim and shooting with the bow, that is, promising to keep the law, and openly saying, All that the Lord hath said unto us we will do and hear, turned back in the day of battle, when they said unto Aaron, Make us gods to worship. They failed in the day of battle, that is, in the day of temptation; for the prophet Hosea saith: Ephraim is as a silly dove that hath no heart. For it is not hearing, but temptation, that puts to the proof the promise of obedience."

12. ZOAN. Its Greek name was Tanis. It "lay near the Eastern border of Lower Egypt, . . . on the east bank of the canal which was formerly the Tanitic branch" (of the Nile). "Zoan is mentioned in connection with the plagues in such a manner as to leave no doubt that it is the city spoken of in the narrative in Exodus, as that where Pharaoh dwelt. The wonders were wrought 'in the field of Zoan,' which may either denote the territory immediately round the city, or its nome, or even a kingdom. This would accord best with the shepherd-period." See the article ZOAN, in the *Dict. of the Bible*, by Mr. R. S. Poole. May not "the field of Zoan" be the rich plain which, as he tells us, "anciently extended due east as far as Pelusium, about thirty miles distant," and the whole of which, "about as far south and west as Tunis, was anciently known as 'the Fields' or 'Plains,' 'the Marshes' or 'Pasture-lands,' and which is now almost covered by the great Lake Menzeleh"? The name only occurs once in the Pentateuch, in Num. xiii. 22. (See the passage discussed in the article just quoted.)

It is remarkable that, after beginning in this verse to speak of the wonders *in Egypt*, the Psalmist drops all mention of them till ver. 43 (which is a resumption of this verse), and turns aside to dwell on the wonders *in the wilderness* (see Introduction).

13. Now follows the exemplification, in certain detailed instances, of the faithlessness and disobedience, and forgetfulness of their fathers in the wilderness. First, in ver. 13—16, some of God's wonders wrought on their behalf are mentioned, and then, ver. 17—20, the thankless and perverse spirit in which these wonders were regarded.

AS AN HEAP; borrowed from Ex. xv. 8. See note on xxxiii. 7.

15. ROCKS. The word *tsur* shows that the Psalmist is thinking in this verse of the miracle at Horeb, recorded in Ex. xvii. (See note on ver. 16.) The plural does not necessarily imply that the two great instances in which this miracle was performed, the one in the first and the other in the last year of the wandering, are here brought together (Ex. xvii. and Num. xx.); for both

And gave them drink as it had been the great deeps.[e]
16 He brought forth streams also out of the cliff,
And caused waters to run down like the rivers.

17 Yet they went on still to sin more against Him,
To rebel against[f] the Most High in the desert.
18 And they tempted God in their heart,
Asking food for their lust,
19 Yea, they spake against God;
They said, "Can God prepare a table in the wilderness?
20 Lo, He smote the rock, that waters gushed out,
And torrents rushed along:
Can He give bread also?
Will He provide flesh for his people?"

that and the verb, which (being here without the Vau consecutive) is apparently the aorist of repeated action, may only be used in the way of poetic amplification. The miracle seems as if ever repeated.

AS IT HAD BEEN THE GREAT DEEPS, lit. "and gave them, as it were, the great deep to drink" (or, "as from the depths in abundance"). De Wette calls this a "gigantic" comparison. But "the deep" here may mean, perhaps, not the sea, but the great subterranean reservoir of waters from which all fountains and streams were supposed to be supplied, as Deut. viii. 7. Comp. xlii. 7 [8], and note there.

16. The word here used (*Selâ*) "is especially applied to the cliff at Kadesh, from which Moses brought water, as *Tsur* is for that struck in Ex. xvii."—STANLEY, *Sinai and Palestine*, App. § 29. See also Chap. I. Part II. p. 95.

17. YET THEY WENT ON TO SIN. In the verses immediately preceding no special instance of transgression is recorded, though such is implied in the mention of the miracle of the water, when they murmured against God. Hence the murmuring for flesh is described as *a further and fresh* instance of sin. Hupfeld thinks it may be only a phrase borrowed from the Book of Judges, where it is commonly prefixed to each fresh act of disobedience (as in iii. 12, &c.); but there the formula is quite in place, as it follows the narration of previous transgression.

18. THEY TEMPTED GOD, *i.e.* demanded, in their unbelief, signs and wonders, to put His power to the proof, instead of waiting in faith and prayer for its exercise (repeated ver. 41, 56 as a kind of refrain, see also cvi. 14). The original is Ex. xvii. 3, 7, where also the name Massah, "tempting," is given to the spot.

19, 20. The words here put into the mouth of the people are only a poetical representation of what they said, not differing materially from the historical narrative, Ex. xvi. 3, &c., xvii. 2, 3, 7; Num. xi. 4, &c., xx. 3, &c.

19. PREPARE A TABLE, lit. "set out in order," the same phrase as in xxiii. 5.

20. WATERS GUSHED OUT occurs also cv. 41; Is. xlviii. 21.

PROVIDE, or "prepare," as in lxv. 9 [10], lxviii. 10 [11].

FLESH: the word is a poetical one. "Bread and flesh" are used in the same way of the manna and the quails, in Ex. xvi.

21 Therefore Jehovah heard (that), and was wroth,
And a fire was kindled in Jacob,
And anger also went up against Israel;
22 Because they believed not in God,
And put not their trust in His salvation.
23 He commanded also the clouds above,
And opened the doors of heaven;
24 And He rained manna upon them to eat,
And gave them the corn of heaven;
25 Bread of the mighty did they eat every one,
He sent them meat to the full.
26 He led forth the east wind in the heaven,

21—29. The awful punishment of their sin. He gives the bread which they ask (ver. 21—25), and then the flesh (ver. 26—29), but His granting of their desire is in itself the most terrible of chastisements. The representation is freely borrowed from the two accounts in Ex. xvi.; Num. xi.; more particularly the last.

21. A FIRE, with allusion to the "fire of Jehovah" in Num. xi. 1 (whence the name of the place was called Tab'erah, "burning"), where also occurs the similar expression, "And when Jehovah heard (it), His anger was kindled."

ALSO. This does not mark that the fire of God's wrath was added to the natural fire; for the last was but the expression of the first. But the particle belongs, logically, to the verb WENT UP, and denotes the retributive character of this fiery scourge. See the same use of the particle, for instance, Is. lxvi. 4.

22. HIS SALVATION, as already shown in the deliverance from Egypt.

24. RAINED. Hence the expression in the preceding verse, "opened the doors," &c. as in Gen. vii. 11; 2 Kings vii. 2; Mal. iii. 10. In the same way the manna is said to be "rained" from heaven in Ex. xvi. 4. (Every expression used shows plainly that it was a miraculous gift, and not a product of nature.) Hence, too, it is called CORN OF HEAVEN, for which we have "bread of heaven" in cv. 40; Ex. xvi. 4; John vi. 31. So again

25. BREAD OF THE MIGHTY (see the marginal rendering of the E.V.) probably means "Angels' bread," LXX. ἄρτον ἀγγέλων, not as if angels were nourished by it, or as if it were food worthy of angels, but as coming from heaven, where angels dwell. The word MIGHTY is nowhere else used of the angels, though they are said in ciii. 20, to be "mighty in strength." Hence many would render here "bread of nobles or princes" (such is the use of this word in Job xxiv. 22, xxxiv. 20), *i.e.* the finest, the most delicate bread.

26. LED FORTH, lit. "made to journey, or go forth." The verb is again the aorist of repeated action, as in ver. 15.

GUIDED (like a flock). The two verbs occur below, ver. 52, where they are used of God's conduct of His people. The usage here is borrowed from the Pentateuch, where both verbs are said of the wind, the first in Num. xi. 31, the second in Ex. x. 13. The winds are thus conceived of as God's flock, which He leads forth and directs at His pleasure.

EAST WIND . . . SOUTH WIND.

And by His power He guided the south wind,
27 And He rained flesh upon them as the dust,
And winged fowls like as the sand of the seas ;
28 And He let it fall in the midst of their camp,
Round about their habitations.
29 So they did eat and were well filled,
Seeing that He gave them their own desire.
30 They were not estranged from their desire ;—
Whilst their food was yet in their mouth,
31 The anger of God went up against them,

These may be mentioned poetically, without being intended to describe exactly the quarter from which the quails came. In Num. xi. 31, it is merely said that, "there went forth a wind from Jehovah, and brought quails from *the sea*," which Hupfeld too hastily asserts must be the Red Sea (*i.e.* as he evidently means, the gulf of Suez); and that consequently the quails must have been brought by a west wind. But Kibroth-hattaavah was probably not far from the western edge of the gulf of Akabah. And the quails at the time of this event were, as Mr. Houghton has remarked (see QUAILS, in *Dict. of the Bible*), on their spring journey of migration *northwards*. "The flight which fed the multitude at Kibroth-hattaavah might have started from Southern Egypt, and crossed the Red Sea near Ras Mohammed, and so up the gulf of Akabah into Arabia Petræa." In this case, the wind blowing from the south first, and then from the east, would bring the quails.

27. RAINED FLESH : as before, "rained manna," from Ex. xvi. 4, 8, 13.

28. LET IT FALL. The word aptly describes the settling of these birds, unfitted for a long flight, and wearied by their passage across the gulf. Pliny, *Nat. Hist.* x. 33, says that quails settle on the sails of ships by night, so as to sink sometimes the ships in the neighbouring sea. And Diod. Sic. i. p. 38, τὰς θηρὰς των ὀρτύγων ἐποιοῦντο ἐφέροντό τε οὗτοι κατ' ἀγέλας μείζους ἐκ τοῦ πελάγους. The verse follows Ex. xvi. 13 ; Num. xi. 31.

29. WERE WELL FILLED, *i.e.* even to loathing, as follows, ver. 30 (see Num. xi. 18—20). So in ver. 25, "to the full," from Ex. xvi. 3, 12.

THEIR DESIRE, the satisfaction of their fleshly appetite. The word (*taavah*) no doubt alludes to Kibroth-*hattaavah*, "the graves of desire, or fleshly appetite." Num. xi. 4, 34.

30. THEY WERE NOT ESTRANGED, or, as it may be rendered, "(Whilst) they were not (yet) estranged," *i.e.* whilst they still found satisfaction and enjoyment in this kind of food, whilst it was yet in their mouths, the anger of God went up, &c. Thus the two verses, 30, 31, stand in the relation of protasis and apodosis. The passage is manifestly borrowed from Num. xi. 33, "And while the flesh was yet between their teeth, ere it was chewed, the wrath of Jehovah was kindled against the people, and Jehovah smote the people with a very great plague ;" and so closely borrowed as to be evidence that this portion of the Pentateuch already existed in writing. But, unfortunately, we cannot draw hence any argument for the age of the whole Pentateuch in its present form.

31. WENT UP. See above, ver 21, and xviii. 8 [9].

And slew the fattest of them,
And smote down the young men of Israel.
32 For all this, they sinned yet more,
And believed not His wondrous works.
33 Therefore did He make their days vanish in a breath,
And their years in terror.
34 When He slew them, then they enquired after Him,
Yea, they turned again and sought God;
35 And they remembered that God was their Rock,
And the Most High God their Redeemer.
36 But they flattered Him with their mouth;
And they lied unto Him with their tongue;
37 For their heart was not steadfast with Him,
Neither were they faithful in His covenant.
38 But He, in His tender mercy, covereth iniquity, and destroyeth not;

31. THE FATTEST: it may mean either the strongest, or the noblest. Comp. xxii. 29 [30]. On these and the young men, the flower of the people, the judgement especially falls.

32. The allusion seems to be to Num. xiv. 11, "How long will it be ere they believe Me, for all the signs which I have showed among them;" the words of God to Moses after the return of the spies. And this is the more likely, because the next verse alludes to that cutting short of the life of the people, which was the consequence of their rebellion at that time. Num. xiv. 28—34.

33. IN A BREATH, or possibly, "*as* a breath," the prep. merely introducing the predicate. See xxxix. 5, 6 [6, 7], and the complaint of Moses, xc. 9, though the word there used is different.

34. The passage which follows, to the end of ver. 39, is a most striking and affecting picture of man's heart, and God's gracious forbearance, in all ages:—man's sin calling for chastisement, the chastisement producing only temporary amendment, God's goodness forgotten, and yet God's great love never wearied, and God's infinite compassion ever moved afresh by man's weakness and misery.

36. FLATTERED. Comp. Is. xxi. 13, lvii. 11, lix. 13. "This returning to God, at least so far as the majority were concerned, was not from any love of righteousness, but only from the fear of punishment."—*Lyra.*

37. THEIR HEART WAS NOT STEADFAST, &c. This is the ever-repeated complaint, see ver. 8, 22. There is no permanence, no stability in the reformation which has been produced. Comp. Hos. vi. 4.

38. The verbs in the first clause are present, and should be so rendered. It destroys the whole beauty of the passage to render, "But He *was* so merciful, &c., as if the reference were only to a particular occasion. God's mercy is like Himself, everlasting, and ever the same.

BUT HE. The words are emphatic, and the allusion is to Ex. xxxiv. 6; Num. xiv. 18, 20.

Yea, many a time turneth He His anger away,
And stirreth not up all His fury.
39 And He remembered that they were (but) flesh,
A wind that goeth and cometh not again.

40 How often did they provoke Him in the wilderness,
And grieve Him in the desert:
41 Yea, again and again they tempted God,
And dishonoured [g] the Holy One of Israel.
42 They remembered not His hand,
Nor the day when He redeemed them from the adversary.
43 How He had set His signs in Egypt,
And His wonders in the field of Zoan,
44 And turned their rivers into blood,
So that they could not drink of their streams.
45 He sent among them flies which devoured them,
And frogs which destroyed them.

39. Compare Gen. vi. 3, viii. 21: Job vii. 7, 9, x. 21; Ps. ciii. 14—16; and for the word "goeth" or "passeth away" of the wind, Hos. vi. 4, xiii. 3.

40. After thus celebrating God's tender compassion in striking contrast with the perpetual rebellion and ingratitude of the people, the Psalmist resumes the sad tale afresh. But instead of mentioning other instances of rebellion in the wilderness (ver. 40), he passes from that topic to dwell on the wonders wrought in Egypt, the lively recollection of which ought to have kept the people from these repeated provocations. Thus he takes up again the thread dropped at ver. 12.

The second principal portion of the Psalm begins with this verse. It is occupied, first, with the narrative of the plagues in Egypt, the Exodus, and Israel's entrance into the Promised Land, ver. 40—55. It then touches briefly on the history under the Judges, the Philistine invasion in the time of Eli, which was God's chastisement for transgression, the disaster at Shiloh, whereby Ephraim was robbed of his ancient honours, and which led to the choice of Zion, the ascendency of the tribe of Judah, and the union of the kingdom under David, ver. 56—72.

41. DISHONOURED, or perhaps "provoked." Others, "limited," *i.e.* set bounds to His power. See Critical Note.

43. In the enumeration of the plagues, the Psalmist does not follow the order of the history, except as regards the first and the last, and omits all mention of the third (the lice), the fifth (murrain of cattle), the sixth (boils and blains on man and beast), and the ninth (darkness).

44. The first plague. Comp. Ex. vii. 17, &c.

45. The fourth plague (Ex. viii. 20, &c.), and the second plague (Ex. viii. 1, &c.).

FLIES. The LXX. and Sym. **κυνόμυιαν.** The rendering of the

46 He gave also their increase unto the caterpiller,
(And) their labour unto the locust.
47 He killed their vines with hail,
And their sycomore-trees with frost :
48 He gave up their cattle also to the hail,
And their flocks to hot thunder-bolts.
49 He let loose upon them the burning of His anger,
Wrath and indignation and distress,
A letting loose of evil angels [h] (among them).

E.V. "*divers sorts* of flies," (Aq. πάμμικτον), comes from a wrong derivation of the word from a root signifying *to mix*.

46. CATERPILLER, or possibly the word means some particular species of locust, or the locust in its larva state. See *Dict. of the Bible*, III. App. xxxix. This word is not used in the Pentateuch, but in Joel i. 4, it is joined with the locust, as here.

47, 48. The seventh plague, that of the hail mingled with fire (Ex. ix. 13), with its effects, both on the produce of the land and on the cattle. As belonging to the former, vines and sycomores are here mentioned, as in cv. 33, vines, and fig-trees. De Wette and Hupfeld assert that the writer, as a native of Canaan, ascribes too much prominence to the vine, the cultivation of which was but little attended to in Egypt, and which is not said in the Pentateuch to have suffered. But this is an unfounded assertion. Mr. R. S. Poole, in his learned article on Egypt, in the *Dict. of the Bible*, says : "Vines were extensively cultivated, and there were several different kinds of wine, one of which, the Mareotic, was famous among the Romans." (Vol. i. p. 497.) Pharaoh's chief butler dreams of the vine, Gen. xl. 9—11, and the vines of Egypt, as well as the figs and pomegranates, are thought of with regret by the Israelites in the wilderness (Num. xx. 5). The mural paintings at Thebes, at Beni-Hassan, and in the Pyramids, contain representations of vineyards. Boys are seen frightening away the birds from the ripe clusters, men gather them and deposit them in baskets, and carry them to the wine-press, &c.

47. FROST, or, as this is unknown in Egypt, perhaps, rather, "huge hailstones," but the word occurs nowhere else, and its meaning is uncertain.

48. HOT THUNDER-BOLTS, or "lightnings ; " the same word as in lxxvi. 3 [4], "*lightnings* of the bow," where see note, the allusion being to the fire which ran along the ground, Ex. ix. 23. Comp. cv. 32.

49. This verse expresses generally the whole work of devastation wrought by the Divine ministers of evil in the land of Egypt, and so strikingly introduces the final act of judgement, the destruction of the first-born, which follows in ver. 50, 51. I see no reason for supposing, as Hupfeld and Delitzsch do, that there is any allusion to the fifth plague, that of the murrain among cattle.

A LETTING LOOSE, or, "a mission," "embassage"; this is a noun, in apposition with the preceding nouns, and further describing the action of the verb, "He let loose." The Poet lifts the veil and shows us the wrath of God as the source, and angels as the ministers in the destruction.

EVIL ANGELS. Others render,

50 He made a free path for His anger ;
He spared not their soul from death,
But gave their life over to the pestilence ;
51 And smote all the first-born in Egypt,
The firstlings of (their) strength in the tents of Ham.
52 But He made His own people to go forth like sheep,
And guided them in the wilderness like a flock.
53 And He led them safely so that they did not fear ;
And as for their enemies, the sea covered (them).
54 And He brought them to His holy border,
To yon mountain which His right hand had purchased.
55 He drove out also the nations before them,
And allotted them for an inheritance by line,
And made the tribes of Israel to dwell in their tents.
56 But they tempted and provoked the Most High God,

"angels or messengers, (the word may mean either, as ἄγγελος, in Greek) of evil," *i.e.* who work evil. So Hengstenberg and Delitzsch, who adopt the view of Ode, in his work *De Angelis*, that God makes use of good angels to punish bad men, and of evil angels to buffet and chasten good men. But this cannot be maintained : see 1 Sam. xvi. 14 ; 1 Kings xxii. 21, &c. However, whichever rendering is preferred, it comes to the same thing, for "evil angels" would not mean here what was commonly understood by evil spirits, but angels sent upon an evil mission—a mission of destruction. There can be no doubt of this, because the expression must have been suggested by "the detroyer" in Ex. xii. 13, 23.

50. MADE A FREE PATH, lit. "levelled a path," as Prov. iv. 26, v. 6.

51. FIRSTLINGS OF THEIR STRENGTH, lit. "beginning of strengths," the plural being used poetically for the singular, which is found in the same phrase, Gen. xlix. 3 ; Deut. xxi. 17.

TENTS OF HAM. So "land of Ham," in cv. 23, 27, cvi. 22. Comp. Gen. x. 6.

54. YON MOUNTAIN, *i.e.* Zion, the building of the temple there being represented, as in lxviii. 16 [17], as the great crowning act to which all else pointed ; unless the noun is used here collectively = "these mountains," *i.e.* this mountain-land of Palestine, as in Ex. xv. 17, "the mountain of Thine inheritance." Comp. Is. xi. 9. This last it may be said, is favoured by the parallelism.

55. AND ALLOTTED THEM, lit. "made them fall," in allusion to the *throwing* of the lot. The pronoun "them" is used somewhat incorrectly (the nations having been just spoken of as driven out), instead of "their land." Comp. Josh. xxiii. 4, "See, I have allotted (made to fall) unto you these nations," &c. Num. xxxiv. 2, "the land which *falleth* to you as an inheritance."

BY LINE. See note on xvi. 6.

56—58. The renewed disobedience of the nation, after their settlement in the land during the time of the Judges.

56. TEMPTED AND PROVOKED,

And kept not His testimonies ;
57 But turned back and dealt faithlessly, like their fathers :
They were turned aside like a deceitful bow.
58 And they angered Him with their high places,
And moved Him to jealousy with their graven images.
59 When God heard (this), He was wroth,
And greatly abhorred Israel ;
60 So that He rejected the tabernacle in Shiloh,
The tent which He pitched among men.
61 And He gave His strength into captivity,
And His beauty into the adversary's hand.
62 Yea, He gave over His people to the sword,
And was wroth with His inheritance.
63 Their young men the fire devoured,
And their maidens were not praised[i] in the marriage-song:

repeated from ver. 17, 18, and 41 ; here the special act of provocation being the worship of idols in the high places. Comp. Jud. ii. 11, &c.

57. A DECEITFUL BOW, *i.e.* one which disappoints the archer, by not sending the arrow straight to the mark (not "a *slack* bow, as some would explain, referring to Prov. x. 4, "a slack hand").

60. The tabernacle was at Shiloh during the whole period of the Judges (Josh. xviii. 10; Jud. xviii. 31 ; 1 Sam. iv. 3). God rejected and forsook it when the Ark was given into the hands of the Philistines, 1 Sam. iv. The Ark was never brought back thither, and the Tabernacle itself was removed first to Nob (1 Sam. xxi.), and subsequently to Gibeon (1 Kings iii. 4). Jeremiah when warning the nation against the superstitious notion that the Temple would be a defence, reminds them how God had forsaken and rejected the place of the first Tabernacle : "For go now to My place which was in Shiloh, where I made My name to dwell at the first, and see what I have done to it, because of the wickedness of My people Israel." (Jer. vii. 12. See also ver. 14, and chap. xxvi. 6.) These passages do not, perhaps, necessarily imply a destruction of Shiloh by enemies, certainly nothing of the kind meets us in the history,—but a desolation which followed on the removal of the sanctuary. Calvin observes: "The mode of expression is very emphatic ; that God was so offended with the sins of His people, that He was forced to forsake the one place in the whole world which He had chosen."

PITCHED, lit. "caused to dwell." Comp. Josh. xviii. 1, xxii. 19.

61. HIS STRENGTH (or perhaps, "glory"). . . . HIS BEAUTY. The Ark is so called as being the place where God manifested His power and glory. Comp. 1 Sam. iv. 3, 21, and Ps. cxxxii. 8.

63, 64. The utter desolation of the land strikingly pictured by its *silence*. Neither the joyous strains of the marriage-song, nor the sad wail of the funeral chant fall upon the ear. It was a land of silence, a land of the dead. Comp. Jer. xxii. 18 ; Ezek. xxiv. 23 ; Job xxvii. 15. There is perhaps, an allusion in

64 Their priests fell by the sword,
And their widows made no lamentation.

65 Then the Lord awaked, as one out of sleep,
Like a mighty man that shouteth by reason of wine;
66 And He smote His adversaries backward,
He put them to a perpetual reproach.
67 And He rejected the tent of Joseph,
And chose not the tribe of Ephraim;
68 But chose the tribe of Judah,
The mount Zion which He loved.
69 And He built His sanctuary like high places,
Like the earth which He hath founded for ever.
70 He chose David also, His servant,
And took him from the sheep-folds;
71 As he was following the ewes giving suck, He brought him,
To feed Jacob His people,
And Israel His inheritance.
72 So he fed them according to the integrity of his heart,
And led them with the skilfulness of his hands.

ver. 64 to the death of Hophni and Phinehas.

65, 66. God punishes and then delivers. The reference is to the long series of victories over the Philistines under Samuel, Saul, and David.

65. AS ONE OUT OF SLEEP, lit. "as a sleeper." Comp. vii. 6 [7], xliv. 23 [24].

LIKE A MIGHTY MAN: comp. Is. xlii. 13.

68. THE TRIBE OF JUDAH, though the sanctuary was planted, not "in Judah only, or in Benjamin only, but on the confines of both (comp. Josh. xv. 63 with Jud. i. 21); so that whilst the altars and the holy place were to stand within the borders of the one tribe, the courts of the Temple were to extend into the borders of the other tribe, and thus the two were to be riveted together, as it were, by a cramp, bound by a sacred and everlasting bond."—Blunt, *Undesigned Coincidences*, &c. p. 181.

69. LIKE HIGH PLACES, &c., or as we might say, "high as heaven, and sure as the solid earth."

70—72. The faithful shepherd of the flock became the faithful shepherd of the nation; just as the obedient fishermen in the Gospel history became the successful fishers of men.

On the figure here employed, see lxxvii. 20 [21], and the remarks in Introduction to Vol. I. p. 97.

[a] See above on xxxix. note [a], and l. note [a].

[b] אֲשֶׁר. The relative may refer to what precedes. Or it may form with the suffix ־ֵם following, a neuter = *quæ;* the relative clause, contrary to rule, being placed before the antecedent. "(The things) which we know . . . (those things) we will not hide." For a similar indefinite use of the suffix see xxxix. 7.

[c] נוֹשְׁקֵי רוֹמֵי ק׳. (LXX. ἐντείνοντες καὶ βάλλοντες τόξον.) This is a compound phrase which has perplexed the commentators. For the two words in the stat. constr. are not, as is usual in such cases, in construction, the first with the second, and the second with the noun following, but are each in construction with the noun קֶשֶׁת, for we have נוֹשְׁקֵי ק׳, 1 Chron. xii. 2; 2 Chron. xvii. 17, meaning "armed with bows," and רוֹמֵי ק׳, Jer. iv. 29, "shooting with bows." Hence Hupfeld calls it "a hybrid phrase," and would strike out one of the words as a gloss; but we have an exact parallel in Jer. xlvi. 9, תֹּפְשֵׂי דֹּרְכֵי ק׳, as he admits. The phrase בַּת בְּתוּלַת צִיּוֹן, lit. "the virgin of Zion, the daughter of Zion," is another instance of the same construction. Maurer, in a note on Jer. xlvi. 9, has drawn attention to this construction, which, as he observes, has escaped the notice of the grammarians. נשק means properly *adjungere, applicare, conserere* (as in נֶשֶׁק, *armour,* as that which fits together), and then *prehendere* (manu), *tenere, tractare.*

[d] יְבַקַּע. Hupf. speaks of this merely as "a pret. without ו consec., as frequently in this Psalm, alternating with imperf. cons., vers. 26, 45, 47, 49, 50." But I prefer regarding it as an aor. of repeated action, not "continuance of an action," as Phillips—who, however, well explains the use of the tense, "as often as water was wanted by the Israelites in the wilderness, the rock was cleft."

[e] כִּתְהֹמוֹת רַבָּה. The plur. noun is apparently used for the sing. (comp. Gen. vii. 11; Ps. xxxvi. 7), like בְּהֵמוֹת ,חָכְמוֹת, &c. Hence the adj. is in the sing. The Chald. changes the adj. into the plur., in order to make it agree with the noun. The LXX. ἐν ἀβύσσῳ πολλῇ. So the older Verss., generally, take the two words as in concord. Others consider רַבָּה to be an adverb, as lxii. 3, lxxxix. 8. "The imperf. consec. [at the beginning of the verse] marks the consequence, which is here contrary to expectation." (De Wette.)

[f] לַמְרוֹת, as Is. iii. 8. Inf. Hiph. for לְהַמְרוֹת, from מרה (as cvi. 7; comp. for other instances lxxiii. 20, Is. xxiii. 11), construed sometimes with acc., as here and ver. 40, 56, sometimes with בְּ or with עִם.

[g] הִתְווּ. The Hiph. occurs again in Ezek. ix. 4 in the sense of "putting a mark" (on the forehead). This has been explained in two ways: (1) "they put boundaries (marks) limits" to the power of God. Or (2), as Hengst., Del., and others, "they branded with reproach" (Del. *brandmarkten*). But we may perhaps connect it with the Syr. ܬܘܳܐ, *pœnituit eum, doluit.* So the LXX. παρώξυναν. Vulg. *exacerbaverunt.* Jerome, *concitaverunt.*

h מַלְאֲכֵי רָעִים. This is commonly rendered "angels (or messengers) of evil," *i.e.* causing evil, generally of the object, as in Prov. xvi. 4, "messengers of death," and רָעִים is supposed to be a neuter = רָעוֹת, "evil things." This may perhaps be defended by נְגִידִים, *nobilia*, Prov. viii. 6, though Hupf. contends that אֲמָרִים must be supplied there, as with the adjectives in ver. 9 of the same chapter; to which it may be replied that the noun has immediately preceded, and would therefore be easily understood in ver. 9, which is not the case in ver. 6. However, it is better to explain מ׳ ר׳ as "angels (belonging to the class) of evil ones," i.e. *evil angels*. (So the LXX. πονηρῶν; Symm. κακούντων.) Comp. the same use of the adj. after the constr. in Num. v. 18, "waters (belonging to the class) of bitter (waters)." Jer. xxiv. 2, "figs of the early ones." See also Is. xvii. 6; 1 Kings x. 15.

i הוּלָּלוּ. This is not (as Schnurr.) pret. Hoph. of ילל = *ejulare factæ sunt*, i.e. *ejularunt*; for that must mean "they *were* lamented." It is merely by incorrect writing for הֻלָּלוּ (Aq. ὑμνήθησαν; Symm. Th. ἐπηνέθησαν), "were sung with praises," *i.e.* at the marriage feast. (Comp. הִלּוּלִים, "of the harvest feast," Jud. ix. 21, with xvi. 24; Lev. xix. 24, and the Rabb. בית הלולא, "marriage house," דבי הלולי, T. B. *Berachoth* 6b).

PSALM 79

This Psalm is a lamentation over the same great national calamity which, as we have already seen, is bewailed in terms so pathetic in the Seventy-fourth. The two Psalms have, indeed, some points of difference as well as of resemblance. The great features in the scene of misery are presented in the two with a different degree of prominence. In the one, the destruction of the Temple occupies the foreground; in the other, the terrible carnage which had made the streets of Jerusalem run with blood is the chief subject of lamentation. In the former, the hope of deliverance and triumph breaks out strongly in the very midst of the sorrow and the wailing (lxxiv. 12, &c.). In the latter, the tone of sadness prevails throughout, with the exception of the short verse with which the Psalm concludes. There is also a marked difference in style. The Seventy-fourth Psalm is abrupt, and sometimes obscure: the Seventy-ninth, on the contrary, flows smoothly and easily throughout.

But these differences are balanced by resemblances not less observable. Thus, for instance, we may compare lxxix. 5, "how long for ever," with lxxiv. 1, 10; lxxix. 1, the desecration of the

Temple, with lxxiv. 3, 7; lxxix. 2, the giving up to the wild beast, with lxxiv. 19; lxxix. 12, the reproach of the God of Israel with lxxiv. 10, 18, 22; lxxix. 13, the comparison of Israel to a flock, with lxxiv. 1. There is the same deep pathos in both Psalms; in both, the same picturesque force of description; both the one and the other may be called, without exaggeration, the funeral anthem of a nation.

There can, therefore, be little doubt that both Psalms, even if not written by the same poet, yet bewail the same calamity. It is equally certain that there are but two periods of the national history to which the language of either could properly apply. But in attempting to draw our inference from this Psalm, the same difficulties meet us which have already met us in our attempts to determine the date of Psalm lxxiv. Does the Psalm deplore the destruction of Jerusalem by Nebuchadnezzar, or is it a dirge over the sack of the city by Antiochus Epiphanes?

That the history of the Canon does not exclude the later of these periods, I must still maintain, notwithstanding the positive and contemptuous manner in which Dr. Pusey has recently expressed himself on this subject (*Lectures on Daniel*, pp. 56, 292, &c.). There is not a shadow of proof (as I have pointed out in the Introduction to Vol. I., pp. 18, 19) that the Canon was closed before the Maccabean era. We are therefore at liberty to form our opinion as to the probable date of the Psalm purely on internal evidence. And, indeed, it is on this ground that Hengstenberg undertakes to show that the Psalm refers to the Chaldean invasion. Let us examine his arguments.

(1) He contends that there are no traces of any special reference to the Maccabean times. To this it may be replied, that it is almost impossible to find in any Psalm language so precise as to fix at once the date and the occasion for which it was written. But in this instance the fact that the desecration, and not the destruction of the Temple is lamented, is certainly more easily explained on the Maccabean hypothesis than on the Chaldean. Antiochus Epiphanes defiled the Temple, Nebuchadnezzar destroyed it.

(2) He asserts that the language used in ver. 1, "They have made Jerusalem an heap of stones," and so general a slaughter as that described in ver. 2, 3, are not applicable to the history of the Maccabean age. It is sufficient answer to say, that the first chapter of the First Book of the Maccabees altogether refutes such an assertion. The desolation of Jerusalem, and the slaughter there spoken of, might adequately, and without exaggeration, be described in the language of the Psalm: the difference is only the difference between poetry and prose.

(3) He objects that in the Psalm (ver. 6) "kingdoms and nations" are spoken of, whereas in the Syrian period the Jews had to do with only one kingdom. But it is obvious that in the one struggle was involved the whole principle of the antagonism to the heathen world at large. And nothing is more common than for the prophets and poets to extend their range of vision beyond the single enemy, or the immediate conflict, so as to embrace a larger issue.

There is one expression in the Psalm, and one only, which may seem to favour the Babylonish exile: "Let the sighing of the prisoner come before Thee" (ver. 11). But even this might be used equally well of the captives who were carried away by the army of Antiochus (1 Macc. i. 32). So far, then, there is no positive evidence—and this Delitzsch cordially admits—in favour of one period rather than of the other.

We now come to difficulties of a more formidable kind. Two passages in the Psalm are found elsewhere; the one in Jeremiah and the other in the First Book of Maccabees.

Verses 6 and 7 stand almost word for word in Jer. x. 25. Does the Prophet quote from the Psalmist, or the Psalmist from the Prophet?

In favour of the former supposition it may be said: (1) That it is Jeremiah's habit to quote largely from other writers, especially from Job and the Psalms; (2) That in his prophecy the verse immediately preceding the 24th verse of the chapter, is a quotation from the Sixth Psalm; (3) That the words occupy a more natural position in the Psalm than they do in the Prophecy, inasmuch as the *prayer* that God would punish the heathen follows immediately on the *complaint* that His wrath burns like fire against Israel; and also inasmuch as the word "pour out" seems to have been employed designedly with reference to the use of the same verb in ver. 3, "they have poured out" (E.V. "they have shed"); (4) That the difficult singular, ver. 7 (see note), is changed in Jeremiah into the plural, and the passage further altered and expanded by the addition, "and they have devoured him and consumed him," which is quite in the style of Jeremiah, who rarely quotes without some alteration of the kind.

The first and the last of these reasons are certainly not without force.

On the other hand, Hupfeld argues with regard to (3), that the passage, as it stands in Jeremiah, is anything but out of place; that the language there, on the contrary, is more definite, the contrast being this, that God would correct His own people with judgement, *i.e.* in measure, but that He would pour out all His fury without measure upon their enemies. He contends that this (expressing the same contrast which occurs elsewhere in chap. xxx. 11, xlvi. 28) must be the original passage. However, this question of coherence does not go for much. Considering the abruptness of transition natural to lyric poetry, even a want of close connection would be no proof that the passage was borrowed by the Psalmist. And, on the other hand, the connection for which Hupfeld contends, does not seem to be closer or more obvious than that in the Psalm.

There is, however, another and a very serious difficulty. This Psalm, supposing it to refer to Nebuchadnezzar, must have been written during the Exile—probably some time after the destruction of the Temple. Psalm Seventy-four, in like manner, which speaks of "the everlasting desolations," must have been composed at a comparatively late period of the Captivity. But when were the passages in Jeremiah's prophecy written, which connect them with these Psalms? Jeremiah, in chap. x. 17, 18, predicts the Captivity, and hence that part of his prophecy seems to be in time prior to the Psalm; and Hengstenberg can only evade this difficulty by the supposition that this chapter was not *written* in its present form till after the destruction of Jerusalem. This however is a mere assumption, without a shadow of proof.

Another difficulty still remains. Ver. 3 is quoted in 1 Macc. vii. 16. The quotation is introduced by the formula κατὰ τὸν λόγον ὃν ἔγραψε (in the Syriac, "according to the word which the prophet has written"). This, Hengstenberg says, is the usual mode of citing from the Canonical Scriptures, and hence he contends that the quotation could not be from a Psalm written at the time of the persecution of Antiochus. But this does not follow, even if the use of ἔγραψε be as limited as he would make it. As I have remarked, it cannot be shown that the Canon was completed before the age of the Maccabees, and *the writer* of the Book lived long after the events which he narrates. Hence it would be quite natural for him to refer to a Poem which had sprung out of the very circumstances of his history. Delitzsch even (i. 557) thinks that the aorist ἔγραψε sounds as if the quotation were from some work which was produced under the pressure of the calamities which the author is describing.

It has not I believe been noticed, and yet it appears to me almost certain, that the prayer of Daniel (ix. 19) contains allusions to the language of this Psalm: "for our sins and for the iniquities of our fathers (comp. ver. 8 of the Psalm, where, though the word 'forefathers' is different, the thought is the same), Jerusalem and Thy people are become a reproach to all that are about us" (comp. ver. 4 of the Psalm).

Still the question must remain an open one whether the passage in Jeremiah or in the Psalm is the original. Unless this question can be positively settled, we have no clue to guide us as to the age of the Psalm. Its language would apply almost equally well either to the time of Nebuchadnezzar or to that of Antiochus Epiphanes. This seems to have been felt by some of the earlier commentators, who, without venturing to bring it down in point of actual composition so low as the latter period, have supposed it to be a prophecy of that calamitous time. So Cassiodorus: "Deplorat vero Antiochi persecutionem tempore Maccabeorum factam, tunc futuram, scilicet in spiritu prophetico quasi præteritam propter certitudinem eventus."

The Psalm can hardly be said to have any regular strophical divisions.

It consists, first, of a complaint (ver. 1—4); and then of a prayer that God would visit His people again in mercy and pour out His vengeance upon their enemies (ver. 5—12); whilst a closing verse announces the gratitude with which God's mercy will be acknowledged (ver. 13).

[A PSALM OF ASAPH.]

1 O GOD, the heathen are come into Thine inheritance;
They have defiled Thy holy temple;
They have made Jerusalem a heap of stones.

1—4. Lament over the terrible calamities which have befallen the nation.

HEATHEN. I have retained in this Psalm the rendering of the E.V. "heathen," because the enemies of Jerusalem are here so designated not merely as consisting of different nations (though the Chaldean army was thus composed), but as *profane* intruders upon the sacred soil. A religious idea is evidently associated with the use of the word. Elsewhere I have thought it better to keep "nations" uniformly as the rendering of the Hebrew word, *Goyim*.

THINE INHERITANCE, the holy land and the holy people (comp. lxxiv. 2, lxxviii. 62, 71, holy as the abode of God (as Exod. xv. 17), itself a sanctuary. The same idea of profanation, as connected with foreign conquests, occurs frequently in the Prophets (see Joel iii. [iv.] 17; Nah. i. 15 [ii. 1]; Is. xxxv. 8, lii. 1, and especially, as parallel with this passage, Lam. i. 10).

DEFILED. Although to a pious Jew this defilement would be a thing of not less horror than the destruction of the holy house, still it is remarkable that if the Chaldean invasion be meant, the profanation only, and not the destruction of the Temple (as in lxxiv.) should be lamented.

A HEAP OF STONES, or rather plur. "heaps of stones," "ruins." Thus was the prophecy of Micah fulfilled, which he uttered in the time of Hezekiah (iii. 12). See also

2 They have given the dead bodies of Thy servants
To be meat unto the fowls of the heaven,
The flesh of Thy beloved unto the beasts [a] of the earth.
3 They have poured out their blood like water round about Jerusalem;
And there was none to bury [b] (them).

Jer. xxvi. 18, where the prophecy is quoted. In both passages the same word is used, and in the E. V. rendered "heaps." It occurs also in the sing., Mic. i. 6, "I will make Samaria a *heap* of the field." The LXX. have ὀπωροφυλάκιον, "a garden-lodge," which is explained by a scholion of the *Cod. Vatic.* 754 (quoted by Delitzsch) as λιθολόγιος τόπος, ὅπου τὴν σκηνὴν ἔχει ὁ τὰς ὀπώρας φυλάσσων. The Vulg. *in pomorum custodiam*, in the same sense, probably, as Cassiodorus explains, with reference to Is. i. 8, "as a lodge in a garden of cucumbers." Lyra says: "Id est in acervum lapidum, custodes enim pomorum faciunt magnum acervum lapidum, ut desuper ascendentes videant per totum pomœrium." But the word employed in this sense is a different word. See Hos. xii. 11 [12].

2. That which the Psalmist here laments was threatened by Jeremiah, vii. 33, "And the carcases of this people shall be meat for the fowls of the heaven and for the beasts of the earth," &c. See also viii. 2; ix. 22; xv. 3; xvi. 4; xix. 7; the original passage being Deut. xxviii. 26.

THE BELOVED, or, "Thy godly ones." See on xvi. 10. Vaihinger argues that such a designation of the people is a proof that the Psalm cannot belong to the Chaldean invasion: for then the nation was utterly evil and corrupt. But in l. 5, the same title is given to the whole nation as in covenant with God, at the very time when they are charged with breaking that covenant. So Habakkuk, after complaining of the corruption of his people, and seeing that their sins will bring God's judgement upon them, still speaks of them as "righteous," in contrast with the Chaldeans, who are "wicked" (Hab. i. 13). So it may be here; unless, indeed, the Psalmist is thinking rather of "the faithful few," the "holy seed," than of the many whose sins had called for chastisement.

Some of those who regard this as a Maccabean Psalm have seen in the word *Chasîdîm* an allusion to the 'Ασιδαῖοι who were slain by Alcimus, 1 Macc. vii.

3. This verse is quoted, but not exactly (probably therefore from memory), from the version of the LXX., in 1 Macc. vii. 16, 17, the Greek translator of the First Book of the Maccabees, being familiar with the Greek Psalter, as Ewald has shown (*Jahrb.* vi. 25). For the bearing of this quotation on the age of the Psalm see the Introduction.

THEY HAVE POURED OUT. And so again in ver. 10, "which is poured out." For it is the same word which occurs also in ver. 6, "*Pour out* Thy fury," &c.; and there may perhaps be, as Hengstenberg thinks, a designed antithesis in the repetition of the word. "As they have poured out our blood, as do Thou pour out upon them Thy fury."

NONE TO BURY, this being according to the deep-rooted feeling of all ancient nations, a great aggravation of the calamity. Comp. Jer. xiv. 16, xxii. 18, 19.

4 We are become a reproach to our neighbours.
A scorn and derision to them that are round about us.

5 How long, O Jehovah, wilt Thou be angry for ever?
Shall Thy jealousy burn like fire?
6 Pour out Thy fury on the heathen which know Thee not,
And upon the kingdoms which have not called upon Thy Name.
7 For they have devoured [c] Jacob,
And laid waste his pasture.
8 Oh remember not against us the iniquities of (our) forefathers; [d]

4. With the exception of the first word, this is an exact repetition of xliv. 13 [14], where see note. (That Psalm, as we have seen, may perhaps be of the Maccabean age.) Comp. also lxxx. 6 [7].

NEIGHBOURS. Such as the Edomites, for instance (see cxxxvii. 7, Lam. iv. 21, 22), if the earlier date be preferred.

5—7. God may make use of the heathen as "the rod of His anger," wherewith to chasten His people, but nevertheless, when His purpose is accomplished, then His wrath is turned against the oppressor. Comp. Ps. x. 5, &c. It is in this conviction that the Psalmist prays, ver. 6, "Pour out," &c. The ground of his prayer is not only that they have not called upon God's name, but that they have *devoured Jacob.* Hence He asks for a righteous retribution. Precisely in the same spirit Habakkuk long before had said of the Chaldeans: "O Jehovah, for judgement Thou hast ordained them, and, O Thou Rock, for correction Thou hast appointed them" (i. 12); and then, after pourtraying the work of judgement wrought by that "bitter and hasty nation," he tells of "the parable" and "taunting proverb" which shall greet their utter overthrow (ii. 6, &c.). The same law of righteous retribution is frequently recognised by the Prophets. See for instance Is. x. 12, 24—26, and elsewhere.

5. FOR EVER. On this, as joined with the question, see on xiii. 2.

LIKE FIRE. Comp. lxxviii. 21, and the original passage, Deut. xxxii. 22.

6. This verse and the next are repeated with slight variation in Jer. x. 25. As to the question whether the Psalmist borrowed from the Prophet, or the Prophet from the Psalmist, see Introduction.

7. PASTURE; or, "habitation of shepherds." Such is the proper meaning of the word (not *sanctuary*, as the Chald.—but see 2 Sam. xv. 25). Comp. lxxxiii. 12 [13]; Ex. xv. 13 (where "His holy pasture" may = "His holy border," lxxxiii. 54); Jer. xxv. 30. The figure is thus *suggested*, which is afterwards more fully expressed in ver. 13, where, however, the word rendered "pasture" is a different one in the Hebrew. It is a favourite image in all this group of Psalms. See Introduction to Vol. I. p. 97.

8. AGAINST US, lit. "with respect to us," *i.e.* so that we should thereby suffer. Daniel ix. 16 combines in some measure the language of this verse and ver. 4. The Prophet confesses that Jerusalem and his people have become "a reproach unto all that are round about," not

Let Thy tender mercies speedily come to meet us,
For we are brought very low.
9 Help us, O God of our salvation, for the glory of Thy Name,
Yea, deliver us, and cover our sins for Thy Name's sake.
10 Wherefore should the heathen say, Where is their God?
Let there be made known [e] among the heathen in our sight

only because of their own sins, but for "*the iniquities of their fathers.*" This heritage of sin and its curse in indeed fully recognised in Holy Scripture. God Himself publishes it in the Law (Ex. xx. 5, comp. xxxiv. 7). See also Lam. v. 7, and 2 Kings xxiii. 26. Hengstenberg, Delitzsch, and Hupfeld are all at pains to argue that the iniquities of the fathers are not visited upon the children, except when the children themselves are guilty. In proof, they appeal to Deut. xxiv. 16, 2 Kings xiv. 6, Ezek. xviii. 20. But only the last of these passages is in point; the other two, the latter of which is merely a quotation from the former, only lay down the rule by which human tribunals are to be bound. Fully to discuss this question in a note would be quite impossible; it would require a volume. I will only remark, (1) That as a simple matter of fact, the innocent do suffer for the guilty. Children receive from their parents their moral and physical constitution, and both the taint and the chastisement of sin are transmitted. To this Scripture and experience alike bear witness. (2) That there is a mysterious oneness of being, a kind of perpetual existence which manifests itself in every family and every nation. Each generation is what all previous generations have been tending to make it. The stream of evil gathers and bears along an ever-increasing mass of corruption; so that upon the last generation comes the accumulated load of all that went before (Matt. xxiii. 35). But (3) Scripture nowhere teaches that a man is guilty in the sight of God for any sins but his own. Sinning himself, he allows the deeds of his fathers; he is a partaker in their iniquities; he helps to swell the fearful catalogue of guilt which at last brings down God's judgement; but his condemnation, if he be condemned, is for his own transgression, not for those of his fathers.

COME TO MEET. E.V. "prevent" God's mercy must anticipate, come to meet man's necessity.

9. Twice the appeal is made "for Thy Name's sake;" that revelation of God which He had made of Himself to Moses, when he passed by and proclaimed the Name of Jehovah. Ex. xxxiv. 6, 7. Comp. Ps. xx. 1 [2], xxiii. 3, xxix. 2.

COVER, or, "make atonement for," and so "forgive," as the word is commonly rendered. See xxxii. 1. The sins have provoked God's wrath, and from that wrath He only can hide them.

10. The first clause of the verse is borrowed nearly word for word from Joel ii. 17, and this Hengstenberg thinks rests on Ex. xxxii. 12, Num. xiv. 15, 16, Deut. ix. 28. It is repeated cxv. 2.

HEATHEN. See on ver. 1.

IN OUR SIGHT, lit. "before our eyes." There can hardly be an allusion to Deut. vi. 22, as has been supposed. The expression suggests a feeling of joy and satisfaction in beholding the righteous judgement of God. Comp. lii. 6 [8], and note there.

The revenging of the blood of Thy servants which
is poured out.
11 Let the sighing of the prisoner come before Thee,
According to the greatness of Thy power spare Thou
those that are appointed unto death,
12 And render unto our neighbours sevenfold into their
bosom
Their reproach wherewith they have reproached Thee,
O Lord.
13 So we Thy people and the sheep of Thy pasture will
give thanks unto Thee for ever;
To all generations we will tell forth Thy praise.

THE REVENGING OF THE BLOOD, &c.: comp. Deut. xxxii. 43.

11. THE SIGHING OF THE PRISONER and THOSE THAT ARE APPOINTED UNTO DEATH (Heb. "the sons of death"), are expressions found again in cii. 20 [21], a Psalm written, there can be no doubt during the Exile. By "the prisoner" must be meant, if this Psalm refers to the same time, the whole nation, whose captivity in Babylon, as well as their bondage in Egypt, is regarded as an imprisonment. If, on the other hand, the Psalm is Maccabean, the allusion will be to those who were carried captive by Antiochus Epiphanes.

THY POWER. Heb. "Thine arm." Comp. Num. xiv. 17, Deut. iii. 24.

12. UNTO OUR NEIGHBOURS. Because their scorn was more intolerable, and also more inexcusable, than the oppression of distant enemies. Comp. ver. 4. SEVENFOLD as in Gen. iv. 15, 24. INTO THEIR BOSOM. Comp. Is. lxv. 7, Jer. xxxii. 18.

[a] חַיְתוֹ. On this form see l. note [e], cxiii. note [a], cxiv. note [b].

[b] קוֹבֵר. In Jer. xiv. 16 the same expression occurs, but there the verb is in the Piel, and is followed by לְ. Gesen. (*Thes. in v.*) says that the Qal is used of the burial of *one* (except Ez. xxxix. 12), and the Piel of *many*. But here the Qal is used of many.

[c] אָכַל. It seems unnecessary to suppose, with Ewald, Hupf., and others, that the sing. is here written by mistake for the plur., although sixteen of Kennicott's MSS., and nine of De Rossi's have the latter, and it is also found in the parall. passage, Jer. x. 25. The use of the sing. has been explained by supposing (1) that the Psalmist had some particular enemy before his eyes: but the objection to this is that he immediately returns to the plur. Or (2), as Delitzsch, that the great world-monarchy is here regarded as one mass, subject to one despotic will. But it may be merely the impersonal use of the verb, lit. "one hath devoured," (see on lvii. note [h]) with which the plur. might readily alternate. See the same interchange of sing. and plur. Is. xvii. 13, xxii. 7, 8.

[d] רִאשֹׁנִים. This might be an adj. qualifying עֲוֹנֹת, "former sins," the masc. instead of the fem., as in Is. lix. 2, עֲוֹנוֹת מַבְדִּילִים, and it is so taken by the ancient Verss. But it is better to regard 'ע as in construction with 'ר, just as we have in Lev. xxvi. 45, בְּרִית ר', "covenant with the fathers." So here, "sins of the fathers," lit. "of those who were at the first, or, were before us." We have the full expression in Jer. xi. 10, ע' אֲבוֹתָם הָרִ', "the iniquities of their fathers who were at the first." Comp. Ex. xx. 5, Lev. xxvi. 39.

[e] יִוָּדַע. Masc. verb with fem. noun following, as often. (See Ges. § 144.) From overlooking this came the wrong rendering of the A. V. The P. B. V. is correct.

PSALM 80

As in the case of most of the historical Psalms, so in the case of this, it is impossible to say with certainty at what period it was written. The allusions are never sufficiently definite to lead to any positive conclusion. It is not a little remarkable that even the mention of the tribes in ver. 2, so far from being a help, has rather been a hindrance to interpretation. The prayer which recurs so often, ver. 3, 7, 14, 19, would seem to imply that the people were in exile; but it may be a prayer, not for restoration to their land, but only for restoration to prosperity, the verb "turn us again" being capable of either explanation. All that is certain is, that the time was a time of great disaster, that the nation was trampled down under the foot of foreign invaders. The Poet turns to God with the earnest and repeated prayer for deliverance, and bases his appeal on the past. God had brought a vine out of Egypt and planted it in Canaan. How could He give up that vine to be devastated by the wild beasts? Will He not appear at the head of the armies of Israel, as once He went before her sons in the desert with a pillar of fire? Will He not, as of old, lift up the light of his countenance upon them?

The mention of the three tribes, "Ephraim, Benjamin, and Manasseh," may, perhaps, denote that this is a Psalm, for the northern kingdom. Some have supposed it to have been a prayer of the Ten Tribes in their captivity in Assyria, and it has been conjectured that the Inscription of the LXX., ὑπὲρ τοῦ Ἀσσυρίου, is to be taken in this sense. Calvin, on the other hand, thinks that it is a prayer *for* the Ten Tribes, by a poet of the southern kingdom.*

* See Introduction to Psalm lxxxv.

He reminds us that even after the disruption prophets were sent from Judah to Israel, and that Amos (vi. 6) rebukes those in Judah who do not "grieve for the wound of Joseph." That Benjamin cannot be mentioned as the representative of the southern kingdom, and Ephraim and Manasseh of the northern, is perfectly clear. Had the object been to describe the nation by its two principal divisions, Judah would have been mentioned, and not Benjamin. It is quite true that Benjamin remained steadfast in its allegiance to the house of Solomon when Jeroboam revolted (see 1 Kings xii. 21), and also that Jerusalem, the capital of the southern kingdom stood partly in the borders of Benjamin; but neither the one circumstance nor the other would account for the mention of Benjamin instead of Judah; still less can the insertion of Benjamin between Ephraim and Manasseh be explained on this hypothesis. Hengstenberg attempts to argue that Benjamin really belonged to the Ten Tribes, because Ahijah only promises to Rehoboam *one* tribe (1 Kings xi. 18, 32, 36); but as the Prophet at the same time divides his mantle into twelve parts, and gives Jeroboam ten, he thus leaves *two* for Rehoboam: one of these Rehoboam is supposed to have already, and hence Ahijah only offers to give him one more. Still, in the course of time a portion of Benjamin may have become incorporated into the northern kingdom. The children of Rachel, Joseph (= Ephraim and Manasseh), and Benjamin, would naturally be drawn together. Benjamin, the tribe of Saul and Ishbosheth, and at one time the leading tribe, would not readily submit to the supremacy of Judah; a jealousy existed which was not extinguished in David's reign (2 Sam. xix., xx., xxi.), and which may have been revived later. It is, moreover, in favour of this view, that in the previous verse *Joseph* is mentioned, and not Judah; and hence the whole Psalm refers, apparently, only to the kingdom of Israel.

Hupfeld, however, argues that the designations here made use of are intended to describe the whole nation, and not a particular portion of it. He observes (*a*) that the use of the first person plural in ver. 2, 3 [3, 4], shows that the whole nation is meant (an argument which is of no force, if the Psalm was written by a native of the northern kingdom); (*b*) that, as regards the mention of Joseph, this is only what we find in lxxxi. 4, 5 [5, 6], where Israel and Joseph denote the whole nation, and in lxxvii. 15 [16], where Jacob and Joseph are employed in the same way, and in both passages with reference to the Mosaic times. So again in Obad. 18, "the house of Joseph" is mentioned with "the house of Jacob," in opposition to "the house of Esau," Jacob's brother. This remarkable usage of later writers has received different explanations. Rashi accounts for it by Joseph's position in Egypt as a second father and protector of the nation; Qimchi, by the blessing pronounced on Ephraim and Manasseh, Gen. xlviii. 16, and by the statement in 1 Chron. v. 1, that "the birthright was given unto the sons of Joseph the son of Israel." Others again suppose that Joseph is mentioned, because, as being pre-eminent above all his brethren, he might be regarded as a fourth patriarch, and Benjamin, because he was a son of the same mother. Hupfeld admits that the phenomenon may be partially explained on these grounds, but sees in this prominence given to the northern tribes by the poet of Judah (for such he holds the writer of the Psalm to be) a hope implied of the re-union and restoration of all the tribes. After the dispersion of the Ten Tribes, and when calamities fell heavy upon the two, the old animosities were forgotten, and the one desire of Prophets and Psalmists was to see the breach healed, and the ancient unity restored. Hence the use of the Catholic names "Israel" and "Jacob," and hence, also, the mention of "Joseph," the best-beloved son of Jacob, even when Judah only was left.*

But it is strange that Hupfeld entirely passes over, without remark, that particular association of the three tribes which most favours his view. In the journey through the wilderness these three tribes were ranged side by side, and in the order of march followed immediately behind the Ark (Num. ii. 17—24). This explains their mention in the Psalm. The prayer of the Psalmist is, that God would again lead His people, again go forth at the head of their armies as He did of old. All the allusions in the Psalm favour this interpretation. God is addressed as the Shepherd of Israel who led Joseph "like a flock," with manifest reference to the journeys through the wilderness (see lxxvii. 20 [21]). The petition is, that He who "is throned above the Cherubim would shine forth." Here the allusion is to the Ark, and the manifestations of the Divine glory. Then naturally comes the mention of those tribes whose position was directly behind the Ark. Hence the whole prayer may be regarded as a prayer for national restoration, and for the same Divine succour which had been so signally vouchsafed to their fathers in the wilderness.

Still, whilst on this ground I am disposed to believe that the whole nation is the object of the Psalmist's hopes and prayer, I am also inclined to think that the prominence given to Joseph and Benjamin may best be accounted for by supposing that the Psalmist was either

* Hupfeld appeals, in support of his view, to such passages as Hos. i. 10, 11 [ii. 1, 2]; iii. 5; Am. ix. 8—11; Is. xi. 11—13; Jer. xxx. xxxi. (where there is a transition from "Jacob," chap. xxx. to "Israel and Ephraim," chap. xxxii.); Ezek. xxxvii. 15—28; Zech. x. 6; comp. Ps. lx. 7 [9]; lxviii. 26, 27 [27, 28].

a native of the northern kingdom, or that he had some strong sympathy with his brethren in Israel. In the 77th, 78th, and 81st Psalms, we meet with a similiar peculiarity in the form of the national designation, and in all it may indicate some special relation on the part of the writer to the kingdom of Israel.

The strophical division of the Psalm is marked by the refrain, ver. 3, 7, 19, with a variation of it in ver. 14. The strophes are thus of very unequal length. The first has three verses; the second four; the third twelve; though this last, again, is partially broken by the imperfect refrain in ver. 14. The first two of these strophes are, in fact, introductory, containing the cry for help, and the lamentation over disaster. The third constitutes the principal part of the Psalm, where, under the figure of a vine, the history of Israel is pourtrayed. In the refrain we have even more emphatically repeated the burden of the Psalmist's prayer, the emphasis being each time deepened by the name given to God; first, "God;" then, "God of Hosts;" lastly, "Jehovah, God of Hosts."

[FOR THE PRECENTOR. ACCORDING TO "THE LILIES—A TESTIMONY." A PSALM OF ASAPH.[a]]

1 O THOU Shepherd of Israel, give ear,
Thou that leadest Joseph like a flock;
Thou that sittest (throned above) the Cherubim, shine forth.
2 Before Ephraim, and Benjamin, and Manasseh,
Stir up Thy might and come to save us.

1. SHEPHERD OF ISRAEL. On the figure as common to this group of Psalms, bearing the name of Asaph, see on lxxviii. 52. There is an allusion to Gen. xlviii. 15, "the God who was my Shepherd" [E.V. "who fed me"], and xlix. 24. In both passages Jacob blesses *Joseph* and his sons. So here it follows: "Thou that leadest *Joseph* like a flock."

(THRONED ABOVE) THE CHERUBIM: as in xcix. 1. Comp. xxii. 3 [4], "throned above the praises of Israel," where see note. The expression denotes the dwelling of God in His temple and the manifestation of His presence there, as is evident from the verb following.

SHINE FORTH, appear in all Thy Glory and Majesty for our help. See l. 2, where the same word is used of God's coming forth from His Sanctuary in Zion to execute judgement.

2. TO SAVE US. Heb. "for our salvation."

BEFORE EPHRAIM, &c. The three tribes are mentioned together with reference to the position which they occupied in the march through the wilderness, where they followed in the order of procession immediately behind the Ark. See Num.

3 O God, turn us again,
And show the light of Thy countenance, that we may be saved.

4 O Jehovah, God (of) hosts,
How long wilt Thou be angry with Thy people that prayeth?

ii. 17—24. [The prep. "before" is used thus of the order in processions. See 2 Sam. iii. 31, Job xxi. 33.] This falls in with the language of the previous verse, "Thou that sittest throned *above the Cherubim*, shine forth. So Lyra: "Hoc dicitur quia istæ tres tribus figebant tentoria ad occidentalem plagam tabernaculi. In parte vero occidentali tabernaculi erat sanctum sanctorum, ubi erat propitiatorium, in quo dabantur divina responsa." It is strange how completely this fact, which is the obvious explanation of the mention of these three tribes together, has been overlooked by nearly all the recent German interpreters. Bear this in mind, and it becomes evident that, whatever the national disaster here deplored, the prayer is, that these tribes may be restored to their ancient position, united as of old, and as of old led by God Himself, with the visible symbols of His Presence.

3. TURN US AGAIN, or "restore us," either from the Exile (as the Chald.), supposing the Psalm to have been written after the captivity of the Ten Tribes; or in the more general sense of recovery from disaster, as in lx. 1 [3].

SHOW THE LIGHT OF THY COUNTENANCE. Again an allusion to the history of the people in the wilderness, Num. vi. 25. See on lxvii. 1 [2], iv. 6 [7].

4. GOD (OF) HOSTS: see on lix. 5 [6]. On this repetition of the Divine Names Hengstenberg remarks: "In prayer all depends upon God, in the full glory of His being, walking before the soul. It is only into the bosom of such a God that it is worth while to pour out lamentations and prayer. 'Jehovah,' corresponding to the 'Shepherd of Israel,' ver. 1, points to the fulness of the love of God toward His people: and 'God, (God of) Hosts,' corresponding to 'throned above the Cherubim,' to His infinite power to help them."

HOW LONG WILT THOU BE ANGRY, &c., lit. "How long *hast* Thou *smoked*." The preterite after the interrogative in this sense is unusual. But the full form of expression would be, "how long hast Thou been . . . and wilt continue to be . . . angry." Comp. Ex. x. 3, xvi. 28. This use of the verb "to smoke," said of a person, is also without parallel. The usual phrase would be, "will Thine anger smoke." Comp. lxxiv. 1; xviii. 8 [9] (where see note); Deut. xxix. 20 [Heb. 19]. But the figure is bolder here than in the other passages, as it is applied immediately to God *Himself*. Such figures, remarks Delitzsch, would be impossible, were not the power of the Divine wrath to be regarded as belonging essentially to the very nature of the Divine Being. God, who is Light and Love, is also "a consuming fire."

WITH THY PEOPLE THAT PRAYETH, lit. "*in* (*i.e.* during, or it may be, notwithstanding,) the prayer of Thy people:" (Jerome *ad orationem*), not as the E.V., Hengst. and others, "*against* the prayer of Thy people:" for that is not the object of God's displeasure. That which seems so mysterious, that which calls for the expostulation and the entreaty is, that even whilst they pray, *in spite of* that prayer, God's wrath is hot against them. Some

5 Thou hast fed them with tears as bread,[b]
And hast made them to drink of tears in large measure.[c]
6 Thou makest us a strife unto our neighbours,
And our enemies mock (us) at their pleasure.
7 O God (of) hosts, turn us again,
And show the light of Thy countenance, that we may be saved.

8 Thou broughtest [d] a vine out of Egypt,
Thou didst drive out the nations and plant it;
9 Thou madest room before it,
And when it had taken root, it filled the land:

have seen here an implied opposition between the smoking of God's wrath, and the prayer which ascends like the smoke of incense (see cxli. 2, Rev. v. 8, viii. 3). But this seems fanciful.

6. A STRIFE, *i.e.* not an object of contention amongst themselves, but rather an object which they vied with one another in assailing.

UNTO OUR NEIGHBOURS, not the great powers, such as the Assyrians, Chaldeans, and Egyptians, but the petty states which bordered on Judea, who were always ready to exult over every misfortune that befel the Israelites. Comp. lxxix. 12.

AT THEIR PLEASURE, lit. "for themselves," *i.e.* for their own satisfaction, the pronoun being used to mark the reflex nature of the action, as for instance in Is. xxxi. 9. It cannot mean "among themselves," as E.V., nor is this the indirect use of the pronoun for the direct, as in lxiv. 5 [6].

8. THOU BROUGHTEST OUT, or, "transplantedst." The word is used of rooting up a tree out of its soil, Job xix. 10. And so here. (In lxxviii. 52 it is applied to the people in the literal sense of "making to depart.") Delitzsch quotes from Shemoth Rabbah, c. 44. "When cultivators wish to improve a vine, what do they do? They root it up out of its place, and transplant it to another." See also Vayyikra Rabbah, c. 36.

A VINE. The same comparison is found in other passages: Is. v. 1—7; xxvii. 2—6; Jer. ii. 21; xii. 10; Ezek. xvii. 5—10. In some of these passages the figure of a vineyard is mixed with that of the vine, and such is partly the case here: see ver. 12. That there is a reference to the blessing of Joseph (see above on ver. 1) can hardly be doubted. Observe especially the word "son," ver. 15 (E.V. "bough") compared with Gen. xlix. 22, "Joseph is a fruitful son," (E.V. "a fruitful bough"). Cassiodorus, remarking on the aptness of the figure, says: "Vinea ecclesiæ aptissime comparatur. Quoniam sicut illa inter folia caduca necessarios infert fructus, sic et ista inter umbras turbatiles peccantium ornatur fruge sanctorum; qui seculi hujus afflictione tanquam torcularibus pressi saporem norunt emanare dulcissimum."

THOU DIDST DRIVE OUT, &c. Comp. xliv. 2 [3].

9. MADEST ROOM, by destroying the Canaanites, as the soil is prepared for planting, by "gather-

10 The mountains were covered with the shadow of it,
And the boughs thereof were (like) the cedars of God.
11 She sent out her branches unto the sea,
And her young shoots unto the river.

12 Why hast Thou broken down her hedges,
So that all they which pass by the way do pluck her?
13 The boar out of the wood [e] doth root it up,
And the wild beasts of the field devour it.
14 O God (of) hosts, turn again, we beseech Thee,
Look down from heaven, and see,
And visit this vine;
15 And protect [f] that which Thy right hand hath planted,

ing out the stones," &c. Comp. Is. v. 2.

10. CEDARS OF GOD. See on xxxvi. 6 [7]. Hengst. and others, who find the comparison exaggerated, supply the verb from the first clause, and render: "And the cedars of God (were covered) with the boughs thereof." But thus the expression "cedars of God" is meaningless; and after all, the hyperbole in the figure is at least not greater than in Ezek. xxxi. 3, &c. Comp. Joel iii. 18 [iv. 18]; Am. ix. 13.

11. SEA . . . RIVER, *i.e.* from Gaza on the Mediterranean to Euphrates. Comp. lxxii. 8. The allusion is to the time of Solomon, of whom it is said, that "he had dominion over all the region on this side the river, from Tiphsah (*i.e.* Thapsacus, on the western bank of the Euphrates) even to Assah (or Gaza)," 1 Kings iv. 24. Comp. Deut. xi. 24, "Every place which the soles of your feet shall tread upon shall be yours: from the wilderness and Lebanon, from the river, the river Euphrates, even unto the west sea shall be your boundaries." See also Gen. xxviii. 14; Josh. i. 4.

12. Portions of this verse are repeated in lxxxix. 40, 41 [41, 42]. Comp. also Is. v. 5. The verb PLUCK occurs again only in the Song of Sol. v. 1.

13. THE BOAR OUT OF THE WOOD, as in Jer. v. 6, "the lion out of the wood." It has been supposed that some particular enemy is meant, such as the Assryrian monarch or Nebuchadnezzar, but this is negatived by the indefinite expression in the parallel clause, "the wild beasts of the field," or more literally, "that which moveth in the field,'' as in l. 11, the only other place where the phrase occurs. Lyra finds a particular reason why Nebuchadnezzar should be meant, "who is so called because he had for a long time his dwelling among the wild beasts!"

14. This verse is a reminiscence, so to speak, of the refrain with which the first two strophes close in verses 3 and 7. It stands, moreover, where it might naturally have formed the conclusion of a third strophe, which, as consisting of seven verses, would have been of the same length as the other two together. But the verse is too closely connected with what follows to be regarded properly as the end of a strophe.

15. PROTECT. The E.V. takes the word, which occurs only here, as

And the son whom Thou madest strong for Thyself.

16 It is burnt with fire, it is cut down ;
They perish at the rebuke of Thy countenance.
17 Let Thy hand be over the man of Thy right hand,
Over the son of man whom Thou madest strong for Thyself :

a noun, "the vineyard ;" and so the P.B.V. "the place of the vineyard." Others, "stock" or "stem." But it may be a verb, as the LXX. have rendered it. See more in the Critical Note.

THE SON. Ewald and others render, "the branch," or "shoot," referring to Gen. xlix. 22, where the word no doubt occurs in this sense (see above on ver. 8), a sense which would be very suitable here with reference to the figure of the vine. But the expressions in ver. 17, "son of man," "son of Thy right hand," seem rather to indicate that here, too, the figure is dropt. The ambiguous word may, however, have been chosen designedly, the more readily to connect the figure with what follows. THE SON evidently means the nation of Israel, as in Ex. iv. 22 ; Hos. xi. 1.

THOU MADEST STRONG, *i.e.* whom Thou didst carefully rear till he reached maturity. Comp. Is. lxiv. 14, where the same word is used of a tree. See also lxxxix. 21 [22], and similar expressions in Is. i. 2, xiii. 4.

16. IT IS CUT DOWN. The word occurs again only in Is. xxxiii. 12, of thorns cut down that they may be burned. In this verse the lamentation over the present condition of the nation is resumed. In the first clause the figure of the vine reappears ; in the second there is an abrupt transition to the nation of whom the vine is the figure. Hence Schröder conjectured that this verse ought to follow ver. 13, and this is approved by Hupfeld, for then, he says : (1) the second member, which now refers awkwardly to the Israelites, might refer to the "boar" and "the wild beasts," and be rendered as the expression of a wish. "Let them perish," &c. ; and (2) the latter portion of the Psalm, from ver. 8, would thus consist of three equal strophes of four verses each. He takes ver. 14 as a variation of the refrain in ver. 3, 7, and as the conclusion of a strophe.

17. MAN OF THY RIGHT HAND. This has been explained (1) "one whom Thy right hand protects," one who is the object of Thy special care and love ; or (2) "one whom Thou hast won for Thyself by Thy right hand" (in allusion to God's putting forth His power on behalf of Israel) ; or (3) with reference to ver. 15, one whom God's right hand planted. This last is perhaps best, as thus the two clauses of ver. 17 answer to the two of ver. 15. Israel has been both *planted* and *made strong* by God, and on both grounds asks God's protecting care. Some see in this title, together with that of "son of man" in the next clause, a designation of the Messiah, who in the same sense is said, in cx. 1, 5, to sit on the right hand of God. [Hupfeld, in mentioning this view, quotes xvi. 8, cxxi. 5, as parallels, but in those places God is said to be on the right hand of David and of Israel, *i.e.* to protect them, whereas the Messiah is said to be on the right hand of God, as Himself invested with kingly dignity.] But the obvious relation of this verse to ver. 17 rather leads to the conclusion that the nation of Israel, the vine spoken of before, is meant. And so Calvin understands it.

18 So will we not go back [g] from Thee :—
Do Thou quicken us, and we will call upon Thy Name.
19 O Jehovah, God (of) hosts, turn us again,
Show the light of Thy countenance, that we may be saved.

18. The first clause of this verse may perhaps be connected with the previous verse, and be rendered, "and who (*i.e.* the son of man) hath not gone back from Thee." See Critical Note.

SO WILL WE NOT, &c. Cassiodorus says: "Quæ enim semel mente concepimus cordis oculis jugiter intuemur. Quæ autem sit utilitas ab ipso non discedere consequenter exponitur; cum dicitur, vivificabis nos." And on these last words Augustine, "ut tecum non terrena amemus in quibus prius mortui eramus."

QUICKEN US, *i.e.* restore us to a *new* life. Comp. lxxi. 20; lxxxv. 6 [7].

[a] See notes on the Inscriptions of xlv., lx., lxix.

[b] On the construction of this clause, see note on lx., note [c], Vol. I., p. 476. In the next clause the construction is apparently changed. Properly speaking, the verb השקה takes a double accus. (of the person and the thing), whereas here we have the prep. בְּ instead of the second accus., "Thou makest them to drink *of* (בְּ, lit. *with*) tears." As there is no other instance of such a construction, Hengst. takes שָׁלִישׁ as the second accus. and renders, "Thou makest them to drink a measure *consisting of* tears;" the measure, he says, is the thing given them to drink; "of tears," denotes the contents of the measure. But the former construction is the most simple and obvious, in spite of the absence of an exact parallel, and so apparently the LXX.: ποτιεῖς ἡμᾶς ἐν δάκρυσιν ἐν μέτρῳ. Sym. ἐπότισας ἡμᾶς μετὰ δακρύων μέτρῳ.

[c] שָׁלִישׁ. The word (which only occurs again Is. xl. 12) means, evidently, a vessel of a particular size for measuring liquids: lit. "a third," *i.e.* of course of some larger measure, as we say a quart. Comp. the Latin *triental.* Jerome renders *tripliciter*, "in threefold degree," a definite for an indefinite number. The Chald. "(Thou hast made us drink) wine, two-thirds of which consists of tears." But Hupfeld argues that the word denotes not a measure of large size, but one of the *usual* size, such as would commonly be used for the purpose of drinking. He explains it thus: "Thou hast made them drink of tears as in (or from) a cup (the accus. describing the manner of an action), as wine is commonly drunk from a cup." Hence the phrase would signify that tears were their *daily* portion (see xlii. 4). Bunsen accepting this says, the idea of abundance can only be derived from the contrast between the tears falling drop by drop, and the cup full of tears.

[d] תַּפִּיעַ. It seems impossible to render this except as a past, though Ewald and Olsh. adopt the present. Hupfeld merely remarks, that in the

passage beginning here, "the earlier acts of God are described partly in perfects, partly in imperfects, with or without Vau conv., as in lxxviii." But he overlooks the peculiarity here, which is, that the tense is used as an imperf., without any perfect tense having preceded. In lxxviii. 9, on the other hand, where the Psalmist begins his narrative of the past, he uses first the preterite, then the fut. with Vau consec., and then the simple fut. as the aor. or imperf., describing past action. And this is undoubtedly the rule. See xviii. 5 (pret.), 7 (fut.), and then a frequent interchange throughout the Psalm. In fact, so regular is this usage, that Delitzsch makes the use of יָבוֹא, in Habak. iii. 3 a reason for concluding that the Prophet cannot be speaking of the past: otherwise, he argues, a pret. must have preceded. The fact that the vision *opens* with the fut. tense compels us to regard the Theophany as relating, not to the past (though its images are borrowed from the past), but to the future, or rather the vision itself is *present* to the Prophet's eye—"*God cometh*," &c.—whilst it pourtrays the future. The occurrence, however, of the fut. (imperf.) in this Psalm at the *beginning* of a past narrative seems to show that such an argument as that of Delitzsch is not of itself convincing; though he is, I believe, right in thinking that Habakkuk's vision regards the future, not the past.

[e] יַעַר. The suspended ע has had all kinds of fanciful meanings attached to it by the Rabbinical writers: the seventy years of the Babylonish captivity, the hanging of the Messiah on a tree; or, according to the Talmud, the middle letter of the Psalms, as similarly a large letter denotes the middle letter of the Pentateuch, &c.

[f] כַּנָּה. This has been taken (1) as a noun in the sense of "plant" (Chald., Syr., Ibn Ez., Qimchi, Jerome, *radicem*) or "vineyard" (E. V.), Chald. עובדא, in which case the whole of ver. 16 depends on the verb פְּקֹד, which is thus construed first with the accus., and then with the prep. עַל. But it is better, perhaps, to take the word as a verb in the imperat. So the LXX. *κατάρτισαι*, as if it were = כּוֹנְנָה, from כּוּן. There can be little doubt, however, that J. D. Mich. is right in deriving it from a root כנן (allied to גנן, *to hedge about*, *to protect*, and the Arab. كَنَّ), construed with עַל, as verbs of "covering" commonly are. There is still a difficulty about the vocalization. The proper form of the imperat. Qal with ה paragogic would be כֹּנָּה. But we have *órah* for *orrah*, Num. xxii. 6, and we find ă instead of ō in verbs ע"ע, as גַּל, cxix. 22. כַּנָּה, therefore, is of the same form as גַּל, with ה paragog.

[g] נָסוֹג. This is usually taken as fut. Qal 1 plur. with the vowel ō instead of ū. Hupf. objects to this (though so slight a variation of the vowel need not trouble us), and alleges, further, that the verb never occurs in the Qal except in the part. liii. 4, Prov. xiv. 14. He contends, therefore, that it is perf. Niph. 3 sing., and that the first clause of this verse must be joined closely with what precedes, as a kind of further relative clause, "the son of man (whom) Thou madest so strong for Thyself, and (who) hath not gone back from Thee."

PSALM 81

THIS Psalm was apparently intended to be sung at one or more of the great national Festivals. There has, however, been much difference of opinion as to the particular Festival or Festivals for which it was originally composed.

1. The Jewish interpretation is, for the most part, in favour of the Feast of Trumpets at the New Year. According to the Targum, the Talmud (see especially Babli *Rosh hash-Shana*), the Midrash, and the Book Zohar, this is a New Year's Psalm. It was to be sung, as it still is, in the Synagogue, on the first day of the month Tishri, the new moon which, beyond all others, was celebrated by the blowing of cornets. But this view can only be maintained by giving to the word *Keseh,* in ver. 3 [4], the meaning, not of "the full moon," but either of "the new moon," or, more generally, of "an appointed time."

2. Others are of opinion that there is no allusion to the new moon, and that the Festival intended must be one celebrated at the full moon, and therefore either the Feast of Tabernacles or the Passover.

3. According to De Wette, Hengstenberg, and others, this Psalm was intended to be sung at the Passover. Hengstenberg's main argument rests upon the language of ver. 5, where the feast is described as one which was instituted at the time of the Exodus, and as appears in verses 6—10, instituted with special reference to that event. He contends, accordingly, that the word *chodesh,* in ver. 3, must be rendered, not "new moon," but "month"—"Blow the cornet in *the month,*" that month which is emphatically the first and chief in the year, the month in which the Passover occurred. Comp. Exod. xii. 1, 2, "And the Lord said to Moses and Aaron in the land of Egypt, this month shall be to you the *chief* of months, it shall be the *first* month of the year to you." "In the full moon," of the second clause, defines exactly the time in the sacred month in which the Festival fell. Just as it is said in Levit. xxiii. 5, "In the first month, on the fourteenth day of the month, is the passover of the Lord," so here the note of time is the same: "in the month . . . . on the full moon." "Month," says Hengstenberg, and not "new moon," is the meaning of the word throughout the Pentateuch. But all festivals, indeed all holy convocations, were regarded as memorials of the deliverance out of Egypt. And the tradition of the Second Temple makes this a New Year's Psalm.

4. A fourth view, and that which is now maintained by some of the most eminent critics (Ewald, Delitzsch, and Hupfeld), combines the first and second interpretations; for it supposes that the exhortation of the Psalm refers both to the Feast of Trumpets on the first of the month, and to the Feast of Tabernacles, which lasted from the fifteenth to the twenty-first or twenty-second. This would explain the mention both of "the new moon" and of "the full moon," both marking important Festivals, and Festivals occurring in the same month. Both would be kept with loud expressions of joy. The blowing of cornets, and the apparatus of musical instruments, by which the first is to be announced, were apparently not usual at the Passover, whereas they would be perfectly in keeping with so joyous an occasion as the Feast of Tabernacles. The music in Hezekiah's celebration of the Passover (2 Chron. xxx. 21, &c.), to which Hengstenberg refers, may have been exceptional. The peculiar circumstances under which the Feast was then kept, and the great joy which it called forth, would sufficiently account for this mode of celebration, but there is no hint given that musical instruments were employed, as the Passover was originally observed; and the general character of the Feast is against such a supposition.* On the other hand, the direction, in Num. x. 10, that the trumpets should be blown "in the day of your gladness and *in your solemn days*, and in the beginnings of your months," may be taken as evidence that on *all* Festivals and therefore on the Passover, music accompanied the observance of the Feast. It is, however, a further evidence that the Feast of Tabernacles is meant, that it is styled so emphatically "our feast." See note on ver. 4.

On the relation of the *two* Festivals which, on this supposition, are combined, more will be found in the note on that verse.

Ewald observes that there is so much resemblance between this Psalm and Psalms lxxvii. and xcv. that, but for certain peculiarities by which this is marked, all might be assigned to the same author. And Delitzsch thinks that Psalm lxxxi. "unites the lyric element of Psalm lxxvii. with the didactic element of Psalm lxxviii." "All these three Psalms," he observes, "have the same character: all end in the same abrupt manner. The author rises to the height of his subject, and then suddenly drops it. Again, in lxxvii. the nation is spoken of as 'the sons of Jacob and Joseph,' in lxxviii. as 'the sons of Ephraim,' and here simply as 'Joseph.' Like lxxix., this Psalm rests upon the history of the Pentateuch, upon Exodus and Deuteronomy."

---

* Hence Tholuck conjectures that this Psalm was composed for Hezekiah's celebration.

Properly speaking there are no strophical divisions. The Psalm consists of two parts :—

I. In the first the Psalmist summons his nation to the Festival, bidding them keep it with loud music and song, and every utterance of joy, because it was ordained of God, and instituted under circumstances worthy of everlasting remembrance. Ver. 1—5.

II. In the next he abruptly drops his own words. What those circumstances were, what the meaning of God's revelation then given, the people had forgotten; and it is for him, in his character of Prophet, as well as Poet, to declare. It is for him to show how that voice from the past had its lesson also for the present; how every festival was God's witness to Himself, how it repeated afresh, as it were, in clear and audible accents, the great facts of that history, the moral of which was ever old and yet ever new. But the Psalmist conveys this instruction with the more imposing solemnity, when, suddenly breaking off his exhortation, he leaves God Himself to speak.

It is no more the ambassador, it is the Sovereign who appears in the midst of His people, to remind them of past benefits, to claim their obedience on the ground of those benefits, and to promise the utmost bounties of grace, on the condition of obedience, for the future. Ver. 6—16.

There could be no grander conception of the true significance of the religious feasts of the nation than this. They are so many memorials of God's love and power, so many monuments set up to testify at once of His goodness, and of Israel's ingratitude and perverseness, so many solemn occasions on which he comes as King and Father to visit them, to rekindle anew their loyalty and their affection, and to scatter amongst them the treasures of His bounty. To give this interpretation to the Festivals, to put in its true light the national joy at their celebration, appears to have been the object of the Psalmist. If so, it is a matter of secondary importance what particular Festival or Festivals were chiefly before his eye.

[FOR THE PRECENTOR. UPON THE GITTITH.[a] (A PSALM) OF ASAPH.]

1 SING joyfully unto God our strength,
Shout aloud unto the God of Jacob.

Ver. 1—5. The Festivals are to be kept with the loudest expressions of joy and thanksgiving, as Israel's special privilege, as instituted by God Himself, and as a great me-memorial of His redemption.

1. SHOUT ALOUD. There may be (as Delitzsch suggests) an allusion in this verb to the expression in Num. xxix. 1, where the noun employed is from the same root (rendered in the E.V., "it is a day

2 Raise a song, and bring hither [b] the timbrel,
The pleasant harp with the lute.
3 Blow the cornet in the new moon,
At the full moon,[c] on our (solemn) feast.[d]

of *blowing the trumpets*." On the first day of the seventh month (Tishri) two silver trumpets (at a later period 120, see 2 Chron. v. 12) were to be blown.

2. RAISE A SONG, &c., or "*take music*" (the noun is used both of the human voice and of instrumental music), "and *strike* the timbrel." See Critical Note.

3. THE CORNET. "The *shophar* is especially remarkable as being the only Hebrew instrument which has been preserved to the present day in the religious services of the Jews. It is still blown, as in time of old, at the Jewish new year's festival, according to the command of Moses (Num. xxix. 1)." (Engel, *Hist. of Music*, p. 292.) These instruments are commonly made of rams' horns; they differ somewhat in shape, some being much more curved than others, and the tube not being round but flattened. Engel mentions one in the Great Synagogue in London, which has this verse of the Psalm inscribed on it. He also quotes David Levi (*Rites and Ceremonies of the Jews*), as saying that the trumpet is made of a ram's horn, in remembrance of Abraham's sacrifice (Gen. xxii. 12, 13), which, according to the Jewish tradition, was on the new year's day, "and therefore we make use of a ram's horn, beseeching the Almighty to be propitious to us, in remembrance and through the merits of that great event."

IN THE NEW MOON. Strictly speaking, this might be any new moon; for in the beginnings of their months they were to blow with trumpets over their burnt offerings, &c., Num. x. 10; but perhaps the new moon of the seventh month, the new year's day, is especially meant. See Num. xxix. 1. And so the Chald. paraphrases, "in the month of Tishri."

AT THE FULL MOON. Such is apparently the meaning of the word here, and of the similar Aramaic form in Prov. vii. 20 (though the E.V. has in both passages "the appointed time"). If, then, the new moon is that of the seventh month, "the full moon" must denote the Feast of Tabernacles, which began on the 15th of the same month. Accordingly there follows—

ON OUR (SOLEMN) FEAST, *i.e.* the Feast of Tabernacles, which was also called pre-eminently "the Feast," 1 Kings viii. 2, 65 (where the E.V. has "*a* feast," wrongly), xii. 32; Ezek. xlv. 25; Neh. viii. 14; 2 Chron. v. 3, vii. 8. Josephus calls it *ἡ ἑορτὴ ἡ ἁγιωτάτη καὶ μεγίστη* (*Antt.* viii. 4), and Plutarch, *ἑορτὴ μεγίστη καὶ τελειοτάτη τῶν Ἰουδαίων* (*Sympos.* iv. 6, 2).

But are we to understand that both Festivals, that at the new moon and that at the full, were to be ushered in with the blowing of cornets? Such seems to be the meaning. Ewald, Rosenm., Hitzig, and Delitzsch, all think that the music was a part of the celebration of both the feasts. Delitzsch thus explains, I think rightly, the reference to the two. Between the Feast of Trumpets on the 1st of Tishri, and the Feast of Tabernacles, which lasted from the 15th to the 21st or 22nd, lay the Great Day of Atonement on the 10th of the month. This circumstance gave a peculiar significance to the Feast of Tabernacles—made it, in fact, the chief of all the Feasts, inasmuch as it was the expression of the joy of forgiveness and reconciliation declared by the High Priest to the nation on that solemn day. Hence it was kept with more

4 For it is a statute for Israel,
An ordinance of the God of Jacob:
5 He appointed it as a testimony in Joseph,
When He went forth against the land of Egypt,

than ordinary rejoicing. And hence the Psalmist would have the gladness of the new moon repeated "at the full moon, on the day of our solemn feast." The first was but a prelude to the last; the one looked forward to the other; and therefore the loud music of the one was to usher in the other also. Hupfeld suggests that the very change of preposition in the last clause, "*for* (rather than *on*) our feast-day," may have been designed to mark that that feast, the Feast of Tabernacles, was chiefly in the Psalmist's mind, so that the blowing of the cornets at the new moon was merely *preliminary to*, and intended as *a preparation for*, this feast. Then the words "at the full moon," denote, not the time of the blowing of the cornets, &c., but the time when the feast was held, so that the two clauses of the last member of the verse might be transposed, "for our feast-day at the full moon." But this is unnecessary when we remember what a feast of gladness the Feast of Tabernacles was, and long continued to be. Plutarch, in his time, terms it a bacchanalian festival. And the later Rabbis were wont to say, that one who had not witnessed the celebration of this feast did not know what joy was ("had not seen joy in his days").

4. FOR. The festivals are thus joyfully to be kept because they are of *Divine* appointment, and a special and distinguishing privilege of the nation. The same preposition before "Israel" marks them as the recipients, before "God" denotes that He is the Author and Giver of the law. Hengstenberg's explanation is unnecessarily artificial here.

IT IS. The pronoun is used generally, in a neuter sense, referring either to *the mode of celebration* described in ver. 1—3, or to the *feast* itself; but the latter was more particularly enjoined in the Law.

ORDINANCE, or "custom" (the word usually elsewhere translated "judgement"); for the word in this sense, see xviii. 22 [23], Gen. xl. 13, &c.; and

5. TESTIMONY, used of a single law, not, as usually, of the whole body of laws. See note on xix. 7. It was a great *witness* and *memorial* set up of God's power and love.

JOSEPH (or as it is here written, "Jehoseph," as elsewhere we find Jehonadab for Jonadab, Jehochanan for Jochanan, &c.). Hupfeld remarks that it is used after "Israel" and "Jacob" in the preceding verse, merely as another designation of the whole nation, as in lxxx. 1 [2]. Hengstenberg says, "Joseph occupies the place of Israel here, because during the whole period of their residence in the land of Egypt the nation owed everything to Joseph, 'the crowned one among his brethren,' Gen. xlix. 26. Their oppression began with the king who knew not Joseph, and this name could only belong to them with reference to that time." And similarly Calvin. But it is far more natural, surely, to see in the use of this name here, as in Psalm lxxx., an indication that the writer belonged to the northern kingdom.

AGAINST THE LAND OF EGYPT, wrongly rendered by the Ancient Verss. "*from* the land of Egypt," (a meaning which it need scarcely be said the prep. cannot bear,) because they supposed that "the going forth" could only be that of Israel out of Egypt. Hengstenberg, retaining the same subject, renders: "When he (Joseph) went forth *before* the land of Egypt." He refers for this use of the preposition to Job xxix. 7, "when I went out to

Where I heard a language [e] that I knew not :

the gate before (along) the city." [A better instance is Gen. xli. 45, where the E.V. has "and Joseph went out over all the land of Egypt."] Thus is denoted, he thinks, Israel's triumphant march *before the very eyes* of the Egyptians, who were unable to prevent their departure. See Num. xxxiii. 3, where they are said to have gone out "with a high hand *in the sight of* all the Egyptians." Similarly Calvin: "populum, præeunte Deo, libere pervagatum fuisse per terram Egypti, quia fractis ac pavefactis incolis datus est transitus." But it is simpler to retain the usual meaning of the preposition, and to refer the pronominal suffix, not to Israel, but to God : "When He (God) went forth *against* the land of Egypt," as in the slaying of the first-born (Exod. xi. 4, "I will *go forth* through the midst of Egypt"), and in all that He did for the deliverance of His people.

As this verse connects the institution of the Feast with a particular event, namely, the departure from Egypt, it does unquestionably furnish a strong argument to those who, like Hengstenberg, believe that the allusion is to the Passover. For no other Feast was then instituted. This difficulty is usually got rid of by saying that the note of time is not to be pressed, and that the Feast of Tabernacles did belong to the earlier legislation, Exod. xxiii. 16; xxxiv. 22. But I confess this is, to my mind, not quite satisfactory. On the other hand, both the Jewish tradition and the manner of celebration as here described are against the Passover. I incline, therefore, to think that the "new moon" and "full moon" are put for *any* feasts that were held at those times respectively, all of which, *beginning with the Passover*, might thus be spoken of as dating from the Exodus, from which the Jews date all their festivals, and to which they are all held to refer.

I HEARD. The verb is properly an imperfect. The LXX. and Vulgate have the third person, "he heard," &c., whence it has passed into our Prayer-book Version, not incorrectly as regards the sense. But the first person is used because the Psalmist speaks in the name of his people, identifying himself with them.

A LANGUAGE THAT I KNEW NOT. What was this unknown tongue? Two interpretations have been given. It has been explained (1) *Of the language of the Egyptians*, which was a foreign tongue to the Hebrews, who were "strangers in the land of Egypt." Comp. cxiv. 1, "the people of strange language," with Deut. xxviii. 49: Is. xxxiii. 19: Jer. v. 15. Accordingly, this fact is mentioned as one of the aggravations of their condition in Egypt, like the toiling with "the burden" and "the basket." Calvin, who takes this view, remarks that the redemption of Israel from a people of foreign language was a special mark of God's favour, inasmuch as the want of that common language, which is the bond of society, made foreigner and enemy synonymous terms : "Quia enim lingua est veluti character mentis ac speculum, non secus ac sylvestres feræ, invicem alieni sunt qui carent linguæ usu." (Comp. the curse in Deut. xxviii. 49.) It is no objection to this view that the words of God follow abruptly. See lxxv. 2. (2) *Of the voice of God*, a voice which the people had heard as uttered in His judgements upon the Egyptians, and in His covenant made with themselves, but had not understood (comp. Acts vii. 25). This language is then given in substance in a poetical form by the Psalmist, who seems suddenly to hear it, and to become the interpreter to his people of the Divine voice. He here places in a fresh light, gives a new application to, the earlier revelation, the meaning and purpose of which were not then understood.

6 "I removed his shoulder from the burden,
His hands were quit of the basket.
7 Thou calledst in distress, and I delivered thee,
I answered thee in the secret place of the thunder,
I proved thee by the waters of Meribah: [Selah.]

Hupfeld supposes it to be called an "unknown" language, merely because it is Divine, unlike the every-day *known* language of men. Ibn Ezra sees a reference to the words of God uttered on Sinai. So also Delitzsch, who would explain the expression by reference to Exod. vi. 2, &c. "It was the language of a known, and yet unknown, God, which Israel heard from Sinai. God, in fact, now revealed Himself to Israel in a new character, not only as the Redeemer and Saviour of His people from their Egyptian bondage, but also as their King, giving them a law which bound them together as a people, and was the basis of their national existence."

The latter interpretation, which regards the language here spoken of as the voice of God, and as virtually given in the following verses, is now that most commonly adopted. It is that of Mendelssohn, Ewald, Delitzsch, and Hupfeld.

6. The words of God follow without any indication of a change of speakers. The Prophet identifies himself with, and becomes the organ of, the Divine voice. He reminds Israel of that fact in connexion with which the Festival was instituted.

It is as though, amidst all the gladness of the Feast, and all the music and the pomp of its celebration, other thoughts arose, not to check, but to guide the current of a holy exultation. The sound of trumpet and timbrel and sacred song must be hushed, while Jehovah speaks to tell His forgetful people the lesson of their past history associated with that festival, the warning and the expostulation suggested by their own perverseness. If they would praise Him aright, it must be with hearts mindful of His goodness, and sensible of their own unworthiness and ingratitude. For the spirit in which all festivals should be kept, see on the offering of the first-fruits, Deut. xxvi. 1—11.

BURDEN, in allusion to Ex. i. 11; v. 4, 5; vi. 6; where the same word occurs in the plural.

THE BASKET. This word is not found in Exod., and its meaning is doubtful. It may either mean (1) a *basket*, in which heavy burdens were carried, such as are now seen pourtrayed on the monuments at Thebes; so it is interpreted by the LXX., and Jerome has *cophino;* or (2), *an earthen pot*, with reference to the work in clay which the Israelites were compelled to perform. Hence the E.V. renders, "his hands were delivered from making *the pots*."

WERE QUIT OF, or, "left toiling with." (E.V. "were delivered,") lit. "passed." The LXX., with a very slight change in a single letter, "served" (ἐδούλευσαν), but this involved also a change of the preposition; "in" or "with" instead of "from."

7. THE SECRET-PLACE OF THE THUNDER, is the dark mass of the thunder-cloud in which God shrouds His Majesty. (Comp. xviii. 11 [12]; Hab. iii. 4.) Here is probably a special reference to the cloud from which Jehovah looked forth in the passage through the Red Sea, Exod. xiv. 19 (comp. the note on lxxvii. 16); as there follows the mention of the second great miracle, the giving the water from the rock.

I PROVED THEE. Deut. xxxiii. 8. The mention of Israel's sin here, which did not of itself belong to an account of the institution of the

8 'Hear, O my people, and let Me testify unto thee ;
O Israel, if thou wouldest hearken unto Me,
9 That there should be in thee no strange god,
And that thou shouldest not bow down unto the god of the stranger!
10 —I am Jehovah thy God,
Who brought thee up out of the land of Egypt,
Open thy mouth wide, and I will fill it.'
11 But My people hearkened not unto My voice,
And Israel was not willing to obey Me.
12 So I gave them up unto the stubbornness of their heart,
That they should walk after their own counsels.
13 Oh that My people would hearken unto Me,
That Israel would walk in My way!
14 I would soon put down their enemies,
And turn My hand against their adversaries.
15 The haters of Jehovah should crouch before him,

feasts, prepares the way, as Hengstenberg points out, for the exhortation which follows.

8—10. This is a discourse within a discourse. It is the language which God held with His people when He proved them.

8. LET ME TESTIFY UNTO, or, "I will testify against." Comp. Deut. vi. 4, and see the note Ps. l. 7.

IF THOU WOULDEST, or "Oh that thou wouldest." The particle is used in the expression of a wish, the apodosis being omitted.

9. GOD OF THE STRANGER, or, "alien god." I have varied the phrase, because the Hebrew words are different in the two lines of the verse. For the former, comp. xliv. 21, Is. xliii. 12 ; for the latter, Deut. xxxii. 12, where the appeal is the same.

10. Comp. Deut. v. 1, 6, &c.

11. Luther remarks: "It is something dreadful and terrible that He says, *My* people. If it had been a stranger to whom I had shown no particular kindness," &c.

12. SO I GAVE THEM UP. The word is used of the letting go of captives, slaves, &c. ; of giving over to sin, Job viii. 4. This is the greatest and most fearful of all God's punishments. Comp. lxxviii. 29.

STUBBORNNESS. The word occurs once in the Pentateuch, Deut. xxix. 18, and several times in Jeremiah. The E.V. renders it here "lusts," and in all the other passages "imagination," but wrongly.

13. A transition is here made from the Israel of the past to the Israel of the present, because the history of the former is repeated in the history of the latter.

14. AND TURN MY HAND. There is no need to supply any ellipse or explain the phrase as meaning "*again* turn." It is used as in Is. i. 25 ; Am. i. 8.

15. CROUCH BEFORE, or, "feign submission" ; see on xviii. 44, lxvi. 3. HIM, *i.e.* Israel (for "the haters of Jehovah" are the enemies

And *their* time should be for ever.
16 He would feed thee[f] also with the fat of wheat,
And with honey out of the rock should I satisfy thee."

of Israel); and hence with the usual change from the collective sing. to the plural, "*their* time" in the next clause is "the time of Israel."

TIME, in the general sense of duration merely, and not implying prosperity. Indeed the word may be used of times of adversity as well as prosperity (see xxxi. 16). Hence Ibn Ezra and Rashi suppose the time *of the enemy* to be meant (and so Theodoret); but the predicate "for ever" is against this.

16. The form of the promise is borrowed from Deut. xxxii. 13, &c. Comp. Ezek. xvi. 19.

HE WOULD FEED THEE. The 3d person instead of the 1st, which recurs again in the next clause. These abrupt interchanges of persons are by no means uncommon in Heb. poetry. Comp. xxii. 26 [27]. The 3d person follows, as Hupfeld observes, from the mention of Jehovah just before, instead of the pronominal suffix of the 1st person.

FAT OF WHEAT, as cxlvii. 14, Deut. xxxii. 14; comp. Gen. xlix. 20. So "fat of the land," Gen. xlv. 18; of fruits, Num. xv. 12, 29, as denoting the best of the kind.

HONEY OUT OF THE ROCK; another image of the abundance and fertility which would have been the reward of obedience.

[a] See the note on the Inscription of Psalm viii.

[b] תְּנוּ־תֹף. Gesen. explains this, *give forth* a sound by striking *the timbrel*, i.e. "*strike* the timbrel," after the analogy of נָתַן קוֹל, "to give forth, utter a sound, the voice," &c. But the analogy is anything but perfect, and there is no instance of a really parallel usage. I have therefore followed Mendelssohn and Zunz in preferring the other rendering.

[c] כֶּסֶה. The Jewish tradition as to the meaning of this word, Delitzsch observes, is uncertain. According to the Talmud (*Rosh hash-Shana*, 8[b], Bêtza, 16[a]) it is the day on which the new moon hides itself, *i.e.* is scarcely visible in the morning in the far west, and in the evening in the far east. Rashi, Qimchi, and others again derive it from כסה = כסס, *computare*, in the sense of a "computed," and so "fixed time." And similarly the LXX. ἐν εὐσήμῳ ἡμέρᾳ, and the Vulg. *in insigni die*. Hence the E. V. "in the appointed time." But it is, perhaps, more probably explained by the Syr. *Keso*, which means "the full moon" (lit. "the *covering* (Heb. כסה) or filling up of the orb of the moon"), or more generally, "the middle of the month," or rather the whole period from the full moon to the end of the month; for in the Peshito Vers. of 1 Kings xii. 32 it is used of the 15th day of the month, and in 2 Chron. vii. 10 of the 23rd, but not, as Delitzsch asserts, in both instances of the Feast of Tabernacles; for in Kings the reference is to Jeroboam's spurious festival on the 15th of the *eighth* month; and in Chronicles the people *are sent away* on the 23rd, the Feast of Dedication, which lasted for seven days, having followed the

Feast of Tabernacles. The Syr. here renders: "sound with horns at the new moons (beginning of the month), and at the full moons (wrongly rendered in Walton's Polygl. *noviluniis*) on the feast days." An analogous Aramaic form occurs Prov. vii. 20, where Aquila has ἡμέρα πανσελήνου. Jerome renders there *in die plenæ lunæ*, and here *in medio mense.*

d חַגֵּנוּ. There can be little doubt that this is the better reading. It has the support of the LXX. and is found in the best texts, but the Syr., Chald., and several of Kenn's and De-R.'s MSS. have the plural חַגֵּינוּ.

e שְׂפַת. The stat. constr. with the verb following, as in vii. 16 (comp. xvi. 3, where the noun stands in construction with a sentence), the verb being here, what the second noun usually is, equivalent to an adjective. There is no need to explain the phrase elliptically, "the language *of one whom* I knew not," though grammatically this would be allowable, as lxv. 5, Job xviii. 21, xxix. 16.

Hengstenberg thinks that שָׂפָה could not be used to denote the voice or speech of God, but can only be employed of a language; but why may not ש׳ ל׳ י׳ א׳ mean "unintelligible words," as שׂ׳ אֱמֶת, Prov. xii. 19, means "true words"?

f וַיַּאֲכִילֵהוּ. The change to the 3d pers. presents no difficulty, but the use of the ו consec. does. It is out of the question to take this, as the LXX. and Syr. do, as an historic tense. A condition is clearly implied. What is meant is, that if the Israel of to-day would be obedient, then the miracles of God's love manifested of old should be repeated. Strictly speaking, if the ו *consec.* is retained, we ought to render "He would *have fed*," as if to intimate that not now only, but even from the first, God would have done this, had His people been obedient.

PSALM 82

THIS Psalm is a solemn rebuke, addressed in prophetic strain, to those who, pledged by their office to uphold the Law, had trampled upon it for their own selfish ends. It is a "Vision of Judgement," in which no common offenders are arraigned, as it is no earthly tribunal before which they are summoned.

God Himself appears, so it seems to the prophet, taking His stand in the midst of that nation whom He had ordained to be the witness of His righteousness, amongst the rulers and judges of the nation who were destined to reflect, and as it were to embody in visible form, the majesty of that righteousness. He appears now not, as in the 50th Psalm, to judge His *people*, but to judge *the judges* of that people; not to reprove the congregation at large for their formality and hypocrisy, but to reprove the rulers and magistrates for their open and shameful perversion of justice.

As in the presence of God, the Psalmist takes up his parable against these unjust judges: "How long will ye judge a judgement which is iniquity (such is the exact force of the original), and accept the persons of the ungodly?" These men have scandalously desecrated their office. They had been placed in the loftiest position to which any man could aspire. They were sons of the Highest, called by His name, bearing His image, exercising His authority, charged to execute His will, and they ought to have been in their measure His living representatives, the very pattern and likeness of His righteousness and wisdom. But instead of righteousness they had loved unrighteousness. They had shown favour to the wicked who were powerful and wealthy. They had crushed the poor, the defenceless, the fatherless, whose only protection lay in the unsullied uprightness and incorruptibility of the judge, and whom God Himself had made their charge.

A witness of these wrongs, the Psalmist appeals to them to discharge their duty faithfully and uprightly: "Do justice to the miserable and fatherless," &c. (ver. 3, 4). But the appeal is in vain. They have neither feeling nor conscience. Morally and intellectually, intellectually because morally, they are corrupt. The light that is in them is darkness. And thus, venal, unscrupulous, base, hard-hearted, the judges and magistrates have loosened the bonds of law, and the consequence is that the foundations of social order are shaken, and the whole fabric threatened with dissolution. Such is the terrible picture of a disorganized society, the very fountains of justice defiled and poisoned, suggested to us by the words in which the Psalmist here addresses the judges of Israel. He himself had thought, he tells us, that their high dignity and the representative character of their office, placed them so far above other men that they were like beings of a different race, but he warns them that the tyrannous exercise of their power will not last for ever, that, as in the case of other rulers of the world, it may only accelerate their fall. And then, finally, he turns to God, and appeals to Him who is the Judge, not of Israel only, but of the world, to arise and execute judgement in the earth, which they who bore His name had perverted.

Ewald, De Wette, Hitzig, and others suppose the expostulations of the Psalm to be addressed, not to Israelitish but to heathen rulers, satraps, &c., by a poet who lived towards the end of the Exile, in Babylon, and who, witnessing the corruption which was fast undermining the Babylonish empire, lifted up his voice against it. This view rests mainly upon the appeal to God (in ver. 7) as the Ruler and Judge of *all nations*, not of Israel exclusively. But the Psalmists so frequently take a wider range than their own nation, so constantly, in a true prophetic spirit, recognize the special rule and revelation of God in Israel, as only a part of His universal dominion (compare, for instance, vii. 6—8 [7—9]), that there is no need to depart from the more common view that Israelitish judges are meant; especially as this is confirmed by the general tenour of the Psalm. Besides, as Stier and Hupfeld have pointed out, the names "gods," and "sons of the Highest," are never given to heathen monarchs in Scripture. The former says: "We look in vain for a passage where a heathen king, or even an Israelitish, except David and Solomon, as types of the Messiah, is thought worthy of this name (Son of God)."

Hupfeld and Bleek (who have been followed by Bunsen) maintain (and I believe that they are almost the only modern expositors who do so) that the "gods" of the Psalm are not human judges, but angels, that the Psalmist sees a vision of judgement going on in heaven (which is conceivable, inasmuch as the angels are not pure in God's sight), and that he poetically applies the circumstances of this judgement to its parallel upon earth. Hence the rebuke addressed to the angels is intended for human judges, and this explains how it is that the angels are charged with human delinquencies, with accepting persons, and crushing the poor. So also when angels are threatened with death (a threat which Hupfeld argues has no meaning when uttered to human beings), this is a mode merely of threatening them with degradation; the language being figurative, and borrowed from the sentence of degradation pronounced on the First Man (Gen. ii. 17; iii. 19, 20). Bleek carries this notion so far as to suppose that the angels are the guardian angels to whom is entrusted the government of the several nations of the world (see Dan. x. 13, 20, 21; xii. 1; and Deut. xxxii. 8, in LXX.), a trust which they have betrayed.

Of such an interpretation it is enough to say with Calvin, *Ad angelos trahere frigidum est commentum*, not to mention that it seems difficult to reconcile such a view with our Lord's use of the Psalm in John x. 34, which Hupfeld passes over without any notice whatever. His objections to the common view that men are not called "gods," and "sons of the Highest," in Scripture, and that there is no meaning in saying to *human* judges, "Ye shall die like men," &c. will be found substantially answered in the notes.

The language of the Psalm is so general that it might belong to any period of the history; and the history itself and the utterance of the prophets show us that the evil here denounced was not the evil of any one age, but of all. It was the accusation brought against the sons of Samuel; the last who bore the venerable title of Judges before the establishment of the monarchy, that they "turned aside after lucre and took bribes, and perverted judgement" (1 Sam. viii. 3). And a long line of prophets repeats the same complaint. See Amos v. 12, 15; Micah vii. 3; Is. i. 17; iii. 13—15; Jer. xxi. 12; Zech. viii. 9, 10. The passages which approach most nearly to the Psalm in their general character are (1) one of those already quoted from Isaiah (iii. 13—15):

"Jehovah standeth up to plead, and standeth to judge the people. Jehovah will enter into judgement with the ancients of His people and the princes thereof: for ye have eaten up the vineyard, the spoil of the poor is in your houses. 'What mean ye that ye beat My people to pieces, and grind the faces of the poor?' saith the Lord, Jehovah of hosts:"—and (2) Jehoshaphat's charge to his judges which "he set in the land, throughout all the fenced cities of Judah, city by city" (2 Chron. xix. 5—7):

"Take heed what ye do; for ye judge not for men, but for Jehovah *who is with you in the judgement.* Wherefore now let the fear of Jehovah be upon you; take heed and do it: for there is no iniquity with Jehovah our God, nor respect of persons, nor taking of gifts." (Cf. Deut. i. 17; x. 17.)

The Psalm has no regular strophical division, but the arrangement is natural, and presents no difficulty. It has been already sufficiently indicated. The general strain is like that of Psalm lviii.

For certain peculiarities, which mark it in common with other Psalms ascribed to Asaph, see General Introduction, vol. i. pp. 97—99, where however the view is taken that God is Himself the speaker in this Psalm.*

[A PSALM OF ASAPH.[a]]

1 GOD standeth in the congregation of God:
In the midst of the gods doth He judge.

1. Earthly rulers and judges are not, as they are too ready to think, supreme, independent, irresponsible. There is One higher than the highest. As Jehoshaphat reminds the judges of Israel, God is with them in the judgement. Calvin quotes, to the like effect, the words of Horace,

"Regum timendorum in proprios greges,
Reges in ipsos imperium est Jovis," &c.

Men cannot see God with their bodily eyes, but He is present with the king on his throne (hence Solomon's throne is called the

* In the Second Temple this was the Psalm for Tuesday.

2 How long will ye give wrong judgement,

throne of Jehovah, 1 Chron. xxix. 23), with the judge on the judgement-seat, with all who hold an authority delegated to them by Him.

STANDETH, more literally, "taketh His stand." The word *nitzâbh* denotes a deliberate and formal act, connected with a definite purpose. 1 Sam. xix. 20. It is distinct from the more usual word *'oméd*, which is merely *standing* as opposed to *sitting*. But see the use of both words in reference to the act of judgement, Is. iii. 13.

IN THE CONGREGATION OF GOD, *i.e.* in the midst of Israel itself (called in Num. xxvii. 17; xxxi. 16; Josh. xxii. 16, 17, "the congregation of Jehovah"), and not only in the midst of the people who are the witnesses of His righteousness, but amidst the judges of the people, who are the representatives of His righteousness. They are called

GODS, not merely as having their authority from God (or as Calvin, quibus specialem gloriæ notam insculpsit Deus), but as His vicegerents, as embodying in themselves the majesty of the Law, as those in whom men look to find the most perfect earthly pattern of Divine attributes, of truth and justice, and mercy and impartiality. This name "gods" is applied to the judges of Israel in the Pentateuch. See Exod. xxi. 6; xxii. 8, 28 [27]. There, I agree with Delitzsch in thinking, Elohim does not mean God, in whose name judgement is pronounced (as Knobel and Hupfeld understand), but the judges themselves acting in His name and by His authority. Even if in Exod. xxii. 28 [27], we render, "thou shalt not revile *God*, nor curse the ruler of thy people," rather than "thou shalt not revile *the judges*," &c., still it is implied that the ruler bears the image of God, and that every insult offered to such a representative of God in His kingdom is an insult against God (as Hengstenberg remarks). The use of the name "gods" may have been intended to remind the world how near man, created in God's image, is to God Himself. So in the 8th Psalm it is said, "Thou hast made him a little lower than God." (See note there on ver. 5.) This would hold especially of those high in office. Thus God says to Moses in reference to Aaron, "Thou shalt be to him instead of God" (Exod. iv. 16). And again, "See I have made thee a god to Pharaoh" (vii. 1). In 1 Sam. xxviii. 13, the witch of Endor says of Samuel, "I saw a god ascending out of the earth" (in allusion either to his majestic appearance or possibly to his office as judge). In Ps. xlv. 6, the king is called God (see note there). But it was in connection with the office of judge that the stamp of divinity was most conspicuous. "The judgement is God's," Deut. i. 17; whoever comes before it comes before God. So, again, Moses uses the phrase, "When ye come to *me*, to inquire of *God*," Exod. xviii. 15. The same idea is found in heathen writers. Seneca (*de Clementia*, i. 1) makes Nero say: "Electus sum qui in terris Deorum vice fungerer: ego vitæ necisque gentibus arbiter, qualem quisque sortem statumque habeat in manu mea positum est."

2. It is usual to consider what follows, to the end of ver. 6, as the words of God as He appears, in vision, pleading with the judges of His people. To me it seems preferable to regard the passage as a rebuke addressed, in the true prophetic strain, by the poet himself, to those whose iniquity called for the protest (somewhat in the same strain as in lviii. 1, 2 [2, 3]); ver. 6, in particular, is thus more forcible, and the address to God in ver. 7 less abrupt.

HOW LONG, like Cicero's "Quousque tandem"; the abuse having become intolerable, because of its long standing.

GIVE WRONG JUDGEMENT, lit. "judge iniquity"; "give a judgement which is iniquity itself";

And accept the persons of the wicked? [Selah.]
3 Judge the miserable and fatherless,
Do justice to the afflicted and needy;
4 Rescue the miserable and poor,
Deliver them from the hand of the wicked.

5 They know not, and they understand not,
In darkness they walk to and fro:
All the foundations of the earth are out of course.
6 I myself have said, Ye are gods,

(the opposite being "judging uprightness," lviii. 1 [2]). Comp. Lev. xix. 15.

ACCEPT THE PERSONS. Such, there can be no doubt, is the meaning of the phrase here, and so it is understood by the LXX. Comp. Prov. xviii. 5; Lev. xix. 15. Sometimes a different verb is employed, as in Lev. xix. 15; Deut. i. 17; xvi. 19; Prov. xxiv. 23; xxviii. 21; where such partiality is straitly forbidden. Jehoshaphat in his address to the judges (2 Chron. xix. 7) reminds them that "with the Lord our God is no respect of persons, nor taking of gifts."

3. MISERABLE. See note on xli. 1. NEEDY or "destitute:" the word (*râsh*), Delitzsch observes, does not occur in Hebrew literature earlier than the time of David. It is persons such as these who most of all need the protection of the judge. Their very existence depends on his integrity. The orphan who has lost his natural protectors, the humble who have no powerful friends, the poor who can purchase no countenance, to whom shall they look but to God's vicegerent? And if he violates his trust, God who is the "God of the widow and the fatherless" (lxviii. 6), and who in the Law declares, "Cursed be he who perverteth the cause of the stranger, the fatherless, and the widow" (Deut. xxvii. 19), will not leave him unpunished.

DO JUSTICE TO, lit. "justify," *i.e.* give them their due.

5. Those expositors who consider verses 2—6 to contain the words of God, suppose that here, either the Psalmist introduces his own reflections, or that a pause takes place after ver. 4, during which God waits to see whether those whom He rebukes will listen to His rebuke. But the transition from the 2d person to the 3d is so common, as to render either exposition unnecessary. It is one strain continued, only that now the infatuation, as before the moral perversion, of the judges is described.

The expostulation falls dead without an echo. The men are infatuated by their position, and blinded by their own pride.

THEY KNOW NOT, absolutely, as in liii. 5 [6]; lxxiii. 21 [22]. Comp. Is. i. 3. Moral blindness is the cause of all sin.

IN DARKNESS, Prov. ii. 13.

THEY WALK TO AND FRO, such is the force of the Hithp., denoting generally the conversation, manner of life, &c.; here, according to Delitzsch, their carnal security and self-seeking.

ALL THE FOUNDATIONS, &c. See note on xi. 3, and comp. lxxv. 3 [4]. The dissolution of society is the inevitable result of corruption in high places.

6. I HAVE SAID. The pronoun is emphatic. If these are the words of God, as most interpreters suppose, then in pronouncing judgement upon the judges, He declares that it was He Himself who called

And ye are all sons of the Most High.
Yet surely like (other) men shall ye die,
And fall like one[b] of the princes.

7 Arise, O God, judge Thou the earth,
For Thou hast all the nations for Thine inheritance.[c]

them to their office, and gave them the name, together with the dignity which they enjoy. (This interpretation falls in readily with our Lord's words in John x. 34.) If, on the other hand, the Psalmist speaks, he expresses his own feelings and convictions. "There was a time when I myself thought that your office and dignity clothed you with something of a superhuman character, but you have degraded it, and degraded yourselves; you are but mortal men, your tenure of office is but for a little while." He does not add what naturally suggests itself to us, and what Calvin inserts here, that they must shortly give an account before the bar of God. If this is implied in ver. 7, it is not after death.

Our Lord appeals to this verse in His argument with the Jews when they charged Him with blasphemy, "because He being a man, made Himself God." John x. 34—38. His words are: "Is it not written in your Law, 'I said ye are gods'? If it called them gods to whom the word of God came—and the Scripture cannot be broken—say ye of Him whom the Father sanctified, and sent into the world, Thou blasphemest, because I said, I am the Son of God?" The argument is one *a minori ad majus*. How could they charge Him with blasphemy in claiming to be *the Son of God* when their own judges had been styled *gods?* They moreover were *unrighteous* judges (the worthy ancestors, it is implied, of the unrighteous Pharisees and members of the Synhedrin, who were our Lord's bitterest opponents), whereas He was One whom the Father had *sanctified*, and sent into the world, and whose life and works were a witness to His righteousness. By nature they had no right to the name of Elohim, "gods," nor had they proved themselves worthy of it by their character. He was, in character as in nature, Divine. To them *the word* of God *had come* (πρὸς οὓς ὁ λόγος τοῦ Θεοῦ ἐγένετο), by which they had been appointed to their office. He was *Himself the Word* of the Father. Their office was but for a time, they were mortal men, yet wearing, by Divine permission, a Divine name. He had been with the Father before He came into the world, was by Him sealed and set apart (ἡγίασεν), and sent to be not a judge, but the Christ—not one of many sons, but emphatically the Son of God, the King of an everlasting kingdom. Both in His office and in His person He has far more right to the title "Son of God," than they have to that of "gods." There is moreover further implied in this argument that the Old Testament does contain hints, more or less obscure, preludes and foreshadowings, which might have arrested the thoughtful reader, as mysteriously prefiguring that close and real union between God and man which was afterwards fully exhibited in the Incarnation.

[a] See General Introduction, pp. 97, 98.

[b] כְּאַחַד: for this Ewald reads כְּאֶחָד, and translates: "And fall, O ye princes, *together*" (lit. like one man), referring to Is. lxv. 25; Ezra iii. 9;

vii. 20, in support of his emendation. He makes this change on the ground that the opposition here is not between princes and gods, but between mortal men and gods. At the same time he admits that the other expression "as one of the princes," *i.e.* like a common prince, is a genuine Hebrew phrase. Comp. 2 Sam. ix. 11; Jud. xvi. 7, 11; 1 Kings xix. 2.

[c] The verb נחל is construed here with בְּ instead of the accus. after the analogy of verbs of *ruling*, &c., like משל, בעל, the word itself being employed to denote that, whilst Israel is God's peculiar *inheritance*, נַחֲלָה, He has the same right, makes the same claim, to all the nations.

PSALM 83

We know of no period in the history of Israel when all the various tribes here enumerated were united together for the extermination of their enemy. The annals have preserved no record of a confederacy so extensive. Hence it has been assumed that the enumeration in the Psalm is merely designed to subserve the purposes of poetry, to heighten the colouring, to represent the danger as even greater and more formidable than it really was. It may have been so. Divine inspiration does not change the laws of the imagination, though it may control them for certain ends. Or it may have been that the confederacy as originally formed, and as threatening Israel, was larger than that which actually advanced to the struggle. The wider the alliance, and the more heterogeneous its elements, the more probable it is that some would drop off, through dissensions, or jealousies, or the working of timid counsels. But as this Psalm helps us to complete the narrative in Judges of the defeat of the Midianites (see note on ver. 11), so it may itself supplement the narrative of the particular event which called it forth. It may describe some event which we read in the history, but which there assumes less formidable proportions, and in so doing it may help us to complete the picture. If so, there can be very little doubt with what portion of the history it best synchronizes. The confederacy must be that which threatened Judah in the reign of Jehoshaphat, the account of which is given in 2 Chron. xx. There, as in the Psalm, Moab and Ammon, "the children of Lot" are the leading powers; and though there is some doubt about the reading, "other beside the Ammonites," in ver. 1, the Edomites are mentioned as forming a part of the invading army. These might naturally include bordering Arabian tribes, mentioned more in detail in the Psalm. The great hiatus in the narrative (supposing this to be the occasion to which the Psalm refers) is that it omits all mention of the Western nations as joining the confederacy. But on the hypothesis of any other historical reference at all, some hiatus will be found to exist. It is so if, with Hitzig, Olshausen, Grimm, and others, we refer the Psalm to the events mentioned in 1 Macc. v. 1—8, where only Edomites, Ammonites, and Bajanites (a name as yet unexplained), are mentioned ; nor is the difficulty got over even if, with Hitzig, we add to this the subsequent campaign of Judas Maccabeus, recorded in the same chapter, ver. 3—54. Those who, like Ewald, place the Psalm in Persian times, and suppose it to be aimed at the attempts of Sanballat, Tobias, and others, to prevent the rebuilding of Jerusalem, are not more successful. The former of these views compels us to take Assyria (Asshur) as a name of Syria ; the latter as a synonym for Persia. In neither case do "the children of Lot" occupy the prominent place ; nor can we account for the mention of Amalekites, either in the time of Nehemiah, or in the time of the Maccabees. (See 1 Chron. iv. 43.) The more common opinion which connects the Psalm with Jehoshaphat's struggle is certainly preferable to either of the views just mentioned.

One expression in Jehoshaphat's prayer bears a close resemblance to the language of the Psalm in ver. 11, when he prays, "Behold, I say, how they reward us to come to cast us out of Thy possession which Thou hast given us to inherit." (2 Chron. xx. 11.) The remark with which the narrative ends : "And the fear of God was on all the kingdoms of those countries when they had heard that the Lord fought against the enemies of Israel," is almost like a recorded answer to the prayer with which the Psalm closes.

It has been conjectured, as the Psalm is said to be a "Psalm of Asaph," that it may have been composed by Jahaziel, the "Levite of the sons of Asaph," who encouraged Jehoshaphat's army before it went out to battle ; and that the Psalm itself may have been chanted by the band of singers whom the king appointed to precede the army on its march. (Ibid. ver. 21.) But no argument can be built upon the title. (See General Introduction, Vol. I. pp. 96, 97.) One thing, however, is clear, the confederacy of which the Psalm speaks was formed before Assyria became a leading power. Moab and Ammon hold the foremost place, while Asshur joins them only as an ally : "they are an arm to the children of Lot." The Poet is fully alive to the danger which threatens his nation. Look where he may, the horizon is black with gathering clouds. Judah is alone, and his enemies are compassing him about. The hosts of invaders are settling like swarms of locusts on the skirts of the land. East, south, and west, they are mustering to the battle. The kindred but ever hostile tribe of Edom on the border, issuing from their mountain fastnesses; the Arab tribes of the desert; the old hereditary foes of Israel, Moab and Ammon; the Philistines, long since humbled and driven back to their narrow strip of territory by the sea, yet still apparently formidable, even Tyre forgetting her ancient friendship,—all are on the march, all, like hunters, are hemming in the lion who holds them at bay.

It is against this formidable confederacy that the Psalmist prays. He prays that it may be with them as with the other enemies of Israel, with Jabin and Sisera, in days of old. But he prays for more than deliverance or victory. He prays that the Name of Jehovah may be magnified, and that all may seek that Name. Two expressions, in fact, give the key to the Psalm—show us the attitude of the Poet in presence of the danger: ver. 5, "They are confederate against *Thee;*" ver. 18, "Let them know that *Thou* art most high over all the earth."

The Psalm consists of two principal divisions :—

I. The first describes the magnitude of the danger, and enumerates the foes who are gathering on all sides, hemming in Judah, and intending by mere force of numbers utterly to crush and destroy it. Ver. 1—8.

II. The next contains the prayer for their complete overthrow, with an appeal to God's former mighty acts on behalf of His people when threatened by their enemies. Ver. 9—18.

[A SONG. A PSALM OF ASAPH.[a]]

1 O GOD, keep not silence,
Hold not Thy peace, and be not still, O God.
2 For lo, Thine enemies make a tumult,
And they that hate Thee have lifted up (their) head.

1. KEEP NOT SILENCE, lit. "Let (there) not (be) silence to Thee," as in Is. lxii. 7. In both places the LXX. have made the same blunder, rendering here τὶς ὁμοιωθήσεταί σοι, and there οὐκ ἔστιν ὅμοιος. On the general sense of this verse see note on xxviii. 1.

2. THINE ENEMIES, in itself a ground of appeal and of consolation.

MAKE A TUMULT, lit. "roar like the waves of the sea." See the same word in xlvi. 3 [4].

HAVE LIFTED UP (THEIR) HEAD. Comp. iii. 3 [4]; xxvii. 6; and Jud. viii. 28.

3 Against Thy people they plot craftily,[b]
And take counsel together against Thy hidden ones.
4 They say, "Come, let us cut them off that they be no
more a nation,
And that the name of Israel be no more in remembrance."
5 For they have taken counsel with (one) heart together,
Against Thee they are confederate—
6 The tents of Edom, and the Ishmaelites,
Moab and the Hagarenes;
7 Gebal and Ammon, and Amalek,

3. PLOT CRAFTILY, lit. "make crafty (their) plot, or secret consultation."

THY HIDDEN ONES, or "treasured ones," those whom God holds in the hollow of His hand; those to whom He is a wall of fire round about them, that none may do them hurt—those of whom He says, he that toucheth you toucheth the apple of Mine eye. Comp. xvii. 8; xxvii. 5; xxxi. 20 [21].

4. THAT THEY BE NO MORE A NATION. Comp. Jer. xlviii. 2; Is. vii. 8; and similar phrases in xvii. 1: xxv. 2. They would in their fury blot out Israel from the map of the world, or, as Calvin says: "It is as if they had formed the design of subverting the counsel of God on which the continued existence of the Church had been founded."

5. WITH (ONE) HEART TOGETHER. The adverb seems to be used almost as an adjective (LXX. ἐν ὁμονοίᾳ ἐπιτοαυτό), so that the phrase would answer to that in 1 Chron. xii. 38. But perhaps it would be simpler and more certain, with Hupf. and Hengst., to render: "They have taken counsel in (their) heart together," (Jerome, *corde pariter*,) the heart being the source of their machinations. Comp. v. 9 [10]; lxiv. 6 [7].

AGAINST THEE, as in ver. 3, "against Thy people." God and His people are one. So our Lord says to Saul, "Why persecutest thou Me?"

6—8. The enumeration of the confederate tribes. First, those on the south and east. Then, those on the west, Philistia and Tyre. Lastly, the Assyrians in the north, not yet regarded as a formidable power, but merely as allies of Moab and Ammon.

6. THE TENTS, as properly descriptive of the nomad Arabian tribes.

EDOM. So in 2 Chron. xx. 2, "Edom" should be read instead of "Aram" (Syria), the confusion of the two words being discernible elsewhere.

THE ISHMAELITES, according to Gen. xxv. 18, were spread over the whole tract of country south of Palestine, lying between Egypt and the Persian Gulf. Part of this territory is occupied by Amalekites in 1 Sam. xv. 7.

THE HAGARENES dwelt to the east of Palestine in the land of Gilead. They were driven out by the tribe of Reuben in the time of Saul (1 Chron. v. 10, 18—20).

7. GEBAL, usually supposed to denote the mountainous country south of the Dead Sea, in the neighbourhood of Petra (Arab. *Dgebel*). Mr. Ffoulkes, indeed, in Smith's *Dict. of the Bible*, identifies

Philistia, with them that dwell at Tyre.
8 Asshur also is joined with them,
They have been an arm to the children of Lot.

9 Do Thou to them as unto Midian,
As unto Sisera, as unto Jabin at the torrent of Kishon,
10 Who were destroyed at En-dor,
Who became dung for the land.

it with the Gebal of Ezekiel (xxvii. 9), a maritime town of Phœnicia. He says, "Jehoshaphat had in the beginning of his reign humbled the Philistines and Arabians (2 Chron. xvii. 9, 10), and still more recently had assisted Ahab against the Syrians (ibid. ch. xviii.). Now, according to the poetic language of the Psalmist, there were symptoms of a general rising against him. On the south the Edomites, Ishmaelites, and Hagarenes; on the south-east Moab; and north-east Ammon. Along the whole line of the western coast (and, with Jehoshaphat's maritime projects this would naturally disturb him most), (see 2 Chron. xx. 36), the Amalekites, Philistines, or Phœnicians and inhabitants of Tyre, to their frontier town Gebal; with Assur, *i.e.* the Syrians or Assyrians, from the more distant north. It may be observed that the Asshurites are mentioned in connexion with Gebal no less (ver. 6) in the prophecy than in the psalm." But the objection to this identification is the position which Gebal here occupies in the enumeration of the tribes.

8. ASSHUR. If the Psalm was written in Jehoshaphat's reign, this is the first mention of the Assyrians since the days of Nimrod, and here evidently they hold a subordinate place. We do not hear of the Assyrian kingdom as a great power formidable to Israel till the time of Menahem, who "was reduced to the necessity of buying off an invasion of the Assyrians (the first incursion of that people), under Pul." (2 Kings xv. 19.)

THEY HAVE BEEN AN ARM. Comp. xliv. 4; Is. xxxiii. 2. This agrees with the statement in Chronicles that Moab and Ammon were the leaders of the confederacy.

9. MIDIAN, mentioned by anticipation with reference, not to the example which immediately follows, but to that in ver. 11. The victory of Gideon over the Midianites was one of the most glorious in the national history, one the memory of which was fondly cherished. When Isaiah would describe the victories which are to precede the peaceful reign of Messiah, he can compare the overthrow of the enemy to nothing so well as to that on "the day of Midian." The allusion to it here may also have been suggested by the fact, that many of the enemies now arrayed against Israel were the same as on that occasion; for with the Midianites were the "Amalekites and all the children of the East." Jud. vi. 36. See Is. ix. 4 [3]; x. 26; Hab. iii. 7.

SISERA . . . . JABIN. See the history in Jud. iv. v.

THE TORRENT OF KISHON, which swept away the corpses of the enemy, Jud. v. 21. Others, "the valley or Wâdi of Kishon:—the Hebrew word means both.

10. EN-DOR is not mentioned in Judges, but the Psalm shows us that tradition associated with that spot the death of the two chiefs. It is a considerable but now deserted village, 4 m. south of Tabor.

11 Make them, their nobles, like Oreb and like Zeeb;
Yea, all their princes, like Zebah and like Zalmunna,
12 Who said: "Let us take to ourselves
The pastures of God in possession."
13 O my God, make them as the whirling dust,
As stubble before the wind.
14 As a fire that burneth a forest,
And as a flame that setteth the mountains in a blaze,

The name occurs besides, Josh. xvii. 11; 1 Sam. xxviii. 7.

11. OREB AND ZEEB, the two "princes," or probably "generals of the army," whilst Zebah and Zalmunna have the title of "kings." Jud. vii. 25; viii. 5, 6. The allusions here and in Is. x. 26 help us to complete the narrative in Judges. Isaiah implies that the slaughter must have been awful beyond anything that history records, for "he places it in the same rank with the two most tremendous disasters recorded in the whole of the history of Israel—the destruction of the Egyptians in the Red Sea, and of the army of Sennacherib." Here the discomfiture and flight of the Midianites is prominent. "In imagery both obvious and vivid to every native of the gusty hills and plains of Palestine, though to us comparatively unintelligible, the Psalmist describes them as driven over the uplands of Gilead like the clouds of chaff blown from the threshing-floors; chased away like the spherical masses of dry weeds which course over the plains of Esdraelon and Philistia — flying with the dreadful hurry and confusion of the flames, that rush and leap from tree to tree and hill to hill when the wooded mountains of a tropical country are by chance ignited." See the article OREB, by Mr. Grove, in Smith's *Dict. of the Bible.*

12. PASTURES. Others, "habitations," which Gesen. gives as the first meaning. But there is no reason to depart from the usual signification. See on lxxix. 7, Comp. xxiii. 2. Israel is God's flock lying down in *His* pastures. The figure accords with the usage of Psalms ascribed to Asaph. See General Introduction, Vol. I. pp. 96—98.

13. AS THE WHIRLING DUST. The same word is rendered by the E.V. in the parallel passage, Is. xvii. 13, "a rolling thing."

> And (they) shall be chased as the chaff of the mountains before the wind,
> And like a rolling thing before the whirlwind.

Here both the A.V. and P.B.V. have "as a wheel," and so all the Ancient Versions, and this Hupfeld maintains is the only correct rendering. But the parallel rather suggests "spherical masses of weeds" (as Mr. Grove renders), chaff, dust, anything driven in rolling masses by the wind. And so Gesenius, Ewald, Delitzsch, &c. Reuss: "Comme le tourbillon."

14. The image in this verse is also found in Isaiah. See chap. ix. 18 [17]; x. 17, 18; and comp. Zech. xii. 6.

Hupfeld connects this with the preceding verse, and so supposes a confusion in the figure (such as he finds also in xxi. 9), the sense being, "O my God, make them as a forest which is burned with fire." But it is far better to take ver. 14 and ver.

15 So pursue them with Thy tempest,
And with Thy hurricane make them afraid.
16 Fill their face with confusion,
That they may seek Thy Name, O Jehovah.
17 Let them be ashamed, and afraid for evermore,
Yea, let them be confounded and perish,
18 And let them know that Thou, (even) Thy Name Jehovah alone,
Art most high over all the earth.

15 as the two members of the comparison, and then there is no need to resort to such metonymy.

15. With this verse and what follows comp. xxxv. 4—6.

16. The object with which the Psalmist prays for the Divine judgement upon the foes who are gathering to swallow up his people is remarkable. It is "that they may seek the name of Jehovah, that they may know (ver. 18) that He is most High over all the earth." This is the nobler aspiration which mingles with the prayer for vengeance. The man in danger, feeling his own and his country's peril, desires to see his enemies destroyed with a slaughter as terrible, a discomfiture as complete, as that on "the day of Midian." The man who loves and fears Jehovah desires to see others, even his enemies, love and fear Him too. A pious Englishman in Lucknow, or Delhi, or Cawnpore, during the Indian mutiny, might have understood how possible it was to reconcile the two parts of the prayer.

The prayer in v. 18 might indeed only mean that by their overthrow they should be forced to acknowledge the power and greatness of Jehovah, an external subjection as in xxxi. 17 [18], but the prayer that they should *seek His Name* must mean more than this. The end of all God's judgements, as of all history, is the same, that all should confess that Jehovah is One, and His Name One, Zech. xiv. 9.

18. THOU, THY NAME, *i.e.* Thou who dost reveal Thyself as Jehovah. Calvin observes that the pronoun is emphatic, because there is implied a comparison between the true God, the God of Israel, and all false gods, "as though the prophet had said, Lord, make them feel that their idols which they have made for themselves are nothing." The construction is that of a double nominative. See note on xliv. 2.

[a] See General Introduction, Vol. I. p. 96.

[b] סוֹד, here used in a bad sense, as in lxiv. 3, is the object of the verb, the constr. being the same as in lv. 14 [15], "to make counsel sweet;" so here, "to make counsel crafty." In other places, it is true, the Hiph. of this verb occurs intransitively, and so Hengst. would take it here, "*they act craftily* in reference to their counsel;" but this is unnecessary. See on xiv. 1. In the next clause the Hithp. יִתְיָעֲצוּ, which occurs only here, expresses the *mutual* deliberation.

PSALM 84

In its general character this Psalm very nearly resembles Psalm xlii.—xliii. Like that, it is the ardent outpouring of a man of no common depth and tenderness of feeling, the expression of a devoted love for the house and worship of Jehovah. Like that, it is written under circumstances of suffering and depression, at a time when the Psalmist was in exile, or at a distance from the Sanctuary. Like that, it touches, and even more fully, on the celebration of the national feast, and pictures the crowd of pilgrims on their way to the Holy City. In both Psalms there is the same deep pathos, the same "exquisite delicacy and tenderness of thought," in both the same strain of remembrance and of anticipation, half sad, half joyful. Certain turns of expression are the same in both. Compare ver. 2 here with xlii. 1, 2; ver. 4 [5] here, "they will still (or *yet*) praise Thee," with xlii. 5, "for I shall yet praise Him;" the name of God as "the Living God," ver. 2 here, and xlii. 2 (occurring nowhere else in the Psalter); the phrase, "appear before God," ver. 7 here, and xlii. 2; "Thy dwellings" or "tabernacles," ver. 1, here, and xliii. 3. But with all these resemblances, there is this difference, that here nothing is said to define exactly the locality in which the Psalm was written; nor is there any allusion to the taunts of enemies, to "men of deceit and wrong," such as meets us in xlii., xliii.

From the general likeness in structure, and sentiment, and colouring of language, and yet perfect distinctness and originality, of the two Poems, Ewald is doubtless right in concluding that both are by the same author. Whether he is right in inferring from ver. 9 [10] of this Psalm that the author was a king, has been questioned. The form of expression points that way, and scarcely admits of a different explanation (see note on the verse). Ewald supposes the king to have been Jehoiachin (or Jeconiah), "who, according to Jer. xxii. 28, &c. was no contemptible person, and who, after having been long in exile (and in confinement), was at last restored to a place of honour, 2 Kings xxv. 27—30." But see more in the Introduction to Psalm xlii.

The former part of this Psalm may also be compared with Psalm lxiii., and there are expressions which connect it with Psalms xxvii. and lxv.

Hengstenberg, who is a zealous upholder of the inscriptions, maintains that the Psalm was composed by some member of the

Levitical family of the Korahites who accompanied David when he fled from Absalom to the east side of the Jordan. But his explanation of the fact is not very intelligible. He says: "The ninth verse renders it evident that the speaker is the Anointed of the Lord. This fact can be reconciled with the title, which ascribes the Psalm to the sons of Korah, only by the supposition that it *was sung from the soul of the Anointed.*"

Mr. Plumptre, who gives reasons for concluding that all the Korahite Psalms were written during the reign of Hezekiah by members of that Levitical family, considers the Psalm to have been written on the same occasion as Psalm xlii., and supposes that "a devout Levite or company of Levites was hindered by the presence of Sennacherib's army from going up at the appointed seasons to take their turn in the ministrations of the Temple." He draws attention to "the touch which indicates the possible familiarity with the Temple precincts. The Levite minstrel remembers 'the sparrow and the swallow' that fluttered about the courts of the Sanctuary there, and built their nests upon its eaves, as they now love to haunt the enclosure of the Mosque of Omar." He observes what new force the Psalmist's words acquire, "I had rather be a door-keeper in the house of my God," &c., if we regard them not as the vague indeterminate wish of any devout worshiper, but remember that they fell from the lips of one of those sons of Korah "whose special function it was to be '*keepers of the gate of the tabernacle*' in the time of David (1 Chron. ix. 19), and sure to be appointed therefore to an analogous service in the Temple." And he concludes "that this Psalm, like Psalm xlii., was written by some Levite detained against his will 'in the land of Jordan' and 'on the slopes of Hermon,' somewhere, *i.e.*, in the upland Gilead country, and that then the recollection of past journeys to Jerusalem would bring back the scenes of travel through the valley of the Jordan, which, with its deep depression and tropical climate, had from the earliest date been famous for its balsam-weeping trees. Some parched rock-ravine on the way would be that which the Psalmist would think of as having been watered by the tears of pilgrims." (*Biblical Studies*, pp. 163—166.)

The Psalm consists of two principal divisions; the first of which dwells on the blessedness of God's service in His House, the supreme happiness of those who are permitted to take their part in it, ver. 1—7: the second consists of a prayer that the Psalmist himself, though shut out from access to the Sanctuary, may nevertheless find God to be his sun and shield, ver. 8—12. Or we may divide the whole into three parts, thus: ver. 1—3 (or 4); ver. 4 (or 5) to 7; ver. 8—12. If we make the first strophe end with ver. 3, then the first strophe and the last resemble one another in structure so far, that both begin and end with the same address to God, "O Jehovah of Hosts" (slightly varied in ver. 8). On the other hand, ver. 4 completes the subject of the first strophe (see note on the verse).

Hupfeld, Delitzsch, De Wette, and others, follow the division suggested by the Selah, and arrange the strophes accordingly: ver. 1—4; ver. 5—8; ver. 9—12. But it is quite impossible to regard ver. 8 as the natural conclusion of the second strophe.*

[FOR THE PRECENTOR. UPON THE GITTITH.[a] A PSALM OF THE SONGS OF KORAH.[b]]

1 How lovely are Thy dwellings, O Jehovah (of) Hosts!
2 My soul longeth, yea even fainteth, for the courts of
Jehovah;
My heart and my flesh cry aloud to the living God.

1. THY DWELLINGS. The plural may either be used to denote *the several parts* of the sanctuary (see on lxviii. 35), or perhaps rather, poetically, instead of the singular. Comp. xliii. 3, xlvi. 4, [5] cxxxii. 5, 8. And the same may be said of the plural "courts," in the next verse (which Mendelssohn renders by the singular, *Vorhof*.) But see General Introduction, Vol. I. p. 99.

2. By the COURTS, that part of the building is meant which was for the people at large. (So in Is. i. 12, "Who hath required this at your hand to tread my *courts*." Comp. lxv. 4 [5], cxvi. 19.) No inference can be drawn from the plural, that the reference is to the court of the people and the court of the priests in the Temple (as the Rabbis explain), and that consequently the Temple was already built.

On this intense expression of personal affection to God and His worship, see note on lxiii. 1.

SOUL . . . HEART . . . FLESH. Even more strongly than there (where "heart" is omitted) marking the whole man, with every faculty and affection. The verbs are also very expressive. The first, LONGETH, means literally, "hath grown pale," as with the intensity of the feeling; the second, FAINTETH, is more exactly "faileth," or "is consumed" (Job xix. 27).

CRY ALOUD. The verb in this conjugation is used elsewhere of a *joyful* utterance, and some would retain this meaning here, as if, even amidst the sadness of exile, there mingled with his longing a joy as he remembers, and anticipates, in spite of all that is adverse, communion with God in Zion. Mendelssohn, keeping to this meaning of the verb, renders: "My soul . . ., fainteth for the court of the Eternal. (where) heart and flesh shout aloud (*jauchzen*) to the God of life." But this ignores the pronominal suffixes. However, the cry of *prayer* may be all that is meant. So the noun from the same root is frequently used, and so the verb (in the Qal conjug.) of the cry of distress, Lam. ii. 19.

LIVING GOD. See note on xlii. 2, the only other place in the Psalms where God is so named. This particular form of expression *'El Chây*

* All the Sephardim synagogues use this Psalm as introductory to the Afternoon Prayer.

3 Yea the sparrow hath found a house,
And the swallow a nest for herself where [c] she hath laid her young,
(Even) [d] Thine altars, O Jehovah (of) Hosts,
My King and my God!

occurs but twice beside in the Bible, Josh. iii. 10, Hos. i. 10. The similar name, *Elohim Chayyîm*, is found, Deut. v. 26 (the first use of the epithet); 1 Sam. xvii. 26, 36; Jer. x. 10; xxiii. 36; and the corresponding Chaldee, Dan. vi. 26. A third combination of the noun and adjective, *Elohim Chây*, occurs in 2 Kings xix. 4, 16, and the corresponding passage in Is. xxxvii. 4, 17. In the New Testament the name "Living God" is found in St. Matthew's and St. John's Gospels, in the speech of Paul and Barnabas in the Acts (xiv. 15), in several of St. Paul's Epistles, four times in the Epistle to the Hebrews, and once in the Revelation.

3. MY KING AND MY GOD. Thus joined also in v. 2. It will be seen from my rendering of this verse, which coincides with that of the E.V., that I do not find in it that "insuperable difficulty" which has presented itself to some of the modern commentators. The Psalmist, at a distance from Zion, envies the birds who are free to build their nests in the immediate precincts of the Temple. They have a happiness which he cannot enjoy. They are nearer to God, so it seems to him in his despondency, than he is. This is all that is meant. Nor can I see anything "trivial" in such a thought. "Thine altars" is a poetical way of saying "Thy house." It is manifestly a special term instead of a general. Yet it has been seriously argued, that no birds could or would ever be suffered to build their nests on the altar. Surely this sort of expression, which is hardly a figure, is common enough. *A parte potiori fit denominatio*. We say, "There goes a sail." What should we think of a man who should argue that a sail cannot go? The altars mean the Temple. There was

"No jutty frieze,
Buttress, nor coigne of vantage, but these birds
Had made their pendant bed,"

not to mention that trees grew within the sacred enclosure, where birds might have built their nests. The comparison between the lot of the birds, happy in their nearness to the house of God, and the Psalmist far removed and in exile, is suggested rather than developed; but it is sufficiently obvious. Hence there is no need to adopt any of the different interpretations of the last clause of the verse which have been proposed, in order to escape a purely imaginary difficulty,—such as (1) "Oh for Thine altars, O Jehovah," &c., as if the meaning were: "The birds have their nests, their homes, their shelter: Oh that I could find my place of refuge and shelter in Thy temple!" Or (2) supposing an ellipsis or omission of certain words, "The sparrow hath found an house, &c. . . . *but I would find* Thine altars," &c., or, "*When shall I come* (as in xlii. 6) to Thine altars?" Or (3) by a transposition (which Hupfeld proposes), so that the last two clauses of ver. 3 [4] would stand after the first clause of ver. 4 [5]:

"Blessed are they that dwell in Thy house,
(Even) Thine altars (or, by Thine altars), O Jehovah of Hosts,
My King and my God;
They will be alway praising Thee."

(4) The most improbable view of all is that of Hengstenberg and Delitzsch—no doubt following the

4 Blessed are they that dwell in Thy house!
They will be still praising Thee. [Selah.]
5 Blessed are the men whose strength is in Thee,
In whose heart are (the) ways,[e]

Rabbis, who say that "the bird" is Israel (a mere 'Agadah)—who suppose that the Psalmist speaks of himself under the figure of a bird. If that be so, what is the meaning of the allusion to the young ones? They are a pointless addition to the figure. Again, what is the force of the particle "yea" (גַּם) with which ver. 3 opens, unless it be to institute a comparison and a conclusion *à minori?* Lastly, how can the Psalmist express this longing for God's house in ver. 2, and in ver. 3 say that he *has found* (observe the perfect tense) a home and a rest there? This has been well argued by Hupfeld, who however himself misses the simple and obvious explanation of the verse.

4. It is doubtful whether this verse should be regarded as closing the first strophe, or commencing the second. The Selah has been urged in favour of the former view, but no stress can be laid upon this, as in the very next Psalm it is inserted in the middle of a strophe, and in some instances, as has been noticed elsewhere, even in the middle of a verse. The chief argument in favour of that division is that thus the thought of ver. 3 is completed. Even the birds are happy, who find shelter beneath that sacred roof; far more happy—truly blessed are they who dwell there, rendering the reasonable service of a thankful heart. *The* blessedness of God's house is that there men *praise* Him. This it was that made that house so precious to the Psalmist. And what Christian man can climb higher than this,—to find in the praise of God the greatest joy of his life?

THEY WILL BE STILL PRAISING THEE, *i.e.* "always, continually." Others, who suppose that a contrast is implied between the gloomy present and the more hopeful future, render, "They will *yet* praise Thee," taking the particle in the same sense as in xlii. 5 [6], 10 [11].

5—7. But not only blessed are they who dwell in the holy place in God's city, and near to His house; blessed are they who can visit it, with the caravan of pilgrims at the great national festivals. They cherish the remembrance of such seasons. Every spot of the familiar road, every station at which they have rested, lives in their heart. The path may be dry and dusty, through a lonely and sorrowful valley, but nevertheless they love it. The pilgrim band, rich in hope, forget the trials and difficulties of the way: hope changes the rugged and stony waste into living fountains. The vale blossoms as if the sweet rain of heaven had covered it with blessings. Hope sustains them at every step; from station to station they renew their strength as they draw nearer to the end of their journey, till at last they appear before God, present themselves as His worshipers, in His sanctuary in Zion.

Such appears to be the general scope of the passage, though the meaning of the second clause, "In whose heart are the ways," has been much questioned. (1) The Chaldee renders the verse: "Blessed is the man whose strength is in Thy word, who has *confidence* (in Thee, or in it, *i.e.* Thy word), in his heart." This preserves the parallelism, "strength" . . . . . "confidence." It probably rested on a figurative interpretation of the word "highways," roads carefully constructed being firm, strong, safe, and hence an image of confidence. (2) Others again, as Qimchi (Joseph), understand by "the ways," those of the knowledge "of God" (in

6 Who passing through the Vale of Weeping, make it a
place of springs;
Yea, the early rain [f] covereth (it) with blessings.
7 They go from strength to strength,

which men are said to walk), and these are in their heart, because they love and meditate thereon. (3) Hengstenberg explains the ways or roads constructed in the heart as the second condition of salvation (the first being that a man has his strength in God), and thinks that the expression designates zealous moral effort, righteousness, &c.; the heart of man being naturally like a pathless and rocky wilderness, in which roads are levelled by repentance. He quotes Ps. l. 23; Prov. xvi. 17; Is. xl. 3, 4.

But these interpretations do not fall in with the general strain and tenour of verses 5—7. The WAYS (lit. "highways") are those traversed by the caravans of pilgrims—the ways to the sanctuary. No wonder that in all ages men have rejoiced to find in this beautiful picture an image of the Christian life. To what can that so aptly be compared as to a pilgrimage in a vale of tears? Is it not by the hope of appearing before God in the heavenly Jerusalem that the Christian is sustained? Does he not find fountains of refreshment in the wilderness of the world? Does not God's grace visit him like the sweet refreshing shower from heaven? Does he not advance from strength to strength, from grace to grace, from glory to glory, till he reaches his journey's end?

6. THE VALE OF WEEPING. The meaning of the word "Baca" is doubtful, but all the Ancient Versions render it by "weeping," and according to the Massoreth it is the same as "Bakhah," *weeping*, the word being written here only with א. Comp. xxiii. 4, "valley of the shadow of death." Burckhardt tells us that he found a valley in the neighbourhood of Sinai, which bore the name of "the valley of weeping."

Others, as Delitzsch and Ewald, take Baca to be the name of a tree, as it is in 2 Sam. v. 24; 1 Chron. xiv. 4; and either (as the E.V. there renders) "a mulberry-tree," or more probably some species of balsam-tree, dropping its tears of balm, and so taking its name from the Hebrew root which signifies "weeping." In this case some sandy valley is meant, where these trees grew, and which took its name from them. "With the love for detecting allusive and, as it were, ominous meanings in proper names, which was characteristic of Hebrew thought at all times . . . . the Psalmist plays upon its etymological significance."—Plumptre, *Biblical Studies*, p. 165.

The meaning of the verse is, that the faith and hope and joy of the pilgrims make the sandy waste a place of fountains, and then (this is the Divine side of the picture) God from heaven sends down the rain of His grace. The word denotes the soft, gentle autumnal rain (Joel ii. 23) which fell after the crops were sown. Thus the Vale of Weeping becomes a Vale of Joy. "Compare for the use of the same figure in a simpler form, Is. xxxv. 7; Hos. ii. 15 [17 Heb.]. The entrance into Palestine is, as a matter of fact, waste and arid."—*Ewald.*

A PLACE OF SPRINGS. This is the strict meaning of the word, rather than "a spring" or "fountain." Comp. cvii. 35.

7. FROM STRENGTH TO STRENGTH, ever renewing it, in spite of the toils of the way, and in view of the journey's end, as Is. xl. 31. Comp. Joh. i. 16, and 2 Cor.

(Every one of them) appeareth before God in Zion.

8 O Jehovah, God (of) Hosts, hear my prayer,
Give ear, O God of Jacob. [Selah.]

9 See, O God our shield,
And look upon the face of Thine Anointed ;

10 For a day in Thy courts is better than a thousand (elsewhere) ;
I had rather be a door-keeper in the house of my God,
Than dwell in the tents of wickedness.

11 For Jehovah God is a sun and a shield,
Jehovah giveth grace and glory,
No good thing doth He withhold from them that walk uprightly.

iii. 18, and similarly Rom. i. 17, ἐκ πίστεως εἰς πίστιν, from "first to last of faith, and nothing but faith."

APPEARETH. See note on xlii. 2. Comp. especially Exod. xxiii. 17, xxxiv. 23.

8. The Psalmist has pictured to himself the blessedness of those who dwell in the holy city, in immediate proximity to God's house, the blessedness of those who can join the pilgrim-caravans. Now, he pours out a prayer for himself that he, though distant, may share the same blessing.

9. SEE (absol. as in lxxx. 14 [15]).

OUR SHIELD, and again ver. 11 ; so God is called in iii. 3, where see note ; xxviii. 7, &c.

LOOK UPON THE FACE OF THINE ANOINTED. This following immediately upon the words in ver. 8, "hear *my* prayer," favours the supposition that the Psalm was written by the king. So also does the use of the pronoun of the first person in ver. 10, introduced by the conjunction "for." Another might, however, offer the prayer on his behalf. See xx., xxi., lxi. 6 [7].

10. BE A DOOR-KEEPER, lit. "lie on the threshold" (LXX. παραρριπτεῖσθαι), or "busy oneself on the threshold ;" the lowest place, the meanest office in God's house is a happiness and an honour beyond all that the world has to offer. Delitzsch sees in the comparison with "tents" rather than "palaces," an intimation that the Ark of God was still in a tent, and the Temple not yet built.

11. JEHOVAH GOD (Elohim). This form of the Divine Name is characteristic, as is well known, of the section, Gen. ii. 14—iii. 24, where it first occurs. We find it again in Exod. ix. 30, and in David's prayer, 2 Sam. vii. 22. This is the only passage in the Psalter where it is employed. In lxviii. 18 [16] it is the shorter form "Jah Elohim." In lxxxv. 8 the order of the two names is different, "The Elohim Jehovah." In lxxi. 5, and in a large number of passages in the Prophets where the E.V. has "the Lord God," this represents the Hebrew "Adonai Jehovah."

A SUN. This is the only place where God is directly so called. In other passages we have the more general name of "Light," as in xxvii. 1. Comp. however, Is. lx. 19, 20 ; Rev. xxi. 23 ; and the expression, "Sun of Righteousness," as applied to the Messiah, Mal. iii. 20 [iv. 2 in E.V.].

Instead of "Jehovah God is a sun and a shield," the LXX. and

12 O Jehovah (of) Hosts,
Blessed is the man that trusteth in Thee.

Theod. have, "The Lord God loveth mercy and truth."

UPRIGHTLY, lit. "in perfectness;" see xv. 2. To such persons God will show His salvation, all that is comprised in those two great words, "grace" and "glory," whether they can enter His earthly house or not.

And the Psalmist rises at last to the joyful conviction, not only that they are blessed who dwell in God's house (ver. 4), or they who swell the festal throng on their way to that house (ver. 5), but they who, whether they worship in it or not, are one with Him by faith: "Blessed is the man that *trusteth* in Thee."

[a] See on the Title of Psalm viii., and General Introduction, Vol. I. p. 88.

[b] See on Title of xlii., and General Introduction, Vol. I. p. 98.

[c] אֲשֶׁר, *where*, as in xcv. 9, Num. xx. 13. The two names of birds here mentioned are found together also in Prov. xxvi. 2. The Chald. render "dove" and "turtle," but the rendering as above is preferable. See the words in Ges. *Thes.*

[d] אֶת־מ׳. The אֶת may be as I have taken it, the sign of the accus. (in appos.), or it may be a preposition, *by*, *near*. In this last sense it is taken by the Syr., and so Ewald.

[e] מְסִלּוֹת. As the word stands, it can only mean *highways*, *roads*, and here, the roads leading to the Sanctuary. So the LXX. seeing a reference to the caravans going up to the yearly feast, render, ἀναβάσεις ἐν τῇ καρδίᾳ αὐτοῦ διέθετο. The Syro-hex. supplies the pronoun: "*Thy* path is in their heart." The Chald., we have seen, gives the word a figurative meaning, *confidence*. This meaning Hupfeld thinks is required by the parallelism, and he proposes to read כְּסָלוֹת, the plur. of the noun כִּסְלָה, which occurs in this sense, Job iv. 6. The plur. of abstract nouns is frequently used for the sing., and this plur. is found in a proper name, Josh. xix. 22.

[f] מוֹרֶה. The same word occurs in Joel ii. 23 (*bis*), of the *autumnal rain* (elsewhere יוֹרֶה); here, perhaps, any rain as softening and fertilizing. The older Verss. generally took the word in the sense of *teacher*, *lawgiver*. LXX. ὁ νομοθετῶν. Sym. ὁ ὑποδείκτης. E′. ὁ φωτίζων. S′. ὁ διδάσκων. Jer. *doctor*, and so the Rabbis, but Aquila has πρώϊμος. Herder understands by it *the leader* of the caravan.

יַעְטֶה. Hiph. with double accus. (the nearer object being here omitted) as in lxv. 13. Hengst. makes it Qal (as in Lev. xiii. 45, Jer. xliii. 12), and insists that מוֹרֶה means *teacher*, as in 2 Kings xvii. 28, Is. xxx. 20, Prov. v. 13, and so renders: "the teacher (*i.e.* David himself) shall even be covered with blessings." In this he follows Jerome: *Benedictionibus amicietur doctor;* but the whole beauty of the image is thus destroyed.

בְּרָכוֹת. Some with the change of a single vowel read בְּרֵכוֹת, *pools.* Hence the E. V.: "The rain also filleth the pools." But the LXX. follow our present pointing: *καὶ γὰρ εὐλογίας δώσει ὁ νομοθετῶν*, and so does Sym. The accusative is placed first in the sentence as emphatic, whilst the part. גַּם, *yea, also,* shows that the rain produces its effect *also* in blessing, as well as the springs in the valley: "Yea with blessings doth the rain cover it."

The Chaldee paraphrase of this verse is singular enough to be worth quoting: "The sinners who pass through the depths of Gehenna, greatly weeping, make it a fountain; but [God] shall cover with blessings those that return to the doctrine of His law."

PSALM 85

THERE seems every reason to conclude that this Psalm was written after the return of the exiles from the Babylonish captivity. It opens with an acknowledgement of God's goodness and mercy in the national restoration, in terms which could hardly apply to any other event. But it passes immediately to earnest entreaty for deliverance from the pressure of existing evils, in language which almost contradicts the previous acknowledgement. First we hear the grateful confession, "Thou hast turned the captivity of Jacob;" and then we have the prayer, "Turn us, O God of our salvation." If the third verse contains the joyful announcement, "Thou hast withdrawn all Thy wrath," &c., the fifth pleads as if no such assurance had been given: "Wilt Thou for ever be angry with us? Wilt thou draw out Thine anger to all generations?"

The most probable way of explaining this conflict of opposing feelings is by referring the Psalm to the circumstances mentioned by Nehemiah (chap. i. 3). The exiles on their return, he learnt, were "in great affliction and reproach." And when he obtained leave to go to Jerusalem himself, it was only in the midst of perpetual opposition and discouragement (chap. iv.) that he was able to carry on his work of restoration. The bright prospect which was opening before them had been quickly dashed. They had returned indeed, but it was to a desolate land and a forsaken city, whose walls were cast down, and her gates burned with fire; whilst jealous and hostile tribes were ever on the watch to assail and vex them. Hence it is that the entreaty for mercy follows so hard upon the acknowledgement that mercy has been vouchsafed. The 126th Psalm is conceived in a somewhat similar strain. In the latter portion of this Psalm (from ver. 8) the present misery is forgotten in the dawning of a glorious future. The prayer has been uttered; the storm of the soul is hushed; in quietness and resignation the Psalmist sets himself to hear what God will say, and the Divine answer is given, not in form, but in substance in ver. 9—12. It is a glowing prophecy of Messianic times, most naturally connecting itself with the hopes which the return from Babylon had kindled afresh, and well fitted to enable those who heard it to triumph over the gloom and despondency of the present. Delitzsch traces in the Psalm the influence of the later portion of Isaiah's prophecy (chaps. xl.—xlvi.) It is one of the many Psalms which were inspired, he says, by the unsealing of that great book, and which in their flowing, graceful, transparent style, their figurative allegorizing language, and their great prophetic thoughts of consolation, remind us of the common source whence they draw.

Mr. Plumptre, who holds that all the Korahite Psalms belong to the time of Hezekiah, thinks that this Psalm refers to the Assyrian invasion. He reminds us that the language of Isaiah in reference to that invasion is that "the cities shall be wasted without inhabitant," that "the Lord shall remove men far away" (Is. vi. 11, 12); that he speaks not only of "the remnant of Israel," "the remnant of Jacob" as returning (x. 29), but in terms hardly less strong, at the very crisis of Sennacherib's invasion, of "the remnant that is escaped of the house of Judah" (xxxvii. 32). After the overflow of Sennacherib, and when the alliance of Hezekiah was courted by Babylon, there would be ample opportunities for many of those who had been carried into exile to return to the land of their fathers. "The vision of mercy and truth, righteousness and peace, is the same with the Psalmist as with the Prophet." It may be added, he remarks, that the prayer, "Turn us, O God of our salvation" (in ver. 4), is identical with the ever-recurring burden of Psalm lxxx., which clearly refers to the captivity of "Ephraim and Benjamin and Manasseh" *i.e.* of "Jacob" rather than of "Judah." (*Biblical Studies*, pp. 166-7.)

It is not surprising, considering the bright picture which the latter verses contain, that this Psalm should have been appointed by the Church for the services of Christmas Day.

According to Hupfeld, the Psalm falls into two nearly equal portions:—

(1) The Prayer of the people, or for the people, ver. 1—7; (2) the Divine Promise, ver. 8—13. Ewald and Olshausen suppose

that the first was intended to be sung by the congregation, the second by the Priest, who after prayer seeks and receives the Divine answer.

[FOR THE PRECENTOR. A PSALM OF THE SONS OF KORAH.[a]]

1 THOU art become favourable, O Jehovah, unto Thy land,
Thou hast brought back the captivity of Jacob.
2 Thou hast taken away the iniquity of Thy people,
Thou hast covered all their sin. [Selah.]
3 Thou hast withdrawn all Thy wrath,
Thou hast turned [b] from the fierceness of Thine anger.

4 Turn us, O God of our salvation,
And cause Thine indignation towards us to cease.
5 Wilt Thou for ever be angry with us?
Wilt Thou draw out Thine anger to all generations?
6 Wilt not THOU quicken us again,
That Thy people may rejoice in Thee?
7 Show us Thy loving-kindness, O Jehovah,
And grant us Thy salvation.

8 I will hear what God Jehovah will speak,

1—3. The acknowledgement of God's goodness to His people in their restoration from the Babylonish captivity. It is not necessary to translate the tenses as aorists, "Thou *didst* become" (as Ewald and others); for though the restoration is a past event, we need not regard it as long past.

1. THOU HAST BROUGHT BACK, &c. See on xiv. 7, and on lxviii. 18. Others, "Thou hast returned to."

2. TAKEN AWAY . . . COVERED. Both words are used in xxxii. 1, where see notes.

5. FOR EVER. The emphatic word placed first, because there seemed to be no end to their calamities. Even the return to their own land had brought them apparently no rest, no consolation, no hope for the future.

6. THOU. The pronoun is emphatic; for God alone can thus revive the sad hearts and broken hopes of His people.

QUICKEN, &c. Comp. lxxi. 20, lxxx. 19.

IN THEE. Not in any earthly blessings, even when they are vouchsafed; not in corn, or wine, or oil; not in the fatness of the earth or the dew of heaven; but in Him who giveth all these things, who giveth more than all these, Himself.

8. I WILL HEAR, or, "let me hear." Having uttered his sorrows and his prayer for better days, he would now place himself in the attitude of calm and quiet expecta-

For He will speak peace to His people and His beloved,
Only let them not turn again to folly.
9 Surely His salvation is nigh them that fear Him,
That glory may dwell in our land.
10 Loving-kindness and truth have met together;
Righteousness and peace have kissed (each other).
11 Truth springeth out of the earth,
And righteousness hath looked down out of heaven.
12 Jehovah will give that which is good,

tion. Like Habakkuk, he will betake him to his watch-tower, and wait to hear what the Lord will speak. "He might have said," Calvin observes, "what the Lord will *do*; but since God's benefits to His church flow from His promises, the Psalmist mentions His mouth rather than His hand (os potius quam manum posuit), and at the same time teaches us that patience depends on the calm listening ear of faith."

GOD JEHOVAH, lit. "the God Jehovah," the two nouns being in apposition.

PEACE: that is God's great word, which in fact sums up and comprises all else, peace with Him declared to all who are HIS BELOVED, the objects of His loving-kindness (see on xvi. 10) having the privileges of their covenant relation to Him.

HIS BELOVED or, "His godly ones." See on iv. 3 [4] note [b], and lxxxvi. 2.

ONLY LET THEM NOT TURN, or "that they turn not."

FOLLY: so the infatuation of sin is spoken of. Comp. xiv. 1, xlix. 13 [14]. Or, perhaps, idolatry may be meant, and especially if the reference is to the Babylonish captivity.

9. GLORY, *i.e.* the manifested Presence of God tabernacling visibly amongst them, as of old. This hope was destined to have its fulfilment, but in a better and a higher sense, when He who was the brightness of the Father's glory tabernacled in human flesh, and men "beheld His glory, the glory as of the only-begotten of the Father."

10. The four virtues here mentioned are, as Calvin remarks, the four cardinal virtues of Christ's kingdom. Where these reign amongst men, there must be true and perfect felicity. He adds, however, "If any one prefers to understand, by the loving-kindness and truth here mentioned, attributes of God, I have no objection to such a view." But the truth is, the last are the basis and source of the first.

11. The earth brings forth truth, as she brings forth the natural fruits, and righteousness looks down from heaven like some approving angel on the renewed and purified earth. Or, as Calvin more generally explains: "Tantumdem valet ac si dixisset utramque fore sursum et deorsum ubique diffusam, ut cœlum et terram impleant. Neque enim seorsum illis aliquid diversum tribuere voluit." The figures are designed in both verses to show that these virtues are not regarded merely in their separate aspect, but as meeting, answering one another, conspiring in perfect harmony to one glorious end. For this mutual blessing from the heaven above and the earth beneath, comp. Is. xlv. 8, Hos. ii. 23—25.

12. The Psalmist passes from spiritual to temporal blessings. "If any one objects to this mixing of the two, the answer is easy: there

And our land will give her increase.
13 Righteousness shall go before Him,
And shall follow His footsteps in the way.[c]

is nothing to shock us, if God, whilst He blesses the faithful with spiritual blessings, should vouchsafe to them also some taste of His fatherly love in the good things of this world; for St. Paul assures us that godliness hath the promise of this life as well as of that which is to come."—*Calvin*. He adds an important remark: "This verse, moreover, shows us that the power of fruitfulness was not once for all bestowed on the earth (as men of no religion choose to imagine, that God at the creation gave to the several parts of His universe their several office, and then left them alone to pursue their own course), but that every year it is fertilized by the secret virtue of God, according as He sees fit to testify to us His goodness."

13. Righteousness shall be both His herald and His attendant.

[a] See above on the Title of Psalm xlii., and General Introduction, Vol. I. p. 98.

[b] הֵשִׁיב. The Hiph., which elsewhere is used with the accus. (lxxviii. 38, cvi. 23, Job ix. 13, &c.), is here used like the intrans. Qal, with מִן, see Exod. xxxii. 12, Jon. iii. 9. There is apparently here a confusion of the two constructions, the phrase being borrowed from the passage in Exod., with the substitution of Hiph. for Qal. See a similar case in Ezek. xviii 30, 32.

[c] The constr. is literally "and maketh His footsteps for a way," *i.e.* in which to follow Him. So apparently the LXX. καὶ θήσει εἰς ὁδὸν τὰ διαβήματα αὐτοῦ, and Sym. κ. θ. εἰς ὁδ. τοὺς πόδας αὐτοῦ. Others, as Del. explain: "and (righteousness) setteth (her feet) in the way of His steps," a possible rendering, perhaps, but against the accents. Strictly speaking, יָשֵׂם is the optat. form, and therefore the whole verse ought rather to be rendered, "*Let* righteousness go before Him," &c. So the Talmud, *Berachoth* 14[a], though giving a different interpretation, "Let righteousness precede a man, and then let him put his footsteps in the way (*i.e.* go about his daily business)."

PSALM 86

THIS Psalm, which is inserted amongst a series of Korahite Psalms, is the only one in the Third Book ascribed to David. That it was written by him we can hardly suppose. Many of the expressions are, no doubt, such as we meet with in his Psalms, but there are also many which are borrowed from other passages of Scripture. Indeed, the numerous adaptations of phrases employed by other writers may reasonably be taken as evidence of a much later date. Further, the style is, as Delitzsch remarks, liturgical rather than poetical, and is wholly wanting in that force, animation, and originality for which David's poems are remarkable. The Psalm is stamped by the use of the Divine Name, Adonai, which occurs in it seven times.

There is no regular strophical division, nor is it always easy to trace clearly the connexion between the several parts of the Psalm. Hupfeld denies that there is any. Tholuck has traced it far more carefully than any commentator I am acquainted with, and in the notes I have given the substance of his remarks.

The introductory portion (ver. 1—5) consists of a number of earnest petitions, based on several distinct pleas—the suffering (ver. 1), the faith (ver. 2), the continued and earnest supplication (ver. 3, 4) of the Psalmist, and the mercy and goodness of God (ver. 5).

In the next part (ver. 6—13) he resumes his petition; expresses his confidence that God will hear him, comforting himself with the majesty and greatness of God, who is able to do all that he asks (ver. 8—10); prays for guidance and a united heart, mixing with his prayer resolves as to his conduct, and thanksgiving for deliverance (ver. 11—13).

Finally (ver. 14—17) he speaks of the peril by which he has been threatened, turns to God with affectionate confidence as to a gracious God, and casts himself fearlessly upon His mercy.

[A PSALM OF DAVID.]

1 BOW down Thine ear, O Jehovah, answer me!
For I am afflicted and poor.
2 Keep my soul, for I am one whom Thou lovest;
O THOU my God, save Thy servant,
Who putteth his trust in Thee.

1. BOW DOWN, &c. Comp. lv. 1, 2.

AFFLICTED AND POOR: alleged in the same way as a reason, xl. 17 [18]. This is not the highest ground which can be taken in pressing for an answer to our prayer, but it is a ground which God suffers us to take, both because He declares Himself to be the helper of the needy (comp. xii. 5 [6]), and because it is the sense of their need and misery which drives men to God. Comp. for the same epithets xxxv. 10, xxxvii. 14, lxxiv. 21.

2. ONE WHOM THOU LOVEST, or, who has been graciously dealt with by Thee. The first plea was his need; now he pleads his own covenant relation to God; for this is implied in the adjective here used, *châsîd*. Comp. iv. 3 [4] note [b], and the note on xvi. 10. It is unfortunate that the E.V. renders:

3 Be gracious unto me, O Lord,
For upon Thee do I call all the day long.
4 Rejoice the soul of Thy servant,
For unto Thee, O Lord, do I lift up my soul.
5 For Thou, Lord, art good, and ready to forgive,
And plenteous in loving-kindness to all them that call upon Thee.
6 Give ear, O Jehovah, unto my prayer,
And hearken unto the voice of my supplications.
7 In the day of my distress, I will call upon Thee,
For Thou wilt answer me.
8 There is none like unto Thee among the gods, O Lord,
Neither are there (any works) like unto Thy works.

"for I am *holy*." (The margin gives the true rendering.) The appeal is not to anything in himself, but to God's goodness. This is clear from ver. 5. At the same time he does not hesitate to say what the attitude of his heart is towards God, and to urge his simple absolute confidence in God, as well as his unceasing earnest prayer, as reasons why he should be heard. This is the language of honest straightforward simplicity, not of self-righteousness.

4. I LIFT UP MY SOUL, as in xxv. 1. Comp. cxxx. 6.

5. READY TO FORGIVE. The adjective occurs nowhere else. The general sentiment of the verse (repeated in 15) is borrowed from such passages as Exod. xx. 6; xxxiv. 6, 9; Num. xiv. 18, 19.

It is on the broad ground of God's mercy, and of that mercy as freely bestowed on *all* who seek it, that he rests. He applies the general truth (ver. 5) to his own case (ver. 6). In ver. 7 he pleads again the need, under the pressure of which he cries to God: it is no unmanly, petulant, peevish complaint that he utters. The calamity is real, and there is but One who has power to deliver him.

6. Comp. v. 2, xxviii. 2, cxxx. 2. The peculiar form of the word SUPPLICATIONS occurs only here.

7. Comp. xx. 1; l. 16; lxxvii. 2 [3]; xvii. 6.

8—10. There are two kinds of doubt which are wont in the hour of temptation to assail the soul; the doubt as to God's *willingness*, and the doubt as to God's *power*, to succour. The first of these the Psalmist has already put from him: he now shows that he has overcome the second. God is able as well as willing to help, and every being on the face of the earth who receives help, receives it from the hand of Him who is the only God, and who shall one day be recognized (so speaks the strong prophetic hope within him, ver. 9) as the only God. This hope rests on the fact that God has created all men ("all nations whom *Thou hast made*"), and nothing can be imagined more self-contradictory than that the spirit which has come from God should remain for ever unmindful of its source. In ver. 8 it might seem as if God were merely compared with the gods of the nations. In ver. 10 they are plainly said to be "no gods," though they "be called gods." There is but one God: "Thou art God alone."

8. The first half of the verse is

9 All nations whom Thou hast made
Shall come and bow themselves down before Thee, O Lord,
And shall give glory to Thy Name.
10 For Thou art great, and doest wondrous things;
Thou art God alone.
11 Teach me, O Jehovah, Thy way,
I will walk in Thy truth:
Unite my heart to fear Thy Name;
12 I will give thanks unto Thee, O Lord my God, with my whole heart,
And I will glorify Thy Name for ever.

borrowed from Exod. xv. 11. Comp. lxxxix. 8 [9], lxxi. 19, &c. With the econd half comp. Deut. iii. 24.

9. Nearly as in xxii. 27 [28]. Comp. lxvi. 4; Is. lxvi. 18, 23; Zech. xiv. 9, 16.

10. Comp. lxxvii. 13, 14 [14, 15] with Exod. xv. 11. See also lxxxiii. 18 [19]; 2 Kings xix. 15, 19; Neh. ix. 6.

11. The first clause is word for word as in xxvii. 11. Comp. xxv. 4.

Walk in thy truth, xxvi. 3. Although in a great strait, and in fear of his enemies, the Psalmist, like all who pray aright, offers first the petition, "Hallowed be Thy Name," before he asks, "Give us this day our daily bread," and "deliver us from evil." He confesses that his spiritual eye is not yet perfectly enlightened, his heart not yet perfect with God. And while he rejects every other way, every other rule of life, but the eternal rule of God's truth, he prays first that he may more clearly discern that way, and then that all the various desires, interests, passions, that agitate the human heart, may have no hold upon him, compared with the one thing needful—"to fear God's name."

Unite my heart—suffer it no longer to scatter itself upon a multiplicity of objects, to be drawn hither and thither by a thousand different aims, but turn all its powers, all its affections in one direction, collect them in one focus, make them all one in Thee. The prayer derives a special force from the resolve immediately preceding: "I will walk in Thy truth." The same integrity of heart which made the resolve could alone utter the prayer. The nearest Old Testament parallels are: the "one heart," Jer. xxxii. 39; "And I will give them one heart and one way, that they may fear Me for ever;" and the "whole heart" of love to God, Deut. vi. 5, x. 12. Our Lord teaches us how needful the prayer of this verse is. Comp. what He says of "the single eye," the impossibility of serving two masters, the folly and the wearisomeness of those anxious cares by which men suffer themselves to be hampered and distracted, and in contrast with all this the exhortation, "Seek ye first the kingdom of God," &c. (Matt. vi. 19—34.) See also the history of Martha and Mary, Luke x. 38—42.

12. Why does he offer this prayer for a "united heart"? That he may then with his "whole heart" give thanks to God for all His infinite loving-kindness. God's mercies

13 For Thy loving-kindness is great toward me,
And Thou hast delivered my soul from the unseen world beneath.
14 O God, proud men are risen up against me,
And an assembly of violent men have sought after my soul,
And have not set Thee before them.
15 But Thou, O Lord, art a God full of compassion and gracious,
Long-suffering and plenteous in loving-kindness and truth.
16 O turn unto me, and be gracious to me,
Give Thy strength unto Thy servant,
And save the son of Thy handmaid.
17 Show me a sign for good,
That they who hate me may see and be ashamed,
Because Thou, Jehovah, hast holpen me, and comforted me.

are a motive to greater thankfulness, and to a more whole-hearted undivided service. Briefly, the connexion in ver. 11, 12, is this: "Teach me Thy way, (and then) I will walk, &c. Unite my heart, (and then) I will give thanks."

13. Comp. lvii. 10 [11]; lvi. 13 [14]; cxvi. 8.

THE UNSEEN WORLD BENEATH, *i.e.* under the earth. Comp. Exod. xx. 4 with Phil. ii. 10. For similar phrases see Ezek. xxxi. 14, 16, 18; Ps. lxiii. 9 [10]; cxxxix. 15; Ezek. xxvi. 20; xxxii. 18, 24; Is. xliv. 23, and Ps. lxxxviii. 6 [7]; Lam. iii. 55.

14. Now at last he comes to the peril, and now (ver. 15) his appeal lies even more fully than in ver. 5 to God's glorious Name by which He made Himself known to Moses, Exod. xxxiv. 6. This verse explains what the peril was, and what he means by the deliverance from Hades. The words are borrowed, with a slight variation ("proud men" instead of "strangers"), from liv. 3 [5].

VIOLENT, or rather "overbearing." Aq. κατισχυρευομένων.

16. SON OF THY HANDMAID, as in cxvi. 16.

17. A SIGN, *i.e.* not a *miraculous* sign, but an *evident* proof of Thy good-will towards me, such as shall force even my haters to acknowledge that Thou art on my side.

"Is it not the fact," says Tholuck, "that the more we recognize in every daily occurrence God's secret inspiration guiding and controlling us, the more will all which to others wears a common every-day aspect, to us prove a sign and a wondrous work?"

FOR GOOD. Comp. Neh. v. 19, xiii. 31, and often in Jeremiah.

PSALM 87

This Psalm presents us with one of those startling contrasts to the general tone of Jewish sentiment and belief which meet us in various passages of the Prophetical writings. The Jewish nation was, even by its original constitution, and still more by the provisions of the Law of Moses, an isolated nation. Shut in by the mountains, the sea, the desert, it was to a great extent cut off from the world. And the narrowness of its spirit corresponded to the narrowness of its geographical position. It was pervaded by a jealous exclusiveness which was remarkable even among the nations of antiquity, and which derived its force and sanction from the precepts of its religion. The Jews were constantly reminded that they were a separate people, distinct, and intended to be distinct, from all others. Their land was given them as a special gift from Heaven. Both they and their country belonged to God, in a sense in which no other people and country belonged to Him. It was a holy Ark which no profane hands might dare to touch; or if they did, they must perish in the attempt. As a natural consequence of this belief, the Jewish people, for the most part, regarded their neighbours as enemies. Judaism held out no hope of a brotherhood of nations. The Jewish Church was not a missionary church. So far as the Jews looked upon the world around them, it was with feelings of antipathy, and with the hope, which was never quenched in the midst of the most terrible reverses, that finally they, as the chosen race, should subdue their enemies far and wide, and that, by the grace of Heaven, one sitting on David's throne should be king of the world. Psalmists and Prophets shared the feeling. They exulted in the thought that the king who ruled from Zion would dash the nations in pieces like a potter's vessel, fill the places with dead bodies, and lead rival kings in the long array of his triumph.

But mingling with these anticipations, and correcting them, there were others of a nobler kind. The Prophets speak not only of victories, but of voluntary submission. The vision which rises before them is not only of a forced unity of nations, such as that which was achieved by the iron hand of Roman dominion, but of a unity of faith and love. They see the mountain of the Lord's house exalted above the hills, and all nations flowing to it with one impulse, not led thither in the conqueror's train, but attracted by its glory, longing to taste its peace (Is. ii. 2—4). They see Gentiles coming to the light of Jerusalem, and kings to the brightness of her rising. They foretell a time when all wars and all national antipathies shall cease, when "the root of Jesse" shall be as a standard round which all nations shall flock, and the temple of Jehovah the centre of a common faith and worship.

It is this last hope which expresses itself in this Psalm, but which expresses itself in a form that has no exact parallel in other passages. Foreign nations are here described, not as captives or tributaries, not even as doing voluntary homage to the greatness and glory of Zion, but as actually incorporated and enrolled, by a new birth, among her sons. Even the worst enemies of their race, the tyrants and oppressors of the Jews, Egypt and Babylon, are threatened with no curse, no shout of joy is raised in the prospect of their overthrow, but the privileges of citizenship are extended to them, and they are welcomed as brothers. Nay more, God Himself receives each one as a child newly born into His family, acknowledges each as His son, and enrols him with His own hand in the sacred register of His children.

It is this mode of anticipating a future union and brotherhood of all the nations of the earth, not by conquest, but by incorporation into one state, and by a birthright so acquired, which is so remarkable. In some of the Prophets, more especially in Isaiah, we observe the same liberal, conciliatory, comprehensive language toward foreign states, as Tyre and Ethiopia, and still more strikingly toward Egypt and Assyria (chap. xix. 22—25). But the Psalm stands alone amongst the writings of the Old Testament, in representing this union of nations as a new birth into the city of God.

This idea gives it a singular interest, and clearly stamps it as Messianic. It is the Old Testament expression of the truth which St. Paul declares, when he tells us that in Jesus Christ "there is neither Greek nor Jew, barbarian, Scythian, bond nor free;" or when he writes to the Gentile Church at Ephesus, "Now therefore ye are no more strangers and foreigners, but fellow-citizens with the saints, and of the household of God."

It is the first announcement of that great amity of nations, or rather of that universal common citizenship of which heathen philosophers dreamt, which was "in the mind of Socrates when he called himself a citizen of the world," which had "become a commonplace of the Stoic philosophy," which Judaism tried finally to realize by the admission of proselytes, through baptism, into the Jewish community; which Rome accomplished, so far as the external semblance went, first by subduing the nations, and then by admitting them to the rights of Roman citizenship. But the true fulfilment of this hope is to be found only in that kingdom which Christ has set up. He has gathered into His commonwealth all the kingdoms of the earth. He has made men one, members of the same family, by teaching them to feel that they are all children of the same Father. He has made it evident that the hope of the Jewish singer is no false hope ; that there is a Father in heaven who cares for all, whatever name they bear. Thus the Psalm has received a better and higher fulfilment than that which lies on the surface of its words. It was fulfilled in Christ. When He came, "the city of God, of which the Stoics doubtfully and feebly spoke, was set up before the eyes of men. It was no insubstantial city, such as we fancy in the clouds, no invisible pattern, such as Plato thought might be laid up in heaven, but a visible corporation, whose members met together to eat bread and drink wine, and into which they were initiated by bodily immersion in water. Here the Gentile met the Jew, whom he had been accustomed to regard as an enemy of the human race; the Roman met the lying Greek sophist, the Syrian slave the gladiator born beside the Danube. In brotherhood they met, the natural birth and kindred of each forgotten, the baptism alone remembered, in which they had been born again to God and to each other." *

There are two principal epochs to which the Psalm may be referred :—

I. Its tone, as has been already observed, falls in with that of some of the prophecies of Isaiah. Hence it has been referred, not without reason, to the reign of Hezekiah. Some have supposed that it was a song of triumph, written, like Psalms xlvi. and xlviii., after the defeat of Sennacherib ; others, more probably, that it was a hymn composed for some solemn reception of proselytes into the Church, "the Psalmist and his brother Levites exulting in this admission of converts as they would do in a national victory." Mr. Plumptre gives several reasons in favour of this view. He refers (1) to the similarity between the opening verse and the language of Psalm xlviii. 2 (written, as we have seen, in Hezekiah's reign), compared with Is. xxv. 6, 7, and ii. 3. (2) He thinks the use of the name "Rahab" as designating Egypt is almost sufficient to fix the date of the Psalm. For the use of the word in this sense is characteristic of Isaiah, as in li. 9, "Art thou not it that hath *cut Rahab* (*i.e.* smitten Egypt) and wounded the dragon?" And again, Is. xxx. 7, "The Egyptians shall help in vain. . . . They are *Rahab*

---

* *Ecce Homo*, p. 136.

(proud, mighty, ferocious as the monstrous forms of their own river), and yet they sit still." (3) The hope thus expressed, that Egypt and Babylon shall be enrolled among the worshipers of Jehovah, is a hope identical with that in Isaiah xix. : "In that day shall Israel be the third with Egypt and with Assyria, even a blessing in the midst of the land," &c. And Babylon is substituted for Assyria in the Psalm, because of the greater intercourse with the former kingdom, and the seeming overthrow of the latter towards the close of Hezekiah's reign. Babylonish ambassadors came to Hezekiah, and Isaiah's prophecies in chaps. xiii., xiv., xxxix., are evidence that Babylon was prominent at this time. (4) The mention of Philistia, Tyre, and Ethiopia also synchronizes with Hezekiah's reign. As Isaiah had foretold (xiv. 29), he subdued the Philistines (2 Kings xviii. 3). This was a token that the Lord "had founded Zion." His reign witnessed a renewal of the intercourse with Tyre, and this was accompanied by a partial conversion, and by gifts and tribute in token of it. Ethiopia, too, had come at the same time into fresh prominence in connexion with Judah (see Isaiah xxxvii. 9, and comp. Zeph. iii. 10). (5) Hezekiah was conspicuous for his catholic spirit. He not only seeks to effect the re-union of Israel and Judah (2 Chron. xxx.), but also brings with them into fellowship, "the *strangers* that came out of the land of Israel," as distinct from the "congregation" (ver. 26). In 2 Chron. xxxii. 23, other nations are said to have brought gifts for the Temple. (6) Traces of this admission of proselytes meet us in the latter history of the kingdom of Judah. Isaiah pronounced a solemn blessing on "the *sons of the strangers* that *join themselves to the Lord*," who are to be made joyful in the "holy mountain" (Is. lvi. 7). Comp. also Is. lv. 1, and Jerem. xxxviii. 7.—*Biblical Studies*, pp. 167—171.

II. Calvin and others refer the Psalm to a time subsequent to the return from the captivity. It was designed, as Calvin thinks, to console the exiles, whose hearts must have died down within them as they thought of the present enfeebled, impoverished, defenceless state of the city; who sighed as they looked at their temple, so far inferior in beauty and stateliness, as well as in the imposing splendour of its worship, to the house which their fathers remembered; and who, dispirited and girt by enemies, needed every encouragement for the future. A study of the earlier chapters of Zechariah, and the later chapters of Isaiah, in connexion with this Psalm, may lead us to adopt this view. But our conclusion must depend to a great extent on the date which we are disposed to assign to the later chapters of Isaiah (xl.—lxvi.).

The outline of the Psalm is as follows :—

It opens with an outburst of intensely national feeling, celebrating the glory of Zion as the city of God. Ver. 1—3.

But the patriotic sentiment is too large and too grand to suffer any narrow jealousy to interfere with it, and therefore all nations are said to be gathered to her as children to one mother. It lends more force and dignity to this idea, that God Himself appears as the speaker, declaring of one and another, foreign and hostile nations, that their true birthplace is *there*, in Zion. Finally, one brief, obscure verse tells of the joy and happiness of the holy city, welcoming new children on all sides, and making them partakers in her joy. Ver. 7.

[OF THE SONS OF KORAH.[a] A PSALM. A SONG.]

1 HIS foundation [b] upon the holy mountains doth Jehovah love,
2 (He loveth) the gates of Zion more than all the dwellings of Jacob.
3 Glorious things [c] are spoken of thee,
O city of God ! [Selah.]
4 "I will mention Rahab and Babylon among them [d] that know Me ;

1—3. The same deep affection and admiration for the holy city are expressed here which are expressed in Psalm xlviii. But there is nothing in the language employed to lead us to suppose that the city had just escaped from the horrors of war. The "gates" are mentioned, not as a part of the fortifications, but as one of the most prominent features of the city—the place of concourse, of judgement, &c.

Every word is emphatic. His FOUNDATION, the city and the temple which *He*, Jehovah Himself, hath built ; UPON THE HOLY MOUNTAINS, consecrated by His immediate and manifested Presence ; which Jehovah LOVETH with a special and distinguishing affection, as compared not only with other nations, but even with other parts of the Holy Land itself.

UPON THE HOLY MOUNTAINS. The plural is used with reference to the mountainous character of the whole country. "Jerusalem was on the ridge, the broadest and most strongly marked ridge of the backbone of the complicated hills which extend through the whole country from the Desert to the plain of Esdraelon." — STANLEY, *Sinai and Palestine*, chap. iii. p. 176. He compares its position in this respect to that of Rome, that "each was situated on its own cluster of steep hills" (p. 175).

3. GLORIOUS THINGS: not earthly splendour or victories, but such a gathering of nations into her bosom as follows in the next verse.

4. I WILL MENTION. The words are the words of God. We have the same abrupt introduction of the Divine Speaker in other Psalms. Comp. xiv. 4; perhaps xxxii. 8;

Lo Philistia and Tyre, with Ethiopia:
'This one is born there.'"
5 And of Zion it is said:
"One after another [e] is born in her,
And the Most High Himself shall stablish her."

lxxv. 2 [3]; lxxxi. 6 [7]; and (according to some expositors) lxxxii. 2.

RAHAB. Originally the word denotes pride, ferocity. So in Job ix. 13, "the helpers of pride (*Rahab*) do stoop under him." Possibly even there, and certainly in Job xxvi. 12, it is the name of some fierce monster of the deep, probably the crocodile: "He divideth the sea by His power, And by His understanding He smiteth the proud monster (*Rahab*)," where the LXX. have κῆτος. In Ps. lxxxix. 10 [11], there can be no doubt of the reference to Egypt: "Thou hast broken Rahab in pieces," the crocodile of the Nile being there taken as the symbol of that kingdom. So too in Is. li. 9, "Art thou not it that hast *cut Rahab* (*i.e.* smitten Egypt) *and wounded the dragon?*" and xxx. 7, "The Egyptians shall help in vain, &c. . . . . they are Rahab *i.e.* proud, mighty, &c." The name, then, is applied to Egypt as a vast and formidable power, of which the crocodile might naturally be regarded as the symbol. Ewald supposes it to be connected with the Egyptian name Rîf, and refers to Burckhardt's *Nubia*, p. 457.

AMONG THEM THAT KNOW ME, lit. "as *belonging to* (the number of) them that know Me." See Critical Note. The verb *to know* is here used in that deeper and wider sense in which it frequently occurs in Scripture, both of God and of man. Comp. i. 6 (where see note), and xxxvi. 10 [11]; John x. 14, 15. It is the knowledge of friendship, the knowledge which springs of intimate acquaintance, the knowledge of parent and child.

PHILISTIA, TYRE, ETHIOPIA. Of all these nations it shall be said, that one and another of them ("this one," as if pointing to them) has become a worshiper of Jehovah, and an adopted citizen of Zion, "born *there*." With regard to these nations, see the prophecies of Isaiah quoted in the Introduction, and comp. lxviii. 31 [32]. THERE, so Zion is designated even before she is named. Others refer THERE to the countries mentioned before, and explain: "Only a few are to be found there; great numbers, many a one (see next ver.) in Zion."

5. AND OF ZION, or "*to* Zion," it is said, ONE AFTER ANOTHER, lit. "man and man," *i.e.* vast multitudes are born in her, as the nations one after another become incorporated as her children. The LXX. here render, not "it shall be said to Zion," but "Mother Zion shall say" (Μήτηρ Σιὼν ἐρεῖ), and Zion is spoken of as a mother Is. lxvi. 7; liv. 1—3; lx. 4, 5; but the sense here is different (other copies of the LXX. read μὴ τῇ Σιών; and so the Syro-hex. and the Psalt. Gall. *Numquid Sion*). It is remarkable that the figure of a new birth is used to express the admission of the different nations to the rights of citizenship in Zion. So Cicero speaks of his restoration to his privileges and honours on his return from banishment as "a regeneration:" "Amicorum literæ nos ad triumphum vocant, rem a nobis, ut ego arbitror, propter hanc παλιγγενεσίαν nostram, non negligendam" (*Ep. ad Att.* vi. 6, § 4).

"Clearly Zion stands in opposition to the countries mentioned before, the one city to the whole of the different countries, the one city of God to all the kingdoms of the world." — *Delitzsch.* These kingdoms one after another lose their

6 Jehovah shall reckon when He writeth the peoples,
"This one is born there." [Selah.]
7 Both they that sing and they that dance,[f]
All my fountains, are in thee.[g]

population, cease to be kingdoms, whilst their inhabitants all contribute to swell the population of that city which God's own right hand establishes and makes glorious.

6. WHEN HE WRITETH, *i.e.* takes a census of the nations (E′ ἐν ἀπογραφῇ λαῶν, comp. the figure of Ezek. xiii. 9, Is. iv. 3, and see note on Ps. lxix. 28), the most glorious thing that He can say of each of them, the crown of all their history, shall be this, not the record of their separate national existence or polity or dominion, but the fact that they have become members by adoption of the city of God. Zion shall be the metropolis of the world.

THIS ONE IS BORN THERE. The words are repeated, as by God Himself, as He enters one after another in the register of His city.

7. Great shall be the joy, great the pomp of festival and music, when Zion welcomes her new inhabitants. This is doubtless the sense; but the compressed brevity of this verse makes it extremely obscure. It has been rendered:—

(1) "Both they that sing and they that dance (or, as others, *play the flute*) say: 'All my fountains (of salvation, or of delight) are in thee (O city of God).'"

(2) "Both they that sing and they that dance, All my fountains of (delight), are in thee;" meaning that every source of pleasure, music, singing, &c., was to be found in Zion.

(3) By a change in the reading "They both sing and dance, all who dwell in thee (or, all my dwellers in thee)."

Of these, (2) is clearly preferable. The verse might be arranged thus:—

(In *thee*) are they that sing and they
that dance.
In thee are *all* my living springs.

This is abrupt, but still a natural touch of genuine poetic feeling.

Milton, in his Paraphrase, gives a similar interpretation:—

"Both they who sing and they who
dance
With sacred songs are there;
In thee fresh brooks and soft
streams glance,
And all my fountains clear."

[a] See General Introduction, Vol. I. p. 99, and p. 347.

[b] יְסוּדָה. This is not the part. pass. (as Hengst. and others maintain), "*the founded city*," but a subst., as is clear from the use of the suff.; and although the word occurs nowhere else, it is fully supported by the analogy of מְלוּכָה, יְשׁוּעָה, &c. Comp. מוּסָד, of Zion, Is. xxviii. 16. So the LXX. οἱ θεμέλιοι αὐτοῦ. Sym. θεμελίωσις αὐτοῦ. The suff. evidently refers, not to Zion, but to God. Rashi refers the suff. apparently to the Psalm itself: "its theme (the foundation on which it rests) is on the holy mountains." This clause would thus be a sort of prelude describing the nature of the Psalm. But it seems to me better, instead of taking ver. 1 as a separate clause, "His (or its) foundation is upon the holy mountains,"

to connect this clause with ver. 2, and to consider the words אֹהֵב י״י as belonging to the first member. The verb can then readily be repeated with the second. If we follow the accents, ver. 1, 2 will be arranged as follows :—1. His foundation is on the holy mountains. 2. Jehovah loveth the gates of Zion, More than all the dwellings of Jacob.

[c] נִכְבָּדוֹת, not an adv., as נוֹרָאוֹת in cxxxix. 14, nor an accus. as in lxv. 5 (see note [f] there), as Ewald, Hengst., and others explain, taking מְדֻבָּר as an impersonal : "*it is said of thee = men say of thee* glorious things;" but fem. plur. = neut. (as in xlv. 5), joined irregularly with the masc. sing. part., not however to be defended by such passages as those quoted by Hupf., Gen. xxvii. 29 ; Is. iii. 12 ; Prov. iii. 18, where the sing. part. is used *distributively;* better on the principle which he suggests, that the part. is regarded as a kind of neuter noun : "*that which is spoken of thee*, is glorious," lit. glorious things. He quotes, as similar, lxxiii. 28 ; Prov. xi. 23 ; Gen. xlix. 15, where the masc. טוֹב is used as the predicate of a fem. noun, and Is. xvi. 8, שַׁדְמוֹת אֻמְלַל. The last is an exact parallel. But the simplest way is to regard all such instances as covered by the general principle that the predicate is frequently in the masc. sing. (not only when it stands first), whilst the subject is fem. or plural, or both, as here. (Gesen. § 144.) Comp. Is. viii. 22, וַאֲפֵלָה מְנֻדָּח.

[d] לְיֹדְעָי. The לְ is here used in the sense of *belonging to*, not as marking merely apposition, as Hupf. and others explain. The constr. cannot be compared with that of לְ in such phrases as היה ל, *to become*, חשב ל, *to reckon as*, nor with such a usage as that in Exod. xxi. 2, or Ps. vii. 14, לדלקים, "he maketh his arrows (*for, as*) fiery arrows," where the verb determines the sense in which the לְ occurs.

The LXX. render μνησθήσομαι Ῥαὰβ καὶ Βαβυλῶνος τοῖς γινώσκουσί με. Neither Aq. nor Sym. takes Rahab as a proper name, and they understand the construction differently. Aq. ἀναμνήσω ὁρμήματος καὶ Βαβυλῶνος τοὺς γινώσκοντάς με. Sym. ἀν. ὑπερηφανίαν καὶ Βαβ. τοῖς εἰδόσι με.

[e] אִישׁ וְאִישׁ, lit. "man and man," i.e. *every man* (Gesen. § 106. 4), as in Lev. xvii. 10, Esth. i. 8, or perhaps more exactly, *one man after another*, as it were in a series extended indefinitely. Hofmann compares the phrases דּוֹר וָדוֹר, *one generation after another*, and מִי וָמִי, Exod. x. 8.

[f] חֹלְלִים for מְחֹלְלִים, *dancers* engaged in the sacred solemnities, as maidens who celebrated a victory, and as David himself danced before the Ark, 2 Sam. vi. 16. The prefixed כְּ must be supplied also before שָׁרִים, "*as well* singers *as* dancers." Or better, as Hupf. (following Is. and Dathe), who takes the participles as finite verbs, "They shall sing and leap for joy," viz. all they that dwell in thee (see next note). Gesen. and others regard ח' as a denom. from חָלִיל, *flute-players*. Aq. has, καὶ ᾄδοντες ὡς χοροί, πᾶσαι πηγαί μου ἐν σοί. Sym. καὶ αἰνέσουσιν ὡς ἐν αὐλοῖς πᾶσαι αἱ πηγαὶ ἐν σοί. Jerome and the LXX. read שָׂרִים, and connect it with the preceding verse, καὶ ἀρχόντων τούτων τῶν γεγεννημένων ἐν αὐτῇ, and then render the last clause ὡς εὐφραινομένων πάντων ἡ κατοικία ἐν σοί. See next note, and Hupfeld's rendering based on this.

[8] כָּל־מַעְיָנַי בָּךְ. According to the existing punctuation this can only mean, "all my fountains are in thee" (and so Aq. and Sym. among the ancients), which has been variously explained. Many interpreters suppose these to be the words of the nations keeping festival with songs and dances, and saying, in the joy of their new birth into the city of God: "All my fountains of salvation (comp. Is. xii. 3) are in thee." But there is nothing in the context to favour this paraphrase of the word "fountains." Hence Ewald would connect it with a root עון cognate with similar Arab. and Syr. roots, meaning *to help*, *to be of service*, and take מָ וֹן in the sense of *place of refuge*, or something *useful*, and hence *an art*. Accordingly he renders, "singers as well as flute-players, all My arts are in thee." Hupfeld, on the other hand, follows the guidance of the LXX., who have *κατοικία*. He would read מְעִינֵי, Hiph. part. constr. of עוּן, *to dwell*, or rather מְעִינַי, "*My dwellers*, i.e. those who dwell with Me" (as spoken by God). Hofmann also (*Schriftb.* II. 2. 526) supposes the words to be spoken by God, and renders: "all My *fountains* are in thee," and explains this by reference to such passages as lxviii. 27, "the fountain of Israel" (comp. Prov. v. 18), or Is. xlviii. 1, "the waters of Judah," and Zech. ix. 1, "the fountain of Adam (the source of man) is Jehovah." Hence, according to this view, Jehovah here says that all His fountains are in Zion, that is, all His children are born there. Hofmann connects this with the previous words thus: singers as they join in the dance repeat these words, as the words of a song in which Jehovah says of Zion, "all My fountains," &c.

PSALM 88

THIS is the darkest, saddest Psalm in all the Psalter. It is one wail of sorrow from beginning to end. It is the only Psalm in which the expression of feeling, the pouring out of the burdened heart before God, fails to bring relief and consolation. In every other instance, however heavy the gloom, however oppressed and dejected the spirit of the sufferer, prayer and supplication are mingled with thanksgiving, the accents of lamentation are changed into the notes of triumph, the darkness of midnight gives way to the brightness of faith's morning-dawn. The deeper the sorrow at the opening, the greater the joy at the close. But here the darkness continues to the end. There is no confidence expressed that prayer will be heard no hope uttered, much less any triumph. The Psalm ends with complaint, as it began. Its last word is "darkness." One ray of light only struggles through the gloom, one star pieces that thick midnight blackness; it is the name by which the Psalmist addresses

God: "O God of *my salvation*." That he can address God by that name is a proof that faith and hope are not dead within him: it is the pledge of his deliverance, though he cannot yet taste its comfort. There is but one such Psalm, as if to teach us that our Father's will concerning us is not to leave us in our dejection, but, in answer to the prayer of faith, to lift us out of it; there is one, that we may remember that even His truest servants may be called upon "to walk in darkness and have no light," that thus they may be the better trained, like a child holding his father's hand in the dark, "to trust in the name of the Lord, to stay themselves upon their God."

The older expositors commonly interpreted the Psalm of Christ and of His Passion either in Gethsemane or on the Cross. And our Church has, in a measure, sanctioned this application by appointing this as one of the Psalms for Good Friday.

As to the author, and the circumstances under which the Psalm was written, various conjectures have been made, but they are really worth nothing. One thing only is clear, that it is not a national Psalm, and that it does not deplore the Babylonish captivity, or any other *national* calamity. It is, throughout, personal and individual. Uzziah when smitten with leprosy, Jeremiah in the dungeon, Hezekiah in his sickness, Job in his sufferings—to all these in turn has the authorship of the Psalm been assigned. But neither the thoughts nor the expression of the thoughts favour one of these hypotheses more than another, except that, in one or two instances, the language has some affinity with that of the Book of Job, whereas the language of ver. 15, "I am afflicted from my youth up," is, to say the least of it, very exaggerated language in the mouth of any of these persons, and hardly to be justified by any pressure of sorrow.

Delitzsch goes so far as to draw hence the inference, that Heman the Ezrahite was the author of the Book of Job; but the words which he quotes as common to this Psalm and Job are to be found in other places of Scripture: they cannot be called characteristic words, and therefore the argument built upon them falls to the ground.

[A SONG. A PSALM OF THE SONS OF KORAH. FOR THE PRECENTOR. "AFTER MACHALATH L'ANNOTH." A MASKIL OF HEMAN THE EZRAHITE.[a]]

1 O JEHOVAH, God of my salvation,
I have cried day [b] and night before Thee.

1. GOD OF MY SALVATION. "Deum *salutis suæ* vocans, quasi injecto freno, cohibet doloris intemperantiam, desperationi januam claudit, seque ad crucis tolerantiam munit et comparat."—*Calvin.*

2 Let my prayer come before Thee,
Incline Thine ear to my cry.

3 For my soul is full of troubles,
And my life draweth nigh to the unseen world.
4 I am counted [c] with them that go down into the pit,
I am become as a man that hath no strength,
5 Among the dead, cast away,[d]
Like the slain, lying in the grave,
Whom Thou rememberest no more,
But they are cut off from Thy hand.
6 Thou hast laid me in the lowest pit,
In darkness, in the deeps.
7 Upon me Thy fury lieth hard,
And Thou hast afflicted (me) with all Thy waves.[e]
[Selah.]

3. The greatness of his affliction, which has brought him to the very edge of the grave, is urged as a reason why God should hear him. Comp. vi. 4, 5 [5, 6]; xxx. 3 [4]; Is. xxxviii. 10, 11.

IS FULL OF TROUBLES, lit. "is satiated with evils." Comp. cxxiii. 4; Lam. iii. 15, 30.

4. THAT HATH NO STRENGTH, *i.e.* not merely as worn out with pain and suffering, which would be an anti-climax, but, as the parallelism shows, like the unsubstantial shadowy phantoms which people the unseen world.

5. CAST AWAY, or as the E.V. "free," *i.e.* left alone, with none to care for me, in that unseen world whenc even God's Presence seemed to be withdrawn. Calvin suggests that such a mode of expression may be accounted for, either "ex vulgi sensu . . . quia ad futuram vitam, quæ abscondita est, nonnisi gradatim conscendimus," or rather on the principle that the Prophet spoke "ex turbulento afflicti hominis sensu." "Nec mirum est," he adds, "hominem Spiritu Dei præditum, ubi prævaluit mœror, quasi attonitum fuisse, ut vocem parum consideratam emitteret."

But it is the same strain of feeling which we have already had in vi. 5 [6], xxx. 9 [10], where see notes. His eye is looking down into the darkness, he sees himself already numbered with the dead. But what are the dead? Beings who "know not anything," "clean forgotten, out of mind," beings whom God Himself remembers not. "The living, the living, he shall praise Thee:" this was the feeling, not of Hezekiah only, but of all the Old Testament saints, in seasons of gloom and despondency. It could not be otherwise till the bright light of Christ's resurrection was cast upon the grave and the world beyond.

6. IN THE LOWEST PIT. See on lxiii. 9 [10]; lxxxvi. 13. Comp. Lam. iii. 55, and Ezek. xxvi. 20.

IN DARKNESS, lit. "in dark places," as in lxxiv. 20; Lam. iii. 6.

IN THE DEEPS, usually said of the sea, as in lxviii. 22 [23]; Exod. xv. 5; here of Hades.

7. WITH ALL THY WAVES. On this Calvin beautifully remarks:

8 Thou hast removed my familiar friends far from me,
Thou hast made me an abomination unto them ;
I am shut up, so that I cannot go forth.
9 Mine eye wasteth away because of affliction ;
I have called upon Thee, O Jehovah, every day,
I have stretched forth my hands unto Thee.
10 Wilt Thou show wonders unto the dead ?
Shall the shades below[f] arise and give Thee thanks ?
[Selah.]
11 Shall Thy loving-kindness be told in the grave,
Thy faithfulness in destruction ?
12 Shall Thy wonders be known in the dark ?
And Thy righteousness in the land of forgetfulness ?
13 But as for me—unto Thee, O Jehovah, have I cried,

"Jam quum tam horribile diluvium Prophetam non impedierit quominus cor suum et vota ad Deum extolleret, discamus, ejus exemplo, in omnibus naufragiis nostris ancoram fidei et precum in cœlos jacere."

8. THOU HAST REMOVED, as before, "*Thou* hast laid," &c., thus directly tracing all to God's will and fatherly hand.

MY FAMILIAR FRIENDS. The word expresses close intimate friendship, more than the mere "acquaintance" of the E.V. He is like one shut up in prison—these cannot come in to him, nor he go forth to them. Delitzsch thinks that, according to Levit. xiii., this sounds like the complaint of a leper, the leprosy moreover being just that death in life (Num. xii. 12) which is so pathetically described as the Psalmist's condition.

The cry here is repeated in ver. 18.

AN ABOMINATION, lit. "abominations," the plural intensifying and enlarging the idea. Comp. note on lxviii. 35.

10. Ewald takes this and the two following verses as the words of the prayer implied in saying, "I have stretched forth my hands unto Thee," and cited from some former Psalm.

ARISE, *i.e.* "rise up," not "rise again from the dead" (comp. lxxviii. 5 [6]). The language refers to what takes place in the unseen world, not at the resurrection. Comp. Is. xiv. 9.

The expostulation is like that of Job : "If a man die, shall he live again ?" There is no question of the general resurrection, but only the improbability that God should restore to life one who was already dead. Calvin observes that this state of feeling "cannot be excused, inasmuch as it is not for us to prescribe to God when He shall give us succour ; for we wrong His power, if we are not assured that it is as easy for Him to restore life to the dead, as to prevent and avert the last extremity. And of a truth the constancy of the saints has ever shown some traces of the weakness of the flesh, so that God's fatherly indulgence has had to make allowance for the defects which are mingled even with their very virtues."

13. BUT AS FOR ME, emphatic ; though thus at the very edge of

And in the morning my prayer cometh to meet Thee.
14 Why, O Jehovah, castest Thou off my soul?
(Why) hidest Thou Thy face from me?
15 I am afflicted, and ready to die from my youth [g] up,
I have suffered Thy terrors (till) I am distracted.[h]
16 Over me Thy fierce wrath hath passed;
Thy horrors have cut me off.[i]
17 They have compassed me like waters all the day long,
They have come round about me together.
18 Thou hast removed lover and friend far from me,
My familiar friends—are darkness.[j]

death, though bowed down with the heavy load of affliction, still I look to Thee. This unwearied "continuing instant in prayer" is the victory of faith in the midst of trials which, but for this, would end in despair. It had been one life-long suffering *from his youth up*, yet still his earnest pleading had never ceased. Such prayers are those "unutterable groanings" of which St. Paul speaks.

COMETH TO MEET, or as E.V. "preventeth." Sym. προφθάνει σε.

16. THY HORRORS: a frequent expression in the Book of Job, vi. 4; ix. 34; xiii. 21, &c.

18. DARKNESS, lit. "the place of darkness," the dark kingdom of the dead, is now all I have to look to, instead of friends, or, as we might say, The grave is now my only friend. Similar expressions occur in Prov. vii. 4, and in Job xvii. 14, "I have said to the grave, Thou art my father," &c. Or perhaps the sense is rather, "I have no friends. When I look for them, I see nothing but darkness." "The Psalm ends with an energetic expression of its main thought—the immediate vicinity of death. The darkness is thickest at the end, just as it is in the morning before the rising of the sun."—Hengstenberg. But here, at least, the sun does not rise.

[a] עַל־מַחֲלַת: see on liii. note [a].

לְעַנּוֹת has been interpreted either (1) *for chastisement;* or (2) *for singing* (as in Exod. xxxii. 18; Is. xxvii. 2).

Heman the Ezrahite, celebrated, together with Ethan (to whom the next Psalm is ascribed), for his wisdom, 1 Kings iv. 31 [v. 11], including reputation as a writer and a poet. In 1 Chron. vi. 18, 29 (33, 42 in E.V.), both are mentioned as Levitical singers.

The Inscription is a double one, and is evidently derived from two different sources. This is plain, because the Psalm is ascribed to different authors; in the one instance to the Korahites, in the other to Heman; and is differently described, in the first as "a song, a Psalm," and in the second as "a Maskil." Besides, לַמְנַצֵּחַ always stands *at the beginning* of the Title. Hence one Title was "A song, a Psalm of the sons of Korah;" the other, "For the Precentor. After '*Machalath l'annoth.*' A Maskil of Heman the Ezrahite."

[b] יוֹם־צָעַקְתִּי. Grammatically, this can only be explained, "in the day (when) I cry," and the next clause must then be rendered, "in the night is my crying before Thee, or I am before Thee." But this would be placing a peculiar emphasis on the night, and the whole sentence is lame. (Unless, indeed, we could take יוֹם צ׳ as merely equivalent to "when I cry," and carry on the construction into the next verse, "when I cry in the night before Thee, let my prayer, &c.") But it would seem that "day" and "night" are used as marking the unceasing character of the cry, as we find often elsewhere; xxii. 3, lv. 18, lxxvii. 3, &c. Hence it is probable that we ought to read יוֹמָם, *in the daytime.*

[c] נֶחְשַׁבְתִּי עִם; a mixed constr. compounded of two expressions, *to be considered as* (כְּ, as xliv. 23), and *to be made equal with,* as in xxviii. 1, cxliii. 7.

[d] חָפְשִׁי. This may be either (1) a noun with pron. suff. from חֹפֶשׁ (Ezek. xxvii. 20), *my bed, my couch;* or (2) an adj. *free, let loose,* which occurs usually in a good sense, of freedom from chains, wounds, burdens, and the like, or freedom as of a slave from a master, Ex. xxi. 3, 26, &c.; so of one set free by death, Job iii. 19. The LXX. and Aq. both have ἐλεύθερος, Symm. ἀφεὶς ἐλεύθερος. Here in a bad sense: either (*a*) *forsaken, neglected, uncared for;* or (*b*) *separated, cut off,* i.e. from human companionship. Comp. בֵּית חָפְשִׁית, "a separate house," 2 Kings xv. 5, a hospital or asylum for lepers, &c.; or (*c*) *set free, discharged,* from the cares and duties of life, from communion with God and intercourse with men (Chald., Rashi, Ibn 'Ezra., Calv., Del., Hengst.). Others, again, would connect the word with the Arab. خفش, *to be weak, prostrate,* which would accord with רְפָאִים, v. 11.

[e] עִנִּיתָ. Against the common explanation of the constr. that the accus. of the pers. pron. is understood, and that כָּל־מ׳ is the accus. of the instrument, "Thou hast afflicted (me) (with) all Thy waves," Hupf. objects first, that such a constr. is unheard of with עִנָּה, and next, that the accent forbids it. He accordingly supplies the verb from the first clause, and inserts the relative, "And all Thy waves (lie upon me) *with which* Thou hast afflicted me," referring to the constr. in li. 10, "the bones *which* Thou hast broken," where the accent is the same. Others (as Ew. and Del.), "Thou hast hurled down (lit. *bowed down*) upon me (like a cataract) all Thy waves." So the LXX., πάντας τοὺς μετεωρισμούς σου ἐπήγαγες ἐπ' 'μέ. But Symm., ταῖς καταιγίσι σου ἐκάκωσάς με. And Jerome, *fluctibus tuis afflixisti me;* and in answer to Hupf. it may be said that the use of the accus. instrum. is common with all verbs, as well as the omission of the personal object, and that the accent is not an infallible guide.

[f] רְפָאִים: here "the spirits of the departed" (εἴδωλα καμόντων). Comp. Is. xxvi. 14, Prov. xxi. 16, &c., but in other places used of "the race of giants." Many attempts have been made to connect the two significations (see Ges. Thes. in v.), but perhaps Hupfeld's is the most plausible. He connects the word, as the Jewish interpreters had done before him, with the root רפה, *to be relaxed,* and so (*a*) *weak, feeble,* as "the shades," and

on the other (*b*) *extended*, at a vast length, *immania corpora*, like "the giants." Jerome here has *gigantes*. The LXX. ἰατροί (as also in Is. xxvi.), connecting it curiously with the root רפא, *to heal*.

[g] נֹעַר, abstr. from נַעַר, *youth*, as Prov. xxix. 21, Job xxxiii. 25; and not from נער, *excutere*, *expellere*, which derivation has led some to explain it *propter concussionem*.

[h] אָפוּנָה, only here, and both the root and the form occasion difficulty. Usually connected with the Arab. أفن, *infirma mente et consilii inops fuit*. LXX. ἐξηπορήθην. Jer. *conturbatus sum*. Hupf. would read אָפוּגָה, in the sense of *growing cold* (spoken of the cessation of physical and spiritual life). The paragog. form is to be explained of *an inner necessity*, as in lv. 2; see note [c], there.

[i] צִמְּתוּתֻנִי. Such a reduplication of the *termination* is unexampled. The dagesh in the 2d rad. makes it look like a Piel (as in cxix. 139, where the 3d fem sing. occurs), whereas the reduplication of the last rad. points to a Pilel form. Besides, the Qibbutz instead of Sh'va defies all grammar, and the form cannot be compared with סְחַרְחַר and such forms. It would be better to suppose that there is a play upon the form צְמִיתוּת, Lev. xxv. 23, 30 (as Köst. and Hengst. suppose), or that it is the mistake of a copyist for צִמְּתוּנִי (see Hupfeld), or that the original צִמְּתָנִי was emended into צִמְּתוּנִי, and both afterwards remained.

PSALM 89

THERE can be little doubt that this Psalm was written in the latter days of the Jewish monarchy, when the throne of David had fallen or was already tottering to its fall, and when the prospect for the future was so dark that it seemed as if God had forgotten His covenant and His promise. Tholuck's conjecture is not improbable that the king of whom the Psalm speaks (ver. 45) [46] is the youthful Jehoiachin, who after a reign of three months was deposed and imprisoned by Nebuchadnezzar, and of whom it was said, that no man of his seed should "prosper, sitting on the throne of David." The lamentation over him in Jeremiah xxii. 24—29, may be taken as evidence that he was beloved by his subjects, and the Prophet and the Psalmist indulge in a similar strain as they behold the last hope of David's house perish.

There is no reason to conclude from ver. 47 [48], that the king himself is the author of the Psalm (see note there); and from ver. 18 [19] indeed, the contrary perhaps may be inferred.

The Psalm opens by a reference to the Promise given to David, 2 Sam. vii. 8, &c. This Promise, and the attributes of God on which the Promise rests, and which are the great pledge of its fulfilment, form the subject of the Poet's grateful acknowledgement, before he passes to the mournful contrast presented by the ruin of the house of David, and the blighting of his people's hopes. He turns to the glorious past, that by its aid he may rise out of the grief and discouragement of the present. He takes the Promise, and turns it into a song. He dwells upon it, and lingers over it. He dwells on that which is the ground and pillar of the Promise—the faithfulness of God—and then he first lifts his loud lament over the disasters which have befallen his king and people, speaking out his disappointment, till his words sound like a reproach; and next pleads earnestly with God that He would not suffer his enemies to triumph.

Certain words and thoughts run through the Psalm, and give it a marked character. Such are, especially, the constant reference to the "faithfulness of God," in confirming His covenant and promise, ver. 1, 2, 5, 8, 14, 24, 33, 49 (comp. also the use of the participle "faithful," ver. 28, 37); the phrase "I will not lie," ver. 33, 35, "I have sworn," ver. 3, 35, 49; and the "covenant," ver. 3, 28, 34, 39.

[A MASCHIL OF ETHAN THE EZRAHITE.[a]]

1 I WILL for ever sing of the loving-kindnesses [b] of Jehovah,
I will make known Thy faithfulness with my mouth to all generations.
2 For I have said, for ever shall loving-kindness be built up,

1, 2. The loving-kindness and the faithfulness of Jehovah are the source of the Promise. We are led to the source, that thence we may track the stream.

1. FOR EVER. The position of these words before the verb has been supposed to indicate that the Psalmist is not speaking in his own name, but in the name of the Church which abideth "ever." But they may refer to the everlasting continuance of God's love and faithfulness, as pledged to David and his seed.

LOVING-KINDNESSES, plural, as in Is. lv. 3, "The sure mercies [faithful loving-kindnesses] of David." For the same union of these two attributes of God, see xxxvi. 5 [6].

2. FOR I HAVE SAID, *i.e.* this is the conviction whence springs the resolve in ver. 1.

BE BUILT UP, like some stately

In the heavens shalt Thou establish Thy faithfulness.
3 "I have made a covenant with My chosen,
I have sworn unto David My servant;
4 For ever will I establish thy seed,
And build up thy throne to all generations." [Selah.]
5 And the heavens shall praise Thy wondrousness, O Jehovah,
Thy faithfulness also, in the assembly of the holy ones.
6 For who in the sky can be compared with Jehovah,
(Who) is like unto Jehovah among the sons of the mighty?

palace, rising ever greater and fairer, stone by stone, before the wondering eyes of men, knowing no decay, never destined to fall into ruin. Grätz: "The world is built (created) in love." *Koheleth*, Gloss. p. 193.

IN THE HEAVENS, lit. "The heavens, Thou shalt establish Thy faithfulness in them." The heavens are the type of unchangeableness and perpetuity, as compared with the restless vicissitudes, the ever-shifting shows of earth. Comp. cxix. 89.

3, 4. These are the words of God, the sum of His promise as given in 2 Sam. vii. They are introduced with remarkable abruptness, standing alone in their forcible brevity, while the Psalmist passes on to celebrate at length the might and faithfulness of the Promiser. In the 19th verse, he returns to the promise, and then expands and dwells upon it.

Most of the expressions, "David My servant," "establish," "for ever," "build," the parallelism of "seed" and "throne," "My chosen," are taken, either directly or indirectly, from the original passage in 2 Sam.

MY CHOSEN. The LXX. have the plural τοῖς ἐκλεκτοῖς μου, but all the other Versions follow the Heb. and retain the singular. See Critical Note [e] on ver. 19.

5. At first sight the passage which follows to ver. 18 appears to break the train of thought. But the object of the Psalmist is to place in the strongest light those attributes of God on which the *fulfilment* of His promise depends, for "in a promise everything depends upon the person who promises." The question therefore occurs, "Has he the will and the power to fulfil the promise?"—*Hengstenberg*. Hence the Psalmist dwells first upon God's power as exhibited and confessed in creation, then upon his righteousness, goodness, and truth, as manifested especially to His people, of whom and whose king He is the protector.

THY WONDROUSNESS (lit. wonder): either (1) "Thy wondrous works," as in lxxxviii. 10, 12 [11, 13]; or (2) "Thy wonderful mysterious nature and being," as separate and distinct from that of all created beings. The word occurs in Is. ix. 6 [5], as one of the names of Messiah (comp. also Jud. xiii. 18).

ASSEMBLY OF THE HOLY ONES, *i.e.* the angels, to which corresponds in the next verse, "the sons of the mighty," comp. xxix. 1. They are called an "assembly" or "congregation," as the church above, which, like the church below, worships and praises God. In this second clause the verb must be repeated from the

7 A God very terrible in the council of the holy ones,
And to be feared above all them that are round about Him?
8 O Jehovah, God of Hosts,
Who is mighty [c] as Thou, O Jah!
And Thy faithfulness is round about Thee.

9 THOU rulest the pride of the sea;
When the waves thereof arise,[d] THOU stillest them.
10 THOU hast crushed Rahab, as one that is slain;
With Thy mighty arm Thou hast scattered Thine enemies.
11 Thine are the heavens, Thine also is the earth;
THOU hast founded the world and the fulness thereof.
12 THOU hast created the north and the south;
Tabor and Hermon shout for joy in Thy Name.

first: "Thy faithfulness also is praised," &c.

7. A GOD. It is more forcible to regard this as a predicate, or as standing in a kind of free apposition with "Jehovah," than to take it as the subject of a fresh sentence: "God is very terrible," &c.

8. WHO IS MIGHTY, or, "Who is like unto Thee, a mighty one, O Jah."

AND THY FAITHFULNESS. Or as Ewald: "And what faithfulness is like Thy faithfulness," &c.

ROUND ABOUT THEE, God's attributes being personified, as in ver. 14 and lxxxv. 13 [14]. Then follow proofs and instances, first, of God's might, ver. 9—13, and next of His faithfulness, ver. 14—18.

10. RAHAB: here probably, as in lxxxvii. 4 (where see note), a name of Egypt. God's power as ruling the sea would naturally be connected in the Psalmist's mind with that great manifestation of His power in the deliverance from Egypt. Compare the same association of ideas in lxxiv. 13—17. Others take the word in the more general sense of *pride* (*i.e.* our proud foes), as in Job ix. 13, xxvi. 12. In the context of both passages in Job, God's power over the sea is magnified, but the Book is too far removed from the circle of Israelitish history to allow of our seeing any reference there to the passage of the Red Sea.

AS ONE THAT IS SLAIN. The particle of comparison must not be pressed. The sense is: "Thou hast crushed Egypt, so that it lies fallen, like one who has received a deadly wound."

11. THOU HAST FOUNDED, &c.; lit. "The world and the fulness thereof, Thou hast founded them." And so in the next verse: "The north and the south, Thou hast created them."

12. TABOR AND HERMON do not denote merely the West and East, as most interpreters explain. They are mentioned rather as conspicuous mountains in a mountain land. Tabor, "remarkable for the verdure, which climbs—a rare sight in Eastern scenery—to its very summit" (STANLEY, *Sinai and Palestine*, p. 350): Hermon, as its name imports, "The lofty prominent peak," crowned with snow, the most striking of all the mountains of

13 Thine is an arm clothed with might;
Strong is Thy hand, exalted is Thy right hand.
14 Righteousness and judgement are the foundation of Thy throne;
Loving-kindness and Truth go to meet Thy face.
15 Blessed are the people that know the joyful sound,
That walk, O Jehovah, in the light of Thy countenance.
16 In Thy name do they exult all the day,
And in Thy righteousness are they exalted.
17 For THOU art the excellency of their strength,
And in Thy favour dost Thou exalt our horn:
18 For our shield belongeth to Jehovah,
And to the Holy One of Israel our king.
19 Then Thou spakest in vision to Thy beloved,[e] and saidst,

Palestine, are fit representatives of the whole country; open, as it were, the loud hymn of praise. See lxxii. 3; xcviii. 8.

FOUNDATION. Others render "pillar," but Aq. has *ἕδρασμα* and Sym. *βάσις*. The LXX. *ἑτοιμασία*. The same word occurs in xxxiii. 14, where the renderings are similar. The E.V. has "place" there (in 1 Kings viii. 13, "settled place,") and "habitation" here, but in the margin "establishment."

GO TO MEET. See on lxxxviii. 13.

15—18. Such is the God, so full of majesty and power, who has given the promise. Blessed, therefore, are the people who have Jehovah for their God. They may well rejoice in their privilege.

These verses are recited in the Jewish synagogues on New Year's Day after the sounding of the trumpet (*shophar*). The Ashkenazim recite only ver. 15.

15. THE JOYFUL SOUND, *i.e.* the loud music of trumpets, &c., in the festivals, especially on the New Year's Day, Lev. xxiii. 24, or on extraordinary occasions, Num. x. 1—10; xxix. 1; Josh. vi. 5, 20, &c. See on xxvii. 6; lxxxi. 1 [2]. This Israel only knows, because Israel only is the people of God. They are blessed, because they, and they only, of all nations, can keep these solemn feasts to His praise.

UP. The Midrash says: Because Israel only understands how to move their God by the sound to go *up* from the throne of judgement to the throne of mercy, as it is written, God is gone up, &c.

18. OUR SHIELD, *i.e.* as is evident from the parallelism, the king. Comp. xlvii. 9 [10]. The rendering "Jehovah is our shield," is against grammar. Some would render the second member of the verse, Even to the Holy One of Israel our King (*i.e.* who is our king).

19. The mention of the king in the preceding verse leads now to the resumption and expansion of the promise given to David. The two aspects of God's relation to David and his house and kingdom are herein presented to us, an outward and an inward, corresponding to the two great attributes of God which are praised in ver. 1—18, His omnipotence and His faithfulness. To the first of these belong: (*a*) David's exaltation to the throne, ver. 19; (*b*) God's constant aid, and hence his victory over his foes, ver. 21—23, and extended dominion,

"I have laid help[f] upon a mighty man,
I have exalted one chosen out of the people.
20 I have found David My servant,
With My holy oil have I anointed him ;
21 With whom My hand shall be established ;
Mine arm also shall strengthen him.
22 No enemy shall exact[g] upon him,
No son of wickedness shall afflict him.
23 And I will beat down his adversaries before his face,
And plague them that hate him.
24 My faithfulness also and My loving-kindness shall be with him,
And in My Name shall his horn be exalted.
25 And I will set his hand on the sea,
And his right hand on the rivers.
26 He shall call Me, 'THOU art my Father,
My God, and the Rock of my salvation.'
27 Also I will make him My first-born,

ver. 21, 25. To the second, which is the most prominent, God's fatherly relation to David's seed, which is shown in (*a*) the exaltation to the dignity of a son, who is also the first-born, and therefore holds the pre-eminence above all kings, ver. 26, 27 ; accordingly (*b*) an *everlasting* covenant made with him and his seed, and an everlasting kingdom, ver. 28, 29 ; hence, too, (*c*) the transgressions of his sons do not make the covenant void, ver. 33, 34 ; (*d*) and the assurance is finally repeated, that this covenant, which God has once confirmed by an oath, cannot lie, and that therefore the seed as well as the throne of David must endure as the very heavens. For this outline of the connection I am indebted to Hupfeld.

THEN, referring to the time when the promise was given.

THY BELOVED. On this word see note on xvi. 13. David is evidently meant, though the revelation was made in vision, not to him, but to Nathan (2 Sam. vii. 4, 17). If we adopt the plural, which is the reading of many MSS., then the revelation is made to the nation at large.

A MIGHTY MAN. Comp. 2 Sam. xvii. 10.

22. SON OF WICKEDNESS. This clause is taken verbatim from the words of the promise in 2 Sam. vii. 10.

25. THE SEA . . . THE RIVERS, *i.e.* the Mediterranean Sea and the Euphrates, with reference, no doubt, to the extent of Solomon's dominion. See above on lxxx. 11. Or the range of hope may be wider, as in lxxii. 8. The plural "rivers" is in accordance with poetic usage, and need not be explained of the Euphrates and its separate channels, or the Euphrates and Tigris, &c.

27. MY FIRST-BORN. As he calls Me "Father," so I not only acknowledge him as My son, but as

Highest of the kings of the earth.
28 For ever will I keep for him My loving-kindness,
And My covenant shall stand fast with him.
29 And I will make his seed (to endure) for ever,
And his throne as the days of heaven.
30 If his children forsake My law,
And walk not in My judgements,
31 If they profane My statutes,
And keep not My commandments,
32 Then will I visit their transgression with the rod,
And their iniquity with stripes.
33 But My loving-kindness will I not break off [h] from him,
Nor suffer My faithfulness to fail :
34 I will not profane My covenant,
Nor alter the thing that is gone out of My lips ;
35 Once have I sworn by My holiness ;
I will not lie unto David :
36 His seed shall be for ever,
And his throne as the sun before Me :
37 He shall be established for ever as the moon,

My first-born, and therefore My heir. (So Israel is called the first-born, Ex. iv. 22, and Ephraim, Jer. xxxi. 9.)

28. SHALL STAND FAST, lit. "is *faithful*," the word being the same as in ver. 37, "the *faithful* witness."

30. There follows a paraphrase of 2 Sam. vii. 14. The chastisement is a necessary part of the paternal relationship, Heb. xii. The sins of individuals will be punished by God's fatherly correction, but the covenant cannot cease, the promises made to the seed as a whole cannot be withdrawn. Their unfaithfulness cannot make the faithfulness of God of none effect (Rom. iii. 3). But see, as presenting a different view, 1 Kings viii. 25.

32. THE ROD . . . STRIPES. In 2 Sam. vii. qualifying expressions are added : "rod of men," "stripes of the children of men :" not meaning "such punishments as all men because all are sinners, are exposed to" (Hengstenberg) ; but either (1) chastisements such as men (comp. for similar phraseology Hos. vi. 7, Job. xxxi. 33), human fathers, employ, for the correction, not the destruction of their children ; "for what son is there whom his father chastiseth not?" or (2) chastisements fitted to the measure of man's endurance (comp. 1 Cor. x. 13).

35. ONCE, *i.e.* "once for all" (LXX. ἅπαξ). Or, as others, "one thing."

BY MY HOLINESS, as in Amos iv. 2. Other formulæ are "by Myself," Is. xlv. 23 ; "by My name," Jer. xliv. 26. For the general sentiment of the verse comp. Rom. xi. 29 ; "the gifts and calling of God are without repentance."

37. THE FAITHFUL WITNESS. This according to the parallelism,

And (as the) faithful witness in the sky."
38 But THOU hast cast off and rejected,
Thou hast been wroth with Thine anointed.
39 Thou hast made void [i] the covenant of Thy servant,
Thou hast profaned his crown (even) to the ground.
40 Thou hast broken down all his hedges,
Thou hast made his strongholds a ruin.
41 All they that pass by the way have spoiled him,
He is become a reproach to his neighbours.
42 Thou hast exalted the right hand of his adversaries,
Thou hast made all his enemies to rejoice.
43 Yea, Thou hast turned back the edge [j] of his sword,
And hast not made him to stand in battle.
44 Thou hast made his splendour [k] to cease,
And hast cast his throne down to the ground ;

must be "the moon." Luther and others have supposed the rainbow to be meant. Others, again, think that the witness is God Himself, and render, "And a faithful witness is in heaven." But the moon is more for certain seasons than any other orb : in all countries she has been the arbiter of festivals, and the Jewish festivals were regulated by her.

38. But now comes the mournful contrast. This covenant, made by the Almighty and all-faithful God, confirmed and ratified by an oath, eternal as the heavens are eternal, sure as the order of the Universe is sure—what has become of it? Has it not failed, or is it not in danger of failing? Appearances are against its perpetuity, against the truth of God. The expostulation of the Psalmist is nothing less than a reproach. God has with His own hand cast down the throne of David, and annulled the covenant : so it seems to one who measures promise and performance by a human standard.

The boldness of the expostulation has scandalized the Jewish interpreters. Ibn 'Ezra (on. v. 1) tells the story of a learned and pious Jew in Spain, who would never read nor listen to this Psalm. He (Ibn 'Ezra) and others would get rid of the offence by taking ver. 38--45 as expressing the scoff of enemies, not the reproach of the Psalmist. But see the exactly similar language in xliv. 9—22, and notes there.

40. HIS HEDGES. The pronouns in this and the next verse refer grammatically to the king, but in sense to the people, who are regarded as one with their monarch. The expressions are borrowed from lxxx. 12 (13).

43. HAST TURNED. Although there is a change here to the present tense in the Heb. which is probably due to the poetic imagination vividly bringing the past before the eye, it is better, perhaps, to render it as a perfect. See on xviii. note [c].

44. SPLENDOUR, lit. "purity," and thus "brightness," "lustre," and the like. The literal rendering of the clause is, "Thou hast made (him) to cease from his brightness, or splendour." See Critical Note.

45 Thou hast shortened the days of his youth,
Thou hast covered him with shame. [Selah.]
46 How long, O Jehovah, wilt Thou hide Thyself for ever?
Shall Thy fury burn like fire?
47 O remember how short a time[l] I have to live!
For what vanity hast Thou created all the sons of men!
48 What man is he that liveth and shall not see death,
That can deliver his soul from the hand of the unseen world? [Selah.]
49 Lord, where are Thy former loving-kindnesses,
Which Thou swarest unto David in Thy faithfulness?
50 Remember, Lord, the reproach of Thy servants,
How I bear in my bosom [the reproach of] many peoples,[m]

45. THOU HAST SHORTENED, &c. This has been explained by Grotius and others of the short reigns of the later sovereigns of Judæa. But if spoken of an individual monarch, the expression would naturally mean that he had grown old before his time; comp. Hos. vii. 9: if of the family of David, it would be a figure denoting its failing strength before it attained to the glory and dominion promised. In this latter sense the clause is understood by Hupfeld and Hengstenberg; and so Rosenm.: "Quum regnum Judæ vix ad maturitatem aliquam perductum, et quasi in ipso flore extinctum sit, neque enim ad quingentos annos pervenit Davidicæ stirpis regnum."

46. The transition from expostulation to pleading, which of itself shows how the expostulation is to be understood. It is human weakness discovering to God its inmost heart. There *is* a sense of wrong, and the true man says that he feels it, speaks it out, and asks God to set it right. It is an example of the perpetual clash between convictions and facts. See Hab. i. 2, 3.

The pleading consists of two parts, each comprised in three verses. The argument of the first is the shortness of human life; that of the second, the dishonour cast upon God by the triumph of His enemies.

HOW LONG . . . FOR EVER. See note on xiii. 1, and comp. lxxix. 5.

47. HOW SHORT A TIME: a frequent ground of appeal to God's forbearing mercy, xxxix. 5; Job. vii. 6, xiv. 1, &c.

For the sentiment in this and the two following verses, see note on lxxxviii. 10. The occurrence of the pronoun of the first person singular can only be explained by its being intended to describe a fact of common experience, for in ver. 17, 18 the people speak in the first person *plural*, and the Anointed is always spoken of in the third person. The "I" is the expression of personal feeling, measuring others by itself. Or ver. 47—49 may mean, "Let *me*, even *me*, see Thy restoring love."

49. FORMER LOVING-KINDNESSES; not the promise itself, but the manifold proofs of its fulfilment in past times.

50. I BEAR IN MY BOSOM. The phrase elsewhere signifies "cherish-

51 Wherewith Thine enemies have reproached, O Jehovah,
Wherewith they have reproached the footsteps of Thine anointed.

52 Blessed be Jehovah for evermore.
Amen and Amen.

ing with tender care and affection," Num. xi. 12; Deut. i. 31; Is. xl. 11; xlvi. 3, a signification which is here, of course, quite out of the question. See more in the Critical Note. It is rather the expression of an intense sympathy with the Anointed as the representative of Jehovah, and is urged as a plea why God's faithfulness should be vindicated.

51. FOOTSTEPS, *i.e.* as we might say "every step he takes." Comp. xvii. 11; xxii. 16 [17]; xlix. 5 [6]. The Targum interprets this as a reproach, because of the *tarrying* of the footsteps of the Messiah. And so Qimchi: "He delays so long in coming, that they say He will never come."

Thus ends the Third Book of the Psalter, like the First and Second, with a Messianic Psalm.

52. The Doxology is no part of the original Psalm, but was added subsequently, to mark the close of the Book.

[a] Ethan the Ezrahite. The Greek Verss. differ, the LXX. rendering τῷ Ἰσραηλίτῃ, another τῷ Ζαραίτῃ, and another, τῷ Ἐζραΐτῃ. (See note [a] on lxxxviii.) Compare 1 Kings iv. 31 [v. 11]; 1 Chron. ii. 6. An Ethan or Jeduthun, a Levite, is also mentioned 1 Chron. vi. 29 (44 in E.V.), xv. 17, 19, whom some hold to be the same person. He and Heman, according to Hengst., are called Ezrahites as belonging to the family of Serah, the א being *Aleph prosthetic*. At the same time, as they were Levites, he thinks they were incorporated into the family of Serah, the son of Judah. So Elkanah the Levite, 1 Sam. i. 1, is called an Ephramite. Comp. Jud. xvii. 7.

[b] חֲסָדֵי, with *Dagesh lene*, contrary to the rule, here and in Lam. iii. 22.

[c] חֲסִין, not constr., but like the forms גְּבִיר, יָדִיד, עֲוִיל. Perhaps ה׳ יָהּ may be a special designation, as it occurs only here, "the strong Jah."

[d] שׂוֹא, either infin. = נְשׂוֹא, xxviii. 2, Is. i. 14 (instead of שְׂאֵת) or infinitival noun, like שִׂיא, Job xx. 6.

[e] חֲסִידְךָ. The sing. refers clearly to David, but many of De-Rossi's and Kenn.'s MSS., 16 Edd., and all the Greek Verss. (LXX. τοῖς υἱοῖς σου, the others τοῖς ὁσίοις σου, except S'. which has τοῖς προφήταις σου), the Chald., Syr., and Jerome, *sanctis tuis*, the Bab. and Jerus. Talmud (perhaps, though not certainly, as the י with them may be only a *mater lectionis*), and the Rabbis have the plur., which would refer to the people. See the same various reading in xvi. 10, and the double reference below in ver. 41.

[f] עֵזֶר. Hupf. objects to the word as inapplicable, and would read either נֵזֶר, *a crown* (comp. ver. 40), or עֹז, *majesty*. But the ancient Verss. vouch for the present reading.

[g] יַשִּׁיא, the Hiph. usually means *to deceive, lead astray, vex* (and so here Symm. ἐξαπατήσει, J. H. Mich. Maur., Del.), but, construed with בְּ, it is better to take it in the sense in which it occurs in Qal, *to act as a creditor, to exact.*

[h] אָפִיר. Both the form and the meaning of this word occasion some difficulty. פרר, to which it is commonly referred, means properly *to break, violate*, a covenant, &c., and hence could only be used improperly here; and besides, the fut. Hiph. of that verb would be אָפֵר. Hence we must either refer it to a root פור, as Gesenius does (*Thes. v.* פרר), or read אָסִיר, *I will take away*, from the parallel passages, 2 Sam. vii. 15, 1 Chron. xvii. 13.

[i] נֵאַרְתָּה. The word occurs only here (LXX. κατέστρεψας) and Lam. ii. 7 (LXX. ἀπετίναξε). It seems to be cognate with נער.

[j] צוּר. The only place where it occurs in this sense, "*edge* of a sword," but the sense is amply justified by the cogn. Arab. حار, an onomatopoetic root, used of sharp, shrill, grinding, grating noises, &c., as Fleischer has elaborately shown in a note to Delitzsch's commentary; as well as by the use of צֹר, Exod. iv. 25, denoting a *sharp* stone, or some sharp instrument. Hence it is quite unnecessary to translate, "O Thou Rock" (Olsh.), or, "the rock of his sword" (Hengst.), in a metaphorical sense, "the *strength*, &c., of his sword." LXX. τὴν βοήθειαν τῆς ῥομφαίας αὐτοῦ.

[k] מִטְּהָרוֹ. This is the reading of Norcia, Heidenheim, and the best Christian editors. The Jewish interpreters (as Ib. 'Ez., Qimchi, &c.) assume a noun מִטְּהָר, with euphonic Dagesh, as in מִקְּדָשׁ, Ex. xv. 17. The anomalous compound Sh'va is defended by such a form as בַּסְּעָרָה, 2 Kings ii. 1. But it is better to take the מ as the prep. *from*, "Thou hast made (him) to cease from his splendour." Nor is it necessary to have recourse to a form טְהָר or טְהָר (if we read with some MSS. מִטְהָרוֹ), like אֱיָל, כְּתָב, &c. It may be a heteroclite from טֹהַר, instead of טָהֳרוֹ, with rejection of the first syllable instead of the second. Dr. Schiller-Szinessy, however, in his Catalogue of Hebrew MSS. in the University Library at Cambridge (I. pp. 22, 26, &c.), draws attention to the fact that in olden times (in Ashkenazic MSS. mostly) the Qametz Chatuph was always represented by a Chateph Qametz; so that מִטְּהָרוֹ only represents מִטָּהָרוֹ.

[l] אֲנִי מ' ח'. MSS. vary considerably (see in Davidson's *Hebrew Text*), and editors have troubled themselves with explanations, but there is really no difficulty. The pronoun stands emphatically first instead of מֶה ח' אֲנִי, *ego quantilli sim ævi.* See on xxxix. 4 [5], note [c]. The LXX. μνήσθητι τίς ἡ ὑπόστασίς μου. Sym. (Syro-hex.) μν. τί εἰμι ζῶν· πρὸς ἡμέραν (s. ἐφήμερος) εἰμί. Jerome, *memento mei de profundo* (Aq. ἐκ καταδύσεως).

[m] The whole of the latter clause of ver. 50 [51] presents difficulties such as render the correctness of the existing text questionable: (1) the singular number, when the plural has just preceded (for the reading עבדך of some MSS., and the Syr., looks as if altered on purpose to meet the difficulty); (2) the sense in which the phrase *to bear in the bosom* is here used, contrary to that in which it elsewhere occurs; (3) the strange collocation of כָּל רַבִּים, *all many*, which cannot be defended by Ez. xxxi. 6, where כל stands in appos. with גּוֹיִם ר׳, following; (4) the position of the adj. רַבִּים before its noun, which in a common phrase of this kind is indefensible, and derives no support from Jer. xvi. 16, to which Maurer refers, as רַבִּים is there emphatically placed first. It seems necessary to repeat the word *reproach* from the first member of the verse, as the object of the verb in the second, either making this second clause a relative one, as the LXX. οὗ ὑπέσχον ἐν τῷ κόλπῳ μου πολλῶν ἐθνῶν (Symm. without the relative or the personal pron., ἐβάσταζα ἐ. τ. κ. παμπολλῶν ἐθ.), "which I bear from [the whole of] many nations;" or supplying חֶרְפַּת after כָּל, "all the reproach of many nations." Aquila may have had some other word instead of רַבִּים, for he renders αἴροντός μου ἐν κόλπῳ πάσας ἀδικίας λαῶν, and so Jerome, *portavi in sinu meo omnes iniquitates populorum.* This would remove all difficulty.

Delitzsch gives a different interpretation. He renders, "That I carry in my bosom all the many nations," and supposes the Psalmist to complain, as a member of the body politic, that his land is full of strangers, Egyptians and their allies (he assigns the Psalm to the time of Shishak's invasion), whose outrages and taunts fill his heart with sorrow.

The literal rendering of the present text can only be: "How I bear in my bosom all the many nations."

THE PSALMS

BOOK 4

Psalms 90—106

PSALM 90

"THE 90th Psalm," says Isaac Taylor, "might be cited as perhaps the most sublime of human compositions, the deepest in feeling, the loftiest in theological conception, the most magnificent in its imagery. True is it in its report of human life as troubled, transitory, and sinful. True in its conception of the Eternal,—the Sovereign and the Judge, and yet the refuge and the hope of men who, notwithstanding the most severe trials of their faith, lose not their confidence in Him; but who, in the firmness of faith, pray for, as if they were predicting, a near-at-hand season of refreshment. Wrapped, one might say, in mystery, until the distant day of revelation should come, there is here conveyed the doctrine of Immortality: for in this very plaint of the brevity of the life of man, and of the sadness of these his few years of trouble, and their brevity and their gloom, there is brought into contrast the Divine immutability; and yet it is in terms of a submissive piety; the thought of a life eternal is here in embryo. No taint is there in this Psalm of the pride and petulance, the half-uttered blasphemy, the malign disputing or arraignment of the justice or goodness of God, which have so often shed a venomous colour upon the language of those who have writhed in anguish personal or relative. There are few, probably, among those who have passed through times of bitter and distracting woe, or who have stood the helpless spectators of the miseries of others, that have not fallen into moods of mind violently in contrast with the devout and hopeful melancholy which breathes throughout this Ode. Rightly attributed to the Hebrew Lawgiver or not, it bespeaks its remote antiquity, not merely by the majestic simplicity of its style, but negatively, by the entire avoidance of those sophisticated turns of thought which belong to a late—a lost age, in a people's intellectual and moral history. This Psalm, undoubtedly, is centuries older than the moralizing of that time, when the Jewish mind had listened to what it could never bring into a true assimilation with its own mind—the abstractions of the Greek Philosophy."—*Spirit of the Hebrew Poetry*, pp. 161-3.

Two objections have been urged by Hupfeld against the Mosaic authorship of the Psalm, neither of which can be regarded as very weighty. (1) The first of these is, that the Psalm contains no clear and distinct reference to the circumstances of the Israelites in the wilderness. (2) The next is, that the span of human life is limited to threescore and ten or fourscore years, whereas not only Moses himself, but Aaron, Joshua, and Caleb, are all said to have reached a period of life considerably beyond this (Deut. xxxiv. 7; Num. xxxiii. 39; Josh. xxiv. 29; xiv. 10).

As regards the first objection, it is sufficient to reply that the language of the Psalms is in almost every case general, not special, and that all that can be reasonably demanded is that there be nothing in the language at variance with the supposed circumstances, or unsuitable to the person, the time, the place, to which a particular Psalm is alleged to belong. Hupfeld himself admits that the general strain of thought and feeling is in every respect worthy of a man like Moses, as well as in perfect accordance with the circumstances under which this Psalm is commonly believed to have been written, viz. towards the close of the forty years' wandering in the wilderness.

The second objection seems at first sight of more force. Yet there is no evidence that the average duration of human life at that period was as extended as that of the few individuals who are named. On the contrary, if we may judge from the language of Caleb, who speaks of his strength at eighty-five as if it were quite beyond the common lot (Josh. xiv. 10), the instances mentioned must rather be regarded as exceptional instances of longevity. The life of the majority of those who died in the wilderness must have fallen short of fourscore; and there is no reason to suppose that their lives were prematurely cut short. Not this (as Hupfeld asserts), but the forty years' wandering in the wilderness was their punishment; and this limit seems to have been placed to their desert sojourn, because thus all the generation who left Egypt, having reached man's estate, would, not exceptionally, but *in the natural course of things,* have died out.

All the ablest critics, even those who, like Ewald and Hupfeld, deny the Mosaic authorship of the Psalm, nevertheless admit, that in depth and loftiness of thought, in solemnity of feeling, and in majesty of diction, it is worthy of the great Lawgiver and Prophet. "The Psalm," writes Ewald, "has something uncommonly striking, solemn, sinking into the depths of the Godhead. In subject-matter and style it is original, and powerful in its originality, and would be rightly attributed to Moses, the man of God (as the later collector calls him, comp. Deut. xxxiii. 1; Ezra iii. 2), if we knew more exactly the historical grounds which led the collector to this view." It is strange that Ewald's one reason for bringing down the Psalm to a later time, the ninth or eighth century B.C., is the deep sense of human infirmity and transitoriness which pervades it, and which he imagines could not have been felt at an earlier period of the history.

"There are important *internal* reasons," says Hengstenberg, "which may be urged in favour of the composition of the Psalm by Moses, as announced in the title. The poem bears throughout the stamp of high antiquity;* there is no other Psalm which so decidedly conveys the impression of being the original expression of the feelings to which it gives utterance. There is, moreover, no other Psalm which stands so much *by itself*, and for which parallel passages furnish so little kindred matter in its characteristic peculiarities. On the other hand, there occurs a series of striking allusions to the Pentateuch, especially to the poetical passages, and above all others to Deut. xxxii., allusions which are of a different kind from those which occur in other passages in the Psalms, and which do not appear, like them, to be *borrowed*. Luther remarks in the Psalm another peculiarity; 'Just as Moses acts in teaching the law, so does he in this prayer. For he preaches death, sin, and condemnation, in order that he may alarm the proud who are secure in their sins, and that he may set before their eyes their sin and evil, concealing, hiding nothing.' The strong prominence given to the doctrine of *death as the wages of sin*, is characteristic of the Psalm, a doctrine of not frequent occurrence in Holy Scripture, and especially not in the Psalms, and which is proclaimed as distinctly and impressively as it is here only in the Pentateuch, Gen. ii. iii., and in those ordinances of the ceremonial law which threaten death."

The points of resemblance between the language of the Psalm and expressions occurring in parts of the Pentateuch, and more particularly in Deuteronomy, will be found mentioned in the notes. To those who believe, as I do, that Deuteronomy was written by Moses, they furnish an argument for the Mosaic authorship of the Psalm.

"This Psalm, then, is one of the oldest of the inspired utterances. It is the prayer which is read over the mortal dust of some hundreds of the children of men, every week, in London alone. And so used, none of us finds it antiquated. The lapse of 3,000 years has not made it necessary to discard this clause and that. Words that described the relation of the children of Israel to the eternal God,

---

* So Herder calls it "that ancient Psalm, that hymn of eternity."

serve still to express the devotion of English hearts turning to God in their sorrow. As these grand words are uttered, the curtain that hangs round our life seems to draw back, and we see, beyond, depths that we dreamt not of. From time and the slow succession of events, from the minutes and the hours that seem so long and so many, we turn to God, whose eternal nature was as it now is even when the world was formed, and to whom a thousand years are no more than the middle watch of the night is to a sound sleeper. Nations that seem established for ever are carried off down the roaring cataract of time; men full of pride, and glory, and power, grow and perish like grass; and God alone remains unchangeable, the same yesterday, and to-day, and for ever."—ARCHBISHOP OF YORK'S *Sermons preached at Lincoln's Inn*, p. 2.

The Psalm has no strophical division, nor even any regular rhythmical arrangement. It consists of two principal parts :—

I. The first is a meditation on the eternity of God, as it stands in contrast with the weakness and transitoriness of man (ver. 1—12); and here we have, first, the contrast stated (ver. 1—6), and then the reason of this transitoriness, viz. man's sin, and God's wrath as following thereon, together with the prayer for wisdom to turn to a practical account these facts of human life (ver. 7—12).

II. The second (ver. 13—17) is a prayer that God—who, notwithstanding Israel's sin, and notwithstanding the chastisement that sin has provoked, is still Israel's Hope and Refuge—would now at last have compassion upon His people, give them joy for sorrow (ver. 13—15), and crown all their labours with success (ver. 16, 17).

[A PRAYER OF MOSES, THE MAN OF GOD.]

1 LORD, Thou hast been our dwelling-place
In all generations.

Ver. 1—6. The eternity and unchangeableness of God contrasted with the transitoriness of man.

THOU HAST BEEN, or "hast proved Thyself to be." It is the record of a past experience, not merely the statement of what God is in His own nature. It is the acknowledgement of what God had been to Abraham, to Isaac, and to Jacob, when they had no fixed dwelling-place, but "confessed that they were strangers and pilgrims," of what He had been both to their fathers and to themselves.

OUR DWELLING-PLACE, or "a place of refuge for us." The word, which occurs Deut. xxxiii. 27, combines both ideas, and would have a peculiar force of meaning for the Israelites in the wilderness. For Israel was without a country and

2 Before the mountains were brought forth,
Or ever Thou gavest birth to[a] the earth and the world,
Yea from everlasting to everlasting, Thou art God.
3 Thou turnest frail man to dust,[b]
And Thou sayest: Return, ye children of men.
4 For a thousand years in Thy sight
Are (but) as yesterday, when it passeth,[c]
And as a watch in the night.

without *a home*, finding here and there only a brief resting-place beside the well and under the palms of the desert. And Israel was without *a refuge*, exposed to enemies and a thousand perils.

IN ALL GENERATIONS, lit. "in generation and generation," a phrase which occurs Deut. xxxii. 7

2. THOU GAVEST BIRTH TO. Perhaps the passive rendering, which involves only a very slight change in a single vowel-point (see Critical Note), is to be preferred: "Or ever the earth and the world were formed."

EARTH . . . WORLD. The former is the more common and general word; the latter, which is exclusively used in poetry, denotes, according to its etymology, the *fruitful* earth (comp. Prov. viii. 31; Job xxxvii. 12).

3. TO DUST: lit. "to the state of one who is crushed, reduced to dust," with allusion, no doubt, to Gen. iii. 19.

RETURN. As men perish by the breath of God, so by His word He calls others into being: "one generation goeth, and another cometh." This is the sense given in the P.B.V. "again Thou sayest: Come again, ye children of men." Others suppose the second clause of the verse to be merely a repetition of the first:

"Thou turnest men to destruction,
And sayest, Turn (*i.e.* to destruction), ye children of men."

But if an emphatic repetition were designed, the form of the sentence would rather have been:

"Thou sayest, Turn to destruction, ye children of men,
And they are turned."

Besides, the fut. consec. "and sayest," would indicate that the act in the second clause of the verse is to be regarded as a consequence of that in the first, or at least as subsequent to, and not merely as parallel with it. Others, again, interpret the word "return" of a moral returning or conversion; or of the return of the spirit to God who gave it; or even of the resurrection. But none of these explanations harmonizes with the context.

4. YESTERDAY. To a Hebrew, the new day began in the evening. . . . A WATCH IN THE NIGHT. The night was anciently divided into three, later into four watches. There is a climax; for the past day, short as it seems, was, whilst it was passing, capable of measurement: it had its hours and its minutes, its thoughts and its acts, and its memories. But the night-watch "is for us as though it were not; we sleep through the watch of the night, living, but observing nothing." "In those words, 'a thousand years in Thy sight are but as yesterday,' &c. the Psalmist has thrown a light upon the nature of God such as a volume of reasoning could not have kindled. With God there are no measures of time. With us time is the name we give to the duration of a certain succes-

5 Thou sweepest them away (as with a flood);[d] they are
(as) a sleep:
In the morning they are as grass which springeth
afresh,[e]
6 In the morning it flourisheth and springeth afresh,
In the evening it is cut down[f] and withereth.
7 For we have been consumed by Thine anger,
And by Thy fury have we been terrified;
8 Thou hast set our iniquities before Thee,

sion of thoughts and efforts, each of which for a moment held full possession of us, each of which cost us a certain pain, and contributed a little to that weariness which at last took shelter in repose. The Most High does not and cannot so govern the world. He does not look away from the earth to add fuel to the sun; He does not leave one nation of the earth neglected whilst He works mighty social changes in another. . . . All that we mean by time must now be left out of the account. . . . It would be a longer and more tedious task, if a man were the worker, to build a world than to guide a wayward nation through its fortunes; but what means longer or shorter, where there is no labour, nor waiting, nor weariness, but only the streaming forth of an omnipotent will? Dare we say that it cost more to construct the universe than to guide the footsteps of one man during the short year that has just closed!"—ARCHBP. OF YORK'S *Sermons*, pp. 6—8.

The sentiment of the verse is repeated by S. Peter, who gives also the converse, 2 Pet. iii. 8.

5. THOU SWEEPEST, &c. Or the two clauses may be dependent upon one another, as in the P.B.V.: "As soon as Thou hast swept them away, they are (or, become) as a sleep."

IN THE MORNING. This can hardly mean "in early youth," as some of the Rabbis explain. The words, strictly speaking, are a part of the comparison ("they are as grass which springeth afresh in the morning"), and are only thus placed first to give emphasis to the figure. In the East, one night's rain works a change as if by magic. The field at evening was brown, parched, arid as a desert; in the morning it is green with the blades of grass. The scorching hot wind (James i.11) blows upon it, and again before evening it is withered.

6. IT IS CUT DOWN, or, "it is dried up." The P.B.V. gives both meanings: "it is *cut down, dried up*, and withered." Ewald observes that the beauty of the comparison consists in the fact that the flower which was so lovely in the morning fades away *of itself* the same day in the scorching heat of the sun. But "cut down" may have this sense, not "cut down by the scythe," but "cut down by the hot blast, or by the fierceness of the sun's heat."

7. FOR: explanatory, not argumentative. The reason of all this transitoriness is to be found in Israel's sin, which has provoked God's heavy displeasure against His people. The statement is not a general one of human sinfulness and frailty. The use of the first person, and the past tenses, shows that the writer is dealing with the facts of his own history and that of his people.

HAVE BEEN TERRIFIED, or, "utterly confounded." See the same word xlviii. 5 (note), "driven away in panic terror."

8. OUR SECRET SINS (this is

Our secret (sins) in the light of Thy countenance.
9 For all our days are passed away in Thy wrath,
We have spent our years as a thought:
10 The days of our years are threescore years and ten,
Or (perchance) by reason of much strength,[g] fourscore years;
And their pride is (but) labour and vanity,
For it passeth swiftly,[h] and we have fled away.

favoured by the parallelism) or, "our secret (heart);" for the word is singular. The whole inner being, that which is in man (John ii. 25), the pollution and sinfulness of which is hidden from a man himself, till it is set in the light of God's countenance.

LIGHT, or more properly, "luminary," the same word which is found in Gen. i., used of the heavenly bodies, but nowhere else used in this particular phrase. (It is always *'ōr* not *m'ōr*.) There seems, however, to be a special reason for this. The light of God's countenance is everywhere else spoken of as a light of love and approbation. (Hence, the Syriac renders the second clause "make us grow young again in the light of Thy countenance.") Here it is a revealing light. The "light" or rather "sun" of God's countenance shines down into the dark abysses of the human heart, bringing out its hidden evils into strong and painful relief. The nearest parallel expression occurs in Prov. xv. 30, where the same word is used, rendered in the E.V. "the *light* of the eyes." It means "that which contains and gives the light, as the sun, a lamp, &c."

9. ARE PASSED AWAY, lit. "are turned," or "have declined," cf. Jer. vi. 4, "the day turns," *i.e.* declines. The same word is used in Ps. xlvi. 5 [6], of the *turning*, *i.e.* dawn of the morning.

AS A THOUGHT. The same comparison is found in Homer, as an emblem of speed: *ὡσεὶ πτερὸν ἠὲ νόημα.* And Theognis speaks of the years of youth as fleeing like a thought: *αἶψα γαρ ὥστε νόημα παρέρχεται ἄγλαος ἥβη.* But perhaps we ought to render, "as a *sigh* or *sound*," a meaning which the word has in the two other passages where it occurs, Job xxxvii. 2 (E.V. *sound*,) Ezek. ii. 10 (E.V. *mourning*). Referring to this passage in Ezek., Kay renders here: "sad reverie." But the root idea of הגה is rather *to think aloud*. Hence the word may mean "a brief passing utterance," "a fleeting sound." Others again, "as a *breath*." So the Chald., "as the breath of the mouth in winter." (Comp. xxxix. 5, 6 [6, 7], where, however, the word is different.) The LXX. and the Syr. have "as a *spider*." On this rendering and its probable origin, information will be found in Rosenmüller's note.

10. THE DAYS OF OUR YEARS (a common expression in Genesis). The literal rendering of this clause is, "The days of our years (nom. absol.)—in them are seventy years."

OR (PERCHANCE). More literally, "or if they (the years) be with much strength."

THEIR PRIDE, *i.e.* the pride of the years, meaning all in which men make their boast, as health, strength, honour, riches, &c.

FOR IT PASSETH, &c. Words which come with double force from the lips of one now standing himself on the extreme verge of life, and looking back on the past. Comp. the language of S. John, "The world passeth away and the lust thereof," &c.

11 Who knoweth the power of Thine anger,
And Thy wrath, according to the fear that is due unto Thee ?
12 So teach us to number our days,
That we may gain a heart of wisdom.

13 Return, O Jehovah !—how long ?—
And let it repent Thee concerning Thy servants.

11. WHO KNOWETH, *i.e.* "regardeth, considereth aright." This must be repeated with the next hemistich, "Who regardeth Thy wrath, according," &c.

12. TEACH US, lit. "To number our days, *so* teach us," i.e. *in this manner* teach us, give us *this* kind of instruction. The position of the words and the accents justify this interpretation. Others take *so* (כֵּן) in the sense of *accordingly*. Others, as meaning *rightly*. And others again connect it with what goes before : "*So*, i.e. according to the fear due unto Thee ;" or, in accordance with all the previous meditation. Of the need of this Divine arithmetic Calvin well says : "Nam qui optimus erit arithmeticus, et myriades myriadum distincte ac subtiliter tenebit ac excutiet, non tamen poterit octoginta annos supputare in propria vita. Hoc certe prodigio simile est homines extra se ipsos metiri omnia intervalla, cognoscere quot pedibus distet luna a centro terræ, quam longis inter se spatiis planetæ dividantur, denique omnes cœli et terræ dimensiones tenere, quum in seipsis septuaginta annos non numerent."

THAT WE MAY GAIN, gather, bring in as a harvest, the fruit of the earth, &c. Comp. the use of the same word, 2 Sam. ix. 10, Hagg. i. 6: a heart of wisdom, a wise heart is the fruit which we are to gather from the Divine instruction.

13. The prayer which follows springs from the deep source of the preceding meditation. God is everlasting, man transitory and sinful. Man does not consider his sin aright, even when God lays His hand upon him. He needs Divine instruction that he may take to heart the lesson both of his sinfulness and of his transitoriness. But Moses does not forget that, in spite of all, God has been and still is the home of His people. He is a compassionate God, as well as a God that punisheth transgression. And therefore he asks not only that he and his people may learn the lesson of Divine wisdom, but that the God who had chastened them would visit them with His lovingkindness, that the night of sorrow may flee away, and the morning of gladness dawn. God's love, God's personal manifestation of Himself, His blessing descending upon them as they enter upon their new life in the promised inheritance,—for this, and not for anything less, he prays. "And the prayer is a presage of the end of their pilgrimage, and of their forgiveness, and their settlement in the land that God had given them."

RETURN. This may mean, as in Exod. xxxii. 12, "Turn from Thine anger," or, as in vi. 4 [5], "Turn to Thy people."

HOW LONG. See notes on vi. 3, 4.

LET IT REPENT THEE, or, "show compassion towards." The fuller expression is found in Exod. xxxii. 12, "Let it repent Thee of the evil," &c. The phrase occurs frequently in the Prophets.

14 Oh satisfy us in the morning with Thy loving-kindness,
That we may sing for joy and be glad all our days.
15 Make us glad according to the days[i] wherein Thou hast afflicted us,
The years wherein we have seen evil.
16 Let Thy work appear unto Thy servants,
And Thy majesty upon their children.
17 And let the graciousness of Jehovah our God be upon us;
And the work of our hands do Thou establish upon us;
Yea, the work of our hands establish Thou it.

14. IN THE MORNING, when the night of sorrow is spent. Comp. xlvi. 5 (note), cxliii. 8.

15. AFFLICTED US, or, "humbled us," the same word which is used in Deut. viii. 2, where this "humbling" is said to have been God's purpose in those forty years' wandering.

16. THY WORK. The word is used both of God's judgements and of His acts of grace. Some Edd. have the plural, "Thy works," but the sing. is most common in the Psalms when the reference is to God. Comp. lxxvii. 12 [13], xcii. 4 [5], xcv. 9, and Hab. iii. 2. Here, the bringing of Israel into his inheritance is meant. The noun occurs nowhere in the Pentateuch, except in Deuteronomy. See, for instance, Deut. xxxii. 4.

"Quia Deus Ecclesiam suam deserens, quodammodo alienam personam induit, scite Moses *proprium ejus opus* nominat protectionis gratiam quam pollicitus fuerat, filiis Abrahæ. . . . Hac ratione Paulus (Rom. ix. 23) Dei bonitatem gloriæ titulo specialiter insignit."—CALVIN.

THY MAJESTY. "Notandum est," says Calvin, "*decoris et pulchritudinis* nomen, unde colligimus quam incomparabilis sit erga nos Dei amor. Quamvis enim suis donis nos ornans, nihil sibi acquirat, liberaliter tamen nobiscum agendo splendere vult, et decorem suum palam facere; ac si forma ejus obscura esset, ubi nos sua beneficentia prosequi cessat."

UPON, as coming down out of heaven, and so descending *upon*. Comp. Is. xl. 1, 2; but this is not certain, as the prepositions אֶל and עַל are often interchanged.

17. GRACIOUSNESS, or "favour." This is perhaps a better rendering here than "beauty," which I have retained in xxvii. 4, where see note; but see Prov. iii. 17, Zach. xi. 7.

THE WORK OF OUR HANDS, another expression which runs all through Deuteronomy.

The order deserves notice. *God's* work is first to appear, His Majesty to be revealed; then *man's* work, which is God's work carried out by human instruments, may look for His blessing. Referring to the use of this Psalm in the office for the Burial of the Dead, Mr. Housman observes: "It is remarkable how not only this but the 39th Psalm, as well as the Lesson (1 Cor. xv.) all close with the same thought,—*work;* as though the one great use of the shortness of life, and the coming on of death, were to stir us up to use the very utmost of the time that is left."—*Readings on the Psalms*, p. 189.

[a] וַתְּחוֹלֵל. (1) According to the existing punctuation, this is active (Pilel); but it may be either 2 pers. masc., as in the E. V., or it may be 3 fem., as the Syr. takes it: "or ever it" (*i.e.* the earth) "was in travail" or "brought forth," viz. plants, animals, &c. (comp. Gen. i. 11, 24). So Ewald: *eh' kreiste Erd' und Land.* Hupf., Del. and Bunsen adopt the former rendering, which makes God the subject of the verb, appealing to Deut. xxxii. 18, where the same verb is used of God in reference to Israel. The act of creation, says Del., is compared to the pangs of travail. There is, however, greater harshness in the application of such a figure to the origin of the material universe, than in its application to describe the relation of His people to God. But (2) a very slight change of punctuation will give us the passive, תְּחוֹלַל, which accords with the pass. יֻלָּדוּ before, and which is the rendering of the Chald., LXX. πλασθῆναι, Aq. and Symm. ὠδινηθῆναι, and Jerome, who says that this is what the Hebrew had in his time, and all the Versions, "illud autem, quod et Hebraicum habet et omnes alii interpretes: *Antequam montes nascerentur, et parturiretur terra.*" Then the rendering will be: "Or ever the earth and the world were formed," lit. "born."

[b] דַּכָּא, according to Ewald, fem. subst., for דַּכָּה, the termination in א being found early, Num. xi. 20. (Comp. Deut. xxiii. 2, where the reading varies between the form in ה and that in א.) The form, however, is rather that of the adj. (xxxiv. 19, Is. lvii. 15), either in a neuter sense, *contritum, comminutum,* i.e. *dust* (comp. Gen. iii. 19), or as a predicate, *eo ut fiat contritus,* "to the condition of one who is crushed" (comp. for the constr. Num. xxiv. 24). LXX. εἰς ταπείνωσιν. Sym. (Syro-hex.) *ad condemnationem contritionis.* Chald. "Unto death." And so the Tal., &c., דכדובה של נפש.

[c] כִּי יַעֲבֹר. This can neither be rendered "when it *is* past" (as the E. V.), nor "when it *shall have* past" (as De Wette): grammatically it can only be "when it passeth" or "is passing" (so Ewald, who observes, "it is at evening when the day is just passing away that it seems the shortest," but?), or "*because* it passeth;" but neither of these yields a satisfactory sense: we want the rendering of the E.V., "when *it is* past." Hupfeld therefore would take אֶלֶף שׁ' as the subject of יַעֲבֹר, "For a thousand years are in Thy sight when they pass (or, because they pass) but as yesterday." We have אֶלֶף with the sing. verb in xci. 7, but there the verb stands first in the sentence (and the verb may be in the sing. when it *precedes* a plur. subject), and אֶלֶף is without a substantive.

[d] זְרַמְתָּם. The verb occurs only here and lxxvii. 18, formed from the noun זֶרֶם. The preterite may stand in the protasis as the condition of what follows: "(When) Thou hast swept them away with a flood, they become as a sleep," &c., like the shadowy image of a dream which leaves no trace behind. Hupfeld connects בַּבֹּקֶר with this clause: "they become as a sleep in the morning" (comparing lxxiii. 20, Is. xxix. 7). No doubt this gives a good sense, and there is a difficulty in explaining the

Masoretic text, "In the morning they are as grass," &c., for "the morning" cannot mean the morning of human life, or youth, as Qimchi and others understand. But on the other hand, Hupfeld's arrangement of the clauses leaves the second miserably lame: "As the grass passeth away." [On the question whether כְּ can thus be construed with the verb, see on xlii. note [b] (3).] On the whole, it is better to assume an incorrectness of expression, and to take "in the morning they are," &c. as: = "they are as grass which *withereth* [or *springeth afresh*, see below] in the morning."

[e] יַחֲלֹף. Two exactly opposite interpretations have been given of this verb, both proceeding from the same radical idea, that of *change*, *transition* from one place or condition to another; but the one implying the change of new life, growth, &c., the other that of decay and death. The first meaning is common in the Hiph. of this verb (comp. Is. ix. 9; xl. 31; xli. 1; and of plants, Job xiv. 7; xxix. 20), but is nowhere else found in the Qal (though Gesen. gives this sense in Hab. i. 11, but wrongly). Hence Ewald, Hupf., Bunsen, and others, adopt the second meaning of *passing away*, in the sense of *perishing* (so the LXX. has παρέλθοι, and Jerome, *quasi herba pertransiens*). According to this view, the first member of ver. 6 contains the whole figure, the latter part of which is then repeated and expanded in the second member:—

> In the morning it flourisheth, and (then) perisheth,
> In the evening it is dried up and withered.

Gesenius, on the other hand (*Thes. in v.*), gives to חלף, in this passage, the sense of *viret*, *revirescit*. Zunz's Bible has *sprosset*, Delitzsch *schosset wieder*. And amongst the older interpreters, the Chald. and Syr. render similarly. Hupf. and others object to the repetition involved in this rendering, but that exists on either interpretation, and the repetition is merely emphatic, as for instance in xcii. 10.

[f] יְמוֹלֵל. According to the punctuation, Palel, act., which is usually taken as an impers. instead of the passive: "one cuts down," instead of "it is cut down." Ewald, Hupfeld, and others give to the verb מוּל the sense of *withering*, here and in xxxvii. 2; and this sense of the root may be defended by reference to Deut. xxiii. 26, where מְלִילוֹת is "the ripe, *sun-dried*, ears of corn." But perhaps here the pass., with the same slight change of the vowel as in note [a], is preferable.

[g] בִּגְבוּרֹת. "Poet. plur. for sing. The word, an abstract from גִּבּוֹר, occurs nowhere else in this sense, but always of physical strength as *exercised*, *put forth*, as for instance in warlike prowess: so of the war-horse, cxlvii. 10, Job xxxix. 19 (comp. חַיִל, Ps. xxxiii. 16), of the sun at his rising, Judg. v. 31 (comp. Ps. xix. 6). The plural in particular is always used of deeds of valour, of the mighty acts of God or of men. The notion of physical strength, natural vigour, &c., is usually expressed by בַּכֹּחַ, בְּעֹז, and the like."—*Hupfeld.*

[h] גָּז, not from גזז, in a pass. sense, *is cut off*, as Symm., τμηθέντες, but to be connected with גּוז, Aram. and Syr., *to pass by*. See on lxxi. note [b], where, however, גָּז is spoken of as the part. It is better, as the Vau consec. follows, to take it as the pret.

[i] יְמוֹת, only here and Deut. xxxii. 7, instead of יְמֵי; the following שְׁנוֹת, poet. plur. for שְׁנֵי, occurs first in the same passage of Deut. Both are in construct. with the verbal clauses following, Ges. § 114, 3.

PSALM 91

THIS Psalm, which in the Hebrew has no inscription, is by the LXX., apparently without sufficient reason, ascribed to David. It celebrates, with considerable variety and beauty of expression, God's loving and watchful care, and the perfect peace and security of those who make Him their refuge. "Can the Providence of God," asks Herder, "be taught in a more trustful or a more tender spirit? The language is the language of a father, growing ever more fatherly as it proceeds, till at last the Great Father Himself takes it up and declares His truth and faithfulness."

Mr. Plumptre speaks of it as "an echo, verse by verse almost, of the words in which Eliphaz the Temanite (Job v. 17—23) describes the good man's life."—*Biblical Studies*, p. 184.

There is no reason to suppose that the Psalm was written during the prevalence of a pestilence (such for instance as that mentioned in 2 Sam. xxiv. 15),* for the variety of figures employed shows that the Psalmist is thinking of peril of every kind, coming from whatever source, and that he paints all dangers and fears vividly to the eye of his mind, in order to express the more joyfully his confidence that none of these things can move him, that over all he is more than conqueror. It is St. Paul's fervid exclamation, "If God be for us, who can be against us?" expressed in rich and varied poetry.

The structure of the Psalm is in some respects peculiar. The writer speaks at one time of or from, at another to, himself; he is both subject and object; now he utters his own experience, and now he seeks to encourage himself with Divine promises; and the transitions are so abrupt, that various attempts have been made to soften

---

* Stier mentions that some years ago an eminent physician in St. Petersburg recommended this Psalm as the best preservative against the cholera.

or explain them. A full account of these will be found in the Critical Note on verse 2.

There is no strophical arrangement, but the general structure of the Psalm rests on the common principle of pairs of verses, except that the two concluding groups consist of three verses each, thus: 1, 2; 3, 4; 5, 6; 7, 8; 9, 10; 11—13; 14—16.

1 HE that sitteth in the secret place of the Most High,
That resteth under the shadow of the Almighty,
2 Saith[a] of Jehovah, He is my refuge and my fortress,
My God, in whom I trust.
3 For HE shall deliver thee from the snare of the hunter,
From the devouring pestilence.
4 With His feathers shall He cover thee,
And under His wings shalt thou find refuge,
His truth shall be a shield and a buckler.
5 Thou shalt not be afraid for any terror by night,

1. In the first edition this verse was rendered as if it were complete in itself:

"He that sitteth in the secret place of the Most High
Resteth under the shadow of the Almighty."

But it cannot be denied that such a rendering is open to the charge of tautology. It is better to take the second clause, as only a variation of the first, in accordance with the common principle of Hebrew parellelism. There is no reason for affirming that the verb RESTETH (lit. "lodgeth, passeth the night"), is used in any emphatic sense, such as is implied by the rendering of the E.V., "He that dwelleth, &c. . . . shall *abide*," *i.e.* constantly and permanently continue. Hence the reading of the LXX., who in ver. 2 have the 3rd per. ἐρεῖ, *he shall say*, instead of the 1st, *I will say*, has much to commend it, and I have now adopted it.

In each clause of verses 1, 2, God is spoken of by a different name. God is "Most High," far above all the rage and malice of enemies; "Almighty," so that none can stand before His power; "Jehovah," the God of covenant and grace, who has revealed Himself to His people; and it is of such a God that the Psalmist says in holy confidence, He is "my God," in whom I trust.

2. SAITH, or "will say." In the Hebrew text the 1st person stands, "I will say." See more in Critical Note.

3. FOR. Well may such a man thus speak of Jehovah, for He, &c.

SNARE OF THE HUNTER. Comp. xviii. 5 [6], cxxiv. 7, Hos. ix. 8.

DEVOURING PESTILENCE. For the epithet, see Critical Note on ver. 9 [10].

4. WITH HIS FEATHERS or "pinion." See the beautiful passage, Deut. xxxii. 11, and note on Ps. xvii. 8; lxiii. 7.

5. TERROR BY NIGHT (comp. Song of Sol. iii. 8, Prov. iii. 23–26), in allusion, probably, to night-attacks like those of Gideon (Judg. vii.), a favourite artifice of Oriental warfare; or perhaps to a destruction like that of Sennacherib.

(Nor) for the arrow that flieth by day,
6 For the pestilence that walketh in darkness,
(Nor) for the sickness that wasteth [b] at noon-day.
7 A thousand shall fall at thy side,
And ten thousand at thy right hand;
(But) it shall not come nigh thee.
8 Only with thine eyes shalt thou behold
And shalt see the reward of the wicked.
9 For Thou, O Jehovah, art my refuge:—
Thou hast made the Most High thy habitation;
10 (Therefore) there shall no evil befall thee,
Neither shall any plague come nigh thy tent;
11 For He will give His angels charge over thee,
To keep thee in all thy ways;

7. IT SHALL NOT COME NIGH THEE. The singular refers to any and every one of the evils mentioned in ver. 5, 6. "As the general who carries within him the conviction that he is called to a great work, whilst the bullets fall thick as hail about him, stands with calm eye and firm foot, and says: I know that the bullet is not yet cast which can strike me, so stands the man of prophetic faith in the hour of danger, with the conviction that the thunderbolt will turn aside from his head, and the torrent dry up at his feet, and the arrows fall blunted from his breast, *because the Lord wills it*."—*Tholuck*.

9. The change of persons is again perplexing. The Psalmist suddenly interrupts the address to himself which had been continued in one strain from ver. 3 (and which is resumed again in the second clause of this verse, "Thou hast made," &c.), to express his own trust in God. This difficulty is not lessened by the rendering of the E.V. "Because thou hast made the Lord which is my refuge, even the Most High thy habitation." In such a construction (which is very harsh), the natural form of expression would have been, "*Thy* refuge." It is better to look upon the first member of this verse, "For Thou, O Jehovah, art my refuge," as parenthetical, with a reference to the words of ver. 2. But whether we suppose the address in ver. 3—8, and again that which, beginning with the second member of ver. 9, extends to the end of ver. 13, to be the words of the Psalmist himself, or whether they are put into some other mouth with a view to musical effect—in either case the words are really a voice from Heaven, the promise of God uttered to and appropriated by the soul.

10. TENT. An instance of the way in which the Patriarchal life became stereotyped, so to speak, in the language; cf. Mal. ii. 12. There is an allusion, perhaps, to Israel's exemption from the plagues of Egypt, Exod. xii. 23.

11. ANGELS: not as "guardian angels," but as God's ministers in the government of the world, and especially as "sent forth to minister for them that shall be heirs of salvation." Comp. xxxiv. 7. By the "lion and adder" there is no need to understand exclusively, or chiefly, the powers of darkness, the evil spirits (as Del. thinks). As by "a stone" all hindrances, so by "the

12 On (their) hands they shall bear thee (up),
Lest thou dash thy foot against a stone.
13 Upon the lion and adder shalt thou tread,
Thou shalt trample the young lion and serpent under thy feet.
14 "Because he hath set his love upon Me,
Therefore will I deliver him;
I will set him on high, because he knoweth My Name.
15 When he calleth upon Me, I will answer him.
I will be with him in trouble,
I will deliver him and honour him;
16 With long life will I satisfy him,
And show him My salvation."

lion and dragon" all hostile powers, are denoted, more particularly in the natural world. This may be illustrated from histories like those of Samson, David, Daniel, &c., and especially in the N. T. by the history of the Temptation, Mark i. 13.

What a prophecy of the victory of faith over the material as well as over the spiritual world, and that not only by miraculous, but by non-miraculous means! Comp. Mark xvi. 18; Luke x. 19; John xiv. 12.

The LXX. render ver. 11, 12, *ὅτι τοῖς ἀγγέλοις αὐτοῦ ἐντελεῖται περὶ σοῦ, τοῦ διαφυλάξαι σε ἐν πάσαις ταῖς ὁδοῖς σου. Ἐπὶ χειρῶν ἀροῦσίν σε, μήποτε προσκόψῃς πρὸς λίθον τὸν πόδα σου.* The quotation both in Matt. iv. 6, and Luke iv. 10, 11, is made from the LXX., but the former omits the whole of the clause "to keep thee," &c., and the latter the words "in all thy ways," so that it would seem that the omission of this last was designed in the mouth of the tempter. The "ways" spoken of in the Psalm are the "ways" of obedience and duty, not the "ways" of presumption or self-seeking. S. Bernard, speaking of the temptation, says: "Non est via hæc, sed ruina, et si via, tua est, non illius."

"Quanquam autem de singulis Ecclesiæ membris agit Propheta, non temere hoc diabolus aptavit ad personam Christi. Nam utcunque semper ei sit propositum pervertere et corrumpere veritatem Dei, in generalibus tamen principiis speciosum colorem adhibet, satisque acutus est theologus."—*Calvin.*

14—16. God's answer to the soul which trusts in Him. "God Himself comes forward to establish the faith of His servant, writes deeper in the soul so great a consolation, and confirms the testimony to His servant. 'He hath set his love upon Me—he knoweth My Name—he calleth upon Me'—these are the marks of a true servant of God. God draws nigh to one who so draws nigh to Him." Compare with this passage l. 15, 23.

16. LONG LIFE, lit. "length of days."

The special promise of long life at the close, as a temporal blessing, is in accordance with the general character of the Old Testament. Still it is possible that men like the Psalmist, full of faith in God, attached a deeper and more spiritual meaning to promises and hopes like these, than was attached to them by the majority of their countrymen.

[a] אֹמַר. This, as it stands, can only be the 1st pers. fut., which is embarrassing as the 3rd pers. precedes. This and other abrupt changes of person in the Psalm have given rise to every variety of explanation.

Delitzsch thinks that the Psalm is dramatic in character, and that it must be distributed between three voices, and may have been possibly so sung in Divine service. The first voice utters ver. 1, "He that sitteth in the secret place, That abideth in the shadow of the Almighty," and is taken up by the second voice, which sings ver. 2, "I will say," &c. The first voice resumes at the beginning of ver. 3, and continues to the end of ver. 8. The second voice then utters the first clause of ver. 9, "For Thou, O Jehovah, art my refuge." And the first voice begins with "Thou hast made the Most High thy habitation," and goes on to the end of ver. 13. The third voice, which utters the words of God Himself, is heard in ver. 14—16.

Perhaps this on the whole is the simplest explanation of the change of speakers in the Psalm, but ver. 1 may have been sung by the choir rather than by a single voice.

Tholuck's arrangement is the same, except that he makes ver. 1 complete in itself, and that he gives ver. 1, ver. 3—8, and 9*b*—13 to the Precentor; ver. 2 and 9*a* to the Choir, and supposes 14—16 (the Divine words) to be sung by the Precentor and Choir together.

Herder in like manner distributes the Psalm between two voices, but gives ver. 1, 2, and 9*a* to the first voice, and the rest of the Psalm to the second.

Ewald has a different conception of the structure of the Psalm. Partly, he thinks, the Poet expresses his own feelings as from himself, and partly as if they were uttered by another. He seems to listen to the thoughts of his own spirit, till they become clear and distinct, like some prophetic words, or some Divine oracle speaking to him from without, and giving him thus the assurance and the consolation afresh which had already sprung up in his heart.

Hupfeld, who is followed by Bunsen, alters the text. He would supply אַשְׁרֵי at the beginning of ver. 1, and read אֹמֵר instead of אֹמַר in ver. 2. He renders ver. 1, 2:

"[Blessed is he] who sitteth in the hiding-place of the Most High,
Who passeth the night in the shadow of the Almighty,
Who saith to Jehovah, my refuge," &c.

Again in ver. 9 he supplies אָמַרְתָּ:

Because [thou hast said] "Thou Jehovah art my refuge,"
(And) hast made the Most High thy habitation.

(So S. Pagnini, "Quoniam tu *dixisti*, Domine, spes mea.").

Such alterations may no doubt "get rid of all difficulty at a stroke," but they are purely conjectural, and have no support from MSS. or Verss. The difficulty is older than any of the existing versions. The LXX. either had a different text, or felt the awkwardness of the change from the 3rd pers. in ver. 1 to the 1st in ver. 2, and hence they have the 3rd pers., ἐρεῖ, in ver. 2. Jerome likewise has *dicens* in ver. 2, as if he read אֹמֵר. The Syr. also has the

3rd pers. instead of the 1st. The Chald. distributes the Psalm between three speakers. On any view there is much difficulty in determining the relation of the first verse to what follows. Taken by itself it is tautological—the second clause is merely a repetition of the first, for the verb יִתְלוֹנָן is not, as Mich. and others suppose, emphatic. It would seem better, therefore, with the Syr., LXX., and Jerome, to retain the 3rd pers. in ver. 2, and to read either אֹמֵר or יֹאמַר, the change in either case being very slight. The latter is preferable, as in the former both the subject and predicate would be participial. Ewald, however, thinks the Poet is himself the subject in both verses, first, as *looking at* himself (hence 3rd pers.), then, as *speaking of* himself (1st pers.): "The man who sitteth . . . who resteth, &c. . . . even I say," &c. He refers to Job xii. 4. See also Is. xxviii. 16.

[b] יָשׁוּד for יָשׁוֹד from שׁדד. Comp. for similar forms Prov. xxix. 6, Is. xlii. 4. The LXX. καὶ δαιμονίου, from a false reading וְשֵׁד.

PSALM 92

THIS Psalm is called a Psalm for the Sabbath-day, and, as we learn from the Mishnah, *Tamîd* vii. 4, was appointed to be used in the Temple service on that day. It was sung in the morning when, on the offering of the first lamb, the wine was poured out as a drink-offering unto the Lord (Num. xxxviii. 9). At the evening sacrifice one of the three passages, Ex. xv. 1—10, 11—19, Num. xxi. 17—20, was sung. From the T. B. *Rosh hash-Shana* 31[a] we learn that the following was the selection of Psalms for the service, each day of the week, in the second Temple. On the first day, Ps. xxiv.; on the second, Ps. xlviii.; on the third, Ps. lxxxii.; on the fourth, Ps. xciv.; on the fifth, Ps. lxxxi.; on the sixth, Ps. xciii.; on the seventh "A Psalm *or song for the Sabbath-day*, i.e. A Psalm or song for the future age (the age of the Messiah), all of which will be Sabbath." In *Rosh hash-Shana*, however, the question is raised whether the Psalm refers to the Sabbath of Creation (R. Nehemia), or the final Sabbath of the world (R. Akiba). The title in the Targum, "Of the first Adam," favours the former, as does also the opinion of the older Rabbis (see Midrash Rabbah, on Gen. cap. 22, on Eccles. i. ver. 1 and 2; Pir'qê de Rabbi Eliezer, cap. 19, *Shocher Tôb* on Ps. xcii.), who tell us that this Psalm "was said by the First Man, who was created on the eve of the sabbath, and when he awoke early in the morning of the Sabbath, uttered this Psalm. Athanasius supposes the latter to be intended, αἰνεῖ ἐκείνην τὴν γενησομένην ἀνάπαυσιν. Better Augustine, "Dicit unde solent perturbari homines, et docet te agere sabbatum in corde tuo." It cannot be said, however, that there is anything in the contents of the Psalm which, as pointing either to the future or the present rest, would account for its selection as the Sabbatical Psalm.*

It celebrates in joyful strain the greatness of God's works, and especially His righteous government of the world, as manifested in the overthrow of the wicked, and the prosperity and final triumph of the righteous. The *apparent* success of the ungodly for a time is admitted, but this is a mystery which worldly men, whose understanding has become darkened, cannot penetrate (ver. 6). The Psalm therefore touches upon the same great principles of the Divine government which are laid down in such Psalms as the first, the thirty-seventh, the forty-ninth, and the seventy-third. But here there is no struggle with doubt and perplexity, as in the seventy-third; the Poet is beyond all doubt, above all perplexity; he has not fallen down to the low level of the brutish man (comp. lxxiii. 22 with ver. 6 of this Psalm); he is rejoicing in the full and perfect conviction of the righteousness of God.

The strophical arrangement of the Psalm is doubtful. Hupfeld groups the first three verses and the last four together, and disposes the intermediate verses in pairs. Delitzsch is clearly wrong when he distributes the Psalm into five groups, each of three verses. I believe that we have two principal divisions, ver. 1—7, and ver. 9—15, each division consisting of seven verses, separated by a verse (the eighth), which, unlike all the rest, is comprised in a single line. Each seven is again subdivided into a three and four. The whole scheme, therefore, stands thus 1—3, 4—7, (8) 9—11, 12—15. All the joy of the Psalmist culminates in that great fact, that Jehovah is throned on high for evermore; from that flows the overthrow of the wicked and the triumph of the righteous.

[A PSALM. A SONG FOR THE SABBATH DAY.]

1 It is a good thing to give thanks unto Jehovah,

1—3. Introduction, expressive of real delight in God's service.

IT IS A GOOD THING, *i.e.* a delightful thing, not merely

* Now both on Sabbath eve (Friday night) and Sabbath morning the next Psalm (xciii.), which is the proper Psalm for Friday is used; and they were perhaps early sung together, *i.e.* first xcii., and then xciii. This and all the Psalms which follow, as far as the 100th, are liturgical in character, and were evidently intended for use in the Temple service. They bear also some resemblance to one another in point of style, especially in the anadiplosis, xcii. 9 [10]; xciv. 1, 3; xcvi. 13. Compare also xciii. 1 with xcvi. 10, and the recurrence of the same expression in xcv. 3; xcvi. 4; xcvii. 9.

And to sing psalms unto Thy Name, O Most High,
2 To declare Thy loving-kindness in the morning,
And Thy faithfulness every night,
3 With a ten-stringed instrument and with the lute,
With sound of music [a] upon the harp.

4 For Thou hast made me glad, O Jehovah, because of that Thou hast done,
I will sing for joy because of the works of Thy hands.
5 How great, O Jehovah, are Thy works!
Very deep are Thy thoughts.
6 A brutish man [b] knoweth not,
And a fool doth not consider this.
7 When the wicked spring as the green herb,
And all the workers of iniquity do flourish,
It is that they may be destroyed [c] for ever.

8 And Thou, O Jehovah, art (throned) on high for evermore.

acceptable to God, but a real joy to the heart.

4. The great reason of all this joy. The Psalmist has witnessed the manifestation and the triumph of the eternal righteousness of God.

THAT THOU HAST DONE, or "Thy doing;" not here God's power in creation (a misunderstanding which may have led to this Psalm being associated with the Sabbatical rest of creation), but God's moral government of the world. So also in the next clause THE WORKS OF THY HANDS, as in cxliii. 5. The Rabbis, however, understand it both of the appointment of the earthly Sabbath, and also of the future Sabbatical rest in the Kingdom of the Messiah (Mishnah, *Tamid* vii. 4).

5. HOW GREAT; not as in lxxiii., "it was a trouble in mine eyes." Faith wonders and adores. Men's thoughts on such subjects are but folly. It is as though they considered not (ver. 6). Faith is the true interpreter of the world (ver. 7).

VERY DEEP. Comp. xxxvi. 6 [7]; xl. 5 [6]; cxxxix. 17; Rom. xi. 33.

6. A FOOL; in the same sense as in xiv. 1. "Stultos autem vocat omnes incredulos, ac tacite eos fidelibus opponit, quibus Deus per Verbum suum et Spiritum illucet. Nam peræque omnium mentes occupat hæc inscitia et cæcitas, donec cœlesti gratia oculati reddamur."—*Calvin.*

8. This verse, consisting of but one line, expresses the great central fact on which all the doctrine of the Psalm rests. This is the great pillar of the universe and of our faith. "Hoc elogium non tantum honoris causa ad Dei essentiam refertur, sed ad fidei nostræ fulturam: ac si dictum esset, quamvis in terra anxie gemant fideles ac trepident, Deum tamen, qui custos est vitæ ipsorum, in sublimi manere et eos protegere virtute æterna."—*Calvin.*

ON HIGH. The word only occurs here as a predicate of God. Lit. "height," or "in the height" (accusative). Comp. the adverbial use

9 For lo, Thine enemies, O Jehovah,
For lo, Thine enemies shall perish,
All the workers of iniquity shall melt away.
10 But Thou hast exalted my horn like (the horn of) a wild ox ;
I am anointed [d] with fresh oil.
11 Mine eye also hath seen (its desire) upon them that lie in wait for me,[e]
And my ear hath heard (its desire) of the evil-doers who rise against me.

12 The righteous shall spring as the palm,
He shall grow like a cedar in Lebanon.
13 They that are planted in the house of Jehovah
Shall spring in the courts of our God ;

of the same word in lvi. 2 [3], where see note. Elsewhere God is said "to inhabit the height," Is. lvii. 15, to be "glorious in the height," xciii. 4, and in Mic. vi. 6 we have "God of height," *i.e.* "God on high," or "God in heaven."

9. SHALL MELT AWAY, lit. "shall separate themselves, disperse," breaking up as it were without the application of any external force.

10. FRESH OIL, or "green oil," as in Latin, *oleum viride*, said of the best oil.

11. MINE EYE, &c. See for this expression liv. 7 [9], lix. 10, &c. ; the one which follows in the next clause, of the ear hearing with satisfaction of the overthrow of his enemies, seems to have been expressly framed to correspond to the other: it occurs nowhere else in this sense.

THEM THAT LIE IN WAIT FOR ME; the same whom in ver. 9 he calls "*Thine* enemies." Sure of the triumph of the kingdom of God, he is sure also of his own triumph.

12—15. What is true of the Psalmist is true of all who are partakers of the same faith. The date-palm and the cedar are selected as the loveliest images of verdure, fruitfulness, undecaying vigour and perpetuity. "Throughout the year, in the winter's cold, as in the summer's heat, the palm continues green: not by years, but by centuries is the cedar's age reckoned."—*Tholuck*. There is also a contrast: "The wicked spring as the green herb, or, grass" (ver. 7), which soon withers away, "The righteous spring as the palm," which is ever green and ever fruitful.

Besides this, there are only two passages in the Old Testament where the palm is used in comparison,—Song of Sol. vii. 7, where it is said of the bride, "Thy stature is like to a palm-tree ;" Jer. x. 5, where the idols are said to be "upright as a palm-tree ;" and one in the Apocrypha, Ecclus. xxiv. 14, "I was exalted like a palm-tree in Engaddi." This, as Dr. Howson (Smith's *Dict. of the Bible*, art. PALM-TREE) has noticed, is remarkable, considering the beauty of the tree, and its frequent recurrence in the scenery of Palestine.

13. The figure need not be so far pressed as to imply that such trees actually grew in the Temple-court (see on lii. 8). Still it is by no means improbable that the

14 They shall still bear fruit in old age,
They shall be full of sap and green,
15 To declare that Jehovah is upright,
My rock in whom there is no unrighteousness.[f]

precincts of the temple, like the Haram es-Sherif, contained trees.

14. THEY SHALL BEAR FRUIT, in allusion probably to the great fruitfulness of the date-palm, which, when it reaches maturity, produces three or four hundred pounds' weight of fruit, and has been known even to produce six hundred pounds' weight.

15. TO DECLARE, &c. Thus in the end God's righteous government of the world will be manifested. The flourishing of the workers of iniquity has been but for a moment (ver. 7, 9, 11); the joy and prosperity of the righteous is for ever. This is the signal proof of God's righteousness: this is the justification of the Psalmist's confidence resting ever on that unshaken "Rock."

[a] הִגָּיוֹן. As this word occurs in the midst of others signifying musical instruments, it seems most natural to suppose that it also means an instrument of some kind. But usage and the derivation of the word are rather in favour of Gesenius's interpretation, *noise, sound* (ad strepitum cithara factum; comp. ix. 16 [17]); nor does the prep. עֲלֵי militate against this. It may mean not only *upon* but *accompanying*. Hupf. renders "zum Spiel mit der Harfe," and Del., "auf sinnigem Spiel mit Cither."

[b] אִישׁ־בַּעַר, "a brute-man," a compound expression, like פֶּרֶא אָדָם, Gen. xvi. 12, Ezek. xxxvi. 38.

[c] לְהִשָּׁמְדָם. An instance of the periphrastic use of the infin., with לְ for the future (see on lxii. note [g]); but perhaps the apodosis begins with וַיָּצִיצוּ, "then all the workers of iniquity flourish to their everlasting destruction."

[d] בַּלֹּתִי. 1 Perf. sing. anomalously with the accent on the last syllable (as cxiv. 6, Is. xliv. 16). The former is rather that of the inf. with suffix, and so it was taken, against the context, by the older translators. LXX. τὸ γῆράς μου. Symm. ἡ παλαίωσίς μου. Jerome, *senecta mea*. But this requires a verb to be supplied, on the principle of zeugma, from the first clause. "Thou hast exalted (= refreshed) my old age with fresh oil." It is preferable therefore to take the word as 1 perf. sing., here apparently intrans., though elsewhere trans. (cf. Gen. xi. 7, 9); and it *may* be trans. here, if we supply the object, *the horn*, or, *the head*. Qimchi leaves it an open question whether the verb is trans. or intrans.

[e] שׁוּרָי, similar participial forms occur Num. xxxv. 32, Jer. xvii. 13 (Q'ri סוּרַי), Mic. ii. 8. שׁוּר = שׁוֹרֵר v. 9, and the construction with the suffix may be compared with קָמַי xviii. 40, but שׁוּר takes the acc. in Num. xxiii. 9.

[f] עֹלָתָה, to be read עֹלָתָה, as in Job v. 16, from עוֹלָה, Is. lxi. 8, fem. of עָוֶל (by contraction of the original diphthong *au* into *ô*), instead of the more common עַוְלָה, which the Q'ri prefers (עַוְלָתָה, as cxxv. 3).

PSALM 93

THE sum and substance of this Psalm is contained, as Hitzig has remarked, in the eighth verse of the preceding Psalm. It celebrates the Majesty of Jehovah as Ruler of the Universe. He is Creator of the world. He has been its King from everlasting; it rests upon Him, and is stayed by His might. All the powers of nature obey Him, however lawless they may seem, as all the swelling and rage of men, of which those are but a figure, must obey Him. But His Majesty and His Glory are seen, not only in controlling the powers of nature, and whatsoever exalteth and opposeth itself against Him, but in the faithfulness of His word, and in the holiness of His house.

As the Psalm speaks of a particular manifestation of Jehovah's kingly rule, of a time when He has taken to Himself His great power and reigned (see note on ver. 1), it may in this sense be termed Messianic. For, as Delitzsch has pointed out, the Old Testament prophecy concerning the kingdom of God consists of two series of predictions, the one of which speaks of the reign of the anointed of Jehovah out of Zion, the other of the reign of Jehovah Himself as the great King over all the earth. These two lines of prophecy converge in the Old Testament, but never meet. Only here and there do we discern an intimation (as in xlv. 7) that the two are one.

The LXX. (Codex *B*) have the Inscription, *εἰς τὴν ἡμέραν τοῦ προσαββάτου, ὅτε κατῴκισται ἡ γῆ, αἶνος ᾠδῆς τῷ Δαυίδ*. The latter part of this title is probably merely conjectural. The former agrees with the Jewish tradition (Mishnah, *Tamid* vii. 4), according to which this is the Friday Psalm, and as is said in T. B. Rosh ha-Shana, 31*a*, "because God on the sixth day had finished His work, and begun to reign over His creatures." Perhaps this is what is meant also by the *ὅτε κατῴκισται* (or *κατῴκιστο*), "when the earth was peopled with living creatures," of the LXX.

1 JEHOVAH is King, He hath clothed Himself with majesty;

1. IS KING. More exactly, "hath become King," as if by a solemn coronation (comp. the same expression of a new monarch ascending the throne, 2 Sam. xv. 10; 1 Kings i. 11; 2 Kings ix. 13). He has been

Jehovah hath clothed, He hath girded, Himself with
strength.
Yea, the world is established that it cannot be moved.
2 Thy throne is established of old;
Thou art from everlasting.

3 The floods have lifted up, O Jehovah,
The floods have lifted up their voice,
The floods lift up their roaring.
4 More than the voices of many waters,
The glorious [a] breakers of the sea,
Jehovah on high is glorious.

King from everlasting, but now His kingdom is visibly set up, His power and His majesty fully displayed and acknowledged; as it is said in the Apocalypse of the final manifestation, "The kingdoms of this world are become the kingdoms of our Lord and of His Christ."

HATH CLOTHED . . . HIMSELF. Comp. civ. 2, Is. li. 9, Job xl. 10. In the second member of the verse the verb is rhythmically repeated, and the noun "strength" really belongs to both verbs. (So the LXX.) For the further description of this girding with strength, see Is. lix. 17, lxiii. 1; Dan. vii. 9.

YEA, THE WORLD, &c. The effect of the Divine rule and power, as in xcvi. 10. The reference is apparently not merely to the creation of the world and its providential administration, but to these as representing in a figure the moral government of God. For the throne of God in ver. 2 denotes, as Calvin says, His righteous sway and government, and the language of ver. 3 is to be understood figuratively as well as literally.

3. THE FLOODS. The word commonly signifies *streams, rivers*, but occasionally also is used of the sea in poetic parallelism, as in xxiv. 2; Jon. ii. 3 [4]; Jer. xlvi. 7, 8.

HAVE LIFTED UP. The use of the past tense had led some commentators to see a reference to some historic event, some gathering of hostile powers who are described under the figure of the sea and the waves roaring. But the change in the last clause of the verse to the present tense renders this doubtful.

Hupfeld infers from the use of the word "floods" (comp. Hab. iii. 8), the epithet of "glorious," or "mighty" in next verse, which is used of waters besides only in Exod. xv. 10, and the "lifting up the voice," as in Hab. iii. 10 (comp. lxxvii. 17, 18), that there is an allusion to the passage of the Red Sea.

THEIR ROARING, lit. "their blow," or "beating," said of the dashing of the surf in thunders upon the shore. The word occurs only here; in the next verse the plural "voices" is used here only of the sea, elsewhere always of the thunder. Hence some have supposed a comparison, "Louder than the thunders."

4. This verse is the answer to ver. 3, and may have been sung antiphonally. The construction is not very clear. For the different renderings see Critical Note.

GLORIOUS, or "mighty." An epithet of the waves in Ex. xv. 10, of God in Is. xxxiii. 21.

JEHOVAH ON HIGH. Comp. xcii. 8 [9], xxix. 10.

5 Thy testimonies are very faithful.
Holiness becometh Thy house, O Jehovah, for ever.

5. The transition is abrupt, from the Majesty of God as seen in His dominion in the world of nature, to His revelation of Himself in His word. At the same time there is a connection between the two, as in xix. God who rules the world, He whose are the kingdom, and the power, and the glory, for ever, has given his testimonies to His people, a sure and faithful word, and has Himself come to dwell among them, making His house and His people holy.

FOR EVER, lit. "for length of days," as in xxiii. 6.

[a] אַדִּירִים. According to the common accentuation, this adj., though standing before its noun, is not a predicate, but an attribute, "the glorious, or mighty breakers of the sea," and Hupf. would defend this by xcii. 12, where, however, the case is not parallel, the participle, with the pron. and noun following, being so closely connected as to form as it were one word, בַּקָּמִים עָלַי מְרֵעִים, or where at least the latter word might be regarded as in appos. with the former. Perhaps, however, as it has been suggested that there מְרֵעִים is a gloss, so in like manner here מִשְׁבְּרֵי יָם may have crept into the text. There is a similar ambiguity arising from the place of the adj. in Is. xxviii. 21, זָר מַעֲשֵׂהוּ . . . נָכְרִיָּה עֲבֹדָתוֹ, commonly rendered as in E.V. "His strange work . . . His strange act," although many there insist on retaining the predicate: "His work is strange . . . His act is strange," &c. So in Is. xxxiii. 21, the adj. (and it is the same adj. as here in the Psalm, אַדִּיר) may be a predicate, "Jehovah in His glory"; though Del. takes the two words in apposition, "a glorious one, even Jehovah," referring to Is. x. 34. The adj. however stands first as an attribute apparently, Is. liii. 11, צַדִּיק עַבְדִּי, "My righteous servant." But instead of *Merca* with אַדִּירִים, or *Tarcha*, as Ben-Asher reads, Ben-Naphtali has *Dechî*, and according to this we may take both adjectives as qualifying מַיִם, and then repeat the prep. from the first clause before מִ׳ יָ׳. "More than the voices of many mighty waters, (even) the breakers," &c. Or we may take the prep. מִן, not as expressing comparison, but as causal, and then two renderings are open to us, either (*a*) "Because of the voices of many waters, mighty are the breakers of the sea; Jehovah on high is mighty" [and this is supported by the LXX., except that perhaps they intended ἀπὸ φωνῶν ὑδάτων πολλῶν to be joined with the previous verse]: or (*b*) "By reason of the voices of many mighty waters, even the breakers of the sea, Jehovah is mighty;" *i.e.* these great phenomena of nature show forth His glory and His majesty.

There is yet another explanation of the construction possible. The Psalmist may have begun with a comparison and then have broken it off in order to bring the 2d and 3d members into more forcible juxtaposition. Above the voices of many waters,—Glorious are the breakers of the sea, Jehovah on high is glorious.

PSALM 94

By the LXX. this is called "A lyric Psalm of David, for the fourth day of the week" (τετράδι σαββάτου). It is probably not a Psalm of David, but the latter part of the Inscription accords with the Talmudic tradition (see Introduction to Ps. xcii.).

The Psalm opens with an appeal to God to execute righteous vengeance on wicked rulers or judges who oppress and crush the helpless, whilst in their folly they dream that His long-suffering is but the supineness of indifference. It concludes with the expression of a calm confidence that God's righteousness will be finally manifested. The righteous, taught by God's fatherly discipline, and upheld by Him, can wait for the end, when the wicked shall reap the reward of their wickedness, and shall be utterly destroyed.

The conviction thus expressed of the righteousness of God's government is similar to that in Ps. xcii., except that here this conviction is grounded more directly on personal experience.

The Psalm may be thus divided :—

1. An Introduction, consisting of an appeal to God. Ver. 1, 2.

2. The reason for this appeal, namely, the insolence and oppression of the wicked. Ver. 3—7.

3. The blindness and folly of such conduct, as a virtual contempt of God. Ver. 8—11.

4. In contrast with this the blessedness of those who are taught of God, and who can therefore in their confidence possess their souls. Ver. 12—15.

5. The strong personal conviction of Jehovah's righteousness, based upon past experience. Ver. 16—19.

6. A conviction which extends also to the future, and by virtue of which the Psalmist sees righteous retribution already accomplished upon the wicked. Ver. 20—23.

1 O Jehovah, Thou God to whom vengeance belongeth,
Thou God to whom vengeance belongeth, shine forth.[a]

1. God to whom, &c. : lit. "God of vengeances." Comp. ix. 12 [13]; Jer. li. 56. For the anadiplosis, see again ver. 3, 23, and xciii. 1, 3.

2 Lift up Thyself, Thou judge of the earth,
Render a reward to the proud.

3 How long shall the wicked, O Jehovah,
How long shall the wicked triumph?
4 They belch out (and) speak arrogant things,
All the workers of iniquity carry themselves proudly.[b]

5 Thy people, O Jehovah, they crush,
And Thine inheritance do they afflict.
6 They slay the widow and the stranger,
And they murder the fatherless;
7 And they say: "Jah seeth not,
Neither doth the God of Jacob consider."

8 Consider, O ye brutish among the people!
And ye fools, when will ye be wise?

3. With this verse begins the complaint, the expostulation with God, and therefore clearly the first strophe. Delitzsch and others wrongly join this with the two preceding verses as forming part of the Introduction. So far from that, it is quite possible, with the E.V., to regard ver. 4 as continuing the question of ver. 3. "(How long) shall they pour forth," &c.

4. THEY BELCH OUT (AND) SPEAK, two verbs having one noun as the object (as in xciii. 1) = "they pour forth hard, or, proud (xxxi. 18 [19], 1 Sam. ii. 3) speeches." The first verb is rendered "they belch out" in lix. 7.

5. CRUSH: Prov. xxii. 22; Is. iii. 5.

6. The LXX. has transposed the words "fatherless" and "stranger," and rendered the last "proselyte" (προσήλυτον). The widow and the fatherless are mentioned, as often, as particular instances of those whose misery ought to excite compassion, but whose defencelessness makes them the easy prey of the wicked. There is no abbreviated comparison, as Hengstenberg maintains—"Thy people who are as helpless as the widow," &c. But the language shows that domestic tyrants, not foreign enemies, are aimed at.

7. JAH SEETH NOT. Comp. x. 11, lix. 7 [8]. Not that they deliberately utter such blasphemy, but their conduct amounts to this, it is a practical atheism. See on xiv. 1.

8. The utter folly of this denial of a Divine Providence, because judgement is not executed speedily. The argument which follows is from the perfections of the creature to those of the Creator. The very nature of God and of man convicts these fools of their folly. "Can anything," says Herder, "more to the point be urged, even in our time, against the tribe of philosophers who deny a purpose and design in Nature? All that they allege of the dead abstraction which they term 'nature,' the heathen ascribed to their gods: and what the Prophets say against the one, holds against the other."

AMONG THE PEOPLE, *i.e.* of Israel. "Gravius est autem vocare *stultos in populo*, quam simpliciter stultos: eo quod minus excusabilis sit talis amentia in filiis Abrahæ, de quibus dictum fuerat à Mose, Quis popu-

9 He that planteth the ear, shall He not hear?
Or He that formeth the eye, shall He not see?
10 He that instructeth the nations, shall not He reprove,
(Even) He that teacheth man knowledge?
11 Jehovah knoweth the thoughts of man,
That they are vanity.
12 Blessed is the man whom Thou instructest, O Jah,
And teachest out of Thy law,
13 To give him rest from the days of evil,

lus tam nobilis, &c. Deut. iv. 7."
—*Calvin.*

10. In the English Bible this is broken up into two questions, and a clause is supplied in the second member which does not exist in the Hebrew, "Shall not He know?" But this is incorrect. There is a change in the argument. Before, it was from the physical constitution of man; now it is from the moral government of the world. He who is the great Educator of the race ("who nurtureth the heathen," P.B.V.), who gives them all the knowledge they possess, has He not the right which even human teachers possess of chastening, correcting, reproving? He may not always exercise the right, but it is His. This, which I believe to be the true interpretation of the verse, is that of the LXX.: Ὁ παιδεύων ἔθνη, οὐχὶ ἐλέγξει; ὁ διδάσκων ἄνθρωπον γνῶσιν; or there may be a change in the appeal, a breaking off of the question, as one he need not ask. The Psalmist was going to say at the end of ver. 10, "Shall not He know?" finishing his question as in the preceding verses, but instead of that he gives the answer directly in ver. 11, "He knoweth," &c. Hengstenberg remarks, that the doctrine of an influence exercised by God upon the consciences of the heathen is of comparatively rare occurrence in the Old Testament, a fact to be explained by the very depraved condition of such of the heathen as were the near neighbours of the Israelites, and among whom few traces of such an influence could be seen. On this Divine education see Rom. i. 20, ii. 14, 15.

11. So far from "not seeing," "not regarding," as these "brutish" persons fondly imagine, Jehovah reads their inmost thoughts and devices, as He reads the hearts of all men, even though for a time they are unpunished. The verse is quoted in 1 Cor. iii. 20, ὁ Κύριος γινώσκει τοὺς διαλογισμοὺς τῶν σοφῶν ὅτι εἰσὶν μάταιοι, which only deviates from the version of the LXX. in the substitution of the special σοφῶν, as more suitable to the Apostle's argument, for the general ἀνθρώπων.

VANITY, lit. "a breath," as in xxxix. 5, 6 [6, 7].

The second clause of the verse is ambiguous. The pronoun "they," although masc., *may* refer to the noun "thoughts" (fem.), but perhaps rather to the collective "man." Probably the best rendering of this clause would be, "*For* they (*i.e.* men) are but a breath;" this vanity, weakness, and emptiness of men being alleged as a reason why God sees and understands their thoughts: they are finite, whereas He is infinite.

12. The Psalmist turns to comfort the individual sufferer. God who educates the heathen (ver. 10), educates also the Israelite, giving him a better instruction (comp. Deut. viii. 5; Job v. 17), inasmuch as it is that of a direct Revelation. On this ver. see T. B. *Berachoth*, *5a*.

13. TO GIVE HIM REST. This is

Till the pit be digged for the wicked.
14 For Jehovah will not thrust away His people,
Neither will He forsake His inheritance.
15 For judgement must turn unto righteousness,
And all the upright in heart shall follow it.

16 Who will rise up for me against the evil-doers?
Who will set himself up for me against the workers of iniquity?
17 Unless [c] Jehovah had been my help,
My soul had soon dwelt in silence.
18 (But) when I said, My foot hath slipt,
Thy loving-kindness, O Jehovah, held me up.
19 In the multitude of my anxious thoughts within me,
Thy comforts refreshed my soul.

the end of God's teaching, that His servant may wait in patience, unmoved by, safe FROM, THE DAYS OF EVIL (comp. xlix. 5 [6]), seeing the evil all round him lifting itself up, but seeing also the secret, mysterious retribution, slowly but surely accomplishing itself. In this sense the "rest" is the rest of a calm, self-possessed spirit, as Is. vii. 4, xxx. 15, xxxii. 17, lvii. 20, and "to give him."="that Thou mayest give him." Others interpret the "rest" of external rest, deliverance from sufferings (comp. Job iii. 13, 17); then "to give" would be="so as to give," &c.

14. FOR. God will give peace to the man whom he teaches, *for* he is a partaker of the covenant, one of that PEOPLE and that INHERITANCE which He cannot forsake, and He cannot forsake them till righteousness ceases to be righteousness.

15. FOR JUDGEMENT, &c., or, "For judgement shall come back unto righteousness with all them that are upright in its train," *i.e.* with the approval of all good men. Judgement cannot always be perverted, cannot always fail. It must appear in its true character at last as very righteousness. This, no doubt, was what Luther meant by his forcible rendering,

"Denn Recht muss doch Recht bleiben."

SHALL FOLLOW IT, lit. "(shall be) after it," *i.e.* shall give in their adhesion to it, openly avow their attachment to it. For the phrase, see 1 Sam. xii. 14; 2 Sam. ii. 10; 1 Kings xiv. 8.

16—19. Application to himself, and record of his own experience.

AGAINST, lit. "with;" but we need not suppose that it = "to fight with," as Hupfeld explains. See note on lv. 18 [19].

SET HIMSELF UP, in battle, as in ii. 2; 2 Sam. xxxiii. 10, 12.

17. SILENCE, *i.e.* of the grave, or the unseen world, as in xxxi. 18, cxv. 17.

19. ANXIOUS THOUGHTS, or "perplexities," lit. "*divided* or *branching* thoughts," whether doubts or cares. Kay: "busy thoughts." The word occurs, as here, with the

20 Can the throne of iniquity have fellowship with Thee,[d]
Which frameth mischief by statute?
21 They gather themselves in troops against the soul of the righteous,
And condemn the innocent blood.
22 But Jehovah hath been a high tower for me,
And my God the rock of my refuge.
23 And He hath requited them their own iniquity,
And shall destroy them through their own wickedness:
Jehovah our God shall destroy them.

r inserted, in cxxxix. 23, and the simpler form in Job iv. 13.

20—23. This strophe, like the last, applies the general doctrine of the Psalm to the individual case, the personal security of the Psalmist, and the righteous retribution visited upon the evil-doers. But for "Jehovah *my* God," in ver. 22, we have in ver. 23, "Jehovah *our* God," as if to remind us that his personal welfare does not stand apart from, but is bound up with, that of the nation. Comp. ver. 14.

20. THE THRONE or "judgement-seat." The word is purposely employed, as Calvin observes, to show that he is inveighing, not against common assassins or thieves, but against tyrants who, under a false pretext of justice, oppressed the Church. The throne of the king, the seat of the judge, which is consecrated to God, they stain and defile with their crimes.

INIQUITY, or, perhaps, "destruction." It is scarcely possible to give the word an adequate rendering here. It occurs v. 9 [10] ("yawning gulf"), where see Critical Note; xci. 3, where, as the latter of two nouns, it may be rendered as an adjective, "devouring."

HAVE FELLOWSHIP WITH THEE. Comp. for the Hebrew expression v. 4 [5]; Gen. xiv. 3. "Judges and magistrates ought to exercise their authority as God's vicegerents, so that in this their unrighteousness they might seem to be claiming God Himself as their ally. Comp. l. 16."—*Bunsen.*

BY STATUTE. They claim to be acting according to law, seeking to hide their unrighteousness by a holy name. This seems, on the whole, the best rendering of the words, though others would render "*against* the law" (Symm *κατὰ προστάγματος*).

21. GATHER THEMSELVES IN TROOPS, like bands of brigands. For the word see xxxi. 13 [14], xxxv. 15, lv. 18 [19].

CONDEMN THE INNOCENT BLOOD, *i.e.* "condemn the innocent to death;" comp. Matt. xxvii. 4. Delitzsch wrongly explains, that because the blood is the life, the blood is the same as the person.

23. HATH REQUITED, lit. "hath caused to return," as vii. 16 [17], liv. 5 [7]. The preterites here express, not so much what has already taken place, as the confidence of faith which looks upon that which shall be as if already accomplished. Hence the interchange with the futures which follow.

[a] הוֹפִיעַ, imperat. but irregular; it should be either הוֹפִיעָה, the full form, as in lxxx. 2; or הוֹפַע, the shorter form; see Ges. § 64, 1*c*. It may,

however, be the pret., as in l. 2. So the LXX. ἐπαρρησιάσατο. And so Hengst., who refers to xciii., xcvii., xcix., as also beginning with the preterite.

[b] יִתְאַמְּרוּ, only here, not the Hithp. of אמר, "they say to themselves, or among themselves;" but more probably, as Schultens, connected with the Arab. أَمَرَ, *to command*, تَأَمَّرَ, *to carry oneself as ruler* (comp. أَمِير *Emir*). In Heb. the root appears in אָמִיר, *a high branch*, and אֱמֹרִי, *dweller in the mountains*, cognate with ימר, the Hithp. of which occurs Is. lxi. 6, rightly rendered by Jerome, *superbietis*.

[c] לוּלֵי. We must supply הָיָה, *nisi fuisset*, or *esset*, the apodosis being *propemodum*, or *cito* (see on ii. 12, note [f]) *occubuisset*. As regards the construction, comp. cxix. 92, cxxiv. 1—5; Is. i. 9; and for the pret. with כִּמְעַט lxxiii. 2, cxix. 87 (with the fut. lxxxi. 15).

[d] יְחָבְרְךָ, not Pual for יְחֻבַּרְךָ, with substitution of ŏ for ŭ, for this would still leave unexplained the dropping of the Pathach, but Qal with transposed vowel for יַחְבָּרְךָ. Comp. יָחְנְךָ (Gen. xliii. 29, Is. xxx. 19) for יָחָנְךָ, and תְּאָכְלֵהוּ (Job xx. 26) for תֹּאכְלֵהוּ. The same law holds, as Hupf. observes, in such forms as תְּאֵהֲבוּ for תְּאֶהָ', Prov. i. 22, &c. The ŏ in יְחָבְרְךָ points to a form יַחְבֹּר, which ought however to be יֶחְבַּר, as the root is intrans., and therefore must be pointed חָבֵר; but comp. יֶחְפַּץ and יַחְפֹּץ from חָפֵץ. For the construction, comp. יְגֻרְךָ, v. 5.

PSALM 95

THIS Psalm is one of a series,* as has been already observed, intended for the Temple worship, and possibly composed for some festal occasion. Both the joyfulness of its opening verses, and its general character, in which it resembles the 81st Psalm, would render it suitable for some of the great national feasts.

As to the date of its composition nothing certain can be said. The LXX. call it a Psalm of David; and the writer of the Epistle to the Hebrews, in making a quotation from the Psalm, uses the expression "in David," but this is evidently only equivalent to saying "in the Psalms." In the Hebrew it has no Inscription.

In Christian liturgies the Psalm has commonly been termed the Invitatory Psalm. We are all familiar with it, as used in the Morning Service of our Church; and it has been sung in the Western churches

* This *series* has preceded (from time immemorial) the Sabbath Psalms on Friday evening; they form the "reception of the Sabbath" (קבלת שבת).

from a very remote period before the Psalms of the Nocturn or Matins. (Palmer, *Orig. Liturg.* i. 221.)

"We may think of this Psalm as we sing it in our daily worship as prophetic of a better worship still, even of the perpetual adoration of that heavenly city, wherein the Apostle saw no temple, 'for the Lord God Almighty and the Lamb are the Temple of it.'"—Housman, *Readings on the Psalms*, p. 198.

It consists of two very distinct parts:—

I. The first is an invitation to a joyful public acknowledgement of God's mercies. Ver. 1—7.

II. The second (beginning with the last member of ver. 7 to the end) is a warning to the people against the unbelief and disobedience through which their fathers had perished in the wilderness.

1 O COME, let us sing joyfully unto Jehovah,
Let us shout aloud to the Rock of our salvation;
2 Let us go to meet His face with thanksgiving,
With psalms let us shout aloud unto Him.
3 For Jehovah is a great God,
Yea, a great King above all gods.

1—7. The character of the invitation here given, to worship God, not with penitence and brokenness of heart, but with loud thanksgiving, is the more remarkable, when we recollect in what a strain the latter part of the Psalm is written.

1. UNTO JEHOVAH. Augustine lays stress on this: "He invites to a great feast of joy, of joy not unto the world, but unto the Lord." And in the next clause, where the Latin has *jubilemus*, he explains it of a joy which runs beyond all words.

ROCK OF OUR SALVATION, as in lxxxix. 26 [27]. Comp. "rock of my refuge," xciv. 22.

2. GO TO MEET. Such is the proper and strict rendering of the word. See the same phrase xvii. 13, lxxxix. 14 [15]. The verb is used in the same sense as here, Micah vi. 6. In both places the E.V. has "come before," which does not sufficiently express the forwardness, the ready alacrity, which are really denoted by the verb.

WITH PSALMS. The LXX. ἐν ψαλμοῖς ἀλαλάξωμεν. The Syro-hex. adds "with the trumpet."

3. A threefold reason is given why this worship should be offered with glad hearts and loud thanksgivings—that Jehovah is a King more glorious than all "who are called gods, and who are worshipt," that He is the Creator of the world, that He is the watchful shepherd of His own chosen people.

ABOVE ALL GODS: not the angels, but all the gods of the heathen. Comp. Exod. xviii. 11. xv. 11, &c. It cannot be inferred from this language that the Psalmist supposed the heathen deities to have any real power, or real existence (comp. xcvi. 5). He is merely contrasting heathen objects of worship, clothed in the imagination of their worshipers with certain attributes, and the one true supreme object of worship, who *is* really all, and more than all, which the heathen think their gods to be. See more in the note on xcvii. 7.

4 (Even He) in Whose hands are the deep places[a] of the earth:
And the heights[b] of the mountains are His.
5 Whose is the sea,—and He made it,
And His hands formed the dry land,
6 O come let us worship and bow down,
Let us kneel before Jehovah our Maker.
7 For He is our God,
And we are the people of His pasture and the sheep of His hand.

To-day oh that ye would hear His voice:

6. O COME. Again the invitation to lowliest adoration and worship, called forth afresh by the remembrance of God's revelation to and covenant with Israel.

OUR MAKER, and ver. 7, OUR GOD, thus asserting the personal covenant relationship of God to His people (so Moses speaks of "the Rock who begat thee, the God who made thee," Deut. xxxii. 18); and here, as so often elsewhere, God's majesty as seen in Creation is linked with His love as seen in Redemption. See on xix. 7, xxiv. 1, 2.

7. PEOPLE OF HIS PASTURE, Hupfeld would correct, "people of His hand, and sheep of His pasture." But this is as dull as it is unnecessary. The subject of comparison and the figure are blended together.

The last member of this verse belongs clearly to what follows. It may however be rendered (1) either as the expression of a wish (as in the text), "Oh that," &c., lit. "*if* ye will hear . . . (then it shall be well with you)," the apodosis being understood: or (2), as in the LXX., Jerome, the E.V., and others, this clause may be the protasis, "if ye will hear His voice," ver. 8 introducing the apodosis, "harden not your hearts." So also in Heb. iii. 7, the writer of the Epistle, as usual, following the LXX. (3) A third interpretation, however, is possible, which is that of Ibn' Ezra, and others, according to which the first two members of ver. 7 are to be taken parenthetically, and the last member joined with ver. 6: "Let us kneel before Jehovah . . . to-day, if ye will hear His voice." In any case there is the same solemn strain of warning and expostulation breaking in upon the very joy and gladness of the Temple worship, as we have already observed in lxxxi. 6 [7]. Psalms like these seem to have had a double purpose. They were not only designed to be the expression of public devotion, the utterance of a nation's supplications and thanksgivings, but they were intended also to teach, to warn, to exhort. They were sermons as well as liturgies. Hence, too, the prophetic character which marks them. The Psalmist, like every true preacher, comes as an ambassador from above, speaking not his own words, but the words which God has given him, the words which God himself has uttered.

The warning here rests, as in lxxviii., lxxxi., &c., on the example of their fathers in the desert.

TO-DAY, the present moment, as critical and decisive, the day of

8 "Harden not your heart as at Meribah,
As in the day of Massah [trial] in the wilderness,
9 When your fathers tried Me,
Proved Me, yea [c] saw My work.
10 Forty years (long) was I grieved with (that) generation.[d]
And I said, 'It is a people that do err in (their) heart,

grace which may be lost; or the reference may be, and probably is, to some special circumstances under which the Psalm was composed. It "stands first," as Bleek observes, "with strong emphasis, in contrast to the whole past time during which they had shown themselves disobedient and rebellious against the Divine voice, as for instance during the journey through the wilderness, alluded to in the following verses: 'to-day' therefore means '*now;*' '*nunc tandem.*'" "To-day" may, however, apply not only to a particular historical crisis, but (as Alford on Heb. iii. 7 remarks) to every occasion on which the Psalm was used in public worship. "Often as they were faithless, the 'to-day' sounded ever anew; for 'the gifts and calling of God are without repentance.'"—*Tholuck.*

8. HARDEN NOT. Bleek asserts that this is the only place where to "harden the heart" is spoken of as *man's* act, elsewhere it is said to be God's act; but this is not correct. Man is said to harden his own heart, Exod. ix. 34; 1 Sam. vi. 6 (where the verb is כבד in the Piel); Prov. xxviii. 14, where the same verb is used as here, קשה; Deut. xv. 7; 2 Chron. xxxvi. 13 (where the verb אמץ is in the Piel).

MERIBAH, "striving" or "provocation." MASSAH, "temptation" or "trial." From Exod. xvii. 1—7 it would appear that *both* names were given to the same locality. But according to Num. xx. 1—13, the names were given to two different places on different occasions. Comp. also Deut. xxxiii. 8, "thy Holy One whom thou didst prove at Massah, and with whom thou didst strive at the waters of Meribah." The LXX., in this Psalm only, give παραπικρασμός as the equivalent of "Meribah:" elsewhere they have λοιδόρησις (Exod. xvii. 7); λοιδορία (Num. xx. 24); ἀντιλογία (Num. xx. 13, xxvii. 14; Deut. xxxii. 51, xxxiii. 8; Ps. lxxx. 8, cv. 32 [Heb. lxxxi. 7 [8]; cvi. 32]); the only places where they have preserved the proper name being Ezek. xlvii. 19, xlviii. 28 (see Alford on Heb. iii. 8).

IN THE WILDERNESS, of Sin, near Kadesh, where the second murmuring against Moses and Aaron for want of water took place (Num. xx. 1).

9. TRIED ME. In allusion to Massah, "trial," in ver. 8.

MY WORK. Whether miracles of deliverance, or acts of judgement, all that I did. See in Critical Note.

10. FORTY YEARS. These words in the quotation in Heb. iii. 9 are joined, as in the Syriac, with the preceding verse, and the word "wherefore" is inserted after them. This departs both from the Hebrew and the LXX. The alteration is evidently intentional, because the passage is afterwards quoted iii. 17 as it stands in the Psalm.

WAS I GRIEVED. The word is a strong word, expressive of *loathing* and *disgust.*

A PEOPLE THAT DO ERR, lit. "a people of wanderers in heart." There may be, as Hupfeld suggests, an allusion to the *outward* wandering in the wilderness as the punish-

And they do not know My ways;'
11 So that [e] I sware in Mine anger,
They shall not enter into My rest."

ment of this *inner* wandering. The same word is used of the former, cvii. 4.

AND THEY DO NOT, &c. This is almost equivalent to "*for* they do not," &c. Their ignorance of the straight way of God, "the king's highway" (as Bunsen calls it), is the reason that they wander in crooked by-paths.

11. I SWARE. The reference is to Num. xiv. 21, &c., 28, &c.

THEY SHALL NOT, lit. "if they shall enter," this elliptical form of the oath being equivalent to a strong negative. Hence in the LXX. and Heb. iii. 11, &c., *εἰ εἰσελεύσονται.*

MY REST, strictly "place of settlement," as the abode of God (comp. cxxxii. 8, 14), but used also of the land of promise (Deut. xii. 9), as a place of *rest* after the wandering in the wilderness.

The author of the Epistle to the Hebrews (iv. 6—9) argues, from the use of the word "to-day" in ver. 7, that the language of the Psalm is applicable not merely to the times of the Law, but also to the Gospel dispensation; and from the reference to God's rest here, "in David" (*i.e.* in the Book of Psalms), that Canaan was not the true rest. Joshua did not bring the people into God's rest, he says, otherwise we should not find in a Psalm written so long after the settlement of the people in Canaan, a warning addressed to them not to sin as their fathers, lest they also through unbelief should fail of God's rest. Hence, he argues, the rest must be still future, *ἀπολείπεται ἄρα σαββατισμός.* This, however, is not clear on the face of the Psalm, as the words "they shall not enter into My rest" seem to refer to the *past*, not the *present*, history of Israel. Hence Calvin remarks on the quotation in the Epistle to the Hebrews: "subtilius disputat quam ferant prophetæ verba."

[a] מֶחְקְרֵי א׳ Sym. rightly *κατώτατα γῆς.* But Aq. *ἐξιχνιασμοί*, and Jer. *fundamenta.* The LXX., (perhaps reading מרחקי), *τὰ πέρατα*, unless they gave this merely as an equivalent in sense.

[b] תּוֹעֲפוֹת (from יעף, *κάμνειν, κοπιᾶν*), according to its etymology, "*the weariness* that comes of hard labour," but not found in this sense. In Num. xxiii. 22, xxiv. 8, spoken of the buffalo, it can only mean *strength;* in Job xxii. 25, it is used of "silver as obtained by *toil* and *labour* from the mine." So Böttcher here would explain ת׳ ה׳, "mines in the mountains," parallel with "deep places of the earth;" others, "*treasures* of the mountains as obtained by labour." Others, again, following the LXX., *τὰ ὕψη τῶν ὀρέων*, "the *heights* of the mountains," a meaning of the word which is supposed to spring from "the *effort* and *weariness* with which men climb to the top of mountains" (cacumina montium, quia defatigantur qui eo ascendunt), an explanation etymologically unsatisfactory. The choice lies between the first and the last of these meanings. The first is supported by the passage in Numbers, the last has the parallelism in its favour.

[c] גַּם רָ' פָּ'. This has been explained (1) "*Although* they had seen all the wonders I had wrought in their behalf." (2) "*Yea* (not only did they prove Me, but) they saw My judgements, felt My chastisements." (So Hupf., Ewald, and Bleek.) The objection to the former is that גַּם does not elsewhere mean *although;* it is not necessary so to render it in Is. xlix. 15, to which Del. refers, though no doubt post-Biblical writers employ it in this sense. On the other hand, "My *work*" is more naturally understood of God's great redemptive acts than of acts of punishment, although it occurs in the latter sense lxiv. 10; Is. v. 12; Hab. i. 5.

[d] דּוֹר, without the article (LXX. *τῇ γενεᾷ ἐκείνῃ*), perhaps, as Del. explains, "not *hac* but *tali generatione*," the purely ethical notion being predominant in the word. But the absence of the article may be only poetical usage. The Targum has "with the generation in the wilderness."

[e] אֲשֶׁר, *so that,* as in Gen. xi. 7.

PSALM 96

THIS grand prophetic Psalm looks forward with joyful certainty to the setting up of a Divine kingdom upon earth. But it is only indirectly Messianic. It connects the future blessings, not with the appearance of the Son of David, but with the coming of Jehovah. And it has already been pointed out (in a note on Psalm lxxii. 17) that there are in the Old Testament two distinct lines of prophecy, culminating in these two advents. Their convergence and ultimate unity are only seen in the light of New Testament fulfilment. The same hopes, however, gather about both, as may be seen, for instance, by a comparison of this Psalm with such a passage as Isaiah xi. 1—9. Calvin, in his introduction to the Psalm observes, that it is "An exhortation to praise God, addressed not to the Jews only, but to all nations. Whence (he adds) we infer that the Psalm refers to the kingdom of Christ; for till He was revealed to the world, His name could not be called upon anywhere but in Judæa."

The LXX. have a double inscription :—

(1) *ὅτε ὁ οἶκος ᾠκοδομεῖτο μετὰ τὴν αἰχμαλωσίαν*, which is probably correct, as indicating that the Psalm was composed after the Exile, and for the service of the second Temple.

(2) *ᾠδὴ τῷ Δαυίδ*, which seems to contradict the other, but was no doubt occasioned by the circumstance that this Psalm, together with

portions of Psalm cv. and cvi., is given, with some variations (which will be found in the notes), by the author of the Book of Chronicles, as the great festal hymn which "David delivered into the hand of Asaph and his brethren to thank the Lord" on the day when the Ark was brought into the sanctuary in Zion.

The Psalm consists of four strophes (of which the first three are perfectly regular, consisting of three lines each):—

I. Jehovah is to be praised in all the world and at all times. Ver. 1—3.

II. He alone is worthy to be praised, for all other objects of worship are nothing. Ver. 4—6.

III. Let all the heathen confess this, and give Him the honour due to his name. Ver. 7—9.

IV. Let all the world hear the glad tidings that Jehovah is King, and even things without life share the common joy. Ver. 10—13.

Supposing the Psalm to have been sung antiphonally, verses 1 and 2, 4 and 5, 7 and 8, may have been sung by two bands of Levites alternately, the whole choir taking up the concluding verses of each stanza, verses 3, 6, 9. Then in the last strophe, verses 10, 11, 12 would be sung antiphonally, the whole choir taking up the grand solemn close of ver. 13, with fullest expression of voice and instrument.

1 O SING unto Jehovah a new song,
Sing unto Jehovah, all the earth.
2 Sing unto Jehovah, bless His name,
Publish His salvation from day to day.
3 Declare His glory among the nations,
His wonders among all the peoples.

4 For great is Jehovah, and highly to be praised,
He is to be feared above all gods;

1. A NEW SONG. See on xxxiii. 3. The new song is not the Psalm itself, but one which shall be the fit expression of all the thoughts and hopes and triumphs of the new and glorious age which is about to dawn. It is the glad welcome given to the King when He enters His kingdom. Comp. with this verse Is. xlii. 10, lx. 6, lxvi. 19.

2. PUBLISH, or "tell the tidings of." See lxviii. 11 [12], xl. 9 [10]. LXX. εὐαγγελίζεσθε.

4. The manifestation of God's glory. Comp. cxlv. 3, xlviii. 1 [2].

ABOVE ALL GODS (as in xcv. 3;

5 For all the gods of the peoples are idols,
But Jehovah made the heavens.
6 Honour and majesty are before Him,
Strength and beauty [a] are in His sanctuary.
7 Give unto Jehovah, O families of peoples,
Give unto Jehovah glory and strength;
8 Give unto Jehovah the glory due unto His name,
Bring presents, and come into His courts.
9 Bow yourselves before Jehovah in holy attire,
Tremble before Him, all the earth.
10 Say ye among the nations: Jehovah is King,—
Yea the world is established that it cannot be moved,—

see note on xcvii. 7). Here, as is plain from what follows, the heathen deities, which are IDOLS, lit. "nothings;" a favourite word in Isaiah for idols, but occurring also as early as Lev. xix. 4, xxvi. 1. See the strong assertions of their absolute nothingness in Is. xli., xliv.

5. JEHOVAH MADE THE HEAVENS. So has He manifested His power and majesty as the Creator in the eyes of all the world; but the chief manifestation of His glory is in Israel, "in His sanctuary." Compare the same strain in xcv. 3—7.

7—9. The families of the nations (see xxii. 27 [28]), themselves are called upon to take up the song in which Israel has made known to them the salvation of Jehovah. Comp. Zeph. iii. 9.

These three verses are taken partly from xxix. 1, 2.

7, 8. GIVE. We go into God's courts, it has been truly remarked, to *give* rather than to *get*. This is the principle of all true prayer, ascription more than petition.

PRESENTS (the collective sing. for the plural), in allusion to the Oriental custom which required gifts to be brought by all who would be admitted to the presence of a king. Compare xlv. 12 [13]; lxviii. 29 [30]; lxxii. 10.

INTO HIS COURTS. In 1 Chron. xvi. 29, "before Him," meaning the same thing. Comp. the parallelism above in ver. 6.

9. ATTIRE, or "array," but the word rather denotes *all* that lent solemnity and impressiveness to the service. See xxix. 2. 2 Kings viii. 22.

10. The glad tidings which the world is to hear. The world's largest hopes are to be fulfilled. A new era is to begin, a reign of righteousness and peace, a time so blessed that even the inanimate creation must be partakers of the joy. Comp. Is. xxxv. 1, xlii. 10, xliv. 23, xlv. 8, xlix. 13, lv. 12. With the coming of Jehovah and the setting up of His kingdom all the broken harmonies of creation shall be restored. Not "the sons of God" only, but the whole creation is still looking forward to this great consummation. (Rom. viii. 21.)

JEHOVAH IS KING, lit. "hath become King;" hath taken to Himself His great power and reigned. See xciii. 1; Rev. xi. 17. The LXX. rightly, *ὁ Κύριος ἐβασίλευσε*, with the addition in some copies of *ἀπὸ τοῦ ξύλου*, whence the Itala *Dominus regnavit a ligno*, on which Justin, Tertullian, Augustine, and others, lay great stress, although it is obviously opposed to the whole scope and character of the Psalm.

YEA THE WORLD, &c. This

He shall judge the peoples in uprightness.
11 Let the heavens rejoice, and let the earth be glad,
Let the sea thunder and the fulness thereof;
12 Let the field be joyful, and all that is therein.
Then shall all the trees of the wood sing for joy
13 Before Jehovah, for He cometh,
For He cometh to judge the earth ;
He shall judge the world in righteousness,
And the peoples in His faithfulness.

clause is introduced somewhat abruptly, and quasi-parenthetically, from xciii. 1. It describes one of the elements in Jehovah's government, but is it to be understood in a physical or a moral sense? It may be that the fact that God has so established the *natural* order of the world is alleged as showing His power and His right *as Creator* to rule. (So Rosenm) Or the meaning may be that the *nations of the world* (the inhabited earth), shaken and torn by war and anarchy, are now safe and peaceful under Jehovah's righteous sway. (So Delitzsch.)

Calvin has well combined the two senses: "Notatu vero dignum est quod subjicit de *stabilitate orbis*. Etsi enim scimus naturæ ordinem ab initio divinitus fuisse positum, eundem semper solem, lunam, et stellas resplenduisse in cælo, iisdem alimentis quibus fideles sustentatos fuisse incredulos, et eundem traxisse spiritum vitalem; tenendum est omnia esse confusa, et horribilem ἀταξίαν instar diluvii mundum in tenebris demersum tenere quamdiu impietas hominum animos occupat: quia extra Deum quid stabile esse potest? Non immerito igitur docet hic locus stabiliri orbem ut amplius non nutet, ubi rediguntur homines sub manum Dei. Unde etiam discendum est, quamvis suum officium peregant singulæ creaturæ, nihil tamen esse in mundo ordinatum, donec regiam sedem sibi Deus figat regendis hominibus." He refers to Ps. xlvi. 5 [6].

It may be owing to the abruptness of this clause that the Chronicler has transposed some of the clauses in his adaptation of the Psalm. His arrangement (1 Chron. xvi. 30—33) is as follows: "Tremble before Him all the earth, yea the world is established that it cannot be moved. Let the heavens rejoice, and let the earth be glad, and let them say among the nations, Jehovah is King. Let the sea thunder, and the fulness thereof. Let the field exult, and all that is therein. Then shall the trees of the wood shout for joy before Jehovah, for He cometh to judge the earth."

13. [This verse may have been sung antiphonally by the choir in some such way as is suggested in the Introduction to the Psalm.] HE COMETH. The repetition is full of force and animation. The participle is used to express more vividly the coming of Jehovah, as if actually taking place before the eyes of the Psalmist. It is a coming to judgement, but a judgement which is to issue in salvation. This judgement in righteousness and faithfulness, and the peace which follows thereon, are beautifully portrayed in Is. xi. 1—9.

[a] הוֹד וְגו׳. Instead of this the Chronicler has עֹז וְחֶדְוָה בִּמְקוֹמוֹ, "Strength and joy are in His place," חֶדְוָה being a late word formed from a verb which occurs in the Pentateuch, Exod. xviii. 9. Whether, as Del. suggests, the Chronicler put "in His place" instead of "in His sanctuary," because the Temple was not yet built, seems very doubtful.

PSALM 97

THE advent of Jehovah, and His righteous rule over the whole earth, is the subject of this Psalm, as of the last. Here, however, it would seem as if some great display of God's righteousness, some signal deliverance of His people, had kindled afresh the hope that the day was at hand, yea had already dawned, when He would take to Himself His great power and reign.

"Jehovah is King." Such is the glad assurance with which the Psalm opens. He has come to take possession of His throne with all the awful majesty with which He appeared on Sinai. All nature is moved at His presence. The heavens have uttered their message, telling of His righteousness, and all the nations of the world have seen His glory. His empire must be universal. Already the idols and the worshipers of idols are ashamed: and Zion rejoices in the coming of her King. He is near, very near. The first flush of the morning is already brightening the sky. They who love His appearing may look for Him, in holy abhorrence of evil and in faithfulness of heart, waiting till they enter into the joy of their Lord. Such is briefly the purport of the Psalm.

"If the bringing in of an everlasting worship gives its distinctive colouring to the foregoing Psalm, the final casting out of evil is the key-note of this: if the thought of the Great King bringing salvation to His people is foremost in that, in this it is the trampling down of His enemies: there he comes 'to diadem the right,' here 'to terminate the evil.'"—*Housman*, p. 203.

The coming of Jehovah as King and Judge is described almost in the same terms as the theophany in the Eighteenth and Fiftieth Psalms. The use of the past tenses in ver. 4—8, and in particular the vivid language in ver. 8, where Zion and the daughters of Judah rejoice in presence of Jehovah's judgements, are most naturally explained as occasioned by some historical event, some great national deliverance or triumph of recent occurrence; such, for instance, as the overthrow of Babylon and the restoration of the theocracy (so Ewald). The structure of the Psalm, like the last, consists of strophes of three verses.

I. In the first, the coming of Jehovah is portrayed as if actually present. Ver. 1—3.

II. In the second, its effects are described on nature, and its purposes with reference to the world at large. Ver. 4—6.

III. The third speaks of the different impression produced on the heathen and on Israel, and the exaltation of God above all earthly power as the final result. Ver. 7—9.

IV. The fourth is an exhortation to the righteous, and also a promise full of consolation. Ver. 10—12.

1 JEHOVAH is King: let the earth be glad,
Let the multitude of the isles rejoice.
2 Cloud and darkness are round about Him,
Righteousness and judgement are the foundation of His throne.
3 A fire goeth before Him,
And devoureth His adversaries round about.

4 His lightnings gave shine unto the world,

1. The strain of the preceding Psalm, xcvi. 10, 11, is here resumed. Comp. also Is. xlii. 10—12, li. 5.

JEHOVAH IS KING. Augustine, who understands this directly of Christ's advent, writes: "Ille qui stetit ante judicem, ille qui alapas accepit, ille qui flagellatus est, ille qui consputus est, ille qui spinis coronatus est, ille qui colophis cæsus est, ille qui in ligno suspensus est, ille cui pendenti in ligno insultatum est, ille qui in cruce mortuus est, ille qui lancea percussus est, ille qui sepultus est, ipse resurrexit. *Dominus regnavit.* Sæviant quantum possunt regna; quid sunt factura Regi regnorum, Domino omnium regum, Creatori omnium sæculorum?"

MULTITUDE OF THE ISLES, lit. "the many isles," or "many as they are." (Comp. Is. lii. 15.) The word rendered "isles" is used strictly of the islands and coasts of the Mediterranean Sea (as in lxxii. 10), but perhaps here, as in the later chapters of Isaiah, in a wider sense, of heathen countries at large.

2. The coming of God is thus frequently described by later prophets and psalmists in images borrowed from the theophany on Sinai (Exod. xix. 9, 16, xx. 21; Deut. iv. 11, v. 23); as in xviii. 9 [10].

THE FOUNDATION OF HIS THRONE: the word is singular, and means strictly "support." Comp. lxxxix. 14 [15].

3. A FIRE, as in l. 3. Comp. also Hab. iii. 5, and the whole description in that chapter, so solemn and so majestic, of God's coming to judgement.

4. GAVE SHINE UNTO. See on

The earth saw, and trembled.
5 The mountains melted like wax at the presence of Jehovah,
At the presence of the Lord of the whole earth.
6 The heavens have declared His righteousness,
And all the peoples have seen His glory.

7 Ashamed are all they that serve graven images,
That boast themselves in idols:
Bow down before Him, all ye gods.

lxxvii. 18 [19], whence the first member of this verse is taken: with the second compare lxxvii. 16 [17].

5. THE MOUNTAINS MELTED: comp. Judg. v. 5, Micah i. 4, and Ps. lxviii. 2 [3].

THE LORD OF THE WHOLE EARTH. This name of God occurs first in Joshua iii. 11, 13, where the Ark (at the passage of the Jordan) is called "the ark of Jehovah the Lord of the whole earth," as if emphatically, then when the people were about to occupy their own land, to distinguish Jehovah their God from the merely local and national gods of the heathen. The name is found again in Micah iv. 13; Zech. iv. 14, vi. 5.

6. HAVE DECLARED HIS RIGHTEOUSNESS. This is the end and purpose of God's coming (as in l. 6). He comes to judge, and the act of judgement is one which the whole world shall witness, as in lxxvii. 14 [15], lxxix. 10, xcviii. 3. Comp. the language used of the great deliverance from Babylon, Is. xxxv. 2, xl. 5, lii. 10, lxvi. 18.

7. This and the next verse describe the twofold result of the Divine judgement—the impression produced on the heathen and on Israel, the confusion of all worshipers of idols, and the joy and exultation of the people of God.

ASHAMED, a word frequently employed with the same reference by the prophet Isaiah. It is a shame arising from the discovery of the utter vanity and nothingness of the objects of their trust.

On this Augustine says: "Nonne factum est? Nonne confusi sunt? Nonne quotidie confunduntur? . . . Jam omnes populi gloriam Christi confitentur: erubescant qui adorant lapides. . . . Hanc gloriam ipsius cognoverunt populi; dimittunt templa, currunt ad ecclesias. Adhuc quærunt adorare sculptilia? Noluerunt deserere idola: deserti sunt ab idolis."

ALL YE GODS. The LXX. (προσκυνήσατε αὐτῷ πάντες ἄγγελοι αὐτοῦ) and the Syr. both understand these to be angels. But this is contrary both to usage (see note on viii. 5) and to the context. The Chald. paraphrases: "all who worship idols." But doubtless heathen deities are meant. As all the worshipers are confounded, so must all the objects of their worship be overthrown, as Dagon was before the Ark of the Lord; all must yield before Him who is the Lord of the whole earth. If this be the meaning, the line may be taken as a sarcastic, contemptuous challenge to the idols of the heathen. If so, we need not enter into the question whether angels or spiritual beings were the real objects of worship, idols being only their representatives. Augustine supposes a heathen excusing himself when charged with idol-worship by saying that he does not worship the image but

8 Zion heard and rejoiced,
And the daughters of Judah were glad,
Because of Thy judgements, O Jehovah.
9 For THOU, Jehovah, art most high above all the earth,
Thou art greatly exalted above all gods.

10 O ye that love Jehovah, hate evil ;
He keepeth the souls of His beloved,
He delivereth them from the hand of the wicked.
11 Light is sown [a] for the righteous,

"the invisible deity which presides over the image," and argues that this is a plain proof that the heathen worship not idols but demons, which is worse. He quotes in support of this view the language of St. Paul in 1 Cor. x. 19, 20, viii. 4. But, he continues, if the pagans say we worship good angels, not evil spirits, then the angels themselves forbid such worship : "Let them imitate the angels and worship Him who is worshipt by the angels ;" and then he cites the passage in the Latin Version, *Adorate eum omnes angeli ejus.* Calvin here, as in the two preceding Psalms, xcv. 3, xcvi. 5, understands by "gods" both angels and also those creatures of the human imagination, the projected images of their own lusts and fears, which men fall down and worship. "Quanquam proprie in angelos id competit, in quibus relucet aliqua Deitatis particula, potest tamen improprie ad deos fictitios extendi, acsi dixisset : Quicquid habetur pro Deo, cedat et se submittat, ut emineat Deus unus." Delitzsch refers to the addition made by the LXX. to the text of Deut. xxxii. 43, *καὶ προσκυνησάτωσαν αὐτῷ πάντες ἄγγελοι Θεοῦ*, which is quoted in Heb. i. 6, perhaps with a reference also to the Septuagint Version of this Psalm, and applied to the worship which the angels shall give to the first-born of God when He comes again [of course taking *ὅταν πάλιν εἰσαγάγῃ* to mean, "When He shall have brought in a second time into the world," &c.] to judge the world : "where it is implied that it is Jesus in whom Jehovah's universal kingdom is gloriously perfected."

8. HEARD AND REJOICED : borrowed from xlviii. 11 [12], where see note, and the opposite to "the earth saw and trembled," ver. 4. Although the coming of Jehovah has been portrayed in images full of awe and terror, yet here, as in the two preceding Psalms, it is described as a coming to be welcomed with jubilant gladness by His Church. In the same spirit our Lord, when speaking of the signs of fear which shall be the precursors of His second coming, says, "When ye shall see these things begin to come to pass, then lift up your heads : for your redemption draweth nigh."

10. The Psalm closes with a practical application, because the King and Judge is drawing near, a warning against the evil which is in the world, and an assurance of Divine protection and blessing to those who "hate evil." Comp. xxxiv. 14—22, xlv. 7 [8], cxxxix. 21, 22, 2 Cor. vi. 14—18.

11. LIGHT IS SOWN. The figure has been understood to mean that the prosperity of the righteous is future, just as seed is cast into the earth, and only after a time springs

And joy for the upright in heart.
12 Rejoice in Jehovah, O ye righteous,
And give thanks to His holy Name.

up and bears fruit. But it is far simpler to take the verb "sown" in the sense of "scattered," "diffused."

Milton uses the same figure of the dew:

"Now Morn her rosy steps in th' Eastern clime
Advancing, sow'd the earth with Orient pearl."

12. HOLY NAME, lit. "Holy Memorial."

The first member of the verse corresponds nearly with xxxii. 11*a*; the second is exactly the same as xxx. 4 [5]*b*. where see note.

[a] זָרֻעַ. The LXX. ἀνέτειλε, *hath sprung up*, *arisen*, and so the other Ancient Versions, as if they read זרח, as in cxii. 4, but the change is unnecessary. In Prov. xiii. 9, "the light of the righteous *rejoiceth*," it has been proposed in like manner to read יִזְרַח.

PSALM 98

THIS Psalm is little more than an echo of Psalm xcvi. Its subject is "the last great revelation, the final victory of God, when His salvation and His righteousness, the revelation of which He has promised to the house of Israel, shall be manifested both to His own people and to all the nations of the earth."

The Inscription of the Psalm in the Hebrew is only the single word *Mizmor*, "Psalm" (whence probably the title "orphan Mizmor" in the Babylonian Talmud, *Abodah Zara*, 24*b*. Comp. Tosaphoth (Additamenta) of the North French, South German, and English Rabbis twelfth and thirteenth centuries). In the Syriac the inscription runs, "Of the Redemption of the people from Egypt." Both the beginning and the end of the Psalm are taken from Psalm xcvi. The rest of it is drawn chiefly from the latter portion of Isaiah.

This Psalm follows the reading of the First Lesson in our Evening Service. It was first inserted there in 1552, though it had not been sung among the Psalms of Vespers or Compline.

[A PSALM.]

1 SING unto Jehovah a new song,
For He hath done marvellous things;
His right hand and His holy arm hath gotten Him salvation.
2 Jehovah hath made known His salvation,
Before the eyes of the nations hath He revealed His righteousness.
3 He hath remembered His loving-kindness and His faithfulness to the house of Israel;
All the ends of the earth have seen the salvation of our God.

4 Make a loud noise to Jehovah, all the earth;
Break forth and sing joyfully, and play,—
5 Play unto Jehovah with the harp,
With the harp and the voice of a psalm;
6 With trumpets and the voice of the cornet,
Make a loud noise before Jehovah, the King.

7 Let the sea thunder, and the fulness thereof,
The world and they that dwell therein.

1. The first two lines are taken from xcvi. 1; the last line, and ver. 2, 3, from Is. lii. 10, lxiii. 5.

HATH GOTTEN HIM SALVATION, or, "the victory," as in E.V. Comp. xliv. 4 [5] (and note); Is. lix. 16, lxiii. 5. I have preferred here the former rendering, because in the next verse the noun occurs from the same root, and there the rendering "salvation" is, I think, preferable to "victory."

2. BEFORE THE EYES, &c.; language especially applied (as in Isaiah) to the great deliverance from Babylon. See xcvii. 6.

RIGHTEOUSNESS, parallel with "salvation," as so frequently in the latter portion of Isaiah. See note on lxxi. 15.

3. LOVING-KINDNESS . . . FAITHFULNESS, the two attributes expressive of God's *covenant relationship* to His people.

4. BREAK FORTH AND SING, as in Is. lii. 9, though the more common phrase is "break forth into singing" (Is. xiv. 7; xliv. 23; xlix. 13; liv. 1).

5. VOICE OF A PSALM, as in Is. li. 3.

6. TRUMPETS, "*Chatzotzeroth*:—here only in the Psalter. They were the straight trumpets (such as are seen on the Arch of Titus) used by the priests for giving signals, Num. x. 2—10; 1 Chron. xv. 24, 28, &c. The *shofar* was the ordinary curved trumpet, cornet, or horn."—*Kay*.

7. Compare xcvi. 11 and xxiv. 1.

8 Let the streams clap their hands,
Together let the mountains sing for joy,
9 Before Jehovah, for He cometh to judge the earth.
He shall judge the world with righteousness,
And the peoples with uprightness.

8. CLAP THEIR HANDS. The same phrase occurs Is. lv. 12; elsewhere a different verb is used, as in xlvii. [2]; 2 Kings xi. 12. On the next verse see xcvi. 13.

PSALM 99

THIS is the last of the series of Royal Psalms, of Psalms which celebrate the coming of Jehovah as King. The first of the series is the 93rd. This opens with the announcement that "Jehovah is King," passes on to tell that His throne has been from everlasting, that He made the world and that He rules it—rules the rage of the elements and the convulsions of political strife, of which that is the figure—and then concludes with one brief glance at His revelation of Himself to His people, and the distinguishing glory of the house in which he deigns to dwell, "*Holiness* becometh Thine house for ever."

The 95th Psalm* ascribes glory to Him as "a great King above all gods" (ver. 3). The 96th would have the glad tidings run far and wide that "Jehovah is King," that "He shall judge the people righteously" (ver. 13). The 97th opens "Jehovah is King," speaks of the glory of His advent, and of the joy with which it is welcomed by His people. The 98th calls upon all lands to break forth into loud shouts "before the King Jehovah," to go forth to meet Him with glad acclaim, with the voice of harp and cornet and trumpet, as men go forth to meet a monarch who comes in state to take possession of the throne of his fathers. The 99th, like the 93rd and the 97th, opens with the joyful announcement that "Jehovah is King," and then bids all men fall down and confess His greatness, and

* The 94th Psalm seems out of place in the series; it does not, like the rest, speak of the reign of Jehovah; and the number seven, if we take the 100th Psalm as the closing Doxology, is complete without it.

worship Him who alone is *holy*. Both the first and the last of the series, the 93rd and the 99th, celebrate the kingly majesty and the holiness of Jehovah, and also the holiness of His worship.

All these Psalms, then, alike tell of the setting up of a Divine kingdom upon earth. All alike anticipate the event with joy. One universal anthem bursts from the whole wide world to greet the advent of the righteous King. Not Zion only and the daughters of Judah are glad, but the dwellers in far-off islands and the ends of the earth. Even inanimate nature sympathises with the joy; the sea thunders her welcome, the rivers clap their hands, the trees of the wood break forth into singing before the Lord. In all these Psalms alike, the joy springs from the same source, from the thought that on this earth, where might has no longer triumphed over right, a *righteous* King shall reign, a kingdom shall be set up which shall be a kingdom of *righteousness*, and judgement, and truth.

In this Psalm, not only the righteous sway of the King, but His awful holiness, forms the subject of praise; and the true character of His worshipers as consecrated priests, holy, set apart for His service, is illustrated by the examples of holy men of old, like Moses, Aaron, and Samuel.

The two principal divisions of the Psalm are marked by the greater refrain with which each closes, "Exalt ye Jehovah our God," &c. (ver. 5, 9). But the thrice-repeated lesser refrain, "He is holy," more full, as at the close (in ver. 9), "Jehovah our God is holy," marks also a strophical division, and is, in the words of Delitzsch, "an earthly echo of the Seraphic *Trisagion*" (comp. Is. vi. 3). We have thus three strophes or Sanctuses, ver. 1—3, ver. 4—5, ver. 6—9, the first and second consisting each of six lines. In each of these Jehovah is acknowledged in His peculiar covenant relation to His people. In the first, He is "great in *Zion*" (ver. 2); in the second He has "executed righteousness in *Jacob*" (ver. 4), and He is "Jehovah *our* God" (ver. 5); in the third, the great examples of this covenant relationship are cited from Israel's ancient history; and again God is twice claimed as "Jehovah *our* God" (ver. 8 and 9). In each there is the same exhortation to worship (ver. 3, ver. 5, ver. 9), and in each the nature of the worship and the character of the worshipers is implied, because the character of God is in each exhibited, "He is holy." But in the third Sanctus this is brought out most fully. The priestly character of all true worship is declared. All who call upon Jehovah call upon Him as His priests, all anointed with the same holy oil, all clothed in the same garments of holiness, "for Jehovah our God is holy."

Bengel (quoted by Delitzsch), recognizing this threefold partition of the Psalm, explains the subject somewhat differently. "The 99th Psalm," he says, "has three parts, in which the Lord is celebrated as He who is to come, as He who is, and He who was, and each part is closed with the ascription of praise, He is holy."—*Erklärte Offenb.*, S. 313.

1 JEHOVAH is King, the peoples tremble;
He sitteth throned upon the cherubim, the earth is moved.[a]
2 Jehovah in Zion is great,
And He is exalted above all the peoples.
3 Let them give thanks unto Thy great and fearful name:
He is holy.

4 And the King's strength loveth judgement;
THOU hast established uprightness,
THOU hast executed judgement and righteousness in Jacob.

1. IS KING, lit. "hath become King," *regnum capessivit.* See note on xcvii. 1.

HE SITTETH. This is a participle, and is, strictly speaking, not so much an independent clause as a further description of the manner of God's kingly rules: He rules sitting throned, &c. It also suggests "not only the *identity* of the heavenly King with the God who is worshipt in Zion, but also His *presence* in His temple."—*Moll.*

UPON THE CHERUBIM. See note on lxxx. 1 [2].

3. LET THEM GIVE THANKS, or the words may be taken as the utterance of the Psalmist's hope that God's "great and fearful Name" (Deut. x. 17) which is known in Israel shall be glorified in all the world: "they shall give thanks," &c. But the optative form of expression accords best with the exhortation in ver. 5, 9.

HE IS HOLY. This might be rendered "*It* is holy," *i.e.* the Name of God, mentioned just before. The meaning is the same in either case, for God's name "is God Himself in His revealed holiness," as Delitzsch observes. I have preferred the more immediately personal rendering, because it is obviously required in the repetition of the same words afterwards, ver. 5, 9.

4. AND THE KING'S STRENGTH, &c. This rendered as an independent clause is awkward, though it is so rendered by most of the Ancient Versions. But the Chald., Ibn Ez., Del., and others take the two last words of this member of the verse as a relative clause; Ibn Ez. renders: "It is strength and honour in a King who loves judgement." Del.: "And the strength of a King, who loveth judgement, Thou hast established in uprightness." Others carry on the construction from the last verse, taking the words "He (or, it) is holy," as parenthetical, thus: "They shall praise Thy great and fearful Name (it is holy), and the might of the King who (or, which) loveth righteousness." It must be confessed

5 Exalt ye Jehovah our God,
And bow down at His holy footstool :
He is holy.

6 Moses and Aaron among His priests,
And Samuel among them that call upon His Name—
They called upon Jehovah, and HE answered them.

that but for the words of the refrain, which it is awkward to take thus parenthetically, the sense and the construction are better preserved by this rendering. Certainly the use of the conj. "and" at the beginning of this verse is far more natural on either of these views than on the other. At present it is otiose, supposing ver. 4 to begin a fresh sentence. It is possible, I think, that the words "He is holy" did not stand at the end of ver. 3 in the original Psalm, and that they were subsequently introduced in order to complete the *Ter Sanctus.* The correspondence between the two greater refrains, the natural introduction of the words there, and their abruptness here, all render such a supposition at least not wholly improbable.

THE KING'S STRENGTH ; the same King who is mentioned ver. 1, Jehovah. His might is no arbitrary power, like that of earthly tyrants, but a judgement-loving might. His power only expresses itself in righteousness. He has "established uprightness" as the great eternal law of His government, the inner principle of His sway, and He has manifested it in all His acts : "He has *executed* judgement and righteousness in Jacob."

5. FOOTSTOOL : properly, the lower part or step of the throne (as Is. lxvi. 1, Ezek. xliii. 7) put for the throne itself. In cxxxii. 7 it is spoken, apparently, of the sanctuary, "His dwellings, or tabernacles," being in the parallelism. So the sanctuary is called "the place of My feet," Is. lx. 13. In 1 Chron, xxviii. 2 it is used of the ark of the covenant ; in Lam. ii. 1 of the holy city (or perhaps the Temple) ; in Is. lxvi. 1 (comp. Matt. v. 35) of the whole earth. Here it seems doubtful whether the earthly or the heavenly sanctuary is meant.

6. The apparent abruptness of the transition in this verse—which, however, is very natural in lyric poetry—to the examples of Moses, and Aaron, and Samuel, has led to a variety of explanations. Rosenmüller proposes to join this with ver. 4, the refrain in ver. 5 being regarded as parenthetical ; and takes this ver. as containing a fresh instance of God's goodness in hearing the prayers of His people. Delitzsch sees in it an appeal to the great men of old, and their experience as to the "absolute life and kingly rule of Jehovah." No explanation that I have seen satisfies me. I have already hinted, in the Introduction to the Psalm, at what I believe to be the train of thought. The great subject of the Psalmist's praise is the *holiness* of God. It is a *holy* God whom he calls upon all men to worship. It is "a holy footstool," "a holy mountain," before which they bow down ; it is therefore a holy worship which they must render. Such was the worship of His saints of old : and then likewise Jehovah manifested His holiness both in "forgiving" and in "taking vengeance" (ver. 8).

MOSES . . . AMONG HIS PRIESTS. The priestly office was exercised by Moses in the sprinkling of the blood of the covenant, Exod. xxiv.

7 In the pillar of a cloud He spake unto them;
They kept His testimonies and the statute that He gave them.
8 Jehovah, our God, THOU didst answer them,
A forgiving God wast Thou to them;
And (yet) taking vengeance of their doings.
9 Exalt ye Jehovah our God,
And bow down before His holy mountain;
For Jehovah our God is holy.

6—8, and again in the whole ritual for the consecration of Aaron and his sons, Levit. viii., as well as in the service of the sanctuary, before that consecration took place, Exod. xl. 22—27. So likewise he "called upon the Lord" as "a priest," in intercession for His people, Exod. xvii. 11, 12, xxxii. 30—32 (comp. Ps. cvi. 23); Num. xii. 13. Samuel also, though not here classed with the priests, but mentioned as a great example of prayer, not only like Moses discharged priestly functions, but also like Moses interceded for the people. We find him at Ramah offering sacrifices in the high place, and his independent priestly position so recognized by the people, that they would not partake of the sacrifice till he had blessed it (1 Sam. ix. 12, 13). We find him on the occasion of a battle offering a whole burnt-offering unto Jehovah (1 Sam. vii. 9), at the same time that he sternly rebukes Saul for presuming to do the same thing (1 Sam. xiii. 11—13). For the efficacy of his prayers and intercessions—on which, and not on sacrifices, the stress is here laid—see the instances in 1 Sam. vii. 8, 9, xii. 16—18. Comp. Ecclus. xlvi. 16, 17.

7. IN THE PILLAR OF A CLOUD. Strictly this applies only to Moses, or at the most only to Moses and Aaron: see Num. xii. 5.

THEY KEPT HIS TESTIMONIES; an evidence of the holiness of those who called on Jehovah, and whom He answered. This latter clause might be disposed in two lines, thus:—

"They kept His testimonies,
And He gave them a statute (statutes)."

This verse would then, like all the others in this strophe, consist of three lines.

8. WAST THOU, or "didst Thou prove thyself to be," LXX. εὐίλατος ἐγίνου αὐτοῖς. Cf. Ez. xxxiv. 7.

TAKING VENGEANCE. As it is clear that this cannot refer to all the three great examples cited above, certainly not to Samuel, the pronouns in this verse (and perhaps, as Calvin and others think, in ver. 7) must refer to the people at large, who, though not mentioned, are in the Psalmist's thoughts, as he goes back to their ancient history.

[a] תָּנוּט. The verb occurs only here instead of the more usual מוט. In most of the Ancient Verss. it is rendered, as well as יִרְגְּזוּ in the previous member, as an optative. The LXX. have ὀργιζέσθωσαν . . . σαλευθήτω; Jerome, *commoveantur . . . concutiatur*. But Mendels., Hupf., and Del. render the verbs as presents, which appears to me to be preferable. The two verbs describe the effects which immediately and necessarily follow from the inauguration and establishment of Jehovah's kingdom. For the sequence of tenses, cf. xlvi. 7.

PSALM 100

If we are right in regarding the Psalms xciii.—xcix. as forming one continuous series, one great prophetic oratorio, whose title is "Jehovah is King," and through which there runs the same great idea, this Psalm may be regarded as the Doxology which closes the strain. We find lingering in it notes of the same great harmony. It breathes the same gladness: it is filled with the same hope, that all nations shall bow down before Jehovah, and confess that He is God.

"This last Jubilate," says Delitzsch, "is the echo of the first—that, namely, which occurs in the first half of Psalm xcv. There we find all the thoughts which recur here. There it is said, ver. 7, 'He is our God, and we are the people of His pasture and the sheep of His hand.' And in ver. 2, 'Let us come before His presence with thanksgiving; let us sing joyfully to Him with Psalms.'"

"Among the Psalms of triumph and thanksgiving this stands pre-eminent, as rising to the highest point of joy and grandeur. No local restrictions, no national exclusiveness, can find place in the contemplation of God as the common Creator and Father of man: hence it is that no hymn or psalm in any subsequent age has found a readier response than this first appeal to the whole world to unite in worshiping Jehovah on the ground of common sonship and humanity." *

This Psalm is recited in the Jewish synagogues every day, except on Sabbaths and Festivals.

[A PSALM FOR THE THANK-OFFERING.[a]]

1 SHOUT aloud unto Jehovah, all the earth;

1. SHOUT ALOUD: used of the welcome given to a king who enters his capital, or takes possession of the throne, as in xcviii. 4, 6, lxvi. 1.

ALL THE EARTH. As in all the preceding Psalms, xciii.—xcix., so here, the hope of the Psalmist goes far beyond the narrow limits of his own people and country. The blessing of Abraham is become the heritage of the Gentiles. The whole world is to acknowledge Jehovah, and to rejoice before Him. So Augustine: "Et tamen hanc vocem audivit universa terra. Jam jubilat Domino universa terra, et quæ adhuc non jubilat jubilabit. Pertendens enim benedictio incipiente Ecclesia ab Jerusalem per omnes gentes, impietatem ubique prosternit, pietatem ubique construit. Et mixti sunt boni malis; et mali

* *The Psalms Chronologically Arranged*, p. 321.

2 Serve ye Jehovah with gladness,
Come before His presence with a song of joy.
3 Know ye that Jehovah, He is God:
He hath made us and we are His,[b]
We are His people and the sheep of His pasture.
4 O enter into His gates with thanksgiving,
Into His courts with praise:
Give thanks unto Him, bless His Name.
5 For Jehovah is good, His loving-kindness is everlasting;
And His faithfulness (endureth) unto all generations.

per omnem terram, et boni per omnem terram. In malis murmurat omnis terra; in bonis jubilat omnis terra."

2. SERVE YE. Comp. ii. 11; where, however, in accordance with the warlike character ascribed to the monarch, it is added "with fear," instead of "with joy" as here. "Libera servitus est apud Dominum," remarks Augustine, "libera servitus; ubi non necessitas, sed caritas, servit."

3. KNOW YE, *i.e.* learn by experience, as Theodoret explains, δι' αὐτῶν μάθετε τῶν πραγμάτων.

HATH MADE US: *i.e.* not merely "hath created us," but hath made us what we are, viz. His people. Comp. 1 Sam. xii. 6: "It is Jehovah that made (E. V. advanced) Moses and Aaron." See also Deut. xxxii. 6, 15; Ps. xcv. 6. And so Israel is called "the work (lit. *making*) of Jehovah," Is. xxix. 23, lx. 21.

WE ARE HIS. For the justification of this rendering see Critical Note, and comp. xcv. 7. Dr. Kay, observing that Psalms xciii.—c. are full of parallelisms to Is. xl.—lxvi., points out that this reading (that of the Q'ri) is supported by Is. xliii. 1: "And now saith the Lord *that created thee*, *O Jacob*, and *formed thee*, *O Israel*, fear not, for I have redeemed thee, I have called thee by My name; *Mine art thou*."

4. The knowledge that Jehovah has chosen Israel to be His inheritance and the sheep of His pasture is not to tend to the exclusion of others from the same privileges. On the contrary, all nations are to flow to Jerusalem, and worship in the Temple. What in Is. ii. 2, 3 appears in the form of prediction, is here invitation, as in Is. ii. 5. "His temple is open to all. They may enter in; and when they enter may expect great things; 'For Jehovah is gracious, and His loving-kindness and truth never fail,' according to the repeated expression of the Hallelujah-Psalms and Psalms of Thanksgiving." — *Delitzsch.*

5. GOOD, *i.e.* "gracious," "kind," as in xxv. 8, xxxiv. 8 [9].

[a] לְתוֹדָה. The expression is used apparently in a liturgical sense (like the analogous titles of xxxviii., lxv., xcii.), to denote that the Psalm was to be sung during the offering of thank-offerings. Compare זֶבַח ת', cvii. 22, cxv. 17, which is also termed simply תּוֹדָה, lvi. 13, 2 Chron. xxix. 31.

[b] וְלֹא א'. So the K'thîbh; the sense being, as it is commonly explained, "He hath made us (chosen us to be His people), and not we ourselves,"

—*i.e.* it was not of merit on our part, but of His grace. So the LXX., *αὐτὸς ἐποίησεν ἡμᾶς, καὶ οὐχ ἡμεῖς*, the Vulg., and the Syr. And the Midrash (Bereshith Rabba, c. 100, *ad init.*) finds in this confession the opposite to Pharaoh's boast, "I have made myself," Ezek. xxix. 3 (where, however, the rendering probably is as in E.V., "I have made it (the Nile) for myself"). But it is very doubtful if such a meaning would be thus expressed in Hebrew. Hence Symm. (who adopts the K'thîbh) gives a different explanation, *αὐτὸς ἐποίησεν ἡμᾶς οὐκ ὄντας*, and similarly Rashi.

But the Q'ri וְלוֹ, has the support of the Chald., Jerome, and Saadia, the Talmud and Midrash have it, it is found in nineteen MSS. of De R. and nine of Kenn., yields the best sense, is more in accordance with the parallel passage, xcv. 7, and has been adopted by the ablest modern critics, Ewald, Hupfeld, Delitzsch, &c. The Massoreth reckons fifteen passages in which לֹא is written, and לוֹ ought to be read: Ex. xxi. 8; Lev. xi. 21, xxv. 30; 1 Sam. ii. 3; 2 Sam. xvi. 18, xix. 7; Is. ix. 2, xlix. 5, lxiii. 9; Ps. c. 3; Job vi. 21, xiii. 15; Prov. xix. 7, xxvi. 2.

PSALM 101

THIS Psalm has been styled "the godly purposes and resolves of a king." It might also be described as "Speculum Regis," a mirror for kings and all that are in authority. It opens with the joyful contemplation of God's mercy and justice as kingly virtues, in their measure and degree to be manifested in earthly kings. It then records the king's pious resolve to keep his own heart and life unspotted, and to remove from him all that might lead him astray. Yet scarcely has he uttered the resolve, when, reflecting on all that such a resolve implies, he breaks forth in the earnest cry that God Himself would come to him and take up His dwelling with him, giving him grace to walk in "a perfect way." Thus having consecrated himself and his house, he declares further how he will provide for the purity of his court. With jealous care he will exclude those who are the bane of kings' houses—the slanderer, the proud, the deceitful, the liar. None but the faithful, none but those who, like himself, walk in a perfect (*i.e.* blameless) way, shall be admitted to places of honour and trust about his person. Finally, the work of zealous reformation shall extend to his capital, the city of Jehovah, and to the utmost borders of the land, that he may see realized under his sway the great ideal, "Ye shall be to Me a kingdom of priests and *a holy nation.*"

All this falls in admirably with the early part of David's reign, and the words are just what we might expect from one who came to the throne with a heart so true to his God. If the words "When wilt Thou come unto me?" may be taken to express, as seems most natural, David's desire to see the Ark at length fixed in the Tabernacle which he had prepared for it on Zion, the Psalm must have been written whilst the Ark was still in the house of Obed-edom (2 Sam. vi. 10, 11). "Zion was already David's royal seat, and the Tabernacle of Jehovah was there; but all had not yet been accomplished that was necessary for the proper ordering and administration of the kingdom. The new state had still to be organized, and the great officers of state and of the household to be chosen, men upon whose character so much always depends, and especially in despotic monarchies like those of the ancient world. David himself was standing at the threshold of the most critical period of his life, and, fully aware of the greatness of his responsibilities, did not feel himself as yet equal to the task which devolved upon him, to the burden which he was henceforth to bear. Still at this first period of his reign in Jerusalem, in the flush of victory, in the full splendour of his newly-acquired dominion over the whole of Israel, at a time when lesser princes would so easily have been dazzled by the deceitful sunshine of prosperity, or would have been terrified at the responsibility, David is only the more earnest in praising Jehovah and calling to mind His attributes, in striving to purify his own heart, and to form wise measures for the conduct of a strong and righteous rule, and in the resolution to keep far from him all that would bring a reproach upon himself or a stain upon his court. For the very sanctity of that city which had just been chosen as the dwelling-place of Jehovah required that nothing unholy should be tolerated therein. One who begins his reign with thoughts and resolutions such as these may well look for a happy termination of it, and nothing shows us more clearly the true nobleness of David's soul than this short Psalm. It is the spontaneous, inartificial expression of feelings long restrained; feelings and purposes, however, which form in themselves a whole, and which therefore naturally, and without effort, appear as a whole in the Psalm, and give it the unity which it possesses."*

* The passage in inverted commas is taken in substance from Ewald.

[A PSALM OF DAVID.]

1 OF loving-kindness and judgement will I sing,
Unto Thee, O Jehovah, will I sing psalms.
2 I will behave myself wisely [a] in a perfect way.
—When [b] wilt Thou come unto me?—
I will walk with a perfect heart within my house.
3 I will not set any vile thing before mine eyes;

1. LOVING-KINDNESS AND JUDGEMENT. These can only be the theme of praise as *Divine* attributes. But it is as a king who would frame his own rule and his kingdom after the Divine pattern that David makes these attributes the burden of his song. He meditates on the mercy and the righteousness of God, that he may learn the lesson of that mercy and righteousness himself. He meditates on them till his heart glows with the thought of their surpassing excellence, as seen in the Divine government, and with the earnest desire that the same kingly virtues may be transferred into his own life and reign. See note on lxxxv. 10.

SING PSALMS, or perhaps, rather, "play," *i.e.* upon the harp or other musical instruments. "Quum dicit, *Tibi, Jehovah, psallam,*" says Calvin, "Dei beneficio se agnoscit ad tam præclarum et honorificum munus esse destinatum; quia superbæ temeritatis fuisset ultro se ingerere. Non abs re autem regias virtutes duabus his partibus complectitur, clementia et judicio; quia sicuti præcipuum regis munus est suum cuique jus reddere, ita sollicitus erga suos amor et humanitas in eo requiritur. Nec abs re dicit Solomo: Clementia stabiliri solium (Prov. xvi. 12)."

2. I WILL BEHAVE MYSELF WISELY IN, or, "I will give heed to" (see Critical Note). The expression shows his sense of his own responsibility. The possession of absolute power too often dazzles and blinds men. An Eastern despot might have cast off all restraint, or at least might have allowed himself large license in the indulgence of his passions or his follies, almost without scandal or hatred. The nobler, therefore, is this resolve.

WHEN WILT THOU COME. It would be possible to render: "I will behave myself wisely in a perfect way when Thou comest unto me;" but the question is far more expressive. It bursts forth from the heart, moved and stirred to its inmost centre, as it thinks of all the height and depth of that resolve to "walk in a perfect way." How shall a frail son of man keep his integrity? The task is too great for his own strength, honest and sincere as the resolution is, and therefore he cries, "When wilt Thou come unto me?"—come to be my abiding guest—come not only to dwell in Zion, in Thy tabernacle, but with me Thy servant, in my house and in my heart (comp. John xiv. 23), giving me the strength and the grace that I need? The expression is no doubt remarkable as occurring in the Old Testament; though if it be understood as referring to the removal of the Ark to Zion (see Introduction to the Psalm), it would be but a claiming of the promise in Exod. xx. 24: "In all places where I record My Name *I will come unto Thee,* and bless thee.

WITH A PERFECT HEART, lit. "in the perfectness, or integrity, of my heart." So "a perfect way" might be rendered "the way of integrity."

3. SET BEFORE MINE EYES, *i.e.* as

I hate the sin of unfaithfulness [c]; it shall not cleave unto me.

4 A froward heart shall depart from me;
A wicked person I will not know.

5 Whoso privily slandereth [d] his neighbour, him will I destroy.
Whoso hath a high look and proud heart, him I will not suffer.

an example to imitate. According to Calvin, he speaks in the previous verse of the manner in which he will regulate his private life; in this of his duties as a king.

VILE THING, lit. "thing of villany." The noun is that which is wrongly rendered in the A.V. of the Historical Books, "Belial," as if it were a proper name. It is really a compound noun meaning "that which profiteth not." Comp. Deut. xv. 9. See on Ps. xli. 8.

THE SIN OF UNFAITHFULNESS, lit. "the doing of turnings aside" (if we take the noun as an abstract), or, "the doing of them that turn aside," *i.e.* I hate to act as they do (if we take the word as an adjective). The alliteration of the sibilants in the three words is noticeable. See more in the Critical Note.

All such deviations from truth, from integrity, from that Divine law by which he rules himself, shall not "cleave" to him. Temptations to such a course may beset him. The whisper might come, Policy requires this course, craft must be met by craft, power is given to be used, kings are above law, and the like. But he refuses to listen to the whisper of the serpent, and when it would fasten its fangs in him, he shakes it off.

4. First David proves himself, laying down the rule for his own guidance; then he determines what his court and household shall be.

In this verse he repudiates generally "the froward heart" and "the wicked person." In the following he enters more into detail.

A WICKED PERSON, or "wickedness;" but the former accords better with "the froward heart" (comp. Prov. xi. 20) in the parallelism.

5. The secret slanderer, seeking to ingratiate himself into his prince's favour by pulling down others, and the haughty, over-bearing noble (ver. 6), would be no uncommon characters in any court, least of all an Oriental court. Such persons would David destroy. Thus he exercised the kingly virtue of "judgement" (ver. 1). "As a private individual he could never have ventured on such a measure; but when he was placed on the throne, he received from God's hand the sword with which he was to punish wrongdoing."

A HIGH LOOK &c., lit. "whoso is lofty of eyes and wide of heart," the latter denoting a heart puffed up and blown out with pride (comp. Prov. xxi. 4, xxviii. 25). Elsewhere the phrase, "a wide heart," occurs in a very different sense. It is said of Solomon that God gave him "a wide heart," *i.e.* comprehensiveness, a large grasp, the power not only of gathering facts, but the power of seeing their mutual relation,—breadth of sympathy, and breadth of understanding. In cxix. 32, Is. lx. 5, the phrase denotes a feeling of liberty and of joy. In this last sense, the expression "my heart is dilated" occurs constantly in the "Arabian Nights." Comp. 2 Cor. vi. 11: Ἡ καρδία ἡμῶν πεπλάτυνται (where see Stanley's note).

I WILL NOT SUFFER, or "I cannot away with," Is. i. 13; Jer. xliv. 22.

6 Mine eyes are upon the faithful in the land, that they
may dwell with me.
Whoso walketh in a perfect way, he shall minister unto me.
7 He that worketh deceit shall not dwell within my house,
He that speaketh lies shall not be established in my
sight.
8 Morning by morning will I destroy all the wicked of the
land,
That I may cut off all the workers of iniquity from
the city of Jehovah.

6. MINE EYES ARE UPON. Comp. xxxii. 8, xxxiv. 15 [16], lxvi. 7. His ministers shall be chosen, not for high birth, or gifts of fortune, or talents, or accomplishments, or flattering lips, or supple compliance, but for incorruptible fidelity ; the word "faithful" implying that faithfulness to God is the basis of such fidelity to their king.

WHOSO WALKETH IN A PERFECT WAY, *i.e.* with evident reference to ver. 2, "whoever has laid down for himself the same rule of integrity, is actuated by the same purity of motive as I myself am."

7. WORKETH DECEIT, as in lii. 2 [4].

BE ESTABLISHED, or "abide," "continue :" comp. cii. 28 [29].

8. MORNING BY MORNING. Fast as the evil springs under shelter of the darkness, it shall be destroyed with the returning light. This is the common explanation, but I believe that the allusion, beyond all question, is to the Oriental custom of holding courts of law in the early morning. (See the same allusion in Jer. xxi. 12, "Execute judgement in the morning, and deliver him that is spoiled," &c. ; Zeph. iii. 5, "Morning by morning doth He bring His judgement to light." See also 2 Sam. xv. 2, and comp. Luke xxii. 66 ; John xviii. 28.)

Day by day will he exercise his work of righteous judgement, purging out all ungodliness from the Holy City. His zeal is like the zeal of Phinehas, a zeal for God and for His honour. He will have a pure state, a pure city, as the writer of the 104th Psalm hopes to see a pure earth (civ. 35), without spot or stain of sin. It is like the dream which fascinated the Roman poet of an *Astræa redux*. It is a hope which finds its accomplishment in the Apocalyptic vision, in that new Jerusalem into which "there shall in no wise enter any thing that defileth, or worketh abomination, or maketh a lie." (Rev. xxi. 27.)

[a] אַשְׂכִּילָה. See Critical Note on xli. 1 [2]. According to Hupf. with prep. (as here, and Dan. ix. 13, with בְּ, and elsewhere with אֶל, עַל, לְ), it can only have the meaning of *to regard*. But in Dan. i. 4 we have the Hiph. part. followed by בְּ, apparently in the other sense of *behaving wisely*, and hence the rendering of the E.V., "I will behave myself wisely," may be defended. Delitzsch explains the verb by the noun מַשְׂכִּיל in xxxii. 1, xlvii. 8, as expressing "poetic meditation," *will dichtend ehren.*

[b] מָתַי ת'. The rendering given in the text is the most obvious. It is that of the LXX., Πότε ἥξεις πρὸς μέ ; and has been adopted by the E.V.

It would be possible, however, (1) to take מָתַי, not as an interrogative, but as a conjunction, *when, as often as:* compare the similar usage in Arab. and Syr., and that of other interrogative words, as for instance מִי, xxv. 12, xxxiv. 13. (2) תָּבוֹא may be 3d fem., referring to דֶּרֶךְ or תָּמִים (so Maur.), "may it come to me," *i.e.* become my possession. But to speak of "a way," or even of "perfectness"—taking תָּמִים as a neut. noun (see on xv. 2, note [a])—as "coming" to a person, is a strange expression, to which the words "within my house" in the next line form no real parallel.

[c] עֲשֹׂה, inf. constr. for עֲשׂוֹת, as in Gen. xxxi. 28; l. 20; Prov. xxi. 3: comp. רְאֹה, Gen. xlviii. 11, and perhaps בְּזֹה, Is. xlix. 7.

סֵטִים. It seems most natural to take this as an abstract = שֵׂטִים, Hos. v. 2 (see note on xl. 5), after the analogy of זֵדִים, xix. 14. The verb almost requires this, lit. "the doing of apostasies or faithlessnesses." Ewald admits that this is the simplest construction, but thinks that the passage in Hosea is against it, as well as the sing. יִדְבַּק. Hence he renders, "the doing of the false," *i.e.* so to act as the false do, taking סֵט as an adjective.

[d] מְלוֹשְׁנִי (K'thîbh), Part. Po., with the connecting vowel of the old stat. constr. (Ges. § 93. 2, Ew. § 211 *b*). According to Hupf. the Q'ri is Piel for מְלַשְּׁנִי, like תְּרַצְּחוּ, lxii. 4; but it may only be the shortened form of the Poel with Kametz Chatûph instead of Cholem, in which case it will be read *m'loshni.*

PSALM 102

THIS Psalm must have been written by one of the exiles in Babylon, probably towards the close of the Captivity, when the hope of a return seemed no longer doubtful. In mournful strains he describes his bitter lot. Sorrow and pain had been very busy with him. His very heart was smitten within him, as the grass is withered in the hot eye of the sun. He was alone, with no friend to comfort him; his enemies turned his misery into a proverb; his life was drawing to a close under the heavy wrath of God.

But when he has time to look away from his sorrow, a prospect so bright and so glorious opens before him, that in the thought of it all else is swallowed up and forgotten. Zion's deliverance is at hand. Her God has not forsaken her. The grounds on which his hope rests are broad and manifold; for Jehovah is the everlasting King (ver. 12); the time fixed in His counsels is come (ver. 13); the hearts of her children are moved with a more passionate longing for her restoration (ver. 14); the prayer of His suffering people has prevailed, the sighing of the prisoner has entered into His ears (ver. 17, 19, 20). A new nation shall be born in Zion, and other nations and kingdoms shall be gathered into her to praise Jehovah (ver. 18, 21, 22).

Once again, as for a moment, the sadness of the exile and the sufferer prevails. His life is ebbing away, his heart and his flesh fail. Shall he be permitted to look upon that glory with the thought of which he has been comforting himself, the vision of which has been passing before his eyes? "O my God, take me not away in the midst of my days!" is the natural and touching petition which breaks from his lips, as he fears lest his eyes should be closed in death before that glory appears. And then suddenly, as if every cloud of apprehension were dispelled, he triumphs in the thought that there is One who changeth not; that though the solid frame of the universe itself should crumble into dissolution, yet He is the same "yesterday, to-day, and for ever," the one Hope and Stay of His children now and in all generations to come.

On the Messianic character of the Psalm, and the quotation made from it in the Epistle to the Hebrews, see the remarks at the end on ver. 25—27. It is strange that this quotation should have been passed over without any notice not only by commentators like De Wette and Hupfeld but even by Calvin, Tholuck, and Hengstenberg.

This Psalm is clearly individual, not national, and must have been intended for private rather than liturgical * use, as the Inscription seems designed to inform us. This Inscription is peculiar; it stands quite alone among the Tities prefixed to the Psalms; for it describes the character of the Psalm, and marks the circumstances under which it should be used. In all other instances the Inscriptions are either musical or historical.

Besides the prologue, ver. 1, 2, and the Epilogue, ver. 23—28, the Psalm consists of two main divisions, the Complaint, ver. 3—11, and the Consolation, ver. 12—22.

[A PRAYER OF THE AFFLICTED, WHEN HE IS OVERWHELMED, AND BEFORE JEHOVAH POURETH OUT HIS COMPLAINT.]

1 O JEHOVAH, hear my prayer,
And let my cry come unto Thee.

1, 2. The opening words are such as are found in other Psalms: comp. xviii. 6 [7]; xxxix. 12 [13]; xxvii. 9 ("hide not Thy face"); lix. 16 [17] ("in the day when I was in distress"), and xviii. 6 [7]; xxxi. 2 [3] ("incline Thine ear unto me"); lvi. 9, [10] ("in the day when I

* Since the beginning of the seventeenth century however, and perhaps from an earlier date, it has been used in the Jewish synagogues as the introductory Psalm to "the little Day of Atonement," *i.e.* the Eve of the New Moon.

2 Hide not Thy face from me; in the day when I am in distress;
Incline Thine ear unto me;
In the day that I call, answer me speedily.

3 For my days are consumed in smoke,
And my bones are burnt up as a firebrand.
4 My heart is smitten [a] like grass and withered,
For I have forgotten to eat my bread.
5 Because of the voice of my groaning,
My bone cleaveth to my flesh.
6 I am like a pelican of the wilderness,
I am become like an owl of the ruins.
7 I have watched, and have been [b]

call"); lxix. 17 [18], cxliii. 7 ("answer me speedily"). But all these are forms of expression which would easily pass into the common language of prayer.

2. This verse may admit of a different arrangement of its clauses:—

Hide not, &c. . . . in the day of my distress,
Incline, &c. . . . in the day that I call;
Answer me speedily.

So Hupfeld; but I have followed the accents.

3. IN SMOKE, as in xxxvii. 20. There is no need to adopt the reading of some MSS., "*as* smoke;" nor again is it necessary to render in the next clause, "as *with* a firebrand" (Hupfeld). The bones are burned (see on lxix. 3) as the brand is when placed on the fire. Comp. xxii. 15 [16], xxxi. 10 [11], xxxii. 3.

4. SMITTEN, as by a sun-stroke. Comp. cxxi. 6; Hos. ix. 16; Jon. iv. 8.

I HAVE FORGOTTEN, in the sorrow of my heart, as in cvii. 18; Job xxxiii. 20; 1 Sam. i, 7, 8, xx. 34; 1 Kings xxi. 4; Dan. vi. 18. [19]. So too in Homer, *Il.* xxiv. 129.

5. MY BONE. The Heb. has the singular, and the E.V. retains the singular in Job xix. 20, but the sing. may perhaps be collective, for the plural.

TO MY FLESH. More naturally in Lam. iv. 8, "my bones cleave to my *skin;*" the expression denoting extreme emaciation. In Job xix. 20, however, it is, "my bone cleaveth to my skin and to my flesh," which may refer to a state of weakness and relaxation brought on by severe pain, in which the bones have lost their power of motion.

6. A PELICAN . . . AN OWL. Both are mentioned Lev. xi. 17, 18, and the former as inhabiting the wilderness, Zeph. ii. 14; Is. xxxiv. 11. The LXX. have πελεκάν and νυκτικόραξ. The owl is called in Arabic, "mother of the ruins."

7. I HAVE WATCHED, sleep having been driven away by sorrow. With the next clause of the verse may be compared Virg. *Æn.* iv. 462:—

"Solaque culminibus ferali carmine bubo
Visa queri, et longas in fletum ducere voces."

And *Georg.* i. 403:—

——"de culmine summo
Nequicquam seros exercet noctua cantus."

Ovid also has—

"In adverso nocturnus culmine bubo."

Like a lonely bird on the house-top.
8 All the day long have mine enemies reproached me,
They that are mad against me[c] have made their oaths by me.
9 For I have eaten ashes like bread,
And mingled my drink with weeping;
10 Because of Thine indignation and Thy wrath;
For Thou hast taken me up and cast me away.
11 My days are like a shadow that declineth,
And I am withered like grass.

12 But THOU, O Jehovah, sittest throned for ever,
And Thy memorial is to all generations.

8. MADE THEIR OATHS BY ME, *i.e.* when they curse, choose me as an example of misery, and imprecate upon themselves or others my misfortunes—say, "God do to me, to thee, as He has done to this man." Comp. Is. lxv. 15; Jer. xxix. 22.

9. ASHES LIKE BREAD, Lam. iii. 16. Comp. Ps. xlii. 3 [4], "my tears are my food," lxxx. 5 [6].

10. "The acknowledgement is the same as in xc. 7–9. It is sin which has thus provoked God's displeasure; the two nouns, 'indignation' and 'wrath,' are in the Hebrew the strongest which the language possesses."—*Delitzsch.*

THOU HAST TAKEN ME UP, &c. God's wrath has seized and whirled him aloft, only to cast him, as worthless, away. So in Is. xxii. 18, "He will toss thee like a ball into a large country." Comp. Job xxvii. 21, xxx. 22; Is. lxiv. 6; Ezek. iii. 14. Others explain, "only to dash him the more forcibly to the ground;" but the verb properly means *to cast away*, as in li. 11 [13]; Job xviii. 7.

11. THAT DECLINETH. The word is used properly of the day at its close (as in Jud. xix. 9), or the sun as setting, and so here transferred to the evening shadows (comp. cix. 23), which would strictly be said to *lengthen*. The figure describes the near approach of death.

12. BUT THOU. This is the great consolatory thought by which he rises above his sorrow. He, the individual, may perish, but Zion's hopes rest on her Eternal King. And yet this might seem, as Calvin remarks, a far-fetched consolation. What is it to us that God changeth not, that He sitteth King for ever, if meanwhile our own condition is so frail and feeble that we cannot continue for a moment in one stay? His unchangeable peace and blessedness do but make our life seem the more complete mockery. But the Psalmist recalls God's promises to His Church, especially that great covenant promise, "I will dwell in the midst of you" (Exod. xxv. 8). Resting on this, he feels sure that God's children, however miserable their state, shall have their share in that heavenly glory wherein God dwelleth. Because God changes not, His promise and covenant change not, and therefore we may ever lift our eyes to His throne in heaven, from which He will surely stretch forth His hand to us.

SITTEST THRONED, as in ix. 7 [8], xxix. 10.

THY MEMORIAL, as in Exod. iii. 15. Some MSS. read "Thy *throne*:" which, however, may have come from the parallel passage, Lam. v. 19.

13 THOU wilt arise (and) have compassion upon Zion,
For it is time to have pity upon her,[d]
For the set time is come.
14 For Thy servants find pleasure in her stones,
And have pity upon her dust.
15 And the nations shall fear the Name of Jehovah,
And all the kings of the earth Thy glory,
16 Because Jehovah hath built Zion,
He hath appeared in His glory;
17 He hath turned to the prayer of the poor-destitute,
And hath not despised their prayer.
18 This shall be written for the generation to come,
And a people new-created shall praise Jah.

13. Because God is eternal, therefore He will have compassion on Zion. Or we may connect this verse with the following: THOU, Jehovah, the covenant God and our Father, wilt rebuild the walls of Zion, for even *we* her children love her very dust.

HAVE PITY UPON, lit. "be gracious unto," or as the E.V. "favour."

THE SET TIME. See on lxxv. 2. It is not necessary to understand this definitely of the seventy years prophesied by Jeremiah, xxv. 11, 12, xxix. 10. It is rather the time when her warfare is accomplished.

14. STONES . . . DUST. It is strange that Luther and others should have understood these of the materials for building the new city. They evidently denote the ruins of the old (Neh. iii. 34 [E.V. iv. 2], iv. 4 [E.V. iv. 10]. It is not less strange that Hengstenberg should assert that we have here only a *figure* representing the low and ruinous condition of Zion, because in the Psalm there are no traces of the destruction of Jerusalem.

HAVE PITY UPON HER DUST (the same verb as in verse 13). Zion was not only dear to them in her glory, when the splendour of her Temple riveted every eye; but her very dust is sacred, her very ruins are dear. To this day pious Jews have the dust of Jerusalem (or of Palestine) cast on their bodies before burial. "Quamvis subversum sit templum, et deformis tantum vastitas illuc appareat, fideles tamen, in ejus amore manere defixos, in putridis lapidibus et corrupto cæmento agnoscere Dei gloriam." — *Calvin.* And then he applies all this to the spiritual Zion, the Church, bidding us remember that the more mournful her desolations, the less should we cease to love her; yea, rather the more earnestly should our sighs and prayers go up on her behalf.

15. The effect produced on the heathen world by the manifestation of God's glory, as seen in the redemption and restoration of His people, which is not only the accomplishment of a sovereign purpose, but vouchsafed in answer to prayer.

17. POOR-DESTITUTE. I have retained this rendering of the P.B.V. because the word expresses utter nakedness and destitution. It only occurs here and Jer. xvii. 6.

18. SHALL BE WRITTEN. The only place in the Psalms where the memory of great events is said to be preserved in writing: elsewhere (as in xxii. 30 [31], xliv. 1 [2], lxxviii. 2 [3]) it is left to oral transmission.

A PEOPLE NEW-CREATED, or "a people to be created," as in xxii. 31

19 For He hath looked down from His holy height,
From heaven hath Jehovah beheld the earth,
20 To hear the sighing of the prisoner,
To set at liberty those that are doomed unto death;
21 That men may declare the name of Jehovah in Zion,
And His praise in Jerusalem;
22 When the peoples are gathered together,
And the kingdoms to serve Jehovah.

23 He hath brought down my strength [e] in the way,
He hath shortened my days.
24 I said, O my God, take me not away in the midst of
my days;—
Thy years are to all generations.

[32], "a people that shall be born." There is, as Calvin remarks, an implied antithesis between the new creation of the people and their present destruction. "The return from the Captivity was like a second birth." It was a *παλιγγενεσία*. See the quotation from Cicero in the note on lxxxvii. 5. "The passage strikingly teaches that even when the Church seems dead it can be created anew when God wills. Let us never therefore despair, but rest assured that He who created a world out of nothing, can also bring His Church out of the darkness of death."

19. HE HATH LOOKED. Comp. Deut. xxvi. 15.

20. DOOMED UNTO DEATH. Heb. "sons of death." See on lxxix. 11.

22. On this gathering of the nations in Jerusalem comp. xxii. 27 [28], lxviii. 32 [33]; Is. xlv. 14. It is a fulfilment of the prophecy in Gen. xlix. 10.

Verses 18—22 express again in a somewhat different form what has already been said in verses 13—17: Thus, "Thou wilt arise," &c., ver. 13, answers to ver. 19, each describing the first movement of the Divine compassion. Again, ver. 17, like ver. 20, ascribes God's merciful interference to the prayer of His people. Ver. 15, like verses 21, 22, speaks of the effect to be produced on the world at large.

23. Again he returns to the contrast between his own weakness and the brevity of human life, on the one hand, and the eternity and unchangeableness of God on the other (see above, ver. 11, 12), finding in this list his perfect satisfaction and rest.

IN THE WAY, *i.e.* in the journey of life. Those who suppose the Psalm to express the feelings rather of the nation at large than of the individual, see here an allusion to the journey through the wilderness, as in Exod. xviii. 8; Num. xvii. 12, 13 [27, 28]. xx. 14.

24. The abrupt transition in this verse is full of pathetic beauty. The prayer that his life may not be prematurely cut short seems to spring in this instance not merely from a natural clinging to life (as in Hezekiah's case, Is. xxxviii. 10, 11), but from the intense desire to see God's glory manifested in Israel's restoration. Then, having uttered that prayer, without waiting for the answer, he magnifies God's eternity and unchangeableness. He

25 Of old Thou hast laid the foundation of the earth,
And the heavens are the work of Thy hands:
26 They shall perish, but Thou remainest,
Yea, all of them shall wax old as a garment,
As a vesture shalt Thou change them, and they shall be changed;
27 But THOU art the same,
And Thy years shall have no end.
28 The children of Thy servants shall continue,

finds in these his strength in weakness; he feels that he can rest on the Everlasting Arms. He draws his highest consolation from the thought, that though he himself may perish, cut off in the midst of his days, though the heavens and the earth may be changed, and wax old as a garment, yet He who created them is ever the same, that His purposes cannot be frustrated, that His Church, the children of His servants, shall abide, the witness and the monument of His love.

25. The *creation* of the world implies its transitoriness. That which had a beginning shall have an end. He alone who created all cannot change. Comp. Is. li. 6, liv. 10. Elsewhere the order of nature is spoken of as unchanging, as in cxlviii. 6. Comp. Gen. viii. 22. And such expressions occur as "the everlasting mountains," "the everlasting heavens:" but as *compared with God* all that is most abiding has upon it the impress of decay and death. On the other hand, there is nothing here which contradicts the promise made elsewhere of "new heavens and a new earth" (2 Peter iii. 13).

27. THOU ART THE SAME, lit. "Thou art He." Comp. the same form of expression, Is. xli. 4, xlvi. 4; Job iii. 19. Or, in a different sense, as in Deut. xxxii. 39, "I am He," *i.e.* I am God, I am Jehovah, the only true God: comp. Is. xliii. 10, 13, xlviii. 12, lii. 6; and see Neh. ix. 6, "Thou art He, Jehovah alone,' &c.

28. CONTINUE, lit. "dwell," *i.e.* in the land, as in xxxvii. 29, lxix. 36 [37], where the full expression occurs.

Verses 25—27 are quoted in the Epistle to the Hebrews (i. 10—12) as addressed to Christ, and form a part of the writer's proof from the Old Testament that He, as the Son of God, is higher than the angels. The quotation stands between two others, one from the 45th, the other from the 110th Psalm, bearing on the same argument. But these are, both of them Messianic Psalms and the principle on which the quotation rests is sufficiently obvious. It is by no means so easy to understand why the words of this Psalm should have been quoted, as it does not seem at first sight to be a Messianic Psalm. It may be observed, however, (1) that it is in this sense Messianic, that it looks forward to Israel's redemption from captivity, and the future glory of Zion; (2) that, as has been observed in the note on Ps. lxxii., and in the General Introduction, Vol. I. p. 54, there are two great lines of Messianic hope running through the Psalms, the one human, the other Divine; the one of which the reign of the Son of David, the other of which the advent of Jehovah, is the great end and object. Here the Psalmist is occupied with the latter, the appearing of Jehovah in His glory. (3) This identification of the Jesus of the New Testament with the Jehovah of the Old is what we find elsewhere; comp. John xii. 41

And their seed shall be established before Thee.

with Is. vi. (Isaiah sees the glory of Jehovah, St. John tells us it was the glory of Christ), and John xix. 37, "they shall look on Him whom they pierced," which in Zech. xii. 10 is language used directly of Jehovah. The difference between these quotations in St. John and the one in the Ep. to the Hebrews is, that *the argument* in the latter *requires* that the Messianic character of the Psalm should be conceded. (4) Not only the revelation, the *appearing* of Jehovah in Zion, but also the creation of the world (ver. 25) would point to the Great Mediator, the Eternal Word, as the Person here spoken of, and on this last ground, especially, the quotation in the Epistle to the Hebrews seems to rest.

[a] חוּכָּה, incorrect writing for הֻכָּה, as in Hos. ix. 16. See on xlv. note [l].

[b] וָאֶהְיֶה. If the reading is correct, it is clear that the accent (Athnâch) is misplaced. Olsh. ingeniously conjectures וָאֶהֱמֶה (comp. lv. 18). Instead of בּוֹדֵד many MSS. of Kenn. and De R. have נוֹדֵד, *wandering*, as the Syr. also renders (the Chald. gives both), but contrary to the Massoreth on Is. xiv. 31, Hos. viii. 9.

[c] מְהֹלָלַי, Po. part. pass. (occurring also Eccl. ii. 2), with the objective suffix. Comp. for a similar constr. וַיִּלָּחֲמוּנִי, cix. 3; but the part. lends itself more readily to this kind of construction, as the suffix may be regarded, in a measure, as possessive; comp. קָמַי, xviii. 40.

[d] לְחֶנְנָהּ, Inf. Qal. The not unusual expanded form of this verb, as for instance in Is. xxx. 18, with Segol, instead of Chiriq or Pathach.

[e] כחו. The Q'ri is כֹּחִי, which in this instance seems preferable, as more in accordance with the parallelism; but if we retain the K'thîbh we may render either (1) "he hath brought down," or 'humbled," or "afflicted with his strength, He hath shortened," &c.; or (2) "His strength hath humbled, it hath," &c.

PSALM 103

THIS beautiful Psalm is the outpouring of a full heart in thanksgiving to Jehovah for His grace and compassion, both as experienced by the Psalmist in his own life, and also as manifested to his nation in their history. It celebrates especially God's mercy in the forgiveness of sin, and that tender pity, as of a human father, wherewith He remembers the frailty, and stoops to the weakness, of His children. It is a hymn of which the text and motto are to be found in that revelation of Himself which God gave to Moses when He proclaimed Himself as "Jehovah, tenderly compassionate and gracious, long-suffering, and abundant in goodness and truth" (Exod. xxxiv. 6).

Nothing certain can be said as to the author and date of the Psalm, though various conjectures have been hazarded. The Hebrew title gives it to David, the Syriac still more definitely assigns it to his old age. Rosenmüller supposes it to have been written after his sin in the matter of Uriah, a supposition which appears to me to be wholly without foundation. De Wette places the Psalm near the end of the Exile, on the ground that the Poet celebrates so largely God's grace and long-suffering, manifested to His people in spite of their sins and their idolatry. Not one word, however, hints at idolatry as the sin of which they had been guilty, nor is there a word to connect the Psalm with the Exile.

The argument built on the supposed later (Aramaic) forms which this Psalm has in common with Psalms cxvi., cxxiv., cxxix., cxxxix., is not absolutely conclusive for a post-Exile date, for the same forms occur in 2 Kings iv. 1—7. Still, such forms do not occur in David's time, or in Psalms in the earlier Books ascribed to him, and they must fairly be regarded either as marking a dialectic variation (see Critical Note on ver. 3), or a time when Aramaic influence had begun to make itself felt.

Ewald, who thinks that this and the next Psalm were written by the same author, regards both as Temple-Psalms, composed after the Exile, the first praising Jehovah as the Redeemer of His people in the various circumstances of their history, the second praising Him as the Creator and Ruler of the world. There is little, however, to connect the two Psalms, except that both begin and end with the same self-exhortation, "Bless Jehovah, O my soul."

Others, again, attempt to connect this with the preceding Psalm. So Rieger observes : "To feel sin and death, and with this feeling to wrestle for grace and reconciliation, and to seek after the kingdom of God and His righteousness, is the subject of the 102nd Psalm ; to feel sin and death, and then to have received reconciliation and the Spirit which quickeneth, and so to praise God, and in faith and patience to join oneself to all God's saints, is the subject of the 103rd Psalm." Delitzsch, who quotes this with approbation, takes the same view.

The Psalm consists of three parts:—

I. A prelude, in a strain of trustful gladness, in which the Psalmist seeks to stir up gratitude within him, by the review of God's mercies to him as an individual. Ver. 1—5.

II. The body of the Poem, in a more reflective tone, full of a quiet, tender, pathetic, even melancholy beauty, in which, after a brief allusion to the facts of the national history, the great covenant relationship of God to His people forms the prominent ground of hope amid human sins and transitoriness. Ver. 6—18.

III. A triumphant conclusion. Joy in the remembrance of God's goodness to himself and his people predominates over every other feeling. Such a joy must utter itself in praise. Praise seems its natural employment, and therefore the natural employment of all other creatures which it summons to a holy sympathy and fellowship with itself. Ver. 19—22.

[(A PSALM) OF DAVID.]

1 BLESS Jehovah, O my soul,
And all that is within me (bless) His Holy Name.
2 Bless Jehovah, O my soul,
And forget not all His benefits ;
3 Who forgiveth all thine iniquity,[a]
Who healeth all thy diseases,

1. ALL THAT IS WITHIN ME ; not as opposed to outward or mere lip service, but expressing the desire to enlist every thought, faculty, power, the heart with all its affections, the will, the conscience, the reason, in a word the whole spiritual being, all in man that is best and highest, in the same heavenly service.

2. FORGET NOT. This touches the secret spring of so much ingratitude :—forgetfulness, the want of recollection, or gathering together again of all the varied threads of mercy. Comp. Deut. vi. 12, viii. 11, 14. "Si oblivisceris, tacebis."

3. FORGIVETH, the first and greatest of all the Divine benefits to the soul burdened with a sense of guilt and defilement : therefore also that which calls first for acknowledgement. "God's benefits will not be before our eyes, unless our sins be also before our eyes." —*Augustine.*

DISEASES or "sicknesses," primarily, at least, of body, as in Deut. xxix. 21 ; 2 Chron. xxi. 19 : and this agrees with what follows ; though possibly the maladies of the soul may be included. "Even when sin is forgiven," says Augustine, "thou still carriest about with thee an infirm body . . . . Death is not yet swallowed up in victory, this corruptible hath not yet put on incorruption, still the soul herself is

4 Who redeemeth thy life from the pit,
Who crowneth thee with loving-kindness and tender mercies,
5 Who satisfieth thy mouth [b] with good (things),
(So that) thy youth reneweth itself [c] as the eagle.

6 Jehovah executeth righteousness

shaken by passions and temptations. . . . [But] thy sicknesses shall all be healed, doubt it not. They are great, thou wilt say; but the physician is greater. To an Omnipotent Physician no sickness is incurable; only suffer thyself to be healed, thrust not away His hand; He knoweth what He doeth. . . . A human physician is mistaken sometimes; why? Because he did not make that which he undertakes to heal. God made thy body. God made thy soul; He knoweth how to re-create that which He created; He knoweth how to re-form that which he formed; only be thou still under the hands of the Physician . . . suffer thou His hands, O soul that blesseth Him, forgetting not all His benefits; for He healeth all thy sicknesses."

4. FROM THE PIT (see on xvi. 10); including death, the grave, Hades. The Targum renders, "from Gehenna."

CROWNETH. The love of God not only delivers from sin, disease, and death. He makes His children kings, and weaves their crown out of His own glorious attributes of loving-kindness and tender mercies.

5. SATISFIETH. Giving Himself to us as the bread of life; as Athanasius says: *Τῶν πνευματικῶν ἡμᾶς ἐνέπλησεν ἀγαθῶν, ἑαυτὸν ἡμῖν ἄρτον ὄντα ζωῆς ἐπιδιδούς.* And Augustine, observing that every creature has its own good: "Seek thine own good, O soul. *None is good but one, that is God.* The highest good, this is thy good. What, then, can he want who hath the highest good? . . . God is this good. What kind of good who can say? Behold we cannot say, and yet we are not permitted to be silent."

AS THE EAGLE, *i.e.* so that in strength and vigour, thou art like the eagle. The rendering of the E.V., "so that thy youth is renewed like the eagle's," is grammatically justifiable, but very unnecessarily makes the Psalmist responsible for the fable of the eagle's renewing its youth (see at end of Critical Notes). Neither this passage nor Is. xl. 31 countenances any such fable. There is an allusion, no doubt, to the yearly moulting of the feathers of the eagle and other birds, the eagle being selected as the liveliest image of strength and vigour. The P.B.V. gives the sense rightly: "Making thee young and lusty as an eagle." And so Reuss: "Et te fait rajeunir comme l'aigle."

6. He passes from his own experience to that of the Church at large: God's mercies to the individual are only a part of that vast circle of mercy which embraces all Israel. The connection is thus traced by Sanchez in his paraphrase:—

"Thou hast shown mercy to me, Thou hast on various occasions executed judgement on those who have persecuted and oppressed me, and others of Thy people. These are Thy ways which Thou didst show to Moses, and to Thy people in the wilderness.—The Book of Deuteronomy from the 4th to the 10th chapter, and again from the 27th to the 31st, teaches nothing else but this, that Jehovah is full of compassion and long-suffering." *Los Salmos*, tomo ii. p. 34.

RIGHTEOUSNESS AND JUDGEMENT. The words are in the plural,

And judgement for all that are oppressed.
7 He made known His ways unto Moses,
His acts unto the children of Israel.
8 Jehovah is full of compassion and gracious,
Long-suffering and plenteous in loving-kindness.
9 He will not alway be contending,
Neither keepeth He (His anger) for ever.
10 Not according to our sins hath He dealt with us,
Neither according to our iniquities hath He requited us;
11 For as high as the heaven is above the earth,
So great [d] is His loving-kindness upon them that fear Him.
12 As far as the East is from the West,
So far hath He removed our transgressions from us.
13 Like as a father hath compassion on (his) children,
So Jehovah hath compassion on them that fear Him.
14 For He knoweth our frame,
He remembereth [e] that we are dust.

which therefore must either be used intensively for the singular (see note on lxviii. 35), or perhaps rather to denote *the several acts* in which Jehovah had displayed His righteousness.

ALL THAT ARE OPPRESSED; the Church of God being a suffering Church.

7. HIS WAYS, in allusion to the prayer of Moses, Exod. xxxiii. 13: "If I have found grace in Thy sight, make known to me Thy way, and let me know Thee."

8. The verse is taken from Exod. xxxiv. 6. Comp. lxxxvi. 5, 15, cxi. 4, cxlv. 8; Joel ii. 13; Nehem. ix. 17, 31.

9. Compare Is. lvii. 16, "For not for ever will I contend, and not perpetually will I be angry; for the spirit would fail before Me, and the souls that I have made."

KEEPETH. See the same absolute use of the verb, Lev. xix. 18, "Thou shalt not keep (*i.e.* cherish any grudge) against the children of thy people;" Nah. i. 2; and of the synonymous word (*shâmar*) Jer. iii. 5, 12. Calvin compares the French phrases *il lui garde*, *il me l'a gardé*.

11. The expressions in xxxvi. 5 [6], lvii. 10 [11], are similar. God's love is like Himself, infinite. It cannot be measured by all the measures of the universe.

12. REMOVED OUR TRANSGRESSIONS. The forgiveness of sin (as in ver. 3) is the great proof of God's love. "The expression describes, in language which might be that of the N.T., the effects of justifying grace."—*Del.* Comp. Micah vii. 19, "Thou wilt cast all their sins into the depths of the sea;" Is. xxxviii. 17, "Thou hast cast all my sins behind Thy back."

14—16. Man's weakness and transitoriness is itself an appeal to God's fatherly compassion. Compare Gen. viii. 21, and see the same ground taken in Ps. xxxix. 5 [6], 13 [14], lxxviii. 39; Job vii. 7.

14. OUR FRAME, lit. "our *fash-*

15 As for frail man, his days are as grass,
As a flower of the field, so he flourisheth.
16 For the wind passeth over it, and it is gone,
And the place thereof knoweth it no more.
17 But the loving-kindness of Jehovah is from everlasting to everlasting upon them that fear Him,
And His righteousness unto children's children ;
18 To such as keep His covenant,
And to those that remember His precepts to do them.

19 Jehovah hath established His throne in the heavens,
And His kingdom ruleth over all.
20 O bless Jehovah, ye His angels,
That are mighty in strength, that execute His word,
Hearkening[f] to the voice of His word.

ioning," as in Gen. ii. 7, "And He *fashioned* (formed) man of the dust," &c. ; or as a potter moulds and fashions the clay, Is. xxix. 16, xlv. 9, 11 ; Job. x. 8.

15. Compare, for the figures in this and the next verse, xxxvii. 2, 10, 36, xc. 5, 6 ; Is. xl. 6—8, li. 12 ; Job xiv. 2 ; and for the phrase, "the place thereof knoweth it no more," Job vii. 10.

17. The same contrast between man's transitoriness and God's unchangeableness which occurs in Psalm xc. For the third time God's mercy and loving-kindness is said to be upon "them that fear Him," comp. ver. 11, 13, as if to remind us that there is a love within a love, a love which they only know who have tasted that the Lord is gracious, who fear Him and walk in His ways, as well as a love which "maketh the sun to shine, and sendeth rain upon the just and the unjust." In the next verse there is the same limitation, "To such as keep His covenant," and to those who not only know but "*do*" His will. The blessings of the covenant are no inalienable right ; *manicipio nulli datur ;* children's children can only inherit its blessings by cleaving to it. Comp. Exod. xx. 6, xxiv. 7 ; Deut. vii. 9.

FROM EVERLASTING TO EVERLASTING. "Ab æterno, ob prædestinationem ; in æternum, ob beatificationem ; altera principium, altera finem nesciens."—*S. Bernard.*

19. The concluding portion of the Psalm extols the greatness and majesty of Him who has thus stooped in pity to His children. The Psalmist had begun by calling upon his own soul to bless Jehovah for His goodness ; he had associated with himself, as partakers in that goodness, all who feared the Lord. Now he concludes by calling on the angels in heaven and all creation, inanimate as well as animate, to ascribe blessing and honour and power to Him who sitteth upon the throne. Lastly, from all that vast congregation of worshipers praising God, he turns to himself, that his voice may not be wanting in the mighty anthem, "Bless thou Jehovah, O my soul."

20. MIGHTY IN STRENGTH, or "strong *warriors*" (see note on lii. 1), as afterwards "all His *hosts*," by

21 Bless Jehovah, all ye His hosts,
Ye ministers of His, that do His pleasure.
22 Bless Jehovah, all ye His works,
In all places of His dominion.
Bless Jehovah, O my soul.

which not the stars but the angels are meant, as is plain from the parallelism, " ye ministers of His that do His pleasure." Compare the λειτουργικὰ πνεύματα of Heb. i. 14. See also Ps. civ. 4 ; Dan. vii. 10.

22. ALL HIS WORKS. In the same way in Ps. cxlviii. first the angels and then the whole creation is called upon to praise God.

On the closing words, " Bless Jehovah, O my soul," J. H. Michaelis observes, " Magnum πάθος habet hic Psalmi finis, in quo Psalmista per epanalepsin ad animam suam revertitur."

[a] עֲוֹנֵכִי . . . תַּחֲלוּאָיְכִי. These forms of the fem. suffix, *ēchi* in the sing. and *ây'chi* in the plural are commonly regarded as later Aramaic forms. In the Psalter they occur, it is true, only in the later Psalms, as in cxvi. 7, 19 (where in ver. 12 occurs also the pure Chaldee masc. suffix, ־וֹהִי), cxxxv. 9, cxxxvii. 6. But they are rather to be regarded as instances of a return to the original fuller form of the 2d pers. fem. (corresponding to the original form אַתִּי, afterwards shortened into אַתְּ), a return due, perhaps, to Aramaic influence. It is, however, remarkable that these same forms are found (in the K'thîbh) in a passage in the history of Elisha, 2 Kings iv. 1—7, a fact which certainly seems to suggest a dialectic, *i.e.* North Palestinian variation. The only other passage in which (according to Del.) this form of suffix occurs is Jer. xi. 15.

[b] עֶדְיֵךְ. It is difficult to determine the meaning of the word here. In xxxii. 9 I have adopted the rendering *trapping*, *harness*. Hupfeld contends for a similar meaning here : he takes it to denote the whole *apparatus* of external means by which life is maintained, all, whether in the way of ornament or of use, which is to a man what trappings are to a horse ; all that he may be said, figuratively, to *put on* (עדה), just as men are said, for instance, to put on strength, pride, &c. But as Hitz. pertinently observes the verb "satisfy" is wholly against such an interpretation. Hengst. also renders the word *ornament* or *beauty*, but supposes it to be used, like the word *glory* elsewhere, for *the soul*, and tries to obviate the objection to this, viz. that the soul is addressed in ver. 1, by saying that in what precedes the idea of the whole person has imperceptibly taken the place of the soul. Maurer and Köster keep to the same rendering, viz., *ornament*, but think that *the body* is meant, spoken of by anticipation as restored to youth and beauty.

In Ezek. xvi. 7, where the dual form of the word occurs, the A.V. has "ornaments," but Hitz. contends for the sense of "cheeks," which certainly accords better with the dual.

Of the older interpreters, the Syr. has *thy body*, the LXX. *desire* (ἐπιθυμίαν), the Chald. *old age* (either as connecting the word with עַד, *time* or as parallel to *youth* in the next member), and this last is followed by De Wette and by Gesen. in his Lex., though in his Thes. he prefers the more general sense of *ætas*, and thinks that youth rather than old age is meant. Finally, there is the interpretation of Ibn 'Ezra, Qimchi, and others, who here, as in xxxii. 9 (see Critical Note there), give the sense *mouth*, lit. *cheek* [just as Cicero uses *bucca* in the same general way, *quicquid in buccam venerit, scribito*, "whatever comes into your *head*"]. There are thus, in short, three meanings assigned to the word: (1) *that which is put on*, *ornament*, *beauty*, &c., according to which the rendering would be, "Who satisfieth all *that thou hast about thee;*" the awkwardness of this it is impossible not to feel: (2) *time* (whether *youth* or *old age*), a rendering to which Hupf. would incline, if it were allowable to set aside usage, and to go back to the root עָד, *ætas:* (3) *mouth*, for which may be alleged the interpretation of the older versions in xxxii. 9, and the Arabic cognate. This last, which in xxxii. 9 has Ewald's support (though here he has "deinen *Muth*"), is perhaps, on the whole, simplest, though I give it with some hesitation. Hitz. has "deine Backe;" Reuss: "ta bouche."

[c] תִּתְחַדֵּשׁ: 3 fem. sing. with plur. noun, according to the well-known rule, Ges. § 146, 3. There is no reason to render this verb as a passive. The proper reflexive meaning is far more lifelike and expressive.

[d] גבר with עַל, in the same sense, cxvii. 2. Elsewhere the phrase has a different meaning, Gen. xlix. 26; 2 Sam. xi. 23. Hence Hupf. would here read גבה.

[e] זָכוּר, strictly a passive *infixus*, but according to Ges. § 50, Obs. 2 = *infixum* (*menti*) *habens*.

[f] לִשְׁמֹעַ; gerundial = *obediendo*.

The fable of the eagle's renewing its youth has received different embellishments. The version of Saadia, given by Qimchi, is as follows: The eagle mounts aloft into heaven till he comes near to the seat of central fire in the sun, when, scorched by the heat, he casts himself down into the sea. Thence he emerges again with new vigour and fresh plumage, till at last in his hundredth year he perishes in the waves. Augustine's story is more elaborate and far less poetical. According to him, when the eagle grows old, the upper curved portion of the beak becomes so enlarged, that the bird is unable to open its mouth to seize its prey. It would die of hunger, therefore, did it not dash this part of its beak against a rock till the troublesome excrescence is got rid of. Then it can devour its food as before, vigour is restored to its body, splendour to its plumage, it can soar aloft; a kind of resurrection has taken place. Thus it renews its youth. And then, wonderful to say, having told this story gravely, he makes Christ the rock, adding, "in Christ thy youth shall be renewed as the eagle's."

PSALM 104

THE general argument of this Divine Ode of Creation has been well expressed by Calvin. "This Psalm," he says, "differs from the last, in that it neither treats of God's special mercies bestowed on His Church, nor lifts us to the hope of a heavenly life; but painting for us in the frame of the world, and the order of nature, the living image of God's wisdom, power, and goodness, exhorts us to praise Him, because in this our frail mortal life He manifests Himself to us as a Father." It is a bright and living picture of God's creative power, pouring life and gladness throughout the universe.

There are several points in the Psalmist's treatment of his subject which deserve especial notice.

1. First there is here, what is not to be found to the same extent, if at all, in any other ancient poetry, the distinct recognition of the absolute dependence of the universe, as created, upon the Creator: "He is before all things, and by Him all things subsist." This truth is throughout implied. It forms the very basis, and so to speak, main thread of the poem.

2. Secondly, the great work of creation is here regarded not as a thing of the past merely: the Universe is not a machine once set a-going, and then left to its fate, or to inexorable laws. The Great Worker is ever working.* "The world and all things owe their past origin and their present form to the continuous operation" of God. Creation ever repeats itself; death is succeeded by life. He who made, renews the face of the earth. It is the same profound view of the relation of the Kosmos to the Creator, which St. Paul exhibits in his speech on Mars' hill. He, too, is careful not to separate the past from the present. "God, who *made* (past, ὁ ποιήσας) the world," did not then leave the work of His fingers: the streaming forth of His Omnipotence and His love was not checked or stayed; on the contrary, every part of His creation rests at every moment on His hands; "He *giveth* (present, διδοὺς) to all life and breath, and all things (Acts xvii. 25).

3. Thirdly, in its main outline the Poem follows the story of creation contained in the first chapter of Genesis. There manifestly

---

* See the excellent remarks on the importance of this view of nature in reference to miracles, in the Rev. D. J. Vaughan's valuable work, *Christian Evidences and the Bible*, p. 97.

is the source whence the Psalmist drew. Meditating on that sublime description, itself a poem, he finds in it his subject and his inspiration. And yet the Psalm is not a mere copy of the original. Breathing the same lofty spirit, it has a force and an originality of its own. In some respects the Psalm, even more strikingly than the early record, exhibits the infinite greatness, the order, the life of the Universe. "It is remarkable," says a Spanish commentator, "how the lyric verse, while losing nothing of its freedom and fire (*bizarría ed entusiásmo*), contrives at the same time to preserve all the force and simplicity of the picture of nature presented to us in Genesis." * But the creation of Genesis is a creation of the past; the creation of the Psalm is a creation of the present. The one portrays the beginning of the eternal order, the other its perpetual, living spectacle. Hence, too, the Ode has far more animation than the Record. The latter is a picture of still life; the former is crowded with figures full of stir and movement. How vivid are the images which it calls up,—the wild ass roaming the sands of the wilderness, stooping to slake his thirst at the stream which God has provided; the birds building their nests, and breaking forth into song in the trees which fringe the margin of the torrent-beds; the wild goats bounding from rock to rock, and finding their home in the inaccessible crags; the young lions filling the forest by night with their roar, and "seeking from God their prey;" and the sea with the same plentitude of life, its depths peopled with huge monsters and swarming myriads of lesser fish, and its surface studded with sails, the image of the enterprise, the traffic, the commerce of the world; and lastly, in fine contrast with this merely animal activity of creatures led by their appetites, the even tenor, the calm unobtrusive dignity of man's daily life of labour: take all these together, and we have a picture which for truth and depth of colouring, for animation, tenderness, beauty, has never been surpassed.

It is not surprising that this great Hymn of Creation should have called forth the warmest expressions of admiration from those who have studied it, and that they should have vied with one another in praising it as a masterpiece which has rarely been exceeded. One writer † "prefers it to all the lyric poetry of the Greeks and Romans." Another ‡ declares that "in Hebrew poetry there is little that can compare with it in precision of outline, and in the delicacy of its transitions, as well as in its warm sympathy with nature, and in the beauty of its images." A third § says, "The Psalm is delightful,

---

* Sanchez, *Los Salmos*, ii. 36. † Amyraldus. ‡ Hupfeld. § Sanchez.

sweet and instructive, as teaching us the soundest views of nature (*la mas sana fisica*), and the best method of pursuing the study of it, viz., by admiring with one eye the works of God, and with the other God Himself, their creator and preserver." The great philosopher and naturalist, A. von Humboldt, writes: "It might almost be said that one single Psalm represents the image of the whole Cosmos. . . . We are astonished to find in a lyrical poem of such limited compass the whole universe—the heavens and earth—sketched with a few bold touches. The contrast of the labour of man with the animal life of Nature, and the image of omnipresent, invisible Power, renewing the earth at will, or sweeping it of inhabitants, is a grand and solemn poetical creation."—*Cosmos*, vol. ii. part. i. (p. 413, Bohn's edition). "With what an eye of gladness," says Herder, "does the Poet survey the earth! It is a green mountain of Jehovah, which He lifted above the waters; a paradise which He established for the dwelling-place of so many living creatures above the seas. The series of pictures which the Poet here displays is in fact the natural history of the earth."

The Psalm is without any strophical division, but its main outline, as has been said, follows the first chapter of Genesis. The Poet begins with the light, and the heaven with its clouds and storms, ver. 2—4, corresponding to the works of the First and Second Days, Gen. i. 3—8. Then he passes to the earth, first describing its original chaotic state, and the separation of earth and water by the voice of God. ver. 5—9, in accordance with Gen. i. 9, 10 (first portion of the Third Day's work); and then the varied adornment of the earth as the dwelling-place of living creatures, in a strain which goes far beyond the narrative in Gen. i. 11, 12. The mention of the heavenly bodies follows, ver. 19—23 (Fourth Day's work), but with a more direct reference to the life of men and animals than in Gen. i. 14—18. Then, after a short exclamation of admiring gratitude, ver. 24, the Poet, who has already woven into his verse so happily some portion of the creative wonders of the Fifth and Sixth Days, the birds, and beasts, and creeping things, and man, Gen. i. 20—26, turns back again, ver. 25, 26, to speak of the sea and its life, Gen. i. 21. Finally, after expressing in vivid phrase the absolute dependence of all this vast and manifold creation upon its Maker, ver. 27—30, he longs to see the bright original restored, to find himself and all God's creatures parts of the mighty harmony, that a new sabbath of creation may dawn, a rest of God, in which He shall rejoice in His works and they in Him, and the world become a temple filled with the anthem of praise, ver. 31—35.

1 BLESS Jehovah, O my soul!
O Jehovah my God, Thou art very great,
Thou art clothed with honour and majesty.
2 Thou coverest Thyself with light as with a robe,
Thou spreadest out the heavens like a curtain.

1. CLOTHED, comp. xciii. 1.

2. THOU COVEREST THYSELF, lit. "covering Thyself" (and in the next member "spreading out"), if we connect these participial clauses with what precedes, or "covering Himself" if we join them with what follows. This participial construction (of which we have further instances in ver. 10, 13, 14, ciii. 3—5; see also Is. xliv. 24, 25, xlv. 7; Jer. x. 12; Am. iv. 13) gives a present force to God's creative action, teaches us to regard it not merely as a thing of the past, but as still operative. The fifth verse, on the other hand, opening with a past tense, takes us back to the original creation of all things.

WITH LIGHT. This is the First Day. At the creation God *said*, "Let there be light." Here, where the creation is an ever-continued work, He *apparels* Himself with light. The final revelation tells us that "God is Light," 1 John i. 5; comp. John i. 4—9.

"In comparing the light to a robe," says Calvin, "he signifies that though God is invisible, yet His glory is manifest. If we speak of His essential being, it is true that He dwelleth in light inaccessible; but inasmuch as He irradiates the whole world with His glory, this is a robe wherein He in some measure appears to us as visible, who in Himself had been hidden. . . . It is folly to seek God in his own naked Majesty . . . let us turn our eyes to that most beautiful frame of the world in which He would be seen by us, that we may not pry with idle curiosity into the mystery of His nature." And Herder asks, "Is there in the universe a created thing more worthy to be the robe of Jehovah, whose very being is such that He dwelleth in darkness?"

SPREADEST OUT THE HEAVENS. The same figure in Is. xl. 22 (comp. xlii. 5; xliv. 24). This describes briefly the work of the Second Day, Gen. i. 6—8. The heavens are the firmament, the expanse (as the Hebrew word literally means) which is spread out to separate the waters. And in the waters above God lays, as it were, the floor of His palace.

LIKE A CURTAIN, *i.e.* the curtain of a tent, "ac si diceret regium esse tentorium."

"Because the Hebrews conceived of heaven as a temple and palace of God, that sacred azure was at once the floor of His, the roof of our, abode. Yet methinks the dwellers in tents ever loved best the figure of the heavenly tent. They represent God as daily spreading it out, and fastening it at the extremity of the horizon to the pillars of heaven, the mountains: it is to them a tent of safety, of rest, of a fatherly hospitality in which God lives with His creatures."—*Herder*.

Both Athanasius and Augustine observe, that in the use of this figure the Psalmist designs to mark not merely the form of the heaven, but the ease with which God works. "For easy as it is," says the former, "for a man to stretch out a skin, so easy it is for God to create the heaven which did not exist before." Augustine: "What infinite labour, and toil, and difficulty, and continued effort it costs to spread out one little room; there is no effort of this kind in the works of God. Thou art not to think that God spread out the heaven as thou spreadest out the roof of thy house;

3 Who layeth the beams of His chambers in the waters,
Who maketh the clouds His chariot,
Who walketh upon the wings of the wind;
4 Who maketh the winds His messengers,

but as easy as it is for thee to spread out a single skin, so easy was it for God to spread out that vast heaven. . . . Nay, God did not spread out the heaven as thou spreadest out the skin. For let a skin, wrinkled or folded, be placed before thee, and command it to be unfolded and stretched out; spread it out by thy word. 'I cannot,' thou wilt reply. See then how far thou comest short of the ease with which God worketh."

3. WHO LAYETH THE BEAMS. The figures, as Calvin remarks, are all designed to teach the same truth, viz.. that we are not to pierce heaven in order to discover God, because He meets us in His world and presents everywhere living pictures to our eyes. We must not suppose that anything was added to Him by the creation of the world; it is for our sakes that He puts on this garment.

HIS CHAMBERS, lit. "upper chambers," ὑπερῷα, built on the flat roof of the Eastern houses. For the literal use of the word, see for instance 2 Kings iv. 10; for the figurative, as here, Jer. xxii. 13, 14, and comp. Am. ix. 6. Clericus cites from Ennius, "cœnacula maxima cœli;" and from Plautus, *Amph.* iii. 1—3, where Jupiter says of himself, "in superiore qui habito cænaculo."

IN THE WATERS, *i.e.* the waters above the firmament, Gen. i. 7. It is impossible not to admire the boldness of the figure.

WALKETH UPON THE WINGS. *Δείκνυσιν ὡς οὐδε ἡ τῶν ἀνέμων φορὰ εἰκῇ φέρεται, ἀλλ' αὐτός ἐστιν ὥσπερ τις ἡνίοχος αὐτῶν γινόμενος, διὰ τὸ ταῖς αὐτῶν ἐπιβαίνειν πτέρυξιν.—Athanasius.*

4. In former editions this verse was rendered, "Who maketh His messengers winds, His ministers a flaming fire." I admitted that the other rendering, which I have now adopted, seemed to be the natural sense of the words, and that which harmonized best with the context: God has His palace in heaven, He makes the clouds His chariot, the winds and the lightning His avant-couriers and His train. But I then thought there were insuperable grammatical difficulties in the way of this interpretation, both in the plural predicate in the second member, and in the inversion of order in both members of the verse. As regards the first, the plural predicate we ought to have either, "flames of fire His ministers," or, "the flaming fire His minister." The plural predicate, however, is not wholly unexampled (see Prov. xvi. 14, "the wrath of the king is messengers of death," where the E.V. inserts the particle of comparison); and it may be accounted for here, as an accommodation to the plural predicate "messengers" in the first member of the verse (so Hitz. and Hupf.); though I think it more likely that as by "the flaming fire" the lightnings are meant, the subject itself is conceived of as plural. But the greater difficulty of the inversion of order in the subject and predicate which remained, and which seemed insuperable to so acute a critic as Bishop Thirlwall (see his remarks in the Critical Note), is no longer an obstacle. The natural order, no doubt, in Hebrew as in English, is verb, object, predicate, and I had seen no proof that any other was possible. But since the last edition of this work was published, I have met with other instances of the inverted order of the object and predicate after the verb, which I have given in the Critical Note, and which fully justify the rendering I have now adopted. It is no longer necessary therefore to adopt either of

His ministers the flaming fire.[a]
5 He established the earth upon the foundations thereof,
That it should not be moved for ever and ever.
6 Thou coveredst it [b] with the deep as with a garment ;

the explanations suggested in former editions ; such as (*a*) " He maketh His messengers winds, &c., *i.e.* He clothes His messengers with the might, the swiftness, the all-pervading subtilty of wind and fire ;" or still less (*b*) [as in First Edition] that God's messengers (or angels) are the secret agents who assume the forms of wind and lightning, in order to accomplish His will ; that what we see working around us are not blind forces of nature, but beings to whom natural objects are a veil concealing their operation. This view has no apparent support in Scripture, though it has been illustrated with great beauty of language by Dr. Newman in his Sermon on the Feast of St. Michael: " But how do the wind and water, earth and fire move? Now, here Scripture interposes, and seems to tell us that all this wonderful harmony is the work of Angels. Those events which we ascribe to chance as the weather, or to nature as the seasons, are duties done to that God who maketh His Angels to be winds, and His Ministers a flame of fire. . . . Thus, whenever we look abroad, we are reminded of those most gracious and holy Beings, the servants of the Holiest, who deign to minister to the heirs of salvation. Every breath of air, and ray of light and heat, every beautiful prospect, is, as it were, the skirts of their garments, the waving of the robes of those whose faces see God in heaven." [But why " deign," when this is their mission and their duty?]

On the rendering of the verse by the LXX., and the quotation in the Ep. to the Hebrews, i. 7, more will be found in the Critical Note. Calvin observes that we are not bound in this and similar instances to regard the application of a passage in the New Testament as settling the question of its meaning where it occurs in the Old.

HIS MESSENGERS. Hitz. illustrates the expression by reference to Babr. *Fab.* 1, where an arrow is called " the messenger of the huntsman," and to Xen. *Mem.* iv. 3 § 4, where Socrates speaks of the winds and the lightning as " servants of the gods."

5. The work of the Third Day in its two great divisions : first, the separation of the land and water (ver. 5—9) ; next, the clothing of the earth with grass, herbs, and trees (ver. 10—18). The Poet, however, ranges beyond the first creation, and peoples the earth with the living creatures of the Fifth Day. It is not a picture of still life like that in Genesis, but a living, moving, animated scene.

HE ESTABLISHED. God's order is itself the surest prop.

UPON THE FOUNDATIONS THEREOF. Comp. Job xxxviii. 4—6 ; Prov. viii. 29. On the other hand, in Job xxvi. 7, God is said to " hang the earth upon nothing." Mendelssohn gets rid of the figure here by rendering " Thou hast established the earth in herself," but it must be a dull mind which needs thus to be guarded against misapprehension. Yet it is curious to see how these obvious figures have been strained, and a hard, literal, prosaic sense given to what is manifestly poetry. This was one of the passages which, according to Father Sanchez, was most strongly relied upon in the controversy with Galileo.

6—8. These verses hang together in construction, and are a poetical expansion of Gen. i. 9.

6. The original chaos is described not according to the heathen notion,

Above the mountains did the waters stand.
7 At Thy rebuke they fled,
At the voice of Thy thunder they were scattered;
8 They went up by the mountains, they sank down into the valleys,

as a confused mass, earth and water mingled together, but the earth as already formed, yet completely enveloped in the water, ἐξ ὕδατος καὶ δι' ὕδατος, 2 Pet. ii. 5. This vast, swelling, tumultuous sea hears the "rebuke" of God, and sinks to its appointed place; the earth appears, emerges from her watery covering, and shows her surface diversified with mountain and valley.

So Milton:—

"The earth was formed, but in the womb as yet
Of waters, embryon immature involved,
Appear'd not: over all the face of earth
Main ocean flow'd."

7. Comp. lxxvii. 17—19. AT THY REBUKE; comp. xviii. 15 [16]; lxxvi. 6 [7]; Is. l. 2, and Matt. viii. 26.

There is some doubt as to the construction of the clauses of this verse. I should see no objection to that which the LXX. and Jerome have adopted, according to which the two clauses are immediately connected (ἀναβαίνουσιν ὄρη καὶ καταβαίνουσι πεδία εἰς τόπον ὃν ἐθεμελίωσας αὐτοῖς, Ascendent montes, et descendent campi ad locum quem fundasti eis), but that the subject of the next verse is evidently again that of ver. 6, the waters. Ewald and Hupfeld take the first member as parenthetical, and connect the second with the previous verse, "At the voice of Thy thunder the waters fled to the place," &c.; and there may be a reference to Gen. i. 9, "Let the waters be gathered *into one place*." Del. says this reference is undeniable, but his own rendering, "the mountains rose, (the water) sank down into the valleys," is as improbable as it is artificial and unnecessary. The rendering of the Chald., "They (*i.e.* the waters) go up to the mountains, they sink down into the valleys," which has been followed by our translators both in the Bible and in the P.B.V. (the margin gives the other rendering), is grammatically admissible, and has a certain picturesque force, carrying on, as it does, the image of the preceding verse—the rush and confusion of the waters fleeing at the rebuke of God. It has also the advantage of retaining the same subject throughout verses 6—9. And further it is supported by the very similar construction in cvii. 26. But with the present tense, "they go up by the mountains; they go down by the valleys unto the place," &c., the rendering does not harmonize well with ver. 6, or with the narrative in Genesis. The verbs here, as in the previous verse, are true aorists or imperfects, and the reference is still to the original creation. Hence Jun. and Trem. rightly, "Conscenderunt per montes, descenderunt per valles; in locum quem fundaveras ipsis."

The other explanation, "The mountains rose, the valleys sank," *i.e.* the mountains seemed to rise as the waters subsided, may be illustrated by Ovid, *Met.* i. 43:

"Jussit et extendi campos, subsidere valles,
Fronte tegi sylvas, lapidosos surgere montes;"

and 244,

"Flumina subsidunt, montes *exire videntur*,
Surgit humus, crescunt loca, decrescentibus undis."

And Milton:—

"Immediately the mountains huge appear

(Even) to the place which Thou hadst established for them.
9 Thou hast set them a bound that they cannot pass,
That they turn not again to cover the earth ;
10 Who sendest forth springs along the torrent-beds;
They flow between the mountains ;
11 They give drink to all the beasts of the field;
The wild asses quench their thirst.
12 Above them the fowls of the heaven have their habitation,
(And) sing among the branches.

Emergent, and their broad bare backs upheave
Into the clouds, their tops ascend the sky;
So high as heaved the tumid hills, so low
Down sunk a hollow bottom, broad and deep,
Capacious bed of waters," &c.
Paradise Lost, book vii.

The words of the first member occur again cvii. 26, where, as Ewald remarks, they are strictly in place ; whereas here he thinks they may have been no part of the original poem.

9. A BOUND separating the sea from the land, as in Job xxxviii. 8—11. See for a wider view, extending still further this separation of the elements, xxvi. 8—10, Prov. viii. 27, 29, and comp. Ps. cxlviii. 6. Delitzsch says it might almost seem as if the poet who wrote these words did not suppose the flood to be universal, but it is far more probable that he is not thinking of the Flood, but only of the everlasting order first established at the creation, and afterwards confirmed in the covenant made with Noah, Gen. ix. 9—16.

10. The loving care, the tender sympathy with which God, clothing the earth with beauty, provides at the same time for the wants of all His creatures. Even the wild ass which shuns the approach of man, and the birds of heaven, which have no keeper, are not left unprovided for.

WHO SENDEST FORTH. The article with the participle carries on the construction, Jehovah being the great subject throughout the Psalm.

THE TORRENT-BEDS. The word (*nachal*) denotes both the torrent and the valley through which it flows, corresponding to the Arabic *Wady*. Ewald and Hupfeld render, "Who sendeth forth springs into brooks." The latter argues (1) that the word never means *the valley* only, without the stream, and (2) that the subject of the next clause, "They flow," &c., cannot be *the springs*, but must be *the streams*. But in answer to (1) it may be said, that the torrent-bed is not here supposed to exist apart from the torrent, but rather to be produced by the action of the torrent; and in answer to (2), that the general subject of "water" is easily supplied from the preceding clause, as the LXX. have seen.

11. QUENCH THEIR THIRST, lit. "break their thirst," a phrase which occurs only here. Comp. the Latin *frangere sitim;* and the Welsh, "a dorrant eu syched."

12. ABOVE THEM, or, "beside them." The banks of the streams and the valleys would first be clothed with trees, and there the foliage would be most luxuriant.

THE FOWLS OF THE HEAVEN, a frequent expression in Genesis, as in i. 30, ii. 19, &c.

SING AMONG, lit. "give voice from."

13 He watereth the mountains from His chambers;
The earth is satisfied with the fruit of Thy work.
14 He maketh grass to grow for the cattle,
And green herb for the service of man;
That He may bring forth bread from the earth,
15 And wine that maketh [d] glad the heart of man;

13. God waters the earth not only by the fountains and torrents, but by the rain. Comp. Gen. ii. 5 and 10.

HE WATERETH, lit. "He giveth drink to," the same word as in ver. 11. The MOUNTAINS are mentioned not only because on them the clouds rest, from them the streams descend, but because Palestine was a mountain-land. Comp. Deut. xi. 11, "a land of mountains and of valleys; of the rain of heaven it drinketh water" (unlike Egypt, which was watered by the Nile). Thus doubly watered, from above and from beneath (comp. Gen. xlix. 25), the earth brings forth grass for the cattle, and its various fruits, corn and wine and oil for the use of men—for the cattle what they need, for man more than he needs—that which makes his heart glad and his countenance bright.

HIS CHAMBERS, *i.e.* the clouds, as in ver. 3, where they are built on the waters.

THE FRUIT OF THY WORK, *i.e.* apparently the rain, as seems to be required both by the parallelism and by the expression "the earth is satisfied," for with the "mountains" in the first clause, "the earth" can hardly stand here by metonymy, for "the dwellers on the earth," viz. cattle and men. The rain may perhaps be called "the fruit of God's work," as the result of His operation, as elsewhere it is called "the brook of God," lxv. 9, 10.

14. GRASS . . . GREEN HERB. Comp. Gen. i. 11, 29, 30; iii. 18, 19; Ex. x. 12, the latter comprising not vegetables only, but corn, &c.

FOR THE SERVICE OF MAN. This seems the most natural interpretation, corresponding to "for the cattle," in the first member, and may be supported by the use of the word in 1 Chron. xxvi. 30. Others render, "for the *labour* or tillage of man" (as the same word in ver. 23); but though we may speak of tilling *the ground*, we can hardly speak of tilling *the green herb*. Some connect the next clause with this: "that he (*i.e.* man by his labour in cultivating the earth) may bring forth bread from it." (So Ibn. Ez.). But it is an objection to this, that the whole passage speaks of *God's* works and gifts, and there is nothing in it to suggest man's co-operation.

THAT HE MAY BRING FORTH, or perhaps, "in that He brings forth," for the construction is somewhat loose, and it can hardly be said that *purpose* is clearly marked. If we adopt the latter rendering, then ver. 15 must be taken as an independent statement. See Critical Note.

BREAD in this verse seems to be used in its most general signification to denote all by which man is nourished. In the next verse it is mentioned in its proper sense, together with wine and oil, as the three most important products of the soil, the three essential elements of an Eastern banquet, the object being to set forth the *bounty* of God's provision for man. He furnishes no scanty table, He gives with no niggard hand.

15. From the satisfying of the earth by the precious rain, the Poet's thoughts turn to the satisfying of man by the earth. Not that man is the main subject, but rather the herbs and the trees; only he

That he may make (his) face to shine with oil,
And that bread may strengthen man's heart.
16 The trees of Jehovah are satisfied,
The cedars of Lebanon which He hath planted;
17 Where the birds make their nests:
As for the stork, the cypresses are her house.
18 The high mountains are for the wild goats;
The steep precipices are a refuge for the conies.

19 He hath made the moon for seasons;
The sun knoweth his going down:

passes for a moment from them to their chief uses, viz. for man, and for fowls, and for beasts.

WITH OIL, the face being mentioned rather than the head which was anointed, because the radiancy of joy is seen in the face.

The construction of the verse is very doubtful. See Critical Note.

STRENGTHEN MAN'S HEART, Gen. xviii. 5; Jud. xix. 5. Comp. Ps. cv. 16.

16. THE TREES OF JEHOVAH, so called as planted, not by human hand, but by God himself (as in the next member), trees of the forest and the mountain, in opposition to those which come under human cultivation, such as the vine and the olive, which are implied in ver. 15. See note on xxxvi. 6.

ARE SATISFIED, *i.e.* with the rain, as in ver. 13.

17. These trees have their use; they are a home and a shelter for the birds—probably the larger birds are specially intended, as the stork is named, the smaller tribes of singing-birds having already been mentioned, ver. 12.

THE STORK. The word means in Hebrew, "the pious, or affectionate bird," called in Babrius, *Fab.* xiii., πτηνῶν εὐσεβέστατον ζώων, and by Petronius, 55, 6, *pietaticultrix.*

18. THE HIGH MOUNTAINS and PRECIPICES or "cliffs" are mentioned, because they, like the trees, are a *shelter* for the wild animals. God provides food, and God provides shelter for His creatures.

CONIES. I have left the word as in the E.V., though incorrect. The creature meant is the *hyrax Syriacus.* See Knobel on Lev. xi. 5, and Smith's *Dict. of the Bible.*

19. Transition to the work of the Fourth Day, but still so contrived as to introduce another picture of life upon the earth, and the contrast between the life of the night and the life of the day.

THE MOON mentioned first, because to the Hebrew mind the night naturally preceded the day, as throughout Gen. i., "And there was evening and there was morning." Hence we have first the night-scene, ver. 20, 21, and then the day-scene, ver. 22, 23.

FOR SEASONS, as in Gen. i. 14. Others would render in both passages, "for festivals"; comp. Sir. xliii. 7, ἀπὸ σελήνης σημεῖον ἑορτῆς, but there is no reason so to restrict it. See note on lxxv. 2 ("set time"), and comp. Lev. xxiii. 4.

KNOWETH HIS GOING DOWN. Comp. Job xxxviii. 12; Jer. viii. 7. This mention of the sunset prepares the way for the night-picture which follows.

20 Thou makest darkness—and it is [e] night,
Wherein all the beasts of the forest do move.
21 The young lions roar after their prey,
And seek their food from God :
22 The sun ariseth,—they get them away,
And lay them down in their dens.
23 Man goeth forth to his work,
And to his labour until the evening.
24 How manifold are Thy works, O Jehovah !
In wisdom hast Thou made them all :
The earth is full of Thy riches.
25 Yonder is the sea, great and broad,

20—23. Even the night has its busy life ; the beasts of prey are abroad, and they, too, wait upon the providence of God. The whole picture is finely conceived, and the contrast is perfect between the restless movement and roaring of the wild beasts, and man's calm life of labour, continued in the quiet light of day from morning till evening. All the other creatures wait upon God, in simple dependence upon Him ; man must *labour*, as well as gather what God gives him, if he would be satisfied with good.

20. DO MOVE. The word is strictly used of the movements of reptiles and fishes. In Gen. i. 21, and in Ps. lxix. 34 [35] the verb, and in ver. 25 of this Psalm the noun, "things moving," are used of creatures in the sea. In Gen. i. 24, 25, the noun denotes things *creeping* upon the earth. Here, as applied to the beasts of the forest, the word may have been chosen to express their *stealthy* movements in pursuit of their prey, or it may be used of any kind of motion, as it is in Gen. vii. 21, "all flesh that moved upon the earth :" see also Gen. ix. 2.

24. Having thus come to man, the crown of all creation, and so touched, as it were, by anticipation, on the work of the Sixth Day, the Psalmist pauses to review with grateful wonder the multitude of God's works, and the wisdom which is manifest in creation.

Athanasius beautifully remarks on the sense of rest and refreshment which is produced by this change of strain, the Psalmist passing from the narration of God's works of providence to praise and glorify Him who is the Creator of all : τὸν περὶ τῆς προνοίας διεξελθὼν λόγον ἐπὶ ὕμνον τοῦ κτίσαντος τὸν λόγον μετέβαλεν, διαναπαύων ὥσπερ διὰ τούτου τὴν ἀκοήν.

RICHES, lit. "possessions." Others giving a different meaning to the root render "creatures."

25. Then he remembers that there is one vast field of creative wonders of which as yet he has said nothing. The sea, too, has its life, a life in its depths of things small and great, a life of the coral insect as well as of the whale, and also a life on its surface, where "go the ships" carrying the thoughts and the passions, the skill and the enterprise of human hearts.

The way in which the sea is mentioned indicates a writer not living on the coast. It is visible, perhaps, but at a distance. Its monsters are not familiar objects, but are vaguely described as "leviathan."

BROAD, lit. "wide of two hands,"

Wherein are things moving without number,
Beasts both small and great.
26 There go the ships,
(And there) leviathan whom Thou hast formed to take his pastime therein.
27 All of them wait upon Thee,
That Thou mayest give them their food in its season.
28 That Thou givest them, they gather;
Thou openest Thine hand, they are satisfied with good;
29 Thou hidest Thy face, they are troubled;
Thou takest away their breath, they die,
And turn again to their dust.
30 Thou sendest forth Thy breath, they are created,

i.e. "on both sides," and so in all directions, a phrase used elsewhere of a land or country, as Gen. xxxiv. 21; Jud. xviii. 10; Is. xxii. 18.

26. LEVIATHAN; not here as in lxxiv. 14; Job xi. 25 [E.V. xli. 1], "the crocodile," but a general term for all "sea-monsters."

THEREIN, *i.e.* in the sea, the pronoun referring to the more remote noun. It is strange that Ewald should render "whom Thou hast made to play with him," and appeal to Job xl. 29 [E. V. xli. 5], as supporting the rendering. The Jewish tradition does indeed make Leviathan the plaything of the Almighty, but there is nothing of the kind in Scripture.

27, 28. In allusion, probably, to Gen. i. 29, 30.

27. WAIT UPON THEE. The verb (which is more usual in Aramaic) occurs in the same sense and with the same construction, cxlv. 15.

IN ITS SEASON. Or the suffix may refer distributively to the animal (not to the food): "to each in his season," "at the fitting time," "in due season" as the E.V. renders.

28. GATHER. The word denotes properly "to pick up objects from the ground," as stones, flowers, ears of corn, grapes, wood, &c.; here, provender. There is no allusion (as Hengst.) to the gathering of the manna.

29, 30. God is not only the liberal and provident householder, the gracious father of a family; He is the Fountain of Life to His creatures. Comp. xxxvi. 8, 9 [9, 10].

29. THOU HIDEST THY FACE; a phrase elsewhere used to express God's wrath or displeasure; here in a physical sense, the withdrawal of His care.

TROUBLED. See the same expression, xxx. 7 [8], and comp. Job xxiii. 15.

THOU TAKEST AWAY, or perhaps rather "Thou withdrawest," "drawest in," correlative to "sendest forth," ver. 30. Comp. cxlvi. 4 with Job xxiv. 14.

THEY DIE, lit. "breathe out their life," *exhalare animam*, *exspirare*, the same word as in Gen. vi. 17, vii. 21, though there is no need to assume any allusion to the deluge.

TURN AGAIN TO THEIR DUST, as in Gen. iii. 19; Job xxxiv. 15.

30. The reference can hardly be (as Hupf.) to Gen. ii. 7, where the

And Thou renewest the face of the ground.
31 Let the glory of Jehovah be for ever!
Let Jehovah rejoice in His works!
32 Who looketh on the earth, and it trembleth,
When He toucheth the mountains, they smoke.
33 Let me sing to Jehovah, as long as I live,
Let me play unto my God, while I have any being.
34 Let my meditation be sweet unto Him;
As for me, I will rejoice in Jehovah.
35 Let sinners be consumed out of the earth,

inbreathing of life is confined exclusively to the creation of man, but rather to i. 2, where the Spirit of God is the great vivifying Agent in all Creation.

THOU SENDEST FORTH. Comp. Acts xvii. 25. THY BREATH. The same word in Hebrew may be rendered "breath" or "spirit." As the reference is here only to physical life, I have retained the former, especially as the same word is employed in the previous verse, where there can be no doubt as to the meaning. Comp. Job xxxiii. 4, xxxiv. 14, 15, Eccl. xii. 7, with Ps. cxlvi. 4. God is called "the God of the spirits of all flesh," Num. xvi. 22, xxvii. 16, Heb. xii. 9, and He "in whom we live, and move, and have our being," Acts xvii. 28.

THOU RENEWEST; life ever succeeding death, and all life being, as it were, a new creation.

"States fall, arts fade, but Nature
does not die."

31. The Psalm closes with the prayer that the glory of that God who has thus manifested His glory in creation may endure for ever, and that He who looked with loving approbation upon His works when they were first created, pronouncing all "very good," may ever rejoice in them; for He is a God awful in His majesty, One whose look makes the earth tremble, One whose touch consumes the mountains, One who could in a moment blot out the creation He has made.

33. The same words occur in cxlvi. 2. And as the Psalmist utters the devout wish that God may rejoice in His works, so he utters the wish for himself that he may ever rejoice in God, that his thoughts and words may find acceptance with Him. This is the truest, highest harmony of creation; God finding pleasure in His creatures, His reasonable creatures finding their joy in Him. But this harmony has been rudely broken; the sweet notes of the vast instrument of the Universe are "jangled out of tune." Sin is the discord of the world. Sin has changed the order (κόσμος) into disorder. Hence the prophetic hope (35) that sinners shall be consumed, that the wicked shall be no more, that thus the earth shall be purified, the harmony be restored, and God once more, as at the first, proncunce His creation "very good." In the prospect of such a consummation, the Poet calls upon his own soul, and upon all around him, to bless and praise Jehovah.

35. HALLELUJAH, or "Praise ye Jah." I have had considerable difficulty in deciding which mode of rendering to adopt. Something is lost by not translating uniformly "Praise ye Jah," especially in Psalms where the verb occurs several times with a different object. On the other hand, Hallelujah is

And let the wicked be no more.
Bless Jehovah, O my soul!
Hallelujah.[f]

almost like the titles of some of the Psalms, and like Amen, has become current in our language. The Talmud (B. Berakhoth, 91,) and Midrash observe that this is the first Hallelujah in the Psalter, and that the way in which it is connected with the prospect of the final overthrow of the wicked is remarkable and full of meaning.

[a] The LXX. render the verse: *ὁ ποιῶν τοὺς ἀγγέλους αὐτοῦ πνεύματα, καὶ τοὺς λειτουργοὺς αὐτοῦ πῦρ φλέγον* (*πυρὸς φλόγα* in the Cod. Alex., which is followed in Heb. i. 7, where the passage is quoted), making the first nouns objects, and the second predicates. This is no doubt supported by the construction in the previous verse, where the same order is observed; "Who maketh the clouds His chariot." As regards the English translation it may be remarked, that the two words *ἀγγέλους* and *πνεύματα* being both ambiguous, it is just as correct to render *messengers* and *winds*, as to render *angels* and *spirits;* and the whole passage shows that *winds*, not *spirits*, is the proper meaning of *πνεύματα* here. But as has been already remarked in the note on ver. 4, most of the modern commentators abandon the rendering of the LXX., and invert the order of the object and predicate, "Who maketh the winds His messengers, the flaming fire His ministers."

There are, however, two difficulties, as I have said, in the way of this interpretation. First, there is the plural predicate in the second member, and next there is the inversion of order.

Hoffmann, who has discussed the passage carefully (*Schriftb.* I. 325), urges the first difficulty, and contends, moreover, that עשה, followed by a double accus., means not to make a thing to be something else, but to exhibit a thing as something (*etwas als etwas herstellen*). So in Gen. vi. 14 the meaning is not "Thou shalt make the ark, already constructed, into cells or compartments," but, thou shall construct it as (of) a number of compartments. So again, "male and female created He them" (Gen. i. 27), *i.e. as* male and female; and "he made the altar of planks of acacia-wood" (Ex. xxxviii. 1), is, says Hoffmann, not essentially different. [Here, however, the second noun is not so much a predicate describing the form or manner in which the thing appears, as the material out of which it is made.] He renders therefore, "making His messengers as winds, His ministers as a flaming fire," so that the passage does not describe the purpose to which God applies winds and fire, but the form which He gives to those whom He, riding upon the clouds, makes use of to announce His presence, and to execute His will. And such is the traditional Jewish view: as for instance in Shemoth Rabbah, f. 25, "Deus dicitur Deus Zebaoth, quia cum angelis suis facit quæcunque vult. Quando vult, facit ipsos sedentes, Jud. vi. 11. Aliquando facit ipsos stantes, Isa. vi. 2. Aliquando facit similes mulieribus, Zech. v. 9. Aliquando viris, Gen. xviii. 2. Aliquando facit ipsos spiritus (why not *ventos?*), Ps. civ. 4. Aliquando ignem, Ib." Del. partially adopts this view, but takes the second accus., that is, the predicate, as denoting *the material out of which* a thing is made (as in Ex. xxxviii. 1). Accordingly he renders, "Who maketh His messengers of winds, His servants of flaming fire," which he says may either mean that God makes wind and fire of service to Him for special missions (comp. cxlviii. 8), or that God gives to His angels wind and fire as means whereby they may work, forms in which they may clothe themselves in order to execute His will in the world. But the former of these meanings comes to the same thing exactly as the rendering, "Who maketh winds His messengers," &c.

But as regards the plural predicate, this may be defended by Prov. xvi. 14. חֲמַת־מֶלֶךְ מַלְאֲכֵי־מָוֶת. In the Psalm the parallelism accounts in some measure for the use of the plural.

Next, there is the difficulty that lies in the order of the words. Can a Hebrew writer place the verb first, then the predicate, and then the object? The Bishop of St. David's [the late Bishop Thirlwall], who kindly allowed me to make use of the remarks which he sent me on this passage, after observing that he could recall no instance of such an inversion of the natural order of words in a sentence, continues: "*A priori*, I should have thought it incredible that the language should have been left in such a state as to make it immaterial as to the sense whether you wrote 'Who maketh the clouds His chariot,' or, 'Who maketh His chariot the clouds,' and that the reader should have to infer the author's meaning not from the order of his words, but from extrinsic considerations, such as those which you have discussed. I cannot help thinking that more attention should have been paid to this question, and that it should have taken precedence of every other: because if in this respect the rule of Hebrew syntax was the same as our own, the only remaining doubt would be in what sense we are to understand the words 'He maketh His messengers winds, His ministers a flaming fire,' which would then be the only possible rendering. And in itself it would give a very good sense as meaning: 'He endows His messengers with the might of the winds, His ministers with the all-pervading subtilty of fire'—or as any one might paraphrase it better. But it would be only the irresistible compulsion of a grammatical necessity that would induce me to adopt this rendering; because, however satisfactory in itself, it appears to me quite foreign to the context. The Psalmist is evidently speaking of God's doings in the visible creation, not of the secret agency by which He accomplishes His ends. It was, therefore, very much to the purpose to say that wind and fire are His servants and do His pleasure; but not at all to say that He has unseen servants who act as wind and fire."

Happily, I am now able (Fourth Edition) to remove this difficulty. I can produce two passages from Isaiah which illustrate this inversion of order, xxxvii. 26, וּתְהִי לְהַשְׁאוֹת גַּלִּים נִצִּים עָרִים בְּצֻרוֹת; lx. 18, וְקָרָאת יְשׁוּעָה חוֹמֹתַיִךְ and show indisputably that the rule of Hebrew syntax was in this respect not the same as our own. I no longer therefore feel any hesitation in adopting the rendering in the text, which has the support of many of the ablest of the modern commentators. The passages quoted in the first edition of this work, Gen. i. 27, Ex. xxv. 39, in which the predicate stands first, are not to the point, because there the predicate stands *before* the verb. In Am. iv. 13, the only passage which Del. quotes, there is no reason whatever for assuming an inversion of the order.

[b] כִּסִּיתוֹ, abbr. for כִּסִּיתָהוּ. The masc. suffix may refer to אֶרֶץ, according to Del., by attraction, as in Is. ix. 18, lxvi. 8. Others, in order to avoid the sudden change of gender in אֶרֶץ, render "As for the deep (nom. absol.), as a garment Thou coverest it" (*i.e.* placest it as a covering over the earth). But thus the verb "to cover" appears without an object, and תְּהוֹם, moreover, is generally like אֶרֶץ, fem., except in Job xxviii. 14, Jon. ii. 6. In other cases where it occurs with a masc. verb, the verb precedes, and this proves nothing as to gender; when the verb precedes, all fem. nouns may be construed with a masc. verb.

[c] יַעַמְדוּ. The imperf. (after the perf. or pluperf.) as describing the then condition of things (relative preterite), and so again in the next verse, instead of historic tenses with ו consec.

[d] The construction presents much difficulty. If we connect this verse with the last clause of the preceding, then as we have the inf. with לְ twice followed by the fut., the four lines might alike denote the purpose of God, "That he may bring forth bread, &c. And that wine may make glad, &c. That he may make his face to shine with oil, And that bread may strengthen, &c.,"—this change of construction from the infin. to the fut. being in accordance with a well-known principle of the language. But the position of יַיִן in ver. 15 is against this explanation. The difficulty lies in the subordinated form of (*b*) in ver. 15 (if the object were to mention oil as well as bread and wine as one of the chief products of the soil), as well as in the mention of bread a second time in (*c*).

Ibn Ezra says: "He mentions bread and wine, for these two are the life of man, and because he has mentioned the effect of the wine, he mentions the effect of the bread." It is clear, therefore, how he understood the passage generally, though he has given no explanation of (*b*). The effect of the wine is to gladden man's heart, to make his face shine more than oil (so he must have understood this clause as a part of the effect produced by the wine); the effect of the bread is to stay man's heart. Rashi, on the other hand, gives oil a place with bread and wine among the things which God is here said to bring out of the earth. He says: "Wine which maketh glad the heart of man, that also He brought forth from the earth, and oil wherewith to make his face shine, and bread which strengtheneth man's heart."

Ewald gives to מִן in ver. 15 the comparative meaning *more than*, and takes the infin. with לְ as gerundial merely: "Bringing bread out of the earth, Wine to gladden man's heart, More than oil making his face to shine, Bread to strengthen man's heart:" but this, though it seems to be the most obvious construction of the words, places in too subordinate a position what must have been designed to be prominent; *oil* and *wine* are commonly joined together as principal products of the soil of Palestine; Jud. ix. 9—13, Deut. xii. 17, Jer. xxxi. 12, &c.

Hitz.: "And wine gladdens man's heart, So that it makes his face shine more than oil (shines), And bread supports man's heart."

Hupfeld takes ver. 15 as unconnected in construction with the preceding: "And wine maketh glad the heart of man, Whilst oil makes his face to shine (lit. "whilst he maketh his face to shine with oil"), and bread strengthens man's heart."

[e] וַיְהִי . . . תָּשֶׁת. The apocopated forms are used as marking protasis and apodosis: "(When) Thou makest darkness, (then) it is night;" or the first may be pret. (as in xviii. 12), and the second denote purpose, object, &c. (as in xlix. 10).

[f] The Hallelujah is written differently in different MSS., sometimes הַלְלוּ־יָהּ, at others הַלְלוּ יָהּ, without the *Makkef*, or again הַלְלוּיָהּ, one word, but always, unless by mistake, with the *He mappic*. When it appears as one word, יָהּ is not regarded as strictly the Divine name, but only as strengthening the meaning of הַלְלוּ, as in the reading במרחביה, cxviii. 5. —GEIGER, *Urschrift u. Uebers. der Bibel*, S. 275.

PSALM 105

THIS Psalm, like the 78th and the 106th, has for its theme the early history of Israel, and God's wonders wrought on behalf of the nation; but it differs from both those Psalms in the *intention* with which it pursues this theme. The 78th Psalm is didactic; its object is to teach a lesson; it recalls the past, as conveying instruction and warning for the present. The 106th Psalm is a Psalm of penitential confession. The history of the past appears in it only as a history of Israel's sin. In this Psalm, on the other hand, the mighty acts of Jehovah for His people from the first dawn of their national existence are recounted as a fitting subject for thankfulness, and as a ground for future obedience. Those interpositions of God are especially dwelt upon which have a reference to the fulfilment of His promise, which exhibit most clearly His faithfulness to His covenant. Hence the series begins with the covenant made with Abraham, tracing all the steps in its fulfilment to the occupation of the Promised Land. This is commenced as the theme of the Psalm in ver. 8—11.

Hengstenberg has inferred, from the length at which the history of Joseph and the plagues in Egypt are dwelt upon, that the design of the Psalmist was to encourage the exiles in the Babylonish captivity, which by Psalmists and Prophets is so often compared with the bondage of the nation in Egypt. But although this is evidently one of the later Psalms, and, like the two which follow (both of which contain allusions to the Exile), may have been written after the Return from the Captivity, still there is nothing in its language to justify the view which Hengstenberg takes. There is no hint of any comparison or contrast between those two great periods of national exile, and, in particular, the very slight allusion to the circumstances of the *deliverance* from Egypt—nothing being said either of the passover or of the passage of the Red Sea—is unfavourable to the supposition that any such contrast is implied.

The first fifteen verses are found in 1 Chron. xvi. 8—22 (with some slight variations), as the first portion of the festal song which, on the day when the Ark of God was brought to its resting-place on Zion, was delivered by David into the hands of Asaph and his brethren, "to give thanks unto Jehovah." The second part of that song consists of Psalm xcvi., the first verse of Psalm cvii., and the forty-seventh and forty-eighth verses of Psalm cvi. The last of these is the doxology which closes the Fourth Book, and was evidently a late addition. It seems, therefore, impossible to doubt that the song in the Chronicles is a combination from other sources. It is a striking proof how little a question like this, which is purely a critical question, can be fairly perverted into a question of orthodoxy, that whilst Hitzig holds the Psalm in Chronicles to be the original, Delitzsch maintains that it is a compilation, though he observes that the writer of the Book may not have compiled it himself, but have found it in its present shape in the Midrash of the Book of the Kings, which was his principal authority, and the source of his materials.

Like the last Psalm, this closes with a Hallelujah. It is the first of a number of Psalms beginning with the word הוֹדוּ (*Hodu*), "Give thanks" (cv., cvii., cxviii., cxxxvi.), which Delitzsch styles "Hodu-Psalms," or *Confitemini*, just as those that begin with Hallelujah may be called Hallelujah Psalms (cvi., cxi.—cxiii., cxvii., cxxxv., cxlvi.—cl.).

1 O GIVE thanks to Jehovah, call upon His Name,

1—6. The greatness of God's love, as manifested to His people in their history, calls for the fullest acknowledgement. The Psalmist would have Israel sound forth His praises among all nations. They are not to sit down in idle satisfaction with their own privileges. His "doings" (ver. 1), His "wondrous works" (ver. 2, 5), His "tokens,"

Make known among the peoples His doings.
2 Sing unto Him, play unto Him ;
Meditate of all His wondrous works.
3 Make your boast of His holy Name,
Let the heart of them rejoice that seek Jehovah.
4 Enquire ye after Jehovah and His strength;
Seek His face evermore.
5 Remember His wondrous works that He hath done,
His tokens, and the judgements of His mouth,
6 O ye seed of Abraham His servant,
Ye children of Jacob, His chosen.
7 He, Jehovah, is our God ;
His judgements are in all the earth.
8 He hath remembered His covenant for ever,
The word which He confirmed to a thousand generations ;
9 (The covenant) which He made with Abraham,

"the judgements of His mouth" (ver. 5), "His holy Name" (ver. 3), as the revelation of His character and attributes,—all these are to form the subject of loud thanksgiving, —all these are to become, through Israel, the heritage of the world.

1. Taken word for word from Is. xii. 4.

5. TOKENS . . . JUDGEMENTS; the miracles in Egypt are chiefly meant, as these are chiefly dwelt upon afterwards.

6. SEED OF ABRAHAM: in 1 Chron. xvi. 13, "seed of Israel." HIS CHOSEN, plural, referring to the people, not to Jacob. It is on this ground, because they are Abraham's seed, because they are God's chosen, because they are Jacob's children, heritors of the covenant and the promises, that they are bound beyond all others to "remember" what God has done for them. On the other hand, God, who made the covenant with their fathers, "remembers" it (ver. 8), "for His part will surely keep and perform" it.

7. The Psalmist begins himself that praise of God to which he has exhorted his people. And first he extols "the covenant," "the word" (or promise), the "oath" by which God had bound Himself to the patriarchs, and which He "remembered," *i.e.* fulfilled, when He brought them into the land of Canaan.

OUR GOD, by covenant, but also, as follows in the next hemistich, Judge and Ruler of all nations.

8. HE HATH REMEMBERED: in 1 Chron. xvi. 15, "remember ye."

CONFIRMED: for this, the original meaning of the word, see Ex. xviii. 23, "If thou wilt do this thing, then shall God confirm thee, and thou shalt be able to stand." Num. xxvii. 19, "Confirm," or "set him before thine eyes." In both these passages the word is joined with the same verb which occurs in ver. 10 of this Psalm, "establish," lit. "make to stand."

TO A THOUSAND GENERATIONS: from Deut. vii. 9.

9. The verb MADE (lit. "cut," as

And the oath which He sware unto Isaac;
10 And He established it unto Jacob for a statute,
Unto Israel for an everlasting covenant;
11 Saying, "Unto thee will I give the land of Canaan,
The line of your inheritance;"
12 When they were [a] (but) a small number,
Very few, and sojourners therein;
13 And they went to and fro from nation to nation,
From (one) kingdom to another people;
14 He suffered no man to oppress them,
And reproved kings for their sakes, (saying,)
15 "Touch not Mine anointed ones,
And to My prophets do no harm."

in *icere fœdus*) seems to require that the relative should refer to "covenant" in the first hemistich, rather than to "word" in the second, of ver. 8. But the phrase to "make (lit. "cut") a word" occurs in Hag. ii. 5, and therefore the relative may refer to the nearer noun.

UNTO ISAAC, in allusion to Gen. xxvi. 3, where God says to Isaac, "To thee and to thy seed will I give all these countries, and I will perform the oath which I sware unto Abraham thy father": comp. Gen. xxii. 16.

11. THE LINE, *i.e.* an inheritance measured out by line, as in lxxviii. 55; see note on xvi. 6.

12—15. The Divine protection by which the small beginnings of the nation were shielded.

12. A SMALL NUMBER, lit. "men of number," as in Gen. xxxiv. 30; see also Deut. iv. 27, xxvi. 5; Jer. xliv. 28. So Horace says, "Nos numerus sumus."

VERY FEW, lit. "as (it were) a little," or "as little as possible," ὅσον ὀλίγον. Comp. Prov. x. 20.

13. NATION . . . PEOPLE. "The former denotes the mass as bound together by a common origin, language, country, descent; the latter as united under one government." —*Delitzsch*.

14. HE SUFFERED, as in Ex. xxxii. 10.

KINGS. viz. of the Egyptians, Gen. xii., and of the Philistines, Gen. xx., xxvi.

15. TOUCH NOT, with allusion, perhaps, to Gen. xxvi. 11.

MINE ANOINTED, *i.e.* specially set apart and consecrated. The poet uses, as Ros. observes, the language of his own time, not that of the patriarchs, who were never anointed. But inasmuch as in David's time priests and prophets were anointed (1 Kings xix. 16), when he would say that the patriarchs are priests of the true God, and therefore to be regarded as sacred, he gives them the epithet "anointed," as in the next hemistich "prophets," a name which God bestows upon Abraham, Gen. xx. 7, when he says to Abimelech, "And now give the man back his wife, for he is a prophet; and if he pray for thee, thou shalt live."

MY PROPHETS. A good instance of the wide signification of this word. It is derived from a root signifying *to boil, to bubble up*. The prophet is one in whose soul there rises a spring, a rushing stream of

16 And He called for a famine upon the land;
He brake the whole staff of bread.
17 He sent before them a man;
Joseph was sold for a slave.
18 They afflicted his feet with fetters;
He was laid in iron (chains).

Divine inspiration. In the later language he not only receives the Divine word, but he is made the *utterer of it*, the organ of its communication to others. But in the earlier instances, as in that of Abraham, his official character does not distinctly appear, though doubtless, like Noah, he was "a preacher of righteousness," and taught his own family (and through them ultimately the whole world) the way of the Lord. See Gen. xviii. 19. Here the prophet means little more than one to whom God speaks, one with whom He holds converse, whether by word, or vision, or dream, or inner voice. (Comp. Num. xii. 6—8.) We approach nearest to what is meant by styling the patriarchs prophets, when we read such passages as Gen. xvii. 17, "And Jehovah said, Shall I hide from Abraham that thing which I do?" or again, the pleading of Abraham for Sodom, in ver. 23—33, of the same chapter. It is, indeed, as pleading with God *in intercession* that Abraham is termed a "prophet" in Gen. xx. 7. The title is thus very similar to that of the "Friend of God," Is. xli. 8; 2 Chron. xx. 7; James ii. 23.

16. From this point, as far as ver. 38, the history of the nation in Egypt is followed, with a recognition of the Divine Hand fashioning it at every step, and at every step accomplishing the fulfilment of the promise.

16—22. First the preliminary steps in the history of Joseph. The famine in Canaan was no chance occurrence; God called for it. (Comp. 2 Kings viii. 1; Am. v. 8; Hag. i. 11.) Joseph's position in Egypt was no accident; God had sent him thither; so he himself traces the hand of God, Gen. xlv. 5, l. 20.

16. STAFF OF BREAD. The figure occurs first in Lev. xxvi. 26; comp. Is. iii. 1. The same figure is suggested in civ. 15, "bread that strengtheneth (stayeth) man's heart."

18. This is a much harsher picture of Joseph's imprisonment than that given in Genesis xxxix. 20—23, xl. 4. But it may refer to the earlier stage of the imprisonment, before he had won the confidence of his gaoler, or it may be tinged with the colouring of poetry.

WITH FETTERS. Heb. "with the fetter." The word occurs only here and cxlix. 8.

HE WAS LAID IN IRON. I have here followed the paraphrase of the E.V. In the margin, however, the literal rendering of the Hebrew is correctly given: "His soul came into iron," ("his soul," merely a periphrasis of the person="he," as in lvii. 4 [5], xciv. 17), *i.e.* he was a prisoner, bound with chains. So the Syr. and the LXX. σίδηρον διῆλθεν ἡ ψυχὴ αὐτοῦ. Jerome, "in ferrum venit anima ejus." The more picturesque but incorrect rendering of the P.B.V., "the iron entered into his soul," follows the Vulg., "ferrum pertransiit animam ejus." (The Chald. led the way in this interpretation, and it has been recently adopted by Moll.) The force of the expression has made it stereotyped in our language. It is a striking instance of the supremacy of the P.B.V. in our Church. Probably not one reader in a hundred of those who are familiar with that version

19 Until the time that his word came,
The saying of Jehovah tried him.
20 The king sent and loosed him,
The ruler of the peoples, and let him go free.
21 He made him lord over his house,
And ruler over all his substance;
22 To bind his princes at his will,
And to teach his elders wisdom.

ever thinks of any other translation of the verse, or is aware that the Bible version is different.

19. HIS WORD. This may be (1) "the word of *Joseph*," *i.e.* either (*a*) his interpretation of the dreams of the king's officers in the prison, which finally led to his own liberation, Gen. xli. 12 (so Rosenm. De Wette, Hupf.); or (*b*) the word revealed to him in dreams of his own future exaltation, Gen. xlii. 9 (Ibn Ez.); or (2) "the word of *Jehovah*," viz. that which first foretold, and then fulfilled the promise of, his exaltation; or (3) "his cause," *i.e.* his trial, in which case the verb must be rendered "came on," *i.e.* for hearing, an interpretation which seems at least very doubtful. If we adopt (1), then the meaning is, Joseph lay in prison till his interpretation of the dreams came to pass.

CAME, *i.e.* was fulfilled, a word used in the same way of the fulfilment of prophecies, Jud. xiii. 12, 17 ("come to pass," E.V.); 1 Sam. ix. 6; Jer. xvii. 15. Delitzsch, who understands the "word" here mentioned as the word of God, illustrates the passage by reference to cvii. 20; just as there God "sends" His word, so here His word "comes;" it came first as an angel of promise, and then as an angel of fulfilment.

THE SAYING (utterance, promise) OF JEHOVAH. LXX., τὸ λόγιον τοῦ Κυρίου, different from the WORD in the previous verse. This seems most naturally to be understood, not of God's interpretation of the dream (as Hupf. and others), but of God's promise of future exaltation conveyed to him in his dreams. The Divine utterance (*'imrah*) has ascribed to it a living effectual power, as in cxix. 50. It proved him by testing his faith during the years of suffering and imprisonment which intervened between the promise and its fulfilment.

20. With what follows, comp. Gen. xli. 14, 39, 40, 44.

22. TO BIND. The earliest instance of the use of the word in a sense approaching to that which it had later, in the phrase "binding and loosing," although that phrase is always used of *things*, in the Rabbinical writings, never of *persons*. It denotes here generally the exercise of control. "The capability of binding is to be regarded as an evidence of authority; a power of compelling obedience, or in default thereof, of inflicting punishment."—*Phillips*.

Hengstenberg thinks that the figure was occasioned by a reference to ver. 18: his soul, once bound, now binds princes. He illustrates the meaning by Gen. xli. 44, "without thee shall no man move his hand or his foot in all the land of Egypt;" and ver. 40, "thou shalt be over my house, and all my people shall kiss thy mouth."

AT HIS WILL, lit. "in, according to, his soul" (see on xvii. 9), equivalent to "according unto thy word," Gen. xli. 40.

TO TEACH . . . WISDOM; not to

23 Israel also came into Egypt,
And Jacob was a sojourner in the land of Ham.
24 And He caused His people to be fruitful exceedingly,
And He made them stronger than their adversaries.
25 He turned their heart to hate His people,
To deal subtilly with His servants.
26 He sent Moses His servant,
Aaron whom He had chosen.
27 They wrought His signs among them
And tokens in the land of Ham.
28 He sent darkness and made it dark,—

be pressed of literal instruction in the art of politics, but merely expressing in poetical form what is said in Gen. xli. 38, 39.

23. LAND OF HAM, as in lxxviii. 51.

24. Comp. Exod. i. 7; Deut. xxvi. 5. What follows to ver. 38 is a *résumé* of the history as given in the first twelve chapters of Exodus, and especially of the plagues. The fifth and sixth plagues, however, are omitted altogether, and the plague of darkness is placed first: in other respects the order of Exodus is observed. That in lxxviii. 44, &c. is different.

25. HE TURNED. This direct ascription of the hostility on the part of the Egyptians to God as its author gave early offence. Hence the Chald. and Arab. render, "their heart was turned." Grotius and others would soften the expression as meaning only that God suffered this hostility, arising from the increase of the people. But the difficulty is exactly of the same kind as when it is said that God hardened Pharaoh's heart, or as we find in Is. vi. 9, 10; Mark iv. 12; John xii. 39, 40; Rom. xi. 8. See notes on li. 4, lx. 3.

TO DEAL SUBTILLY; the same word as in Gen. xxxvii. 18 (where E. V. "they conspired against"). Compare Exod. i. 10, "Come and let us deal wisely with them:" the reference is to the putting to death the male children.

26. WHOM HE HAD CHOSEN, viz. as His priest.

27. AMONG THEM, the Egyptians. Comp. lxxviii. 43; Exod. x. 2, "My signs which I have done (lit. set, placed) among them."

WROUGHT HIS SIGNS, lit. "set the words of His signs;" comp. lxv. 3 [4] (where see note), cxlv. 5, perhaps as facts that speak aloud (Del.), or as announced beforehand, so that they were, in fact, prophetic words (Hupf.), Exod. iv. 28, 30.

28. The ninth plague (Exod. x. 21—29) mentioned first,—why, it is difficult to see. Hengstenberg thinks because "darkness is an image of the Divine wrath," and "the Egyptians were in this sense covered with darkness from the first to the last plague." But this is far-fetched: more probably to embrace all other terrors between the two awful images of darkness and death. The variation in the order of the plagues from the narrative in Exodus may be paralleled by the variation in the order of the commandments as quoted by our Lord in Matt. xix. 18, 19; Mark x. 19: Luke xviii. 20,—passages in which the order and enumeration differ from one another as well as from the original in Exod. xx.

MADE IT DARK: causative, as in cxxxix. 12; Am. v. 8; but the in-

And they rebelled not against His words.
29 He turned their waters into blood,
And made their fish to die.
30 Their land swarmed with frogs
In the chambers of their kings.
31 He spake the word, and there came flies,
Gnats in all their border.
32 He gave them hail for rain,
Flaming fire in their land.
33 He smote also their vines and their fig-trees,
And brake the trees of their border.
34 He spake the word, and the locusts came,
And grasshoppers without number,
35 And devoured all the green herb in their land,
And devoured the fruit of their ground.
36 And He smote all the first-born in their land,
The beginning of all their strength.
37 And He brought them forth with silver and gold,

transitive rendering, "and it was dark," is also defensible; see Jer. xiii. 16.

AND THEY REBELLED NOT, *i.e.* Moses and Aaron, who, and not the Egyptians, must here be the subject, if the reading is correct. The LXX. omit the negative, καὶ παρεπίκραναν τοὺς λόγους αὐτοῦ (and so also the Syr., Arab., and Ethiop.), whence in the P.B.V., "and they were not obedient unto His word." The Vulg. retains the negative, but puts the verb in the singular, "Et non exacerbavit sermones suos." The obedience of Moses and Aaron to the Divine command may here be made prominent, with reference to the unwillingness of Moses in the first instance, and also to the subsequent disobedience of both, Num. xx. 24, xxvii. 14.

The Q'ri unnecessarily substitutes the sing. "word," for the plural "words."

29. The first plague, Exod. vii. 14—25; in the next verse, the second, Exod. viii. 1—14 [vii. 26—viii. 11].

31. The fourth plague, that of flies, Exod. viii. 20—24 [16—20], and the third, that of gnats, or mosquitoes (E. V. "lice"), Exod. viii. 16—19 [12—15].

32, 33. From the third plague he passes to the seventh, Exod. ix. 13—35.

34, 35. The eighth plague, Exod. x. 1—20, where only one kind of locust is mentioned (*arbeh*). Here we have also *yeleq*, "grasshopper" (a species of locust, winged, Nah. iii. 16, and hairy, Jer. li. 27), as in lxxviii. 46, *châsîl*, "caterpillar," in the parallelism: see Knobel on Levit. xi. 22.

36. The fifth and sixth plagues are omitted, and the series closed with the last, in language borrowed from lxxviii. 51.

37. WITH SILVER AND GOLD: Exod. xii. 35.

And there was none among their tribes that stumbled.

38 Egypt was glad when they went forth;
For their terror had fallen upon them.

39 He spread a cloud for a covering,
And fire to lighten the night.

40 They asked and He brought quails,
And satisfied them with the bread of heaven.

41 He opened the rock and the waters flowed;
They went in the dry places like a river.

42 For He remembered His holy word,
(And) Abraham His servant;

43 And He brought forth His people with gladness,
His chosen with a song of joy.

44 And He gave them the lands of the nations,
And they took possession of the labour of the peoples;

THAT STUMBLED. See the same phrase, as descriptive of vigour, Is. v. 27, "none shall be weary or stumble among them;" and for the general sense comp. Exod. xiii. 18.

38. WAS GLAD: Exod. xii. 31—33. THEIR TERROR: Exod. xv. 14—16; Deut. xi. 25.

39—41. Three of the principal miracles in the wilderness, which sum up the period between the departure from Egypt and the entrance into the Promised Land. But it is remarkable that the great miracle of the passage of the Red Sea, a favourite theme with poets and prophets, is not even alluded to.

39. SPREAD A CLOUD: not, as in Ex. xiv. 19, as a protection against their enemies, but rather over their heads, as a protection against the burning sun. See the use of the same verb, Exod. xl. 19, of the tabernacle; Joel ii. 2, of a cloud; and comp. Is. iv. 5, 6.

LIGHTEN. See note on lxxvii. 19 [20].

40. See on lxxviii. 24, 27.

THEY ASKED. The verb is in the sing., referring to the people.

41. ROCK. The word is *tsur*, and therefore the miracle at Horeb is intended; see on lxxviii. 15.

42—45. Conclusion, giving, first the reasons why God had thus dealt with Israel, viz. His own promise, and the faith of His servant Abraham, as in ver. 8, 9; next, the result in their history, that by virtue of this covenant they had taken possession of the land of Canaan; lastly, the great purpose designed by all that marvellous guidance, "That they might keep His statutes, and observe His laws."

43. WITH GLADNESS, alluding, probably, to the song of triumph after the overthrow of Pharaoh and his captains in the Red Sea. Comp. Is. xxxv. 10; "And the redeemed of Jehovah shall return and come to Zion with a song of joy, and everlasting gladness shall be on their head," &c.

44. LABOUR; not only cultivated lands, but cities, treasures, &c.

45 That they might keep His statutes,
And observe His laws.
Hallelujah.

45. THAT THEY MIGHT KEEP. This was God's purpose, that Israel should be a holy nation in the midst of other nations, a priesthood representing the world, and claiming it for God as His world.

[a] בִּהְיוֹתָם. There is some difficulty as to the construction in this and the two next verses. In 1 Chron. xvi. 19 this verse is joined with what goes before, the suffix being changed to that of the 2d pers., "when *ye* were," and so the Chald. and Syr. here. Del. finds the protasis here, and the apodosis in ver. 14. He takes ver. 13 as a part of the protasis, according to the common rule, that a sentence beginning with the infinitive recurs to the use of the finite verb: "When they were few, and sojourners, and went to and fro, &c. . . . (then) He suffered no man to harm them." Ewald connects both ver. 12 and ver. 13 with what precedes. Hupfeld thinks that ver. 12 is loosely subjoined to what precedes, but makes of ver. 13 and ver. 14 independent sentences: "they went from nation to nation," . . . "He suffered no man," &c.

PSALM 106

THIS is the first of a series of Hallelujah Psalms; Psalms of which the word Hallelujah is, as it were, the Inscription (cvi., cxi.—cxiii., cxvii., cxxxv., cxlvi.—cl.). As in the last Psalm, so here, the history of Israel is recapitulated. In that it was turned into a thanksgiving; in this it forms the burden of a confession. There God's mighty acts for His people were celebrated with joy; here His people's sin is humbly and sorrowfully acknowledged. Nothing is more remarkable in these great historical Psalms than the utter absence of any word or sentiment tending to feed the national vanity. All the glory of Israel's history is confessed to be due, not to her heroes, her priests, her prophets, but to God; all the failures which are written upon that history, all discomfitures, losses, reverses, the sword, famine, exile, are recognized as the righteous chastisement which the sin of the nation has provoked. This is the strain of such Psalms as the 78th, the 105th, the 106th. This is invariably the tone assumed by all the divinely-instructed teachers of the people, by the prophets in their great sermons, by the poets in their contributions to the national liturgy. There is no other poetry in the world of a popular and national kind so full of patriotic sentiment, and yet at the same time marked by so complete an abstinence from all those themes which are commonly found in poetry written for the people. There is not a single ode in honour of Moses or Aaron, or Joshua or David; there is not one which sings the glory of the nation, except as that glory is given it of God. The history of the nation, whenever referred to, is referred to almost invariably for the purpose of rebuke and upbraiding, certainly not for the purpose of commendation or self-applause. A similar review of the past history of Israel, joined in the same way with a confession of the sins of the nation during their history, occurs in the prayer of the Levites on the occasion of the solemn fast proclaimed after the return from the Captivity (Nehem. ix.). But the earliest specimen of this kind of confession is the prayer which is directed to be used at the offering of the first-fruits, Deut. xxvi. Solomon's prayer at the consecration of the Temple, 1 Kings viii., is not itself a prayer of confession, so much as a pleading with God that He would hear His people whenever, having sinned, they should come to Him confessing their sins. All these instances differ from the Psalm in being prose, not poetry. Still the Psalm is not free, as Delitzsch observes, from certain peculiarities found in the others, such as (1) the fondness for rhyme, especially in the use of suffixes having the same sound (see, for instance, ver. 4, 5, 8, 35—41): (2) the fondness for synonyms, as in ver. 21, 22, "great things," "wonderful things," "terrible things;" (3) the direct, even tautological expansion of the thought, as in ver. 37, 38, to the comparative neglect of the usual principle of parallelism.

From ver. 47 it may be fairly inferred that the Psalm is of the date of the Exile, or was written shortly after the return of the first company of exiles. It is, however, remarkable that both that verse and the closing doxology, together perhaps with the first verse of this Psalm, form the concluding portion of the Psalm which, according to the author of the Book of Chronicles, was sung by David when he removed the ark to Mount Zion, 1 Chron. xvi. 34—36. On this point, see more in the Introduction to Ps. cv., and the note on ver. 48.

The Psalm has no strophical division. It consists of an Introduction, ver. 1—5. It then follows the history of Israel as a history of perpetual transgressions, first, from Egypt through the wilderness, ver. 7—33, and then in the Holy Land, 34—46, and concludes with a prayer for deliverance from the present calamity, viz. the captivity in Babylon, ver. 47.

1 HALLELUJAH!
Give thanks unto Jehovah, for He is good,
For His loving-kindness (endureth) for ever.
2 Who can utter the mighty acts of Jehovah,
(Or) tell forth all His praise?
3 Blessed are they that keep judgement,
He that doeth righteousness at all times.
4 Remember me, O Jehovah, with the favour Thou bearest unto Thy people,
O visit me with Thy salvation;

1–5. The first five verses seem to stand alone, and to have little or no direct connection with the rest of the Psalm. Hupfeld regards the first three verses, in particular, as nothing but a general introduction, and one quite at variance with the strain of the Psalm as a confession of sin. But this is a hasty and superficial view. The first verse, no doubt, is of the nature of a doxological formula, such as we find in some other of these later Psalms. But the second and third verses have an immediate bearing on what follows. What so fitting to introduce the confession of a nation's sin and ingratitude, as the rehearsal of God's goodness manifested to it, and the acknowledgement of the blessedness of those who, instead of despising that goodness, as Israel had done, walked in the ways of the Lord, keeping judgement and doing righteousness (ver. 3)? Or, again, what more natural than that the sense of the national privilege, the claim of a personal share in that privilege, should spring in the heart and rise to the lips of one who felt most deeply the national sin and ingratitude?

The fourth and fifth verses are clearly the expression of *personal* feeling. It is strange that some commentators should have seen here a personification of the people, when the fifth verse so expressly distinguishes, in every clause, between the individual who speaks and the people of which he is a member. Nor is there any reason to assume that the Psalmist speaks in the name of the people. There is the same blending of personal feeling and personal experience with the national life which we find, for instance, in lxv. 3 [4]. The hope expressed is, that when God looks again with favour upon the nation, when He delivers them from the hand of the heathen (see ver. 47), then the Psalmist himself may share in the general joy.

1. The Psalm begins with the liturgical formula which was in use in Jeremiah's time, xxxiii. 11 (under Zedekiah), and which became afterwards more frequent, 1 Macc. iv. 24. It is not, therefore, quite so certain that 1 Chron. xvi. 34 was taken from the beginning of this Psalm, as that the two following verses, 35, 36, were taken from its close.

GOOD, *i.e.* not so much in reference to His own nature, as in His gracious dealing with men. The LXX., rightly, χρηστός.

2. THE MIGHTY ACTS are all that He has done for His people, as HIS PRAISE is all the glory which He has thus manifested, and which calls for praise from them.

4. In this and the next verse the same suffix recurs, almost with the effect of rhyme; "the peculiarity," says Delitzsch, "of the T'phillah-style." In ver. 6 the same thing is observable, which is characteristic

5 That I may see the prosperity of Thy chosen,
That I may be glad with the gladness of Thy nation,
That I may make my boast with Thine inheritance.

6 We have sinned with our fathers,
We have done iniquity, we have dealt wickedly.
7 Our fathers in Egypt considered not Thy wonders;
They remembered not the multitude of Thy loving-kindnesses,
But rebelled at the sea, at the Red Sea.
8 And (yet) He saved them for His Name's sake,
To make His might to be known.
9 And He rebuked the Red Sea, and it was dried up,
And He made them go through the depths as (through) the wilderness.
10 And He saved them from the hand of the hater,
And ransomed them from the hand of the enemy.

of these prayers of confession (*Vidduy*, in the later Hebrew, from the verb, "to confess," Lev. xvi. 21), 1 Kings viii. 47.

5. NATION. The word in the plural is always used of the heathen, but in the singular sometimes of the nation of Israel, and even with the pronominal suffix, as here, and Zeph. ii. 9.

6. The language is borrowed evidently from that of Solomon's prayer, 1 Kings viii. 47. Comp. Dan. ix. 5; Bar. ii. 12, where in the same way several words are used in confession as if to express both the *earnestness* of deep conviction, and also the sense of *manifold* transgressions.

WITH OUR FATHERS. The nation is thus regarded as a whole, one in guilt and one in punishment. See note on lxxix. 8. Not only the "fathers in Egypt" (ver. 7) are meant, because the generation in Canaan are also mentioned (ver. 34—36).

7. OUR FATHERS IN EGYPT. These words are connected together by the accents, but the words "in Egypt" belong to the whole sentence. The "wonders" are wonders wrought in Egypt, the impression of which, great as they were, had so quickly faded, that they were forgotten even when the people stood on the shore of the Red Sea. Again in ver. 13, 21, this *forgetfulness* is censured. Comp. lxxviii. 11; Deut. xxxii. 18; and see note on Ps. ciii. 2.

REBELLED (the verb is here used absol., elsewhere with the accus.), with reference to the occurrence in Ex. xiv. 10—13.

This is the first act of transgression of which confession is made.

8. HIS MIGHT TO BE KNOWN, as in lxxvii. 14 [15].

9. Compare, for the form of expression, Nah. i. 4; Is. l. 2, li. 10, lxiii. 13. The word rendered "wilderness" denotes not the sandy waste but "the pasture-ground;" and the figure means that God led His people through the sea as the shepherd leads his sheep along the

11 And the waters covered their adversaries,
Not one of them was left.
12 And they believed His words,
They sang His praise.

13 Very soon they forgat His doings,
They waited not for His counsel;
14 But lusted for themselves a lust in the wilderness,
And tempted God in the waste.
15 And He gave them their request,
And sent leanness (withal) into their soul.

16 And they were jealous against Moses in the camp,
Against Aaron, the holy one of Jehovah.

well-known, well-tracked sheep-paths.

11. NOT ONE OF THEM WAS LEFT. Comp. Ex. xiv. 28.

12. THEY BELIEVED . . . THEY SANG, with evident reference to Ex. xiv. 31, xv. 1; "And Israel saw the great act (lit. hand) which Jehovah had done against Egypt, and the people feared Jehovah, and they *believed* on Jehovah and His servant Moses. Then *sang* Moses and the children of Israel this song." Both the faith and the song are mentioned, not in praise of their conduct, but only as still further proof, that whatever impressions were produced, whether by God's judgements or His mercies, were but temporary and on the surface. The goodness of Israel was like the dew, early gone.

13—33. The confession of Israel's sins in the wilderness. On the first of these, the lusting for food, comp. lxxviii. 18, 29, and Ex. xv. 22—24, xvii.2. See also Ex. xvi. and Num. xi.

13. VERY SOON, lit. "they made haste, they forgat." WAITED NOT; they were not content to exercise a patient dependence upon God, leaving it to Him to fulfil His own purposes in His own way, but would rather rule Him than submit themselves to His rule.

14. LUSTED FOR THEMSELVES A LUST; the expression is taken from Num. xi. 4.

15. HE GAVE THEM THEIR REQUEST. See on lxxviii. 21, 29.

LEANNESS. Comp. Is. x. 16, xvii. 4. The LXX., πλησμονήν, "satiety," and so the Syr. and Vulg., but wrongly. This LEANNESS and sickness (phthisis) may refer to the loathing of the food, followed by great mortality (the "blow of God"), Num. xi. 20, 33, the SOUL being here used only in a physical sense of the life. But the figurative sense is equally true and equally pertinent. The very heart and spirit of a man, when bent only or supremely on the satisfaction of its earthly desires and appetites, is always dried up and withered. It becomes a lean, shrunk, miserable thing, always craving more food, yet drawing thence no nourishment, "magnas inter opes inops."

16—18. The second great sin in the wilderness was the insurrection against their divinely-appointed leaders. The reference is to Num. xvi., xvii.

16. THE HOLY ONE. Aaron is so called on account of his priestly office. It was this, as an exclusive privilege, which was assailed by Korah and his company, on the

17 (Then) the earth opened and swallowed up Dathan,
And covered the congregation of Abiram;
18 And a fire was kindled in their congregation,
A flame burned up the wicked.

19 They made a calf in Horeb,
And bowed themselves before the molten image,
20 And they bartered their glory,
For the likeness of an ox that eateth grass.
21 They forgat God their Saviour,
Who had done great things in Egypt;
22 Wondrous things in the land of Ham,
Fearful things by the Red Sea.
23 Then He said He would destroy them,

ground that all the congregation were "holy," *i.e.* set apart and consecrated to God as His priests.

17. OPENED. In Num. xvi. 30, 32, xxvi. 10, the fuller expression occurs, "opened her mouth." COVERED, as in Num. xvi. 33.

Dathan and Abiram only are mentioned, and this is in strict agreement with Num. xxvi. 11, where it is said, "Notwithstanding *the children of Korah* died not." And the same thing is at least *implied* in Num. xvi. 27, where it is said that, just before the catastrophe took place, "Dathan and Abiram" (there is no mention of Korah) "came out and stood in the door of their tents." See this noticed and accounted for in Blunt's *Veracity of the Books of Moses*, Part I. § 20, p. 86.

18. The other punishment, the destruction by fire, befell the 250 princes of the congregation who offered incense before the Lord, Num. xvi. 2, 35.

THE WICKED, as in Num. xvi. 26, "Get ye up from the tents of these wicked men."

19. The third instance of transgression, the worship of the calf; see Ex. xxxiii. There is probably also a reference to Deut. ix. 8—12, where Moses reminds the people of their sin, especially as *Horeb* (which is the common name in Deuteronomy), and not Sinai, is here the name of the mountain.

20. THEIR GLORY, *i.e.* their God, who had manifested Himself to them in His glory: glory, like light, being used in Scripture to denote the Divine perfections. Others understand by the expression the God who was the source and fountain of their glory, or that revelation of God to them which distinguished them from all other nations. Comp. Deut. iv. 7, "For what nation is there so great, who hath God so nigh unto them, as the Lord our God is in all things that we call upon Him for?" But the closest parallel is Jer. ii. 11, "Hath a nation bartered their gods, which are yet no gods? But my people have *bartered their glory* for that which doth not profit."

LIKENESS, properly "model" or "figure." See the same word in Deut. iv. 16, 17, 18.

21. FORGAT GOD; with reference, perhaps, to the warning, Deut. vi. 12, "beware lest thou forget Jehovah."

22. LAND OF HAM as in cv. 23, 27. Comp. lxxviii. 51, "tents of Ham," peculiar to those historical Psalms.

23. THEN HE SAID, lit. "And He

Had not Moses His chosen stood in the breach before
Him,
To turn away His fury from destroying (them).

24 And they rejected the desirable land,
They believed not His word.
25 And they murmured in their tents,
They hearkened not to the voice of Jehovah.

26 Then He lifted up His hand unto them,
That He would make them fall in the wilderness;
27 And that He would make their seed fall among the
nations,
And scatter them in the lands.

28 They were yoked also unto Baal-peor,
And ate the sacrifices of the dead.

said (resolved, uttered His word), to destroy them," Deut. ix. 13. Comp. Ex. xxxii. 10; and for the construction, Ezek. xx. 8, 13, 21.

IN THE BREACH. The intercession of Moses is compared to the act of a brave leader, covering with his body the breach made in the walls of his fortress. Comp. Ezek. xxii. 30, "And I sought for a man among them, that should make up the hedge, and stand in the gap (*breach*, as here) before Me for the land that I should not destroy it."

24—27. A fourth act of sin,—the rebellion which followed on the report of the spies, Num. xiii., xiv.

24. THE DESIRABLE LAND, so called also in Jer. iii. 19; Zech. vii. 14 (in E.V. "pleasant land"). The other expressions in this and the next verse are from the Pentateuch: "they rejected," Num. xiv. 31; "murmured in their tents," Deut. i. 27; "lifted up His hand," as in Ex. vi. 8; Deut. xxxii. 4; "make them fall," as in Num. xiv. 29, 32. The phrase, "to lift up the hand," refers to the custom in the taking of an oath. Comp. Gen. xiv. 22. The threat of exile (ver. 27), of which nothing is said in Num. xiv., is taken, doubtless, from Lev. xxvi.; Deut. xxviii. Comp. the same expression Exek. xx. 23, "I lifted up Mine hand unto them also in the wilderness, that I would scatter them among the heathen, and disperse them through the countries."

27. MAKE FALL; here *projicere*, in the same sense almost as "scattered," in the parallelism.

28. THEY WERE YOKED; a fifth transgression in the wilderness, recorded in Num. xxv. The same verb is used there, ver. 3, 5, with reference to the prostitution which accompanied the worship of Baal-peor, "the Moabite Priapus." Comp. 1 Cor. vi. 16, 17, and with the next clause ATE THE SACRIFICES. 1 Cor. x. 18—21, with Num. xxv. 2. The LXX., for "they were yoked," have ἐτελέσθησαν, "they were initiated."

THE DEAD. Two interpretations have been given: (1) that idols are meant, as opposed to "the *living* God." Comp. Jer. x. 10, 11, and the contemptuous expression "car-

29 And they gave provocation with their doings,
And a plague brake in upon them.

30 Then stood (up) Phinehas and did judgement,
And (so) the plague was stayed;

cases of their kings" (probably said of idols, as rivals of the One true King of Israel), in Ezek. xliii. 7, 9. Comp. Lev. xxvi. 30; Jer. xvi. 18. (2) Usage, however, is rather in favour of some allusion to necromantic rites, as in Deut. xviii. 11, "one who seeketh to the dead;" Is. viii. 19, "should a people seek to the dead (by the aid of necromancers, consulting them as Saul consulted the Witch of Endor), on behalf of the living?" So Selden, *De Diis Syris*, i. 5, understands this place of sacrifices offered *Dîs manibus*. Hupfeld objects that in Num. xxv. 2 the same sacrifices are called "sacrifices of their *gods*," and that sacrifices to the dead would scarcely be accompanied by sacrificial feasts. This last objection has no force.

This 28th verse, as Delitzsch remarks, is of historical importance, as having given rise to the prohibition of flesh offered in sacrifice to idols. In the *T. B. 'Abodah Zarah*, Pereq 29*b*, in a comment on the words of the Mishnah, "The flesh which is intended to be offered to idols is allowed (to derive a profit from), but that which comes from the temple is forbidden, because it is like sacrifices of the dead," it is observed, *ib.* 32*b*: "R. Jehudah b. Bethêra said, 'Whence do I know that that which is offered to idols pollutes like a dead body? From Ps. cvi. 28. As the dead pollutes everything which is with him under the same roof, so also does all which is offered in sacrifice to idols.'" St. Paul teaches that the pollution, when it exists, is not in the meat which has been offered in sacrifice, but in the conscience of the eater. 1 Cor. x. 28, 29.

29. GAVE PROVOCATION. The verb used absol., without a case, as other verbs in ver. 7, 32, 43, a peculiarity of the writer of this Psalm.

A PLAGUE. The word is used of a Divine judgement, more commonly of sickness, but here, as in Num. xxv. 8, 9, 18, of the slaughter accomplished by human instruments. Comp. Ex. xxxii. 35.

BRAKE IN, or "made a breach" (for the verb is from the same root as the noun in ver. 23). Comp. Ex. xix. 24.

30. STOOD. See the similar expression, Num. xxv. 7, "And when Phinehas saw it, he *rose up*;" and the same verb as here, Num. xvi. 48 [xvii. 13], of Aaron's intercession. It is a picture of the one zealous man rising up from the midst of the inactive multitude, who sit still and make no effort.

DID JUDGEMENT, not, as in P.B.V., following the Chald. and Syr. "prayed" (*i.e.* interceded), a meaning which the verb never has in this conjugation (Piel), but only in the Hithpael. The LXX. give the sense only when they render ἐξιλάσατο (Vulg. *placavit*). This righteous act of judgement, like the intercession of Aaron, was propitiatory; it appeased and turned away the wrath of God; "and the plague was stayed;" words borrowed from Num. xxv. 8; comp. Num. xvi. 48 [xvii. 13]. The two figures, Aaron standing with the incense, and with the true priestly heart, between the dead and the living, and making atonement, and Phinehas as the minister of righteous vengeance turning away wrath, form a striking and instructive contrast. The one makes atonement in saving life, the other in destroying it.

31 And it was counted unto him for righteousness,
Unto all generations for evermore.

32 They angered (God) also at the waters of Meribah,
And it went ill with Moses for their sakes.
33 For they rebelled against His Spirit,
And he spake unadvisedly with his lips.

34 They did not destroy the peoples,
As Jehovah had said unto them;

31. IT WAS COUNTED UNTO HIM FOR RIGHTEOUSNESS; it was looked upon as a righteous act, and rewarded accordingly. The same thing is said of the *faith* of Abraham, Gen. xv. 6; a striking instance of the fearlessness of expression which is to be found in the Scriptures, as compared with the dogmatic forms of modern controversial theology. This verse has given occasion to whole disquisitions on the subject of justification, with which it really has nothing to do, though at least the language is in perfect accordance with that of St. James (ii. 20—26).

The reward of this righteousness was the perpetual continuance of the priesthood in his family (Num. xxv. 12, 13).

UNTO ALL GENERATIONS, &c. lit. "for generation and generation, to (all) eternity," a remarkable instance of the hyperbolic way in which this and similar phrases are employed, and one which is a warning against hastily building doctrines upon mere words.

32. The sixth instance of transgression — the rebellion against Moses and Aaron at Meribah, in the fortieth year of the wandering, Num. xx. 2—13

IT WENT ILL WITH. This must be the meaning here (though elsewhere the same phrase means "it grieved, or displeased," as in Neh. ii. 10, xiii. 8; Jon. iv. 1). Comp. Deut. i. 57, iii. 26, "also Jehovah was angry with me *for your sakes*." The reason why Moses was forbidden to enter the Promised Land is here stated more distinctly than in the narrative. It was the exasperation into which he suffered himself to be betrayed in uttering the words in Num. xx. 10; though the impatient spirit was shown also in striking the rock twice.

33. THEY REBELLED AGAINST HIS SPIRIT. Three explanations of this line have been given. (1) By "his spirit" has been understood the spirit of Moses, and accordingly the line has been rendered in the E.V. "they *provoked* his spirit." This, however, is to give a meaning to the verb which it never has. Hence De Wette, "they strove against his spirit." (2) The words have been understood of disobedience against God: "They rebelled against His (God's) Spirit." Comp. Is. lxiii. 10, "But they rebelled and vexed His Holy Spirit," with Ps. lxxviii. 40. But (3), retaining this last explanation, it is still a question what is the subject of the verb. It *may* be said of Moses and Aaron, that *they* rebelled (see Num. xx. 24, xxvii. 14), but it is better to assume that the people are the subject, the two clauses of ver. 33 thus answering to the two of ver. 32.

34. Disobedience in the land of Canaan itself, especially in not rooting out the nations (as enjoined) Ex. xxiii. 32, 33, and often repeated, Josh. xxiii. 12, 13, and the adoption of their idolatrous worship.

AS JEHOVAH HAD SAID, the construction may be either (1) "Which thing Jehovah had said unto them;" or (2) "Concerning whom Jehovah

35 But they mixed themselves with the nations,
And learned their works;
36 And they served their idols,
And they became unto them a snare:
37 And they sacrificed their sons and their daughters to false gods;
38 And they shed innocent blood,
The blood of their sons and their daughters,
Which they sacrificed to the idols of Canaan;
And the land was polluted with bloodshed.
39 And they were defiled with their works,
And went a-whoring with their doings.

40 Then the anger of Jehovah was kindled against His people,
And He abhorred His own inheritance.
41 And He gave them into the hand of the nations,
And their haters ruled over them.
42 And their enemies oppressed them,
And they were bowed down under their hand.
43 Many a time did He deliver them,
But they rebelled (against Him) in their counsel,
And were brought low through their iniquity.

had commanded them," as in the E.V.

36. A SNARE, as the warning ran, Ex. xxiii. 33, xxxiv. 12; Deut. vii. 16. Of the abominations of the heathen, that of human sacrifices, as in the worship of Moloch, is especially dwelt upon. This was an offering to FALSE GODS (Heb. *Shêdîm*), lit. "lords," like *Bealim*, *'Adonim*, and then applied to gods (as the forms *Shaddai*, *'Adonai*, were confined to Jehovah); see the same word Deut. xxxii. 17, for which in Jud. ii. 11, *Bealim*. The LXX. render δαιμονίοις, and Jerome *dæmonibus*, whence the E.V. has "devils."

38. POLLUTED. The strongest word, taken from Num. xxxv. 33; comp. Is. xxiv. 5. The land, the very soil itself, was polluted and accursed, as well as the inhabitants (ver. 39).

40—43. The terrible and repeated judgements of God.

42. THEY WERE BOWED DOWN, elsewhere said of the enemies of Israel, Jud. iii. 30, iv. 23, viii. 28, xi. 33.

43. IN THEIR COUNSEL, as in lxxxi. 12 [13]; Jer. vii. 24, emphatically opposed to the counsel and purpose of God.

WERE BROUGHT LOW, Lev. xxvi. 39.

44 But He looked upon their distress,
When He heard their cry.
45 And He remembered for them His covenant,
And pitied them according to the greatness of His loving-kindness.
46 And He made them to find compassion
In the presence of all who carried them captive.
47 Save us, O Jehovah our God,
And gather us from the nations,
That we may give thanks unto Thy Holy Name;
That we may glory in Thy praise.

48 Blessed be Jehovah, the God of Israel,
From everlasting even to everlasting.
And let all the people say, Amen!
Hallelujah!

44. The Psalmist turns now to the other side of God's dealings with His people. It was not all anger. If they forgot His covenant, He remembered it. Even in the land of their captivity, He softened the hearts of their captors.

THEIR CRY. The word which is often used of the song of joy, here, as in 1 Kings viii. 28, of the cry of distress.

45. PITIED THEM, or "repented," as in xc. 13.

46. MADE THEM TO FIND, &c., lit. "Made them for (an object of) compassions, or tender mercies." There is a reference to Solomon's prayer, 1 Kings viii. 50. Comp. Neh. i. 11; Dan. i. 9. For the construction, see Gen. xliii. 14.

47. The grace of God, already shown to His people, leads to the prayer of this verse—a supplication for which the whole Psalm has prepared the way. The language would seem to indicate that the Psalm was written in exile, though the same prayer might also have been uttered by one of those who returned in the first caravan, on behalf of his brethren who were still dispersed.

GLORY IN THY PRAISE, or "deem ourselves happy in that we can praise Thee." The verb is the reflexive form (Hithpael), which occurs only in this Psalm.

48. The last verse is merely a Doxology added at a time subsequent to the composition of the Psalm, to mark the close of the Book. The first line varies but slightly from that at the end of lxxii., "Blessed be Jehovah God, the God of Israel."

The Chronicler who quotes this verse (see Introduction to this Psalm and cv.), changes the wish "Let all the people say, Amen," into the historic tense, "And all the people said Amen, and praised Jehovah" (1 Chron. xvi. 36). The fact that he has incorporated this verse as well as the preceding in his Psalm, is a proof that already in his time the Psalter was divided, as at present, into Books, the Doxology being regarded as an integral portion of the Psalm.

THE PSALMS

BOOK 5

Psalms 107—150

PSALM 107

It has already been observed in the General Introduction to this work (Vol. I. p. 71) that there is no obvious reason why, in the division of the Psalter into Five Books, the doxology marking the close of the Fourth Book should have been placed at the end of the 106th Psalm. On the contrary, the 106th and 107th Psalms seem to have certain links of connection, and many critics have supposed that they are the work of the same author.

Not only are the opening words of the two Psalms identical, but what is the subject of prayer in the one is the subject of thanksgiving in the other. In cvi. 47 the Psalmist prays that God would gather Israel from the heathen: in cvii. 3 he exhorts Israel to give thanks to Him who has brought them back from their captivity.*

Some expositors have even gone so far as to maintain that the four Psalms, civ.—cvii., were designed to constitute a complete tetralogy arranged in chronological order, beginning with the narrative of creation (Ps. civ.), going on to the history of the patriarchs and the early history of Israel (Ps. cvi.), pursuing the fortunes of the nation in the Promised Land, and even down to the time of the Captivity (Ps. cvi.), and finally celebrating the deliverance from Babylon, and the return of the exiles (Ps. cvii.). But the connection between Ps. civ. and those which follow it is by no means so close as that between the three Psalms, cv.—cvii.

"These three anonymous Psalms," says Delitzsch, "form a trilogy in the strictest sense, and are in all probability a tripartite whole from the hand of one author." Philipson takes the same view, remarking that the Poet has shown consummate art in the form which he has given to the whole, and the disposition and grouping of his materials. He thus traces the connection: "In the first part (Ps. cv.) the Poet has set forth the benefits of God, and the effect produced by them: in the second (Ps. cvi), only the sins of Israel, and the loss and suffering thereby incurred; in the third (Ps. cvii.), the deliverance, into the picture of which he has skilfully introduced both the sufferings

* On these grounds both Ewald and Hengstenberg regard these two Psalms as closely connected.

of his people and also their return to their God. The first part is bright with praise and thanksgiving, the second gloomy and terrifying, the third full of exhortation and encouragement. And how skilful is the transition from one part to another! At the close of the first division (cv. 45), an intimation is given that Israel had not accomplished the purpose for which Canaan had been given him as an inheritance; at the close of the second (cvi. 45), we already see the dawn of approaching redemption."

Delitzsch, who traces the connection in a similar way, points to the three following passages as confirming it: "He gave them *the lands* of the heathen" (cv. 44); "He threatened to cast forth their seed among the heathen, and to scatter them *in the lands*" (cvi. 27); "And He hath gathered them *from the lands*, from the East, and the West," &c. (cvii. 3). Other expressions, he observes, occur which link the three Psalms together. Egypt is called in them "the land of Ham," cv. 23, 27, cvi. 22, and Israel "the chosen of Jehovah," cv. 6, 43, cvi. 5 (comp. 23). In cv. 19, cvii. 20, there is an approach to the hypostatic sense of the "word" of God.* In cvi. 14, cvii. 4, *y'shîmon* is the word used to describe the waste, the wilderness. To these characteristics may be added the use of the Hithpael conjugation in all the Psalms, cv. 3, cvi. 5, cvi. 47, cvii. 27. In all alike there is the same absence of strophical arrangement.† In all there is evidence of a partiality for the later chapters of Isaiah (xl.—lxvi.) and the Book of Job. This is more especially noticeable in the 107th Psalm, where the Poet is more at liberty, as he is no longer recapitulating the history of his nation.

But ingenious as all this is, it rests on the assumption that the 107th Psalm, like the other two, is historical, and is designed chiefly to celebrate the return from the Babylonish captivity. The second and third verses of the Psalm are supposed to mark the occasion for which it was written, and the rest of the Psalm is held to exhibit, by means of certain examples of peril and deliverance, either in a figure the miseries of the Exile, or literally the various incidents of the homeward journey.

Such an interpretation, however, can scarcely be maintained. No doubt the deliverance from Babylon is uppermost in the Psalmist's thoughts (ver. 2, 3), and this suggests the various instances of God's providential care. Wanderers in the desert, captives, the sick and

---

* See, however, the notes on those passages.

† This can hardly be maintained with regard to Ps. cvii. At least to the end of ver. 32 the strophical arrangement is clearly marked by the double refrain, "Then they cried unto Jehovah," &c., and "Let them thank Jehovah for His loving-kindness," &c.

suffering, the merchant and the mariner have experienced that care, and have had reason to acknowledge it with gratitude. But it is unnatural to regard these various examples, taken from every-day experience, as a figurative description of the Exile; it is quite impossible, in particular, that the picture of the seafarers should represent the sufferings of captivity, though it certainly might form one part of the story of the return; for the exiles are here described, not merely as coming back from Babylon, but from all the countries of their dispersion (comp. Jer. xvi. 15, xl. 12; Dan. ix. 7).

It is obvious that this Psalm is not historical. It describes various incidents of human life, it tells of the perils which befall men, and the goodness of God in delivering them, and calls upon all who have experienced His care and protection gratefully to acknowledge them; and it is perfectly general in its character. The four (or five) groups, or pictures, are so many samples taken from the broad and varied record of human experience.

Such a Psalm would have been admirably adapted to be sung in the Temple-worship, at the offering of the thank-offerings.

But, whatever may have been the circumstances under which the Psalm was written, or the particular occasion for which it was intended, there can be no doubt as to the great lesson which it inculcates. It teaches us not only that God's providence watches over men, but that His ear is open to their prayers. It teaches us that prayer may be put up for temporal deliverance, and that such prayer is answered. It teaches us that it is right to acknowledge with thanksgiving such answers to our petitions. This was the simple faith of the Hebrew Poet.

It is needless to say how readily such a faith is shaken now. First, there is the old and obvious objection that *all* such prayers, even when offered by men of devout mind, are *not* answered. Calvin notices the difficulty, quoting the story of the wit, who when he entered the temple, and observed the votive tablets suspended there by merchants, recording their escape from shipwreck by the favour of the gods, sarcastically remarked, "I see no record of those who perished in the sea, and yet the number of them must be immense." Calvin replies, as might be expected, that though a hundred-fold more are lost than escape, still God's goodness is not obscured; that He exercises judgement as well as mercy; that all deserve destruction, and that therefore His sovereign mercy ought to be acknowledged in every instance where it is displayed. It would have been better, surely, to have replied, that answers to prayer are not all of one kind; and that God as really answers His children's supplication when He gives them strength and resignation in prison or in sickness, as when

He "breaks in pieces the bars of iron," or "sends His word and heals them"; when He suffers them to sink beneath the raging waters, with heaven open to their eyes, as when He "brings them to their desired haven." Closely akin to this, there arises another question. Does God ever answer prayer by *direct* action upon the material world? Are not the laws of the universe the expression of His will? Are they not, therefore, unchangeable? And is it not both presumptuous and selfish to ask him to change the phenomena, which are the result of those laws: presumptuous, because we thus dictate to Him what is best for us; selfish, because the blessing we crave may be at the expense of injury and loss to others? I conceive it may be replied, that it is not for the most part by immediate action in the material world that God grants our petitions. Even if we were forced to concede that now, since the age of miracles is past, God *never* so acts, still this should not trouble us, seeing how wide the region is in which *indirectly* our prayers even for temporal blessings may be answered. "Thus, for instance" (I venture to repeat what I have said elsewhere*), "we pray that the cholera or the murrain may be stayed. God does not with His own hand take away the plague; but He puts it into the heart of some physician to find the remedy which will remove it. He does not hush the storm in a moment; but He gives the mariner courage and skill to steer before it till he reach the haven. He does not shower bread from heaven in a famine; but He teaches the statesman how, with wise forethought and patient endeavours, at least to mitigate the calamity. How often we speak of happy inspirations, little knowing what we mean when we speak thus! And how unable we are to trace the chain! We cannot see God's Spirit prompting the prayer, or suggesting the remedy which shall be the answer to the prayer. But the antecedent and the consequent are as really there, the links of the chain are as essential as they are in any of the phenomena of the material world, which present themselves to our bodily senses. And thus the answer comes not by direct interference with the laws of nature, but in accordance with the laws of the spiritual world, by the Divine action on the heart of man." If so, then the answer may be acknowledged with devout thanksgiving, and men may praise the Lord for His goodness.

The Psalm consists of six groups, with a preface (ver. 1—3), and a conclusion (ver. 43). The preface and the conclusion alike give the theme or key-note of the Psalm. The first four groups are marked

---

* *The Feast of Harvest.* A Sermon preached in St. Peter's Church, Carmarthen, p. 19. [I have discussed the subject still more fully in a Sermon on "Prayer and Natural Law" in a volume of sermons recently published by Isbister and Co., 1874.]

by the double refrain, the two last have but a slight connection with the others (see note on ver. 33). The grammatical structure is peculiar. In the first part of the Psalm the strophes, except the first, begin with a particle or adjective of the subject, the predicate being virtually contained in the verb of the refrain: *Let them give thanks.*

1 "O GIVE thanks unto Jehovah, for He is good,
For His loving-kindness (endureth) for ever,"
2 Let the ransomed of Jehovah say (so),
Whom He hath ransomed from the hand of the adversary.
3 And gathered them out of the lands,
From the East and from the West,
From the North and from the South.[a]
4 They wandered in the wilderness, in a pathless waste;[b]
A city where men dwell they found not:

1. The Psalm opens with the same doxological formula as cvi., only here it is put into the mouth of the exiles returned from Babylon. For a similar opening see cxviii. 1—4. In earlier Psalms where phrases of the kind occur, they do not stand at the beginning of the Psalm, and the verb "say" precedes the doxology instead of following it; see xxxv. 27, xl. 16 [17].

It is the old liturgical doxology which, as in Jer. xxxiii. 11, is to be heard in the mouth of the captives restored to their own land.

2. RANSOMED OF JEHOVAH; as in Is. lxii. 12 (whence it may have been borrowed), lxiii. 4; comp. xxxv. 9, 10.

THE ADVERSARY, the oppressor in Babylon; or the word may mean, as in ver. 6, "distress." (So Ibn Ez. and Qimchi.) "From the hand of distress" might be said in Hebrew, in the same way as "from the hand of the dog" (xxii. 20).

3. GATHERED THEM, as in cvi. 47, and generally in the Prophets (comp. Is. xi. 12, lvi. 8, and often) of the return from the Captivity. For the same picture see Is. xliii. 5, 6, xlix. 12. The exiles free to return are seen flocking, not from Babylon only, but from all lands, "like doves to their windows." Cf. cv. 44, cvi. 27.

THE SOUTH, lit. "the sea" (if the text is correct), which everywhere else means the West (the Mediterranean Sea), but must obviously here denote the South. Hence the Chald. understands by "the Sea," the Southern Sea (*i.e.* the Arabian Gulf); others again, the Southern (Indian) Ocean; but as these explanations are contrary to usage, there is reason to question the correctness of the text. See more in Critical Note.

4. The first example: the caravan which has lost its way in the desert. The interpretation of the verse will vary according to the view we take of its connection with the preceding.

(i.) We may take "the ransomed of Jehovah" (ver. 2) as the subject

5 Hungry and thirsty,
    Their soul fainted in them :
6 Then they cried unto Jehovah in their trouble,
    (And) He delivered them out of their distresses ;
7 He led them by a straight way,
    That they might go to a city where men dwell.

of the verb ; and then (*a*), by those who adopt the historical interpretation of the Psalm, the picture which follows has been held to be a description either (1) of what befell the Jews who (Jer. xliii.) fled into the wilderness to escape the Chaldeans after the taking of Jerusalem ; or (2) of the perils encountered by the caravans of exiles as they crossed long tracts of sandy desert on their return ; or (3) intended to set forth in a figure the miseries of the Exile itself. Or (*b*) "the ransomed of Jehovah" may be taken in a wider sense, as denoting, not the captives at Babylon, but all Jews exposed to the risks and hardships of foreign travel. So Calvin : "Et primo ad gratitudinem hortatur qui ex longinqua et difficili peregrinatione, adeoque ex servitute et vinculis, domum incolumes reversi sunt. Tales autem vocat *redemptos Dei*, quia per deserta et invias solitudines vagando sæpius a reditu exclusi essent, nisi Deus, quasi porrecta manu, ducem se illis præbuisset."

(ii.) The subject of the verb may be changed, and this, either because (*a*) the Psalmist, having begun to speak of God's goodness to the exiles, restored by His hand to the land of their fathers, goes on to speak of other instances in which His goodness has been manifested. Or (*β*), because the first three verses were a liturgical addition, framed with particular reference to the return from Babylon, and prefixed to a poem originally designed to have a wider scope.

THEY WANDERED. The subject of the verb (see last note) may be "men" generally. The incident described was doubtless not uncommon. The usual track of the caravan is lost—obliterated, perhaps, by the sandstorm.

A CITY WHERE MEN DWELL, lit. "a city of habitation" (as E.V.). No particular city is meant, as P.B.V., "the city where they dwelt," much less is Jerusalem intended, but any inhabited city, as opposed to the uninhabited wilderness. The expression recurs in verses 7, 36.

5. FAINTED, lit. "covered itself," as with darkness, sorrow, and the like, as in lxxvii. 3 [4], cxlii. 3 [4], cxliii. 4 ; Jon. ii. 7 [8].

6. THEN THEY CRIED. So it ever is : only the pressure of a great need forces men to seek God. Prayer is not only the resource of good men, but of all men in trouble. It is a natural instinct even of wicked men to turn to God at such times : "Si graviori in discrimine versentur, etiam sine certa meditatione, ad Deum invocandum natura duce et magistra impelli."—*Calvin.*

JEHOVAH. Hengstenberg alleges the use of this Name instead of the more general one, Elohim, God, in proof that the Psalmist is speaking not of men at large, but only of Jews (and that hence the Psalm refers to the return from the Captivity at Babylon). The heathen, he objects, would not be said to call upon *Jehovah*. But surely a Jew even when speaking of the general providence of God, would have Jews chiefly before his mind as embraced in that providence, and as naturally would use the name of God which was dearest to him as a

8 Let them give thanks to Jehovah for His loving-kindness,
And for His wonders to the children of men :
9 For He satisfieth the longing soul,
And filleth the hungry soul with good.

10 They that sat in darkness and the shadow of death,
Being bound in affliction and iron,
11 Because they rebelled against the words of God,
And despised the counsel of the Most High,
12 And He brought down their heart with labour,
They stumbled, and there was none to help;
13 Then they cried unto Jehovah in their trouble,
(And) He saved them out of their distresses ;
14 He brought them out of darkness and the shadow of death,
And brake their bonds asunder ;—

Jew. The distinction between Jew and Gentile would be lost sight of altogether.

8. Others render, "Let them praise His loving-kindness before Jehovah, and His wonders before the children of men," *i.e.* let them confess His goodness before God and man. The parallelism may perhaps be more accurately preserved by this rendering, but grammatically it is not necessary. It is also doubtful whether we have here the expression of a wish, "*Let them give* thanks ;" or the statement of a past fact, "*they gave* thanks." In support of the latter rendering may be alleged the frequent use of the same tense in the Psalm as a past ("a relative preterite," Hupf.) ; see on xviii., note [c]. But the analogy of ver. 2, which is clearly optative, makes the former the more probable.

9. There is a reference to ver. 5 ; "longing" answers to "thirsty," as in Is. xxix. 8.

10—16. The second example—that of prisoners.

10. DARKNESS, &c. The same expression occurs Is. xlii. 7, xlix. 9 ; Micah vii. 8, of the gloom of the prison-house. Comp. Virgil. *Æn.* vi. 734, "Neque auras Respiciunt, clausæ tenebris et carcere cæco."

AFFLICTION AND IRON. Comp. the fuller phrase Job xxxvi. 8, "bound in fetters, and holden in cords of affliction."

11. WORDS . . . COUNSEL. The commandments of God as given in the Law, and His counsel as declared by his prophets, are chiefly meant ; for throughout the passage language is employed which implies the theocratic position of Israel. But the reference may be wider. The law written in the conscience, the instruction given by inner revelation (comp. xvi. 7) need not be excluded. So the verb THEY DESPISED is used both in the theocratic sense of blasphemy (Num. xiv. 11, 23, xvi. 30 ; Deut. xxxi. 20), and also in a more general sense, as in the rejection of the counsels of wisdom (Prov. i. 30, v. 12, xv. 5).

12. AND HE BROUGHT, &c. Some would begin the apodosis here, "So He brought," &c., or "Therefore He brought," &c. ; but in that case, as on any interpretation, the participles in ver. 10 must be a *nominativus pendens,* the

15 Let them give thanks to Jehovah for His loving-kindness,
And for His wonders to the children of men :
16 For He brake the doors of brass,
And cut the bars of iron in sunder.

17 Foolish men, because of the way of their transgression,
And because of their iniquities, bring affliction upon themselves ;
18 Their soul abhorreth all manner of food,
And they draw near to the gates of death :

construction not being completed till ver. 15, see note on that verse. Hitz. with more probability makes the nominative in ver. 10 taken up in ver. 13, verses 11 and 12 being parenthetical : "They that sat in darkness, &c. (because they rebelled, &c.), they cried unto Jehovah."

15. The construction of the whole passage, beginning with ver. 10, is only completed here. The participial subject, "they that sat, or sit," &c., finds here its verb. The intervening verses, 11—14, are to a certain extent parenthetical, ver. 11, 12 giving the reason, and ver. 13, 14 the consequences, of the chastisement. The verbs in ver. 10, 13, 14, might all be rendered as presents.

16. The expressions are apparently taken from Is. xlv. 2.

17—22. Third example : sick persons brought by their sickness to the edge of the grave.

17. FOOLISH MEN so called because of the moral infatuation which marks their conduct, as in xiv. 1, where see notes ; men of earthly, sensual, selfish minds, who turn a deaf ear to warning, and despise counsel (comp. Prov. i. 7, xii. 15, xiv. 3, 9, xv. 5, xxvii. 22), and who can only be brought to reason by chastisement. The expression seems quite to exclude the notion that the allusion is to "a party of sick exiles, enfeebled probably by labours, or by uncongenial climates, so that their soul abhorred all manner of meat, and they were hard at death's door."—*Liddon.* Such persons would not be decribed as "foolish," but rather as objects of pity. The noun "foolishness," xxxviii. 5 [6], is from the same root, and is used in the same ethical sense. See note there.

THE WAY OF THEIR TRANSGRESSION. The expression is used to denote the course of conduct, the habit of the life, and is not merely pleonastic.

BRING AFFLICTION UPON THEMSELVES. The proper reflexive signification of the conjugation is by all means to be retained. It most expressively marks how entirely a man brings upon himself his own punishment. The same form of the verb is used, but with a somewhat different shade of meaning, in 1 Kings ii. 26. There it rather denotes the involuntary submission to suffering. [Delitzsch would give this sense here, and in 1 Kings ii. 26 explains the Hithp., "geflissentlich leiden." He is quite right in adding, "reines Passivum *affligebantur* ist es nicht."] I have here, and in what follows, after the example of our translators, preferred the present tense to the past. This change of tense exists in the Hebrew, and the rendering gives more force and animation to the picture ; though it would certainly be possible to continue the use of the past tense throughout. See on xviii., note [c].

18. Comp. the similar passage, Job xxxiii. 20—22.

19 Then they cry unto Jehovah in their trouble,
He saveth them out of their distresses:
20 He sendeth His word, and healeth them,
And rescueth them from their graves.
21 Let them give thanks to Jehovah for His loving-kindness,
And for His wonders to the children of men:
22 And let them sacrifice sacrifices of thanksgiving,
And tell of His works with a song of joy.

23 They that go down to the sea in ships,

20. HE SENDETH HIS WORD. The same expression occurs in cxlvii. 15, 18; see also cv. 19, and comp. Is. ix. 8 [7], lv. 11. We detect in such passages the first glimmering of St. John's doctrine of the agency of the personal Word. The Word by which the heavens were made (xxxiii. 6) is seen to be not merely the expression of God's will, but His messenger mediating between Himself and His creatures. It is interesting to compare with this the language of Elihu in the parallel passage of Job xxxiii. 23, where what is here ascribed to the agency of the Word is ascribed to that of the "mediating angel, or messenger." Theodoret observes: *'Ο Θεὸς Λόγος ἐνανθρωπήσας καὶ ἀποσταλεὶς ὡς ἄνθρωπος τὰ παντοδαπὰ τῶν ψυχῶν ἰάσατο τραύματα, καὶ τοὺς διαφθαρέντας ἀνέρρωσε λογισμούς.* Too much stress, however, must not be laid on the use of the verb "sendeth." Comp. cxi. 9, "He *sent* redemption unto His people."

GRAVES. The word may be taken in this sense, in allusion to their nearness to death, ver. 18; others understand by it "pits" metaphorically, the pit of suffering into which they have sunk. (So Delitzsch, referring to Lam. iv. 10, and the similar form in Prov. xxviii. 10.) Hitz. *from their sins* (Dan. vi. 5) into whose powers they have given themselves (Job viii. 4), which have taken hold of the doer of them (Ps. xl. 13); *i.e.* the consequences of their sins. He therefore connects the word with שחת in the sense of corruption, as the LXX. *ἐκ τῶν διαφθορῶν αὐτῶν.*

23—32. Fourth example: seafarers tossed and driven by the tempest, and brought at last safe into port. The description may be compared with the language of Jonah i., ii. It is the most highly finished, the most thoroughly poetical of each of the four pictures of human peril and deliverance. It is painted as a landsman would paint it, but yet only as one who had himself been exposed to the danger could paint the storm — the waves running mountains high, on which the tiny craft seemed a plaything, the helplessness of human skill, the gladness of the calm, the safe refuge in the haven.

Addison remarks, that he prefers this description of a ship in a storm before any others he had ever met with, and for the same reason for which "Longinus recommends one in Homer, because the poet has not amused himself with little fancies upon the occasion, as authors of an inferior genius, whom he mentions, had done, but because he has gathered together those circumstances which are the most apt to terrify the imagination, and which really happened in the raging of a tempest." By the way, he adds, "how much more comfortable as well as rational is this system of

That do business in great waters,
24 These men have seen the works of Jehovah,
And His wonders in the deep.
25 For He commandeth and raiseth a stormy wind,
Which lifteth up the waves thereof.
26 They mount up to the heaven,
They go down (again) to the depths;
Their soul melteth away because of (the) trouble.
27 They reel to and fro, and stagger like a drunken man,
And are at their wits' end:

the Psalmist, than the pagan scheme in Virgil and other poets, where one deity is represented as raising a storm, and another as laying it! Were we only to consider the sublime in this piece of poetry, what can be nobler than the idea it gives us of the Supreme Being thus raising a tumult among the elements, and recovering them out of their confusion; thus troubling and becalming nature?"—*Spectator*, No. 489.

23. GO DOWN TO THE SEA, as in Is. xlii. 10; Jon. i. 3.

BUSINESS. There is no need to restrict this to the management of craft by seamen. It includes the occupations of fishermen, traders, persons on a voyage, &c.

24. THE WORKS OF JEHOVAH, AND HIS WONDERS, *i.e.* His rule of the elements: how at His word the storm raises the billows high as heaven, how at His words it sinks down hushed and gentle as the soft breath of summer.

25. FOR HE COMMANDETH, lit. "and He said," the phrase which occurs so often in Gen. i. to describe God's creative fiat. Compare the use of the same word in cv. 31, 34.

THE WAVES THEREOF, *i.e.* of the sea, the pronominal suffix referring to the remote noun in ver. 23, as is not uncommonly the case in Hebrew. (See for a still more remarkable instance of this, cxi. 10, where the plural pronoun "them" can only refer to the word "statutes" in ver. 7.) In sense it may also refer to the noun "deep" in ver. 24, but not in grammar, this noun being feminine.

26. THEY MOUNT UP, *i.e.* not "the waves," but "the seafarers." The same expression occurs, but in a different sense, in civ. 8, where see note.

27. REEL TO AND FRO, or, even more exactly, "spin round and round."

ARE AT THEIR WITS' END, lit. "all their wisdom (skill, resources, &c.) swalloweth itself up," or, "cometh of itself to nought."* (Comp. Is. xix. 3, "I will bring his counsel to nought.") The Hithpael occurs only here. Possibly the figure may

* The whole description up to this point finds a striking parallel in Ovid, *Trist.* i. 2:—

"Me miserum quanti montes volvuntur aquarum:
Jamjam tacturos sidera summa putes.
Quantæ diducto subsidunt æquore valles:
Jamjam tacturos Tartara nigra putes.
Rector in incerto est, nec quid fugiatve petatve
Invenit: ambiguis ars stupet ipsa malis."

28 Then they cry unto Jehovah in their trouble,
And He bringeth them out of their distresses;
29 He husheth the storm to a gentle air,
So that the waves thereof are still.
30 Then are they glad because they be quiet,
And He leadeth them to their desired haven.
31 Let them give thanks to Jehovah for His loving-kindness,
And for His wonders to the children of men;
32 Let them exalt Him also in the assembly of the people,
And praise Him in the seat of the elders.

33 He turneth rivers into a wilderness,
And water-springs into a thirsty ground;
34 A fruitful land into a salt-marsh,
Because of the wickedness of them that dwell therein.

have been taken from the Syrtes, or a whirlpool.

29. A GENTLE AIR. This, and not absolute "stillness," "calm" (Symm. γαλήνη), seems to be the meaning of the word, or they could not move on to the haven. Comp. 1 Kings xix. 12, and so the LXX. and Aq. αὖρα. J. D. Mich. quotes Virgil's *æquatæ spirant auræ.*

THE WAVES THEREOF, lit. "*their* waves," but the plural suffix must refer to the sea, and may perhaps have been occasioned by the plural "great waters" in ver. 23. See note on ver. 25. Others refer the plural pronoun to the seafarers: "*their* waves," *i.e.* those on which they are tossed, and which threaten to engulf them.

30. BE QUIET. A word used of the quiet of the sea after a storm, Jon. i. 11, 12, and only once besides, Prov. xxvi. 20, of the ceasing of contention.

HAVEN. This is probably the meaning of the word, but it occurs nowhere else. Ibn Ezra renders "shore," "coast." Others explain: "sight (fr. חזה) of their desire," *i.e.* the desired object, the land or haven in sight.

32. SEAT or "assembly," *concessuss.* See note on i. 1.

33. The character of the Psalm changes at this point. We have no longer distinct pictures as before: the beautiful double refrain is dropped, the language is harsher and more abrupt. Instead of fresh examples of deliverance from peril, and thanksgiving for God's mercies, we have now other instances of God's providential government of the world exhibited in two series of contrasts. The first of these is contained in ver. 33—39, and expresses a double change—the fruitful well-watered land smitten, like the rich plain of Sodom, with desolation, and changed into a salt-marsh (LXX. εἰς ἅλμην, Jer. *in salsuginem;*) and anon, the wilderness crowned with cities, like Tadmor (of which Pliny says, *vasto ambitu arenis includit agros*), and made fertile to produce corn and wine: the second is contained in ver. 40, 41, and expresses the changes in the fortunes of *men* (as the last series did those of *countries*), viz. how the poor and the humble are raised and the rich and the proud overthrown.

35 He turneth a wilderness into a pool of water,
And a dry land into water-springs.
36 And there He maketh the hungry to dwell,
And they build a city to dwell in;
37 And sow fields, and plant vineyards,
Which may yield the fruit of (yearly) produce.
38 And He blesseth them so that they multiply greatly,
And He suffereth not their cattle to be minished.
39 And again they are minished and brought low
Through oppression, evil, and sorrow.
40 ' He poureth contempt upon princes,

35. HE TURNETH, &c. The language is borrowed from Is. xli. 18, 19, and hence it has been supposed that the allusion here is to historical events; that ver. 33 depicts the desolation of the land whilst the Jews were captives in Babylon, ver. 35 the change which took place on their return (comp. with this the language of cxxvi. 4, "Turn again our captivity, as the streams in the south"). But the passages in Isaiah (comp. besides that already quoted, xxxv. 6, 7, xlii. 15, 16, xliii. 19, 20, xliv. 27, l. 2) refer not to the Holy Land, but to the deserts through which the exiles would pass on their return; and further, the language employed is far too general to be thus limited to one event. It describes what frequently has occurred. The histories of Mexico and of Holland might furnish examples of such a contrast.

37. WHICH MAY YIELD (lit. "and they yield"). This rendering is in accordance with the common usage of the verb and noun. Others however render: "and they (men) get their fruit of increase," or the like. So Mendels., "Jährlich Früchte sammeln."

39. It is possible that this verse and ver. 40 stand to one another in the relation of protasis and apodosis: "When theyare minished &c. . . . He poureth contempt, &c." Another reverse is described as befallen those who had just risen into prosperity. It may have happened, says the Poet, that the prosperity of this race, living at peace amid its herds and flocks, and the labours of its hands, has provoked the envy and the cupidity of some neighbouring tyrant. He destroys their harvest, and burns their homestead, and drives off their flocks; but God pours contempt upon him, leads him astray in the wilderness to perish, and restores the victims of his tyranny to more than their former fortune. But it is more probable that, as verses 33, 34 present one picture of which the contrast is given in verses 35—37, so verses 38 and 39 are in opposition to each other, and again ver. 40 and 41. We thus have three successive contrasts, the second (ver. 38, 39) being in the reverse order to the other two. The play on the word "minished" in ver. 38 and 39 indicates a close connection between the two. On the other hand, here, as in verse 4, the subject may not be found directly in what precedes, but may be general: "They, *i.e.* men, whoever they may be, are minished," &c.

40. This verse is a quotation from Job xii. 21, where it stands in a series of participial sentences describing the method of God's government. Here it is introduced not only as forming a direct anti-

And maketh them to wander in the waste where there
is no way.'
41 And He setteth the poor on high out of affliction,
And maketh families like a flock.
42 The upright see (it) and are glad,
And all iniquity hath shut her mouth.
43 Who is wise that he should observe these things,
And that they should understand the loving-kindnesses
of Jehovah?

thesis to the following verse, but as suggesting also an antithesis to ver. 36.

41. LIKE A FLOCK: a figure expressive of large increase, as in Job xxi. 11.

42. The impression produced by these acts of Divine Providence. Comp. Job. v. 16.

43. The conclusion, in the form of a question, such as that with which Hosea concludes his prophecy, xiv. 10.

This verse might, however, also be rendered, either (1) "Who is wise and will observe these things? Let them understand, &c.," or, (2, "Whoso is wise will observe, &c., and they shall understand, &c."

[a] יָם everywhere else (unless possibly in Is. xlix. 12, where it is opposed to צָפוֹן) means *the West*, the "Sea" being the Mediterranean. That evidently cannot be the meaning here, where another word is already used for *West*. Perhaps, therefore, we ought to read מִיָּמִין (Köst.) or מִתֵּימָן, as in Is. xliii. 5.

[b] יְשִׁימוֹן דֶּרֶךְ. It seems unnecessary, with Olsh. and others, to read לֹא דֶרֶךְ, as in ver. 40. The negative is implied in the word יְשִׁימוֹן. The noun "way" is the accus. of nearer definition, as it is called (Ges. § 118, 3), "Waste as to way" = "a region where there is no way," "a pathless desert." The LXX., Syr., Vulg., join דֶּרֶךְ with what follows, "a way to a city of habitation," &c. Others would join it with תָּעוּ (*errarunt a via*), which, however, is too remote.

PSALM 108

THIS Psalm consists of portions of two others, the first half of it being taken from the 57th Psalm, ver. 7—11 [8—12], and the latter half from the 60th, ver. 5—12 [7—14]. It bears the name of David, because the original passages both occur in Psalms ascribed to him as their author. But there is no reason for concluding that these fragments were thus united by David himself. Some later Poet probably adapted them to circumstances of his own time; possibly wished thus to commemorate some victory over Edom or Philistia. The change in the tenth verse, as compared with the corresponding passage in the 60th Psalm, may be held to favour this view. There are a few other not very important variations of the text which will be pointed out in the notes.

For the interpretation at large, the notes on the other two Psalms may be consulted.

[A SONG. A PSALM OF DAVID.]

1 My heart is steadfast, O God;
I will sing and play, yea, even my glory.
2 Awake, lute and harp,
I will wake the morning-dawn.
3 I will give thanks unto Thee among the peoples, O Jehovah,
And I will play unto Thee among the nations.
4 For great above the heavens is Thy loving-kindness,
And Thy truth (reacheth) unto the skies.
5 Be Thou exalted above the heavens, O God,
And Thy glory above all the earth.

6 That Thy beloved may be delivered,

1. MY HEART IS STEADFAST. In lvii. 7 [8] this is repeated. In the next member of the verse, MY GLORY has been made a second subject, "I, (even) my glory," instead of being joined with the following imperative, as in lvii. 8 [9].

MY GLORY, *i.e.* "my soul," with all those powers and faculties which belong to the rational being, as created in the image of God. See Gen. xlix. 6.

3. JEHOVAH. In lvii. "Adonai" (Lord).

4. ABOVE: comp. cxiii. 4. In xxxvi. 5 [6] the form of expression is somewhat different; "*in* the heavens . . . *unto* the clouds:" see also Jer. li. 9.

6—13. These verses are taken from Ps. lx. The passage consists of two lines of the first strophe of that Psalm, and the second and third strophes complete.

6. The construction of this verse is different from that in lx. 5 [7]. Here it forms a complete sentence in itself, the first clause depending on the second. The verse was evidently necessary to soften the abruptness of the transition from the former passage to this.

Save with Thy right hand, and answer me.
7 God hath spoken in His holiness:
Let me exult, let me portion out Shechem,
And the valley of Succoth let me mete out.
8 Mine is Gilead, mine Manasseh,
Ephraim also is the defence of my head;
Judah is my sceptre:
9 Moab is my washpot;
Upon Edom will I cast my shoe;
Over Philistia will I shout (in triumph).
10 Who will conduct me into the fenced city?
Who hath led me unto Edom?
11 Hast not Thou, O God, cast us off?
And wilt not go forth, O God, with our hosts?
12 O give us help from the adversary,
For vain is the salvation of man.
13 Through God we shall do valiantly,
And HE shall tread down our adversaries.

ANSWER ME; here in the text, and not the Massoretic correction, as in lx.

9. On the change in this verse, instead of "Because of me, O Philistia, cry aloud," the principal variation in the Psalm, see note on lx. 8.

10. FENCED. The more common word *mibtsar* is used instead of *mâtsōr* in ix.

The omission of the copula in ver. 9*a*, and of the pronoun in ver. 11, are the only other variations of any note.

PSALM 109

THIS is the last of the Psalms of imprecation, and completes the terrible climax. The remarks already made in the Note on xxxv. 22, in the Introduction to lxix. and the Note on ver. 22, and in the General Introduction to Vol. I., pp. 62—65, may be consulted here.

This Psalm differs from the 96th in being levelled against one enemy chiefly, not against many. This circumstance may partly account for the even more intensely-wrought and detailed character of the curse. In the awfulness of its anathemas, the Psalm surpasses everything of the kind in the Old Testament. Who the person was who was thus singled out for execration, it is in vain to conjecture. Those who hold, in accordance with the Inscription, that the Psalm was written by David, suppose that Doeg or Cush, Shimei or Ahithophel, is the object of execration.

In Acts i. 20, St. Peter combines a part of the 8th verse of this Psalm, " his office let another take," with words slightly altered from the 25th [Heb. 26th] verse of the 69th Psalm, and applies them to Judas Iscariot. Hence the Psalm has been regarded by the majority of expositors, ancient and modern, as a prophetic and Messianic Psalm. The language has been justified not as the language of David, but as the language of Christ, exercising His office of Judge, or, in so far as He had laid aside that office during His earthly life, calling upon His Father to accomplish the curse. It has been alleged that this is the prophetic foreshadowing of the solemn words, " Woe unto that man by whom the Son of man is betrayed ; it were good for that man if he had not been born" (Matt. xxvi. 24). The curse, in the words of Chrysostom, "is a prophecy in form of a curse" (προφητεία ἐν εἴδει ἀρᾶς).

The strain which such a view compels us to put on much of the language of the Psalm ought to have led long since to its abandonment. Not even the woes denounced by our Lord against the Pharisees can really be compared to the anathemas which are here strung together. Much less is there any pretence for saying that those words, so full of deep and holy sorrow, addressed to the traitor in the Gospels, are merely another expression of the appalling denunciations of the Psalm. But terrible as these undoubtedly are,—to be accounted for by the spirit of the Old Dispensation, not to be defended by that of the New,—still let us learn to estimate them aright. This is the *natural* voice of righteousness persecuted. These are the accents of the martyr, not smarting only with a sense of personal suffering, but feeling acutely, and hating nobly, the triumph of wickedness.*

---

* Calvin defends the imprecations on this ground partly, but goes further : " Tenendum est," he says, " Davidem quoties diras istas vel maledictionis vota concepit, nec immodico carnis affectu fuisse commotum, nec privatam causam egisse, nec zelo inconsiderato fuisse accensum. Hæc tria diligenter notanda sunt." He then warns us not to allege the example of David when we are hurried away by our own passions,—for Christ's answer to His disciples will apply to us, " Ye know not of what spirit ye are,"—and severely comments on the sacrilege of the monks, and particularly the Franciscans, who could be hired to recite this Psalm as a curse against an enemy. He mentions as a fact coming within his own knowledge, that a lady of quality in France had hired some Franciscans to curse her only son in the words of this Psalm.

The strains of this Psalm are strains which have lingered even in the Christian Church, not softened by "the meekness and gentleness of Christ." Let any one read the closing passage of Tertullian's treatise *De Spectaculis*, in which he does not hesitate to speak of the joy and exultation with which, at the day of judgement, he shall look upon the agonies of the damned, of the delight with which he shall see the kings of the earth, and the rulers who persecuted the Name of the Lord, melting in flames fiercer than those which they lighted for the Christians, philosophers burning with their disciples, tragic actors shrieking with real pain, the charioteer red upon his fiery wheel, and the wrestler tossing in the flames, till the fierce invective ends in a perfect shout of triumph as he thinks of the grandeur of the spectacle—let any one, I say, read passages such as this, let him remember how long it was held a sacred duty by Christian Fathers and Bishops to persecute, and then let him pause before he passes a too sweeping judgement on "the fierce vindictiveness" of the Jew.

A mode of interpretation has, however, sometimes been advocated which would get rid of the difficulty connected with the imprecations, by supposing them not to be uttered by the Psalmist, but to be merely cited by him as the words of his enemies directed against himself. We have only at the end of ver. 5 to supply the word "saying" which is so commonly omitted in Hebrew before quotations (see for instance ii. 2, xcv. 7, 10), and all that follows to the end of ver. 19 may be regarded as the malediction of the Psalmist's enemies. This is the view of Kennicott and of Mendelssohn, and it has been recently revived by Mr. Taylor (*Gospel in the Law*, p. 244, &c.), who has also attempted to apply the same method in explaining Ps. lxix. (*ib.* p. 225, &c.), though I cannot think successfully. For not to mention that other passages of vindictive and imprecatory character remain, of which no such solution is possible, he is obliged to give an interpretation of ver. 20 of this Psalm, which, to say the least of it, is strained and improbable (see note on the verse). It is moreover somewhat difficult to understand how the imprecations of the *Psalmist's enemies* could be cited by St. Peter, Acts i. 20, as prophetically descriptive of the fate of Judas. Would not this almost imply that the Psalmist himself was a kind of Old Testament Judas? Moreover, if we could account for *every* imprecation in the Psalms on the principle advocated by Mr. Taylor, what are we to say of such passages as the closing verses of Ps. lviii., or cxxxix. 19, or cxlix. 5—9?

Since the last edition of this work appeared, the view in question has been maintained with very great ability by the Rev. Joseph Hammond in a paper entitled *An Apology for the Vindictive Psalm*, which appeared in the *Expositor*, vol. ii. pp. 225—360. He maintains the Davidic authorship of the Psalm, and thinks that it is directed against Shimei. He argues that the Psalm is admirably illustrated by the narrative in 2 Sam. xvi., always remembering that the Psalmist has forewarned us that the charges brought against him were "lying" and "deceitful" (verse 2). Verses 1—5 of the Psalm "would describe exactly the words and deeds of Shimei." He has traced step by step each point in the narrrative in 2 Sam. which illustrates the language of the Psalm, and it must be admitted has made out a very strong case for the view that in verses 6—19 of the Psalm, David is quoting Shimei's curses against himself, and not indulging in curses of his own. He lays stress (*a*) on the change from the plural to the singular in ver. 6, and on the change back again from the singular to the plural in ver. 20; (*b*) on the verbal coincidences between the first and second sections of the Psalm; on the change between the tone and form of expression from ver. 20, and the resumption here of the complaint of the first section, that the Psalmist's adversaries "spoke evil against his soul"—that evil having meanwhile been put before us in the intervening section, 6—19. "The whole of this concluding section," he observes, "harmonizes, as it seems to me, with the first part, and is alien from the spirit of the second." I cannot, however, do more here than refer thus briefly to his able and exhaustive paper, which will well repay perusal.

In a series of papers in the third volume entitled *The Vindictive Psalms Vindicated*, he has discussed the whole subject of the Imprecations in the Psalms with a learning and a candour and a grasp of the subject of which it is impossible to speak too highly. I hope to advert more fully to these papers in the Appendix to this volume, but meanwhile I am sure my readers will thank me for directing their attention to them.

[FOR THE PRECENTOR. A PSALM OF DAVID.]

1 O GOD of my praise, be not silent!
2 For a wicked mouth and a deceitful mouth have they
opened against me;

1. GOD OF MY PRAISE, *i.e.* the object of my praise (Jer. xvii. 14). "The name contains the ground of the prayer. The God whom the Psalmist has hitherto found reason to praise will now also give him fresh reason for praise. In this faith he offers the prayer: 'Be not silent' (comp. xxviii. 1, xxxv. 22). God speaks when he interferes to judge and to save."—*Delitzsch.*

2. A WICKED MOUTH, &c., lit. "a

They have spoken against me with a false tongue.
3 Yea with words of hatred have they compassed me about,
And fought against me without a cause.
4 For my love they are adversaries unto me,
But I (give myself unto) prayer.
5 They have requited me also evil for good,
And hatred for my love.

6 Set Thou a wicked man over him,
And let an adversary stand at his right hand.

mouth of the wicked, and a mouth of deceit." For the first, some would read, by a slight change of the vowels, "a mouth of wickedness," so as to bring the two clauses into harmony. Stier, however, thinks that the expression "mouth of the wicked" may have been purposely employed with reference to the wicked man against whom the Psalmist prays. Hence, too, the play upon the word in ver. 6.

4. THEY ARE ADVERSARIES UNTO ME, or "withstand me," (as in xxxviii. 20 [21]); the verb is from the same root as the noun in ver. 6, "an adversary," "a Satan;" see also ver. 20, 29. It is used like διαβάλλω, διάβολος, of malicious accusation.

I (GIVE MYSELF UNTO) PRAYER, lit. "I am prayer," *i.e.* one who prays, having recourse to no other means of defence. So in cxx. 7, "I am peace;" cx. 3, "Thy people are freewillingness." To supply "for them," as if the prayer were for his enemies, as the Syriac translator and others do (influenced probably by the language of xxxv. 13), is against the tenor of the Psalm. The sense is, rather, "I find refuge in prayer, committing myself and my cause to thee." Comp. lxix. 12, 13.

5. For the sentiment comp. xxxv. 12, xxxviii. 20 [21].

6. Leaving the mass of his enemies, the Psalmist (if these are his words, and not those of his enemies, which he is quoting), suddenly singles out one, on whom he pours forth the terrible curse which follows. See a similar transition in lv. 12 [13]. Ver. 1—5 do not give the whole grounds for the curse; they are resumed in ver. 16—18.

SET, *i.e.* in an official capacity (comp. the use of the noun from the same root, "office," in ver. 8). Here, "appoint as judge," or "set over him with power and authority to punish." For the construction, comp. Lev. xxvi. 16.

AN ADVERSARY, or, "SATAN," (the LXX. διάβολος, Jerome, *Satan*). Let him have not only an unrighteous judge, but a malicious accuser. On the whole, I prefer the more general word "adversary," which is that of the margin of the E.V., especially as the same root occurs several times in the Psalm; see note on ver. 4. It is not indeed certain from the language of ver. 7 that the process is supposed to take place before a human tribunal; for the "prayer" there spoken of is prayer to God, not supplication to the human judge. But, on the other hand, "a wicked man" in the parallelism, and the general tenor of what follows, are rather in favour of the rendering "adversary." In Zech. iii. 1, where there is the same form of expression,—"and he shewed me Joshua the High Priest standing before the angel of Jehovah, and the adversary (or, the Satan) *standing at his right hand* to be an adversary unto him," Satan himself is doubtless meant,

7 When he is judged let him go forth condemned,
And let his prayer be turned into sin.
8 Let his days be few ;
His office let another take.
9 Let his children be orphans,
And his wife a widow.
10 Let his children also be continually vagabonds and beg ;
(Driven) from their ruined houses [a] let them seek (their bread).
11 Let the extortioner lay snares for all that he hath ;
And let strangers spoil his labour.

for the whole scene is that of a vision, as also in Job i. 6—13. This last passage shows how comparatively early the name occurred as a proper name. There is no pretence, therefore, for saying that the use of the name as that of the Evil Spirit is later than this Psalm.

7. WHEN HE IS JUDGED, &c. When his case is tried let him GO FORTH, leave the court, with sentence pronounced against him (lit. "guilty," comp. the verb from the same root "to condemn, to pronounce guilty," xxxviii. 33).

HIS PRAYER, not addressed to the human judge for mitigation of the sentence, but here, as always, prayer to God. The criminal looking in vain for pity or justice at the hands of man, turns in his extremity to God; but even there, at the very fount of mercy, let mercy fail him, let his prayer aggravate his guilt. The utterance of such a wish is the most awful part of the imprecation. That prayer may thus draw down not forgiveness but wrath, see Is. i. 15 ; Prov. xxviii. 9 ("He that turneth away his ear from hearing the law, even his prayer shall be abomination"), xv. 8, xxi. 27. But it is one thing to recognize this as a fact in the Divine government of man, it is another thing to imprecate it.

8. HIS OFFICE, implying that the person held a position of some importance. The LXX. ἐπισκοπή, whence in Acts i. 20 the passage is applied to Judas. In this verse a double loss is imprecated, the loss of life, "let his days be few," and the loss of honour, "let another take his office;" in ver. 11 a third is added, the loss of property.

9. The curse passes in accordance with the Mosaic Law ("visiting the iniquity of the fathers upon the children") to the family of the offender. This has occasioned considerable perplexity to those who take the whole Psalm as prophetic, and aimed throughout at Judas Iscariot. It is painful to see an expositor like Stier driven to maintain that from this point the curse is directed against the Jews at large, rather than against Judas Iscariot, and that "wife" and "mother" are used figuratively to denote city, land, &c. Others have inferred from the passage that Judas must have left a wife and children.

10. BEG. The form of the verb is intensive or frequentative. The object, "bread" (comp. xxxvii. 25 : Prov. xx. 4), must be supplied here, and with the verb "seek" in the next member.

FROM THEIR RUINED HOUSES, lit. "from, out of, their ruins."

11. EXTORTIONER, lit. "creditor," LXX. δανειστής. But Symm. has the stronger word πράκτωρ. LAY SNARES FOR, admirably descriptive

12 Let there be none to continue kindness unto him ;
Neither let his fatherless children have any to favour (them).[b]
13 Let his posterity be cut off;
In the next generation let their name be blotted out.
14 Let the iniquity of his fathers be remembered with Jehovah
And let not the sin of his mother be blotted out.
15 Let them always be before Jehovah,
That He may cut off the memory of them from the earth.
16 Because he remembered not to show kindness,
But persecuted the afflicted man and the poor,
And the broken in heart, to put (them) to death ;

of the arts of the usurer, never resting till he has robbed his victim of "all that he hath."

12. CONTINUE KINDNESS to himself in distress, or to his children. See the same phrase xxxvi. 10 [11].

14, 15. The curse goes backward as well as forward. The whole race of the man is involved in it ; root and branch he is accursed. Not the guilt of the individual only, but the guilt of all his guilty ancestors, is to be remembered and visited on his posterity. For the great law, comp. Matt. xxiii. 32—36. Hupfeld objects that the curse on "the fathers" is pointless, as it could no longer reach them ; but if I see rightly, the object is to heighten the effect of the curse as it falls upon *the children* mentioned in ver. 13. So in our Litany : "Remember not our offences, nor the offences of our forefathers."

16. HE REMEMBERED NOT : therefore "let his iniquity be *remembered*," ver. 14.

TO PUT TO DEATH. The intensive form of the verb (Poel instead of Hiphil) denotes the eagerness, the relentless cruelty of the persecutors. The construction of this and the three following verses admits of some question.

(i.) Ver. 16 may be connected with ver. 15, as giving the reason for the prayer of that verse, "Let them always be," &c., "because he remembered not," &c. Then ver. 17, 18 stand alone describing the man's wickedness and the retribution it brought upon him. The man's own curse, aimed at others, has fallen back upon himself. What he has sown, *that* he has also reaped. Thus the figures "as with a garment," "like water," "like oil," would denote the penetrating, clinging nature of the curse, or, as Stier expresses it : "As the man has sinned through and through his whole being, so is his whole being cursed through and through."

But there are two objections to this explanation. (*a*) The figures in a Hebrew writer would more naturally denote what is refreshing than what is hurtful (comp. Job xv. 16, xxxiv. 7, Prov. iii. 7, 8, and xvii. 22). (*b*) The change to the expression of a wish, when the figures employed are so much weaker, has almost the effect of an anti-climax. This is only partially obviated, even if, with Delitzsch, we make the verb "covereth" emphatic = "envelopeth."

(ii.) We may take ver. 16—18 as the protasis, and ver. 19 as the

17 And he loved cursing, and it came unto him,
And he had no delight in blessing, and it was far from him;
18 Yea, he clothed himself with cursing as with his raiment,
And it came like water into his bowels,
And like oil into his bones;
19 Let it be unto him as the garment (wherewith) he covereth himself,
And as the girdle that he is always girded withal.
20 This is the reward of mine adversaries from Jehovah,
And of them that speak evil against my soul.

apodosis: "Because he persecuted the poor, because cursing was as water to his thirsty soul, as marrow and fatness to his bones, let it be unto him as a garment, let it wrap him round, and envelope him, covering him from head to foot, and clinging to him like a girdle which never leaves his loins."

The verbs cannot be rendered in verses 17, 18, as in the E.V., as optatives. The tenses are past tenses, and have been rightly so rendered by the LXX.

20. Two explanations of this verse are possible, according to the view we take of the former part of the Psalm. (1) It may mean, "My enemies may curse me thus (as in ver. 19) but after all this cursing returns upon themselves. This is the reward (for this meaning of the Hebrew word, see Is. xlix. 4), they themselves receive from the hand of the righteous Judge" (comp. vii. 15, 16 [16, 17]). (2) Those who take the passage ver. 6—19, not as the words of the Psalmist, but as the words of his enemies, suppose the genitive here to be subjective; "This is mine adversaries' award unto me: this the sentence they would procure against me from Jehovah, when they pray, Set Thou a wicked man over him," &c. So Mr. Taylor explains (*Gospel in the Law*, p. 249), and illustrates this use of the genitive by such expressions as "the wages *of* sin," *i.e.* the wages sin gives (Rom. vi. 23); "children are an heritage *of* the Lord," *i.e.* which the Lord bestows (Ps. cxxvii. 3); "*My* reward is with me" (Rev. xxii. 12). Comp. also Is. xl. 10. But the addition "from Jehovah" renders the first explanation far the more probable: "This is the reward which my adversaries receive from Jehovah." The sentence is clear and intelligible. But on the other interpretation we should have expected, not "from Jehovah" meaning "supplicated from Jehovah," but rather the personal pronoun which can hardly be omitted, "This is mine adversaries' reward *unto me*." Mr. Hammond however gets rid of this difficulty by taking פְּעֻלָּה in its original sense of "work" or "labour," not in its derived sense of "wages," or "reward." This primary sense, being given both by the LXX. τοῦτο τὸ ἔργον τῶν ἐνδιαβαλλόντων με παρὰ Κυρίου, and the Vulg. "Hoc opus eorum qui detrahunt mihi apud Dominum." He explains accordingly, "This—the string of imprecations just quoted—is the work of mine adversaries from the Lord." This he would no doubt consider to be equivalent to David's words in 2 Sam. xvi. "Let him curse; *for the Lord hath bidden him.*"

21 But THOU, O Jehovah Lord, deal with me for Thy Name's sake;
For Thy loving-kindness is good : deliver Thou me.
22 For I am afflicted and poor,
And my heart is wounded within me.
23 As a shadow, when it lengtheneth, am I gone hence,
I have been driven away as the locust.
24 My knees are become weak through fasting,
And my flesh hath failed [d] of fatness.
25 As for me,—I am become a reproach unto them;
When they see me, they shake their head.
26 Help me, O Jehovah my God,
Save me according to Thy loving-kindness.
27 And let them know that this is Thy hand;
Thou, Jehovah, hast done it.
28 Though *they* curse, yet THOU blessest;
They arose and were put to shame,
But Thy servant rejoiceth.
29 Mine adversaries are clothed with confusion;
They cover themselves with their own shame (as with) a mantle.

21. BUT THOU. He turns from his adversaries to God, from their curses to His loving-kindness. The emphatic pronoun, and the double name of God, both mark the earnestness of the appeal. See the use of these two names in lxviii. 20 [21], cxl. 7 [8], cxli. 8; Hab. iii. 19. The second member of the verse might be rendered, "Deliver me, because Thy loving-kindness is good;" or, again, the imperative, "Deliver me," might be transferred to the beginning of ver. 22.

23. AS A SHADOW, &c.: comp. cii. 12.

AM I GONE HENCE, or, more literally, "am I made to go hence." This passive form (which only occurs here) denotes external compulsion.

I HAVE BEEN DRIVEN AWAY, lit. "I have been shaken out," as from a cloth, or mantle, or the deep folds of an Eastern robe. See the use of the verb in Neh. v. 13, where the shaking out of the upper part of the robe is symbolical of the Divine judgement. See also Job xxxviii. 13.

AS THE LOCUST, as easily terrified and driven away. Comp. Job xxxix. 20; Exod. x. 19.

25. SHAKE THEIR HEAD. See on xxii. 7.

27. At the close of the Psalm the individual persecutor drops out of sight, and a return is made to the plural number, as in ver. 2—5.

28. The emphatic position of the pronoun before the second verb makes the rendering as given in the

30 I will greatly give thanks unto Jehovah with my mouth,
And in the midst of a multitude will I praise Him.
31 For He standeth at the right hand of the poor,
To save (him) from them that judge his soul.

text more probable than the optative rendering of the E. V., "Let them curse," &c.

30, 31. The Psalm closes with the confident and joyful anticipation that the prayer in ver. 26, 27 is heard and answered.

There is, further, a remarkable contrast between these verses and verses 6, 7. There, the adversary stands at the right hand of the wicked man to accuse him; here, Jehovah, at the right hand of the poor, defenceless victim, to protect him. There, the persecutor finds no mercy at the hands of the human judge, into whose hands he has fallen; here, the Great Judge of all rescues "the poor" from "those that judge his soul."

[a] מֵחָרְב׳, "*from*, i.e. out of, away from, *their ruins*, i.e. the ruins of their homes." The LXX. have ἐκβληθήτωσαν ἐκ τῶν οἰκοπέδων αὐτῶν, whence it has been conjectured that they read גֹּרְשׁוּ (as in Exod. xii. 39; Job xxx. 5) instead of דָּרְשׁוּ.

[b] חוֹנֵן, *a benefactor*. This is the form everywhere, except in Prov. xiv. 21, where it is מְחוֹנֵן. Like the verb, it is always construed with the accus. of the person, consequently לְית׳ is not governed by חוֹנֵן, but belongs to יְהִי.

[c] יְהִי לה׳. On this periphrastic future or optative, see on lxii., note [g].

[d] כחש (Qal. only here, elsewhere Piel), lit. *hath lied* or *become faithless*, i.e. *is changed* (as LXX. and Symm. ἠλλοιώθη) *from fatness*, so as no longer to be fat. Or it may be rendered *hath fallen away* (hath become faithless) *from fat*. שֶׁמֶן here, as in Is. v. 1, xxviii. 1, *fat*, not *oil*. The LXX. δι' ἔλαιον, Symm. ἀπὸ ἀναλειψίας, "my flesh has changed, grown lean for (want of) oil;"—but wrongly.

PSALM 110

THIS Psalm claims emphatically to be the fruit and record of a Divine revelation. The words of the Poet, though shaped in the Poet's heart, come to him from the very sanctuary of the Most High. It is an oracle, an utterance of Jehovah which he has heard, and which he is to declare to others. It is an oracle which concerns a king who reigns in Zion; it is addressed to one to whom the Poet does homage, calling him "Lord;" it assures him of the high favour of Jehovah, who lifts him to a share in His own regal dignity, giving him the victory over all his enemies. The Poet then pictures the king going forth to battle, surrounded by his youthful warriors, bright and numberless as the dew-drops on a summer's morn, willing to shed their hearts' blood in his service, each one robed as a priest, each one a soldier of God.

As he gazes on the vision which has been called up by the first word from heaven, another Divine word sounds in his ear, the word confirmed by the oath of Jehovah, that the king shall also be A PRIEST FOR EVER AFTER THE ORDER OF MELCHIZEDEK.

Then he follows the king in imagination to the war, sees him winning victory after victory with great slaughter, aided by God Himself in the fight, and securing the fruits of his victories by a pursuit of his enemies which knows no check even in the burning heat of an Eastern sun.

If we were at liberty to adopt in this Psalm the same principles of interpretation which we have already adopted with regard to all the other Messianic Psalms, it would present no special difficulty. We might suppose it to have been written by some Poet of David's time, who would naturally speak of David himself as his lord. In the first and lowest sense his words would apply to David as the theocratic king; in their ultimate and highest sense they would be fulfilled in David's great Descendant, in Him who was both David's son and David's lord. But we seem to be precluded from this method of interpretation here by the argument which, according to the first three Evangelists, our Lord, in disputing with the Pharisees, builds upon the first verse of the Psalm. "When the Pharisees were gathered together," St. Matthew tells us, "Jesus asked them, saying, What think ye of Christ? whose son is He? They say unto Him, The son of David. He saith unto them, How then doth David in spirit call Him lord, saying, The Lord said unto my lord, Sit Thou on My right hand till I make Thine enemies Thy footstool? If David then call Him lord, how is He his son?" (xxii. 41—45). In St. Mark's Gospel still more emphatically: "And Jesus answered and said, while He taught in the Temple, How say the scribes that Christ is the son of David? (For) *David himself* said *by the Holy Ghost*, The Lord said to my lord, Sit Thou on My right hand, till I make Thine enemies Thy footstool. David (therefore) himself calleth Him lord, and whence is He his son?" (xii. 35—37). In St. Luke the quotation is introduced by "David himself saith in the Book of Psalms," but there is no other variation of any importance.

Now in this argument all turns on these two points; first, that David himself wrote the Psalm, and the next, that in writing he was moved by the Holy Ghost. David himself, in a confessedly Messianic Psalm, is speaking not of himself, but of his great Descendant, and, so speaking, calls Him his *lord*. David was able to do this, was able in faith to recognize the true Divine greatness of One who, according to the flesh, would be his son, because he spake as the organ of a Divine revelation, as "he was moved by the Holy Ghost." This is clearly the scope of our Lord's argument. And if so, then it is plain that there can be no lower reference of the Psalm to David or any other Jewish monarch. It is a prediction, and a prediction of the Christ as the true King, as the everlasting Priest after the order of Melchizedek. Nor is there anything to startle us in such a conclusion, unless we are prepared to deny altogether the possibility of a revelation of the future. The real difficulty is this, that, taking this view of the Psalm, it differs from all the other prophetic Psalms which, in their first intention at least, refer to David or Solomon, or some other Jewish monarch. And further, the language of the latter part of the Psalm is such as to be only fairly applicable to an earthly king literally reigning in Zion, and literally engaged in fierce and bloody war with his enemies; and therefore it becomes the more difficult to understand on what principle the former part of the Psalm can be detached from a primary reference to some reigning monarch.

Attempts have consequently been made to reconcile a primary reference in the Psalm with our Lord's argument as given by the Evangelists. It has been said, for instance, that the Psalm may have been written, not by David, but by Nathan or some other poet, in honour of David, without either impugning our Lord's veracity or affecting His argument. We are reminded that our Lord in His human nature does not claim omniscience, and that, in so trifling a matter as the authorship of a particular poem, there is no reason why any supernatural illumination should have been vouchsafed Him. In matters of literature and criticism, His knowledge was the knowledge of His time.* It is conceivable, therefore, that He might have adopted, as man, the popular view respecting the authorship of the Books of Holy Scripture. Or, as Neander puts it: "If Christ really named David as the author of the Psalm, we are not reduced to the alternative of detracting from His infallibility and unconditional truthfulness, or else of admitting that David really wrote it. The question of the authorship was immaterial to his purpose; it was no part of His divine calling to enter into such investigations." (*Life of Christ*, Bohn's ed. p. 403.)

* So Meyer, *Evang. des Matthäus*, kap. xxii. 43.

But whilst we may freely admit that our Blessed Lord's human knowledge was subject to limitation, since this is implied in the Gospel narrative, and we have His own express declaration to the same effect, it does not follow that we are justified in deciding for ourselves where the line is to be drawn—when it is that He speaks only as man, when it is that His divine nature operates. Surely on so mysterious a subject it is wiser and more reverent to abstain from speculation, wiser and more reverent, to say the least, not lightly to charge Him with error to Whom we look as the Source and Fountain of truth. But apart from this, how does the argument hold, if the Psalm was not written by David, but by some one else? Neander contends that it is not invalidated. "Its principal point," he says, "is precisely that of the Psalm; the idea of the Theocratic King, King and Priest at once, raised up to God, and looking with calm assurance for the end of the conflict with his foes, and the triumphant establishment of his kingdom. This idea could never be realized in any *man;* it was a prophecy of Christ, and in HIM it was fulfilled. This idea went forth necessarily from the spirit of the Old Dispensation, and from the organic connection of events in the old Theocracy; it was the blossom of a history and a religion that were in their very essence prophetical. In this regard it is a matter of no moment whether David uttered the Psalm or not. History and interpretation, perhaps, may show that he did not. But whether it was a conscious prediction of the royal Poet, or whether some other, in poetic but holy inspiration, seized upon this idea, the natural blossom and offshoot of Judaism, and assigned it to an earthly monarch, although in its true sense it could never take form and shape in such an one, still it was *the* idea by which the Spirit, of which the inspired seer, whoever he may have been, was but the organ, pointed to Jesus." All very true, except that it does not show how it is possible for our Lord's argument to stand if we reject the Davidic authorship of the Psalm. If we hold ourselves at liberty to assume, that our Lord was mistaken on this point, then His argument might certainly still be of force as against the Pharisees, who, like Himself, held the Psalm to be David's, but has no force whatever for ourselves. For the very hinge of the argument turns on the circumstance, that David wrote the Psalm. "The Messiah, you admit, is David's son. How then doth David in spirit call Him lord?" Suppose the Prophet Nathan or some Poet of David's time to have written the Psalm in honour of David, and the argument falls to the ground.*

---

* But see the remarks of Bishop Thirlwall, quoted in the note at the end of the Psalm, p. 313.

It has been suggested by others, in order to escape from the embarrassment in which the argument involves them, that our Lord's object, in this instance, was not to establish any particular doctrine, as He had before established against the Sadducees the doctrine of a Resurrection, but only to silence His adversaries. It was quite unnecessary for Him, therefore, to do more than argue from the premisses admitted by the Pharisees, that the Psalm was a Messianic Psalm, and that it was written by David. But this distinction is too subtle. As in His conflict with the Sadducees He proved the doctrine of the Resurrection from the Pentateuch, so in His conflict with the Pharisees He showed from the Psalms that the Messiah must be not only the Son of Man, but the Son of God. His object was in each case to establish a truth which had been gainsaid by His opponents.

It seems to me, then, that we are shut up to the conclusion, that in this lofty and mysterious Psalm, David, speaking by the Holy Ghost (ἐν ἁγίῳ πνεύματι), was carried beyond himself, and did see in prophetic vision that his son would also be his lord. Nor is it altogether strange, altogether inconsistent with the course of God's providence, that such a vision should be vouchsafed to one to whom so clear a promise was given that the Messiah should come of his seed, and who in his "last words" pictured in such glowing terms the Righteous Ruler and the blessings of His righteous reign.*

Whilst, however, we maintain what our Lord's argument compels us to maintain, that the Psalm is a prediction, we cannot tell to what extent it was a conscious prediction. We do not know how far David himself needed an interpretation of the vision in which he saw the majestic figure of the priestly king. His words may have been higher than his thoughts: they may have been pregnant with a meaning which he did not see. Unless we deny all inspiration, we must be prepared to admit this. At the same time, he is not wholly lifted out of his own age and time. If he speaks of a Messiah to come and so far sees something of His greatness as to call Him "lord," he is still suffered to conceive of Him, partially at least, as an earthly

---

* It is impossible not to feel how not only our Lord's argument but also that of the Epistle to the Hebrews fails, if we suppose the Psalm to have a first reference to David. If the writer of the Epistle had supposed that David himself was a priest after the order of Melchizedek, what would have become of his argument that the abrogation of the Levitical priesthood was signified by the fact that the priesthood of Christ was after the order of Melchizedek? For if David, who raised the Levitical priesthood to a pitch of importance and splendour which it had never before possessed, was a priest after the order of Melchizedek, it is not clear how the priesthood of Christ was a proof that the Levitical priesthood had come to an end, or that the one positively excluded the other.

monarch fighting bloody battles with his enemies. The Psalm thus sinks down towards its close into—must we not say?—a lower key. The image which it presents to us is an image partly of fine gold, but partly of clay. We may indeed think ourselves at liberty to take the earthly words as symbols of spiritual truths. We may understand the victories of the Messiah as won in the kingdom of mind and heart, not as won with sword and spear. But we cannot suppose that it was with any such meaning that David wrote "He shall judge among the nations, filling them with corpses." To his eye the struggle was one of flesh and blood, the victory such as he had himself obtained, the triumph that of an earthly conqueror.

Again, as we may allow that the prediction was partially at least unconscious, or that the vision was obscure, so we may also admit that it was vouchsafed in connection with circumstances and events to which it would stand in some definite relation. Prophecy—and the inspired songs of Psalmists are often prophecies—never seems wholly to forsake the ground of history. However extended the vista which stretches before him, that vista begins at the Prophet's feet. The present is his home and his starting-point, though he may make "all the ages" his own. So we must look to some occurrence in David's life for the secret impulse of his song; and none seems so naturally and obviously to associate itself with the language of the Psalm, as that marked occurrence to which, in all probability, many other Psalms are due, the bringing up of the Ark of God into the Tabernacle which he had prepared for it in Zion. David on that occasion danced before the Ark, girded with a linen ephod, offered burnt-offerings and peace-offerings, and blessed the people in the name of the Lord of hosts;* and thus, though but in a passing and temporary manner, prefigured in his own person the union of the kingly and priestly offices. Zion had become, by the removal of the Ark thither, the seat of Jehovah's visible Presence. The king, therefore, who made Zion his abode, was himself in some sense the assessor of Jehovah on His throne. Jerusalem, tradition said, was the ancient Salem, the capital of Melchizedek, and the memories which thus lingered about it and hallowed it may have helped David to

---

* See 2 Sam. vi. 14--18. I own I cannot see any evidence in this passage that "David was recognized as the head of the priesthood," or that "the union of priesthood and kingship in David was more complete than in any other sovereign in Judah." We read of no repetition of such acts as those here recorded; the occasion itself was peculiar; and certainly no stress can be laid upon the expression "he offered burnt-offerings and peace-offerings before the Lord," for the same might be said of any one who brought the victims to the priests to sacrifice, *e.g.* Solomon and all the congregation, 1 Kings viii. 5.

understand how the true Ruler, Priest as well as King, should be Priest, not after the ancient and venerable order of Aaron, but after the order, still more ancient and more venerable, of Melchizedek. It may, however, have been wisely ordered not only with a view to the future Antitype, but with regard to the present relation between the king and the priesthood, that no hint should be given of any unwarranted assumption on the part of the one of the duties belonging to the other. David did not interfere with the Levitical priesthood as existing in his own day; he pointed to a time when that priesthood would be superseded by a higher.

It may throw still further light on some of the expressions in the Psalm, if we recollect in what a spirit and with what resolves David had begun his reign, how jealously he desired to maintain the purity of his household and of his court (see Psalm ci.), how firm his determination was to have recognized under his sway the great ideal to which Israel was called, "Ye shall be unto Me a kingdom of priests and a holy nation." For the people of the king in the Psalm who offer themselves willingly to fight his battle are priestly soldiers. If the king is henceforth to be a priest on his throne, he is so as embodying in his own person the priestly character of the people. He is not only the military chief, he is the religious head of the nation, the representative both of Church and State.

It has been said, that it is of importance for the right understanding of the Psalm, and especially of the fourth verse of the Psalm, to bear in mind the military character of the Hebrew priesthood. It is perhaps of more importance to bear in mind, that the whole nation was at once a nation of soldiers and a nation of priests. They were the soldiers of God pledged to a crusade, a holy war; pledged to the extermination of all idolatry and all wickedness, wherever existing. The character of the war marked the character of the soldiers. They were God's "sanctified ones." They were set apart as priests for His service. That zeal for God should have manifested itself chiefly in the priesthood, and that they should not have hesitated to draw the sword, is readily accounted for by the fact that in them the ideal of the nation culminated: they were in every sense its representatives.

The Psalm is not only quoted by our Lord as Messianic in the passages already referred to; it is more frequently cited by the New Testament writers than any other single portion of the ancient Scriptures. Comp. besides those passages in the Gospels, Acts ii. 34, 35; 1 Cor. xv. 25; Heb. i. 13, v. 6, vii. 17, 21, x. 13.

In later Jewish writings nearly every verse of the Psalm is quoted as referring to the Messiah.

In the Midrash Tehillim on Ps. xviii. 36, on the words, "Thy gracious condescension shall make me great," we read: "R. Yoden, in the name of R. Chama, said: 'In the age to come [*i.e.* the new Messianic dispensation] the Holy One—blessed be He!—makes King Messiah to sit on His right hand (for it is said, The Lord said unto my Lord, Sit on my right hand), and Abraham on His left. But his (Abraham's) face grows pale, and he says, The son of my son sitteth on the right hand, but I on the left. But the Holy One—blessed be He!—appeases him, and says, The son of thy son is on My right hand, but I am at thy right hand,' as is intimated in the words, 'The Lord is at thy right hand.'" According to R. Martini, this passage was also in his *Bereshith Rabba* as the commentary of R. Mosheh Haddarshan on Gen. xviii. 1.

Again, Martini quotes a passage from the Midrash Tehillim on Ps. ii. 7, in which this verse is cited, together with Exod. iv. 22, Is. lii. 13, xlii. 1, and Dan. vii. 13, as having, like Psalm ii. 7, a Messianic sense. According to Martini, the passage in the Midrash begins, מסופרים הם עניני של משיח. According to the printed text of the Midrash it is simply מספרים הם. Consequently, in a recent work, this quotation of Martini's (found also in Schöttgen) is held up as a palpable mistake; and we are told that no Messianic explanation is given by the M.T. on Ps. ii. 7, and that "it would be strange if it were, for the comment of the Midrash on the verse is expressly intended as תשובת לימינים,* an answer to the heretics [*i.e.* Christians], and does its best to refute the Messianic exegesis." But how do we know that there has been no alteration in the text since Martini's time? and why does the attempt to do away with the *Christian* Messianic interpretation, show that there could be no Messianic interpretation originally in the Jewish sense? In the Zohar, Raya Mahemra (*Numb.* fol. 112*b*, col. 448), it is said: "Jacob put his hand cleverly and put the ox (*i.e.* Messiah ben Joseph) on his right, and the lion (*i.e.* Messiah ben David) on his left; and therefore the Lord said unto my lord, 'Sit thou at My right hand, O righteous one, over against Messiah, the son of Joseph' (thus rectifying Jacob's mistake by reversing the place of each), and he said unto him, 'Sit at My right hand, the arm of Abraham, in the dispersion of Israel, until I make thine enemies thy footstool.'"

R. Saadyah (not the Gaon, but another Rabbi later than Rashi),

---

* The words really are "an answer to them that say that there is a Son to Him. And do Thou answer them, He saith not 'Thou art a Son to Me,' but 'Thou art My Son.'"

commenting on Dan. vii. 13, "And behold there came with the clouds of heaven one like unto the Son of Man," writes (I give the quotation from Martini): "This is the Messiah our Righteousness, as it is written, 'Jehovah said unto my lord' (Ps. cx.); 'And He gave unto Him power' (Dan. v. 14); as it is written (Ps. ii. 7), 'But I have set my king,' &c."

Ver. 2. According to Bereshith Rabba, cap. 85 (on Gen. xxxviii. 18), the sceptre of the kingdom which the Lord sends out of Zion is the King Messiah of whom Isaiah (xi. 1) speaks: "There shall go forth a rod out of the stem of Jesse." So according to Bemidbar Rabba (cap. 18, near the end), "The rod of Aaron is preserved, that it may be in the hand of King Messiah, which is the meaning of 'the rod of Thy strength.'" And according to Yelamdenu (*Yalqut Shime'oni*), the Messiah will smite the nations with the same rod or sceptre.

Ver. 3. The words "From the womb of the morning," &c., are applied in Bereshith Rabba to the Messiah, as follows: "R. Borachia says: God spake to the Israelites: 'Ye say unto Me, We are orphans and have no father (Lam. iv. 3). The Redeemer (*Goel*) likewise, whom I shall raise up for you, hath no father,' for it is said (Zech. vi. 12), 'Behold a man whose name is the Branch (*Zemach*), and he shall branch out of his place.' And so saith Isaiah (liii. 2): 'He groweth up before Him as a shoot.' It is of the same also that David speaks in Ps. cx. 3, 'From the womb of the morning Thou hast the dew of Thy youth'" (Martini, fol. 594).

Ver. 4. In Bereshith Rabba, on Gen. xiv. 18 (Martini, fol. 654), it is remarked of Melchizedek, king of Salem, "This is what the Scripture says (Ps. cx. 4), 'The Lord hath sworn and will not repent, Thou art a priest for ever after the order of Melchizedek.' And who is this? It is the King righteous, and bringing salvation—the King Messiah, as in Zech. ix. 9, 'Behold thy King cometh to thee: He is righteous, and bringing salvation.' But what means, 'He brought forth bread and wine'? It is the same as Ps. lxxii. 16, 'There shall be abundance of corn in the land;' and this it is which is written, 'He was a priest of the Most High God.' The Targum on this verse runs: "For Thou hast been appointed prince of the age to come, and that for Thy merit's sake, because Thou art a righteous King." *

* These passages are not in the work commonly known as the Bereshith Rabba. But Martini quotes from the B. R. of Rabbi Moses Haddarshan, and a Jewish convert, Hieronymus a S. Fide, "quotes also from a *Genesi magno antiquissimo*," and his quotations, though varying in some minor points, agree in the main with those of Martini. Pusey, Introduction to "Jewish Interpreters of Isaiah liii," p. xxxii.

Ver. 6. On the words "He will judge among the nations," it is said in the book Zohar (*Gen.* fol. 38[b], 39[a]), "The Holy One—blessed be He!—hath determined to clothe himself with purple garments, *i.e.* dyed with the blood of the slain righteous among Israel, that he may judge the nations, as the Psalm saith, 'He shall judge.'" See also R. 'Aqibah.

Ver. 7. The Midrash Tehillim on "He shall drink of the brook in the way" is, "In the time to come [the age of the Messiah], streams of blood shall flow from the wicked, and the birds shall come to drink of the stream of blood, as it is written, 'He shall drink.'" See the authorities in Raym. Martini, *Pugio Fidei;* Schöttgen, *De Messiâ*, p. 246.

It is not surprising, however, to find that by many of the Rabbis this line of interpretation was abandoned. So long as the Psalm was admitted to be a Messianic Psalm, the argument based upon it by our Lord and His Apostles was irresistible. Accordingly, we find as early as the second century that the interpretation common among the Jews was that which explained the Psalm of Hezekiah. Both Justin Martyr in his Dialogue with Trypho (§ 33, 83), and Tertullian in his Treatise against Marcion (lib. v. cap. 9), set themselves to meet this as the then current Jewish application. The Rabbis of Justin's days interpreted the words "sit thou on My right hand" as a command to Hezekiah to sit on the right side of the Temple, safe under the Divine protection, when the messengers of the king of Assyria came to him with the threat of their master's vengeance.* Chrysostom tells us that the Jews of his time held that these words were addressed, not to the Messiah, but to Abraham, or Zerubbabel, or David. The Rabbis of the middle ages all agree in repudiating the Messianic interpretation. Rabbi Solomon Isâki (Rashi) mentions that some of the earlier Rabbis expounded the Psalm of Abraham, whom in Gen. xxiii. the children of Heth called "my lord." He himself attempts to carry out this exposition in the most extraordinary way; interprets the "enemies" of ver. 2 of the four kings mentioned Gen. xiv. (because of their connection with the history of Melchizedek), and finds an allusion in the "corpses," ver. 6, first to the carcases of the animals which Abraham divided, Gen. xv., and then to the dead bodies of the Egyptians at the Red Sea, Exod. xiv. Immediately after he suggests another application of the Psalm to David, and on ver. 6 yet another to Hezekiah and the destruction of the Assyrians.

---

* Conf. Tertullian (*ut supra*): "Dicunt denique (Judæi) hunc Psalmum in Ezechiam cecinisse, quia is sederit ad dextram templi, et hostes ejus averterit Deus et absumpserit; *Propter ea* igitur etc. *ante luciferum ex utero generavi te*, in Ezechiam convenire, et in Ezechiæ nativitatem."

Ibn 'Ezra and Qimchi argue that David is the subject of the Psalm, explaining the Inscription to mean not "of David," but "*for* or *concerning* David." The former sees a reference to the war with the Philistines, 2 Sam. xxi. 15—17, when David, having nearly lost his life, his men sware unto him, saying, "Thou shalt not go forth with us any more to battle, that thou quench not the light of Israel." In accordance with this, Ibn 'Ezra explains the address in the first verse of the Psalm to mean, "Remain safe in thy stronghold of Zion, trusting in My help; go not forth to battle; I will subdue thine enemies for thee, even when thou art not present in the battle."

[PSALM OF DAVID.]

1 THE oracle [a] of Jehovah unto my lord:
"Sit Thou at My right hand,

1. SIT THOU AT MY RIGHT HAND, *i.e.* on My throne. The expression denotes that the person thus honoured occupied the second place in the kingdom, taking rank immediately after the king, and also sharing as viceroy in the government. The custom was a common one in antiquity. We find allusion to it both amongst the Arabs and the Greeks. The viceroys of the ancient Arab kings sat on the right hand of the king. Ibn Cotaiba says: "The *Ridafat* is the dignity of sitting next to the king. But the *Radaf* (he who holds rank after the king) sits on his right hand, and if the king drinks, the Radaf drinks next, before all others, and if the king goes out upon an expedition, the Radaf sits on his seat and acts in his room till he returns, and if the king's army goes forth to war, the Radaf receives a fourth part of the booty."—EICHHORN, *Monum. Antiquiss. Hist. Arabum*, p. 220.

Similarly the Greek Poets spoke of their gods as σύνεδροι, πάρεδροι σύνθρονοι with Zeus. So Pindar (*Fragm.* Ed. Schneider, p. 55) speaks of Minerva as associated with Zeus in his sovereignty, and receiving his commands for the other gods: δεξιὰν κατὰ χεῖρα τοῦ πατρὸς καθεζομένην, τὰς ἐντολὰς τοῖς θεοῖς ἀποδέχεσθαι, on which Aristides observes that Minerva was ἀγγέλου μείζων, and that she τῶν ἀγγέλων ἄλλοις ἄλλα ἐπιτάττει, πρώτη παρὰ τοῦ πατρὸς παραλαμβάνουσα. And Callimachus *Hymn. in Apoll.* ver. 28) says that Apollo is able to reward the chorus, if they sing to please him, because he sits at the right hand of Zeus. δύναται γάρ, ἐπεὶ Διὶ δεξιὸς ἧσται. In both these passages it is clear that this session at the right hand of Zeus indicates not merely a mark of honour conferred, but actual participation in the royal dignity and power.

It is true that we have no exactly parallel instance in the O.T. When Solomon placed Bathsheba on his throne, and gave her a seat at his right hand (1 Kings ii. 19), this was done as a mark of honour, not as associating her with himself in the government. So also in Ps. xlv. 6 [10], the queen consort stands at the right hand of the king as the place of honour—though possibly there the expression may denote more than this, may signify her joint sovereignty, for the Tyrians are said to entreat her favour with gifts, ver. 12 [13]. The same mark of honour was conferred by the king of Syria on Jonathan, 1 Macc. ii. 19. There is a more nearly

Until I make Thine enemies Thy footstool."
2 The sceptre of Thy strength shall Jehovah stretch forth
out of Zion (saying):

parallel passage in Matt. xx. 20, &c. (comp. Mark x. 35, &c.), where the mother of Zebedee's children asks for her two sons that they may sit one on the right hand and the other on the left of our Lord in His kingdom. Ewald indeed supposes that the king is represented as sitting in the war-chariot, at the right hand of Jehovah. This no doubt agrees with the martial character of the Psalm, but it does not agree so well with the language of ver. 2. It is evident that in the Psalm not an occasional honour, but a permanent dignity is meant, for Jehovah is to aid the King in effecting the subjugation of his enemies: he is to sit at Jehovah's right hand till that subjugation is effected.

If, then, this be the meaning, if the solemn address "Sit Thou at My right hand" is equivalent to saying, "Be Thou associated with Me in My kingly dignity, in My power and universal dominion," then the best comment on the passage is to be found, as even some of the Jewish interpreters have seen, in Dan. vii. 13, 14, where "one like the Son of Man comes with the clouds of heaven, and is brought unto the Ancient of Days, and there is given Him dominion, and glory, and a kingdom, that all people, nations, and languages should serve Him." The two passages, the one from the Psalm and the other from Daniel, are, in fact, combined by our Lord Himself, when standing before the high priest He says, "Hereafter ye shall see the Son of Man sitting on the right hand of God, and coming in the clouds of heaven." The same interpretation is given by St. Peter, Acts ii. 34—36. Comp. Ephes. i. 20—22; Heb. i. 13, 14.

UNTIL. St. Paul, in 1 Cor. xv. 24—28, gives a limitation to the meaning of the passage which does not lie on the surface. He argues from the words of this verse that Christ must reign until (*i.e.* only until) He has put all enemies under His feet, and that then His mediatorial reign will cease, and He will give up the kingdom to God, even the Father. But this sense is not necessarily conveyed by the use of the conjunction "until." It does not follow that what takes place *until* a certain limit is reached must cease immediately afterwards. Thus, for instance, in cxii. 8, "He shall not be afraid *until* he see his desire upon his enemies;" Gen. xxviii. 15, "I will not leave thee *until* I have done that which I have spoken to thee of;" Deut. vii. 24, "There shall no man be able to stand before thee, *until* thou have destroyed them,"—the "until" is clearly not to be pressed as if it were equivalent to "only until, not afterwards." See also Gen. xlix. 10. The context must determine in each case whether the "until" is inclusive or exclusive of a time subsequent to the limit mentioned, and here the general tenour of the Psalm does not seem to favour a restriction to previous time. This is accordingly one of those instances in which a peculiar turn is given in the N.T. to the language of the Old. See the remarks of Calvin quoted in the notes on xcv. 11, civ. 3.

THY FOOTSTOOL, lit. "a stool for Thy feet," an emblem of complete subjection; comp. viii. 6 [7], xviii. 38 [39]. The allusion is probably to the custom of conquerors placing their feet on the necks of the conquered. See Josh. x. 24, 25.

2. Having announced the oracle which he has received by Divine revelation, the Poet turns to address the King, and declares by what means he is to conquer, viz. by the help of God, and the willing courage and self-sacrifice of his own people.

"Rule Thou in the midst of Thine enemies."
3 Thy people[b] offer themselves willingly in the day that
Thou warrest.

The Son of David has His royal seat in Zion, the city of David. Thence, by the grace of God, He shall give laws to the world, for Jehovah Himself, whose vicegerent He is, in whose strength He rules, holds and sways His sceptre. So the throne of even the earthly king is in like manner called the throne of Jehovah, 1 Chron. xxviii. 5, xxix. 23.

THE SCEPTRE OF THY MIGHT, *i.e.* of "Thy kingly majesty," as in Jer. xlviii. 17; Ezek. xix. 14. Chrysostom plays upon the word ῥάβδος (LXX.) as a rod of strength and consolation, as in xxiii. 4; a rod of chastisement, as in ii. 9, 1 Cor. iv. 21; a symbol of kingly rule, as in Is. xi. 1, Ps. xlv. 6 [7]. It was by this rod, he says, that the disciples wrought when they subdued the world in obedience to the command, "Go and make disciples of all nations;" a rod far more powerful than that of Moses, "for that divided rivers, this brake in pieces the ungodliness of the world." And then with profound truth he adds, "Nor would one err who should call the Cross the rod of power; for this rod converted sea and land, and filled them with a vast power. Armed with this rod, the Apostles went forth throughout the world, and accomplished all that they did, beginning at Jerusalem." The Cross, which to men seemed the very emblem of shame and weakness, was, in truth, the power of God.

RULE THOU, or, "Have dominion," the same word as in lxxii. 8. The imperative contains in itself a prediction or promise of fulfilment. See for the same use of the imperat. xxxvii. 3, Gen. xx. 7. These words are probably (as many of the best commentators suppose) addressed by Jehovah to the King. Others think that the Poet himself thus speaks.

IN THE MIDST OF THINE ENEMIES. Rosenmüller well explains: "Hostes tuos non quidem protinus delebit Jova, sed *tuæ potentiæ metu injecto continebit.* Qui Davidem hac oda cani existimant, illi vicinos Palæstinæ populos indicari volunt, hoc sensu: imperabis, quamvis circum circa hostes, Philistæi, Ammonitæ, Moabitæ, alii, sint; coll. 2 Sam. iii. 18. *In medio i.e.* medios inter hostes, ut sensus sit: quamvis terrarum orbis hostibus tuis repletus sit, non tamen hi impedire poterunt, quominus regnum tuum in eorum medio propagetur."

3. THY PEOPLE. In the midst of His enemies, the King has His own faithful adherents. God, who holds the sceptre of His Anointed, and assures Him of victory, has also given Him a willing people, working in their hearts by His Spirit joyfulness and courage, and ready self-sacrifice. Comp. Is. xxviii. 5, 6, "In that day shall the Lord of hosts be for a crown of glory .... and for strength to them that turn the battle to the gate."

OFFER THEMSELVES WILLINGLY, lit. "are free-will offerings," *i.e.* give, devote themselves as a willing sacrifice. Comp. for the form of expression cix. 4, "I am prayer," and for the sacrificial sense of the word Exod. xxxv. 29, Lev. xxii. 18, 21, 23, Am. iv. 5. This interpretation harmonizes best with the priestly character assigned both to the warriors and to their leader. Otherwise the word often loses its sacrificial meaning; and so here many render, "Thy people are most willing," lit. "are willingnesses," (plur. for sing. as more emphatic, comprising every possible aspect of the idea contained in the word, alacrity, readiness,

In holy attire;
(As) from the womb of the morning,
Thou hast the dew of Thy youth.

devotion in every form). They are no hireling soldiery; they serve not of constraint nor for filthy lucre. For this sense of the word, see the notes on li. 12 [14], liv. 6 [8], and comp. Hos. xiv. 4 [5], "I will love them *freely*." The reflexive form of the verb from the same root is used in like manner in Jud. v. 2, 9, of the people "willingly offering themselves" for the war against Jabin and Sisera.

IN THE DAY THAT THOU WARREST, lit. "in the day of Thy *host*," *i.e.* in the day Thou musterest Thy host to the battle; or we may render, "in the day of Thy *power*," for the word occurs in both significations; for the former, see for instance Exod. xiv. 28, Deut. xi. 4, 2 Kings vi. 15; for the latter Ps. xviii. 32 [33], 39 [40].

IN HOLY ATTIRE. Comp. xxix. 2, xcvi. 9. The youthful warriors who flock to the standard of the king are clad in holy attire, combatants in a holy war. Comp. Is. xiii. 3, 4, "I have commanded *My sanctified ones*, I have also called My mighty ones for Mine anger. . . . . The Lord of hosts mustereth the host of the battle." (See also 1 Sam. xxv. 28; Jer. vi. 4, "*Sanctify* ye war against her;" li. 27, "Raise a standard, blow a trumpet among the nations, *sanctify* the nations against her.") But more is implied perhaps than this. The "holy garments" are priestly garments. They who wear them are priestly warriors, in the train of a priestly leader. If so, the imagery is the same as in Rev. xix. 14, where it is said that "the armies in heaven followed Him (whose name is called the Word of God) upon white horses, *clothed in fine linen, white and clean.*" The garments of Aaron and the priests were of linen, Exod. xxviii. 39, 42, Lev. vi. 10 [3], xvi. 4, and they were called "holy garments," Exod. xxviii. 4, Lev. xvi. 4. The Hebrew word there rendered *garments* is different from that employed in this, and the two parallel passages in the Psalms, but apparently the same thing is intended. Some have supposed that the allusion is to a solemn religious service held before going out to battle, but we have no evidence of the existence of any such custom.

Instead of "in holy attire," another reading found in several MSS. is "on the holy mountains." This reading, which only involves the slightest possible change in a single letter, is as old as Jerome, who has *in montibus sanctis*. It would describe the armed host as going forth to the battle from the mountain ridge on which Zion lay (see on lxxvi. 4), and from which Jehovah stretches out the sceptre of His Anointed.

FROM THE WOMB OF THE MORNING. According to the Massoretic punctuation, these words belong to the preceding member, "In holy attire, from the womb of the morning," the principal accent being after "Thou warrest," and the next chief accent after "morning." It is clear, however, that they belong to the figure of the dew, and the only question is, whether the words "in holy attire" should be connected with the previous noun, "Thy people," or with the following, "Thy young men,"—a question of little importance. Another rendering of the words is possible. A comparison may be implied, "*More than* the dew from the womb," &c., the construction being the same as in iv. 7 [8], where see note.

DEW OF THY YOUTH, or, "Thy youthful dew." Elsewhere the word (*yalduth*) means *the time of youth*, as in Eccl. xi. 9, 10; and so it has been understood here, the object being thus to mark the vigour and

4 Jehovah hath sworn, and will not repent:

prowess of the leader, as the dew denotes fresh and early beauty. But the parallelism requires us to take "Thy youth" here in a collective sense, = "Thy young men," "thy youthful warriors." Ibn 'Ezra makes the parallelism yet more complete by rendering *n'dâbhoth* "willingnesses" ver. 3, as if it were *geshem n'dâbhoth*, "a bountiful rain" lxviii. 9 [10], and explains "If Thou needest to make war, Thy people shall go forth to Thee as plentiful showers." [It would be quite possible to render the line "Thy youth is (or, cometh) to Thee as the dew."] This has been adopted by Mendelssohn. His disciple, Joel Brill, in his *Biur*, or Commentary on Mendelssohn's translation, observes: "The force of the figure is, that they shall flow to Him, and hasten to serve Him, as fruitful showers do the field. The meaning is repeated in the next hemistich, which is as if the Psalmist had said, 'In the day of Thy battle Thy young men are to Thee (as) dew from the womb of the morning.' And how beautiful is the figure which likens the act of men who make to the battle to drops of rain, and the act of young men who are anxious to try their strength in battle to drops of dew, which are smaller and finer than rain."

The dew which, especially in the East, falls so copiously, is most probably employed here as a figure denoting *infinite multitude*. Comp. the use of the figure in 2 Sam. xvii. 11, 12, "Therefore I counsel that all Israel be gathered to thee . . . *as the sand* that is by the sea *for multitude* . . . . and we will light upon him *as the dew* falleth on the ground," &c. Others find the point of comparison here in the *brightness* and *freshness* of the dew; and this may be suggested by the figure as well as multitude. In Mic. v. 7 [6] the point of comparison seems to be different: "And the remnant of Jacob shall be in the midst of many people as a dew from Jehovah, as showers upon the grass that turneth not for man nor waiteth for the sons of men." Here the point is, that the dew, like the rain, is a wonderful gift of God, with which man has no concern.

The Greek and Latin Fathers, following the rendering of the LXX. and Vulg. (see Critical Note), build on this verse the doctrine of the eternal generation of the Son, and His oneness of nature with the Father.

4. This verse contains the great central revelation of the Psalm. How weighty it is, and of how vast import, may be inferred from the solemnity of the introduction "Jehovah hath sworn" (see on the Divine oath, Heb. vi. 13, 17, 18), and this is carried to the very highest pitch by the addition of the words "And will not repent," *i.e.* the decree is absolutely immutable (for God Himself is said to have repented, Gen. vi. 6). It is the solemn inauguration of the Messiah in time to the priestly office. It is the first intimation of the union of the kingly and priestly functions in His person. See the latter typical representation of the same truth in Zech. vi. 12, 13. The writer of the Epistle to the Hebrews dwells on the significance of each expression in this verse: "with an oath"—"for ever"—"after the order of Melchizedek."

(1) He lays stress on the fact that this solemn inauguration into the priestly office was by an oath, which was not the case with the institution of the Levitical priest. This, he observes, is a proof that Christ is Mediator of a better covenant than that of Moses, Heb. vii. 20—22.

(2) He argues that as the priesthood rests on an unchangeable *foundation*, so it is in its *nature* unchangeable: a Priest *for ever*. "He, because He abideth for ever, hath His priesthood unchangeable," vii. 23, 28.

(3) He enlarges upon all those

"Thou art a priest for ever
After the order[c] of Melchizedek."
5 The Lord at Thy right hand

points in which Melchizedek, rather than Aaron, was the most fitting type of Christ; passing over, however, in entire silence that which in the Patristic and Romish expositors holds a prominent place, the bringing forth of bread and wine. Another and essential feature of the type which is implied in Heb. vii. is too often overlooked, viz. that the priesthood of Melchizedek was not only before the law, but was a Gentile priesthood, and therefore the most fitting type of a universal priesthood.

5—7. The martial strain of ver. 2—4 is resumed. There the might of the King and his army were described, here the conflict and the victory. It is remarkable how these earthly images, this warlike tone predominates, considering the language of ver. 4. The priestly character of the monarch, the very name of Melchizedek, who was not only king of righteousness, but king of Salem, that is, king of peace (Heb. vii.), would have led us to expect anything but the picture of a battle-field covered with corpses and a leader in full pursuit of his enemies. Still it must not be forgotten that we have a parallel example in the New Testament. See Rev. xix. 11—16.

5. THE LORD (Adonai). This form of the plural is never used except as a Divine Name. The Targum gives as the equivalent here "the Shekhinah of Jehovah." Is this name here applied to Jehovah or to the King? Many expositors argue that the King must be meant; for (1) it is hardly probable that in so short a Psalm the King should first be said (ver. 1) to be at the right hand of Jehovah, and then that in ver. 5 Jehovah, on the contrary, should be said to be at the right hand of the King. (2) There is apparently no change of subject to the end of the Psalm, and in the 7th verse it is quite clear that the King is the subject: it is he, and not Jehovah, who drinks of the brook in the way. Hence it has been inferred that as the Messiah is called Adonai, we have here a testimony to His divine nature.

On the other side it has been argued that (1) the name Adonai is never elsewhere given to the Messiah, or to any but God: (2) that the expression "in the day of His wrath" is more naturally to be interpreted of God than of the Messiah; see ii. 12, where that is threatened which is here fulfilled; (3) that when, in ver. 1, the King *sits* at the right hand of Jehovah, this is a session on the throne, indicating equal rank and honour; whereas in ver. 5 Jehovah is said to *stand* at the right hand of the King, a different phrase altogether, and one denoting help, succour, and the like, both phrases being legitimately employed to express a distinct meaning; (4) that the change of subject (in ver. 6 or 7), though abrupt, is only what is found in other Psalms, and is characteristic of Hebrew poetry.

Where the arguments are so nearly balanced, it is difficult to decide, although most of the recent expositors—even those who hold to the Messianic interpretation—understand by Adonai, ver. 5, not the Messiah, but Jehovah. It should be observed, however, that there is no reason why the King who is called Elohim (God) in Ps. xlv., should not be called Adonai (Lord) in this Psalm. On the other hand, to assume a change of subject, whether that change is to be introduced at the beginning of ver. 6 or ver. 7 (see below), is perfectly justifiable; and it is more justifiable in this instance, because Jehovah and the King are so closely

Hath smitten through kings in the day of His wrath.
6 He shall judge among the nations,
He hath filled (them) with corpses,[d]
He hath smitten through the heads over wide lands.[e]
7 Of the brook shall He drink in the way;
Therefore shall He lift up (His) head.

associated, that what the one does the other may be said to do. It is Jehovah's throne on which the King sits, it is Jehovah's hand which wields the King's sceptre: Jehovah discomfits the King's enemies, and the King pursues them in their flight. It may be remarked, further, that throughout the Psalm the address is directed to the King and Priest, and that in cix. 31, Jehovah "stands at the right hand" of the poor to succour and defend him, as here at the right hand of the King.

Taking this view, however, it is still difficult to say whether the King is the subject of both verses 6 and 7, or only of ver. 7. Hupfeld, Bunsen, and Ewald think that the King is not introduced till ver. 7, which they regard as a single scene taken from the war. But I confess Reinke's objection to this view appears to me to be weighty, viz. that such a scene standing by itself has no meaning. We must first see the warrior in the battle, or we cannot understand why he should drink of the brook in the way. I prefer, therefore, regarding the King as the subject of ver. 6.

KINGS. There may, perhaps, be an allusion to the glorious victories of old, such as that of Moses, Num. xxi.; of Joshua, Josh. x.; of Deborah, Jud. v. 3, 19; of Gideon, Jud. viii. Comp. Ps. lxviii. 12 [13]. If so, this would account for the use of the past tense "*hath* smitten through," all God's judgements having been judgements executed on behalf of His Anointed. But as the future tenses are interchanged with the past in the next two verses, it seems better to regard the former as indicating that the victory is yet future, while the latter imply that it is represented so vividly to the Poet's eye that he can conceive of it as already accomplished.

6. THE HEADS. The word is singular, but used apparently in a collective sense, either literally as in lxviii. 21 [22], or metaphorically of *rulers, princes*. See the same ambiguity in Hab. iii. 14. The older expositors, adhering to the singular, "the head over the wide earth," suppose Satan to be meant, who is called "the god of this world," others, "over a great country." On the construction, see in Critical Note. Some interpreters, as Mendelssohn and Delitzsch, take "Rabbah" here as a proper name, supposing that David's war with Ammon was the historical occasion of the Psalm. The former renders: (He shall judge the nations) . . . . who hath but now smitten the head of Rabbah: the latter, He breaks in pieces the head over the land of Rabbah. But the land of Ammon would no more be called the land of Rabbah, than the land of Judæa would be called the land of Jerusalem.

7. OF THE BROOK, or, "torrent." The victorious leader, who has made so terrible a slaughter that the field of battle is covered with corpses, is now seen pursuing his enemies. Wearied with the battle and the pursuit, he stops for a moment on his way to refresh himself by drinking of the torrent rushing by, and then "lifts up his head," derives new vigour to continue the pursuit.

[a] נְאֻם. The word is used in almost every instance of the immediate utterance of God Himself, more rarely of that of the prophet or inspired organ of the Divine revelations, as of Balaam, Num. xxiv. 3, 15; of David, 2 Sam. xxiii. 1. Once only is the word used apparently in a catachrestic sense of the evil inspirations of the wicked man, xxxvi. 1 [2], where see note [a].

[b] This verse has been altogether misinterpreted by the LXX. They render: Μετὰ σοῦ ἡ ἀρχὴ ἐν ἡμέρᾳ τῆς δυνάμεώς σου, ἐν ταῖς λαμπρότησι τῶν ἁγίων σου· ἐκ γαστρὸς πρὸ ἑωσφόρου ἐγέννησά σε. They must have read עִמְּךָ for עַמְּךָ, יְלִדְתִּיךָ, as in ii. 7, for יַלְדֻתֶךָ, מִשַּׁחַר for מִשְׁחָר, and קָדְשֶׁיךָ for קֹדֶשׁ. The words לְךָ טַל they have passed over altogether. In rendering נְדָבוֹת by ἀρχή, *rule, dominion,* they connected it with נָדִיב, *a prince.* Etymologically this is defensible, for the two ideas of *nobleness* and *freedom* are readily and naturally connected. But the noun נְדָבוֹת can only mean either *willingness* (plur. and sing.) or *free-will offerings.* The Vulg. carried the blunder further by translating ἀρχή *principium:* "Tecum principium in die virtutis tuæ in splendoribus sanctorum: ex utero ante luciferum genui te." The Syr. confounding טַל with טָלֶה, *the young* of an animal (1 Sam. vii. 9), *a young child,* Is. lxv. 25, has: "In the splendour of holiness have I begotten thee as a child (son) from the womb of old" (reading like the LXX. מִשַּׁחַר, and interpreting it as = מִקֶּדֶם). All these renderings point to the eternal generation of the Messiah as the Son of God, and have so been explained by the Greek and Latin Fathers. Jerome follows Symmachus (ἐν ὄρεσιν ἁγίοις) in adopting the reading בְּהַרְרֵי ק׳, which has the support of many MSS. and some editions (the interchange of ד and ר being very common), and is preferred by some of the ablest critics, though, I think, on hardly sufficient grounds. He renders: "Populi tui spontanei erunt in die fortitudinis tuæ: in montibus sanctis quasi de vulva orietur tibi ros adolescentiæ tuæ." The latter part of the verse is rendered by Aquila: ἀπὸ μήτρας ἐξωρθρισμένης [ἐξ ὠρθρισμένου] σοι δρόσος παιδιότητός σου. Symm. ὡς κατ᾽ ὄρθρον σοι δρόσος ἡ νεότης σου. Th. ἐκ μήτρας ἀπὸ πρωΐ (σοι δρόσος) νεότητός σου. S΄. ἐκ γαστρὸς ζητήσουσί σε, δρόσος νεανικότητός σου, which seems to anticipate the more recent interpretations.

[c] עַל־דִּבְרָתִי, the old form of the stat. constr. with the connecting vowel, for עַל דִּבְרַת, which occurs in Eccles. iii. 18, vii. 14, viii. 2, and in the Chald. of Dan. ii. 30, iv. 14, instead of the earlier and more usual עַל דְּבַר. For the termination of the stat. constr. in *î*, see on cxiii. note [a]. In the other passages where it occurs, the phrase ע׳ ד׳ means *because of,* a meaning which Hupfeld would retain here, "because of Melchizedek," *i.e.* so far as the type is the ground of the antitype. Others (as Herder and Geiger, *Urschrift,* &c. p. 29) take the final *î* as a suffix: "Thou art a Priest for ever—I swear it by My word—a (second) Melchizedek." It is however, far simpler and more natural, although no other instance of like usage can be adduced, to take ע׳ ד׳ in the sense of the LXX. κατὰ τὴν τάξιν. So the Syr. and so Jerome, *Secundum ordinem.* Except in this phrase and in the passages above quoted, דִּבְרָה only occurs once in the Bible, Job v. 8, though it is common enough in Rabbinical literature.

[d] מָלֵא גְ׳. The second accus. is understood, אֹתָם. "He hath filled them (*i.e.* the nations) with corpses," the verb being transitive, as often. Others make of מָלֵא an adjective governing גְּוִיּוֹת, "(it, *i.e.* the field of battle, or the land, is) full of corpses, as in lxv. 10, מ׳ מָיִם, "full of water."

[e] עַל א׳ ר׳. The prep. may either depend on the verb, "He hath smitten over a wide extent of country," &c., or it may depend on רֹאשׁ, "head over, *i.e.* prince over a wide territory," like נָגִיד עַל, &c., but here the former is clearly to be preferred.

A. I subjoin the following paraphrase of the Psalm :—

"Thus saith Jehovah,—it is His revelation that I hear, it is His word addressed to one who, though He be my son, is yet my Lord—'I give Thee honour and dignity equal to my own, I associate Thee with Myself in kingly rule and dominion, until I have subdued every enemy who shall dare to lift himself against Thee.'"

Then turning to the King who has thus been solemnly placed on the throne of Jehovah, and who rules as His vicegerent in Zion, the Psalmist says : "From Zion, Thy royal seat, shall Jehovah Himself, on whose throne Thou sittest, stretch out the sceptre of Thy dominion. So close shall be the fellowship between Him and Thee. Thou shalt sit on His throne, He shall wield Thy sceptre, His might shall be Thy might, His kingdom shall be Thy kingdom, and Thou shalt not only subdue Thine enemies, but before they are yet vanquished Thou shalt rule in the midst of them. When Thou goest forth to war, Thine own people shall flock with glad and willing hearts to Thy standard. They shall come clad, not in armour, but in holy vestments as ministering priests, for Thou hast consecrated them to be Thy priestly soldiers. They shall come a youthful host, in numbers numberless as the dew, bright and fresh as the dew from the womb of the morning.

"Yet another solemn word concerning Thee have I heard. It is a word confirmed by an oath, the oath of the Most High, which cannot be broken. By that oath He hath made Thee Priest as well as King; King Thou art, Priest Thou shalt be henceforth; Priest not after the law of a carnal commandment, or by descent through the Levitical priesthood, but after the order of Melchizedek,—Priest therefore not of the Jew only, but of the Gentile also,—Priest not for a time, but for ever."

Then, looking on the leader, the host, the conflict, the Poet exclaims: "The Lord, the God of hosts who is with Thee, O King, who is at Thy right hand to succour and give Thee the victory in the battle, hath already crushed the rival monarchs that dispute Thy sway. Thou shalt be a judge and ruler among the nations whom He has given Thee as Thine inheritance. The vast battle-field is strewn with the corpses of Thy foes. Far and wide hast Thou extended Thy conquests, vanquishing one leader after another; and Thou shalt reap the fruit of Thy victories like a warrior who, pressing hotly on the rear of his enemies as they flee before him, scarcely pauses for a moment to snatch a hasty draught from the wayside brook, and then with renewed ardour, with head erect and kindling eye, continues the pursuit. Thus shall victory be crowned, and not a foe remain."

B. The Bishop of St. David's [*i.e.* the late Bishop Thirlwall] has favoured me with the following valuable remarks on this Psalm, which he has kindly allowed me to publish :—

"I think it will be convenient first to consider the Psalm by itself, just as if no reference had been made to it in the New Testament, and then to see how our conclusions about it must be modified by our Lord's language.

"(i.) I think there can be no doubt that, whoever was the author, it must be considered as a Messianic Psalm, a picture of a state of things which had not been fully realized either in the literal or the spiritual sense, before the coming of Christ. This character of the Psalm, as manifested by its contents, would not be more strongly marked if it is considered as the work of David: and the only question is whether, without some special revelation, beyond what would have been required for any other author, he could have spoken of the person described in it as his 'Lord.' I will only say that it does not appear to me inconceivable, but quite natural, that he should so style one who answered to the description given of the future victorious King. Only I am not sure that there is anything in that description that might not be accounted for without any peculiarly distinct *consciousness—some* consciousness the writer must have had, whoever he was—in David's mind, partly by the promises which he had received (2 Sam. vii.), and partly by traditional expectations of the coming Great One.

"(ii.) How, then, is the case altered by our Lord's reference to the Psalm? Here we find ourselves in the presence of two opposite theories as to our Lord's ordinary intellectual state. According to that which invests Him with the fulness of divine as well as human knowledge, there is, of course, no room for doubt about the authorship of the Psalm. You, however, seem willing to admit that of

Neander, Meyer, and others (among the rest, Pressensé, *Vie de Jésus*), that our Lord was not habitually conscious of facts, such as 'matters of literary criticism,' which did not fall within the range of His human knowledge. But then arises the question whether, even on this theory, we are not compelled to suppose that He would not have argued as He does with the Pharisees on the Psalm, if a certain knowledge of its real authorship had not been supernaturally infused into Him for the special occasion. This leads us to inquire what His argument was. And here it is to be observed that, strictly speaking, it was no *argument* at all. Still less was it an argument proving that the Christ was foreseen by David to be the Son of God. As far as our Lord's words go, they are simply questions, and questions which might have been put by one who wished to suggest to the Pharisees that they were mistaken in believing that David was the author of the Psalm. Nothing of course could be farther than that from our Lord's intention (though I see from Alford that De Wette actually thought so). But if He did not take, but stand on, the same intellectual level, in this respect, with the Pharisees, can it be said that His question, if David was not really the author of the Psalm, tended to mislead them, and therefore that this was a case in which, if He had needed a supernatural revelation of the truth, He must have received one? I must own, that is not at all clear to me. But that which most perplexes me is the difficulty I find in understanding the precise drift of our Lord's questions, or why they should have had the effect of putting the Pharisees to silence. One would think that they could have been at no loss for an answer, according to the current Messianic notions of the day. They knew that Messiah was to be of the lineage of David. They also believed that He was to be a greater than David, though the precise degree of His superiority might be open to doubt. But this might suffice to remove the appearance of inconsistency between David's language and His relation to the expected Messiah. Nor does it appear elsewhere that the question between our Lord and His opponents was, who and what the Messiah was to be, but whether He was the Messiah. If the Pharisees had not believed that the Psalm related to the Messiah, the question would have been futile. The argument, whatever it may have been, turns upon that, quite as much as it does upon David's authorship, and though the title of *Lord* implied a dignity higher than David's, it can hardly be said to carry so much as the sitting on Jehovah's right hand, or even as the everlasting priesthood. But if so, the alleged occasion for a supernatural infusion of superhuman knowledge seems to lose almost all its importance, as the only result would be the addition of a title, which could have no such meaning except in the mouth of David, but which is thrown into the shade by other attributes which do not depend on the supposition of his authorship.

"On the whole, the conclusion to which I am led, as far as the great obscurity and imperfection of the data permit me to draw any, is that we are left very much in the same position with regard to the Psalm as if our Lord had not asked those questions about it; and that though we may be at liberty, we are not 'compelled' to attach any greater weight to it than it would have if it was not written by David. All that 'falls to the ground' in our Lord's 'argument' is a particular which does not seem to have any bearing upon doctrine, and to be indeed immaterial."

PSALM 111

THIS Psalm and the next are framed exactly on the same model. They are both alphabetical Psalms. In both, the letters of the alphabet mark not only the beginning of verses, as in other Psalms, but the beginning of each several clause of the verses. In both, there are exactly twenty-two lines, each line consisting usually of three words, and in both the order of the alphabet is strictly preserved, which is not the case in other alphabetical Psalms (see, for instance, xxv., xxxiv., xxxvii.). Finally, so exactly does the structure of the two Psalms correspond, that the first eight verses in both consist each of two lines, and the last two verses of three lines.

But the Psalms answer to one another not only in structure, but in thought. The same significant phrases occur in both, and occur in such a way as to mark the mutual relation of the two Poems. In the 111th the mighty deeds, the glory, the righteousness of Jehovah are celebrated in the assembly of the upright. In the 112th the righteousness, the goodness, the blessedness of the upright themselves are described and enlarged upon. The one sets forth God, His work and His attributes; the other tells us what are the work and character of those who fear and honour God. Thus in cxi. 3 it is said of Jehovah that "His righteousness standeth fast for ever;" in cxii. 3, the same thing is affirmed of the man that feareth Jehovah. In cxi. 4, it is declared of Jehovah that "He is gracious and of tender compassion;" in cxii. 4, the same character is given of the upright. In the 111th Psalm the faithfulness of Jehovah to His covenant is magnified (ver. 5, 9), in the 112th the faithfulness of the righteous man, his trust in Jehovah is exhibited (ver. 7, 8).

In spite of the acrostic arrangement by which the writer has chosen to fetter himself, this Psalm is more than a mere string of gnomic sentences. The thoughts have a real inner connection. The Psalmist begins by declaring that with his whole heart he will give thanks to God, and because to keep his thankfulness and his ascription of praise to himself would be to rob God of half His honour, therefore will he give utterance to his feelings, and give utterance to them in the fitting place, "in the congregation of the upright." Abundant subject for such praise is to be found in the works of God: the more these are studied, the more will their marvellous and unsearchable character be seen, and the greater the delight which will be experienced in the study. Everywhere the glory of God will be traced, everywhere will the footsteps of His unchangeable righteousness be discovered. At all times His works testify of Him, rebuking the apathy and forgetfulness of men, and calling them to Him who is "gracious and of tender compassion."

He has shown His goodness in never failing to supply the need of His people: He gave them manna in the wilderness, He gave them the spoil of the heathen in Canaan: He thus kept with them the covenant which He had made of old with their fathers. Not unmindful of other nations, it is to His people that He has specially revealed Himself; He has given them their promised inheritance. As in His works so in His commandments, as in His providence so in His word, the same truth and faithfulness are visible. Therefore His commandments cannot fail; they remain the sure everlasting pillars of His kingdom. The great seal of all is the redemption which He accomplished for His people. He who brought them out of Egypt will never suffer His covenant to fail.

Is it not the highest wisdom to fear such a God as this, so great in His works, so true in His word, so faithful to His covenant? To fear God and to keep His commandments is the whole of man, to praise Him man's highest employment both now and for ever.*

1 HALLELUJAH!
א I will give thanks unto Jehovah with (my) whole
heart,

* With this Psalm begins another series of Hallelujah Psalms, cxi. cxiii., cxv.—cxvii.

ב In the council of the upright and in the congregation.
2 ג Great are the works of Jehovah,
ד Sought out [a] of all them that have delight therein.
3 ה His doing is honour and majesty,
ו And His righteousness standeth fast for ever.
4 ז He hath made a memorial for His wonderful works;
ח Gracious and of tender compassion is Jehovah.
5 ט He hath given meat to them that fear Him,

1. COUNCIL. See on xxv. note [g]. A narrower and more intimate circle is implied than in the word "congregation" which follows. In xxv. 14 the word occurs in the sense of "secret," *i.e.* "secret converse," and in lv. 14 [15] in a similar sense. See note on this last passage.

2. THE WORKS OF JEHOVAH, *i.e.* specially His mighty deeds on behalf of His people. These are said to be—

SOUGHT OUT, the objects of earnest and devout meditation and study, studied that they may be known, studied that they may be lived. The same law holds of God's revelation in His word as of His revelation in nature. They only who *search* diligently and who have a *delight* therein can discover His wonders either in the one or the other. For if what Origen says of the final revelation is true, ἐπέμφθη γὰρ οὐ μόνον ἵνα γνωσθῇ, ἀλλ' ἵνα καὶ λάθῃ (*Contr. Cels.* ii. 67), it is no less true, λανθάνει ἵνα γνωσθῇ.

3. HIS RIGHTEOUSNESS STANDETH FAST FOR EVER. Comp. cxii. 3, where the same is said of the righteousness of the man who fears Jehovah, and hath delight in His commandments. See also xix. 9.

4. A MEMORIAL. Comp. Num. xvi. 40, [xvii. 5]; Josh. iv. 6, 7.

FOR (or "belonging to") HIS WONDERFUL WORKS. By means of all that He has so marvellously wrought on behalf of Israel, He has reared, so to speak, a monument to His glory.

5. MEAT, or "food," as in Prov. xxxi. 15, Mal. iii. 10, often in the sense of "prey" or "booty." "The use of this word," says Mr. Grove, "especially when taken in connection with the words rendered 'good understanding' in ver. 10, which should rather be as in the margin, 'good success,' throws a new and unexpected light over the familiar phrases of this beautiful Psalm. It seems to show how inextinguishable was the warlike predatory spirit in the mind of the writer, good Israelite and devout worshiper of Jehovah as he was. Late as he lived in the history of his nation, he cannot forget 'the power' of Jehovah's 'works' by which his forefathers acquired the 'heritage of the heathen;' and to him, as to his ancestors when conquering the country, it is still a firm article of belief that those who fear Jehovah shall obtain most of the spoil of His enemies—those who obey His commandments shall have the best success in the field."—*Dict. of the Bible*, Art. MEAT.

To the above may be added the probable allusion to the deliverance from Egypt, and the occupation of Canaan in ver. 9. It is doubtful, however, whether the rendering "good success" in ver. 10 is correct.

Delitzsch, on the other hand, supposes that by the "memorial" is meant the Festivals, which were instituted to keep alive the remembrance of God's mighty works in the days of Moses, and by the "food," the meal accompanying the sacrifices, and the Paschal feast.

י He remembereth His covenant for ever.
6 כ The power of His works hath He shewed to His people,
ל To give them the heritage of the nations.
7 מ The works of His hand are truth and judgement;
נ Faithful are all His statutes;
8 ס They are upheld for ever and ever,
ע They are done in truth and uprightness.
9 פ He hath sent redemption to His people;
צ He hath commanded His covenant for ever;
ק Holy and fearful is His Name.
10 ר The fear of Jehovah is the beginning of wisdom,
ש A good understanding have all they that do them:

[It is with reference to this verse, doubtless, that Luther calls the Psalm "an Easter or Paschal Psalm."] Theodoret, Augustine, and others understand by this "food," in the N. T. sense, the Eucharist, and the Psalm has been accordingly used as a Eucharistic Psalm. It is a curious instance of the way in which a word may draw to itself a whole train of thought with which it has really no connection.

6. TO GIVE, or, the infin. may be used gerundially, as often "giving."

8. UPHELD, not however by any external prop, but by their own inherent power: comp. the use of the word cxii. 8; Is. xxvi. 3 (where the E. V. has "stayed").

UPRIGHTNESS. The neuter adj. used thus in connection with a noun preceding is peculiar (see cvii. 20).

9. HE HATH SENT. There is, probably, an allusion to the redemption from Egypt, and in the next member to the Sinaitic covenant. Then Jehovah revealed Himself as the holy and the awful God. But here, and throughout the Psalm, I have rendered the past tenses as perfects, because the reference is evidently not exclusively to the past, but also to the still present results of the "redemption" and the "covenant."

HE HATH COMMANDED. The verb is used, as in cv. 8, in its original sense of *appointing, establishing*.

10. THE BEGINNING, or, "chief part, principal thing." Comp. Job xxviii. 28; Prov. i. 7, ix. 10. Augustine beautifully says, "Pro deliciis autem omnibus hujus sæculi, quales vel expertus es, vel augere ac multiplicare augendo potes, immortalium deliciarum matrem concupisce sapientiam: sed *Initium sapientiæ timor Domini*. Delectabit illa, et ineffabiliter procul dubio delectabit castis atque æternis veritatis amplexibus: sed prius tibi donanda sunt debita, quam præmia flagitanda. *Initium* ergo *sapientiæ*," &c.

A GOOD UNDERSTANDING, or perhaps rather "understanding of, insight into, that which is good." Comp. Prov. iii. 4, xiii. 15; 2 Chron. xxx. 22.

THEY THAT DO THEM. The reference of the plur. pron. "them" can only be to the "statutes" mentioned in ver. 7, 8. See the note on

ת His praise endureth for ever.

cvii. 25. The P.B.V. "thereafter." Augustine lays stress on this "doing." "*Bonus est intellectus*," he says; "quis negat? Sed intelligere et non facere periculosum est. *Bonus* ergo *facientibus*."

[a] דְּרוּשִׁים, pass. part. only here; not merely *worthy of being sought out*, as in other passive forms, like נֶחְמָד, חָמוּד, *sought*, but the subject of diligent investigation, earnest pursuit, &c. לְכָל־חֶפְצֵיהֶם, not "according to all their desires" (as the sing., 1 Kings ix. 11), *i.e.* so that they find in it their highest satisfaction; for the plur. of חֵפֶץ does not mean *wishes*, *desires*, but *precious things* (Prov. iii. 15, viii. 11), and לְ after a pass. can only point out the author or subject. Hence this is plur. of חָפֵץ. It is true this appears elsewhere in the form חֲפֵצֵי', as xxxv. 27, xl. 15, but that is really an incorrect form of the stat. constr., with the vowel retained, contrary to the rule (Gesen. § 133, Rem. 1, 2). In like manner we have שְׂמֵחֵי, Is. xxiv. 7, and שְׂמֵחֵי, Ps. xxxv. 26. There is, indeed, no parallel case where the first radical takes Segol. Usually a guttural first radical has Pathach or short Chireq, as חַנְפֵי, עִמְקֵי, &c., but this is of no importance, as the guttural in other forms is found with a Segol. Besides, though the long vowel might be retained in the stat. constr., it would naturally fall away before the grave suffix ־הֶם. The rendering given in the text is supported by the Syr., Chald., Jerome, Qimchi, Luther, Calv., Ges., &c." The LXX. *ἐξεζητημένα εἰς πάντα τὰ θελήματα αὐτοῦ*. Chrysost.: Ἄλλος· *ἐξηκριβωμένα*, *et paulo post:* Τί δέ ἐστιν, *ἐξεζητημένα* κ.τ.λ.; Ἠκριβωμένα, φησὶ, καθάπερ καὶ ἕτερος ἑρμηνευτὴς εἶπε, παρασκευασμένα, ἀπηρτισμένα κ.τ.λ. Ἀ. scrutata ab omnibus qui complacuerunt sibi in iis. E. *scrutata* ἐν πάσῃ τῇ χρείᾳ αὐτῶν. Vulg. "Exquisita in omnes voluntates ejus." Jer. "Exquirenda in cunctis voluntatibus suis."

PSALM 112

On this Psalm, see the Introduction to Psalm cxi. In its general character it resembles Psalms i. and xxxvii. In the Vulgate the title is "Conversio Aggæi et Zachariæ."

1 HALLELUJAH!
א Happy is the man that feareth Jehovah,
ב That delighteth greatly in His commandments.
2 ג His seed shall become mighty in the earth,

1. Comp. i. 1, 2.

2. MIGHTY. The word is commonly used of *warlike* strength and prowess, but sometimes also in a

ד The generation of the upright shall be blessed.
3 ה Wealth and riches are in his house,
ו And his righteousness standeth fast for ever.
4 ז There ariseth a light in the darkness for the upright;
ח (He is) gracious, and of tender compassion, and righteous.

5 ט Well [a] is it with the man who dealeth graciously and lendeth,
י He shall maintain his cause in judgement;
6 כ For he shall not be moved for ever;
ל The righteous shall be in everlasting remembrance.

more general sense of wealth, substance, &c. So Boaz is called "a mighty man of wealth," Ruth ii. 1; and Kish, 1 Sam. ix. 1; see also 2 Kings xv. 20.

3. WEALTH AND RICHES. So in the Proverbs these are said to be the gift of Wisdom to them that love her. See iii. 16, viii. 18, xxii. 4. So even in the New Testament: see Mark x. 29, 30.

HIS RIGHTEOUSNESS, &c. It seems a bold thing to say this of anything human, and yet it is true; for all human righteousness has its root in the righteousness of God. It is not merely man striving to copy God. It is God's gift and God's work. There is a living connection between the righteousness of God and the righteousness of man, and therefore the imperishableness of the one appertains to the other also. Hence the same thing is affirmed here of the human righteousness which, in cxi. 3, is affirmed of the Divine.

4. A LIGHT FOR THE UPRIGHT. Comp. xcvii. 11, "Light is sown for the upright."

In the next clause of the verse the three adjectives occasion some difficulty. Although they are in the singular number, whilst "the upright" in the preceding line is plural, it seems most natural to take them as intended further to describe the character of the upright. The first two epithets, elsewhere applied only to Jehovah, are so applied in cxi. 3, and the relation of the two Psalms makes it almost certain, therefore, that they are here applied to His servants. See also Matt. v. 45, 48; Is. lviii. 7. The change from the plural to the singular is certainly unusually harsh, as the three epithets are loosely strung together, without anything to mark their reference; but this may be accounted for in some measure by the requirement of the alphabetical arrangement.

Others take the three attributes as in apposition with the noun "light" in the preceding clause, God Himself being the "Light" (as in xxvii. 1: comp. Is. x. 17, lx. 1—3; Mal. iv. 2 [iii. 20]): "There hath arisen a Light, viz. He who is gracious," &c.

5. LENDETH, see xxxvii. 21, 26, HE SHALL MAINTAIN, &c.: mentioned as an instance of his happiness, which is then confirmed by what follows, ver. 6, cxxxiii. 5, in the courts of judgement, cxliii. 2, Prov. xvi. 10.

6. IN EVERLASTING REMEMBRANCE (comp. Prov. x. 7), or, "shall have an everlasting memorial," see cxi. 3.

7 מ Because of evil tidings he shall not fear;
נ His heart is established, trusting in Jehovah.
8 ס His heart is upheld, he cannot fear,
ע Until he see his desire upon his adversaries.
9 פ He hath dispersed, he hath given to the poor,
צ His righteousness standeth fast for ever;
ק His horn shall be exalted with glory.
10 ר The wicked shall see (it) and be grieved,
ש He shall gnash his teeth and melt away;[b]
ת The desire of the wicked shall perish.

7. Further evidence of the happiness of such a man—a clear conscience and a heart that trusts not in itself but in God, and thus is raised above all fear. The epithets "established," "trusting," "upheld," are all strikingly descriptive of the true attitude of faith, as that which *leans upon* and *is supported by* God. The two last are combined also in Is. xxvi. 3.

9. HE HATH DISPERSED. The verb occurs in Prov. xi. 24 in the same way, of the free and active exercise of charity. This verse is quoted by St. Paul when exhorting the Corinthians to liberal contributions on behalf of the poor, 2 Cor. ix. 9.

HIS HORN. See on lxxv. 5 [6].

10. BE GRIEVED, filled with vexation, irritated. SHALL GNASH HIS TEETH, as in xxxv. 16, xxxvii. 12.

MELT AWAY, *i.e.* through jealousy and annoyance.

[a] טוֹב, here not in a moral sense *good*, but rather in a physical sense *fortunate, happy*, as in Is. iii. 10; Jer. xliv. 17; Eccl. viii. 12, 23. It is not necessary, however, to make it a noun, as Qimchi does (as in xxv. 13). The expression 'ט' א is exactly equivalent to 'אַשְׁרֵי א, ver. 1, and the article is absent before אִישׁ, in both cases, because it is defined by the attributes which follow.

[b] נָמָס, 3 pret. Niph. pausal form (as in Ex. xvi. 21) of נָמַס or נָמֵס. Usually the pausal substitute for Tsere is Pathach; here we have Qametz, probably as lengthened from the form נָמֵס, as in the plur. נָמֵסּוּ. Comp. also the use of the suffixes ָם and ֵם, instead of ֵם, cxviii. 10.

PSALM 113

WITH this Psalm begins "the Hallel" which was sung at the three Great Feasts, at the Feast of Dedication, and at the New Moons. At the Feast of the Passover it was divided into two parts, the first of which, consisting of Psalms cxiii., cxiv., was sung before the meal, that is, before the second cup was passed round; and the second, consisting of Psalms cxv.—cxviii., after the meal, when the fourth cup had been filled. This last, probably, was "the hymn" which our Lord and His Apostles are said to have sung (ὑμνήσαντες, Matt. xxvi. 30, Mark xiv. 26), after His last Passover.

Paulus Burgensis styles Psalms cxiii.—cxviii. *Alleluia Judæorum magnum*, and this has been a very usual designation. But according to the ancient Jewish tradition this series of Psalms is called simply "the Hallel," or sometimes "The Egyptian Hallel," whereas the name "Great Hallel" is given to Psalm cxxxvi. (See Delitzsch, from whom the above is taken.)

The Psalm may be said to be a connecting link between the Song of Hannah and the Magnificat of the Virgin.

It may be viewed as consisting of three strophes.

1. The first exhorts to the praise of Jehovah as the one great object of praise. Ver. 1—3.
2. The second sets forth His greatness. Ver. 4—6.
3. The third magnifies His condescension. Ver. 7—9.

The second and third of these divisions, however, are closely connected, and, in fact, run into one another.

1 HALLELUJAH!
Praise, O ye servants of Jehovah,
  Praise the Name of Jehovah.
2 Blessed be the Name of Jehovah
  From this time forth and for evermore.

1. SERVANTS OF JEHOVAH; all Israel as a nation consecrated to His service; comp. lxix. 36 [37], cxxxv. 1 (where this same verse is found, but with the clause transposed), cxxxvi. 22.

The rhythm of this verse is that of xxix. 1.

3 From the rising of the sun unto the going down of the
same
The Name of Jehovah be praised.

4 Jehovah is lifted up above all nations,
His glory is above the heavens.
5 Who is like Jehovah our God
Who setteth His throne on high,[a]
6 Who stoopeth down to see
(What is) done in the heaven and in the earth?
7 He raiseth the miserable from the dust,
(And) lifteth up the poor from the dunghill,
8 That He may set (him)with princes,
(Even) with the princes of His people,
9 Who maketh the barren woman to keep house,

3. BE PRAISED. This rendering seems preferable in the context, though we might render "is praised," or "is worthy to be praised," as in xviii. 3 [4], xlviii. 1, "greatly to be praised"; but here the participle depends on the verb in the jussive.

4. ABOVE THE HEAVENS. De Wette remarks that this goes beyond what we find elsewhere in describing the exaltation of Jehovah; that in Ps. xviii., for instance, He inhabits the lower atmospheric heaven, and in Ps. lxviii., He is throned in Zion, whereas here He is lifted high above the sphere of creation. But he must have forgotten such passages as viii. 1 [2], and lvii. 5 [6], 11 [12].

5. SETTETH HIS THRONE ON HIGH, lit. "maketh high to sit;" as in the next verse, "maketh low to see." The same antithesis occurs cxxxviii. 6. It denotes not merely the omniscience of God, but His greatness and his condescension. Comp. viii. 4 [5], and the striking expansion of the same thought, Is. lvii. 15.

6. STOOPETH DOWN TO SEE, &c. This verse might also be rendered, "Who looketh low down,—vaileth or lowereth his regard,—upon the heavens and the earth," the construction of the verb and prep. (רָאָה בְּ) being the same as in Gen. xxxiv. 1, Jud. xvi. 27. Some commentators would connect the second hemistich of this verse with the first clause of ver. 5, "Who is like Jehovah our God in the heaven and in the earth?" (as in Deut. iii. 24), taking the two intervening clauses as parenthetical; but this is quite unnecessary. The rendering given above may be adopted, or the ellipsis may be supplied as it is in the E.V.

7. This and the next verse are almost word for word from the Song of Hannah, 1 Sam. ii. 8.

9. The curse of barrenness was so bitter a thing in Jewish eyes, that its removal was hailed as a special mark of Divine favour. The allusion to it here was suggested, doubtless, by Hannah's history, and by the strain of Hannah's song already quoted: see 1 Sam. ii. 5.

MAKETH THE BARREN WOMAN,

As a joyful mother of children.[b]
Hallelujah!

&c.: lit. "maketh her who is the barren of the house to dwell," *i.e.* maketh her who through barrenness has no family to have a family, and so a fixed, settled habitation in the land. A barren woman might be divorced, or another taken besides her; but, having children, her position in the house is sure. The use of the phrase in lxviii. 6 [7] is somewhat different, as there the word "house" means *the place of abode;* here, the *family*. Compare the expression "to make a house," Ex. i. 21; 2 Sam. vii. 11.

[a] הַמַּגְבִּיהִי. The final Chireq, *Yod* or *Chireq compaginis* as it is called, or long connecting vowel, in this and the two following participles, and also in the Hiph. infin. לְהוֹשִׁיבִי (ver. 8), is the vowel originally employed to mark the relation of the genitive. The old form of the stat. constr. had for its termination either Cholem, as in חַיְתוֹ אֶרֶץ, Gen. i. 24, or Chireq, as in the compound names מַלְכִּי־צֶדֶק, אֱלִיעֶזֶר, and many others, in the participle אֹסְרִי לַגֶּפֶן, Gen. xlix. 11, חַכְלִילִי עֵינַיִם, *ib.* 12, and in some prepositions, as בִּלְתִּי, זוּלָתִי, מִנִּי (poet).

The termination *i* is found (*a*) with the first of two nouns in the stat. constr., whether masc., as in Deut. xxxiii. 16, Zech. xi. 17, or fem. as in Gen. xxxi. 39; Ps. cx. 4. It is found also (*b*) when the stat. constr. is resolved by means of a prep. prefixed to the second noun, as in the passage already quoted, Gen. xlix. 11; in Ex. xv. 6; Obad. 3; Hos. x. 11; Lam. i. 1; Ps. cxxiii. 1, and in the K'thîbh, Jer. xxii. 23, li. 13; Ezek. xxvii. 3. It occurs (*c*) even where a word intervenes between the two which stand in the genitival relation, as in ci. 5; Is. xxii. 16; Mic. vii. 14. The fact that this long vowel usually draws to it the accent shows that it is no mere euphonic (paragogic) addition, but that it is really a connecting vowel marking the relation of the gen. case. Hence it may be regarded as a connecting link between the Semitic and Indo-Germanic languages.

In this and other late Psalms (see for instance cxxiii. 1, cxiv. 8, where we have both the Chireq and the Cholem, and perhaps cxvi. 1) an attempt seems to have been made to bring back the old termination, but without regard always to its original signification. Thus in ver. 8 of this Psalm it is appended even to the Hiph. infin., a form which occurs nowhere else.

[b] הַבָּנִים. Hupfeld and Olsh. condemn the article as incorrect. Delitzsch says: "The Poet brings the matter so vividly before him, that he points, as it were, with his finger to the children with which God blesses her."

According to Ibn. 'Ez. עֲקֶרֶת in the first hemistich is not in construction, but absolute. If so we may render: "Who setteth the barren woman in a house."

PSALM 114

THIS is perhaps the most beautiful of all the Psalms which touch on the early history of Israel. It is certainly the most graphic and the most striking in the boldness of its outlines. The following remarks may perhaps illustrate the connection and plan of the Poem.

1. In structure it is singularly perfect. This rests upon the common principle of pairs of verses, and thus we have four strophes, each consisting of two verses: each of these verses, again, consists of two lines, in which the parallelism is carefully preserved.

2. The effect is produced, as in Psalm xxix., not by minute tracing of details, but by the boldness with which certain great features of the history are presented.

3. A singular animation and an almost dramatic force are given to the Poem by the beautiful apostrophe in ver. 5, 6, and the effect of this is heightened in a remarkable degree by the use of the present tenses. The awe and the trembling of nature are a spectacle on which the Poet is looking. The parted sea through which Israel walks as on dry land, the rushing Jordan arrested in its course, the granite cliffs of Sinai shaken to their base—he sees it all, and asks in wonder what it means?

4. Then it is that the truth bursts upon his mind, and the impression of this upon the reader is very finely managed. The name of God, which has been entirely concealed up to this point in the poem (even the possessive pronoun being left without its substantive, "Judah was His sanctuary, Israel was His dominion"), is now only introduced after the apostrophe in ver. 5, 6.

"The reason seems evident, and the conduct necessary, for if God had appeared before, there could be no wonder why the mountains should leap and the sea retire; therefore, that this convulsion of nature may be brought in with due surprise, His name is not mentioned till afterward; and then, with a very agreeable turn of thought, God is introduced all at once in all His majesty." *

We have no clue to guide us to the age of the Psalm, or the occasion for which it was written, except that perhaps the forms in ver. 8, which are found in other late Psalms, may be taken to indicate a date after the Exile.

* *Spectator*, No. 461.

1 WHEN Israel went forth out of Egypt,
The house of Jacob from a people of strange language,
2 Judah became [a] His sanctuary,
Israel His dominion.

3 The sea saw and fled,
Jordan turned backwards;
4 The mountains skipped like rams,
The hills like young sheep.

5 What aileth thee, O thou sea, that thou fleest;
Thou Jordan, that thou turnest backwards?
6 Ye mountains, that ye skip like rams;
Ye hills, like young sheep?

7 Before the Lord tremble, O earth,
Before God (the God) of Jacob.
8 Who changed [b] the rock into a pool of water,

1, 2. The Introduction sets forth at once both the great redemptive act and also the end of the redemption, viz. that God Himself might dwell among and rule His people.

This sanctifying of the nation, as a nation to Himself, took place in the wilderness before the Law was given: "Ye shall be unto Me a kingdom of priests and a holy nation" (Exod. xix. 6).

A PEOPLE OF STRANGE LANGUAGE, lit. "a stammering (*i.e.* an unintelligible) people." Comp. Deut. xxvii. 49; Is. xxviii. 11, xxxiii. 19; Jer. v. 15. LXX. λαοῦ βαρβάρου.

2. HIS SANCTUARY. Comp. Exod. xv. 17, where the Promised Land is called "the Sanctuary, O Lord, which Thy hands have established."

HIS DOMINION or kingdom; comp. Num. xxiii. 21. The noun is in the plural, which is here used poetically as a plural of amplification. Comp. xliii. 3, xlvi. 4 [5], lxviii. 35 [36] (where see note).

3. THE SEA SAW, viz. God, whose name and whose presence are still purposely concealed. Comp. lxxvii. 16 [17], xcvii. 3; Hab. iii. 10.

The passage of the Red Sea and of the Jordan are combined, not only as miracles of a similar character, but as marking the beginning and the end of the great deliverance — the escape from Egypt, the entrance into the Promised Land.

4. The reference is probably to the terrors which accompanied the giving of the Law on Sinai (Exod. xix. 18, "and the whole mount quaked greatly"), although these convulsions of nature form a part of every Theophany, or manifestation of God. Comp. xviii. 7 [8], lxxvii. 18 [19]; Hab. iii.; Is. lxiv. 1—3. For the figure see Ps. xxix. 6.

8. THE ROCK (*tsûr*), referring to

The flint-stone into a fountain of waters.

the miracle in Exod. xvii. 6. THE FLINT-STONE (or perhaps "the steep cliff;" LXX. τὴν ἀκρότομον) seems to be placed here poetically for the other characteristic word (*sela'*), which marks the scene of the miracle at Kadesh. See notes on lxxviii. 15, 16.

These miracles are selected as the most striking proofs of "God's absolute creative omnipotence, and of the grace which changes death into life." They are, moreover, parallel miracles like the two mentioned in ver. 3, and thus the poetical effect is heightened.

[a] הָיְתָה. "Judah" is here feminine, in accordance with the general principle that *lands* and *nations* are feminine.

[b] הַהֹפְכִי. On the termination see xciii. note [a]. The final Chireq, however, in this instance, is not strictly that of the stat. constr., for the participle here has the article prefixed, and therefore cannot be in construction. But it is one of the instances in which, as has been remarked in the note referred to, the later language adopted the termination without regard to its original use.

In לְמַעְיְנוֹ, on the other hand, we have a genuine instance of the old termination of the stat. constr. This final Cholem, however, is by no means so widely used as the final Chireq. With the exception of this place, and Num. xxiv. 3, 15, בְּנוֹ בְעֹר, it is found only in the phrase חַיְתוֹ אֶרֶץ (or חַ׳ הַשָּׂדֶה), which first occurs Gen. i. 24.

PSALM 115

THIS is evidently one of the later liturgical Psalms. It was probably composed for the service of the Second Temple, whilst yet the taunts of their heathen adversaries were ringing in the ears of the returned exiles, and whilst yet contempt for the idolatries which they had witnessed in Babylon was fresh in their hearts.

The Psalm opens with a confession of unworthiness and a prayer that God would vindicate His own honour against the scoff of the heathen. Ver. 1, 2.

It exalts Him, the Invisible, Omnipotent, absolutely Supreme Ruler of the Universe, and pours contempt upon the idols and their worshipers. Ver. 3—8.

It bids all Israel, both priests and people, put their trust in Him who is alone worthy of trust, the help and shield of His people. Ver. 9—12.

It promises that Jehovah shall give His blessing to them that thus trust in Him, and calls upon them in return to give Him thanks for ever. Ver. 12—18.

Ewald's conjecture that the Psalm was intended to be sung whilst the sacrifices were offered, and that at ver. 12 the voice of the priest declares God's gracious acceptance of the sacrifice, is not improbable. He gives ver. 1—11 to the congregation, ver. 12—15 to the priest, ver. 16—18 to the congregation. But it seems more likely that the change of voices comes in at ver. 9, and that, as Tholuck supposes, in each of the verses 9, 10, 11, the first line was sung as a solo, perhaps by one of the Levites, and the second by the whole choir.

The LXX., Syriac, Arabic, and Ethiopic have strangely enough, and in defiance of all probability, joined this with the preceding Psalm, and then have restored the balance by dividing Psalm cxvi. into two parts. Even in some Hebrew MSS. Psalms cxiv. and cxv. are found written as one Psalm. But the very structure of Psalm cxiv., its beauty and completeness in itself, are sufficient to make us wonder what caprice could have led to such an arrangement.

(*The Congregation.*)

1 NOT unto us, O Jehovah, not unto us,
But unto Thy Name, give glory,
Because of Thy loving-kindness, because of Thy truth.
2 Wherefore should the nations say:

1. NOT UNTO US. The repetition of the words expresses the more vividly the deep sense of unworthiness, the unfeigned humility which claims nothing for itself.

LOVING-KINDNESS . . . TRUTH. The two great characteristic attributes of God, even in the Old Testament; though in contrast with the Law as given by Moses, St. John could say, ἡ χάρις καὶ ἡ ἀλήθεια διὰ Ἰησοῦ Χριστοῦ ἐγένετο, John i. 17.

Both these attributes of God would be assailed if the taunt of the heathen should be allowed to pass unsilenced. It is God's glory which is at stake. "Deo itaque," says Calvin, "gratiam suam objiciunt (fideles), deinde fidem, quarum utramque manebant impiæ calumniæ, si populum quem æterno fœdere sibi devinxerat, et quem adoptaverat gratuita misericordia, frustratus esset."

2. NOW is not a particle of time,

"Where now is their God?"

3 But our God is in the heavens;
He hath done whatsoever He pleased.
4 Their idols are silver and gold,
The work of men's hands.

as might be inferred from the rendering of the E.V., but an interjection used in taunt as well as in entreaty, &c.

3. BUT, or "and yet." See the same use of the conjunction in ii. 6. The answer to the taunt of the heathen, who, seeing no image of Jehovah, mocked at His existence. First, He is *in heaven*, invisible indeed, yet thence ruling the universe; next, *He doeth what He will*, in fine contrast with the utter impotence of the idols of the heathen. The last expression denotes both God's almighty power and His absolute freedom. This, truthfully accepted, does away with all *à priori* objections to miracles.

4. SILVER AND GOLD, *i.e.* however costly the material, this adds no real value to the image; it is, after all, man's workmanship. This seems to be the thought: otherwise the Psalmist would have said "wood and stone" rather than "silver and gold." This agrees also with what follows. "*Though* they may be of costly materials, they are but of human workmanship; *though* they may have the form and members of man, they are lifeless."

De Wette remarks that "the Jew, who was accustomed to see no image of the Deity, fell into the error (often perhaps purposely) of confounding the idols of the heathen with the gods whom they represented, and of which they were only the symbols. The Israelite of the ten tribes, who had his symbols of Jehovah Himself, could not have made such a mistake." But it may be replied, in the first place, that the Jew would not have admitted that the gods had any real existence; they were as much the creatures of man's imagination as the idols were of his art. In the next place, the heathen worship itself was not careful to maintain the difference between the symbol and the thing symbolized, and the great mass of worshipers probably drew no distinction between them. "Non habent Siculi deos ad quos precentur," says Cicero. On which Calvin remarks: "Barbare hoc diceret, nisi hæc infixa fuisset opinio vulgi animis, deorum cœlestium figuras sibi ante oculos versari in ære, vel argento, vel marmore." Even the refined teaching of the Church of Rome does not save the ignorant and the unlettered from absolute idolatry.

Augustine has here some admirable remarks on idol-worship, and the various attempts made to distinguish between the image and the deity it represented. But he concedes the real existence of the gods as demons: "Aliis itaque locis et contra ista divinæ Literæ vigilant ne quisquam dicat, cum irrisa fuerint simulacra, Non hoc visibile colo, sed numen quod illic invisibiliter habitat. Ipsa ergo numina in alio psalmo eadem Scriptura sic damnat: *Quoniam dii gentium*, inquit, *dæmonia; Dominus autem cælos fecit*. Dicit et Apostolus: *Non quod idolum sit aliquid, sed quoniam quæ immolant gentes, dæmoniis immolant, et non Deo*," &c. The whole passage is well worth reading as a masterly analysis of idol-worship.

We have the same description of these dumb and deaf and dead gods in cxxxv. 15—18, probably bor-

5 A mouth have they, but they speak not;
Eyes have they, but they do not see.
6 They have ears, but they hear not;
A nose have they, but they do not smell.
7 They have hands, but they handle not;
Feet have they, but they walk not;
They do not utter any sound with their throat.
8 Like unto them are they that make them,
Every one that putteth his trust in them.

(*Levites and Choir.*)

9 O Israel, trust in Jehovah!
He is their help and their shield.

rowed from this passage. Comp. Deut. iv. 28, and the sarcastic picture in Is. xliv. 9—20.

5. A MOUTH. The picture is of a single image.

7. THEY HAVE HANDS, lit. "As for their hands, they handle not (with them); As for their feet, they do not walk (therewith:)" or, "With their hands they handle not; With their feet they walk not." The construction is changed, and we have nominative absolutes, followed by the conjunction introducing the apodosis. See for the same construction Gen. xxii. 24; Prov. xxiii. 24; Job xxxvi. 26.

UTTER ANY SOUND. The verb may mean only *to speak*, as in xxxvii. 30; Prov. viii. 7; but the rendering in the text approaches more nearly to the root-signification of the word, "do not utter even an inarticulate sound." So Ibn. 'Ezra and Qimchi.

8. LIKE UNTO THEM. So true it is, not only that as is man so is his god, but the reverse also, as is the god so is his worshiper. Comp. Is. xliv. 19, where what is elsewhere said of the idols is said of the worshipers, that they are "emptiness" (*tôhû*); and observe the use of the verb "to become vain," 2 Kings xvii. 15; Jer. ii. 5, applied in like manner to idolaters. They who, turning away from God's witness of Himself in the visible creation, worshipt the creature rather than the Creator, received in themselves the sentence of their own degradation, "their foolish heart became darkened." They became blind and deaf and dumb and dead, like the idols they set up to worship.

ARE, or "become." By the LXX., Jerome, and the Syriac the verb is rendered as an optative, "May they become," &c., which, however, is less forcible.

9. The change in the strain of the Psalm here must unquestionably have been accompanied by a change in the music. And it appears highly probable, as has been said, that the first line of this and the two following verses was sung as a solo by some of the Levites, and the second line, or refrain, which occurs in each verse, "He is their help and their shield," by the choir.

TRUST IN JEHOVAH, in contrast with the "trust" of the previous verse. Trust in Jehovah, for He is not like the idols, He is the living

10 O house of Aaron, trust ye in Jehovah!
He is their help and their shield.
11 Ye that fear Jehovah, trust in Jehovah!
He is their help and their shield.

(*The Priest.*)

12 Jehovah (who) hath been mindful of us will bless,—
He will bless the house of Israel,
He will bless the house of Aaron.
13 He will bless them that fear Jehovah,
Both small and great.
14 Jehovah increase you more and more,
You and your children!
15 Blessed be ye of Jehovah,
The Maker of heaven and earth.

(*The Congregation.*)

16 The heavens are Jehovah's heavens;

God, "the help and the shield" (comp. xxxiii. 20) of them that trust in Him. Trust in Jehovah, for He *hath been* mindful of us in times past, He *will* bless us in time to come (ver. 12). The threefold division, Israel—house of Aaron—they that fear Jehovah, is the same as in cxviii. 2, 3, 4. In cxxxv. the house of Levi is added.

10. First the people at large are exhorted to this trust, then the priests—because to them was confided the worship of Jehovah, with them it rested to keep it pure, and they might naturally be expected to lead the people in the path of holy trust.

11. YE THAT FEAR JEHOVAH. This has been understood of proselytes of the gate, in accordance with the later Jewish and New Test. usage, as in the Acts, *σεβόμενοι τὸν Θεόν*, or simply *σεβόμενοι*. Comp. Acts xiii. 43, 50. But in other places in the Psalms the phrase occurs of all Israel; see xxii. 23 [24], ciii. 11, 13, 17, and it is better to understand it so here.

12. (WHO) HATH BEEN MINDFUL . . . WILL BLESS. So the LXX. *μνησθείς*, and Jerome *recordatus*, and so Ibn. 'Ez. takes זכרנו as a relative. The past is the pledge of the future. Again the same three classes are mentioned as in the three preceding verses.

This blessing, thus promised (ver. 12, 13) and thus supplicated (ver. 14, 15), was sung, as Ewald conjectures, by the priest. But see Introduction to Ps. cxviii.

14. INCREASE YOU. Comp. Gen. xxx. 24; Deut. i. 11; 2 Sam. xxiv. 3.

15. MAKER OF HEAVEN AND EARTH. The title has reference to the impotent idols before described.

16. The words in this and in the next verse are simple enough, but

But the earth hath He given to the children of men.
17 The dead praise not Jah,
Neither all they that go down into silence ;
18 But *we* will bless Jah
From henceforth even for ever,
Hallelujah !

their connection with the rest of the Psalm is not very clear. Perhaps it may be traced thus: In ver. 15 Jehovah is said to have made heaven and earth. Then in ver. 16 these are distributed: heaven is His abode; earth is the abode of man. But the mention of heaven and earth suggests the thought of another region, that unseen world below where none can praise God as they do on this fair earth which He has given to the children of men. But what the dead cannot do, *we* will do,—we to whom our God has given the earth, we to whom He has been a help and a shield, we whom He has blessed and will bless, we with thankful hearts will never cease to show forth His praise.

17. Comp. cxviii. 17; Is. xxxviii. 18, 19.

PSALM 116

In this Psalm one who has been in peril of death (ver. 3, 9, 15) gives thanks to God with a full heart for the deliverance which has been vouchsafed to him. Beginning with the expression of a love to God called forth by His mercy, the Psalmist then passes in review all God's goodness, till he feels that it surpasses infinitely not only all his deserts, but all adequate power of acknowledgement (ver. 12); and he concludes by declaring that in the most public manner, before the assembled congregation, he will confess how great the debt he owes, and bind himself solemnly to the service of Jehovah.

The Psalm is evidence of the truth and depth of the religious life in individuals after the return from the Exile ; for there can be little doubt that it must be assigned to that period. Many words and turns of phrases remind us of earlier Psalms, and especially of the Psalms of David. His words must have laid hold in no common degree of the hearts of those who were heirs of his faith, and have sustained them in times of sorrow and suffering ; and nothing would be more natural than that later Poets should echo his strains, and mingle his words with their own when they poured forth their prayers and praises before God.

1 I LOVE (Him) because Jehovah heareth
My voice and my supplications,
2 Because He hath inclined His ear unto me,
Therefore as long as I live will I call (upon Him).
3 The cords of death compassed me,
And the pains [a] of the unseen world gat hold upon me.
I found distress and sorrow :
4 Then I called upon the name of Jehovah,
"O Jehovah, I beseech Thee,[b] deliver my soul."
5 Gracious is Jehovah and righteous ;
Yea, our God showeth tender compassion.
6 Jehovah preserveth the simple :
I was in misery and He saved [c] me,
7 Return unto thy rest,[d] O my soul,
For Jehovah hath dealt bountifully with thee.

1. I LOVE. The verb stands alone without any expressed object, as if the full heart needed not to express it. The object appears as subject in the next clause, from which it is readily supplied : "I love Jehovah, for He heareth," &c. The writer is fond of this pregnant use of the verb without an object expressed. See ver. 2, "I call," and ver. 10, "I believe." For the sentiment, comp. xviii. 1 [2], "Tenderly do I love Thee." The rendering, "I am well pleased that," &c. has no support in usage.

On this first verse Augustine beautifully says : "Cantet hoc anima quæ peregrinatur a Domino, cantet hoc ovis illa quæ erraverat, cantet hoc filius ille qui mortuus fuerat et revixit, perierat et inventus est ; cantet hoc anima nostra, fratres et filii carissimi."

2. AS LONG AS I LIVE, lit. "in my days." The phrase, "in my days will I call," is certainly hard, and 2 Kings xx. 19 (Is. xxxix. 8), to which Del. refers, is not a real parallel. Still, as the LXX. and Jerome evidently had the reading, it is probably the true one, and we need not adopt any of the conjectural emendations which have been proposed.

3. The later Psalmists would naturally often use David's words as the best expression of their own feelings, especially in seasons of peril and sorrow. See xviii. 1—6 [2—7].

GAT HOLD UPON, lit. "found," as in cxix. 143.

5. Instead of saying directly "Jehovah answered me," he magnifies those attributes of God which from the days of His wonderful self-revelation to Moses (Ex. xxxiv. 6), had been the joy and consolation of every tried and trusting heart. See Introduction to ciii. The epithet "righteous" is added here, as in cxii. 4.

6. THE SIMPLE. LXX. τὰ νήπια. The very simplicity which lays them most readily open to attack is itself an appeal for protection to Him who "showeth tender compassion."

7. The deliverance vouchsafed in answer to prayer stills the tumult of the soul. The REST is the rest of confidence in God.

8 For Thou hast delivered my soul from death,
Mine eye from tears,
My foot from stumbling.
9 I will walk before Jehovah
In the land of the living.
10 I believe;—for I must speak; [e]
I was greatly afflicted.
11 I said in my confusion,
"All men are liars."

12 How shall I repay unto Jehovah
All His bountiful dealings [f] with me?
13 I will take the cup of salvation,
And call on the name of Jehovah.

9. THE LAND OF THE LIVING, lit. "the lands," but the plural may be only poetic amplification. In xxvii. 13 (comp. lvi. 13 [14]), we have the singular.

10. The E.V., "I believed, therefore have I spoken," follows the LXX. *ἐπίστευσα, διὸ ἐλάλησα*, a rendering which is also adopted by St. Paul, 2 Cor. iv. 13, in illustration of the truth that a living faith in the heart will utter its convictions with the mouth. But the Hebrew will not admit of such a rendering. For the various explanations, see Critical Note. That given in the text may be thus explained: "I believe"—emphatic, *i.e.* I do believe, I have learnt trust in God by painful experience—"for I must speak"—I must confess it, "I even I (pron. emphatic) was greatly afflicted; I myself (pron. emphatic as before) said," &c. This gives the due prominence to the repeated pronoun, and moreover a satisfactory sense is obtained. Kay renders: "I believed in that I spake."

The Psalmist declares that he *stays himself* upon God ("I believe"), for he had looked to himself, and there had seen nothing but weakness; he had looked to other men and found them all deceitful, treacherous as a broken reed. Comp. lx. 11 [13], lxii. 9 [10], cxviii. 8, 9. There is an allusion to this passage in Rom. iii. 4.

11. The first member is the same as in xxxi. 22 [23].

CONFUSION, or, "rashness."

13. THE CUP. Many see in the word an allusion to the "cup of blessing" at the Paschal meal (Matt. xxvi. 27), and this would accord with the sacrificial language of ver. 14, 17. It is true there is no evidence of any such custom at the celebration of the Passover in the Old Test.; but as the custom existed in our Lord's time, the only question is as to the *time* of its introduction. If it was introduced shortly after the Exile, this Psalm may very well allude to it. It may however have been earlier, there being, according to the Rabbis, no sacrificial gift (Korban) without libations (the two are joined in Joel i. 9). They tell us, that the saying that wine was that which cheereth God and man (Jud. ix. 13) was the blessing pronounced emphatically over the cup. Others understand by "the cup," in a figurative sense, the portion allotted to man, whether of prosperity, as in xvi. 5 [6], xxiii. 5, or of adversity, as

14 My vows unto Jehovah will I pay,
Yea, in the presence of[g] all His people let me (pay them).

15 Precious in the sight of Jehovah
Is the death of His beloved.
16 I beseech Thee, O Jehovah—for I am Thy servant,
I am Thy servant, the son of Thine handmaid;
Thou hast loosed my bonds.[h]
17 I will sacrifice unto Thee the sacrifice of thanksgiving,
And I will call upon the Name of Jehovah.
18 My vows will I pay unto Jehovah,
Yea, in the presence of all His people let me (pay them),
19 In the courts of Jehovah's house,
In the midst of Thee, O Jerusalem!
Hallelujah!

in xi. 6 [7], lxxv. 8 [9]. So the Arabs speak of "the cup of death," "the cup of love," &c. Then the meaning of the verse will be, "I will accept thankfully and with devout acknowledgement the blessings which God gives me as my portion."

14. LET ME (PAY THEM). I have endeavoured thus to render here, and in ver. 18 (the refrain), the interjection which is used in beseeching. It is a part of the same interjection which occurs in ver. 4 and 16, and which is there rendered "I beseech Thee." A fondness for these forms is characteristic of the Psalm.

15. PRECIOUS . . . . IS THE DEATH, *i.e.* it is no light thing in the sight of God that His servants should perish. The more obvious form of expression occurs lxxii. 14, "precious is their blood in His eyes."

16. SON OF THINE HANDMAID. Comp. lxxxvi. 16; 2 Tim. i. 5.

[a] מְצָרֵי; a later word, which occurs besides in the sing. הַמֵּצַר, cxviii. 5, and in the plur. הַמְּצָרִים, Lam. i. 3. In these other passages it means *narrowness*, *straitness*, as of a narrow *place*, whereas here an abstract sense is required. The word does not also seem very suitable to שְׁאוֹל. In the original passage חֶבְלֵי is the word employed, and hence Hupf. would read here מְצָדֵי, *nets*, referring to similar forms in Job xix. 6; Eccl. vii. 26.

[b] אָנָּה with ה, as in five other places, instead of א, compounded of אָהּ and נָא. It is accentuated both Mil'el and Milr'a. Properly speaking, in beseeching it is *annâ*, Mil'ra; in asking questions, *ânnah*, Mil'el.

[c] יְהוֹשִׁיעַ. For this form, with the ה retained, see lxxxi. 5 [6].

[d] מְנוּחָיְכִי. The plur. masc. occurs only here, the plur. fem. in two other places instead of the sing. The noun means primarily *a resting-place.* and then *rest* (xxiii. 2). The plur. is used to denote *rest in its fulness.* On the form of the fem. suffix in this word, and in עָלָיְכִי in the same verse, and again in בְּתוֹכֵכִי, ver. 19, see on ciii. note [a].

[e] האמנתי כי א׳. The construction of this clause is extremely difficult. In all other instances where כִּי follows the Hiph. of אמן it means "that," but in all other instances the subject of the verb in the subordinate clause is different from that in the principal clause; *e.g.* Ex. iv. 5, "that they may believe that Jehovah hath appeared," &c. But we could not render here, "I believe that I should speak." Hence various renderings have been proposed: (1) "I believe when I speak," *i.e.* when I break forth into the complaint which follows in the next clause. (So Hupfeld.) Similarly Ewald: "I have faith, when I speak." For this use of the verb *speak,* comp. xxxix. 3 [4]. (2) "I believed when I spoke (thus);" the next hemistich, "I was greatly afflicted," being independent, and not an expression of what he said. (3) "Credidi, quum hæc loquuturus essem," Jun. and Trem. (4) Delitzsch remarks that the rendering "I have believed, that I should yet speak," *i.e.* yet have to praise God's goodness (דִּבֵּר, as in xl. 6), would yield a good sense, that in his deepest affliction he yet kept his faith, which was first silent and then spake, whereas unbelief first speaks and at last is silent, yet this interpretation is not satisfactory because it leaves the connexion between the parallel members too slight and loose. And as כִּי can only mean either "that" (Job ix. 16) or "suppose that" = "if" (Hab. i. 5) or "for," nothing is left but to render, "I have believed, for I spake (or must speak)." This, however, gives a suitable sense. If he looked at himself (obs. the emphatic pron. אֲנִי), he found himself in the deepest affliction, unable to help himself: if he looked to men he must confess to himself (obs. the repetition of the pers. pron. אֲנִי) that all confidence placed in man was vain. Hence, despairing alike of himself and of other men, he believed in God. האמנתי thus stands absolutely, "I stayed myself upon God, in the depth of my own misery, and in the absence of human help." Hitz. rejecting such renderings as those of Ew.: Ich habe Glauben, wann ich rede, of Del: Ich fasste Glauben, denn ich musste sprechen, &c., as contrary to grammar, thinks that the construction here is like that in Jer. xii. 1: "Thou art (too) righteous that (כִּי) I should plead with thee." He appeals to similar constructions in Arabic and in Greek writers. So here he renders: 10. Ich vertraue als dass ich spräche: ich bin gebeugt sehr. 11. Ich hatte gedacht in meiner Bestürzung alle Menschen sind Lügner. He connects this with ver. 9 thus: I shall live through God's mercy, and I confide therein so that in what may befall me, I will not suffer myself to be led away into any expression of faint-heartedness. I have too much faith in Him to complain how I am bowed down." Before this, on the contrary, he had been in a state of trepidation (ver. 11): I had thought that all men are liars;—I had lost all confidence in men; but Jehovah dealt bountifully

with me (ver. 7), and how can I repay Him (ver. 12)? Reuss renders: Je croyais, bien que je dusse dire: Je suis dans un profond abaissement. Je disais dans mes alarmes, Tous les hommes sont trompeurs. Rejecting the interpretation of the LXX. on grammatical grounds, he observes: "L'auteur veut évidemment affermer sa foi, ferme malgré la situation dans laquelle il se trouvait et malgré l'impossibilité de s'en rapporter aux hommes. Pour compléter sa pensée il faut ajouter: et ma confiance n'a point été trompée." Of the Verss. the Syr.-Hex. has in the text, ܗܝܡܢܬ ܥܠ ܗܘ ܡܠܠܬ . "I have believed; therefore have I spoken;" but in the margin, ܐ. ܗ . ܗܝܡܢܬ ܡܛܠ ܕܐܡܠܠ, "I believed that I should speak," or, perhaps, "because I must speak." The LXX. ἐπίστευσα, διὸ ἐλάλησα. Jerome: Credidi propter quod [h. quia] locutus sum. The Syr. has merely the conjunction, "I believed and I spake, and I was greatly afflicted."

[f] תַּגְמוּלוֹהִי. This Aramaic plural suffix occurs only here in Biblical Hebrew (Ges. § 91, 2, Obs. 2).

[g] נֶגְדָה. The form seems adapted to the following נָא, to express the inward earnestness of wish; see the same form ver. 18, and again the use of אָנָּה, ver. 16. It is more difficult to account for the termination *-ah* in הַמָּוְתָה, ver. 15, which, as an accusatival termination, can have no force. Del. calls it "a pathetic form" for מָוֶת, but the fondness for this termination is a peculiarity of the writer.

[h] לְמוֹסֵרָי. The prep. לְ instead of the accus. after the trans. verb is an Aramaic construction, but not necessarily one of the signs of the later date of the Psalm, as the construction occurs sometimes in the earlier Books.

PSALM 117

THIS short Psalm may have been a doxology intended to be sung after other Psalms, or perhaps at the beginning or end of the Temple service. In many MSS. and editions it is joined with the following Psalm, but without any sufficient reason.

1 O PRAISE Jehovah, all ye nations,
Laud Him, all ye peoples! [a]
2 For His loving-kindness is mightily shown towards us,

2. LOVING-KINDNESS . . . TRUTH. These two great attributes of God (see on cxv. 1), as manifested to Israel, "*towards us*," are to be the subject of praise for the heathen, an indication of those wider sympathies which appear to have manifested themselves after the Exile. Hence the first verse is quoted by St. Paul, Rom. xv. 11, together with

And the truth of Jehovah is for ever.
Hallelujah!

Deut. xxxii. 43, "Rejoice, ye Gentiles, with His people," as showing that in the purpose of God the Gentiles were destined to be partakers, together with the Jews, of His mercy in Christ.

IS MIGHTILY SHOWN. Comp. ciii. 11.

[a] אֻמִּים. The only instance of this form in Biblical Hebrew. Elsewhere, either אֻמּוֹת (Gen. xxv. 16; Num. xxv. 15), or more commonly לְאֻמִּים.

PSALM 118

IT is evident that this Psalm was designed to be sung in the Temple worship, and was composed for some festal occasion. Its liturgical character is shown by the formula with which it opens and closes, "O give thanks unto Jehovah," &c.; by the introduction of different voices, which may be inferred in ver. 2—4; and by the frequent repetition of certain lines as a refrain in the former half of the Psalm, which can leave little doubt that it was constructed with a view to antiphonal singing. The allusions in the latter part, and especially ver. 24, "This is the day which Jehovah hath made," &c. point to some great festival as the occasion for which it was written. Its general character, and the many passages in it borrowed from earlier writers, render it probable that it is one of the later Psalms, and we may assume that it was composed after the return from the Captivity.

Four different occasions have been suggested for which it might have been written:—

1. The first celebration of the Feast of Tabernacles in the seventh month of the first year of the Return, when nothing but the altar had, as yet, been erected for the worship of God, Ezra iii. 1—4. (Ewald.)

2. The laying of the foundation-stone of the Second Temple in the second month of the second year, Ezra iii. 8—13. (Hengstenberg.)

3. The completion and consecration of the Temple in the twelfth month of the seventh year of Darius, Ezra vi. 15—18. (Delitzsch.)

4. The extraordinary celebration of the Feast of Tabernacles after the completion of the Second Temple, recorded in Neh. viii. 13—18. (Stier.)

The following conclusions may help us to decide :—

1. The use of the Psalm in the ritual of the Second Temple leads to the conclusion that it was composed originally for the Feast of Tabernacles. For the words of the 25th verse were sung during that Feast, when the altar of burnt-offering was solemnly compassed; that is, once on each of the first six days of the Feast, and seven times on the seventh day. This seventh day was, and is to this day, called "the great *Hosannah*" (*Save now*, ver. 25); and not only the prayers for the Feast, but even the branches of willow-trees, the myrtles, and the "Citron" (fruit of the tree of Hadar), or Ethrag, together with the palm-branch (*Lulab*), were called "Hosannas" (הושענות). On the seventh day, after the three מינים (kinds of plants, *i.e.* Ethrag, myrtle, and palm-branch) are laid aside, the "Hosha'nah" still plays a part.

2. In the next place, it seems equally clear that the Psalm supposes the completion of the Temple. The language of verses 19, 20, "Open me the gates of righteousness," "This is the gate of Jehovah," and the figure employed in ver. 22, "The stone which the builders rejected is become the head stone of the corner," cannot be easily explained on any other supposition. The allusions in verses 8—12 to the deceitfulness of human help and the favour of princes, as well as to the active interference of troublesome enemies, are exactly in accordance with all that we read of the circumstances connected with the rebuilding of the Temple. The most probable conclusion therefore is, that the Psalm was composed for the first celebration of the Feast of Tabernacles, after the completion of the Second Temple. (Nehemiah viii.)

Dr. Plumptre, who, like Ewald, supposes the Psalm to have been originally composed for the first Feast of Tabernacles after the Return, suggests that it may subsequently have been used with adaptations at the later great gatherings of the people. He thus in fact combines the different views which have been held as to the occasion for which the Psalm was written. He thinks it may possibly have been written by one of the two prophets of that time, and draws attention to the prominence in Zechariah of parables and illustrations drawn from the builder's work: the "stone" of iii. 9, iv. 7; the "house" and "timber" of v. 4. 11; the "line" of i. 16; the "carpenters" of i. 20; the "measuring-line for the walls of Jerusalem" of ii. 1; the "plummet" in the hand of Zerubbabel of iv. 10. "The Prophet lives as it were among the works of the rising Temple." (*Biblical Studies*, p. 274.) Comp. ver. 19 and 22 of the Psalm.

Ewald distributes the Psalm between different voices, giving ver. 1—4 to the choir, ver. 5—23 to the leader of the choir, ver. 24, 25 to the choir, ver. 26, 27 to the priest, ver 28 to the leader of the choir, ver. 29 to the choir. But, as Delitzsch observes, the priests took no part in the singing of the service; they blew with the trumpets, but the singers and the players on the stringed and other instruments of music were Levites. The Psalm, therefore, should be distributed between the Levites and the congregation, the lines containing the refrains being probably sung antiphonally by the latter. Delitzsch thinks it more certain that the Psalm consists of two parts, the first of which, ver. 1—19, was sung by the festal procession, led by priests and Levites, on the way to the Temple; the second, ver. 20—27, by the Levites, who received the procession at the Temple gate. Finally, ver. 28 would be the response of those who had just reached the Temple, and ver. 29 would be sung by all, both Levites and those who formed the procession.

A similar arrangement of the Psalm is suggested in the Midrash (*Shocher tobh,*) but there "the men of Judah" form the procession, which is received by "the men of Jerusalem." In Tal. B. *Pesachim* 119*a* the Psalm is assumed to be intended for antiphonal singing.

The congregation speak of themselves sometimes in the singular, sometimes in the plural, but it is not necessary to assume that in the former case the words were always sung by a single voice and in the latter by many. It is more probable that in some portions of the Psalm, although it was intended for public worship, the personal feelings of the writer were uppermost. There is the same change, for instance, in the "Te Deum," and such variations are perfectly natural. On the other hand, we may take it for granted, that in the first four verses the lines would be sung antiphonally, the precentor, perhaps, singing the first line of each verse, and the choir taking up the refrain, "For His loving-kindness," &c.

1 O GIVE thanks to Jehovah, for He is good,
For His loving-kindness (endureth) for ever.
2 Let Israel now say,
That His Loving-kindness (endureth) for ever.

1—4. Comp. Ezra iii. 11, where the same refrain is found as the burden of the psalmody which was sung at the laying of the foundations of the second Temple. This is so far in favour of Hengstenberg's view as to the occasion on which the Psalm was first sung. See introduction to the Psalm.

2. THAT or rather "for" as in ver. 1. It is the same particle. The words "for His loving-kindness endureth for ever," are in fact a quotation, a refrain such as

3 Let the house of Aaron now say,
That His loving-kindness (endureth) for ever.
4 Let them now that fear Jehovah say,
That His loving-kindness (endureth) for ever.
5 Out of (my) straitness I called upon Jah,
Jah answered [a] me (and set me) in a large place.[b]
6 Jehovah is on my side, I am not afraid;
What can man do unto me?
7 Jehovah is on my side, to help me,
Therefore I shall see my desire upon them that hate me.
8 It is better to find refuge in Jehovah,
Than to put any trust in man:
9 It is better to find refuge in Jehovah,
Than to put any trust in princes.

10 All nations compassed me about;
In the name of Jehovah will I cut them off.[c]
11 They compassed me about, yea, they compassed me about;
But in the name of Jehovah will I cut them off.
12 They compassed me about like bees,
They were extinguished like a fire of thorns:

Jehoshaphat's singers were directed to sing, 2 Chron. xxv. 21.

6. Borrowed from lvi. 9, 11 [10, 12].

7. TO HELP ME, or "as my Helper." Comp. liv. 4 [6], where see note. Exod. xviii. 4.

8, 9. See lxii., xxxiii. 16—19, and comp. cxlvi. 3.

The allusion is probably to the hostility of the Samaritans and the Persian satraps during the building of the Temple. The Jews had learnt by painful experience how little they could trust in princes, for the work which had been begun under Cyrus had been threatened under Cambyses, and had been suspended under the pseudo-Smerdis, and it was not till Darius came to the throne that they were allowed to resume it (Ezra iv.).

10. ALL NATIONS, *i.e.* the neighbouring tribes, who harassed the returning exiles, the four times repeated "compassed me about" marking their close and pertinacious hostility.

12. LIKE BEES. See the same figure, Deut. i. 44.

WERE EXTINGUISHED. Others "they blazed up" (so Leeser), the Pael being taken here in the privative sense which the Piel sometimes has, as for instance in li. 7 [9], Is. v. 2. So the LXX. ἐξεκαύθησαν ὡς πῦρ ἐν ἀκάνθαις. Vulg. *exarserunt.*

FIRE OF THORNS, quickly blazing up and as quickly dying out. Comp. lviii. 9 [10].

In the name of Jehovah will I cut them off.
13 Thou didst thrust sore at me, that I might fall,[d]
But Jehovah helped me.
14 Jah is my strength and my song ;[e]
And He is become my salvation.
15 The voice of joyous song and salvation
Is in the tents of the righteous :
The right hand of Jehovah doeth valiantly.
16 The right hand of Jehovah is exalted,[f]
The right hand of Jehovah doeth valiantly.
17 I shall not die but live,
And I shall tell forth the works of Jah.
18 Jah hath chastened me sore,
But He hath not given me over unto death.
19 Open to me the gates of righteousness,
I will enter into them, I will give thanks to Jah.

13. THOU DIDST THRUST SORE, or perhaps "Thou didst *indeed* thrust, &c. . . . *but*," for the emphasis in the repetition of the verb (infin. absol.) belongs, as Hupf. remarks, not merely to the idea contained in the verb, but rather to the whole sentence, and implies an opposition, as here in what follows. The words are an apostrophe to the enemy, here addressed as an individual.

14. In the first line there is a reminiscence of Israel's song of triumph at the Red Sea, Ex. xv. 2 (comp. Is. xii. 2).

15. TENTS. "We can imagine," says Dr. Plumptre, "with what special force the words [of this verse] would come to those who then were, or had but recently been keeping their Feast of Tabernacles, dwelling in the temporary huts which they constructed of the branches of the olive and the fir-tree, the myrtle and the palm, and rejoicing in the great deliverance which God had given them."—*Biblical Studies*, pp. 274, 275. But the word for these temporary huts is always *succah*, "booth," not *ohel*, "tent."

17. "Ad se redit, lætusque exclamat," remarks Rosenmüller. And certainly the personal feeling of the Psalmist seems here to predominate, though the Psalm is so manifestly liturgical, and therefore intended to represent the feelings of the congregation, that the personal experience includes that of the nation at large. Each one of those redeemed captives may take up the words and utter them as his own, and the whole nation as one man may adopt them also. Nationally and individually they are alike true.

19. THE GATES OF RIGHTEOUSNESS. The gates of the Temple are so called with reference to the service of God, and the character He requires of His worshipers. This is evident from the next verse, "The *righteous* shall enter into it." Comp. v. 4 [5], "Evil cannot dwell with Thee," *i.e.* in Thy house ; xv. 1, 2, "Who may dwell on Thy holy mountain ? He that walketh perfectly and worketh *righteousness*,"

20 This is the gate of Jehovah;
The righteous shall enter into it.
21 I will give thanks unto Thee, for Thou hast answered me,
And art become my salvation.
22 A stone which the builders rejected
Is become the head (stone) of the corner.

&c. See also xxiv. 3—6. What David had declared to be the necessary condition of all acceptable worship in Zion was felt to be perpetually true.

The demand "Open to me," may be understood either (1) literally, in which case it is best explained as the words of the singers in the festal procession when they reach the Temple gates (see Introduction to the Psalm); or (2) figuratively as implying the readiness and alacrity with which the Psalmist will go to the house of God, there to offer his sacrifices and to utter his thanksgivings. Comp. Is. xxvi. 2, "Open ye the gates, that the righteous nation may enter in," where righteousness is made the condition of entrance into "the strong city" or God's building, as here into the holy place.

To this day, the words of this verse are used at the dedication of a new synagogue.

22. A STONE. The imagery is drawn obviously from the building of the Temple. "Some incident in the progress of the works had probably served as the starting-point of the parable. Some stone—a fragment, we may conjecture, of the Old Temple, rescued from its ruins—has seemed to the architects unfit for the work of binding together the two walls that met at right angles to each other. They would have preferred some new blocks of their own fashioning. But the priests, it may be, more conversant with the traditions of the Temple, knew that that was the right place for it, and that no other stone would answer half as well. The trial was made, and the issue answered their expectations. Could they fail to see that this was a type and figure of what was then passing in the history of their nation? Israel had been rejected by the builders of this world's empire, and seemed now about to be once more 'the head of the corner.'" (*Biblical Studies*, p. 275.) They had been despised by their heathen masters, but now, by the good hand of their God upon them, they had been lifted into a place of honour. They, rejected of men, were chosen of God as a chief stone of that new spiritual building which Jehovah was about to erect, the temple of the world, the foundation of which was to be laid in Zion. In Matt. xxi. 42—44 (Mark xii. 10, 11, Luke xx. 17), our Lord applies the words of this and the next verse to Himself. The quotation was, it would seem, purposely taken from the same Psalm from which the multitude had just before taken their words of salutation (see on ver. 25, 26), as they went forth to meet Him and conduct Him in triumph into Jerusalem. But there is more than an application of the words. Israel is not only a figure of Christ, there is an organic unity between Him and them. Whatever, therefore, is true of Israel in a lower sense, is true in its highest sense of Christ. Is Israel God's "first-born son?" the name in its fulfilment belongs to Christ (Matt. ii. 15); if Israel is "the servant of Jehovah," he is so only as imperfectly representing Him who said, "My meat is to do the will of Him who sent me, and to finish His work." If Israel is the rejected stone made the head of the corner, this is far

23 This is Jehovah's doing,
It is marvellous in our eyes.[g]
24 This is the day which Jehovah hath made,
Let us exult and be glad in it.
25 We beseech Thee, O Jehovah, save now,
We beseech Thee, O Jehovah, send now prosperity.

truer of Him who was indeed rejected of men, but chosen of God and precious; the corner-stone of the one great living temple of the redeemed, whether Jews or Gentiles. (Comp. Eph. ii. 20.) See the use of the same figure in its application to our Lord by St. Peter, Acts iv. 11; 1 Pet. ii. 7.

The passage which forms the connecting link between this Psalm and the N.T. quotations is Isaiah xxviii. 16, "Behold, it is I who have laid securely in Zion a stone, a tried precious corner-stone, most securely laid: he that believeth (i.e. *resteth thereon*) shall not flee (through fear of any evil)." In this passage the Messianic reference is still more direct, even if we suppose a primary reference to the house of David. (The Targum interprets it of David, Jesse, his wife and children; and Rashi of Israel and the nations.) In marked contrast with this, it is said of Babylon, Jer. li. 26, "They shall not take of thee a stone for a corner, nor a stone for a foundation."

23. The change in Israel's destiny, the restoration to their land, the rebuilding of their Temple, the future that was opening before them—these things are a miracle; Jehovah's hand alone could have accomplished it. Comp. Josh. xi. 20.

24. THIS IS THE DAY, *i.e.* perhaps the great day of festival with reference to which the Psalm was composed. It is possible, however, that this verse is rather to be connected with the previous verse, so that "the day" is not the Feast-day, but the day (the time) on which Jehovah had wrought for Israel: "This is Jehovah's doing . . . this is the day which He hath made." The prayer of the next verse falls in best with the latter interpretation.

25. WE BESEECH THEE. Comp. cxvi. 4, 16.

SAVE NOW, or rather, "Save, I pray" (*Hosanna*). The particle of entreaty is repeated in each member of this verse, so that altogether it occurs four times, as if to mark the earnestness of the petition. The English word "now" is not, therefore, a particle of time, but a particle of entreaty.

With this word "Hosanna," and words from the next verse, "Blessed be He that cometh," &c., the multitude welcomed Jesus as the Messiah, the Psalm being perhaps already recognized as a Messianic Psalm. According to the Midrash, the first hemistich of this verse was said by "the men of Jerusalem from within," "welcoming the men of Judah," *i.e.* the caravans of pilgrims coming up to the feast: the second, by "the men of Judah from without," in reply. So in the next ver. the men of Jerusalem say the first hemistich: "Blessed be He," &c., and the men of Judah, "We have blessed you," &c. [In this case we must interpret the latter part of the clause, You that are of the house of Jehovah.] In ver. 27, the men of Jerusalem say, "Jehovah is God," and the men of Judah from without answer, "And He showeth us light:" the one say, "Bind the sacrifice," &c., and the others, "My God, I will exalt Thee." Then both together open their mouth and praise and glorify God, saying, "Oh give thanks," &c. (ver. 29).

26 Blessed be he that cometh in the name of Jehovah,
We have blessed you from the house of Jehovah.
27 Jehovah is God, and He showeth us light;
Bind the sacrifice with cords,
Even unto the horns of the altar.
28 Thou art my God, and I will give Thee thanks,
(Thou art) my God, (and) I will exalt Thee.
29 Oh give thanks to Jehovah, for He is good,
For His loving-kindness (endureth) for ever.

26. According to the accents the rendering would be "Blessed in the name of Jehovah be he that cometh," the formula being the same as in the priestly blessing, Num. vi. 27; Deut. xxi. 5; 2 Sam. vi. 18. Comp. Ps. xxxiv. 8.

FROM THE HOUSE OF JEHOVAH, the priests standing there to bless those who entered.

27. SHOWETH US LIGHT, in allusion to the priestly blessing, "Jehovah make His face *shine* (lighten, the same verb as here) upon thee." Comp. iv. 6 [7].

THE SACRIFICE. The word commonly denotes *the feast;* here, in Ex. xxiii. 18, Mal. ii. 3, *the victim* offered at the feast. The E.V. gives this sense in Is. xxix. 11.

UNTO THE HORNS OF THE ALTAR. The expression is apparently a pregnant one, and the sense is, "Bind the victim with cords till it is sacrificed, and its blood sprinkled on the horns of the altar." Delitzsch, on the other hand, renders "as far as the horns of the altar." Supposing the Psalm to have been written for the dedication of the Second Temple, he refers to Ezra vi. 17, where mention is made of the vast number of animals slaughtered on the occasion; hence he explains that the victims (taking the word *sacrifice* in a collective sense) were so numerous that the whole court of the priests was crowded with them, and that they reached as far as the horns of the altar. "The meaning is," he says, "bring your hecatombs and have them ready for sacrifice."

But on this interpretation there is nothing appropriate in the mention of *the horns* of the altar. These have always a reference to the blood of the sacrifice.

Luther has "Deck the feast with garlands (or boughs)," following the LXX. *συστήσασθε ἑορτὴν ἐν τοῖς πυκάζουσιν.* Symm. has *συνδήσατε ἐν πανηγύρει πυκάσματα*, and Jerome *frequentate solennitatem in frondosis*—all renderings which imply a belief, that the Psalm was intended for the Feast of Tabernacles. As regards this rendering, the word translated in the text *cords* may mean *thick boughs*, *πυκάσματα* (see Ezek. xix. 11; xxxi. 3, 4), but the verb *bind* cannot mean *deck* or *wreath.*

[a] עָנָנִי. This (and not עֲנָנִי) is the usual vocalization, whether in pause or not; comp. 1 Sam. xxviii. 15, where it stands with *Munach.* Baer says here that עָנָנִי is "with *Rebia Mugrash*, and the *Nun* has Qametz according to the best MSS." The construction with בַּמֶּרְחַבְיָה is an instance of what is called the *constructio prægnans.* Comp. lxxiv. 7; 2 Sam. xviii. 19; Jer. xli. 7. Symm. *ἐπήκουσέ μου εἰς εὐρυχωρίαν.*

[b] According to the Massoreth יָהּ is not a separate word, but we are to read בַּמֶּרְחַבְיָה, this being one of several instances in which the final syllable יָה merely intensifies the form of the word, and the ה is expressly said to be without Mappik. Cf. Jos. xv. 28, 2 Sam. xii. 25, Jer. ii. 31, 1 Chr. iv. 18 (bis), viii. 24, 27. Song of Sol. i. 7, viii. 6, and see note on הללויה, Ps. civ. 35.

[c] אֲמִילַם. Hiphil (only here) of מול, which means elsewhere to *circumcise*, in Qal and Niphal. Hengst. would retain the signification here, as if the victory over the heathen, "the uncircumcised," were described under the figure of a compulsory circumcision. Such a form of expression does occur in the later Jewish history (Joseph. *Arch.* xiii. 9, 1, 11, 3). Compare also the allusions in Gal. v. 12, Phil. iii. 2, and the forcible circumcision as a token of victory, 1 Sam. xviii. 25, 2 Sam. iii. 14. But this is quite out of the question here. The Hiph. may have the more general meaning *to cut off*, which is found in the Pilel, xc. 6, and in the Hithpael, lviii. 8. Hupf. would read אֲכִילֵם (from כול, *sustinere*), "I will repel them," in accordance with the rendering of the LXX. ἠμυνάμην.

As regards the punctuation, the correct texts of Solomon of Norcia, Heidenheim, and others, have אֲמִילֵם, and so Gesen. would read, the Pathach in pause being the representative of the Tzere. Delitzsch observes, that such a change of vowel is remarkable, and he would account for it by supposing that, in such cases, as the vowel is already long and cannot be lengthened, it is sharpened (pointed) instead.

The affirmative כִּי stands before this verb (instead of at the beginning of the sentence), as in cxxviii. 2. Compare the position of אִם, lxvi. 18. Its use may be explained by an ellipse = "know that," "be sure that," as in an oath, 1 Sam. xiv. 44. See also Num. xiv. 3, &c.

[d] לִנְפֹּל, with *Nun* expressed (as in Is. xxix. 2) and *Pe dagess.*, whereas with כ and ב the aspirate is left, with but few exceptions, such as Gen. xxxv. 22.

[e] זִמְרָת. See on xvi. note [k].

[f] רוֹמֵמָה. Not an adj., as if from רמם, a root which does not exist, but either (1) 3 pret. Pal., or (2) Part. Pal. with loss of the מְ (as שֹׁמֵם, Dan. viii. 13, עוֹלֵל, Is. iii. 12, and elsewhere), and retention of the vowel ֵ, as in pause. The objection to (1) is, that then the accentuation ought to be רוֹמֵמָת.

[g] נִפְלָאת. For other instances of this form comp. Gen. xxxiii. 11; Deut. xxxi. 29; Jer. xliv. 23; Is. vii. 14. הָיְתָה זֹּאת, rhythmic *Mile'el* with *Dagesh* in the following word, as for instance in Gen. xix. 38; Ex. xvi. 24; 1 Sam. vi. 9; Prov. vii. 13, &c.

PSALM 119

THIS is the longest and the most elaborate of the Alphabetical Psalms. It is arranged in twenty-two stanzas, according to the number of letters in the Hebrew alphabet. Each stanza is composed of eight verses, each verse consisting of two members only, and each beginning with the same letter of the alphabet. Thus each of the first eight verses begins with the letter Aleph, each of the next eight with the letter Beth, and so on throughout the alphabet. In the third chapter of the Lamentations of Jeremiah a similar arrangement is adopted, but there the stanzas or groups consist only of three verses, each beginning with the same letter. Other instances of this acrostic arrangement occurring in the Psalter will be found enumerated in the Introduction to Psalm xxv. (See also the Introduction to Psalm cxi.)

The great subject of the Psalmist's praise is the Law of God. In this respect the Psalm may be said to be an elaborate expansion of the latter part of Psalm xix. The Massoretes observe, that in every verse but one, the 122nd, there is direct reference to the Law under some one of the ten names (supposed to allude to the Ten Commandments [Hebrew, Words]) *word, saying, testimonies, way, judgement, precept, commandment, law, statute, faithfulness* (or according to another reading, *righteousness*). In the 132nd verse, the word "judgement" occurs in the Hebrew, although apparently not as a synonyme of the Law: see note on the verse. In ver. 121, "judgement and righteousness," if not denoting the Law immediately, are employed with reference to the requirements of the Law.

The date of the Psalm cannot be fixed with anything like certainty, though it may probably be referred to a time subsequent to the return from the Babylonish captivity.

(*a*) The allusion to "princes" (ver. 23) and "kings" (ver. 46) who do not share the faith of the Psalmist, may be taken to denote that the Jews were subject at this time to foreign dominion.

(*b*) The Law of which he speaks as his daily study, as his delight and his counsellor, must obviously have been the written Law, and it may be inferred that it was now in the hands of the people. Whether this was the case to any extent before the Exile, we have now no means of ascertaining. After the Exile, copies of the Scriptures were multiplied. The efforts of Ezra and Nehemiah, which were directed in the first instance to the collection of the Sacred Books (2 Macc. ii. 13), must have been directed eventually to their dissemination. Accordingly, we find that copies of "the books of the Law," or of "the book of the Covenant," were in the possession of the people at the time of the Maccabees (1 Macc. i. 55, 56). In the Psalm, the writer perhaps includes in "the word" of God, not only the Law, but other writings regarded as sacred. In Zech. vii. 12, "the former Prophets" are joined with "the Law."

(*c*) The general character of the Psalm, which is a meditation rather than a poem, as well as its place in the Collection, favours the supposition that it is one of the later Psalms.

(*d*) The alphabetical arrangement, it has also been argued, forbids our assigning it to an earlier period: "adapted for didactic rather than for lyric expression, it belongs," it has been said, "to an age no longer animated by the soul of poetry, but struggling to clothe its religious thoughts in a poetic form."* It is, however, far from certain that this acrostic device is of itself evidence of the decline of the poetic spirit. Some of the oldest poems in our own language are constructed on the principle of alliteration. It is the same in Welsh poetry. And unless the different stages of Hebrew poetry were more clearly marked than they are at present, its acrostic character can hardly be taken as settling the question of the date of any single Psalm.

The circumstances of the Psalmist may be inferred in some measure from the language of the Psalm itself. He is suffering from persecution. His enemies are men of rank and authority (ver. 21, 23), having both the power and the will to crush him (ver. 61, 69). His constancy is severely tried. He is exposed to reproach and contempt on account of his religion, and has reason to fear lest his hope and trust in God should be put to shame (ver. 6, 22, 31). He is solicited to give up his faith for gain, and even perhaps invited to join in idolatrous worship (ver. 36, 37). These things make him sad (ver. 25, 28), but he stays himself upon the word and promise of God. That word in all its varied aspects of law and promise, of precepts and judgements, had been his comfort in his affliction, his most precious possession, dearer to him than all earthly treasures; he had meditated upon it day and night; it had been a lamp to his feet and a light to his path. He had taken it for his rule of life, he longed to know it better, he prayed to have the veil taken off his eyes that he might behold its hidden wonders. These thoughts, and thoughts like these, recur again and again. He is never wearied of declaring

* *The Psalms Chronologically Arranged*, by Four Friends, p. 383.

his love of God's Law, or of praying for more light to understand it, more power to keep it, to keep it with his "whole heart." The frequency of this last expression is striking evidence of the earnestness of the writer: see on ver. 2. But there does not seem to be any thing like continuity, or progress of thought, or of recorded experience, in the several stanzas of the Psalm.*

Still, "if we would fathom the depth of meaning in the written Law of Israel, if we would measure the elevation of soul, the hope, the confidence even before princes and kings, which pious Jews derived from it, we must turn to this Psalm. Here is an epitome of all true religion, as conceived by the best spirits of that time. To such a loving study and meditation on the Law the Alphabetical arrangement is not inappropriate, and if the poem be necessarily somewhat cramped, it is nevertheless pervaded by the glow of love, and abounds in spiritual life." †

Delitzsch thinks that the Psalm must have been written by a young man, and appeals to ver. 9, and ver. 99, 100, as supporting this view. But the language of ver. 9 is rather that of one who, looking back on his own past life, draws the inference which he seeks to impress upon the young, that youthful purity can only be preserved by those who from their early years take God's word for their guide. Just so in Ecclesiastes xii. 1, it is the man of mature age and large experience who gives the wise and friendly counsel, "Remember thy Creator in the days of thy youth." The lesson in each case comes with double force, because it comes from the lips of one who speaks with the authority of experience. When it is said in verses 99, 100 of this Psalm, that the Psalmist is wiser than his teachers, wiser than the aged, the only conclusion that can be drawn is that he is not advanced in life. It is plain that the writer is not an old man, as Ewald would have us believe, or he would not compare his knowledge of the law with the knowledge of the aged. But it does not follow that he is a young man. The teachers whom he has outstript may have been those whose disciple he once was, not those whose disciple he still is; or he may refer to authorized teachers to whom he listened because they sat in Moses' seat, though he felt that they had really nothing to teach him. Indeed the whole strain of the Psalm, in the depth and breadth of spiritual life, and the long

---

* Delitzsch thinks that he discovers a leading idea in each stanza, and thus endeavours to link the several stanzas together, but his analysis does not appear to me to be very successful. To a certain extent, freedom of thought and expression must have been fettered by the requirements of the alphabetical order. But, after all, what is rhyme but a fetter?

† *The Psalms Chronologically Arranged*, p. 385.

acquaintance which is everywhere implied in it with the word of God, can leave us in no doubt that it was written by a man who was no longer young, who had at least reached "the middle arch of life."

Aleph.

1 א BLESSED are the perfect in the way,
Who walk in the law of Jehovah.
2 א Blessed are they that keep His testimonies,
That seek Him with the whole heart,
3 א (Who) also have done no iniquity,
(Who) have walked in His ways.
4 א Thou hast commanded Thy precepts,
That we should keep (them) diligently.
5 א O that[a] my ways were established
To keep Thy statutes.
6 א Then shall I not be ashamed,
While I have respect unto all Thy commandments.
7 א I will give thanks to Thee with uprightness of heart,
When I learn Thy righteous judgements.
8 א I will keep Thy statutes:
O forsake me not utterly.

Beth.

9 ב Wherewithal shall a young man cleanse his path?
By taking heed (thereto) according to Thy word,[b]
10 ב With my whole heart have I sought Thee:
O let me not wander from Thy commandments.

2. WITH THE WHOLE HEART. An expression characteristic of this Psalm. Comp. ver. 10, 34, 58, 69, 145.

6. ASHAMED, *i.e.* put to shame, my hope being frustrated. This is the shame meant, not shame of conscience in comparing a man's life with the requirement of the Law.

HAVE RESPECT UNTO, lit. "look upon," *i.e.* with care and thought, so as to make them the rule of life.

7. JUDGEMENTS; here and throughout this Psalm not used of God's acts of judgement, but merely as the equivalent of "law," "precepts," and the like, utterances as of a Judge and Lawgiver, and found in this sense even in the Pentateuch, Ex. xxi. 1, xxiv. 3; Lev. xviii. 4, 5.

11 ב In my heart have I laid up Thy word,
That I might not sin against Thee.
12 ב Blessed art Thou, O Jehovah :
Teach me Thy statutes.
13 ב With my lips have I told
Of all the judgements of Thy mouth.
14 ב In the way of Thy testimonies I have rejoiced,
As much as in all manner of riches.
15 ב I will meditate in Thy precepts,
And have respect unto Thy paths.
16 ב In Thy statutes will I delight myself;
I will not forget Thy word.

Gimel.

17 ג Deal bountifully with Thy servant that I may live,
So will I keep Thy word.
18 ג Open Thou mine eyes,
That I may behold wondrous things out of Thy law.
19 ג I am a sojourner in the earth :
Hide not Thy commandments from me.
20 ג My soul breaketh for the longing [c]
(That it hath) unto Thy judgements at all times.

11. IN MY HEART. See Luke ii. 19—51. It is to me no merely outward rule of conduct : it is a power and a life within.

WORD, or rather "saying," "speech," distinct from the word employed, for instance, in ver. 9, lxxvii. 18. Both words are constantly interchanged throughout the Psalm.

14. ALL MANNER OF RICHES. Comp. what is said of the incomparable worth of wisdom, Prov. ii. 4, iii. 13—15, viii. 10, 11, 19, xvi. 16, xxii. 1 ; Job xxviii. 15—19.

17. THAT I MAY LIVE : or the construction may be, " Let me live (or, if I live), so will I," &c. The gift of life, if vouchsafed, shall be devoted to the keeping of God's word.

18. WONDROUS THINGS ; an acknowledgement of treasures in the Divine word not seen by common eyes, needing, indeed, spiritual discernment and heavenly unveiling ; hence "Open *Thou.*"

19. A SOJOURNER, here therefore but for a short time (see on xxxix. 12), and needing for that time Divine teaching. Hence the prayer " Hide not," *i.e.* reveal, show me the inner sense and true application of, " Thy commandments."

20. BREAKETH, lit. "is broken," as expressive of the intensity of the desire, which seems to pervade the

21 ג Thou hast rebuked the proud that they are cursed,
Which do wander from Thy commandments.
22 ג Remove [d] from me reproach and contempt;
For I have kept Thy testimonies.
23 ג Princes also have sat and talked against me,
But Thy servant meditateth in Thy statutes.
24 ג Thy testimonies also are my delight,
And my counsellors.

Daleth.

25 ד My soul cleaveth unto the dust:
Quicken Thou me according to Thy word.
26 ד I have told my ways, and Thou answeredst me:
Teach me Thy statutes.
27 ד Make me to understand the way of Thy precepts,
So shall I meditate of Thy wondrous works.
28 ד My soul melteth away for heaviness:
Stablish Thou me according unto Thy word.
29 ד Remove from me the way of falsehood,
And with Thy law be gracious unto me.

whole man, and leave him crushed and powerless in its grasp. Bp. Taylor speaks somewhere of "the violence of the desire, bursting itself with its fulness into dissolution."

21. THAT THEY ARE CURSED. The adjective is a predicate marking the effect of God's rebuke. There is another division of the verse which has the support of the LXX. and Jerome :—

Thou hast rebuked the proud,
Cursed are they that, &c.

And so the P.B.V.

22. REMOVE FROM ME, lit. "take off, strip, from me," shame being regarded as a cloak or mantle covering the person. LXX. περίελε.

23. TALKED, or "spoken one with another." The verb (Niphal) is reciprocal, as in Ezek. xxxiii. 30.

25. CLEAVETH UNTO THE DUST. See on xliv. 25 [26].

26. I HAVE TOLD MY WAYS. I have laid before Thee severally, numbering them as it were, all the acts and events of my life. Cf. xxii. 17 [18], "I may tell all my bones."

28. MELTETH, lit. "droppeth," weeps itself away, so to speak.

STABLISH, lit. "set me up again," the meaning being nearly the same as in the often-repeated prayer, "quicken me."

29. THE WAY OF FALSEHOOD, *i.e.* not falsehood in the common sense of the term, but "unfaithfulness" to God, to which, in the next verse, "the way of faithfulness" is opposed.

WITH THY LAW, or "Graciously impart Thy law unto me." The construction is that of the double accusative. See Gen. xxxiii. 5.

30 ד I have chosen the way of faithfulness;
Thy judgements have I laid (before me)
31 ד I have stuck unto Thy testimonies:
O Jehovah, put me not to shame.
32 ד I will run the way of Thy commandments,
When Thou shalt enlarge my heart.

He.

33 ה Teach me, O Jehovah, the way of Thy statutes,
And I shall keep it unto the end.
34 ה Give me understanding, that I may observe Thy law,
That I may keep it with my whole heart.
35 ה Make me to walk in the path of Thy commandments;
For therein do I delight.
36 ה Incline my heart unto Thy testimonies,
And not to covetousness.
37 ה Turn away mine eyes from seeing vanity;
In Thy way quicken Thou me.
38 ה Confirm Thy promise unto Thy servant,
Who is (devoted) to Thy fear.
39 ה Turn away my reproach which I am afraid of;
For Thy judgements are good.

32. ENLARGE MY HEART, *i.e.* expand it with a sense of liberty and joy, as in Is. lx. 5; 2 Cor. vi. 11, 13. See on ci. 6.

36. MY HEART, to which answers in the next verse "mine eyes," as representing the senses through which the forbidden desire is kindled in the heart. Comp. Is. xxxiii. 15; Job xxxi. 1, 7.

COVETOUSNESS, or, rather, "gain unjustly acquired." LXX. πλεονεξίαν. Stanley, on 1 Cor. v. 10, thinks that from the connection of πλεονεξία with idolatry, it may be used in the sense of *sensuality*, which so often accompanied idolatry, and he sees a similar connection here, *vanity* in the next verse being a term of *idolatry*. However, the Hebrew word בֶּצַע can only mean *plunder, rapine, unjust gain*.

37. TURN AWAY, lit. "make to pass on one side" of the object.

FROM SEEING, *i.e.* being attracted by, and so finding pleasure in (Is. xxxiii. 15) VANITY, all which, as being against God, or without God, is unreal and unstable: but perhaps *idols* are especially meant.

38. PROMISE, or "saying." See on ver. 11. The second member of the verse might also be rendered: "Which (promise) is for Thy fear," *i.e.* either (*a*) is given to them that fear Thee; or (*b*), which has the fear of Thee for its aim and object (cxxx. 4), tends to cherish a holy fear.

39. The train of thought seems

40 ה Behold, I have longed after Thy precepts:
In Thy righteousness quicken Thou me.

Vau.

41 ו Let Thy loving-kindness also come unto me, O Jehovah,
Thy salvation, according to Thy saying.
42 ו So shall I have wherewith to answer him that reproacheth me;
For I trust in Thy word.
43 ו And take not the word of truth utterly out of my mouth;
For I have waited for Thy judgements.
44 ו So shall I keep Thy law continually,
(Yea) for ever and ever.
45 ו And I shall walk at liberty;
For I have sought Thy precepts.
46 ו And I will speak of Thy testimonies before kings,
And will not be ashamed.
47 ו And I will delight myself in Thy commandments,
Which I love.
48 ו My hands also will I lift up unto Thy commandments, which I love;
And I will meditate in Thy statutes.

to be: Keep me from the reproach of breaking Thy commandments, for those commandments are not grievous, but good, sweet, and full of blessing to one who longs after them as I do. Or "the reproach" may be that of his enemies (ver. 42), who taunt him as the servant of God.

41. The vowel-points both of the verb and the noun suggest a plural, although the *Yod* of the plural is wanting in the noun. Similarly in ver. 43 the vowels suggest the plur. "judgements." See Critical Note [b].

43. The sense seems to be, "Give me the power faithfully to witness for Thy truth, and so to answer him that reproacheth me" (ver. 42).

45. AT LIBERTY, lit. "in a wide space," where there is nothing to check or hinder freedom of action, as in cxviii. 5.

46. BEFORE KINGS. It may be inferred that the Psalm was written whilst Judæa was in subjection to foreign rule. The viceroys of the Persian king may be meant.

48. MY HANDS WILL I LIFT UP. The expression denotes the act of prayer, as in xxviii. 2, lxiii. 4 [5], cxxxiv. 2, cxli. 2. Comp. Lam. iii. 41, "Let us lift up our heart with our hands." Here it would seem

Zain.

49 ז Remember the word unto Thy servant,
Upon which Thou hast caused me to hope.
50 ז This is my comfort in my affliction,
For Thy word hath quickened me.
51 ז The proud have had me greatly in derision;
(Yet) have I not swerved from Thy law.
52 ז I have remembered Thy judgements of old, O Jehovah,
And have comforted myself.
53 ז Burning indignation hath taken hold upon me,
Because of the wicked that forsake Thy law.
54 ז Thy statutes have been my songs
In the house of my pilgrimage.
55 ז I have remembered Thy name in the night, O Jehovah,
And have kept Thy law.

to denote figuratively reverence, devotion of heart, and the like; unless we suppose it to be a *locutio prægnans* = "I will pray to Thee for grace to keep Thy commandments."

49. THE WORD, apparently some special word of promise which had been his stay in his affliction, and had roused him to new hope and courage (ver. 50).

UPON WHICH, or perhaps, "seeing that," "because."

50. MY COMFORT. Comp. Job vi. 10, the only other place where the word occurs. It is the "word" (ver. 49) which is his comfort. Others render the ver. "This is my comfort, &c. . . . *that* Thy word hath quickened me."

WORD, lit. "saying." See on ver. 11. Or the construction may be: "This is my comfort . . . that Thy word," &c. Here, as is evident from the mention of "affliction"—and indeed throughout the Psalm—the verb "quicken" is used not merely in an external sense of "preservation from death" (Hupf.), but of "reviving the heart," "imparting fresh courage," &c.

51. HAVE HAD ME IN DERISION, *i.e.* probably both on account of his misery and his trust in God. The verb is from the same root as the noun "scorners," "mockers," in i. 1. Comp. for the same connection between the spirit of *pride* and the spirit of *irreligious scoffing*, Prov. xxi. 24.

52. JUDGEMENTS, in the same sense as throughout the Psalm, God's righteous laws which He revealed OF OLD, which are ever true and ever in force.

53. BURNING INDIGNATION. See on xi. note [c]. Kay connects it with זעף the ל being inserted, "fainting," "drooping," &c. LXX. ἀθυμία, Vulg. *defectio*. The action of the Simûm may either be regarded as a *burning*, parching wind, or in its *effects*, as producing faintness.

54. PILGRIMAGE, or rather, "sojourning," from the same root as the noun in ver. 9, where see note. In this earth I am but a passing

56 ז This I had,
Because I kept Thy precepts.

Cheth.

57 ח "Jehovah is my portion,"
I said that I would keep Thy words.
58 ח I entreated Thy favour with (my) whole heart;
Be gracious to me according to Thy promise.
59 ח I thought on my ways,
And turned back my feet unto Thy testimonies.
60 ח I made haste, and delayed not
To keep Thy commandments.
61 ח The cords of the wicked have been wound about me,
(But) Thy law have I not forgotten.
62 ח At midnight I will rise to give thanks unto Thee,
Because of Thy righteous judgements.
63 ח I am a companion of them that fear Thee,
And of them that keep Thy precepts.
64 ח The earth, O Jehovah, is full of Thy loving-kindness:
Teach me Thy statutes.

Teth.

65 ט Thou hast dealt well with Thy servant,
O Jehovah, according unto Thy word.

guest, as at some wayside inn. Comp. Gen. xlvii. 9.

56. THIS I HAD. It is not clear to what "this" refers. If to what goes before, it may be to the remembrance of God's Name. Otherwise we must render: "This has been (vouchsafed) to me, this has been my reward, *that* I have kept Thy precepts," *i.e.* such has been the gift of Thy grace.

57. This is the arrangement according to Baer's text. According to others, "I said" belongs to the first member: Jehovah is my portion, I said, that I might keep, &c., the verb "I said" being thrown in parenthetically, as in Is. xlv. 24; Lam. iii. 24, and like *inquam* in Latin.

THAT I WOULD KEEP, or "in keeping."

58. I ENTREATED THY FAVOUR. Comp. xlv. 12 [13].

61. WOUND ABOUT, or "entangled," so the LXX. περιεπλάκησαν. Jer. *implicaverunt.* Vulg. *circumplexi sunt.*

66 ט Teach me good perception and knowledge,
For I have believed Thy commandments.
67 ט Before I was afflicted I went astray,
But now do I keep Thy saying.
68 ט Thou art good, and doest good:
Teach me Thy statutes.
69 ט The proud have forged a lie against me;
I, with (my) whole heart, will keep Thy precepts.
70 ט Their heart is gross as fat:
As for me, in Thy law do I delight.
71 ט It is good for me that I have been afflicted,
That I might learn Thy statutes.
72 ט The law of Thy mouth is better unto me
Than thousands of gold and silver.

Yod.

73 י Thy hands have made me and fashioned me:
Give me understanding, that I may learn Thy commandments.
74 י They that fear Thee will be glad when they see me;
For in Thy word have I hoped.
75 י I know, O Jehovah, that Thy judgements are righteous,
And that in faithfulness Thou hast afflicted me.
76 י Let, I pray Thee, Thy loving-kindness be for my comfort,

66. GOOD PERCEPTION, lit. "goodness of perception" or discernment; the fine taste and delicate feeling which are like a new sense. So St. Paul prays for the Church at Philippi, that their "love may abound more and more in *knowledge* and in all *perception*," ἐν ἐπιγνώσει καὶ πάσῃ αἰσθήσει. The two words correspond to the two Hebrew words here; but the latter, αἴσθησις, marks in the Epistle (chap. i. 9) the *delicate tact* by which Christian love should be characterised. Here the Psalmist prays rather for a *fine sense* or apprehension of God's words.

69. THE PROUD. The same overbearing, tyrannical oppression already mentioned ver. 51, 61.

HAVE FORGED, lit. "have patched up." Comp. Job xiii. 4, xiv. 17.

70. FAT. For the figure as expressive of want of feeling, see xvii. 9 [10], lxiii. 6 [7]; Is. vi. 10.

71. IT IS GOOD FOR ME. See ver. 67.

75. RIGHTEOUS, lit. "righteousness."

76. Even when a man recognises that affliction is sent in "faithfulness," that God has a wise purpose of love in sending it, still it is in itself bitter, and therefore

According to Thy saying unto Thy servant.

77 ו Let Thy tender mercies come unto me, that I may live;
For Thy law is my delight.

78 ו Let the proud be ashamed, for they have subverted me by falsehood:
As for me, I meditate in Thy precepts.

79 ו They that fear Thee will turn unto me,
And they shall know Thy testimonies.

80 ו Let my heart be perfect in Thy statutes,
That I be not ashamed.

Caph.

81 כ My soul hath failed for Thy salvation;
In Thy word have I hoped.

82 כ Mine eyes have failed for Thy word,
Saying, "When wilt Thou comfort me?"

83 כ For I am become like a bottle in the smoke:
(Yet) do I not forget Thy statutes.

84 כ How many are the days of Thy servant?
When wilt Thou execute judgement on them that persecute me?

he prays that he may have God's "loving-kindness" and His "tender mercies" as his comfort in the midst of affliction. Comp. Heb. xii. 11.

79. WILL TURN, or there may be the expression of a wish, "Let them turn."

THEY SHALL KNOW, *i.e.* by their own experience. Such is the reading of the present text, but if we accept the Masoretic correction the second member of the verse will be: "And they that know Thy testimonies."

80. PERFECT, *i.e.* whole, undivided.

83. A BOTTLE IN THE SMOKE, *i.e.* a skin bottle for wine. The figure is generally supposed to denote the misery and affliction of the Psalmist who compares himself to one of these wine-skins blackened and shriveled and rendered useless by the smoke of the fire in which it is hung. Rosenm. sees a reference to the custom of the ancients to hang skins full of wine in the smoke, in order to mellow the wine. In this case, the figure would denote the mellowing and ripening of the character by affliction. But the first interpretation is the more probable.

84. HOW MANY. Comp. xxxix. 4 [5]. It is an argument why God should take *speedy* vengeance on his enemies, that he may see it executed before he dies.

85 כ The proud have digged pits for me,
Who are not after Thy law.
86 כ All Thy commandments are faithfulness:
They persecute me wrongfully; help Thou me.
87 כ They had almost consumed me upon earth;
But as for me, I forsook not Thy precepts.
88 כ Quicken me after Thy loving-kindness,
So shall I keep the testimony of Thy mouth.

Lamed.

89 ל For ever, O Jehovah,
Thy word is settled in heaven.
90 ל Thy faithfulness is unto all generations;
Thou hast established the earth, and it standeth fast.
91 ל For Thy judgements, they stand fast (unto) this day;
For all things are Thy servants.
92 ל Unless Thy law had been my delight,
I should then have perished in my affliction.
93 ל I will never forget Thy precepts;
For by them Thou hast quickened me.
94 ל Thine I am, save me;
For I have sought Thy precepts.
95 ל The wicked have waited for me to destroy me;
(But) Thy testimonies do I consider.
96 ל I have seen an end of all perfection;
Thy commandment is exceeding broad.

89. IN HEAVEN, as marking its unchanging, everlasting character, as in lxxxix. 2 [3].

91. FOR THY JUDGEMENTS, *i.e.* "with reference to Thine ordinances or laws, they (*i.e.* heaven and earth) stand fast."

ALL THINGS, lit. "the whole," *i.e.* the universe.

96. ALL PERFECTION. If this rendering is correct, the meaning is obvious. There is nothing upon earth to which there does not cleave some defect. But perhaps the clause should rather be rendered: "I have seen an end, a limit, to the whole range (or compass) of things;" a meaning which may be defended by the use of the similar word in Job xxvi. 10, xxviii. 3, and which harmonizes with the next clause: "Thy commandment is exceeding

Mem.

97 מ O how I love Thy law:
It is my meditation all the day.

98 מ Thy commandments make me wiser[e] than mine enemies;
For they are ever with me.

99 מ I have more understanding than all my teachers;
For Thy testimonies are my meditation.

100 מ I understand more than the aged;
For Thy precepts have I kept.

101 מ I have refrained my feet from every evil path,
That I might keep Thy word.

102 מ From Thy judgements have I not turned aside;
For THOU hast taught me.

103 מ How sweet are Thy sayings unto my taste,
(Yea, sweeter) than honey to my mouth.

104 מ Through Thy precepts I get understanding;
Therefore I hate every path of falsehood.

Nun.

105 נ Thy word is a lamp unto my foot,
And a light unto my path.

106 נ I have sworn, and am steadfastly purposed
That I will keep Thy righteous judgements.

107 נ I am afflicted very greatly;
Quicken me, O Jehovah, according unto Thy word.

broad," has no limits, whilst all other things are bounded by a narrow compass.

BROAD. Comp. Job xi. 7—9.

98. MAKE ME WISER, *i.e.* teach me a different wisdom and a better wisdom than theirs; not one which consists in policy, or craft, or human prudence. So, too, as he is wiser than his enemies, he is wiser than his teachers (ver. 99), wiser than the aged (ver. 100), and his wisdom is that practical wisdom which consists in the fear of the Lord, and which leads him to eschew all evil (ver. 101).

FOR THEY *i.e.* Thy commandments.

102. THOU HAST TAUGHT ME. This is the secret of all the previous boast, this is the source of all his wisdom.

103. SAYINGS. The verb is plural, see on ver. 41, and note [b].

108 נ Accept, I beseech Thee, O Jehovah, the freewill offerings of my mouth,
And teach me Thy judgements.
109 נ My soul is continually in my hand;
Yet I do not forget Thy law.
110 נ The wicked have laid a snare for me;
Yet have I not strayed from Thy precepts.
111 נ Thy testimonies have I taken as an heritage for ever
For they are the rejoicing of my heart.
112 נ I have inclined mine heart to perform Thy statutes
For ever, (even unto) the end.

Samech.

113 ס I hate them that are of double mind,
But Thy law do I love.
114 ס THOU art my hiding-place and shield:
I have hoped in Thy word.
115 ס Depart from me, ye evil doers,
That so I may keep the commandments of my God.
116 ס Uphold me according unto Thy saying, that I may live,
And let me not be ashamed of my hope.
117 ס Hold Thou me up, and so I shall be saved,
And have respect unto Thy statutes continually.
118 ס Thou hast made light of all them that wander from Thy statutes;
For their deceit is falsehood.

109. MY SOUL IS IN MY HAND. He has been faithful even in constant peril of death. Comp. Judg. xii. 13; 1 Sam. xix. 5, xxviii. 21; Job xiii. 14.

111. God's law is an everlasting possession (comp. ver. 98), more truly so than the land of Canaan itself, which was given to Israel for an everlasting heritage. Comp. xvi. 5, 6, where the Psalmist claims God Himself as an heritage.

113. OF DOUBLE MIND. See the noun from the same root, 1 Kings xviii. 21, "How long halt ye between two opinions?" and comp. the ἀνὴρ δίψυχος of St. James (i. 8).

116. SAYING or "promise," as in ver. 172. See on ver. 11, 38.

118. FALSEHOOD, *i.e.* self-decep-

119 ס Thou hast put away all the wicked of the earth like
dross;
Therefore I love Thy testimonies.
120 ס My flesh trembleth for terror of Thee,
And because of Thy judgements I am afraid.

Ain.

121 ע I have done judgement and righteousness;
Leave me not to mine oppressors.
122 ע Be surety for Thy servant for good;
Let not the proud oppress me.
123 ע Mine eyes fail for Thy salvation,
And for Thy righteous saying.
124 ע Deal with Thy servant according to Thy loving-
kindness,
And teach me Thy statutes.
125 ע I am Thy servant, give me understanding,
That I may know Thy testimonies.
126 ע It is time for Jehovah to act;
(For) they have broken Thy law.
127 ע Therefore I love Thy commandments
Above gold, yea, above fine gold.

tion: they rely upon their deceitful artifices in vain, and only to their own confusion.

119. LIKE DROSS, *i.e.* by the fire of Thy judgement. Comp. Jer. vi. 28—30; Ezek. xxii. 18—20; Mal. iii. 2, 3.

120. TREMBLETH or "shuddereth," strictly used of the hair as standing erect in terror (comp. Job iv. 15).

121. JUDGEMENT AND RIGHTEOUSNESS, apparently terms employed with reference to the Law. It is equivalent to saying, "I have kept Thy law."

122. BE SURETY, as in Is. xxxviii. 14; Job xvii. 3. This and ver. 132 are the only two verses in the Psalm which contain no allusion to the Law. The Talmud, however, understands by "good" in this ver. "the Law." (T. B. *Berachoth* 5[a]).

126. TO ACT. The verb is used absolutely of God's acts of judgement, as in Jer. xviii. 23: Ezek. xxxi. 11. So the LXX. καιρὸς τοῦ ποιῆσαι τῷ Κυρίῳ, which has been rendered, "it is time to sacrifice to the Lord," in defiance of all usage, as well as the whole character of the Psalm. It ought not to be necessary to say that ποιεῖν in Greek of itself no more means *to sacrifice* than "make" in English.

128 ע Therefore I esteem all Thy precepts concerning all
(things) to be right;
(And) I hate every false way.

Pe.

129 פ Wonderful are Thy testimonies;
Therefore hath my soul kept them.
130 פ The revelation of Thy words giveth light,
It giveth understanding unto the simple.
131 פ I opened my mouth and panted;
For I longed for Thy commandments.
132 פ Turn Thee unto me, and be gracious to me,
As Thou usest to do unto those that love Thy
Name.
133 פ Establish my steps in Thy saying,
And let no iniquity have dominion over me.
134 פ Redeem me from the oppression of man,
That I may keep Thy precepts.
135 פ Make Thy face to shine upon Thy servant,
And teach me Thy statutes.
136 פ In rivers of water mine eyes run down,
Because they keep not Thy law.

Tsaddi.

137 צ Righteous art Thou, O Jehovah,
And upright are Thy judgements.

128. CONCERNING ALL THINGS. These words are doubtful. See Critical Note.

130. REVELATION, lit. "door," "opening," i.e. *unfolding* or *unveiling*, not *entrance*, as in E.V.

131. I OPENED MY MOUTH, an expression denoting eager desire, as in Job xxix. 23. Like one oppressed with burning heat, and longing for some cool spring of water, or some fresh breeze to fan his brow.

132. AS THOU USEST, lit. "according to the judgement of (belonging to) them that love Thy Name," which may mean "as is just to them." But the word *mishpat* "judgement" is frequently used in the sense of "custom," a sense readily derived from that of "law," "enactment," &c.

133. HAVE DOMINION, as in xix. 13 [14].

136. IN RIVERS OF WATER: see the same phrase Lam. iii. 48, and for the construction Gesen. § 138, 1, Obs. 9

138 צ Thou hast commanded Thy testimonies in righteousness
And exceeding faithfulness.
139 צ My zeal hath consumed me;
Because mine adversaries have forgotten Thy words.
140 צ Thy saying is tried to the uttermost,
And Thy servant loveth it.
141 צ I am small and despised;
(Yet) do not I forget Thy precepts.
142 צ Thy righteousness is an everlasting righteousness,
And Thy law is truth.
143 צ Distress and anguish have gotten hold upon me;
Thy commandments are my delight.
144 צ Thy testimonies are righteousness for ever;
Give me understanding, that I may live.

Koph.

145 ק I called with (my) whole heart:
"Answer me, Jehovah, so will I keep Thy statutes."
146 ק I called upon Thee: "Save me,
So will I keep Thy statutes."
147 ק Early in the morning twilight did I cry;
I hoped in Thy word.
148 ק Mine eyes prevented the night-watches,
That I might meditate in Thy promises.
149 ק Hear my voice according unto Thy loving-kindness;

138. IN RIGHTEOUSNESS AND FAITHFULNESS. The nouns may either be used adverbially, or they may be accusatives in apposition, "as righteousness," &c.

139. Comp. lxix. 9 [10].

140. TRIED, lit. "fined," as metals are in the furnace, and hence pure, free from all admixture of dross, true. Comp. xii. 6 [7].

147. EARLY, lit. "I was beforehand in the twilight." The verb means "to anticipate," "to go to meet," with the accus. (as in xvii. 13); and used absolutely, as here, it must mean "I rose early." It is the same word as the word rendered "prevented" in the next verse. It is difficult to find an English expression suitable for both. We might say: "I was beforehand with the dawn." "Mine eyes were before-hand with the night-watches."

O Jehovah, quicken me according to Thy judgements.
150 ק They draw nigh that follow after mischief;
They are far from Thy law.
151 ק THOU art nigh, O Jehovah,
And all Thy commandments are truth.
152 ק Long since do I know from Thy testimonies
That Thou hast founded them for ever.

Resh.

153 ר Look upon mine affliction, and deliver me;
For I do not forget Thy law.
154 ר Plead my cause, and ransom me;
Quicken me according to Thy word.
155 ר Salvation is far from the wicked;
For they have not sought Thy statutes.
156 ר Many are Thy tender mercies, O Jehovah,
Quicken me according to Thy judgements.
157 ר Many are my persecutors and mine adversaries;
I have not swerved from Thy testimonies.
158 ר I saw the faithless and was grieved,
Because they kept not Thy saying.
159 ר See how I love Thy precepts;
Quicken me, O Jehovah, according to Thy lovingkindness.
160 ר The sum of Thy word is truth,
And every one of Thy righteous judgements (endureth) for ever.

151. They are *nigh* (ver. 150) to persecute and destroy me; Thou art *nigh* to help me.

154. ACCORDING TO. For the use of the preposition comp. Is. xi. 3.

155. FAR. A masc. predicate prefixed, the noun being fem., as in 137 a singular predicate is prefixed when the noun is in the plural. For other instances of anomalous usage of gender see ver. 115, 151.

158. WAS GRIEVED (pausal aorist), lit. "felt loathing." Comp. cxxxix. 21.

BECAUSE, or "who," viz. "the faithless."

160. THE SUM, as in cxxxix. 17. Jerome, "*Caput* verborum tuorum."

Schin.

161 ש Princes have persecuted me without a cause;
But my heart standeth in awe of Thy word.
162 ש I rejoice because of Thy saying,
As one that findeth great spoil.
163 ש As for falsehood, I hate and abhor it;
Thy law do I love.
164 ש Seven times a day do I praise Thee,
Because of Thy righteous judgements.
165 ש Great peace have they which love Thy law,
And there is no stumbling-block unto them.
166 ש I have hoped for Thy salvation, Jehovah,
And have done Thy commandments.
167 ש My soul hath kept Thy testimonies,
And I love them exceedingly.
168 ש I have kept Thy precepts and Thy testimonies;
For all my ways are before Thee.

Tau.

169 ת Let my cry come near before Thee, O Jehovah;
Give me understanding, according to Thy word.
170 ת Let my supplication come before Thee;
Deliver me according to Thy promise.
171 ת Let my lips pour forth praise;
For Thou teachest me Thy statutes.

The LXX. wrongly, *ἀρχὴ τῶν λόγων σου*. Still less defensible is the E.V., "from the beginning."

165. NO STUMBLING-BLOCK. LXX. *οὐκ ἔστιν αὐτοῖς σκάνδαλον*. Comp. the words of St. John, *σκάνδαλον οὐκ ἔστιν ἐν αὐτῷ* (1 John ii. 10). So we may supply here, "no stumbling-block *in them*," or "in their path." When God's law is loved, instead of being struggled against, the conscience is at peace, and the inward eye is clear; a man sees his duty and does it, free from those stumbling-blocks which are ever occasion of falling to others.

166. I HAVE HOPED. Comp. the words of Jacob, Gen. xlix. 18.

168. FOR ALL MY WAYS. In saying "I have kept Thy precep s," I make no vain boast, I say it as in Thy sight, who seest all my life.

170. PROMISE, lit. "saying," and again in ver. 172.

172 ת Let my tongue sing of Thy promise,
For all Thy commandments are righteousness.
173 ת Let Thine hand be a help unto me;
For I have chosen Thy precepts.
174 ת I have longed for Thy salvation, O Jehovah,
And Thy law is my delight.
175 ת Let my soul live, and praise Thee,
And let Thy judgements help me.
176 ת I have gone astray like a lost sheep; seek Thy servant;
For I do not forget Thy commandments.

172. SING OF, or perhaps "repeat," "echo."

176. According to the accents, the rendering would rather be, "I have gone astray; seek Thy servant as a lost sheep." In what sense can one who has so repeatedly declared his love of God's word, who has asserted that he has kept God's precepts, make this confession? The figure cannot be employed here in the same sense, for instance, in which it is employed in our Lord's parable. He who is the lost sheep here is one who does not forget God's commandments. The figure, therefore, seems in this place to denote the helpless condition of the Psalmist, without protectors, exposed to enemies, in the midst of whom he wanders, not knowing where to find rest and shelter. But in the "I have gone astray," there is doubtless the sense of sin as well as of weakness, though there is also the consciousness of love to God's law, "I do not forget Thy commandments." Comp. with this xix. 12—14 [13—15]. The word rendered "lost" may be rendered "ready to perish."

[a] אַחֲלַי (whence אַחֲלֵי, 2 Kings v. 3), compounded of אָח and לֵי (לְוַי) = *o si.*

[b] כִּדְבָרֶךָ. Many MSS. and Edd. have the plural, and again ver. 16, 17, 25, 28, 42, 101. The same is the case with אִמְרָתֶךָ, ver. 11, 103, 148, 162. But there is no doubt that the sing. is to be preferred. It is otherwise with מִשְׁפָּטֶךָ, which is clearly a defective form, instead of the plur. ־ֶיךָ, 43 and 149. Comp. 37, 41, for similar forms.

The construction in לִשְׁמֹר is that of the gerund.

[c] תַּאֲבָה, only here, instead of תַּאֲוָה, and so also the verb תאב occurs only in this Psalm, ver. 40, 174.

[d] גַּל, not instead of גֹּל, from גלל, *to roll away*, as De Wette and others, referring to Josh. v. 9, but the same word as in ver. 18, from גִּלָּה (Piel), to *uncover*, which occurs with a twofold construction; either (1) with the accus. of the thing uncovered, as in ver. 18, "to uncover the eyes;" or (2) with accus. of the covering which is taken off, as in Is. xxii. 8, Nah. iii. 5, and so here: "uncover," *i.e.* take off from me, the reproach which lies upon me "as a cloak."

[e] תְּחַכְּמֵנִי, 3 sing. fem., not 2 masc. For this use of the sing. verb with the plur. noun see Ges. § 143, 3. The following הִיא shows that the law is regarded *as a whole;* "it maketh me wiser." However, the plur. punctuation of the noun may be an error. See note [b]. The Verss. generally take the verb as the E.V. does as 2d pers. "Thou through Thy commandments," &c.

[f] כָּל פִּקּוּדֵי כֹל. This is usually rendered, "All (Thy) precepts concerning all (things)," and is defended by Ez. xliv. 30, "All firstlings of all (sorts)." See a similar expression, Num. viii. 16. The case, however, is not really analogous, as the phrase here does not mean "all precepts of all sorts;" and, besides, the absence of the pronoun is awkward: we want "*Thy* precepts." Hence the reading ought probably to be כָּל־פִּקּוּדֶיךָ; and so Houb., Ew., Olsh., Hupf. And this is supported by the LXX., *πρὸς πάσας τὰς ἐντολάς σου κατωρθούμην*, and Jerome, *in universa præcepta tua direxi.* Others explain, "all precepts concerning the whole of things," *i.e.* all moral, universal laws in contradistinction to those of temporary character, as political, ceremonial, &c.

PSALM 120

WITH this Psalm begins a series of fifteen Psalms, all bearing the same title, "Songs of the goings-up" (E.V. "Songs of degrees"), and constituting originally, no doubt, a separate hymn-book—a Psalter within a Psalter. The different interpretations which have been given of the name will be found mentioned in the Introduction to Vol. I. p. 87.* Of these, the most probable is that which supposes that the Psalms to which this title is prefixed were intended to be sung by the caravans of pilgrims "going up" to keep the yearly feasts at Jerusalem. The collection in its present form must have been made after the return from Babylon, some of the songs containing manifest allusions to the Captivity as still fresh in the recollection of the writers. All these odes have certain features in common. With one exception (the 132nd) they are all short—the utterance of a single thought or feeling, a sigh, a hope, a joy. They are alike in tone, in diction, in rhythm, the climactic form of the last recurring so often as to have led Gesenius to suppose that the title, "Song of ascents," was given to them owing to this peculiarity. They are all pervaded by the

* Mr. Armfield (*The Gradual Psalms*) has discussed the question anew, with special reference to the Jewish tradition. I hope to recur to it in the Appendix to this Volume.

same quiet, graceful, tender beauty, the charm of which was so felt by a Spanish commentator, that he does not hesitate to say, that this collection is to the rest of the Psalms what Paradise was to the rest of the world at its first creation.

The first in the collection is a prayer against the lying tongues of treacherous neighbours, whom the Poet compares, for their cruelty and perfidy, to the savage hordes of the Caucasus or of the Arabian desert. But whether the Psalmist thus pictures the heathen among whom he dwells in exile, or the wild tribes with whom no treaty can be kept, by whom he is beset on his way back from Babylon to Palestine, or the Samaritans,* Arabians and others, who after their return attempted, by false representations to the Persian monarch, to thwart the rebuilding of the Temple (Ezra iv.) and the fortification of the city (Nehem. ii.—iv.), it is impossible to say. The allusions are brief and obscure. Reuss says: "Ce psaume, le seul qui soit difficile à expliquer parmi ces chants de pélerinage, peut être regardé comme l'un des plus obscurs de tout le Psautier. Les idées y sont à peine indiquées, les images sont peu transparentes, et les allusions historiques sont pour nous autant d'énigmes."

[A PILGRIM SONG.]

1 UNTO Jehovah, when I was in distress,[a]
I called, and He answered me.
2 O Jehovah, deliver my soul from the lying lip,
From the deceitful tongue.[b]
3 What shall He give[c] unto thee, and what shall He add unto thee,
O thou deceitful tongue?

1. CALLED . . . ANSWERED. The verbs are in the past tense, but do not refer merely to a past occasion. Past experience and present are here combined. From the past he draws encouragement for the present.

3. GIVE . . . ADD. The phrase seems to mean: "What calamities shall He (or *it*) heap upon thee? How shall punishment upon punishment visit thee? Compare the somewhat similar expression in the formula of cursing, "God do so to

* It is indeed doubtful whether the Chaldee letters in Ezra iv. do relate to the obstacles offered by the Samaritans to the rebuilding of the Temple, or whether they are not rather to be referred to the opposition made to the rebuilding of the city walls under Xerxes and Artaxerxes, at a much later period, Neh. ii. &c. The chief enemies of the Jews at this time were not the Samaritans, but persons of other tribes,—Moabites, Ammonites, Philistines, all perhaps comprised under the general name of Arabians. See Neh. ii. 10, 12, iv. 7.

4 Sharp arrows of the mighty,
With coals of broom.
5 Woe [d] is me that I have sojourned in Meshech,

me, and more also," 1 Sam. iii. 17, xx. 13, and often. In that formula, however, the first verb is *do*, not *give*.

It is not necessary to regard Jehovah as the subject of the verbs in this verse. They may be taken impersonally: "What shall be given unto thee, what more shall be done unto thee?" See more in Critical Note.

4. The expressions of this verse may either (1) describe further the treacherous tongue ("thou that art as sharp arrows," &c.), as in lvii. 4 [5], "whose teeth are spears and arrows, and their tongue a sharp sword," lxiv. 3 [4], "who have sharpened their tongue like the sword, and have aimed their arrow, even a bitter word"—see also lv. 21 [22], lix. 7 [8]; or (2) the punishment of the tongue, a punishment according with its character. As the lying tongue is a sharp sword (lvii. 4 [5]), as it is a sharp arrow (Jer. ix. 8 [7]), as it is set on fire of hell (James iii. 6), so shall the man who employs it be destroyed by the arrows and the fire of the Mighty One, *i.e.* God. (But see below.) So in the B. Talmud, *'Erachin* 15*b*, it is said, "The Mighty is none other but God Himself." Comp. cxl. 9, 10 [10, 11], "Let the mischief of their own lips cover them, let burning coals fall upon them, let them be cast into the fire," &c. Such is the law of the Eternal Nemesis: "*What* a man soweth, *that* shall he also reap."

It is in favour of the first interpretation that it falls in with the general scope of the Psalm, in which the Poet complains that, loving peace himself, he meets with nothing but hostility and treachery. On the other hand, that he should burst forth into an imprecation of God's judgements on the head of these treacherous neighbours is quite in accordance with what we find in other Psalms, where the circumstances are similar. Comp. for instance Ps. lviii. For other explanations see Critical Note.

THE MIGHTY. Even if we take this verse as describing the punishment of the lying tongue, we need not take "the mighty" to mean God, as the Talmud does. The expression may only mean "sharp arrows," as of a *warrior*. Comp. cxxvii. 4; Jer. 1, 9.

BROOM, not as E. V., following Jerome, "juniper." The shrub meant is the *genista monosperma* (Arab. *retem*), the root of which, according to Burckhardt (*Itin.* ii. p. 791), is used for fires in the desert, and has the property of retaining the heat for a considerable time. The same shrub is mentioned 1 Kings xix. 4; Job xxx. 4. The latter passage may mean, not that the root of the genista was used for food, which seems unlikely as it is very bitter, but, perhaps, that it was used for fire, "to warm them" (comp. Is. xliv. 15). Wonderful stories are told by Jerome (*De mansionibus Israel ad Fabiolam* xv.), and in the Midrash Tehillim, how travellers, having cooked their food with a fire made of the juniper-wood (which they suppose to be the wood here meant), and returning a year after to the same spot, still found the embers alive.

These COALS are an image either of the burning, devouring character of the tongue, or of its punishment. "Arrows WITH (*i.e.* together with) coals," not, as others, "fiery arrows," or "arrows sharpened and made hard by means of fire," which would have been differentiy expressed.

5. MESHECH, probably the Moschi of Herodotus (iii. 94), mentioned, together with Tubal,

That I have dwelt beside the tents of Kedar.
6 My soul hath too long [e] had her dwelling
With him that hateth peace.
7 I am (for) peace,
But when I speak,[f] they are for war.

Gen. x. 2, Ezek. xxvii. 13; a barbarous tribe situated south-east of the Caucasus, between the Black Sea and the Araxes; and

KEDAR, one of the predatory hordes roaming the Arabian Desert. By the names of these remote and barbarous tribes, the one to the north, the other to the south of Palestine, the Psalmist intends to mark the savage character of those who surround him. We might speak in the same way, says De Wette, of Turks and Hottentots.

7. The literal rendering of the first clause is, "I (am) peace," as in cix. 4, "I (am) prayer." The pronoun in each clause is emphatic.

[a] צָרָתָה; the fuller form for צרה, as in ii. 3, xliv. 27. Comp. xviii. 7.

[b] לָשׁוֹן ר׳, absol. instead of constr. (comp. lii. 6); unless we take רְמִיָּה (as Del. suggests) as an adj. (see Mic. vi. 12). But the expression may be explained on the principle of apposition, "a tongue which is deceit," as in Prov. xxii. 21, אֲמָרִים אֱמֶת, "words which are truth," Zech. i. 13.

[c] מַה יִּתֵּן. The interpretations of this verse are various.

Is the "giving," &c. to be understood in a good or a bad sense? Does it mean "What doth it profit thee?" or "What doth it harm thee?" And who is addressed,—the lying tongue, *i.e.* the liar, or God, or the Psalmist himself, or some third person indefinitely?

1. Supposing the words to be taken in a bad sense, they can mean harm, injury, which the deceitful tongue works to others, or punishment which it brings upon itself. In the first case "the tongue," in the second "Jehovah," is the subject. So far as the grammar goes, there is nothing against either interpretation; for the verb standing before the fem. noun can be masc. (Ges. § 147), and thus "the tongue" may be the subject; and, on the other hand, the masc. pron. "to thee" may refer not immediately to the *tongue*, but to the *person* whose the tongue is (§ 121, Rem. 1).

(*a*) It is in favour, however, of the interpretation which makes the tongue addressed, and Jehovah the subject ("What shall *He* give to thee," &c.), that a very similar phrase is used several times in adjuration. "So Jehovah do unto me, and more also," *i.e.* so let Him punish me (1 Sam. iii. 17, xiv. 44, xx. 13, and often). Then the punishment threatened is further described in the next verse: "What shall He give thee?" "Sharp arrows of the mighty," &c. Hupf. objects to this interpretation, that here the formula is not employed in an oath, and that it is doubtful whether it denotes punishment, inasmuch as the principal verb here is not יַעֲשֶׂה, but יִתֵּן. Those who make Jehovah the subject are again divided when they come to the next verse; for, instead of seeing in that verse the manner of punishment, some see in it a further description of the character of the tongue itself, as elsewhere the tongue is compared to a sharp sword, &c.

(*b*) Hence others take *the tongue* as the subject, and suppose that the person whose the deceitful tongue is, is addressed. The sense will then be: "What does a false tongue profit thee (O thou liar)?" So far from that, thou only doest harm to others; and this harm is then expressed figuratively in the next verse, "for thou art as sharp arrows," &c. So the Chald., Qimchi, Calv., De Dieu, most of the older interpreters, Ros., De W. Here the pron. "thee" is taken generally of any one who speaks deceit.

2. Others refer the pron. to Jehovah. "What can a deceitful tongue profit Thee?" the argument being similar to that in such questions as in xxx. 9 [10], and ver. 4 again giving the reply: so far from profit, it is a pestilent mischief.

3. Once more, the pronoun may refer to the Poet himself, or some third person indefinitely, "What can the false tongue give thee? *i.e.* what harm can it inflict upon thee?" the poet turning this question upon himself, and the answer being that in ver. 4, "Surely much harm, for it is as sharp arrows," &c. According to this, נתן is = עשׂה, *to work*, in a bad sense, as Lev. xxiv. 19, 20; Prov. x. 10, xiii. 10, xxix. 25. But it may be questioned if נתן with לְ can have this meaning. In Lev. xxiv. it is followed by בְּ, in the other passages it stands absol., *to effect*, and therefore proves nothing.

Hupfeld, rejecting all these interpretations, separates ver. 3 entirely from ver. 4. To the former he gives the meaning: "What (real) good can a false tongue bring thee, how can it help thee, O thou who employest its arts?" and supposes (1) that not a slanderer, but a false friend or neighbour is pointed at, and (2) that the Poet is speaking not to himself so much as to a third person, and uttering a general sentiment. In ver. 4 he would read אָהֳלֵי instead of גַּחֲלֵי, and would either understand רְתָמִים as a proper name, the name of a tribe or a locality in which the broom was plentiful (as Rithmah, Num. xxxiii. 18, 19, one of the stations of the Israelites, doubtless took its name from the broom which grew there), or else that by *tents of broom* are meant poor hovels formed of broom, as a shelter for some needy desert-horde. He takes the verse, not in appos. with the preceding, but as an independent sentence: "Sharp are the arrows of the warrior, by the tents of the Rethamim," which of course is to be understood figuratively as expressive of the hostility of the neighbours of the Poet.

[d] אוֹיָה, only here with the termination ָה, used pathetically. There is no need in such an interjection as this to assume, with Hupf., that it is an accus. termination like הַמָּוְתָה, for instance, cxvi. 15, in accordance with later usage.

גּוּר, with the accus., as in v. 5; Is. xxxiii. 15; Jud. v. 17.

[e] רַבַּת. See the same form lxv. 10, cxxiii. 4, cxxix. 1, 2. It belongs chiefly to the later language. Comp. 2 Chron. xxx. 17, 18.

[f] וְכִי אֲדַבֵּר. The verb here stands absolutely, as in xxxix. 4, cxvi. 10; there is no need to supply the object, "when I speak of peace." Nor is Ewald's rendering, "As for me, when I speak of peace," at all probable; for even if כִּי can thus stand in the middle of the sentence, as in cxviii. 10, 11, cxxviii. 2 (comp. עַד, cxli. 10), it is very unlikely that וְכִי should occupy such a position. The construction is the same as in cix. 4, where see note.

PSALM 121

THIS beautiful Psalm is the trustful expression of a heart rejoicing in its own safety under the watchful eye of Him who is both the Maker of heaven and earth, and the Keeper of Israel. The Creator of the Universe, the Keeper of the nation, is also the Keeper of the individual. The one ever-recurring thought, the one characteristic word of the Psalm, is this word *keep*. Six times it is repeated in the last five verses of this one short ode. The beauty of this repetition is unfortunately destroyed in the Authorized Version by the substitution in the last three instances, in verses 7 and 8, of the verb "preserve" for the word "keep." For the use of the same word in the original is evidently designed,—designed to mark by this emphasis of iteration the truth of God's loving care for the individual, and so to banish all shadow of doubt, fear, anxiety, lest in the vast sum the unit should be forgotten.

Under what circumstances the Psalm was written is doubtful. Some (as Ewald and De Wette) suppose it to have been written in exile. The Psalmist turns his longing eyes towards the hills of his native land, or the hills which bounded his sight in the direction in which it lay, as Daniel opened his windows towards Jerusalem when he prayed. Others (as Hupfeld) understand by "the mountains" in ver. 1, not the mountains of Palestine at large, but the one mountain or mountain-group of Zion, as the dwelling-place of God, the plural being used as in cxxxiii. 3, lxxxvii. 1, and leave it an open question whether the Psalmist was in exile, or merely at a distance from the sanctuary.

Others, again, have conjectured that this was the song sung by the caravans of pilgrims going up to the yearly feasts, when first they came in sight of the mountains on which Jerusalem stands. At evening, as they are about to make preparations for their last night's encampment, they behold in the far distance, clear against the dying light of the western sky, the holy hill with its crown of towers. The sight fills them with a sense of peace and security, and from the midst of the band a voice begins: "I will lift up mine eyes to the mountains," &c. And another voice answers, "Surely He will not suffer thy foot to be moved. Surely He that keepeth thee will not slumber." And anon the whole company of pilgrims take up the strain: "Behold He that keepeth Israel shall neither slumber nor sleep; Jehovah shall keep," &c.

To-morrow, in the words of the next Psalm, they will sing, "Our feet are standing within thy gates, O Jerusalem."

It is not, however, absolutely necessary to assume different voices in the Psalm; there may be one voice only, the voice of the Poet speaking to his own heart,—speaking to it, in words that are not his own, heavenly strength and courage. That he is at a distance from the sanctuary, if not from Palestine, is clear. It is almost equally certain that there is no reference to "the special dangers of the desert" as encountered by the exiles on their return. The baneful influence of the sun and the moon (ver. 6) would not be peculiar to the desert, and I can see no allusion to "perils from lawless tribes by night" in ver. 3, 4. The expression, "thy going out and thy coming in," would surely describe naturally, not the life of a traveller passing through the desert, but the settled home life, with its usual occupations, whether in Palestine or in Babylon. Beyond this, and the words of ver. 1, we have nothing to guide us.

The Psalm has no marked divisions, but falls naturally into pairs of verses. The Inscription, "A song *for* the goings up," differs slightly from that which is prefixed to other odes of this collection.

[A PILGRIM-SONG.]

1 I LIFT up mine eyes unto the mountains;
Whence should my help come?

1. THE MOUNTAINS, as already remarked in the Introduction, either those of Palestine, as in Nahum i. 15 [ii. 1] and in Ezekiel, "the mountains of Israel;" or, the ridge on which lay Jerusalem and the Temple. Comp. for the plural, lxxxvii 1, cxxxiii. 3; and for the expectation of help from Zion, xiv. 7, "Oh that the salvation of Israel were come out of Zion;" xx. 2 [3], "Jehovah send thee help from the sanctuary, and uphold thee out of Zion."

WHENCE. It is better to take this as an interrogative than as a

2 My help (cometh) from Jehovah,
The Maker of heaven and earth.
3 Surely He[a] will not suffer thy foot to be moved;
He that keepeth thee will not slumber.
4 Behold, He doth neither slumber nor sleep
That keepeth Israel.
5 Jehovah is thy Keeper,
Jehovah is thy shade upon thy right hand.
6 The sun shall not smite thee by day,
Nor the moon by night.

relative. In Josh. ii. 4, the only passage where the word occurs as a relative, it is really an indirect interrogative.

2. MAKER OF HEAVEN AND EARTH; a name of God occurring especially in these Pilgrim odes, and other later Psalms, as in cxv. 15, cxxiv. 8, cxxxiv. 3, cxlvi. 6. God's creative power and majesty were, especially during the Exile, impressed upon the heart of the nation, in contrast with the vanity of the gods of the heathen. Comp. Jer. x. 11, "Then shall he say unto them(*i.e.* the Jews to the Chaldeans), The gods that have not made the heavens and the earth, even they shall perish from the earth, and from under these heavens."

3. The Psalmist turns to address himself. First he utters the wish that God's watchful care may be extended to him; then the conviction that the Keeper of Israel, He who has been the God of his fathers, whose Hand has led the nation through all its eventful history, doth not—will not, cannot—slumber or sleep. Comp. cxxxii. 4; 1 Kings xviii. 27; Is. v. 27; Job vii. 20.

SURELY HE SHALL NOT, as expressing the conviction of the speaker (see Critical Note). It must be confessed that the optative rendering is somewhat weak. It does not seem very pertinent to express the wish that God may not slumber. Or if we assume that the Psalm was designed for antiphonal singing, then ver. 4, is the answer to ver. 3, "you need not fear that He should sleep. He cannot slumber."

4. SLUMBER . . . SLEEP. There is no climax in these words, as some have supposed. Etymologically, the first is the stronger word, and it occurs lxxvi. 5 [6] (where see note) of the sleep of death. In this instance there is no real distinction between the two. Possibly there may be an allusion to the nightly encampment, and the sentries of the caravan.

5. THY SHADE, as a protection against the burning rays of the sun. Comp. xci. 1, "shall abide under the shadow of the Almighty;" Is. xxv. 4, "Thou hast been a shadow from the heat;" xxxii. 2, "As the shadow of a great rock in a weary land."

UPON THY RIGHT HAND. This is not part of the former figure: it does not denote the south side (as some would explain), as that on which the sun would be hottest, and therefore protection most necessary. It is rather a separate figure, denoting generally succour, help, &c. (as in cix. 31, cx. 5), *i.e.* Jehovah standing upon thy right hand to defend thee is thy shade.

6. Sun-stroke, a special danger of the East. See 2 Kings iv. 18—20; Jon. iv. 8; and comp. Ps. cii.

7 Jehovah shall keep thee from all evil,
He shall keep thy soul.
8 Jehovah shall keep thy going out and thy coming in
From this time forth and for evermore.

4 [5], where the heart is said to be *smitten* like grass. In the same way the influence of the moon was considered to be very injurious to the human frame, in hot climates more particularly. De Wette refers to Andersen's *Eastern Travels*, Ewald to Carne's *Life and Manners in the East*, in proof that this opinion is commonly entertained. Delitzsch mentions having heard from Texas that the consequence of sleeping in the open air when the moon was shining was dizziness, mental aberration, and even death. The names given to persons of disordered intellect, σεληνιαζόμενοι, *lunatici*, "lunatics," arose of course from the wide-spread belief in the effects of the moon on those who were exposed to its influence. At the same time, this is only a popular belief. The injury is due not to the light of the moon, which is innocuous, but to the raw vapour and chilling mists after the intense heat of the day.

8. THY GOING OUT AND THY COMING IN; a phrase denoting the whole life and occupations of a man. Comp. Deut. xxviii. 6, xxxi. 2; 1 Sam. xxix. 6, &c. The threefold expression, "shall keep *thee* . . . *thy soul* . . . *thy going out* and *thy coming in*" marks the completeness of the protection vouchsafed, extending to all that the man is and that he does. Comp. 1 Thess. v. 23, καὶ ὁλόκληρον ὑμῶν τὸ πνεῦμα, καὶ ἡ ψυχὴ καὶ τὸ σῶμα . . . τηρηθείη.

[a] אַל = μή, and must not, therefore, be rendered as if it were merely οὐ. Ewald takes it interrogatively, as μή is also used, "Surely He will not suffer thy foot to be moved?" Delitzsch takes it similarly, but without a question, as expressing the subjective view of the speaker. Such a rendering, "Surely He will not suffer," &c., is, I think, to be preferred to the optative rendering, "May He not," &c., which I adopted in former editions. See on xxxiv. 5, and l., note [b] (Vol. I. p. 411). On the other hand, the optative rendering may be defended, especially as we have a similar transition from one form of the negative to the other in xxv. 1—3, where see note.

PSALM 122

THIS Psalm, more emphatically than any in the collection to which it belongs, merits the title of a Pilgrim song. It was evidently composed with immediate reference to one of the three yearly festivals, when the caravans of pilgrims "went up" to the Holy City. The Poet is living in the country. As the time of the Feast draws near, his friends and neighbours come to him, inviting him to join them in their visit to Jerusalem. It is with this picture that he begins his Poem. He tells us how his heart filled with joy as they bade him come with them "to the house of Jehovah." We see the procession starting; we see beaming eyes and happy faces, and hear the music of gladness with which the pilgrims beguile the tediousness of the journey. The next verse transports us at once to the Holy City itself. "Our feet have stood within thy gates;" the few words are enough. They have reached their journey's end; they are in the city which they love. Then the Poet tells us, first, the impression made upon his mind by her stateliness and her beauty, and next, how there comes crowding upon his memory the scenes of her earlier grandeur, the thought of all she had been as the gathering-place of the tribes of Jehovah, the royal seat of David and of his house.

Filled with these thoughts, inspired by these memories, he bursts forth into hearty, fervent prayer—the prayer of one who loved his country as he loved his God, with no common devotion—for the welfare of that city so glorious in her past history, that city with which all hopes for the future were so intimately bound up. And so the beautiful ode closes.

The Psalm is called in the title a Song of David. It is certainly possible that Psalms written by him might be comprised in a collection which formed a hymn-book for the pilgrims. It is possible, also, that David himself, although there was still a sanctuary at Gibeon, even after the Ark was brought to Zion, may nevertheless have encouraged the people to regard Jerusalem as the true centre of worship, and that the custom of keeping the annual feasts there may have begun during his reign. In fact, this seems most natural and most probable, when we remember how great and joyful an event was the bringing up of the Ark to Zion. There, henceforth, must have been "the heart of the Israelite religion." The expression in ver. 3 might also be explained very naturally of Jerusalem as it was in David's time,—"a city beautifully built, well compacted, adorned with palaces, and fortified." Still, in spite of Hengstenberg's remarks to the contrary, I cannot think that the expression "thrones of the house of David" would be a natural one in David's lips. The phrase points, surely, to a dynasty which has long been established: verses 4 and 5 are clearly a retrospect. "The great argument against the Davidic authorship," remarks Mr. Cox, very pertinently, "is the general tone of the second strophe (ver. 4, 5). Here the Poet uses the historic tenses, and is manifestly recalling a time long past in which the tribes went up to Jerusalem, to give thanks to the name of the Lord. But Jerusalem was only wrested from the Jebusites by

David. How then could *he* speak of it as the place in which for generations past, the Hebrew tribes had come before Jehovah?"*

As most, if not all, of these Psalms belong to a period subsequent to the Captivity, we turn more naturally to that time as furnishing the occasion for the composition of this ode. But, even if we fix upon that as the most probable date, still the question arises, Is the whole Psalm a retrospect, or does it spring out of the new life of the people? Does it paint only the recollection of former pilgrimages in the days of Zion's first glory, or does it paint the feelings of one who sees the old state of things revived, and who joins the pilgrims going up now as they went up of yore?

Ewald supposes it to be a blessing on a party of pilgrims uttered by an old man returned from the Exile, himself unequal to a journey across the desert. "The departure of his friends reminds him of the alacrity with which he too had once obeyed a similar summons; his spirit is fired by sympathy with their enthusiasm, and he pours forth the praises of that city which from the earliest times had been recognized as the key-stone of the national unity, the civil and religious metropolis of the tribes."† Delitzsch takes a somewhat similar view, except that he supposes the Poet to be still in exile. But the Psalm is too bright, the pictures are too fresh, to lend any colour to either interpretation. There is none of that "deep sighing" of the exile or the old man looking back on a departed glory which must have made itself felt, none of that melancholy which breathes, for instance, in such a Psalm as the Forty-second, and even the Eighty-fourth. The gladness of the first verse is a gladness still warm at the heart of the Poet; the picture of the second is one the lines of which are not yet effaced from the eye of his mind. The reminiscences of the past, as he has heard the tale from others, or as he has read it in the words of other Psalmists and Prophets, mingle with the present, and Jerusalem, rising from her ashes, seems to him fair and stately, her bulwarks strong, and her palaces magnificent, as of old.

[A PILGRIM-SONG OF DAVID.]

1 I WAS glad when they said [a] unto me,
Let us go into the house of Jehovah.

1. I WAS GLAD WHEN; or, more lit. "I rejoiced over, or because of, them that were saying unto me." THE HOUSE OF JEHOVAH. His

---

* *The Pilgrim Psalms*, p. 64. I gladly refer to this work as a really valuable contribution to our exegetical literature on this portion of the Psalter.

† *The Psalms Chronologically Arranged*, by Four Friends, p. 292.

2 Our feet have stood [b]
Within thy gates, O Jerusalem.
3 Jerusalem that art built,
As a city which is compact [c] together!
4 Whither the tribes went up, the tribes of Jah,

joy was that he should worship *there* "in the presence of Jehovah." Ex. xxiii. 17.

2. HAVE STOOD. This may be a strict perfect, implying that they are *still standing*. It is the lively expression of the satisfaction and delight of one who finds himself on this high day of festal joy within the sacred walls, mingling with the throng of worshipers who crowd the courts of the Temple, and taking his part, with a full sense of his privileges as an Israelite, in the solemn services of the Feast.

The rendering of the E.V., "shall stand," is clearly wrong. The only other possible rendering (see Critical Note) is one that would throw the whole scene into the past, "our feet once stood." It is the uncertainty attaching to this form which occasions so much difficulty in the interpretation of the Psalm.

3. BUILT. This has been explained in three different ways. (1) It has been closely joined with what follows, "built as a city which," &c. (2) It has been taken in the sense of "well-built, stately." (3) It has been understood emphatically to describe the city as *rebuilt* after the Exile, "which is built again," or, "O thou that art built again." Of these, the last is preferable: (1) injures the parallelism, and (2) has no support in usage.

COMPACT. This has been understood by some to refer to the natural conformation of the ground on which the city stood. So Stanley, speaking of "those deep ravines which separate Jerusalem from the rocky plateau of which it forms a part," observes that they must have not only "acted as its natural defence, but must also have determined its natural boundaries. The city, wherever else it spread, could never overleap the valley of the Kedron or of Hinnom. . . . . The expression of *compactness* was still more appropriate to the original city, if, as seems probable, the valley of Tyropæon formed in earlier times a fosse within a fosse, shutting in Zion and Moriah into one compact mass, not more than half a mile in breadth."—*Sinai and Palestine*, pp. 172, 173.

Others, as Herder, suppose the epithet to mark the well-built city with its fine streets and long rows of contiguous houses, such an epithet being peculiarly appropriate and very natural in the lips of one who, accustomed only to the scattered dwellings of country villages, is struck with the compact line of stately buildings which form so imposing a feature of the capital. "This," he exclaims, "is indeed a city:"

"Urbem quam dicunt Romam, Melibœe, putavi
Stultus ego huic nostræ similem."

Herder accordingly renders,—

"Jerusalem, du dicht-gebaute Stadt!
Wohnung an Wohnung ist in dir."

So the peasants and fishermen of Galilee were struck with admiration, and expected their Master to share it with them as they exclaimed, "See what manner of stones and what buildings are here!" (Mark xiii.)

If, however, the Psalm refers, as is probable, to the city as rebuilt after the Exile, then the epithet alludes to the reconstruction of walls and houses; the city is compact, because there are no more waste places, no more gaps and heaps of ruin.

4. The Poet glances here, and in the next verse, at the earlier times,

A testimony unto Israel,
To give thanks to the Name of Jehovah.
5 For there were set thrones for judgement,
The thrones of the house of David.

6 O pray for the peace of Jerusalem:
They shall prosper that love thee.
7 Peace be within thy bulwarks,
Prosperity within thy palaces.

when Jerusalem had been the great religious and political centre of the nation, the dwelling-place of Jehovah, to whose Temple all the tribes were gathered at the three great Feasts, and the seat of government of kings of the house of David.

This had been its double glory. It may be inferred, that he was living at a time when all was changed. There was still one sanctuary, but all Israel was not united under one sceptre. It was no longer all the tribes who went up, as they had done of old; there was now no throne of the house of David. In fact, even after the disruption of the kingdom under Jeroboam, the tribes did not go up to keep the yearly Feasts in Jerusalem. It was a part of "the Machiavellian policy" of that prince to put a stop to this custom, lest such occasions should be made the means of restoring the national unity (1 Kings xii. 26).

TESTIMONY. The word seems almost equivalent to "law" or "statute," but there is in it also the sense of a "witness" to the people of their covenant relation to God. The "law" is that, according to which all males were to appear before the Lord three times in the year: Ex. xxiii. 17, xxxiv. 23; Deut. xvi. 16; comp. Ps. lxxxi. 4, 5 [5, 6].

The words "a testimony for Israel," are grammatically in apposition with the previous clause, "the tribes went up," &c.

5. FOR. Jerusalem had become the religious capital of the nation, because it was already the civil capital. The law had enjoined that the supreme tribunal should be in the same place as the sanctuary (Deut. xvii. 8, 9). But Jerusalem was first the civil metropolis, "the city of David" (2 Sam. v. 9, vi. 12, 16), before it became "the city of God." To a Jewish mind, however, the religious and the political importance of the city were not so much contrasted as identical; Church and State were not two, but one.

WERE SET, lit. "sit," more commonly used of those who sit on the throne, but the verb may be used of things without life to describe their position; as of mountains, cxxv. 1; in many passages, of cities; and even of countries (Jer. xvii. 6; Joel iv. 20).

THRONES FOR JUDGEMENT. The king was also the judge: see on lxxii. 1. Comp. 2 Sam. xv. 2; 1 Kings iii. 16, 17.

THE HOUSE OF DAVID. The expression plainly points to successors of David, not to members of his family associated with himself in government, administration of justice, &c.

6. PEACE . . . PROSPER, and in the next verse PEACE . . . PROSPERITY, with a play of words in the original (*shâlôm*, *shalvah*), with an allusion to the name of Jerusalem (Yerushalaim).

7. BULWARKS . . . PALACES, as in xlviii. 13 [14].

8 For my brethren and friends' sakes,
Let me now wish [d] thee peace.
9 For the sake of the house of Jehovah our God,
I will seek thy good.

8. The last four verses of the Psalm breathe a spirit of the noblest, most unselfish patriotism. Not for his own sake, but for the sake of his brethren—the people at large—and for the sake of his God, His temple and His service, he wishes peace to Jerusalem, and calls upon others to wish her peace. With love to Israel, and love to Jehovah, there is naturally united a warm affection for Jerusalem, a hearty interest in her welfare.

[a] בְּאֹמְרִים. Strictly, this means, "I rejoiced *in*, *over*, *because of* them that were saying unto me." The difference in sense between this and בְּאָמְרָם, "when they said," is that with the part. the *persons* who speak become more prominent, and the continuance of the action is marked The LXX. rightly, ἐπὶ τοῖς εἰρηκόσι μου.

שָׂמַחְתִּי may be either past (as all the older interpreters) or present.

[b] עֹמְדוֹת הָיוּ. This compound tense may either be an imperfect, "were standing," "used to stand;" or a strict perfect, "have been standing, and now are standing." In this last case it may even be rendered as a present.

(1) היה, with the part., is an imperfect, either (*a*) of habit, as Gen. xxxii. 22, "Whatever they did (part.) there, he *was doing*," *i.e.* was in the habit of doing; Jud. i. 7, "seventy kings *were gathering* (*i.e.* were in the habit of gathering) their meat under my table:" or (*b*) of continued past action simply, as Job i. 14, "the herd *were ploughing*."

(2) היה, with the part., is a strict perfect in Is. lix. 2, "Your sins *have been separating*," *i.e.* have separated, and still do separate; Jer. v. 8, where מְשֻׁכָּים הָיוּ probably means either "they have strayed," or "they have been fed to the full" (see Neumann, *in loc.*). In Is. xxx. 20 the same construction is used to express a *prophetic* future, *i.e.* a perfect transferred into the future, in which case it is followed by a future: "Your eyes have *been seeing* (*i.e.* assuredly shall see) . . . and your ears shall hear (fut.)."

[c] שֶׁחֻבְּרָה. The verb is used of the *putting together* of the coverings of the tabernacle, Ex. xxvi. Comp. חבשׁ in Is. iii. 7, and נקשׁר, Neh. iii. 38. The prefixed שֶׁ is not a later form of the pron., for it is found in the song of Deborah. לָהּ is the reflexive pron. used emphatically, as in cxx. 6.

[d] אֲדַבְּרָה ב׳. This has been rendered (1) "Let me speak peace concerning thee," as lxxxviii. 3. LXX. περὶ σοῦ. So Del. who compares Luke xix. 42, τὰ πρὸς εἰρήνην αὐτῆς. (2) As Hupf. "let me speak peace in thee," *i.e.* in all my words, prayers, &c. wish that peace may be in thee; and God is said "to speak peace," lxxxv. 9; comp. Esth. x. 3, where the prep. אֶל or לְ is used; "to speak good," Jer. xii. 6, 2 Kings xxv. 28. (3) "Let me speak: 'Peace be in thee.'" Hengst., Olsh.

PSALM 123

ALSTED beautifully entitles this Psalm *Oculus Sperans*, "The Eye of Hope." "This," says Luther, "is a deep sigh of a pained heart, which looks round on all sides, and seeks friends, protectors, and comforters, but can find none. Therefore it says, 'Where shall I, a poor despised man, find refuge? I am not so strong as to be able to preserve myself; wisdom and plans fail me among the multitude of adversaries who assault me; therefore I come to Thee, O my God, to Thee I lift my eyes, O Thou that dwellest in the heavens.' He places over against each other the Inhabitant of heaven and the inhabitants of the earth, and reminds himself that, though the world be high and powerful, God is higher still. What shouldest thou do, then, when the world despises and insults thee? Turn thine eyes thither, and see that God with His beloved angels and His elect looks down upon thee, rejoices in thee, and loves thee."

This Psalm is either the sigh of the exile, towards the close of the Captivity looking in faith and patience for the deliverance which he had reason to hope was now nigh at hand; or it is the sigh of those who, having already returned to their native land, were still exposed to "the scorn and contempt" of the Samaritans and others, who favoured by the Persian government, took every opportunity of harassing and insulting the Jews. Comp. Nehem. ii. 19, "They laughed us to scorn and despised us," with ver. 4 of the Psalm, "The scorn of them that are at ease, the contempt of the proud."

In structure the Psalm is noticeable for its number of rhymes, or rather (for these do not always mark the ends of lines or half lines) for the repetition at short intervals of the same terminal syllable (e.g. *'eyneynu, eloheynu, y'chonnênu*, &c.). These, however, are apparently accidental, not intentional; rhyme, though frequent in modern Hebrew poems, being no characteristic of ancient Biblical poetry.

But "the Psalm needs no singular or exceptional charm. It is perfect as it stands. It is a little gem, cut with the most exquisite art. Few poems, inspired or uninspired, have been more admired or beloved. It has the charm of unity. It limits itself to one thought, or rather it expresses a single mood of the soul—the upward glance of a patient and hopeful faith. . . . This unity, moreover, is blended with and enhanced by variety of expression. While the first strophe sounds and illustrates the single theme of the Psalm, the second, to use a musical term, is a variation upon it."—Rev. S. Cox, *The Pilgrim Psalms*, p. 69.

[A PILGRIM-SONG.]

1 UNTO thee do I lift up mine eyes,
O Thou that art throned [a] in the heavens!
2 Behold, as the eyes of slaves unto the hand of their masters,
As the eyes of a maiden unto the hand of her mistress;
So our eyes (look) unto Jehovah our God,
Until He be gracious unto us,
3 Be gracious unto us, O Jehovah, be gracious unto us,
For we are exceedingly [b] filled with contempt.
4 Our soul is exceedingly filled
With the scorn [c] of them that are at ease,
With the contempt of the proud.[d]

1. Comp. cxxi. 1.

2. AS THE EYES OF SLAVES, watching anxiously the least movement, the smallest sign of their master's will. The image expresses complete and absolute dependence. Savary (in his *Letters on Egypt*, p. 135), says: "The slaves stand silent at the bottom of the rooms with their hands crossed over their breasts. *With their eyes fixed upon their master* they seek to anticipate every one of his wishes." Comp. the Latin phrases, *a nutu pendere*, *a vultu*, *ore*, &c. Plautus (*Aulul.*) uses the expression of a slave, "oculos in oculis heri habere;" and Terence (*Adelph.*), "oculos nunquam ab oculis dimovere." In those passages, however, the ready *obedience* of the slave may also be denoted by his attitude. In the Psalm the eye directed to the hand of God is the *oculus sperans*, the eye which waits, and hopes, and is patient, looking only to Him and none other for help.

3. EXCEEDINGLY FILLED, or perhaps "has long been filled," lit. "has been filled to itself," the reflexive pronoun marking the depth of the inward feeling. (Comp. cxx. 6.) This expression, together with the earnestness of the repeated prayer, "Be gracious unto us," shows that the "scorn" and "contempt" have long pressed upon the people, and their faith accordingly been exposed to a severe trial. The more remarkable is the entire absence of anything like impatience in the language of the Psalm. From the expression of trustful dependence with which it opens, it passes to the earnest, heartfelt *kyrie eleison* in which it pours out in a few words the trouble whence springs the prayer.

[a] הַיֹּשְׁבִי. On this form, with the *Chireq compaginis*, see cxiii. note [a].

[b] רַבַּת = רַב, ver. 4, and cxx. 6, and is the older form of this word in its adverbial use. See Gen. xlv. 28; 2 Sam. xxiv. 16; 1 Kings xix. 4.

[c] הַלַּעַג. The noun apparently in stat. constr. with the art., which is unusual, though according to Ges. § 108, 2, *a.c.*, Ewald, § 290, *d.e.*, this is allowable in certain instances, viz. either when the demonstrative power of the article is required, or when the connection between the noun and the following genitive is somewhat loose, so that the first forms a perfect idea by itself, while the second conveys only a supplemental idea relating to the material or purpose. It is on this latter principle that the art. stands here.

[d] גאיונים. According to the Q'ri, this is to be read as two words גְּאֵי יוֹנִים, "proud ones of oppressors" (which, however, as גְּאֶה does not occur, ought rather to be גְּאֵי, from גֵּאֶה), but quite unnecessarily. It is one word, a plur. from a form גַּאֲיוֹן (from גַּאֲוָה), as Gesenius, or גְּאֵיוֹן, as Ewald takes it, like רַעְיוֹן. The adjective, however, occurs nowhere else. According to Hupf., this is substantially the same form as the שַׁאֲנָן above, the terminations וֹן and ָן being originally adverbial, and formed from a *nunnated* accusative.

PSALM 124

THE last Psalm was the sigh of an exile in Babylon, waiting in absolute trust and dependence upon God for the deliverance of himself and his people from captivity. This Psalm is the joyful acknowledgement that the deliverance has been vouchsafed. The next Psalm (the 125th) describes the safety of the new colony, restored to its native land, and girt round by the protection of Jehovah. Here, then, we have three successive pictures, or rather three parts of one and the same picture; for they are not only linked together, as representing successive scenes in one history, but they are also pervaded by one great master-thought, which lends its unity to the whole group. In each there is the same full recognition of Jehovah's grace and power as working both for the deliverance and the security of His people. In the 123rd Psalm, "The eye waits upon Jehovah, till He be gracious." In the 124th, "If Jehovah had not been on our side, men had swallowed us up alive. . . . Our help is in the name of Jehovah." In the 125th, "The mountains are about Jerusalem, and Jehovah is round about His people."

There can be little doubt that this Psalm (the 124th) records the feelings of the exiles when the proclamation of Cyrus at length permitted them to return to their native land. Yet the figures employed are somewhat startling. The swelling waters rising till they threaten to sweep all before them is an image expressing, far more strongly than anything in the history would seem to warrant, the hostility of their conquerors to the Jews. The bird escaped from the broken snare is an image rather of sudden, unlooked for deliverance, than of a return so deliberate, so slow, in some instances apparently so reluctant, as that of the Jews from Babylon. The figures remind one rather of the earlier deliverance from Egypt. The Egyptians did "rise up" against them. Pharaoh and his chariots and his horsemen followed hard after them, and did seem as if about to swallow them up, when they were entangled in the wilderness. The waves of the Red Sea overwhelming their enemies might have suggested naturally the figure by which the might of those enemies was itself compared to swelling waters. The hasty flight might well be likened to the escape of the bird from the broken snare; the blow struck in the death of the first-born to the breaking of the snare.

Still the language of poetry must not be too closely pressed. Individuals may have felt strongly their oppression in Babylon. How keenly some had reason to remember their captive condition, we see from the 137th Psalm. And the providential means by which their deliverance was at last effected were unlooked for, and may have well taken them by surprise. The power of Babylon had been broken by Cyrus, and the conqueror had set them free. "When Jehovah turned again the captivity of Zion, then were we like unto them that dream." Moreover, we know how constantly both Prophets and Psalmists are in the habit of comparing the return from Babylon to the deliverance from Egypt. Twice had the nation been in bondage to other nations, in a strange land: twice had the yoke of its masters been broken; and, unlike as the circumstances may have been under which the two great acts of national redemption were accomplished, still the one was naturally associated in the minds and thoughts of the people with the other. And hence a Poet celebrating the one might almost unconsciously borrow his imagery from the other.

Mr. Cox, however, remarks: "In the ancient Oriental world, Babylon was much what the France of the first Napoleon was in the modern European world; and its capture by the hardy Persians of Cyrus was even more astonishing than the defeat of Napoleon by the English. It was the great military empire of antiquity, 'that fierce and impetuous nation, which marched across the breadths of the earth, to seize upon dwelling-places that were not its own.' . . . That it should be overthrown by the poor hill tribes of Persia led by Cyrus had indeed been predicted by Isaiah, but was nevertheless well nigh as great a marvel to the Jews as to other Eastern races. That the Lord should 'stir up the spirit of the king of Persia' to proclaim Jehovah 'the God of heaven,' to affirm 'the Lord God of heaven, who hath given me all the kingdoms of the earth, hath charged me to build Him an house at Jerusalem,' and to set free as many of His people as were willing to 'go up to Jerusalem and build the house of the Lord God of Israel'—all this was so strange, so unexpected, so far beyond the reach of hope, that when the Hebrew captives heard it, they 'were like unto them that dream,' and could not believe for wonder and joy. 'This was the Lord's doing,' none but He *could* have done it, and it was marvellous in their eyes.' "

The exquisite beauty of the Poem consists not only in the striking figures which are employed, but in the way in which these are repeated and return upon themselves. "The effect is indefinitely enhanced by the lingering repetition of phrase after phrase." And "the whole Psalm is alive with joy, the joy of an escape, of a triumph as wonderful as it was unexpected."

The title, which gives the Psalm to David, is evidently of no authority. Delitzsch conjectures that the recurrence of certain words found in the genuine Davidic Psalms may have led the collector to assign this ode to him. In the LXX. and the Syriac it is anonymous.

But apart from the Aramaic colouring of the diction, which points to a later time, the theme of the Psalm is obviously such a captivity as David never experienced.

[A PILGRIM-SONG. OF DAVID.]

1 IF Jehovah had not [a] been on our side,—
Let Israel now say—
2 If Jehovah had not been on our side,
When men rose up against us;
3 Then [b] had they swallowed us up alive,
When their anger was kindled against us;

3. SWALLOWED US UP ALIVE. Comp. lv. 15 [16]; Prov. i. 12; with Num. xvi. 32, 33, where the phrase is used of the company of Korah.

Or the figure may refer to the ravening beast swallowing its prey, the figure being repeated in ver. 6, "a prey to their teeth." If so, we have three images. "The Babylonian beast had lost its prey,

4 Then had the waters overwhelmed us,
The stream [c] had gone over our soul;
5 Then there had gone over our soul
The proudly-swelling [d] waters.
6 Blessed be Jehovah,
Who hath not given us as a prey to their teeth.
7 Our soul is escaped as a bird from the snare of the fowlers;
The snare is broken, and we are escaped.
8 Our help is in the name of Jehovah,
The Maker of heaven and earth.

the Babylonian torrent its victim, the Babylonian fowler his prize."

4. THE STREAM, *i.e.* the mountain-torrent as swollen by the rains and the melting of the snow in spring. For the figure comp. xviii. 16 [17], lxix. 1, 2 [2, 3], cxliv. 7, and the still more exact parallel, Is. viii. 7, 8; Hab. i. 11.

5. PROUDLY-SWELLING. Comp. xlvi. 3 [4], lxxxix. 9 [10], and the ποταμὸς ὑβριστὴς of Æschylus. *Prom. V.* 717.

8. This verse resumes the theme of verses 1, 2, as well as of ver. 6. The deliverance so marvellous, so unexpected, comes not from man, but from Israel's covenant God.

[a] לוּלֵי, followed both in protasis and apodosis by preterite. See xxvii., note [b].

שֶׁהָיָה. The use of the relative here is commonly accounted for by an ellipse of the verb היה, "If (it had not been) Jehovah who was on our side," &c. But Hupf. observes, that such an ellipse of the verb after a conjunction is unheard of (in xciv. 17 it is virtually supplied in the predicate), and supposes therefore that שֶׁ is here used pleonastically after לוּלֵי as a conjunction, in the sense of "that." He compares the use of the English *if that* and the pleonastic use of שֶׁ in Cant. iii. 4, Eccles. vi. 3. The LXX., too, render εἰ μὴ ὅτι. Delitzsch compares the Aram. (דְ) שֶׁ לְוַאי, *o si* (lit. *o si quod*).

[b] אֲזַי. According to Hupf., the genuine old Hebrew (not Aram.) form, instead of the more common אָז, here introducing the apodosis (as in cxix. 92), and rightly rendered by the LXX. ἄρα. Del., on the other hand (following Ewald, § 103, *e*), holds it to be a shortened form of the Aram. אֱדַיִן. It here introduces the apodosis instead of the affirmative כִּי, which is employed in the older language to introduce the apodosis after לוּלֵי, Gen. xxxi. 42, xliii. 10.

[c] נַחְלָה, in many MSS. and Edd., with the accent on the last syllable, as if it were fem., but properly on the antepenultimate (as the Massora and Qimchi, and the majority of MSS.), to distinguish it from the same word as *Milra*, meaning, "an inheritance," and thus masculine, as the

verb requires, with the old accus. termination, as cxvi. 15 (comp. cxx. 6, and Is. viii. 23, אַרְצָה, where the accent is on the antepenultimate), which, however, has lost its meaning. In Num. xxxiv. 5, on the other hand, it is a real accusative, *to the stream.*

[d] זֵידוֹנִים, only here, a later adjective form for the more common זֵדִים (but not Aramaic), bearing the same relation to זָדוֹן that גְּאֵיוֹן (see note [c] on last Psalm) does to גָּאוֹן.

PSALM 125

THE exiles had been restored to their own land (see Introduction to last Psalm), but fresh perils awaited them there. Not only were they perpetually molested by the Samaritans and others in the rebuilding of the Temple and of the city walls, but they were troubled with internal dissensions. Ezra found the "abominations of the heathen" countenanced by the intermarriages of the Jews who returned from the Captivity with "the people of those lands," and was dismayed when he learnt that "the hand of the princes and the rulers had been chief in this trespass." Nehemiah, at a later period, had to contend against a faction within the city who had taken the bribes of the Samaritans. In rebuilding the walls, he did not trust the priests, the nobles, or the rulers, till he had begun the work (Neh. ii. 16, vi. 17). Even the prophets took part with his enemies against him. Shemaiah, he found, had been hired by Tobiah and Sanballat, and "the prophetess Noadiah and the rest of the prophets" had joined the plot, and sought "to put him in fear," and so to hinder his work (vi. 10—48).

To these plots and this defection on the part of many of the Jews themselves there is probably an allusion in ver. 3 and 5. On the other hand, the faith of the Psalmist rises above all these dangers. There is One who is the sure defence of His people, who is their bulwark as the mountains are the bulwark of Jerusalem.

[A PILGRIM-SONG.]

1 THEY that trust in Jehovah are as Mount Zion
Which cannot be moved,

1, 2. Two images of the security of those who trust in Jehovah : (1) they stand firm as Zion itself, they are like a mountain which cannot

(But) is seated for ever.
2 As for Jerusalem, the mountains are round about her,
And Jehovah is round about His people,
From this time even for evermore.
3 For the rod of wickedness shall not rest upon the lot of the righteous,

be shaken ; (2) they are girt as by a wall of mountains—a natural bulwark against all enemies.

1. IS SEATED, lit. "sitteth ;" as spoken of a mountain "lieth" or "is situated," but here, with the following "for ever," used in a still stronger sense. Milton :—

"From their foundations loosening to and fro,
They plucked the *seated* hills."

See on the use of this verb cxxii. 5.

2. MOUNTAINS ARE ROUND ABOUT HER. "This image is not realized," says Dean Stanley, "as most persons familiar with our European scenery would wish and expect it to be realized. Jerusalem is not literally shut in by mountains, except on the eastern side, where it may be said to be inclosed by the arms of Olivet, with its outlying ridges on the north-east and south-east." Viewed from any other direction, Jerusalem always appears "on an elevation higher than the hills in its immediate neighbourhood. Nor is the plain on which it stands inclosed by a continuous though distant circle of mountains like that which gives its peculiar charm to Athens and Innsbruck. The mountains in the neighbourhood of Jerusalem are of unequal height, . . . only in two or three instances . . . rising to any considerable elevation. Even Olivet is only 180 feet above the top of Mount Zion. Still they act as a shelter; they must be surmounted before the traveller can see, or the invader attack, the Holy City ; and the distant line of Moab would always seem to rise as a wall against invaders from the remote east." It is of these distant mountains that Josephus speaks (*Bell. Jud.* vi. v. 1) as "the surrounding mountains," *συνήχει δὲ ἡ περαία καὶ τὰ πέριξ ὄρη*.—*Sinai and Palestine*, pp. 174, 175.

AND JEHOVAH, instead of "so Jehovah," &c., the comparison being formed by merely placing the two objects side by side, as so frequently in the Proverbs.

IS ROUND ABOUT HIS PEOPLE. Comp. Zech. ii. 4, 5 [8, 9], "Jerusalem shall be inhabited as towns without walls, for I, saith Jehovah, will be unto her a wall of fire round about."

3. FOR introduces an example of God's protecting care—an example not taken from the past, but which faith anticipates and is sure of, as if already accomplished.

THE ROD OF WICKEDNESS. The expression may refer to the Persian rule under favour of which the Samaritans and others annoyed the Jews. The *rod* or *sceptre*, De Wette urges, could not apply to the Samaritans, for they did not *rule* over the Jews. But it was through them that the tyranny of the Persian court made itself felt; and they contrived, moreover, to gain over a considerable part, and that the most influential part, of the Jews to their side. The fear was, as the next clause shows, lest in this state of things the defection should spread still more widely.

REST, *i.e.* "lie heavy," so as to oppress, as in Is. xxv. 10, with a further sense of continuance of the oppression.

THE LOT OF THE RIGHTEOUS is the Holy Land itself ; comp. xvi. 5, 6. The consequence of a long continuance of this oppressive rule

That the righteous put not forth their hands unto
iniquity.
4 Do good, O Jehovah, to them that are good,
And to them that are upright in their hearts.
5 But as for those who turn aside to their crooked paths,
Jehovah shall make them go their way with the workers
of iniquity.
Peace be upon Israel.

would be that THE RIGHTEOUS, the sound and true part of the nation, would itself be tempted to despair of God's succour, and so be drawn away from its steadfastness (comp. xxxvii. 7, 8, xlix. 13 [14], lxxiii. 13, 14 [14, 15]; Job. xv. 4).

4, 5. The Psalm ends with a confident assertion of righteous requital—first in the form of a prayer, and then in the utterance of a hope, both springing from the same faith in the righteousness of God.

5. TURN ASIDE TO THEIR CROOKED PATHS. This may be, if we take the participle transitively, "bend their crooked paths," *i.e.* turn their paths aside so as to make them crooked. Comp. Jud. v. 6. But in Num. xxii. 23; Is. xxx. 11, the participle is used intransitively, and so here we may explain "who turn aside in, or to, crooked paths." The expression does not necessarily denote a going over to heathenism: it would describe the conduct of those who, in the time of Nehemiah, made common cause with the enemies of Israel (Neh. vi. 10—14, xiii. 28—31).

MAKE THEM GO THEIR WAY, *i.e.* so as to perish. Comp. the use of the same verb in lviii. 8 [9] (Hithpael), cix. 22 [23] (Niphal). Those who begin with being crooked, double, deceitful, will at last walk openly with the wicked, and this is Jehovah's doing, because it is His law of righteous retribution.

PEACE UPON ISRAEL. Comp. the conclusion of cxxviii. So LXX. εἰρήνη ἐπὶ τῷ Ἰσρ. Jer. and Vul. *pax super Israel*, but in the 128th Ps. *pacem.*

PSALM 126

THE first colony of exiles had returned to Palestine. The permission to return had been so unexpected, the circumstances which had led to it so wonderful and so unforeseen, that when it came it could hardly be believed. To those who found themselves actually restored to the land of their fathers it seemed like a dream. It was a joy beyond all words to utter. God, their fathers' God, had indeed wrought for them, and even the heathen had recognized His hand.

It is with these thoughts that this beautiful Psalm opens. But, after all, what was that little band of settlers which formed the first caravan? It was but as the trickling of a tiny rill in some desert waste. Hence the prayer bursts from the lips of the Psalmist, Bring back our captives like mighty streams, which swoln by the wintry rains, descend to fertilize the parched and desolate wilderness. Then comes the thought of the many discouragements and opposition which the first settlers had to encounter; it was a time of sowing in tears (Ezra iv. 11—24). Still faith could expect a joyful harvest. He who had restored them to the land would assuredly crown His work with blessing.

[A PILGRIM-SONG.]

1 WHEN Jehovah brought back the returned[a] of Zion,
We were like unto them that dream.
2 Then was our mouth filled with laughter,
And our tongue with songs of joy.
3 Then said they among the nations,
"Jehovah hath done great things for them."
4 (Yea) Jehovah hath done great things for us;
(Therefore) were we glad.

5 Bring back, O Jehovah, our captives,
As the streams in the South.

1. LIKE UNTO THEM THAT DREAM, *i.e.* so unexpected and so wonderful was our redemption from the Exile, that we could scarcely believe it was true, and not a dream.

In Neale's Commentary there is an apt and striking parallel, which is quoted from Livy, xxxiii. 32, where the Greeks, after the defeat of the Macedonians by Flamininus, receive the announcement at the Isthmian games that the Romans would allow them to retain their liberty. "The joy was too great for men to take it all in. None could well believe that he had heard aright, and they looked on one another in wonder like the empty show of a dream; and as for each person singly, having no confidence in their own ears, they all questioned those standing near them."

2. FILLED WITH LAUGHTER, as in Job viii. 21.

3. JEHOVAH HATH DONE GREAT THINGS, lit. "hath magnified to do with (towards) these," as in Joel ii. 20. THEM, lit. "these," δεικτικῶς.

4. WERE WE GLAD. Or perhaps present, "we *are* glad;" the construction of the verb and participle is the same as in cxxii. 2.

5. STREAMS, or rather "channels" (watercourses). THE SOUTH, *i.e.* the south country, the Negeb, is the image of a dry and thirsty land, which wanted springs. Comp. Judg. i. 15.

Palestine without her people has been like the south country parched with the drought of summer: the return of her inhabitants will be grateful as the return of the mountain torrents when, swoln by the

6 They that sow in tears
Shall reap with songs of joy.
7 He may go weeping as he goeth,
Bearing (his) store of seed;
8 He shall come, he shall come with songs of joy,
Bearing his sheaves.

wintry rains, they flow again along the beds of the watercourses, carrying with them life and verdure and fertility. We find the expression of the same feeling under a different figure Is. xlix. 18, where the land, like a bereaved mother, waits for her children, whose return will fill her heart with joy. . . . The verse is a prayer that *all* may be brought back. There is a great past, may the future be great also.

6. THEY THAT SOW IN TEARS. The sowing is a season of trouble and anxiety, but the rich harvest makes amends for all. So though the new colonists were exposed to many trials, yet a glorious future was before them. That time of labour, and trouble, and opposition, and discouragement, and anxious waiting, should by no means lose its reward. The weeping should be changed into joy; the weeping should be the path of joy. Comp. for the contrast between the sowing and the reaping, Haggai ii. 3—9, 17—19.

7, 8. These verses are merely an expansion of the image in ver. 6, with the common substitution of the singular for the plural, to bring out more clearly the figure of the individual sower.

7. This verse might perhaps be more exactly rendered: "He who beareth the handful of seed may indeed weep every step that he goes."

7. GO WEEPING, or, yet more strongly, "take no step of his way without weeping," the double infinitive being employed to mark the continued nature of the action. Comp. 2 Sam. iii. 16; Jer. i. 4; Gesen. § 131, 3*b*.

STORE OF SEED, lit. "that which is drawn," out of the store-house and placed in the vessel or fold of the robe to be scattered on the field. Hence a sower is called "a drawer of seed." Amos ix. 13.

[a] שְׁבַת צ׳, generally rendered, after the LXX., *τὴν αἰχμαλωσίαν Σιών*, though perhaps unnecessarily. For the construction, comp. Deut. xxx. 3, Ps. xiv. 7.

שִׁיבָה is formed from שׁוּב, as קִימָה from קוּם (Lam. iii. 63), and signifies "the return," and so "those who return," just as שְׁבוּת or שְׁבִית, "the captivity," and hence "the captives," גָּלוּת, "the exile," and so "the exiles." To this Hupf. objects that it is hardly likely that a form שִׁיבָה should be found as well as שׁוּבָה, which occurs in the same sense "return," Is. xxx. 15. Hence he maintains that שִׁיבַת is an old mistake for שְׁבִית or שְׁבוּת.

That בְּשׁוּב refers to the past is quite certain, from the following הָיִינוּ and Jerome is right, "quum converteret . . . facti sumus."

אָז introduces emphatically the apodosis, and the verbs which follow are proper *imperfects*: "then our mouth *began to be filled*," &c. . . . *then they were saying*, &c.

PSALM 127

THIS and the next Psalm form two bright companion pictures of social and domestic life, and of the happiness of a household which, trained in the fear of God, is blessed by His providence. "These pictures," says Isaac Taylor, "are mild and bright; humanizing are they in the best sense: they retain certain elements of Paradise, and yet more the elements of the Patriarchal era, with the addition of that patriotism and of that concentration in which the Patriarchal life was wanting. The happy religious man, after the Hebrew pattern, possessed those feelings and habitudes which, if they greatly prevail in a community, impart to it the strength of a combination which is stronger than any other; uniting the force of domestic virtue, of rural, yeomanlike, agricultural occupations, of unaggressive defensive valour, and of a religious animation which is *national* as well as authentic and true. Our modern learning in Oriental modes of life and its circumstances and scenery may help us to bring into view either of two gay pictures;—that of the Hebrew man in mid-life, at rest in his country home, with his sturdy sons about him; his wife is still young; her fair daughters are like cornices sculptured as decorations for a palace: or else the companion picture, with its group on their way Zionward, resting for the sultry noon-hour under the palms by the side of a stream, and yet home, happy home, is in the recollection of the party; but the Hill of God, 'whereunto the tribes of the Lord go up,' is in the fervent purpose of all; and while they rest they beguile the time with a sacred song and with its soothing melody. Happy were the people while their mind was such as this, and such their habits, and such their piety!"—*Spirit of the Hebrew Poetry*, pp. 165, 166.

There is not a word in either Psalm to guide us as to the time of its composition. The title gives the 127th to Solomon (only one other in the entire Psalter, the 72nd, being ascribed to him), but it may be doubted whether with sufficient reason. In form, in rhythm, in general tone and character, it resembles all the others in this collection. It has been conjectured that the proverb-like structure of the Psalm, the occurrence in it of several words and phrases also occurring in the Proverbs, and possibly a supposed allusion to the name Jedediah in ver. 2, "His beloved" (*y'dîdo*), and to the building of the Temple in ver. 1, may have led some collector to conclude that the Psalm was Solomon's. In the Septuagint it is anonymous.

In the Syriac it is said to have been spoken by David concerning Solomon; but also concerning Haggai and Zechariah, who urged the building of the Temple. Many, both ancient and modern interpreters have, in the same way, discovered in the Psalm an allusion to the circumstances of the people after the return from the Captivity, to the rebuilding of the Temple, and the guarding of the newly-erected walls in ver. 1, and to the numerical increase of the people in ver. 4, 5, which at such a time would possess especial importance in the eyes of a patriotic Hebrew. But the "house" in ver. 1 is clearly not the Temple, but any house which men build, for the whole Psalm is a picture of daily life, social and domestic; and, as De Wette very truly observes, to build houses, to guard the city, to be diligent in labours, would be just as important at any other period as after the return from the Exile; and the Jews at all times of their history esteemed a large family one of the chief of blessings.

A want of unity, an abruptness, in the transition, from the first part to the second part of the Psalm has been alleged, but without sufficient reason. "The first part is engaged with *the Home* and *the City;* the second part with *the Children* who are the strength and joy of the Home, and with *the Men* who are the crown and defence of the City. In both, in our home life and in our civic life, we are wholly dependent on the providence and bounty of God."

The great moral of the Psalm is, that without God's blessing all human efforts and human precautions are in vain; that man can never command success; that God gives and man receives. There is a passage in Tennyson's "Lotos Eaters," the strain of which is not unlike that of ver. 3 of the Psalm, except that there is a shadow of sadness and weariness on the words of the modern Poet which finds no response in the spirit of the Hebrew bard:—

"Why are we weigh'd upon with heaviness,
And utterly consumed with sharp distress,
While all things else have rest from weariness?
All things have rest: why should we toil alone?
We only toil who are the first of things,
And make perpetual moan,
Still from one sorrow to another thrown:
Nor ever fold our wings,
And cease from wanderings;
Nor steep our brows in slumber's holy balm;
Nor hearken what the inner spirit sings,
'There is no joy but calm!'
Why should we only toil, the roof and crown of things?"

[A PILGRIM SONG. OF SOLOMON.[a]]

1 EXCEPT Jehovah build a house,
They labour thereat in vain that build it;
Except Jehovah watch over a city,
The watchman waketh (but) in vain.
2 Vain is it for you, ye that rise up early, ye that late take rest,[b]
That ye eat the bread of toil:
So[c] He giveth His beloved sleep.[d]

1, 3. The truth seems obvious and undeniable that all success is from God, "An Gottes Segen ist alles gelegen": yet practically this is by most men forgotten. The spirit of the Chaldean invader of whom the Prophet says, "This his strength is his God," the *Dextra mihi Deus*, is in the heart, if not on the lips, of others besides the atheist.

1. A HOUSE, not "the Temple," as some explain, nor "the family," as others, but the structure itself, as is evident from the context. WATCHMAN, lit. "keeper," *i.e.* by night, as in cxxi. 3, 4.

THEY LABOUR, or rather "they have laboured." It is the strict perfect; the writer places himself at the end of the work, sees its result, "they have spent their labour in vain;" and so in the next verse, "the watchman hath waked."

2. YE THAT RISE. The Hebrew expression runs literally: "making early to rise, making late to sit (down)," *i.e.* going forth early to labour, and returning late at night to take rest. It is an artificial lengthening of the natural day. Others render the latter clause as in the E.V. "sit up late," appealing to Is. v. 11, where, however, the construction is different, the participle being followed not as here by the infinitive, but by a noun with the preposition, and the expression being lit. "that make late in the evening," *i.e.* no doubt that prolong their revels into the night.

BREAD OF TOIL, or perhaps rather "of wearisome efforts." Comp. Prov. v. 10, "and thy wearisome efforts (*i.e.* what thou hast gotten with labour and toil) be in the house of a stranger." There is an allusion, no doubt, to Gen. iii. 17, "in sorrow (or weariness) thou shalt eat of it all the days of thy life."

GIVETH SLEEP. Most follow Luther in rendering "He giveth it, *i.e.* bread, the necessaries of life, in sleep." What others obtain only with such wearing toil, such constant effort, with so much disappointment and so much sorrow, God gives to the man whom He loves as it were *while he sleeps*, i.e. without all this anxiety and exertion. This is the interpretation now perhaps commonly adopted; but it seems to me very questionable (though I accepted it in the First Edition) for the following reasons: (1) it is necessary to supply "bread," not "bread of toil," in this clause; and (2) I am not satisfied that the rendering of the accusative "*in sleep*" is justifiable. The alleged parallel instances (see Critical Note), expressing parts of time, are not really parallel. I am inclined, therefore, to prefer the rendering, "So He giveth His beloved sleep," though it is no doubt difficult to explain the reference of the particle "so." I suppose it

3 Behold, sons are a heritage from Jehovah,
The fruit of the womb is (His) reward.
4 Like arrows in the hand of a mighty man,
So are the sons of (a man's) youth.
5 Happy is the man who hath filled his quiver with them,

refers to the principle laid down in the previous verse, there being a tacit comparison, "as all labour is vain without God's providence, as He builds the house, as He watches the city, so He gives the man who loves Him and leaves all in His hands, calm refreshing sleep."

There is no discouragement here, it is needless to say, to honest labour. It is undue anxiety, a feverish straining, a toiling, as if toil of itself could command success, the folly of which is condemned. Comp. for a similar sentiment Prov. x. 22, "The blessing of Jehovah maketh rich, and toil can add nothing thereto." The teaching is that of our Lord in the Sermon on the Mount, "Wherefore I say unto you, Be not anxious (*μὴ μεριμνᾶτε*) for your life, what ye shall eat and what ye shall drink, neither for your body, wherewith ye shall be clothed," &c., Matt. vi. 25—34. See also Luke x. 41; 1 Pet. v. 7. God's "beloved" are not exempted from the great law of labour which lies upon all, but the sting is taken from it when they can leave all results in a Father's hand, with absolute trust in His wisdom and goodness.

3. BEHOLD, as drawing particular attention to one marked example of God's good gifts; which none can question is emphatically His *gift*; on this the Poet lingers, "allured by the charm of the subject," for such there was, especially to an Oriental, to whom a numerous progeny was the first of blessings, giving value and stability to all others.

A HERITAGE, or perhaps here, in a wider sense, "a possession."

4. SONS OF YOUTH, *i.e.* sons of early married life (as in Prov. v. 18, Is. liv. 6, "a wife of youth" is one married when a man is young). On the other hand, in Gen. xxxvii. 3, "a son of old age" is one born when his father is old.

These sons of a man's youth are particularly mentioned, because they would naturally grow up to be a support and protection to their father in his old age, when he would most need their support.

5. THEY. The pronoun cannot be referred, with Calvin and many expositors, to the sons, for it is clearly the father whose cause is supposed to be at stake, and who in the emergency finds his sons ready to defend him. Others, with more probability, suppose it to include both father and sons. But it may refer only to the father. Hupfeld calls the change of number harsh (from singular to plural), but it is not more so than in cvii. 43, "Who is wise that *he* should observe . . . and that *they* should understand," &c. When the singular means the genus, the transition is easy to the plural.

THEIR ENEMIES. The pron. is inserted by the LXX. *τοῖς ἐχθροῖς αὐτῶν*, Jer. *inimicis suis*. Cf. Job v. 4.

IN THE GATE, here mentioned chiefly as the place of judgement (Deut. xxi. 19; Is. xxix. 21; Amos v. 12), as well as of all public acts. See on ix. 14. The allusion is to lawsuits, in which, if unjustly accused or brought before an unrighteous judge, a man need not fear lest he should be "put to shame," *i.e.* lose his cause; his stalwart sons would not suffer might to prevail against right.

The phrase "speak with their enemies," in the sense of defending

They shall not be ashamed, when they speak with (their)
enemies in the gate.

their cause, may be illustrated by Josh. xx. 4, Gen. xlv. 15, "And he (the manslayer who has fled) shall stand in the entrance of the gate of the city, and shall *speak his words* (*i.e.* plead his cause) in the ears of the elders of that city." Comp. 2 Sam. xix. 30; Jer. xii. 1.

Others understand by speaking with enemies in the gate a battle fought with besiegers at the gates. So apparently Ewald, who refers to Gen. xxii. 17, "thy seed shall possess the gate of his enemies;" and xxiv. 60, "let thy seed possess the gate of those which hate them." This certainly harmonizes better with the warlike figure of the quiver full of arrows: but can "to speak with enemies" mean to fight with them? If so, it must be an idiom something like that of "looking one another in the face," 2 Kings xiv. 8, 11. But it may be understood of "parleying with them," as Rabshakeh for instance with the captains and ministers of Hezekiah.

With the sentiment of ver. 4, 5, compare Soph. *Antig.* 641—644:

τούτου γὰρ οὕνεκ' ἄνδρες εὔχονται γονὰς
κατηκόους φύσαντες ἐν δόμοις ἔχειν,
ὡς καὶ τὸν ἐχθρὸν ἀνταμύνωνται κακοῖς,
καὶ τὸν φίλον τιμῶσιν ἐξ ἴσου πατρί.

So, too, in Ecclus. xxx. 5, 6, it is said of a father that "while he lived, he saw and rejoiced in him (his son); and when he died, he was not sorrowful. He left behind him an avenger against his enemies, and one that shall requite kindness to his friends." The coincidence of expression in the last two passages is remarkable.

[a] The following coincidences of expression have been supposed to justify the title. עֲצָבִים, *wearisome efforts*, ver. 2, occurs also Prov. v. 10; מְאַחֲרֵי, *making late*, in Prov. xxiii. 30. As in ver. 4 of the Psalm בְּנֵי הַנְּ׳, *sons of youth*, so in Prov. v. 18 אֵשֶׁת נ׳, *wife of youth*. Ver. 5, *in the gate*, as in Prov. xxii. 22, xxiv. 7. And the whole Psalm may be considered an expansion of Prov. x. 22.

[b] שֶׁבֶת, opposed to קוּם as cxxxix. 2, Lam. iii. 63, as also are the two participles in the stat. constr. Aquila, rightly, βραδυνοῦσι καθῆσθαι.

[c] כֵּן, *so*, *i.e.* with just the same result. So in the passages cited by Del.: Num. xiii. 33, "we were *so*, *i.e.* just the same in their sight;" Is. li. 6, כְּמוֹ־כֵן, *as so*, *i.e.* in like manner; Job ix. 35, "for it is not so with me (as you think)," *i.e.* I am not guilty, as you assert; 2 Sam. xxiii. 5 may be interrogative, "For is not my house so with God that He hath made an everlasting covenant with me?" In all these instances Del. would take כֵּן as meaning *small*, or *as nothing* (*gering*, *wie nichts*), which can only be justified if we suppose the word to be used δεικτικῶς.

[d] שֵׁנָא, with Aramaic termination, for שֵׁנָה, here it is said not acc. of the object, but of time, as frequently in other words, such as בֹּקֶר, עֶרֶב, &c., Ges. § 118, 2; but, as I have said in the note on ver. 2, I do not think these can be regarded as really parallel instances, because שֵׁנָא is not a word of time but of state.

PSALM 128

THE Introduction to the preceding Psalm may be consulted on this, which is a sunny picture of the family happiness of one who fears God, and leads a holy life.

Luther says: "In the former Psalm the prophet treated of both kinds of life, that is, both of national life and domestic life (*politia et œconomia*). The same thing almost he doth in this Psalm, but yet after another sort. For although here also he joineth the two together, and wisheth the blessing of God and peace unto them both, yet hath he more respect to household government or matrimony, because it is, as it were, the fountain and source of civil government For the children whom we bring up and instruct at home, these will, in time to come, be the governors of the state. For of houses or families are made cities, of cities provinces, of provinces kingdoms. Household government, then, is with reason called the fountain of policy and political government, for if you destroy the one, the other cannot exist.

"Wherefore to this Psalm we will give this title, that it is an Epithalamium or Marriage Song, wherein the Prophet comforteth them that are married, wishing unto them and promising them from God all manner of blessings."

The Psalm consists of two parts:—

I. The description of the happy life. Ver. 1—4.

II. The good wishes and promises for him who has entered upon it. Ver. 5, 6.

[A PILGRIM-SONG.]

1 HAPPY is every one that feareth Jehovah,
That walketh in His ways.
2 For[a] the labour of thy hands shalt thou eat,
Happy art thou, and it (shall be) well with thee.

2. THE LABOUR OF THY HANDS. This is the first part of the blessing, —the quiet peaceful life of a thriving, prosperous yeoman in the country, with no fear that the harvest will be trodden down by the invader before it is ripe, or the cattle swept off by some roving predatory tribe. The opposite condition is threatened as a curse in the Law: "Ye shall sow your seed in vain, for your enemies shall eat it," Lev. xxvi. 16; "Thou shalt build an house, and thou shalt not dwell therein; thou shalt plant a vineyard, and shalt not gather the grapes

3 Thy wife[b] (shall be) like a fruitful vine, in the inner part
of thy house;
Thy children, like olive-plants, round about thy table:
4 Behold, thus shall the man be blessed that feareth Jehovah.
5 Jehovah bless thee out of Zion,
And see thou the prosperity of Jerusalem
All the days of thy life,
6 And see thy children's children.—
Peace be upon Israel.

thereof, &c., Deut. xxviii. 30—33, 39, 40. See also Am. v. 11; Micah vi. 15; Eccles. vi. 1, 2; and for a contrast in this respect, between the lot of the righteous and that of the wicked, Is. iii. 10, 11.

3. The comparison would perhaps be brought out more clearly by arranging the verse as follows:—

Thy wife shall be in the inner part
of thy house
Like a fruitful vine;
Thy children round about thy table
Like the shoots of the olive.

IN THE INNER PART, lit. "the sides of thy house," as in Am. vi. 10, *i.e.* the women's apartments, as marking the proper sphere of the wife engaged in her domestic duties, and also to some extent her seclusion, though this was far less among the Jews than among other Orientals.

The VINE is an emblem chiefly of *fruitfulness*, but also of gracefulness and dependence, as needing support; the OLIVE of vigorous, healthy, joyous life. The same figure is employed by Euripides, *Herc. Fur.* 839, *Med.* 1,098.

5. Looking on the beautiful family picture, the Poet turns to greet the father of the household, and to wish him the blessing of which he has already spoken in such glowing terms.

OUT OF ZION, as the dwelling-place of God, His earthly throne and sanctuary, whence all blessing comes, cxxxiv. 3, xx. 2 [3].

Then follows the truly patriotic sentiment—the wish that he may see *the prosperity of Jerusalem*, as well as that he may live long to see his children and grandchildren. The welfare of the family and the welfare of the state are indissolubly connected.

SEE, THOU, an imperative following the optative, and therefore to be understood as expressing a wish, and even more, a promise, as in xxxvii. 3, where see note[b].

6. CHILDREN'S CHILDREN. So Virgil: "Adspicies . . . natos natorum et qui nascentur ab illis."

[a] כִּי is sometimes thus placed after other words instead of standing first in the sentence: comp. cxviii. 10—12; Gen. xviii. 20. Hupfeld contends that it retains its usual meaning *for*, but he would transpose the two clauses of the verse: "Happy art thou, and it is well with thee, *For* thou shalt eat," &c. Del. on the other hand, following Ew., takes it as emphatic, *surely;* in German *ja.* Hupf. says כִּי never has this sense; but surely it may be used elliptically, = "be assured *that*, &c.; הֲלֹא כִּי, 1 Sam. x. 1; אָמְנָם כִּי, Job xii. 2; and the common expression אַף כִּי, &c.

[b] אֶשְׁתְּךָ; only here with this punctuation, instead of אִשְׁתְּךָ. פֹּרִיָּה is for פֹּרָה, as בֹּכִיָּה, Lam. i. 6, for בֹּכָה, Ew. § 189, *e*.

PSALM 129

THE nation, delivered from the Babylonish Captivity, may well look back to all her past history, and trace in it the same great law of suffering, and the same ever-repeated tokens of God's mercy. The record is a record of conflict, but it is also a record of victory (ver. 2). The great principle on which Israel's final deliverance rests is the *righteousness* of Jehovah (ver. 4). That has been manifested, as often before, so now in cutting asunder the cords by which the people had been bound in Babylon. Full of thankfulness at this deliverance, the Poet draws thence an augury and a hope for the overthrow, complete and final, of their oppressors.

The Psalm consists, accordingly, of two stanzas, each of four verses; the first containing the record of the past, the second the prayer (which is also a hope, and almost a promise) for the future.

In subject, style, and rhythmical structure, it most nearly resembles Psalm cxxiv., so nearly indeed that there can be no doubt that both are by the same author. Observe how exactly the opening of the two corresponds in form, and how in each Psalm two principal figures are wrought out.

[A PILGRIM-SONG.]

1 GREATLY have they fought against me, from my youth up—
Let Israel now say—
2 Greatly have they fought against me, from my youth up,
(But) they have not also [a] prevailed against me.
3 The ploughers ploughed upon my back,
They made long their furrows.[b]

1. GREATLY, or "long:" the same word as in cxx. 6, cxxiii. 4.

FOUGHT AGAINST ME, lit. "have been adversaries unto me."

FROM MY YOUTH UP. The youth of the nation was in Egypt, at which time God speaks of His relation to Israel as "love of youth," "espousals of youth," &c. Hos. ii. 15; Jer. ii. 2, xxii. 21; Ezek. xxiii. 3.

2. HAVE NOT PREVAILED. This is the point of the Psalm. The New Testament parallel is 2 Cor. iv. 8—10, and the whole history of the Christian Church is an echo of the words.

3. FURROWS. Deep wounds, such as those made by the lash on the back of slaves. Comp. Is. i. 6, and a different but not less expressive image li. 23. Isaiah, a *town* poet,

4 Jehovah is righteous,
He hath cut asunder the cord of the wicked.

5 Let them be ashamed and turned backward,
As many as hate Zion.
6 Let them be as the grass on the housetops,
That withereth afore [c] it be plucked up : [d]
7 Wherewith the mower filleth not his hand,
Nor he that bindeth sheaves his bosom ;
8 Neither do they which go by say,
"The blessing of Jehovah be upon you."
"We bless you in the name of Jehovah."

takes his image of the same oppression from the street : "Thou madest thy back like the ground, and like the street to them that go over it" (li. 23). But the rural poet in the Psalm takes his image from the farm, from the deep furrow driven by the ploughshare.

4. THE CORD. The figure is probably taken from the yoking of oxen : when the traces are cut, the bullock is free. Or "the cord" may be, in a wider sense, an image of slavery, as in ii. 3.

6. GRASS ON THE HOUSETOPS, easily springing up, but having no root. The flat roofs of the Eastern houses "are plastered with a composition of mortar, tar, ashes, and sand," in the crevices of which grass often springs. The houses of the poor in the country were formed of a plaster of mud and straw, where the grass would grow still more freely : as all the images are taken from country life, it is doubtless to country dwellings that the Poet refers. Comp. 2 Kings xix. 26 ; Is. xxxvii. 27.

7, 8. These two verses are a poetic expansion of the figure, an imaginative excursus, exactly parallel to that which occurs in ver. 4, 5, of the 127th Psalm. "The charm of the subject allures" the Poet in each instance.

The picture of the harvest-field is like that in Ruth ii. 4, where in like manner we have the greeting and counter-greeting. "And behold Boaz came from Bethlehem and said unto the reapers, Jehovah be with you. And they answered him, Jehovah bless thee."

[a] גַּם. According to Ew. § 354 *a*, in this and other passages, such as cxix. 24, Ezek. xvi. 28, Eccl. vi. 7, the particle is equivalent to the Greek ὅμως, *nevertheless*. Hupf. denies this, and argues that there is no need to depart from the usual signification in any case : thus here, "They have fought . . . they have not *also* prevailed." Comp. Gen. xxx. 8, xxxviii. 24, Job ii. 10.

[b] לְמַעֲנוֹתָם. So the K'thîbh, rightly, the word being plur. of מַעֲנָה, which occurs besides only in 1 Sam. xiv. 14. The לְ, marking the object, is not necessarily an Aramaism, though found more frequently in the later Psalms. Comp. lxix. 6, cxvi. 16. Here, however, the construction may be explained by the form of the verb as = "*have made length to* their furrows."

c שֶׁקַּדְמַת, a doubly Aramaic form; for (1) the relative שֶׁ belongs to the verb, *which withereth*, and (2) קַדְמַת occurs elsewhere only in Chald., Ezra v. 11, Dan. vi. 11, but not as here, immediately before a verb.

d שָׁלַף, *to draw out*, used of drawing out a weapon, &c., here impersonal for the passive, *before one pulls up*, i.e. *before it is pulled up*. So the LXX., Th., and the Quinta, πρὸ τοῦ ἐκσπασθῆναι, and so Gesen. *Thes. in v.*, Hupf., De W., &c. Others render *before it shoot up*, or *be grown* so as to blossom (the blossom coming out of the sheath, as it were). So according to Theodoret, some copies of the LXX. ἐξανθῆσαι, Aq. ἀνέθαλεν. But it is extremely doubtful whether שָׁלַף can be taken thus intransitively: no other instance of such usage has been alleged. Symm. has ἐκκαυλῆσαι, which may mean *has come to a stalk*, or perhaps be equivalent to ἐκκαυλίζειν, *root up*.

PSALM 130

THIS Psalm is a cry to God for the forgiveness of sin. The Psalmist pleads that he has long waited upon God, trusting in His word. Out of his own experience, he exhorts all Israel in like manner to hope, and wait, and look for God's mercy and redemption, which will assuredly be vouchsafed.

"When Luther, in the year 1530, was in the fortress of Coburg, on four occasions during the night there seemed to pass before his eyes burning torches, and this was followed by a severe headache. One night he saw three blazing torches come in at the window of his room, and he swooned away. His servant coming to his assistance, poured oil of almonds into his ear and rubbed his feet with hot napkins. As soon as he recovered, he bade him read to him a portion of the Epistle to the Galatians, and during the reading fell asleep. The danger was over, and when he awoke, he cried out joyfully: 'Come, to spite the devil, let us sing the Psalm *De profundis*, in four parts.'

"Being asked on one occasion which were the best Psalms, he replied, 'The Pauline Psalms' (*Psalmi Paulini*); and being pressed to say which they were, he answered: 'The 32d, the 51st, the 130th, and the 143d. For they teach us that the forgiveness of sins is vouchsafed to them that believe without the law and without works; therefore are they Pauline Psalms; and when David sings, "With Thee is forgiveness, that Thou mayest be feared," so Paul likewise saith, "God hath concluded all under sin, that He may have mercy

on all." Therefore none can boast of his own righteousness, but the words, "That Thou mayest be feared," thrust away all self-merit, teach us to take off our hat before God and confess, *gratia est non meritum, remissio non satisfactio*—it is all forgiveness, and no merit.'"
—*Delitzsch.*

This is the sixth of the seven Penitential Psalms, as they are called.

Delitzsch notices that several of the words and phrases of this Psalm occur also in Psalm lxxxvi., but there are few of them of a marked kind. It may be taken as evidence of the late date of the Psalm that the word rendered "attentive," ver. 2, occurs besides only in 2 Chron. vi. 40, vii. 15, and the word "forgiveness," ver. 4, only in Dan. ix. 9, Neh. ix. 17.

[A PILGRIM-SONG.]

1 OUT of the depths have I called upon Thee, O Jehovah!
2 Lord, hear my voice:
Let Thine ears be attentive to the voice of my supplications.

3 If Thou, O Jah, shouldest mark iniquities,
O Lord, who shall stand?
4 But with Thee is forgiveness,

1. OUT OF THE DEPTHS. Deep waters, as so often being an image of overwhelming affliction: comp. lxix. 2 [3], 14 [15]; Is. li. 10.

"Unde clamat?" says Augustine. "De profundo. Quis est ergo qui clamat? Peccator. Et qua spe clamat? Quia qui venit solvere peccata, dedit spem etiam in profundo posito peccatori. . . Clamat sub molibus et fluctibus iniquitatum suarum. Circumspexit se, circumspexit vitam suam; vidit illam undique flagitiis et facinoribus cooperatam: quacunque respexit, nihil in se bonum invenit, nihil illi justitiæ serenum potuit occurrere."

HAVE I CALLED, a strict perfect (not a present), as marking a long experience continued up to the present moment: comp. ver. 5.

2. LET THINE EARS BE ATTENTIVE. The same expression occurs 2 Chron. vi. 40.

3. MARK, lit. "keep," or "watch," so as to observe: the same word as in ver. 6, but used in the sense of *marking, observing*, Job x. 14, xiv. 16 (comp. for the sense Ps. xc. 8); and with the further sense of *keeping in memory*, i.e. in order to punish, Jer. iii. 5; Amos i. 11.

WHO SHALL (OR CAN) STAND? Comp. lxxvi. 7 [8]; Nah. i. 6; Mal. iii. 2. "Non dixit, ego non sustinebo; sed, *quis sustinebit?* Vidit enim prope totam vitam humanam circumlatrari peccatis suis, accusari omnes conscientias cogitationibus suis, non inveniri cor castum præsumens de sua justitia."—*Augustine.*

4. BUT, or rather FOR, the conjunction referring to what is *implied* in the previous verse. The sentiment expanded would be: "If Thou shouldest mark iniquities, none can stand: but Thou dost

That Thou mayest be feared.[a]

5 I have waited for Jehovah, my soul hath waited;
And in His word have I hoped.

not mark them, *for* with Thee is forgiveness."

FORGIVENESS, lit. "*the* forgiveness" (either the common use of the article before abstract nouns, or possibly with reference to something not expressed, *e.g.* "the forgiveness we need"). This noun occurs besides only in two later passages, Neh. ix. 17, Dan. ix. 9; and the adjective from the same root only in Ps. lxxxv. 5 [6]; but the verb occurs frequently, both in the Pentateuch and the later books.

THAT THOU MAYEST BE FEARED. God freely forgives sin, not that men may think lightly of sin, but that they may magnify His grace and mercy in its forgiveness, and so give Him the fear and the honour due unto His Name. So in xxv. 11, the Psalmist prays, "For Thy Name's sake pardon mine iniquity;" and lxxix. 9, "Purge away our sins for Thy Name's sake," *i.e.* that God's Name may be glorified as a God who pardoneth iniquity, transgression, and sin. This forgiveness is a far more powerful motive than any other to call forth holy fear and love and self-sacrifice. Luther says: "Why doth he add, 'That Thou mayest be feared?' . . . It is as if he should say, I have learned by experience, O Lord, why there is mercy with Thee, and why of right Thou mayest challenge this title unto Thyself, that Thou art merciful and forgivest sins. For in that Thou shuttest all under free mercy, and leavest nothing to the merits and works of men, therefore Thou art feared. But if all things were not placed in Thy mercy, and we could take away our sins by our own strength, no man would fear Thee, but the whole world would proudly contemn Thee. For daily experience shows that where there is not this knowledge of God's mercy, there men walk in a presumption of their own merits. . . . The true fear of God, the true worship, the true reverence, yea, the true knowledge of God, resteth on nothing but mercy, that through Christ we assuredly trust that God is reconciled unto us. . . Christian doctrine doth not deny or condemn good works, but it teacheth that God willeth not to mark iniquities, but willeth that we believe, that is, trust, His mercy. For with Him is forgiveness, that He may be feared and continue to be our God. Whoever, then, do believe that God is ready to forgive, and for Christ's sake to remit, sins, they render unto God true and reasonable service; they strive not with God about the law, works, and righteousness, but, laying aside all trust in themselves, do fear Him because of His mercy, and thus are made sons who receive the Holy Ghost, and begin truly to do the works of the law. So in these two lines, David sets forth to us the sum and substance of all Christian doctrine, and that Sun which giveth light to the Church."

5. I HAVE WAITED. This has been the attitude of soul in which God's mercy has come to me.

IN HIS WORD, on the ground of His promises I have claimed that mercy, and now my soul "is unto the Lord," that I may ever find fresh mercy, and grace for all my n ed. This waiting, hoping attitude is the attitude of a true heart, of one not easily discouraged, of one that says, "I will not let Thee go, except Thou bless me."

Luther, taking the verbs as presents, "I wait," &c. traces the connection somewhat differently. "The Psalmist," he observes, "first prays to be heard (ver. 2), then, obtaining mercy, he perceiveth that he is heard. Now, therefore, he addeth

6 My soul (looketh) for the Lord,
More than watchmen (look) for the morning,[b]
(I say, more than) watchmen (look) for the morning.

7 O Israel, hope in Jehovah;
For with Jehovah is loving-kindness,
And with Him is plenteous redemption.
8 And HE will redeem Israel
From all his iniquities.

an exhortation whereby he stirreth himself up constantly to persevere in this knowledge of grace. As if he had said, I know that there is mercy with the Lord. This principal article I have in some part now learned. Now this remaineth for me to do, to wait upon the Lord, that is, to trust in the Lord, that I may continue in this knowledge, and hold fast this hope of mercy for ever."

6. MY SOUL (LOOKETH) FOR, lit. "my soul is unto the Lord" (as in cxliii. 6, "my soul is unto Thee"), as the eyes of watchers through the long and weary night look eagerly for the first streaks of the coming day. Delitzsch quotes in illustration of the expression the words of Chr. A. Crusius on his death-bed, when lifting up his eyes and hands to heaven he exclaimed: "My soul is full of the grace of Jesus Christ, *my whole soul is unto God.*"

WATCHMEN, as in cxxvii. 1. The allusion here is probably to the night-watch of the Temple (see Introduction to Ps. cxxxiv.) anxiously expecting the moment when they would be released from their duties. But sentinels watching a city or an encampment might also be included in the term, and indeed all who, from whatever cause, are obliged to keep awake. No figure could more beautifully express the longing of the soul for the breaking of the day of God's loving mercy.

7. He has not been disappointed of his hope, and therefore he can bid Israel hope. "Here he hath respect," says Luther, "to that great conflict, wherein the mind, oppressed with calamities, beginneth to doubt of the mercy of God. In this conflict, because the mind doth not so soon feel those comforts which the word promiseth and faith believeth, as it would do, it is ready to despair. Against this temptation David armeth us, and warneth us to be mindful that we must wait upon the Lord, and never depart from the word or believe anything against the word, and he showeth the cause why. For with the Lord is mercy. . . . In myself I perceive nothing but wrath, in the devil nothing but hatred, in the world nothing but extreme fury and madness. But the Holy Ghost cannot lie, which willeth me to trust because there is mercy with the Lord, and with Him is plenteous redemption."

PLENTEOUS REDEMPTION, or more literally, "redemption plenteously" (the inf. absol. being used as an adverb). He calls it plenteous, as Luther says, because such is the straitness of our heart, the slenderness of our hopes, the weakness of our faith, that it far exceeds all our capacity, all our petitions and desires.

8. HE emphatic, He alone, for none other can.

FROM HIS INIQUITIES, not merely from the punishment (as Ewald and Hupfeld). The redemption includes the forgiveness of sins, the breaking of the power and dominion of sin, and the setting free from all the consequences of sin.

[a] לְמַעַן תִּוָּרֵא. The words seem to have been a stumbling-block to the Greek translators. The LXX. render as if it were לְמַעַן שִׁמְךָ, joining these words with what follows, ἕνεκεν τοῦ ὀνόματός σου ὑπέμεινά σε, Κύριε. Aq. Th., ἕνεκεν τοῦ φόβου. Symm., ἕνεκεν τοῦ νόμου (possibly taking *the fear* of Jehovah to be a name of the Law, as in xix. 10). Another has ἕνεκεν τοῦ γνωσθῆναι τὸν λόγον σου; and another ὅπως ἐπίφοβος ἔσῃ, this last alone being a rendering of the Hebrew. Jerome goes equally astray: "Quia tuum est propitiatio, *cum terribilis sis*, sustinui Dominum." The Fathers, of course following the Greek or the Vulgate, "propter legem tuam sustinui te, Domine," miss the whole scope of the passage.

[b] This is clearly the construction: "My soul is unto the Lord," Aq. ψυχή μου εἰς Κύριον. The construction in the E.V., "more than they that watch for the morning," is not supported by usage: שֹׁמֵר followed by לְ never means *to watch for*.

PSALM 131

WHETHER written by David, to whom the title gives it, or not, this short Psalm, one of the most beautiful in the whole Book, assuredly breathes David's spirit. A childlike simplicity, an unaffected humility, the honest expression of that humility as from a heart spreading itself out in conscious integrity before God—this is what we find in the Psalm, traits of a character like that of David. Delitzsch calls the Psalm an echo of David's answer to Michal, 2 Sam. vi. 22, "And I will become of still less account than this, and I will be lowly in mine own eyes." At the same time, with the majority of interpreters, he holds it to be a post-exile Psalm, written with a view to encourage the writer himself and his people to the same humility, the same patient waiting upon God, of which David was so striking an example.

"Few words, short lines, sober images, all conspire to place in striking relief that virtue which certainly was not a characteristic of the Jewish nation, but which has been sanctioned and consecrated by the Gospel."—*Reuss.*

[A PILGRIM-SONG. OF DAVID.]

1 JEHOVAH, my heart is not haughty,

1. "All virtues together," it has been said, "are a body whereof humility is the head." It is this chief crowning virtue to which the Poet lays claim; "for Jehovah hath respect unto the lowly," cxxxviii. 6,

Nor mine eyes lifted up:
Neither do I busy myself in things too great,[a]
And in things too wonderful for me.
2 But [b] I have stilled and hushed my soul;
As a weaned child with his mother,
As the weaned child [c] (I say) is my soul within me.

and "dwelleth with him that is of an humble spirit," Is. lvii. 15. The remarkable thing is that the Poet can assert his own lowliness without losing it. "To claim this virtue is as a rule to forfeit it, but David contrives to *claim humility with humility*. His words have no taint of pride in them;" they are not like the prayer of the Pharisee, God, I thank thee that I am not as other men are: there is no comparison with others. "We feel that he is alone with God; that he is showing God his heart as it really is; that he is virtually thanking God for the meek and quiet spirit which He has given."—Cox, *Pilgrim Psalms.*

MINE EYES LIFTED UP, as in xviii. 27 [28], ci. 5; therefore a Davidic expression. Pride has its seat in the heart, looks forth from the eyes, and expresses itself in the actions.

I BUSY MYSELF, lit. "walk," a common figure for the life and behaviour. The perfects denote strictly past action continued to the present moment (as in cxxx. 1, 5), and the intensive form of the verb (Piel), the busy, continual action.

TOO GREAT . . . TOO WONDERFUL, here probably in a practical sense, "I have not aimed at a position above me, involving duties and responsibilities too heavy for me." Though the lesson applies also to speculation on abstruse mysteries. He had not sought "for some great thing to do, or secret thing to know." Comp. for the phrase, Gen. xviii. 14, "Is anything too wonderful for Jehovah?" Deut. xvii. 8, "When a matter is too wonderful (too hard) for thee for judgement:" xxx. 11, "For this commandment . . . is not too wonderful for thee, it is not far off."

2. I HAVE STILLED MY SOUL, *i.e.* the pride and passions which were like the swelling waves of an angry sea. The word is used in Is. xxviii. 25, of *leveling* the ground after the clods have been broken by the plough. The E. V. uses "behaved" in the old sense of restraining, managing, as for instance in Shakespeare's *Timon of Ath.*, "He did behave his anger ere 'twas spent."

The next two clauses of the verse would be more exactly rendered:—

"As a weaned child *upon* his mother"

(*i.e.* as he lies resting upon his mother's bosom);

"As the weaned child (I say), lies
my soul upon me."

The figure is graceful, touching, original, beautifully expressive of the humility of a soul chastened by disappointment. It expresses both the cost at which he gained rest, for the child is not weaned without much pain and strife, and also the purity and unselfishness of the rest he gained. As the weaned child when its first fretfulness and uneasiness are past no longer cries, and frets, and longs for the breast, but lies still and is content, because it is with its mother; so my soul is weaned from all discontented thoughts, from all fretful desires for earthly good, waiting in stillness upon God, finding its satisfaction in His presence, resting peacefully in His arms.

"The weaned child," writes a mother, with reference to this passage, "has for the first time

3 O Israel, hope in Jehovah,
From henceforth even for ever.

become *conscious of grief*. The piteous longing for the sweet nourishment of his life, the broken sob of disappointment, mark the trouble of his innocent heart: it is not so much the *bodily* suffering; he has felt that pain before, and cried while it lasted; but now his *joy and comfort are taken away*, and he knows not why. When his head is once more laid on his mother's bosom, then he trusts and loves and rests, but he has learned the first lesson of humility, he is cast down, and clings with fond helplessness to his one friend."

At a time when the devices of our modern civilization are fast tending to obliterate the beauty of this figure, mothers no longer doing their duty by their children, it seems the more necessary to draw attention to it.

3. Prayer, as at the close of the last Psalm, that the experience of the individual may become the experience of the nation, that they too may learn to lie still, and trust, and wait, in that hope which, like faith and love, abideth for ever (1 Cor. xiii. 13).

[a] It is doubtful whether the comparison מִמֶּנִּי belong to both the adjectives. Perhaps the rendering of the E.V. "in great things, and in things too wonderful" is to be preferred.

[b] אִם לֹא, not conditional, with the apodosis beginning at כְּגָמֻל, nor interrogative, as if = הֲלֹא, but either an asseveration, *surely* (commonly so used after words of swearing, but also without the adjuration, Num. xiv. 35, Is. v. 9, and often in Job), or serving to introduce an opposition to what precedes, as in Gen. xxiv. 38, Jer. xxii. 6, Ezek. iii. 6; but even in these instances, the force of the particles is rather that of emphatic assertion than of mere opposition. "God do so to me, *if* I do *not* this or that," is the formula always implied in their use.

[c] כַּגָּמֻל. The article is clearly the article of reference, *i.e.* it resumes the word in the previous line: "As *a* weaned child . . . as *the* weaned child, I say." And this resumption of the previous expression is in entire accordance with the common rhythmical structure of so many of these Pilgrim-Songs. Hupf. most unnecessarily takes the double כְּ as correlative, and explains, "*As* a weaned child, *so* is that which is weaned in me, viz. my soul." There is, I think, a designed parallel in the use of the prep. עַל in the two lines (though Del. denies this): As the weaned child lies *upon* its mother's breast, so my soul lies *upon* me; the soul being for the moment regarded as separate from the man, as that part which is the seat of the affections, passions, &c.

PSALM 132

THIS Psalm is a prayer that God's promises made to David may not fail of fulfilment, that He will dwell for ever in the habitation which He chose for Himself in Zion, and that the children of David may for ever sit upon his throne. It opens with a recital of David's efforts to bring the Ark to its resting-place; it ends with a recital of the promises made to David and to his seed.

There has been much difference of opinion as to the occasion for which the Psalm was written.

1. The majority of the ancient interpreters regard it as a prayer of David's, either at the consecration of the Tabernacle after the removal of the Ark thither, or at the time when he formed the design of building the Temple, and received in consequence the promise in 2 Sam. vii., or at the dedication of Araunah's threshing-floor, 2 Sam. xxiv. But the petition in ver. 10, "For Thy servant David's sake, turn not away the face of Thine Anointed," does not seem natural in the mouth of David. In the mouth of one of his descendants, whose confidence and hope rested on the promise made to his ancestor, and who could plead David's faithfulness to the covenant, such a petition becomes much more intelligible. In any case, it is clear that the Psalm could not have been composed till after the promise had been given to David in 2 Sam. vii., to which it contains a distinct reference, and therefore was not intended to be sung at the consecration of the Tabernacle on Mount Zion.

2. Others, with more probability, have thought that the Psalm was written in commemoration of the completion and dedication of the Temple, either by Solomon himself, or by some Poet of his time. On such a view, this ode is seen to be harmonious and consistent throughout. It is perfectly natural that Solomon, or a Poet of his age writing a song for such an occasion, should recur to the earlier efforts made by his father to prepare a habitation for Jehovah. On the completion of the work, his thoughts would inevitably revert to all the steps which had led to its accomplishment. It is no less natural that at such a time the promise given to David should seem doubly precious, that it should be clothed with a new interest, a fresh significance, when David's son sat upon his throne, and when the auspicious opening of his reign might itself be hailed as a fulfilment of the promise. It is, moreover, in favour of this view that ver. 8—10

of the Psalm form, with one slight variation, the conclusion of Solomon's prayer at the dedication of the Temple, according to the version of that prayer given in the Chronicles (2 Chron. vi. 41, 42).*

3. Many of the more recent expositors, starting with the prejudice that all these Pilgrim Songs belong to a period subsequent to the Exile, suppose the Psalm to have been written for the dedication of the Second Temple, or in order to encourage Zerubbabel, the chief representative at the time of David's family, "whose spirit God had stirred to go up to build the house of the Lord" (Ezra i. 5). But the title of "the Anointed" would hardly have been given to Zerubbabel. He never sat on the throne. The crowns which Zechariah was directed to make were to be placed not on the head of Zerubbabel, but on the head of Joshua, the son of Josedech, the high priest: the sovereignty was to be with him; "he shall bear the glory, and shall sit and rule upon his throne" (Zech. vi. 10—13). It is possible, of course, that a Poet in these later times might have transported himself in imagination into the times of David, and that his words might borrow their colouring and glow from the brighter period which inspired his song. Yet it is hardly probable that there should have been no allusion to the existing depression of David's house, no lamentation over its fallen fortunes, as in Ps. lxxxix. for instance, no hint of any contrast between its past and its present condition.† Such entire sinking of the present in the past is hardly conceivable.

Still less probable does it appear to me, that some prince of the House of David, at a still later period of the history, should be the Anointed of the Psalm, or that it is to be brought down to the age of the Maccabees.

---

* It is at least evidence that the compiler of the Book supposed the Psalm to have been written with reference to that event. The passage does not occur at all in Solomon's prayer as given in 1 Kings viii. This, of itself, makes it probable that the Chronicler borrows from the Psalmist, not the Psalmist from the Chronicler. Besides, the variations in the Chronicles are such as would be made in changing poetry into prose, especially the *explanation* given of ver. 10 in the Psalm: "Remember the mercies of David Thy servant." We have already seen, in the Introduction to Ps. cv., that the writer of that book allows himself some liberty in quoting from the Psalms.

† I confess I can see no indication in the Psalm of any such contrast, though it has been assumed by many interpreters, both ancient and modern. The mention of the Ark does not prove that the Psalm was not intended for the dedication of the Second Temple, for although it may be inferred from Josephus (*Bell. Jud.* v. § v. 5), and from the Mishnah (*Yoma*, v. 2)—where we are told that the place of the Ark was an altar-stone three fingers' height above the ground, on which the High Priest placed the censers on the Day of Atonement—that the Ark had perished in the destruction of the First Temple, still the exiles might have used, without changing them, the words which were sung at Solomon's dedication.

Reuss argues for the later date. He contends that the Anointed (ver. 17) is one of the priest-princes of the post-exile history, and that the *diadem* (ver. 18) is the distinctive mark of the spiritual chief, representing the theocratic power (Ex. xxix. 6, &c.) before it became the mark of royalty. He is right, I believe, in saying that the main and dominant thought of the Psalm is to be found in the last strophe, the fulfilment, namely, of the promise and the oath to David, the first two strophes being merely the historical prelude clothed in the forms of poetry. No doubt we have "a poetic ideal, and not a simple narrative in exact conformity with history." But neither this fact, nor the other arguments which Reuss has adduced, satisfy me that he is right in his inference as to the age of the Psalm.

4. It may be mentioned that Origen, Theodoret, and some other of the Greek fathers, hold the Psalm to be a prayer of the exiles in Babylon, longing for the rebuilding of the Temple, and the restoration of David's dynasty.

5. Finally, Maurer would refer the Psalm to the time of Josiah, and conjectures that it may have been written after the reformation which he introduced in accordance with the law of Moses.

The Psalm consists of three strophes. The first, ver. 1—5, is a grateful acknowledgment of the completion of the Temple, the crowning of the purpose which had been in David's heart. The second, ver. 6—10, traces briefly the history of the Ark and its wanderings, till it was brought to its final resting-place in the Temple, and recalls the prayer which was uttered on the occasion. The third, ver. 11—18, is virtually the Divine answer to the prayer, and echoes each petition, only that the answer is larger.

[A PILGRIM-SONG.]

1 O JEHOVAH, remember for David
All his anxious cares;

1. REMEMBER, *i.e.* so as to fulfil Thy promise made to him: comp. 2 Chron. vi. 42.

FOR DAVID. "The Temple was built in David's heart before it was built by Solomon's hands; and Solomon asks, not that *his* toil may be accepted, but that his father's devotion may be remembered." —Cox, *Pilgrim Psalms*, p. 271.

ALL HIS ANXIOUS CARES, lit. "all his being afflicted" (the infin. Pual used as a noun). See the same word cxix. 71; Is. liii. 4. David had *tormented* himself with his anxiety to prepare a suitable earthly dwelling-place for Jehovah. First, the building of the Tabernacle on Mount Zion, and the solemn bringing up of the Ark there, had engaged his thoughts. The prayer in ci. 2, "O when wilt Thou come unto me?" is the best comment on David's *afflictions* and *anxious cares* till his purpose was accomplished. In contrast with this, he says himself, "We did not seek it (did not trouble ourselves about it) in the day of Saul," 1 Chron. xiii. 3. Next, if we suppose the Psalm to

2 How he sware unto Jehovah,
(And) vowed to the Mighty One of Jacob:
3 " I will not come into the tent of my house,
I will not go up to the couch of my bed,
4 I will not give sleep [a] to mine eyes,
Nor slumber to my eyelids,
5 Until I find a place for Jehovah,
A dwelling for the Mighty One of Jacob."
6 Lo, we heard of it in Ephrathah,

take a wider range, there may also be included in these "anxious cares" his earnest desire to build the Temple, and the great preparations which he made with that object, by collecting the materials, furnishing the design to his son, and making provision for the service and worship of God on a scale of unexampled magnificence.

2. HOW HE SWARE, lit. "who sware."

MIGHTY ONE OF JACOB. This name of God (repeated in ver. 5) occurs first in Gen. xlix. 24, in the mouth of the dying Jacob. It is found besides only in three passages: in Is. i. 24 ("Mighty One of *Israel*"), xlix. 26, lx. 16. "Jacob is mentioned here for two reasons: (1) because he is the first-mentioned of those who *vowed*, and (2) for his having erected a *pillar* for a *House of God:* comp. v. 5."

3. TENT OF MY HOUSE, *i.e.* "the tent which is my house" (as in the next clause, "the couch which is my bed"), a good instance of the way in which the associations of the old patriarchal tent life fixed themselves in the language of the people.

4. SLEEP TO MINE EYES. See the same proverbial expression, Prov. vi. 4.

5. A DWELLING, lit. "dwellings;" but see on the plur. lxxxiv. 1. This has been referred (1) to David's intention of building the Temple, 2 Sam. vii., and the preparatory consecration of the threshing-floor of Araunah, 2 Sam. xxiv.; (2) to the placing the Ark in a *fixed* abode on Zion, after its many wanderings: comp. lxxviii. 68, 69. The latter is the more probable.

6. This verse is extremely obscure, but it seems at any rate to describe in some way the accomplishment of David's purpose. There are three principal points in it to be considered :—

(1) To what does the feminine pronoun "it," which is the object of the two verbs "heard," "found," refer? Either (*a*) it is an indefinite neuter, "We heard of *the matter*," or as Bunsen more precisely explains, "We heard it, viz. the joyful cry in ver. 7, Let us go to the Temple on Zion." The objection to taking the pronoun in this way is, that the second verb, "we found," is not very suitable on either explanation. Or (*b*) the pronoun refers to the Ark, which has already been tacitly brought before us in ver. 5 (where "a dwelling for *Jehovah*" is a dwelling for the *Ark*, as the symbol of His presence), and is expressly mentioned in ver. 7. The noun is fem. as well as masc., and, by a not uncommon Hebrew usage, the pronoun anticipates the mention of the object to which it points. G. Bauer (in a note to De Wette) objects that Hebrew usage will not allow of the rendering "We heard *of* it," and that the only proper translation is "We heard it," viz. the rumour. But in Jer. xlvi. 12, we have the

We found it in the field of the wood :[b]

same construction (the verb with the accus.), "The nations have heard of thy shame."

(2) In the use of the verbs "heard" . . . "found" is the parallelism synonymous or antithetical? Do they describe two parts of the same action, "We heard it was, &c. and there we found it"? or do they mark two distinct and opposed actions, "We heard it was in one place, we found it in another"? The answer to this question must depend on the interpretation we give to the proper names which follow.

(3) What are we to understand by Ephrathah and "the field of the wood"?

(*A*) To take the latter expression first. This may be either an appellative or a proper name. In the last case it may be rendered, "fields of Jaar," *Jaar* being a shortened form of Kirjath-*Jearim*, "the city of woods," for Jearim, "woods," is only the plural of Jaar, "wood." The name of this city, as it happens, appears in a variety of different forms; in Jer. xxvi. 20, as Kirjath-hajearim (*i.e.* with the article) and apocopated, Kirjath-'arim, Ezra ii. 25 (comp. Josh. xviii. 28); it is also called Kirjath-baal, Josh. xv. 60, and Baalah, xv. 9, 1 Chron. xiii. 6 (comp. Josh. xv. 10, "the mountain of Jearim," with 11, "the mountain of Baalah"); and apparently Baale-judah, 2 Sam. vi. 2. There is no reason why, poetically, it should not be called Jaar; and when we further remember that the Ark, after having been captured by the Philistines and restored by them, remained for twenty years at Kirjath-jearim (1 Sam. vii. 2), it is at least probable that, in a passage which speaks of the removal of the Ark to Zion, there may be some allusion to the place of its previous sojourn.

(*B*) Ephrathah, as the name of a place, only occurs elsewhere as the ancient name of Bethlehem, Gen. xxxv. 16, 19, xlviii. 7; Ruth iv. 11. In Micah v. 2 [1], the two names are united, Bethlehem-Ephrathah. Hengstenberg maintains that the usage is the same here, "We, being in Bethlehem, heard." There, he says, David spent his youth while as yet he had only heard of the Ark of the covenant. It was known only by hearsay, no one went to see it, it was almost out of mind; comp. Job xlii. 5; Ps. xviii. 44, 45 (and David's words in 1 Chron. xiii. 3). But the pronoun "we" must surely refer, not to David, but to the people at large. And besides, although the construction "We in Bethlehem heard it" may possibly be defended by Matt. ii. 2, "We in the East saw His Star," yet here the parallelism seems rather to require the sense, "We heard that it was at Ephrathah, we found it at Kirjath-jearim." [Reuss recently takes the same view: "It was at Ephratah, *i.e.* Bethlehem, where they lived, that they heard of his project. It was at Ja'ar, *i.e.* Qiryat-Ie'arim, that they found the holy Ark."]

Other explanations have accordingly been given of the name.

(*a*) Although *Ephrathah* is only an ancient name for Bethlehem, yet since Ephrathite as frequently denotes an Ephraimite as a Bethlehemite, so it is possible that Ephrathah here may be a name for Ephraim. In that case, the allusion is to the first resting-place of the Ark in Shiloh, which was the capital of Ephraim: "We *heard* in ancient story that the Ark was placed in Shiloh; we *found* it, when at last it was to be removed to its new abode, at Kirjath-jearim." The word *found* would naturally suggest the many vicissitudes and wanderings of the Ark in the interval.

(β) It has been supposed that Ephrathah is not a proper name, but denotes, in accordance with its etymology, *the fruitful land*, by way of contrast with the *fields of the wood*, i.e. the forest district; the former denoting the southern part

7 " Let us come into His dwelling,
Let us bow ourselves before His footstool.
8 Arise, O Jehovah, into Thy resting-place,

of Palestine, as the more cultivated, the latter the northern, and especially the woody ranges of Lebanon. Thus the whole land would be poetically summed up under the two heads of the fertile and the woody regions, and the meaning would be, " From all parts of the land we flocked at the summons of our king, to bring up the holy Ark to its dwelling-place in Zion." In this case, the verbs "heard" . . . "found" cannot be taken as describing different and contrasted acts, but as referring to one and the same event.

(γ) Ephrathah has been conjectured (also with reference to its etymological meaning of "the *fruitful* country") to be a name for Beth-shemesh, the spot where the Ark was first deposited by the Philistines, and whence it was subsequently removed to "the fields of the wood," *i.e.* Kirjath-jearim. According to this interpretation, which is that of Hupfeld, the verse would mean,

"We heard that the Ark was brought
to Beth-shemesh first,
We found it at Kirjath-jearim."

(δ) Lastly, Delitzsch identifies Ephrathah with the district about Kirjath-jearim, and on these grounds: Caleb had by Ephrath, his third wife, a son named Hur (1 Chron. ii. 19). By the descendants of this Hur Bethlehem was peopled (1 Chron. iv. 4); and from Shobal, a son of this Hur, the inhabitants of Kirjath-jearim were descended (2 Chron. ii. 50). Kirjath-jearim then is, as it were, a daughter of Bethlehem. Bethlehem was originally called Ephrathah, and this latter name was afterwards given to the district about Bethlehem, whence in Micah v. 2 [1] we find the compound name Bethlehem-Ephrathah. Kirjath-jearim belonged to Caleb-Ephrathah (1 Chron. ii. 24), which is probably to be distinguished as the northern part of the territory from Negeb Caleb, "the south of Caleb" (1 Sam. xxx. 14).

On the whole, whichever interpretation we adopt, the general scope of the passage seems to be: Remember Thy servant David, remember all his efforts to build Thee an habitation for Thy Name; he gave himself no rest till he had brought the Ark to Zion. We heard where the Ark was, we went to fetch it, saying one to another as we brought it to its new abode, "Let us come into His dwelling," &c. And now, by the memory of David, by the memory of Thy covenant with him and his faithfulness to that covenant, we plead with Thee. Reject not the prayer of our king who is David's son, grant him the request of his lips, fulfil all his desires. (Comp. xx. 1—4.)

The Poet by what is scarcely a figure of speech identifies himself and his contemporaries with the generation of David. In the time of Solomon, many would be living who had taken part in the ceremonies attending the removal of the Ark of Zion. Reuss, who brings the Psalm down to Maccabean times, remarks: "The Jews, eight centuries later, say: *We* found the Ark at Qiryat-Ie'arim, just as Frenchmen of to-day might say, *We* gained the battle of Bouvines."

7. HIS DWELLING, or "tabernacle," the house which David calls "curtains," 2 Sam. vii. 2, purposely repeated from ver. 5. On the plural form of the word see on lxxxiv. 1.

HIS FOOTSTOOL. See on xcix 5.

8. As in ver. 7 we have the expression of the feelings of the congregation in David's time, so in ver. 8 there may be a transition to

Thou, and the Ark of Thy strength.
9 Let Thy priests be clothed with righteousness,
And let Thy saints shout for joy.
10 For Thy servant David's sake,
Turn not away the face of Thine Anointed."

11 Jehovah hath sworn unto David,
It is truth,[c] He will not depart from it,—
"Of the fruit of thy body will I set upon thy throne.
12 If thy sons will keep My covenant,
And My testimony [d] that I shall teach them,

the language of the people in Solomon's time. To the Poet's thoughts the congregation is one, and the utterance of their feelings is one. He blends together the song which was raised when the Ark was carried up to Zion, with the song which was raised when it was again moved from Zion to its final resting-place in the Temple, 2 Chron. v. 2—5, vi. 41.

ARISE. The words are taken from the old battle-cry of the nation, when the Ark set forward, "to search out *a resting-place* for them" (Numb. x. 33—36). Comp. Ps. lxvii. 1 [2].

ARK OF THY STRENGTH. The only place in the Psalms where the Ark is mentioned. The designation occurs only here and in 2 Chron. vi. 41.

9. LET THY PRIESTS. The blessing of God's presence in its effects both upon the priests and the people.

RIGHTEOUSNESS. In the promise, ver. 16, which corresponds to this prayer, SALVATION is the equivalent word: see on lxxi. 15.

SAINTS, or "beloved," as also in ver. 16. See on xvi. 10. From this verse are taken the petitions in our Liturgy: "Endue Thy ministers with righteousness. And make Thy chosen people joyful."

10. TURN NOT AWAY THE FACE, *i.e.* refuse not the prayer. See the same phrase 1 Kings ii. 16, 17, 20; 2 Kings xviii. 24, where the E.V. renders "deny me not, say me not nay."

THINE ANOINTED. This cannot be David (as Hengst., Hupf., and others). It would be extremely harsh to say, "For David's sake refuse not the prayer of David." Obviously the Anointed here must be Solomon (or some one of David's descendants), who pleads David, and the promises made to David, as a reason why his prayer should not be rejected. In 2 Chron. vi. 42, the verse stands somewhat differently: "O Jehovah God, turn not away the face of Thine Anointed: remember the loving-kindnesses of David Thy servant." The last clause most probably means, "Thy loving-kindnesses *to* David," but others render "the goodness or piety of David Thy servant," the meaning of the Hebrew word *chesed* being ambiguous. The prayer is a prayer for the fulfilment of the promise. Hence the promise is quoted, ver. 11, 12. Others suppose that the subject of the prayer is to be found in ver. 8, 9.

11. HATH SWORN . . . WILL NOT DEPART, marking the unchangeableness of the promise, as is cx. 4, "Jehovah hath sworn and will not repent." Comp. lxxxix. 34—37 [35—38]. The substance of the promise follows, as given in 2 Sam. vii.

Their sons also for evermore
Shall sit upon thy throne."
13 For Jehovah hath chosen Zion,
He hath desired it as an abode for Himself.
14 This is My resting-place for evermore,
Here will I abide, for I have desired it.
15 I will abundantly bless her provision,
Her poor I will satisfy with bread.
16 Her priests also will I clothe with salvation,
And her saints shall shout aloud for joy.
17 There will I make the horn of David to bud,
I have prepared a lamp for Mine Anointed.
18 His enemies will I clothe with shame,
But upon himself shall his crown shine.

13. The choosing of Zion as the seat of the sanctuary is mentioned as being closely and intimately connected with the choosing of David as King, and the tribe of Judah as the ruling tribe. The connection is: Jehovah has given the sovereignty to David and to David's house; *for* He hath chosen Zion to be His own dwelling-place. The religious centre and political centre of the people are one and the same: exactly as in cxxii. 4, 5. Comp. lxxviii. 67—71. "He chose the tribe of Judah, the Mount Zion which he loved . . . He chose David also His servant," &c.

14. The answer to the petition in verse 8. MY RESTING-PLACE. Shiloh had been abandoned; for a time the Ark was at Bethel, Jud. xx. 27; then at Mizpah, Jud. xxi. 5; afterwards, for twenty years, at Kirjath-jearim, 1 Sam. vii. 2; and then for three months in the house of Obed-Edom, before it was finally brought to its last resting-place.

16. The answer to the petition in ver. 9.

17. The answer to the petition in ver. 10. MAKE THE HORN . . . TO BUD. Giving ever new strength to his house and victory over all ene mies. See on lxxv. 5 [6], and comp. Ezek. xxix. 21.

We might render "I will make an horn to bud for David," (as in ver. 1 "remember for David,") but "David" is here put for the house of David, and therefore the rendering in the text is perhaps preferable.

A LAMP. See on xviii. 28 [29]. Comp. 1 Kings xi. 36, "And unto his son will I give one tribe, that David My servant may have a lamp always before Me in Jerusalem, the city which I have chosen Me to put My Name there."

18. SHINE, lit. "blossom." On the etymological connection between the two ideas, see Gesenius, *Thes. in v.*

[a] שְׁנָת for שֵׁנָה. Hupf. correctly explains this as apocopated from the fuller form שְׁנָתִי, like זִמְרָת, נַחֲלָת (see on xvi. note [k]), as he says is plain from the rejection of the first vowel, which cannot otherwise be explained. Del., following Ewald (*Lehrb.* § 173 *d*), regards the termination as Aramaic. תְּנוּמָה, he observes, is always said of the *eyelids*, Gen. xxxi. 40, Prov. vi. 4.

Eccl. viii. 16, never of the *eyes*, and this distinction is carefully maintained even in the post-biblical T'phillah style; but the word only occurs in one passage which he quotes, Prov. vi. 4, and this is the only place where it is found with the word *eyelids*.

[b] שְׂדֵי. This may be the construct state *singular*, from the poetic form שָׂדַי; and except the LXX. (ἐν τοῖς πεδίοις) most of the ancient Versions have the sing. Aq. and Sym. ἐν χώρᾳ, with which Kay compares the ἐν τῇ χώρᾳ used of the same locality in Luke ii. 8. The Quinta ἐν ἀγρῷ. Jer. *in regione*.

[c] אֱמֶת. This is not the object of the verb נִשְׁבַּע, "He hath sworn a faithful oath." Del. makes it an adverbial accus., and claims the support of the accents, the *Pazer* (distinctive) marking the close of the first member of the verse. But it is better to take אֱמֶת independently, as standing at the beginning of a parenthetical clause: "It (*i.e.* the oath) is truth, He will not depart from it."

[d] עֵדֹתִי, either sing. for עֵדוּתִי, like תַּחֲנֹתִי for תַּחֲנוּתִי, 2 Kings vi. 8, or plur. with the suffix of the singular, as for instance Deut. xxviii. 59, Ges. § 89, 3.

PSALM 133

HERDER says of this exquisite little song, that "it has the fragrance of a lovely rose." Nowhere has the nature of true unity—that unity which binds men together, not by artificial restraints, but as brethren of one heart—been more faithfully described, nowhere has it been so gracefully illustrated, as in this short Ode. True concord is, we are here taught, a holy thing, a sacred oil, a rich perfume which, flowing down from the head to the beard, from the beard to the garment, sanctifies the whole body. It is a sweet morning dew, which lights not only on the lofty mountain-peaks, but on the lesser hills, embracing all, and refreshing all with its influence.

The title of the Psalm gives it to David. Hence it has been conjectured that it may refer to the circumstances attending his coronation at Hebron, when, after eight years of civil war, "all the tribes of Israel," laying aside their mutual animosities, came to David unto Hebron, and spake, saying, "Behold, we are thy bone and thy flesh" (2 Sam. v. 1). The picture of a united nation is given still more vividly in the narrative of the Chronicles: "All these men of war that could keep rank came with a perfect heart to Hebron, to make David king over all Israel: and all the rest also of Israel were of one heart to make David king. And there they were with David three days eating and drinking; for their brethren had prepared for them. Moreover, they that were nigh them, even unto Issachar, and Zebulun, and Naphtali, brought bread on asses, and on camels, and on mules, and on oxen, and meat, meal, cakes of figs, and bunches of raisins, and wine, and oil, and oxen, and sheep abundantly: for there was joy in Israel." (1 Chron. xii. 38—40.)

Others have supposed, that the Psalm was suggested by the sight of the multitudes who came up from all parts of Palestine to be present at the great national Feasts in Jerusalem.

Again, others, and perhaps the majority of commentators, refer the Psalm to the time of the return from the Captivity, when, there being no longer any division of the kingdom, the jealousies of the tribes had ceased, and all who returned, of whatever tribe, were incorporated in one state. That at this time there was a real unity of heart and mind in the nation may be inferred from the narratives in Ezra and Nehemiah. Thus, for instance, we read in Ezra iii. 1, that "when the seventh month was come, and the children of Israel were in the cities, the people gathered themselves together *as one man* to Jerusalem." And in Nehem. viii. 1: "And all the people gathered themselves together *as one man* into the street that was before the Water Gate, and they spake unto Ezra the scribe to bring the book of the Law of Moses, which the Lord had commanded to Israel."

But in truth there is not a syllable in the Psalm which can lead us to any conclusion respecting its date. Such a vision of the blessedness of unity may have charmed the Poet's heart and inspired the Poet's song at any period of the national history. And his words, though originally, no doubt, intended to apply to a state, would be equally true of a smaller circle, a family, or a tribe.

[A PILGRIM SONG. OF DAVID.]

1 BEHOLD how good and how pleasant (it is)
For brethren to dwell together (in unity).

1 BEHOLD draws attention to an important truth. Augustine says of this first verse, that the very sound of it is so sweet that it was chanted even by persons who knew nothing of the rest of the Psalter. He also says that this verse gave birth to monasteries: it was like a trumpet-call to those who wished to dwell together as *brethren* (*fratres* or friars).

FOR BRETHREN TO DWELL TOGETHER. The exact force of the Hebrew is, "for them who are brethren *also* to dwell together, *i.e.* that those who are of one race and

2 It is like the precious oil upon the head,
Which descended upon the beard, (even) Aaron's beard,

one stock should live in peace and harmony together as living members of the same body, filled with the same spirit, seeking, in mutual forbearance and sympathy, the same ends."

2. The first figure is taken from the oil which was poured on the head of the High Priest at his consecration (Ex. xxix. 7; Lev. viii. 12, xxi. 10). The point of the comparison does not lie in the *preciousness* of the oil, or in its *all-pervading fragrance;* but in this, that being poured on the head, it did not rest there, but flowed to the beard, and descended even to the garments, and thus, as it were, consecrated the whole body in all its parts. *All the members participate in the same blessing.* Comp. 1 Cor. xii. This is the point of the comparison. Other thoughts may be suggested by it, as that the spirit of concord, both in a state and in a family, will descend from those who govern to those who are governed; or again, that concord is a holy thing, like the holy oil, or that it is sweet and fragrant, like the fragrant oil; but these are mere accessories of the image, not that which suggested its use. If, as is commonly assumed, the point of comparison lay in the all-pervading fragrance of the oil, the addition to the figure, "which descended upon *the beard* . . . which descended to the *edge of his garments*," would be thrown away. But understand this as typifying the consecration of *the whole man*, and the extension of the figure at once becomes appropriate and full of meaning. Luther remarks: "In that he saith 'from the head,' he showeth the nature of true concord. For, like as the ointment ran down from the head of Aaron the High Priest upon his beard, and so descended unto the borders of his garment, even so true concord in doctrine and brotherly love floweth as a precious ointment, by the unity of the Spirit, from Christ the High Priest and Head of the Church, unto all the members of the same. For by the beard and extreme parts of the garment he signifieth, that as far as the Church reacheth, so far spreadeth the unity which floweth from Christ her Head."

THE PRECIOUS OIL, lit. "the good oil," *i.e.* the sacred oil, for the preparation of which special directions were given, and which was to be devoted exclusively to the consecration of holy things and persons, Ex. xxx. 22—23. Hence the image implies not only that the whole body is united, but that the whole body is *consecrated.*

AARON, named not because he only was thus anointed, but as the representative of all priestly anointing: see Ex. xxviii. 41, xxx. 30, xl. 15.

WHICH DESCENDED. I have followed the Hebrew in retaining the same word in the three successive lines. The LXX. have throughout καταβαίνειν, Jerome and the Vulg. *descendere.* In the second line, "Which descended to the edge of his garments," there is considerable doubt to what the relative refers. Is it *the oil* (as in the previous line), or is it *the beard*, which descends to the edge of the garments? Some of the recent interpreters understand it of *the beard*, as a kind of connecting link between the head and the garments: the oil descended on the beard, the beard touched the garments, and so imparted to them the sanctification which it had itself received from the oil (so De W., Stier, Hengst., Del., Hupf.). But the other interpretation, which has the support of all the ancient Versions, and the majority of interpreters, is certainly to be preferred, and is even required by the rhythmical structure of the Psalm. We have here, as in so many of the Pilgrim

Which descended to the edge of his garments;
3 Like the dew of Hermon which descended upon the mountains of Zion;
For there Jehovah commanded the blessing,
(Even) life for evermore.

Songs, the repetition of the same word in connection with the same subject. See the repetition of the word "keep" in cxxi., and the same rhythmical figure in cxxiii. 3, 4, cxxiv. 1, 3, 4, &c.

EDGE, or rather "collar," lit. "mouth," "opening," as the mouth of a sack. The word is used Ex. xxviii. 32, xxxix. 23, of the opening at the top of the robe of the ephod. The image does not represent the oil as descending to the skirts, the lower edge of the garment. It is enough that it touch the robe to sanctify it. [According to the Law, the garments of the priests were sprinkled with the holy oil, Ex. xxix. 21; Lev. xiii. 30.]

3. The second image expressive of the blessing of brotherly concord is taken from the dew. Here again it is not the *refreshing* nature of the dew, nor its *gentle*, *all-pervading* influence, which is the prominent feature. That which renders it to the Poet's eye so striking an image of brotherly concord, is the fact that *it falls alike on both mountains:* that the same dew which descends on the lofty Hermon descends also on the humbler Zion. High and low drink in the same sweet refreshment. Thus the image is exactly parallel to the last; the oil descends from the head to the beard, the dew from the higher mountain to the lower. (Hermon in the north, and Zion in the south, may also further suggest the union of the northern and southern tribes.) Luther says: "Whereas the mountains often seem, to those that behold them afar off, to reach up even unto heaven; the dew which cometh from heaven seemeth to fall from the high mountains unto the hills which are under them. Therefore he saith that the dew descendeth from Hermon unto Mount Zion, because it so seemeth unto those that do behold it afar off. And this clause, after my judgement, pertaineth to civil concord, like as the former similitude pertaineth to the Church, because God through peace and concord maketh commonwealths and kingdoms to flourish; even as seeds, herbs, and plants are fresh and flourish through the morning dew. The beginning of this peace cometh from the princes and magistrates, as from Mount Hermon: from whom it floweth unto every particular person, and to the whole commonwealth, which is refreshed thereby."

THERE. In Zion the blessed fruits of this brotherly concord may chiefly be looked for, for Jehovah Himself has made it the great centre of all blessing and all life.

This last verse lends some colour to the view, that the Psalm was intended to be sung at the gathering of the tribes for the great national Feasts. Comp. cxxviii. 6, cxxxiv. 4.

The similitude of the dew has taken shape in a legend.

An old pilgrim narrates, that every morning at sunrise a handful of dew floated down from the summit of Hermon, and deposited itself upon the Church of St. Mary, where it was immediately gathered up by Christian leeches, and was found a sovereign remedy for all diseases: it was of this dew, he declares, that David spoke prophetically in this Psalm.—*Itinerary of St. Anthony.*

PSALM 134

"THREE things are clear with regard to this Psalm," says Delitzsch. "First, that it consists of a greeting, ver. 1, 2, and a reply, ver. 3. Next, that the greeting is addressed to those Priests and Levites who had the night-watch in the Temple. Lastly, that this Psalm is purposely placed at the end of the collection of Pilgrim Songs in order to take the place of a final blessing."

That the address is not to any persons in the habit of frequenting the Temple is evident, because it was only in rare and exceptional cases (Luke ii. 37) that such persons could be found in the Temple at night. And, further, the word "stand" in ver. 1. is the common word to express the service of the Priests and Levites, who had their duties by night as well as by day (1 Chron. ix. 33).

The Targum, too, explains the first verse of the Temple watch.

"The custom in the Second Temple appears to have been this. After midnight the chief of the door-keepers took the key of the inner Temple, and went with some of the Priests through the small postern of the Fire Gate (שער בית המוקד). In the inner court this watch divided itself into two companies, each carrying a burning torch; one company turned west, the other east, and so they compassed the court to see whether all were in readiness for the Temple service on the following morning. In the bakehouse, where the *Mincha* ('meat-offering') of the High Priest was baked, they met with the cry, 'All well.' Meanwhile the rest of the Priests arose, bathed themselves, and put on their garments. They then went into the stone chamber (one half of which was the hall of session of the Synhedrin), and there, under the superintendence of the officer who gave the watch-word and one of the Synhedrin, surrounded by the Priests clad in their robes of office, their several duties for the coming day were assigned to each of the Priests by lot (Luke i. 9)."

Accordingly it has been supposed by Tholuck and others, that the greeting in ver. 1, 2, was addressed to the guard going off duty by those who came to relieve them; and who in their turn received the answer in ver. 3. Others conjecture that the greeting was interchanged between the two companies of the night-watch, when they met in making their rounds through the Temple. Delitzsch, however thinks that the words of ver. 1, 2, are addressed by the congregation to the Priests and Levites who had charge of the night-service, and that ver. 3 is an answer of blessing from them to the congregation who were gathered on the Temple-mount.

[A PILGRIM SONG.]

(*The Greeting.*)

1 BEHOLD, bless ye Jehovah, all ye servants of Jehovah,
Which by night stand in the house of Jehovah.
2 Lift up your hands to the sanctuary,[a]
And bless ye Jehovah.

(*The Answer.*)

3 Jehovah bless thee out of Zion,
(Even He who is) the Maker of heaven and earth.

1. BEHOLD. The word draws attention here to a duty, as at the beginning of the last Psalm it drew attention to a truth at once important and attractive.

SERVANTS OF JEHOVAH. The expression of itself might denote the people at large, but the next clause limits it (as in cxxxv. 2) to the Priests and Levites.

BY NIGHT. Lit. "in the nights." This cannot mean merely "night as well as day," and therefore "at all times," as Hupfeld maintains. In xlii. 8 [9], and xcii. 2 [3], to which he refers, "the morning" is expressly mentioned as well as "the night," and in v. 3 [4], where "the morning" only is mentioned, the morning only is meant. Even if there were no other mention of a night-service in the Temple, considering how meagre the notices are, we should not be justified in setting this aside: but we have express reference to a night-service in 1 Chr. ix. 33.

STAND. A common word for the service of the Priests and Levites, Deut. x. 8, xv. 2, 7; 1 Chr. xxiii. 30; 2 Chr. xxix. 11.

3. BLESS THEE. The singular instead of the plural "bless *you*," because the words are taken from the form used by the High Priest in blessing the people, Numb. vi. 24.

OUT OF ZION. See on cxxxv. 21.

MAKER OF HEAVEN AND EARTH. As in cxxi. 2, cxxiv. 8.

[a] קֹדֶשׁ. The accusative of direction, as frequently; and so the LXX. *εἰς τὰ ἅγια*, Jer. *ad sanctum*, Vulg. *in sancta*. In v. 8, xxviii. 2, we have the full phrase. For the constr. Del. compares Hab. iii. 11. But it may be rendered "in holiness." So Symm. *ἁγίως*. יְדֵכֶם is merely an incorrect form for יְדֵיכֶם.

PSALM 135

A PSALM intended for the Temple service, and one of the Hallelujah Psalms, though not placed in the same series with the rest. It is, like Ps. cxxxiv, an exhortation to the Priests and Levites who wait in the sanctuary to praise Jehovah, both because of His goodness in choosing Israel to be His people, and because of His greatness and the almighty power which He has shown in His dominion over the world of nature, and in the overthrow of all the enemies of His people. Then His abiding Majesty is contrasted with the nothingness of the idols of the heathen. The Psalm is almost entirely composed of passages taken from other sources. Compare ver. 1 with cxxxiv. 1; ver. 3 with cxlvii. 1; ver. 6 and 15—20 with cxv.; ver. 7 with Jer. x. 13; ver. 14 with Deut. xxxii. 36; ver. 8—12 with cxxxvi. 10—22.

Delitzsch not inaptly describes the Psalm, on this account, as a species of mosaic, applying to its structure the expression of the old Roman poet Lucilius: "Quam lepide lexeis compostæ ut tesserulæ omnes." The prophecies of Jeremiah furnish many instances of a similar composite diction. Zephaniah takes his words and phrases almost entirely from Jeremiah. Many sentences in the Book of Proverbs would naturally appear in other writers, and a collector of proverbial wisdom must, by the very nature of the case, compose a mosaic instead of painting a picture. Several of the Psalms are specimens of this composite work. The diction of the 97th and 98th Psalms in particular is a series of coloured fragments, as it were, from the later chapters of Isaiah. The *tesserulæ* of this Psalm, on the other hand, are gathered from the Law, the Prophets, and the Hagiographa.

HALLELUJAH!
1 Praise ye the Name of Jehovah,
Praise (it), O ye servants of Jehovah.
2 Ye that stand in the house of Jehovah,
In the courts of the house of our God,

1. The opening of the Psalm resembles the opening of cxxxiv.

2. IN THE COURTS. See on lxxxiv. 2 [3]. The mention of these

3 Praise ye Jah, for Jehovah is good ;
Sing psalms unto His Name, for it is lovely.
4 For Jah hath chosen Jacob to Himself,
Israel for His peculiar treasure.
5 For I know that Jehovah is great,
And that our Lord is above all gods.
6 Whatsoever Jehovah pleaseth that hath He done,
In heaven and in earth,
In the seas and in all deeps.

"courts" is no evidence that the exhortation is addressed not merely to the Priests, but to the people. Nor can this be inferred from the formula in ver. 19, 20, which is common to these liturgical Psalms; comp. cxv. 9—11. The address is, as in cxxxiv. 1, to the Levites who sang Psalms and played on the different musical instruments which were used in the service of God, and to the Priests who blew with the trumpets and repeated the liturgical prayers and the blessings.

The thrice-repeated Jehovah, followed by Jah—Jehovah—Jah, may have a reference to the form of the priestly blessing in which they "put the Name of Jehovah upon the children of Israel," Num. vi. 22—27. Thrice the Priests uttered the Name; thrice, and yet thrice again, the congregation echoed it back in their song.

3. JEHOVAH IS GOOD. "Breviter uno verbo," says Augustine, "explicata est laus Domini Dei nostri : *bonus Dominus.* Sed bonus, non ut sunt bona quæ fecit. Nam fecit Deus omnia bona valde ; non tantum bona, sed et valde. Cœlum et terram et omnia quæ in eis sunt bona fecit, et valde bona fecit. Si hæc omnia bona fecit, qualis est ille qui fecit? Et tamen, cum bona fecerit, multoque sit melior qui fecit quam ista quæ fecit non invenis melius quod de illo dicas nisi *quia bonus est Dominus :* si tamen intelligas proprie bonum, a quo sunt cætera bona. Omnia enim bona ipse fecit: ipse est bonus quem nemo fecit. Ille bono suo bonus est, non aliunde participato bono : ille seipso bono bonus est, non adhærendo alteri bono. . . . Ineffabili dulcedine teneor cum audio *bonus Dominus;* consideratisque omnibus et collustratis quæ forinsecus video, quoniam ex ipso sunt omnia, etiam cum mihi hæc placent, ad illum video a quo sunt, ut intelligam *quoniam bonus est Dominus.*"

IT IS LOVELY. According to the parallelism, this will refer either to the Name of Jehovah, or to Jehovah Himself, "for *He* is lovely." But according to the analogy of cxlvii. 1 (comp. Prov. xxiii. 8) the subject is the song: "for it is pleasant, viz. thus to sing praise."

4. Then follow the several grounds of this praise. First, because He has chosen Israel. Next, because He is higher than all the gods of the heathen, as He has shown in His absolute supremacy over the world of nature, ver. 5—7. Then, because He redeemed His people from Egypt, ver. 8, 9. Lastly, because, vanquishing all their enemies, He gave them the Promised Land, ver. 10—12.

5. I KNOW. The pron. is emphatic, and the phrase marks a strong personal conviction (sometimes, as in xx. 6 [7], one newly gained).

6. WHATSOEVER HE PLEASETH. This absolute supremacy of God over all the forces and phenomena of the natural world is stated in the

7 He bringeth up vapours from the end of the earth,
He hath made lightnings for the rain,
He sendeth forth [a] the wind out of His treasuries.
8 Who smote the firstborn of Egypt,
Both of man and beast;
9 (Who) sent signs and wonders into the midst of thee,[b]
O Egypt,
Upon Pharaoh and upon all his servants;
10 Who smote many nations,
And slew mighty kings.
11 Sihon,[c] king of the Amorites,
And Og, the king of Bashan,
And all the kingdoms of Canaan;
12 And gave their land as an heritage,
An heritage unto Israel His people.
13 O Jehovah, Thy name (endureth) for ever,
Thy memorial, O Jehovah, to all generations.
14 For Jehovah judgeth His people,
And repenteth Himself concerning His servants.
15 The idols of the nations are silver and gold,
The work of men's hands.

same way as in cxv. 3, with reference more particularly to the weakness of the gods of the nations, as also in this Psalm, ver. 15—18.

7. The verse occurs almost word for word in Jer. x. 13, li. 16.

VAPOURS, or perhaps "clouds," as formed of masses of vapour.

FROM THE END OF THE EARTH. *i.e.* either from the horizon on which they seem to gather, or from the sea; or, perhaps, as Augustine says, because "unde surrexerint nescis."

FOR THE RAIN, *i.e.* so that the rain follows the lightning; see Is. x. 13, li. 16. The lightning is supposed to precede the rain. A common Arabic proverb says of a man who turns out other than was expected of him, that he lightens but does not rain. The LXX., ἀστραπὰς εἰς ὑετον εποίησεν.

HIS TREASURIES. Comp. Job xxxviii. 22. "Occultis causis, unde nescis."—*Augustine.*

8. BOTH OF MAN AND BEAST. Lit. "from man unto beast."

13. Comp. Exod. iii. 15.

14. Borrowed from Deut. xxxii. 36. Comp. for the second clause of the verse Ps. xc. 13.

FOR. Here is the proof and evidence that Jehovah's Name and memorial abide for ever; that He will manifest, as in the past, so in the future, His righteousness and His mercy to Israel.

JUDGE, *i.e.* see that they have right, which is in fact the consequence of His "repenting concerning," or "having compassion of," His servants.

15—18. Borrowed with some variation from cxv. 4—8.

16 They have a mouth, and speak not ;
Eyes have they, and see not.
17 They have ears, and (yet) they hear not,
Yea, they have no breath at all[d] in their mouths.
18 They that make them shall be like unto them,
Every one that putteth his trust in them.
19 O house of Israel, bless ye Jehovah :
O house of Aaron, bless ye Jehovah :
20 O house of Levi, bless ye Jehovah :
Ye that fear Jehovah, bless Jehovah.
21 Blessed be Jehovah out of Zion,
Who dwelleth in Jerusalem.
Hallelujah !

19, 20. Precisely as in cxv. 9—11, cxviii. 2—4, only that here "the house of Levi" is added.

21. As in cxxviii. 5, cxxxiv. 3, Jehovah blesses out of Zion, so here, on the other hand, His people bless Him out of Zion. For there they meet to worship Him ; there not only He, but they, may be said to dwell (Is. x. 24) ; and thence accordingly His praise is sounded abroad.

[a] מוֹצֵא, either incorrect for מוֹצִיא, the accent being drawn back after the analogy of the fut. conv., or, as the participle is somewhat lame after עָשָׂה, perhaps it is merely an error for וַיּוֹצֵא, which is found in the parallel passages, Jer. x. 13, li. 16.

[b] בְּתוֹכֵכִי. For this form see on ciii. note [a].

[c] The לְ after הרג is not necessarily due to Aramaic influence. It occurs not only in 2 Sam. iii. 30 (where Del. alleges that ver. 30, 31, and 36, 37, are a later addition, and therefore not exempt from Aramaic tendencies), but also in Job v. 2. We have it also again in cxxxvi. 19, 20. Maurer explains that with the accus. it is *interficere aliquem*, and with לְ *cædem facere alicui.* For other instances of the לְ after the active verb see xxxv. 7, lxix. 6, cxvi. 16, cxxix. 3, cxxxvi. 23. With the exception of this use of the לְ and the שֶׁ, the whole colouring and language of ver. 10—12 is that of Deuteronomy.

[d] יֵשׁ, constr., and quite superfluous after אֵין. It occurs also 1 Sam. xxi. 9, where, however, according to Del., the punctuation should be אִין and אִין יֵשׁ = Aram. אִין אִית, *num* (*an*) *est*, אִין being a North Palestine Aramaising form of the Heb. interrog. אִם.

PSALM 136

THIS Psalm is little more than a variation and repetition of the preceding Psalm. It opens with the same liturgical formula with which the 106th and 108th Psalms open, and was evidently designed to be sung antiphonally in the Temple worship. Its structure is peculiar. The first line of each verse pursues the theme of the Psalm, the second line, "For is loving-kindness endureth for ever," being a kind of refrain or response, like the responses, for instance, in our Litany, breaking in upon and yet sustaining the theme of the Psalm : the first would be sung by some of the Levites, the second by the choir as a body, or by the whole congregation together with the Levites. We have an example of a similar antiphonal arrangement in the first four verses of the 118th Psalm; but there is no other instance in which it is pursued throughout the Psalm. The nearest approach to the same constant repetition is in the "Amen" of the people to the curses of the Law as pronounced by the Levites, Deut. xxvii. 14.

In the Jewish liturgy (see T. B. Pesachim 118) this Psalm, with its twenty-six responses, is called "the Great Hallel," by way of distinction from "the Hallel," simply so called, which comprises Psalms cxiii.—cxviii., though there is some uncertainty as to the former designation; for according to some "the Great Hallel" comprises cxxxv. 4—cxxxvi., and according to others, cxx—cxxxvi.

According to an old rule of writing observed in some of the most ancient MSS., the two lines of the verses ought to be arranged each in a separate column, or, as the phrase runs, "half-brick upon half-brick, brick upon brick."

It may be observed that the verses are grouped in threes as far as ver. 18, and then the Psalm concludes with two groups of four verses each. It is possible (as Delitzsch suggests) that ver. 19—22 did not originally belong to this Psalm, being introduced from the previous Psalm, and that there were thus, in the first instance, 22 lines, corresponding to the number of letters in the Hebrew Alphabet.

1 O GIVE thanks unto Jehovah, for He is good,
For His loving-kindness (endureth) for ever.
2 O give thanks unto the God of gods,
For His loving-kindness (endureth) for ever.
3 O give thanks unto the Lord of lords,
For His loving-kindness (endureth) for ever.
4 To Him who alone doeth great wonders,
For His loving-kindness (endureth) for ever.
5 To Him who by understanding made the heavens,
For His loving-kindness (endureth) for ever.
6 To Him that stretched out the earth above the waters,
For His loving-kindness (endureth) for ever.
7 To Him who made great lights,
For His loving-kindness (endureth) for ever.
8 The sun to rule the day,
For His loving-kindness (endureth) for ever.
9 The moon and (the) stars to rule the night,
For His loving-kindness (endureth) for ever.
10 To Him that smote Egypt in their firstborn,
For His loving-kindness (endureth) for ever.
11 And brought forth Israel from the midst of them,
For His loving-kindness (endureth) for ever.
12 With a mighty hand and a stretched-out arm,
For His loving-kindness (endureth) for ever.
13 To Him who divided the Red Sea into parts,
For His loving-kindness (endureth) for ever.

2, 3. GOD OF GODS . . . LORD OF LORDS, from Deut. x. 17.

5. BY UNDERSTANDING, as in Prov. iii. 19. Comp. civ. 24; Prov. iii. 19; Jer. x. 12, li. 15.

6. STRETCHED OUT; from the same root as the word *firmament* or expanse in Gen. i. Comp. Is. xlii. 5, xliv. 24.

ABOVE THE WATERS: comp. xxiv. 1 [2].

7. LIGHTS. The word is employed here strictly, instead of the corresponding word in Gen. i. 14—16, which means not *lights*, but *luminaries;* the bodies, that is, which hold the light.

9. TO RULE, lit. "for dominions over;" the plural, poetically, instead of the singular, as in the preceding verse, and in Gen. 1.

10—22. Almost word for word as in cxxxv. 8—12.

13. DIVIDED; the same word as in 1 Kings iii. 25 and the noun PARTS (lit. "divisions," from the

14 And made Israel to pass through the midst of it,
For His loving-kindness (endureth) for ever.
15 And overthrew Pharaoh and his host in the Red Sea,
For His loving-kindness (endureth) for ever.
16 To Him who led His people through the wilderness,
For His loving-kindness (endureth) for ever.
17 To Him who smote great kings,
For His loving-kindness (endureth) for ever.
18 And slew mighty kings,
For His loving-kindness (endureth) for ever.
19 Sihon king of the Amorites,
For His loving-kindness (endureth) for ever.
20 And Og the king of Bashan,
For His loving-kindness (endureth) for ever.
21 And gave their land for a heritage,
For His loving-kindness (endureth) for ever.
22 An heritage unto Israel His servant,
For His loving-kindness (endureth) for ever.
23 Who remembered us in our low estate,
For His loving-kindness (endureth) for ever.
24 And set us free from our adversaries,
For His loving-kindness (endureth) for ever.
25 He giveth food to all flesh,
For His loving-kindness (endureth) for ever.
26 O give thanks to the God of heaven,
For His loving-kindness (endureth) for ever.

same root), as in Gen. xv. 17. A different word is used of the dividing of the Red Sea, Ex. xiv. 16, 21. See also Ps. lxxviii. 12 [13].

15. OVERTHREW, lit. "shook out," as in Ex. xiv. 27.

19. The occurrence of the preposition לְ at the beginning of this verse before the object is the more remarkable because hitherto throughout the Psalm it has been employed at the beginning of the verse to connect some fresh attribute or work of God with the verb "Give thanks" in the first verse. So in ver. 4, "(Give thanks) unto Him who doeth great wonders;" in ver. 5, "(Give thanks) to Him who made the heavens;" and so on, ver. 6, 7, 10, 13, 16.

PSALM 137

THERE can be no doubt whatever as to the time when this Psalm was written. It expresses the feeling of an exile who has but just returned from the land of his captivity. In all probability the writer was a Levite, who had been carried away by the armies of Nebuchadnezzar when Jerusalem was sacked and the Temple destroyed, and who was one of the first, as soon as the edict of Cyrus was published, to return to Jerusalem. He is again in his own land. He sees again the old familiar scenes. The mountains and the valleys that his foot trod in youth are before him. The great landmarks are the same, and yet the change is terrible. The spoiler has been in his home, his vines and his fig-trees have been cut down, the House of his God is a heap of ruins. His heart is heavy with a sense of desolation, and bitter with the memory of wrong and insult from which he has but lately escaped.

He takes his harp, the companion of his exile, the cherished relic of happier days,—the harp which he could not string at the bidding of his conquerors by the waters of Babylon ; and now with faltering hand he sweeps the strings, first in low, plaintive, melancholy cadence pouring out his griefs, and then with a loud crash of wild and stormy music, answering to the wild and stormy numbers of his verse, he raises the pæan of vengeance over his foes.

He begins by telling in language of pathetic beauty the tale of his captivity. He draws first the picture of the land—so unlike his own mountain land—the broad plain watered by the Euphrates and intersected by its canals, their banks fringed with willows, with no purple peak, no deep, cool glen to break the vast, weary. monotonous expanse ; and then he draws the figure of the captives in their deep despondency, a despondency so deep that it could find no solace even in those sacred melodies which were dear to them as life—"As for our harps, we hanged them up on the willows by the water-side." Next, his verse tells of the mocking taunt of their captors, "Sing us one of the songs of Zion ;" and the half sad, half proud answer of the heart, strong in its faith and unconquerable in its patriotism, "How shall we sing Jehovah's song in a strange land ?" It were a profanation, it were a treachery. Sooner let the tongue fail to sing than sing to make the heathen mirth ; sooner let the hand lose he cunning than tune the harp to please the stranger.

No wonder that then, brooding over the memory of the past, brooding over his wrongs, and seeing around him in blackened ruins and wasted fields the footsteps of the invader, the Poet should utter his wrath. No wonder that the Psalm concludes with that fierce outburst of natural resentment, a resentment which borrows almost a grandeur from the religious fervour, the devoted patriotism, whence it springs. Terrible have been the wrongs of Jerusalem: let the revenge be terrible. Woe to those who in the day of her fall took part with her enemies and rejoiced in her overthrow, when they ought rather to have come to her aid. Woe to the proud oppressors who have so long held her children captive, and made their hearts bitter with insult and wrong. "Blessed shall he be who taketh thy little ones, and dasheth them against the rock."

What a wonderful mixture is the Psalm of soft melancholy and fiery patriotism! The hand which wrote it must have known how to smite sharply with the sword, as well as how to tune his harp. The words are burning words of a heart breathing undying love to his country, undying hate to his foe. The Poet is indeed

> "Dower'd with the hate of hate, the scorn of scorn,
> The love of love."

1 BY the rivers of Babylon, there we sat down, yea, we wept,
When we remembered Zion
2 Upon the willows in the midst thereof
We hanged up our harps.
3 For there they that led us captive demanded of us songs,
And they that spoiled us [a] (demanded of us) mirth,
(Saying) "Sing us (one) of the songs of Zion,"
4 How should we sing Jehovah's song
In the land of the stranger?
5 If I forget thee, O Jerusalem,

3. SONGS. Heb. "words of song," or subjects of song, as in lxv. 3 [4] "words of iniquities."

4, 5. How sing a *holy* song on a strange, *profane* soil? How sing a song of *joy* when the city and Temple of our God lay in ruins? Compare the words of Nehemiah, "Wherefore the King said unto me, Why is thy countenance sad, seeing thou are not sick? And I said, Let the King live for ever: why should not my countenance be sad when the city, the place of my father's sepulchres, lieth waste, and the gates thereof are consumed with fire?" (Neh. ii. 2, 3.)

5. FORGET. Probably there is

Let my right hand forget (her cunning).
6 Let my tongue cleave to the roof of my mouth,
If I remember thee not;
If I prefer not Jerusalem above my chiefest joy.
7 Remember, O Jehovah, the children of Edom
In the day of Jerusalem,
Who said, Down with[b] it, Down with it, even to the foundation thereof.

an aposiopesis; or we may supply either, as the E.V., "her cunning," *i.e.* her skill with the harp, or, more generally, "the power of motion."

6. MY CHIEFEST JOY, lit. "the top of my joy." Comp. Exod. xxx. 23; Song of Sol. iv. 14. Others, "the sum of my joy."

7. This verse may also be rendered:

Remember for (against) the children of Edom.
The day of Jerusalem--

the construction being the same as in cxxxii. 1. As he broods over his wrongs, as he looks upon the desolation of his country, as he remembers with peculiar bitterness how they who ought to have been allies took part with the enemies of Jerusalem in the fatal day of her overthrow, there bursts forth the terrible cry for vengeance; vengeance first on the false kindred, and next on the proud conquerors of his race.

"Deepest of all was the indignation roused by the sight of the nearest of kin, the race of Esau, often allied to Judah, often independent, now bound by the closest union with the power that was truly the common enemy of both. There was an intoxication of delight in the wild Edomite chiefs, as at each successive stroke against the venerable walls they shouted, 'Down with it! down with it! even to the ground.' They stood in the passes to intercept the escape of those who would have fled down to the Jordan valley; they betrayed the fugitives; they indulged their barbarous revels on the Temple hill. Long and loud has been the wail of execration which has gone up from the Jewish nation against Edom. It is the one imprecation which breaks forth from the Lamentations of Jeremiah; it is the culmination of the fierce threats of Ezekiel; it is the sole purpose of the short, sharp cry of Obadiah; it is the bitterest drop in the sad recollections of the Israelite captives by the waters of Babylon; and the one warlike strain of the Evangelical Prophet is inspired by the hope that the Divine Conqueror should come knee-deep in Idumæan blood. (Lam. iv. 21, 22; Ezek. xxv. 8, 12—14; Obad. 1—21; Jer. xlix. 7—22; Is. lxiii. 1—4)."—STANLEY, *Jewish Church*, ii. p. 556.

In later times, Edom and Bozrah were used as typical names to denote Rome, Christian and pagan, as the destroyer of Jerusalem and the temple, and the persecutor of the Jews. So Qimchi, "While he was prophesying with regard to the Babylonish captivity, he saw by the Holy Spirit, the captivity of the Second House which was effected by the hands of Edom; for Titus destroyed it who was of the kingdom of Rome, which is of the sons of Edom." And Abarbanel in his Commentary on Obad., says that the prophecy is directed not merely against the literal Edom, but against "the Nazarene people who are of the sons of Edom, whose beginning and origin is the city of Rome."

8 O daughter of Babylon that shalt be destroyed,[c]
Happy shall he be that rewardeth thee
As thou hast served us.
9 Happy shall he be that taketh and dasheth thy little ones
Against the rock.

8. THAT SHALT BE DESTROYED, or, perhaps, "doomed to destruction." Others, "that art laid waste," as if referring to the taking of Babylon by Cyrus. The LXX. ambiguously, ἡ ταλαίπωρος. See more in Critical Note. Compare for the sentiment, Jer. li. 56, "Because the spoiler is come upon her, even upon Babylon, and her mighty men are taken, every one of their bows is broken: for Jehovah is a God of recompenses, He shall surely requite." See also for the same principle of *retribution* in the overthrow of Babylon, Is. xlvii. 1—9.

AS THOU HAST SERVED US, lit. "the requital wherewith thou hast requited us."

9. LITTLE ONES, lit. "sucklings." With such barbarous cruelty wars were carried on, even by comparatively civilised nations. Comp. for Biblical examples 2 Kings viii. 12, xv. 16; Is. xiii. 16; Hos. x. 14, xiii. 16 [xiv. 1]; Nah. iii. 10. So Homer, painting the sack of a city, mentions, as one of its features, νήπια τέκνα βαλλόμενα προτὶ γαίῃ. And again, Andromache addressing her child says, σὺ δ' αὖ τέκος, ἢ ἐμοὶ αὐτῇ . . . Ἕψεαι . . . ἤ τις Ἀχαιῶν Ῥίψει, χειρὸς ἑλὼν ἀπὸ πύργου, λυγρὸν ὄλεθρον. At a far later period, Athenæus tells us, such inhuman barbarity was to be found even among the Greeks, that in one insurrection the populace wreaked their fury on the upper classes by throwing their children to be trampled under the feet of oxen, and when the aristocracy in their turn got the upper hand, they took their revenge by burning their enemies alive, together with their wives and children. (Tholuck.)

But we need not turn only to the history of the past. We have had in our own times the awful records of Turkish atrocities on the one hand, and Bulgarian atrocities on the other. In all conflicts between antagonistic races, where the antagonism has been exasperated by religious animosities, or where the keen sense of humiliation in a subject race held down under the yoke of foreign masters has roused them to revolt, there have been these bloody reprisals. In our own Sepoy War in India, men of humanity and Christian principle showed a sternness little less than that of the Jewish poet. The historian of that war writes: "And now there lay before them (the English) the great question, the most difficult, perhaps, which soldiers and statesmen ever have the responsibility of solving—whether after such convulsions as have been illustrated in these pages true righteousness and true wisdom consisted in extending the hand of mercy and aiming at conciliation, or in dealing out a stern and terrible retribution. Our soldiers and statesmen in June, 1857, at Allahabad, solved the question in practice *by adopting the latter course.* Sir J. Kaye's *Hist. of the Sepoy War*, vol. ii. p. 268. See also p. 236, and pp. 269-271, &c.

[a] תּוֹלָלֵינוּ. The LXX. οἱ ἀπαγαγόντες ἡμᾶς, and similarly the Chald. and Syr. "our plunderers," the word being regarded as an Aram. form, with ת for שׁ, instead of שׁוֹלָלֵינוּ. There is a twofold objection, however, to

this: first, that שׁוֹלָל only occurs as a *passive;* and next, in Aram. the form is שׁלל, not תלל, in this sense. Hence it seems probable that we ought to read שׁוֹלְלֵינוּ. Otherwise we must derive the word from a root ילל, "to howl" (after the analogy of תּוֹשָׁב, from ישׁב); then the abstract "howling" will stand by metonymy for the torture, punishment, &c. which occasions it, and this, again concrete, for the torturers. In the abstract sense, Abulwal., Qimchi. In the concrete, Ges., De W., Win., and others, and so Jerome, *qui affligebant nos.*

[b] עָרוּ. Imp. Piel, with a drawing back of the accent to the penult. because of the pause, Ges. § 29, 4, *b*, *c*. ערה, "to make bare, shave smooth, &c., reduce to a flat, level surface." Comp. Hab. iii. 13, and the noun in Is. xix. 7.

[c] הַשְּׁדוּדָה. This cannot be active with the present punctuation, *Thou that wastest* (Symm. ἡ λῃστρίς, but it is a further objection to this that the root does not mean *to plunder*).

(1) If we give the active meaning, which certainly seems very suitable, the punctuation must be הַשֹּׁדוֹדָה, like בָּגוֹדָה, Jer. iii. 7, 10 (with immovable Qametz), or at any rate הַשֹּׁדְדָה, Ew. § 152 *b*.

(2) In its existing form it is a pass. part., as Aq. προνενομευμένη, Jerome *vastata.* But (3) it has been rendered as a part. fut. pass., *vastanda.* Theod., διαρπασθησομένη. And so Röd. in Gesen. *Thes.*, but Del. objects that though the Niph. part. (*e.g.* xxii. 32, cii. 19) and the Pual (xviii. 4) may have this meaning, it is not found in the Qal. However, he would himself give the meaning *vastationi devota*, which he defends by Jer. iv. 30, where שָׁדוּד is used hypothetically = "when thou art wasted." So he says the sense is here: "O daughter of Babylon, that art wasted, blessed shall he be who, when this judgement of wasting shall come upon thee, shall take thy sucklings," &c. Hupf., on the other hand, contends for the simple passive rendering, *thou that art wasted*, which he explains of the capture of the city by Cyrus.

PSALM 138

According to the Hebrew title, this is a Psalm of David. The LXX. have added to this title the names of Haggai and Zechariah (τῷ Δαυὶδ, Ἀγγαίου καὶ Ζαχαρίου), which would seem to show that the translators were not satisfied with the traditional view as to the authorship of the Psalm, and would rather refer it to a time subsequent to the Exile. So far as the Psalm itself is concerned, we have no clue to guide us; neither the language nor the allusions will warrant any conclusions as to date or authorship. The mention of the Temple in ver. 2 does not prove that the Psalm was not written by David, for the word rendered "Temple" might be used of a structure like the Tabernacle (see on Ps. v. 7). Nor does the hope or prophecy concerning the kings of the earth in ver. 4 necessarily point to a post-Exile time, for hopes of a similar kind are found also in earlier Psalms (see note on that verse).

The Psalm consists of three strophes :—

(1) In the first the Poet encourages himself to praise God both because of His goodness and faithfulness and His great promises, and also because he himself had had his prayers answered. Ver. 1—3.

(2) He utters the hope, the prophecy, that the kings of the earth shall acknowledge the greatness of Jehovah,—His greatness chiefly in this, that He does not measure by any human standard of great and small, of high and low. Ver. 4—6.

(3) The application of all that he has learnt of Jehovah's character to his own individual experience in prospect of trouble and danger Ver. 7, 8.

[(A PSALM) OF DAVID.]

1 I WILL give thanks unto Thee with my whole heart,
Before the gods will I sing praise unto Thee.
2 I will bow myself before Thy holy Temple,
And I will give thanks to Thy Name, because of Thy loving-kindness and Thy truth,

1. UNTO THEE. The Being who is addressed is not named till ver. 4. The LXX. have thought it necessary to insert a Κύριε, and in this have been followed by the Vulg. and by our P. B. V. The absence of the vocative is, however, more emphatic. It is as though in the Psalmist's heart there could be but one object of praise, whether named or unnamed.

BEFORE THE GODS. This has been variously explained. (1) The LXX., who are followed by Luther, Calvin, and others, understand it of the *angels*. But though the angels are called upon to praise God, they are nowhere in the O.T. regarded as witnesses of, or sharers in, the worship of men. (2) The Chald., Syr., Rabb., and many recent interpreters suppose that *kings* or *judges* are meant (see on lxxxii.). (3) Ewald and others would render "before God," and consider this as equivalent to "before the Ark," or "in the sanctuary." But the extreme awkwardness of such a phrase here, "Before God I will give thanks to thee, O Jehovah," is sufficient to condemn the interpretation. (4) It is far more probable that "the gods" are the false gods, the objects of heathen worship, in the very presence of whom, and to the confusion of their worshipers, the Psalmist will utter his praise of the true God. See xcv. 3, xcvi. 4, 5, cxv. 3—8.

2. THY WORD, or "promise." Comp. lvi. 10 [11], lx. 6 [8], lxii. 11 [12]. No particular promise is meant.

For Thou hast magnified Thy word above all Thy Name.

3 In the day that I called, Thou answeredst me,
Thou madest me courageous [a] with strength in my soul.

4 All the kings of the earth shall give thanks unto Thee, O Jehovah;
For they have heard the words of Thy mouth.
5 And they shall sing of [b] the ways of Jehovah;
For great is the glory of Jehovah.
6 For Jehovah is high, yet He seeth the humble;
And the proud He knoweth [c] afar off.

The same word occurs frequently in cxix. See note on ver. 25 of that Psalm.

ABOVE ALL THY NAME. The expression seems to mean that to the soul waiting upon God, and trusting in His word, the promise becomes so precious, so strong a ground of hope, that it surpasses all other manifestations of God's goodness and truth; or in the promise may here also be included the fulfilment of the promise. Many interpreters have stumbled at the expression, and Hupfeld objects that "it is contrary to all analogy. The name of God cannot be surpassed by any individual act or attribute of God, for every such separate act is only a manifestation of that Name; nor can it be limited to *past* manifestations of God's character, or taken as equivalent to *calling upon* His Name. On the other hand, *to make great* (magnify) is only said of God's acts, of His grace, His salvation, and the like, and could scarcely be said of His word or promise. One would rather expect, *Thou hast magnified Thy Name above all Thy word;* it surpasses all that Thou hast promised."

The difficulty has been felt from the first. The LXX. ἐμεγάλυνας ἐπὶ πᾶν τὸ ὄνομα τὸ ἅγιόν σου, "Thou hast magnified, Thy Holy Name above all." The Chald. "Thou hast magnified the words of Thy praise above all Thy Name." Hupfeld would follow Clericus in reading "above all Thy heavens," which involves only a very slight change of the text. But all the Ancient Versions had the present reading.

4. ALL THE KINGS OF THE EARTH. See the expression of the same feeling in lxviii. 29—32 [30—33], lxxii. 10, 11, cii. 15 [16].

FOR THEY HAVE HEARD. This sounds in the Old Testament almost like an anticipation of St. Paul's words: "But I say have they not heard? Yea verily, their sound is gone forth into all the world." It is to be explained by the deep conviction in the Psalmist's heart that *God's* words cannot be hidden, must be published abroad. Others, however, render, "When they (shall) have heard."

5. SING OF THE WAYS. Having heard the tidings, "the words of God's mouth," they will joyfully celebrate His mighty acts. Comp. ciii. 7, where "His ways" correspond to "His acts" in the parallelism. The second clause may also be rendered, "*That* great is," &c. Ibn Ezra says: "They shall no more sing of love or war, but of the glory of the Lord."

6. IS HIGH. Comp. cxiii. 5, 6.

HE KNOWETH AFAR OFF. This

7 If I walk in the midst of trouble, Thou wilt quicken me :
Against the wrath of mine enemies Thou wilt stretch out Thine hand,
And Thy right hand shall save me.
8 Jehovah will perfect that which concerneth me
Jehovah, Thy loving-kindness (endureth) for ever :
Forsake not the works of Thy hands.

is the only proper rendering of the clause ; but the expression is somewhat remarkable. (1) It has been explained by reference to cxxxix. 2 ("Thou understandest my thoughts afar off"), which would mean, God knows (observes) the proud, distant as they may think themselves to be from His control. (2) Or, God knows them (regards them) only at a distance, does not admit them into His fellowship : He does not "see" them as He "seeth the humble." (3) Or it would be possible to explain, He knows them *so as to keep them* at a distance. (4) Or, again, God from afar (parallel to "high" in the first member) knows the proud, just as he sees the humble.

7. IF I WALK. Compare xxiii. 4, and lxxi. 20.

QUICKEN ME, or perhaps "keep me alive."

8. PERFECT, *i.e.* accomplish the work He has begun. See the same word in lvii. 2 [3], and comp. the ἐπιτελεῖν of Phil. i. 6.

FORSAKE NOT, or "relax not," turning into a prayer what he had just before expressed as a conviction of his own mind. For the word see Nehem. vi. 3.

[a] תַּרְהִבֵנִי. LXX. πολυωρήσεις. De-Rossi says that he found in several MSS. and Edd. תַּרְחִיבֵנִי, which is also expressed by Jerome, *dilatabis.* But the change is not necessary : the root רהב means strictly *to be proud.* Is. iii. 5, "behave himself proudly" (in a bad sense). Prov. vi. 3, "*press* (make sure, E.V.) thy neighbour." Song of Sol. vi. 5, "for they (thine eyes) have *overcome* me" (Hiph. as here), or perhaps "have *dazzled* or *bewildered* me." If we trace the shades of meaning, we shall see that the root-meaning is *to act with spirit.* This applies both in Is. iii. 5 and in Prov. vi. 3, and so here, "*Thou hast infused spirit into me,*" a sense which would not be unsuitable in Song of Sol. vi. 5. The tense obtains a *past* signification, because it follows a fut. with Vau consecutive.

[b] בְּדַרְכֵי י׳. The prep. denotes the object as often with analogous verbs as דבר, הלל, הגה, &c.

[c] יֵידַע, fut. Qal, apparently formed after the analogy of the Hiph'il forms, יֵילִיל, Is. xvi. 7, יֵיטִיב, Job xxiv. 21, and originating in the effort to restore the sound of the first radical, which in the Hiph, coalesces with the preceding vowel, and in the Qal is lost altogether.

PSALM 139

NOWHERE are the great attributes of God—His Omniscience, His Omnipresence, His Omnipotence, set forth so strikingly as they are in this magnificent Psalm. Nowhere is there a more overwhelming sense of the fact that man is beset and compassed about by God, pervaded by His Spirit, unable to take a step without His control; and yet nowhere is there a more emphatic assertion of the personality of man as distinct from, not absorbed in, the Deity. This is no pantheistic speculation. Man is here the workmanship of God, and stands in the presence and under the eye of One who is his Judge. The power of conscience, the sense of sin and of responsibility, are felt and acknowledged, and prayer is offered to One who is not only the Judge, but the Friend; to One who is feared as none else are feared, who is loved as none else are loved.

Both in loftiness of thought and in expressive beauty of language the Psalm stands pre-eminent, and it is not surprising that Aben Ezra should have pronounced it to be the crown of all the Psalms.

The Psalm both in the Hebrew and the LXX. is ascribed to David. In some copies of the latter it is also said to be a Psalm of Zechariah (Ζαχαρίου), with the further addition by a second hand of the words, "in the dispersion" (ἐν τῇ διασπορᾷ), which Origen tells us he found in some MSS. Theodoret, on the other hand, says that he had not found the addition either in the Hebrew or the LXX., or in any of the other interpreters. The strongly Aramaic colouring of the language certainly makes it more probable that the Psalm was written after the Exile than before, unless, indeed, this tendency to Aramaisms is to be regarded as evidence of a variation merely of dialect, perhaps the dialect of Northern Palestine,—a supposition which seems not to be wholly without foundation.

The rhythmical structure is, on the whole, regular. There are four strophes, each consisting of six verses; the first three strophes containing the proper theme of the Psalm, and the last the expression of individual feeling.

I. In the first strophe the Poet dwells on the omniscience of God, as manifested in His knowledge of the deepest thoughts and most secret workings of the human heart. Ver. 1—6.

II. In the second, on His omnipresence; inasmuch as there is no corner of the universe so remote that it is not pervaded by God's presence, no darkness so deep that it can hide from His eyes. Ver. 7—12.

III. The third strophe gives the reason for the profound conviction of these truths of which the Poet's heart is full. No wonder that God should have so intimate a knowledge of man, for man is the creature of God: the mysterious beginnings of life, which none can trace; the days, all of which are ordered before the first breath is drawn,—these are fashioned and ordered by the hand of God. Ver. 13—18.

IV. In the last strophe the Psalmist turns abruptly aside to express his utter abhorrence of wicked men—an abhorrence, no doubt, deepened by the previous meditation on God and His attributes, and called forth probably by the circumstances in which he was placed; and then closes with a prayer that he himself may, in his inmost heart, be right with that God who has searched him and known him and laid his hand upon him, and that he may be led by Him in the way everlasting. Ver. 19—24.

[FOR THE PRECENTOR. A PSALM OF DAVID.]

1 O JEHOVAH, Thou hast searched me, and known (me).
2 THOU knowest my downsitting and mine uprising,
Thou understandest my thought [a] afar off.
3 Thou hast examined [b] my path and my lying down,[c]
And art acquainted with all my ways.
4 For before a word is yet on my tongue,
Lo,[d] O Jehovah, Thou knowest it altogether.
5 Behind and before hast Thou beset me,
And laid Thine hand upon me.

1. KNOWN (ME). The form of the verb marks a consequence of the previous action.

2. AFAR OFF. However great the distance between us. See on cxxxviii. 6. The P.B.V. "long before."

3. THOU HAST EXAMINED, lit. "Thou hast winnowed," or "sifted."

4. FOR BEFORE A WORD. This is probably the better rendering (see Critical Note), though that of the E.V., "For there is not a word . . . but lo, O Lord, Thou knowest it altogether," is not certainly wrong.

5. BESET ME, or "shut me in." Comp. Job iii. 23, xiii. 27, xiv. 5, 13, 16, xix. 8. The P.B.V., "fashioned me," follows the LXX., ἔπλασας Jer. *formasti*, but these renderings depend upon a wrong derivation of the word from יצר.

LAID THINE HAND. Job xiii. 21, xxxiii. 7. Therefore, in the utmost exercise of his freedom, man is only accomplishing what God's counsel and foreknowledge have determined.

With the general sentiment of

6 (Such) knowledge is too wonderful[e] for me,
It is too high, I cannot attain unto it.

7 Whither shall I go from Thy Spirit?
Or whither shall I flee from Thy presence?
8 If I climb up[f] into heaven, THOU art there,
If I make my bed in hell, behold, Thou art there;
9 If I take the wings of the morning,
If I dwell in the uttermost parts of the sea,
10 Even there shall Thy hand lead me,
And Thy right hand shall hold me.
11 And should I say, Only let darkness cover[g] me,
And the light about me be night;

the first strophe compare Acts xvii. 28, "In him we live, and move, and have our being."

6. (SUCH) KNOWLEDGE. See a similar strain of acknowledgement at the close of the third strophe, ver. 17, 18, and compare Rom. xi. 33, "O the depth of the riches both of the wisdom and knowledge of God! How unsearchable are His judgements, and His ways past finding out!"

7. WHITHER SHALL I GO. It was this and the following verses, in all probability, which led a Spanish commentator (Father Sanchez) to ascribe this Psalm to the Prophet Jonah. Comp. Jon. i. 3, "But Jonah rose up to *flee* unto Tarshish *from the presence of Jehovah.*"

THY SPIRIT. "The word *Spirit*," says Calvin, "is not put here simply for the power of God, as commonly in the Scriptures, but for His mind and understanding. For inasmuch as the spirit in man is the seat of understanding, the Psalmist transfers the same to God; which is clearer from the second member, where the word *face* (*presence*) is put for knowledge or sight." He then remarks that the passage has been wrongly applied to prove the infinite nature of God (*ad probandam essentiæ Dei immensitatem*); for it is not with metaphysical conceptions that the Psalmist is employed, but with the practical truth that by no change of place or circumstance can *man* escape from the eye of *God*. There is further implied, too, in the thought of *escape*, and in the thought of *darkness*, a sense of sin and the terror of an awakened conscience, which of itself would lead a man to hide himself, if it were possible, from his Maker.

8. MY BED IN HELL, lit. "Should I make the unseen world (*Sheol*) my bed." Comp. Is. lviii. 5. For the same thought see Prov. xv. 11; Job xxvi. 6—9.

9. If I could fly with the same swiftness from east to west as the first rays of the morning shoot from one end of heaven to the other.

WINGS OF THE MORNING. So the sun is said to have wings, Mal. iv. 2.

UTTERMOST PARTS OF THE SEA, *i.e.* the furthest west.

11. AND THE LIGHT ABOUT ME. The apodosis does not begin here, as in E.V., "even the night shall be light about me," but with the next verse, where it is introduced by the particle "even," as in ver. 10. The predicate "night" stands first in the Hebrew, as is not unusual.

12 Even darkness cannot be too dark for Thee,
But the night is light as the day;
The darkness [h] and light (to Thee) are both alike.

13 For THOU hast formed my reins,
Thou didst weave me together in my mother's womb.
14 I will give Thee thanks for that I am fearfully and wonderfully made;
Wonderful are Thy works,
And my soul knoweth (it) right well.
15 My frame was not hidden from Thee,
When I was made in secret,
(When) I was curiously wrought [i] (as) in the lower parts of the earth.
16 Thine eyes did see my substance [j] yet being imperfect,

12. CANNOT BE TOO DARK FOR THEE, lit. "cannot be dark (so as to hide) from Thee;" or we may retain, both in this and in the next clause, something of the causative meaning of the verbs, and render "make darkness" . . . "give light."

13. "Who can have a truer and deeper knowledge of man than He who made him?"

FORMED. The connection and parallelism seem to show that this must be the meaning of the word here, as in Deut. xxxii. 6, "Is not He thy Father that *formed* thee?" where E.V. has "that *bought* thee;" and Gen. xiv. 19, "*Maker* of heaven and earth," where E.V. has "*possessor.*"

MY REINS. See on xvi. 7. It seems to denote the sensational and emotional part of the human being, as afterwards "the bones" denote the framework of the body.

WEAVE ME TOGETHER, as in Job x. 11, "Thou has woven me together (E.V. fenced me) with bones and sinews."

15. MY FRAME, or, "my strength" (and so Symm. ἡ κραταίωσίς μου), but there evidently meaning the bony framework of the body.

CURIOUSLY WROUGHT, Aq. ἐποικίλθην. The verb is used of some kind of parti-coloured work, but whether woven or embroidered is doubtful. Gesenius, who discusses the question at large in his *Thesaurus*, decides for embroidery. On the other hand, it has been denied by Hartmann that the Hebrews possessed this art. Camp. explains well: "Velut tapetum e nervis et venis contextus."

IN SECRET. Comp. Æsch. *Eumen.* 665, ἐν σκότοισι νηδύος τεθραμμένη.

IN THE LOWER PARTS OF THE EARTH. Elsewhere the phrase denotes "the unseen world," comp. lxiii. 9 [10], lxxxvi. 13. Here, as the parallelism shows, it is used in a figurative sense to describe the womb as a region of darkness and mystery.

16. MY SUBSTANCE YET BEING IMPERFECT. One word in the original which means strictly anything *rolled together* as a ball, and hence is generally supposed to mean here the fœtus or embryo. Hupfeld, however, prefers to understand it of the ball of life, as consisting of a number of different threads ("the days" of ver. 16) which are first a

And in Thy book were they all of them [k] written,—
The days which were ordered, when as yet there was none of them.
17 And how precious unto me are Thy thoughts, O God,
How great is the sum of them!
18 If I would tell them, they are more in number than the sand:
When I awake, I am still with Thee.

19 Oh that Thou wouldest slay the wicked, O God!
Depart from me, ye bloodthirsty men.

compact mass, as it were, and which are then unwound as life runs on.

ALL OF THEM, *i.e.* the days mentioned in the next verse. Or, "all the parts of the one mass, the various elements of the embryo yet undeveloped." If the reference be to them, then we must render the next clause "the days that (*i.e.* during which) they were ordered."

17. He breaks off in wonder and admiration and holy thankfulness, as before in ver. 14; these expressions of personal feeling lending not only much beauty and force, but also much reality, to the contemplation of God's attributes. Comp. xxxvi. 7 [8], xcii. 5 [6]; Rom. xi. 33.

HOW PRECIOUS, or perhaps (in accordance with the root-meaning of the word) "how hard to understand" (lit. "how heavy, or weighty"), in which case it would correspond with the ἀνεξερεύνητα of Rom. xi. 33.

SUM, lit. "sums," an unusual plural, denoting that the investigation and enumeration extend in many directions.

18. MORE IN NUMBER. Comp. xl. 5 [6].

WHEN I AWAKE, lit. "I have waked," *i.e.* as often as he awakes from sleep, he finds that he is again in the presence of God, again occupied with thoughts of God, again meditating afresh with new wonder and admiration on His wisdom and goodness. Others explain, "Waking and sleeping, day and night, I think of Thee, and find ever the same inexhaustible depth and fulness." Others again would interpret the "awaking" as awaking out of a reverie in which the Psalmist had lost himself while meditating upon God. But the first explanation is the simplest and most probable.

19. How strangely abrupt is the turning aside from one of the sublimest contemplations to be found anywhere in the Bible, to express a hope that righteous vengeance will overtake the wicked. Such a passage is startling,—startling partly because the spirit of the New Testament is so different; partly too, no doubt, because "our modern civilization has been so schooled in amenities" that we hardly know what is meant by a righteous indignation. It is well, however, to notice the fact, for this is just one of those passages which help us to understand the education of the world. Just because it startles us is it so instructive. The 63rd Psalm presents us, as we have seen, with a similar contrast. There, however, the feeling expressed is of a more directly personal kind. David is encompassed and hard pressed by enemies who are threatening his life. He has been driven from his

20 Who rebel[l] against Thee with (their) wicked devices,
(Who) lift up[m] themselves against Thee[n] in vain.
21 Should I not hate them which hate Thee, O Jehovah.
And should I not be grieved with them that rise up[o] against Thee?
22 With perfect hatred do I hate them,
I count them mine enemies.
23 Search me, O God, and know my heart:
Try me, and know my thoughts;
24 And see if there be any wicked way in me,

throne by rebels, and the deep sense of wrong makes him burst forth in the strain of indignation and of anticipated victory. "They that seek my life to destroy it shall be cast into the pit," &c. Here, apparently, the prayer for the overthrow of the wicked does not arise from a sense of wrong and personal danger, but from the intense hatred of wickedness as wickedness, from the deep conviction that, if hateful to a true-hearted man, it must be still more intensely hateful to Him who searcheth the hearts and trieth the reins. The soul, in the immediate presence of God, places itself on the side of God, against all that is opposed to Him. Still, the prayer, "Oh that Thou wouldest slay the wicked," can never be a Christian prayer.

20. WHO REBEL. Either the construction is changed from the second person in the preceding verse ("Depart from me") to the third in the relative clause; or the last clause of ver. 19 must be regarded as parenthetical, which is natural enough in a strong outburst of personal feeling, and then the construction proceeds regularly: "Wilt Thou not slay the wicked, who rebel," &c.

WITH WICKED DEVICES . . . IN VAIN. The parallelism would be better preserved by taking both words as adverbs: "wickedly" . . . "foolishly."

23. SEARCH ME. "That man must have a rare confidence," says Calvin, "who offers himself so boldly to the scrutiny of God's righteous judgement." And then he remarks that such a prayer is no evidence of self-ignorance, or a presumptuous spirit, but of integrity of heart and the absence of all hypocrisy. It is connected with what precedes in this way: that, having declared his utter separation from, and aversion to, the wicked, he prays that this may be no mere outward separation; he remembers that, even whilst he seems most opposed to the wicked, the All-seeing Eye may discern in him some way of evil and sorrow; that only as God holds his hand, and leads him, can he walk in the way of life.

24. WICKED WAY, or rather "way of pain," *i.e.* leading to pain, such pain and smart being the consequences of sin, as in Is. xiv. 3. Others, "way of *idols*," as in Is. xlviii. 5, "the way of idolatry" being opposed to "the way of Jehovah," xxv. 4. Comp. also Am. viii. 14, and the use of ὁδός Acts xix. 23, xxii. 4.

WAY EVERLASTING, *i.e.* the one true abiding way, which leads to the true and everlasting God. Calvin, who translates *via seculi*, supposes merely the course of life in this world to be meant, and that the Psalmist prays God to be with him to the end ("ac si peteret Deum sibi

And lead me in the way everlasting.

esse ducem stadii sui usque ad metam"); but the Hebrew *'olam* (*αἰών*) has not of itself this meaning. Others render "the *old* way," *i.e.* the true religion, the religion of his fathers, as in Jer. vi. 16, "the old paths," xviii. 15.

[a] רֵעִי only here: רֵעַ = Chald. רְעוּת frequent in Ecclesiastes (from root רְעָה = רצה), properly "will," here "thought." The לְ prefixed to the obj. is perhaps an Aramaism (comp. cxvi. 25, cxxix. 3, cxxxv. 11), but not necessarily, as the לְ may denote the *direction* of the thought.

[b] זֵרִיתָ (cognate with זרה, זרע), *Thou hast spread out*, and so *winnowed.* LXX. ἐξιχνιάσας, *tracked;* Jerome, *eventilasti.*

[c] רִבְעִי. Another apparently Aram. or later form for רִבְצִי, and another ἅπ. λεγ. This and the preceding word are properly two infinitives, "my walking and my lying down." Though the noun אֹרַח is Hebrew, the verb occurs only here and in Job xxxiv. 8, a passage which has also an Aram. tincture.

[d] הֵן. The construction of this verse has been taken in two ways: (1) There is no word on my tongue (which) Thou dost not know altogether; (2) A word is not (yet) upon my tongue, (but) lo! Thou knowest it altogether. This last is the rendering of Qimchi, Calvin, and others, and the הֵן favours it, as Hupf. observes. Comp. Is. xl. 24. [But הֵן in later writers = אִם. See Gesen. *Lex.* Can it here be used after a negative in the sense of *nisi* or *quin?*]

[e] פלאיה. Fem. of the adj. פְּלִאִי (as the K'thîbh, Jud. xiii. 18), and therefore to be read פְּלִאִיָּה, and not as the Q'rî, פְּלִיאָה.

On יכל לְ see xiii. 5.

[f] אֶסַּק (only here) from נְסַק, Aramaic (for the usual Heb. עלה), but only used in fut. imperat. inf. Qal and Aphel. The alternate form is סְלֵק, but we must not therefore assume, with Ges., Ew., and others, that אֶסַּק is for אֶלְסַק, and this again by transposition for אֶסְלַק. The roots are distinct, though cognate. Comp. also הַנְסָקָה, Dan. vi. 24.

[g] ישופני. In the two other passages where the same word occurs, Gen. iii. 15, Job ix. 17, it means "to bruise," "to crush," a meaning evidently not applicable here, though the LXX. have καταπατήσει. Hence Umbreit would connect it with שאף, in the sense *inhiare, insidiari* (comp. LXX. τηρεῖν), and so *invadere*, "to fall upon." Even this, however, gives but a poor meaning, as Hupfeld truly remarks. Either, therefore, we must connect it with another root, נֶשֶׁף, "the darkness shall be gloomy, thick, about me"—so the Targ., Se'adyah, Rashi, Qimchi, &c., and so Symm. ἐπισκεπάσει με, another Greek Vers. καλύψει, Jerome, *operient*—or we must adopt a different reading, such as יְעוּפֵנִי, which Böttcher proposes, comparing Job xi. 17; or יְשׂוּכֵנִי, as Ewald suggests, from שׂךְ = סךְ, *to cover*, as יָשׁוּר, for יָשֹׁר, xci. 6.

[h] חֲשֵׁיכָה, a fem. with a superfluous ׳ inserted, but not otherwise an uncommon form, whereas the fem. אוֹרָה only occurs besides Esth. viii. 16, and is a later and Aram. form.

[i] רֻקַּמְתִּי (Pu'al only here). The root means to *variegate*, ποικίλλειν. The body of the fœtus is described as woven together of so many different-coloured threads, like a cunning and beautiful network of tapestry—"velut tapetum e nervis et venis contextus,"—Camp.—similar therefore to the use of סכך, ver. 13; Job x. 11.

[j] גָּלְמִי from גלם, *to roll together*, 2 Kings ii. 8, whence גְּלוֹם, *a mantle*, Ezek. xxvii. 24. The word גֹּלֶם occurs here only in the O.T., but is used in the Mishnah of any unformed, unshapen mass. So the LXX., Aq., have here ἀκατέργαστόν μου, Symm. ἀμόρφωτόν με, as describing the embryo. Hupfeld, however, understands it not of the embryo, but of the yet undeveloped course of life, the days of which are so many *threads* which as yet are rolled together *in a ball*, and which are unwound as life goes on. So that גָּלְמִי would mean *my ball of life*, just as in classical and other writers we have *the thread of life*, *the web of life*, &c. Comp. Catull., "Currite ducentes subtemina, currite, Parcæ."

[k] כֻּלָּם. To what does the suffix refer? Some suppose that the yet undeveloped *members* in the embryo are alluded to, as so many threads rolled and twisted together, and fashioned day by day. But the pronoun must rather be anticipative of the following plur. *days*; these are so many threads of life (comp. Is. xxxviii. 12) which were written (imperf.) in God's book. For other instances of this anticipative use of the pronoun see ix. 13, lxxxvii. 1, cxxxii. 6; Job vi. 29; Is. viii. 21, xiii. 2.

In the following וְלֹא the K'thîbh is obviously right; though the Rabb. attempt to explain the Q'rî וְלוֹ, "to Him (*i.e.* God) they are as one day."

[l] יֹמְרוּךָ. This cannot be "speak against Thee," from אמר, with omission of the א (of which there is only one instance in this verb, 2 Sam. xix. 14, though other elisions of the א may be cited, civ. 29; 2 Sam. xx. 9. xxii. 40; Is. xiii. 20), for this must have been expressed by דִּבֶּר, with the prep. עַל or בְּ; nor "speak of Thee," as the Chald. paraphrases "swear by Thy name wickedly." There is no other instance in which אמר with the accus. means "to speak of a person." Passages like Gen. xliii. 27, Num. xiv. 31, Lam. iv. 20, have been alleged as other instances of this usage, but in each of these cases the object is the relative אֲשֶׁר, "with respect to whom," and the thing said follows, so that they are not real parallels. The correct reading is probably יַמְרוּךָ (as the Quinta renders, παρεπίκρανάν σε) "Provoke Thee," "rebel against Thee," this verb being construed with the accus. Then the following לִמְזִמָּה is used adverbially like לַשָּׁוְא in the next member, as further explaining the nature of the provocation or rebellion, for לַשָּׁוְא may mean *foolishly*, i.e. *wickedly*, as well as *in vain*, *to no purpose*.

[m] נָשׂוּא, an anomalous form, after the analogy of verbs ל׳ ה with prosthetic א. It ought to be נָשְׂאוּ (comp. Jer. x. 5; Ezek. xlvii. 8). The same mode of writing is found (Jer. x. 5) in the Niph'al.

For this absolute use of the verb comp. lxxxix. 10; Hab. i. 3, וּמָדוֹן יִשָּׂא, "and contention *lifteth itself up*."

n עָרֶיךָ. This is generally rendered *Thine enemies*, and as the verse begins with the relative אֲשֶׁר, a second subject is thus awkwardly introduced. So the Chald. and so Aq., ἀντίζηλοί σου, Symm., οἱ ἐναντίοι σου, Jerome, *adversarii tui* (but rendering the relative preceding by *quia*). Some, feeling the awkwardness of the double subject, render, "And they have lifted up Thine enemies (*i.e.* raised them to honour) in vain." Others, again, would explain נ׳ ל׳, with reference to Ex. xx. 7, "they have uttered lies, sworn falsely;" or would read שְׁמֶךָ for עָרֶיךָ, so as to bring the passage into a closer resemblance to Ex. xx. 7. But it is a slighter and simpler change to read עָלֶיךָ, a change which ought perhaps to be made also in 1 Sam. xxviii. 16. Seven MSS. Kenn., and twenty De-R., have here עָדֶיךָ, *unto Thee.* עָרֶיךָ is usually taken to be an Aramaic form for צָרֶיךָ. Otherwise it must mean *Thy cities* (ix. 7, Is. xiv. 21), a sense which is unsuitable here, though it is given by the LXX., λήψονται εἰς ματαιότητα τὰς πόλεις σου, and also by the Syr. and Vulg.

o תְּקוֹמְמֶיךָ. The only instance of an apocop. Hithp. part. Either the מ is omitted incorrectly, or, as Buxtorf conjectures, in order to avoid the concurrence of four *servile letters* at the beginning of the word. For the objective affix comp. xvii. 7.

PSALM 140

THIS Psalm is a prayer for protection against enemies who were at once violent and crafty and unscrupulous in the use of their tongues. The general strain of the Psalm is like that of many which occur in the earlier Books, and like them it is ascribed to David. In tone and language it resembles Psalms lviii. and lxiv., but we have no means of testing the accuracy of the Inscription. The chief peculiarity of the Psalm is, that it has several words which occur nowhere else. Ewald would refer this and the two following Psalms,—but, as it appears to me, without any sufficient reason,—to the age of Manasseh. The impression left upon the mind in reading them, I think, is that they are cast in David's vein and in imitation of his manner rather than written by David himself; but it would be absurd to dogmatize in a matter where we are really left with nothing to guide us, unless we are disposed to accept the tradition from which the title has sprung.

The strophical division of the Psalm is, on the whole, regular. There are four strophes, consisting each of three verses, except that the third, instead of consisting of three verses of two members, consists of two verses of three members, so that the length of each strophe is in fact the same. There is also a concluding strophe of two verses. The close of the first three strophes is marked by the Selah.

[FOR THE PRECENTOR. A PSALM OF DAVID.]

1 DELIVER me, O Jehovah, from the evil-man,
From the violent man preserve[a] me.
2 Who have imagined evil things in (their) hearts;
All the day they stir up[b] wars.
3 They have sharpened their tongue like a serpent,
Adder's poison is under their lips. [Selah.]

4 Keep me, O Jehovah, from the hands of the wicked,
From the violent man preserve me.
Who have purposed to thrust aside my steps.
5 The proud have hidden a snare for me, and cords,
They have spread a net by the side of the road,
They have set gins for me. [Selah.]

6 I said to Jehovah, THOU art my God,
Give ear, O Jehovah, to the voice of my supplications.
7 O Jehovah Lord, Thou strength of my salvation,
Thou hast covered my head in the day of battle.
8 Grant not, O Jehovah, the desires[c] of the wicked;
Further not his wicked device, that they be not lifted up.[d] [Selah.]

1. EVIL MAN, or "evil men" . . . "violent men" (the sing. being used collectively for the plur.), which is more in accordance with the plural in the next verse.

THE VIOLENT MAN, lit. "the man of violences," as in 2 Sam. xxii. 49, instead of "man of violence," as in Ps. xviii. 48 [49].

3. SHARPENED THEIR TONGUE. Comp. lii. 2 [4]. And for the next clause, lviii. 4 [5], x. 7.

4. The opening of the second strophe is a repetition with slight variation of the opening of the first.

5. THE PROUD HAVE HIDDEN, or the adjective may be a predicate, and the subject the same as before: "who have hidden in their pride," &c.

7. COVERED MY HEAD, *i.e.* as with a helmet. Comp. lx. 7 [9].

BATTLE, lit. "armour," as in 1 Kings x. 25; 2 Kings x. 2; Ezek. xxxix. 9, 10.

9 [When they lift up] the head that compass me[e] about,
Let the mischief of their own lips cover them.[f]
10 Let hot burning coals fall[g] upon them,
Let them be cast into the fire,
Into floods of water[h] that they rise not again.
11 An evil speaker shall not be established in the earth,
The violent man—evil[i] shall hunt him to overthrow (him).

12 I know that Jehovah will maintain the cause of the afflicted,
The right of the poor.
13 Surely the righteous shall give thanks unto Thy Name;
The upright shall dwell in Thy presence.

9. WHEN THEY LIFT UP. The verb should probably be transferred here from the end of the previous verse (see Critical Note). In the next clause, and verses, 10, 11, I have followed the E.V. in preferring the optative to the future. But the LXX., Jerome, and the majority of modern commentators give the future: "Though they that compass me may lift up the head, the mischief of their own lips *shall* cover them; hot burning coals *shall* fall upon them," &c.

10. LET THEM BE CAST, lit. "let one cast them," or perhaps Jehovah may be the subject of the verb, "May He cast them."

11. AN EVIL SPEAKER, lit. "a man of tongue;" not, however, used here in the sense of "a talkative man;" as the similar phrase, "a man of lips" (E.V. "a man full of talk"), in Job xi. 2, but with the further notion of *evil* speaking, as in ver. 3.

13. DWELL IN THY PRESENCE. See xi. 7, xvi. 11.

[a] תִּנְצְרֵנִי. The full form, as in lxi. 8, lxxviii. 7, &c.

[b] יָגוּרוּ. The verb is usually intrans. "gather themselves," in a hostile sense, as in lvi. 7. So it is commonly taken here, the prep. אֶל or לְ being understood, or the accus. being regarded as the accus. of direction. Qimchi, however, makes the verb trans. here *gather wars*, i.e. gather the materials for war. Perhaps it is better to take נור = גרה, *to stir up*, as the Chald., Syr., and others. In the next verse עַכְשׁוּב is a ἅπ. λεγ.

[c] מַאֲוַיֵּי (only here, instead of אַוַּת, תַּאֲוַת). Constr. plur. of מַאֲוֶה (not of מַאֲוַי, or מַאֲוָי, as Gesen.), for the termination ֶה is a contraction from *ai*—a false formation, with euphonic doubling of the third radical, according to the analogy of מַחֲמַדִּים, מַשְׁמַנִּים, &c., here transferred to 3 Yod, contrary to rule. It would be better to write מַאֲוָיֵי, like the constr. forms גְּדָיֵי (Gen. xxvii. 9, 16); לְחָיֵי (Is. xxx. 28, instead of גְּדָיֵי, &c.), after the analogy

of the termination יָאִי. This is proposed by Abulwalid, who found it in his MS., and Qimchi (*Mikhlol*), and Kenn. and Shelomoh Yedidyah of Norcia mention having found it in some MSS.; but the form does not occur elsewhere. (See Hupfeld.) זְמָם is another ἅπ. λεγ.

[d] יָרוּמוּ. This is commonly taken as loosely subjoined to the previous sentence, either as governed by the preceding negative, LXX., μήποτε ὑψωθῶσι, Symm. ἵνα μὴ ἐπαρθῶσι (comp. Is. xiv. 21, בַּל יָקֻמוּ), or as describing the consequences of their success, "they will lift themselves up." But it is impossible not to feel that in all probability the word is misplaced before the Selah, and that it belongs to the following verse, especially as the first clause of that verse requires a verb to make sense: "They that surround me have lifted up the head." It is true that רוּם in the Qal is not trans., and therefore רֹאשׁ must either be the accus. of reference, "as to the head," or perhaps we ought to read יָרִימוּ. For the fluctuations between Qal and Hiph. in this word comp. lxxxix. 18, 26, cxlviii. 13.

[e] מְסִבָּי, usually taken as part. Hiph.: but the Hiph. of this verb is never intransitive, not even in Josh. vi. 11, 2 Sam. v. 23. It must therefore be from an abstract מֵסַב, whence plur. constr. מְסִבּוֹת, used adverbially, and מְסִבֵּי, 2 Kings xxiii. 5; and here with suffix = סְבִיבֹתַי, xxvii. 6.

[f] יכסומו. The K'thîbh is plur., referring to the *lips* as the subject (Ges. § 148, 1). The correction to the sing. in the Q'rî is therefore unnecessary.

[g] ימיטו. The K'thîbh can only refer to an indefinite subject: "*Let them* (men) *cast* hot burning coals," &c., which is equivalent to a passive: *Let hot burning coals* (which may perhaps mean *lightnings*, as in xviii. 13, 14) *be cast*, &c. See on lvi. note [e]. The Q'rî, however, substitutes the Niph. יִמּוֹטוּ, which is contrary to the usage in the Niph. Hupf. therefore would read יַמְטִיר (comp. xi. 6), making Jehovah the subject here, as in the next clause.

[h] מַהֲמֹרוֹת, only here. Ibn Ez. and Qimchi explain it to mean *deep pits*, but without any reason. It is probably to be explained by the cogn. Arab. همر, *to pour out water*, هَمْرَةٌ, *a cataract.*

[i] רָע. The accent is clearly wrong, for this is not an adjective to אִישׁ ח׳, *a wicked, violent man*, but a noun, which is the subject of the following verb, as the Chald., the LXX., the Rabb., and others have taken it. The Athnach should therefore be transferred to חָמָס.

PSALM 141

This Psalm presents some peculiar difficulties of interpretation, which, however, are due neither to the words employed, nor to the grammatical construction, but to the extreme abruptness with which in verses 5—7 the thoughts follow one another, and the extreme obscurity which hangs over the allusions. To translate each sentence by itself is no difficult matter, but it is almost hopeless either to link the sentences plausibly together, or to discover in them any tangible clue to the circumstances in which the Psalmist was placed. As all the Ancient Versions must have had substantially the same text, the deviations in any of them being very slight, it is hardly probable that, as Olshausen and Hupfeld maintain, the text is corrupt: it is more likely that our entire ignorance of the circumstances under which the Psalm was written prevents our piercing the obscurity of the writer's words.

It has been usual to accept the Inscription which assigns the Psalm to David, and to assign it to the time of his persecution by Saul. Ver. 5 has generally been supposed to allude to David's generous conduct in sparing the life of his foe when he was in his power (see 1 Sam. xxiv., and comp. the note on ver. 6 of this Psalm), but it is quite impossible on this supposition to give any plausible interpretation to ver. 7.

Delitzsch, with more probability, refers the Psalm to the time of Absalom's rebellion. He sees an allusion to David's distance from the sanctuary and the worship of the sanctuary in ver. 2, and he explains ver. 6 of the punishment which shall overtake the rebel leaders, and the return of the people to their allegiance.

Ewald would assign this, as well as the preceding and following Psalms, to a time subsequent to the Assyrian invasion,—perhaps the reign of Manasseh. He supposes that in the persecution to which the true worshipers of Jehovah, and especially the leading men amongst them, were exposed, the Psalmist, who was apparently a man of some distinction (cxlii. 7 [8]), had himself suffered. He had been assailed by threats (cxl. 3 [4], 9 [10]), and by flatteries (cxli. 4); and if these failed in drawing him away, his destruction was resolved upon (cxl. 5 [6], cxli. 9, 10, cxlii. 3 [4]). But undaunted by threats, unseduced by flatteries, he cleaves with the most resolute faith and love to his God, and will rather submit to reproof from the true-hearted than suffer himself to be cajoled and led astray by the wicked (cxli. 5). And when at last his enemies, enraged at his firmness, seize him and cast him into prison, leaving him there to perish (cxlii. 7 [8]), he does not give way, but still cries to Jehovah for help, and trusts in His power and faithfulness.*

Maurer thinks that this Psalm was written at a time when idolatry had become prevalent, especially among men of the highest rank and station, and that in consequence the faithful servants of Jehovah were exposed to bitter persecution. We thus obtain a suitable meaning, he says, for the whole Psalm, of which he thus sketches the outline :—" There are three strophes : (1) Hear my prayer, O Jehovah : suffer me not to speak any word against Thee, nor to fall away to the wicked, allured by their luxurious banquets (ver. 1—4). (2) Why should I not rejoice in my God? Nay, if their leaders are overthrown, the men shall gladly hear me raising a song of joy and triumph, though now our bones cover the earth (ver. 5—7). (3) Keep me, O Jehovah, from the devices of the wicked. Let them be snared in their own nets, whilst I escape " (ver. 8—10).

It is curious that, whilst De Wette, describing the Psalm as "a very original, and therefore difficult, Psalm," holds it to be one of the oldest in the collection, Maurer, almost on the same grounds ("oratio maxime impedita ac talis in qua manifeste cum verbis luctetur vates"), sets it down as belonging to a comparatively late period.

[A PSALM OF DAVID.]

1 O JEHOVAH, I have called upon Thee, haste Thee unto me;
Give ear to my voice when I call upon Thee.

---

* I subjoin Ewald's rendering and explanation of ver. 5—7 : "Let the righteous smite me in love and chastise me ; let no oil for the head soften my head ! For still—my prayer is uttered in their misfortunes. Their judges have been hurled into the rifts of the rock ; so shall they hear how sweet my words are ! As though one should furrow and cleave the earth, our bones have been scattered for the jaws of death." That is, "So far am I from partaking of the dainties of the wicked, I will rather turn to the righteous, and welcome their reproofs for my past coldness. I will not even anoint my head," for that would be a sign of joy and festivity, whereas now they are in suffering, and I can only pray. The chiefest among them have already perished, " but the righteous who have escaped the general persecution shall hear my words of sympathy and my prayers " (such, for instance, as we have in this Psalm) ; and then, as if deeply sympathising with the judges, the princes who have been slain, he counts himself in their number, "*Our* bones lie scattered," &c., as on a field of battle (liii. 5 [6].)

2 Let my prayer be set forth (as) incense before Thee,
The lifting up of my hands as the evening sacrifice.
3 Set a watch,[a] O Jehovah, before my mouth,
Keep the door [b] of my lips.
4 Incline not my heart to any evil thing,
To busy itself [c] in wicked doings with men [d] that work iniquity;
And let me not eat of their dainties.

5 Let a righteous man smite me, it shall be a kindness;
And let him reprove me, it shall be as oil upon (my) head,
Let not my head refuse [e] (it):
For yet is my prayer [f] against their wickednesses.

2. LIFTING UP OF MY HANDS. *i.e.* evidently, as the parallelism requires, in prayer: comp. xxviii. 2. Others, as the Syr., and recently Ewald and Hengstenberg, explain it of bringing an offering. This, however, is against both the parallelism and the comparison with the evening sacrifice.

EVENING SACRIFICE. The sacrifice here meant is strictly the offering consisting of fine flour with oil and frankincense, or of unleavened cakes mingled with oil, which was burnt upon the altar (Heb. *minchah*, E.V. "meat-offering"): see Lev. ii. 1—11. This, however, like the "incense," was only added to the burnt-offering, the lamb which was offered every morning and evening (Ex. xxix. 38—42; Num. xxviii. 3—8). It would seem, therefore, that these two, "the incense" and "the offering of fine flour," &c., stand for the morning and evening sacrifices; and the sense is, "Let my daily prayer be acceptable to Thee as are the daily sacrifices of Thine own appointment." (The *minchah* is used 1 Kings xviii. 29, 36, of the whole evening sacrifice, and of the morning sacrifice, 2 Kings iii. 20.) The incense may be mentioned because, as ascending in a fragrant cloud, it was symbolical of prayer (Rev. v. 8, viii. 3, 4); and the same would hold also of the "meat-offering," of which it is said that the priest was to burn a part as "a memorial," "a *sweet savour* unto Jehovah" (Lev. ii. 9).

3. SET A WATCH. Comp. xxxiv. 13 [14], xxxix. 1 [2]; Prov. xiii. 3, xxi. 23. The prayer is apparently directed against the temptation to indulge in rash and foolish words such as wicked men would indulge in (see next verse). Others suppose that he prays to be kept from the temptation to break out into bitter words against his persecutors (as against Saul, if the Psalm be David's); or into murmurs and complaints against God.

4. INCLINE NOT. See note on li. 4.

DAINTIES. It is unnecessary to explain this of things sacrificed to idols (Ros., Del.), as if the Psalmist were surrounded by heathen: comp. xvi. 4. The temptation is rather to an easy, luxurious, sensual life, as in lxxiii.

5. According to the rendering I have preferred of this verse, the sense will be: "I will gladly welcome even the reproofs of the good (comp. Prov. xxvii. 6; Eccl. vii. 5), and I will avail myself of prayer (as in ver. 2—4) as the best defence

6 (When) their judges have been hurled down the sides of
the rock,
Then they shall hear my words that they are sweet.

against the wickedness of my persecutors." The last member of the verse may be rendered, "For even *in* their wickedness (whilst it continues and whilst I suffer from it) shall my prayer continue." So Mendels. "Ich bete noch da jene Schandthat üben." Aq. *ὅτι ἔτι καὶ προσευχή μου ἐν κακίαις αὐτῶν.* It is possible, however, that this last clause refers not to his enemies, but to the righteous, in which case it must be rendered, "For still my prayer shall be offered *in their misfortunes.*" (So Ewald.)

Again, the first two clauses have been rendered: "Let a righteous man smite me in love (*accus.*) (LXX. ἐν ἐλέει), and reprove me. Such oil upon the head let not my head refuse." (Delitzsch.) But nothing is gained by this, and the balance of the members is not so well preserved. Others again (as Maur., Hengst.) understand by "the righteous," God, appealing to Is. xxiv. 16—where, however, "the righteous" means not God, but "the righteous nation."

In ver. 4 he had prayed that he might not be led astray by the evil he saw around him, nor allured by the blandishments and luxurious prosperity of the wicked. Now he says, on the contrary, "let me ever be ready to welcome even reproof from the righteous," which, however harsh, is salutary. The wounds of a friend are faithful, and better than the kisses of an enemy.

6. This verse, difficult in itself, is still more difficult, because it has no very obvious connection either with what precedes or with what follows. The allusions are so obscure that it is impossible to do more than guess at the meaning.

THEIR JUDGES must be in a general sense the "rulers" or "princes" of "the wicked;" for the pronoun must refer to them. (Ewald, however — see Introduction to the Psalm—supposes the leading men amongst the righteous to be meant, who are the principal sufferers in the time of persecution.) The verse apparently describes a punishment which has been, or will be inflicted upon them (see for this mode of punishment 2 Chron. xxv. 12; Luke iv. 29). The verb HURLED DOWN is the same which is used, 2 Kings ix. 33, of the throwing down of Jezebel from the window.

THE SIDES OF THE ROCK, lit. "along," or "by the sides (Heb. *hands*) of the rock or precipice.' Comp. cxl. 5 [6], "by *the side* of the path"; Jud. xi. 26, "by the sides (E. V. *coasts*, Heb. *hands*) of Arnon." Others, "into the hands (*i.e.* the power) of the rock," with the same notion of punishment, but rather, as in cxxxvii. 9, being hurled against the rock. (The preposition employed favours the latter explanation; see Lam. iv. 14.)

THEY SHALL HEAR, *i.e.* of course not the "judges," but either *their followers* who have been led astray by their pernicious influence, or perhaps more generally, *men* shall hear. If the Psalm is to be referred to Absalom's rebellion, or any similar occasion, the sense will be, "When the leaders in the insurrection meet with the fate they deserve, then the subjects of the king will return to their allegiance." And the expression, "they shall hear my words that they are sweet," would be a throughly Oriental mode of describing the satisfaction with which they would welcome the gracious amnesty pronounced by their offended sovereign.

Others, who suppose that the Psalm alludes to David's magnanimity in sparing Saul when he was in his power (1 Sam. xxiv.), explain "When their leaders (meaning

7 As when one furroweth [g] the earth (with the plough),
Our bones have been scattered at the mouth of the grave.
8 For unto Thee, O Jehovah, the Lord, are mine eyes,
In Thee have I found refuge, O pour not out [h] my soul.

Saul) were let go (suffered to escape) along the sides of the rock, they heard my words that they were sweet,"—recognized, that is, my forbearance and generosity in sparing my enemy, instead of taking his life.

7. AS WHEN ONE FURROWETH, &c., lit. "as one who furroweth and cleaveth in the earth" (the participle absolute being used for the finite verb). The allusion is as obscure as in the previous verses, and the point of the comparison is differently explained. The bones scattered are compared either (1) to the clods broken by the ploughshare, or (2) to the seed scattered in the earth turned up by the plough. Maurer finds the point of the comparison in the *length* of the furrow: "Quemadmodum qui terram arat, *longas* facit *series* sulcorum, sic ossa nostra, longa serie sparsa, prostrata sunt orci in prædam." But the emphasis is laid by the use of the double verb on the *breaking-up* of the clods. There is no reason to supply a different object, as the E.V., "As when one cutteth and cleaveth *wood* upon the earth." The explanation first given is the most probable. In 2 Chron. xxv. 12, where ten thousand Edomites are said to have been cast down from the top of the rock (*sela'*, as here), the same verb is used to describe their destruction which is here used of *cleaving* the earth by the plough.

AT THE MOUTH, or perhaps "*for* the mouth," *i.e.* so as to be swallowed up by it.

THE GRAVE. Heb. Sheol, the abode of the dead, though here perhaps nothing more than the grave may be meant. The verse thus describes a complete and disastrous overthrow and apparently of the whole nation; for now we have the pronoun of the first person, "*our* bones." It is true that in some of the Ancient Versions the pronoun of the third person is found. So in the LXX. although τὰ ὀστᾶ ἡμῶν is the original reading yet *B* has an alternate reading αὐτῶν, and this is found in *A* (by a second hand) and in the Syr., Arab., and Æthiop. Böttcher insists upon this as the correct reading, and explains "*their* bones" of the bones of the judges hurled down the rock. Hengst. and Delitzsch, on the other hand, find here a figure expressive of hope and consolation. The bones, according to them, are compared to seed scattered in the upturned earth, from which a harvest may be expected. So here a national resurrection (the first germ of what is expressed in Is. xxvi. 19; Ezek. xxxvii.), a new life, is anticipated. But if this be the point of comparison, it is very strangely expressed: it certainly does not lie on the surface of the words.

8. FOR. The conjunction does not refer to what immediately precedes, but either to what is said in ver. 4, 5 (so Maurer), or perhaps rather to the whole of the former part of the Psalm, so far as it consists of petition: "Listen to my prayer,—keep me from temptation, —*for* unto Thee are mine eyes."

POUR NOT OUT MY SOUL, *i.e.* give not my life up to destruction. Comp. the use of the same verb Is. liii. 12, "He poured out His soul unto death."

But the rendering of the E.V., "leave not my soul destitute" is in accordance with the root signifi-

9 Keep me from the snare which they have laid for me,
From the gins of the workers of iniquity.
10 Let the wicked fall into their own nets,
Whilst that I withal[i] escape.

cation of the word, and therefore may be right.

9. FROM THE SNARE, lit. "from the hands of the snare." So we have in xxii. 20 [21], "from the hand of the dog;" in Job v. 20, "from the hand of the sword;" Is. xlvii. 14, "from the hand of the flame."

INTO THEIR OWN NETS. The pronoun is singular, used distributively,—"Each one of them into his own net." For the sentiment comp. vii. 15 [16].

[a] שָׁמְרָה. The noun occurs only here. Qimchi (after R. Mosheh, Hakkohen, Ib. Giqitilla) defends it by forms such as חָכְמָה, עָצְמָה. Hupf. finds a difficulty in admitting this abstract noun from a transitive verb, especially as we have another noun, מִשְׁמָר, in this sense; and is inclined therefore to take the word as the imperative with ה paragog., in the same construction with לְפִי, as in xxxix. 2, where, however, it is followed by the accus. מַחְסוֹם. Like Ibn 'Ezr., he supposes that the writer intended to imitate the construction in xxxix. 2, but to break it up into שִׁית מ׳ לְפִי and שָׁמַר, but then either omitted מ׳ or dropped the construction he had begun. It is so far in favour of this view, that נִצְּרָה is of the same imperat. form (Qal with euphon. Dagesh, as in Prov. iv. 13); here followed by עַל (which it is nowhere else), after the analogy of שמר. Some, however, would make נִצְּרָה, like שָׁמְרָה, a noun.

[b] דַּל, another ἅπ. λεγ., instead of the fem. דֶּלֶת.

[c] הִתְעוֹלֵל. This Hithp. (denom. from עֲלִילָה) occurs only here.

[d] אִישִׁים. This plur. form occurs also Is. liii. 3; Prov. viii. 4. מַנְעַמִּים, in the next line, is another ἅπ. λεγ.

[e] יָנִי for יָנִיא, as אָבִי for אָבִיא, Micah i. 15, written defectively, perhaps because optative or jussive. See lv. note [1]; Ges. § 73, Rem. 4, § 74; Rem. 21 *c*. The rendering of the LXX., μὴ λιπανάτω τὴν κεφαλήν μου, with which Jerome and the Syr. agree, cannot be defended. There is, indeed, an Arab root, نَيِ, *to become fat*, but said only of *camels*, and there is no active formation from it "to make fat," and no such root in Hebrew.

[f] כִּי עוֹד וּתְ׳. The ו must introduce the apodosis, and the sentence is elliptical: "For (so it is) still, *that* my prayer," &c. With this elliptical use of עוֹד ו compare עוֹד אֲשֶׁר, "it will still be that," Zech. viii. 20, and אַחַר ו, Prov. xxiv. 27, "afterwards it shall be that," &c.

[g] פֹּלֵחַ is taken by some of the ancient interpreters as = a noun, "husbandman," and as the subject of the sentence. Sym. ὥσπερ γεωργὸς ὅταν ῥήσσῃ τὴν γῆν οὕτως ἐσκορπίσθη κ.τ.λ. Jer. *Sicut agricola cum scindit*

terram. The root is of course the same as that of the common Arabic word *Fellah.*

[h] תְּעַר for תְּעָר (Ges. § 75, Rem. 8), Pi'el, or incorr. for תַּעַר, Hiph., which is found in Is. liii. 12. The root is used of *emptying* a vessel, Gen. xxiv. 20; a chest, 2 Chron. xxiv. 11; then it gets the sense of *pouring out*, as Maurer observes: "Quod evacuandi verba facillime a vasis transferuntur ad id quod vasis continetur." But it is better perhaps to keep to the root meaning of making bare, destitute, empty.

[i] יַחַד. Some would join this to the previous hemistich: "into their own nets together." Maurer considers it to be = כֹּל יַחַד, and supposes it to refer to *the nets*, and to be the object of the verb: "Whilst I escape them all." But it is better to take יַחַד here in the sense of *at the same time* (comp. iv. 9, xxxiii. 15), and עַד (*whilst*, as in Job viii. 21) as merely placed second in the sentence (comp. cxxviii. 2), in order that the emphatic word may occupy the first place.

PSALM 142

THIS is the last of the eight Psalms which, according to their Inscriptions, are to be referred to David's persecution by Saul. Like the 57th Psalm, it is supposed to describe his thoughts and feelings when he was "in the cave," though whether in the cave of Adullam (1 Sam. xxii. 1) or in that of Engedi (1 Sam. xxiv. 3) is not clear. (See Introduction to Psalm lvii.) The general strain of the Psalm is that of the earlier Books. It expresses in language liket hat of David the cleaving of the heart to God, the deep sense of loneliness, the cry for deliverance, the confidence that that deliverance will call forth the sympathy and the joy of many others. But whether it is written only in imitation of David's manner, or whether it is a genuine work of David's extracted perhaps from some history, and added, at a time subsequent to the Exile, to the present collection, it is impossible now to determine.

[A MASCHIL[a] OF DAVID WHEN HE WAS IN THE CAVE. A PRAYER.]

1 WITH my voice to Jehovah will I cry,
With my voice to Jehovah will I make supplication.
2 I will pour out before Him my complaint;
My trouble before Him will I make known.

3 When my spirit is overwhelmed within me,
THOU knowest my path:
In the way wherein I walk,
Have they hidden a snare for me.
4 Look [b] on the right hand and see,
There is none that will know me;
Refuge hath failed me;
There is none that seeketh after my soul.

5 I have cried unto Thee, O Jehovah,
I have said, THOU art my refuge,
My portion in the land of the living.
6 Attend unto my cry,
For I am brought very low:
Deliver me from my persecutors,
For they are too strong for me.
7 Bring forth my soul out of prison,

3. WHEN MY SPIRIT. The first member of this verse is, perhaps, to be connected with the preceding verse, precisely as the same words are found connected in the title of Ps. cii. (So Hupfeld and Bunsen.)

IS OVERWHELMED, lit. "darkens itself." See on lxxvii. 3 [4].

WITHIN ME, lit. "upon me." See on xlii. note [d].

THOU: lit. "and THOU." If the existing arrangement of the text is right, the conjunction only serves to introduce the apodosis. But if the first clause, "when my spirit," &c., belongs to the previous verse, then we must render here, "And Thou knowest," &c.

4. LOOK. There is no contradiction in this prayer to the previous statement of belief in God's omniscience, "Thou knowest my path," as has been alleged. Such appeals to God, to see, to regard, &c., are common enough, "and are bound up with the very nature of prayer, which is one great anthropomorphism."

ON THE RIGHT HAND, as the direction in which he would naturally look for succour (a παραστάτης). See xvi. 8, cix. 6, 31, cx. 5, cxxi. 5.

THAT WILL KNOW, lit. "that recognizes me." Comp. Ruth ii. 10, 19.

HATH FAILED, as in Am. ii. 14; Jer. xxv. 35; Job xi. 20.

SEEKETH AFTER, *i.e.* "troubleth himself concerning," "careth for," as in Deut. xi. 12; 2 Sam. xi. 3; Job x. 6; though according to the analogy of Jer. xxx. 17, it would be possible also to render, "My soul hath none that seeketh (it);" or "seeker" may here mean "avenger," as Hammond explains, *vindex et servator sollicitus*. Comp. for this use of the verb x. 13.

5. MY PORTION. Comp. xvi. 5, lxxiii. 26.

THE LIVING, or "life." See xxvii. 13.

7. OUT OF PRISON. This is clearly to be understood figuratively. Comp. the parallel passage, cxliii. 11.

That I may give thanks unto Thy Name.
The righteous shall come about[c] me,
Because Thou dealest bountifully with me.

COME ABOUT ME, *i.e.* sympathising in my joy, though elsewhere the word is used in a hostile sense. The P.B.V. "then shall the righteous resort unto my company."

[a] See on xxxii. note [a], and Introduction to lvii.

[b] הַבִּיט. This can only be imperat. (like the following רְאֵה) for הַבֵּט, as in Job xxxv. 5. See on lxxvii. note [c], xciv. note [a]. The Ancient Versions, nearly without exception, have here the first person. LXX. κατενόουν καὶ ἐπέβλεπον. Similarly the Chald. and Syr., and the Rabb. commentators, and so the E.V., evidently taking the forms as infinitive absolutes, which would hold of הַבִּיט, but not of רְאֵה, for the apparent inf. constr. הֱיֹה, Ezek. xxi. 15, proves nothing as it follows לְמַעַן. Ewald would read רָאֹה, but no change is necessary. Jerome is quite right in keeping the imperative, *Respice . . . et vide.*

[c] יַכְתִּרוּ. The verb, both in Hiph. and Pi'el, is elsewhere used in a hostile sense, and with the accus. Here it must be expressive of sympathy, though neither this meaning nor the constr. with בְּ is to be found elsewhere. Others, following the LXX. and Aq., render "shall *wait* for me;" but then it must be Pi'el, as in Job xxxvi. 2, where it is also followed by לְ. Others again take the word as a denom. from כֶּתֶר, and explain *crown*, or *put on a crown*, in a figurative sense, *i.e.* triumph in me, boast themselves of me as of a crown. Del. compares Prov. xiv. 18. Symm. τὸ ὄνομά σου στεφανώσονται δίκαιοι. Jerome, *in me coronabuntur justi.* The following כִּי is rendered in the E.V. *for.* The LXX. have ἕως οὗ ἀνταποδῷς μοι. Jer. *cum retribueris mihi.* Symm. ὅταν εὐεργετήσῃς με.

PSALM 143

THIS is the last of the seven Penitential Psalms, as they are called. (See Introduction to Vol. I. p. 23.) In the Hebrew it is styled a Psalm of David; in some copies of the LXX. it is further said to have been written when he had to flee from his son Absalom. It is probable that the deep tone of sorrow and anguish which pervades the Psalm, and the deep sense of sin, led to the belief that it must be referred to that occasion. The spirit and the language, it is true, are not unworthy of David; yet the many passages borrowed from earlier Psalms make it more probable that this Psalm is the work of some later Poet. Delitzsch says very truly, that if David himself did nor write it—and he admits that the many expressions derived from other sources are against such a supposition—still the Psalm is " an extract of the most precious balsam from the old Davidic songs." Like other post-exile Psalms (such, for instance, as the 116th and 119th), it is a witness to us of the depth and reality of the religious life in the later history of the nation, and an evidence also of the way in which that life was upheld and cherished by the inspired words of David and other Psalmists and prophets of old.

The Psalm consists of two parts, each of which is of six verses, the conclusion of the first being marked by the Selah. The first portion contains the complaint (ver. 1—6); the second, the prayer founded on that complaint (ver. 7—12).

[A PSALM OF DAVID.]

1 O JEHOVAH, hear my prayer,
Give ear to my supplications.
In Thy faithfulness answer me, (and) in Thy righteousness.
2 And enter not into judgement with Thy servant;
For before Thee no man living is righteous:

1. IN THY FAITHFULNESS ... IN THY RIGHTEOUSNESS. It is to God's own character that the appeal is made. It is there first, and not in his own misery, that the sinner finds the great argument why his prayer should be answered. It is precisely the same ground which St. John takes: " If we confess our sins, He is *faithful* and *righteous* (true to His promise and true to His revealed character) to forgive us our sins."

2. ENTER NOT INTO JUDGEMENT, as in Job ix. 32, xxii. 4. He traces his suffering to his sin: the malice of his enemies is the rod of God's chastisement, calling him to repentance.

BEFORE THEE, *i.e.* at thy bar, in the judgement.

IS RIGHTEOUS. Our translators are not consistent in their rendering of this verb. Here they follow the LXX. οὐ δικαιωθήσεται, "shall not be justified." But in Job ix. 15, x. 15, xv. 14, xxii. 3, xxxii. 1, xxxiv. 5, xxxv. 7, xl. 8, they give as the equivalent "to be righteous;" so, too, in Ps. xix. 9 [10]. But in Ps. li. 4 [6] they have "justify," as here; and so in Job xi. 2, xiii. 18, xxv. 4; whereas in iv. 17, xxxiii. 12, they render "to be just."

In many of the passages referred to in Job we see the same deep sense of man's unrighteousness before a righteous God which the Psalmist here expresses. Yet it is that very righteousness before which he trembles, to which he appeals, which he needs, in which alone he can stand before his Judge. The passage clearly shows, says Calvin, that he is justified who is considered and accounted just before God, or whom the heavenly Judge Himself acquits as innocent.

3 For the enemy hath persecuted my soul,
He hath smitten my life down to the earth,
He hath made me dwell in darkness as those that are for ever dead.
4 And my spirit is overwhelmed in me,
My heart within me is desolate.
5 I have remembered the days of old,
I have meditated on all Thou hast done;
On the work of Thy hands do I muse.
6 I have spread forth my hands unto Thee,
My soul (thirsteth) after Thee as a thirsty land.
[Selah.]

3. FOR THE ENEMY. This is the reason why he turns to God so earnestly. The outward suffering, the persecution, the chastisement laid upon him—it may have been through some guilt of his own—had purged the spiritual eye, had made him look within, had shown him his own heart, its sinfulness and its misery, as he had never seen it before; and this deep sense of sin and misery had led to the prayer in ver. 2. Hence his deliverance from his enemy and the forgiveness of his sin are naturally connected in his mind.

IN DARKNESS, lit. in "darknesses," or "dark places," as in lxxxviii. 6 [7], where it is used of the abode of the dead.

Comp. with this verse vii. 5 [6]; Lam. iii. 6; Ps. lxxxviii. 3—6 [4—7].

FOR EVER DEAD. The dead are so called as "fixed in an eternal state," as those who can never return again to this world.

4. IS OVERWHELMED. The same word as in lxxvii. 3 [4], cvii. 5 (where see note), cxlii. 3 [4]. "Having spoken of his outward troubles," says Calvin, "he now confesses the weakness of his spirit, whence we gather that this was no stony fortitude (*non saxeam fuisse ejus fortitudinem*), but that, whilst overwhelmed with sorrow so far as his natural feelings were concerned, he stood and was supported only by faith and the grace of the Spirit."

IS DESOLATE, or rather "is full of amazement," lit. "astonies itself;" seeks to comprehend the mystery of its sufferings, and is ever beaten back upon itself in its perplexity: such is the full force of the reflexive conjugation here employed. The form occurs besides Is. lix. 16, lxiii. 5; Dan. viii. 27; Eccl. vii. 16. This and the next verse are an echo of lxxvii. 3—6 [4—7], 11, 12 [12, 13]. See notes there.

6. I HAVE SPREAD FORTH MY HANDS, as the weary child stretches forth its hands to its mother, that on her bosom it may be hushed to rest.

THIRSTY, lit. "weary," "languishing," but used as here Is. xxxii. 2. The construction is doubtful. According to the accents it would be, "My soul is a land thirsting after Thee." But as the adjective is used both of the soul, Prov. xxv. 25, and of a land, Ps. lxiii. 1 [2], it is probable that it here belongs to both words. "In great heat we see the earth cracking and gaping, as though with open mouth she asked for the rain from heaven."—*Calvin.*

AFTER THEE. "Observe how he binds himself to God alone, cuts off every other hope from his soul, and,

7 Make haste to answer me, O Jehovah,
  My spirit faileth:
Hide not Thy face from me,
  That so I become like them that go down into the pit.
8 Cause me to hear Thy loving-kindness in the morning,
  For in Thee have I trusted;
Cause me to know the way in which I should walk,
  For unto Thee have I lifted up my soul.
9 Deliver me from mine enemies, O Jehovah,
  Unto Thee have I fled to hide me.[a]
10 Teach me to do Thy will,
  For Thou art my God;
    Let Thy good [b] Spirit lead me in a plain country.

in short, makes his very need a chariot wherewith to mount up to God."

7. In the second half of the Psalm many of the expressions are borrowed from earlier Psalms. With the prayer in this verse comp. lxix. 17 [18], xxvii. 9, cii. 2 [3]; with the second clause comp. lxxxiv. 2 [3], where the ardent longing for God is expressed in the same way.

THAT SO I BECOME, &c., is word for word as in xxviii. 1; comp. lxxxviii. 4 [5].

8. IN THE MORNING, *i.e.* early, soon. Comp. Moses' prayer, xc, 14. Various interpretations have been given, which are thus summed up by Calvin: "Adverbium *mane* frigide quidam restringunt ad sacrificia. Scimus enim quotidie bis sacrificia offerre solitos, matutinum et vespertinum. Alii subtilius accipiunt, quod Deus mitius agens cum suis servis dicatur formare novum diem. Alii metaphoram esse volunt et notari prosperum lætumque statum: sicut triste et calamitosum tempus sæpe notatur per tenebras. Sed miror in hac voce quæri extraneos sensus, qua simpliciter repetit quod prius dixerat *festina.* Mane ergo tantundem valet ac tempestive vel celeriter."

THE WAY IN WHICH I SHOULD WALK. Comp. xxv. 4, cxlii. 3 [4], with Exod. xxxiii. 13.

LIFTED UP MY SOUL, as in xxv. 1, lxxxvi. 4.

9. FLED TO HIDE ME, lit. "unto Thee have I hidden (myself)." But the phrase is very peculiar and its meaning doubtful. See in Critical Note.

10. TO DO THY WILL, not merely to *know* it; hence the need of the Holy Spirit's aid, His quickening, guiding, strengthening, as well as His enlightening influence. "Necesse est Deum nobis *non mortua tantum litera* magistrum esse et doctorem, sed arcano Spiritus instinctu, imo tribus modis fungitur erga nos magistri officio: quia verbo suo nos docet; deinde Spiritu mentes illuminat: tertio cordibus nostris insculpit doctrinam, ut vero et serio consensu obediamus."

THY WILL, lit. "Thy good pleasure," as in ciii. 21. P.B.V., "The thing that pleaseth Thee."

THY GOOD SPIRIT, as in Neh. ix. 20; comp. Ps. li. 11 [13].

IN A PLAIN COUNTRY, lit. "in a level land," or "on level ground," where there is no fear of stumbling and falling, LXX. *ὁδηγήσει με ἐν τῇ εὐθείᾳ*, Sym. *διὰ γῆς ὁμαλῆς.* The word *mîshōr* is constantly used of the plain (champaign) country. See

11 For Thy Name's sake, O Jehovah, quicken me,
In Thy righteousness bring my soul out of distress.
12 And of Thy loving-kindness cut off mine enemies,
And destroy all the adversaries of my soul;
For I am Thy servant.

for instance Deut. iv. 43. Comp. Is. xxvi. 7, "The path of the righteous is level. Thou makest level (even, as if adjusted in the balance) the road of the righteous." It is unnecessary with Hupf. to correct the text, and substitute "path" for "land," for we have a similar expression in Is. xxvi. 10, "the land of uprightness."

Comp. with this verse generally xxvii. 11, xxxi. 3 [4], xl. 8 [9], ciii. 21.

11. OUT OF DISTRESS. Comp. cxlii. 7 [8].

The series of petitions in ver. 8—12 may thus be grouped:—

(1) Prayer for God's mercy or loving-kindness, as that on which all hangs, and then for guidance (ver. 8).

(2) For deliverance from enemies, and then still more fully for a knowledge of God's will, and the gifts of His Spirit, that he may obey that will (ver. 9, 10).

(3) For a new life, and deliverance from suffering, and now not only for deliverance from his enemies, but for their destruction (ver. 11, 12).

Hence the second petition in (1) answers to the second petition in (2); the first in (2) to the second in (3).

Further, in ver. 8—10, the ground of the petition in each case is the personal relation of the Psalmist to God: "In Thee have I trusted," "Unto Thee have I lifted up my soul," "Unto Thee have I fled," "Thou art my God;" and so also at the close of ver. 12, "I am Thy servant." On the other hand, in ver. 11, and the first member of ver. 12, the appeal is to God and His attributes, "For Thy Name's sake," "In Thy righteousness," "of Thy loving-kindness."

12. I AM THY SERVANT. "Tantundem hoc valet acsi Dei se clientem faciens, ejus patrocinio vitam suam permitteret."—*Calvin*.

[a] אֵלֶיךָ כִסִּתִי. It is not easy to explain the construction. The Syr. omits the words altogether. The LXX. render *ὅτι πρός σε κατέφυγον*, from which it might seem that they read חָסִיתִי, were it not that elsewhere they render נוּס, and not חסה (comp. חוּס), by *καταφυγεῖν*. The Targum paraphrases, "Thy word have I counted as a Redeemer," whence it might be inferred that they read כַּסֹּתִי (see this verb, Ex. xii. 4). Jerome apparently had our present text, only that he changed the vocalization, making it passive instead of active, *Ad Te protectus sum* (כֻּסֵּיתִי). Qimchi would explain the phrase as a *locutio prægnans:* "I cried unto Thee in secret, and so as to hide it from men." Similarly Ibn 'Ez., who remarks that "*to hide to* a person" is exactly opposite to the expression "*to hide from* a person" (Gen. xviii. 17), and means, therefore, to reveal to him what is hidden from others. J. D. Mich. (*Supplem.* p. 1317) takes the same view, and so does Rosenm., "Tibi in occulto revelavi quod homines celavi." Se'adyah, who is followed by Ewald, Maurer, Hengst. and others, takes the verb in a reflexive sense, "Unto Thee (*i.e.* with Thee) have I hidden myself," which they defend by the use of the Pi'el in Gen. xxxviii.

14, Deut. xxii. 12, Jon. iii. 6. The last of these, however, proves nothing, as עָלָיו is to be supplied from the preceding מֵעָלָיו, and then the construction will be "he covereth sackcloth, *i.e.* he puts it as a covering, upon him," the construction being exactly the same as in Job xxxvi. 32, Ezek. xxiv. 7. In the other two passages Hupf. would adopt the somewhat arbitrary method of substituting the Hithpa'el for the Pi'el. Delitzsch more probably explains the use of the Pi'el in these passages as elliptical, Gen. xxxviii. 14, "And she put a covering with a veil (before her face);" (Deut. xxii. 12, "Wherewith thou puttest a covering (on thy body)." Hence they do not justify our taking כִּסִּיתִי here in a reflexive sense. Hupf., Olsh., and others, would read חָסִיתִי; but the objection to this is, that this verb is elsewhere always followed by בְּ, not by אֶל.

[b] טוֹבָה. The art. is omitted occasionally with the adj. after a definite noun, Ges. § 111, 2 *b*. He quotes 2 Sam. vi. 3, Ezek. xxxix. 27. In the very same expression, Neh. ix. 20, we have the article with the adj. LXX. *τὸ πνεῦμα σου τὸ ἀγαθόν.*

PSALM 144

THIS is a singularly composite Psalm. The earlier portion of it, to the end of ver. 11, consists almost entirely of a cento of quotations, strung together from earlier Psalms; and it is not always easy to trace a real connection between them. The latter portion of the Psalm, ver. 12—15, differs completely from the former. It bears the stamp of originality, and, with the exception of the last line, which occurs also in xxxiii. 12, is entirely free from the quotations and allusions with which the preceding verses abound. It is hardly probable, however, that this concluding portion is the work of the Poet who compiled the rest of the Psalm: it is more probable that he has here transcribed a fragment * of some ancient Poem, in which were portrayed the happiness and prosperity of the nation in its brightest days,—under David, it may have been, or at the beginning of the reign of Solomon.

His object seems to have been thus to revive the hopes of his nation, perhaps after the return from the Exile, by reminding them how in their past history obedience to God had brought with it its full recompense.

* The latter portion of the Psalm is plainly a fragment, and has not even a verbal connection or link with what precedes. Yet in all MSS. and Editions and Versions, ancient and modern, it is joined to the first part as one Psalm.

Qimchi, who holds the Psalm to be David's, refers it to the events mentioned in 2 Sam. v., when having been acknowledged by all the tribes of Israel as their King (see ver. 2 of the Psalm, "who subdueth my people under me"), and having completely subjugated the Philistines, he might look forward to a peaceful and prosperous reign.

In some copies of the LXX. the Psalm is said to have been composed in honour of David's victory over Goliath; which may perhaps be due to the Targum on ver. 10, which explains "the hurtful sword" as the sword of Goliath. It is scarcely necessary to remark how improbable such a view is.

Others, again, have conjectured that the Psalm was directed against Abner (2 Sam. ii. 13, &c.), or against Absalom.

Theodoret supposes it to be spoken in the person of the Jews who, after their return from Babylon, were attacked by the neighbouring nations.

Another Greek writer, mentioned by Agellius, would refer the Psalm to the times of the Maccabees.

But the language of ver. 1—4, as well as the language of ver. 10, is clearly only suitable in the mouth of a king, or some powerful and recognized leader of the nation; and it is difficult to find a person of rank in the later history in whose mouth such a Psalm as this would be appropriate.

The Psalmist recounts glorious victories in the past, complains that the nation is now beset by strange, *i.e.* barbarous, enemies, so false and treacherous that no covenant can be kept with them, prays for deliverance from them by an interposition great and glorious as had been vouchsafed of old, and anticipates the return of a golden age of peace and plenty.

[(A PSALM) OF DAVID.]

1 BLESSED be Jehovah my rock,
Who traineth my hands for war,
My fingers for the battle.
2 My loving-kindness and my fortress,

The first two verses are taken from Ps. xviii. 2 [3], 46 [47], 34 [35].

2. MY LOVING-KINDNESS. A singular expression for "God of my loving-kindness," lix. 10 [11], 17 [18]; Jon. ii. 8 [9]. "Deum . . . bonitatem suam nominat, ab eo manare intelligens quicquid possidet bonorum."—*Calvin.*

My high tower and my deliverer,
My shield, and He in whom I find refuge,
Who subdueth my people under me.

3 Jehovah, what is man, that Thou takest knowledge of him?
A son of man, that Thou makest account of him?
4 As for man, he is like a breath;
His days are as a shadow that passeth.
5 Bow Thy heavens, O Jehovah, and come down,
Touch the mountains that they smoke.
6 Shoot out lightning, and scatter them,

MY DELIVERER, lit. "my deliverer for me," as the expression is found in the other version of Ps. xviii. in 2 Sam. xxii. 2. On the heaping together of epithets and titles of God Calvin remarks, that "it is not superfluous, but designed to strengthen and confirm faith; for men's minds are easily shaken, especially when some storm of trial beats upon them. Hence, if God should promise us His succour in one word, it would not be enough; in fact, in spite of all the props and aids He gives us, we constantly totter and are ready to fall, and such a forgetfulness of His loving-kindness steals upon us, that we come near to losing heart altogether."

WHO SUBDUETH, as in xviii. 47 [48]; only there we have "peoples" instead of "my people," as here. Some indeed would correct the text here, or regard the form as an imperfect plural. The Syr. and Chald. have the plural, and it is found in some MSS. It is certainly not easy to understand how any but a despotic ruler, or one whose people had taken up arms against him, could thus celebrate God as subduing his own nation under him. Delitzsch suggests that the words may have been the words of David after he had been anointed, but before he had ascended the throne. And similarly Calvin, supposing this to be one of David's Psalms, "Postquam ergo David quas adeptus erat victorias contra exteros Deo ascripsit, simul etiam gratias agit de ordinato regni statu. Et certe quum esset ignobilis, deinde falsis calumniis exosus, vix credibile fuit posse unquam tranquillum imperium consequi. Quod ergo præter spem repente se populus dedidit, tam admirabilis mutatio præclarum fuit Dei opus." In any case, the Psalmist is not triumphing in the exercise of despotic power, but gratefully acknowledges that the authority he wields comes only from God.

3. This and the next verse are again borrowed from other passages. The weakness of man seems here to be urged as a reason why God should come to his succour against his enemies. Ver. 3 is a variation of viii. 4 [5]. Ver. 4 resembles xxxix. 5, 6 [6, 7]: compare cii. 11 [12]; Job viii. 9, xiv. 2.

5. Here begins the direct prayer for the overthrow of his enemies. The Psalmist longs for a Theophany, a coming of God to judgement, which he describes in language again borrowed from xviii. 9 [10], 14—16 [15—17].

TOUCH THE MOUNTAINS, as in civ. 32, with allusion perhaps to Exod. xix. 18, xx. 18.

6. SHOOT OUT LIGHTNING, lit. "lighten lightning." The verb occurs nowhere else, and the verb

Send forth Thine arrows, and discomfit them.
7 Send forth Thine hand from above,
Rid me, and deliver me from many waters,
From the hand of the sons of the alien,
8 Whose mouth hath spoken falsehood,
And whose right hand is a right hand of lies.

9 O God, a new song will I sing unto Thee,
Upon a ten-stringed lute will I play unto Thee,
10 Who giveth victory unto kings,
Who riddeth David His servant from the hurtful sword.
11 Rid me, and deliver me from the hand of strange persons,
Whose mouth hath spoken falsehood,
And whose right hand is a right hand of lies.

12 We whose [a] sons are as plants
Grown up in their youth;

translated "rid" in the next verse is found only here in this sense (which is the meaning of the root in Aramaic and Arabic), so that even a writer who borrows so largely as this Psalmist has still his peculiarities. Comp. with this verse, xviii. 14.

7. THINE HAND. Many MSS. and editions have the singular, and so have all the ancient versions, though the received text has the plural.

SONS OF THE ALIEN, as in xviii. 44 [45].

8. A RIGHT HAND OF LIES, denoting faithlessness to a solemn covenant, the right hand being lifted up in the taking of an oath.

9. The prayer for deliverance is followed by the promise of thankfulness for the aid vouchsafed. The "new song," however, is not given.

O GOD. "The *Elohim* in this verse is the only one in the last two Books of the Psalter, except in Ps. cviii., which is a composite Psalm formed of two old Davidic Elohistic Psalms, and therefore clearly a weak attempt to reproduce the old Davidic Elohistic style."—*Delitzsch.*

A NEW SONG. Comp. xxxiii. 3, xl. 3 [4]. UPON A TEN-STRINGED LUTE, xcii. 3 [4].

10. DAVID HIS SERVANT. Mentioned here apparently as an example of all kings and leaders, but with obvious reference to xviii. 50 [51].

11. This verse is repeated as a refrain from ver. 7, 8.

12. The passage which follows to the end is, as has already been remarked, altogether unlike the rest of the Psalm.

For its grammatical construction see Critical Note; on its connection with the preceding verses something has been said in the Introduction to the Psalm.

AS PLANTS. In a striking sermon

Our daughters as corner-pillars,
Sculptured to grace a palace ;
13 Our garners [b] full,
Affording all manner of store ;
Our sheep multiplying in thousands,
In ten thousands in our fields ;
14 Our oxen [c] well laden ;
No breach and no sallying forth,[d]
And no cry (of battle) in our streets.

on this verse, the late Archdeacon Hare says of the figure here employed, "There is something so palpable and striking in this type, that, five-and-twenty years ago, in speaking of the gentlemanly character, I was led to say, 'If a gentleman is to grow up, he must grow like a tree : there must be nothing between him and heaven.'"

This figure marks the native strength and vigour and freedom of the youth of the land, as the next does the polished gracefulness, the quiet beauty, of the maidens. They are like the exquisitely-sculptured forms (the Caryatides), which adorned the corners of some magnificent hall or chamber of a palace.

CORNER-PILLARS, lit. "corners," Zech. ix. 15.

TO GRACE A PALACE, lit. "(after) the mode of structure of a palace."

13. ALL MANNER OF STORE, lit. "from kind to kind." The word is a late Aramaic word.

MULTIPLYING, lit. "bringing forth thousands, multiplied into ten thousands," or "made ten thousands."

FIELDS. This (and not "streets," E.V.) is the meaning of the word here, as in Job v. 10, Prov. viii. 26 ; and this is in accordance with the root-meaning, "places *outside* the city." "Field" is used in this sense in English : "By the civil law the corpses of persons deceased were buried *out of the city in the fields*."—Ayliffe, *Parergon.*

14. Every expression in this verse is of doubtful interpretation.

LADEN, or perhaps "our cattle great with young," *i.e.* "fruitful," which accords better with the preceding description of the sheep. See more in Critical Note.

NO BREACH. This is the obvious meaning of the word : see on lx. 1, 2 [2, 3].

NO SALLYING FORTH, lit. "going out," which has been interpreted either of "going forth to war," or "going forth into captivity." This and the previous expression, taken together, most naturally denote a time of profound peace, when no enemy lies before the walls, when there is no need to fear the assault through the breach, no need to sally forth to attack the besiegers. Comp. Amos v. 3. The LXX. have διέξοδος Symm. ἐκφορά, Jerome *egressus.* Ainsworth, "none going out, *i.e.* no cattle driven away by the enemy. See Amos iv. 3."

CRY (OF BATTLE). Such seems the probable meaning from the context ; and so Calvin, *clamor qui ex subito tumultu exoritur,* and Clericus, *pugnantium ;* or it may mean, generally, "cry of sorrow," as in Jer. xiv. 2.

STREETS, broad open places, πλατεῖα. In Jer. v. 1, the E.V. has "broad places."

The whole passage, 12—15, is a picture of the most perfect, undisturbed peace and tranquillity.

15 Happy is the people that is in such a case;[e]
Happy is the people which hath Jehovah for its God.

15. HAPPY. The temporal blessing of prosperity, as a sign of God's favour, is natural enough under the Old Dispensation. Calvin, however, says truly: "Si quis objiciat nihil nisi crassum et terrenum spirare, quod de felicitate hominum æstimat ex caducis commodis; respondeo, hæc duo conjunctim legenda esse, beatos esse qui in sua abundantia Deum sibi propitium sentiunt; et sic ejus gratiam degustant in benedictionibus caducis ut de paterno ejus amore persuasi, aspirent ad veram hæreditatem."

[a] אֲשֶׁר. The relative at the beginning of this verse is very perplexing. (1) The LXX., with their rendering ὧν οἱ υἱοί, would seem to refer it to the enemy, "the strange persons" of the preceding verse. But it is clear, from ver. 15, that the picture of ver. 12—14 is a picture of the felicity of the Jewish nation under the protection of Jehovah. (2) Hence De Wette and others would give to the relative the meaning of "in order that," "so that," as in Gen. xi. 7, Deut. iv. 40, 1 Kings xxii. 16; but then it must be followed by the finite verb, whereas here we have nothing but participles. (3) It has been suggested, therefore, to take the relative in the sense of "for," "because," as in Gen. xxxi. 49, Deut. iii. 24; but it is not clear how what follows in this and the next verse can be alleged *as a reason* for the prayer of the previous verse. (4) Bunsen refers the relative to God, and supplies a verb: "Who maketh our sons like plants," but does not attempt to defend the rendering. (5) Maurer joins the relative with the suffix of the following noun—certainly the most obvious construction—but finds here the expression of a wish, to which the form of the sentence (in participles) does not lend itself. He connects the verses thus: "Save me, Thy people, even us (ver. 11); whose sons, may they be as plants," &c. (6) Ewald also keeps to the common use of the relative, but connects it with ver. 15, "We, whose sons are, &c. . . . O happy is the people that is in such a case." And, supposing that the relative is to be retained, this is, on the whole, the most satisfactory. Hupfeld, however, and others, consider the whole passage, 12—15, as a fragment belonging to some other Psalm, and here altogether out of place. Delitzsch suggests, that perhaps ver. 11, where the refrain is repeated, ought to be struck out. In this case, however, the relative would naturally refer to God, and then we should expect some verb to follow it.

[Kay renders, "what time;" but though אֲשֶׁר may mean this, such a sense is doubtful with the participle. The only other passage in which אֲשֶׁר stands with the participle, so far as I am aware, is Eccl. viii. 12, where Dr. Ginsburg, after a careful discussion of the use of the particle, renders "because." That sense, however, would not be suitable here, and I am now inclined (3rd Edit.) to suggest the rendering "whereas," as best suiting the context and the participle.]

[b] מְזָוֵינוּ, a ἅπ. λεγ., from a sing. מָזֶו or מְזוּ (Ew.), and in either case shortened from מְזָוָה. The Aram. זַן in the next line occurs again 2 Chron. xvi. 14, instead of מִין, which is the older word.

[c] אַלּוּפֵינוּ מְ׳. The word means elsewhere "princes," "leaders," and Maur., Fürst, and others, would retain this meaning here: "Our princes are set up, *i.e.* full of power and dignity." They appeal, for this sense of מְסֻבָּלִים, to the Chald. form in Ezra vi. 3. This interpretation accords with what follows, but not with what precedes. After the mention of "sheep" (צֹאונֵנוּ, a form in which the ו is evidence of late writing), it is more natural to take אַלּוּפִים here as the representative in the later language of the older אֲלָפִים (viii. 8) *oxen*. But assuming this to be the case, the meaning of מס׳ is still doubtful. It means *laden* or *burdened*, but how? (1) It has been explained to mean "capable of bearing burdens," *laboris patientes, robusti* (so the Chald. and Qimchi), but it is doubtful whether the pass. part. can bear this meaning. (2) "*Laden*, *i.e.* with the fruits of the land," as an image of plenteousness; or "laden with fat or flesh," and so "strong," which comes to pretty much the same thing as (1). So the LXX. παχεῖς, and so the Syr., Jer., and most of the older interpreters. (3) *Pregnant* (laden with the fruit of the womb), as descriptive of the fruitfulness of the herds: so Ros., Ges., De W., Ew., Hitz., Hupf. The chief objection to this is the masc. form of the noun, but אַלּוּף, like בָּקָר, may be epicene.

[d] יוֹצֵאת. App. here used as a noun, though strictly speaking the fem. participle as in Deut. xxviii. 57.

[e] שֶׁכָּכָה. The same form occurs again Song of Sol. v. 9. The שׁ prefixed to יְהוָֹה is a solitary instance.

PSALM 145

THIS is the last of the Alphabetical Psalms, of which there are eight in all, if we reckon the 9th and 10th Psalms as forming one. Like four other of the Alphabetical Psalms, this bears the name of David, although there can in this case be no doubt that the Inscription is not to be trusted. As in several other instances, so here, the acrostic arrangement is not strictly observed. The letter *Nun* (נ) is omitted. The LXX. have supplied the deficiency by intercalating a verse, Πιστὸς (נאמן, as in cxi. 7) Κύριος ἐν τοῖς λόγοις αὐτοῦ, καὶ ὅσιος ἐν πᾶσι τοῖς ἔργοις αὐτοῦ; but the latter part of this is taken from ver. 17, and none of the other Ancient Versions except the Syr. and those which follow the LXX. recognize this addition.

This is the only Psalm which is called a *Tehillah*, *i.e.* "Praise" or "Hymn," the plural of which word, *Tehîllim*, is the general name for the whole Psalter. The LXX. render it αἴνεσις, Aquila ὕμνησις, Symmachus ὕμνος, and "Hymn" is given as the equivalent in the Midrash on the Song of Solomon. In the Talmud Babli (*Berakhoth*, 4*b*) it is said: "Every one who recites the Tehillah of David thrice a day may be sure that he is a child of the world to come. And why? Not merely because the Psalm is alphabetical (for that the 119th is, and in an eightfold degree), nor only because it celebrates God's care for all creatures (for that the Great Hallel does, cxxxvi. 25), but because it unites both these qualities in itself."

[A HYMN OF DAVID.]

1 א I WILL exalt Thee my God, O King,
And I will bless Thy Name for ever and ever.
2 ב Every day will I bless Thee,
And I will praise Thy Name for ever and ever.
3 ג Great is Jehovah, and highly to be praised,
And His greatness is unsearchable.
4 ד One generation to another shall laud Thy works,
And shall declare Thy mighty acts.
5 ה Of the glorious honour of Thy majesty,
And of Thy wondrous works will I meditate.
6 ו And men shall speak of the power of Thy terrible acts,
And I will tell of Thy greatness.[a]
7 ז The memory of Thine abundant goodness[b] they shall utter,
And sing aloud of Thy righteousness.

1. FOR EVER AND EVER. Not merely, as Calvin, *etiamsi plura secula victurus est:* but the heart lifted up to God, and full of the thoughts of God, can no more conceive that its praise should cease, than that God Himself should cease to be.

3. GREATLY TO BE PRAISED, or "greatly praised;" but see on xviii. 3.

5. OF THE GLORIOUS HONOUR, &c., or "of the majesty of the glory of thine honour."

THY WONDROUS WORKS, lit. "the words of Thy wondrous works." Comp. lxv. 3 [4].

MEDITATE, or perhaps "rehearse," *i.e.* in poetry. The E.V. commonly renders the word "talk of."

6. AND I WILL TELL, &c., lit. "and as for Thy greatnesses (or great acts), I will tell of every one of them."

7. UTTER, lit. it is "pour forth," the same word as in xix. 2 [3], lix. 7 [8], where see Note.

8 ח Gracious and of tender compassion is Jehovah,
Long-suffering and of great loving-kindness.
9 ט Jehovah is good unto all,
And His tender compassions are over all His works.
10 י All Thy works give thanks to Thee, O Jehovah,
And Thy beloved bless Thee.
11 כ They talk of the glory of Thy kingdom,
And speak of Thy might.
12 ל To make known to the sons of men His mighty acts,
And the glorious majesty of His kingdom.
13 מ Thy kingdom is a kingdom for all ages,
And Thy dominion for all generations.

14 ס Jehovah upholdeth all them that fall,
And raiseth up all those that be bowed down.
15 ע The eyes of all wait upon Thee,
And Thou givest them their food in its season;
16 פ Opening Thine hand,
And satisfying the desire of every living thing.
17 צ Jehovah is righteous in all His ways,
And loving in all His works.
18 ק Jehovah is nigh to all them that call upon Him,
To all that call upon Him in truth.
19 ר He fulfilleth the desire of them that fear Him,
And when He heareth their cry He helpeth them.

14. The glory, the majesty, the eternity of God's kingdom, of which so much has been said—how are they manifested? Where is the conspicuous excellence of that kingdom seen? Not in the symbols of earthly pride and power, but in gracious condescension to the fallen and the crushed, in a gracious care which provides for the wants of every living thing. (We have here a resumption and expansion of the thoughts in ver. 8, 9.)

ALL THEM THAT FALL. Others, "them that are ready to fall:" but see xxxvii. 24.

15. This verse, and the first clause of the next, are taken from civ. 27, 28.

16. SATISFYING THE DESIRE, lit. "satisfying every living thing with (the object of) its desire," or, "satisfying every living thing with favour," see Deut. xxxiii. 23; but in the 19th ver. of this Psalm it seems quite clear that "desire" is the proper rendering. The P.B.V. has "with plenteousness."

20 ש Jehovah keepeth all them that love Him,
But all the wicked will He destroy.
21 ת Let my mouth speak the praise of Jehovah,
And let all flesh bless His holy Name for ever and ever.

[a] גדלותיך. The K'thîbh is in the plur., which has been very unnecessarily corrected to the sing., because of the following singular suffix, which, however, is not uncommon with the plur. (see for instance 2 Kings iii. 3, x. 26), and here, moreover, can be readily explained as distributive, especially as the sing. suffix follows.

[b] רַב־טוּבְךָ. The adj. is irregularly prefixed, possibly, as Hengst. suggests, because it forms one word with the noun following = *much-goodness*. Qim., Ros., Olsh., Del., would take רב as a subst., for רֹב; but according to the analogy of xxxi. 20, Is. lxiii. 7, it must be an adj.

PSALM 146

THIS Psalm is the first of another series of Hallelujah Psalms, with which the Book closes. Certain of the words and phrases seem to connect it with the 145th; others are borrowed from the 104th and 118th. The LXX. ascribe it, as they do the 138th and the next two Psalms (or the next three, according to their reckoning, for they divide the 147th into two), to Haggai and Zechariah (Ἀλληλούια· Ἀγγαίου καὶ Ζαχαρίου). It is by no means improbable that this Inscription represents an ancient tradition, for nothing would be more natural than that these Prophets should directly or indirectly have contributed to the liturgy of the Second Temple, to which these Psalms so evidently belong. Later they formed, together with Psalms cxix. and cl., a portion of the daily morning prayer; they also had the name of "Hallel," though expressly distinguished from "*the* Hallel," which was to be sung at the Passover and the other Feasts.

The Psalm bears evident traces, both in style and language, and also in its allusions to other Psalms, of belonging to the post-Exile literature; and the words of verses 7—9 are certainly no inapt expression of the feelings which would naturally be called forth at a time immediately subsequent to the return from the Captivity.

It has an exhortation to trust not in man (ver. 3, 4), but in Jehovah alone (ver. 5),—an exhortation enforced by the exhibition of Jehovah's character and attributes as the one really worthy object of trust (ver. 6—9), and confirmed by the fact that His kingdom does not contain the seeds of weakness and dissolution, like all earthly kingdoms, but is eternal as He is eternal (ver. 10).

HALLELUJAH!

1 PRAISE Jehovah O my soul!
2 I will praise Jehovah as long as I live,
I will play (on the harp) unto my God while I have any being.

3 Trust not in princes,
(Nor) in the son of man, in whom there is no help.
4 His breath goeth forth; he turneth to his earth,
In that very day his thoughts perish.
5 Happy is he that hath the God of Jacob for his help,
Whose hope (resteth) upon Jehovah his God,
6 Who made heaven and earth,
The sea, and all that therein is;
Who keepeth truth for ever;

2. WHILE I HAVE ANY BEING, lit. "while I yet (am)." See civ. 33. Not in this song only will he utter His praise, but "his life shall be a thanksgiving unto the Power that made him."

3. TRUST NOT IN PRINCES. A warning which might be called forth by the circumstances of the nation after their return from Babylon. See on cxviii. 8, 9.

NO HELP, or "no salvation." Comp. xxxiii. 16, lx. 11 [13].

4. HIS BREATH, &c., or, "When his breath goeth forth, he turneth," &c., the two apocopated forms indicating perhaps that the two clauses are protasis and apodosis.

HIS BREATH. Comp. civ. 29. And, with his breath HIS THOUGHTS or "purposes," or "schemes," though this is a modern word in this sense (a Chald. word for which we have the Hebrew equivalent Job xii. 5), however grand the conception, however masterly the execution, all come to an end. The science, the philosophy, the statesmanship of one age is exploded in the next. The men who are the masters of the world's intellect to-day are discrowned to-morrow. In this age of restless and rapid change they may survive their own thoughts: their thoughts do not survive them. There is an almost exact parallel in 1 Macc. ii. 63.

5. FOR HIS HELP. The predicate is introduced by the preposition (the *Beth essentiæ*, as the grammarians term it), as in xxxv. 2, for instance.

6. WHO MADE (as in cxv. 15, cxxi. 2, cxxiv. 8, cxxxiv. 3, this designation of God being characteristic of the later Psalms). First, He is an *Almighty* God, as the

7 (Who) executeth judgement for the oppressed,
(Who) giveth bread to the hungry :
Jehovah looseth the prisoners,
8 Jehovah openeth the eyes of the blind,
Jehovah raiseth up them that are bowed down ;
Jehovah loveth the righteous ;
9 Jehovah keepeth the strangers,
He setteth up the widow and the fatherless,
But the way of the wicked He turneth aside.
10 Jehovah shall be King for ever,
Thy God, O Zion, unto all generations.
Hallelujah !

Creator of the universe; next, He is a *faithful* God ("who keepeth truth for ever") ; further, He is a *righteous* God (ver. 7), a *bountiful* God (*ib.*), a *gracious* God (ver. 7—9).

WHO KEEPETH. In the series of participles marking the several acts or attributes of God in this and the next two verses, this only has the article prefixed, perhaps because the Psalmist designed to give a certain prominence or emphasis to this attribute of God, that He is One "who keepeth truth for ever." It is, in fact, the central thought of the Psalm. For on this ground beyond all others is God the object of trust. He is true, and His word is truth, and that word He keeps, not for a time, but for ever.

7—9. These verses portray God's character as a ruler. It is such a God who is Zion's King, ver. 10. Such an One men may trust, for He is not like the princes of the earth, ver. 3.

7. LOOSETH THE PRISONERS. Comp. Is. lxi. 1. Delitzsch quotes a curious instance of the allegorical interpretation of these words from Joseph Albo, who in his *Dogmatics* (bearing date 1425), sect. ii. cap. 16, maintaining against Maimonides that the ceremonial law was not of perpetual obligation, appeals to the Midrash Tanchuma, which interprets this loosing of the prisoners as an allowing of what had once been forbidden.

8. OPENETH THE EYES, lit. "openeth the blind," *i.e.* maketh them to see. The expression may be used figuratively, as a remedy applied either to physical helplessness, as Deut. xxviii. 29, Is. lix. 9, 10, Job xii. 25 ; or to spiritual want of discernment, as Is. xxix. 18, xlii. 7, 18, xliii. 8. Here the context favours the former.

RAISETH UP. This word only occurs once besides, cxlv. 14.

9. THE STRANGERS . . . THE WIDOW . . . THE FATHERLESS, the three great examples of natural defencelessness. "Valde gratus mihi est hic Psalmus," says Bakius, "ob Trifolium illud Dei : Advenas, Pupillos, et Viduas, versu uno luculentissime depictum, id quod in toto Psalterio nullibi fit."

SETTETH UP, the same word as in cxlvii. 6.

HE TURNETH ASIDE, rendered by the E.V. in Ecclesiastes, "made crooked." That which happens in the course of God's Providence, and as the inevitable result of His righteous laws, is usually ascribed in Scripture to His immediate agency.

10. SHALL BE KING. See Introduction to xcix.

PSALM 147

LIKE the last Psalm, and like those which follow it, this is evidently an anthem intended for the service of the Second Temple. It celebrates God's almighty and gracious rule over His people and over the world of nature, but mingles with this a special commemoration of His goodness in bringing back His people from their captivity and rebuilding the walls of Jerusalem. In the allusions to these events in ver. 2, 3, and ver. 13, 14, we shall probably be justified in seeing the occasion of the Psalm. It may have been written for the dedication of the wall of Jerusalem, which, as we learn from Nehem. xii. 27, was kept "with gladness, both with thanksgivings and with singing, with cymbals, psalteries, and with harps." It is indeed not improbable, as Hengstenberg suggests, that not this Psalm only, but the rest of the Psalms to the end of the Book, are all anthems originally composed for the same occasion. The wall had been built under circumstances of no ordinary difficulty and discouragement (Neh. ii. 17—iv. 23): its completion was celebrated with no common joy and thankfulness; "for God had made them rejoice with great joy; the wives also and the children had rejoiced: so that the joy of Jerusalem was heard even from afar off." See Neh. xii. 27—43.

The Psalm cannot be said to have any regular strophical arrangement, but the renewed exhortations to praise in ver. 7, 12, suggest a natural division of the Psalm. It is a *Trifolium* of praise.

The LXX. divide the Psalm into two parts, beginning a new Psalm at ver. 12.

1 HALLELUJAH!
For it is good to sing [a] unto our God,
For it is sweet; comely is the hymn of praise.
2 Jehovah doth build up Jerusalem,
He gathereth together the outcasts of Israel;

1. This verse might perhaps be better rendered with the change of a single consonant: "Praise ye Jah, for He is good; sing unto our God, for He is lovely; comely is the hymn of praise." Comp. cxxxv. 3, xxxiii. 1. See more in Critical Note.

2. DOTH BUILD UP. With reference to the rebuilding of the walls after the Captivity, as in cxxii. 3.

3 Who healeth the broken in heart,
And bindeth up their wounds;
4 Who telleth the number of the stars,
He giveth names unto them all.
5 Great is our Lord, and of great power,
His understanding is infinite.
6 Jehovah setteth up the afflicted,
He casteth the wicked down to the ground.

GATHERETH TOGETHER. A verb found in this conjugation only, Ezek. xxii. 20 [21], xxxix. 28, and in the latter passage with the same reference as here.

OUTCASTS, lit. "those who are thrust out, driven away." Symm. ἐξωσμένους, whereas the LXX. express the sense more generally, τὰς διασποράς. It is the same word as in Is. xi. 12, lvi. 8.

3. BROKEN IN HEART. As in xxxiv. 18 [19], Is. lxi. 1, where, however, the participle is Niph'al.

4. WHO TELLETH THE NUMBER, lit. "apportioneth a number to the stars." This is adduced as a proof of the omniscience and omnipotence of God, and hence as a ground of consolation to His people, however they may have been scattered, and however they may have been oppressed. Surely He must know, He must be able to succour, human woe, to whom it is an easy thing to count those stars which are beyond man's arithmetic (Gen. xv. 5).

The argument is precisely the same as in Is. xl. 26—29, "Lift up your eyes and see: Who hath created these things? It is He that bringeth out *their host by number*, who *calleth them all by name. For abundance of power*, and because He is *mighty in strength*, not one faileth. Why sayest thou, O Jacob, and speakest, O Israel, My way is hid from Jehovah, and my cause is passed away from my God? Hast thou not known, hast thou not heard? An everlasting God is Jehovah, who created the ends of the earth. He fainteth not, neither is weary: *there is no searching of His understanding*. He giveth to the weary strength, and to them that have no power He increaseth might," &c. The passages in italics will show how evidently the words of the Prophet were in the mind of the Psalmist.

GIVETH NAMES, an expression marking not only God's power in marshalling them all as a host (Is. xl. 26), but also the most intimate knowledge and the most watchful care, as that of a shepherd for his flock, John x. 3. For the idiom see Gen. ii.

5. OF GREAT POWER, lit. "abounding in power," as in Is. xl. 26, "mighty in strength," though there perhaps the epithet applies to the stars, unless indeed we may take the use of the phrase here as deciding its application there.

HIS UNDERSTANDING IS INFINITE, lit. "to (of) His understanding there is no number," apparently in the Heb. a play on ver. 4, where it is said "He telleth the number," &c., whereas both in cxlv. 3 and Is. xl. 28 it is, "there is no searching." Comp. Rom. xi. 33, ἀνεξιχνίαστοι αἱ ὁδοὶ αὐτοῦ.

6. The same Lord who with infinite power and unsearchable wisdom rules the stars in their courses, rules also the world of man. The history of the world is a mirror both of His love and of His righteous anger. His rule and His order are a correction of man's anarchy and disorder.

7 Sing unto Jehovah with thanksgiving,
Play upon the harp unto our God;
8 Who covereth the heaven with clouds,
Who prepareth rain for the earth,
Who maketh grass to grow upon the mountains;
9 (Who) giveth to the cattle their fodder,
(And) to the young ravens which cry.
10 Not in the strength of an horse doth He delight,
Not in the legs of a man doth He take pleasure;
11 Jehovah taketh pleasure in them that fear Him,
In them that hope for His loving-kindness.

12 Laud Jehovah, O Jerusalem,
Praise thy God, O Zion;
13 For He hath strengthened the bars of thy gates,
He hath blessed thy children in the midst of thee;
14 Who maketh thy border peace,
(And) satisfieth thee with the fat of wheat;

7. A fresh burst of praise because of God's fatherly care, as shown in His provision for the wants of the cattle and the fowls of the air. And as He feeds the ravens (comp. Luke xii. 24), which have neither storehouse nor barn, but only cry to Him for their food (Job. xxxviii. 41), so amongst men (ver. 10) His delight is not in those who trust in their own strength and swiftness, but in those who look to *Him*, fear *Him*, put their trust in *His* goodness.

In ver. 8 the LXX. have added, from civ. 14, "and herb for the service of men," whence it has found its way into our P. B. V. But here this addition is out of place, and disturbs the order of thought. It is not till ver. 10, 11, that *man* is introduced.

9. WHICH CRY, or, "when they cry."

12. Again the Psalmist begins his hymn of praise, and now with a direct reference to the rebuilding of Jerusalem, and the bright prospect which seemed to dawn upon the nation after its restoration.

13. HATH STRENGTHENED THE BARS OF THY GATES. The expression might certainly denote figuratively (as Hupfeld says) the security of the city, but as the Psalm so evidently refers to the return from the Captivity and the rebuilding of Jerusalem (ver. 2), there can be little doubt that there is here a direct and literal reference to the setting up of the gates as described in Neh. vii. 1—4.

With the latter part of the verse comp. the promise in Is. lx. 17, 18, "I will also make thy officers peace . . . violence shall no more be heard in thy land, wasting nor destruction within thy borders, but thou shalt call thy walls Salvation, and thy gates Praise."

14. FAT OF WHEAT. See on lxxi. 16 [17].

15 Who sendeth forth His commandment upon earth:
His word runneth very swiftly;
16 Who giveth snow like wool,
(And) scattereth the hoarfrost like ashes;
17 (Who) casteth forth His ice like morsels:
Who can stand before His frost?
18 He sendeth His word, and melteth them,
He causeth His wind to blow, (and the) waters flow.
19 He declareth His word unto Jacob,
His statutes and His judgements unto Israel.
20 He hath not dealt so with any nation;
And as for (His) judgements, they do not know them.
Hallelujah!

15—18. This repeated reference to God's power as manifested in the world is certainly remarkable, and is characteristic of these later Psalms. It may perhaps be accounted for by the fact that never had so strong a conviction laid hold of the national heart, of the utter impotence of all the gods of the heathen as after the return from the Exile; never, therefore, so triumphant and living a sense of the dominion of Jehovah, not in Israel only, but throughout the universe.

15. HIS COMMANDMENT, or "*saying*," with reference perhaps to the creative fiat, "And God *said*:" comp. xxxiii. 9. God is said to "send" this as His messenger, as in ver. 18 of this Psalm, and cvii. 20, where see note.

16. SNOW LIKE WOOL, &c. The point of the comparison is probably merely in the general resemblance of the snow, frost, ice, to the different objects mentioned, not in "the ease with which God accomplishes the greatest things as man does the least, such as causing some locks of wool to fly, or scattering a few ashes." (Hengst.)

19. God's works in Nature are for all men; "He maketh His sun to rise on the evil and on the good, and sendeth rain on the just and on the unjust" (Matt. v. 45) but there is a special privilege belonging to His chosen people. They, and they alone in the world, have received the lively oracles of His mouth. Comp. Rom. iii. 1, 2. "What advantage then hath the Jew? . . . Much, every way: first, because that unto them were committed the oracles of God."

[a] זַמְּרָה. This, as it stands, must be a fem. infin. Pi'el, and as such it is usually defended by יַסְּרָה, Lev. xxvi. 18, the only other instance of such a form; but Hupf. contends that such fem. infin. in the Pi'el and Hiph. ought to be of the forms קַטָּלָה and הַקְטָלָה, as in Aramaic. He also objects that כִּי טוֹב cannot mean "for *it* is good," but "for *He* is good," the adjective being always predicated of God, and he appeals especially to the parallel passage, cxxxv. 3. Further, according to the usual rendering, the second hemistich of the verse consists of two verses

dependent on כִּי, yet unconnected with one another; and in the next verse the construction is carried on with a participle, which implies that Jehovah is already the subject of the previous verse. Hence, unless זַמְּרָה is imperat. paragog. sing., instead of plur. (which here would be a harsh enallage of number), we must either read זַמְּרוּ (so Ven., Olsh.) or אֲזַמְּרָה, with the same change from the 3rd pers. to the 1st as in cxlv. 6. The Athnach is wrongly placed: it should clearly stand with נָעִים, not with אֱלֹהֵינוּ.

PSALM 148

In this splendid Anthem the Psalmist calls upon the whole creation, in its two great divisions (according to the Hebrew conception) of heaven and earth, to praise Jehovah. Things with and things without life, beings rational and irrational, are summoned to join the mighty chorus. The Psalm is an expression of the loftiest devotion, and embraces at the same time the most comprehensive view of the relation of the creature to the Creator. Whether it is exclusively the utterance of a heart filled to the full with the thought of the infinite majesty of God, or whether it is also an anticipation, a prophetic forecast, of the final glory of creation, when, at the manifestation of the sons of God, the creation itself shall also be redeemed from the bondage of corruption (Rom. viii. 18—23), and the homage of praise shall indeed be rendered by all things that are in heaven and earth and under the earth, is a question into which we need not enter. The former seems to my mind the more probable view; but the other is as old as Hilary, who sees the end of the exhortation of the Psalm to be, "Ut ob depulsam sæculi vanitatem creatura omnis, ex magnis officiorum suorum laboribus absoluta, et in beato regno æternitatis aliquando respirans Deum suum et læta prædicat et quieta, et ipsa secundum Apostolum in gloriam beatæ æternitatis assumpta."

Isaac Taylor says: "It is but faintly and afar off that the ancient liturgies (except so far as they merely copied their originals) come up to the majesty and the wide compass of the Hebrew worship such as it is indicated in the 148th Psalm. Neither Ambrose, nor Gregory, nor the Greeks, have reached or approached this level; and in tempering the boldness of their originals by admixtures of what is more Christianlike and spiritual, the added elements sustain an injury which is not compensated by what they bring forward of a purer or less earthly kind: feeble, indeed, is the tone of these anthems of the ancient Church; sophisticated or artificial is their style. Nor would it be possible,—it has never yet seemed so,—to Christianize the Hebrew anthems, retaining their power, their earth-like richness, and their manifold splendours—which are the very splendours and the true riches and the grandeur of God's world—and withal attempered with expressions that touch to the quick the warmest human sympathies. And as the enhancement of all these there is the *nationality*, there is that fire which is sure to kindle fire in true human hearts—

> 'He showeth His word unto Jacob,
> His statutes and His judgements unto Israel.
> He hath not dealt so with any nation;
> As for His judgements, they have not known them.'

[From the close of the 147th Psalm]."—*Spirit of the Hebrew Poetry*, pp. 157, 158.

The earliest imitation of this Psalm is "The Song of the Three Children," interpolated by the LXX. into the 3rd chapter of Daniel. The Hymn of Francis of Assisi, in which he calls upon the creatures to praise God, *propter honorabilem fratrem nostrum solem*, has also been compared with it, though there is really no comparison between the two. The same Francis, who thus calls the sun our "honourable brother," could also address a cricket as his sister, "Canta, soror mea cicada, et Dominum creatorem tuum jubilo lauda." But neither in this Psalm, nor elsewhere in Scripture, is this brotherly and sisterly relation of things inanimate and irrational to man recognized or implied.

The Psalm consists of two equal parts:

I. The praise of God in heaven. Ver. 1—6.

II. The praise of God on earth. Ver. 7—12.

1 HALLELUJAH!
O praise Jehovah from the heavens,
Praise Him in the heights.

1. FROM THE HEAVENS. This first verse is not to be restricted merely to the angels. It is the prelude comprising all afterwards enumerated, angels, sun, and moon, &c.

2 Praise ye Him, all His angels,
Praise Him, all His host.
3 Praise Him, sun and moon,
Praise Him, all ye stars of light.
4 Praise Him, ye heavens of heavens,
And ye waters, that be above the heavens.
5 Let them praise the Name of Jehovah,
For HE commanded, and they were created;
6 And He made them to stand (fast) for ever and ever,
He hath given them a decree, and they transgress it not.

7 O praise Jehovah from the earth,
Ye sea-monsters and all deeps;
8 Fire and hail, snow and vapour,
Stormy wind fulfilling His word;

2. HIS HOST. Here, as is plain from the parallelism, "the angels," as also in 1 Kings xxii. 19, though elsewhere the expression is used of the *stars*, and some would so understand it here.

4. HEAVENS OF HEAVENS. A superlative, according to the common Hebrew idiom, denoting "the highest heavens;" comp. 2 Cor. xii. 2. Others take it as a poetical way of expressing the apparently boundless depth of the heavens. So Luther, "Ihr Himmel allenthalben;" Maurer, "Omnia cœlorum spatia utut vasta et infinita"; an interpretation which perhaps derives some support from the phrase, "the heaven and the heaven of heavens," Deut. x. 14; 1 Kings viii. 27.

WATERS . . . ABOVE THE HEAVENS, as in Gen. i. 7. This is usually explained of the clouds, though the form of expression cannot be said to favour such an explanation, nor yet the statement in Genesis, that the firmament or expanse was intended to separate the waters above from the waters below. Taken in their obvious meaning, the words must point to the existence of a vast heavenly sea or reservoir. However, it is quite out of place, especially when dealing with language so evidently poetical as this, to raise any question as to its scientific accuracy.

5. HE COMMANDED. The LXX. add here from the parallel passage, xxxiii. 9, the other clause, "He spake, and it was done," or, as they render, ". . . and they were made."

6. AND THEY TRANSGRESS IT NOT, lit. "and none of them transgresses it;" for the verb is in the singular, and therefore distributive. Others, as the E.V., following the LXX., Jerome, the Syriac, &c., "a law which shall not pass," or "shall not be broken." The objection to this is, that the verb is never used elsewhere of the passing away of a law, but always of the transgression of a law.

7. The second great division of created things,—that is, according to the Old Test. view, THE EARTH.

SEA-MONSTERS, mentioned first, as at the bottom of the scale in creation, as in Gen. i. 21.

8. FIRE, *i.e.* "lightning," as in

9 Mountains and all hills,
Fruit-trees and all cedars;
10 Beasts and all cattle,
Creeping things and winged fowl;
11 Kings of the earth and all peoples,
Princes and all judges of the earth;
12 Both young men and maidens,
Old men and children;
13 Let them praise the name of Jehovah,
For His Name only is exalted,
His majesty above earth and heaven.
14 And He hath lifted up the horn of His people,
—A praise to all His beloved,—
(Even) to the children of Israel, a people near unto Him.

Hallelujah!

xviii. 12 [13], where it is in like manner joined with hail.

VAPOUR, or perhaps rather "smoke," answering to "fire" as "snow" to "hail."

STORMY WIND, as in cvii. 25.

11, 12. Man mentioned last, as the crown of all. The first step (see ver. 7) and the last are the same as in Gen. i. In the intervening stages, with the usual poetic freedom, the order of Genesis is not adhered to.

13. LET THEM PRAISE, exactly as at the close of the first great division of the anthem, ver. 5; and, in the same way as there, the reason for the exhortation follows in the next clause. But it is a different reason. It is no longer because He has given them a decree, bound them as passive unconscious creatures by a law which they cannot transgress. (It is the fearful mystery of the reasonable will that it can transgress the law.) It is because His Name is exalted, so that the eyes of men can see and the hearts and tongues of men confess it; it is because He has graciously revealed Himself to, and mightily succoured, the people whom He loves, the nation who are near to Him. If it be said, that what was designed to be a Universal Anthem is thus narrowed at its close, it must be remembered that, however largely the glory of God was written on the visible creation, it was only to the Jew that any direct revelation of His character had been made.

EXALTED. Is. xii. 4, &c., xxx. 13.

14. LIFTED UP THE HORN. See on lxxv. 6, others "hath lifted up a horn unto His people," the horn being the house of David.

A PRAISE. This may either be (1) in apposition with the whole previous sentence, viz. the lifting up of the horn is "a praise," a glory, to His beloved (comp. Is. lxi. 3, 11, lxii. 7); or (2) in apposition with the subject of the previous verb, God Himself is "a praise (*i.e.* object of praise) to," &c. So the LXX. ὕμνος, Jerome *laus*. So the P.B.V. gives the sense: "all His saints shall praise Him."

NEAR UNTO HIM, as a holy people, Deut. iv. 7. Comp. Lev. x. 3.

PSALM 149

THE feelings expressed in this Psalm are perfectly in accordance with the time and the circumstances to which we have already referred the whole of this closing group of Hallelujah-Psalms, beginning with the 146th. It breathes the spirit of intense joy and eager hope which must have been in the very nature of things characteristic of the period which succeeded the return from the Babylonish captivity. Men of strong faith and religious enthusiasm and fervent loyalty must have felt that in the very fact of the restoration of the people to their own land was to be seen so signal a proof of the Divine favour, that it could not but be regarded as a pledge of a glorious future yet in store for the nation. The burning sense of wrong, the purpose of a terrible revenge, which was the feeling uppermost when they had first escaped from their oppressors (as in Psalm cxxxvii.), was soon changed into the hope of a series of magnificent victories over all the nations of the world, and the setting up of a universal dominion. It is such a hope which is expressed here. The old days of the nation, and the old martial spirit, are revived. God is their King (ver. 2), and they are His soldiers, going forth to wage His battles, with His praises in their mouth and a two-edged sword in their hands. A spirit which now seems sanguinary and revengeful had, it is not too much to say, its proper function under the Old Testament, and was not only natural but necessary, if that small nation was to maintain itself against the powerful tribes by which it was hemmed in on all sides. But it ought to require no proof that language like that of ver. 6—9 of this Psalm is no warrant for the exhibition of a similar spirit in the Christian Church.

"The dream that it was possible to use such a prayer as this, without a spiritual transubstantiation of the words, has made them the signal for some of the greatest crimes with which the Church has ever been stained. It was by means of this Psalm that Caspar Sciopius in his 'Clarion of the Sacred War' (*Classicum Belli Sacri*), a work written, it has been said, not with ink but with blood, roused and inflamed the Roman Catholic Princes to the Thirty Years' War. It was by means of this Psalm that, in the Protestant community, Thomas Münzer fanned the flames of the War of the Peasants. We see from these and other instances, that when in her interpretation of such a Psalm the Church forgets the words of the Apostle, 'the weapons of our warfare are not carnal' (2 Cor. x. 4), she falls back upon the ground of the Old Testament, beyond which she has long since advanced,—ground which even the Jews themselves do not venture to maintain, because they cannot altogether withdraw themselves from the influence of the light which has dawned in Christianity, and which condemns the vindictive spirit. The Church of the Old Testament, which, as the people of Jehovah, was at the same time called to wage a holy war, had a right to express its hope of the universal conquest and dominion promised to it, in such terms as those of this Psalm; but, since Jerusalem and the seat of the Old Testament worship have perished, the national form of the Church has also for ever been broken in pieces. The Church of Christ is built up among and out of the nations; but neither is the Church a nation, nor will ever again one nation be the Church, κατ' ἐξοχήν. Therefore the Christian must transpose the letter of this Psalm into the spirit of the New Testament."—*Delitzsch.*

1 HALLELUJAH!
O sing to Jehovah a new song,
His praise in the congregation of (His) beloved.
2 Let Israel rejoice in Him that made him,[a]
Let the children of Zion be joyful in their King;
3 Let them praise His Name in the dance,
With tabret and harp let them play unto Him;
4 For Jehovah taketh pleasure in His people,
He beautifieth the afflicted with salvation.

5 Let (His) beloved exult with glory,

1. A NEW SONG. As expressive of all the new hopes and joys of a new era, a new spring of the nation, a now youth of the Church bursting forth into a new life.

(HIS) BELOVED, or "them that love Him;" see on xvi. 10. A name repeated ver. 5 and 9, and therefore characteristic of the Psalm.

2. IN THEIR KING. God again is claimed emphatically as the King of the nation, when they had no longer a king sitting on David's throne. Such a King will not leave them under foreign rule; He will break the yoke of every oppressor from their neck.

4. TAKETH PLEASURE, as has been shown by their restoration to their own land. Comp. Is. liv. 7, 8.

BEAUTIFIETH. Comp., as having the same reference to the change in the condition of the nation, Is. lv. 5; lx. 7, 9, 13; lxi. 3.

5. WITH GLORY, or it might be rendered "*because of* (the) glory (put upon them)."

UPON THEIR BEDS. Even there,

Let them sing for joy upon their beds;
6 With the high [b] (praises) of God in their mouth,
And a two-edged sword in their hand;
7 To execute vengeance on the nations,
(And) punishments on the peoples;
8 To bind their kings with chains,
And their nobles with iron fetters;
9 To execute upon them (the) judgement written,
It is an honour for all His beloved.
Hallelujah!

even when they have laid themselves down to rest, let them break forth into joyful songs at the thought of God's high favour shown to them, in the anticipation of the victories which they shall achieve. This appears to me to be the obvious and most simple explanation. Maurer, "Tam privata quam publica sit lætitia." Hengstenberg, "*Upon their beds*,—where before, in the loneliness of night, they consumed themselves with grief for their shame." Comp. Hos. vii. 14.

6. A revival of the old military spirit of the nation, of which we have an instance Neh. iv. 17 [11], "With the one hand they did their work, and with the other they held the sword." But a still better parallel is 2 Macc. xv. 27, *ταῖς μὲν χερσὶν ἀγωνιζόμενοι, ταῖς δὲ καρδίαις πρὸς τὸν Θεὸν εὐχόμενοι.*

MOUTH. Heb. "throat," probably intended to express the *loud* utterance.

9. (THE) JUDGEMENT WRITTEN. This has been explained to mean the judgement written in the Law, and that either (1) the extermination of the Canaanites, as a pattern for all future acts of righteous vengeance (Stier); or (2), in a more general sense, such judgements as those threatened in Deut. xxxii. 40—43. Comp. Is. xlv. 14; Ezek. xxv. 14, xxxviii., xxxix.; Zech. xiv. But the extermination of the Canaanites could not be regarded as a typical example, for the Jews were not sent to exterminate other nations, nor is any such measure hinted at here. Nor, again, if by "written" we understand "prescribed in the Law," is the allusion to Deut. xxxii. 40—44 and similar passages more probable; for in those passages vengeance on the enemies of Israel is not *enjoined*, but God speaks of it as His own act.

Hence others understand by "a judgement written" one in accordance with the Divine will as written in Scripture, as opposed to selfish aims and passions (so Calvin). But perhaps it is better to take it as denoting a judgement fixed, settled —as committed to writing, so as to denote its permanent, unalterable character—written thus by God Himself. As in Is. lxv. 6 God says, "Behold it is written before Me: I will not keep silence, but will recompense, even recompense into their bosom."

IT IS AN HONOUR. That is, the subjection of the world described in the previous verses. But perhaps it is better to take the pronoun as referring to God: "He is a glory to all," &c.: *i.e.* either (1) His glory and majesty are reflected in His people; or (2) He is the author and fountain of their glory; or (3) He is the glorious object of their praise.

[a] עֹשָׂיו. This has been usually taken as a plur., adapting itself to אֱלֹהִים: but it is rather sing. (with the usual substitution of י for ה, in verbs ל״ה), and particularly in this participle, Job xxxv. 10, Is. liv. 5. So Hupf. and Ewald, *Lehrb.* § 256 *b*, and so also Gesen. in the latest editions of his Grammar.

[b] רוֹמְמוֹת, infin. subst. from רוֹמֵם: see on lxvi. note [f].

PSALM 150

THE great closing Hallelujah, or Doxology of the Psalter, in which every kind of musical instrument is to bear its part as well as the voice of man, in which not one nation only, but "everything that hath breath," is invited to join. It is one of those Psalms which "declare their own intention as anthems, adapted for that public worship which was the glory and delight of the Hebrew people; a worship carrying with it the soul of the multitude by its simple majesty and by the powers of music, brought in their utmost force to recommend the devotions of earth in the ears of heaven." "Take it," says Isaac Taylor, "as a sample of this class, and bring the spectacle and the sounds into one, for the imagination to rest in. It was evidently to subserve the purposes of *music* that these thirteen verses are put together: it was, no doubt, to give effect first to the human voice, and then to the alternations of instruments,—loud and tender and gay,—with the graceful movements of the dance, that the anthem was composed and its chorus brought out,

> 'Let everything that hath breath praise the Lord !
> Praise ye the Lord !'

And so did the congregated thousands take up their part with a shout, 'even as the voice of many waters.'"—*Spirit of the Hebrew Poetry*, pp. 156, 157.

1 HALLELUJAH !
O praise God in His sanctuary,
Praise Him in the firmament of His strength.

1. IN HIS SANCTUARY. This may be either the earthly or the heavenly Temple. The character of the Psalm, as a liturgical anthem, would seem to show that the former is meant; the parallelism would favour the latter. See xi. 4, where there is the same ambiguity.

2 Praise Him for His mighty acts,
Praise Him according to His excellent greatness.
3 Praise Him with the sound of the cornet,
Praise Him with lute and harp.
4 Praise Him with tabret and dance,
Praise Him upon the strings and pipe.
5 Praise Him upon the clear cymbals,
Praise Him upon the loud cymbals.
6 Let everything that hath breath praise Jah!
HALLELUJAH!

FIRMAMENT OF HIS STRENGTH, *i.e.* the heaven in which His kingly power and majesty are displayed. Comp. lxviii. 34 [35].

3. CORNET, properly the curved instrument made of a ram's horn (see on lxxxi. 3), and distinct from the straight metal trumpet, though in the Talmud it is said that after the destruction of the Temple the distinction of names was no longer observed.

4. TABRET, or "tambourine." The Hebrew *tōph* is the same as the Arab. *dūff;* and the Spanish *adufe* is derived, through the Moorish, from the same root.

STRINGS. This is probably the meaning, as in Syriac. See on xlv. note [h].

PIPE, properly "shepherd's flute," Gen. iv. 21; but not elsewhere mentioned as an instrument employed in sacred music.

5. CYMBALS. The Hebrew word is onomatopoetic, intended to describe the *clanging* of these instruments. It occurs in sacred music, 2 Sam. vi. 5, LXX. *κύμβαλα*. The distinction between the two kinds mentioned is, probably, that the first, as smaller, had a clear, high sound; the latter, as larger, a deep, loud sound. (So Ewald, *Jahrb.* viii. 67.) Others render, "castanets."

6. LET EVERYTHING THAT HATH BREATH, and, above all, the voice of man, as opposed to the dead instruments mentioned before.

What more fitting close than this of the great "Book of Praises"?

APPENDIX 1

MESSIANIC INTERPRETATION

PSALM ii.—In former editions of this work, I had quoted in the note on ver. 4 of this Psalm a passage from the *Mechilta* (the most ancient Jewish Commentary on Exodus), which not only seemed to be evidence of the early Messianic interpretation of this Psalm, but even to show that the doctrine of a persecuted and suffering Messiah was not unknown to the Rabbis. In the *Yalqut Shimeoni* (ii. *f.* 90, i.), the comment on the words of the Psalm, "Against Jehovah, and against His anointed" is, "Like a robber who was standing and expressing his contempt behind the palace of the king and saying, 'If I find the son of the king, I will seize him and kill him, and crucify him, and put him to a terrible death;' but the Holy Spirit mocks thereat, and says, 'He that dwelleth in heaven shall laugh.'"

As the Psalm is admitted by the Jews to be Messianic, this certainly looked like a Messianic interpretation; and as in some of the early Rabbinical writings, there are distinct traces of a belief in a suffering Messiah, such a belief might have found expression here This seemed the less improbable because in the comment which follows on the words, 'But I have set my King' in ver. 6, after various explanations have been given of the verb 'I have set,' we are told that R. Huna in the name of R. Acha, says: "Chastisements are divided into three portions; one for David and for the fathers, and one for our own generation, and one for King Messiah Himself; for it is written, 'He was wounded for our transgressions, he was bruised for our iniquities'" (Is. liii. 5).* It is however somewhat startling to read not only that the Messiah was to be persecuted, but that the death with which He was threatened was a death by crucifixion. And when we turn to the *Mechilta*, from which the comment of the

* This comment of R. Huna's is quoted again with slight variations in the *Yalqut* (ii. *f.* 53) on Is. lii. 14; in the *Midrash Tillim* on Ps. ii. 7, and in the *Agadah Shemuel*, xix.

Yalqut on ver. 4 is taken, we find that the words are applied not to the Messiah, but to the nation of Israel in Egypt. The 'robber' is Pharaoh, the king's son is Israel. It is Pharaoh who thus threatens to destroy the nation, and whose proud boast is derided by Him who sitteth in the heavens. "Five words," says the Mechilta, "did Pharaoh utter blasphemously in the midst of the land of Egypt. 'The enemy said, I will pursue, I will overtake; I will divide the spoil; my lust shall be satisfied upon them; I will draw my sword; my hand shall destroy them' (Ex. xv. 9). And the Holy Spirit answered him in five corresponding words, and said: 'Thou didst blow with thy wind, the sea covered them, they sank as lead in the mighty waters; thy right hand, O Lord, dashed in pieces the enemy; and in the greatness of thy majesty thou didst overthrow them that rose against thee; thou didst send forth thy wrath which consumed them as stubble; thou stretchedst out thy right hand." And then follow the words quoted in the *Yalqut*, as given already, "Like a robber (ληστής in Hebrew letters) who was standing," &c. *Massichta deshiretha*, Parashah vii. (ed. Weiss, Wien, 1865, p. 49). Nor is the passage cited *as Messianic* in the *Yalqut.* The subsequent reference to a Messianic interpretation in ver. 6, and the acknowledged typical character of the nation in accordance with which the prophecies which have their first application to Israel find their final fulfilment in the Messiah, may be held to justify such an interpretation. But as no such sense is put on the passage either in the *Yalqut* or in the *Mechilta,* I have not felt myself at liberty to make use of it as an illustration of the Jewish Messianic explanation of the Psalm.

In the Talmud Babli, *Succah,* 52*a,* there is the following comment on ver. 8 of the Psalm: "God says to Messiah the Son of David who is about to appear—may it be soon, in our days!—'Ask of me and I will give thee,' as it is said, 'I will tell the decree . . . I have this day begotten thee.' 'Ask of me and I will give.' And when he (*i.e.* Messiah the son of David) sees that Messiah the son of Joseph has been slain, then he says before Him, 'Lord of the Universe, I ask of Thee nothing but life,' and God says to him, 'Life! Before thou saidst that, David thy father prophesied concerning thee, for it is said, 'He asked life of thee, thou gavest it him.' "

PSALM xxii.—Although, as I have said in the Introduction to this Psalm, it has been explained by the Rabbis as having a reference to the nation in exile and not to the Messiah, it is interesting to observe that the doctrine of a suffering Messiah is distinctly acknowledged in Jewish Rabbinical literature, even before and apart from the notion of the two Messiahs, the Messiah, the son of Ephraim, who was to be persecuted and put to death, and the Messiah, the son of David, who was to reign and triumph.

Thus there is a story in the Talmud Babli (*Synhedrin*, 98*b*), which tells us how different Rabbis of different schools gave each a name to the Messiah; one saying his name is Shiloh; and another Yinnôn—in allusion to the word in the 17th verse of the 72nd Psalm, *His name shall be continued* (or, *propagated*, Heb. ינון *yinnôn*) *before the sun*;—and another, the Comforter. But others said, His name is the Leprous One of the house of Rabbi, the proof being taken from the 53rd chapter of Isaiah, *He hath borne our sickness, and carried our sorrows, though we esteemed him smitten of God*. For this word *smitten* was applied by the Jews to the case of the leper, in whose affliction they saw the evident hand of God, and it is rendered in the Latin version of Jerome *quasi leprosum*. It enhances the interest of the story when we remember that the Rabbi to whose house the Messiah is said to belong, had himself been grievously afflicted for thirteen years, and that it was believed commonly that his sufferings had a vicarious efficacy; for during those years, it was alleged, there had been no untimely birth. It argues surely a deep conviction of the clinging taint, the deep ineradicable pollution of sin, as well as of the shame and degradation and suffering to which the Messiah must stoop in taking it upon himself to put it away, that a name otherwise so opprobrious should have been given him.

In the Midrash Rabbah on Ruth (cap. v.) the words of Boaz to Ruth are thus explained: "This passage speaks of King Messiah. *Come thou hither* means, Draw near to the kingdom, *and eat of the bread* means, the bread of kingly rule, *and dip thy morsel in the vinegar* means, affliction and chastisements, for it is said, *He was wounded for our iniquities*."

Such a comment as this is no doubt fanciful in the extreme. It departs altogether from the plain sense of the text, from the obvious literal and historical meaning. But it has notwithstanding, it has even on this very account, its value. The mind must have been saturated with a belief in a suffering Messiah, or it would not have fastened it on a passage such as this; it would not have hung the doctrine upon so slender a thread. It is with such comments, as it is with their direct offspring in patristic and mediæval glosses. We may deplore the injury done to the plain sense of Scripture, and the license given to violent dealing with it by these ingenious conceits. We may feel that they have thrown back, perhaps for centuries, a truer, a healthier, a more rational exposition, that they have really impoverished the mind while professing to enrich it, that they have encouraged men to treat Scripture as a book of riddles in which every man may exercise his fancy to the uttermost to see what meaning can be extracted from it, or thrust upon it, instead of taking the meaning that obviously presents itself; that in the search after some mysterious hidden sense men have lost the richer and more fruitful lessons which lay on the surface; but still we must admit that the heart was full of Christ which could see Him in Ruth's morsel dipt in vinegar, or in Samson's rude feats of strength, or in the scarlet thread of Rahab.

I quote two more striking passages from the *Pesiqta Rabbathi*,* xxxvi., xxxvii., because they contain a reference to this Psalm the more remarkable that many of the later Rabbis have refused to recognise the Messianic interpretation.

(i.) "The congregation of Israel spake before the Holy One (blessed be He!), Lord of the world, for the sake of the Law which Thou hast given me, and which is called the Fountain of Life, I shall delight myself in Thy light. What is the meaning of these words (Ps. xxxvi. 10), *In Thy light shall we see light?* This is the light of the Messiah; for it is said, *And God saw the light that it was good.* This teaches us that the Holy One (blessed be He!) had respect to the generation of the Messiah and to His works, before the world was created, and treasured it up for Messiah and for his generation under His throne of glory. Satan said before the Holy One (blessed be He!), Lord of the world, for whom is the light that is treasured up under Thy throne of glory? He replied, It is for him who will turn thee back, and put thee to confusion and shame of face. (Satan) said to Him, Lord of the world, shew him to me. God said, Come and see him. And when he had seen him, he was overwhelmed with terror, and fell on his face and said, Truly this is he that shall cast me and all the nations into Gehenna; for it is said, *He will swallow up death for ever, and the Lord God will wipe away tears from all faces* (Is. xxv. 8). In the same hour the nations were moved and said before Him, 'Lord of the world, who is this into whose hands we are to fall? What is his name and what is his nature?' The Holy One (blessed be He!) replied, His name is Ephraim, my righteous Messiah, and he shall make high his stature and the stature of his nation, and shall enlighten the eyes of Israel, and shall save his people. No nation nor language shall be able to stand against him; for it is said, *The enemy shall not exact upon him, nor the son of wickedness afflict him* (Ps. lxxxix. 22 [23]). All his enemies and adversaries shall be afraid and flee before him; for it is said, *And I will beat down his foes before his face* (ver. 23 [24]); and even

* They are quoted also with slight variations in the *Yalqut Shimeoni* (on Is. lx), ii. f. 56[b], col. 2, § 359.

the rivers that empty themselves in the sea shall cease (before him); for it is said, *I will set his hand also in the sea, and his right hand in the rivers* (ver. 25 [26]). When they (the nations of the world) fled, the Holy One (blessed be He!) began to make conditions with him. He said to him, 'Those whose sins are treasured up beside thee will bring thee under a yoke of iron, and make thee like this calf whose eyes are dim, and will torment thy spirit with a yoke [or, will stifle thy breath through iniquity]: and because of the sins of these, *thy tongue shall cleave to the roof of thy mouth* (Ps. xxii. 15 [16]). Dost thou consent to this?' Messiah answered before the Holy One (blessed be He!), Lord of the world, is this affliction to last many years? The Holy One (blessed be He!) said, By thy life, and by the life of thy head, I have decreed upon thee one week (Dan. ix. 27). If it grieves thy soul, I will expel them now. He answered, 'Lord of the world, with joy and cheerfulness of heart, I will take this upon myself; on condition that not one of Israel be lost, and that not only the living shall be saved in my day, but also those that are treasured up in the dust; and not only the dead shall be saved (who died) in my days, but also the dead who died from the days of the first Adam until now; and not these only, but also the untimely births shall be saved in my days; and not only the untimely births, but also all that Thou intendest to create and have not yet been created: Thus I consent, and on these terms I will take this upon myself.'"

(ii.) In the next quotation it will be observed that the whole Psalm is referred to the sufferings of the Messiah. "Our Rabbis have taught [this shows] that the Patriarchs will rise (from the dead) in the month Nisan (the Paschal or Easter month) and will say to him, 'O Ephraim, our righteous Messiah, though we are thy fathers, yet art thou [better] greater than we, for thou hast borne the iniquities of our children, and there have passed upon thee hard destinies such as have not passed on them that were before, neither (shall pass) on them that come after. Thou hast been a scorn and derision among the nations for the sake of Israel; thou hast sat in darkness and gloom; and thine eyes have not seen the light, and thy skin hath cleaved to thy bones, and thy body hath been dried up like wood, and thine eyes have been darkened through fasting, and thy strength is dried up like a potsherd, and all this because of the iniquities of our children. Is it thy good pleasure that our children should have their portion in the prosperity which the Holy One (blessed be He!) bestoweth upon Israel? Perchance by reason of the suffering which thou hast suffered exceedingly on account of them when they bound thee in the prison-house, thy mind will not be favourable unto them.'

He said unto them, 'O ye Patriarchs, all that I have done, I have not done it but for your sakes, and for the sake of your children that they may have their portion in the prosperity which the Holy One (blessed be He!) bestoweth upon Israel.' The Patriarchs say unto him, 'O our righteous Messiah, let thy mind be appeased; for thou hast appeased the mind of thy Lord and our mind.'"

R. Simeon b. Pazzi said, "In the selfsame hour the Holy One (blessed be He!) exalts Messiah unto the heaven of heavens, and spreads over him the splendours of His glory before [or, because of] the nations of the world, before [or, because of] the wicked Persians saying unto him, 'O my righteous Messiah, be thou judge over these, and do with them that which thy soul desireth, for but that fulness of compassion had prevailed towards thee, already would they have destroyed thee from the world as in a moment,' &c., for it is said *Is not Ephraim a dear son to me?* &c. (Jer. xxxi.); why (does it say) 'should have compassion on him' twice? * but this means compassion in the hour when he was bound in the prison-house, seeing that every day *they*, *i.e.* the nations of the world, were gnashing their teeth at him, and winking with their eyes, and shaking their heads, and shooting out their lips; for it is said, *All they that see me laugh me to scorn, they shoot out the lip, they shake the head* (Ps. xxii. 8),—and the whole Psalm. 'I will have compassion upon him' in the hour that he goeth forth out of the prison-house; for not one or two kingdoms are coming against him, but a hundred and forty kingdoms will compass him about. But the Holy One will say unto him, Ephraim, My righteous Messiah, be not afraid of them, for all these shall be slain by the breath of thy lips; for it is said, *And with the breath of his lips shall the wicked be slain.*"

Psalm xlv.—The great difficulty of the 6th verse (in the Hebrew the 7th verse) of this Psalm is acknowledged on all hands.† If the vocative rendering is retained—and it certainly seems the most natural, and is that of the great majority of the Ancient Versions—then it is not easy to explain how the king, who is certainly spoken of as an earthly monarch (see, for instance, verses 9 and 16) should be addressed directly as God. This difficulty may not present itself to those who suppose that the mystery of the Incarnation was clearly revealed under the Old Testament dispensation, though even then

* In allusion to the repetition of the verb in the Hebrew idiom, רחם ארחם.

† Except indeed in *The Speaker's Commentary*, which merely says of the vocative rendering: "This is the literal and grammatical construction," and dismisses such a rendering as "thy throne (is a throne of) God" with the remark, "it is certain that no such explanation would have been thought of, had not a doctrinal bias intervened."

the strange blending of the literal and the allegorical interpretation must be admitted, but to those who believe that in its primary sense the Psalm refers to a human monarch sitting upon David's throne, the title "Elohim" given to him is not a little startling and perplexing, however he may be regarded as glorified in the light of the promise given to David and to his seed. I am not aware that there is an exact parallel to this elsewhere. Elohim is, however, used of others beside the Supreme Being, and Ibn Ezra, though not adopting the explanation himself, remarks, "there are some who say that it is used here as in the expression, 'thou shalt not revile the Elohim.' But the Gaon (Seadyah) says, 'God shall establish thy throne:' but according to my view, the word כסאך is used (once) instead of repeating it, [thy throne the throne of God,] as in הנבואה עודד הנביא," [where Ibn Ezra means us to understand that the first word having the article, and not being in the construct state, the noun must be repeated in the construct state,] which is equivalent to, 'the prophecy, viz., the prophecy of Oded.' And in the same way here, 'Thy throne, a throne of God,' as it is said, 'And Solomon sat on the throne of Jehovah.'" Ibn Ezra therefore seems to prefer the rendering "thy throne which is God's throne," or simply "thy Divine throne is for ever," &c., thus making "for ever and ever" the predicate of the sentence.

A larger number of interpreters, however, prefer the other order, "Thy throne is a throne of God for ever and ever," which is defended by such a passage as Song of Sol. i. 15, "thine eyes are doves," *i.e.*, "thine eyes are like the eyes of doves." That such a construction is possible can hardly be questioned. But it is not the natural or obvious construction, and can only be justified by the exegetical difficulty of taking "Elohim" in the sense of "judge," "prince," and the like.

This difficulty, however, did not present itself to Rashi. He writes:—"Thy throne, O prince and judge, is for ever and ever, in the same sense as it is said 'I have made thee a god (*Elohim*) unto Pharaoh' (Exod. vii. 1); and why? Because the sceptre of thy kingdom is a right sceptre and thou art worthy to be king."

Qimchi, on the other hand, argues as follows against the vocative interpretation, in a polemical passage against the Christians, which, having been struck out by the Papal Censor in the first edition of Qimchi's Commentary, is not to be found now in the printed text.

"The mistaken Christians who apply the Psalm to Jesus of Nazareth and who say that the daughters of the king are to be taken figuratively, meaning the nations that have been converted to his religion, allege in proof what is said (before) *Thy throne,*

O God, seeing that he calls him in one place King, and in another, God. There are two answers to be given. (1) The words כסאך אלהים [*thy throne, O God*, which Qimchi explains, 'thy throne is the throne of God']; and even if we were to take it as a vocative addressed to God [not to the king], O Lord, may Thy throne be for ever and ever. (2) But how could we apply to God the expression, *the oil of joy, above thy fellows*, or how can we explain the word שגל (shêgāl, the queen-consort), even in a figure, of a relation to God, seeing that it implies the matrimonial usus; and how can it be said, *Instead of thy fathers thou shalt have children?* If they say God has children, as we find it said in Deuteronomy of them that believe in Him, *Children are ye unto the Lord your God*, then answer them, If he has children, he has not fathers, and if they appeal to their doctrine of a Trinity, in explanation, Father, Son, and Holy Ghost, then we have already answered this in our commentary on the Second Psalm. And, moreover, there is a further answer, for if they could say according to their view 'father,' they could not say 'fathers' in the plural."

Many other passages of a polemical character directed against the Christians have in the same way been struck out of the early editions. Dr. Schiller-Szinessy, however, is preparing a critical edition of Qimchi's *Commentary on the Psalms* in which these passages will appear. I am indebted to his kindness for the following account of a copy of the *Editio Princeps* of the Commentary in the University Library at Cambridge:—

1. The copy in question was printed in 1477, *sine loco*, but the type is that of Bologna.

2. It was in the possession of Abraham de Portaleone, the uncle of the author of the שלטי הגבורים (of the same name), and who was consequently Abraham b. Eliezer b. Binyamin, the Hebrew Knight (הפרש העברי), Physician to Ferdinand I. of Aragon, King of Naples. The book belonged subsequently to his son Shelomoh, and no doubt remained in the family till 1640-42. It then came into the possession of R. Yitzchaq b. Menachem, after whose death, about 1646-7, it was bought and presented by the House of Commons in 1647 to the University.

3. There are two Censors' entries on leaf 152^b, Domenico Gerusolomitano, 1595, and Alessandro Scipione, 1597. To judge from the ink (but Dr. S. S. is not quite certain), it was the former Censor, a Jewish convert, who struck out the passages in question, but this was not done very completely, or a sponge was passed over the erasure, so that the text is legible beneath.

Psalm cii.—The directly Messianic interpretation of this Psalm in the Epistle to the Hebrews (i. 10—12) is somewhat remarkable, verses 25—27 [26—28], which are an address to God as the Creator of the world, being quoted in proof of the Divinity of Christ. It is plain, therefore, that the Alexandrine author of that Epistle considered the address here, like the address in Psalm xlv., "Thy throne, O God, is for ever and ever," to be made to the Eternal Word who became incarnate in the person of Jesus Christ. Yet there is no evidence, so far as I am aware, that the Psalm has ever been held by the Jews to be directly or personally a Messianic Psalm. The most ancient Rabbinic commentators have interpreted it of the congregation of Israel towards the close of the Captivity. In this sense, as looking forward to the deliverance and rebuilding of Zion, and the glory that should follow, the Psalm had indirectly a Messianic reference. But that its words should have been so immediately applied, and that, moreover, in an argument addressed to Jews, in support of the Divine nature of the Christ, seems to show that there was a Jewish exegetical school in Alexandria, which differed in its interpretation of the Scriptures from the Palestinian.

Psalm cx.—As I have already remarked I have omitted in this edition some passages alleged by R. Martini in his *Pugio Fidei* as evidence that the Jews put a Messianic interpretation upon this Psalm. That they did so is indisputable; but there is much reason to suspect the genuineness of the passages which he professes to quote from the *Bereshith Rabbah* of R. Moses Haddarshan; though why he should have thought it necessary to forge them is a mystery. With abundance of genuine material at hand, it is strange that he should have had recourse to such artifices, except that there are some natures which delight in this sort of ingenuity for its own sake. However, the question it may be hoped will shortly be set at rest by the publication of the *Bereshith Rabbah* from the unique MS. at Prague which Jellinek has undertaken to edit.

I subjoin some of Qimchi's remarks on this Psalm.

He supposes it to have been written "when the men of David sware unto him, saying: 'Thou shalt no more go out with us to battle;' and the words *Sit on my right hand* mean, 'Sit in my house, *i.e.* the Tabernacle, and serve me; and there will be no occasion for thee to go into the battle for I will fight thy battles.'"

"*The dew of thy youth*, &c. Thou art predestined from the very day of thy birth to have this dew of blessing. *From the womb of the morning*. The morning of thy birth was then, and the dew of thy birth was then."

With regard to the priesthood of Melchizedek, he observes that the priesthood ought to have gone in the direct line from Shem, who, according to the Jewish tradition, was Melchizedek; but they said because Melchizedek blessed Abraham first, and not God first, therefore the priesthood was taken from him.

Qimchi * also charges the Christians with having corrupted the text of the Psalm in two places. In the first verse they have נ׳ אֲדֹנָי לָאדֹנָי writing אדני twice with Qametz as showing that two Persons of the Trinity are here mentioned, God (the Father) says to God (the Son), the Spirit being the Third. Another error is that in ver. 3 they had עִמְּךָ instead of עַמְּךָ. Curiously enough, he charges the first error upon Jerome.† "Jerome, their translator, made a mistake; for we must read לַאדֹנִי . . . . and how can they uphold the error of one man against the great majority? From the rising of the sun to the setting thereof, go where you will, you will find the *Chireq* under the *Nun*, and so likewise you will find in all MSS. עַמְּךָ." Then he refers to the argument in support of the Divinity of Christ drawn from this Psalm: "If the Father and the Son are Gods, the one does not stand in need of the other, because you cannot call any one God who stands in need of another. How (then) can the Father say to the Son, *Sit on my right hand till I make thine enemies thy footstool?* For if this be so, he stands in need of his help, and if he does need it, there must be weakness; and if there be weakness, he cannot be God, for God cannot be lacking in power. And besides how could He have said to him, Thou art a *cōhēn* ‡ for ever, that is, 'a noble and great one;' but if so, was he not noble and great before? But if they (the Christians) should say to this, the sense here is more definitely that he should be 'a priest,' that henceforth from the coming of Jesus the priesthood shall be after a different manner, that there shall be no more sacrifices of flesh and blood, but only of bread and wine such as Melchizedek offered; for it is said that Melchizedek brought forth bread and wine; then give them this answer: To whom does he say, *Thou art a priest?* Does he say this to the Son, who is addressed in the beginning of the verse and from this verse to the end of the Psalm, and is it he who is the minister that sacrifices? But God is not one who brings sacrifices; on the contrary, they bring sacrifices to Him.

---

* This passage is in the printed text, but more correctly in MS. 114 in the Paris Library.

† In the existing text of Jerome, however, we have: "Dixit Dominus Domino meo," and there is no variation apparently in the MSS.

‡ The Hebrew word, commonly rendered "priest," is sometimes used in a wider and less restricted sense of persons holding any office of dignity. Such at least is the opinion of Qimchi, and of many other interpreters.

But if they should say the words are addressed to any one indefinitely, 'I have founded a new priesthood,' without saying to whom, as they have no priestly families, any one may be consecrated to the office; if so, to whom does this apply, *The Lord hath sworn*, &c.? And moreover, why has God changed His will? First He desired sacrifices of flesh, and now He is satisfied with bread and wine; and how can He add, *And will not repent*, when in this very thing he shows that He did repent? And Malachi, the seal of all the Prophets, says: Remember ye the Law of Moses my servant, and he says, *Behold I send my messenger*. Elijah is not come yet, and will not come till the time of the Messiah. And Malachi says that they shall remember the Law to do it as *he* commanded, not as Jesus commanded. From this thou canst see that the Law has never been altered: as it was given to Moses, so it shall remain for ever.

"Again, Where are the battles that he fought? and where are the kings whom he conquered? and how can he say, *He shall rule among the nations full of corpses?* Surely he came (*i.e.* according to their view) to judge *souls*, and to save them, and so the phrase, *he lifts up the head;* and hereby he has not lifted up the head. Let the blind ones open their eyes and confess, Our forefathers have inherited an untruth."

The above is a good specimen of Qimchi's polemics against the Christians of his time, and is very instructive as showing the nature of the difficulties which presented themselves to a cultivated Rabbi in the Middle Ages.

APPENDIX 2

THE MASSORETH

As frequent references occur in the Notes to the Massoreth, and as the widest misapprehension exists with respect to it, and to what is familiarly known as the Massoretic text, it may not be out of place to make a few remarks upon the subject in this Appendix.

What is the Massorah? The word *Massorah*, or, as it ought to be written, *Massoreth*, means tradition. The text in our printed Bibles is commonly supposed to be the text as settled by a certain body of men called Massoretes, who were the custodians of this tradition. No mistake could be greater. The Massoretes were not a single body of men or a single school; the Massoreth is not a single collection of marginal glosses establishing for ever one uniform text. On the contrary, the Massoretes were learned annotators, belonging to many schools, and their marginal annotations vary considerably in different copies. The Eastern Recension differs from the Western, and the different families of MSS. belonging to the latter, French, German, Italian, and Spanish, present more or less considerable variations. The critical value of these glosses consists in the fact that the labours of the Massoretes were directed to the careful enumeration of all the words and phrases of the Bible. The marginal note tells us exactly how often each particular grammatical form and each phrase occurs in the whole Bible and in the several books, and also in what sense it is employed. It is obvious, therefore, at a glance that no new reading could creep into a passage without being immediately detected. The scribe may make a blunder, but the Massoreth checks it; for the Massoreth is not the compilation of the scribe who copies it, but is taken from model codices of a much earlier date.

The extreme minuteness of this verbal criticism has so multiplied, and has been carried to such an extent, that Elias Levita says in his work on the Massoreth, that he believes that if all the words of the Great Massoreth which he had seen in the days of his life were written down and bound up in a volume, it would exceed in bulk all the twenty-four books of the Bible. Only two attempts have till very lately been made to collect these scattered notes and glosses —the one in the well-known work entitled *Ochlah-ve-Ochlah*, the other in Yakob ben Chayyim's Rabbinic Bible published at Venice in 1526. Another scholar is now, however, labouring in the same field. Dr. Ginsburg for the last eighteen years has devoted himself to the task, and has already accomplished far more than his predecessors. With infinite pains and labour he has collected and digested this vast mass of textual criticism. For the first time the Hebrew scholar will really know what the Massoreth is. Hitherto it has been scattered in a number of different MSS., often written in the form of an ornamental border to the text, in minute characters and with numerous abbreviations, and in many cases requiring not only great patience, but a wide acquaintance with the peculiarities of the Massoretic scribes, for its decipherment. Now, all these various editions of the text, all these traditional notes, will be classified and arranged under the head of the several MSS. to which they belong, in parallel columns, so that the eye will see at a glance how far the MSS. agree, the additions in one case, the deficiencies or variations in another.

It is a special advantage attending Dr. Ginsburg's labours that he has been able to make use of the Eastern or Babylonian recension of text and Massoreth for comparison with the Western. It was well known that a divergence did exist between these two recensions, and that as there was very early a different system of vocalisation, as well as a difference in traditions between the Eastern and Western Jews, so there was also a difference in their MSS. of the Bible. But before the year 1840 the only record of that difference that had been preserved was the list of variations given in Yakob ben Chayyim's Bible, which was extremely defective. Now, however, a very important discovery has been made. Among the MSS. recently acquired by the Imperial Library at St. Petersburg, there is, besides a fragment of the Pentateuch, a MS. containing the whole of the later Prophets, exhibiting the Eastern recension; and as this MS. has also the Massoreth, we are enabled thereby to ascertain the Oriental reading of a large number of passages in other books of the Bible, besides those which are comprised in the MS. We thus get a recension of the text which is very much earlier than any existing MS. of which the age is undisputed.

It must always be a matter of the deepest regret that no Hebrew MS. of the Bible of any antiquity has come down to us; for on how many dark passages might light be cast, if a codex were discovered even as ancient as the most ancient MSS. of the New Testament? It must always enhance our regret to reflect that Christian barbarism is to a large extent responsible for this calamity. The savage and unrelenting persecution of the Jews has left an indelible blot on the pages of Christian history from the beginning of the eleventh century to the middle of the sixteenth. There is not a European nation, scarcely a European town of any magnitude, the annals of which are not disgraced by the intolerable cruelties practised on this people. Popes, Fathers, and Councils vied with one another in denouncing them. Edict after edict was issued against them. No insult was too coarse for them; Jew and devil were synonymous terms in the Christian vocabulary; they were outside the pale of humanity. Again and again the fury of the populace, stirred up often by renegades of their own nation, was let loose upon them; their houses were plundered, their property confiscated, their wives and children violated before their eyes. The tale of "Christian Atrocities" in those ages reads in many exact particulars like the tale of "Turkish Atrocities" with which we have all of late been familiar. Thousands of Jews were compelled to abjure their faith and to submit to baptism; thousands more were banished from the cities or countries in which they had settled; great multitudes were tortured and cruelly put to death. Their *Selichoth* or Synagogue hymns for centuries were one great wail going up to heaven, a cry like the cry of the souls pleading beneath the altar, "Lord, how long?" a bitter lamentation, a burden of weeping and great mourning as of Rachel weeping for her children and refusing to be comforted.

In these outbursts of religious fanaticism we know that many precious books and MSS. perished. Synagogues were plundered, burnt, razed to the ground, and the rolls of the Law torn to pieces and strewed in the streets. On the 17th of June, 1244, twenty-four cartloads of MSS. were burnt in Paris alone. "I have not a single book left," writes a French Rabbi to R. Meir of Rothenburg; "the oppressor has taken from us our treasures." Many books were thrown into wells; many were buried in the earth to conceal them from Christians. The possessor of one Codex thanks God that he and not the earth has been the means of preserving it. "We are forbidden," writes Abr. ibn Ramoch, at the close of the fourteenth century, "to have the Torah (the Law) in our possession, and other books which they have carried off into the churches." Another complains that the holy books were disfigured by the ruthless hand of the Christian scribe, and many a fair parchment cut to pieces and made to serve for repairing the boots of the Nazarene. It is the persecution of Antiochus Epiphanes repeated, intensified, prolonged, through centuries.

Add to all this the fact, that it has been the practice of the Jews themselves to consign to oblivion all imperfect copies of their Scriptures. The Talmud enacts that if a copy of the Law have two errors in a page, it shall be corrected; if three, it shall be stowed away. The act by which this is done is called *Genizah.* By the Karaite Jews the receptacle itself in which incorrect or mutilated copies of the Bible were placed were called Genizah, but it is not so called in the Talmud. The receptacles in which all imperfect or injured MSS. of the kind are placed are called by the German Jews "Shemoth-boxes," in allusion to the names (*Shemoth*) of God, because every scrap on which that name might chance to be written, as might be the case with any leaf of the Bible, was held too sacred to be destroyed, and must, therefore, be solemnly deposited in the receptacle prepared for it. No Hebrew MS. consequently was preserved by the Jews merely on the ground of antiquity, and taking this circumstance into connexion with the wholesale destruction of MSS. by Christians during the Middle Ages, to which we have already referred, it can no longer appear surprising that our oldest MSS. are so comparatively late.

Thus Jews and Christians have conspired together for the destruction of these precious documents. The earliest known MS. of the Old Testament (which is in the University Library at Cambridge) only dates from the middle of the ninth century. A fragment belonging to the beginning of the same century is in the Library at St. Petersburg. The beautiful MS. of the Later Prophets in the same Library, already referred to, bears the date A.D. 916. We must not, therefore, indulge unreasonable expectations. It is scarcely probable that even Dr. Ginsburg's collations will furnish us with a *large* harvest of important textual variations. But his work is one of which it is scarcely possible to exaggerate the value notwithstanding. It will give us, what we have never had before, a really accurate collation of all the best MSS. of the Old Testament, together with a complete view of the Massoreth of each. We shall at least have all the evidence with which we are ever likely to be furnished now, for constructing a critical text of the Hebrew Scriptures.

GENERAL INDEX

A.

D.

E.

F.

G.

H.

I.

J.

N.

O.

P.

Q.

R.

T.

U.

V.

W.

X.

Y.

Z.

GRAMMATICAL AND CRITICAL INDEX

Other Valuable Resources for Biblical Studies

COMMENTARY ON ZECHARIAH: HIS VISIONS AND PROPHECIES — **David Baron**

W. H. Griffith Thomas called this ". . . the best available book on Zechariah." A thorough exposition of this prophetic Book.

0-8254-2277-9	566 pp.	paperback
0-8254-2216-7	566 pp.	deluxe hardcover

COMMENTARY ON EZEKIEL — **Patrick Fairbairn**

One of the most valuable works on this important Old Testament book. Fairbairn discusses the person, position, and circumstances of Ezekiel as well as looking at some of the more distinctive features of his prophetic character. This verse-by-verse commentary is a welcome addition to Old Testament studies.

0-8254-2627-8	512 pp.	paperback
0-8254-2630-8	512 pp.	deluxe hardcover

COMMENTARY ON ROMANS — **Robert Haldane**

One of the most authoritative expositions ever to appear on this Epistle. It offers exhaustive exegesis on every sentence in Romans, emphasizing scholarship, theological reflection, and spiritual insight. Special attention is given to the glorious doctrine of justification by faith. Clearly refutes critical attacks on the words and doctrines communicated by Paul.

0-8254-2865-3	754 pp.	paperback
0-8254-2862-9	754 pp.	deluxe hardcover

CHRISTOLOGY OF THE OLD TESTAMENT — **E. W. Hengstenberg**

This volume is one of the greatest works ever written on the messianic prophecies of the Old Testament. Full of profound scholarship, it confirms students in the deep truths of their faith. An indispensable reference work both for scholarship and Bible students, this study is a masterful example of scholarly research based on the integrity and authenticity of the Holy Scriptures. Christ is presented as the center of Old Testament revelation, both in type and in prophecy.

0-8254-2835-1	716 pp.	paperback

THE COMPLETE WORKS OF JOSEPHUS — **Flavius Josephus**

(Translated by William Whiston.) Complete in one volume. The "classic" account of Jewish culture and history which remains the primary extra-biblical reference for biblical studies and archaeology. Additional valuable information in this volume includes: Harmony of Greek and English numbering systems, tables of Jewish weights and measures, Old Testament text parallels to Josephus' histories, 20 full-page illustrations, and a completely updated index. 840 double-column pages. Enlarged-type edition.

0-8254-2952-8	840 pp.	paperback
0-8254-2951-X	840 pp.	hardcover

JOSEPHUS: THE ESSENTIAL WRITINGS **(Translated and edited by Paul L. Maier)**

A newly condensed, illustrated edition of a timeless classic for today's generation. Read and enjoy reading *Jewish Antiquities* and *The Jewish War* which verify so much biblical information. All important passages are included—many word-for-word. Only non-essential or repeated information is omitted. Keyed throughout to Loeb's numbering system. Includes many photos, illustrations, updated indexes, and references.

0-8254-2963-3	416 pp.	hardcover

STUDIES IN LEVITICUS **Samuel Kellogg**

Kellogg staunchly defends Mosaic authorship and ably treats Jewish ceremonial law in all its practical aspects. A classic study of the "law of the priests," the typology of the tabernacle, and the laws governing the daily lives of God's people.

0-8254-3041-0	574 pp.	paperback
0-8254-3043-7	574 pp.	deluxe hardcover

COMMENTARY ON JUDE **Thomas Manton**

An exhaustive, classic exposition. Manton's organization is excellent and his practical observations are valuable. "Manton's work is most commendable." - Spurgeon

0-8254-3239-1	384 pp.	paperback
0-8254-3240-5	384 pp.	deluxe hardcover

SPURGEON ON THE PSALMS **Charles H. Spurgeon**

A faithful condensation by David Otis Fuller of the *Treasury of David*. This work is recognized as one of the finest expositions on Psalms ever produced. Includes an exhaustive compilation of quotations from various expositors.

0-8254-3714-8	704 pp.	paperback